SPECIAL INDIAN EDITION

Services Marketing

Integrating Customer Focus Across the Firm

Eighth Edition

SPECIAL INDIAN EDITION

Services Marketing

Integrating Customer Focus Across the Firm

Eighth Edition

Valarie A. Zeithaml
University of North Carolina at Chapel Hill

Mary Jo Bitner
Arizona State University

Dwayne D. Gremler
Bowling Green State University

Martin Mende
Florida State University

G Shainesh
Indian Institute of Management Bangalore

McGraw Hill Education (India) Private Limited

Published by McGraw Hill Education (India) Private Limited
Registered Office: Anjana Complex No: 5/90 A, Butt Road, St. Thomas Mount, Chennai – 600016

Published by arrangement with McGraw Hill LLC.

Special Indian Edition (SIE) 2025

This edition can be exported from India only by the publishers

Sales Territories: India, Pakistan, Nepal, Bangladesh, Sri Lanka and Bhutan

Print Edition:
ISBN (13): 978-93-6444-955-7
ISBN (10): 93-6444-955-X

E-Book Edition:
ISBN (13): 978-93-6444-614-3
ISBN (10): 93-6444-614-3

1 2 3 4 5 6 7 8 9 D103074 29 28 27 26 25

Printed and bound in India.

Typeset at APS Compugraphics, 4G, PKT 2, Mayur Vihar Phase-III, Delhi 96
and printed at Rajkamal Electric Press, Kundli, Haryana-131 028.

Cover Image Source: Shutterstock
Cover Designer: Neeraj Dayal

Visit us at: www.mheducation.co.in
Write to us at: support.india@mheducation.com
CIN: U80302TN2010PTC111532
Toll Free Number: 1800 103 5875

Aan mijn alleriefste, Jan Benedict Steenkamp—soul mate, inspiration, and biggest supporter.

—V.A.Z.S.

To my husband, Rich, and my very big and wonderful family for the joy they all bring to my life.

—M.J.B.

To my wife, Candy, and daughters, Samantha and Mallory, for their many years of love, support, and encouragement.

—D.D.G.

To Maura and our family in Germany.

—M.M.

To my wife, Leena and our children, Priya and Aditya, with love.

—G.S.

About the Authors

Valarie A. Zeithaml *University of North Carolina–Chapel Hill*

VALARIE ZEITHAML is Distinguished Professor of Marketing Emerita at the Kenan-Flagler Business School of the University of North Carolina at Chapel Hill. She has devoted her career to researching and teaching service quality and services management. She is the co-author of Delivering Quality Service: Balancing Customer Perceptions and Expectations, now in its 20th printing, and Driving Customer Equity: How Customer Lifetime Value Is Reshaping Corporate Strategy. In 2008, Dr. Zeithaml won the Paul D. Converse Award from the American Marketing Association. The award acknowledges enduring contributions to marketing through one or more journal articles, books, or a body of work. In 2009, she received the American Marketing Association/Irwin/McGraw Hill Distinguished Marketing Educator Award for lifetime leadership in marketing education and extensive contributions to the field of marketing. She also won the 2012 Bullard Research Impact Award in recognition of the broad impact of research on the field, industry, and society, and was appointed an American Marketing Association Lifetime Fellow in 2015. The 2014 List of Thomson Reuters included her in the "World's Most Influential Scientific Minds," reflecting citation data that identified those scholars who published the highest impact work.

Mary Jo Bitner *Arizona State University*

MARY JO BITNER is an Emerita Professor of Marketing in the W. P. Carey School of Business, Arizona State University, USA. While at ASU she held the Edward M. Carson Chair in Service Marketing and was the Executive Director of the Center for Services Leadership at ASU. She has contributed over four decades of service research, publishing in leading marketing, service, and management journals and is recognized as one of the pioneers in service research globally. Her primary research foci are customer—employee interactions, technology-delivered service, and customer satisfaction. Dr. Bitner has received a number of awards recognizing her pioneering work in the service discipline including the American Marketing Association's (AMA) SERVSIG recognition for *Career Contributions to the Services Discipline Award*, an IBM Faculty Award, and ISSIP's inaugural Fellow Award for Lifetime Achievement in Service Science. She is an AMA Fellow and served on the AMA's Board of Trustees. She served four years as the editor-in-chief of the *Journal of Service Research.* Dr. Bitner was a founder and board member of the global network for Responsible Research in Business and Management (RRBM), a network committed to societal impact and usefulness in business research, where she remains involved.

Dwayne D. Gremler *Bowling Green State University*

DWAYNE D. GREMLER is professor of Marketing at Bowling Green State University. Dr. Gremler has been teaching Services Marketing courses for almost 30 years and has been identified as having taught more undergraduate classes on this subject during this time than anyone in the United States. He is the recipient of several national teaching awards. In 2015 Dr. Gremler was appointed *Distinguished Teaching Professor* by the Bowling Green State University Board of Trustees and in 2022 was also appointed as *Distinguished Research Professor*. Dr. Gremler has been invited to conduct seminars and present research in more than a dozen countries. He has published over 100 peer-reviewed journal articles, conference papers, and book chapters and has received 16 awards for his research. He has served as an Associate Editor for the *Journal of Service Research* for nearly a decade and as chair of the American Marketing Association's Services Marketing Special Interest Group. Dr. Gremler is a former *Fulbright Scholar*, having received a grant from the U.S. government to teach at the University of Maastricht, Netherlands, in spring 2006. In 2014 he received the *Christopher Lovelock Career Contributions Award* from the AMA's SERVSIG.

Martin Mende *Florida State University*

MARTIN MENDE is Professor of Marketing and Jim Moran Professor of Business Administration at Florida State University. His research focuses on services marketing, consumer-based strategy, and transformative consumer research, and has appeared in the *Journal of Marketing Research, Journal of the Academy of Marketing Science, Journal of Consumer Psychology, Journal of Service Research, Journal of Public Policy & Marketing, Journal of Retailing,* and other leading scholarly journals. Martin serves in various leadership roles in the academy, such as Associate / Area / Guest Editor for the *Journal of the Academy of Marketing Science, Journal of Service Research, Journal of Public Policy & Marketing,* and the *Journal of Retailing*; he also serves on multiple Editorial Review Boards (e.g., *Journal of Marketing, Journal of Marketing Research, Journal of Consumer Psychology*). Martin was recognized by the American Marketing Association as the "*2017 Emerging Scholar*" for both SERVSIG, as well as the Marketing and Society SIG. His research has been recognized globally with various awards, including the AMA-EBSCO-RRBM Award for Responsible Marketing Research. At FSU, Martin has been recognized with college-wide and university-wide teaching awards.

G SHAINESH *Indian Institute of Management Bangalore*

G SHAINESH is Professor of Marketing and Chair of Consumer Insights at the Indian Institute of Management Bangalore (IIMB). With nearly three decades of experience in research, teaching, and academic leadership, he specializes in digital marketing strategy, service innovations, and customer relationship management (CRM). He leads the cross-functional research initiative, *Consumer Insights,* focused on understanding consumer behavior in digital and emerging markets. His award-winning case study, *Narayana Nethralaya: Expanding Affordable Eye Care*, earned global recognition, and his contributions to academia have been honored with accolades such as the CMO Asia Council's Best Professor in Marketing Award. Professor Shainesh has co-authored influential books, including *Marketing Management* (17th Edition, 2025) and CRM in the Digital Age (2025). His research has been published in leading journals such as *MIS Quarterly, Journal of Business Research*, and *Journal of Services Marketing*. At IIMB, he has held key leadership roles, including Dean of Administration and Chairperson of Executive Education, contributing significantly to the institute's global academic initiatives.

Preface

This text is for students and businesspeople who recognize the vital role that services play in the economy and its future. The advanced economies of the world are now dominated by services, and virtually all companies view service as critical to retaining their customers. Manufacturing and product-dominant companies that, in the past, have depended on their physical products for their livelihood now recognize that service provides one of their few sustainable competitive advantages.

We wrote this book in recognition of the ever-growing importance of services and the unique challenges faced by service managers.

WHY A SERVICE MARKETING TEXT?

Since the beginning of our academic careers in marketing, we have devoted our research and teaching efforts to topics in service marketing. This text is unique in both content and structure, and we hope that you will learn as much from it as we have in writing and revising it now for over 30 years. Over this time period we have incorporated major changes and developments in the field, keeping the book up to date with new knowledge, changes in management practice, and the global economic trend toward services.

Content Overview

The foundation of the text is the recognition that services present special challenges that must be identified and addressed by managers. We wrote the text to help students and managers understand and tackle these special challenges of service marketing.

The development of strong customer relationships through quality service (and services) are at the heart of the book's content. The topics covered are equally applicable to organizations whose core product is service (such as banks, transportation companies, hotels, hospitals, educational institutions, professional services, telecommunication) and to organizations that depend on service excellence for competitive advantage (high-technology manufacturers, automotive and industrial products, information-intensive technology firms, and so on). The topics covered also apply equally to large, well-established companies, and to smaller entrepreneurial ventures.

The book's content focuses on knowledge needed to implement service strategies for competitive advantage across industries. Included are frameworks for customer-focused management and strategies for increasing customer satisfaction and retention through service. In addition to standard marketing topics, this text introduces students to foundational topics of service marketing that include management and measurement of service quality, service recovery, the linking of customer measurement to performance measurement, service blueprinting, the cocreation of value by customers, as well as emerging topics in service technologies (e.g., artificial intelligence and service robotics). Each of these topics represents pivotal content for tomorrow's businesses as they structure around process rather than task, engage in one-to-one marketing, mass customize their offerings, cocreate value with their customers, and attempt to build strong relationships with their customers. The cross-functional treatment of issues through integration of marketing with disciplines such as operations information systems, and human resources is a constant underlying theme.

New Features

This eighth edition of the text includes the following new features:

1. New or updated chapter openers in all chapters.
2. New research references and examples in every chapter with greater coverage of new business model examples such as Airbnb and Uber.
3. Greater emphasis on technology and how it is transforming service businesses; for example, the book includes examples from application services ("apps"), the "Gig" economy, and artificial intelligence (AI).
4. Inclusion of current theories and best practices on customer satisfaction and customer retention.
5. Updated coverage of service dominant logic, which focuses on customers as cocreators of value and value in use.
6. Increased and updated coverage of "Big Data" as a source of customer information and data analytics as a service.
7. Updated discussion and examples of strategic service initiatives and service business models in business-to-business firms.
8. New or improved global, technology, and strategic service features in nearly every chapter and updated data in key charts and examples throughout the text.
9. A new chapter dedicated to "Artificial Intelligence and Service Robotics" and the implications for service marketing.

ADDITION TO SPECIAL INDIAN EDITION

The Indian adaptation of the Services Marketing textbook significantly enhances learning outcomes for students and managers in India by embedding rich, localized content across various chapters. The examples cover a wide array of businesses, from traditional and B2B to digital firms, startups, and public organizations. This approach ensures that learners can easily understand how theoretical frameworks translate into real-world business practices within their own market, fostering a deeper comprehension of services marketing principles.

It features engaging chapter openers such as Swiggy – Winning through Customer-Centricity and Zepto – Innovations for Rapid Growth, setting the tone for practical, real-world learning. In-text examples like Oberoi Hotels and Resorts, Zoho, and HDFC Bank's customer focus offer contextual illustrations of core concepts. The Indian Service Strategy Insights section further strengthens relevance by showcasing a diverse mix of companies including Urban Company, cult.fit, Tata 1MG, Licious, Practo, Manipal Hospitals, Jindal Nature Cure Institute, LitmusWorld, Tata Neu, Ginger Hotels, Indian Music Experience Museum, Vande Bharat Express, Apollo's preventive health approach, Zomato, NPCI, ONDC, Air India (AI.g), IndiGo (6Eskai), and Airtel. These examples span consumer and B2B firms, public and not-for-profit organizations, traditional players, and digital disruptors - helping learners understand how service marketing strategies are applied across different sectors.

The book also features a dedicated global perspective through examples like Taj Hotels and Accenture – Strategic Talent Management, providing a comparative lens to Indian practices. The adaptation improves practical application skills through detailed case studies on a diverse range of companies. These case studies allow learners to analyze and solve complex business problems, bridging the gap between theory and practice.

The eight comprehensive case studies deepen this applied learning by exploring the service strategies of Asian Paints Beautiful Home Painting Solutions, Akasa Air, Zerodha, SatSure, ICICI Bank, cult.fit, Nykaa, and PolicyBazaar. These cases highlight themes such as customer centricity, digital transformation, integrated marketing, service innovation, and strategic positioning. Together, these localized and global insights make the textbook highly relevant for learners, enabling them to connect theory with real-world challenges and opportunities in our dynamic service economy. In addition, this practical approach, rich with examples of well-known and successful firms, makes the learning experience more relevant and impactful for students and managers.

WHAT COURSES AND STUDENTS CAN USE THE TEXT?

In our years of experience teaching services marketing, we have found that a broad cross section of students is drawn to learning about services marketing. Students with career interests in service industries as well as goods industries with high service components (such as industrial products, high-tech products, and durable products) want and need to understand these topics. Students with an interest or background in software, technology-based businesses, online applications, and "data as a service" are also drawn to the course since each of these new business models is a form of service, demanding understanding of service concepts and tools. Students who wish to become consultants and entrepreneurs want to learn the strategic view of marketing, which involves not just physical goods but also the myriad services that envelop and add value to these goods. Virtually all students—even those who will work for packaged goods firms—will face employers needing to understand the basics of service marketing and management.

Students need only a basic marketing course as a prerequisite for a service marketing course and this text. The primary target audience for the text is service marketing classes at the undergraduate (junior or senior elective courses), graduate (both masters and doctoral courses), and executive student levels. A subset of chapters would also provide a concise text for use in a quarter-length or mini-semester course. A further reduced set of chapters may be used to supplement undergraduate and graduate basic marketing courses to enhance the treatment of services.

HOW MANY PARTS AND CHAPTERS ARE INCLUDED IN THE BOOK, AND WHAT DO THEY COVER?

The text material includes 17 chapters divided into seven parts and organized around the Gaps Model of Service Quality. Part 1 includes an introduction in Chapter 1 and an overview of the Gaps Model in Chapter 2. Part 2 considers the customer gap by examining customer expectations and perceptions. Part 3 focuses on listening to customer requirements, including chapters covering marketing research for services, building customer relationships, and service recovery. Part 4 involves aligning service strategy through design and standards and includes chapters on service innovation and design, customer-defined service standards, and physical evidence and the servicescape. Part 5 concerns the delivery and performance of service and has chapters on employees' and customers' roles in service delivery, as well as managing demand and capacity. Part 6 focuses on managing services promises and includes chapters on integrated services marketing communications and pricing of services. Finally, Part 7 illustrates the role and relevance of artificial intelligence (AI) and robotics in service, and it examines the financial and economic effect of service quality.

WHAT DO WE PROVIDE EDUCATORS WHO TEACH SERVICES MARKETING?

As a team, we have accumulated more than 100 years of experience teaching the subject of services marketing. We set out to create a text that represents the approaches we have found most effective. We incorporated all that we have learned in our many years of teaching services marketing.

ACKNOWLEDGMENTS

We owe a great deal to the pioneering service researchers and scholars who developed the field of services marketing. They include John Bateson, Leonard Berry, the late Bernard Booms, David Bowen, Stephen W. Brown, Larry Crosby, John Czepiel, the late Pierre Eiglier, Ray Fisk, William George, Christian Gronroos, Steve Grove, Evert Gummesson, the late Eric Langeard, Chuck Lamb, the late Christopher Lovelock, Parsu Parasuraman, Ben Schneider, Lynn Shostack, and Carol Surprenant. We also owe gratitude to the succeeding generations of service researchers who broadened and enriched the services marketing field. The length of that list, too extensive to include here, is testament to the influence of the early pioneers and to the importance that service marketing has achieved both in academia and in practice.

We remain indebted to Parsu Parasuraman and Len Berry, who have been research partners of Dr. Zeithaml's since 1982. The Gaps Model around which the text is structured was developed in collaboration with them, as was the model of customer expectations used in Chapter 3. Much of the research and measurement content in this text was shaped by what the team found in a 15-year program of research on service quality. Dr. Zeithaml is particularly indebted to her long-time colleague A. "Parsu" Parasuraman, who has been her continuing collaborator over the 30 years she has been in academia. An inspiring and creative talent, Parsu has always been willing to work with her as a mentor and partner. He is also her treasured friend. As always, she credits the Marketing Science Institute (MSI), of which she was a researcher and an academic trustee, for the support and ongoing inspiration from the beginning of her service quality journey.

Dr. Bitner expresses special thanks to the W. P. Carey School of Business at Arizona State University, and the Center for Services Leadership staff and faculty. Their support and encouragement have been invaluable throughout the multiple editions of this book. Dr. Bitner also acknowledges the many ideas and examples provided by the member companies of the Center for Services Leadership that are committed to service excellence and from which she has the opportunity to continually learn. She also acknowledges and thanks the Faculty Network members of the Center for Services Leadership from around the world, whose ideas, energy, and creativity keep the discipline current and vital. Finally, Dr. Bitner is grateful to the fine group of Arizona State services doctoral students and MBA students she has worked with, who have shaped her thinking and supported the text.

Dr. Gremler expresses thanks to several people, beginning with his mentor, Steve Brown, for his advice and encouragement over the past three decades. He thanks other Arizona State University faculty who served as role models and encouragers, including John Schlacter, Michael Mokwa, and David Altheide. Dr. Gremler acknowledges the support of fellow doctoral student colleagues from Arizona State University who have gone on to successful careers and who continue to serve as role models and encouragers, including Kevin Gwinner, Mark Houston, John Eaton, and Lance Bettencourt. Finally, a special thanks to Candy Gremler for her unending willingness to serve as copy editor, encourager, wife, and friend.

Martin Mende is grateful to his many friends, coauthors, and mentors in the service community, all of whom are incredibly bright, kind, and hard-working scholars. At the Catholic University of Eichstätt-Ingolstadt (Germany), Bernd Stauss—who held the first Chair for Service Management in Germany—sparked Martin's initial interest in services scholarship. Martin's years at Arizona State University were truly life-changing and he is indebted to his mentors and friends at ASU, Mike Hutt and Beth Walker, as well as Mary Jo Bitner, Ruth Bolton, and Amy Ostrom. Martin is also immensely grateful for the friendship of incredible, inspiring scholars such as Mike Brady and Charlie Hofacker, Mark Houston, Rob Palmatier, John Hulland, Lisa Bolton, Dhruv Grewal, Jenny van Doorn, Stephanie Noble, and Len Berry. These scholars (and many more) are not only important members of Martin's academic family, but they have become the dearest of friends. Finally, literally none of the above would have happened without Maura Scott, who is the sun in Martin's universe.

Professor Shainesh expresses his heartfelt gratitude to his academic advisors, Late Professors P. N. Thirunarayana and M. R. Rao, for their invaluable support and encouragement during his doctoral studies at IIM Bangalore. He is deeply fortunate to have Dr. Jagdish Sheth, Emory University, as his mentor for over two decades, whose guidance has profoundly shaped his academic journey. He acknowledges the meticulous efforts of Irene Aniyan Puthethu, doctoral student at IIM Bangalore, for her dedication in identifying and compiling multiple sources for case studies, ensuring a comprehensive understanding of each topic. Professor Shainesh is also grateful to the business leaders, CEOs, CMOs, and Marketing Heads who generously contributed images and creatives, many of which were tailored exclusively to align with the content on their brands and organizations. Finally, Professor Shainesh extends his sincere thanks to the professional team at McGraw Hill, particularly Navneet Kumar and Sanjeev Jha, for their skillful collaboration and unwavering support in shaping this adaptation. Working with them has been a truly rewarding experience.

All five authors want to thank Dr. Elise Riker for her excellent assistance in revising the instructor's materials for this edition of the book.

Finally, we would like to acknowledge the professional efforts of the McGraw Hill Higher Education staff.

Valarie A. Zeithaml

Mary Jo Bitner

Dwayne D. Gremler

Martin Mende

G Shainesh

PUBLISHER'S NOTE

McGraw-Hill Education (India) invites suggestions and comments from you, all of which can be sent to *support.india@mheducation.com* (kindly mention the title and author name in the subject line).

Piracy-related issues may also be reported.

Contents in Brief

Detailed Contents

PART 2
FOCUS ON THE CUSTOMER 55

Chapter 3
Customer Expectations of Service 56

Chapter 4
Customer Perceptions of Service 82

PART 3
UNDERSTANDING CUSTOMER REQUIREMENTS 115

Chapter 5
Listening to Customers through Research 117

Chapter 6
Managing Customer Relationships 150

Chapter 7
Service Recovery 186

PART 5
DELIVERING AND PERFORMING SERVICE 321

List of Boxes

Part **One**

Foundations for Service Marketing

Part One of this text provides you with the foundations needed to begin your study of services marketing. The first chapter defines services as well as identifies up-to-date trends, issues, and opportunities in service marketing and management as a backdrop for the strategies addressed in the remaining chapters. The second chapter introduces the Gaps Model of Service Quality, the framework that provides the structure for the text. The remaining parts of the book include information and strategies to address specific gaps, giving you the tools and knowledge to become a service marketing leader.

Chapter One

Introduction to Services

This chapter's learning objectives are to:

1. Explain what services are and identify important trends in services.
2. Explain the need for special service marketing concepts and practices and why the need has developed and is accelerating.
3. Explore the profound impact of technology on service.
4. Outline the basic differences between goods and services and the resulting challenges and opportunities for service businesses.
5. Introduce the expanded marketing mix for services and the philosophy of customer focus as powerful frameworks and themes that are fundamental to the rest of the text.

All Businesses are Service Businesses[1]

It is frequently said that "everything is a service" and "all businesses are service businesses". Clearly, no one would argue that brand icons like Disney, Oberoi Hotels, Google, Zoho, Airtel, HDFC Bank, Infosys and Starbucks are service companies – service is the core of their business and service excellence is a key to their success. Companies like Wipro GE Healthcare, Airbus, Xerox, Eureka Forbes and IBM are also service providers. They compete effectively in their industries by providing essential services like training, repair, and distribution associated with their products, but also more sophisticated services like consulting, data and technology services, and business process outsourcing in their areas of expertise. Even consumer product companies like Apple and Samsung are service providers. For these companies, services are embedded in the products themselves, with smart phones and tablets providing essential services and solutions that many of us find critical to our daily lives. Finally, many new business models are service models, which are often based in technology. Some, like Uber and Airbnb, have disrupted entire service industries.

The examples below illustrate the diversity of service companies that we will feature in the text and the kinds of businesses you will learn about.

Oberoi Hotels and Resorts

Oberoi Hotels and Resorts exemplifies service excellence through their foundational philosophy that "the guest is everything," a principle established by founder M.S. Oberoi in 1934 and continued by his successors. The group operates 32 hotels in seven countries under the luxury 'Oberoi' and five-star 'Trident' brand. Other businesses include flight catering, airport restaurants, travel and tour services, car rentals, project management and corporate air charters. The group's reputation stems not just from its beautiful properties and exceptional facilities, but from creating a singular guest experience where each person feels truly seen, heard, and understood. This commitment manifests through personalized attention, anticipation of needs, meticulous detail, and genuine warmth that transforms service into heartfelt gestures. By placing customers first and focusing on exceeding expectations through unrelenting attention to every aspect of service, coupled with extensive staff training through their renowned learning center, has secured them loyal guests and numerous accolades in the global hospitality industry. Being excellent at service – both for customers and employees – has been one of the keys to the Oberoi Group's success for decades.

Salesforce.com

Many large technology firms are service providers to their business customers. Salesforce.com, an American cloud-based software company, is a prime example of such a business-to-business service provider. Salesforce is the global #1 provider for customer relationship management (CRM) software solutions. More than 150,000 companies use Salesforce's CRM platform to optimize their marketing, sales, commerce, service, and IT activities so that they can deliver better service to their own customers. For example, Salesforce software is designed to better engage customers (e.g., with digital marketing), design and scale ecommerce around customer needs, and provide excellent customer service. Importantly, Salesforce's success is driven by its core values around customer success, innovation, integrity, and accountability, which collectively aim to inspire customer trust in Salesforce's promises. As you will learn in this book, many of these values are fundamental factors for the success of service organizations.

Zoho

Zoho is a global technology company that provides a comprehensive suite of cloud-based business applications to organizations of all sizes. Founded in 1996 as AdventNet and rebranded as Zoho in 2009, the company offers over 55 integrated software applications spanning customer relationship management (CRM), enterprise resource planning (ERP), email, collaboration tools, marketing automation, HR management, finance, and project management solutions. Its deeply integrated applications, available on the web and mobile, offer a solution to fit almost every business need. Zoho distinguishes itself through its vertically integrated approach—developing its own technology stack and infrastructure while maintaining affordable pricing compared to competitors. Headquartered in Chennai, India, with offices worldwide, Zoho serves millions of users across 180 countries, emphasizing privacy, data security, and customer autonomy by not relying on advertising revenue. The company is privately held, profitable, and known for its commitment to sustainable growth, employee development, and serving small to medium-sized businesses with enterprise-grade technology. Zoho's commitment to private ownership and bootstrapped growth, deliberately avoiding venture capital to maintain complete autonomy in decision-making and product development allows the leadership to prioritize long-term customer relationships over short-term profits, investing in research and development rather than aggressive promotions. The company embraces a "rural revival" philosophy by establishing offices in smaller communities, creating job opportunities outside major tech hubs while maintaining affordable pricing to democratize access to enterprise-grade software. The company fosters a strong learning culture, investing heavily in employee development through Zoho University, which recruits and trains talent from diverse backgrounds, including those without traditional educational credentials. This holistic approach—balancing business success with social responsibility, employee development, customer-centricity, and technological innovation—has created a sustainable business model that continues to thrive in the competitive global software industry.

Apple

In many industries, products are becoming a vehicle for service provision. Nowhere is this more obvious than in consumer electronics. Every app that you have on your smart phone promises to provide you with information, entertainment, purchasing opportunities, or unique solutions for your everyday life—all of these are services. The phone itself is really just a "container" for the services it provides. Apple continues to stay on the forefront of technology and product design, but it is always geared to providing customers with the innovative services and solutions they have come to expect and depend on from the company. Indeed, Apple is in the process of reinventing itself as a service company (e.g., increasingly focusing on streaming and subscription services related to the App Store, iCloud, Apple Pay, Apple Music, as well as games and video offerings).

Uber

Technology, collaboration, and the sharing economy are giving rise to many new services today. Some are short-lived, while others seem to have real staying power. Uber's rapid rise as a prominent, disruptive business model in the personal transportation industry is one of the best known examples. Technology has made Uber's business model possible, and consumer willingness to collaborate underlies its success. Through technology Uber is able to link individual drivers, driving their own personal cars, with customers who are seeking a ride. The technology tracks locations, availability, payment, and evaluations of both drivers and riders, making the service extremely efficient and yet customized. Although it is facing challenges from regulated taxis and others, Uber's rapid expansion globally is a testament to the robustness of the service model.

As the chapter opener suggests, services are prevalent across industries, service strategies can be very profitable, and technology and digital transformation of companies and industries is driving growth and innovation in services. Yet, the University of Michigan's American Customer Satisfaction Index has consistently shown lower scores for services when compared to other products.[2] Given the economic growth in services, their profit and competitive advantage potential, and the overall lower levels of customer satisfaction for services, it seems that the potential and opportunities for companies that can excel in service marketing, management, and delivery have never been greater.

This book will give you a valuable lens with which to approach the marketing and management of services. What you learn can be applied in a company like Boeing with a traditional manufacturing history or in pure service businesses like Disney, Marriott, or Southwest Airlines. You will learn tools, strategies, and approaches for developing and delivering profitable services that can provide competitive advantage to firms. At the foundation of service marketing and management you will find a strong customer focus that extends across all functions of the firm—thus the subtitle of this book, "Integrating Customer Focus Across the Firm."

WHAT ARE SERVICES?

Put in the most simple terms, *services are deeds, processes, and performances* provided, coproduced, or cocreated by one entity or person for and/or with another entity or person. Our chapter opener and the four company examples illustrate the range of meanings and types of companies that offer services today. Although we will rely on the simple, broad definition of *services,* you should be aware that over time *services* and the *service sector of the economy* have been defined in subtly different ways. The variety of definitions can often explain the confusion or disagreements people have when discussing services and when describing industries that constitute the service sector of the economy. Compatible with our simple, broad definition is one that defines services to include "all economic activities whose output is not a physical product or construction, is generally consumed at the time it is produced, and provides added value in forms (such as convenience, amusement, timeliness, comfort, or health) that are essentially intangible concerns of its first purchaser."[3] The breadth of industries making up the service sector of the Indian economy is illustrated in Figure 1.1.

Service Industries, Service as a Product, Customer Service, and Derived Service

As we begin our discussion of service marketing and management, it is important to draw distinctions between *service industries and companies, service as a product, customer service,* and *derived service.* The tools and strategies you will learn in this text can be applied to any of these categories.

Service industries and companies include those industries and companies typically classified within the service sector where the core product is a service. All of the following companies can be considered pure service companies: Taj Hotels (lodging),

FIGURE 1.1
Contributions of Service Industries to India's Gross Domestic Product (GDP)

Reference: *Ministry of Statistics and Programme Implementation # 12,13;* https://mospi.gov.in/data accessed on April 24, 2025

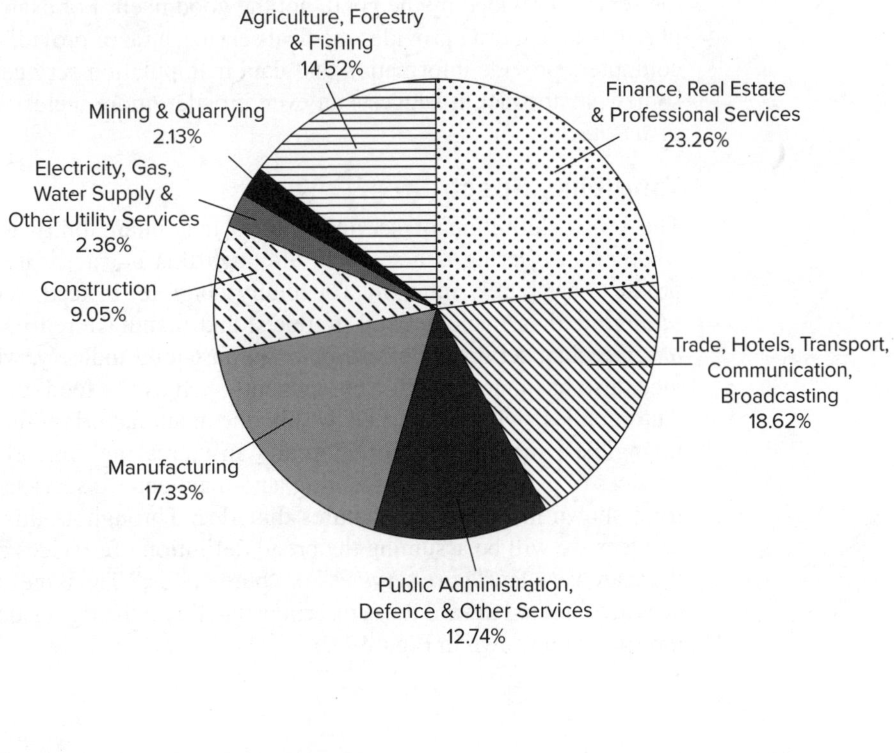

Indigo Airline (transportation), State Bank of India (financial services), and Apollo Hospitals (healthcare). The service sector comprises a wide range of service industries, as suggested by Figure 1.1. Companies in these industries sell services as their core offering.

Service as a product represents a wide range of intangible product offerings that customers value and pay for in the marketplace. Service products are sold by service companies and by nonservice companies such as manufacturers and technology companies. For example, IBM and Hewlett-Packard offer information technology consulting services to the marketplace, competing with firms such as Accenture, a traditional pure service firm. Other industry examples include department stores like Macy's that sell services such as gift wrapping and shipping, pet stores like PetSmart that sell pet grooming and training services, and distributors like VWR who offer services such as instrument calibration, equipment maintenance, and inventory management to their research lab customers.

Customer service is also a critical aspect of what we mean by "service." Customer service is the service provided in support of a company's core products. Companies typically do not charge for customer service. Customer service can occur on-site (as when a retail employee helps a customer find a desired item or answers a question), or it can occur over the phone or via the Internet through chat in real time. Many companies operate customer service call centers, often staffed around the clock. In other cases, customer service is provided remotely, through machine-to-machine communication without any human interaction. Regardless of the method, quality customer service is essential to building customer relationships. It should not, however, be confused with the services provided for sale by the company.

Derived service is yet another way to look at what service means. In their paradigm-shifting and award-winning research, Steve Vargo and Bob Lusch argue for a logic for marketing that suggests that all products and physical goods are valued for the services they provide.[4] Drawing on the work of respected economists, marketers, and philosophers, they suggest that the value derived from physical goods is really the service provided by the good, not the good itself. For example, they suggest that a pharmaceutical drug provides medical service, a razor provides barbering service, and computers provide information and data manipulation service. Although this view is somewhat abstract, it suggests an even broader, more inclusive, view of the meaning of *service*.

Tangibility Spectrum

The broad definition of service implies that intangibility is a key determinant of whether an offering is a service. Although this is true, it is also true that very few products are purely intangible or totally tangible. Instead, services tend to be *more intangible* than manufactured products, and manufactured products tend to be *more tangible* than services. For example, the fast-food industry, while classified as a service, also has many tangible components such as the food, the packaging, and so on. Automobiles, while classified within the manufacturing sector, also supply many intangibles, such as transportation and an increasingly broad portfolio of app-based services (e.g., navigation, streaming, and maintenance services). The tangibility spectrum shown in Figure 1.2 captures this idea. Throughout this text, when we refer to services we will be assuming the broad definition of services and acknowledging that there are very few "pure services" or "pure goods." The issues and approaches we discuss are directed toward those offerings that lie on the right side, the intangible side, of the spectrum shown in Figure 1.2.

FIGURE 1.2 Tangibility Spectrum

Source: L. G. Shostack, "Breaking Free from Product Marketing," *Journal of Marketing* 41 (April, 1977), pp. 73–80, American Marketing Association.

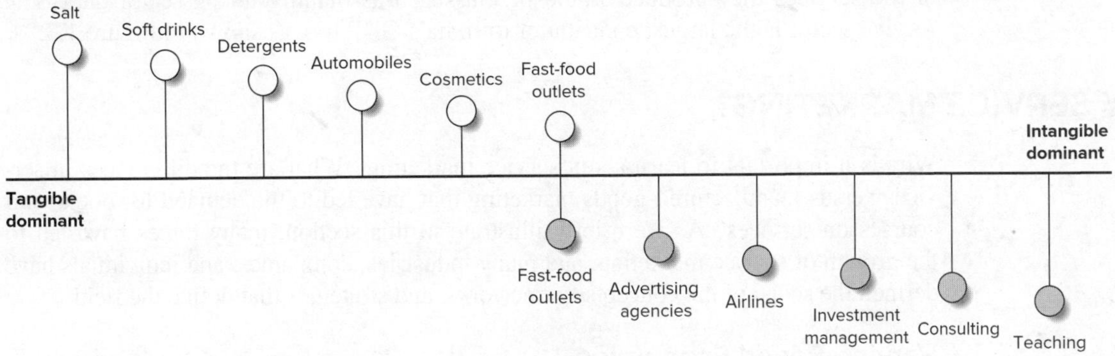

Trends in the Service Sector

Although you often hear and read that many modern economies are dominated by services, the United States and other countries did not become service economies overnight. As early as 1929, 55 percent of the working population was employed in the service sector in the United States, and approximately 54 percent of the gross national product was generated by services in 1948. The trend toward services has continued, until in 2020 services represented nearly 77 percent of the gross domestic product

FIGURE 1.3 Percentage of India's GDP by Sector

Reference: World Bank December 2024; worldbank.org; ID 271329

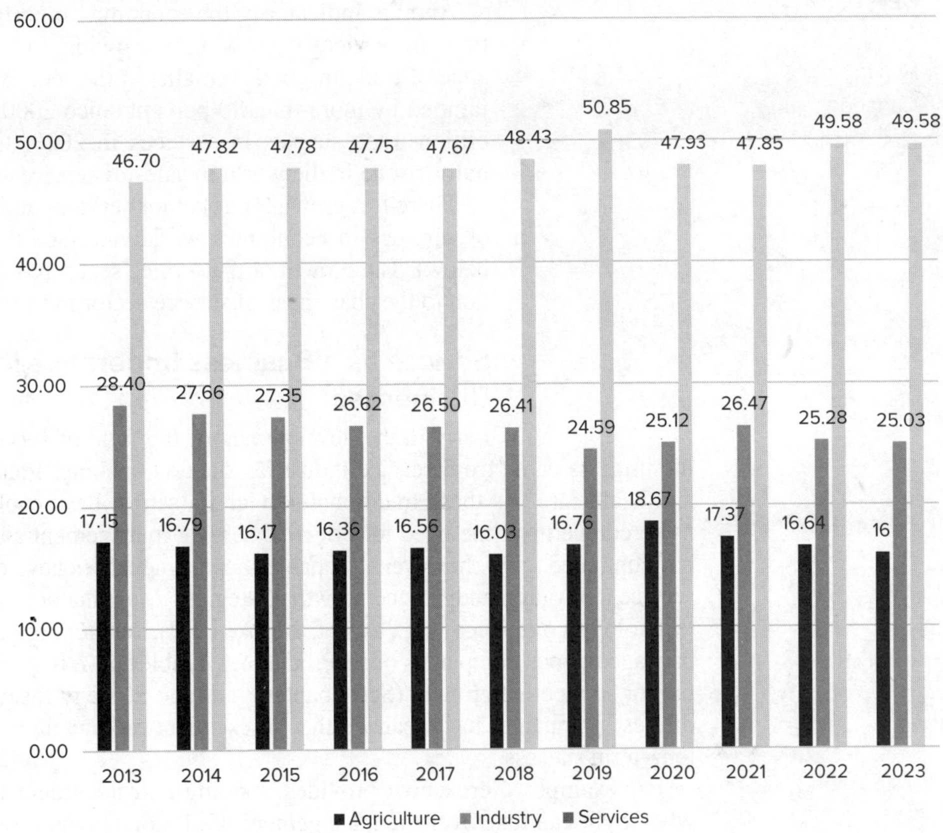

(GDP), and in 2019, 80 percent of employment. Note that these data do not include services provided by manufacturing companies. The number of employees and value of the services they produce would be classified as manufacturing sector data. The service sector is the largest contributor to India's GDP too, as shown in Figure 1.3.

WHY SERVICE MARKETING?

Why is it important to learn about service marketing? What are the differences in services versus manufactured-goods marketing that have led to the demand for books and courses on services? As we briefly illustrate in this section, many forces have led to the growth of service marketing, and many industries, companies, and individuals have defined the scope of the concepts, frameworks, and strategies that define the field.

Service-Based Economies

First, service marketing concepts and strategies have developed in response to the tremendous growth of service industries, resulting in their increased importance to the U.S. and world economies. As was noted, the service sector represented approximately 80 percent of total employment in 2019 and 77 percent of gross domestic product of the United States in 2020. Almost all the absolute growth in numbers of jobs and the fastest growth rates in job formation are in service industries, particularly healthcare and IT professional services.

Another indicator of the economic importance of services is that trade in services is growing worldwide. In fact, while the U.S. balance of trade in goods remains in the red, exports of services have jumped by more than 80 percent since 2000 and there was a $245 billion trade surplus in services in 2020. In fact, the U.S. ranks number one in the world in sales of services abroad.[5,6]

There is a growing market for services and increasing dominance of services in economies worldwide (see the accompanying table below). The growth of the service sector has drawn increasing attention to the challenges of service sector industries worldwide.

Country	Contribution to GDP by Service Sector (in %) as of 2017
United States	80.0
UK	79.2
France	78.8
Singapore	75.2
New Zealand	72.8
Brazil	72.7
Australia	71.2
Canada	70.2
Netherlands	70.2
Japan	68.7
Germany	68.6
Sweden	65.4
Mexico	64.5
India	61.5
China	51.6

Source: *The CIA World Fact Book*, 2021.

Service as a Business Imperative in Goods-Focused Businesses

Early in the development of the field of service marketing, most of the impetus came from service industries such as banking, transportation, hospitality, and healthcare. As these traditional service industries have evolved and become even more competitive, the need for effective service management and marketing strategies has continued. Now, however, companies across industries have discovered the value of service innovation and service growth strategies.[7] Manufacturers (e.g., GE, Caterpillar), technology companies (e.g., Avnet, Xerox, IBM), retailers (e.g., PetSmart), and even packaged goods companies (e.g., Procter & Gamble) have begun to discover the potential for service-led growth. (See Chapter 8 and the Strategy Insight in that chapter.) All of these companies have realized that an excellent product alone is not a guarantee for long-term success.

For example, Xerox now provides imaging and document management services, whereby it can take over the management of all documents (digital and paper) within an organization. This type of service lies far beyond its traditional printer repair and maintenance service business. In a different industry, PetSmart, a very large pet retailer, attributes nearly all of its growth in recent years to its services, including pet hotels, grooming, and training. Procter & Gamble has also begun a push into services tied to a few of its renowned brands, including franchise models for Mr. Clean Car Wash, and Tide Cleaners, which provides laundry and dry cleaning, alterations, as well as shoe cleaning and repair services. Knowing the tremendous value of these brands, Procter & Gamble has been very meticulous and careful in its extension of these brands into services. To expand their service business expertise, many technology companies have partnered with or purchased service businesses (e.g., IBM purchased PricewaterhouseCoopers's entire consultancy business to further develop its own professional services arm, IBM Global Business Services).

Why are all these companies choosing to focus on services? There are a number of reasons.

1. First, the commoditization of products in many industries has resulted in price and margin pressures on many physical goods. Services can help firms to customize their offerings, adding value for customers. Moreover, services often have higher profit margins than products and can thus provide platforms for firm profitability.
2. Second, customers are demanding services and solutions, especially in business-to-business markets. In many situations, customers demand a solution to their problem or challenge that involves multiple products and services. They look to their providers to create and deliver these product-service solutions.
3. Third, as you will learn in later chapters, customer loyalty and customer satisfaction are driven in large part by service quality and service offerings. Again, this knowledge provides firms with another reason to develop services and cement customer loyalty through high-quality service.
4. Finally, many industries are highly competitive today and service can be a differentiator in a crowded market.

As firms transition into services, they often encounter serious challenges in terms of culture change, sales and channel issues, and a need for expertise in designing and delivering services. These companies are typically engineering, technology, science, or operations driven. Their expertise is anchored in what they produce. As these companies transition and seek to grow through service, they find they need a new service logic, and the special concepts and approaches for managing services become increasingly apparent.[8]

Deregulated Industries and Professional Service Needs

Specific demand for service marketing concepts has come from deregulated industries and professional services as both these groups have gone through rapid changes in the ways they do business. In the past several decades many very large service industries, including airlines, banking, telecommunications, and trucking, have been deregulated by the U.S. government. Similar deregulatory moves have taken place in many other countries as well. As a result, marketing decisions that used to be tightly controlled by the government are now partially, and in some cases totally, within the control of individual firms.[9] For example, historically all airline fares, routes, and commissions paid to travel agents were determined and monitored by the government. All of that changed with deregulation, and airlines have been free to set their own pricing structures and determine which routes they will fly. Deregulation created turmoil in the airline industry, accelerating the need for more sophisticated, customer-based, and competition-sensitive marketing.

Providers of professional services (such as physicians, lawyers, accountants, engineers, and architects) have also demanded new concepts and approaches for their businesses as these industries have become increasingly competitive and as professional standards have been modified to allow advertising. Whereas traditionally the professions avoided even using the word *marketing,* they now seek better ways to understand and segment their customers, to ensure the delivery of quality services, and to strengthen their positions amid a growing number of competitors.

Service Marketing Is Different

As the previously mentioned forces coincided and evolved, businesspeople realized that marketing and managing services presented issues and challenges not faced in manufacturing and packaged goods companies. For example, when a firm's core offering is a deed performed by an employee (such as engineering consulting), how can the firm ensure consistent product quality to the marketplace? As service businesses began to turn to marketing and decided to hire marketing people, they naturally recruited from the best marketers in the world—Procter & Gamble, General Foods, Kodak (at the time). People who moved from marketing in packaged goods industries to marketing in healthcare, banking, and other service industries found that their skills and experiences were not directly transferable. They faced issues and dilemmas in marketing services that their experiences in packaged goods and manufacturing had not prepared them for. These people realized the need for new concepts and approaches for managing service businesses.

Service marketers responded to these challenges and began to work across disciplines and with academics and business practitioners from around the world to develop and document marketing practices for services. As the field evolved, it expanded to address the concerns and needs of *any* business in which service is an integral part of the offering.

Service Equals Profits

In the final decades of the 20th century, many firms jumped on the service bandwagon, investing in service initiatives and promoting service quality as ways to differentiate themselves and create competitive advantage. Many of these investments were based on faith and intuition by managers who believed in serving customers well and who believed in their hearts that quality service made good business sense. Indeed, a dedication to quality service has been the foundation for success for many firms, across industries.[10]

Since the mid-1990s firms have demanded hard evidence of the bottom-line effectiveness of service strategies. And researchers have built a convincing case that service strategies, implemented appropriately, can be very profitable.[11] For example, research out of the Harvard Business School built a case for the "service–profit chain," linking internal service and employee satisfaction to customer value and ultimately to profits.[12] And considerable other research shows linkages from customer satisfaction (often driven by service outcomes) to customer loyalty and to profits.[13] From the University of Michigan American Customer Satisfaction Index (ACSI) come data suggesting that customer satisfaction is directly linked to shareholder value. Firms in the top 25 percent of the ACSI rankings show significantly higher shareholder value than do firms in the bottom 25 percent. Research based on ACSI data also shows that the top 20 percent of ACSI firms outperform the Standard & Poor's 500, NASDAQ, and Dow Jones Industrial Average.[14]

An important key to these successes is that the right strategies are chosen and that these strategies are implemented appropriately and well.[15] Much of what you learn from this text will guide you in making correct service strategy decisions and in providing superior implementation. Throughout the text we will point out the profit implications and trade-offs to be made with service strategies. See this chapter's Strategy

Strategy Insight Competing Strategically through Service

Firms can compete profitably through services in a variety of ways. Through our work with companies across industries and through benchmarking other companies, we see four strategic themes emerge as the primary ways that firms can compete through service. Although firms tend to emphasize one or two of these strategic choices at a given time, it may be possible to do more.

EXEMPLARY OUT-OF-THE-BOX CUSTOMER SERVICE

There are some organizations whose competitive advantage is their reputation for out-of-box customer service. Urban Company, cult.fit, Tata 1MG and Mayo Clinic are just a few examples.

- Urban Company (formerly UrbanClap) revolutionized home services by creating a professional marketplace for plumbers, electricians, beauticians, and more. Their quality controls, standardized pricing, and professional training have transformed traditionally unorganized sectors into reliable service experiences.
- At Mayo Clinic, a grand piano in the lobby and doctors who sit physically close to patients, look them in the eye, and truly believe that "the needs of the patient come first."
- cult.fit reimagined fitness services through a hybrid phydigital model offering online classes, gym access, healthy meal deliveries, and mental wellness programs in one subscription. Their data-driven personalization creates tailored fitness and wellness journeys.
- Tata 1MG transformed healthcare access through their delivery platform that combines doctor consultations on chat to online pharmacy and lab tests at home, prescription management, medicine refill reminders, making healthcare more accessible and organized. India's leading digital healthcare platform has delivered over 25 million orders in 1000+ cities till date. The company's mission is to bring "care" to "health" and provide a flawless healthcare experience.

INNOVATIVE, CUTTING-EDGE SERVICES

Other organizations compete through providing innovative, cutting-edge services – being the first and/or the best in their industry or being on the forefront of new inventions, technology or science. Examples here include Licious that revolutionized meat and seafood retail with farm-to-fork traceability, cold chain delivery, and quality assurance in a category traditionally dominated by unorganized vendors. Similarly, Unacademy transformed education access by bringing quality teachers to students anywhere through online courses, live classes, and personalized learning journeys. Amazon.com, the first company to introduce really effective and innovative online retailing. Mayo Clinic falls into this category as well. It is on the leading edge of medicine in the United States and typically sees patients who have hard-to-diagnose or complex problems. The clinic's research-based, team-oriented, consultative model of medicine keeps it on the forefront.

Technology helps firms to expand the possibilities in service and create offerings that become an integral part of customers' lives. For example, Amazon introduced "Amazon One" as a fast, convenient, contactless way for people to use their palm to pay at a store, present a loyalty card, or enter a location like a stadium. This service uses custom-built algorithms and hardware to create a person's unique palm signature.

These businesses have succeeded by identifying pain points in traditional service models and applying technology to create more efficient, accessible, and personalized experiences while maintaining consistently high service standards.

VALUE-ADDED, REVENUE-PRODUCING SERVICES

A major trend in manufacturing, information technology, and other nonservice industries is the introduction of value-added, revenue-producing services. Firms in these industries have recognized that they cannot compete on the sales and margins produced by their manufactured products alone. Many firms, such as IBM, Hewlett-Packard, Siemens, and General Electric, have integrated services into their mix of offerings.

This focus on revenue-producing services also extends to retailers. For example, PetSmart, the largest pet retailer in the United States, has introduced a host of new services in recent years as a way to compete effectively in this relatively low-margin industry. The company targets "pet parents" in its advertising, and its special services include pet training, grooming, and overnight care.

A SERVICE CULTURE THAT DIFFERENTIATES

Finally, a firm can compete by nurturing a service culture that attracts the very best workers in the industry. In attracting the best workers, the company has an advantage over the competition in terms of providing the very best services and thus becoming both the "employer of choice" and the "provider of choice" in its industry. This approach is used, for example, by Southwest Airlines, Mayo Clinic, Disney, and Marriott Hotels. At Marriott, the underlying company philosophy is "take care of your employees and they will take care of your guests." This philosophy permeates all the Marriott brands, from Fairfield Inns to the Ritz Carlton, giving Marriott a worldwide competitive advantage in its industry.

Sources: Center for Services Leadership, W. P. Carey School of Business, Arizona State University (www.wpcarey.asu.edu/csl). https://www.southwest.com/html/about-southwest/index.html; https://www.mayoclinic.org/about-mayo-clinic/mission-values; https://www.zappos.com/about/stories/customer-service-things-to-know; https://www.aboutamazon.com/news/innovation-at-amazon/introducing-amazon-one-a-new-innovation-to-make-everyday-activities-effortless

Reference: https://www.urbancompany.com/about; https://support.cure.fit/support/solutions/articles/25000006131-what-is-cult-; https://www.1mg.com/aboutUs; https://www.licious.in/about-us; https://unacademy.com/about

Insight for four ways that firms successfully and profitably compete through service. In Chapter 17 we will come back to this topic by providing integrated coverage of the financial and profit impact of service.

But "Service Stinks"

Despite the importance of quality service and the bottom-line profit potential for service, consumers perceive that overall the quality of service is not great in many companies and industries.[16] For example, we see *BusinessWeek* magazine blatantly condemning service in its cover story "Why Service Stinks," a *Wall Street Journal* editorial questioning service quality and value that is entitled "We Pay Them to Be Rude to Us," and a *Harvard Business Review* exploring the question: "Why is Customer Service so bad?"[17] And although there are exceptions in every industry, American Customer Satisfaction Index scores for service industries are on average lower than the scores for durable and nondurable products.[18]

This critique of service is troubling when, at some level, service has never been better. For example, think of just one industry—healthcare. The ability to prevent and treat diseases has never been greater, resulting in an ever-increasing life expectancy in the United States and in most other industrialized countries. Or take the communications industries—communicating quickly, effectively, and cheaply with people all over the world has never been easier. Access to vast quantities of information, entertainment, and music is unbelievable compared to what people had just 10 years ago. So clearly, in some ways and in many industries, service is better than ever.

Despite these obvious improvements, there is hard evidence that consumers are not satisfied with the services they receive from many companies and industries today. There are many plausible explanations for why this is the case, including:

- With more companies offering tiered service based on the calculated profitability of different market segments, many customers are, in fact, getting less service than they have in the past.
- Increasing use by companies of self-service and technology-based service is perceived as less service because no human interaction or human personalization is provided.
- Customers update their expectations over time; therefore, customer expectations are higher in all industries because of the excellent service they receive from some companies. Thus, they expect the same from all and are frequently disappointed.
- Organizations have cut costs to the extent that they are too lean and too understaffed to provide quality service.
- The competitive job market results in less-skilled people working in frontline service jobs; talented workers soon get promoted or leave for better opportunities.
- Many companies give lip service to customer focus and service quality, but they fail to provide the training, compensation, and support of employees needed to actually deliver quality service.

These explanations can be debated. But for managers, students, and teachers of service marketing, the message is clear: there is plenty of work to be done. In this text we will provide many examples of best practices—companies that understand how to get it right and are succeeding with service. We will also delineate many tools, concepts, and strategies that can help to reverse the "service stinks" mind-set.

SERVICE AND TECHNOLOGY

The preceding sections examined the roots of service marketing and the reasons the field and business function exist. Another major trend—technology, specifically information technology—is shaping the field and profoundly influencing the practice of service marketing. According to researchers Roland T. Rust and Ming-Hui Huang, information technology is causing a "service revolution," resulting in an expansion of the service sector and increased importance of service in all categories of the economy.[19] In this section we begin to explore trends in technology (positive *and* negative) to set the stage for topics that will be discussed throughout this text before Chapter 16 will provide a detailed examination of how comprehensively technology affects service marketing. In the subsequent chapters you will also find Technology Spotlight boxes that highlight the influence of technology on issues related to the particular chapter.

Technology-Based Service Offerings

Looking to the past, it is apparent how technology was the basic force behind service innovations now taken for granted. Cell phones, cashless payments, self-check-in at airports or self-check-out in hotels as well as grocery stores, and other common services were possible only because of new technologies. Just think how dramatically different your world would be without these basic technology services.

Now, Internet-based companies like Amazon and Google/Alphabet offer services previously unheard of and smart phones offer innumerable service applications that seemed unimaginable in the recent past. The Internet of Things (IoT), a network of physical objects that use sensors, software, and other technologies to exchange data with other devices and systems over the Internet, will further transform how people live, consume, and work in the 21st century. For example, shopping experiences will continue to evolve as people can shop in smart stores where service robots assist customers, smart shelves connect to customers' phones to display customized product pricing while also tracking store inventory levels, and customers buy items on the spot instead of standing in a checkout line (e.g., like in Amazon's Go convenience stores).[20]

Many other new technology services (e.g., in the field of Artificial Intelligence) are evolving as we write this book, and they will continue to explode on the scene at an increasingly rapid rate.[21] For example, the "connected car" allows people to access all kinds of existing and new services while on the road. Not only have cars increased self-driving capabilities, but in-car systems provide recommendations for shopping by informing drivers when they are within a certain number of miles of their preferred retailer. On a road trip, the system may provide weather forecasts and warnings, and when it is time to stop for the night, the car's system can book a room at a nearby hotel, recommend a restaurant, and make dinner reservations. Additionally, cars will offer increasingly sophisticated in-car entertainment (e.g., projected on the windshield and using virtual and augmented reality technology) that will be similar to video-game levels.

Other technological advances are making it possible for medical professionals to monitor patients' conditions remotely and even to provide medical diagnoses, treatment, and surgery guidance via technology interfaces. Similarly, large equipment

Global Feature The Impact of COVID-19 on Service Industries

As one of the worst crises in recent history, COVID-19 has had an unprecedented impact on the world; it disrupted lives and caused a severe negative impact on global economic growth. A report by the Congressional Research Services (2021) projects major advanced economies, which represent 60 percent of global economic activity, to remain operating below their potential output level through at least 2024, with negative consequences for national and individual economic welfare. Beyond its economic impact, the virus caused dramatic human costs (e.g., in terms of disease and fatalities, social unrest, personal lives or careers derailed, jobs lost).

The pandemic hit service industries particularly hard (e.g., healthcare, retail, education, logistics, entertainment, as well as hospitality and tourism). Although some individual service companies benefited from the circumstances created by the pandemic (e.g., online retailers such as Amazon), this crisis caused significant distress for service customers, service employees, and service organizations around the world, and the damage continues to unfold as we prepare this revised edition. For example, millions of employees were furloughed or lost their jobs, and others had to rapidly adjust to working online from home. In fact, the Congressional Research Services (2021, p. 2), observed that quarantines and lockdowns affected service business disproportionately, and that "job losses have been concentrated more intensively in the services sector where workers have been unable to work offsite." Other service workers in so-called essential professions (e.g., employees in healthcare, pharmacies, grocery stores) had to quickly adapt to new professional regimens and rules to fight the spread of the virus. However, as COVID-19 exposed existing vulnerabilities in some service systems, it also allowed service managers to learn from and prevent similar crises in the future. Some, but not all, service sectors were able to use technology to adjust to the circumstances of the pandemic; for example:

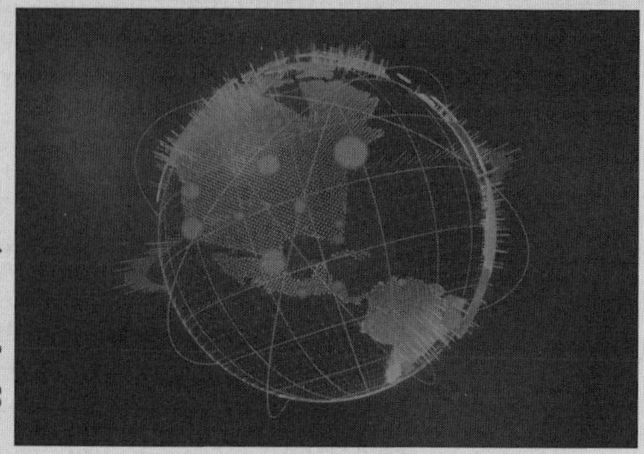

Gregg Vignal/Alamy Stock Photo

- Healthcare: Driven by the pandemic, numerous healthcare systems around the world came close to collapsing because they were not prepared to serve the overwhelming influx of patients. In parallel, many healthcare providers shifted to technology-based services in response to COVID-19. For example, there was a sharp increase in healthcare apps and the adoption of telemedicine, which not only was aligned with social distancing guidelines, but also helped to use stretched healthcare resources more efficiently.
- Education: Many countries closed their educational institutions (e.g., schools and universities) to slow the spread of the virus, which impacted millions of students and their families, as well as educators. Similar to healthcare services, many educational organizations shifted toward technology-based services (e.g., digital and online learning formats) to mitigate the impact on students' learning experience and education.

manufacturers like John Deere and Caterpillar can now remotely monitor and service equipment, as well as provide sophisticated information and data to their clients via the Internet. These services further illustrate that the IoT is generating a plethora of new service opportunities.[22] Finally, as our Global Feature further emphasizes, the COVID-19 pandemic also triggered numerous technology innovations because organizations realized that they had to swiftly adjust the way they provide service in light of the pandemic (e.g., telemedicine). In other words, the pandemic caused an accelerated adoption of emerging technologies across industries (e.g., Artificial Intelligence), which is expected to continue as organizations worldwide return to a "new post-pandemic normal."

New Ways to Deliver Service

In addition to providing opportunities for new service offerings, technology is providing approaches for delivering existing services in more accessible, convenient, and

- Tourism and Hospitality: The global travel, tourism, and hospitality industries were hit very hard. For example, flight operations were sharply restricted, and partially shut down (e.g., for airlines in the United States, passenger volume collapsed by 80 percent by June 2020 relative to the prior year). Similarly, local service businesses in tourist destinations (e.g., hotels, restaurants, museums, sports, entertainment venues) were closed for months. Not surprisingly, countries whose economies are heavily driven by tourism experienced a dramatic economic shock. Importantly, compared to the above examples of healthcare and education, it is much more challenging to use technology to mitigate the impact of the pandemic in the tourism sector (e.g., through e-tourism). However, some hospitality companies use technological innovation in response to the pandemic; for example, some hotels are now using service robots (e.g., in housekeeping and room services) to reduce human-to-human interactions.

SERVICE SHORTCOMINGS AND TECHNOLOGY ADOPTION DRIVEN BY THE PANDEMIC

The pandemic exposed shortcomings in customer service in many companies and industries. For example, a global study conducted by Salesforce among service professionals showed that 86 percent of the participants felt that the pandemic exposed service channel gaps as customers moved away from physical service locations (e.g., stores) and toward digital platforms. A similar percentage (87 percent) realized that their firm's existing policies were not suited for the pandemic circumstances (e.g., cancellation fees for events that were prohibited by public health measures such as concerts, sports events, or airline travel). Other companies were not adequately prepared to manage customer requests as they shifted to having their employees work from home. For example, as lockdowns caused consumers to shift from brick-and-mortar shopping to online and digital service platforms, customer care centers were flooded with unprecedented call volumes, while the service agents were also forced to work from home; not surprisingly, this resulted in decreased service levels (e.g., Forbes reports a +30 percent increase in hold times for customer service calls, Kulkarni 2021). In response to these challenges, many organizations realized that they had to swiftly move their customer service operations to the cloud. In other words, the pandemic has triggered an accelerated adoption of emerging technologies across industries (e.g., Artificial Intelligence), which is expected to continue as organizations worldwide are returning to a "new post-pandemic normal."

In the face of the pandemic, service managers (had to) rethink their established business approaches as they strive to better prepare their organizations for the future beyond COVID-19.

Sources: Congressional Research Service, Global Economic Effects of COVID-19, 2021, Updated June 15, 2021, https://crsreports.congress.govR46270, accessed June 17, 2021; A. Kulkarni, "Covid-19 Drives Contact Center Digitalization and Automation," *Forbes*, 2021, https://www.forbes.com/sites/forbestechcouncil/2021/02/09/covid-19-drives-contact-center-digitalization-and-automation/?sh=34004bb34195, accessed June 17, 2021; M. Taylor, "14 Industries That Have Been Hit Hardest by the Pandemic," *MSN Money*, 2020, https://www.msn.com/en-us/money/news/14-industries-that-have-been-hit-hardest-by-the-pandemic, accessed June 04, 2021; Salesforce.com, Customer Service in 2020 and Beyond: Global Study Reveals the Pandemic's Lasting Impact, https://www.salesforce.com/news/stories/4th-state-of-service/, accessed June 06, 2021; S. Xiang, S. Rasool, Y. Hang, K. Javid, T. Javed, and A. E. Artene, "The Effect of COVID-19 Pandemic on Service Sector Sustainability and Growth," *Frontiers in Psychology* (2021), 12.

productive ways. Technology facilitates basic customer service functions (bill paying, questions, checking account records, order tracking), transactions (both retail and business-to-business), and learning or information seeking. Our Technology Spotlight traces how, through history, evolving technologies have changed one aspect of service, namely, customer service. Companies have moved from face-to-face service to telephone-based service to widespread use of interactive voice response systems to Internet-based customer service and now to wireless service. Interestingly, many companies are coming full circle and now offer human contact as the ultimate form of customer service! For example, in online service encounters, customers might first interact with a Chatbot, but if that machine cannot help, it connects customers to a human employee.

Technology also facilitates transactions by offering a direct vehicle for making purchases and conducting business. In the financial services field, for example, "robo advisors" analyze information investors provide about themselves and their financial

Technology Spotlight The Changing Face of Customer Service

Excellent customer service—the daily, ongoing support of a company's offerings—is critical in creating brand identity and ultimate success for service, manufacturing, and consumer products companies. It includes answering questions, taking orders, dealing with billing issues, handling complaints, scheduling appointments, and similar activities. These essential functions can make or break an organization's relationships with its customers. Because of its importance in creating impressions and sustaining customer relationships, customer service has sometimes been called the "front door" of the organization or its "face."

So how has the "face" of customer service changed with the influx of technology? Long ago all customer service was provided face-to-face through direct personal interaction between employees and customers. To get service you had to visit stores or service providers in person. The telephone changed this, allowing customers to call companies and speak directly with employees, typically Monday–Friday, 8:00 a.m.–5:00 p.m. Customer service became less personal, but without a doubt more efficient, through use of the telephone. With the evolution of computer technology, customer service representatives (CSRs) became even more efficient. Through computer information systems and customer data files, CSRs are able to call up customer records at their workstations to answer questions on the spot.

Over time, because communication and computer technologies allowed it, large organizations began to centralize their customer service functions, consolidating into a few large call centers that could be located anywhere in the country or the world, with calls handled 24/7. But still, in these types of call centers, customer service is, for the most part, an interpersonal event, with customers talking directly, one-on-one with an employee.

The advent and rapid proliferation of the efficient, but much maligned, automated voice response systems changed personal customer service in many organizations into menu-driven, automated exchanges. In almost every industry and any business context, consumers encounter these types of systems, and many are quite frustrating—for example, when a system has a long, confusing set of menu options or when no menu option seems to fit the purpose of the call. Similarly, customers become angered when they cannot get out of the automated system easily or when there is no option to speak to a live person.

Beyond automated telecom systems, the Internet has also dramatically changed customer service for many companies. Service can now be provided on the Internet via e-mails, website robots, FAQs, and online chats. Many firms also integrate artificial intelligence and robotics into their customer service operations as a complement to human service agents such that customers are served by human-machine teams. However, human service representatives are also often replaced by increasingly sophisticated chatbots (systems designed to communicate with human users by means of natural language, frequently based on artificial intelligence). So, in these cases, not only is there no human interaction, but customers actually perform the service (largely) on their own. In other cases, there is no human involvement at all in customer service. For example, many manufacturers in business-to-business settings provide remote monitoring of equipment and automated machine-to-machine service without customer or employee intervention.

With the relentless proliferation of technology solutions, firms are finding that expectations for customer service have changed. Customers are demanding choices in how they get customer service, whether it be via phone, automated voice system, e-mail, Internet self-service, or remote machine-to-machine service. Although customers often enjoy technology-based service and even demand it in many cases, they dislike it when it does not work reliably, when it does not seem to have any advantages over the interpersonal service alternatives, and when there are no systems in place to recover from failures. Interestingly, when things do not work as they are supposed to on an Internet site or through an automated response system, customers are quick to look for more traditional interpersonal (in person or via telephone) options, coming full circle to where they started. Chapter 16 will, more broadly, examine the role of AI and robotics in service.

Sources: L. Xiao and V. Kumar, "Robotics for Customer Service: A Useful Complement or an Ultimate Substitute?," *Journal of Service Research* 24 (February 2021), pp. 9–29; M.-H. Huang and R. T. Rust, "Engaged to a Robot? The Role of AI in Service," *Journal of Service Research*, 24 (February 2021), pp. 30–41; B. Libai, Y. Bart, S. Gensler, C. Hofacker, A. Kaplan, K. Kötterheinrich, and E. Kroll, "Brave New World? On AI and the Management of Customer Relationships," *Journal of Interactive Marketing*, 51 (August 2020), pp. 44–56; J. A. Nickell, "To Voice Mail Hell and Back," *Business 2.0,* July 10, 2001, pp. 49–53; M. L. Meuter, A. L. Ostrom, R. I. Roundtree, and M. J. Bitner, "Self-Service Technologies: Understanding Customer Satisfaction with Technology-Based Service Encounters," *Journal of Marketing* 64 (July 2000), pp. 50–64; S. Ali, "If you want to Scream, Press . . . ," *The Wall Street Journal,* October 30, 2006, p. R4; J. Light, "With Customer Service, Real Person Trumps Text," *The Wall Street Journal,* April 25, 2011, p. B7.

situation and provide digital investment advice and account management services, often for a lower fee than traditional investment advisory services.[23] Technology company Intuit offers technology-based services designed to make customers' financial lives easier, including TurboTax and QuickBooks. Their free Mint app allows customers to pull all their accounts, cards, and investments into one place to track spending, create a budget, and receive bill reminders. Technology has also transformed service delivery and transactions for many business-to-business firms. For example, technology giant Cisco Systems offers virtually all its customer service and ordering functions to its business customers via technology.

Finally, technology, specifically the Internet, provides an easy way for customers to learn, do research, and collaborate with each other. For example, tens of thousands of websites currently offer health-related information. Many provide answers to specific disease, drug, and treatment questions. In a study of online healthcare information usage, the Pew organization found that, among Americans with Internet access, 80 percent had looked for health or medical information on the Web.[24] Technology also facilitates easy and direct communication from companies and individual providers to customers, resulting in new shared services such as Airbnb, Uber, and Fiverr. Collectively these types of services make up the growing "shared economy," sometimes called the Gig Economy.[25]

Enabling Both Customers and Employees

Technology enables both customers and employees to be more effective in getting and providing service.[26] Through self-service technologies, customers can serve themselves more effectively. Via online banking, customers can access their accounts, check balances, apply for loans, shift money among accounts, and take care of just about any banking need they might have—all without the assistance of the bank's employees. Online shopping and more than 1 million service applications available via the Internet and smart phones have transformed the lives of consumers. Through social media, consumers and companies can communicate and collaborate with each other as well.

For employees, technology can provide tremendous support in making them more effective and efficient in delivering service. Customer relationship management and sales support software are broad categories of technology that can aid frontline employees in providing better service. For example, firms can provide their employees with facial-expression recognition software that analyzes customer emotions and allows employees to adjust their service accordingly in real time. By having immediate access to information about their product and service offerings as well as about particular customers, employees are better able to serve them. This type of information allows employees to customize services to fit the customer's needs. They can also be much more efficient and timely than in the old days when most customer and product information was in paper files or in the heads of sales and customer service representatives.

Extending the Global Reach of Services

Technology infusion results in the potential for reaching out to customers around the globe in ways not possible before. The Internet has little to no boundaries, and therefore information, customer service, and transactions can move across countries and across continents, reaching any customer who has access to the Internet. Technology also allows employees of international companies to stay in touch easily—to share information, to ask questions, to serve on virtual teams together. All this technology facilitates the global reach as well as the effectiveness of service businesses.

The Internet *Is* a Service

An interesting way to look at the influence of technology is to realize that the Internet is just "one big service." All businesses and organizations that operate on the Internet are essentially providing services—whether they are giving information, performing basic customer service functions, facilitating transactions, or promoting social interactions among individuals. Even mobile-to-mobile or IoT offerings are all services at their core. Thus, all the tools, concepts, and strategies you learn in studying service marketing have direct application in an Internet or e-business world. Although technology and the Internet have profoundly changed how people do business and what offerings are possible, it is clear that customers still want basic service. They want what they have always wanted: dependable outcomes, easy access, responsive systems, flexibility, apologies, and compensation when things go wrong. But now they expect these outcomes from technology-based businesses and from e-commerce solutions.[27] With hindsight it is obvious that many dot-com start-ups suffered and even failed because of a lack of basic customer knowledge and failure of implementation, logistics, and service follow-up.[28]

The Paradoxes and Dark Side of Technology and Service

Although there is clearly great potential for technology to support and enhance services, there are potential negative outcomes as well. For decades, consumer researchers have pointed out the many paradoxes of technology products and services for consumers.[29] For example, one concern relates to the fact that AI improves a firm's ability to predict customer lifetime value (as further discussed in Chapter 6). This detailed understanding of which customers are most (and least) profitable can then influence the firm's customer acquisition, development, and retention, and points to risks of customer prioritization (of wealthy consumers) and service discrimination.

Relatedly, customer concerns about privacy and confidentiality raise major issues for firms as they seek to learn about and interact directly with customers through the Internet. These types of concerns are what have stymied and precluded many efforts to advance technology applications in the healthcare industry, for example. Nor are all customers equally interested in using technology as a means of interacting with companies. Research exploring "customer technology readiness" suggests that some customers are simply not interested in using or ready to use technology.[30] Employees can also be reluctant to accept and integrate technology into their work lives—especially when they perceive, rightly or wrongly, that the technology will substitute human labor and perhaps eliminate their jobs.

With technology infusion comes a loss of human contact, which many people believe is detrimental purely from a quality of life perspective. Parents may lament that their children spend hours in front of computer and smart phone screens, interacting with games, seeking information, and relating to their friends only through instant messaging, Twitter, and Facebook without any face-to-face human contact. And workers in organizations become more and more reliant on communicating through technology—even communicating via e-mail or online chat sessions with the person in the next office.

Finally, the payback in technology investments is often uncertain. It may take a long time for an investment to result in positive value in terms of productivity or customer satisfaction gains. Sometimes it never happens. For example, an *MIT Sloan Management Review*/Boston Consulting Study (based on a survey of more than 2,500 executives and 17 interviews with leading experts) found that "7 out of 10 companies report minimal or no impact from AI so far."[31]

TABLE 1.1 Comparing Characteristics of Goods and Services

Goods	Services	Resulting Implications
Tangible	Intangible	• Services cannot be inventoried. • Services cannot be easily patented. • Services cannot be readily displayed or communicated. • Pricing is difficult.
Standardized	Heterogeneous	• Service delivery and customer satisfaction depend on employee and customer actions. • Service quality depends on many uncontrollable factors. • There is no sure knowledge that the service delivered matches what was planned and promoted.
Production separate from consumption	Simultaneous production and consumption	• Customers participate in and affect the transaction. • Customers affect each other. • Employees affect the service outcome. • Decentralization may be essential. • Mass production is difficult.
Nonperish-able	Perishable	• It is difficult to synchronize supply and demand with services. • Services cannot be returned or resold. • Services for any given time-period cannot be sold or delivered at a later date.

Source: A. Parasuraman, V. A. Zeithaml, and L. L. Berry, "A Conceptual Model of Service Quality and Its Implications for Future Research." *Journal of Marketing* 49 (Fall 1985), pp. 41–50.

CHARACTERISTICS OF SERVICES

There is general agreement that differences between goods and services exist and that the distinctive characteristics discussed in this section result in challenges (as well as advantages) for managers of services.[32] It is also important to realize that each of these characteristics could be arranged on a continuum similar to the tangibility spectrum shown in Figure 1.2. That is, services tend to be more heterogeneous, more intangible, and more difficult to evaluate than goods, but the differences between goods and services are not black and white by any means.[33]

Table 1.1 summarizes the differences between goods and services and the implications of these characteristics. Many of the strategies, tools, and frameworks in this text were developed to address these characteristics. Recently it has been suggested that these distinctive characteristics should not be viewed as unique to services but that they are also relevant to goods, that "all products are services," and that "economic exchange is fundamentally about service provision."[34] This view suggests that all types of organizations may be able to gain valuable insights from service marketing frameworks, tools, and strategies.

Intangibility

The most basic distinguishing characteristic of services is intangibility. Because services are performances or actions rather than objects, they cannot be seen, felt, tasted, or touched in the same manner that you can sense tangible goods. For example, healthcare services are actions (such as surgery, diagnosis, examination, and treatment) performed by providers and directed toward patients and their families. These services cannot be seen or touched by the patient, although the patient may be able to see and touch certain tangible components of the service (like the equipment or hospital room). In fact, many services such as healthcare are difficult to grasp even mentally. Even after a diagnosis or surgery has been completed the patient may not fully comprehend the service performed, although tangible evidence of the service (e.g., incision, bandaging, pain) may be apparent.

Resulting Marketing Implications Intangibility presents several marketing challenges. Many services cannot be inventoried due to capacity constraints, and therefore fluctuations in demand are often difficult to manage. For example, there is tremendous demand for resort accommodations in Phoenix in February but little demand in July. Yet resort owners have the same number of rooms to sell year-round. Services cannot be easily patented, and new service concepts can therefore easily be copied by competitors. Services cannot be readily displayed or easily communicated to customers, so quality may be difficult for consumers to assess. Decisions about what to include in advertising and other promotional materials are challenging, as is pricing. The actual costs of a "unit of service" are hard to determine, and the price–quality relationship is complex.

Heterogeneity

Because services are performances, frequently produced, consumed, and often cocreated by humans, no two services will be precisely alike. The employees delivering the service frequently are the service in the customer's eyes, and people may differ in their performance from day to day or even hour to hour. Heterogeneity also results because no two customers are precisely alike; each will have unique demands or experience the service in a unique way. Because services are often coproduced and cocreated with customers, customer behaviors will also introduce variability and uncertainties, resulting in heterogeneity of outcomes. Thus, the heterogeneity connected with services is largely the result of human interaction (between and among employees and customers) and human behaviors, as well as all of the vagaries that accompany them. For example, a tax accountant may provide a different service experience to two different customers on the same day depending on their individual needs and personalities and on whether the accountant is interviewing them when he or she is fresh in the morning or tired at the end of a long day of meetings. Although technology can help companies manage some aspects of heterogeneity, this service characteristic still has important managerial implications.

Resulting Marketing Implications Because services are heterogeneous across time, organizations, and people, ensuring consistent service quality is challenging. Quality actually depends on many factors that cannot be fully controlled by the service supplier, such as the ability of the customer to articulate his or her needs, the ability and willingness of personnel to satisfy those needs, the presence (or absence) of other customers, and the level of demand for the service. Because of these complicating factors, the service manager cannot always know for sure that the service is being delivered in a manner consistent with what was originally planned and promoted. Sometimes services are provided by a third party, further increasing the potential heterogeneity of the offering.

Simultaneous Production and Consumption

Whereas most goods are produced first, then sold and consumed, many services are sold first and then produced and consumed simultaneously. For example, an automobile can be manufactured in Detroit, shipped to San Francisco, sold two months later, and consumed over a period of years. But restaurant services cannot be provided until they have been sold, and the dining experience is essentially produced and consumed at the same time. Frequently in service situations like the restaurant this also means that customers are present while the service is being produced and thus view and may take part in the production process as so-called coproducers or cocreators of the service, for example, by

Students in a university class cocreate their educational service experience with each other and the professor.

informing the restaurant about food allergies, or, in medical settings, by describing symptoms to the physician. Simultaneity also means that customers will frequently interact with each other during the service production process and thus may affect each other's experiences. For example, strangers seated next to each other in an airplane may well affect the nature of the service experience for each other. That passengers understand this fact is clearly apparent in the way business travelers will often go to great lengths to be sure they are not seated next to families with small children. Another outcome of simultaneous production and consumption is that service producers find themselves playing a role as part of the product itself and as an essential ingredient in the service experience for the consumer. Interestingly, with the advent of technology, many services can now be produced and consumed at different points in time, resulting in fewer challenges related to this characteristic for some providers.[35] For example, online education allows asynchronous delivery of class lectures and information.

Resulting Marketing Implications Because services often (although not always) are produced and consumed at the same time, mass production is difficult. The quality of service and customer satisfaction will be highly dependent on what happens in "real time," including actions of employees, the interactions between employees and customers, and interactions among customers themselves. Clearly the real-time nature of services also results in advantages in terms of opportunities to customize offerings for individual consumers. Simultaneous production and consumption also means that it is not usually possible to gain significant economies of scale through centralization. Often, operations need to be relatively decentralized, so that the service can be delivered directly to the customer in convenient locations, although the growth of technology-delivered services is changing this requirement for many services. Also because of simultaneous production and consumption, the customer is involved in and observes the production process and thus may affect (positively or negatively) the outcome of the service transaction.

Perishability

Perishability refers to the fact that services cannot be saved, stored, resold, or returned. A seat on an airplane or in a restaurant, an hour of a lawyer's time, or space in a shipping container not used or purchased cannot be reclaimed and used or resold at a later time. Perishability is in contrast to goods that can be stored in inventory or resold another day, or even returned if the consumer is unhappy. Would it not be nice if a bad haircut could be returned or resold to another customer? Perishability makes this action an unlikely possibility for most services.

Resulting Marketing Implications A primary issue that marketers face in relation to service perishability is the inability to inventory. Demand forecasting and creative planning for capacity utilization are therefore important and challenging decision areas. The fact that services cannot typically be returned or resold also implies a need for strong recovery strategies when things do go wrong. For example, although a bad haircut cannot be returned, the hairdresser can and should have strategies for recovering the customer's goodwill if and when such a problem occurs.

Search, Experience, and Credence Qualities

One framework for isolating differences in evaluation processes between goods and services is a classification of properties of offerings proposed by economists.[36] Economists first distinguished between two categories of properties of products: *search qualities*, attributes that a customer can determine before purchasing a product, and *experience qualities*, attributes that can be discerned only after purchase or during consumption. Search qualities include color, style, price, fit, feel, hardness, and smell; experience qualities include taste, wearability, and comfort. Products such as automobiles, clothing, furniture, and jewelry are high in search qualities because their attributes can be almost completely determined and evaluated before purchase. Products such as vacations and restaurant meals are high in experience qualities because their attributes cannot be fully known or assessed until they have been purchased and are being consumed. A third category, *credence qualities*, includes characteristics that the consumer may find impossible to evaluate even after purchase and consumption.[37] Examples of offerings high in credence qualities are appendix operations, brake relinings on a car, and computer software updates. Few consumers possess medical, mechanical, or technical skills sufficient to evaluate whether these services are necessary or are performed properly, even after they have been prescribed and produced by the provider. Consequently, customer trust toward a service provider is particularly important with increasing levels of a service's credence qualities.

Figure 1.4 arrays products that are high in search, experience, or credence qualities along a continuum of evaluation ranging from easy to evaluate to difficult to evaluate. Products high in search qualities are the easiest to evaluate (left end of the continuum). Products high in experience qualities are relatively more difficult to evaluate because they must be purchased and consumed before assessment is possible (center of the continuum). Products high in credence qualities are the most difficult to evaluate because the customer may lack sufficient knowledge to appraise

FIGURE 1.4
Continuum of Evaluation for Different Types of Products

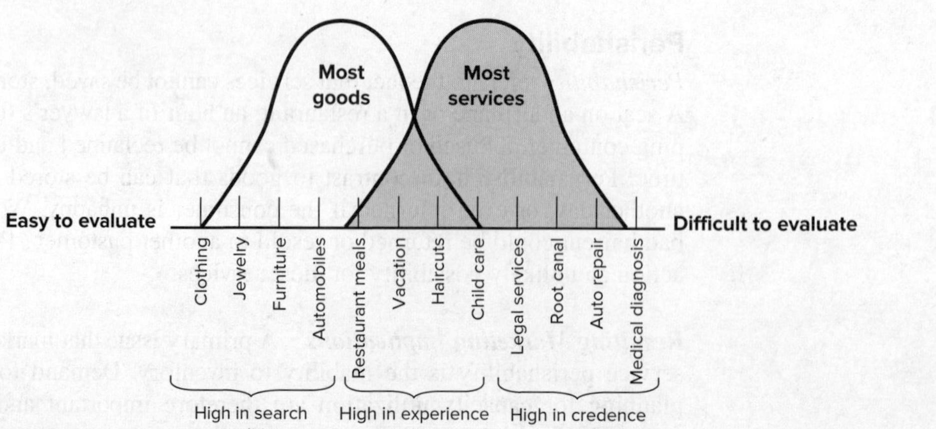

whether the offerings satisfy given wants or needs even after usage and/or consumption (right end of the continuum). Most goods fall to the left of the continuum, whereas most services fall to the right because of the characteristics of services just described. These characteristics make services more difficult to evaluate than goods, particularly in advance of purchase. Difficulty in evaluation, in turn, forces consumers to rely on different cues and processes when deciding upon and assessing services.

Challenges for Service Marketers

Because of the characteristics of services, marketers face some very distinctive challenges. Answers to questions such as the ones listed here still elude managers of services, but you will learn how to overcome these challenges in this book:

- *How can service quality be defined and improved* when the product is intangible and nonstandardized?
- *How can new services be designed and tested effectively* when the service is essentially an intangible process and one that is frequently cocreated with customers and networks of providers?
- *How can the firm be certain it is communicating a consistent and relevant image* when so many elements of the marketing mix communicate to customers and some of these elements are the service providers themselves?
- *How does the firm accommodate fluctuating demand* when capacity is fixed and the service itself is perishable?
- *How can the firm best motivate and select service employees* who, because the service is delivered in real time, become a critical part of the product itself?
- *How should prices be set* when it is difficult to determine actual costs of production and price may be inextricably intertwined with perceptions of quality?
- *How should the firm be organized so that good strategic and tactical decisions* are made when a decision in any of the functional areas of marketing, operations, and human resources may have significant impact on the other two areas?
- *How can the balance between standardization and personalization* be determined to maximize both the efficiency of the organization and the satisfaction of its customers?
- *How does the firm communicate quality and value to customers* when the offering is intangible and cannot be readily tried or displayed prior to the purchase decision?
- *How can the organization ensure the delivery and cocreation of consistent quality service* when both the organization's employees and the customers themselves can affect the service outcome?

SERVICE MARKETING MIX

The preceding questions are some of the many raised by managers of services that will be addressed throughout the text through a variety of tools and strategies. Sometimes these tools are adaptations of traditional marketing tools, as with the service marketing mix presented here. Other times they go beyond the established marketing mix, as in the case of service blueprinting presented in Chapter 8.

Traditional Marketing Mix - the 4 Ps

One of the most basic concepts in marketing is the *marketing mix,* defined as the elements an organization controls that can be used to satisfy or communicate with customers. The traditional marketing mix is composed of the four Ps: *product, place* (distribution), *promotion,* and *price*. These elements appear as core decision variables in any marketing text or marketing plan. The notion of a mix implies that all the variables are interrelated and depend on each other to some extent. Further, the marketing mix philosophy implies an optimal mix of the four factors for a given market segment at a given point in time.

Key strategy decision areas for each of the four Ps are captured in the top four groups in Table 1.2. Careful management of product, place, promotion, and price are clearly also essential to the successful marketing of services. However, the strategies for the four Ps require some modifications when applied to services. For example, traditionally promotion is thought of as involving decisions related to sales, advertising, sales promotions, and publicity. In services, these factors are also important, but because many services are produced and consumed simultaneously, service delivery

TABLE 1.2
Expanded Marketing Mix for Services and Key Strategy Decisions Related to the 7 Ps

Product	Place	Promotion	Price
Physical good features	Channel type(s)	Promotion blend	Flexibility
Quality level	Exposure	Salespeople	Price level
Accessories	Intermediaries	Selection	Terms
Packaging	Outlet locations	Training	Differentiation
Warranties	Transportation	Incentives	Discounts
Product lines	Storage	Advertising	Allowances
Branding	Managing channels	Media types	
Product-support services		Types of ads	
		Sales promotion	
		Publicity	
		Internet/Web strategy	

People	Physical Evidence	Process
Employees	Facility design	Flow of activities
Recruiting	Equipment	Standardized
Training	Signage	Customized
Motivation	Employee dress	Number of steps
Rewards	Web pages	Simple
Teamwork	Other tangibles	Complex
Customers	Reports	Customer involvement
Acquisition	Business cards	Low
Education	Statements	Medium
Training	Guarantees	High
Motivation		
Rewards		

employees (such as clerks, ticket takers, nurses, and phone personnel) are involved in realtime promotion of the service even if their jobs are typically defined in terms of the operational functions they perform.

Expanded Marketing Mix for Services - the 7 Ps

Because services are usually produced and consumed simultaneously, customers are often present in the service firm's "factory" (e.g., a doctor's office, a gym, a university auditorium), interact directly with the firm's personnel, and are actually part of the service production process. Also, because services are intangible, customers will often be looking for any tangible cue to help them understand the nature of the service experience. For example, in the hotel industry the design and decor of the hotel as well as the appearance and attitudes of its employees will influence customer perceptions and experiences.

Acknowledging the importance of these additional variables has led to the *expanded marketing mix* for services shown in the three remaining groups in Table 1.2.[38] In addition to the traditional four Ps, the services marketing mix includes *people, physical evidence,* and *process*, resulting in the 7 Ps of service marketing.

People All human actors who play a part in service delivery and thus influence the buyer's perceptions: namely, the firm's personnel, the customer, and other customers in the service environment.

All human actors participating in the delivery of a service provide cues to the customer regarding the nature of the service itself. Their attitudes and behaviors, how these people are dressed, and their personal appearance all influence the customer's perceptions of the service. In fact, for some services, such as consulting, counseling, teaching, and other professional relationship–based services, the provider *is* the service. In other cases the contact person may play what appears to be a relatively small part in service delivery—for instance, a cable service installer, an airline baggage handler, or an equipment delivery dispatcher. Yet research suggests that even these providers may be the focal point of service encounters that can prove critical for the organization.

In many service situations, customers themselves can also influence service delivery, thus affecting service quality and their own satisfaction. For example, a client of a consulting company can influence the quality of service received by providing needed and timely information and by implementing recommendations provided by the consultant. Similarly, healthcare patients greatly affect the quality of service they receive when they either comply or do not comply with health regimens prescribed by the provider.

Customers not only influence their own service outcomes, but they can influence other customers as well. In a theater, at a ballgame, in a classroom, or online, customers can influence the quality of service received by others—either enhancing or detracting from other customers' experiences.

Physical evidence The physical (and virtual) environment in which the service is delivered and where the firm and customer interact, as well as any tangible components that facilitate performance or communication of the service.

The physical evidence of service includes all the tangible representations of the service such as brochures, letterhead, business cards, reports, signage, equipment; the virtual environment includes a service organization's websites, virtual reality interfaces, as well as its apps. In some cases physical evidence includes the facility where the service is offered—the "servicescape"—for example, a retail bank branch facility. In other cases, such as telecommunication services, the physical facility is irrelevant. In this case other tangibles such as billing statements and appearance of the service vehicle and installer may be important indicators of quality. Especially when consumers have little on which to judge the actual quality of service, they will rely on such cues. Physical evidence cues provide excellent opportunities for the firm to send consistent and strong messages regarding the organization's purpose, the intended market segments, and the nature of the service.

Process The procedures, mechanisms, and flow of activities by which the service is cocreated, delivered, and/or consumed—the service delivery and operating systems.

The delivery steps that the customer experiences, or the operational flow of the service, also give customers evidence on which to judge the service. One way to think about the process design is the question whether a firm seeks to follow a highly standardized production-line approach or whether the service process should be flexible and deliberately customizable to the individual consumer. Neither option is inherently better or worse than another. Rather, the point is that these process characteristics are another form of evidence used by the customer to judge service. For example, two successful airline companies, Southwest and Singapore Airlines, follow extremely different process models. Southwest is a no-frills (no food, no assigned seats), low-priced airline that offers frequent, relatively short domestic flights. All the evidence it provides is consistent with its vision and market position, as illustrated in Exhibit 1.1. Singapore Airlines, on the other hand, focuses on the business traveler and is concerned with meeting individual traveler needs. Thus, its process is highly customized to the individual, and employees are empowered to provide nonstandard service when needed. Both airlines have been very successful.

The three new marketing mix elements (people, physical evidence, and process) are included in the marketing mix as separate elements because they are particularly salient for services, they are within the control of the firm, and any or all of them may influence the customer's initial decision to purchase a service as well as the customer's level of satisfaction and repurchase decisions. The traditional elements as well as the new service marketing mix elements will be explored in depth in subsequent chapters.

STAYING FOCUSED ON THE CUSTOMER

Consistent with contemporary views of marketing that place the customer at the center of strategy, a critical theme running throughout this text is *customer focus.*[39] In fact, the subtitle of the book is "Integrating Customer Focus Across the Firm." From the firm's point of view, this means that all strategies are developed with an eye on the customer, and all implementations are carried out with an understanding of their impact on the customer. From a practical perspective, decisions regarding new services and communication plans will integrate the customer's point of view; operations and human resource decisions will be considered in terms of their impact on customers. All the tools, strategies, and frameworks included in this text have customers at their foundation. The service marketing mix just described is a fundamental tool kit that addresses the uniqueness of services, while keeping the customer at the center.

In this text, we also view customers as assets to be valued, developed, and retained. The strategies and tools we offer thus focus on customer relationship building and loyalty as opposed to a more transactional focus in which customers are viewed as one-time revenue producers. This text looks at customer relationship management not as a software program but as an entire architecture or business philosophy. Every chapter in the text can be considered as a component needed to build a comprehensive customer relationship management system.

Exhibit 1.1 Manipal Hospitals: Aligning People, Processes, and Physical Evidence

Manipal Hospitals is a leading Indian multi-speciality healthcare provider with 37 hospitals across 19 cities and annually serving over 7 million patients with a talented pool of over 5,600 doctors and more than 18,600 employees. It is a part of the Manipal Education and Medical Group (MEMG), a leader in the areas of education and healthcare. Manipal Hospitals has emerged as India's second-largest hospital chain by masterfully integrating the three critical dimensions of service marketing: people, process, and physical evidence. This integration forms the foundation of their service excellence strategy and competitive advantage in the healthcare sector.

- **People** The people component begins with the group's meticulous approach to human resource management. The group implements rigorous selection processes to recruit medical professionals and support staff who possess technical qualifications as well as the interpersonal skills necessary for healthcare delivery. Beyond recruitment, Manipal invests heavily in continuous professional development, offering regular clinical updates, technical training, and soft skills development. This dual focus ensures staff remain at the cutting edge of medical knowledge while maintaining the empathy required for patient-centered care. Manipal further cultivates a culture where every employee, from consultant physicians to housekeeping staff, understands their role in the patient experience journey, creating a unified service approach across all touchpoints.
- **Process** Excellence at Manipal manifests through carefully designed patient pathways that minimize wait times and streamline administrative procedures. The group has implemented standardized clinical protocols across all facilities, ensuring consistent care quality regardless of location. These protocols are regularly reviewed and updated based on emerging evidence and best practices. Manipal's integration of digital technology into service delivery processes represents another significant advancement. Electronic medical records, online appointment systems, and digital diagnostic reporting create seamless information flows that support clinical decision-making while enhancing patient convenience. Quality assurance mechanisms, including regular clinical audits, infection control monitoring, and adherence to international accreditation standards like JCI and NABH, maintain process integrity and drive continuous improvement.
- **Physical evidence** The physical evidence dimension receives equal attention at Manipal facilities, where infrastructure design deliberately balances clinical functionality with patient comfort. Modern buildings featuring spacious waiting areas, private consultation rooms, and well-equipped treatment facilities provide tangible evidence of service quality. The group maintains impeccable cleanliness standards and implements thoughtful touches like clear wayfinding signage, comfortable furnishings, and nature-inspired design elements that create a healing environment. Staff uniforms, identification badges, and consistent branding across all materials from admission forms to discharge summaries further reinforce the professional image. Manipal's digital presence, including their website and patient portal, extends this physical evidence into the virtual realm, offering the same level of professionalism and accessibility.

Shutterstock

What distinguishes Manipal's approach is the alignment between these three dimensions. Their leadership has recognized that excellence cannot be achieved by focusing on any single aspect in isolation. Instead, they've created systems where processes are designed with both staff capabilities and physical constraints in mind. Training programs specifically prepare employees to execute standardized processes within the available infrastructure at different hospitals. Meanwhile, facility renovations and technology investments are prioritized based on their ability to enhance process efficiency or staff effectiveness. This systemic perspective ensures that improvements in one area complement rather than conflict with others.

The outcomes of this integrated approach are evident in Manipal's clinical metrics, patient satisfaction scores, and market growth. Patients experience a cohesive journey where staff interactions, service processes, and physical surroundings collectively communicate competence, care, and reliability. This harmony between people, process, and physical evidence has enabled Manipal to deliver consistently excellent service experiences, building trust among patients and referring physicians alike. As healthcare grows increasingly competitive and consumer-driven, Manipal's strategy of aligning these service dimensions provides a successful model for sustainable excellence.

The group continues to evolve this approach, particularly as digital transformation reshapes healthcare delivery. Telemedicine services, AI-assisted diagnostics, and remote monitoring represent new frontiers where Manipal must maintain the same careful balance between human expertise, efficient processes, and tangible quality indicators. Their ongoing success will depend on preserving this strategic alignment while adapting to emerging healthcare trends and consumer expectations.

Reference: https://www.indiaratings.co.in/pressrelease/75082
Sambit Saha (2024) 'Manipal Hospitals undertakes asset light route to expansion for greenfield ventures' The Telegraph https://www.telegraphindia.com/business/manipal-hospitals-undertakes-asset-light-route-to-expansion-for-greenfield-ventures/cid/2019906
https://www.manipalhospitals.com/about-us/
Shainesh, G. (2024), 'Interview with Dilip Jose, MD and CEO – Manipal Hospitals' https://www.edx.org/learn/marketing/indian-institute-of-management-bangalore-services-marketing-concepts-applications#syllabus

Summary

This chapter has set the stage for learning about service marketing by presenting information on changes in the world economy and business practice that have driven the focus on service: the fact that services dominate the modern economies of the world; the focus on service as a competitive business imperative; specific needs of the deregulated and professional service industries; the role of new service concepts growing from technological advances; and the realization that the characteristics of services result in unique challenges and opportunities for managers. The chapter presented a broad definition of services as deeds, processes, and performances, and it drew distinctions among pure service, value-added service, customer service, and derived service.

Building on this fundamental understanding of the service economy, the chapter presented the key characteristics of services that underlie the need for distinct strategies and concepts for managing service businesses. These basic characteristics are that services are intangible, heterogeneous, produced and consumed simultaneously, and perishable. Because of these characteristics, service managers face a number of challenges in marketing, including the complex problem of how to deliver quality services consistently.

The chapter ended by describing two themes that provide the foundation for future chapters: the expanded marketing mix for services and customer focus as a unifying theme. The remainder of the text focuses on exploring the unique opportunities and challenges faced by organizations that sell and deliver services and on developing solutions that will help you become an effective service champion and manager.

Discussion Questions

1. What distinguishes service offerings from customer service? Provide specific examples.
2. How is technology changing the nature of customer service and service offerings?
3. What are the basic characteristics of services compared with goods? What are the implications of these characteristics for Airbnb, Salesforce, Manipal Hospitals, or the company you work for?
4. One of the underlying frameworks for the text is the expanded marketing mix for services. Discuss why each of the three new mix elements (process, people, and physical evidence) is included. How might each of these communicate with or help to satisfy an organization's customers?
5. Think of a service job you have had or currently have. How effective, in your opinion, was or is the organization in managing the elements of the service marketing mix?
6. Again, think of a service job you have had or currently have. How did or does the organization handle relevant challenges listed in Table 1.1?
7. How can quality service be used in a manufacturing context for competitive advantage? Think of your answer to this question in the context of automobiles, computers, or some other manufactured product you have purchased.

Exercises

1. Roughly estimate your spending for an average month. What percentage of your spending goes for services versus goods? Do the services you purchase have value? In what sense? If you had to cut back on your expenses, what would you cut out?
2. Visit two local retail service providers that you believe are positioned very differently (such as Target and Nordstrom, or Burger King and a fine dining restaurant). From your own observations, compare their strategies on the elements of the service marketing mix.

3. Try a service you have never tried before on the Internet or on your smart phone. Analyze the benefits of this service. Was enough information provided to make the service easy to use? How would you compare this service to other methods of obtaining the same benefits?

Notes

1. Sources for Chapter Opener: S. L. Vargo, and R. R. Lusch, "Evolving to a New Dominant Logic for Marketing," *Journal of Marketing* 68 (January 2004), pp. 1–17; www.sdlogic.net; G. M. Eckhardt, M. B. Houston, B. Jiang, C. Lamberton, A. Rindfleisch, and G. Zervas, "Marketing in the Sharing Economy," *Journal of Marketing* 83, no. 5 (2019), pp. 5–27; D. Leonard and R. Clough, "Move Fast and Break Things," *Bloomberg Businessweek,* March 21–27, 2016, pp. 54–59; Fortune Magazine's World's Most Admired Companies, 2021, Source: https://fortune.com/company/marriott-international/worlds-most-admired-companies/; D. MacMillan, "Saudis Back Uber as Market Heats Up," *The Wall Street Journal,* June 2, 2016, p. A1, https://www.salesforce.com, accessed June 13th, 2021; M. Gurman, "Apple Reinvention as Services Company Starts for Real on Monday," https://www.bloomberg.com/news/articles/2019-03-23/apple-s-reinvention-as-a-services-company-starts-for-real-monday, accessed June 13th, 2021.
2. www.theacsi.org, accessed May 2016.
3. J. B. Quinn, J. J. Baruch, and P. C. Paquette, "Technology in Services," *Scientific American* 257 (December 1987), pp. 50–58.
4. S. L. Vargo, R. F. Lusch, and K. Koskela-Huotari (Eds.), *The SAGE Handbook of Service-Dominant Logic* (Sage, 2018); R. F. Lusch and S. L. Vargo, *The Service-Dominant Logic of Marketing: Dialog, Debate, and Directions* (Routledge, 2014).
5. W. M. Cox, "An Order of Prosperity to Go," *The New York Times,* February 17, 2010.
6. United States Census Bureau, "U.S. International Trade in Goods and Services, 2020," www.census.gov, accessed June 15, 2021; World's Top Export Services, available at https://www.worldstopexports.com/worlds-top-export-services/, accessed June 15, 2021.
7. M. Sawhney, S. Balasubramanian, and V. V. Krishnan, "Creating Growth with Services," *Sloan Management Review* 45 (Winter 2004), pp. 34–43.
8. For research on the topic of goods firms transitioning to services, see: V. A. Zeithaml, S. W. Brown, M. J. Bitner, and J. Salas, *Profiting from Services and Solutions: What Product-Centric Firms Need to Know* (New York, NY, Business Expert Press, 2014). R. Oliva and R. Kallenberg, "Managing the Transition from Products to Services," *International Journal of Service Industry Management* 14 (2003), pp. 160–172; W. A. Neu and S. W. Brown, "Forming Successful Business-to-Business Services in Goods-Dominant Firms," *Journal of Service Research* 8 (August 2005), pp. 3–17; W. Reinartz and W. Ulaga, "How to Sell Services More Profitably," *Harvard Business Review* 86 (May 2008), pp. 90–96; A. Gustafsson, S. Brax, and L. Witell (eds), "Service Infusion in Manufacturing Industries," special issue of the *Journal of Service Management* 21 (2010).
9. R. H. K. Vietor, *Contrived Competition* (Cambridge, MA: Harvard University Press, 1994).
10. L. Berry, *Discovering the Soul of Service* (New York: The Free Press, 1999).
11. R. T. Rust, C. Moorman, and P. R. Dickson, "Getting Return on Quality: Revenue Expansion, Cost Reduction, or Both?" *Journal of Marketing* 66 (October 2002), pp. 7–24.

12. J. L. Heskett, T. O. Jones, G. W. Loveman, W. E. Sasser Jr., and L. A. Schlesinger, "Putting the Service–Profit Chain to Work," *Harvard Business Review* 72 (March–April 1994), pp. 164–174; J. Hogreve, A. Iseke, K. Derfuss, and T. Eller, "The Service-Profit Chain: A Meta-Analytic Test of a Comprehensive Theoretical Framework," *Journal of Marketing* 81, no. 3 (2017), pp. 41–61.
13. E. W. Anderson and V. Mittal, "Strengthening the Satisfaction–Profit Chain," *Journal of Service Research* 3 (November 2000), pp. 107–120; S. Gupta and V. A. Zeithaml, "Customer Metrics and Their Impact on Financial Performance," *Marketing Science* 25 (December 2006), pp. 718–739; A. S. Otto, D. M. Szymanski, and R. Varadarajan, "Customer Satisfaction and Firm Performance: Insights from Over a Quarter Century of Empirical Research," *Journal of the Academy of Marketing Science* 48, no. 3 (2020), pp. 543–564.
14. C. Fornell, S. Mithias, F. V. Morgeson III, and M. S. Krishnan, "Customer Satisfaction and Stock Prices; High Returns, Low Risk," *Journal of Marketing* 70 (January 2006), pp. 3–14; "Economic Indicator," www.theacsi.org, accessed May 11, 2016.
15. J. L. Heskett, W. E. Sasser Jr., and L. A. Schlesinger, *What Great Service Leaders Know and Do* (Oakland, CA: Berrett-Kehler Publishers, Inc., 2015).
16. C. Fishman, "But Wait, You Promised . . . ," *Fast Company,* April 2001, pp. 116–127.
17. D. Brady, "Why Service Stinks," *BusinessWeek,* October 23, 2000, pp. 116–128; P. Noonan, "We Pay Them to Be Rude to Us," *The Wall Street Journal,* August 14–15, 2010, p. A11; A. Dukes and Y. Zhu, "Why Is Customer Service So Bad? Because It's Profitable," *Harvard Business Review*, February 28, 2019.
18. https://www.theacsi.org/about-acsi/key-acsi-findings, accessed March 03, 2021.
19. R. T. Rust and M-H Huang, "The Service Revolution and the Transformation of Marketing Science," *Marketing Science* 33 (March/April 2014), pp. 206–221.
20. D. Grewal, J. Hulland, P. Kopalle, and E. Karahanna, "The Future of Technology and Marketing: A Multidisciplinary Perspective," *Journal of the Academy of Marketing Science* 48 (January 2020), pp. 1–8; M. Taylor, D. Reilly, and C. Wren, "Internet of Things Support for Marketing Activities," *Journal of Strategic Marketing* 28 (February 2020), pp. 149–160.
21. T. H. Davenport & R. Ronanki, (2018). "Artificial intelligence for the real world." *Harvard Business Review*, 96(1), 108–116; Fountaine, T., McCarthy, B., & Saleh, T. (2019). "Building the AI-powered organization." *Harvard Business Review*, 97(4), 62–73.
22. Ibid.
23. Fidelity (2021), Robo Advisors: Affordable, Professional Investment Management, https://www.fidelity.com/learning-center/tools-demos/planning-guidance-tools/robo-advisor-vs-hybrid-robo-advisor, accessed June 14, 2021; M. E. Porter and J. E. Heppelmann, "How Smart Connected Products are Transforming Companies," *Harvard Business Review* 92 (October 2015), pp. 64–88.
24. "The Social Life of Health Information, 2011," *Pew Internet and American Life Project*, www.pewinternet.org; Schneider, Janina Anne, and Christopher Patrick Holland. "eHealth search patterns: a comparison of private and public healthcare markets using online panel data." *Journal of Medical Internet Research* 19.4 (2017): e117.

25. S. Vallas and J. B. Schor, (2020). "What do platforms do? Understanding the gig economy." *Annual Review of Sociology*, 46, 273–294; K. Steinmatz, "Exclusive: See How Big the Gig Economy Really Is," *Time*, January 6, 2016, http://time.com/4169532/sharing-economy-poll/.
26. M. J. Bitner, S. W. Brown, and M. L. Meuter, "Technology Infusion in Service Encounters," *Journal of the Academy of Marketing Science* 28 (Winter 2000), pp. 138–149.
27. M. J. Bitner, "Self-Service Technologies: What Do Customers Expect?" *Marketing Management* 10 (Spring 2001), pp. 10–11.
28. R. Hallowell, "Service in E-Commerce: Findings from Exploratory Research," *Harvard Business School,* Module Note, N9-800-418, May 31, 2000.
29. D. G. Mick and S. Fournier, "Paradoxes of Technology: Consumer Cognizance, Emotions, and Coping Strategies," *Journal of Consumer Research* 25 (September 1998), pp. 123–147. B. Libai, Y. Bart, S. Gensler, C. Hofacke, A. Kaplan, K. Kötterheinrich, and E. Kroll, "Brave New World? On AI and the Management of Customer Relationships," *Journal of Interactive Marketing* 51 (2020), pp. 44–56.
30. A. Parasuraman and C. L. Colby, *Techno-Ready Marketing: How and Why Your Customers Adopt Technology* (New York: The Free Press, 2001); A. Parasuraman and C. L. Colby, "An Updated and Streamlined Technology Readiness Index: TRI 2.0," *Journal of Service Research* 18 (February 2015), pp. 59–74.
31. S. Ransbotham, S. Khodabandeh, R. Fehling, B. LaFountain, and D. Kiron, "Winning With AI," *MIT Sloan Management Review* and Boston Consulting Group, October 2019.
32. Discussion of these issues is found in many services marketing publications. The discussion here is based on V. A. Zeithaml, A. Parasuraman, and L. L. Berry, "Problems and Strategies in Services Marketing," *Journal of Marketing* 49 (Spring 1985), pp. 33–46. For another viewpoint on the subject of goods vs. services, see: C. Lovelock and E. Gummesson, "Whither Services Marketing? In Search of a New Paradigm and Fresh Perspectives," *Journal of Service Research* 7 (August 2004), pp. 20–41. See also: K. Hellen and J. Gummerus, "Re-Investigating the Nature of Tangibility/Intangibility and Its Influence on Consumer Experiences," *Journal of Service Management* 24 (2013), pp. 130–150.
33. For research supporting the idea of goods–services continua, see D. Iacobucci, "An Empirical Examination of Some Basic Tenets in Services: Goods–Services Continua," in *Advances in Services Marketing and Management,* eds. T. A. Swartz, D. E. Bowen, and S. W. Brown (Greenwich, CT: JAI Press, 1992), vol. 1, pp. 23–52.
34. S. L. Vargo and R. F. Lusch, "The Four Service Marketing Myths," *Journal of Service Research* 6 (May 2004), pp. 324–335; S. L. Vargo, K. Koskela-Huotari, and J. Vink (2020), "Service-Dominant Logic: Foundations and Applications." In *The Routledge Handbook of Service Research Insights and Ideas*, pp. 3–23.
35. H. T. Keh and J. Pang, "Customer Reactions to Service Separation," *Journal of Marketing* 74 (March 2010), pp. 55–70.
36. P. Nelson, "Information and Consumer Behavior," *Journal of Political Economy* 78 (1970), pp. 311–329.

37. M. R. Darby and E. Karni, "Free Competition and the Optimal Amount of Fraud," *Journal of Law and Economics* 16 (April 1973), pp. 67–86.

38. B. H. Booms and M. J. Bitner, "Marketing Strategies and Organizational Structures for Service Firms," in *Marketing of Services,* eds. J. H. Donnelly and W. R. George (Chicago: American Marketing Association, 1981), pp. 47–51.

39. See: G. S. Day and C. Moorman, *Strategy from the Outside In: Profiting from Customer Value* (New York: McGraw Hill, 2010); J. Bliss, *Chief Customer Officer 2.0: How to Build Your Customer-Driven Growth Engine* (Hoboken, NJ: John Wiley & Sons, Inc., 2015).

Chapter Two

Conceptual Framework of the Book: The Gaps Model of Service Quality

This chapter's learning objectives are to:

1. Introduce the framework, called the Gaps Model of Service Quality, used to organize this textbook.
2. Demonstrate that the gaps model is a useful framework for understanding service quality in an organization.
3. Demonstrate that the most critical service quality gap to close is the customer gap, the difference between customer expectations and customer perceptions.
4. Show that four gaps that occur in companies, which we call provider gaps, are collectively responsible for the customer gap.
5. Identify the factors responsible for each of the four provider gaps.

Service Quality at Trader Joe's: The Specialty Store with Spirit

Although there is not only one effective way to provide service excellence and value, if you seek an outstanding customer experience in grocery shopping, look no further than Trader Joe's. This whimsical privately held chain of specialty food stores aims to create an outstanding customer experience around the discovery and enjoyment of amazing food and beverages. Selling approximately 85 percent private-label goods and heavily promoting exclusive product favorites (e.g., via the Annual Customer Choice Awards Winners such as the Trader Joe's Mandarin Orange Chicken, Cauliflower Gnocchi, and Dark Chocolate Peanut Butter Cups), Trader Joe's also features its own brand of service excellence unlike any other grocery store.[1]

From the moment you walk in, you feel the distinction. Stores are relatively small with a carefully selected set of fewer than 4,500 SKUs versus the typical 50,000 SKUs.

The employees are virtually all engaged in and having fun doing their jobs. If a customer asks about a product, employees are not supposed to simply point but instead walk the customer over to the location, offering to tear open a package to let the customer sample the product. Walls are decked with cedar planks, signs are hand written, and the flavor of the South Seas pervades all aspects of the stores. Sampling trendy products is happening in many aisles. Bells are ringing rather than intercoms buzzing. And the shelves are packed with innovative, tasty foods under the "Trader Joe's" name. As Beth Kowitt commented in *Fortune* magazine, ". . . Trader Joe's is no ordinary grocery chain. It's an offbeat, fun discovery zone that elevates food shopping from a chore to a cultural experience."[2]

Not only is the experience designed to be outstanding, but the company provides it all to the customer at low prices. Value is the philosophy on which the company bases its positioning—great everyday prices on all of its products. It does this by buying direct from suppliers whenever possible, bargaining hard to get the best price, purchasing in volume, contracting early to get the best prices, eliminating products that do not satisfy customers, and keeping costs in the stores low. All of these approaches result in savings to the customer.

Trader Joe's listens closely to customers using informal, qualitative research. This research is not done through focus groups or contact centers, and the company has neither a toll-free number nor a customer care e-mail address. Instead, employees and managers find out what customers want by talking to them—managers ("Captains") spend most of the day on the floor, where there are always multiple product samplings taking place, and anyone on the sales staff ("Crew Members") can directly e-mail a buyer to tell them what people are liking or not.

Besides being small, the interior of Trader Joe's is unique. Registers do not have conveyor belts and perishables are sold by unit instead of weight, which speeds up checkout. Product placement decisions are made based not on sales or profits but instead on what is best for the shopper. The Crew all wear Hawaiian shirts to evoke the image of the South Seas. The company webpage claims that they wear Hawaiian shirts because they are "traders on the culinary seas, searching the world over for cool items to bring home to [their] customers."[3] The bells are a specialty of Trader Joe's and are a simple system to communicate in the maritime tradition. One bell signals the need to open another register. Two bells indicates that there are additional questions needing to be answered at the checkout. Three bells call over a manager-type person.

How does the company get such engagement from its employees? Trader Joe's views employees as assets to be maximized and this results both in better operational efficiency and customer service, both of which generate better sales. Supervisory crew members ("Merchants" and "Mates") can start at $45,000–$75,000 per year and store managers ("Captains") can earn in the low six figures. To incentivize exceptional performance, Trader Joe's conducts performance reviews for each Crew member twice a year (on average, Crew have the potential to receive a 7 to 10 percent annual increase). The company also makes a contribution equal to 10 percent of annual compensation to retirement plans (without any obligation for Crew Members to make a matching contribution), and it offers comprehensive medical, dental, and vision plans.[4] But compensation is not the whole story. A team atmosphere pervades the Crew. All employees, including Captains, work all aspects of the store, cooperating on a myriad of jobs. Besides offering customers free samples, they hand stickers out to your fidgeting children, and refund your money if you are unhappy with a purchase, all of which is consistent with the goal of employing hard-working, fun people with a passion for food, learning, and creating delight for others.

The company is known for not spending much money on marketing and advertising and deliberately keeps a relatively low profile on social media. Most people hear about Trader Joe's through word of mouth. Virtually all the promotion comes through its zealous fan base acting as brand promoters who feature favorite snacks and experiences in their own social media. The one form of promotion is Trader Joe's Fearless Flyer comic-book-like newsletter, a quirky bulletin with amusing stories and product information.

How does Trader Joe's provide such service excellence and value? We will provide a framework for examining this question in this chapter, which specifies a conceptual framework of the book and—with it—a framework for offering service excellence to customers.

Source: https://www.traderjoes.com/digin/post/11th-customer-choice-winners

Effective service marketing is a complex undertaking that involves many different strategies, skills, and tasks. Executives of service organizations have long been confused about how to approach this complicated topic in an organized manner. This textbook is designed around one approach: viewing services in a structured, integrated way based on the *Gaps Model of Service Quality*.[5] This model systematically organizes the key concepts, strategies, and decisions in service marketing and will guide the structure of this book; sections of the book are tied to each of the gaps described in this chapter.

THE CUSTOMER GAP

The *customer gap* is the difference between customer expectations and perceptions (see Figure 2.1). Customer expectations are standards or reference points that customers bring into the service experience, whereas customer perceptions are subjective assessments of actual service experiences. In assessing a service experience, customers compare their expectations and their perceptions. Customer expectations often consist of what a customer believes should or will happen. For example, when you visit an expensive restaurant, you expect a high level of service, one that is considerably superior to the level you would expect in a fast-food restaurant. Closing the gap between what customers expect and what they perceive is critical to delivering quality service; this goal forms the basis for the gaps model.

Because customer satisfaction and customer focus are so critical to the competitiveness of firms, any company interested in delivering quality service must begin with a clear understanding of its customers. For this reason, we will devote the first

FIGURE 2.1
The Customer Gap

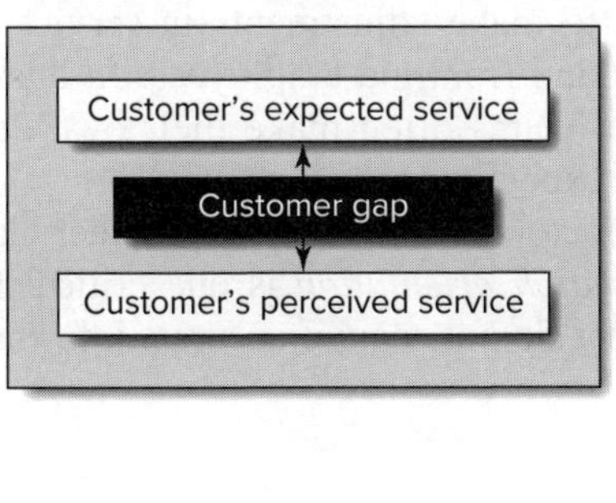

part of the textbook to describing the relevant customer concepts (e.g., customer expectations, perceived service quality, customer satisfaction, and customer loyalty), because the subsequent chapters are all grounded in these concepts. Considerable evidence exists that consumer evaluation processes differ for goods and services and that these differences affect how service providers should market their organizations.

The sources of customer expectations are marketer-controlled factors (such as pricing, advertising, and sales promises) as well as factors that marketers have limited ability to affect (innate personal needs, word-of-mouth communications, and competitive offerings). In a perfect world, expectations and perceptions would be identical: customers would perceive that they have received what they thought they would and should. In practice customer expectations and perceptions are often separated by a gap (as illustrated in Figure 2.1). Broadly, it is the goal of service marketing to close this gap, and we will devote the entire textbook to describing strategies and practices designed to close this customer gap. We will describe customer expectations in detail in Chapter 3 and customer perceptions in Chapter 4.

THE PROVIDER GAPS

To close the all-important customer gap, the gaps model suggests that four other gaps—the *provider gaps*—need to be closed. These four gaps occur within the organization providing the service (hence the term *provider gaps*) and include

Provider Gap 1: The listening gap

Provider Gap 2: The service design and standards gap

Provider Gap 3: The service performance gap

Provider Gap 4: The communication gap

The rest of this chapter is devoted to a description of the gaps model.

Provider Gap 1: The Listening Gap

Provider Gap 1, the *listening gap,* is the difference between customer expectations of service and a company's understanding of those expectations. The primary reason that many firms do not meet customers' expectations is that the firms lack an accurate understanding of exactly what those expectations are. Many reasons exist for managers not being aware of what customers expect: they may not interact directly with customers, they may be unwilling to ask about expectations, or they may be unprepared to address them. When people with the authority to set priorities and the responsibility to do so do not fully understand customers' service expectations, they may trigger a chain of bad decisions and suboptimal resource allocations that result in perceptions of poor service quality. In this text, we broaden the responsibility for the first provider gap from managers alone to any employee in the organization with the authority to change or influence service policies and procedures. In modern organizations, the authority to make adjustments in service delivery is often delegated to empowered teams and frontline employees. In business-to-business situations, in particular, account teams often make their own decisions about how to address their clients' unique expectations.

Figure 2.2 shows the key factors responsible for provider Gap 1, the listening gap. An inadequate *customer research orientation* is one critical factor. When management or empowered employees do not acquire accurate information about customers'

FIGURE 2.2
Key Factors Leading to Provider Gap 1: the Listening Gap

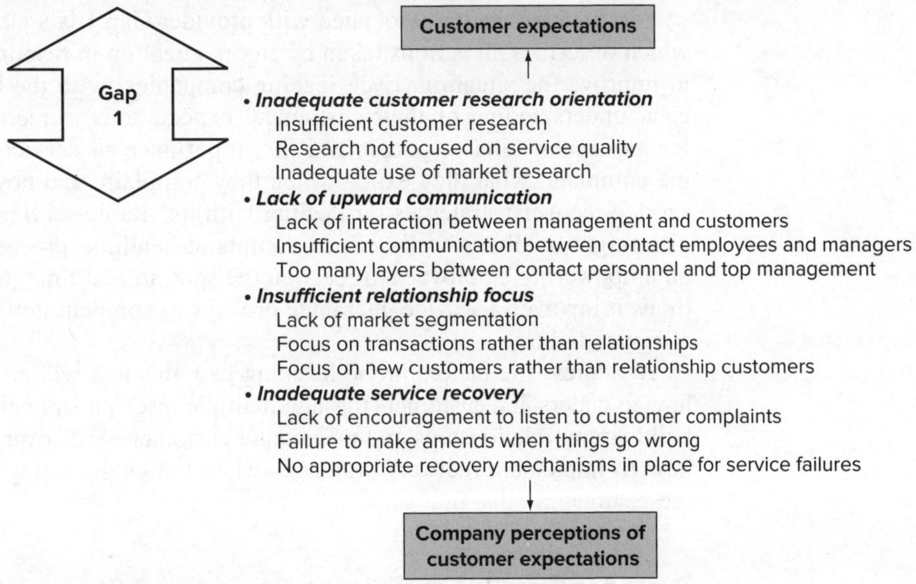

expectations, the listening gap is large. Formal and informal methods to capture information about customer expectations must be developed through customer research. Techniques involving a variety of traditional research approaches—among them customer interviews, survey research, complaint systems, and customer panels—must be used to stay close to the customer. More innovative techniques, often related to increasingly sophisticated algorithms that analyze consumer data, can also provide valuable insights about customer expectations. The Global Feature in this chapter shows how IKEA works to understand customers.

Another key factor that is related to the listening gap is lack of *upward communication*. Frontline employees often know a great deal about customers; if management is not in contact with frontline employees and does not (pro)actively strive to leverage their knowledge, the listening gap widens.

Also related to the listening gap is a lack of company strategies to retain customers and strengthen relationships with them, an approach called *relationship marketing*. When organizations have strong relationships with their customers, provider Gap 1 is less likely to occur. Relationship marketing is distinct from transactional marketing, which emphasizes acquiring new customers rather than retaining them. Relationship marketing has always been a practice of wise business-to-business firms (such as Accenture, IBM, Oracle, or SAP) that recognize that clients have the potential to spend more with them if they provide excellent service. Other business-to-business firms, and many companies that sell to end customers, often take a short-term view and see each sale as a transaction. When companies focus too much on attracting new customers, they may fail to understand the changing needs and expectations of their current customers. Technology affords companies the ability to acquire and integrate vast quantities of customer data, which can be used to build relationships. Customer loyalty programs by airlines, car rental companies, credit card companies, and hotels are among the most familiar examples of these relationship building efforts.

The final key factor associated with provider Gap 1 is a lack of *service recovery*, which describes all actions taken by an organization in response to a service failure to improve the situation. Even leading companies, with the best of intentions and clear understanding of their customers' expectations, sometimes fail. It is critical for an organization to understand the importance of service recovery—why people complain, what they expect when they complain, and how to develop effective service recovery strategies for dealing with inevitable service failures. Such strategies might involve a well-defined complaint-handling procedure and an emphasis on empowering employees to react on the spot, in real time, to fix the failure; other times it involves a service guarantee or ways to compensate the customer related to a service failure.

To address the factors in the listening gap, this text will cover topics that include how to understand customers through multiple research strategies (Chapter 5), how to build strong relationships and understand customer needs over time (Chapter 6), and how to implement recovery strategies when things go wrong (Chapter 7). Through these strategies, this first gap can be minimized.

Provider Gap 2: The Service Design and Standards Gap

Accurate perceptions of customers' expectations are necessary, but not sufficient, for delivering superior service. Another prerequisite is the presence of service designs and performance standards that reflect those accurate perceptions. A recurring theme in service companies is the difficulty experienced in translating customer expectations into service quality specifications that employees can understand and execute. These problems are reflected in provider Gap 2, the difference between company understanding of customer expectations and the development of customer-driven service designs and standards to match these customer expectations. Customer-driven standards are different from the conventional performance standards that companies establish for service in that they are based on pivotal customer requirements that are visible to and measured by customers. They are operations standards set to correspond to customer expectations and priorities rather than to company concerns such as productivity or efficiency.

As shown in Figure 2.3, provider Gap 2—which we call the *service design and standards gap*—exists in service organizations for a variety of reasons. Those people responsible for setting standards, typically management, sometimes believe that customer expectations are unreasonable or unrealistic. They may also believe that the degree of variability inherent in service defies standardization and therefore that setting standards will not achieve the desired goal. Although some of these assumptions are valid in some situations, they are often only rationalizations of management's reluctance to tackle head-on the difficult challenges of creating service standards to deliver excellent service. Technology changes and improvements are particularly helpful in closing this gap, as the Technology Spotlight in this chapter describes.

Because services are intangible, they are difficult to describe and communicate. This difficulty becomes especially evident when new services are being developed. One of the most important ways to avoid provider Gap 2 is to clearly design services without oversimplification, incompleteness, subjectivity, and bias. To do so, tools are needed to ensure that new and existing services are developed and improved in as careful a manner as possible. Chapter 8 describes the tools that are

FIGURE 2.3
Key Factors Leading to Provider Gap 2: the Service Design and Standards Gap

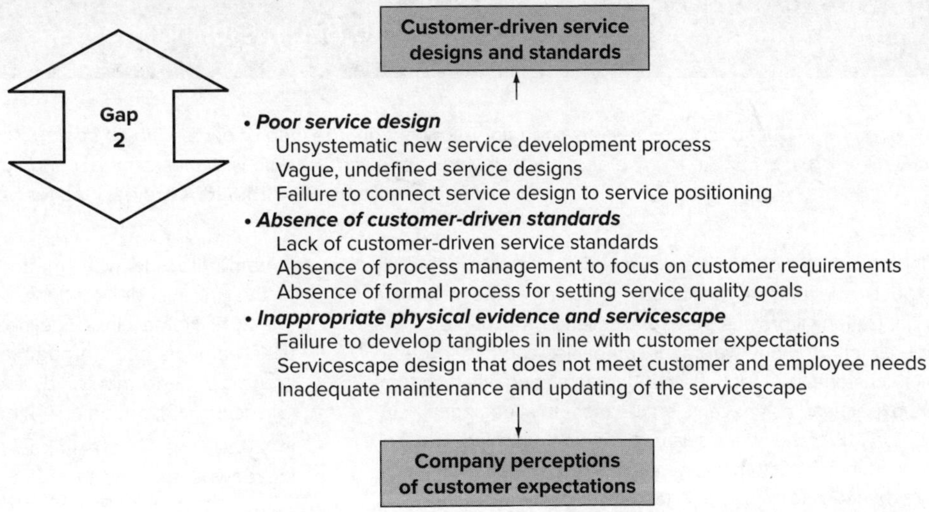

most effective in *service development and design,* including service blueprinting, a unique tool for services.

The quality of service delivered by customer contact personnel is critically influenced by the standards against which they are evaluated and compensated. Standards signal to contact personnel what management priorities are and which types of performance really count. When service standards are absent or when the standards in place do not reflect customers' expectations, quality of service as perceived by customers is likely to suffer. When standards do reflect what customers expect, perceptions of the quality of service they receive are likely to be enhanced. Chapter 9 discusses this topic of *customer-defined service standards* and shows that if they are developed appropriately they can have a powerful positive impact on closing both provider Gap 2 and thereby the customer gap.

In Chapter 10 we focus on the roles of physical evidence in service design and in meeting customer expectations. By *physical evidence,* we mean everything from business cards to reports, signage, Internet presence, equipment, and facilities used to deliver the service. The *servicescape,* the physical setting where the service is delivered, is a particular focus of Chapter 10. Think of a restaurant, a hotel, a theme park, a health club, a hospital, or a school. The servicescape—the physical facility—is critical in these settings in terms of communicating about the service and making the entire experience pleasurable. In Chapter 10, we explore the importance of physical evidence, the variety of roles it plays, and strategies for effectively designing physical evidence and the servicescape to meet customer expectations.

Provider Gap 3: The Service Performance Gap

Once service designs and standards are in place, it would seem that the firm is well on its way to delivering high-quality service. This assumption is true but is still not enough to deliver excellent service. The firm must have systems, processes, and people in place to ensure that service delivery actually matches (or is even better than) the designs and standards in place.

Global Feature How IKEA Explores Customer Needs and Expectations to Begin Closing the Gaps

"Our concept of home is changing – away from the idea of ownership, to seeing it as a service, like many digital platforms have allowed us to do with music, media and cars."
Jamiee Williams, SPACE10/IKEA project lead for Shared Living

Finding out what customers expect today, and what they likely expect in the future, is the first step in closing all the gaps in an organization to provide service excellence. In Chapter 5, we will talk about many ways that companies can use to determine customer perceptions, but understanding what customers expect and desire can often be more challenging.

For IKEA, the world's largest home furnishings retailer, understanding customer expectations is crucial, as the company's mantra is to always put customers first by providing value and service, "always in appreciation for—and solely intended to delight—its customer base" (Pontefract 2016). IKEA expects that environmental and societal shifts (e.g., urbanization, climate change, food security) will have a dramatic influence on how people live, eat, and work in the coming decades; it therefore combines qualitative and quantitative methodologies to further explore how customer expectations are changing:

- One example is IKEA's annual "Life at Home Report" (https://lifeathome.ikea.com/). For this research, the company surveys thousands of people from all-around the world and in different types of homes to explore their at-home life and what matters most to them in terms of their needs, desires, and preferences. For example, the 2018 Home Life Report revealed that people view their home largely through an emotional perspective and expect it to meet five emotional needs: (1) comfort, (2) security, (3) belonging, (4) ownership, and (5) privacy.
- In 2020, due to the impact of the pandemic-related lockdowns around the world, IKEA further enriched its approach to understanding consumers. In addition to surveying more than 38,000 people in 37 countries, the research team also regularly interviewed 20 households in six countries (Sweden, Italy, mainland China and Hong Kong SAR, Australia, USA) over a period of two months to better understand how people in different cultures experienced being locked-down at home. IKEA discovered that the vast majority of people feel emotionally closer to their homes than before the pandemic, and that many are planning to further nurture this newfound closeness to their home (a phenomenon that IKEA calls "The Big Home Reboot"). Accordingly, the 2020 Life

A healthy relationship with home satisfies a particular set of needs

Our research continues to tell us that most people experience the feeling of home when their home meets five fundamental emotional needs. With these needs met, we feel content and happy, and can really thrive in our lives there.

Recently our relationship has been tested

Over the past couple of years, we've seen a gap open up between how people expect their needs to be met by their homes, and their real experience. As a result, more and more of us have looked to social media, messaging apps, parks, friends' houses and community centres to find the feeling of home-bridging the gap our homes couldn't, by looking to the outside world.

2018

we looked beyond our four walls

A third of people all over the world told us there were places where they felt more at home than the space they lived in.

2020

we demanded much more of home

As restrictions limited our access to the outside world, it could no longer meet our needs. We were challenged to rely on home, and only home, to satisfy us. Our homes have never been under such scrutiny and intense demand to fulfil all our needs.

PRIVACY

This is being able to disconnect, reflect and choose how we interact with others. A little 'me-time' with a book or doing some exercise goes a long way.

COMFORT

This isn't about having a comfy bed or a fluffy throw, it's about feeling content and at ease in our surroundings. Knowing we can really relax and be ourselves where we live, means a lot.

OWNERSHIP

Having a sense of control over the space and place where we live is important to us. When we can paint a wall or choose our furniture, a house really starts feeling like a home.

BELONGING

This means feeling part of a group that accepts us, in a place that reflects who we are. We might get this from family or housemates, or even from friends in our community.

SECURITY

More than physical or financial security, this is about feeling safe and grounded when we're at home. When our homes feel like a sanctuary from the uncertainty of the outside world, we can really thrive there.

Back to contents

at Home report summarizes: *"Confined within our four walls all across the world, many of us have come to a realization: we want something different from our lives at home. With new priorities emerging everywhere, and at the same time, the way we will live in the future looks dramatically different."* Some of these differences result in (a) nature being more integrated into home life (e.g., homes will become lighter and greener), and (b) materials will be increasingly chosen for their hygienic properties (e.g., product designs will increasingly incorporate easy-to-clean and smart materials). Research insights such as these help IKEA understand how consumer needs and expectations can influence which products and services they would want to buy.

- Another example is IKEA's collaboration with SPACE10—a Copenhagen-based research and design lab—to better understand how people hope to live, work, and play in their homes in the future and what products they might need or desire to do that. IKEA has identified *shared living* (also called co-living) as one major trend of the future. To develop a deeper understanding of what people might expect from co-living, IKEA and SPACE10 are running "One Shared House 2030" (http://onesharedhouse2030.com). This crowdsourced research approach asks consumers from all around the world to imagine a co-living community in the year 2030, and then to define their preferences for the kinds of people they would wish to live with, the way co-living should be organized, and which home-related goods and services they would be willing to share with co-habitants. Based on respondents from more than 170 countries, the company has learned that co-living is indeed a viable option in response to increasing cost-of-living in urban areas; however, IKEA also realized that it needed to broaden the demographic scope of its thinking, because co-living is not only appealing to affluent millennials, but also to lower-income single parents, or elderly people who can often feel socially isolated.

The above examples illustrate some effective approaches to closing Gap 1 that proved successful for IKEA. The company is an impressive case study for how a sustained customer-focus, a commitment to data-driven research, and a spirit of innovation, creativity, and discovery, are the pathway to exploring, understanding, and predicting customer expectations.

IKEA has also done an excellent job of closing all four provider gaps. For example, the company's supplier network is carefully chosen and managed to ensure quality and consistency. Despite the fact that the company has stores in more than 50 countries, it keeps standards, designs, and approaches very consistent everywhere, thereby reducing the service design and standards gap (Gap 2). The company also makes important changes to its service design. For example, the company introduced a new retail concept by opening small-format stores in vibrant urban areas around the world, to become more accessible by getting closer to where many of its customers live or work. This new format is distinctly different from IKEA's traditional approach of warehouse-style locations in suburban areas, yet it is driven by the ambition to meet customer "needs in better and new ways" (Biron 2020). Regardless of which store format is considered, IKEA's servicescapes—the indoor and outdoor physical environments—are unique and customer focused, further contributing to closing Gap 2.

Volodymyr Kyrylyuk/Shutterstock

IKEA is also well known for its strong employee culture and careful hiring and training—factors that help reduce Gap 3. In Chapter 12, you will learn about another way the company closes Gap 3: its innovative service concept that involves customers in the delivery, assembly, and creation of its products. To accomplish this service, the company educates its customers thoroughly with its script-like catalogs as well as with its websites and apps, thereby helping to close Gap 4.

Sources: P. N. Danziger, "Ikea Imagines the Connected Home of the Future with Innovation Design Lab Space10," *Forbes.com,* July 11, 2020, https://www.ikea.com/kw/en/ideas/co-living-a-new-way-to-live-in-the-city-pub3dcdca71, accessed June 26, 2021; D. Pontefract, "How IKEA Delights Its Customers," *Forbes.com*, June 8, 2016, https://www.forbes.com/sites/danpontefract/2016/06/08/how-ikea-delights-its-customers/?sh=2e55f0f83ca4; https://lifeathome.ikea.com/ and https://about.ikea.com/en/life-at-home/curiosity-box/space10, accessed June 26, 2021; IKEA's future-living research lab, Space10, has launched a research project into the future of co-living, One Shared House 2030, https://www.theurbandeveloper.com/articles/ikeas-new-innovation-lab-researching-future-co-living, accessed June 26, 2021; B. Biron, "IKEA is Opening 50 Small-Format Stores Globally as it Experiments With New Retail Concepts in 'Vibrant Urban Destinations' during the Pandemic," October 6, 2020, https://www.businessinsider.com/ikea-to-open-new-stores-urban-areas-cities-amid-pandemic-2020-10?op=1, accessed June 26, 2021.

Provider Gap 3—the *service performance gap*—is the discrepancy between the development of customer-driven service standards and actual service performance by the company. Even when guidelines exist for performing services well and treating customers correctly, high-quality service performance is not a certainty. Standards must be backed by appropriate resources (people, systems, and technology) and must be enforced to be effective—that is, employees must be measured and compensated on the basis of performance along those standards. Thus, even when standards accurately reflect customers' expectations, if the company fails to provide support for those standards—if it does not facilitate, encourage, and require their achievement—standards do no good. When the level of service delivery falls short of the standards, it falls short of what customers expect as well. Narrowing the performance gap—by ensuring that all the resources needed to achieve the standards are in place—reduces the customer gap.

Research has identified many critical inhibitors to closing the *service performance gap* (see Figure 2.4). These factors include *employees* who do not clearly understand the roles they are to play in the company (i.e., role ambiguity), employees who experience conflict between customers and company management (e.g., role conflict), poor employee selection, inadequate technology, inappropriate compensation and recognition, lack of empowerment and teamwork, and the inadequate use of technology (e.g., in terms of how technology is used to measure performance or improve employee efficiency). These factors all relate to the company's human resource function and involve internal practices such as recruitment, training, feedback, job design, motivation, and organizational structure. To deliver better service

FIGURE 2.4
Key Factors Leading to Provider Gap 3: the Service Performance Gap

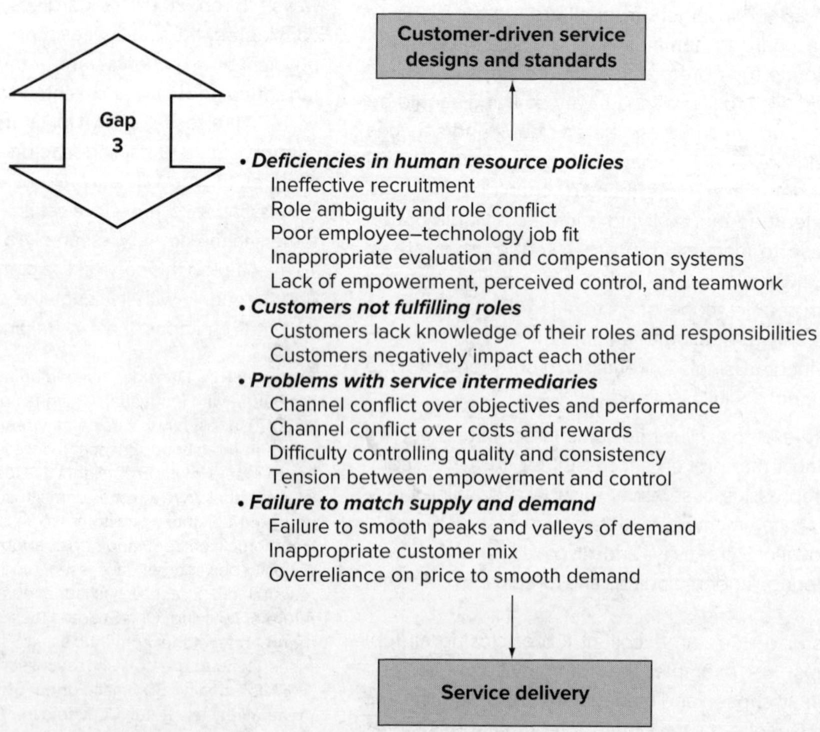

performance, these issues must be addressed across functions (such as marketing and human resources). Beyond human providers, service firms increasingly use technology-based providers (e.g., service robots), which represents a new (but rapidly evolving) area of service performance management.

Another important variable in provider Gap 3 is the *customer.* Even if frontline employees are 100 percent consistent in their service delivery, the uncontrollable behaviors of customers can introduce variability in service delivery. If customers do not perform their roles appropriately—if, for example, they fail to provide all the information necessary to the provider or neglect to read and follow instructions—service quality is jeopardized. Customers can also negatively influence the quality of service received by others if they are disruptive or take more than their share of a service provider's time. Understanding customer roles and how customers themselves can influence service delivery and outcomes is critical.

A third difficulty associated with gap 3 also involves the challenge in delivering service through such *intermediaries* as retailers, franchisees, agents, and brokers. Because quality in service occurs in the human interaction between customers and service providers, company control over the service encounter is crucial, yet it rarely is fully possible. Most service (and many manufacturing) companies face an even more formidable task: attaining service excellence and consistency in the presence of intermediaries who represent them and interact with their customers yet are not under their direct control. Franchisers of services depend on their franchisees to execute service delivery as they have specified it. And it is that execution by the franchisee which the customer uses to evaluate the service quality of the company. With franchisees and other types of intermediaries, someone other than the producer is responsible for the fulfillment of quality service. For this reason, a firm must develop ways to either control these intermediaries or motivate them to meet company goals.

Another issue in the service performance gap is the need in service firms to *synchronize demand and capacity.* Because services are perishable and cannot be inventoried, service companies frequently face situations of over- or underdemand. Lacking inventories to handle overdemand, companies lose sales when capacity is inadequate to handle customer needs. On the other hand, capacity is frequently underutilized in slow periods. Most service companies rely on operations strategies such as cross-training employees or varying the size of the employee pool to synchronize supply and demand. Marketing strategies for managing demand—such as price changes, advertising, promotion, and alternative service offerings—can supplement these approaches for managing supply.

We will discuss strategies to deal with the roles of employees in Chapter 11, customers in Chapter 12, and demand and capacity in Chapter 13.

Provider Gap 4: The Communication Gap

Provider Gap 4, the *communication gap,* illustrates the difference between the actual service delivery and the service provider's external communications. Promises made by a service company through its advertising, sales force, and other communications may raise customer expectations, the standards against which customers assess service quality. The discrepancy between actual and promised services, therefore, can widen the customer gap. Broken promises can occur for many reasons: overpromising in advertising or personal selling, inadequate coordination between operations

Technology Spotlight Technology's Critical Impact on the Gaps Model of Service Quality

Technology has relaxed the fundamental interpersonal, real-time requirements of many services, resulting in increasing accessibility and globalization of services that can now be delivered and consumed anytime, anywhere.

Technology, in particular information technology, has also dramatically influenced the nature of services themselves, how they are delivered, and the practice of service innovation and service management. Consequently, technology has had an impact on each of the gaps in the gaps model, as we will demonstrate here and throughout the book.

TECHNOLOGY'S INFLUENCE ON THE CUSTOMER GAP

Technology advances have significantly influenced the customer gap. First, the nature of services themselves have changed. Now, many services are delivered by technology rather than in person by employees. For example, McDonald's increasingly uses self-service ordering kiosks in many of their locations, thereby reducing the need for frontline employees and interpersonal interactions. Other restaurants in the fast-food and fast-casual segment (e.g., Panera) have also embraced this trend. Some restaurants even experiment with automated chefs (e.g., WhiteCastle is testing a food-preparation robot named "Flippy" that can flip and grill hamburgers). This is just one small example of the proliferation of (self-service) technologies that have changed consumers' service experiences and lives.

Technology has also dramatically changed how customers learn about services. Customers' ability to search the Web and view photos of service locations, compare prices, and even experience services through virtual tours has dramatically changed the amount and type of information customers have prior to purchasing services. The availability of this information has influenced their expectations and ability to compare and judge services. In earlier days, customers found it difficult to gather this type of information and lacked the ability to compare services as easily as they could tangible goods that were displayed side-by-side in a retail store. To some extent the Internet now provides this same type of comparability for services.

TECHNOLOGY'S INFLUENCE ON PROVIDER GAP 1

The primary way technology has influenced provider Gap 1 is in allowing firms to know their customers in ways not imagined in the past. One of the most powerful facilitators of these influences is marketing research conducted through social media such as Twitter, Facebook, and Google. On Twitter, when companies take time to respond to customers' specific tweets, particularly when they mention a problem or issue, customers feel special and that firms listened to them. One of the most important approaches is for companies to provide honest information, whether it is advice customers seek and especially if it is for a specific problem.

If you are on Facebook, you know the incredible ability of the platform to target services directly and individually to you. Facebook and other companies (e.g., Google and Amazon) use sophisticated technologies to automatically show advertisements to people who are most likely to find these ads relevant. For example, the companies can define target audiences based on various criteria (e.g., age, relationship status, ZIP code/location, interests, browsing and purchasing history); in other words, the companies merge user-generated content and personal information to deliver targeted and highly customized advertising.

Other cutting-edge technology allows brick-and-mortar stores to gather critical information about who you are and how you react to their products. For example, Walgreens is testing "smart coolers" that come equipped with digital screens as doors to display targeted ads to in-store shoppers. These smart coolers use sensors and cameras to detect shoppers and scan their faces to estimate their gender and approximate age; the system then combines this information with data about weather, time of day, and other events and delivers customized advertising messages on the digital freezer doors. The system also includes iris-tracking technology that detects which items are looked at, providing further insights into the effectiveness of such on-screen promotions. Finally, these digital screens also allow retailers to adjust their marketing in real-time (e.g., by changing pricing and promotions) in response to customers and their behavior.

TECHNOLOGY'S IMPACT ON PROVIDER GAP 2

The focus of the Design and Standards Gap was on designing interpersonal services and real-time operational processes to meet customer expectations. The variability inherent in interpersonal services made designing and standardizing them quite difficult. There is now increasing focus on technology-enabled services and processes to close provider Gap 2. Increasingly, customer expectations can be met through technology-enabled, highly standardized services provided on the Web. For example, take book sales and services provided online by Amazon (just one of its many product lines). Through its highly sophisticated technology infrastructure, the company is able to provide standardized ordering, payment, tracking, and recommendation services at the individual consumer level. Attempting to provide this level of service in a traditional book sales context to masses of people would be very idiosyncratic, inconsistent, and costly if it were done at the level Amazon performs online.

Technology has been the basic force behind service innovations now taken for granted such as Uber, Airbnb, and various smart services—for example the "connected car," smart meters for monitoring energy consumption, and remote health monitoring services. And established companies have developed brand new services based on information technology. Advances in information technology are also enabling whole suites of services in what is termed the "Internet of Things."

Technology has also facilitated the development of brand new services to meet needs and expectations that weren't even conceived of in prior decades. In healthcare, the ability to monitor patient conditions remotely and to train physicians in simulated surgical techniques via video technology are just two additional examples of technology-based services that meet customer expectations in very new and innovative ways.

TECHNOLOGY'S IMPACT ON PROVIDER GAP 3

Technology advances have allowed customer-contact employees to become more efficient and effective in serving customers. For example, today's technology allows customer service representatives to have several online "chats" with many customers simultaneously; indeed, customers often first interact with fully automated chatbots and are only transferred to a human employee if the bot cannot handle the customer's request. Such capability allows employees to resolve problems much faster, increasing employee efficiency and generally creating a more satisfying customer experience. Thus, many firms today often explore ways that technology can be used to empower employees and close the service performance gap.

Technology has also empowered customers. Through technology customers can be more involved in cocreating and even adding value to their service experience. Self-service technologies—services produced entirely by the customer without any direct involvement or interaction with the firm's employees—have also changed the way companies think about closing provider Gap 3. These technologies have proliferated as companies see the potential cost savings and efficiencies that can be achieved: potential sales growth, increased customer satisfaction, and competitive advantage. Medical websites allow patients access to information about particular diseases, drugs and drug interactions, and specific doctors and hospitals; in this case, technology enables patients to make more informed healthcare decisions. As these examples illustrate, such technological advances have facilitated customer participation in service delivery—changing the way that provider Gap 3 is conceptualized and the thinking of how it can be closed.

TECHNOLOGY'S IMPACT ON PROVIDER GAP 4

Traditional communication channels have been affected by technology infusion. There are a number of new channels that service firms can use for communicating with their customers, including social media, blogs, targeted e-mails, customer communities, and employee chat. The number of channels and modes of communication that must be integrated effectively has exploded, exacerbating the challenge of providing consistent messages across all of them. These new channels are not simply options that service firms can consider—more and more they are becoming *expected* by customers as means of communication.

Online brand communities and easy/quick mass communication via the Internet are channels that, whether provider or customer-controlled, can influence customer expectations for service firms. While it is well known that word-of-mouth (WOM) communication has always been especially important for services (whether business-to business [B2B] or business-to-consumer [B2C]), these avenues of peer-to-peer and customer-to-customer communication make WOM an even more important influence in setting expectations for services today. Technology also results in the potential for reaching out to customers around the globe in ways not possible when, in the not-so-distant past, services were limited to local provision. The Internet itself knows almost no boundaries, and therefore information, customer service, and transactions can move across countries and across continents, reaching any customer who has access to the Web.

This Technology Spotlight illustrates the profound impact of technology in recent decades on strategies associated with closing each of the provider gaps. We covered some of the examples of how technology advances and how these innovations have influenced these strategies. We will further illustrate the fundamental impact of technology on service management in the subsequent chapters, before Chapter 16 provides an even more detailed discussion of this topic.

Sources: O. Effron, "White Castle is Testing a Burger-Grilling Robot Named Flippy," https://www.cnn.com/2020/07/16/business/white-castle-flippy-robot/index.html, accessed June 24, 2021; E. Rensi, "McDonald's Says Goodbye Cashiers, Hello Kiosks," https://www.forbes.com/sites/edrensi/2018/07/11/mcdonalds-says-goodbye-cashiers-hello-kiosks/?sh=b83c1bc6f140, accessed June 24, 2021; T. Ryan, "Walgreens Tests Tech that Sort of Recognizes You In-Store," https://www.retailwire.com/discussion/walgreens-tests-tech-that-sort-of-recognizes-you-in-store/, accessed June 24, 2021; M. J. Bitner, V. A. Zeithaml, and D. D. Gremler, "Technology's Critical Impact on the Gaps Model of Service Quality," in *The Handbook of Service Science,* ed. P. Maglio, J. Spohrer, and C. Kieliszewski (Springer, Berlin, Heidelberg, Germany, 2009).

FIGURE 2.5
Key Factors Leading to Provider Gap 4: the Communication Gap

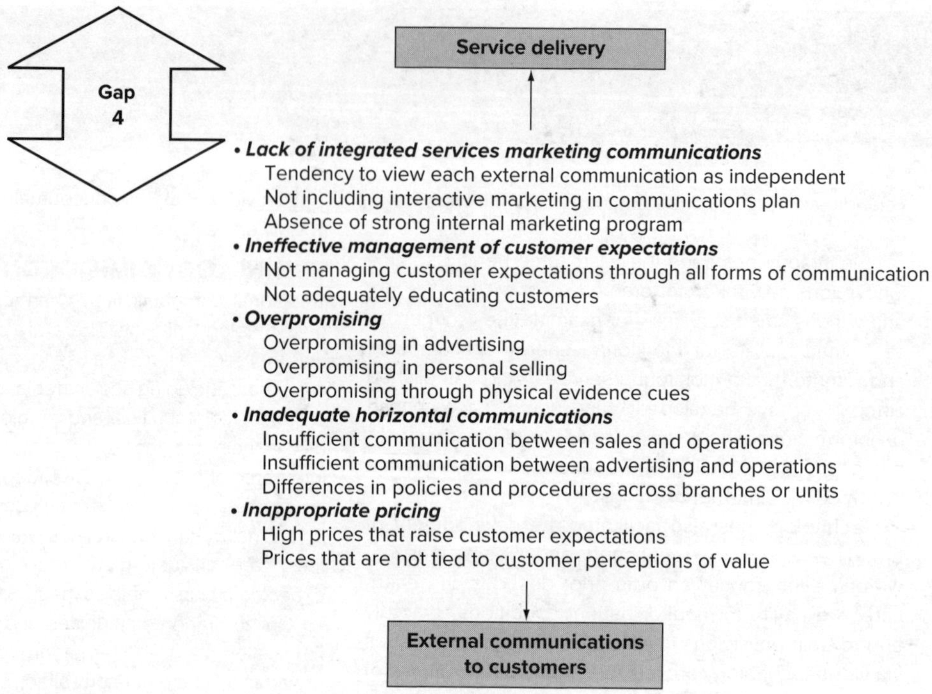

and marketing, differences in policies and procedures across service outlets, and inappropriate pricing of services. Figure 2.5 shows the key factors that lead to the communication gap.

In addition to unduly elevating expectations through exaggerated claims, there are other, less obvious ways in which external communications influence customers' service quality assessments. Service companies frequently fail to capitalize on opportunities to educate customers to use services appropriately. They also neglect to manage customer expectations of what will be delivered in service transactions and relationships.

One of the major difficulties associated with Gap 4 is that communications to consumers involve issues that cross organizational boundaries. Because service advertising promises what people do, and because what people do cannot be controlled the way machines that produce physical goods can be controlled, this type of communication involves functions other than the marketing department. This type of marketing is what we call *interactive marketing*—the marketing between contact people and customers—and it must be coordinated with the conventional types of *external marketing* used in product and service firms. When employees who promote the service do not fully understand the reality of service delivery, they are likely to make exaggerated promises or fail to communicate to customers aspects of the service intended to serve them well. The result is poor service quality perceptions. Effectively coordinating actual service delivery with external communications, therefore, narrows the communications gap and thereby favorably affects the customer gap.

Another issue in Gap 4 is associated with the pricing of services. In packaged goods (and even in durable goods), customers typically possess enough price knowledge before purchase to be able to judge whether a price is fair or in line with competition. With services, customers often have no internal reference points for prices before purchase and consumption. Pricing strategies such as discounting, "everyday prices," and couponing obviously need to be different in service situations in which the customer has little or no initial sense of prices. Techniques for developing prices for services are more complicated than those for pricing tangible goods.

In summary, external communications—whether from marketing communications or pricing—can create a larger customer gap by raising expectations about service delivery. In addition to improving service delivery, companies must also manage all communications to customers, so that inflated promises do not lead to higher expectations. Accordingly, Chapter 14 will discuss integrated service marketing communications, and Chapter 15 will cover pricing to accomplish these objectives.

PUTTING IT ALL TOGETHER: CLOSING THE GAPS

The Gaps Model of Service Quality serves as a framework for service organizations attempting to improve quality service and service marketing. The full conceptual model, shown in Figure 2.6, conveys a clear message to managers wishing to improve their quality of service: the key to closing the customer gap is to close provider Gaps 1 through 4 and keep them closed. To the extent that one or more of provider Gaps 1 through 4 exist, customers perceive service quality shortfalls. The Strategy Insight provides a *service quality gaps audit*, illustrating how the gaps model helps assess and manage an organization's service quality.

The model begins where the process of improving service quality begins: with an understanding of the nature and extent of the customer gap. Given the service organization's need to focus on the customer and to use knowledge about the customer to drive business strategy, this foundational focus on the customer gap is crucial.

FIGURE 2.6 **Gaps Model of Service Quality**

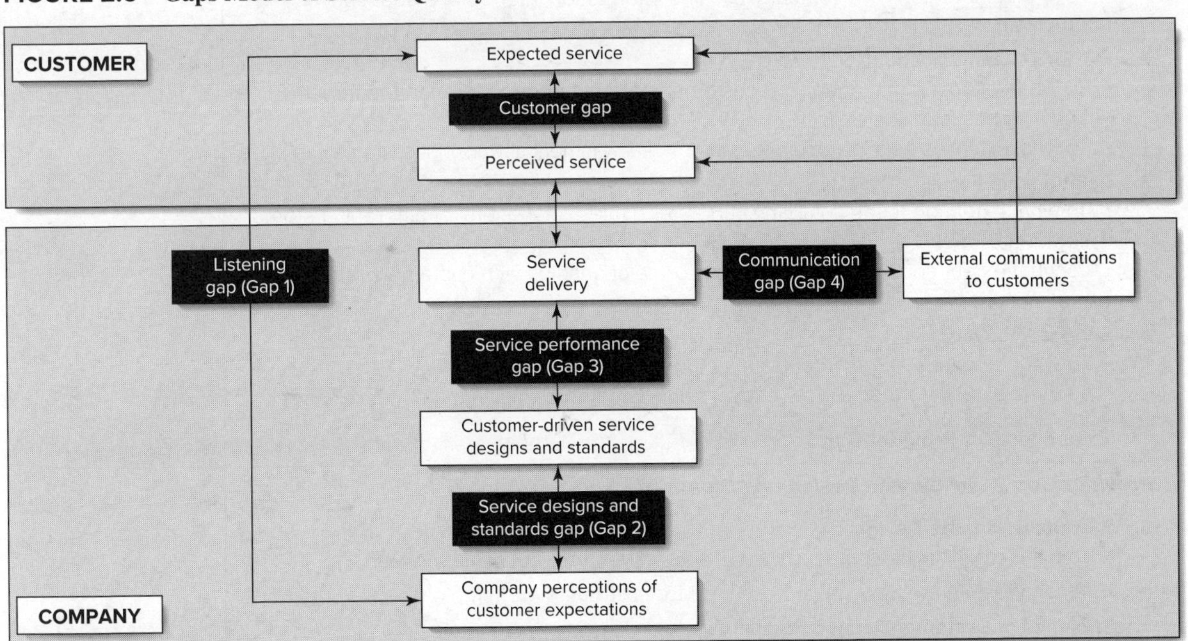

- Gap 1 can be closed through customer research (Ch. 5), relationship marketing (Ch. 6), and service recovery (Ch. 7).
- Gap 2 can be closed through service development and design (Ch. 8), customer-defined service standards (Ch. 9), and managing the physical evidence and servicescape (Ch. 10).
- Gap 3 can be closed through managing the roles of employees (Ch. 11) and customers (Ch. 12), as well as balancing demand and capacity (Ch. 13).
- Gap 4 can be closed through integrated service marketing communications (Ch. 14) and pricing of services (Ch. 15).

Strategy Insight Using the Gaps Model to Assess and Manage an Organization's Service Quality

The gaps model featured in this chapter and used as a framework for this textbook is useful to audit the service performance of an organization. The model has been used by many companies as a service audit tool because it is comprehensive and offers a way for companies to examine all the factors that influence service quality. To use the tool, a company documents what it knows about each gap and the factors that affect the size of the gap. Although you will learn much more about each of these gaps throughout the book, we provide a basic gaps audit below. In Exercise 1 at the end of this chapter, we propose that you use this audit with a company to determine its service quality gaps. As practice, you could evaluate Trader Joe's, the company featured in the opening vignette, to see how its approaches work to close each of the gaps.

Service Quality Gaps Model Audit

For each of the following factors in the gaps, indicate the effectiveness of the organization on that factor. Use a 1 to 10 scale where 10 represents "completely" and 1 represents "not at all"

Customer Gap	**10 = Completely** **1 = Not at all**
1. To what extent does the company understand customer expectations of service quality? 2. To what extent does the company understand customer perceptions of service?	
Provider Gap 1, the Listening Gap	
1. Market Research Orientation • To what extent are the amount and type of market research adequate to understand customer expectations of service? • To what extent does the company use this information in decisions about service provision?	
2. Upward Communication • To what extent do managers and customers interact enough for management to know what customers expect? • To what extent do frontline employees inform management about what customers expect?	
3. Relationship Focus • To what extent does the company understand the expectations of different customer segments? • To what extent does the company focus on relationships with customers rather than transactions?	
4. Service Recovery • To what extent does the organization plan for service failures? • To what extent are the service recovery efforts of the organization effective?	
Total Score for Provider Gap 1	
Provider Gap 2, the Service Design and Standards Gap	
5. Systematic Service Design • To what extent is the company's service development process effective? • To what extent are new services defined for customers and employees well-defined?	
6. Presence of Customer-Defined Standards • To what extent are the company's service standards effective? • To what extent do service standards correspond to customer expectations? • To what extent is the process for setting and tracking service quality goals effective?	

7. **Appropriate Physical Evidence and Servicescape** • To what extent are the company's physical facilities, equipment, and other tangibles appropriate to the service offering? • To what extent are the company's physical facilities, equipment, and other tangibles attractive and effective? **Total Score for Provider Gap 2**	
Provider Gap 3, the Service Performance Gap 8. **Effective Human Resource Policies** • To what extent is the company's recruiting, hiring, training, compensation, and empowerment of employees effective? • To what extent is service quality delivery consistent across employees, teams, units, and branches? **9. Effective Role Fulfillment by Customers** • To what extent do customers understand their roles and responsibilities? • To what extent does the company manage customers to fulfill their roles, especially customers that are incompatible? **10. Effective Alignment with Service Intermediaries** • How well are service intermediaries aligned with the company? • To what extent are objectives and performance, costs and rewards aligned effectively? • To what extent is service quality delivery consistent across the outlets? **11. Alignment of Demand and Capacity** • To what extent is the company able to match supply with demand fluctuations? **Total Score for Provider Gap 3**	
Provider Gap 4, the Communication Gap **12. Integrated Service Marketing Communications** • To what extent do all company communications—including the interactions between company employees and customers—express the same message and level of service quality? • To what extent does the company communicate to customers about what will be provided to them? • To what extent does the company avoid overpromising and overselling? • To what extent do different parts of the organization communicate with each other, so that service quality equals what is promised? **13. Pricing** • To what extent is the company careful not to price so high that customer expectations are raised? • To what extent does the company price in line with customer perceptions of value? **Total Score for Provider Gap 4**	

The score for each gap should be compared to the maximum score possible. Are particular gaps weaker than others? Which areas in each gap need attention? As you work through the rest of the book, you will learn how to improve the factors in each of the gaps.

Indian Service Strategy Insight Practo: Fulfilling Healthcare Stakeholders' Needs

Shashank ND and Abhinav Lal founded Practo in 2007 with a vision to transform healthcare in India. They focused on three core principles:

i. improve access to quality care,
ii. enhance healthcare delivery while ensuring affordability, and
iii. maintain the safety and privacy of all information exchanges.

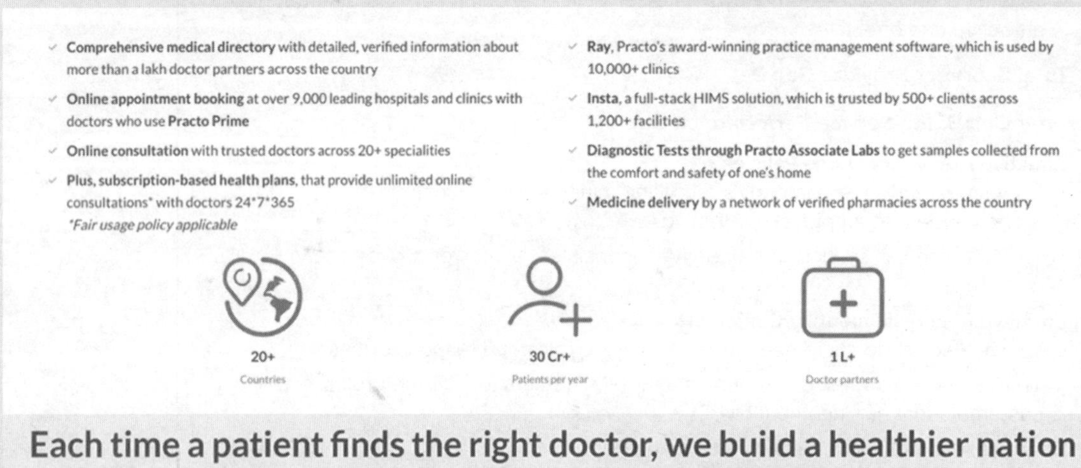

The company has emerged as one of India's leading integrated healthcare platforms, connecting over 300 million patients every year with more than 100,000 verified doctors across 20+ countries. Its growth has been driven by systematically identifying and addressing the needs and expectations of its three primary stakeholder groups: healthcare providers (mostly doctors), patients, and healthcare institutions (hospitals and larger medical facilities).

Initial Problem Identification through Immersion

Practo's approach to understanding healthcare providers' needs began with direct immersion in their daily work environment. Co-founder Shashank spent considerable time in clinics, "interacting with doctors to understand the intricacies and challenges" they faced. This field research revealed that doctors were struggling with administrative burdens that detracted from patient care. As Abhinav explains, they decided to "remove the administrative work to help manage their practice so that the doctors could focus on their expertise."

This on-the-ground research methodology allowed Practo to "look through the cracks to find out the problems in the market" rather than making assumptions sitting in a remote office. By observing clinicians in their natural setting, the founders gained authentic insights into physicians' pain points that informed the development of their first product.

Practo Ray: Responding to Physician's Administrative Burdens

The company's first offering, Practo Ray, was launched in 2008 to address the administrative challenges faced by doctors. The software as a service (SaaS) platform managed appointment scheduling, patient record maintenance, billing, accounting, and analytics for small practices. Dr. Vishwas Madhav Thakur, who has used the platform for over a decade, confirms this value proposition, noting that "Clinic management software has streamlined numerous daily operations for me. With automated appointment scheduling, billing, and patient reminders, I can focus more on patient care."

The platform specifically targeted single-doctor clinics and small practices that were underserved by existing providers of technology solutions. These practitioners needed software tailored to the Indian healthcare context rather than imported solutions designed for a different market context. By focusing on this specific segment, Practo could build customized solutions for a niche with significant unmet needs.

Ensuring Reliability and Performance

Recognizing the critical nature of healthcare operations, Practo prioritized reliability in its offerings. As Abhinav notes, "If Ray stopped working, the business for the doctors would also stop. So, we primarily focused on solving for any redundancies and challenges." This acknowledgment of the high-stakes environment in which healthcare providers operate demonstrated Practo's understanding that software failures could directly impact patient care and provider livelihoods.

Supporting Clinical Decision-Making

Beyond administrative efficiency, Practo also supports clinical decision-making through comprehensive patient data management. Dr. Vishwas emphasizes that "Having instant access to a patient's complete medical history, test results, and previous treatments helps us to make informed decisions quickly. It also helps in identifying health patterns and symptoms more effectively, leading to better outcomes for my patients." The platform's data storage capabilities allow providers to treat "each case as a unique case study for their practice and learning and also to ensure continuity of care."

Enhancing Provider Visibility and Practice Growth

Practo helps doctors expand their practices by increasing their visibility to potential patients. As Dr. Nitin Aherrao notes, "The wide network allows me to reach new patients and maintain a strong online presence." This benefit is particularly valuable for independent practitioners and smaller clinics who may lack resources for promoting their services.

Meeting Patient Expectations and Needs – Reducing Healthcare Access Barriers

From the patient perspective, Practo addresses a fundamental challenge in the Indian healthcare system: limited access to qualified medical professionals. With a doctor-population ratio of 1:834 in India, connecting patients with appropriate healthcare providers is critical. Practo's platform makes discovery and appointment booking significantly easier, particularly for the 20–30 age demographic that represents their largest user segment.

Ensuring Provider Authenticity

Patients need confidence in the qualifications of healthcare providers. Dr. Nitin highlights how Practo addresses this need: "What Practo is doing is ensuring that all good quality doctors who have authentic degrees and qualifications are there on their platform." This verification process creates trust, helping patients navigate a system where "people don't know where to go" by providing "a platform where you get all the options."

Facilitating 24/7 Healthcare Access

Recognizing that health needs do not follow business hours, Practo launched its mobile app around 2012 to "ensure that patients had 24x7 access to healthcare." This always-available approach acknowledges the anxiety that often accompanies healthcare needs and provides reassurance through continuous accessibility.

Creating a Streamlined Patient Journey

Practo maps "the entire journey of a patient, right from booking an appointment, finding a doctor or a diagnostic lab, getting a second opinion, patient experience feedback, medicine reminder, to delivering medicine at the patient's doorstep." This comprehensive approach removes friction from the healthcare experience, addressing patient desires for convenience and simplicity.

Expanding Telemedicine Access

The COVID-19 pandemic accelerated patient demand for remote healthcare options. Practo responded by expanding its telemedicine offerings, which experienced "an average increase of over 100 percent per week" during the early pandemic period. What had previously been "a convenience" rapidly became "a necessity." Particularly important was the platform's reach into underserved areas, with "close to 50 percent of all tele-consult requests" coming from Tier-II and III cities.

Addressing Healthcare Institution Requirements – Integrating with Existing Systems

For larger healthcare institutions like hospitals, system integration capabilities are essential. Practo accommodates this need through "API (application programming interfaces) integration helps connect and solve for online appointment booking and real-time availability, specially for large hospitals." This technical flexibility allows Practo to serve organizations with existing infrastructure while still providing value.

Supporting Data Security and Compliance

Healthcare institutions face stringent regulatory requirements regarding data security. Practo addresses these concerns by encrypting "all data with 256-bit encryption, uses HIPAA-compliant data centers, and is one of the few healthcare companies to be ISO 27001 certified." Dr. Vishwas confirms the importance of this approach, noting that "We keep close watch on data handling and all vital information stored with us like a locker of a bank, safe and secure."

Providing Business Intelligence

Healthcare facilities benefit from the data insights Practo generates. The platform "leverages the data providing valuable insights into patient trends and outcomes," which aids not only in clinical decision-making but also in business operations. These analytics help institutions understand patient flow, appointment adherence, and other key performance indicators.

Balancing Stakeholder Interests Through Platform Design – Two-Sided Market Approach

Practo has designed its business model to balance the needs of its various stakeholders. It has "deeply subsidized the consumer's part of the network" while generating revenue primarily from healthcare providers through SaaS subscription fees. For patients, "the listings are free, and the company doesn't charge any commissions." This approach increases platform adoption while ensuring financial sustainability.

Creating Platform Stickiness

To retain stakeholders, Practo has focused on making its platform "sticky" through data continuity and service breadth. For doctors, the platform's comprehensive patient history capabilities and efficient operations make switching costs high. For patients, "storing health records securely" in a country without "a national system" creates significant value that discourages multi-homing behavior.

Conclusion

Practo's success in addressing diverse stakeholder needs stems from its methodical approach to understanding user requirements before building solutions. By immersing themselves in the healthcare environment, the founders identified genuine pain points rather than assumed problems. They then developed targeted solutions for different stakeholder groups while creating a unified platform that facilitates interaction between these groups.

The company's evolution from a clinic management software provider to a comprehensive healthcare platform demonstrates how deeply understanding stakeholder needs can drive product development and market expansion. By prioritizing reliability, data security, accessibility, and clinical utility, Practo has positioned itself as a trusted intermediary in India's healthcare ecosystem.

With 10 million hours of doctor consultation monthly, Practo has achieved significant scale by consistently addressing the needs and expectations of doctors, patients, and healthcare institutions. As co-founder Abhinav concludes, "Healthcare is a vast space and we can solve a lot of real problems. We have the responsibility to solve them in the right way."

Reference:

https://www.practo.com/company/about
https://yourstory.com/2020/09/product-roadmap-practo-saas-platform-doctors-healthtech-b2c
https://blog.practo.com/the-evolving-relationship-of-doctors-and-patients-in-an-era-of-digital-healthcare/
https://d3.harvard.edu/platform-digit/submission/practo-indias-home-for-health/

Summary

This chapter presented the Gaps Model of Service Quality (shown in Figure 2.6), a framework for understanding and improving service delivery. The entire book will be organized around this model of service quality, which focuses on five pivotal gaps in delivering and marketing service:

The customer gap: the difference between customer expectations and perceptions
Provider Gap 1: the listening gap
Provider Gap 2: the service design and standards gap
Provider Gap 3: the service performance gap
Provider Gap 4: the communication gap

The gaps model positions the key concepts, strategies, and decisions in service marketing in a manner that begins with the customer and builds the organization's tasks around what is needed to close the gap between customer expectations and perceptions; this will be the focus of Chapters 3 through 15. Then, Chapter 16 will further highlight the crucial role of emerging technologies (e.g., AI and robotics) for service management. The final chapter in the book, Chapter 17, discusses the financial implications of service quality, reviewing the research and company data that indicates linkages between service quality and financial performance.

Discussion Questions

1. Think about a service you receive. Is there a gap between your expectations and perceptions of that service? What do you expect that you do not receive?
2. Consider the discussion about IKEA in the Global Feature and its various approaches to understanding customer expectations, needs, and desires. Think about a service that you receive regularly and imagine you need to examine customer expectations in that service context. How would you explore customer expectations and how would you change the service and the way it is provided?
3. If you were the manager of a service organization and wanted to apply the gaps model to improve service, which gap would you start with? Why? In what order would you proceed to close the gaps?
4. Can provider Gap 4, the communication gap, be closed prior to closing any of the other three provider gaps? How?
5. Which of the four provider gaps do you believe is hardest to close? Why?

Exercises

1. Choose an organization to interview, and use the Gaps Model of Service Quality as a framework. Ask the manager whether the organization suffers from any of the factors listed in the figures in this chapter. Which factor in each of Figures 2.2 through 2.5 does the manager consider the most troublesome? What does the company do to try to address the problems?
2. Visit the website of Amazon, Disney, Marriott, Ritz-Carlton, Southwest Airlines, or any other well-known, high-quality service organization. Which provider gaps has the company closed? How can you tell?
3. Interview a nonprofit or public sector organization in your area (it could be some part of your school if it is a state school). Find out if the Gaps Model of Service Quality makes sense in the context of its organization.

Notes

1. Dunnhumby, Trader Joe's Repeats as Top U.S. Grocery Retailer in the dunnhumby Retailer Preference Index, 2019, https://www.businesswire.com/news/home/20190109005221/en/Trader-Joe%E2%80%99s-Repeats-Top-U.S.-Grocery-Retailer, accessed June 20, 2021; A. Felsted and S. Halzack, "The Future of Trader Joe's Looks Bumpy," *Bloomberg*, 2020, https://www.bloomberg.com/opinion/articles/2020-08-21/the-post-pandemic-future-of-trader-joe-s-looks-bumpy, accessed June 20, 2021.
2. B. Kowitt, *Fortune Magazine,* September 6, 2010, p. 87.
3. Trader Joe's webpage www.traderjoes.com, accessed March 29, 2016.
4. www.traderjoes.com/careers, accessed March 8, 2021.
5. The gaps model of service quality that provides the structure for this text was developed by and is fully presented in V. A. Zeithaml, A. Parasuraman, and L. L. Berry, *Delivering Quality Service: Balancing Customer Perceptions and Expectations* (New York: The Free Press, 1990).

Part Two

Focus on the Customer

THE CUSTOMER GAP

The figure shows the part of the Gaps Model of Service Quality that correspond to two concepts—*customer expectations* and *customer perceptions*—that play a major role in service marketing. Customer expectations are the standards of performance or reference points for performance against which service experiences are compared, and they are often formulated in terms of what a customer believes should or will happen. Customer perceptions are subjective assessments of actual service experiences.

The Customer Gap

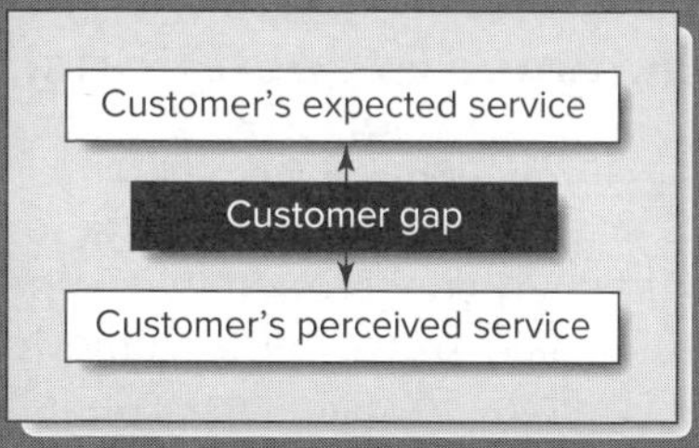

We devote the second part of the textbook to describing this gap and other relevant customer concepts because excellent service marketing requires a focus on the customer. We detail what is known about customer expectations in Chapter 3 and customer perceptions in Chapter 4. Knowing what customers want and how they assess what they receive is the foundation for designing effective, quality services.

Chapter Three

Customer Expectations of Service

This chapter's learning objectives are to:

1. Recognize that customers hold different types of expectations for service performance.
2. Discuss several sources of customer expectations of service.
3. Acknowledge that the types and sources of expectations are similar for end consumers and business customers, for pure service and product-related service, for experienced customers and inexperienced customers.
4. Delineate some important issues surrounding customer expectations.

How Technology and Competition Drive Up Customer Expectations![1]

For many companies, the platform for their success is no longer only their focal products or services; instead, it is the overall customer experience they deliver. Indeed, a study by Gartner found that 81 percent of marketers believe their company competes mostly based on customer experiences. The reason for this strategic focus is that improved customer experiences increase customer loyalty and firm revenue (as we further discuss in Chapter 4). But, it is nearly impossible for organizations to effectively design great experiences if they do not understand their customers' expectations, what influences these expectations, and how these expectations might change over time.

Knowing what customers expect is important for all businesses. Therefore, we underscore the importance of understanding customer expectations, because only if managers know what customers expect can they take steps to meet and exceed these expectations. However, what keeps (even the most excellent) service companies on their toes is the reality that customer expectations are constantly changing, increasingly driven by technological evolution and the competitive landscape, as we briefly illustrate:

1. **Technological evolution:** Based on rapid technological progress, what customers consider cutting-edge products and services today may be barely acceptable in the near future. To illustrate: when online retailers introduced "next day

delivery" a few years ago, customers were delighted by this service. Today, many customers in the United States consider this "normal" and may be disappointed if delivery takes longer than a couple of days. Or, in some European countries, same-day delivery might still delight customers; but in China, Alibaba's supermarket chain Freshippo offers 30-minute delivery for customers who live within a 3 km (~1.9 miles) radius of the nearest Freshippo supermarket. Another technology-driven expectation is the "shareability" of experiences. With the importance of social media, customers increasingly expect to be able to "share" their service experiences by showing friends and families every aspect of it via videos and photos.

2. **Competitive landscape and inter-industry comparison:** In modern marketplaces, where disruptive companies leverage sophisticated technologies (e.g., artificial intelligence, cloud computing, social media) to provide highly personalized, value-driven, convenient, and instant experiences, customers often expect similarly outstanding service from other businesses they interact with. That is, the expectations customers have with one service industry often surface for other service industries. For example, in one study, 62 percent of customers reported that their experiences with one industry influence their expectations of others. Accordingly, the experience people have with a hotel may very well affect the expectations they have toward a hospital. This challenging reality means that customer expectations continue to elevate, and managers must look outside their own industry to understand shifts in customer expectations and emerging benchmarks. One famous example of this phenomenon is the Amazon Effect.
3. **The Amazon Effect and customer expectations:** This effect describes a systematic upshift of customer expectations due to Amazon's way of doing business. Analysts named this effect after Amazon because the company has effectively created the expectation that customers should be able to buy and arrange delivery of their order with just a few clicks and from the comfort of their home. In short: Amazon boosted customer expectations in terms of product availability, speed of delivery, price confidence, and a service culture that errs on the side of the customer. After experiencing Amazon's service, millions of consumers have transferred their high expectations to other companies. This phenomenon turns out to be an effective competitive weapon for Amazon because most of its rivals find it difficult to provide a similar customer experience without undermining their profitability. As a consequence, it is almost always more convenient and cheaper for consumers to order from Amazon. And, the Amazon effect extends beyond online retailing; for example, consumers also expect that they can pre-order their coffee with their phone and then pick it up on their way to work.

Analyzing the current marketplace, one observer concluded: "**There's only one direction that customer expectations go: UP!**" This trend is crucial for managers to note because Salesforce Research found that 76 percent of customers believe it is easier than ever to take their business elsewhere if their current service provider cannot meet their expectations. This insight helps explain why Amazon is so vigorously focused on understanding and exceeding customer expectations; as Amazon founder Jeff Bezos indicates: "Our customers are loyal to us right up until the second somebody offers them a better service."

Source: D. Nas, How Technology is Changing Customer Expectations, Medium.com

Customer expectations are beliefs about service delivery that serve as standards or reference points against which performance is judged. Because customers compare their perceptions of performance with these reference points when evaluating service quality, thorough knowledge about customer expectations is critical to service marketers. Knowing what the customer expects is the first and possibly most critical step in delivering quality service. Being wrong about what customers want can mean losing a customer's business when another company hits the target exactly. Being wrong can also mean expending money, time, and other resources on things that are relatively less important (or even unimportant) to customers. Being wrong can even mean not surviving in a fiercely competitive market.

Among the aspects of expectations that need to be understood for successful service marketing are the following: What types of expectations do customers hold about service? What factors most influence the formation of these expectations? How can a service company meet or exceed customer expectations?

In this chapter we provide a framework for understanding customer expectations.[2] The chapter is divided into three main sections: (1) types of expected service, (2) factors that influence customer expectations of service, and (3) issues involving customers' service expectations.

SERVICE EXPECTATIONS

To say that expectations are reference points against which service delivery is compared is only a beginning. The level of expectation can vary depending on the reference point the customer holds. Although most everyone has an intuitive sense of what expectations are, service marketers need a more thorough and clear definition of expectations to comprehend, measure, and manage them. Therefore, we start this chapter by talking about the types of expectations.

Types of Expectations

Customers hold different types of expectations about service. For purposes of our discussion in the rest of this chapter, we focus on two types. The highest expectations can be termed *desired service*: the level of service the customer hopes to receive—the "wished for" level of performance. Desired service is a blend of what the customer believes "can be" and "should be" provided.[3] For example, consumers who sign up for an online dating service expect to find compatible, attractive, interesting people to date and perhaps even someone to marry. This expectation reflects the hopes and wishes of these consumers. In a similar way, seniors in college are likely to engage the services of their college's placement office as they approach graduation. What are students' expectations of this service? In all likelihood students want the office to help find them a job—the right job in the right place for the right salary—because that is what they hope and wish for.

However, students might also see that the economy may constrain the availability of ideal job openings in companies. And not all companies that students may be interested in have a relationship with their university's placement office. In this situation and in general, customers hope to achieve their service desires but recognize this is not always possible. Thus, we call the threshold level of acceptable service *adequate service*—the minimum level of service the customer will accept.[4] Sometimes when there is a slowdown in the economy, many college graduates who have trained for high-skilled jobs accept entry-level positions at fast-food restaurants or internships for

FIGURE 3.1
Dual Customer Expectation Levels

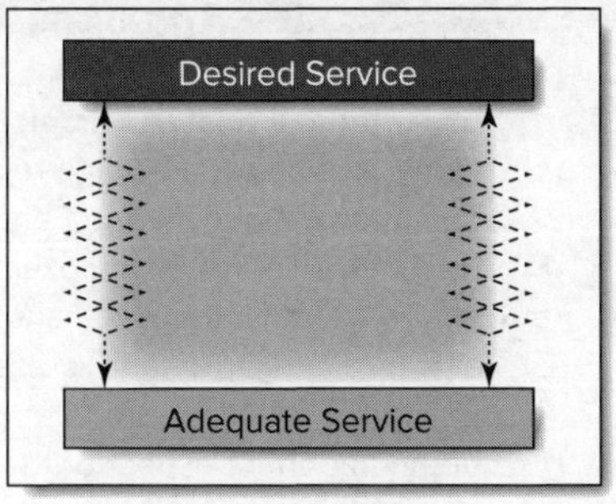

no pay. Their hopes and desires are still high, but they recognize that they cannot attain those desires in the market that exists at the time. Their standard of adequate service from the placement office is much lower than their desired service. Some graduates accept any job for which they can earn a salary, and others agree to nonpaying, short-term positions as interns to gain experience. Adequate service expectations represent the "minimum tolerable expectation,"[5] the bottom level of performance acceptable to the customer.

Figure 3.1 shows these two expectation levels as the upper and lower boundaries for customer expectations. This figure portrays the idea that customers assess service performance on the basis of two boundaries: what they desire and what they deem acceptable; Figure 3.1 also illustrates that these two expectations levels can vary (as depicted by the "dotted springs"). This chapter's Global Feature illustrates some of the challenges firms face in understanding what customers' expectations are, particularly when delivering service to customers in or from another culture.

The Zone of Tolerance

As we discussed in Chapter 1, services are heterogeneous in that performance may vary across providers, across employees from the same provider, and even with the same service employee. The extent to which customers recognize and are willing to accept this variation is called the *zone of tolerance* and is shown in Figure 3.2. If service drops below adequate service—the minimum level considered acceptable—customers will most likely be dissatisfied with the company. If service performance is above the zone of tolerance at the top end—where performance exceeds desired service—customers will be very pleased and maybe pleasantly surprised as well. You might consider the zone of tolerance as the range in which customers do not particularly notice service performance. However, when it falls outside the range (either very low or very high), the service gets the customer's attention in either a positive

FIGURE 3.2
The Zone of Tolerance

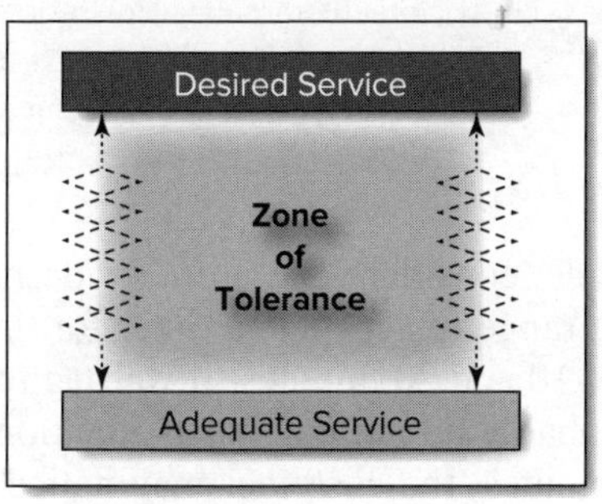

Global Feature Culture and Customer Expectations

This chapter emphasizes the importance of understanding customer expectations for companies to provide effective service. In the global economy, many companies serve customers with different cultural orientations either in international or domestic markets (e.g., consider the increase in migrant workers, students, and tourists). Therefore, managers need to understand how culture can influence customer expectations.

CULTURE AND ITS INFLUENCE ON CUSTOMER EXPECTATIONS

Culture can be described as a set of shared beliefs, norms, and values that influence human behavior and determine the extent to which certain behaviors are acceptable (e.g., shared values related to independence, gender, age).* It is crucial for organizations to understand the cultural expectations and preferences of customers; failing to do that can cost businesses money. Our goal is to pique your curiosity by illustrating some differences in what customers expect in different cultures:

- **Expectations in Service Encounters:** Interpersonal communication matters in many services and culture can influence communication-related expectations. For example, Germans tend to expect a formal tone of communication (e.g., using the formal "Sie or Frau/Herr," which is equivalent to "Ms./Mr."). In contrast, Americans often expect a casual tone in many service settings (e.g., using first names). Moreover, it is a common expectation that store employees in the United States proactively approach customers (e.g., with "How are you? Are you finding everything ok?"), whereas in the United Kingdom customers do not expect to be approached by employees without prompting it.
- **Expectations of "The Customer is King":** Related to communication is the expectation in some cultures that "The Customer is Always Right" or "The Customer is King." This expectation is more common in countries with high levels of consumerism, where customers have more power and therefore expect to be served in a timely manner as well as having the service tailored to their individual needs and preferences. In other countries (e.g., parts of eastern Europe) consumerism is not as prevalent and customers tend to expect that they might have to wait for service and that not all their desires can or will be fulfilled.
- **Expectations related to Colors:** Culture also influences some less-obvious service-related aspects such as colors, because people in different countries perceive certain colors differently. For example, orange is the national color of The Netherlands and it is linked to Dutch Royalty. In contrast, orange is associated with mourning in Egypt. As you will learn later (in Chapter 10), colors can be an important aspect of the physical evidence in servicescapes (e.g., when firms select the color schemes of stores, employee uniforms, or online/social media presence). Managers should note that customers can make inferences about service firms based on how cultural expectations shape the perception of certain colors.

MODELS ON CULTURAL DIMENSIONS AND IMPLICATIONS FOR CUSTOMER EXPECTATIONS

Managers can draw on research-based models to understand cultures. For example, one such model is called the "7 Dimensions of Culture"; it was developed by Trompenaar and Hamden-Turner (https://www3.thtconsulting.com/) who surveyed more than 40,000 managers from 40 countries to better understand how people from different cultures can work together more effectively. Another prominent model was develop by Hofstede based on surveying over 88,000 IBM employees in 72 countries (https://geerthofstede.com). This model distinguishes six dimensions, which allow profiling and comparing countries (see the figure on next page).

Below, we briefly discuss one of Hofstede's dimensions, power distance, in the context of service delivery in Nigeria. With a population of more than 200 million people, Nigeria is Africa's most populous nation. Nigeria is a complex cultural context for companies, yet it offers significant business potential. To succeed, firms must understand how Nigerian culture influences customer expectations.

Power distance describes the extent to which less powerful members of groups, organizations, or institutions expect and accept that power is distributed unequally. In essence, this dimension focuses on how comfortable people are with others being higher or lower than themselves in societal hierarchies. Hofstede's research has discovered that the level of comfort varies considerably between cultures: while low power distance cultures (e.g., Denmark,

or negative way. As an example, consider waiting for a rideshare pickup (e.g., Uber, Lyft). Most customers hold a range of acceptable times for this service encounter—probably somewhere between 10 and 20 minutes. If waiting for the car is within that period of time, customers probably do not pay much attention to the wait. If the car arrives within a couple of minutes, the customer may notice this swift service and judge it as excellent. On the other hand, if a customer has to wait for much longer

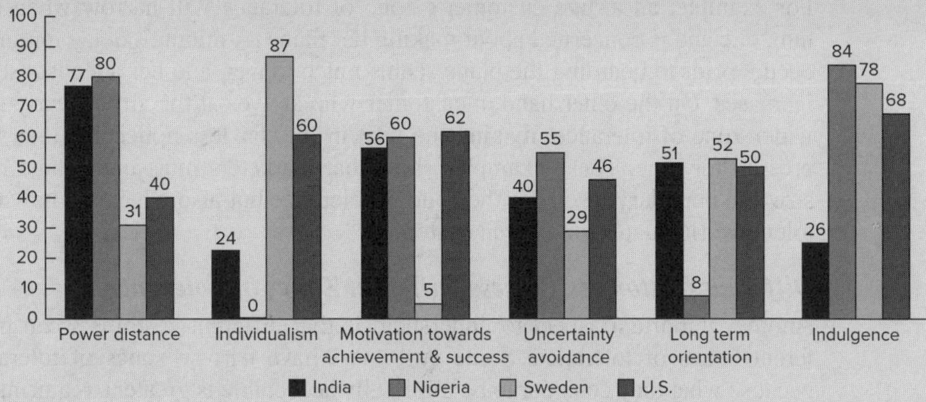

Source: https://www.theculturefactor.com/country-comparison-tool?countries=india%2Cnigeria%2Csweden%2Cunited+states

Sweden) tend to have an aversion toward hierarchies, high power distance cultures (e.g., China, Japan) are more comfortable with hierarchy and authority.

Nigerian culture is characterized by high power distance and people tend to expect hierarchies in business interactions, workplaces, and society. Power distance can influence service expectations in Nigeria in various ways. For example, customers are likely to expect that firms/employees respect and mention the customer's title or social position (e.g., a doctoral degree by addressing the customer as "Doctor"). Or, dissatisfied Nigerian customers are more likely to expect to "speak to the manager" to voice their concerns. In contrast, customers from low power distance cultures (e.g., Sweden) are less likely to ask for the manager, because authority is not as important to them. Therefore, expressing their problem to a frontline employee is equally as valuable as meeting with the manager.

Similarly, consistent with high power distance, in Nigerian culture the elderly enjoy social status as age signifies wisdom and experience, and that is to be respected. Therefore, when an old and a young customer are waiting in line for service delivery, the older customer might expect to be served first; based on the societal power distance, young customers would accept the preferential treatment given to their elders. Related expectations also influence service etiquette:

- Nigerian customers expect to be greeted with a welcoming smile and eye contact.
- Employees are often expected to bow when greeting customers who are older than the employee as a sign of respect.
- As part of a friendly conversation in commercial settings in Nigeria, customers often expect to be asked about their health and well-being as well as their family's well-being.

As this brief overview illustrates, service companies need to understand how culture influences the expectations of their customers to remain competitive. As cultures continue to evolve on an ongoing basis, the effort to understand cultures should be part of service organizations' ongoing market research programs (see Chapter 5).

*Note that a discussion of culture does not intend to promote stereotypes about people. Cultures are permanently evolving and research on culture can provide valuable insights, but it does not suggest a uniform approach to understanding individual people.

Sources: A. Ogechi, I. Adisa, and A. A. Obileye, "Cultural Influence on Customer Service Delivery," In *Customer Service Management in Africa*, pp. 217–226 (Productivity Press, 2020); K. Kulach, "How Cultural Differences Impact Customer Experience," 2018, https://www.cmswire.com/customer-experience/how-cultural-differences-impact-customer-experience/, accessed July 10, 2021; P. van Opzeeland, "Understanding Cultural Diversity in Customer Service," https://www.userlike.com/en/blog/cultural-diversity-customer-service, accessed July 10, 2021; S. Shinomiya, "Culture and the Customer Service Experience," *Berlitz Cultural Insights Series*, www.berlitz.com, accessed July 7, 2021.

than 20 minutes, she may begin to grumble and look at her watch. The more the wait falls below the zone of tolerance (20 minutes in this example), the more frustrated she likely becomes.

Customers' service expectations are characterized by a range of levels (like those shown in Figure 3.2), bounded by desired and adequate service, rather than a single level. This zone of tolerance, representing the difference between desired service and the level of service considered adequate, can expand and contract for a given customer. For example, an airline customer's zone of tolerance will narrow when she is running late and is concerned about making her plane. A minute's delay for anything that occurs prior to boarding the plane seems much longer, and her adequate service level increases. On the other hand, a customer who arrives at the airport early may have a wider zone of tolerance, making the wait in line far less noticeable than when he is pressed for time. These examples show that marketers must understand not just the size and boundary levels for the zone of tolerance but also when and how the zone of tolerance fluctuates for a given customer.

Different Customers Possess Different Zones of Tolerance

Another important aspect to understand is that different customers can possess different zones of tolerance. Some customers have narrow zones of tolerance (often because what they consider to be minimally acceptable is greater), requiring a smaller, but higher-quality, range of service from providers, whereas other customers have a wider range of expectations of service. For example, very busy customers would likely always desire short wait times in general, and hold a constrained range for the length of acceptable wait times. When it comes to meeting plumbers or appliance repair personnel at their homes, customers who work outside the home have a more restricted window of acceptable time duration for that appointment than do customers who work in their homes or do not work at all.

A customer's zone of tolerance increases or decreases depending on a number of factors, including company-controlled factors such as price. When prices increase, customers tend to be less tolerant of poor service. In this case, the zone of tolerance narrows because the adequate service level shifts upward. Later in this chapter we will describe many different factors, some company-controlled and others customer-controlled, that lead to the narrowing or widening of the zone of tolerance.

Typically, the fluctuation in a customer's zone of tolerance is more a function of changes in the adequate service level, which moves readily up and down because of situational circumstances, than in the desired service level, which is less dynamic but tends to move upward incrementally because of accumulated experiences. In other words, desired service is relatively stable compared with adequate service, which moves up and down and in response to competition and other factors. Fluctuation in the zone of tolerance can be likened to an accordion's movement, but with most of the gyration coming from one side (the adequate service level) rather than the other (the desired service level).

Zones of Tolerance Can Vary Across Different Service Dimensions

Customers' tolerance zones can also vary with different service attributes or dimensions. The more important the dimension, the narrower the zone of tolerance is likely to be. In general, customers are likely to be less tolerant about unreliable service (broken promises or service errors) than other service deficiencies, which means that they have higher expectations for this dimension. In addition to higher expectations for the most important service dimensions, customers may relax their expectations for the less important dimensions, making the zone of tolerance for the most important service dimension smaller and the desired and adequate service levels higher.[6] Figure 3.3 portrays the likely difference in zones of tolerance for the most important factor (in this case, reliability) and a factor that might be considered less important (such as empathy) for a given service.[7]

FIGURE 3.3
Differing Zones of Tolerance for Different Service Dimensions

Adapted from L. L. Berry, A. Parasuraman, and V. A. Zeithaml, "Ten Lessons for Improving Service Quality," *Marketing Science Institute,* Report No. 93–104 (May 1993).

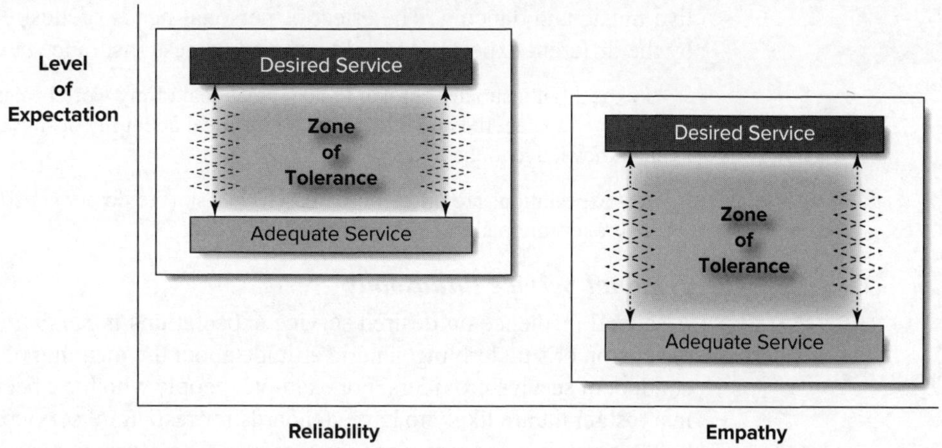

FACTORS THAT INFLUENCE CUSTOMER EXPECTATIONS OF SERVICE

Because expectations play such a critical role in customer evaluation of services, marketers need to understand the factors that shape them. In this section of the chapter we describe some of the key influences on customer expectations.

Sources of Desired Service Expectations

Personal Needs

As shown in Figure 3.4, there are three major influences on the desired service level. The first, *personal needs,* are those states or conditions essential to the physical or psychological well-being of the customer. Personal needs can fall into many categories, including physical, social, psychological, and functional. A fan who regularly goes to baseball games right from work, and is therefore thirsty and hungry (physical needs), hopes and desires that the food and drink vendors will pass by his section frequently, whereas a fan who regularly has dinner elsewhere has a lower level of desired service from the vendors. A customer with high social needs may have relatively high expectations for a hotel's ancillary services, hoping, for example, that the hotel has a bar with

FIGURE 3.4
Factors that Influence Desired Service

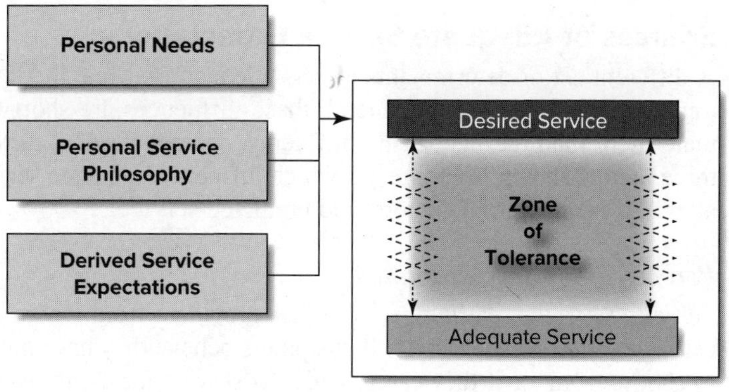

live music and dancing. The effect of personal needs on desired service is illustrated by the different expectations held by two business insurance customers:

> "I expect [an insurance] broker to do a great deal of my work because I don't have the staff . . . I expect the broker to know a great deal about my business and communicate that knowledge to the underwriter."
>
> "My expectations are different . . . I do have a staff to do our certificates, etc., and use the broker minimally."[8]

Personal Service Philosophy

A second influence on desired service expectations is *personal service philosophy*—the customer's underlying generic attitude about the meaning of service and the proper conduct of service providers. For example, people who have been employed as a server in a restaurant are likely to have standards for restaurant service that have been shaped by their training and experience in that role. Therefore, they might believe that servers should not keep customers waiting longer than 15 minutes to take their orders. Knowing the way a kitchen operates, they may be less tolerant of lukewarm food or errors in the order than customers who have not held the role of a server. In general, customers who are themselves in service businesses or have worked for them in the past seem to have especially strong service philosophies.

Derived Service Expectations

Another influence on desired service expectations is called *derived service expectations,* which occur when customer expectations are driven by another person or group of people. A niece from a big family who is planning a 90th birthday party for a favorite aunt is representing the entire family in selecting a restaurant for a successful celebration. Her needs are driven in part by expectations derived from the other family members. A parent choosing a vacation for the family, a spouse selecting a home-cleaning service, an employee choosing an office for the firm—all these customers' individual expectations are intensified because they represent and must answer to other parties who will receive the service. In the context of business-to-business service, customer expectations are driven by the expectations of their own customers. The head of an information technology department in an insurance company, who is the business customer of a large computer vendor, has expectations based on those of the insurance customers she serves: when the computer equipment is down, her customers complain. Her need to keep the system up and running is not just her own desire but is derived from the pressure of her firm's customers.

Sources of Adequate Service Expectations

A different set of determinants affects adequate service, the level of service the customer finds acceptable. In general, these influences are short-term and tend to fluctuate more than the factors that influence desired service. In this section we discuss three factors shown in Figure 3.5 which influence adequate service: perceived service alternatives, situational factors, and predicted service.

Perceived Service Alternatives

Perceived service alternatives are other providers from whom customers can, or perceive they can, obtain service. If customers believe they have multiple service providers to choose from, or if they can provide the service for themselves (such as lawn care or personal grooming), their levels of adequate service are higher than those of customers

FIGURE 3.5
Factors that Influence Adequate Service

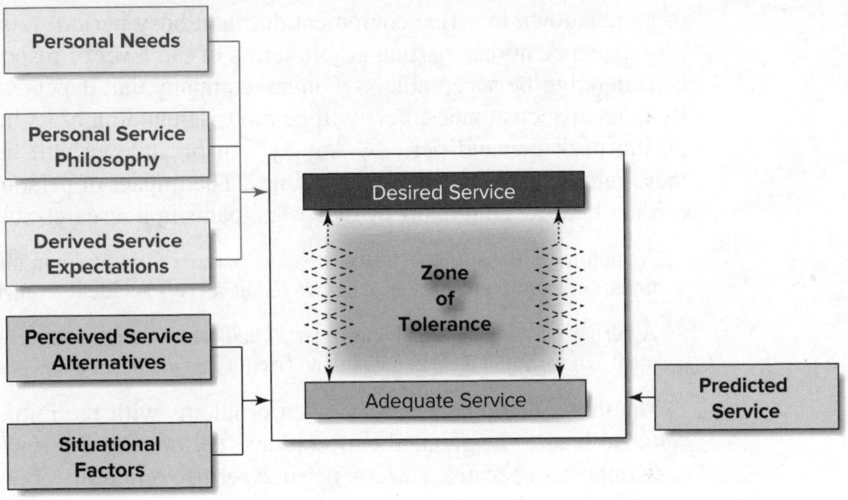

who believe it is not possible to get better service elsewhere. An airline customer who lives in a small town with a tiny airport, for example, has fewer options in airline travel. This customer will likely be more tolerant of the service performance of the carriers in the town because few alternatives exist. She will be more likely to accept the limited schedule of flights and lower levels of service than the customer in a big city who has myriad flights and airlines from which to choose. The customer's perception that service alternatives exist raises the level of adequate service and narrows the zone of tolerance.

It is important that service marketers fully understand the complete set of options that customers view as perceived alternatives. In the small town airport example just discussed, the set of alternatives from the customer's point of view is likely to include more than just other airlines: limousine service to a nearby large city, rail service, or driving. In general, service marketers must identify the alternatives that the customer views as comparable rather than those in the company's competitive set.

Situational Factors

Levels of adequate service are also influenced by *situational factors* that are generally considered contemporary in nature. One type is *uncontrollable situational factors,* which include service performance conditions that customers view as beyond the control of the service provider. For example, catastrophes that affect a large number of people at one time (tornadoes or earthquakes) may lower service expectations for insurance customers in other geographic locations because they recognize that insurers are inundated with demands for their services. To illustrate, when Hurricane Harvey hit the Houston area in 2017, telephone and Internet service was poor because so many people were trying to get in touch with friends and relatives. Similarly, guests in luxury hotels in Houston quickly realized that they should not expect the level of service to which they had become accustomed. Customers of all these services were relatively more forgiving during these days because they understood the source of the problem. Customers who recognize that situational factors are not the fault of the service company may accept lower levels of adequate service, given the context. Situational factors often temporarily lower the level of adequate service, widening the zone of tolerance.

Personal situational factors consist of short-term, individual factors that make a customer more aware of the need for service. Personal emergency situations in which service is urgently needed (such as an accident and the need for automobile insurance or a breakdown in office equipment during a busy period) raise the level of adequate service expectations, particularly in terms of the level of responsiveness required and considered to be acceptable. An online company that depends on network connectivity to receive customer orders will be more demanding of its Internet service provider during peak demand periods. Any system breakdown will be tolerated less during these intense periods than at other times. The impact of personal situational factors is evident in these comments by two participants in a research study:

> An automobile insurance customer: "The nature of my problem influences my expectations; for example, a broken window versus a DWI accident requiring brain surgery."
>
> A business equipment repair customer: "I had calibration problems with the X-ray equipment. They should have come out and fixed it in a matter of hours because of the urgency."[9]

Another situational factor is when problems with the initial service occur, which can also lead to heightened expectations. Performing a service right the first time is very important because customers value service reliability above all other dimensions. In situations when the service fails in the recovery phase, fixing it the second time (i.e., being reliable in service recovery, as further discussed in Chapter 7) is even more critical than it was the first time. Automobile repair service provides a case in point. If a problem with your automobile's brakes sends you to a car repair provider, you expect the company to fix the brakes. If you experience further problems with the brakes after the repair, the level of service you consider to be adequate will increase. In these and other situations where temporary service intensifiers are present, the level of adequate service will increase and the zone of tolerance will narrow.

Predicted Service

The final factor that influences adequate service is *predicted service* (Figure 3.6), the level of service that customers anticipate they are likely to get. This type of service expectation can be viewed as predictions made by customers about what is likely to happen during an impending transaction or exchange and typically is a function of a customer's experiences in the past. Predicted service performance implies some objective calculation of the probability of performance or estimate of anticipated service performance level. If customers predict good service, their levels of adequate service are likely to be higher than if they predict poor service. For example, full-time residents in

FIGURE 3.6
Factors that Influence Desired and Predicted Service

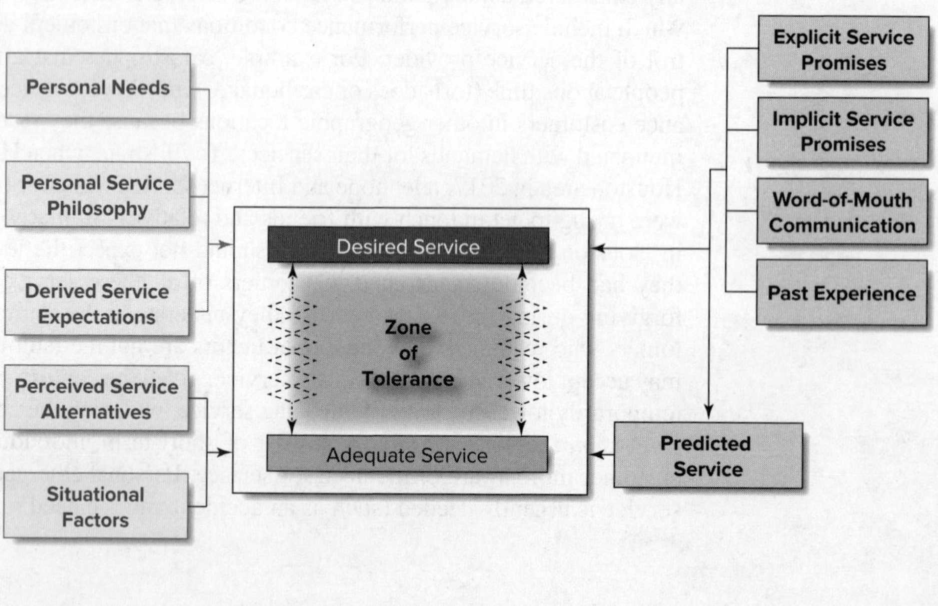

a college town usually predict faster restaurant service during the summer months when students are not on campus. This prediction will probably lead them to have higher standards for adequate service in restaurants during the summer than during school months. On the other hand, customers of cable service providers and utilities in a college town know that installation service from these firms will be difficult to obtain during the first few weeks of school when myriad students are setting up their apartments for the year. In this case, levels of adequate service decrease and zones of tolerance widen.

Predicted service is typically an estimate or a calculation of the service that a customer will receive in an individual transaction rather than in the overall relationship with a service provider. Whereas desired and adequate service expectations are global assessments comprising many individual service transactions, predicted service is almost always an estimate of what will happen in the next service encounter or transaction that the customer experiences. For this reason, predicted service is viewed in this model as an influencer of adequate service.

Sources of Both Desired and Predicted Service Expectations

When potential customers are interested in purchasing services, they are likely to seek or take in information from several different sources. For example, they may call a store, ask a friend, or deliberately track advertisements to find the needed service at the lowest price. They may also receive information through social media, watching television, surfing the Internet, or hearing an unsolicited comment from a colleague about a service that was performed well. In addition to these active and passive types of external search for information, potential customers may also consider (information from) their past service experiences. Thus, this section discusses four factors that influence both desired service and predicted service expectations: explicit service promises, implicit service promises, word-of-mouth communication, and past experience.

Explicit Service Promises

Explicit service promises are personal and nonpersonal statements about the service made by the organization to customers. The statements are personal when they are communicated by the firm's salespeople or service personnel; they are nonpersonal when they come from the company's web pages, social media marketing, advertising, brochures, and other written publications. For example, consider the promises made by the car manufacturer Nissan to its customers. "Our promise is to respect your time and seamlessly deliver a personalized experience tailored to your needs." Explicit service promises are one of the few influences on expectations that are completely within the control of the service provider.

Promising exactly what will ultimately be delivered would seem a logical and appropriate way to manage customer expectations and ensure that reality fits the promises. However, companies and the employees who represent them often deliberately overpromise to obtain business or inadvertently overpromise by stating their best estimates about delivery of a service in the future. In addition to overpromising, company representatives simply do not always know the appropriate promises to make because services are often customized and therefore not easily defined and repeated; the employee may not know when or in what final form the service will be delivered.

All types of explicit service promises have a direct effect on desired service expectations. If a firm's website promises to design an ideal home theater experience for a customer, perform audio and video set-up, and connect all of the customer's various components and home network, the customer's desires for that service (as well as the service of competitors) will be shaped by this promise. Or consider, for example, how a hotel customer describes the impact of explicit promises on expectations: "They get

Nissan's "Customer Promise" is an explicit service promise that influences expectations of desired service and adequate (via predicted) service.

you real pumped up with the beautiful ad. When you go in you expect the bells and whistles to go off. Usually they don't." And in a business-to-business context, a particularly dangerous promise that many companies make to their customers is to provide a "total solution" to their business needs (e.g., sometimes this promise can be the actual product name as is the case for the software "Total Business Solution"). This promise is often very difficult to deliver.

Explicit service promises influence the levels of both desired service and predicted service. They shape what customers desire in general as well as what they predict will happen in the next service encounter with a particular service provider or in a certain service encounter.

A service firm with a "posh" interior is likely to lead to greater (desired and predicted) customer expectations.

Implicit Service Promises

Implicit service promises are service-related cues, other than explicit promises, that lead to inferences about what the service should and will be like. These quality cues are dominated by price and the tangibles associated with the service. In general, the higher the price and the more impressive the tangibles, the more a customer will expect from the service. Consider a customer who shops for insurance, finding two firms charging radically different prices. She may infer that the firm with the higher price should and will provide higher-quality service and better coverage. Similarly, a customer who stays at a posh hotel with a luxurious lobby is likely to desire and predict a higher standard of service than from a hotel with less impressive facilities.

Word-of-Mouth Communication

The importance of *word-of-mouth communication* in shaping expectations of service is well documented.[10] These statements made by parties other than the organization—such as those found on social media and dedicated websites like angi.com—convey to customers what the service will be like and influence both predicted and desired service.[11] Word-of-mouth communication carries particular weight as an information source because it is perceived as unbiased. Word-of-mouth communication tends to be very important in services that are difficult for customers to evaluate before purchase and before having direct experience of them. Experts (e.g., *Consumer Reports*), friends, and family, as well as social media (such as Facebook, YouTube, WhatsApp, Instagram, TikTok, and Twitter) are also important word-of-mouth sources that can affect the levels of desired and predicted service.

Past Experience

Past experience, the customer's previous exposure to service that is relevant to the focal service, is another force in shaping predictions and desires. For example, you probably compare each stay in a particular hotel with all previous stays in that hotel. But past experience with the focal hotel is likely to be a very limited view of your past experience. You may also compare each stay with your experiences in other hotels and hotel chains. Customers also compare across industries: hospital patients, for example, might compare hospital stays against the standard of hotel visits. Cable service customers tend to compare cable service with the standards set by telephone service, one reason cable service is often judged to be poor. Past experience may incorporate previous experience with the focal service provider, typical performance of similar service offerings, and experience with the last service purchased.[12] This chapter's Technology Spotlight illustrates how consumers draw on past experiences with human service employees and self-service technologies to derive their expectations toward service robots.

Notably, the different sources we have discussed vary in terms of their credibility as well as their potential to be influenced by the marketer. The Strategy Insight shows the breakdown of various factors and how service marketers can influence them. Chapter 14 will detail these and other strategies that service marketers can use to match delivery to promises and thereby better manage customer expectations.

ISSUES INVOLVING CUSTOMERS' SERVICE EXPECTATIONS

The following issues represent topics of particular interest to service marketers concerning customer expectations. In this section we discuss frequently asked questions about customer expectations:

- What does a service marketer do if customer expectations are "unrealistic"?
- Should a company try to delight the customer?
- How does a company exceed customers' service expectations?
- Do customers' service expectations continually escalate?
- How does a service company stay ahead of competition in meeting customer expectations?

What Does a Service Marketer Do if Customer Expectations Are "Unrealistic"?

One inhibitor to learning about customer expectations is management's and employees' fear of asking. This apprehension often stems from the belief that customer expectations will be extravagant and unrealistic and that by asking about them a company will set itself up for even loftier expectation levels (that is, "unrealistic" levels). However, compelling evidence, shown in Exhibit 3.1, suggests that customers' main

Technology Spotlight Exploring Customer Expectations of Service Robots

The emergence of service robots is among the most dramatic evolutions in the service arena and customer–robot encounters will be increasingly common (e.g., in retailing, hospitality, and healthcare). For instance, since its launch in 2014, more than 10,000 "Pepper" robots have been sold worldwide. Pepper robots have been used to help sell coffee machines at 1,000 Nescafé stores in Japan and served as waiters at Pizza Hut in Asia. The rise of service robots is consistent with the notion in the business press about how engaging customers through cutting-edge technology helps companies stay competitive.

However, managers who want to use such technology need to consider whether these innovations come with distinct customer expectations. As the figure illustrates, customers often draw on three different categories of expectations as they think about being served by a robot (e.g., in a restaurant, hotel, or airport): (1) expectations related to being served by human frontline employees, (2) expectations related to using self-service technologies (e.g., ATMs, self-check-in/out kiosks), and (3) expectations toward the "ideal" service robot.

MikeDotta/Shutterstock

Pepper is a service robot designed to be friendly and engaging in order to connect with customers.

In terms of the relative importance of these three types of expectations, consumers most frequently draw on their expectations toward human employees to derive expectations toward service robots (e.g., derived from employees' warmth and competence). However, customers also use self-service technologies as a reference point and thus likely understand that service robots may not be different from any other computer built and programmed by humans (e.g., self-service kiosks that customers use in grocery stores, airports, or hotels to check themselves in/out). Finally, customers also consider what they hope the "ideal" service robot can do as a source of their expectations (e.g., based on popular press or even based on how science fiction portrays robots and their abilities). Because many consumers have little (or no) experience with service robots, these idealized expectations may not always be accurate or realistic. At any rate, to be able to *manage* such expectations, companies must first understand these three important sources customer expectations.

Another aspect of robot-related customer expectations concerns how customers expect to interact with robots over time. This interaction is important because many service robots are being developed to form close relationships with people (e.g., robots may serve in the role of teachers in educational settings, or in the role of coaches that help customers with working out or losing

expectations of service are quite simple and basic: "Simply put, customers expect service companies to do what they are supposed to do. They expect fundamentals, not fanciness; performance, not empty promises."[13] Customers want service to be delivered as promised. They want planes to take off on time, hotel rooms to be clean, food to be hot, and service providers to show up when scheduled. Unfortunately, many service customers are disappointed and let down when companies fail to meet these basic service expectations.

A simple way to learn if customers' expectations are realistic is to ask them. Asking customers about their expectations does not so much raise the levels of the expectations themselves but rather heightens the belief that the company will do something with the information that surfaces. Arguably the worst thing a company can do is show a strong

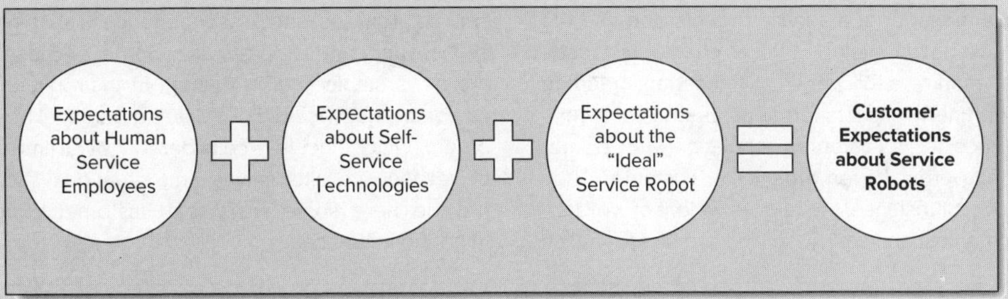

weight). One key assumption for such social robots to be effective is that customers are willing and able to form close relationships with them; thus, it is critical to understand which expectations people have toward robots as partners in social relationships. Consumers have two broad types of expectations: the first type, which captures people's "expectations about a robot as a conversation partner," includes facets such as the desire to chat with a robot about hobbies and art, receiving advice from it, and even discussing topics with it about which people cannot talk with other humans. The second type, which capture people's "expectations for togetherness," directly relates to the idea of forming close social relationships with robots. Accordingly, this category includes emotion-laden expectations such as being able to play with the robot, sharing family dinners with it, or knowing that the robot is devoted, committed, and loyal to its customer (user/owner). Understanding these two main types of expectations is another important platform for robot designers and service firms as they continue to develop service robots for their customers.

Sources: S. Curtis, "Pizza Hut Hires Robot Waiters to Take Orders and Process Payments at its Fast-Food Restaurants," http://www.mirror.co.uk/tech/pizza-hut-hires-robot-waiters-8045172, accessed July 7, 2021; V. N. Lu, J. Wirtz, W. Kunz, S. Paluch, T. Gruber, A. Martins, and P. G. Patterson, "Service Robots, Customers and Service Employees: What Can We Learn From the Academic Literature and Where Are the Gaps?," *Journal of Service Theory and Practice* 30 (July 2020), pp. 361–391; M. Mende, M. L. Scott, J. van Doorn, D. Grewal, and I. Shanks, "Service Robots Rising: How Humanoid Robots Influence Service Experiences and Elicit Compensatory Consumer Responses," *Journal of Marketing Research* 56 (August 2019), pp. 535–556; Nestlé (2014), "Nestlé to Use Humanoid Robot to Sell Nescafé in Japan," 2014, https://www.nestle.com/media/news/nestle-humanoid-robot-nescafe-japan, accessed July 8, 2021; T. Nomura and T. Kanda, "Rapport–Expectation with a Robot Scale," *International Journal of Social Robotics* 8 (January 2016), pp. 21–30; R. M. Stock and M. Merkle, "A Service Robot Acceptance Model: User Acceptance of Humanoid Robots During Service Encounters," In *2017 IEEE International Conference on Pervasive Computing and Communications Workshops* (March 2017), pp. 339–344. IEEE; F. Tobe, "How Is Pepper, Softbank's Emotional Robot, Doing?," https://www.therobot report.com/how-is-pepper-softbanks-emotional-robot-doing/, accessed July 8, 2021.

interest in understanding what customers expect and then never act on the information. At a minimum, a company should acknowledge to customers that it has received and heard their input and that it will expend effort trying to address their issues. The company may not be able to—and indeed does not always have to—deliver to expressed expectations. An alternative and appropriate response would be to let customers know the reasons that desired service is not being provided at the present time or describe the efforts planned to deliver such service in the future. Another approach could be to educate customers about ways to use and improve the service they currently receive. Giving customers progress updates as service is improved to address their needs and desires is sensible because it allows the company to get credit for incremental efforts to improve service.

Strategy Insight How Service Marketers Can Influence Customers' Expectations

How might a manager of a service organization use the information we have developed in this chapter to create, improve, or market services? First, managers need to know the pertinent expectation sources and their relative importance for a customer population, a customer segment, and perhaps even a particular customer. They need to know, for instance, the relative weight of word-of-mouth communication, explicit service promises, implicit service promises, and past experience in shaping desired service and predicted service. Some of these sources are more stable and permanent in their influence (such as personal service philosophy and personal needs) than others, which fluctuate considerably over time (like perceived service alternatives and situational factors). We provide here some ways that customer expectations might be influenced.

Factor	**Possible Influence Strategies**
Personal needs	• Educate customers on ways the service addresses their needs.
Personal service philosophy	• Use market research to profile personal service philosophies of customers and use this information in designing and delivering services.
Derived service expectations	• Use market research to determine sources of derived service expectations and their requirements. Then, focus advertising and marketing strategy on ways the service allows the focal customer to satisfy the requirements of the influencing customer(s).
Perceived service alternatives	• Be fully aware of competitive offerings (as perceived by customers) and, where possible and appropriate, match them.
Situational factors	• Increase service delivery capacity during peak periods or in emergencies. • Use service guarantees to assure customers about service recovery regardless of the situational factors that occur.
Predicted service	• Tell customers when service provision is higher than what can normally be expected, so that predictions of future service encounters will not be inflated.
Explicit service promises	• Make realistic and accurate promises that reflect the service actually delivered rather than an idealized version of the service. • Ask customer contact employees for feedback on the accuracy of promises made in advertising and personal selling. • Avoid engaging in price or advertising wars with competitors because they take the focus off customers and escalate promises beyond the level at which they can be met. • Formalize service promises through a service guarantee that focuses company employees on the promises made to customers and that provides feedback on the number of times promises are not fulfilled.
Implicit service promises	• Ensure that service tangibles are consistent with and accurately reflect the type and level of service provided. • Ensure that price premiums can be justified by higher levels of performance by the company on important service attributes.
Word-of-mouth communications	• Simulate word of mouth in advertising by using testimonials and opinion leaders. • Identify influencers and opinion leaders for the service and concentrate marketing efforts on them. • Use incentives with existing customers to encourage them to say positive things about the service or create positive reviews via social media.
Past experience	• Use marketing research to profile customers' previous experience with similar services.

Exhibit 3.1 Service Customers Want the Basics

Expectation	What This Means to the Customer	Illustrative Service Provider Behaviors
Competency	• "I want everything handled correctly the first time." • "I expect them to know how this works."	• *Appliance Repairman*: Fix the broken refrigerator correctly so that it does not break down again a week later. • *Travel Agent*: Inform the traveler of the visa requirements for each country to be visited.
Explanations	• "I want to know what is happening." • "I want to know how this works."	• *Airline Counter Agent*: Provide passengers frequent updates on the delayed flight's status. • *Insurance Agent*: Clearly explain the policy and answer all questions the customer has about what is (or is not) covered.
Respect	• "I want to feel like a valued customer."	• *Hotel Desk Manager*: Listen to the guest's concerns about his room and act accordingly. • *Healthcare Clinic Receptionist*: Verbally greet each patient and make eye contact upon entrance into the clinic.
Hygiene	• "I expect the facilities to be clean and well kept." • "I expect my home to be kept clean while they are working."	• *Restaurant Manager*: Walk through the dining area every 15 minutes and sweep the floor as needed. • *Plumber*: Wear protective shoe coverings when walking through the customer's house.
Flexibility	• "I would like them to be able to accommodate my situation." • "I expect them to be able to bend the rules a little."	• *Golf Instructor*: Provide concurrent lessons for the customer and his daughter. • *Credit Card Service Representative*: Examine the customer's payment history and waive the late payment fee if this is not a regular occurrence.
Urgency	• "I expect my situation to be taken seriously and addressed quickly."	• *Forklift Service Manager*: Arrange for replacement parts to be delivered and installed for the client by the end of the day. • *Tax Accountant*: Respond within 4 hours to any inquiries from existing customers, within one business day to potential new customers.
Consistency	• "I expect to receive the same level of service each and every time."	• *Dry Cleaner*: Provide the same level of cleanliness and crease the pants in the same spot each and every time. • *Oil Change Technician*: Check and "top off" all six fluids for the customer automobile on every visit.
Hassle-free	• "I want the process to be simple and easy for me."	• *Lawn Care Technician*: Arrive each quarter without being prompted and provide an automatic payment option once service is completed. • *Computer Remote Support Agent*: Complete laptop computer tune-up and install needed software updates without requiring any additional input from the customer.
Promptness	• "I do not want to wait a long time to be served." • "I expect to receive help quickly."	• *Post Office Clerk*: Request assistance/additional help from staff in the back room when the line of customers grows to more than six. • *Financial advisor*: Respond to all telephone calls within 2 (business) hours and emails within 4 hours.
Competence	• "I want some assurance they know what they are doing."	• *Auto Service Repairman*: Explain what was done to the vehicle and demonstrate what was faulty with the old parts. • *Tailor*: Explain the process involved in resizing and altering the dress while the customer is present in the store.
Fairness	• "I expect to receive the same treatment as other customers."	• *Rental Car Agent*: Honor the customer's reservation by holding the car for her even if she is from out of town or a first-time customer.
Empathy	• "I want them to put themselves in my shoes." • "I expect them to be able to see things from my perspective."	• *Retail Clerk*: Use the phrase "I am sorry you have experienced that" and exert visible effort to try to help the customer. • *Veterinarian*: Assume the pet is very important to its owner and show compassion in explaining the pet's medical condition.

Source: Adapted from "Understanding Customer Expectations of Service" by A. Parasuraman, L.L. Berry, and V.A. Zeithaml, *Sloan Management Review* 32 (Spring 1991), pp. 39–48.

Should a Company Try to Delight the Customer?

Some management consultants urge service companies to "delight" customers to gain a competitive edge. The *delight* they refer to is a profoundly positive emotional state that results from having one's expectations exceeded to a surprising degree.[14] One author describes the type of service that results in delight as "positively outrageous service"—that which is unexpected, random, extraordinary, and disproportionately positive.[15]

A way that managers can conceive of delight, as depicted in Figure 3.7, is to consider product and service features in terms of a pyramid.[16] The foundational layer refers to attributes central to the basic function of the product or service, called *musts*. Their provision is not particularly noticeable, but their absence would be. Above the musts is a layer called *satisfiers*: features that have the potential to further satisfy beyond the basic function of the product. At the top and final level are *delights,* or product or service features that are unexpected and surprisingly enjoyable. These features are things that consumers would not expect to find and they are therefore highly surprised and sometimes excited when they receive them. For example, in your classes the musts consist of professors, rooms, syllabi, and class meetings. Satisfiers might include interesting course lectures, professors who are entertaining or friendly, and good audiovisual aids provided in the classroom. Delights might include a free textbook for students signing up for the course or punch and cookies provided for the first day of class.

Delighting customers may seem like a good idea, and can lead to repeat purchasing and customer loyalty,[17] but this level of service provision comes with extra effort and costs to the firm. And, as we will discuss in more detail in Chapter 4, delighting customers does not build their loyalty; what has more influence is providing service that requires customers to put in minimal effort to get a satisfactory solution to their service issue.[18] Therefore, the benefits of providing delight must be weighed. Among the considerations are the staying power and competitive implications of delight.

Staying power involves the question of how long a company can expect an experience of delight to maintain the consumer's attention. If it is fleeting and the customer forgets it immediately, it may not be worth the cost. Alternatively, if the customer

FIGURE 3.7
Musts, Satisfiers, and Delights

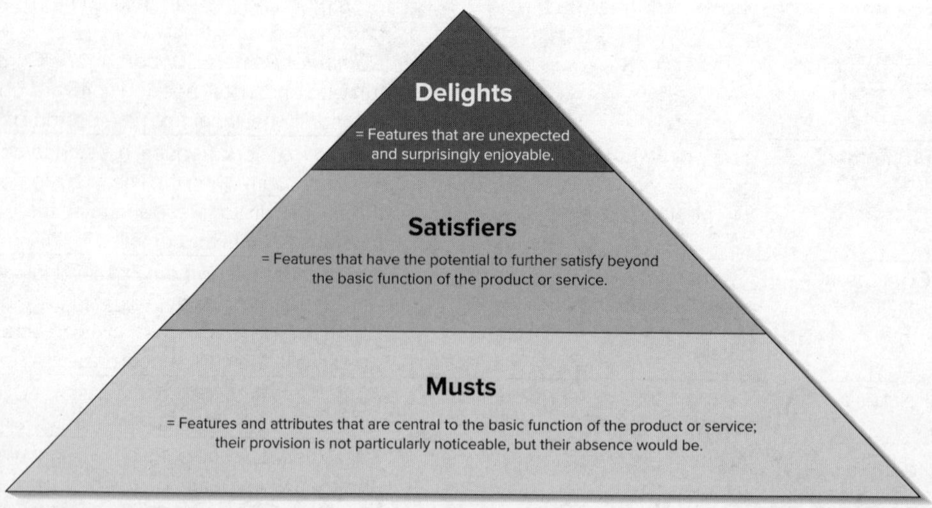

remembers the delight and adjusts her level of expectation upward accordingly, it will cost the company more just to satisfy her, effectively raising the bar for the future. Research indicates that delighting customers does, in fact, raise expectations and make it more difficult for a company to satisfy customers in the future.[19]

The competitive implication of delight relates to its impact on expectations of other firms in the same industry. If a competitor in the same industry is unable to copy the delight strategy, it will be disadvantaged by the consumer's increased expectations. If you were offered that free textbook in one of your classes, you might then expect to receive one in each of your classes. Those classes not offering the free textbook might not have high enrollment levels compared to the delighting class. If a competitor can easily copy the delight strategy, however, neither firm benefits (although the consumer does!), and all firms may be hurt because their costs increase and profits erode. The implication is that, if companies choose to delight, they should do so in areas that cannot be copied by other firms.

How Does a Company Exceed Customer Service Expectations?

Many companies talk about exceeding customer expectations—delighting and surprising them by giving more than they expect (as we will also further discuss in Chapter 4). One such example is Pebble Beach Resort, located along the Pacific coast of Northern California. The golf resort not only talks about exceeding customer expectations, it actually prints the following phrase on the back side of employee business cards: "Exceed the expectations of every guest, by providing a once in a lifetime experience, every time." This philosophy raises the question: Should a service provider try simply to meet customer expectations or to exceed them?

First, it is essential to recognize that exceeding customer expectations of the basics (i.e., adequate service expectations) is virtually impossible. Honoring promises—having the reserved room available, meeting deadlines, showing up for meetings, delivering the core service—is what the company is supposed to do. Companies are *supposed* to be accurate and dependable and provide the service they promised to provide.[20] As you examine the examples of basic expectations of customers in Exhibit 3.1, ask yourself if a provider's doing any of these things would delight you. The conclusion you should reach is that it is very difficult to surprise or delight customers consistently by delivering reliable service.

How, then, does a company delight its customers and exceed their expectations? In virtually any service, developing a customer relationship is one approach for exceeding service expectations. The United Services Automobile Association (USAA), a provider of insurance to military personnel and their dependents, illustrates how a large company that seldom has face-to-face interactions with its customers can surprise and delight them with its personalization of service and knowledge of the customer. Using a state-of-the-art imaging system, all USAA employees can access any customer's entire information file in seconds, giving them full knowledge of the customer's history and requirements and the status of the customer's recent interactions with the company. Expecting a lower level of personalization from an insurance company and from most any service interaction on the telephone, USAA's customers are surprised and impressed with the care and concern that employees demonstrate.

Using a similar type of information technology, Ritz-Carlton Hotels, a two-time recipient of the Malcolm Baldrige Quality Award, provides highly personalized attention to its customers. The company trains each of its employees to note guest likes and dislikes and to record these into a computerized guest history profile. The company has information on the preferences of several hundred thousand repeat Ritz-Carlton guests, resulting in more personalized service. The aim is not simply to meet expectations of guests but to provide them with a "memorable visit." The company uses the guest history information to exceed customers' expectations of the way they will be treated. When a repeat customer calls the hotel's central reservations number to book accommodations, the reservation agent can call up the individual's preference information. The agent then sends this information electronically to the particular hotel at which the reservation is made. The hotel puts the data in a daily guest recognition and preference report circulated to employees. Employees then greet the repeat guest personally at check-in and ensure that the guest's needs/preferences are anticipated and met.[21] How well does this approach work? Quite well. According to an independent survey of luxury hotels conducted annually by J. D. Power and Associates, the Ritz-Carlton is (perennially) a top-rated luxury hotel in terms of customer satisfaction.[22]

Another way to exceed expectations is to deliberately underpromise the service to increase the likelihood of exceeding customer expectations.[23] The strategy is to underpromise and overdeliver. If every service promise is less than what will eventually happen, customers can be delighted frequently. Although this reasoning sounds logical, a firm should weigh two potential problems before using this strategy. First, customers with whom a company interacts regularly are likely to notice the underpromising and adjust their expectations accordingly, negating the desired benefit of delight. Customers will recognize the pattern of underpromising when time after time a firm promises one delivery time ("we cannot get that to you before 5:00 p.m. tomorrow") yet constantly exceeds it (by delivering at noon). Second, underpromising in a sales situation potentially reduces the competitive appeal of an offering and must be tempered by what the competition is offering. When competitive pressures are high, presenting a cohesive and honest portrayal of the service both explicitly (through advertising and personal selling) and implicitly (such as through the appearance of service facilities and the price of the service) may be wiser. Controlling the firm's promises, making them consistent with the deliverable service, may be a better approach.

A final way to exceed expectations without raising them in the future is to position unusual service as unique rather than the standard. On a flight between Raleigh-Durham and Charlotte, North Carolina, one of us experienced an example of this strategy. The flight is extremely short, less than half an hour, and typically too brief for beverage service. On that flight, however, a crew member announced over the intercom that an unusually ambitious crew wanted to try to serve beverages anyway. He warned passengers that the crew may not get to all of us and positioned the service as unique by imploring passengers not to expect beverage service on other flights. In this scenario, passengers seemed delighted but their expectations for regular service were not heightened by the action. (To this day, we have never received beverage service on that route, but are really not expecting it!)

Do Customers' Service Expectations Continually Escalate?

As we illustrated earlier in this chapter, customers' service expectations are dynamic. In both the credit card and mobile telephone industries, as in many competitive service industries, battling companies seek to best each other and thereby raise the level of service above that of competing companies. Service expectations—in this case, adequate service expectations—rise as quickly as service delivery or promises rise. In a highly competitive and rapidly changing industry, expectations can thus rise quickly. For this reason companies need to monitor adequate service expectations continually—the more turbulent the industry, the more frequent is the monitoring needed. Notably, as we will further discuss in Chapters 4 and 5, there are numerous sophisticated research firms that can support companies in tracking overall customer satisfaction across industries and over time (e.g., JD Power, the American Customer Satisfaction Index).

Desired service expectations, on the other hand, are far more stable. Because they are driven by more enduring factors, such as personal needs or personal service philosophy, they tend to be high to begin with and remain high.

How Does a Service Company Stay Ahead of Competition in Meeting Customer Expectations?

All else being equal, a company's goal is to meet customer expectations better than its competitors. Given the fact that adequate service expectations change rapidly in a turbulent environment, how can a company ensure that it stays ahead of competition?

The adequate service level reflects the minimum performance level expected by customers after they consider a variety of personal and external factors (Figure 3.6), including the availability of service options from other providers. Companies whose service performance falls short of this level are clearly at a competitive disadvantage, with the disadvantage escalating as the gap widens. These companies' customers may well be "reluctant" customers, ready to take their business elsewhere the moment they perceive an acceptable alternative exists.

If they are to leverage service quality for their competitive advantage, companies must perform above the adequate service level. This level, however, may signal only a temporary advantage. Customers' adequate service levels, which are less stable than desired service levels, will rise rapidly when competitors promise and deliver a higher level of service. If a company's level of service is barely above the adequate service level to begin with, a competitor can quickly erode that advantage. To develop a true customer franchise—immutable customer loyalty—companies must not only consistently exceed the adequate service level but also reach the desired service level. Exceptional service can intensify customers' loyalty to a point at which they are impervious to competitive options as further discussed in the next chapter.

Firms might also consider how they present their promises to customers relative to the competition. In Chapter 14 we describe various techniques for communicating a firm's promises, but for now consider two options. First, if the salesperson knows that no competitor can meet an inflated sales promise in an industry, he could point that fact out to the customer, thereby refuting the promise made by competitive salespeople. The second option is for the provider to follow a sale with a "reality check" about service delivery. One of us bought a new house from a builder. Typical sales promises were made about the quality of the home, some less than accurate, to make the sale. Before closing on the house, the builder conducted a final check on the house. At the front door, the builder pointed out that each new home has between 3,000 and 5,000 individual elements and that in his experience the typical new home has 100–150 defects. Armed with this reality check, the 32 defects found in the house then seemed to be a relatively small amount.

Summary

Using a conceptual framework of the nature and determinants of customer expectations of service, we showed in this chapter that customers hold two types of service expectations: desired service, which reflects what customers hope to receive, and adequate service, or the minimum level of service customers are willing to accept. The desired service level is less subject to change than the adequate service level. A zone of tolerance separates these two levels of expectations. This zone of tolerance varies across customers and can expand or contract for the same customer.

Customer expectations are influenced by a variety of factors. Desired service expectations are influenced by personal needs, personal service philosophy, derived service expectations, explicit service promises, implicit service promises, word-of-mouth communication, and the customer's past experience. Adequate service expectations are influenced by perceived service alternatives and situational factors. These sources of expectations are the same for end consumers and business customers, for pure service and product-related service, and for experienced customers and inexperienced customers.

Discussion Questions

1. What is the difference between desired service and adequate service? Why would a service marketer need to understand both types of service expectations?
2. Consider a recent service purchase that you have made. Which of the factors influencing expectations were the most important in your decision? Why?
3. Why are desired service expectations more stable than adequate service expectations?
4. How do the technology changes discussed in the Technology Spotlight in this chapter relate to customer expectations? Explain how customers form expectations regarding service robots.
5. Describe several instances in which a service company's explicit service promises were inflated and led you to be disappointed with the service outcome.
6. Consider a small business preparing to buy a computer system. Which of the influences on customer expectations do you believe will be pivotal? Which factors will have the most influence? Which factors will have the least importance in this decision?
7. What strategies can you add to the Strategy Insight in this chapter for influencing the factors?
8. Do you believe that any of your service expectations are unrealistic? Which ones? Should a service marketer try to address unrealistic customer expectations?
9. In your opinion, what service companies have effectively built customer franchises (immutable customer loyalty)?
10. Intuitively, it would seem that managers want their customers to have wide tolerance zones for service. But if customers do have these wide zones of tolerance for service, is it more difficult for firms with superior service to earn customer loyalty? Would superior service firms be better off to attempt to narrow customers' tolerance zones to reduce the competitive appeal of mediocre providers?
11. Should service marketers delight their customers?

Exercises

1. What factors influenced your expectations of this course? Which were the most important factors? How would your expectations change if this were a required course? (Alternatively, if this course *is* required, would your expectations change if this were an optional course?)
2. Keep a service journal for a day and document your use of services. Ask yourself before each service encounter to indicate your predicted service of that encounter. After the encounter, note whether your expectations were met or exceeded. How does the answer to this question relate to your desire to do business with that service firm again?
3. List five incidents in which a service company has exceeded your expectations. How did you react to the service? Did these incidents change the way you viewed subsequent interactions with each of the companies? In what way?

Notes

1. Salesforce.com, "*State of the Connected Customer*," October 2020, https://www.salesforce.com/resources/articles/customer-expectations, accessed August 03, 2021; Qualtrics.com, "*Customer Expectations: 7 Types All Exceptional Researchers Must Understand*," https://www.qualtrics.com/blog/customer-expectations/, accessed August 03, 2021; Gartner.com, "*Key Findings From the Gartner Customer Experience Survey*," https://www.gartner.com/en/marketing/insights/articles/key-findings-from-the-gartner-customer-experience-survey, accessed August 01, 2021; T. Hymes, "*The Amazon Effect - Defining Customer Expectations in eCommerce*," https://tonyhymes.info/2021/02/09/the-amazon-effect-defining-customer-expectations-in-ecommerce/, accessed August 04, 2021.
2. The model on which this chapter is based is taken from V. A. Zeithaml, L. L. Berry, and A. Parasuraman, "The Nature and Determinants of Customer Expectations of Service," *Journal of the Academy of Marketing Science* 21 (Winter 1993), pp. 1–12.
3. See sources such as C. Gronroos, *Strategic Management and Marketing in the Service Sector* (Helsingfors, Sweden: Swedish School of Economics and Business Administration, 1982); R. K. Teas and T. E. DeCarlo, "An Examination and Extension of the Zone-of-Tolerance Model: A Comparison to Performance-Based Models of Perceived Quality," *Journal of Service Research* 6 (February 2004), pp. 272–286; K. B. Yap and J. C. Sweeney, "Zone-of-Tolerance Moderates the Service Quality-Outcome Relationship," *Journal of Services Marketing* 21 (2007), pp. 137–148.
4. R. B. Woodruff, E. R. Cadotte, and R. L. Jenkins, "Expectations and Norms in Models of Consumer Satisfaction," *Journal of Marketing Research* 24 (August 1987), pp. 305–314.
5. J. A. Miller, "Studying Satisfaction, Modifying Models, Eliciting Expectations, Posing Problems, and Making Meaningful Measurements," in *Conceptualization and Measurement of Consumer Satisfaction and Dissatisfaction,* ed. H. K. Hunt (Bloomington: Indiana University School of Business, 1977), pp. 72–91.
6. A. Parasuraman, L. L. Berry, and V. A. Zeithaml, "Understanding Customer Expectations of Service," *Sloan Management Review* 32 (Spring 1991), p. 42.
7. L. L. Berry, A. Parasuraman, and V. A. Zeithaml, "Ten Lessons for Improving Service Quality," *Marketing Science Institute,* Report No. 93–104 (May 1993).
8. A. Parasuraman, L. L. Berry, and V. A. Zeithaml, "Understanding Customer Expectations of Service," *Sloan Management Review* 32 (Spring 1991), p. 7.

9. Ibid., p. 8.
10. D. L. Davis, J. G. Guiltinan, and W. H. Jones, "Service Characteristics, Consumer Research, and the Classification of Retail Services," *Journal of Retailing* 55 (Fall 1979), pp. 3–21; W. R. George and L. L. Berry, "Guidelines for the Advertising of Services," *Business Horizons* 24 (May–June 1981), pp. 52–56; F. v. Wangenheim and T. Bay n, "The Effect of Word-of-Mouth on Services Switching: Measurement and Moderating Variables," *European Journal of Marketing* 38 (2004), pp. 1173–1185; T. J. Brown, T. E. Barry, P. A. Dacin, and R. F. Gunst, "Spreading the Word: Investigating Antecedents of Consumers' Positive Word-of-Mouth Intentions and Behaviors in a Retailing Context," *Journal of the Academy of Marketing Science* 33 (Spring 2005), pp. 123–138. For a meta-analysis of the effect of electronic word-of-mouth communication on services, see A. B. Rosario, F. Sotgiu, K. de Valck, and T. H. A. Bijmolt, "The Effect of Electronic Word of Mouth on Sales: A Meta-Analytic Review of Platform, Product, and Metric Factors," *Journal of Marketing Research* 53 (June 2016), pp. 297–318.
11. M. Trusov, R. E. Bucklin, and K. Pauwels, "Effects of Word-of-Mouth versus Traditional Marketing: Findings from an Internet Social Networking Site," *Journal of Marketing* 73 (September 2009), pp. 90–102.
12. Discussions of the role of past experience in shaping customer expectations of service are included in L. L. Berry, "Cultivating Service Brand Equity," *Journal of the Academy of Marketing Science* 28 (Winter 2000), pp. 128–137; and R. L. Hess Jr., S. Ganesan, and N. M. Klein, "Interactional Service Failures in a Psuedorelationship: The Role of Organizational Attributions," *Journal of Retailing* 83 (January 2007), pp. 79–95.
13. Parasuraman, Berry, and Zeithaml, "Understanding Customer Expectations of Service," p. 40.
14. R. T. Rust and R. L. Oliver, "Should We Delight the Customer?" *Journal of the Academy of Marketing Science* 28 (Winter 2000), pp. 86–94; For a recent overview of the literature, see: D. C. Barnes and A. Krallman, "Customer Delight: A Review and Agenda for Research," *Journal of Marketing Theory and Practice* 27 (Spring 2019), pp. 174–195.
15. T. S. Gross, *Positively Outrageous Service* (Chicago: Dearborn Trade Publishing, 2004); For a more recent exploration of drivers of customer delight, see: A. Parasuraman, J. Ball, L. Aksoy, T. L. Keiningham, and M. Zaki, "More Than a Feeling? Toward a Theory of Customer Delight," *Journal of Service Management* 32 (January 2021), pp. 1–26.
16. J. Clemmer, "The Three Rings of Perceived Value," *Canadian Manager* 15 (Summer 1990), pp. 12–15.
17. T. Keiningham and T. Vavra, *The Customer Delight Principle: Exceeding Customers' Expectations for Bottom-Line Success* (New York: McGraw Hill, 2001); R. Chitturi, R. Raghunathan, and V. Mahajan, "Delight by Design: The Role of Hedonic versus Utilitarian Benefits," *Journal of Marketing* 72 (May 2008), pp. 48–63; D. C. Barnes, M. B. Beauchamp, and C. Webster, "To Delight, or Not to Delight? This Is the Question Service Firms Must Address," *Journal of Marketing Theory and Practice* 18 (Summer 2010), pp. 275–283.
18. M. Dixon, K. Freeman, and N. Toman, "Stop Trying to Delight Your Customers," *Harvard Business Review* 88 (July–August 2010), pp. 116–122.
19. Rust and Oliver, "Should We Delight the Customer?"

20. Parasuraman, Berry, and Zeithaml, "Understanding Customer Expectations," p. 41.
21. "How the Ritz-Carlton Hotel Company Delivers 'Memorable' Service to Customers," *Executive Report on Customer Satisfaction* 6 (March 15, 1993), pp. 1–4; L. A. Dhir, "Top Ten Things Luxury Guests Absolutely Want," http://www.hospitalitynet.org/news/4060166.html, accessed June 28, 2016.
22. J. D. Power and Associates, "North American Hotel Guests Want Breakfast Back, J.D. Power Finds," https://www.jdpower.com/business/press-releases/2021-north-america-hotel-guest-satisfaction-index-nagsi-study, accessed July 24, 2021.
23. W. H. Davidow and B. Uttal, "Service Companies: Focus or Falter," *Harvard Business Review* 67 (July–August, 1989), pp. 77–85; C. Sewell and P. B. Brown, *Customers for Life: How to Turn That One-Time Buyer into a Lifetime Customer* (New York: Random House, 2002).

Chapter **Four**

Customer Perceptions of Service

This chapter's learning objectives are to:

1. Provide a solid basis for understanding what influences customer perceptions of service and the relationships among customer satisfaction, service quality, and individual service encounters.
2. Demonstrate the importance of customer satisfaction—what it is, the factors that influence it, and the significant outcomes resulting from it, such as customer loyalty.
3. Develop critical knowledge of service quality and its key dimensions, both online and offline.
4. Show that service encounters, or the "moments of truth," are the essential building blocks from which customers form their perceptions.

Jindal Nature Cure Institute: Service as a Strategic Differentiator

Established in 1979 by Padma Bhushan Dr. Sitaram Jindal, Jindal Nature Cure Institute (JNI) began as the Institute of Naturopathy and Yogic Sciences (INYS) in Bangalore. Founded under the Sitaram Jindal Foundation, a charitable trust, JNI was conceived as a philanthropic initiative to provide accessible, drug-free healthcare to all sections of society.

Dr. Jindal envisioned a holistic healing center that combined traditional naturopathy with modern scientific methods. The institute's mission is to promote a natural way of life, encouraging individuals to activate their innate ability to fight diseases without relying on drugs. In addition, it aimed to reduce the economic burden of preventable diseases, particularly for the weaker sections of society.

JNI's journey from a 107-bed facility to a renowned 550-bed hospital is a testament to its commitment to service and excellence. Located in the outskirts of Bangalore in a lush green 120-acre campus that oversees a natural lake, its serene, nature-integrated campus promotes peace, mindfulness, and recovery. Combined with well-trained, attentive staff and clear communication, JNI ensures a nurturing atmosphere that enhances healing. In the late 1990s, responding to increasing demand, JNI expanded by adding a 112-bed block catering to the middle-income group. The turn of the millennium saw further growth, with the establishment of Manav Charitable Hospital (MCH), equipped with physiotherapy, acupuncture, and diagnostic services, ensuring comprehensive care for patients.

Today, JNI treats approximately 15,000 patients annually, offering relief, prevention, and healing for various chronic and acute diseases. The institute's approach emphasizes lifestyle modification and disease-specific protocols, empowering patients to maintain health and prevent recurrence.

Service as a Differentiator

Holistic treatment approach – JNI's treatment methodology integrates multiple drug-free therapies, each contributing uniquely to the healing process. Naturopathy serves as the cornerstone, focusing on detoxification and restoring balance through natural elements. Yoga complements this by promoting physical and mental harmony. Diet therapy emphasizes natural, nutritious, and seasonal foods, while acupuncture addresses energy flow imbalances. Physiotherapy aids in physical rehabilitation to enhance mobility and reduce pain.

This multifaceted approach ensures comprehensive care, addressing the root causes of ailments rather than merely alleviating symptoms. It empowers patients to adopt healthier lifestyles, leading to long-term well-being.

Accessibility – JNI's commitment to service is evident in its diverse accommodation options, catering to patients from various socio-economic backgrounds. To ensure accessibility, JNI provides accommodation options for all economic segments – from dormitories and standard rooms to deluxe and VIP suites – while maintaining a consistent treatment quality for all. The wide range of options ensure that financial constraints do not hinder access to quality healthcare. This inclusivity reflects JNI's core value of providing equitable healthcare, aligning with its mission to serve all strata of society.

Patient-centric care – JNI places a strong emphasis on patient education and empowerment. Through personalized treatment plans, patients are guided on lifestyle modifications, dietary changes, and self-care practices. As every patient receives a customized treatment protocol based on her condition, lifestyle, and health goals, it ensures higher efficacy and patient satisfaction as each plan is tailored to individual needs. Such approach fosters a sense of ownership in the healing process, encouraging patients to actively participate in their recovery. This patient-centric model not only enhances treatment outcomes but also instills lasting habits that contribute to sustained health improvements. JNI doesn't just treat; it teaches. Patients are educated on nutrition, stress management, exercise, and sustainable lifestyle practices to prevent relapse and empower long-term self-care.

Technological integration – While rooted in traditional healing practices, JNI embraces modern technology to enhance patient care. The institute employs scientific methods for diagnosis and treatment planning, ensuring that therapies are tailored to individual needs. Its mobile application assists patients in managing their treatment schedules and stay informed about daily activities, further enhancing the patient experience. In addition, online consultation for naturopathy and yoga enables patients connect with JNI's expert naturopaths from home for natural healing and wellness.

JNI's diverse range of services underscores its holistic approach to health. Some of the therapies include –

- Naturopathy: Focuses on detoxification and restoring balance through natural elements.
- Yoga: Promotes physical and mental harmony.
- Diet therapy: Emphasizes natural, nutritious, and seasonal foods.

- Acupuncture: Addresses energy flow imbalances.
- Physiotherapy: Aids in physical rehabilitation, enhancing mobility and reducing pain.
- Hydrotherapy: Utilizes water in various forms to promote healing.
- Massage therapies include techniques like Kairali therapy, mud therapy and herbal massages for relaxation and pain relief.
- Fasting therapy: Guided fasting protocols help detoxify the body and eliminate toxins in the natural way. Doctors recommend a personalized diet, for each patient, with specific soups and juices during the fasting period.

These treatments are designed to work synergistically, addressing the physical, mental, and emotional aspects of every individual patient's health.

Jindal Nature Cure Institute stands as a beacon of holistic healthcare, where service transcends traditional medical treatment. JNI has redefined the standards of naturopathy in India through its comprehensive, drug-free therapies, inclusive approach, patient-centric care, while integrating digital technology. Its unwavering commitment to service continues to inspire and heal, making it a distinguished leader in the field.

Reference

1. https://jindalnaturecure.in/about-us/ Accessed on April 22, 2025
2. Vaidehi Patel (2013), 'Jindal Nature Cure set for global recognition' India Post, July 10 https://indiapost.com/jindal-nature-cure-set-for-global-recognition/ Accessed on April 22, 2025
3. https://www.sitaramjindalfoundation.org/hospitals.php Accessed on April 22, 2025

CUSTOMER PERCEPTIONS

How customers perceive services, how they assess whether they have experienced quality service and whether they are satisfied are the subjects of this chapter. We will be focusing on the *perceived service* box in the gaps model (displayed in Figure 2.1). As we move through this chapter, keep in mind that perceptions are always considered relative to expectations. Therefore, the entire discussion of quality and satisfaction is based on *customers' perceptions of the service*—not some predetermined objective criteria of what service is or should be. Because expectations are dynamic, evaluations may also shift over time—from person to person and from culture to culture. What is considered quality service or the things that satisfy customers today may be different tomorrow.

Satisfaction versus Service Quality

Practitioners and writers in the popular press sometimes use the terms *satisfaction* and *service quality* interchangeably, but researchers have attempted to be more precise about the meanings and measurement of the two concepts.[2] Consensus is that the two concepts

FIGURE 4.1
Customer Perceptions of Quality and Customer Satisfaction

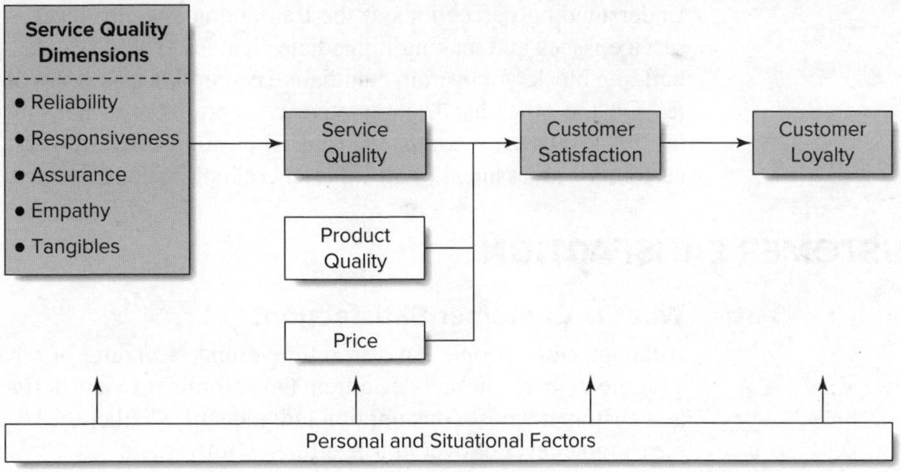

are fundamentally different in terms of their underlying causes and outcomes.[3] Although they have certain things in common, *satisfaction* is generally viewed as a broader concept, whereas *service quality* focuses specifically on dimensions of service. Based on this view, *perceived service quality* is a component of customer satisfaction. Figure 4.1 graphically illustrates the relationship between the two concepts.

As shown in Figure 4.1, service quality is a focused evaluation that reflects the customer's perception of reliability, assurance, responsiveness, empathy, and tangibles.[4] Customer satisfaction, on the other hand, is more inclusive: it is influenced by perceptions of service quality, product quality, and price. For example, service quality of a health club is judged on attributes such as whether equipment is available and in working order when needed, how responsive the staff are to customer needs, how skilled the trainers are, and whether the facility is well maintained. Customer satisfaction with the health club is a broader concept that will certainly be influenced by perceptions of service quality but that will also include perceptions of product quality (such as the quality of products sold in the pro shop), and the price of membership.[5] Moreover, perceived service/product quality, satisfaction, price evaluations, and loyalty can be influenced by personal factors such as the consumer's emotional state, and even uncontrollable situational factors such as weather conditions and experiences driving to and from the health club.[6]

Transaction-specific versus Cumulative Customer Perceptions

In considering perceptions, it is also important to recognize that customers will have perceptions of single, transaction-specific encounters as well as overall perceptions of a company based on all their experiences.[7] For example, a bank customer will have a perception of how he was treated in a particular encounter with an employee at a branch and will form a perception based on elements of the service experienced during that transaction. That perception is at a micro, transaction-specific level. The same bank customer will also have overall perceptions of the bank based on all his encounters over a period of time. The experiences might include multiple in-person encounters at the bank's branches, online banking experiences, and experiences using the bank's customer service (call) centers. At an even more general level, the customer may have perceptions of banking services or the whole banking industry as a result of all his experiences with banks and everything he knows about banking.

Research suggests that it is important to understand all these types of perceptions for different reasons and that the viewpoints are complementary rather than competing.[8]

Understanding perceptions at the transaction-specific level is critical for diagnosing service issues and making immediate changes. These isolated encounters are also the building blocks for overall, cumulative perceptions, as you will learn later in this chapter. On the other hand, cumulative perceptions are likely to be better predictors of overall loyalty to a company. That is, customer loyalty most often results from the customer's assessment of all experiences, not just one encounter.

CUSTOMER SATISFACTION

What Is Customer Satisfaction?

Although most people have an intuitive understanding of what satisfaction is, many struggle to give a formal definition. One prominent view defines customer satisfaction as a customer's post-consumption judgment of whether the service or good provided a pleasurable level of overall usage-related fulfillment.[9]

In less technical terms, we interpret this definition to mean that *satisfaction* is the customer's evaluation of a product or service in terms of whether that product or service has met the customer's expectations. Failure to meet expectations is assumed to result in *dissatisfaction* with the product or service.

In addition to a sense of *fulfillment* in the knowledge that one's expectations have been met, satisfaction can also be related to other types of feelings, depending on the context or type of service.[10] For example, satisfaction can be viewed as *contentment*—more of a passive response that customers may associate with services they do not think a lot about or services that they receive routinely over time. Satisfaction may also be associated with feelings of *pleasure* for services that make the customer feel good or are associated with a sense of happiness. For those services that really surprise the customer in a positive way, satisfaction may mean *delight.* In some situations, where the removal of a negative leads to satisfaction, the customer may associate a sense of *relief* with satisfaction. Finally, satisfaction may even be associated with feelings of *ambivalence* when there is a mix of positive and negative experiences associated with the product or service.

Although customer satisfaction tends to be measured at a particular point in time as if it were static, satisfaction is a dynamic target that may evolve over time, influenced by a variety of factors and by the passage of time itself.[11] Particularly when product usage or the service experience takes place over time, satisfaction may be highly variable, depending on which point in the usage or experience cycle one is focusing on. Similarly, in the case of very new services or a service not previously experienced, customer expectations may be barely forming at the point of initial purchase; these expectations will solidify as the process unfolds and the customer begins to form his or her perceptions. Through the service cycle the customer may have a variety of experiences—some good, some not good—and each will ultimately impact satisfaction.

What Determines Customer Satisfaction?

As shown in Figure 4.1, customer satisfaction is influenced by specific product or service features, perceptions of product and service quality, and price. In addition, personal factors such as the customer's mood or emotional state and situational factors such as family member opinions influence satisfaction.

Product and Service Features

Customer satisfaction with a product or service is influenced significantly by the customer's evaluation of product or service features.[12] For a service such as a resort hotel, important features might include the pool area, access to golf facilities, restaurants, room comfort and privacy, the helpfulness and courtesy of staff, room price, and so forth. In conducting satisfaction studies, most firms determine through some means (e.g., focus groups) what the important features and attributes are for their service and then measure perceptions of those features as well as overall service satisfaction. Research has shown that customers of services make trade-offs among different service features (e.g., price level versus quality versus friendliness of personnel versus level of customization), depending on the type of service being evaluated and the criticality of the service. Other research suggests that customers also increasingly have a "need for speed"; for example, they want to use various forms of automation to enjoy a quick and easy service experience.[13]

Customer Emotions

Customers' emotions can also affect their perceptions of satisfaction with products and services.[14] These emotions can be stable, preexisting emotions. For example, think of times when you are at a very happy stage in your life (such as when you are on vacation), and your good mood and positive frame of mind influence how you feel about the services you experience. Alternatively, when you are in a bad mood, your negative feelings may carry over into how you respond to services, causing you to overreact or respond negatively to any little problem. The effects of emotions on satisfaction are heightened for "high-emotion services" where customers have strong feelings (positive or negative) even before the service begins. Think, for example, of services associated with birth, marriage, illness, or death.[15]

Specific emotions may also be induced by the consumption experience itself, influencing a customer's satisfaction with the service. For example, research done in a river-rafting context showed that the river guides had a strong effect on their customers' emotional responses to the trip and that those feelings (both positive and negative) were linked to overall trip satisfaction.[16] Positive emotions such as happiness, pleasure, elation, and a sense of warm-heartedness enhanced customers' satisfaction with the rafting trip. In turn, negative emotions such as sadness, sorrow, regret, and anger led to diminished customer satisfaction. Overall, in the rafting context, positive

Jupiterimages/Getty Images

River rafters experience many positive emotions, increasing their satisfaction with the service.

emotions had a stronger effect than negative ones. (These positive emotions are apparent in the photo shown on page 85.) In a different context, drawing on emotional contagion theory, researchers found that the authenticity of employees' emotional display directly affected customers' emotions in a video retail and consulting service.[17] In short, as we will further discuss later in this book, employees' positive and negative emotions can affect both the customer's emotional state and ultimate satisfaction.

Attributions for Service Success or Failure

Attributions—the perceived causes of events—influence perceptions of satisfaction as well.[18] When customers have been surprised by an outcome (the service is either much better or much worse than expected), they tend to look for the reasons, and their assessments of the reasons can influence their satisfaction. For example, if a customer of a weight-loss organization fails to lose weight as hoped for, she will likely search for the causes—was it something she did, was the diet plan ineffective, or did circumstances simply not allow her to follow the diet regimen—before determining her level of satisfaction or dissatisfaction with the weight-loss company.[19] For many services, customers (because they are coproducers) take at least partial responsibility for how things turn out.

Even when customers do not take responsibility for the outcome, customer satisfaction may be influenced by other kinds of attributions. For example, research done in a travel agency context found that customers were less dissatisfied with a pricing error made by the agent if they felt that the reason was outside the agent's control or if they felt that it was a rare mistake, unlikely to occur again.[20]

Perceptions of Equity or Fairness

Customer satisfaction is also influenced by perceptions of equity and fairness.[21] Customers ask themselves: Have I been treated fairly compared with other customers? Did other customers get better treatment, better prices, or better-quality service? Did I pay a fair price for the service? Was I treated well in exchange for what I paid and the effort I expended? Notions of fairness are central to customers' perceptions of satisfaction with products and services, particularly in service recovery situations, as further discussed in Chapter 7. Sometimes cases of extreme unfairness result in FTC investigations into company practices. For example, many customers might believe that "throttling" is an unfair tactic. Throttling means that Internet, streaming, or cell phone providers deliberately slow down their service speeds once a customer has used a certain amount of data in a billing cycle. Obviously, this practice can dramatically affect the service experience. However, the Federal Trade Commission (FTC) noted that throttling can be illegal if companies limit their customers' Internet service speeds in an unfair or deceptive manner (e.g., by throttling when customers purchase an "unlimited plan").[22]

Other Customers, Family Members, and Coworkers

In addition to product and service features and one's own feelings and beliefs, customer satisfaction is often influenced by other people.[23] For example, family decisions about a vacation destination and satisfaction with the trip are dynamic phenomena, influenced by the reactions and emotions of individual family members.[24] Later, what family members express in terms of satisfaction or dissatisfaction with the trip will be influenced by stories retold among the family and selective memories of the events. Similarly, the satisfaction of the rafters in the photo is certainly influenced by individual perceptions, but it is also influenced greatly by the experiences, behavior, and views of the other rafters. In a business setting, satisfaction with a new service or technology—for example, a new customer relationship management software service (e.g., Microsoft's Dynamics 365)—will be influenced not only by individuals' personal experiences with the software itself but also by what others say about it in the company, how others use it and feel about it, and how widely it is adopted in the organization.

National Customer Satisfaction Indexes

Because of the importance of customer satisfaction to firms and consumers' overall quality of life, many countries have a national index that measures and tracks customer satisfaction at a macro level.[25] Many public policymakers believe that these measures could and should be used as tools for evaluating the health of the nation's economy, along with traditional measures of productivity and price. Customer satisfaction indexes begin to get at the *quality* of economic output, whereas more traditional economic indicators tend to focus only on *quantity*. The first such measure was the Swedish Customer Satisfaction Barometer introduced in 1989.[26] Later, similar indexes were introduced in Germany (Deutsche Kundenbarometer, or DK, in 1992), the United States (American Customer Satisfaction Index, ACSI, in 1994), and Switzerland (Swiss Index of Customer Satisfaction, SWICS, in 1998).[27] More recently, other countries, including the United Kingdom, India, South Korea, South Africa, Colombia, and Singapore, have adopted the ACSI methodology in creating national customer satisfaction indices (also see the Global Feature in this chapter).[28]

The American Customer Satisfaction Index

The American Customer Satisfaction Index (ACSI),[29] developed by researchers at the National Quality Research Center at the University of Michigan, is a measure of satisfaction with goods and services. The ACSI tracks customer satisfaction not only on a national level and for more than 400 companies/government agencies, but also reports aggregated scores for 10 economic sectors and nearly 50 industries. Within each industry group, major industry segments are included, and within each industry, the largest companies in that industry are selected to participate. For each company/agency, the ACSI conducts 100 to 250 interviews (with a total of roughly 300,000 customers annually), which provide the input to its econometric model that analyzes drivers and outcomes of customer satisfaction. More specifically, each company receives an ACSI score computed from its customers' perceptions of quality, value, satisfaction, expectations, complaints, and future loyalty.[30]

The 2018 and 2020 ACSI results for the 15 highest and 15 lowest ranked industries are shown in Table 4.1.[31] Interestingly, most categories across industries have declined in terms of percentage change. Looking at the table, it is evident that multiple durable and non-durable goods appear in the top section of the table (above 77) and all of the categories in the bottom half are services, with the very lowest being Internet service providers and subscription TV. It is important to point out, however, that these rankings are industry averages. Almost every industry has some strong performers in terms of customer satisfaction. For example, in 2020 scores for airlines ranged from 65 (Spirit) to 79 (Southwest Airlines).

Outcomes of Customer Satisfaction

Why all this attention to customer satisfaction? As mentioned in the previous section, some public policymakers believe that customer satisfaction is an important indicator of national economic health. They believe that it is not enough to track economic efficiency and pricing statistics. Customer satisfaction, they believe, is also an important indicator of well-being. Further, many believe that customer satisfaction is correlated with other measures of economic health such as corporate earnings and stock value.

Global Feature Comparing Customer Perceptions of Service Across Cultures

Customers in different parts of the world perceive, experience, and react to service experiences differently.

SERVICE QUALITY

The original development of the service quality dimensions of reliability, responsiveness, assurance, empathy, and tangibles was based on research conducted across multiple contexts within the United States. As a general rule, reliability comes through as the most important dimension of service quality in the United States, with responsiveness also being relatively important when compared with the remaining three dimensions. But what happens when we look across cultures? Are the same five service quality dimensions still important? Which ones are most important? Answers to these questions can be extremely valuable for companies delivering services across cultures or in multicultural environments.

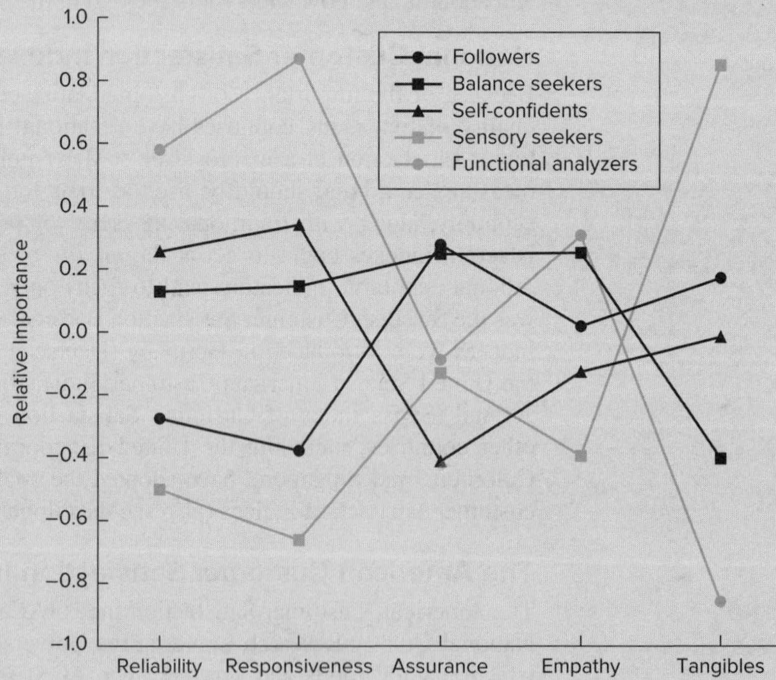

Researchers have used Geert Hofstede's well-established cultural dimensions to assess whether service quality importance would vary across different cultural orientations. For example, *power distance* refers to the extent to which status differences are expected and accepted within a culture. Research has suggested that most Asian countries are characterized by high power distance, whereas many Western countries score lower on power distance measures. Broadly speaking, *individualism* reflects a self-orientation that is characteristic of Western culture, whereas its opposite, *collectivism,* is more typical of the East. Similar comparisons across cultures have been made for the other dimensions: *masculinity, uncertainty avoidance,* and *long-term orientation.* The question is whether these types of cultural differences affect the importance consumers place on the service quality dimensions.

The figure shown here suggests strong differences in the importance of service quality dimensions across clusters of customers defined by different cultural dimensions. The cultural profile of the clusters is described as

Followers: Large power distance, high collectivism, high masculinity, neutral uncertainty avoidance, and short-term orientation.

Balance seekers: Small power distance, high collectivism, neutral masculinity, high uncertainty avoidance, and medium-term orientation.

Through the ACSI data, researchers at the University of Michigan have been able to document a clear relationship between performance of the ACSI stock market portfolio (made up of companies that perform well on the ACSI index) when compared to the S&P 500. This relationship is depicted in Figure 4.2, which shows the ACSI stock portfolio consistently out-performing the S&P 500.[32]

Beyond these macroeconomic implications, however, individual firms have discovered that increasing levels of customer satisfaction can be linked to a variety of a firm's financial performance metrics, such as revenue growth, market share, earnings, and

Self-confidents: Small power distance, high individualism, medium femininity, low uncertainty avoidance, and long-term orientation.

Sensory seekers: Large power distance, medium individualism, high masculinity, low uncertainty avoidance, and short-term orientation.

Functional analyzers: Small power distance, medium individualism, high femininity, high uncertainty avoidance, and long-term orientation.

From this figure it is clear that the service quality dimensions are relevant across cultures, but their relative importance varies depending on cultural value orientation.

GLOBAL CUSTOMER SATISFACTION

Because goods and services are crossing national borders relatively freely in a globalized economy and companies continue to internationalize their operations, marketers need to assess and compare customer satisfaction in increasingly diverse market environments. Therefore, researchers are working toward extending the model of the ACSI into a "Global Customer Satisfaction Index" to inform national policy makers, international organizations, and societal stakeholders. The objective is to combine multiple national indices of satisfaction in a synchronized program that uses comparable measures, methods, and models. The intended result is a Global Customer Satisfaction Index that allows cross-national comparisons of quality of services and goods. Although a truly global index does not yet exist, research groups, quality associations, and universities are working on national satisfaction indices in a range of countries in North and South America, Europe, Asia, and Africa.

For example, the European Union has launched a project to develop models that measure and analyze customer satisfaction in different European countries, across a variety of industries. This project ultimately evolved into the *Extended Performance Satisfaction Index* (EPSI; www.epsi-rating.com), which is based on approximately 300,000 telephone interviews per year conducted with both customers and other stakeholders across Europe. The EPSI program collects, analyzes, and distributes information about customer preferences, perceived quality, and customer loyalty to companies, not-for-profit organizations, and governmental agencies. The EPSI group conducts research predominantly in the United Kingdom, the Netherlands, and the Nordic and Baltic countries of Europe. For example, the EPSI analyzed customer satisfaction with the Telecommunication industry in the Scandinavian countries (2007–2020); the results suggest that, in an era when many human-to-human interactions become more digital, customers increasingly demand stability, connectivity, and functionality from their telecom providers. In parallel, the data also revealed meaningful differences between countries (e.g., overall customer satisfaction with mobile providers was 75.5 in Finland but 69.2 in Sweden, further illustrating that companies need to compare satisfaction across countries and cultures).

Interestingly, as the EPSI continues to evolve, it also examines sustainability as an important part of the customer experience. The corresponding *EPSI Sustainable Development Index* (SDI) measures customers' perceptions of whether a company invests in sustainable growth considering future generations, strives for economic success without the expense of social or environmental factors, and in general demonstrates social, environmental, and financial responsibility. The goal is to understand whether customer perceptions of a firm's sustainability affect customer satisfaction and loyalty. Indeed, the findings show that sustainable development is an important factor that increasingly influences customer experience, satisfaction, and loyalty.

Sources: G. Hofstede, *Cultures and Organizations: Software of the Mind* (New York, McGraw-Hill, 1991); O. Furrer, B. Shaw-Ching Liu, and D. Sudharshan, "The Relationships between Culture and Service Quality Perceptions," *Journal of Service Research* 2 (May 2000), pp. 355–371; www.geert-hofstede.com; C. Fornell, F.V. Morgeson III, G.T.M. Hult, and D. VanAmburg, "*The Reign of the Customer: Customer-Centric Approaches to Improving Satisfaction*," Springer, 2020; www.theacsi.org; www.epsi-rating.com

various metrics of market value.[33] Research also shows that firms that invest in service and excel in customer satisfaction offer excess returns to their shareholders. One study found that firms that did better than their competition in terms of satisfying customers (as measured by the ACSI) generated superior returns at a lower systematic risk.[34] Other research found that portfolios of stocks consisting of firms with high levels and positive changes in customer satisfaction outperform other portfolio combinations.[35]

As illustrated in Figure 4.3, the relationship between customer satisfaction and customer loyalty is particularly strong when customers are very satisfied. Thus, firms

TABLE 4.1 American Customer Satisfaction Index—Ratings by Industry 2018 and 2020

	ACSI Scores		Change
15 Highest Ranked Industries (in 2020)	**2018**	**2020**	**(% 2018 vs. 2020)**
Breweries	85	81	−4
Cell Phones	79	80	1
TVs and Media Players	83	80	−3
Soft Drinks	82	80	−2
Full-Service Restaurants	81	79	−2
Household Appliances	80	79	−1
Apparel	79	79	0
Food Manufacturing	82	79	−3
Online Investments	79	78	−1
Property and Casualty Insurance	81	78	−3
Life Insurance	80	78	−2
Automobiles and Light Vehicles	82	78	−4
Limited-Service Restaurants	80	78	−2
Online Retail	80	78	−2
Consumer Shipping	81	77	−4
	ACSI Scores		**Change**
15 Lowest Ranked Industries (in 2020)	**2018**	**2020**	**(% 2018 vs. 2020)**
Wireless Phone Service	74	74	0
Online News and Opinion	75	74	−1
Ambulatory Care	77	74	−3
U.S. Postal Service	73	73	0
Cooperative Energy Utilities	77	73	−4
Health Insurance	73	72	−1
Investor-Owned Energy Utilities	75	72	−3
Municipal Energy Utilities	75	72	−3
Gasoline Stations	74	71	−3
Landline Phone Service	70	70	0
Social Media	72	70	−2
Hospitals	76	69	−7
Video-on-Demand Service	68	68	0
Internet Service Providers	62	65	3
Subscription Television Service	62	64	2

Source: "American Customer Satisfaction Index—Ratings by Industry," ACSI website, www.theacsi.org.

that simply aim to satisfy customers may not be doing enough to engender loyalty. Xerox Corporation was one of the first, if not the first, companies to pinpoint this relationship. Through its pioneering customer research, Xerox discovered that customers giving Xerox a 5 (very satisfied) on a satisfaction scale were six times more likely to repurchase Xerox equipment than were those giving the company a 4 (somewhat satisfied).[36] Enterprise Rent-A-Car has also learned through its research that customers who give the highest rating to their rental experience are three times more likely to rent again than are those who give the company the second-highest rating.[37] These firm-level insights are consistent with a recent meta-analysis that examined customer satisfaction as a strategic lever for enhancing business performance. Analyzing nearly

FIGURE 4.2 Stock Market Performance of ACSI Stock Portfolio

Source: ACSI website, www.theacsi.org, "National Economic Indicator, Financial Indicator," accessed March 16, 2021.

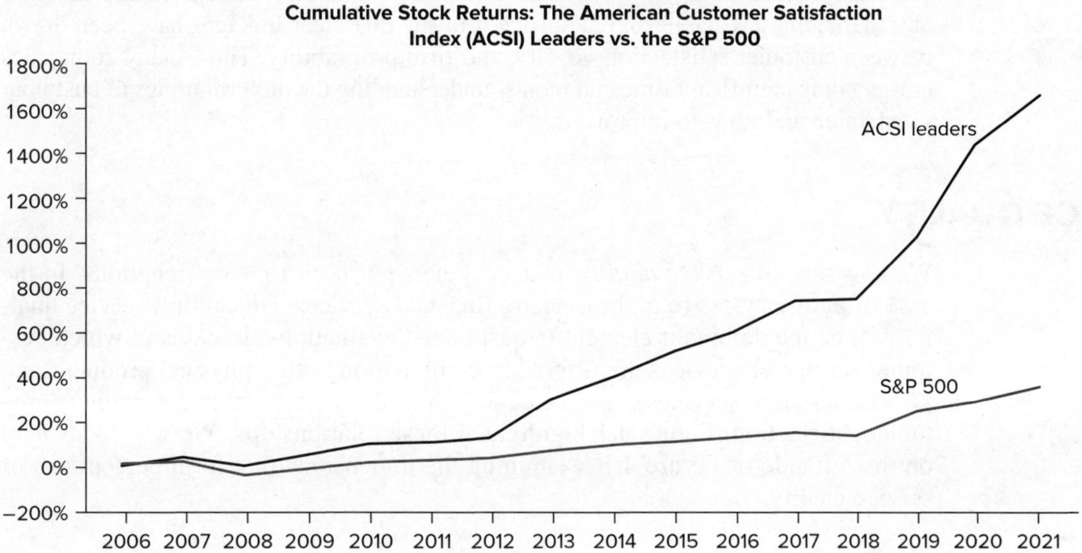

FIGURE 4.3 Relationship between Customer Satisfaction and Loyalty in Competitive Industries

Source: J. L. Heskett, W. E. Sasser Jr., and L. A. Schlesinger, *The Service Profit Chain: How Leading Companies Link Profit and Growth to Loyalty, Satisfaction, and Value* (New York: The Free Press, 1997), p. 83. The Free Press, a Division of Simon & Schuster, Inc.

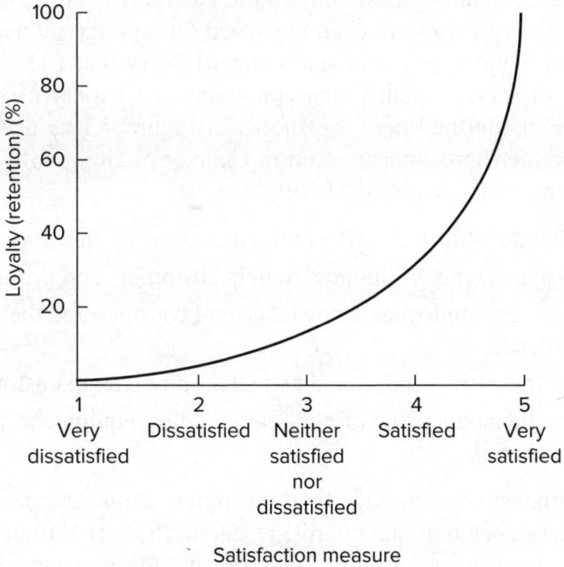

100 empirical studies (spanning from 1991 to 2017), this meta-analysis showed that, in general, customer satisfaction has a positive, significant effect on a firm's financial performance; notably, this effect is particularly strong in service (vs. goods) settings, because satisfied customers are typically more loyal and more profitable in services than goods businesses.[38]

At the opposite end of the satisfaction spectrum, researchers have also found that there is a strong link between dissatisfaction and disloyalty—or defection. Customer loyalty can fall off precipitously when customers reach a particular level of dissatisfaction or when they are dissatisfied with critically important service attributes.[39] We further discuss these relationships and the implications for relationship and loyalty marketing in Chapter 6, but suffice it to say that clear linkages have been drawn between customer satisfaction, loyalty, and firm profitability. Thus, many companies are spending significant time and money understanding the underpinnings of customer satisfaction and ways to improve it.

SERVICE QUALITY

We now turn to *service quality,* a critical element of customer perceptions. In the case of pure services (e.g., healthcare, financial services, education), service quality will be the dominant element in customers' evaluations. In cases in which customer service or services are offered in combination with a physical product (e.g., IT services, auto services), service quality may also be critical in determining customer satisfaction. Figure 4.1 highlighted these relationships. We will focus here on the left side of Figure 4.1, examining the dimensions that form perceptions of service quality.

Service Quality Dimensions

Research suggests that customers do not perceive quality in a unidimensional way but rather judge quality based on multiple factors relevant to the context. The dimensions of service quality have been identified through the pioneering research of Parsu Parasuraman, Valarie Zeithaml, and Leonard Berry. Their research has identified five dimensions of service quality that apply across a variety of service contexts.[40] The five dimensions defined here are shown in Figure 4.1 as drivers of service quality. These five dimensions appear again in Chapter 5, along with the scale developed to measure them, which is called SERVQUAL.

- *Reliability:* the ability to perform the promised service dependably and accurately.
- *Responsiveness:* the willingness to help customers and provide prompt service.
- *Assurance:* the employees' knowledge and courtesy and their ability to inspire trust and confidence.
- *Empathy:* the caring, individualized attention given to customers.
- *Tangibles:* the appearance of physical facilities, equipment, personnel, and communication materials.

These dimensions represent how customers think about service quality. On the basis of exploratory and quantitative research, these five dimensions were found relevant for banking, insurance, appliance repair and maintenance, securities brokerage, long-distance telephone service, automobile repair service, and others. The dimensions are also applicable to retail and business services, and logic suggests they would be relevant for internal services as well (services provided by firms to their own employees through, for example, an internal IT group, the corporate cafeteria, or human resources). Sometimes customers use all the dimensions to determine service quality perceptions, at other times not. For example, for an ATM, empathy is not likely to be a relevant dimension. And in a phone encounter to schedule a repair, tangibles will not be relevant.

Research suggests that cultural differences also affect the relative importance placed on the five dimensions, as discussed in our Global Feature. Interesting differences in service quality dimensions themselves also emerge in country-specific studies. For example, research in Pakistan that builds upon the original service quality dimensions revealed the following dimensions of service quality: tangibles, reliability, assurance, sincerity, personalization, and formality.[41] This study also illustrated that cultural differences may cause the original dimensions to be interpreted slightly differently as well. In Pakistan, "reliability" was not as absolute in its meaning, but rather was interpreted as "promises are mostly kept," "minimum errors are made on reports or statements," and "service is usually available when needed."

In the following pages we expand on each of the five original SERVQUAL dimensions and provide illustrations of how customers judge them.

Reliability: Delivering on Promises

Of the five dimensions, reliability has been consistently shown to be the most important determinant of perceptions of service quality among U.S. customers.[42] *Reliability* is defined as the ability to perform the promised service dependably and accurately. In its broadest sense, reliability means that the company delivers on its promises—promises about delivery, service provision, problem resolution, and pricing. Customers want to do business with companies that keep their promises, particularly their promises about the service outcomes and core service attributes.

One company that has effectively communicated and delivered on the reliability dimension for decades is Federal Express (FedEx). Over many decades, FedEx's service positioning around reliability has been reflected in phrases such as "when it absolutely, positively has to get there," and "the world on time." But even when firms do not choose to position themselves explicitly on reliability, as FedEx historically has done, this dimension is extremely important to consumers and can affect a company's competitiveness.[43] Therefore, all firms need to be aware of customer expectations of reliability. Firms that do not provide the core service that customers think they are buying fail their customers in the most direct way.

Barry Brecheisen/WireImage for NARAS/Getty Images

The Best Buy Geek Squad emphasizes the service quality dimension of responsiveness in its service positioning.

Responsiveness: Being Willing to Help

Responsiveness is the willingness to help customers and to provide prompt service. This dimension emphasizes attentiveness and promptness in dealing with customer requests, questions, complaints, and problems. Responsiveness is communicated to customers by the length of time they have to wait for assistance, answers to questions, or attention to problems. Notably, driven by the continued evolution of technologies, customers tend to have higher expectations that suggest a "need for speed" for the responsiveness of service companies.

To excel on the dimension of responsiveness, a company must view the process of service delivery and the handling of requests from the customer's point of view rather than from the company's point of view. Standards for speed and promptness that reflect the company's view of internal process requirements may be very different from the customer's requirements for speed and promptness. To truly distinguish themselves on responsiveness, companies need well-staffed customer service departments as well as responsive frontline people in all contact positions. The Geek Squad's 24-hour, 365-days-per-year technical assistance for computers, tablets, and other related equipment earned it a reputation for responsive, quick service—"because viruses aren't known for keeping business hours" (see photo on page 93). Responsiveness perceptions are diminished when customers must wait to get through by telephone, are put through to a complex voice mail system, or have trouble accessing the firm's website.

Assurance: Inspiring Trust and Confidence

Assurance is defined as employees' knowledge and courtesy and the ability of the firm and its employees to inspire customer trust and confidence. This dimension is likely to be particularly important for services that customers perceive as high risk or for services of which they feel uncertain about their ability to evaluate outcomes (in other words, services that are high in credence qualities as discussed in Chapter 1)—for example, banking, insurance, brokerage, medical, and legal services.

Trust and confidence may be embodied in the human service provider who links the customer to the company, such as securities brokers, insurance agents, lawyers, or counselors. In such service contexts the company seeks to build trust and loyalty between key frontline employees and individual customers. The "personal banker" concept captures this idea: customers are assigned to one banker who will get to know them individually and who will coordinate all their banking services.

In other situations, trust and confidence are embodied in the organization itself. Large insurance companies such as Allstate ("You're in good hands with Allstate") and State Farm ("Like a good neighbor, State Farm is there") but also smaller companies such as Assured Healthcare, a healthcare staffing agency that uses the tagline "Experience You Can Count On—Healthcare You Can Trust", illustrate efforts to create trusting relationships between customers and the company as a whole.

Empathy: Treating Customers as Individuals

Empathy is defined as the caring, individualized attention that the firm provides its customers. The essence of empathy is conveying, through personalized service, that customers are unique and special and that their needs are understood. Customers want to feel understood by and important to firms that provide service to them. Personnel at small service firms often know customers by name and build relationships that reflect their personal knowledge of customer requirements and preferences. When such a small firm competes with larger firms, the ability to be empathetic may give the small firm a competitive advantage.

In business-to-business services, customers want supplier firms to understand their industries and issues. Many small computer consulting firms successfully compete with large vendors by positioning themselves as specialists in particular industries. Even though larger firms have superior resources, the small firms are perceived as more knowledgeable about customers' specific issues and needs and are able to offer more customized services. However, in response to this reality, large companies often use "Key Account Management" to build close and loyal relationships and provide tailored service to customers that are strategically important to the business.

Tangibles: Representing the Service Physically

Tangibles are defined as the appearance of physical facilities, equipment, personnel, and communication materials. Tangibles typically provide physical representations or images of the service that customers, particularly new customers, will use to evaluate quality; but tangibles can also include virtual environments and websites. Service industries that emphasize tangibles in their strategies include services in which the customer visits the establishment to receive the service, such as restaurants and hotels, retail stores, and entertainment companies.

Although tangibles are often used by service companies to enhance their image, provide continuity, and signal quality to customers, most companies combine tangibles with another dimension to create a service quality strategy for the firm. For example, the financial service firm Capital One® introduced its Cafés in an effort to reimagine banking. The idea is to reinvent the traditional tangibles in a bank and replace them with design spaces with people and their needs in mind, while also attracting new customers.[44] In contrast, firms that do not pay attention to the tangibles dimension of the service strategy can confuse and even undermine an otherwise good strategy.

Table 4.2 provides examples of how customers judge each of the five dimensions of service quality across a variety of service contexts, including both consumer and business services.

E-Service Quality

The growth of e-tailing and e-services has led many companies to wonder how consumers evaluate service quality on the Web and whether the criteria are different from those used to judge the quality of non-Internet services.[45] An early study sponsored by the Marketing Science Institute was conducted to understand how consumers judge e-service quality.[46] In that study, *E-S-QUAL* is defined as the extent to which a website facilitates efficient and effective shopping, purchasing, and delivery. Through exploratory focus groups and two phases of empirical data collection and analysis, this research identified seven dimensions that are critical for core service evaluation (four dimensions) and service recovery evaluation (three dimensions).

The four core dimensions that customers use to judge websites at which they experience no questions or problems are as follows:[47]

- *Efficiency:* the ease and speed of accessing and using the site.
- *Fulfillment:* the extent to which the site's promises about order delivery and item availability are fulfilled.
- *System availability:* the correct technical functioning of the site.
- *Privacy:* the degree to which the site is safe and protects customer information.

The study also revealed three dimensions that customers use to judge recovery service when they have problems or questions:

- *Responsiveness:* the effective handling of problems and returns through the site.
- *Compensation:* the degree to which the site compensates customers for problems.
- *Contact:* the availability of assistance through telephone or online representatives.

TABLE 4.2 Examples of How Customers Judge the Five Dimensions of Service Quality

Industry	Reliability	Responsiveness	Assurance	Empathy	Tangibles
Car repair (consumer)	Problem fixed the first time and ready when promised	Accessible; no waiting; responds to requests	Knowledgeable mechanics	Acknowledges customer by name; remembers previous problems and preferences	Repair facility; waiting area; uniforms; equipment
Airline (consumer)	Flights to promised destinations depart and arrive on schedule	Prompt and speedy system for ticketing, in-flight baggage handling	Trusted name; good safety record; competent employees	Understands special individual needs; anticipates customer needs	Aircraft; ticketing counters; baggage area; uniforms
Medical care (consumer)	Appointments are kept on schedule; diagnoses prove accurate	Accessible; no waiting; willingness to listen	Knowledge; skills; credentials; reputation	Acknowledges patient as a person; remembers previous problems; listens well; has patience	Waiting room; exam room; equipment; written materials
Architecture (business)	Delivers plans when promised and within budget	Returns phone calls; adapts to changes	Credentials; reputation; name in the community; knowledge and skills	Understands client's industry; acknowledges and adapts to specific client needs; gets to know the client	Office area; reports; plans themselves; billing statements; dress of employees
IT Department (internal)	Provides needed information when requested	Prompt response to requests; not "bureaucratic"; deals with problems promptly	Knowledgeable staff; well trained; credentials	Knows internal customers as individuals; understands individual and departmental needs	Internal reports; office area; dress of employees
Internet brokerage (consumer and business)	Provides correct information and executes customer requests accurately	Quick website with easy access and no downtime	Credible information sources on the site; brand recognition; credentials apparent on-site	Responds with human interaction as needed	Appearance of the website as well as flyers, brochures, and other print materials

More recent findings in this dynamic research area further support the idea that E-Service Quality is the function of multiple distinct dimensions, specifically, (1) website design (e.g., information quality, aesthetics, convenience), (2) fulfilment (e.g., time of delivery, order accuracy), (3) customer service (e.g., handling of returns and recovery), and (4) security/privacy. Together these underlying dimensions form customer-perceived E-Service Quality and influence downstream outcomes such as customer satisfaction and repurchase intentions.[48]

SERVICE ENCOUNTERS: THE BUILDING BLOCKS FOR CUSTOMER PERCEPTIONS

We have just finished a discussion of customer perceptions, specifically customer satisfaction and service quality (but also see Exhibit 4.1 for insights about customer effort and service convenience as additional drivers of customer loyalty). As discussed in our Strategy Insight, companies today recognize that they can compete more effectively by distinguishing themselves with respect to service quality, satisfaction, and loyalty. Next, we turn to what have been termed the building blocks for customer perceptions—service encounters, or "moments of truth." Service encounters are where promises are kept or broken and where the proverbial rubber meets the road. It is from these service encounters that customers build their perceptions.

Service Encounters or Moments of Truth

From the customer's point of view, the most vivid impression of service occurs in the *service encounter,* or *moment of truth,* when the customer interacts with the service firm. For example, among the service encounters that a hotel customer experiences are checking into the hotel, being taken to a room by a bellperson, eating a restaurant meal, requesting a wake-up call, and checking out. You could think of the linking of these moments of truth as a service encounter cascade where each individual encounter in the experience cascade has the potential to bolster or undermine perceptions of the service (see Figure 4.4). It is in these encounters that customers assess the organization's service quality, and each encounter contributes to the customer's overall satisfaction and willingness to do business with the organization again. From the organization's point of view, each encounter thus presents an opportunity to prove its potential as a quality service provider and to increase customer loyalty. A sequence of encounters can also be linked to form a customer experience. In the hotel example, all individual encounters would link together to comprise an "end-to-end customer experience," or "customer journey." Such a customer journey could include many encounters and extend over days—or even weeks, in the case of an extended stay.

Some services have few service encounters, and others have many. The Disney Corporation estimates that each of its amusement park customers experiences about 74 service encounters and that a negative experience in any one of them can lead to a negative overall evaluation.

The Importance of Service Encounters

Although some events in the encounter cascade can be especially important (e.g., encounters at the beginning or toward the end of the cascade), *any* encounter can be critical in determining customer satisfaction and loyalty. If a customer is interacting with a firm for the first time, that initial encounter will create a first impression of the organization. In these first encounter situations, the customer frequently has no other basis for judging the organization, and the initial contact with the firm can take on significant importance in the customer's perceptions of quality.

Even when the customer has had multiple interactions with a firm, each individual encounter is important in creating a composite image of the firm in the customer's memory. In today's technology-mediated world, these encounters can occur online through websites, mobile applications, and other Internet-based channels as well as in

Exhibit 4.1 Customer Effort and Convenience as Drivers of Customer Loyalty

Customer effort, and relatedly perceived service convenience, are additional drivers of customer loyalty (distinct from quality or satisfaction) that have attracted considerable attention from businesses and researchers. For example, based on surveys of more than 75,000 business-to-consumer and business-to-business customers about their non-face-to-face service interactions (including live calls, web-based interactions, chat, and e-mail) researchers determined that customer loyalty was based not so much on "delighting" customers or even satisfying them, but rather on minimizing the effort they needed to expend to get their problems solved. The researchers contend that making things difficult and inconvenient (i.e., high effort) for customers will drive them away, while delighting them is not as likely to make them stay. In the context of customer service, when a customer is seeking an answer or solution to a problem with a product or service, this makes total sense. When customers have a problem that needs to be solved, they want it solved quickly with minimal effort on their part. In this context, the researchers suggest that companies should focus on anticipating and heading off the need for follow-up calls, dealing with the emotional side of interactions, minimizing the need for customers to switch to a different service channel to solve their problem, and truly—not just speedily—solving the customer's problem.

More broadly, scholars have studied the effects of service convenience on customer satisfaction and loyalty, and also developed scales to measure how customers assess convenience. In one foundational study, researchers measured service convenience through five dimensions with their SERVCON scale. Specifying these five dimensions, the researchers show that customers perceive time and effort costs associated with (1) service purchase or use decisions (i.e., decision convenience), (2) initiating service delivery and accessing the service location (i.e., access convenience), (3) experiencing the core benefits through identifying and selecting the offering a consumer wishes to buy (i.e., benefit convenience), (4) finalizing the transaction via payment and potential paperwork (i.e., transaction convenience), and (5) reestablishing subsequent contact with the firm for customer service issues such as returns, complaints, or warranty-related requests (i.e., post-benefit/after-sales convenience). Understanding these distinct dimensions helps managers reduce the time and effort related to the corresponding stages of the service experience; this is important because empirical results suggest that service convenience dimensions drive customers' satisfaction and their repurchases.

Many companies today are engaged in measuring customer effort as a way to predict loyalty, and it seems to be a good predictor in customer service situations. The concepts of customer effort and service convenience also seem to be compatible with the five dimensions of service quality and the dimensions of e-service quality, all of which are focused on delivery of the basic service rather than delighting or going above and beyond. That said, there are likely many service situations, outside of basic customer service, where customers are seeking to be delighted (e.g., a long-awaited vacation, a special concert, or a first (or fiftieth) anniversary dinner). In other cases, customers may prefer or expect to expend considerable personal effort to cocreate the service for themselves. In other words, they are not looking to minimize their effort. This is often true of such important service experiences as weddings, educational degrees, or health-related services. For example, one study found that additional effort that patients had to invest into their healthcare experience can, under certain circumstances, elicit a state of "eustress" (i.e., positive stress akin to "rising to a challenge") that can make the service experience more positive for them. Therefore, in some service settings, other elements are likely more important in determining customer loyalty than is effort or convenience. While customers are never looking to waste their time and effort in any situation, they are not always looking to minimize it either.

Sources: Create an Effortless Customer Service Experience, www.gartner.com, accessed September 15, 2021; M. Mende, M.L. Scott, M.J. Bitner, and A.L. Ostrom, "Activating Consumers for Better Service Coproduction Outcomes through Eustress: the Interplay of Firm-assigned Workload, Service Literacy, and Organizational Support," *Journal of Public Policy & Marketing* 36, no. 1 (2017), pp. 137–155; K. Seiders, G.B. Voss, A.L. Godfrey, and D. Grewal, "SERVCON: Development and Validation of a Multidimensional Service Convenience Scale," *Journal of the Academy of Marketing Science* 35, no. 1 (2007), pp. 144–156; M. Dixon, N. Toman, and R. Delisi, *The Effortless Experience: Conquering the New Battleground for Customer Loyalty* (London: Penguin Books, Ltd., 2013); M. Dixon, K. Freeman, and N. Toman, "Stop Trying to Delight Your Customers," *Harvard Business Review* (July–August 2010), pp. 116–122.

person or over the phone. Many positive experiences add up to a composite image of high quality, whereas many negative interactions have the opposite effect. On the other hand, a combination of positive and negative interactions leave the customer feeling unsure of the firm's quality, doubtful of its consistency in service delivery, and vulnerable to the appeals of competitors.

Logic suggests that not all encounters are equally important in building relationships. For every organization, certain encounters are probably key to customer satisfaction.

FIGURE 4.4 **Service Encounters as Building Blocks of Service Quality, Customer Satisfaction, and Loyalty**

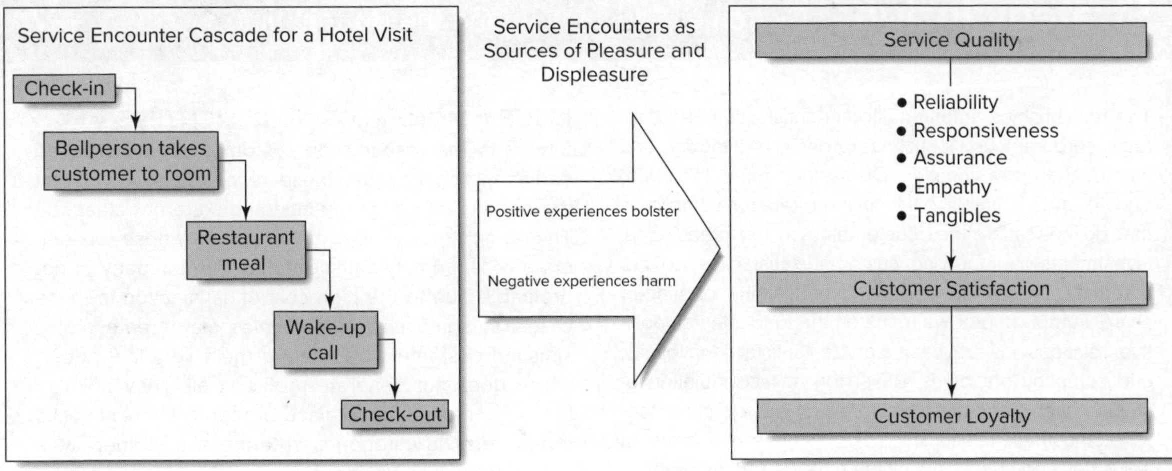

In a hospital context, a study of patients revealed that encounters with nursing staff were more important in predicting satisfaction than were encounters with meal service or patient discharge personnel.[49] Research also suggests that service quality will be influenced by the pattern of events in terms of the timing, frequency, and proximity of negative, or failed service encounters, relative to delightful service encounters.[50] And research in a call center context concludes that, although the average quality of the individual events in a service encounter sequence are important, satisfaction can be enhanced by providing a positive peak experience within the sequence.[51] This and other research suggests that "not all events in an experience sequence are created equal" and that, in fact, there are benefits to be gained by creating truly delightful (or "peak") experiences at predetermined points in the sequence.

Types of Service Encounters

A service encounter occurs every time a customer interacts with the organization. There are three general types of service encounters: *remote encounters, technology-mediated encounters,* and *face-to-face encounters.*[52] A customer may experience any of these types of encounters, or a combination of all three, in his or her interactions with a service firm.

First, encounters can occur without any direct human contact (*remote encounters*), such as when a customer interacts with a bank through the ATM system or with a retailer through its website. Although there is no direct human contact in these remote encounters, each represents an opportunity for the firm to reinforce or establish quality perceptions in the customer. In remote encounters the tangible evidence of the service and the quality of the technical processes and systems become the primary bases for judging quality. Retail purchases, airline ticketing, repair and maintenance trouble-shooting, and package and shipment tracking are just a few examples of services available via the Internet. All these types of service encounters can be considered remote encounters (see our Technology Spotlight).

In many organizations (such as insurance companies, utilities, and telecommunications), the most frequent type of encounter between an end-customer and the firm occurs over the telephone or via simultaneous texting, live chats, or other platforms

Strategy Insight Customer Satisfaction and the Bottom Line

The relationships among customer satisfaction and strategic corporate goals such as growth, profitability, and market share are complex. On the one hand, long-term growth and profitability are very unlikely for companies that do not satisfy their customers. On the other hand, investments in improving customer satisfaction do not automatically pay off in growth, profitability, or market share. In this chapter we focus on the fundamental, positive relationships between service, satisfaction, loyalty, and company outcomes. Based on an accumulation of studies over many decades, research has clearly established that these relationships exist across a wide range of industries and contexts. Multiple reviews and meta-analyses of this research (e.g., the meta-analyses by Otto et al. 2020 and Hogreve et al. 2017) reconfirm the fundamental, core beliefs in these important relationships. Yet no one would deny that there are important nuances, and managers must be cognizant of these. Simply improving customer satisfaction does not ensure bottom-line outcomes, let alone precisely predict the levels of these outcomes.

For example, the nuances and complexities of these strategic relationships were studied by Timothy Keiningham, Sunil Gupta, Lerzan Aksoy, and Alexander Buoye, and reported in the *MIT Sloan Management Review*. This team of researchers demonstrated that the overall direct relationship between customer satisfaction and customer spending is weak, that the return on investments for customer satisfaction is often very low, and that absolute levels of satisfaction are not what truly matters. Instead, what matters is the level of satisfaction relative to competing alternatives.

The researchers raise some issues to consider when determining whether "satisfaction is worth the cost."

ISSUE 1: MONEY-LOSING DELIGHTERS

Similar to the research on customer effort discussed earlier in this chapter, these researchers found that the benefits of delighting customers are not clear cut. They point to a number of companies whose customers are "extremely satisfied," but the company is not profitable due to the high cost of satisfaction in those cases. In some cases companies may create highly satisfied customers by offering them very low prices, which does not generate profits at all. They point to the e-commerce marketplace Groupon, where six of its top-performing categories in terms of customer satisfaction were actually money-losers. A meta-analysis by Hogreve et al. (2017), which included more than 500 empirical studies, further emphasizes this cautionary note as it found that investments in service quality can indeed have a negative direct effect on firm profitability. Thus managers need to look carefully at the potential payback for delighting customers, compared to the costs of doing so.

ISSUE 2: SMALLER OFTEN EQUALS HAPPIER

The idea that high customer satisfaction would correlate positively with market share seems to carry with it some logic. Yet these researchers show that customer satisfaction and market share do not go hand in hand. In fact, some of the highest levels of customer satisfaction are experienced by smaller businesses and non-market-share leaders, and conversely, high market share companies do not necessarily have the highest levels of satisfaction. Examples of this phenomenon include McDonald's and Walmart, which are the market-share leaders in their categories, but which do not

that allow technology-based communication with a real person in real time (*technology-mediated encounters*). The judgment of quality in such technology-mediated encounters is different than in remote encounters because there is greater potential variability in the interaction. Tone of voice and language, employee knowledge, and effectiveness/efficiency in handling customer issues become important criteria for judging service quality in these encounters.

A third type of encounter is the one that occurs between an employee and a customer in direct personal contact (*face-to-face encounters*). For example, in a hospital such as Mayo Clinic, face-to-face encounters occur between patients and reception staff, nurses, doctors, lab technicians, food service workers, pharmacy staff, and others. For a company such as IBM, in a business-to-business setting, direct encounters enjoy the highest levels of satisfaction by any means. The likely explanation is the diverse appeal that these market leaders must have in these broad industry categories. They are serving a diversity of needs and types of customers, resulting in more variability, and lower overall satisfaction. Thus, if market share is a company's primary goal, it must carefully weigh its corresponding customer satisfaction investments.

ISSUE 3: THE IMPORTANCE OF BEING NO. 1

The researchers also found that customer satisfaction is not a good predictor of what a customer will spend with a particular company—that is, their "share of wallet." They show conclusively that customers' share of wallet is related to their relative satisfaction—that is, how do they feel about a particular service brand when compared to others? Absolute satisfaction is therefore not a good predictor of spending or share of wallet. Rather, it is the relative satisfaction that counts.

So What Is a Manager to Do?

First, it is important for all managers to understand that no company will survive very long without satisfied customers. And, having too many truly dissatisfied customers can quickly ruin a business. These are fundamental truths. Yet managers must go into the customer satisfaction business with their eyes open and a clear understanding of their corporate goals, aligning these with their satisfaction strategies.

For example, if the overriding corporate goal is to increase market share and be the market leader, then there needs to be more latitude for customer satisfaction. Often, mass-market brands suffer in terms of customer satisfaction when compared with their smaller, niche, competitors. If the overriding corporate goal is to maximize profits (particularly in the short run), then the costs of investing in customer satisfaction must be carefully considered and balanced with the benefits. Careful segmentation to understand which customers are profitable will also allow for more targeted investments to enhance the satisfaction of the most profitable (or potentially profitable) customers. Finally, managers also need to consider the relevance of the nature of their offering. For example, the meta-analysis by Otto et al. (2020) showed that the effect of customer satisfaction on financial firm performance is stronger in (pure) service settings relative to goods and hybrid (goods-services) settings.

The bottom line: think carefully about customer satisfaction and understand how it fits into the total picture of the company's goals. Then measure it and invest in it accordingly. But never ignore it or dismiss it as unimportant!

Sources: A. S. Otto, D. M. Szymanski, and R. Varadarajan, "Customer Satisfaction and Firm Performance: Insights From Over a Quarter Century of Empirical Research," *Journal of the Academy of Marketing Science* 48 (May 2020), pp. 543–564; J. Hogreve, A. Iseke, K. Derfuss, and T. Eller, "The Service–Profit Chain: A Meta-Analytic Test of a Comprehensive Theoretical Framework," *Journal of Marketing* 81 (May 2017), pp. 41–61; V. Mittal and C. Frennea, "Customer Satisfaction: A Strategic Review and Guidelines for Managers," Marketing Science Institute, 2010; S. Gupta and V. Zeithaml, "Customer Metrics and Their Impact on Financial Performance," *Marketing Science* 25 (November-December 2006), pp. 718–739; T. Keiningham, S. Gupta, L. Aksoy, and A. Buoye, "The High Price of Customer Satisfaction," *MIT Sloan Management Review*, 55 (April 2014), pp. 37–46; T. Keiningham, L. Aksoy and L. Williams, *The Wallet Allocation Rule* (Hoboken, NJ: John Wiley & Sons, Inc., 2015).

occur between the business customer and salespeople, delivery personnel, maintenance representatives, and professional consultants. Determining and understanding service quality issues in face-to-face contexts is the most complex of all. Both verbal and nonverbal behaviors are important determinants of service quality, as are tangible cues such as employee dress and other symbols of service (equipment, informational brochures, physical setting).

Sources of Pleasure and Displeasure in Service Encounters

Because of the importance of service encounters in building perceptions, researchers have extensively analyzed service encounters in many contexts to determine the sources of customers' favorable and unfavorable impressions. The research uses the

Technology Spotlight Customers Love Amazon

rvlsoft/Shutterstock

Amazon.com's website states that the company "seeks to be Earth's most customer-centric company, where customers can find and discover anything they might want to buy online." Jeff Bezos, Founder and former CEO of Amazon, whose company name has become a household word worldwide, has always believed that his customers come first, and in his 2011 letter to shareowners he stated that "the long-term interests of shareowners are perfectly aligned with the interests of customers." Building on this clear focus on customers, relationships, and value, net sales increased 38 percent to $386.1 billion in 2020, compared with $280.5 billion in 2019. Amazon is also one of the world's most valuable brands (e.g., Forbes ranked Amazon #4 most valuable brand in 2020 with a value of more than $135 billion). According to Bezos, "Customers come first. If you focus on what customers want and build a relationship, they will allow you to make money."[53]

In its core business, online book sales, Amazon has taken a historically interpersonally dominated transaction and successfully transformed it into a web-based service experience. Let's take a closer look at what the company is doing in this space and why customers love it so much. Since its inception in July 1995, Amazon has grown to the point where it offers more book titles than any brick-and-mortar bookstore could ever hope to stock, so selection and availability of titles are one key to its popularity with customers. But that is just the beginning. In addition to a wide selection, Amazon has invested significant effort to simulate the feel of a neighborhood bookstore, where a patron can mingle with other customers, discuss books, and get recommendations from bookstore employees.

Over the years, Amazon has incorporated user feedback into product pages and added the "look inside" feature, so that readers can sample books easily. Amazon allows customers to find related books on virtually any topic by simply typing key words and initiating a search of its massive database. Its one-to-one marketing system allows the company to track what individual customers buy and let them know of additional titles that might interest them.

In 2007, Amazon introduced the Kindle, a technology device that allows customers to read books and other print materials on a personal electronic reader. But the Kindle is more than a reading device—it also allows owners to shop for books, read reviews, and purchase and download books in seconds via a wireless connection that operates 24 hours per day. Its trademarked Whispersync technology ensures that customers have their reading library with them wherever they go and that they have all of their highlights, notes, and most recently read pages immediately accessible. In only a few years, sales of books on Kindles overtook those of paper books as the most popular format for Amazon book sales.

As with its other innovations and services, Amazon has designed the Kindle from the customer's perspective, enhancing the design and changing features to ensure the loyalty of serious readers, rather than to keep up with the latest available bells and whistles of technology. The technology that powers the Kindle is invisible to the customer, and the enhancements are made to improve the experience. As Bezos has said, "For the vast majority of books, adding video and animation is not going to be helpful. It is distracting rather than enhancing. You are not going to improve Hemingway by adding video snippets."

Few would deny that Amazon is a master of technology and technology-based services for consumers. The rapid growth of Amazon Web Services (AWS) since its launch in 2006 is a testament to this fact. AWS allows companies to offload data storage and computing to Amazon's cloud,

critical incident technique to get customers and employees to provide verbatim stories about satisfying and dissatisfying service encounters they have experienced (see Chapter 5 for a detailed description and references for the critical incident technique).

On the basis of research that documents thousands of service encounter stories, four common themes—recovery (after failure), adaptability, spontaneity, and coping—have been identified as the sources of customer dis/satisfaction in critical service encounters.[54]

David Ryder/Getty Images

Jeff Bezos, founder and former CEO of Amazon.

and more recently, it has added databases, developer tools, and analytics software to its portfolio of capabilities.

Additionally, in 2015 Amazon expanded into smart home automation technology with its Amazon Echo device. Echo, also known as Alexa, began as a voice-activated speaker that can play music and provide information, such as the latest news, weather, and sports scores. Amazon has continued to build on Echo's capabilities by releasing "skills," which allow the device to communicate with other apps and smart devices in the home, such as Uber, Nest thermostats, Philips Hue lightbulbs, and even Domino's Pizza. By allowing Echo to interact with a wide variety of apps and devices, customers have the flexibility to use the device in a way that best suits their lifestyle.

In addition from its humble beginnings as a free two-day shipping program for avid Amazon customers, Amazon Prime has grown to offer music, movies, books, photo storage, and many other perks, all for a yearly fee.

Continuing its technology innovation, Amazon Robotics conducts scientific research to deliver even more convenient and consistent customer experiences through a variety of technologies (e.g., autonomous mobile robots, language perception, computer vision, and machine learning). Amazon has also secured approval from the United States Federal Aviation Administration to operate its fleet of "Prime Air" delivery drones to deliver packages to customers.

Sources: Amazon.com, www.amazon.com, accessed September 15, 2021; Forbes Most Valuable Brands, www.forbes.com/the-worlds-most-valuable-brands, accessed September 15, 2021; https://amazonrobotics.com, accessed September 15, 2021; A. Palmer, "Amazon Wins FAA Approval for Prime Air Drone Delivery Fleet," https://www.cnbc.com/2020/08/31/amazon-prime-now-drone-delivery-fleet-gets-faa-approval.html, accessed September 15, 2021; A. Penenberg, "The Evolution of Amazon," *Fast Company*, July–August 2009, pp. 66–72, 74; J. Authors, "An Amazing 10-year Amazonian Adventure LONG VIEW," *Financial Times*, April 28, 2007, p. 24; G. Fowler, "Kindle to Go 'Mass Market,'" *The Wall Street Journal*, July 29, 2010, p. 6; S. Woo, "Amazon Grows—at a High Price," *The Wall Street Journal*, January 28, 2011, p. B1; G. A. Fowler, "Amazon's Alexa Listens and Learns," *The Wall Street Journal*, April 14, 2016, p. D1.

Recovery—Employee Response to Service Delivery System Failures

The first theme includes all incidents in which there has been a failure of the service delivery system and an employee is required to respond in some way to consumer complaints and disappointments. The failure may be, for example, a hotel room that is not available, an airplane flight that is delayed six hours, an incorrect item sent from an e-commerce company, or a critical error on a document (e.g., an invoice). The content or form of the employee's response is what causes the customer to remember the event either favorably or unfavorably. The nuances of service recovery, including employee behaviors and customer responses, have been studied extensively by researchers and organizations. You will find an entire chapter in this book, Chapter 7, devoted to service recovery research and best practices.

Adaptability—Employee Response to Customer Needs and Requests

A second theme underlying dis/satisfaction in service encounters is how adaptable the service delivery system is when the customer has special needs or requests that place demands on the process. In these cases, customers judge service quality in terms of the flexibility of the employees and the system. Incidents in this category all contain an implicit or explicit request for customization of the service to meet a need. Such requests might result from "customer deficiencies," including deficiencies of physical capabilities, knowledge, financial resources, and/or time constraints.[55] Much of what customers see as special needs or requests may actually be rather routine from the employee's point of view; what is important is that the customer perceives that something special is being done for her based on her own individual needs. Customers are pleased when the service provider puts forth the effort to accommodate and adjust the system to meet their requirements. On the flip side, they are angered and frustrated by an unwillingness to try to accommodate and by promises that are never followed through. Customer contact employees also see their abilities to adapt the system as being a prominent source of customer satisfaction, and often they are equally frustrated by constraints that keep them from being flexible.

Spontaneity—Unprompted and Unsolicited Employee Actions

Even when there is no system failure and no special request or need, customers can still remember service encounters as being very dis/satisfying. Employee spontaneity in delivering memorably good or poor service is the third theme. Satisfying incidents in this group represent very pleasant surprises for the customer (special attention, being treated like royalty, receiving something nice but not requested), whereas dissatisfying incidents in this group represent unacceptable employee behaviors (rudeness, stealing, discrimination, ignoring the customer).

Coping—Employee Response to Problem Customers

The incidents categorized in this group came to light when *employees* were asked to describe service encounter incidents in which customers were either very satisfied or dissatisfied. In addition to describing incidents of the types outlined under the first three themes, employees described many incidents in which customers were the cause of their own dissatisfaction. Such customers were basically uncooperative—that is, unwilling to cooperate with the service provider, other customers, industry regulations, and/or laws. In these cases nothing the employee could do would result in the customer feeling pleased about the encounter. The term *coping* is used here to describe these incidents because coping is behavior generally required of employees to handle problem customer encounters. Rarely are such encounters satisfying from the customer's point of view. Also of interest is that customers themselves did not relate any "problem customer" incidents. That is, customers either do not see, or choose not to remember or retell, stories of the times when they themselves were unreasonable to the point of causing their own dissatisfaction.

Table 4.3 summarizes the specific employee behaviors that cause dis/satisfaction in service encounters according to the four themes of recovery, adaptability, spontaneity, and coping.

TABLE 4.3 General Service Behaviors Based on Service Encounter Themes—Dos and Don'ts

Theme	Do	Don't
Recovery	Acknowledge problem Explain causes Apologize Compensate/upgrade Lay out options Take responsibility	Ignore customer Blame customer Leave customer to fend for himself or herself Downgrade Act as if nothing is wrong "Pass the buck"
Adaptability	Recognize the seriousness of the need Acknowledge Anticipate Attempt to accommodate Adjust the system Explain rules/policies Take responsibility	Ignore Promise but fail to follow through Show unwillingness to try Embarrass the customer Laugh at the customer Avoid responsibility "Pass the buck"
Spontaneity	Take time Be attentive Anticipate needs Listen Provide information Show empathy	Exhibit impatience Ignore Yell/laugh/swear Steal from customers Discriminate
Coping	Listen Try to accommodate Explain Let go of the customer	Take customer's dissatisfaction personally Let customer's dissatisfaction affect others

Summary

This chapter described customer perceptions of service by first introducing two critical concepts: customer satisfaction and service quality. These critical customer perceptions were defined and discussed in terms of the factors that influence each of them. Customer satisfaction is a broad perception influenced by features and attributes of the product as well as by customers' emotional responses, their attributions, and their perceptions of fairness. Service quality, the customer's perception of the service component of a product, is also a critical determinant of customer satisfaction. Sometimes, as in the case of a pure service, service quality may be the *most* critical determinant of satisfaction. Perceptions of service quality are based on five dimensions: reliability, responsiveness, assurance, empathy, and tangibles.

Another major purpose of the chapter was to introduce the idea of service encounters, or "moments of truth," as the building blocks for both satisfaction and service quality. Every service encounter (whether remote, technology-mediated, or in person) is an opportunity to build customer perceptions of service quality and satisfaction. The underlying themes of pleasure and displeasure in service encounters were also described.

Chapters 3 and 4 have provided you with a grounding in customer issues relevant to services. These two chapters are intended to give you a solid understanding of service expectations and perceptions. Through the rest of the book, we illustrate strategies that firms can use to close the customer gap (between customer expectations and perceptions).

Discussion Questions

1. What is customer satisfaction, and why is it so important? Discuss how customer satisfaction can be influenced by each of the following: product attributes and features, customer emotions, attributions for success or failure, perceptions of fairness, and family members or other customers.
2. What is the ACSI? Do you believe that such national indicators of customer satisfaction should be included as benchmarks of national economic well-being similar to gross domestic product (GDP), price indicators, and productivity measures?
3. Why do service companies generally receive lower satisfaction ratings in the ACSI than nondurable and durable product companies?
4. Discuss the differences between perceptions of service quality and customer satisfaction. When is this distinction particularly relevant?
5. List and define the five dimensions of service quality. Describe the services provided by a firm you do business with (e.g., your bank, your doctor, your favorite restaurant) on each of the dimensions. In your mind, has this organization distinguished itself from its competitors on any particular service quality dimension?
6. Describe a remote encounter, a technology-mediated encounter (phone, texting, or live chat), and a face-to-face encounter that you have had recently. How did you evaluate the encounter, and what were the most important factors determining your satisfaction/dissatisfaction in each case?
7. Describe an "encounter cascade" for an airplane flight. In your opinion, what are the most important encounters in this cascade for determining your overall impression of the quality of the airline?
8. Assume that you are a manager of a health club. Discuss general strategies you might use to maximize customers' positive perceptions of your club. How would you know if you were successful?

Exercises

1. Keep a journal of your service encounters with different organizations (at least five) during the week. For each journal entry, ask yourself the following questions: What circumstances led up to this encounter? What did the employee say or do? How did you evaluate this encounter? What exactly made you evaluate the encounter that way? What should the organization have done differently (if anything)? Categorize your encounters according to the four themes of service encounter satisfaction/dissatisfaction (recovery, adaptability, spontaneity, coping).
2. Interview someone with a non-U.S. cultural background. Ask the person about service quality, whether the five dimensions of quality are relevant, and which are most important in determining the quality of banking services (or some other type of service) in the person's country.
3. Interview an employee of a local service business. Ask the person to discuss each of the five dimensions of service quality with you as it relates to the person's company. Which dimensions are most important? Are any dimensions *not* relevant in this context? Which dimensions does the company do best? Why? Which dimensions could benefit from improvement? Why?
4. Interview a manager, an owner, or a president of a business. Discuss with this person the strategies he or she uses to ensure customer satisfaction. How does service quality enter into the strategies, or does it? Find out how this person measures customer satisfaction and/or service quality.
5. Visit Amazon.com's website. Visit a traditional bookstore. How would you compare the two experiences? Compare and contrast the factors that most influenced

your satisfaction and perceptions of service quality in the two different situations. When would you choose to use one versus the other?

6. Visit the ACSI or EPSI website and examine some of the industry- and firm-specific statistics (over time). Identify and discuss some of the major trends.

Notes

1. https://www.zanes.com/, accessed August 2021; C. Zane, *Reinventing the Wheel* (Dallas, TX: BenBella Books, 2011); "Creating Lifetime Customers," http://www.Christopherzanecom/media/, accessed July 2011; A. Danigelis, "Local Hero: Zane's Cycles," *Fast Company,* September 2006, p. 60; D. Fenn, *Alpha Dogs: How Your Small Business Can Become a Leader of the Pack* (New York: Collins, 2003); Chris Zane presentation at "Compete through Service" Symposium, November 2010, Center for Services Leadership, Arizona State University. Also see excellent YouTube videos of Chris Zane speaking to business audiences about his strategy, accessed 2016.
2. For more discussion of the debate on the distinctions between quality and satisfaction over time, see A. Parasuraman, V. A. Zeithaml, and L. L. Berry, "Reassessment of Expectations as a Comparison Standard in Measuring Service Quality: Implications for Future Research," *Journal of Marketing* 58 (January 1994), pp. 111–124; R. L. Oliver, "A Conceptual Model of Service Quality and Service Satisfaction: Compatible Goals, Different Concepts," in *Advances in Services Marketing and Management,* vol. 2, ed. T. A. Swartz, D. E. Bowen, and S. W. Brown (Greenwich, CT: JAI Press, 1994), pp. 65–85; M. J. Bitner and A. R. Hubbert, "Encounter Satisfaction vs. Overall Satisfaction vs. Quality: The Customer's Voice," in *Service Quality: New Directions in Theory and Practice,* ed. R. T. Rust and R. L. Oliver (Newbury Park, CA: Sage, 1993), pp. 71–93; D. Iacobucci, K. A. Grayson, and A. L. Omstrom, "The Calculus of Service Quality and Customer Satisfaction: Theory and Empirical Differentiation and Integration," in *Advances in Services Marketing and Management,* vol. 3, ed. T. A. Swartz, D. E. Bowen, and S. W. Brown (Greenwich, CT: JAI Press, 1994), pp. 1–67; P. A. Dabholkar, C. D. Shepherd, and D. I. Thorpe, "A Comprehensive Framework for Service Quality: An Investigation of Critical Conceptual and Measurement Issues through a Longitudinal Study," *Journal of Retailing* 76 (Summer 2000), pp. 139–173; J. J. Cronin Jr., M. K. Brady, and G. T. M. Hult, "Assessing the Effects of Quality, Value, and Customer Satisfaction on Consumer Behavioral Intentions in Service Environments," *Journal of Retailing* 76 (Summer 2000), pp. 193–218.
3. See, in particular, Parasuraman, Zeithaml, and Berry, "Reassessment of Expectations"; Oliver, "A Conceptual Model of Service Quality"; and M. K. Brady and J. J. Cronin Jr., "Some New Thoughts on Conceptualizing Perceived Service Quality: A Hierarchical Approach," *Journal of Marketing* 65 (July 2001), pp. 34–49.
4. A. Parasuraman, V. A. Zeithaml, and L. L. Berry, "SERVQUAL: A Multiple-Item Scale for Measuring Consumer Perceptions of Service Quality," *Journal of Retailing* 64 (Spring 1988), pp. 12–40.
5. Parasuraman, Zeithaml, and Berry, "Reassessment of Expectations."
6. Oliver, "A Conceptual Model of Service Quality."
7. See V. Mittal, P. Kumar, and M. Tsiros, "Attribute-Level Performance, Satisfaction, and Behavioral Intentions over Time," *Journal of Marketing* 63 (April 1999), pp. 88–101; L. L. Olsen and M. D. Johnson, "Service Equity, Satisfaction, and Loyalty: From Transaction-Specific to Cumulative Evaluations," *Journal of*

Service Research 5 (February 2003), pp. 184–195; P. C. Verhoef, G. Antonides, and A. N. De Hoog, "Service Encounters as a Sequence of Events: The Importance of Peak Experiences," *Journal of Service Research* 7 (August 2004), pp. 53–64.

8. Olsen and Johnson, "Service Equity, Satisfaction, and Loyalty."
9. R. L. Oliver, *Satisfaction: A Behavioral Perspective on the Consumer* (New York: McGraw-Hill, 1997); also see: A. S. Otto, D. M. Szymanski, and R. Varadarajan, "Customer Satisfaction and Firm Performance: Insights from Over a Quarter Century of Empirical Research," *Journal of the Academy of Marketing Science* 48, no. 3 (2020), pp. 543–564.
10. For a more detailed discussion of the different types of satisfaction, see E. Arnould, L. Price, and G. Zinkhan, *Consumers,* 2nd ed. (New York: McGraw-Hill, 2004), pp. 754–796.
11. S. Fournier and D. G. Mick, "Rediscovering Satisfaction," *Journal of Marketing* 63 (October 1999), pp. 5–23; Verhoef, Antonides, and De Hoog, "Service Encounters as a Sequence of Events"; G. Pizzi, G. L. Marzocchi, C. Orsinger, A. Zammit, "The Temporal Construal of Customer Satisfaction," *Journal of Service Research* 18 (November 2015), pp. 484–497.
12. Oliver, *Satisfaction,* chap. 2.
13. A. Ostrom and D. Iacobucci, "Consumer Trade-Offs and the Evaluation of Services," *Journal of Marketing* 59 (January 1995), pp. 17–28; ACSImatters.com, "3 Up-and-Coming Drivers of Customer Satisfaction," accessed April 22, 2021.
14. For more on emotions and satisfaction, see Oliver, *Satisfaction,* chap. 11; L. L. Price, E. J. Arnould, and S. L. Deibler, "Consumers' Emotional Responses to Service Encounters," *International Journal of Service Industry Management* 6 (1995), pp. 34–63.
15. L. L. Berry, S. W. Davis, and J. Wilmet, "When the Customer is Stressed," *Harvard Business Review*, October 2015, Vol. 93, No. 10, pp. 86–94.
16. L. L. Price, E. J. Arnould, and P. Tierney, "Going to Extremes: Managing Service Encounters and Assessing Provider Performance," *Journal of Marketing* 59 (April 1995), pp. 83–97.
17. T. Hennig-Thurau, M. Groth, M. Paul, and D. D. Gremler, "Are All Smiles Created Equal? How Emotional Contagion and Emotional Labor Affect Service Relationships," *Journal of Marketing* 70 (July 2006), pp. 58–73.
18. For more on attributions and satisfaction, see V. S. Folkes, "Recent Attribution Research in Consumer Behavior: A Review and New Directions," *Journal of Consumer Research* 14 (March 1988), pp. 548–565; and Oliver, *Satisfaction,* chap. 10; and Y. Van Vaerenbergh, C. Orsingher, I. Vermeir, and B. Lariviere, "A Meta-Analysis of Relationships Linking Service Failure Attributions to Customer Outcomes," *Journal of Service Research* 17 (November 2014), pp. 381–398.
19. A. R. Hubbert, "Customer Co-Creation of Service Outcomes: Effects of Locus of Causality Attributions," doctoral dissertation, Arizona State University, Tempe, Az, 1995.
20. M. J. Bitner, "Evaluating Service Encounters: The Effects of Physical Surroundings and Employee Responses," *Journal of Marketing* 54 (April 1990), pp. 69–82.
21. For more on fairness and satisfaction, see E. C. Clemmer and B. Schneider, "Fair Service," in *Advances in Services Marketing and Management,* vol. 5, ed.

T. A. Swartz, D. E. Bowen, and S. W. Brown (Greenwich, CT: JAI Press, 1996), pp. 109–126; Oliver, *Satisfaction,* chap. 7; Olsen and Johnson, "Service Equity, Satisfaction, and Loyalty"; K. Seiders and L. L. Berry, "Service Fairness: What It Is and Why It Matters," *Academy of Management Executive* 12 (May 1998), pp. 8–20.

22. J. Archer, "Disney+ Joins Netflix, Apple, Amazon And YouTube In Throttling Streaming Quality During Coronavirus Outbreak," Forbes.com, accessed April 22, 2021, https://www.forbes.com/sites/johnarcher/2020/03/21/disney-joins-netflix-apple-amazon-and-youtube-in-throttling-streaming-quality-during-coronavirus-outbreak/?sh=261962f7753f.
23. Fournier and Mick, "Rediscovering Satisfaction."
24. A. M. Epp and L. L. Price, "Designing Solutions around Customer Network Identity Goals," *Journal of Marketing* 75 (March 2011), pp. 36–54.
25. C. Fornell, M. D. Johnson, E. W. Anderson, J. Cha, and B. E. Bryant, "The American Customer Satisfaction Index: Nature, Purpose, and Findings," *Journal of Marketing* 60 (October 1996), pp. 7–18; *ACSI 10-Year Report Analysis (1994–2004),* University of Michigan, National Quality Research Center, 2005, www.theacsi.org.
26. E. W. Anderson, C. Fornell, and D. R. Lehmann, "Customer Satisfaction, Market Share, and Profitability: Findings from Sweden," *Journal of Marketing* 58 (July 1994), pp. 53–66.
27. M. Bruhn and M. A. Grund, "Theory, Development and Implementation of National Customer Satisfaction Indices: The Swiss Index of Customer Satisfaction (SWICS)," *Total Quality Management* 11 (2000), pp. S1017–S1028; A. Meyer and F. Dornach, "The German Customer Barometer," http://www.service-barometer.de.or.
28. See www.theacsi.org and F. V. Morgeson III, S. Mithas, T. L. Keiningham, and L. Aksoy, "An Investigation of the Cross-national Determinants of Customer Satisfaction," *Journal of the Academy of Marketing Science* 39 (April 2011), pp. 198–215.
29. Fornell, Johnson, Anderson, Cha, and Bryant, "The American Customer Satisfaction Index"; *ACSI 10-Year Report Analysis.*
30. For a listing of companies and their scores, go to the ACSI website at www.theacsi.org; also see: https://www.theacsi.org/about-acsi/the-science-of-customer-satisfaction.
31. ACSI website, www.theacsi.org.
32. Ibid, "National Economic Indicator, Financial Indicator," ACSI website, accessed October 30, 2021, www.theacsi.org.
33. See C. Fornell, F. V. Morgeson III, G. T. M. Hult, and D. VanAmburg, *The Reign of the Customer: Customer-Centric Approaches to Improving Satisfaction* (Springer Nature, 2020); J. L. Heskett, W. E. Sasser Jr., and L. A. Schlesinger, *The Service Profit Chain* (New York: Free Press, 1997); S. Gupta and V. A. Zeithaml, "Customer Metrics and Their Impact on Financial Performance," *Marketing Science* 25 (November–December 2006), pp. 718–739.
34. C. Fornell, F.V. Morgeson III, G.T.M. Hult, and D. VanAmburg, *The Reign of the Customer: Customer-Centric Approaches to Improving Satisfaction* (Springer Nature 2020).
35. L. Aksoy, B. Cooil, C. Groening, T. L. Keiningham, and A. Yalcin, "The Long-Term Stock Market Valuation of Customer Satisfaction," *Journal of Marketing* 72 (July 2008), pp. 105–122.

36. M. A. J. Menezes and J. Serbin, *Xerox Corporation: The Customer Satisfaction Program,* case no. 591-055 (Boston: Harvard Business School, 1991).
37. F. F. Reichheld, "The One Number You Need to Grow," *Harvard Business Review,* December 2003, pp. 47–54.
38. A. S. Otto, D. M. Szymanski, and R. Varadarajan, "Customer Satisfaction and Firm Performance: Insights from Over a Quarter Century of Empirical Research," *Journal of the Academy of Marketing Science* (May 2020), pp. 543–564.
39. E. W. Anderson and V. Mittal, "Strengthening the Satisfaction–Profit Chain," *Journal of Service Research* 3 (November 2000), pp. 107–120; B. Hindo, "Satisfaction Not Guaranteed," *BusinessWeek,* June 19, 2006, pp. 32–36.
40. Parasuraman, Zeithaml, and Berry, "SERVQUAL: A Multiple-Item Scale." Details on the SERVQUAL Scale and the actual items used to assess the dimensions are provided in Chapter 5.
41. N. Raajpoot, "Reconceptualizing Service Encounter Quality in a Non-Western Context," *Journal of Service Research* 7 (November 2004), pp. 181–201.
42. Parasuraman, Zeithaml, and Berry, "SERVQUAL: A Multiple-Item Scale." C. Zhou, P. Albuquerque, and R. Grewal, "Competition and Firm Service Reliability Decisions: A Study of the Airline Industry," *Journal of Marketing Research* 58 (April 2021), pp. 377–399.
43. Zhou, Chen, Paulo Albuquerque, and Rajdeep Grewal. "Competition and firm service reliability decisions: A study of the airline industry." *Journal of Marketing Research* 58, no. 2 (2021): 377–399.
44. Capital One: "9 Things You Can Do at a Capital One Caf ," https://www.capitalone.com/learn-grow/money-management/explore-capital-one-cafes/, accessed October 20, 2021.
45. For more on customer satisfaction and service quality delivery via the Internet and technology, see: M. L. Meuter, A. L. Ostrom, R. I. Roundtree, and M. J. Bitner, "Self-Service Technologies: Understanding Customer Satisfaction with Technology-Based Service Encounters," *Journal of Marketing* 64 (July 2000), pp. 50–64; V. A. Zeithaml, A. Parasuraman, and A. Malhotra, "Service Quality Delivery through Web Sites: A Critical Review of Extant Knowledge," *Journal of the Academy of Marketing Science* 30 (Fall 2002), pp. 362–375; M. Wolfinbarger and M. Gilly, "Etailq: Dimensionalizing, Measuring and Predicting Etail Quality," *Journal of Retailing* 79 (2003), pp. 183–198; B. B. Holloway and S. E. Beatty, "Satisfiers and Dissatisfiers in the Online Environment," *Journal of Service Research* 10 (May 2008), pp. 347–364.
46. A. Parasuraman, V. A. Zeithaml, and A. Malhotra, "E-S-QUAL: A Multiple-Item Scale for Assessing Electronic Service Quality," *Journal of Service Research* 7 (February 2005), pp. 213–233.
47. M. Blut, "E-Service Quality: Development of a Hierarchical Model," *Journal of Retailing* 92 (December 2016), pp. 500–517; M. Blut, N. Chowdhry, V. Mittal, and C. Brock, "E-Service Quality: A Meta-Analytic Review," *Journal of Retailing* 91 (December 2015), pp. 679–700.
48. Ibid.
49. K. Sivakumar, M. Lei, and B. Dong, "Service Quality: The Impact of Frequency, Timing, Proximity, and Sequence of Failures and Delights," *Journal of Marketing* 78 (January 2014), pp. 41–58.

50. P. C. Verhoef, G. Antonides, and A. N. De Hoog, "Service Encounters as a Sequence of Events: The Importance of Peak Experiences," *Journal of Service Research* 7, no. 1 (2004), pp. 53–64.

51. G. L. Shostack, "Planning the Service Encounter," in *The Service Encounter,* ed. J. A. Czepiel, M. R. Solomon, and C. F. Surprenant (Lexington, MA: Lexington Books, 1985), pp. 243–254.

52. For a complete discussion of the research on which this section is based, see: M. J. Bitner, B. H. Booms, and M. S. Tetreault, "The Service Encounter: Diagnosing Favorable and Unfavorable Incidents," *Journal of Marketing* 54 (January 1990), pp. 71–84; M. J. Bitner, B. H. Booms, and L. A. Mohr, "Critical Service Encounters: The Employee's View," *Journal of Marketing* 58 (October 1994), pp. 95–106; D. Gremler and M. J. Bitner, "Classifying Service Encounter Satisfaction across Industries," in *Marketing Theory and Applications,* ed. C. T. Allen et al. (Chicago: American Marketing Association, 1992), pp. 111–118; D. Gremler, M. J. Bitner, and K. R. Evans, "The Internal Service Encounter," *Journal of Service Industry Management* 5 (1994), pp. 34–56.

53. Bitner, Booms, and Mohr, "Critical Service Encounters."

54. S. E. Beatty, J. Ogilvie, W. M. Northington, M. P. Harrison, B. B. Holloway, and S. Wang, "Frontline Service Employee Compliance with Customer Special Requests," *Journal of Service Research* 19 (May 2016), pp. 158–173.

55. Amazon.com, www.amazon.com, accessed September 5, 2021.

[illegible] Sequence [illegible] analysis [illegible]

[illegible] Signals, [illegible] Bootstrap [illegible]

[illegible] (1989) [illegible]

[illegible]

[illegible] Lecture Notes [illegible]

[illegible]

Part Three

Understanding Customer Requirements

THE LISTENING GAP

Not knowing what customers expect is one of the root causes of not delivering to customer expectations. Provider Gap 1, the listening gap, is the difference between customer expectations of service and company understanding of those expectations. Note that in the accompanying figure we created a link between the customer and the company, showing customer expectations above the line that dissects the model and provider perceptions of those expectations below the line. This alignment signifies that what customers expect is not always the same as what companies believe they expect.

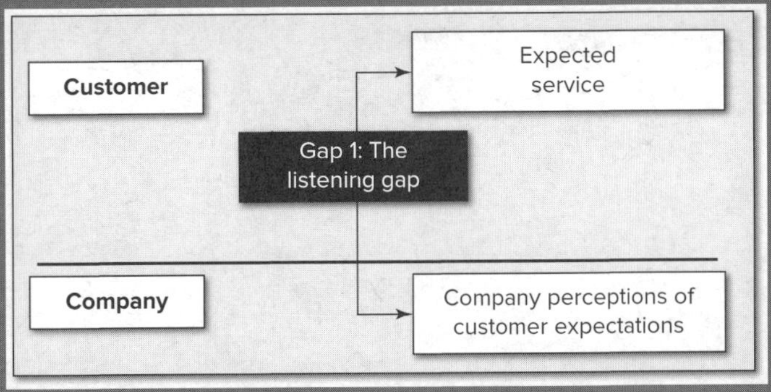

Part Three describes three ways to close provider Gap 1. In Chapter 5, we detail ways companies can listen to customers through research. Both formal and informal methods of customer research are described, including surveys, critical incident studies, and complaint solicitation. Upward communication from frontline employees to managers, another key factor in listening to customers, is also discussed.

Chapter 6 covers company strategies to retain customers and strengthen relationships with them, an approach called relationship marketing. Relationship marketing is distinct from transactional marketing, which tends to focus on acquiring new customers rather than retaining them. When organizations have strong relationships with their customers, opportunities for in-depth listening increase over time, and the listening gap is less likely to occur. A variety of strategies, including the creation of switching barriers and the development of relationship bonds, are suggested as means of relationship development and, ultimately, the cultivation of customer loyalty.

Chapter 7 describes service recovery, another strategy useful in closing provider Gap 1. Service recovery involves understanding why customers complain, what they expect when they complain, and how to deal with, and as much as possible prevent, service failures. Firms engaged in service recovery must, along with other approaches, create a complaint-handling procedure, empower employees to react in real time to fix failures, and guarantee service. Service recovery strategies seek to gain insight from service failures, allowing firms to better understand customers and their expectations.

Chapter Five

Listening to Customers through Research

This chapter's learning objectives are to:

1. Present the types of and guidelines for customer research in services.
2. Show how customer research information can and should be used for services.
3. Describe the strategies by which companies can facilitate interaction and communication between management and customers.
4. Present ways that companies can facilitate interaction between frontline employees and management.

Improving Customer Experiences by Researching Customer Journeys

As you will learn in this chapter, many different research approaches are needed to fully understand customer expectations and perceptions. You will also discover that most of the approaches involve either measuring touchpoints—individual encounters between the customer and the company—or overall service quality/customer satisfaction summary assessments at the end of the service experience. As we will discuss, each of these two major categories has its benefits but each also has its limitations. Measuring customer touchpoints or individual interactions such as a single phone call, service visit, or a sale helps the company understand the performance in that encounter, allowing for process improvements in the interaction and assessment of how employees are performing in that process.

However, the problem with measuring touchpoints in isolation is that each of them can be optimized (even 95 percent satisfaction or higher) while the customer's overall satisfaction can be significantly lower. Consider a service for which customers must make multiple phone calls (to initiate a service, to begin using the service, to question, to report problems, to report additional problems). If short surveys follow each phone call, customers may rate each of the isolated encounters high but because they had to make so many calls for the service, they will evaluate the overall service as tedious, confusing, and unsatisfactory. A summary score on service at the very end of the provision, on the other hand, limits the ability of the company to pinpoint which encounters are the most critical.

An innovative trend is to research the more encompassing "customer journeys," which ultimately form the overall customer experiences. Research experts now know that only by looking at experiences through the customers' own eyes—along the entire experience—can companies really improve service excellence. Customer journeys include clusters of integrated touchpoints that happen before, during, and after the experience of using a service. Examples of such clusters are deciding on a service, beginning to use the service, resolving issues, upgrading a service, or renewing a subscription service. Rather than viewing the multiple touchpoints involved in each cluster as single, isolated events, each with its own metric, journeys are groups of events that customers perceive to be connected. Therefore, they should be measured as linked clusters rather than as individual touchpoints.

So how does a company change to a journey-focused measurement approach? Let us take an example of a purchase that some of you may be making within the next decade or so: a kitchen remodel. How should a remodeling company such as Lowe's or Home Depot tackle this issue? According to McKinsey Consulting, six actions are critical to managing customer experience journeys.

- The first is to step back and identify the nature of the journeys customers take—from *their points of view*.
- The second step is to understand how customers navigate across the touchpoints as they move through the journey.
- Third, the company must anticipate the customers' needs, expectations, and desires during each part of the journey. The company must develop a research approach to determine these in each *cluster* rather than each touchpoint. Instead of conducting simple focus groups, companies must use techniques to deepen empathy for the customer's pain points using customer diaries or ethnographic observation. In these types of approaches, researchers watch or accompany customers in stores, and conduct continual live testing and design iterations with customers during the process.
- The fourth step is to build an understanding of what is working and what is not.
- Fifth, the company must set priorities for the most important gaps and opportunities to improve the journey.
- Sixth, they must fix root cause issues.

Customer research has demonstrated that there are huge benefits to examining the total customer experience rather than individual touchpoints. In one study, for example, McKinsey found that improving a customer experience from merely average to something that wows the consumer can lead to a 30- to 50-percent increase in behavioral measures such as likelihood of purchasing the service or product again. Similarly, academic studies also show that effective customer journey design increases customer loyalty. For example, one study (which included customers in Europe and the United States) showed that effective customer journey design influences customer loyalty directly, and indirectly (because it also increases consumer attitudes toward the brand). Importantly, the same study also found that the magnitude of these direct and indirect effects on customer loyalty are stronger for services than goods (as a function of the characteristics of services, discussed in Chapter 1). Such research further underscores that service managers need to carefully design meaningful customer journeys to improve the customers' brand experience rather than focusing on single touchpoints. Not surprisingly, leading companies (e.g., Apple, Amazon, BMW, and IKEA) are increasingly focused on effective customer journey design.[1]

USING CUSTOMER RESEARCH TO UNDERSTAND CUSTOMER EXPECTATIONS

Despite a genuine interest in meeting customer expectations, many companies miss the mark by thinking inside out—they believe they know what customers *should* want and deliver that, rather than finding out what customers *do* want. When this happens, companies are likely to provide services that do not match customer expectations: important features are left out, and the levels of performance on features that are provided are inadequate. Because services have few clearly defined and tangible cues, this problem may be considerably larger than it is in manufacturing firms. A far better approach involves thinking *outside in*—determining customer expectations and then delivering to them. Thinking outside in uses marketing research to understand customers and their requirements fully. Marketing research, the subject of this chapter, involves far more than conventional surveys. It consists of a portfolio of listening strategies that allows companies to deliver service to customer expectations.

Finding out what customers expect is essential to providing service quality and customer research is a key vehicle for understanding customer expectations and perceptions of services. In services, as with any offering, a firm that does no customer research at all is unlikely to understand its customers. A firm that does customer research, but not on the topic of customer expectations, may also fail to know what is needed to stay in tune with changing customer requirements. Customer research must focus on service issues such as what features are most important to customers, what levels of these features customers expect, and what customers think the company can and should do when problems occur in service delivery. Even when a service firm is small and has limited resources to conduct research, it can explore what customers expect.

In this section we discuss the elements of service marketing research programs that help companies identify customer expectations and perceptions. In the sections that follow, we will discuss how general customer research may need to be adjusted to maximize its effectiveness in services.

Research Objectives for Services

The first step in designing service marketing research is the most critical: defining the problem and research objectives. This is where the service marketer poses the questions to be answered or problems to be solved with research. Does the company want to know how customers view the service provided by the company, what customer requirements are, how customers will respond to a new service introduction, or what customers will want from the company five years from now? Each of these research questions requires a different research strategy. Thus, it is essential to devote time and resources to define the research objective(s) thoroughly and accurately. In spite of the importance of this first stage, many customer research studies are initiated without adequate attention to objectives.

Research objectives should translate into action questions. While many different questions are likely to be part of a customer research program, the following are the most common research objectives in services:

- To discover customer requirements or expectations for service.
- To monitor and track service performance.
- To assess overall company performance compared with that of competition.
- To assess gaps between customer expectations and perceptions.

Indian Service Strategy Insight LitmusWorld – Helping Businesses Enhance their Customer's Experience

LitmusWorld, co-founded in 2015 by Ramesh Natarajan, Ajay Row, and Manish Srivastava, began as an enterprise SaaS platform focusing on customer experience management. The platform helps businesses connect with their customers by enabling them to understand customer expectations and their experiences with their brands through direct conversations. Over nine years, LitmusWorld has helped more than 165 brands across 12 countries understand and improve their customers' journeys. It focuses on making businesses more agile and profitable by improving customer interactions. The company believes that positive customer experiences lead to business success.

The platform serves both external customers and internal employees. LitmusWorld has facilitated over 126 million conversations to help business leaders improve customer centricity. The platform gathers feedback through multiple channels including SMS, emails, QR codes, mobile apps, and websites. It offers comprehensive multi-lingual support across more than 19 languages, including English, Hindi, Tamil, Gujarati, Bengali, and numerous international languages. This multi-lingual capability enables businesses to capture authentic customer emotions in their native language, significantly increasing response rates and gathering more representative feedback. The platform's language versatility has been crucial in their international expansion, allowing them to serve diverse markets effectively. Major brands like Kotak Bank, Eureka Forbes, Bata, Titan, TATA Sky, and Reliance Digital use LitmusWorld to enhance their customer experience.

LitmusWorld operates on a proprietary "Measure, Act, Improve" framework to assess customer experiences through a built-in Net Promoter Score (NPS) mechanism. The **Measure** module gathers customer feedback in real-time at key touchpoints. It integrates with internal systems through APIs to ensure immediate data flow. The platform protects personal information through data masking. This module helps businesses understand what customers are saying at every 'moment of truth'. The technology integration capabilities extend to multiple channels and systems. LitmusWorld seamlessly connects with CRM platforms, ERP systems, and customer service tools. This creates a unified data ecosystem that provides a complete view of the customer journey.

The Act module allows companies to respond quickly to customer feedback. It includes automated workflows to categorize and assign issues to the right teams. The platform aligns with organizational hierarchies to ensure the right departments handle customer concerns. It provides advanced action summaries to track issue resolution times. The Act module also enables cross-functional collaboration through its *Huddle* capabilities. This helps teams work together to address customer needs.

- To identify dissatisfied customers, so that service recovery can be attempted.
- To gauge the effectiveness of changes in service delivery.
- To determine customer expectations for a new service.
- To discover changing customer expectations in an industry.
- To forecast future expectations of customers.
- To appraise the service performance of individuals and teams for evaluation, recognition, and rewards.

These research objectives are similar in many ways to the research conducted for physical products: both aim to assess customer requirements, dissatisfaction, and demand. Service research, however, incorporates additional elements that require specific attention.

First, service research must continually monitor and track service performance because performance is subject to human variability and heterogeneity. Conducting performance research at a single point in time, as might be done for a physical product such as an automobile, would be insufficient in services. A major focus of service research involves

Darshan Mehta – CEO, Reliance Brands acknowledged the platform's value, stating that "LitmusWorld is one great bet that we placed and it has played out very well."

The Improve module transforms data into actionable insights. It offers time series analysis to track changes over time. The platform provides comparative analytics to measure performance across different parameters. It creates leaderboards to recognize high-performing touchpoints. The module includes text analytics to categorize unstructured feedback. Companies can generate detailed reports using multi-parameter filters. All these tools help prioritize organizational changes to enhance business processes. One notable success story comes from Croma, where CHRO Shalini Vohra reported a 50 percent reduction in attrition after implementing LitmusWorld's employee Net Promoter Score (eNPS) system. The platform helped Croma understand employee sentiment and take targeted actions to improve satisfaction.

In a recent development, LitmusWorld merged with RepUp, an AI-driven CX platform from Gurugram. The merged entity will continue to operate under the LitmusWorld brand. This strategic merger combines LitmusWorld's expertise with RepUp's AI capabilities. The unified platform will use advanced AI, Natural Language Processing, and automation to enhance customer engagement. According to CEO Sandip Sen, their vision is to redefine enterprise CX through intelligent and personalized interactions. The merger represents a significant milestone in advancing AI-driven customer experience solutions for enterprises. RepUp founder Pranjal Prashar emphasized that this merger would expand their AI-native social listening capabilities to enterprises across key sectors.

The company has ambitious expansion plans beyond its current operations in 12 countries. LitmusWorld is actively expanding its presence across the Middle East, South-East Asia, and the United States. This geographic expansion strategy aligns with their goal of becoming a global leader in AI-driven customer experience management. The company is investing in localized solutions tailored to regional business practices and consumer behavior, further leveraging their multi-lingual capabilities to serve diverse international markets.

References

https://www.litmusworld.com/platform/
https://litmusworld.com/success-stories
https://litmusworld.com/resources/case-studies/croma-employee-experience
https://litmusworld.com/blog/quantifying-customer-experience
https://litmusworld.com/features/multi-lingual-support
https://litmusworld.com/about/expansion
https://www.ciotechoutlook.com/solutions/customer-experience-management/vendor/2018/litmusworld
https://economictimes.indiatimes.com/small-biz/security-tech/technology/litmus-world-repup-merge-their-operations-launch-an-ai-native-cx-platform-for-enterprises/articleshow/120305388.cms?from=mdr

capturing human performance—at the level of individual employee, team, branch, organization as a whole, and competition. Another focus of service research involves documenting the process by which service is performed. Even when service employees are performing well, a service provider must continue to track performance because the potential for variation in processes associated with service delivery always exists.

A second distinction in service research is the need to consider and monitor the gap between expectations and perceptions. This gap is dynamic because both perceptions and expectations fluctuate. Does the gap exist because performance is declining, because performance varies with demand and supply level, or because expectations are escalating?

Exhibit 5.1 lists a number of service research objectives. Once objectives such as these have been identified, they will point the way to decisions about the most appropriate type of research, methods of data collection, and ways to use the information. The additional columns in Exhibit 5.1 are described in subsequent sections of this chapter.

Exhibit 5.1 Elements in an Effective Customer Research Program for Services

Type of Research	Primary Research Objectives	Qualitative/ Quantitative	Costs of Information		
			Monetary	Time	Frequency
Complaint solicitation	To identify/attend to dissatisfied customers To identify common service failure points	Qualitative	Low	Low	Continuous
Critical incident studies	To identify "best practices" at transaction level To identify customer requirements as input for quantitative studies To identify common service failure points To identify systemic strengths and weaknesses in customer-contact services	Qualitative	Low	Moderate	Periodic
Requirements research	To identify customer requirements as input for quantitative research	Qualitative	Moderate	Moderate	Periodic
Relationship surveys and SERVQUAL surveys	To monitor and track service performance To assess overall company performance compared with that of competition To determine links between satisfaction and behavioral intentions To assess gaps between customer expectations and perceptions	Quantitative	Moderate	Moderate	Annual
Trailer calls or posttransaction surveys	To obtain immediate feedback on performance of service transactions To measure effectiveness of changes in service delivery To assess service performance of individuals and teams To use as input for process improvements To identify common service failure points	Quantitative	Low	Low	Continuous
Social media and other consumer-generated content	To identify/attend to dissatisfied customers To encourage word of mouth To measure the impact of other advertising	Qualitative and quantitative	Low	Moderate	Continuous

Criteria for an Effective Service Research Program

A *service research program* can be defined as the portfolio of research studies and types needed to address research objectives. Many types of research could be considered in a research program. Understanding the criteria for an effective service research program (see Figure 5.1) will help a company evaluate different types of research and choose the ones most appropriate for its research objectives. In this section we discuss some key criteria (but we do not consider more technical aspects such as validity and reliability, which are discussed in dedicated marketing research texts).

Type of Research	Primary Research Objectives	Qualitative/ Quantitative	Costs of Information		
			Monetary	Time	Frequency
Service expectation meetings and reviews	To create dialogue with important customers To identify what individual large customers expect and then to ensure that it is delivered To close the loop with important customers	Qualitative	Moderate	Moderate	Annual
Process checkpoint evaluations	To determine customer perceptions of long-term professional services during service provision To identify service problems and solve them early in the service relationship	Quantitative	Moderate	Moderate	Periodic
Market-oriented ethnography	To research customers in natural settings To study customers from cultures other than America in an unbiased way	Qualitative	Moderate	High	Periodic
Mystery shopping	To measure individual employee performance for evaluation, recognition, or rewards To identify systemic strengths and weaknesses in customer-contact services	Quantitative	Low	Low	Quarterly
Customer panels	To monitor changing customer expectations To provide a forum for customers to suggest and evaluate new service ideas	Qualitative	Moderate	Moderate	Continuous
Lost customer research	To identify reasons for customer defection To assess gaps between customer expectations and perceptions	Qualitative	Low	Low	Continuous
Future expectations research	To forecast future expectations of customers To develop and test new service ideas	Qualitative	High	High	Periodic
Database customer research	To identify the individual requirements of customers using information technology and database information	Quantitative	High	High	Continuous

Include Qualitative and Quantitative Research

Marketing research includes two major types of research, called qualitative research and quantitative research. Qualitative research tends to be "hypothesis generating" whereas quantitative research tends to be "hypothesis testing." Accordingly, qualitative research is exploratory and preliminary and is conducted to clarify problem definition, prepare for more formal research, or gain insight when more formal research is not necessary. Insights gained through qualitative methods such as customer focus groups, critical incidents research (described more fully later in this chapter), and direct observation of service transactions show the marketer the right questions to ask

FIGURE 5.1
Criteria for an Effective Service Research Program

- Include both qualitative and quantitative research.
- Capture both expectations and perceptions of customers.
- Balance the cost of the research and the value of the information.
- Measure priorities or importance of attributes.
- Use appropriate frequency.
- Include measurement of loyalty, behavioral intentions, and actual behavior.

of consumers. Because the results of qualitative research play a major role in designing quantitative research, it is often the first type of research done. However, qualitative research can also be conducted after quantitative research to make the numbers in computer printouts meaningful by giving managers the perspective and sensitivity that are critical in interpreting data and initiating improvement efforts.[2]

One very successful qualitative approach is the Zaltman Metaphor Elicitation Technique (ZMET), an approach developed by Gerald Zaltman and executed by Olson Zaltman, a research and consulting organization. The approach depends on ZMET interviews, which are intense two-hour discussions with customers who are asked to collect visual images that represent their thoughts and feelings about a research topic beforehand and then discuss them in the interview. This storytelling allows the researcher to delve deep into the metaphors that underlie their beliefs and feelings. There are no numbers in this approach, but it results in insightful findings from which a company can build an advertising or marketing campaign.[3]

Quantitative research in marketing is designed to describe the nature, attitudes, or behaviors of customers empirically and to test specific hypotheses. These studies not only are key for quantifying the customers' satisfaction, the importance of service attributes, the extent of service quality gaps, and perceptions of value, but they also provide managers with yardsticks for evaluating competitors. Finally, quantitative studies can highlight specific service deficiencies that can be more deeply probed through follow-up qualitative research.

Capture Both Perceptions and Expectations of Customers

As we discussed in Chapters 3 and 4, customers compare what they perceive they get in a service encounter with their expectations of that encounter. For this reason, a measurement program that captures only perceptions of service is missing a critical part of the service quality equation. Companies also need to incorporate measures of customer expectations.

Measurement of expectations can be included in a research program in multiple ways. First, basic research that relates to customers' requirements—that identifies the service features or attributes that matter to customers—can be considered expectation research. In this form, the *content* of customer expectations is captured, initially in some form of qualitative research such as focus group interviews. Research on the *levels* of customer expectations also is needed. This type of research quantitatively assesses the levels of customer expectations and compares these with perception levels, usually by calculating the gap between expectations and perceptions.

Balance the Cost of the Research and the Value of the Information

An assessment of the cost of research compared with its benefits to the company is another key criterion. One cost is monetary, including direct costs to customer research companies, payments to respondents, and internal company costs incurred by employees collecting the information. Time costs are also important, including the time commitment needed internally by employees to administer the research and the interval between data collection and availability for use by the firm. These costs also need to be considered in light of the frequency with which the focal research is conducted (e.g., on an annual vs. a quarterly basis). These and other costs must be weighed against the gains to the company in improved decision making, retained customers, and successful new product launches.

Measure Priorities or Importance

Customers have many service expectations, but not all are equally important. One of the most common mistakes managers make in trying to improve service is spending resources on the wrong initiatives, only to become discouraged because customer perceptions of the firm's service do not improve! Measuring the relative importance of service dimensions and attributes helps managers to channel resources effectively; therefore, research must document the priorities of the customer.

Use Appropriate Frequency

Because customer expectations and perceptions are dynamic, companies need to institute a comprehensive and systematic service quality research process, not just conduct isolated studies. A single study provides only a "snapshot" view of one moment in time. For full understanding of the marketplace's acceptance of a company's service, customer research must be ongoing. Without a pattern of studies repeated with appropriate frequency, managers cannot tell whether the firm is moving forward or falling behind relative to the competition and which of their service improvement initiatives are working. Just what does "ongoing research" mean in terms of frequency? The answer is specific to the type of service and to the purpose and method of each type of service research a company might do. As we discuss the different types in the following section, you will see the frequency with which each type of research could be conducted.

Include Measures of Loyalty, Behavioral Intentions, and Behavior

An important trend in service research involves measuring the positive and negative consequences of service quality and customer satisfaction in terms of customers' behavioral intentions and their actual behavior. Positive behavioral intentions and customer behaviors include recommending the company to others, remaining loyal, spending more with the company, and paying a price premium. Negative behavioral intentions and customer behaviors include saying negative things to others, doing less business with the company, switching to another company, and complaining to outside organizations such as the Better Business Bureau and to other companies using social media outlets. Other, more specific behaviors differ by service; for example, behaviors related to medical care include following instructions from the doctor, taking medications, and returning for follow-up visits. Tracking customers' behavioral intentions and their actual behavior can help managers estimate the relative value of service improvements to the company and can identify customers who are in danger of defecting.

ELEMENTS IN AN EFFECTIVE SERVICE MARKETING RESEARCH PROGRAM

A good service marketing research program includes multiple types of research approaches. The research program will differ by company because the range of uses for service quality research—from employee performance assessment to advertising campaign development to strategic planning—requires a rich, multifaceted flow of information. If a company were to engage in virtually all types of service research, the portfolio would look like Exhibit 5.1, but few companies do all types of research. The particular portfolio for any company will match company resources and address the key areas needed to understand its customers. So that it will be easier for you to identify the appropriate type of research for different research objectives, we list the objectives in column 2 of Exhibit 5.1. In the following sections, we describe each major type of research and show the way each type addresses the criteria associated with it. The Technology Spotlight discusses some major emerging trends related to conducting customer research.

Complaint Solicitation

You may have complained to employees of service organizations, only to find that nothing happens with your complaint. No one rushes to solve it, and the next time you experience the service the same problem is present. How frustrating! As you will learn in detail in Chapter 7 (Service Recovery), good service organizations take complaints seriously. Not only do they listen to complaints but they also employ *complaint solicitation* (i.e., they proactively aim to increase the percentage of unhappy customers who articulate their dissatisfaction to the firm) as a way of communicating about what can be done to improve their service and their service employees. Vail Resorts, which owns the Vail, Breckenridge, Heavenly, Keystone, and Beaver Creek resorts, has an innovative way to capture complaints and comments of its customers. The resort hires researchers to ride the lifts with skiers and ask and record into handheld computer devices customers' responses to questions about their perceptions of the resorts. Then the researchers ski down the mountain and ride up again with other customers. At the end of the day, the researchers download the results into a computer at the base. The researchers survey 200 skiers per week, looking for patterns of customer comments and complaints. For example, if the researchers receive a number of complaints about certain lift lines or service in one of the restaurants, they will alert managers in those areas so the problems can be resolved quickly. At the end of the week, the data are collected and reported at weekly meetings.

Firms that use complaints as market research collect and document them, then systematically use the information to identify dissatisfied customers, correct individual problems where possible, and identify common service failure points. Although this research is used for both goods and services, it has a critical real-time purpose in services—to improve failure points and to improve or correct the performance of contact personnel. Research on complaints is one of the easiest types for firms to conduct, leading many companies to depend solely on complaints to stay in touch with customers. Unfortunately, there is evidence suggesting that customer complaints alone are a woefully inadequate source of information. As discussed in Chapter 7, only a small percentage of customers with problems actually complain to the company; the rest stay dissatisfied, telling other people about their dissatisfaction. Understanding this reality further highlights the importance of complaint solicitation.

To be effective, complaint solicitation requires rigorous recording of numbers and types of complaints through many channels and then working to eliminate the most frequent problems. Complaint channels include employees at the front line, intermediary organizations like retailers who deliver service, managers, and complaints to third parties such as customer advocate groups. Companies must both solve individual customer problems and identify overall patterns to eliminate failure points. More sophisticated forms of complaint resolution define "complaint" broadly to include all comments—both negative and positive—as well as questions from customers. Firms should build depositories for this information and report results frequently, perhaps weekly or monthly, as discussed in detail in Chapter 7.

Critical Incident Studies

The *critical incident technique* (*CIT*) is a qualitative interview procedure in which customers are asked to provide verbatim stories about particularly satisfying and dissatisfying service encounters they have experienced. With this technique, customers (either internal or external) are asked the following questions:

- Think of a time when, as a customer, you had a particularly *satisfying* (or *dissatisfying*) interaction.
- When did the incident happen?
- What specific circumstances led up to this situation?
- Exactly what did the employee (or firm member) say or do?
- What resulted that made you feel the interaction was *satisfying* (or *dissatisfying*)?
- What could or should have been done differently?

The CIT has been used to study satisfaction in hotels, restaurants, airlines, amusement parks, automotive repair, retailing, banking, cable television, public transportation, and education.[4] The studies have explored a wide range of service topics: consumer evaluation of services, service failure and recovery, employees, customer participation in service delivery, and service experience.[5]

Sometimes contact employees are asked to put themselves in the shoes of a customer and answer the same questions: "Put yourself in the shoes of *customers* of your firm. In other words, try to see your firm through your customers' eyes. Now think of a recent time when a customer of your firm had a particularly *satisfying/unsatisfying* interaction with you or a fellow employee." The stories are then analyzed to determine common themes of satisfaction/dissatisfaction underlying the events. In Chapter 4, we described the four common themes that are sources of pleasure and displeasure in service encounters—recovery (after failure), adaptability, spontaneity, and coping—that have been identified through such research. Individual companies conduct these studies to identify sources of critical levels of satisfaction and dissatisfaction for their firms or industries.

CIT has many benefits. First, data are collected from the respondents' perspective and are usually vivid because they are expressed in consumers' own words and reflect the way they think. Second, the method provides concrete information about the way the company and its employees behave and react, thereby making the research easy

Technology Spotlight Frontiers of Customer Research

Market research is a highly dynamic field that is constantly changing, often driven by technological evolution. According to trend analyses from Qualtrics and QuestionPro, leading edge market research approaches can now shape how service companies listen to their customers. Some key advances include:

1. **Faster and more agile market research:** With markets more dynamic than ever, researchers need to provide insights faster to help managers develop new strategies. In parallel, companies will need to adopt an increasingly "agile" (i.e., iterative) approach to market research that leverages multiple different methodologies and data sources. For example, instead of large, long, and structured research projects, firms are likely to run a series of smaller surveys in an iterative way (i.e., each survey builds off the findings of the one before). Thus, market research will increasingly use high-frequency studies with turnaround times that are very quick (e.g., short surveys can be set up, launched, and analyzed within minutes). To assure good response rates and data quality, researchers will have to design non-intrusive studies that are engaging, fun, and compelling to respond to.
2. **Human and Artificial Intelligence (AI) in market research:** Despite the increasing relevance of market research technology, it will not fully replace human researchers any time soon. Instead, experts expect a blended approach where automated AI is primarily used to collect and analyze data at scale, and where human intelligence and creativity will be vital platforms for managerial flexibility in response to changing customer demands.
3. **Technology in market research:** Market research increasingly relies on technology to be more effective and efficient. Going forward, technology will be even more crucial in collecting and connecting data from multiple sources, and helping researchers to collate, analyze, and communicate their findings to internal and external customers. For example:

   a. **Social listening:** Companies will increasingly track social media to understand consumers. Because social media is highly emotive, it reveals insights related to consumer ideas/trends, their (dis)satisfaction and (re)purchase behaviors, as well as their complaints. Social listening search engines typically screen more than 100 social media sites (e.g., Facebook, Twitter, Google, blogs, videos, and images) for mentions of brands (or brand-related keywords). Marketers can then examine the strength of their brand, how many users are mentioning it, and the sentiment as well as the passion of the conversations related to it.

   b. **Facial recognition and sentiment analysis:** Evolving technology allows market researchers to capture consumer data in novel ways. For example, consumer sentiments can be analyzed based on facial recognition and visual cues that technology can capture. One example is the technology developed by Affectiva Automotive AI. Currently used in cars, this software uses in-vehicle cameras to measure the state of the car's driver and its passengers in real time: the software captures complex emotions (e.g., the driver's mood and anger) and cognitive states (e.g., the driver's drowsiness and distraction). For passengers, the software can improve their comfort by adjusting cabin lighting, temperature, music, or even advertisements in response to their state. Such applications help car manufacturers and other companies (e.g., car sharing services) to optimize aspects related to safety and overall customer experiences, with great potential for conducting real-time market research.

   c. **Biometrics:** Additional biometrics (e.g., brain activity, skin conductance, heart rate) will play a more prominent role in research. For example, Nielsen (an S&P 500 company with operations in over 90 countries) is using neuroscience technology to better predict consumer preferences and behaviors related to

to translate into action. Third, like most qualitative methods, the research is particularly useful when the topic or service is new and very little other information exists. Finally, the method is well suited for assessing perceptions of customers from different cultures because it allows respondents to share their perceptions rather than answer researcher-defined questions.

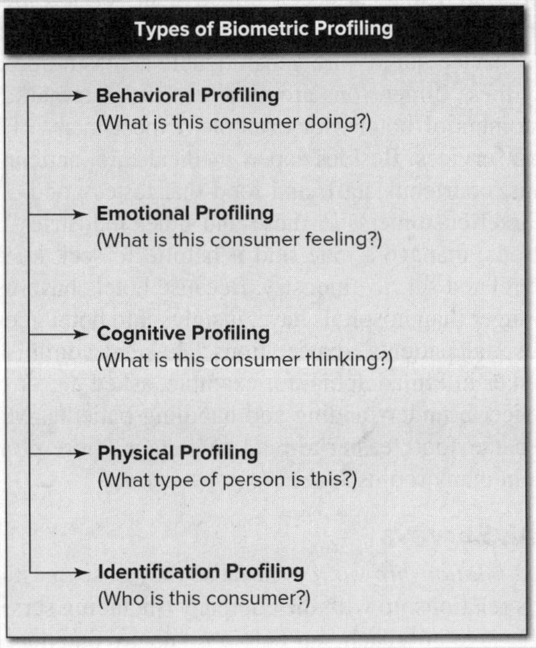

advertising/branding, pricing, and product/service experience. Nielsen has more than 10 labs around the globe (e.g., the United States, Japan, China) to conduct consumer neuroscience studies. Although biometrics has traditionally focused on personal identification/authentication, De Keyser et al. (2020) emphasize that the combination of biometrics with AI allows companies to profile its customers along the five dimensions shown in the figure. These novel biometric profiles provide market researchers with much deeper insights about consumers and a level of understanding that was unrealistic with traditional research methods.

d. **Chatbots and embodied robots as market researchers:** As another evolution of research, companies are now using survey chatbots (e.g., IKEA, Heineken, and Marriott), which can interact with customers in real time and on a one-to-one basis. Because of its conversational nature, customers often perceive chatbot surveys to be easier than traditional surveys; in turn, this allows companies to gain deeper insights by having a conversation (i.e., "chat") with their customers. Looking ahead, it is likely that embodied robots with sophisticated social abilities will also be employed as market researchers. For example, such robots might conduct face-to-face customer satisfaction surveys/interviews. However, robots are not quite ready for prime time (yet). One study showed that the accuracy, quality, and completeness of data collected by a robot was lower than established survey options (e.g., self-report online survey). Reasons for such lower data quality are related to conversational difficulties that might be perceived as awkward or anti-social behaviors (e.g., robots mishearing, robots speaking over humans). Despite such difficulties, there are considerable opportunities where robots can be employed as surveyors in the future (e.g., when elderly consumers may have difficulty with traditional survey approaches, or when a robot with social skills can help reduce the mundanity of completing surveys).

Sources: E. Dean, "Where Will 2021 Take the Market Research Industry?," https://www.qualtrics.com/blog/trends-in-market-research/, accessed October 2, 2021; QuestionPro, "Top 11 Market Research Trends in 2021 to Keep an Eye Out For," https://www.questionpro.com/blog/market-research-trends/, accessed October 2, 2021; S. Heath, J. Liddle, and J. Wiles, "The Challenges of Designing a Robot for a Satisfaction Survey: Surveying Humans Using a Social Robot," *International Journal of Social Robotics* 12 (2020), pp. 519–533, https://www.nielsen.com, accessed October 2, 2021; A. De Keyser, Y. Bart, X. Gu, S. Q. Liu, S. G. Robinson, and P. K. Kannan, "Opportunities and Challenges of Using Biometrics for Business: Developing a Research Agenda," *Journal of Business Research* 136 (November 2021), pp. 52–62.

Requirements Research

Requirements research, also known as "customer needs analysis," involves identifying the benefits and attributes that customers expect in a service. This type of research is essential because it determines the type of questions that will be asked in surveys and ultimately the improvements that will be attempted by the firm. Because these studies are so foundational, qualitative techniques are appropriate to begin them. Quantitative techniques may follow, often in the form of survey research. Individual companies conduct these studies to identify sources of satisfaction and dissatisfaction for their firms or industries.

An approach to requirements research that has been effective in service industries is to examine existing research about customer requirements in similar service industries. The five dimensions of service quality are generalizable across numerous industries, and sometimes the way these dimensions are manifest is also remarkably similar. Hospital patients and customers of hotels, for example, expect many of the same features when using these two services. Besides expert medical care, patients in hospitals expect comfortable rooms, courteous staff, and food that tastes good—the same features that are salient to hotel customers. In these and other industries that share common customer expectations, managers may find it helpful to seek knowledge from existing research in the related service industry. Because hotels have used marketing and customer research longer than hospitals have, insights into hotel guests' expectations can inform about hospital patients' expectations. Hospital administrators at Albert Einstein Medical Center in Philadelphia, for example, asked a group of nine local hotel executives for advice in understanding and handling patients. Many improvements resulted, including better food, easier-to-read name tags, more prominent information desks, and radios in many rooms.[6]

Relationship and SERVQUAL Surveys

One category of surveys are named *relationship surveys* because they pose questions about all elements in the customer's relationship with the company (including service, product, and price). This comprehensive approach can help a company diagnose its relationship strengths and weaknesses.

Relationship surveys typically monitor and track service performance over time, with an initial survey providing a baseline. Relationship surveys are also effective in comparing company performance with that of competitors, often focusing on the best competitor's performance as a benchmark. When used for this purpose, the sponsor of the survey is not identified, and questions are asked about both the focal company and one or more competitors.

A sound measure of service quality is necessary for identifying the aspects of service needing performance improvement, assessing how much improvement is needed on each aspect, and evaluating the impact of improvement efforts. Unlike goods quality, which can be measured objectively by such indicators as durability and number of defects, service quality is abstract and is best captured by surveys that measure customer evaluations of service. One of the first measures to be developed specifically to measure service quality was the *SERVQUAL survey.*

The SERVQUAL scale involves a survey containing 21 service attributes, grouped into the five service quality dimensions of reliability, responsiveness, assurance, empathy, and tangibles (as discussed in Chapter 4). The survey sometimes asks customers to provide two different ratings on each attribute—one reflecting the level of service they would expect from excellent companies in a sector and the other reflecting their perception of the service delivered by a specific company within that sector. The difference between the expectation and perception ratings constitutes a quantified measure of service quality and corresponding gaps. Exhibit 5.2 shows the items on the basic SERVQUAL scale as well as the phrasing of the expectations and perceptions portions of the scale.[7] Data gathered through a SERVQUAL survey can be used for a variety of purposes:

- To assess a company's service quality along each of the five SERVQUAL dimensions.
- To track customers' expectations and perceptions and determine the average gap score (on individual service attributes and/or on the SERVQUAL dimensions) over time.
- To compare a company's SERVQUAL scores against those of competitors.
- To identify and examine customer segments that differ significantly in their assessments of a company's service performance.
- To assess internal service quality (that is, the quality of service rendered by one department or division of a company to others within the same company).

This instrument has spawned many studies focusing on service quality assessment and is used all over the world. Published studies have used SERVQUAL and adaptations of it in a variety of contexts: real estate brokers, physicians in private practice, public recreation programs, dental schools, business school placement centers, tire stores, motor carrier companies, accounting firms, discount and department stores, gas and electric utility companies, hospitals, banking, pest control, dry cleaning, fast food, higher education, and others.

Trailer Calls or Posttransaction Surveys

Whereas the purpose of relationship surveys (such as SERVQUAL) is usually to gauge the overall relationship with the customer, the purpose of transaction surveys is to capture information about key service encounters with the customer. In this method, customers are asked a short list of questions immediately after a particular transaction (hence the name *trailer calls*) about their satisfaction with this transaction and contact personnel with whom they interacted. Because the surveys are administered continuously to a broad spectrum of customers, they are more effective than complaint solicitation (where the information comes only from dissatisfied customers).

For example, a hotel chain can ask customers to answer four or five questions about their stay in the hotel via a text message sent to their phone immediately after their checkout. This approach has obvious benefits over the ubiquitous comment cards left in rooms—the response rate is far higher because the process engages customers and takes only a few minutes. In other companies, transaction surveys are by e-mail (Best Buy, Geek Squad, and Panera Bread). Customers are asked to complete a survey by calling an 800-number or going to a website listed on their receipt. The incentive for completing the survey is a chance to win prizes or coupons from the stores.

A strong benefit of this type of research is that it often appears to customers that the call is following up to ensure that they are satisfied; consequently, the request does double duty as a market research tool and customer service. This type of research is simple and provides management with continuous information about interactions with customers. Further, the research allows management to associate service quality performance with individual contact personnel, so that high performance can be rewarded and low performance corrected. It also serves as an incentive for employees to provide better service because they understand how and when they are being evaluated. However, on a cautionary note, managers should note certain risks of recurring post-transaction surveys. For example, one study (on customer purchase behavior over three years at a large North American automotive dealership) found that repeatedly soliciting a customer's feedback can have detrimental cumulative effects on customer purchases (e.g., amounts and timing).[8] Accordingly, the chapter opener described

Exhibit 5.2 SERVQUAL: A Multidimensional Scale to Capture Customer Perceptions and Expectations of Service Quality

The SERVQUAL scale was first published in 1988 and has undergone numerous improvements and revisions since then. The scale contains 21 perception items that are distributed throughout the five service quality dimensions. The scale also contains expectation items. Although many different formats of the SERVQUAL scale are now in use, we show here the basic 21 perception items as well as a sampling of ways the expectation items have been posed.

PERCEPTIONS

Perceptions Statements in the Reliability Dimension							
	Strongly Disagree						**Strongly Agree**
1. When XYZ Company promises to do something by a certain time, it does so.	1	2	3	4	5	6	7
2. XYZ Company performs the service right the first time.	1	2	3	4	5	6	7
3. XYZ Company provides its services at the time it promises to do so.	1	2	3	4	5	6	7
4. XYZ Company insists on error-free records.	1	2	3	4	5	6	7
Statements in the Responsiveness Dimension							
1. XYZ Company keeps customers informed about when services will be performed.	1	2	3	4	5	6	7
2. Employees in XYZ Company give you prompt service.	1	2	3	4	5	6	7
3. Employees in XYZ Company are always willing to help you.	1	2	3	4	5	6	7
4. Employees in XYZ Company are never too busy to respond to your request.	1	2	3	4	5	6	7
Statements in the Assurance Dimension							
1. The behavior of employees in XYZ Company instills confidence in you.	1	2	3	4	5	6	7
2. You feel safe in your transactions with XYZ Company.	1	2	3	4	5	6	7
3. Employees in XYZ Company are consistently courteous with you.	1	2	3	4	5	6	7
4. Employees in XYZ Company have the knowledge to answer your questions.	1	2	3	4	5	6	7
Statements in the Empathy Dimension							
1. XYZ Company gives you individual attention.	1	2	3	4	5	6	7
2. XYZ Company has employees who give you personal attention.	1	2	3	4	5	6	7
3. XYZ Company has your best interests at heart.	1	2	3	4	5	6	7
4. Employees of XYZ Company understand your specific needs.	1	2	3	4	5	6	7
5. XYZ Company has operating hours that are convenient to all its customers.	1	2	3	4	5	6	7

PERCEPTIONS *(continued)*

Statements in the Tangibles Dimension	Strongly Disagree						Strongly Agree
1. XYZ Company has modern-looking equipment.	1	2	3	4	5	6	7
2. XYZ Company's physical facilities are visually appealing.	1	2	3	4	5	6	7
3. XYZ Company's employees appear neat.	1	2	3	4	5	6	7
4. Materials associated with the service (such as pamphlets or statements) are visually appealing at XYZ Company.	1	2	3	4	5	6	7

EXPECTATIONS: Several Formats for Measuring Customer Expectations Using Versions of SERVQUAL

There are a number of different ways that expectations can be asked in surveys. We present four of these types below: (1) matching expectations statements, (2) referent expectations formats, (3) statements that combine both expectations and perceptions, and (4) statements that cover different types of expectations.

Matching Expectations Statements (Paired with the Previous Perception Statements)

	Strongly Disagree						Strongly Agree
When customers have a problem, excellent firms will show a sincere interest in solving it.	1	2	3	4	5	6	7

Referent Expectations Formats

1. Considering a "world-class" company to be a "7," how would you rate XYZ Company's performance on the following service features?

	Low						High
Sincere, interested employees	1	2	3	4	5	6	7
Service delivered right the first time	1	2	3	4	5	6	7

2. Compared with the level of service you expect from an excellent company, how would you rate XYZ Company's performance on the following?

	Low						High
Sincere, interested employees	1	2	3	4	5	6	7
Service delivered right the first time	1	2	3	4	5	6	7

Combined Expectations/Perceptions Statements

For each of the following statements, circle the number that indicates how XYZ Company's service compares with the level you expect:

	Lower Than My Desired Service Level			The Same as My Desired Service Level			Higher Than My Desired Service Level		
1. Prompt service	1	2	3	4	5	6	7	8	9
2. Courteous employees	1	2	3	4	5	6	7	8	9

(continued)

Exhibit 5.2 (concluded)

Expectations Distinguishing between Desired Service and Adequate Service

For each of the following statements, circle the number that indicates how XYZ Company's performance compares with your *minimum service level* and with your *desired service level.*

	Compared with my *minimum* service level XYZ's service performance is									**Compared with my *desired* service level XYZ's service performance is**								
When it comes to ...	**Lower**			**Same**			**Higher**			**Lower**			**Same**			**Higher**		
1. Prompt service	1	2	3	4	5	6	7	8	9	1	2	3	4	5	6	7	8	9
2. Employees who are consistently courteous	1	2	3	4	5	6	7	8	9	1	2	3	4	5	6	7	8	9

Source: A. Parasuraman, V. A. Zeithaml, and L. L. Berry, "SERVQUAL: A Multiple-Item Scale for Measuring Consumer Perceptions of Service Quality," *Journal of Retailing* 64 (Spring 1988), pp. 12–40.

some limitations of this approach and discussed customer journey measurement as an innovative way to improve upon posttransaction surveys alone.

Service Expectation Meetings and Reviews

In business-to-business situations when large accounts are involved, a form of customer research that is highly effective involves eliciting the expectations of the client at a specified time of the year and then following up later (usually after a year) to determine whether the expectations were fulfilled. Even when the company produces a physical product, the meetings often deal almost completely with the service expected and provided by an account or sales team assigned to the client. Unlike other forms of research we have discussed, these meetings are not conducted by unbiased researchers but are instead initiated and facilitated by senior members of the account team, so that they can listen carefully to the client's expectations. You may be surprised to find that such interaction does not always come naturally to sales teams who are used to talking *to* clients rather than listening carefully to their needs. Consequently, teams have to be carefully trained not to defend or explain but instead to comprehend. One company found that the only way it could teach its salespeople not to talk on these interviews was to take a marketing researcher along to gently kick the salesperson under the table whenever he or she strayed from the format!

The format, when appropriate, consists of (1) asking clients what they expect in terms of 8 to 10 basic requirements determined from focus group research, (2) inquiring what particular aspects of these requirements the account team performed well in the past as well as what aspects need improvement, and (3) requesting that the client rank the relative importance of the requirements. After getting the input, senior account members go back to their teams and plan their goals for the year around client requirements. The next step is verifying with the client that the account plan will satisfy requirements or, when it will not, managing expectations to let the client know what cannot be accomplished. After executing the plan for the year, the senior account personnel then return to the client, determine whether the plan has been successfully executed and expectations met, and establish a new set of expectations for the coming year.

Process Checkpoint Evaluations

With professional services such as consulting, construction, and architecture, services are provided over a long period, and there are no obvious ways or times to collect customer information. Waiting until the entire project is complete—which could last years—is undesirable because myriad unresolvable problems could have occurred by then. In these situations, the smart service provider defines a multi-stage process for delivering the services and then structures the feedback around the various stages of the customer journey, checking in at frequent points to ensure that the client's expectations are being met. For example, a management consulting firm might establish the following process for delivering its services to clients: (1) collect information, (2) diagnose problems, (3) recommend alternative solutions, (4) select alternatives, and (5) implement solutions. Next, it could agree with the client up-front that it will communicate at major *process checkpoints*—after diagnosing the problem, before selecting the alternative, and so on—to make certain that the job is progressing as planned. These process checkpoints are the key milestones along the customer journey.

Market-Oriented Ethnography

Structured questionnaires make key assumptions about what people are conscious of or can recall about their behavior and what they are willing to explain to researchers about their opinions. To fully understand how customers assess and use services, it may be necessary and effective to use other approaches, such as *market-oriented ethnography.* This set of approaches allows researchers to observe consumption behavior in natural settings. The goal is to enter the consumer's world as much as possible—observing how and when a service is used in an actual home environment or consumption environment, such as watching consumers eat in restaurants or attend concerts. Among the techniques used are observation, interviews, documents, and examination of material possessions such as artifacts. Observation involves entering the experience as a participant observer and watching what occurs rather than asking questions about it. One-on-one interviews, particularly with key informants in the culture rather than consumers themselves, can provide compelling insights into culture-based behavior. Studying existing documents and cultural artifacts can also provide valuable insights, especially about lifestyles and usage patterns.[9] ZMET, a technique described earlier in the chapter, is a form of ethnographic research. Research and consulting companies such as IDEO or Envirosell frequently use ethnographic methods to better understand how consumers (want to) use and experience services.

Best Western International used ethnographic research to better understand its senior market. Rather than bringing participants into focus group facilities and asking them questions, the company paid 25 over-55 couples to videotape themselves on cross-country journeys. The firm was able to listen to how couples actually made decisions rather than the way they reported them. The insights they gained from this research were decidedly different from what they would have learned otherwise. Most noteworthy was the finding that seniors who talked hotel clerks into better deals on rooms did not need the lower price to afford staying at the hotel—they were simply after the thrill of the deal, as illustrated in this description:

> The 60-ish woman caught on the grainy videotape is sitting on her hotel bed, addressing her husband after a long day spent on the road. "Good job!" she exults. "We beat the s—t out of the front desk and got a terrific room."[10]

These customers then spent their discount money on better dinners elsewhere, contributing nothing to Best Western. "The degree of discount clearly isn't what it used to be in importance—and we got that right out of the research," claimed the manager of programs for Best Western. This finding would be highly unlikely using traditional research and asking customers directly, for few customers would admit to being willing to pay a higher price for a service.

Mystery Shopping

In this form of research, which is unique to services, companies hire outside research organizations to send people into service establishments and experience the service as if they were customers. These *mystery shoppers* are trained to focus on the service quality criteria important to customers of the focal establishment. They deliver their assessments about service performance by completing questionnaires about service standards or, in other cases, open-ended questions that have a qualitative feel to them. Mystery shopping is common in numerous service industries, such as automotive, financial, fast food, gas station and convenience stores, healthcare, hospitality, and retail. For example, a restaurant chain might send mystery shoppers to its stores to buy meals and then complete questionnaires about the servers, the restaurant, and the food. Servers might be evaluated on standards that include the following:

- Acknowledged within three seconds after reaching first place in line.
- Acknowledged pleasantly.
- Server suggested additional items.
- Server requested payment prior to delivering order.
- Received receipt.
- Received correct change.
- Correct order received.

Companies motivate workers to perform to service standards by using the mystery shopper program as a key element in its compensation and reward system. For example, individual workers who receive positive scores have their names posted on the store's bulletin board and receive letters of congratulations as well as bonuses. Managers whose stores earn high scores can receive on-the-spot bonuses. Perhaps more important, the overall scores received by shift and district managers might qualify them for monthly profit-sharing cash bonuses (e.g., a low score removes them from consideration for a bonus, whereas high numbers lead to good bonuses).

Mystery shopping keeps workers on their toes because they know they may be evaluated at any time. They know they are being judged on the company's service standards and therefore carry out the standards more consistently than if they were not going to be judged. Mystery shopping can be a very effective way of reinforcing service standards.

Customer Panels

Customer panels are groups of customers assembled to provide attitudes and perceptions about a service over time. They offer the company regular and timely customer information—virtually a pulse on the market. Firms can use customer panels to represent large segments of end-customers. The Global Feature in this chapter shows an example of a customer panel.

Customer panels are used, for example, in the entertainment industry to screen movies before they are released to the public. After a rough cut of a film has been created, the movie is viewed by a panel of consumers that matches the demographic target market. In the most basic of these panels, consumers participate in postscreening interviews or focus groups in which they report their responses to the movie. They may be asked questions as general as their reactions to the ending of the movie and as specific as whether they understood different aspects of the plot line. Based on these panels, movies are revised and edited to ensure that they are communicating the desired message and that they will succeed in the marketplace. In extreme situations, entire endings of movies have been changed to be more consistent with customer attitudes. For example, *Titanic* (one of the most successful movies of all time) had a near four-hour runtime and an alternative ending when it was first test-screened for audiences. Based on test-screenings, multiple scenes were either cut back or eliminated altogether, and the alternative ending was abandoned.[11]

Lost Customer Research

This type of research involves deliberately seeking customers who have dropped the company's service to inquire about their reasons for leaving. Some *lost customer research* is similar to exit interviews with employees in that it asks open-ended, in-depth questions to expose the reasons for defection and the particular events that led to dissatisfaction. It is also possible to use more standard surveys on lost customers. For example, a midwestern manufacturer used a mail survey to ask former customers about its performance during different stages of the customer–vendor relationship. The survey also sought specific reasons for customers' defections and asked customers to describe problems that triggered their decreases in purchases.

One benefit of this type of research is that it identifies failure points and common problems in the service and can help establish an early-warning system for future defectors. Another benefit is that it helps firms understand which specific failures *actually* make customers leave (rather than threatening to leave); finally, this approach can be used to calculate the cost of lost customers.

Future Expectations Research

Customer expectations are dynamic and can change rapidly in markets that are highly competitive and volatile. As competition increases, as tastes change, and as consumers become more knowledgeable, companies must continue to update their information and strategies. In dynamic market situations, companies want to understand not just current customer expectations but also future expectations—the service features desired in the future. *Future expectations research* includes different types. First, *features research* involves environmental scanning and querying of customers about desirable features of possible services. Second, *lead user research* brings in customers who are opinion leaders/innovators and asks them what requirements are not currently being met by existing products or services.

The question of customer involvement in expectation studies is often debated. Designers and developers claim that consumers often do not know what they might want, especially in industries or services that are new and rapidly changing. Consumers and marketing researchers, on the other hand, counter that services developed independently of customer input are likely to be targeted at needs that do not exist. To study this question, researchers assessed the contributions made by users compared with professional developers for end-user telecom services. Three groups were studied: users alone, developers alone, and users with a design expert present to provide information on feasibility. Findings showed that users created more original but less producible ideas. However, inviting users to test and explore possibilities once a prototype has been created can produce positive results.[12]

ANALYZING AND INTERPRETING CUSTOMER RESEARCH FINDINGS

One of the biggest challenges facing a customer researcher is converting a complex set of data to a form that can be read and understood quickly by executives, managers, and other employees who will make decisions from the research. For example, "big data" is being adopted as a strategic initiative by many firms (see the Strategy Insight box), but merely having sophisticated data does not ensure that the findings will be useful to managers. Many of the people who use customer research findings have not been trained in statistics and have neither the time nor the expertise to analyze technical research information. The goal in this stage of the customer research process is to communicate information clearly to the right people in a timely fashion. Corresponding key questions include: Who gets this information? Why do they need it? How will they use it? Does it mean the same thing across cultures? When users feel confident that they understand the data, they are far more likely to apply it appropriately. When managers do not understand how to interpret the data, or when they lack confidence in the research, the investment of time, skill, and effort will be lost.

Depicting marketing research findings graphically is a powerful way to communicate research information. Here are samples of graphic representations of the types of marketing research data we have discussed throughout this chapter.

Customer Journey and Experience Maps to Depict Research Insights

As described in the chapter opener, measuring journeys and clusters of steps that form distinct stages of the service experience are on the cutting edge of measurement. By looking at the clusters of the service journey from the customer point of view, companies can completely redesign the journey to be simpler and superior.

Figure 5.2 shows a hypothetical kitchen remodel. The first journey cluster would involve such touchpoints as Internet search, examining magazines, and asking friends or neighbors who have recently made the purchase. This cluster is a particular pain point to customers because of the uncertainty about price and process. In this type of major purchase, customers typically depend on friends and neighbors. In the second cluster, customers visit stores and look at sample kitchens, talk to salespeople, and try to resolve their issues about price and process. During the choosing journey cluster, a company can build a CAD computer model of a kitchen with the attributes that the particular customer desires and give an estimate of cost. It can then also contact the customer with personalized e-mails showing kitchen ideas with their exact specifications and schedules for delivery of the service. This journey cluster could also include provision of a contract with a price cut to motivate the customer to take immediate action. Delivery and installation would be the next cluster, and follow-up would complete the end-to-end experience. In Chapter 8 you will learn (in more detail) how to further analyze and (re-)design customer service journeys with the "blueprinting" technique.

Measurement of this experience, as shown in Figure 5.2, would involve surveys or other approaches at the end of the *journeys,* shown as small stars. A final measure of the entire customer experience is shown as the large seven-sided star. Notably, research also provides companies with easy-to-use scales to measure customer journeys. For

FIGURE 5.2 **Customer Journey and Experience Map for Measurement of a Kitchen Remodel**

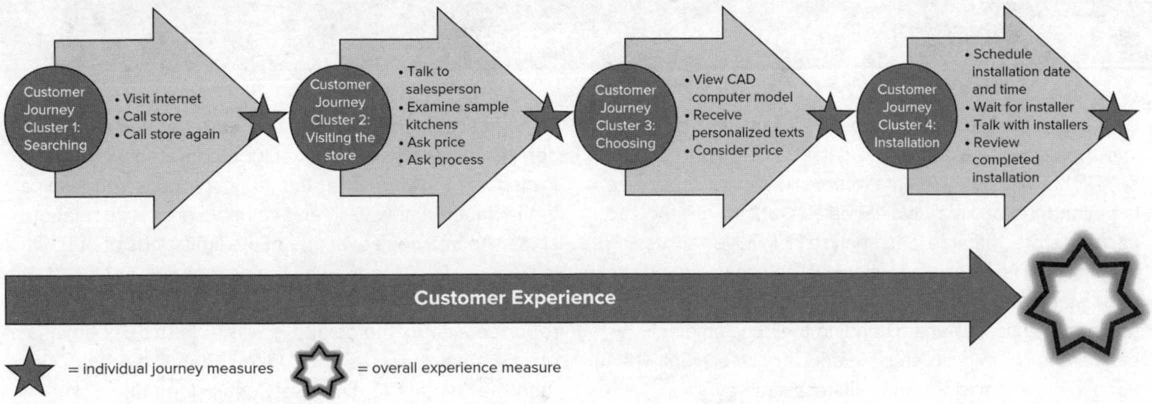

example, one study developed a scale that measures three dimensions of customer journey design as the extent to which consumers perceive clusters of brand-owned touchpoints to be designed in a (1) thematically cohesive way (e.g., "This brand pursues a thematic concept"), (2) consistent way (e.g., "This brand is consistent across different touchpoints"), and (3) context-sensitive way (e.g., "Different touchpoints of this brand are well aligned to my personal circumstances"). This scale includes 12 items that reflect the conceptual definition of these three dimensions and allows companies to evaluate, monitor, and benchmark its customer-perceived journeys over time.[13]

Importance/Performance Matrices

One of the most useful forms of analysis in customer research is the *importance/performance matrix.* This chart combines information about customer perceptions and importance ratings. An example is shown in Figure 5.3. Customer-perceived attribute importance is represented on the vertical axis from high (top) to low (bottom). Customer-perceived performance is shown on the horizontal axis from low (left) to high (right). There are many variations of these matrices: some companies define the horizontal axis as the gap between expectations and perceptions, or as performance relative to competition. The shading on the chart indicates the area of highest leverage

FIGURE 5.3 **Importance/ Performance Matrix**

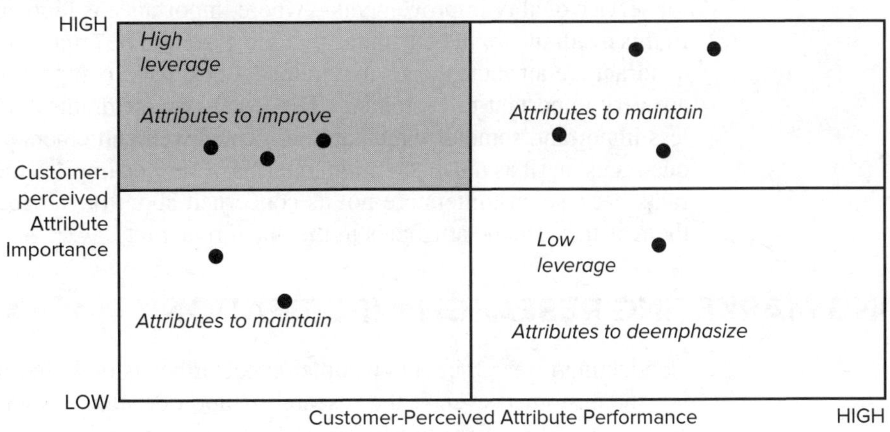

Strategy Insight Big Data, Data Brokers, and Surveillance Economies

One of the tools you hear about frequently as you move into the business world is "big data." According to McKinsey Global Institute, "big data refers to datasets whose size is beyond the ability of typical database software tools to capture, store, manage, and analyze." It involves accessing the vast new flows of information available to companies to understand and link virtually all the information they need, much of it critical to understanding their customers. However, as we will explain later, big data is only relevant when used to make decisions and influence strategy.

You may be familiar with Amazon's big data and algorithms. Not only can Amazon track what you buy, but also what else you view, how you move through the website, how offers and reviews affect you, and even what you will buy next. As Andrew McAfee and Erik Brynjolfsson describe it, big data possesses three pivotal differences from previous analytical approaches:

- **Volume** Think exabytes, not gigabytes. Because of the Internet, companies can now collect petabytes on its customers. A petabyte is one quadrillion bytes (equal to 20 million filing cabinets of text) and an exabyte is 1,000 times that!
- **Velocity** No longer does it take marketing researchers months or weeks to collect data; data collection can now be done in real time, providing virtually instant insights.
- **Variety** Big data includes information from social networks, mobile phones, images, text, locations, sensor readings, and more.

Skeptics say that big data is just that—data—unless companies have ways to use algorithms to make it useful in decision making. The data may spit out relationships in the data but how valid and valuable are those relationships? An infamous example of the limitations of big data is "Google Flu Trends" which was featured in *Nature*, a top scientific journal, a few years ago. At the time, Google reported a coup: the company was able to track an influenza's spread across the United States more quickly than the Centers for Disease Control (one-day delay for Google, a week or more for the CDC). Unfortunately, the following year Google was unable to replicate this feat.

As this example shows, big data is helpful only when it allows managers to reliably make decisions and influence strategy. One team of scholars have written a book to address three important objectives in achieving this, rather than just using data for data's sake. First, they show how big data presents many opportunities for companies to create value but to also demonstrate what they call the "dark side" of big data—issues such as over-investment in unproven data and mistaking correlation (*x* is related to *y*) for causation (*x* causes *y*). Second, they describe the specific analytical approaches that are necessary to get answers from big data. Third, they discuss solutions on how to organize the marketing analytical function within the company to obtain value from the data.

Another key question is whether data-driven companies are better performers than those who make decisions the "old-fashioned" way, through intuition or structured company databases. The Massachusetts

for service quality improvements—where importance is high and performance is low. In this quadrant are the attributes that most need to be improved. In the adjacent upper quadrant are attributes to be maintained, ones that a company performs well and that are very important to customers. The lower two quadrants contain attributes that are less important, some of which are performed well and others poorly. Neither of these quadrants merit as much attention in terms of service improvements as the upper quadrants because customers are not as concerned about the attributes that are plotted in them as they are the attributes in the upper quadrants.

USING MARKETING RESEARCH INFORMATION

Conducting research about customer expectations is only the first part of understanding the customer, even if the research is appropriately designed, executed, and presented. A service firm must also use the research findings in a meaningful way—to

Institute of Technology's Center for Digital Business, along with the Wharton School, found that the more companies characterize themselves as data-driven, the better they performed on financial and operational measures. In fact, they found that companies in the top third of their industry in the use of data-driven decision making were 5 percent more productive and 6 percent more profitable.

Related to improving company performance through better data is the increasing importance of data brokers: **Data brokers** are companies that collect a vast array of detailed and specific consumer information from public records (e.g., census data) and private sources (e.g., social media sites, purchasing histories). They then analyze these data to make inferences about consumers and sell this information to their clients. Although data brokers are unknown to most consumers, they are major actors in the "big data economy." For example, one of the largest companies, Acxiom, reportedly has records on 10 percent of the world's population, with approximately 1,500 data points per consumer. Data brokers are one indicator of the broader emergence of the **surveillance economy**. Former Harvard professor Shoshana Zuboff coined this term to describe an economic system that is based on the commodification of personal data, with the primary objective of using these data for profit generation (e.g., through optimized micro-targeting). On the one hand, such rich data sources in a surveillance economy allow companies to provide better service and products to their customers; indeed, these data might improve consumer well-being (e.g., highly individualized services are delivered at the optimal point in time) and societal well-being (e.g., enabling increasingly smart cities); on the other hand, data brokers might also assemble sensitive or intrusive data about consumers, who typically have little to no control over these data. Therefore, commercializing personal data can also undermine consumer autonomy and result in consumption choices that undermine well-being (e.g., overconsumption that results in financial debt). Responsible business leaders will consider the ethical risks in a surveillance economy and have their customers' best interests in mind.

Even with the advantages big data provides, leaders' and researchers' insights are still needed. As either W. Edwards Deming or Peter Drucker famously first said, "You can't manage what you don't measure." And you must use those measurements wisely to make good strategic decisions.

Sources: J. B. Glasgow, "Data Brokers: Should They Be Reviled or Revered?," *The Cambridge Handbook of Consumer Privacy* (2018), pp. 25–46; S. Zuboff, *The Age of Surveillance Capitalism: The Fight for a Human Future at the New Frontier of Power*, Public Affairs, 2019; P. Verhoef, E. Kooge, and N. Walk, *Creating Value with Big Data Analytics: Making Smarter Marketing Decisions* (New York: Routlege, 2016); A. McAfee and E. Brynjolfsson, "Big Data: the Management Revolution," *Harvard Business Review* 90 (October 2012), pp. 61–67; McKinsey Global Institute, "Big Data—The Next Frontier for Innovation Competition," www.mckinsey .com, 2011; H. Chen, R. H. L. Chiang, and V. C. Storey, "Business Intelligence and Analytics: From Big Data to Big Impact," *MIS Quarterly* 36 (December 2012), pp. 1165–1188.

drive change or improvement in the way service is delivered. The misuse (or even nonuse) of research data can lead to a large gap in *understanding customer expectations*. When managers do not read research reports because they are too busy dealing with the day-to-day challenges of the business, companies fail to use the resources available to them. And when customers participate in research studies but never see changes in the way the company does business, they feel frustrated and annoyed with the company. Understanding how to make the best use of research—to apply what has been learned to the business—is a key way to close the gap between customer expectations and management perceptions of customer expectations. Managers must learn to turn research information and insights into action and to recognize that the purpose of research is to drive improvement and customer satisfaction. With that goal in mind, scholars have examined how marketing research information can best be shared and utilized in companies. For example, one study found that such information is better used when the marketing research department plays five roles as it interacts with

Global Feature Listening to Global Customers in Cross-Cultural Research

Cross-cultural market research remains a major priority in a global economy because service markets are predominately growing in emerging markets such as Africa, Latin and South American, and Asia. For example, China and India are now considered the biggest markets for smart phones and mobile services. Moreover, trade liberalizations (the reduction of restrictions on the free exchange of goods and services between countries) continue to encourage global commerce. Therefore, service companies need to develop high levels of inter-cultural awareness and understanding. Market research is the key platform for service companies to listen to their global customers. As we briefly illustrate next, Airbnb successfully accomplishes that.

How Airbnb Listens to Global Users through Its International Community Panels: A company with a presence in almost 200 countries, Airbnb's services not only must be intuitive for consumers from different cultures to use, but they also must be locally tailored for numerous languages. However, Airbnb's market research was originally focused only on its English-speaking customers. Because multilingual research was more resource-intensive, the company had done very little. Not surprisingly, this created a potential gap in Airbnb's ability to understand the needs, expectations, and perceptions of its non-English-speaking customers. To close this gap, Airbnb launched its International Community Panels (IC Panels), which began as a six-month research project that involved participants in nine non-English-speaking countries and fielded hundreds of questions. The company also formed a "localization team" that was tasked with tailoring the Airbnb service to its various markets. Since its inception, the project has been a success and resulted in multiple improvements to Airbnb's service offering. The company continues its IC Panels and intends to include more countries, languages, and types of community members. Without the IC Panels, Airbnb researchers only gained insights from English-speaking members of its user community, but the IC Panels now allow Airbnb to listen to

360b/Alamy Stock Photo

a broader and deeper portfolio of its customers, illustrating how market research can help close provider Gap 1.

Taj Hotels listens to its global customer base: Taj Hotels has carefully cultivated a global listening strategy that bridges cultural divides while maintaining its signature hospitality excellence. Through its comprehensive Care@Tajness philosophy and customer contact hub, the brand seamlessly integrates digital feedback with meaningful human interactions, creating a continuous loop of insight gathering that informs service refinements across its properties. This internal intelligence network is complemented by Taj's global footprint and robust digital ecosystem – including a website attracting millions of visitors and social media platforms engaging 2 million followers – which together serve as cultural barometers capturing evolving guest expectations across diverse markets in real-time. What truly distinguishes Taj's approach, however, is its nuanced cultural adaptability; the brand does not merely acknowledge cultural differences but embraces them, transforming properties into authentic reflections of their locations while skillfully tailoring experiences to the modern traveler's desire for both technological convenience and genuine human connection. Taj Hotels' properties are deeply integrated with their surroundings, reflecting the local culture, history, and architecture. This thoughtful balance between global consistency and local relevance enables Taj to continuously refine its brand portfolio,

other units within the company, namely that of (1) internal colleague, (2) customer representative, (3) service provider, (4) quality manager, and (5) knowledge broker. Functioning in these roles helps better disseminate and leverage customer and market intelligence, which is one crucial step toward closing Gap 1.[14]

The research plan should specify the mechanism by which customer data will be used. The research should be actionable: timely, specific, and credible. It can also have a mechanism that allows a company to respond to dissatisfied customers immediately.

UPWARD COMMUNICATION

In some service firms, especially small firms, owners or managers may be in constant contact with customers, thereby gaining firsthand knowledge of customer expectations crafting distinct yet cohesive narratives that resonate with various customer segments worldwide, ultimately demonstrating that effective cross-cultural listening is not just about collecting feedback – it is about translating diverse perspectives into personalized experiences that honor both global standards and local traditions.

Future Opportunities and Challenges in Cross-Cultural Customer Research: In light of the dynamics of a worldwide marketplace, service companies need to understand global customers more broadly and consider emerging challenges so that they can prepare their companies for the future. Sheth and Parvatiyar identify several aspects of cross-cultural consumer behavior that are important for service managers; some of which include:

- **Competing against unbranded service competition:** As large service companies enter emerging markets, they often compete against local unbranded service providers. Although these unbranded providers might lack the brand equity of global companies, they can have considerable advantages in terms of costs and access to customers. For example, often the business is owner-managed, which helps to keep overhead costs low. In addition, because these companies are locally owned, the service can be more easily tailored to regional preferences and individual customers' expectations. Market researchers in international service firms need to explore how their companies can compete against such unbranded competition.
- **Understanding lower-income service consumers:** Marketers increasingly recognize the importance of serving lower-income consumers (often referred to as the "bottom-of-the-pyramid") around the globe, as the need for services in these segments is growing rapidly. It is therefore crucial for service organizations to understand key issues related to affordability and accessibility of services for low-income consumers. For example, market research can help identify and develop new solutions to make services (e.g., healthcare, education, financial services) more affordable and accessible in emerging markets such as Africa and Asia.
- **Assuring sustainable growth:** There are increasing concerns whether the planet can sustain a global population of more than 8 billion people, and especially the emergence of a new consumption-focused middle class of almost 3 billion people in China, India, and Africa. Market researchers need to examine the extent to which global consumers are willing and able to adopt more mindful ways of consumption and how service organizations might support this transition to a more sustainable economy (e.g., new services related to reusing and recycling, new services related to sharing resources such as car-sharing).

Sources: J. N. Sheth, and A. Parvatiyar, "Future Directions of Cross-Cultural Marketing Research," in *Handbook on Cross-Cultural Marketing* (Edward Elgar Publishing, 2020), pp. 248–263; "Airbnb's International Community Panels in Translation," https://www.greenbook.org/case-study/airbnb-s-international-community-panels-in-translation/, accessed October 2, 2021; D. Heifa, "Meet the Airbnb Research Org: A Team Leading the Rise of Research," https://medium.com/uxrblog/meet-the-airbnb-research-org-a-team-leading-the-rise-of-research-7d968f0d5d81, accessed October 3, 2021; "Gap Analysis for a University Abroad," https://www.greenbook.org/case-study/gap-analysis-for-a-university-abroad/, accessed October 3, 2021.

References

https://www.ihcltata.com/company/about-us/
https://www.seleqtionshotels.com/en-in/
https://www.hotelierindia.com/leadership/taj-is-an-emotion-a-legend-and-crown-jewel-of-not-only-the-tata-group-but-the-entire-bharat
https://www.ust.com/en/insights/taj-hotels-digital-makeover-enhanced-customer-experiences-increased-online-conversions
https://medium.com/pen-bold-kiln-press/why-taj-is-the-best-customer-service-company-in-the-world-24f24e548574
https://www.modernretail.co/sponsored/brands-are-uncovering-holistic-consumer-insights-with-transaction-data/

and perceptions. But in large service organizations, managers do not always get the opportunity to experience firsthand what their customers want.

The larger a company is, the more difficult it is for managers to interact directly with the customer and the less firsthand information they have about customer expectations. Even when they read and digest research reports, managers can lose touch with customers if they never get the opportunity to experience delivery of the actual service. A theoretical view of how things are supposed to work cannot provide the richness of the service encounter. To truly understand customer needs, management benefits from hands-on knowledge of what really happens in stores, on customer service phone lines, in service queues, and in face-to-face service encounters. If the listening gap is to be closed, managers in large firms need some form of customer contact.

Objectives for Upward Communication

Exhibit 5.3 shows the major research objectives for improving upward communication in an organization. These objectives include gaining firsthand knowledge from and about customers, as well as employees, improving internal service quality, and obtaining ideas for service improvement. These objectives can be met by two types of interactive activities in the organization: one designed to improve the type and effectiveness of communications from customers to management and the other designed to improve communications between employees and management.

Research for Upward Communication

Executive Visits to Customers

This approach is frequently used in business-to-business service marketing. In some visits, executives of the company make sales or service calls with customer contact personnel (salespeople). In other situations, executives of the selling company arrange meetings with executives at a similar level in client companies.

Executive or Management Listening to Customers

Direct interaction with customers adds clarity and depth to managers' understanding of customer expectations and needs. Many companies require executives to perform entry-level jobs to promote understanding of their customers. One vice president from DaVita Inc., a leading dialysis-treatment operator, spent three days helping treat seriously ill patients alongside technicians.[15] A growing number of service companies—including Walt Disney, Continental Airlines, Amazon.com, and Sysco—require that managers spend time interacting with customers and experiencing service delivery. A formal program for encouraging informal interaction is often the best way to ensure that the contact takes place.

Research on Intermediate Customers

Intermediate customers (such as contact employees, dealers, distributors, agents, and brokers) are people the company serves who serve the end-customer. Researching the needs and expectations of these customers *in serving the end-customer* can be a useful and efficient way to both improve service to and obtain information about end-users. The interaction with intermediate customers provides opportunities for understanding end-customers' expectations and problems. It can also help the company learn about and satisfy the service expectations of intermediate customers, a process critical in their providing quality service to end-customers.

Research on Internal Customers

Employees who perform services are themselves customers of internal services on which they depend heavily to do their jobs well. As discussed in Chapter 11, there is a strong and direct link between the quality of internal service that employees receive and the quality of the service they provide their own customers. For this reason, it is important to conduct employee research that focuses on the service that internal customers give and receive. In many companies this focus requires adapting existing employee opinion research to focus on service satisfaction. Employee research complements customer research when service quality is the issue being investigated. Customer research provides insight into what is occurring, whereas employee research

Exhibit 5.3 Elements in an Effective Program of Upward Communication

Type of Research	Research Objective	Qualitative/ Quantitative	Cost of Information		
			Money	Time	Frequency
Executive visits to customers	To gain firsthand knowledge about customers	Qualitative	Moderate	Moderate	Continuous
Executive listenings	To gain firsthand knowledge about customers	Qualitative	Low	Low	Continuous
Research on intermediate customers	To gain in-depth information on end-customers	Quantitative	Moderate	Moderate	Annual
Employee internal satisfaction surveys	To improve internal service quality	Quantitative	Moderate	Moderate	Annual
Employee visits or listenings	To gain firsthand knowledge about employees	Qualitative	Moderate	Moderate	Continuous
Employee suggestions	To obtain ideas for service improvements	Qualitative	Low	Low	Continuous

provides insight into why. The two types of research play unique and equally important roles in improving service quality. Companies that focus service quality research exclusively on external customers are missing a rich and vital source of information. This one-sided focus on external service quality can also be problematic for a firm's financial performance. For example, a recent meta-analysis on the Service-Profit-Chain (discussed in Chapter 4) demonstrates the importance of internal service quality; it finds that internal service quality can influence employee productivity by improving employee skills, enabling operational excellence, and inducing customers to evaluate external service quality more favorably; together, these effects positively influence firm profitability.[16]

Executive or Management Listening Approaches to Employees

Employees who actually perform the service have the best vantage point for observing the service and identifying impediments to its quality. Customer contact personnel are in regular contact with customers and thereby come to understand a great deal about customer expectations and perceptions. If the information they know can be communicated upward, top managers' understanding of the customer may improve. In fact, it could be said that in many companies top management's understanding of the customer depends largely on the extent and types of communication received from customer contact personnel and from noncompany contact personnel (such as independent insurance agents and retailers) who represent the company and its services. When these channels of communication are closed, management may not get feedback about problems encountered in service delivery and about how customer expectations are changing.

Sam Walton, the late founder of the highly successful discount retailer Walmart, once remarked, "Our best ideas come from delivery and stock boys."[17] To stay in touch with the source of new ideas, Walton spent endless hours in stores, working the floor, helping clerks, or approving personal checks, even showing up at the loading dock with a bag of doughnuts for a surprised crew of workers.[18] He was well known for having his plane drop him next to a wheat field, where he would meet a Walmart truck driver. Giving his pilot instructions to meet him at another landing strip 200 miles down the road, he would make the trip with the Walmart driver, listening to what he had to say about the company.

Employee Suggestions

Most companies have some form of formal employee suggestion program whereby contact personnel can communicate to management their ideas for improving work. Suggestion systems have come a long way from the traditional suggestion box. Effective suggestion systems are ones in which employees are empowered to see their suggestions through, supervisors can implement proposals immediately, employees participate for continuous improvement in their jobs, supervisors respond quickly to ideas, and coaching is provided in ways to handle suggestions. In today's companies, suggestions from employees are facilitated by self-directed work teams that encourage employees to identify problems and then work to develop solutions to those problems.

Benefits of Upward Communication

Upward communication of this sort provides information to upper-level managers about activities and performances throughout the organization. Specific types of communication that may be relevant are formal (such as reports of problems and exceptions in service delivery) and informal (like discussions between contact personnel and upper-level managers). Managers who stay close to their frontline employees benefit not only by keeping their employees happy but also by learning more about their customers.[19] Through this important channel, management learns about customer expectations from employees in regular contact with customers and can thereby reduce the size of provider Gap 1.

Summary

This chapter discussed the role of customer research in understanding customer perceptions and expectations. The chapter began by describing criteria for effective service research that should be incorporated into a service marketing research program. Next, we discussed the elements in an effective service marketing research program and indicated how the approaches satisfied the criteria. In addition to the types and techniques of research (shown in Exhibit 5.1), the boxes in this chapter showed how technologies add to the information that managers can collect.

The chapter described key forms of service research, including critical incident studies, mystery shopping, service expectation meetings and reviews, process checkpoint evaluations, and database research. Important topics in researching services—including developing research objectives—were also described. Finally, upward communication, ways in which management obtains and uses information from customers and customer contact personnel, was discussed. These topics combine to help close the listening gap—the gap between customer expectations and company understanding of customer expectations and the first of four provider gaps in the Gaps Model of Service Quality.

Discussion Questions

1. Give five reasons research objectives must be established before customer research is conducted.
2. Why are both qualitative and quantitative research methods needed in a service marketing research program?
3. Why does the frequency of research differ across the research methods shown in Exhibit 5.1?
4. Compare and contrast the types of research that help a company identify common failure points (see column 2 in Exhibit 5.1). Which of the types do you think produces better information? Why?
5. In what situations does a service company need requirements research?
6. What reasons can you give for companies' lack of use of research information? How might you motivate managers to use the information to a greater extent? How might you motivate frontline workers to use the information?
7. Given a specific customer research budget, what would be your recommendations for the percentage to be spent on customer research versus upward communication? Why?
8. What kinds of information could be gleaned from research on intermediate customers? What would intermediate customers know that service providers might not?
9. For what types of products and services would research on the Internet be preferable to traditional research?
10. Which opportunities and challenges come with emerging research techniques such as artificial intelligence and biometrics?

Exercises

1. Choose a local service organization to interview about customer research. Find out what the firm's objectives are and the types of customer research it currently uses. Using the information in this chapter, think about the effectiveness of its customer research. What are the strengths? Weaknesses?
2. Choose one of the services you consume. If you were in charge of creating a survey for that service, what questions would you ask on the survey? Give several examples. What type of survey (relationship versus transaction-based) would be most appropriate for the service? What recommendations would you give to management of the company about making such a survey actionable?
3. If you were the marketing director of your college or university, what types of research (see Exhibit 5.1) would be essential for understanding both external and internal customers? If you could choose only three types of research, which ones would you select? Why?
4. Using the SERVQUAL scale in this chapter, create a questionnaire for a service firm that you use. Give the questionnaire to 10 people, and describe what you learn.
5. To get an idea of the power of the critical incident technique, try it yourself with reference to restaurant service. Think of a time when, as a customer, you had a particularly satisfying interaction with a restaurant. Follow the instructions here, which are identical to the instructions in an actual study, and observe the insights you obtain about your requirements in restaurant service:
   a. When did the incident happen?
   b. What specific circumstances led up to this situation?
   c. Exactly what did the employee (or firm) say or do?

   d. What resulted that made you feel the interaction was satisfying?
   e. What could or should have been done differently?

6. Visit the website of Envirosell (https://envirosell.com/) or IDEO (https://www.ideo.com/), or similar research companies; find and discuss illustrations of market-oriented ethnography.

Notes

1. Sources for the chapter opener include C. Kuehnl, D. Jozic, and C. Homburg, "Effective Customer Journey Design: Consumers' Conception, Measurement, and Consequences," *Journal of the Academy of Marketing Science* 47, no. 3 (2019), pp. 551–568; L. Becker and E. Jaakkola, "Customer Experience: Fundamental Premises and Implications for Research," *Journal of the Academy of Marketing Science* 48, no. 4 (2020), pp. 630–648, H. Fanderl, K. Neher, and A. Pulido, "Are You Really Listening to What Your Customers are Saying?" *McKinsey Newsletter,* March 2016, pp. 1–6; N. Maechler, K. Neher, and R. Park, "From Touchpoints to Journeys: Seeing the World as Customers Do," *McKinsey Newsletter,* March 2016, pp. 1–10; D. Edelman and M. Singer, "The New Customer Decision Journey," *McKinsey Newsletter,* October 2015, pp. 1–3; X. Lhuer, T. Olanrewaju, and H. Yeon, "What It Takes to Deliver Breakthrough Customer Service," *McKinsey Insights,* November 2015, pp. 1–3.
2. A. Parasuraman, L. L. Berry, and V. A. Zeithaml, "Guidelines for Conducting Service Quality Research," *Marketing Research: A Magazine of Management and Applications,* December 1990, pp. 34–44.
3. "Zaltman Metaphor Elicitation Technique," Olson Zaltman, accessed September 25, 2021, www.olsonzaltman.com/zmet; also see: V. A. Zeithaml, B. J. Jaworski, A. K. Kohli, K. R. Tuli, W. Ulaga, and G. Zaltman, "A Theories-in-Use Approach to Building Marketing Theory," *Journal of Marketing* 84 (January 2020), pp. 32–51.
4. This section is based on a comprehensive assessment of the critical incident technique in D. D. Gremler, "The Critical Incident Technique in Service Research," *Journal of Service Research* 7 (August 2004), pp. 65–89.
5. For detailed discussions of the critical incident technique, see J. C. Flanagan, "The Critical Incident Technique," *Psychological Bulletin* 51 (July 1954), pp. 327–358; M. J. Bitner, J. D. Nyquist, and B. H. Booms, "The Critical Incident as a Technique for Analyzing the Service Encounter," in *Services Marketing in a Changing Environment,* ed. T. M. Bloch, G. D. Upah, and V. A. Zeithaml (Chicago: American Marketing Association, 1985), pp. 48–51; S. Wilson-Pessano, "Defining Professional Competence: The Critical Incident Technique 40 Years Later," presentation to the Annual Meeting of the American Educational Research Association, New Orleans, 1988; I. Roos, "Methods of Investigating Critical Incidents," *Journal of Service Research* 4 (February 2002), pp. 193–204; Gremler, "The Critical Incident Technique in Service Research."
6. J. Carey, J. Buckley, and J. Smith, "Hospital Hospitality," *Newsweek,* February 11, 1985, p. 78.
7. See V. A. Zeithaml and A. Parasuraman, *Service Quality,* MSI Relevant Knowledge Series (Cambridge, MA: Marketing Science Institute, 2004) for a complete review of this research, including the many publications by the original authors of SERVQUAL and the extensions by other authors.

8. A. G. Flynn, L. C. Salisbury, and K. Seiders, "Tell Us Again, How Satisfied Are You? The Influence of Recurring Posttransaction Surveys on Purchase Behavior," *Journal of Service Research* 20, no. 3 (2017), pp. 292–305.
9. E. Day, "Researchers Must Enter Consumer's World," *Marketing News,* August 17, 1998, p. 17.
10. G. Khermouch, "Consumers in the Mist," *BusinessWeek,* February 26, 2001, pp. 92–93.
11. D. Dembrow, "15 Movies That Were Drastically Changed Because Audiences Hated Them," https://www.denofgeek.com/movies/movie-endings-changed-by-test-screenings/, accessed September 26, 2021.
12. P. R. Magnusson, J. Mathing, and P. Kristensson, "Managing User Involvement in Service Innovation: Experiments with Innovating End Users," *Journal of Service Research* 6 (November 2003), pp. 111–124; also see: J. Trischler, S. J. Pervan, S. J. Kelly, and D. R. Scott, "The Value of Codesign: The Effect of Customer Involvement in Service Design Teams," *Journal of Service Research* 21, no. 1 (2018), pp. 75–100.
13. C. Kuehnl, D. Jozic, and C. Homburg, "Effective Customer Journey Design: Consumers' Conception, Measurement, and Consequences," *Journal of the Academy of Marketing Science* 47, no. 3 (2019), pp. 551–568.
14. C. Bode and I. Geiger, "Not Just Another Internal Service Provider: How a Firm's Marketing Research Function Influences Uses of Market Research Information," *European Journal of Marketing* 55, no. 2 (2021), pp. 385–419; also see: G. F. Gebhardt, F. J. Farrelly, and J. Conduit, "Market Intelligence Dissemination Practices," *Journal of Marketing* 83, no. 3 (2019), pp. 72–90.
15. J. S. Lublin, "Top Brass Try Life in the Trenches," *The Wall Street Journal,* June 25, 2007, p. B1.
16. J. Hogreve, A. Iseke, K. Derfuss, and T. Eller, "The Service—Profit Chain: A Meta-Analytic Test of a Comprehensive Theoretical Framework," *Journal of Marketing* 81, no. 3 (2017), pp. 41–61.
17. S. Koepp, "Make That Sale, Mr. Sam," *Time,* May 18, 1987.
18. Ibid.
19. Zeithaml, Parasuraman, and Berry, *Delivering Quality Service,* p. 64.

Chapter Six

Managing Customer Relationships

This chapter's learning objectives are to:

1. Explain relationship marketing, its goals, and the benefits of long-term relationships for firms and customers.
2. Explain why and how to estimate customer relationship value.
3. Introduce the concept of customer profitability segments as a strategy for focusing relationship marketing efforts.
4. Present relationship development strategies—including quality core service, switching barriers, and relationship bonds.
5. Identify challenges in relationship management, including the somewhat controversial idea that "the customer is not always right."

Swiggy – Winning through Customer-Centricity

Swiggy is a new age consumer-first firm that offers a convenient platform for food delivery and quick commerce. The company has delivered over 3 billion orders from its 220,000+ restaurant partners in over 680 cities in India through its 520,000+ delivery partners. Its mission revolves around elevating the urban consumer's quality of life through unparalleled convenience. What began as a food delivery service with six delivery partners has transformed into a cultural phenomenon processing millions of daily orders across thousands of restaurants and retail outlets. The company's success stems from its ability to identify emerging consumer needs and rapidly adapt, exemplified by its early adoption of full-stack delivery and quick commerce models. By understanding that consumers want immediate delivery after making purchase decisions, Swiggy has positioned itself at the forefront of the quick commerce revolution. This customer-first mission statement drives all strategic decisions, with Rohit Kapoor, CEO – Food Marketplace emphasizing that the core of their success lies in "the ability to be humble, and the ability to identify the seeds of an idea, and be willing to experiment with it" for customers' benefit.

Customer-centricity is embedded in Swiggy's business model through various strategic initiatives. The platform offers personalized push notifications based on user preferences, streamlined logistics systems to ensure faster deliveries, and subscription services like Swiggy Super for additional benefits. Their communication's approach prioritizes relatability through humorous content, localized promotions, and

Swiggy: a regular at the top of many organizations' customer service award lists.

https://www.swiggy.com/

consistent cross-platform messaging that resonates with their audience. By diversifying beyond food with services like Instamart for groceries and Swiggy Genie for general deliveries, the company continually expands ways to serve customer needs while leveraging its existing infrastructure. Swiggy's strategic vision recognizes changing social dynamics, such as the shift in attitudes toward cooking as a choice rather than an obligation, particularly supporting women who prioritize their time effectiveness to "be the best version of themselves," with Swiggy positioning itself as a partner in enabling that convenience.

The company's dedication to customer satisfaction extends to its organizational culture, where "Consumer comes first" serves as a guiding principle that cascades through all levels of employees. This value is exemplified by quality management teams who develop monitoring programs and standards for customer interactions, constantly exploring unique solutions to improve customer experiences. Syed Waseem, a Quality Manager, highlights how leadership empowers employees to make decisions that result in "building a better customer-centric team." The company fosters a work environment where employees are encouraged to innovate in service delivery, with leaders making time to address issues and aid in formulating customer-focused strategies. Even the delivery partners, often considered the face of the company, are valued for their critical role in fulfilling the customer experience promise, with Swiggy ensuring they have the flexibility and fair compensation needed to provide excellent service. Despite the challenges of maintaining consistent service quality and managing customer expectations, Swiggy measures its success primarily by customer satisfaction, establishing it as the organization's true North Star.

Reference:

https://www.swiggy.com/corporate/
https://yourstory.com/2024/09/swiggys-recipe-for-success-innovation-customer-focus-food-delivery
https://www.business-standard.com/companies/news/swiggy-confident-of-growth-emphasises-strength-in-consumer-insight-124110701176_1.html
https://blog.swiggy.com/life-at-swiggy/crazy-about-customer-care-meet-swiggys-quality-manager/
https://skillcircle.in/swiggy-business-model-marketing-strategy/

Swiggy provides a strong example of an organization that has focused on managing long-term relationships with its members (i.e., customers). Unlike the Swiggy example, however, many companies fail to understand customers accurately because they fail to focus on customer relationships. They tend to fixate on acquiring new customers rather than viewing customers as assets that they need to nurture and retain. By concentrating on new customers, firms can easily fall into the traps of short-term promotions, price discounts, or catchy ads that bring customers in but are not enough to bring them back. By adopting a relationship marketing philosophy, on the other hand, companies begin to understand customers over time and in great depth and are better able to meet their changing needs and expectations. Marketing strategies for understanding customers over time and managing long-term relationships are the subjects of this chapter.

RELATIONSHIP MARKETING

Over the past few decades, many firms have shifted from a transaction focus to a relationship focus in their marketing efforts. Customers have become partners and cocreators as firms have made "long-term commitments to maintaining those relationships with quality, service, and innovation."[1] For example, HDFC Bank explicitly includes its commitment to customer focus in its core values. "The HDFC Bank Way" represents the deliberate culture transformation journey that places customers at the heart of everything they do, alongside culture and conscience as the three powerful enablers that drive success. This customer-focused approach is embedded within the HDFC Bank's six cultural pillars – Integrity, Execution, Innovation, Humility, Inclusion, and Collaboration – which guide the bank's employees in delivering exceptional service experiences. This human-centered framework empowers employees to create meaningful connections with customers while maintaining the highest ethical standards.

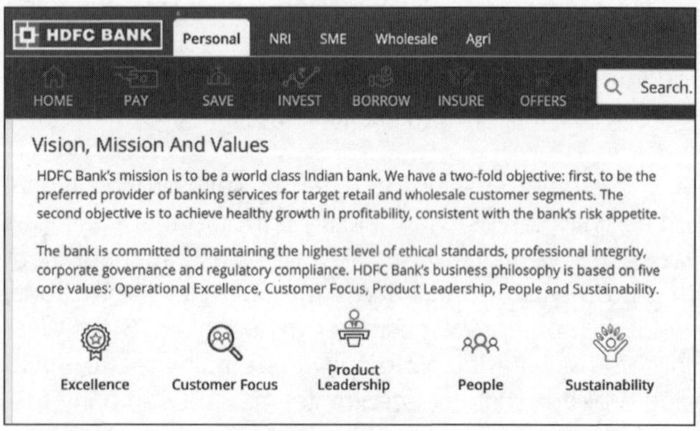

https://www.hdfcbank.com/personal/about-us/overview/who-we-are

The Mission Statement of HDFC bank explicitly defines its commitment to customer satisfaction and to long-term customer relationships.

The integration of the 3Cs – Culture, Conscience, and Customers – ensures that customer-centricity is not just a strategic initiative but a deeply embedded organizational mindset that drives growth and success.[2]

Relationship marketing essentially represents a paradigm shift within marketing—away from an acquisitions/transaction focus toward a retention/relationship focus.[3] Relationship marketing (or relationship management) is a philosophy of doing business, a strategic orientation, that focuses on initiating, *keeping*, and *improving* relationships with current customers rather than on acquiring new customers. This philosophy assumes that many consumers and business customers prefer to have an ongoing relationship with one organization rather than to switch continually among providers in their search for value. Building on this assumption and another that suggests it is usually less expensive to keep a current customer than to attract a new one,[4] successful marketers develop effective strategies for retaining customers. Our opening example shows how Swiggy has built its business around a relationship philosophy.

It has been suggested that firms frequently focus on attracting customers (the "first act") but then pay little attention to what they should do to keep them (the "second act").[5] Ideas expressed in an interview with James Schorr, then executive vice president of marketing at Holiday Inn, illustrate this point.[6] In the interview he referred to the "bucket theory of marketing." By this he meant that marketing can be thought of as a big bucket: it is what the sales, advertising, and promotion programs do that pours customers into the top of the bucket. As long as these programs are effective, the bucket stays full.

FIGURE 6.1 Holes in the Bucket: Why Relationship Development Makes Sense

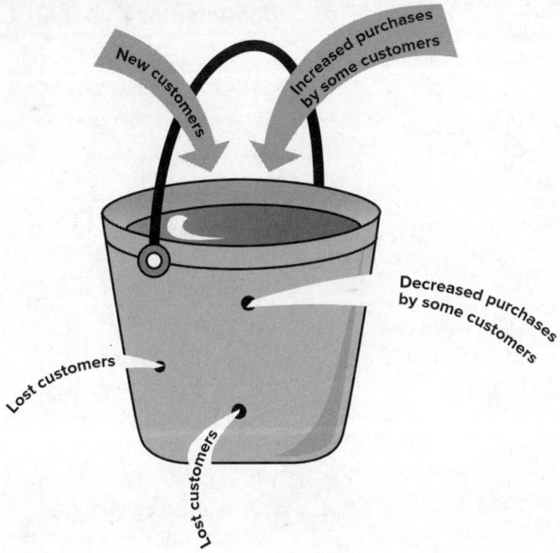

However, "There's only one problem," he said, "there are holes in the bucket." When the business is running well and the hotel is delivering on its promises, any holes are small and few customers are leaving. As indicated in Figure 6.1, when the operation is weak and customers are not satisfied with what they are getting—and therefore the relationship is weak—people start falling out of the bucket through the holes faster than they can be poured in through the top.

The bucket metaphor illustrates why a relationship strategy that focuses on plugging the holes in the bucket makes so much sense. Historically, marketers have been more concerned with acquisition of customers, so a shift to a relationship strategy often represents changes in mind-set, organizational culture, and employee reward systems. For example, the sales incentive systems in many organizations are set up to reward the acquisition of new customers. There are often fewer (or no) rewards for retaining current accounts. Thus, even when people see the logic of customer retention, the existing organizational systems may not support its implementation.

The Evolution of Customer Relationships

Firms' relationships with their customers, like other social relationships, tend to evolve over time. Scholars have suggested that marketing exchange relationships between providers and customers often have the potential to evolve from strangers to acquaintances to friends to partners. Exhibit 6.1 illustrates different issues at each successive level of the relationship.[7]

Customers as Strangers

Strangers are those potential customers who have not yet had any transactions (interactions) with a firm and may not even be aware of the firm. At the industry level, strangers may be conceptualized as customers who have not yet entered the market; at the firm level, they may include customers of competitors. Clearly, the firm has no relationship with the customer at this point. Consequently, the firm's primary goal with these potential customers ("strangers") is to initiate communication with them to *attract* them and *acquire* their business. Thus, the primary marketing efforts directed toward such customers deal with familiarizing those potential customers with the firm's offerings and, subsequently, encouraging them to give the firm a try.

Customers as Acquaintances

Once customer awareness and trial are achieved, familiarity is established and the customer and the firm become *acquaintances,* creating the basis for an exchange relationship. A primary goal for the firm at this stage of the relationship is *satisfying* the customer. In the acquaintance stage, firms are generally concerned about providing a value proposition to customers comparable with that of competitors. For a customer, an acquaintanceship is effective as long as the customer is relatively satisfied and what is being received in the exchange is perceived as fair value. With repetitive interactions, the customer gains experience and becomes more familiar with the firm's offerings. These encounters, over time, can help reduce uncertainty about the

Exhibit 6.1 A Typology of Exchange Relationships

Customers As . . .	Strangers	Acquaintances	Friends	Partners
Product offering	Attractive relative to competitive offerings or alternative purchases.	Parity offering consistent with industry standard.	Differentiated offering tailored to specific market segments.	Individualized offering and dedicated resources fitted to an individual customer.
Source of competitive advantage	Attractiveness	Satisfaction	Satisfaction + trust	Satisfaction + trust + commitment
Buying activity	Interest, exploration, and trial.	Satisfaction drives (re)purchasing and reduces need to search for market information.	Trust in firm evolves over time and further bolsters repurchasing.	Commitment (e.g., mutual information sharing and idiosyncratic investments) allows the creation of truly individualized offerings, which can be further adjusted in response to varying customer needs over time.
Focus of selling activities	Awareness of firm's offerings (encouraging trial) facilitates initial selling.	Repeated interactions lead to familiarity, which reduces customer-perceived risks and facilitates marketing and sales.	Detailed understanding of the needs and situations of customers in a specific market segment facilitates marketing and sales.	Personalized understanding of an individual customer's need and situation and idiosyncratic investments facilitates marketing and sales.
Relationship time horizon	*None:* Buyer may have had no previous interactions with or knowledge of the firm.	*Short:* Often short because customers can switch service providers relatively easily (e.g., low switching costs).	*Medium:* Typically longer than acquaintance relationships because trust takes time to evolve and it is more difficult for competitors to imitate.	*Long:* Typically long because developing the deep understanding of a focal customer's needs and allocating the corresponding resources to fulfill these unique customer needs often takes considerable time.
Sustainability of competitive advantage	*Low:* Generally low, as firm must continually find ways to be attractive, in terms of the value offered, to induce trial.	*Low:* Typically low, but companies vary in their ability to provide unique value to customers through marketing, sales, and/or service even if the offering itself is (merely) industry standard.	*Medium:* Typically medium, but that depends on a firm's ability to identify the various needs and situations of customers in a specific market segment and the ability to turn this knowledge into meaningful, differentiated offerings designed for this market segment.	*High:* Typically high, but that depends on how unique and effective the interconnected activities between customer and service provider become.
Primary relationship marketing goal	*Acquire* the customer's business.	*Satisfy* the customer's needs and wants.	*Retain* the customer's business.	*Enhance* the relationship with the customer.

Source: Adapted from M. D. Johnson and F. Selnes, "Customer Portfolio Management: Toward a Dynamic Theory of Exchange Relationships," *Journal of Marketing* 68 (April 2004), p. 5.

benefits expected in the exchange and, therefore, increase the attractiveness of the company relative to the competition. Repetitive interactions improve the firm's knowledge of the customer, helping to facilitate marketing, sales, and service efforts. Thus, an acquaintance relationship facilitates transactions primarily through the reduction of the customer's perceived risk and the provider's costs.

Customers as Friends

As a customer continues to make purchases from a firm and to receive value in the exchange relationship, the firm begins to acquire specific knowledge of the customer's needs, allowing it to create an offering that directly addresses the customer's situation. The provision of a unique offering, and thus differential value, transforms the relationship from acquaintance to *friendship.* This transition, particularly in service exchange relationships, requires the development of trust.[8] Because customers often cannot assess a service outcome prior to purchase and consumption (as explained through the concepts of "experience and credence qualities" in Chapter 1), they may not be able to discern service performance even after experiencing it and, therefore, must trust the provider to do what is promised. As customers become friends they not only become familiar with the company but also come to trust that it provides superior value.

A primary goal for firms at the friendship stage is customer *retention.* A firm's potential to develop sustainable competitive advantage through friends should be higher than for acquaintances because the offering is more unique (and more difficult for competition to imitate) and the customer comes to trust that uniqueness.[9]

Customers as Partners

As a customer continues to interact with a firm, the level of trust often deepens and the customer may receive more customized product offerings and interactions. The trust developed in the friendship stage is a necessary but not sufficient condition for a customer–firm *partnership* to develop.[10] That is, the creation of trust needs to be accompanied by the creation of commitment as the condition necessary for customers to extend the time perspective of a relationship.[11] The deepening of trust and the establishment of commitment reduce the customer's perceived need to "find a better alternative." Thus, to move the relationship into a partnership stage, a firm must use customer knowledge and information systems to deliver highly personalized and customized offerings.

At the partnership stage, the firm is concerned with *enhancing* the relationship. Customers are more likely to stay in the relationship if they feel that the company understands their changing needs and is willing to invest in the relationship by constantly improving and evolving its product and service mix. By enhancing these relationships, the firm expects such customers to be less likely to be lured away by competitors and more likely to buy additional products and services from the company over time. These loyal customers not only provide a solid base for the organization, they may also represent growth potential. The benefits of such relationship enhancement are illustrated by Swiggy, our opening example in this chapter, whose members' needs for insurance increase over their lifetimes as well as the lifetimes of their children. Other examples abound. A bank checking account customer becomes a better customer when she sets up a savings account, takes out a loan, and/or uses the financial advising services of the bank. And a corporate account becomes a better customer when it chooses to do 75 percent of its business with a particular provider rather than splitting the business equally among three providers. In recent years, in fact, many

Technology Spotlight State-of-the-Art Customer Information Systems Help Hilton Enhance Its Customer Relationship Management

Hilton Worldwide Holdings Inc

The potential of today's customer information systems far exceeds any traditional marketing information system that has gone before. The amount of information about individual customers that can now be captured allows the organization to customize to the individual level what previously would have been undifferentiated services.

HILTON'S OnQ SYSTEM

Hilton Hotels has an integrated technology platform called "OnQ" that provides the basis for its customer relationship management (CRM) system. OnQ centralizes all of the personal profile information that guests provide to Hilton—via hotel or central reservations, their websites, or membership in the HHonors loyalty program—to create a "Guest Profile Manager." Profiles are created for any guest who is an HHonors member or simply visits a Hilton hotel at least four times within a year (HHonors has more than 118 million members). Such a system requires an extraordinary investment in information technology to capture information from Hilton's over 6,600 hotels and more than 1 million rooms in six continents across more than 100 countries and territories worldwide. The information collected via OnQ is combined with the customer's stay history and any prior complaints made during previous visits. The entire packet of information enables many of Hilton's 173,000 employees to recognize and reward guests with appropriate welcome messages, room upgrades, or information related to previous visits.

USING THE INFORMATION TO DEVELOP RELATIONSHIPS WITH CUSTOMERS

OnQ provides a mechanism for Hilton Hotels to learn—and remember—customer interests and preferences. Tim Harvey, former chief information officer for Hilton, describes it this way:

> It's like when your grandmother comes to your house. You know exactly who she is. You know exactly what she eats for breakfast. You know what kind of pillow she likes. You know whether she can climb the stairs or not so you know what room to put her in. We have the same passion about our hotel business. We want to know who our customers are and we want to take care of those customers every time we have an opportunity to touch them. So the value of OnQ is primarily having that information with that in-depth knowledge about customers.

Collecting information on all of its customers is not an easy task, particularly given the many different hotels in the Hilton family of brands: the company owns, manages, or franchises a hotel portfolio of some of the best known and highly regarded brands, including Hilton, Conrad Hotels & Resorts, Doubletree, Embassy Suites, Hampton,

companies have aspired to be the "exclusive provider" of a particular product or service for their customers. Over time these enhanced relationships can increase market share and profits for the organization. Our Technology Spotlight features Hilton Hotels and how the company is successfully using information technology to enhance relationships with their customers.

The Goal of Relationship Marketing

The discussion of the evolution of customer relationships demonstrates how a firm's relationship with its customers might be enhanced as customers move further along this relationship continuum. As the relationship value of a customer increases, the provider

Hilton Garden Inn, Homewood Suites, and the Waldorf-Astoria. OnQ provides a method for capturing and managing information on Hilton customers across a diverse set of properties, differing brands, and various countries with local requirements.

PROVIDING GUESTS WITH OPTIONS

Over the years a large percentage of customers have contacted Hilton via the Internet, and the percentage of rooms reserved in this manner has steadily increased. However, in spite of the lack of face-to-face contact, OnQ has allowed Hilton to create a personal relationship with these customers. Once a customer identifies him- or herself when using the Internet, Hilton knows if the customer is an HHonors member, the customer's preferred room type, and the customer's preferred in-room amenities. OnQ also provides the capability for customers to check into their hotel via the Internet prior to arriving—just as customers do for an airline seat. Customers can view the hotel floor plan, see all of the rooms available, and then pick the room they want—perhaps on the west side of the building for those who like to sleep in late or one close to the pool.

Hilton also allows organizers of relatively small groups to book their entire group event or meeting from start to finish on the Internet—and receive immediate confirmation of their reservation. Potential customers who represent groups requiring 25 rooms or less—such as family reunions, wedding parties, or those attending a sporting event—can see about room availability across all Hilton brands and locations. Through OnQ amateur event planners, small-business owners or family representatives can find a hotel that best fits their needs based on price, room types, and proximity to local attractions. Organizers can reserve guest rooms, meeting spaces, food and beverages, audio/visual equipment, and more up to one year in advance without a request for proposal or a waiting period. Additionally, OnQ enables planners to manage their room block, including instant, online access 24/7 to their group reservation details and guest room information. Planners can instantly see who has booked guest rooms for their event or can reserve rooms on behalf of guests, thus keeping track of the total head count at all times.

THE RESULTS

How well has OnQ worked in managing customer relationships? Hilton was ranked the number 1 hotel company in the United States by the American Customer Satisfaction Index in both 2020 and 2021. And, three of the Hilton brands (Hilton Garden Inn, Embassy Suites, and Homewood Suites) regularly receive the top awards for customer satisfaction in their respective hotel segments by independent research conducted by J. D. Power and Associates. Since 2001, these three brands combined to receive the number 1 ranking more than 30 times. Additionally, Harvey estimated that Hilton's "share of wallet" from its best customers increased from 40 percent to 60 percent once OnQ was fully operational. Hilton's relationship with its many customers has certainly been enhanced through OnQ.

Sources: Tim Harvey, Interview on ZDNet.com, http://www.zdnet.com/article/hilton-hotels-tim-harvey-cio/, accessed February 12, 2016; https://newsroom.hilton.com/assets/HWW/docs/brandFactSheets/HWW_Corporate_Fact_Sheet_FINAL.pdf, accessed October 14, 2021; ACSI, https://www.theacsi.org, accessed October 14, 2021.

is more likely to pursue a closer relationship. Thus, the primary goal of relationship marketing is *to build and maintain a base of committed customers who are profitable for the organization.* Figure 6.2 graphically illustrates the goals of relationship marketing. The overriding goal is to increase (1) the customer's "share of wallet" and (2) "share of heart," consistent with the relationship continuum described above. *Share of wallet* refers to the percentage of a person's total amount spent dedicated to a particular company rather than competing companies; *share of heart* refers to the strength of the emotional bond that customers form with the company (e.g., illustrated by the friendship and partnership stages). From a customer's problem-solving perspective, the formation of satisfaction, trust, and commitment corresponds to the customer's

FIGURE 6.2
The Goal of Relationship Marketing: Increasing the Customer's (1) Share of Wallet and (2) Share of Heart

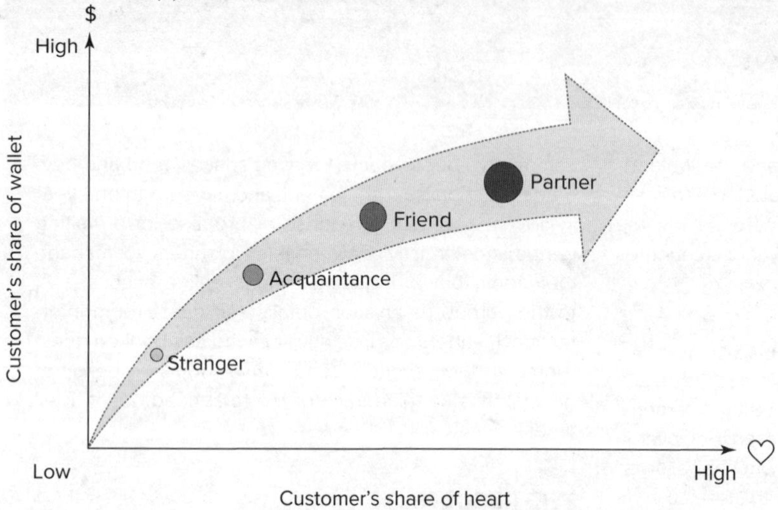

willingness to more fully engage in an exchange relationship as an acquaintance, friend, and partner, respectively. From a firm's resource-allocation perspective, the delivery of differential, and perhaps customized, value corresponds to the extent of its ability and/or desire to create an acquaintance, friend, or partner relationship with the customer. As customers make the transition from satisfaction-based acquaintanceships to trust-based friendships to commitment-based partnerships, increases are required in both the value received and the level of cooperation.

Benefits for Customers and Firms

Both parties in the customer–firm relationship can benefit from customer retention. That is, it is not only in the best interest of the organization to build and maintain a loyal customer base, but customers themselves also benefit from long-term associations.

Benefits for Customers

Assuming they have a choice, customers will remain loyal to a firm when they receive greater value relative to what they expect from competing firms. *Perceived value* represents a trade-off for the consumer between the "give" and the "get" components. (In Chapter 15 we provide an extended discussion of value.) Customers are more likely to stay in a relationship when the "gets" (quality, satisfaction, specific benefits) exceed the "gives" (monetary and nonmonetary costs). When firms can consistently deliver value from the customer's point of view, the customer benefits and has an incentive to stay in the relationship.

Beyond the specific inherent benefits of receiving service value, customers also benefit in other ways from long-term associations with firms. Sometimes these relationship benefits keep customers loyal to a firm more than the attributes of the core service itself. Research has uncovered specific types of relational benefits that customers experience in long-term service relationships including confidence benefits, social benefits, and special treatment benefits.[12]

Confidence Benefits Confidence benefits comprise feelings of trust or confidence in the provider along with a sense of reduced anxiety (e.g., in financial services or healthcare settings) and comfort in knowing what to expect. One customer described his confidence that resulted from having developed a relationship with a service provider:

> There is a comfort [in having] a certain level of experience [with the service provider]. In other words, I know that I am going to be treated right because they know me . . . I don't have any anxiety that I will have a less-than-acceptable experience . . . You know it's going to be good in advance, or if something is wrong it will be taken care of.[13]

Across all the services studied in the relational benefits research, confidence benefits tend to be the most important to customers.[14] Confidence benefits are important to customers because human nature is such that most customers would prefer not to change service providers, particularly when there is a considerable investment in the relationship. The costs of switching are frequently high in terms of dollar costs of transferring business and the associated psychological and time-related costs. Most customers (whether individuals or businesses) have many competing demands for their time and money and are continually searching for ways to balance and simplify decision making to improve the quality of their lives. When they develop confidence in—and can maintain a relationship with—a service provider, they free up time for other concerns and priorities.

Social Benefits Over time, customers develop a sense of familiarity and even a social relationship with their service providers. These ties make it less likely that they would consider switching, even if they learn about a competitor that might have better quality or a lower price. This customer's description of her hair stylist in a quote from the research previously cited illustrates the concept of social benefits:

> I like him. . . . He's really funny and always has lots of good jokes. He's kind of like a friend now. . . . It's more fun to deal with somebody that you're used to. You enjoy doing business with them.[15]

In some long-term customer–firm relationships, a service provider may actually become part of the consumer's social support system.[16] Hairdressers, as in the example just cited, often serve as personal confidants. Less common examples include proprietors of local retail stores who become central figures in neighborhood networks, the health club or restaurant manager who knows her customers personally, the private school principal who knows an entire family and its special needs, and the river guide who befriends patrons on a long rafting trip.[17]

These types of personal relationships can develop for business-to-business customers as well as for end-consumers of services. The social support benefits resulting from these relationships are important to the consumer's quality of life (personal and/or work life) above and beyond the technical benefits of the service provided. Many times the close personal and professional relationships that develop between service providers and clients are the basis for the customer's loyalty. The flip side of this customer benefit is the risk to the firm of losing customers when a valued employee leaves the firm and takes customers with him or her.[18]

Special Treatment Benefits Special treatment includes being given a special deal or price, getting preferential treatment, or perhaps receiving the "benefit of the doubt" from the service provider, as exemplified by the following quotes:

> I think you get special treatment [when you have established a relationship]. My pediatrician allowed me to use the back door to the office so my daughter could avoid contact with other sick children. Other times I have been in a hurry and they take me right back.

> You should get the benefit of the doubt in many situations. For example, I always pay my VISA bill on time, before a service charge is assessed. One time my payment didn't quite arrive on time. When I called them, by looking at my past history, they realized that I always make an early payment. Therefore, they waived the service charge.[19]

Interestingly, in some service industries special treatment benefits, while important, are found to be less important than the other types of benefits received.[20] For example, although special treatment benefits can clearly be critical for customer loyalty in some industries (think of frequent flyer benefits in the airline industry), they seem to be less important to customers in other industries (such as legal services).

Benefits for Firms

The benefits to organizations of maintaining and developing a loyal customer base are numerous. In addition to the economic benefits that a firm receives from cultivating close relationships with its customers, a variety of customer behavior benefits and human resource management benefits are also often received.

Economic Benefits

Jacob Lund/Shutterstock

Satisfied, loyal customers are likely to provide a service provider with strong word-of-mouth endorsements, and they may increasingly do that as influencers on social media, as pictured here.

One of the most commonly cited economic benefits of customer retention is *increased purchases* over time; in many industries customers tend to spend more each year with a particular relationship partner.[21] As customers get to know a firm and are satisfied with the quality of its services relative to that of its competitors, they tend to give more of their business to the firm. Research also suggests that highly satisfied customers are *willing to pay more* for a provider's services.[22]

Another economic benefit for the firm is *lower costs.* Some estimates suggest that repeat purchases by established customers require as much as 90 percent less marketing expenditure.[23] Many start-up costs are associated with attracting new customers, including advertising and other promotion costs, the operating costs of setting up new accounts, and time costs of getting to know the customers. Sometimes these initial costs outweigh the revenue expected from the new customers in the short term, so it is to the firm's advantage to cultivate long-term relationships. In Chapter 17 we provide more specifics on the financial impact of customer retention.

Customer Behavior Benefits The contribution that loyal customers make to a service business can go well beyond their direct financial impact on the firm.[24] Maybe the most easily recognized customer behavior benefit that a firm receives from long-term customers is the free advertising provided through *word-of-mouth communication.* When a product is complex and difficult to evaluate and when risk is involved in the decision to buy it—as is the case with many services—consumers often look to others for advice on which providers to consider. Satisfied, loyal customers are likely to provide a firm with strong word-of-mouth endorsements, both via face-to-face communication and social media. This form of advertising can be more effective than any paid advertising that the firm might use, and it has the added benefit of reducing the costs of attracting new customers.

In addition to word-of-mouth communication, a second customer behavior benefit can be *social support* provided to other customers in the form of friendships or encouragement.[25] At a physical therapy clinic, for example, a patient who is recovering from knee surgery is likely to think more highly of the clinic when fellow patients provide encouragement and emotional support to the patient during the rehabilitation process. Loyal customers may also serve as *mentors* and, because of their experience with the provider, help other customers understand the explicitly or implicitly stated rules of conduct.[26] For example, online communities for people who suffer from chronic diseases (e.g., diabetes) are also platforms to provide and receive social support and mentorship, as illustrated by the online community of the American Diabetes Association (ADA). Inspired by the idea that sometimes "building connections with other people can be the best medicine," the ADA aims to help patients connect with others facing the

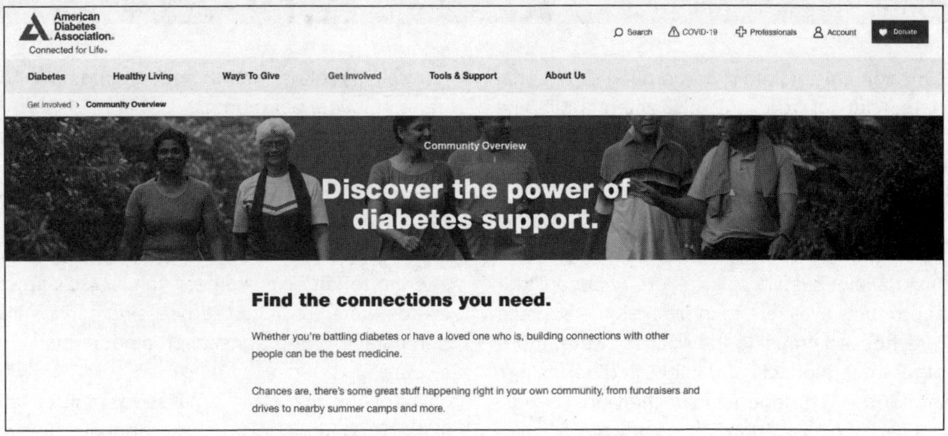

American Diabetes Association

same circumstances, build their confidence, and overcome feelings of isolation. As such, members of the ADA community help prevent diabetes and actively support each other.

Human Resource Management Benefits Loyal customers may also provide a firm with human resource management benefits. First, loyal customers may, because of their experience with and knowledge of the provider, be able to contribute to the coproduction of the service by *assisting in service delivery*; often the more experienced customers can make the service employees' job easier. For example, a regular patient of a medical service provider is likely to know how the system works; she would know to bring her medication with her on a visit, to plan on paying by debit card (having previously learned that the office cannot process personal checks), and to schedule an annual mammogram without waiting for her doctor to prompt her. A second benefit is that customers who are loyal and thus familiar with a firm's processes and procedures are likely to have more realistic expectations of what the firm can achieve for them.[27] A third benefit of customer retention is *employee retention.* It is easier for a firm to retain employees when it has a stable base of satisfied customers. People like to work for companies whose customers are happy and loyal. Their jobs are more satisfying, and they are able to spend more of their time fostering relationships than scrambling to serve new customers. In turn, customers are more satisfied and become even better customers—a positive upward spiral. Because employees stay with the firm longer, service quality improves and costs of turnover are reduced, adding further to profits.

RELATIONSHIP VALUE OF CUSTOMERS

Relationship value of a customer is a concept or calculation that looks at customers from the point of view of their lifetime revenue and/or profitability contributions to a company. This type of calculation is needed when companies start thinking of building long-term relationships with their customers. Just what is the potential financial value of those long-term relationships? Or, to put it another way, what are the financial implications of *losing* a customer? In the next paragraphs we consider some of the factors that influence a customer's relationship value and show some ways it can be estimated. In Chapter 17 we provide more detail on lifetime value financial calculations.

The lifetime or relationship value of a customer is influenced by the length of an average "lifetime," the average revenues generated per relevant time period over the lifetime, sales of additional products and services over time, referrals generated by the customer over time,[28] and costs associated with serving the customer. *Lifetime*

Exhibit 6.2 Calculating the Relationship Value of an Intuit Customer

Customers can sign up for Intuit Corporation's personal finance software, Mint, for free. Intuit also offers a bill-paying service, which is also free. However, the relationship value of a Mint customer to Intuit can be substantially more than zero. How can this be?

First, Mint has a "Ways to Save" feature that suggests new checking, savings, or brokerage accounts. When a customer signs up, Mint earns a referral fee. Also consider the additional products available to Intuit customers. Once a customer gets hooked on using the Mint software, there are several other Intuit products she might find appealing. For example, for \$60–\$120, depending on individual needs, Mint customers can purchase TurboTax, a software product that can automatically use previously created Mint data to help in preparation of federal and state income tax returns.

Intuit also offers QuickBooks—an accounting software product to help self-employed and small business owners keep track of their books—with prices ranging between \$25 and \$180 per month. Customers can also buy checks with matching envelopes and deposit slips for about \$200 (for a pack of 250). Additionally, small business customers may purchase Intuit payroll services starting at \$45 (plus \$4 per employee) per month and ranging up to \$125 (plus \$10 per employee) per month.

If a customer uses all these services, the revenue generated in just one year would be between \$1,042 and \$3,870, and that does not include the referral fees. (Intuit provides several other services, such as more advanced accounting software and a ProAdvisor program, which might be of interest to larger customers. Intuit also offers its business customers a credit card processing service and receives a percentage of the transaction amount plus a small fee per swipe.)

After the first year, a satisfied Intuit customer is quite likely to continue to purchase annual software updates to acquire the latest product features and tax information. Over the course of five years, the revenue generated from this single customer could be between \$5,210 and \$19,350.

Finally, these satisfied customers are likely to refer new customers to Intuit, thus further enhancing the value of the initial customer relationship. Even one new customer referral per year can increase the relationship value potential of the first customer to several thousand dollars in just a few years!

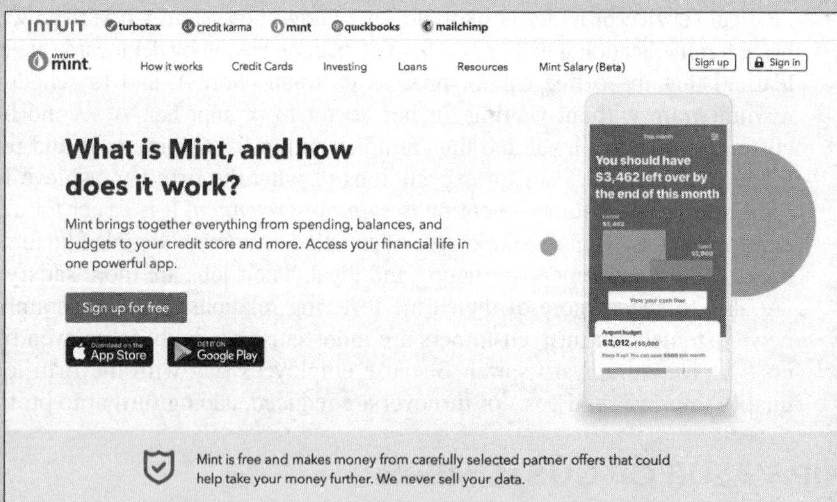

Intuit, Inc.

*Figures in this example are based on 2021 prices as listed on http://www.intuit.com.

value sometimes refers to lifetime revenue stream only; when costs are considered, the more appropriate term to use is *lifetime profitability*. Exhibit 6.2 provides an example of some factors that could be considered when calculating the potential relationship value of a Quicken (personal finance) software customer.

If companies knew how much it really costs to lose a customer, they would be able to accurately evaluate investments designed to retain customers. One way of documenting the dollar value of loyal customers is to estimate the increased value or profits that accrue for each additional customer who remains loyal to the company rather than

TABLE 6.1 Lifetime Value of an Average Business Customer at Telecheck International

Source: J. L. Heskett, W. E. Sasser, L. A. Schlesinger, *The Service Profit Chain: How Leading Companies Link Profit and Growth to Loyalty* (New York: The Free Press, 1997), p. 201.

	Year 0	Year 1	Year 2	Year 3	Year 4	Year 5
Revenue: [a]						
QuickResponse	—	$33,000	$39,600	$47,520	$57,024	$68,429
FastTrack	—	—	5,500	6,600	7,920	9,504
Costs:						
QuickResponse	$6,600	$24,090	$28,908	$34,690	$41,627	$49,953
FastTrack	—	—	4,152	4,983	5,980	7,175
Lifetime customer value:						
QuickResponse profit	($6,600)	$ 8,910	$10,692	$12,830	$15,397	$18,476
FastTrack profit	—	—	1,348	1,617	1,940	2,329
Reduced overhead allocation [b]	—	—	1,155	1,486	1,663	1,995
Profit from referrals [c]	—	—	1,100	1,650	3,300	6,600
Total profit	($6,600)	$ 8,910	$14,295	$17,583	$22,300	$29,400

Note: Product names and data have been disguised. As a result, profit on these products is overstated.
[a]Assuming revenue increases on both products of 20 percent per year.
[b]Declining at the rate of 15 percent per year in relation to revenue, to reflect lower costs of customer relationship associated with both customer and supplier learning curve effects.
[c]Estimated, based on assumptions concerning (1) the importance of referrals to new customers from old customers, (2) the frequency with which satisfied customers refer new customers, (3) the size of customers referred, and (4) the lifetime value calculations for new customers.

defecting to the competition. For example, one study showed that acquiring and retaining the "right" customers garnered a telecom firm an incremental profit of $345,800 with a return-on-investment close to 86 percent.[29]

With sophisticated accounting systems to document actual costs and revenue streams over time, a firm can be quite precise in documenting the dollar value and costs of retaining customers. These systems attempt to estimate the dollar value of *all* the benefits and costs associated with a loyal customer, not just the long-term revenue stream. The value of word-of-mouth advertising, employee retention, and declining account maintenance costs can also enter into the calculation.[30]

For example, Table 6.1 shows how First Data Corporation estimates the lifetime value of an average business customer at its TeleCheck International subsidiary. TeleCheck is a large check acceptance company that provides a range of financial services for business customers related to check guarantees, verifications, and collection services. By including estimates over a five-year lifetime of increased revenues from its core product (QuickResponse), declining per-unit service costs, increasing revenues from a new product (FastTrack), and profit from referrals, the company estimated that an annual increase in revenue of 20 percent on its base product would result in a 33 percent annual increase in operating profit over a five-year customer life.[31]

CUSTOMER PROFITABILITY SEGMENTS

Companies may want to provide all customers with excellent service, but they generally find that customers differ in their relationship value and that it may be neither practical nor profitable to meet (or to exceed) *all* customers' expectations.[32] FedEx Corporation, for example, once categorized its customers internally as "the good, the bad, and the ugly"—based on their profitability. Rather than treating all its customers the same, the company paid particular attention to enhancing their relationships with the good, moving the bad to the good, and discouraging the ugly.[33] Other companies also try to identify segments—or, more appropriately, tiers of customers—that differ in current and/or future profitability to a firm.[34] This approach goes beyond usage or volume segmentation because it tracks costs and revenues for segments of customers, thereby capturing their financial worth to companies. After identifying profitability tiers, the firm offers service levels in line with the identified segments. Building a high-loyalty customer base of the right customers increases profits.[35]

Profitability Tiers—The Customer Pyramid

Although some people may view the FedEx grouping of customers into "the good, the bad, and the ugly" as negative, descriptive labels of the tiers can be useful internally. Labels are especially valuable if they help the company keep track of which customers are profitable. Virtually all firms are aware at some level that their customers differ in profitability and that typically a minority of their customers account for the highest proportion of sales or profit.

One useful approach for thinking of how customers differ in terms of profitability is the four-tier system, shown in Figure 6.3, which includes the following:

1. The *platinum tier* describes the company's most profitable customers, typically those who are heavy users of the product, are not overly price sensitive, are willing to invest in and try new offerings, and are committed customers of the firm.
2. The *gold tier* differs from the platinum tier in that profitability levels are not as high, perhaps because these customers are not as loyal or they want price discounts that limit margins. They may be heavy users who minimize risk by working with multiple providers rather than just the focal company.
3. The *iron tier* contains essential customers who provide the volume needed to utilize the firm's capacity, but their spending levels, loyalty, and profitability are not substantial enough for special treatment.
4. The *lead tier* consists of customers who are costing the company money. They demand more attention than they are due given their spending and profitability and are sometimes problem customers—complaining about the firm to others and tying up the firm's resources.

Note that this classification is superficially reminiscent of, but very different from, traditional usage segmentation. Two differences are crucial. First, in the customer pyramid, profitability rather than usage defines all levels. Second, the lower levels

FIGURE 6.3
The Customer Pyramid

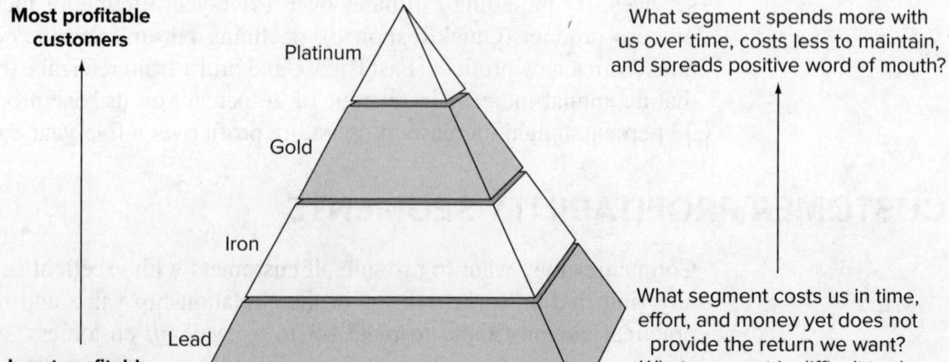

actually articulate classes of customers who require a different sort of attention. The firm must work either to change the customers' behavior—to make them more profitable through increases in revenue—or to change the firm's cost structure to make them more profitable through decreases in costs.

Once a system has been established for categorizing customers, the corresponding levels can be identified, motivated, served, and expected to deliver differential levels of profit. Companies improve their opportunities for profit when they increase shares of purchases by customers who either have the greatest need for the services or show the greatest loyalty to a single provider. By strengthening relationships with the loyal customers, increasing sales with existing customers, and increasing the profitability on each sale opportunity, companies thereby increase the potential of each customer.

The Customer's View of Profitability Tiers

Whereas profitability tiers make sense from the company's point of view, customers do not always understand or appreciate being categorized into a less desirable segment.[36] For example, at some companies (e.g., eTrade), the top clients have their own individual account representative, whom they can contact personally. The next tier of clients may be handled by representatives who each have a limited number (e.g., 100) of clients. Meanwhile, most clients are served by a website, an 800-number, or an automated voice response system. Customers are often aware of this unequal treatment, and may resent it. It makes perfect sense from a business perspective, but customers are often disappointed in the level of service they receive and give firms poor marks for quality as a result. Therefore, it is important that firms communicate with customers so they understand the level of service they can expect and what they would need to do or pay to receive faster or more personalized service. Notably, the fees financial service firms (such as eTrade) charge for the aforementioned individualized, one-on-one advice are considerably higher than the fees related to basic service levels (often provided via websites and robo-advisors).

The ability to segment customers narrowly based on profitability implications also raises questions of privacy for customers. To know who is profitable and who is not, companies must often collect large amounts of individualized behavioral and personal data on consumers. Many consumers today resent what they perceive as an intrusion into their lives in this way, especially when it results in differential treatment.

Making Business Decisions Using Profitability Tiers

Prudent business managers are well aware that past customer purchase behavior, although useful in making predictions, can be misleading.[37] What a customer spends today, or has spent in the past, may not necessarily be reflective of what he or she will do (or be worth) in the future. Banks serving college students know this well—a typical college student generally has minimal financial service needs (i.e., a checking account and a debit card) and tends to not have a high level of deposits. However, within a few years that student may embark on a professional career, start a family, and/or purchase a house, and thus require several financial services and become a potentially very profitable customer to the bank. Generally speaking, a firm would like to keep its consistent big spenders and lose the erratic small spenders. But all too often a firm also has two other groups they must consider: erratic big spenders and consistent small spenders. So, in some situations where consistent cash flow is a concern, it may be helpful to a firm to have a portfolio of customers that includes steady customers, even if they have a history of being less profitable.[38]

Some service providers have actually been quite successful in targeting customers who were previously considered to be unworthy of another firm's marketing efforts.[39]

Paychex, a payroll processing company, became very successful in serving small businesses that the major companies in this industry did not think were large enough to serve profitably. Similarly, Progressive Insurance became very successful in selling automobile insurance to undesirable customers—young drivers and those with poor driving records—that most of the competition did not feel had a sufficient relationship value. As these examples suggest, firms should think carefully and strategically when applying customer value calculations.

RELATIONSHIP DEVELOPMENT STRATEGIES

To this point in the chapter, we have focused on the rationale for relationship marketing, the benefits (to both firms and customers) of the development of strong exchange relationships, and an understanding of the relationship value of a customer. In this section, we examine a variety of factors that influence the development of strong customer relationships and customer loyalty, including the customer's overall evaluation of a firm's offering, switching barriers that customers face if leaving the relationship, as well as relationship bonds created with customers by the firm. These factors, illustrated in Figure 6.4, provide the rationale for specific strategies that firms often use to keep their current customers.

Overall Evaluation of the Core Service

Retention strategies will have little long-term success unless the firm has a solid base of service quality and customer satisfaction on which to build. All the retention strategies that we describe in this section are built on the assumption of competitive quality and value being offered. Clearly, a firm needs to begin the relationship development process by providing a good core service that, at a minimum, meets customer expectations and provides customers with perceived value;[40] it does no good to design relationship strategies for inferior services. Two earlier examples, Intuit and Swiggy, provide convincing support for the argument that excellence in the core service or product offered is essential to successful relationship marketing. Both of these companies have benefited tremendously from their loyal customer base; both offer excellent quality; both use relationship strategies to enhance their success.

FIGURE 6.4
Relationship Development Model

Sources: Adapted from D. D. Gremler and S. W. Brown, "Service Loyalty: Antecedents, Components, and Outcomes," in 1998 *AMA Winter Educators' Conference: Marketing Theory and Applications,* vol. 9, ed. D. Grewal and C. Pechmann (Chicago, IL: American Marketing Association), pp. 165–166.

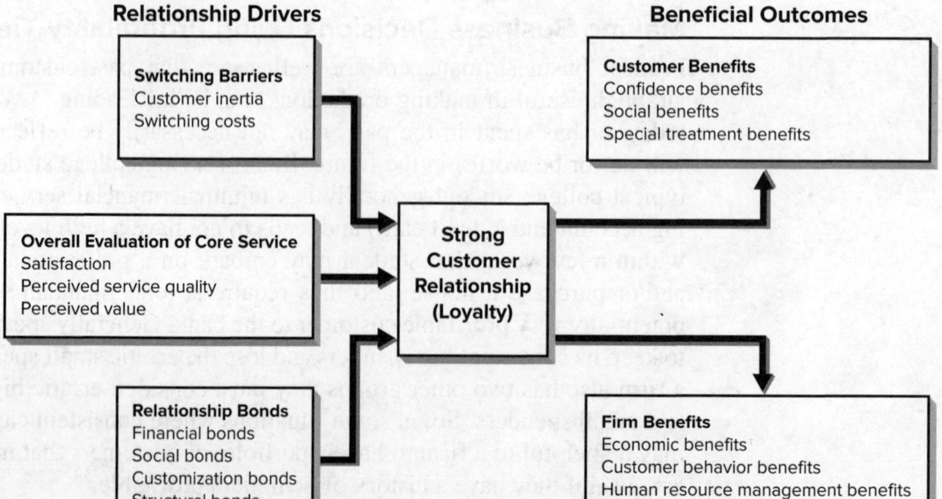

Switching Barriers as Drivers of Customer Loyalty

When considering a switch in service providers, a customer may face a number of barriers that make it difficult to leave one service provider and begin a relationship with another. Literature suggests that these *switching barriers* influence consumers' decisions to exit from relationships with firms and, therefore, help to facilitate customer retention; that is, switching barriers can be considered to be relationship drivers. Important switching barriers are customer inertia and switching costs.[41]

Customer Inertia

One reason that customers stay committed to existing relationships with firms is that a certain amount of effort may be required to change firms. Sometimes consumers simplistically state that "it's just not worth it" to switch providers. *Inertia* may even explain why some dissatisfied customers stay with a provider. In discussing why people remain in relationships (in general) that they no longer find satisfying, scholars suggest that people may stay because breaking the relationship would require them to restructure their life—to develop new habits of living, to refashion old friendships, and to find new ones.[42] All would require effort and a change in behavior—and people do not like to change their behavior.

To retain customers, firms might consider increasing the *perceived effort* required on the part of the customer to switch service providers.[43] If a customer believes that a great deal of effort is needed to change companies, the customer is more likely to stay put. For example, automobile repair facilities might keep a complete and detailed maintenance history of a customer's vehicle. These records remove the customer's burden of having to remember all the services performed on the vehicle and would force the customer to expend considerable effort in providing a complete maintenance history if the vehicle were taken to a new mechanic. Conversely, if a firm is looking to attract a competitor's customers, it might automate the process for switching providers as much as possible to overcome customer inertia.

Switching Costs

In many instances, customers develop loyalty to an organization in part because of costs involved in changing to and purchasing from a different firm. These costs, both real and perceived, monetary and nonmonetary, are termed *switching costs*. Switching costs include investments of time, money, or effort—such as setup costs, learning costs, and contractual costs—that make it challenging for the customer to move to another provider.[44] To illustrate, a patient may incur *setup costs* such as paying for a complete physical when changing doctors or for new X rays when switching dentists. *Learning costs* are those costs associated with learning the idiosyncrasies of how to use a product or service; in many situations, a customer who wishes to switch firms may need to accumulate new user skills or customer know-how. *Contractual costs* arise when the customer is required to pay a penalty to switch providers (e.g., prepayment charges for customer-initiated switching of mortgage companies or mobile telephone services), making it financially difficult, if not impossible, for the customer to initiate an early termination of the relationship.

To retain customers, firms might consider increasing their switching costs to make it difficult for customers to exit the relationship (or at least create the perception of difficulty). Indeed, many firms explicitly specify such costs in the contracts that they require their customers to sign (e.g., mobile telephone services, health clubs). To attract new customers, a service provider might consider implementing strategies designed to

T-Mobile USA, Inc.

T-Mobile advertises that it will cover financial switching costs for some of its new customers.

lower the switching costs of customers not currently using the provider. To reduce the setup costs involved when switching, providers could complete the paperwork required from the customer. Some banks, for example, attempt to decrease perceived switching costs in their marketing communications and others employ "switch kits" that automatically move a customer's online billing information from a competitor's bank; such kits remove the switching costs surrounding one of the biggest barriers preventing customers from changing banks—transferring online bill payments.[45] A related example is T-Mobile paying (financial) switching costs for some of their new customers, as illustrated in some of their advertisements (displayed above). In this specific promotional campaign, T-Mobile offers to reimburse new customers up to $650 (e.g., for early termination fees) customers have to pay when leaving their previous provider.

Relationship Bonds as Drivers of Customer Loyalty

Switching barriers tend to serve as constraints that keep customers in relationships with firms because they "have to."[46] However, firms can engage in activities that encourage customers to remain in the relationship because they "want to"—thus creating relationship bonds and customer loyalty. In this section we present a framework which suggests that relationship marketing can occur at four different levels and that each level results in ties that bind the customer a little closer to the firm—and thus increase the potential for sustained competitive advantage.[47] Figure 6.5 illustrates these four types of relationship bonds. Recall, however, that the most successful retention strategies are built on foundations of core service excellence.

Level 1—Financial Bonds

At level 1, the customer is tied to the firm primarily through financial incentives—lower prices for greater volume purchases or lower prices for customers who have been with the firm a long time. For example, think about the airline industry and related travel service industries like hotels and car rental companies. Frequent-flyer programs provide financial incentives and rewards for travelers who bring more of their business to a particular airline. Hotels and car rental companies do the same. One reason these financial incentive programs flourish is that they are not difficult to initiate and frequently result in at least short-term profit gains. Unfortunately, financial incentives do not generally provide long-term advantages to a firm because, unless combined with

FIGURE 6.5
Levels of Relationship Bonds

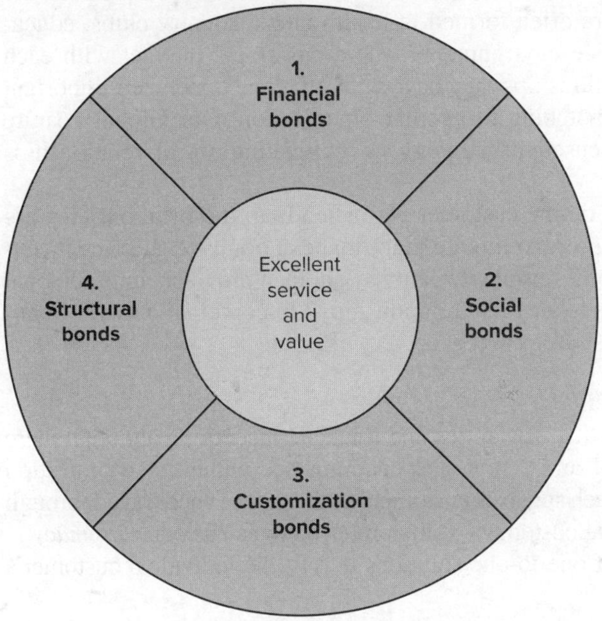

another relationship strategy, they do not differentiate the firm in the long run because they are generally not difficult for competitors to imitate.

Other types of retention strategies that depend primarily on financial rewards are focused on bundling and cross-selling of services. Frequent-flyer programs provide a common example. Many airlines link their reward programs with hotel chains, auto rental, and in some cases credit card usage. By linking airline mileage points earned to usage of other firms' services, customers can enjoy even greater financial benefits in exchange for their loyalty.

Although widely and increasingly used as retention tactics, loyalty programs based on financial rewards merit caution.[48] As mentioned earlier, these programs are often easily imitated. Thus, any increased usage or loyalty from customers may be short-lived. And, these strategies are not likely to be successful unless they are structured to truly lead to repeat or increased usage rather than serving as means to attract new customers and potentially causing endless switching among competitors.

Level 2—Social Bonds

Level 2 strategies bind customers to the firm through more than financial incentives. Although price is still assumed to be important, level 2 strategies seek to build long-term relationships through social and interpersonal bonds.[49] Customers are viewed as "clients," not nameless faces, and become individuals whose needs and wants the firm seeks to understand.

Social, interpersonal bonds are common among professional service providers (lawyers, accountants, teachers) and their clients as well as among personal care providers (hairdressers, counselors, healthcare providers, personal trainers) and their clients.[50] Interpersonal bonds are also common in business-to-business relationships in which customers develop relationships with salespeople and/or relationship managers working with their firms.[51] For example, recognizing the value of continuous relationships in building loyalty, Caterpillar Corporation credits its success to its extensive, stable distribution organization worldwide. Caterpillar is the world's largest manufacturer of mining, construction, and agricultural heavy equipment. Although its engineering and product quality are superior, the company attributes much of its success to its strong dealer network and product support services offered throughout the world. Knowledge of the local market and the close relationships with customers that Caterpillar's dealers provide is invaluable. Caterpillar's dealers tend to be prominent business leaders in their service territories who are deeply involved in community activities; the social bonds formed from these long-term relationships with customers are an important ingredient in the company's success.

wavebreakmedia/Shutterstock

Level 2 strategies create positive social bonds between the client and service provider employees (e.g., a personal trainer and a client).

Sometimes relationships are formed with the organization because of the social bonds that develop *among customers* rather than between customers and the provider of the service.[52] Such bonds are often formed in health clubs, country clubs, educational settings, and other service environments where customers interact with each other. Over time the social relationships they have with other customers are important factors that keep them from switching to another organization. Our Global Feature illustrates how Airbnb has focused its strategy on cultivating social relationships among its customers.

Social bonds alone may not tie the customer permanently to the firm, but they are much more difficult for competitors to imitate than financial bonds (e.g., price incentives).[53] In the absence of strong reasons to shift to another provider, interpersonal bonds can encourage customers to stay in a relationship.[54] In combination with financial incentives, social bonding strategies may be very effective.

Level 3—Customization Bonds

Level 3 strategies involve more than social ties and financial incentives, although there are common elements of level 1 and 2 strategies encompassed within a customization strategy. A customization approach suggests customer loyalty can be encouraged through intimate knowledge of individual customers—often referred to as *customer intimacy*—and through the development of one-to-one solutions that fit the individual customer's needs.

To illustrate customization bonds, consider Pandora—an Internet-based music discovery service that helps its more than 60 million active users find and enjoy music that they like. Based on a huge database that has categorized about a million songs of tens of thousands of different artists based on unique attributes, it customizes its service offering to play music for customers that has the same characteristics of songs or artists they like. A customer can create up to 100 unique "stations" by identifying favorite songs or artists, and then Pandora's expert system analyzes what they like and provides suggestions based on this analysis. To do this Pandora analyzes each song using about 450 distinct musical characteristics, or "genes," by a trained music analyst. Taken together these genes capture the unique and musical identity of a song—everything from melody, harmony, and rhythm to instrumentation, orchestration, arrangement, lyrics, singing, and vocal harmony. Pandora then uses this information to customize music to each customer's unique tastes and interests. The earlier Technology Spotlight illustrates how Hilton Hotels uses technology to customize services to a large number of individual customers.

Cardinal Health

Cardinal Health's ValueLink creates structural bonds with its hospital customers.

Level 4—Structural Bonds

Level 4 strategies are the most difficult to imitate; they can involve structural as well as financial, social, and customization bonds between the customer and the firm. Structural bonds are created by providing services to the client that are designed right into the service delivery system. Often, structural bonds are created by providing customized services to the client that are technology based and make the customer more productive.

An example of structural bonds can be seen in a business-to-business healthcare context with Cardinal Health. By working closely with its hospital customers, Cardinal Health has established ways to improve hospital supply ordering, delivery, and billing that have greatly enhanced its value as a supplier. Many of Cardinal Health's hospital customers use their ValueLink® service, a "just-in-time" distribution program that eliminates their need to maintain and manage large amounts of inventory. Using sophisticated technology and tracking systems to monitor inventory, ValueLink allows Cardinal Health to deliver ready-to-use quantities of supplies as needed—often several times a day—directly to the floors and departments where they are being used. By linking the hospital through its ValueLink service into a database ordering system and by providing enhanced value in the actual delivery, Cardinal Health has structurally tied itself to its more than 200 acute care hospitals in the United States. In addition to the enhanced service that ValueLink provides, Cardinal Health estimates that the system reduces the average customer's inventory costs by 30 to 60 percent per year and labor costs by 25 to 30 percent per year.[55]

RELATIONSHIP CHALLENGES

Given the many benefits of long-term customer relationships, it would seem that a company would not want to refuse to serve or terminate a relationship with any customer. Yet situations arise in which either the firm, the customer, or both want to end (or have to end) their relationship. This final section of the chapter discusses situations in which the *firm* might actually consider ending the relationship and how that might occur; in the next chapter (on Service Recovery) we discuss situations in which the *customer* might decide to terminate the relationship and switch providers.

The Customer Is *Not* Always Right

The assumption that *all* customers are good customers is compatible with the belief that "the customer is always right," an almost sacrosanct tenet of business. Yet any service worker can tell you that this statement is *not* always true, and in some cases it may be preferable for the firm to not continue its relationship with a customer. The following discussion presents a view of customer relationships suggesting that all relationships may not be beneficial and that every customer is not right all the time.

The Wrong Segment

A company cannot target its services to all customers; some segments are more appropriate than others. It would not be beneficial to either the company or the customer for a company to establish a relationship with a customer whose needs the company cannot meet. For example, a school offering a lock-step, daytime MBA program would not encourage full-time working people to apply for its program, nor would a law firm specializing in government issues want to establish a relationship with individuals seeking advice on trusts and estates. In both cases, the organization most likely would struggle to deliver services that meet the expectations of these people. Despite this reality, firms might give in to the temptation to make a sale by agreeing to serve a customer who would be better served by someone else.

Similarly, it would not be wise to forge relationships simultaneously with incompatible market segments. In many service businesses (such as restaurants, hotels, tour package operators, entertainment, and education), customers experience the service together and can influence each other's perceptions about value received. Thus, to maximize service to core segments, an organization may choose to turn away marginally profitable segments that would be incompatible. For example, a conference hotel may find that mixing executives in town for a serious educational program with

Global Feature Developing Loyal Customers at Airbnb

Martin Bureau/AFP/Getty Images

Airbnb relies on the Internet to connect guests with hosts.

Airbnb quickly emerged as a major player in the global hospitality arena. It began in 2007 when roommates Brian Chesky and Joe Gebbia could not afford the rent for their loft in San Francisco. They made their living room into a bed and breakfast, accommodating three guests on air mattresses and providing them breakfast; thus the company was originally called "Airbed & Breakfast." They eventually shortened the name to "Airbnb" and now serve two types of customers, hosts and guests, by being an intermediary that provides an online database of personal properties to rent. Airbnb *hosts* are customers who list properties—which can be single rooms, a suite of rooms, apartments, houseboats, or entire houses—on the Airbnb website with the intent of renting them. The listing is free and hosts decide how much to charge per night, per week, or per month. Travelers (or *guests*) are customers who search the Airbnb database of available properties to rent by entering details about when and where they would like to travel, considering such issues as location, room type (e.g., private room or shared room), price, size, amenities, and host language.

From Airbnb's humble beginnings the company has developed an incredible global presence. Consider the following facts: as of 2021, Airbnb had more than 150 million users, 4 million hosts, more than 7 million listings, and was active in more than 100,000 cities in over 220 countries. Airbnb's revenue for 2020 was $3.4 billion (which was actually a 30 percent loss year-on-year due to the Coronavirus pandemic) and as of December 2020 it was valued at more than $100 billion; this valuation is more than the InterContinental Hotels Group or Hyatt Hotels, making Airbnb the world's largest hospitality brand.

CREATING RELATIONSHIPS WITH CUSTOMERS

A key part of Airbnb's global success has been its ability to develop strong relationships with its customers. To cultivate relationships with hosts and guests from so many different countries, Airbnb ensures that all parties have a sense of trust for how things operate. Hosts must agree to ensure their home is clean and that they are there on time to welcome guests and hand over the keys. In turn, guests must agree to keep the house secure and tidy, and Airbnb agrees to facilitate the whole process and act as an intermediary or source of compensation if anything goes wrong. Before being able to make (or accept) a reservation through Airbnb, each customer (whether a host, a guest, or both) must create a thorough (online) profile to cultivate a sense of accountability. Airbnb encourages customers to upload profile photos that clearly show their faces, and to write detailed descriptions that reveal themselves on a personal level. Additionally, customers can create their own Airbnb symbols, and upload a 30-second profile video to further illustrate who they are to the Airbnb community.

To further develop relationships with its customers, Airbnb includes what it calls "Verified ID" as a safety measure as part of its platform, mandating that customers verify their identity through government documents (such as a passport or driver's license), social accounts (such as Facebook or LinkedIn), and contact information before they can host or stay with another guest. Airbnb also assigns each reservation a "trust score," based on the reservation's details, payment, reviews, and the communication between guest and host. Airbnb uses such capabilities in developing customers' trust and confidence in its service.

FACILITATING SOCIAL BONDS AMONG CUSTOMERS

Airbnb attributes part of its success to understanding well that people want to deal with humans. Customers can access Airbnb's services from their laptop, tablet, or mobile phone, and many feel they are instantly connected with people they can trust. To develop strong social relationships among its customers (i.e., between hosts and guests), Airbnb cultivates interpersonal connections through Airbnb groups, promotes communication between hosts and guests, provides post-reservation reviews, and hosts in-person events. This, along with the other safety precautions mentioned earlier, encourages users to not only trust each other, but to trust in Airbnb's brand as a whole.

CULTIVATING LOYALTY

Airbnb does not offer a traditional rewards program for hosts or guests that hotel chains often do. Instead it focuses on building loyalty with hosts by:

- **Identifying "Superhosts."** Just like PowerSellers on eBay or Google's Trusted Stores, hosts who continually provide a great experience for guests are rewarded with stellar reviews and subsequently become part of the Airbnb Superhost program.

- **Providing Perks.** Those who reach Superhost status receive several perks, including a badge they can put on their listings, priority support, and travel coupons. Their places are also profiled in visible spots such as "Airbnb Picks," appear high in property listings, and are featured in the company's quarterly magazine, *Pineapple.*
- **Creating Local Groups.** Airbnb has created a platform for hosts to form local groups that get together and learn from each other. One event entitled "Airbnb Open" brought 1,500 hosts together face-to-face so that Airbnb could share future plans and product news with them.

When it comes to cultivating loyalty with guests, Airbnb periodically sends out inspirational e-mails and it allows customers to create wish lists of where they would like to go on future trips. It has seen such efforts change people's behavior and actually get them to travel more.

FOCUSING ON THE CORE SERVICE OFFERING

Airbnb believes responsiveness is important to their customers and therefore provides 24/7 coverage in more than 40 languages around the world, making it highly accessible when customers need assistance. It encourages hosts to respond quickly and has a system through which guests can rate hosts on their responsiveness. To help create a great experience for customers, Airbnb has a team that monitors social media to ensure customer service issues are dealt with quickly.

To facilitate good rental experiences, Airbnb encourages each customer (both hosts and guests) to write a review for the other immediately after each stay. This review system creates a sort of quality control to hold both hosts and guests accountable. Reviews not only provide insights into hosts and guests, they also provide "insider tips" about where to visit, have dinner, or experience things that only "locals" would know about. Airbnb feels that hosts can help guests, particularly international ones, get a view into their lives and how they live—creating a more memorable experience.

In the "sharing" economy people are increasingly trusting direct connections with other people (who are often strangers to each other); however, they tend to rely on the intermediary (i.e., Airbnb) when peer trust fails. For that reason, and to provide additional confidence in their services, Airbnb has a $1 million guarantee to protect their hosts. That is, Airbnb guarantees that every booking on its platform is covered by its "Host Guarantee," which states that Airbnb will reimburse hosts for damage to their property up to $1 million—at no cost to them. Nothing is more important to Airbnb than engendering the trust of its customers. Indeed, convincing hosts to entrust complete strangers with their most valuable possessions (their homes and belongings) is the greatest obstacle in the Airbnb business model.

CONTINUOUS IMPROVEMENT AND INNOVATION

Despite its success, Airbnb does not rest on its laurels. Rather, the company always strives to further improve its service, driven by understanding its users' expectations and transforming these into service refinements and innovations. Consider this: In 2020, Airbnb created its "Innovation Council" to better engage with its hosts and partners (e.g., hotel/vacation rental software providers). The objective was to get direct feedback from council members on support they needed, as well as key initiatives and features Airbnb might consider. This drive to innovate remains one key characteristic of Airbnb. In 2021, in response to the shifts in how people traveled after the pandemic, Airbnb released more than 100 innovations and upgrades to improve every aspect of the Airbnb service experience. For example, with regard to its guests, Airbnb placed increased flexibility at the center of its improved browsing and booking experience with three new ways to search on Airbnb (more flexible dates, more flexible matching, and more flexible destinations). In parallel, with regard to its hosts, the company made it even easier to become a host with a simplified onboarding process (reducing the previous process that included dozens of steps to just 10 steps). Finally, Airbnb also improved its community support by doubling the number of support agents and by completely redesigning its Help Center that is now easier to navigate and offers a more personalized support for its hosts and guests.

A SERVICE BASED ON TRUST

Airbnb sees itself as more than just a service; it believes it has created a global community built on trust—and that each transaction is an experience, not merely a purchase. Airbnb has been able to compete in the hospitality industry and develop a loyal customer base internationally because it acts as the safety net that people can trust, which then gives them the confidence to host strangers or sleep in others' homes.

Sources: E. Eyal and A. Fleischer, "The Evolution of Trust in Airbnb: A Case of Home Rental," *Annals of Tourism Research* 75 (March 2019), pp. 279–287; N. Hussain and J. Franklin, "Airbnb Valued at $101.6 bln in Biggest U.S. IPO of 2020," https://www.nasdaq.com/articles/airbnb-valued-at-%24101.6-bln-in-biggest-u.s.-ipo-of-2020-2020-12-10, accessed October 14, 2021; "Airbnb 2021 Release: 100+ Innovations and Upgrades Across Our Entire Service," https://news.airbnb.com/2021-release/, accessed October 14, 2021; K. Jeng, "Trust in the Sharing Economy: 3 Lessons to Learn From Airbnb," https://brandfolder.com/blog/shared-story-3/building-trust/; B. Lyons, "Customer Loyalty: Lessons from Airbnb," http://www.tlsasalestraining.com/content/customer-loyalty-lessons-airbnb.

students in town for a regional track meet is not wise. If the executives are deemed to be key long-term customers, the hotel may choose to pass up the sports group in the interest of retaining the executives.

Not Profitable in the Long Term

In the absence of ethical or legal mandates, organizations will prefer *not* to have long-term relationships with unprofitable customers. Some segments of customers will not be profitable for the company even if their needs can be met by the services offered. Some examples of this situation are when there are not enough customers in the segment to make it profitable to serve, when the segment cannot afford to pay the cost of the service, and when the projected revenue flows from the segment would not cover the costs incurred to originate and maintain their business.

At the individual customer level, it may not be profitable for a firm to engage in a relationship with a customer who has bad credit or who is a high risk for some other reason. Retailers, banks, mortgage companies, and credit card companies routinely refuse to do business with individuals whose credit histories are unreliable. Although the short-term sale may be beneficial, the long-term risk of nonpayment makes the relationship unwise from the company's point of view. Similarly, some car rental companies check into the driving records of customers and reject bad-risk drivers.[56] This practice, while controversial, is logical from the car rental companies' point of view because they can cut back on insurance costs and accident claims (thus reducing rental costs for good drivers) by not doing business with accident-prone drivers.

Beyond the monetary costs associated with serving the wrong customers, there can be substantial time investments in some customers. Everyone has had the experience of waiting in a bank, a retail store, or even an educational setting while a particularly demanding customer seems to use more than his share of the service provider's time. The dollar value of the time spent with a specific customer is typically not computed or calculated into the price of the service; however, if such costs were actually computed, it might reveal that some of these customers are unprofitable for the organization.

In a business-to-business relationship, the variability in time commitment to customers is even more apparent. Some customers may use considerable resources of a service provider through inordinate numbers of phone calls, excessive requests for information, and other time-consuming activities. In the legal profession, clients are billed for every hour of the firm's time that they use because time is essentially the only resource the firm has. Yet in other service businesses, all clients essentially pay the same regardless of the time demands they place on the organization.

Ocean/CORBIS/Getty Images

Some customers may be difficult, if not impossible, to serve.

Difficult Customers

Managers have repeated the phrase "the customer is always right" so often that you would expect it to be accepted by every employee in every service organization. So why isn't it? Perhaps because it simply is not true. The customer is not always right. No matter how frequently it is said, repeating that mantra does not make it become reality, and service employees know it.

In many situations, firms have service encounters that fail because of *dysfunctional customers.* Dysfunctional customer behavior consists of the actions by customers who intentionally, or perhaps unintentionally, act in a manner that in some way disrupts otherwise functional service encounters.[57] Such customers have been described as "customers from hell," "problem customers," or "jay customers." One of us was awakened during a hotel stay at 4:00 a.m. by drunk customers who were arguing with each other in a room above; management eventually called the police and asked them to escort the customers off the property. An Enterprise Rent-A-Car customer demanded that she not be charged for any of the two weeks that she had a car because, near the end of the rental period, she found a small stain in the back seat.[58] Such behavior is considered dysfunctional from the perspective of the service provider and perhaps fellow customers.

Dysfunctional customer behavior can affect employees, other customers, and the organization. Research suggests that exposure to dysfunctional customer behavior can have psychological, emotional, behavioral, and physical effects on employees.[59] For example, customer-contact employees who are exposed to rude, threatening, obstructive, aggressive, or disruptive behavior by customers often have their mood, motivation, or morale negatively affected. Such customers are difficult to work with and often create stress for employees.[60] (See photo above for one example.) Dysfunctional customers can also have an impact on other customers: such behavior can spoil the service experience for other customers, and the dysfunctional customer behavior may become contagious for other customers witnessing it. Finally, dysfunctional customer behavior can create both direct costs and indirect costs for the organization. Direct costs of such behavior can include the expense of restoring damaged property, increased insurance premiums, property loss by theft, costs incurred in compensating customers affected by the dysfunctional behavior of others, and costs incurred through illegitimate claims by dysfunctional customers. Additionally, indirect costs might include increased workloads for staff required to deal with dysfunctional behavior as well as increased costs for attracting and retaining appropriate personnel and, perhaps, for absenteeism payments.

Ending Business Relationships

As suggested in the previous section, firms may identify some customers who are not in their targeted segment, who are not profitable in the long run, or who are difficult to work with or dysfunctional. A company may *not* want to continue in a relationship with every customer. For the effective management of service relationships, managers should not only know how to establish a relationship but also how to end one. However, gracefully exiting a relationship may not be easy. Customers may end up feeling disappointed, confused, or hurt if a firm attempts to terminate the relationship. Our Strategy Insight illustrates how three firms chose to end relationships with their customers.

Relationship Endings

Relationships end in different ways—depending on the type of relationship in place.[61] In some situations, a relationship is established for a certain purpose and/or time period and then dissolves when it has served its purpose or the time frame has elapsed. For example, a house painting service may be engaged with the customer for four days while painting the house exterior, but both parties understand that the end of the relationship is predetermined—the end occurs when the house has been painted and the customer has paid for the service. Sometimes a relationship has a natural ending.[62] Piano lessons for children, for example, often cease as the child gets older and develops interests in other musical areas (such as singing or playing the saxophone); in such situations, the need for the relationship has diminished or become obsolete. In other situations, an event may occur that forces the relationship to end; a provider who relocates to the other side of town may force some customers to select a different company.

Strategy Insight "The Customer Is Always Right": Rethinking an Old Tenet

The old tenet "the customer is always right" has operated as the basic rule in business for so long that for many firms it has become entrenched as an "absolute truth." The practical reality, however, is that sometimes the customer is wrong. When taken to the extreme, the issue for the firm becomes what to do about it. Service managers understand that there are situations when employees should be fired. In some situations, this strategy may need to be applied to customers, too.

SPRINT/NEXTEL FIRES 1,000 CUSTOMERS

On June 29, 2007, Sprint/Nextel sent a letter to about 1,000 of its 53 million customers telling them, in effect, they had been fired from the company. In doing so Sprint was attempting to rid itself of customers who frequented its customer service lines by informing them that it was canceling their service at the end of the next month. In these letters the company stated: "While we have worked to resolve your issues and questions to the best of our ability, the number of inquiries you have made to us during this time has led us to determine that we are unable to meet your current wireless needs."

The customers were told their service agreements were being terminated, they would not owe anything on their final bill, and the company would waive its standard early termination fees. They also were told to switch to another wireless provider by July 30 if they wanted to keep their phone number.

These 1,000 customers had been calling Sprint's customer service an average of 25 times a month, which is 40 times more frequently than a typical customer. Sprint determined these customers were not generating enough revenue to make up for the high cost of serving them. The company conducted an internal review, lasting more than six months, to determine what types of problems these customers had and what information they were seeking when they contacted the customer service department. The review found that these customers often were calling about the same problems over and over after Sprint officials felt they had resolved the issue. Additionally, some callers were repeatedly asking for information about other customers' accounts, which customer service representatives are not allowed to divulge. Sprint indicated that the amount of time being spent to resolve the same issues again and again was affecting their ability to serve other customers.

ximagination/123RF

A disgruntled Sprint/Nextel customer.

The Results

Initially Sprint's move made headlines in the business press, stimulated negative word of mouth from some portion of these 1,000 customers, and may have cost them some new customers in the short run. But it also improved the customer experience for other customers calling customer service. Indeed, customer service improved to the point that just three years later Sprint was named one of the top 40 Customer Service Champions by J. D. Power and Associates.

E-COMMERCE COMPANIES TIGHTEN RETURNS POLICIES TO COMBAT MISUSE BY A FEW CUSTOMERS

The boom in online shopping has also unleashed an unprecedented flood of product returns that has become a logistical and financial nightmare for retailers. Handling these returns costs a lot of money, time and effort in reverse logistics. The process is messy, shipping items back is expensive, and most returned products cannot be sold again for full price. This hits company profits hard. E-commerce firms including Amazon, Flipkart, and Meesho are increasingly tightening their returns policies to combat customer misuse that costs them 15–30% per return. Amazon has implemented a warning system that flags and potentially bans customer accounts with suspicious return patterns, while Flipkart has shortened return

Or an ending may occur because the customer is not fulfilling his obligations. For example, a bank may choose to end the relationship with a customer who regularly has insufficient funds in her checking account. Whatever the reason for ending the relationship, firms should clearly communicate their reasons for wanting (or needing) to terminate it, so that customers understand what is occurring and why.[63]

windows from 30 days to as few as 7 days for many products. Meesho now requires strict verification processes, including video documentation for certain high-value returns, and limits the number of returns allowed per customer within set timeframes.

These changes target specific behaviors that harm company profitability, including "wardrobing" (where customers buy clothing items, wear them once for an event, and then return them), return fraud (returning different or deliberately damaged items), and serial returners (the small percentage of shoppers responsible for a disproportionate number of returns). For example, a customer who repeatedly purchases multiple sizes of the same garment with the intention of keeping just one might now face account warnings on Amazon, while someone attempting to return a non-defective smartphone on Flipkart may encounter restocking fees or shipping charges that did not exist previously.

EVENTS PLANNER TELLS MAJOR CLIENT: "NEVER AGAIN"

Capitol Services Inc. (CSI)—an event planning company in Washington, DC—spent considerable time and money attempting to secure a major automobile company's potentially very lucrative business. In the midst of the first-ever event for the client at a museum in Washington, DC, the person overseeing the event (who was not an employee of the company but working for a third party) became very demanding, degrading, and disrespectful to the CSI staff. Nearly everything the firm did was, in her opinion, not good enough. The entire team, who was in the midst of delivering an event exactly as promised, was being micromanaged. CSI employees felt they were being abused, and for no good reason. David Hainline, company president, approached the client representative and said that CSI would finish the event but would never conduct business again with her—knowing full well this decision might result in the loss of a client with a very high potential relationship value.

The Results

The event was delivered as promised, but the belligerent staff member was not happy. After the event was completed, she demanded that CSI reduce the amount owed for their services—so CSI reduced the amount by $60,000. Months later Hainline had a meeting with the automobile company and began the meeting with an explanation of the situation that had occurred at the Smithsonian. The company understood, and agreed to use CSI to organize future events for them in Washington, DC. And CSI employees felt valued and supported by the management team.

ENDING A CUSTOMER RELATIONSHIP MAY BE THE RIGHT STRATEGIC DECISION

Service providers are not obligated to serve any and all customers, no matter how much revenue they might generate. Although service marketing strategies intended to develop relationships with customers receive much attention—and rightly so—from managers, occasionally selecting a strategy that results in ending a relationship with a customer may be the most prudent approach to take.

Sources: H. Feng, N. A. Morgan, and L. L. Rego, "The Impact of Unprofitable Customer Management Strategies on Shareholder Value," *Journal of the Academy of Marketing Science* 48 (March 2020), pp. 246–269; S. Srivastava, "Sprint Drops Clients over Excessive Inquiries," *The Wall Street Journal,* July 7, 2007, p. A3; L. L. Berry and K. Seiders, "Serving Unfair Customers," *Business Horizons* 51 (January/February 2008), pp. 29–37; D. Hainline, President, Capitol Services Inc., Washington, DC, personal interview, August 15, 2007.

Reference: https://www.sciencedirect.com/science/article/pii/S0969698922002387

https://www.indiaretailing.com/2025/04/30/retailers-stricter-return-policies-e-commerce-margins/

https://timesofindia.indiatimes.com/business/india-business/flipkart-tightens-returns-policy-on-rising-frauds/articleshow/73236225.cms

https://www.reverselogix.com/industry-updates/how-return-fraud-affects-businesses-and-ways-to-prevent-it/

https://www.indianretailer.com/article/technology/digital-trends/fighting-smart-against-policy-abuse-in-online-retail.a7683

Should Firms Fire Their Customers?

A logical conclusion to be drawn from the discussion of the challenges firms face in customer relationships is that perhaps firms should seek to get rid of those customers who are not right for the company. Many companies make these types of decisions based on the belief that troublesome customers are usually less profitable and less loyal and that it may be counterproductive to retain their business.[64] Another

Indian Service Strategy Insight Tata Neu: The Promise of a Super APP

Tata Neu represents a bold strategic vision to unify the conglomerate's diverse digital offerings. Launched in April 2022 with an estimated $2 billion investment, the super app aimed to integrate the Tata group's trusted consumer brands like Titan, Tanishq, Tata Salt, Tata Tea, Westside, Croma, BigBasket, Tata CLiQ, Air India, and Tata 1mg under a single platform. This ambitious initiative would eliminate the overhead of maintaining separate backend systems for each brand while creating cross-selling opportunities across the Tata ecosystem. The appilcation's integrated loyalty program, NeuCoins, was designed as a universal currency (1 NeuCoin = ₹1) to foster customer retention, while the exclusive NeuPass membership promised additional rewards. More recently, the company has doubled down on its commitment with a fresh $1 billion investment and the launch of Neu Flash, an ultra-fast delivery service competing in the growing quick commerce sector.

Despite these aspirations, Tata Neu has faced significant technical and operational challenges. The initial implementation using Adobe Experience Manager revealed limitations in creating a truly flexible, multi-brand experience, as rigid content structures could not accommodate the diverse needs of fashion, electronics, travel, and healthcare verticals. Integration complexities across 20+ different tech stacks led to a fragmented user experience, exemplified by the separate checkout processes for different product categories. These technical issues, combined with market positioning struggles, contributed to disappointing financial performance, with the app missing its first-year revenue targets by 50%. Tata Digital reported widening losses of ₹5,553.11 crore in FY23, signaling the substantial costs of this digital transformation.

For the customer, Tata Neu promised convenience through an all-in-one shopping experience but frequently delivered frustration instead. The app's disjointed interface required users to navigate multiple checkouts for different categories, undermining the very convenience it promised to deliver. Meanwhile, the NeuCoins loyalty program faced skepticism as it failed to provide compelling advantages over existing reward systems at individual Tata brands. Customers who had accumulated points in the Taj Hotels' rewards program or BigBasket's loyalty scheme found little clarity on how these would convert to the new system, creating hesitation rather than excitement about the unified platform.

Customers also struggled to find a compelling reason to switch from established specialized apps. With Google Pay and PhonePe dominating payments, Amazon and Flipkart leading e-commerce, and Zomato and Swiggy controlling food delivery, Tata Neu entered a saturated market without a clear differentiator. The app failed to identify and build a core cohort of users around a distinctive primary service, unlike successful super apps like China's WeChat (messaging) or Indonesia's Gojek (ride-hailing). For value-conscious Indian consumers with low brand loyalty, Tata Neu's offerings simply did not provide sufficient incentives to change established digital habits.

The challenge of creating a successful super app in India is further complicated by the country's unique market characteristics. Unlike the relatively homogeneous markets of China or South Korea, India's diverse population speaks 22 official languages with cultural preferences that "change every 100 km." This diversity demands hyper-personalized and localized experiences that are difficult to deliver at scale. Additionally, Indian consumers have already developed relationships with specialized apps that have spent substantial resources to acquire market share, creating high barriers to switching regardless of the Tata Group's prestigious brand heritage.

Looking forward, Tata Neu's success will depend on finding a balance between company ambitions and customer needs. From the company side, technical improvements to create truly seamless experiences and strategic focus on high-potential verticals like quick commerce could help establish market relevance. From the customer perspective, Tata Neu needs to deliver genuinely superior value propositions – whether through deeper discounts, exclusive products, or innovative services – that overcome inertia and competition. The recent launch of Neu Flash and forays into fintech suggest Tata remains committed to the super app vision despite early setbacks. As India's digital market continues to evolve with greater smartphone penetration and rising disposable incomes, Tata's deep pockets may yet allow it sufficient runway to refine its approach and capture the elusive super app opportunity.

Reference: https://www.financialexpress.com/life/technology-super-app-neu-fails-to-fix-an-old-problem-3684291/

https://www.tata.com/business/tata-digital/tata-neu

https://www.storyboard18.com/brand-marketing/tata-group-enters-ultra-fast-delivery-market-with-neu-flash-46241.htm

https://www.sanity.io/customers/tata

https://medium.com/@chaiwithsai/the-bust-of-super-apps-in-india-mistakes-and-lessons-1a0994f9bd26 reason for "firing" a customer is the negative effect that these customers can have on employee quality of life and morale.

Companies today are making it easier to justify firing customers. Service providers such as Uber, Lyft, and Airbnb, for example, allow drivers and hosts to review and rate customers. If a customer receives low scores or has several complaints from enough people, that customer may not be chosen to receive services or, even more, no longer allowed to use the company's website to schedule services. Similarly, the online restaurant reservation company OpenTable offers a feature to member restaurants where they can make (internal) notes about guests—such as if they frequently send their food back. The website also keeps track of how many reservations a customer misses; those who miss four or more reservations within a year are banned from the site.[65]

Although it may sound like a good idea, firing customers is not that simple and needs to be done in a way that avoids negative publicity or negative word of mouth. Sometimes raising prices or charging for services that previously had been given away for free can move unprofitable customers out of the company. Helping a client find a new provider who can better meet its needs is another way to gracefully exit a nonproductive relationship. If the customer has become too demanding, the relationship may be salvaged by negotiating expectations or finding more efficient ways to serve the client. If not, both parties may need to find an agreeable way to end the relationship.

Summary

In this chapter we focused on the rationale for, benefits of, and strategies for developing long-term relationships with customers. It should be obvious by now that organizations that focus only on acquiring new customers may well fail to understand their current customers; thus, while a company may be bringing customers in through the front door, equal or greater numbers may be exiting. Estimates of lifetime relationship value accentuate the importance of retaining current customers.

The particular strategy that an organization uses to retain its current customers can and should be customized to fit the industry, the culture, and the customer needs of the organization. However, in general, customer relationships are driven by a variety of factors that influence the development of strong customer relationships, including (1) the customer's overall evaluation of the quality of a firm's core service offering, (2) the switching barriers that the customer faces in leaving a relationship, and (3) the relationship bonds the firm has developed with that customer. By developing strong relationships with customers and by focusing on factors that influence customer relationships, the organization will accurately understand customer expectations over time and consequently will narrow Gap 1.

The chapter concluded with a discussion of the challenges that firms face in developing relationships with customers. Although long-term customer relationships are critical and can be very profitable, firms should not attempt to build relationships with just any customer. In other words, "the customer is not always right." Indeed, in some situations it may be best for a firm to discontinue relationships with some customers—for the sake of the customer, the firm, or both.

Discussion Questions

1. Discuss how relationship marketing or retention marketing is different from the traditional emphasis in marketing.
2. Describe how a firm's relationships with customers may evolve over time. For each level of relationship discussed in the chapter, identify a firm with which you have that level of relationship, and discuss how its marketing efforts differ from those of other firms.

3. Think about a service organization that retains you as a loyal customer. Why are you loyal to this provider? What are the benefits to you of staying loyal and not switching to another provider? What would it take for you to switch?
4. With regard to the same service organization, what are the benefits to the organization of keeping you as a customer? Calculate your "lifetime value" to the organization.
5. Describe the logic behind "customer profitability segmentation" from the company's point of view. Also discuss what customers may think of the practice.
6. Describe the various switching barriers discussed in the text. What switching barriers might you face in switching banks? Cellphone service providers? Universities?
7. Describe the four levels of relationship bonds, and give examples of each type. Again, think of a service organization to which you are loyal. Can you describe the reason(s) you are loyal in terms of the different levels? In other words, what ties you to the organization?
8. Have you ever worked as a frontline service employee? Can you remember having to deal with difficult or "problem" customers? Discuss how you handled such situations. As a manager of frontline employees, how would you help your employees deal with difficult customers?

Exercises

1. Interview the manager of a local service organization. Discuss with the manager the target market(s) for the service. Estimate the lifetime value of a customer in one or more of the target segments. To do this estimate, you will need to get as much information from the manager as you can. If the manager cannot answer all of your questions, make some assumptions.
2. In small groups in class, debate the question "Is the customer always right?" In other words, are there times when the customer may be the wrong customer for the organization?
3. Choose a specific company context (your class project company, the company you work for, or a company in an industry you are familiar with). Calculate the lifetime value of a customer for this company. You will need to make assumptions to do this calculation, so make your assumptions clear. Using ideas and concepts from this chapter, describe a relationship marketing strategy to increase the number of lifetime customers for this firm.

Notes

1. F. E. Webster Jr., "The Changing Role of Marketing in the Corporation," *Journal of Marketing* 56 (October 1992), pp. 1–17.
2. https://v.hdfcbank.com/htdocs/common/2022/july/Annual_Report_FY22/social-poeple.html
3. For discussions of relationship marketing and its influence on the marketing of services, consumer goods, strategic alliances, distribution channels, and buyer–seller interactions, see *Journal of the Academy of Marketing Science,* Special Issue on Relationship Marketing (vol. 23, Fall 1995). Some of the early roots of this paradigm shift can be found in C. Gronroos, *Service Management and Marketing* (New York: Lexington Books, 1990); E. Gummesson, "The New Marketing—Developing Long-Term Interactive Relationships," *Long Range Planning* 20 (1987), pp. 10–20. For reviews of relationship marketing across a spectrum of topics, see J. N. Sheth, *Handbook of Relationship Marketing* (Thousand Oaks, CA: Sage, 2000); and R. M. Morgan, J. Turner Parish, and G. Deitz, *Handbook on Research in Relationship Marketing* (Cheltenham, UK: Edward Elgar Publishing, 2015).

4. A commonly mentioned "rule of thumb" suggests that acquiring new customers can cost five times more than satisfying and retaining current customers; see A. E. Webber, "B2B Customer Experience Priorities in an Economic Downturn: Key Customer Usability Initiatives in a Soft Economy," *Forrester Research,* February 19, 2008.
5. L. L. Berry and A. Parasuraman, *Marketing Services* (New York: Free Press, 1991), chap. 8.
6. G. Knisely, "Comparing Marketing Management in Package Goods and Service Organizations," a series of interviews appearing in *Advertising Age,* January 15, February 19, March 19, and May 14, 1979.
7. This discussion is based on M. D. Johnson and F. Selnes, "Customer Portfolio Management: Toward a Dynamic Theory of Exchange Relationships," *Journal of Marketing* 68 (April 2004), pp. 1–17.
8. R. M. Morgan and S. D. Hunt, "The Commitment-Trust Theory of Relationship Marketing," *Journal of Marketing* 58 (July 1994), pp. 20–38; N. Bendapudi and L. L. Berry, "Customers' Motivations for Maintaining Relationships with Service Providers," *Journal of Retailing* 73 (Spring 1997), pp. 15–37; N. Nguyen, A. Leclec, and G. LeBlanc, "The Mediating Role of Customer Trust on Customer Loyalty," *Journal of Service Science and Management* 6 (March 2013), pp. 96–109.
9. Johnson and Selnes, "Customer Portfolio Management."
10. Ibid.
11. See also D. Siredeshmukh, J. Singh, and B. Sabol, "Customer Trust, Value, and Loyalty in Relational Exchanges," *Journal of Marketing* 66 (January 2002), pp. 15–37 and R. W. Palmatier, "Interfirm Relational Drivers of Customer Value," *Journal of Marketing* 72 (July 2008), pp. 77–89.
12. The three types of relational benefits discussed in this section are drawn from K. P. Gwinner, D. D. Gremler, and M. J. Bitner, "Relational Benefits in Service Industries: The Customer's Perspective," *Journal of the Academy of Marketing Science* 26 (Spring 1998), pp. 101–114. For a review of research on relational benefits, see D. D. Gremler and K. P. Gwinner, "Relational Benefits Research: A Synthesis," in *Handbook on Research in Relationship Marketing,* ed. R. M. Morgan, J. Turner Parish, and G. Deitz (Cheltenham, UK: Edward Elgar Publishing, 2015), pp. 32–74.
13. K. P. Gwinner, D. D. Gremler, and M. J. Bitner, "Relational Benefits in Service Industries: The Customer's Perspective," *Journal of the Academy of Marketing Science 26* (Spring 1998), p. 104.
14. D. D. Gremler, Y. Van Vaerenbergh, E. C. Brüggen, and K. P. Gwinner, "Understanding and Managing Customer Relational Benefits in Services: a Meta-Analysis," *Journal of the Academy of Marketing Science* 48 (May 2020), pp. 565–583.
15. K. P. Gwinner, D. D. Gremler, and M. J. Bitner, "Relational Benefits in Service Industries: The Customer's Perspective," *Journal of the Academy of Marketing Science* 26 (Spring 1998), p. 104.
16. See M. B. Adelman, A. Ahuvia, and C. Goodwin, "Beyond Smiling: Social Support and Service Quality," in *Service Quality: New Directions in Theory and Practice,* ed. R. T. Rust and R. L. Oliver (Thousand Oaks, CA: Sage Publications, 1994), pp. 139–172; C. Goodwin, "Communality as a Dimension of Service Relationships," *Journal of Consumer Psychology* 5 (1996), pp. 387–415.

17. E. J. Arnould and L. L. Price, "River Magic: Extraordinary Experience and the Extended Service Encounter," *Journal of Consumer Research* 20 (June 1993), pp. 24–45.
18. N. Bendapudi and R. P. Leone, "How to Lose Your Star Performer Without Losing Customers, Too," *Harvard Business Review* 79 (November 2001), pp. 104–115; L. L. Bove and L. W. Johnson, "Customer Loyalty to One Service Worker: Should It Be Discouraged?," *International Journal of Research in Marketing* 23 (2006), pp. 79–91.
19. K. P. Gwinner, D. D. Gremler, and M. J. Bitner, "Relational Benefits in Service Industries: The Customer's Perspective," *Journal of the Academy of Marketing Science* 26 (Spring 1998), p. 104.
20. Compare Gwinner, Gremler, and Bitner, "Relational Benefits in Service Industries" and T. Hennig-Thurau, K. P. Gwinner, and D. D. Gremler, "Understanding Relationship Marketing Outcomes: An Integration of Relational Benefits and Relationship Quality," *Journal of Service Research* 4 (February 2002), pp. 230–247 with R. Lacey, J. Suh, and R. M. Morgan, "Differential Effects of Preferential Treatment Levels on Relational Outcomes," *Journal of Service Research* 9 (February 2007), pp. 241–256. D. D. Gremler, Y. Van Vaerenbergh, E. C. Brüggen, and K. P. Gwinner, "Understanding and Managing Customer Relational Benefits in Services: a Meta-Analysis," *Journal of the Academy of Marketing Science* 48 (May 2020), pp. 565–583.
21. F. F. Reichheld and W. E. Sasser Jr., "Zero Defections: Quality Comes to Services," *Harvard Business Review* 68 (September–October 1990), pp. 105–111; F. F. Reichheld, *The Loyalty Effect* (Boston: Harvard Business School Press, 1996); S. Gupta and V. Zeithaml, "Customer Metrics and Their Impact on Financial Performance," *Marketing Science* 25 (November–December 2006), pp. 718–739.
22. C. Homburg, N. Koschate, and W. D. Hoyer, "Do Satisfied Customers Really Pay More? A Study of the Relationship between Customer Satisfaction and Willingness to Pay," *Journal of Marketing* 69 (April 2005), pp. 84–96.
23. R. Dhar and R. Glazer, "Hedging Customers," *Harvard Business Review* 81 (May 2003), pp. 86–92.
24. D. D. Gremler and S. W. Brown, "The Loyalty Ripple Effect: Appreciating the Full Value of Customers," *International Journal of Service Industry Management* 10 (1999), pp. 271–291.
25. M. S. Rosenbaum and C. A. Massiah, "When Customers Receive Support from Other Customers: Exploring the Influence of Intercustomer Social Support on Customer Voluntary Performance," *Journal of Service Research* 9 (February 2007), pp. 257–270; Gremler and Gwinner, "Relational Benefits Research: A Synthesis."
26. S. J. Grove and R. P. Fisk, "The Impact of Other Customers on Service Experiences: A Critical Incident Examination of 'Getting Along,' " *Journal of Retailing* 73 (Spring 1997), pp. 63–85.
27. P. J. Danaher, D. M. Conroy, and J. R. McColl-Kennedy, "Who Wants a Relationship? Conditions When Consumers Expect a Relationship with Their Service Provider," *Journal of Service Research* 11 (August 2008), pp. 43–62.
28. I. Garnefeld, A. Eggert, S. V. Helm, and S. S. Tax, "Growing Existing Customers' Revenue Streams Through Customer Referral Programs," *Journal of Marketing* 77 (July 2014), pp. 17–32.
29. V. Kumar and B. Rajan, "Customer Lifetime Value: What, How, and Why," in *The Routledge Companion to Strategic Marketing,* pp. 422–448 (Routledge, 2020); W. Reinartz, J. S. Thomas, and V. Kumar, "Balancing Acquisition and Retention

Resources to Maximize Customer Profitability," *Journal of Marketing* 69 (January 2005), pp. 63–79.

30. Additional frameworks for calculating lifetime customer value that include a variety of other variables can be found in V. Kumar, "A Theory of Customer Valuation: Concepts, Metrics, Strategy, and Implementation," *Journal of Marketing* 82 (January 2018), pp. 1–19; W. J. Reinartz and V. Kumar, "The Impact of Customer Relationship Characteristics on Profitable Lifetime Duration," *Journal of Marketing* 67 (January 2003), pp. 77–99; Dhar and Glazer, "Hedging Customers"; H. K. Stahl, K. Matzler, and H. H. Hinterhuber, "Linking Customer Lifetime Value with Shareholder Value," *Industrial Marketing Management* 32 (2003), pp. 267–279.
31. This example is cited in J. L. Heskett, W. E. Sasser Jr., and L. A. Schlesinger, *The Service Profit Chain* (New York: The Free Press, 1997), pp. 200–201.
32. For more on customer profitability segments and related strategies, see V. A. Zeithaml, R. T. Rust, and K. N. Lemon, "The Customer Pyramid: Creating and Serving Profitable Customers," *California Management Review* 43 (Summer 2001), pp. 118–142.
33. R. Brooks, "Alienating Customers Isn't Always a Bad Idea, Many Firms Discover," *The Wall Street Journal,* January 7, 1999, p. A1.
34. C. Homburg, M. Droll, and D. Totzek, "Customer Prioritization: Does It Pay Off, and How Should It Be Implemented?" *Journal of Marketing* 72 (September 2008), pp. 110–130.
35. A. J. Petersen, V. Kumar, Y. Polo, and F. J. Sese, "Unlocking the Power of Marketing: Understanding the Links Between Customer Mindset Metrics, Behavior, and Profitability," *Journal of the Academy of Marketing Science* 46 (September 2018), pp. 813–836; W. Reinartz, J. S. Thomas, and V. Kumar, "Balancing Acquisition and Retention Resources to Maximize Customer Profitability," *Journal of Marketing* 69 (January 2005), pp. 63–79;
36. D. Brady, "Why Service Stinks," *BusinessWeek,* October 23, 2000, pp. 118–128.
37. Dhar and Glazer, "Hedging Customers."
38. R. Thakur and L. Workman, "Customer Portfolio Management (CPM) for Improved Customer Relationship Management (CRM): Are Your Customers Platinum, Gold, Silver, or Bronze?," *Journal of Business Research* 69 (October 2016), pp. 4095–4102; C. O. Tarasi, R. N. Bolton, M. D. Hutt, and B. A. Walker, "Balancing Risk and Return in a Customer Portfolio," *Journal of Marketing* 75 (May 2011), pp. 1–17.
39. D. Rosenblum, D. Tomlinson, and L. Scott, "Bottom-Feeding for Blockbuster Businesses," *Harvard Business Review* 81 (March 2003), pp. 52–59.
40. M. D. Johnson, A. Herrman, and F. Huber, "The Evolution of Loyalty Intentions," *Journal of Marketing* 70 (April 2006), pp. 122–132.
41. See T. A. Burnham, J. K. Frels, and V. Mahajan, "Consumer Switching Costs: A Typology, Antecedents, and Consequences," *Journal of the Academy of Marketing Science* 32 (Spring 2003), pp. 109–126; F. Selnes, "An Examination of the Effect of Product Performance on Brand Reputation, Satisfaction, and Loyalty," *European Journal of Marketing* 27 (2003), 19–35; M. Colgate, V. T.-U. Tong, C. K.-C. Lee, and J. U. Farley, "Back from the Brink: Why Customers Stay," *Journal of Service Research* 9 (February 2007), pp. 211–228.
42. C. M. Henderson, L. Steinhoff, C. M. Harmeling, and R. W. Palmatier, "Customer Inertia Marketing," *Journal of the Academy of Marketing Science* 49 (March 2021), pp. 350–373; L. White and V. Yanamandram, "Why Customers Stay:

Reasons and Consequences of Inertia in Financial Services," *Managing Service Quality* 14 (2004), pp. 183–194. See also Y. F. Kuo, T. L. Hu, and S. C. Yang, "Effects of Inertia and Satisfaction in Female Online Shoppers on Repeat-Purchase Intention: The Moderating Roles of Word-of-Mouth and Alternative Attraction," *Managing Service Quality* 23 (2012), pp. 168–187.

43. Colgate, Tong, Lee, and Farley, "Back from the Brink."
44. See J. P. Guiltinan, "A Classification of Switching Costs with Implications for Relationship Marketing," in *Marketing Theory and Practice,* ed. T. L. Childers, R. P. Bagozzi, and J. P. Peter (Chicago: American Marketing Association, 1989), pp. 216–220; P. G. Patterson and T. Smith, "A Cross-Cultural Study of Switching Barriers and Propensity to Stay with Service Providers," *Journal of Retailing* 79 (Summer 2003), pp. 107–120; M. A. Jones, K. E. Reynolds, D. L. Mothersbaugh, and S. E. Beatty, "The Positive and Negative Effects of Switching Costs on Relational Outcomes," *Journal of Service Research* 9 (May 2007), pp. 335–355.
45. See D. Pick, "'Switching Is Easy'—Service Firm Communications to Encourage Customer Switching," *Journal of Retailing and Consumer Services* 21 (2014), pp. 502–509; and J. J. Kim, "Banks Push Harder to Get You to Switch—Services Aim to Ease Hassle of Moving Your Accounts," *The Wall Street Journal,* October 12, 2006, p. D1.
46. See Bendapudi and Berry, "Customers' Motivations for Maintaining Relationships with Service Providers"; H. S. Bansal, P. G. Irving, and S. F. Taylor, "A Three-Component Model of Customer Commitment to Service Providers," *Journal of the Academy of Marketing Science* 32 (Summer 2004), pp. 234–250.
47. Figure 6.5 and the discussion of the four levels of relationship strategies is based on Berry and Parasuraman, *Marketing Services,* pp. 136–142.
48. For more information on cautions to be considered in implementing rewards strategies, see J. J. Kim, L. Steinhoff, and R. W. Palmatier, "An Emerging Theory of Loyalty Program Dynamics," *Journal of the Academy of Marketing Science* 49 (January 2021), pp. 71–95; H. T. Keh and Y. H. Lee, "Do Reward Programs Build Loyalty for Services? The Moderating Effect of Satisfaction on Type and Timing of Rewards," *Journal of Retailing* 82 (June 2006), pp. 127–136; L. Meyer-Waarden and C. Benavent, "Rewards That Reward," *The Wall Street Journal,* September 17, 2008, p. R5; J. D. Hansen, G. D. Deitz, and R. M. Morgan, "Taxonomy of Service-based Loyalty Program Members," *Journal of Services Marketing* 24 (2010), pp. 271–282; R. Lacey, "Relationship Marketing Tools: Understanding the Value of Loyalty Programs," in *Handbook on Research in Relationship Marketing,* ed. R. M. Morgan, J. Turner Parish, and G. Deitz (Cheltenham, UK: Edward Elgar Publishing, 2015), pp. 104–122.
49. C. K. Yim, D. K. Tse, and K. W. Chan, "Strengthening Customer Loyalty through Intimacy and Passion: Roles of Customer-Firm Affection and Customer-Staff Relationships in Services," *Journal of Marketing Research* 45 (December 2008), pp. 741–756.
50. Colgate, Tong, Lee, and Farley, "Back from the Brink."
51. Bendapudi and Leone, "How to Lose Your Star Performer Without Losing Customers"; E. Anderson and S. D. Jap, "The Dark Side of Close Relationships," *Sloan Management Review* 46 (Spring 2005), pp. 75–82; R. W. Palmatier, R. P. Dant, D. Grewal, and K. R. Evans, "Factors Influencing the Effectiveness of Relationship Marketing: A Meta-Analysis," *Journal of Marketing* 70 (October 2006), pp. 136–153. However, some scholars have recently questioned the use of the relationship metaphor in business-to-business contexts; see L. A. Bettencourt, C. P. Blocker, M. B. Houston, and D. J. Flint, "Rethinking Customer Relationships,"

Business Horizons 58 (2015), pp. 99–108; C. P. Blocker, M. B. Houston, and D. J. Flint, "Unpacking What a 'Relationship' Means to Commercial Buyers: How the Relationship Metaphor Creates Tension and Obscures Experience," *Journal of Consumer Research* 38 (February 2012), pp. 886–908.

52. Rosenbaum and Massiah, "When Customers Receive Support from Other Customers."
53. W. Ulaga and A. Eggert, "Value-Based Differentiation in Business Relationships: Gaining and Sustaining Key Supplier Status," *Journal of Marketing* 70 (January 2006), pp. 119–136.
54. D. D. Gremler and S. W. Brown, "Service Loyalty: Its Nature, Importance, and Implications," in *Advancing Service Quality: A Global Perspective,* ed. B. Edvardsson, S. W. Brown, R. Johnston, and E. E. Scheuing (Jamaica, NY: International Service Quality Association, 1996), pp. 171–180; H. Hansen, K. Sandvik, and F. Selnes, "Direct and Indirect Effects of Commitment to a Service Employee on the Intention to Stay," *Journal of Service Research* 5 (May 2003), pp. 356–368.
55. A. Andersen, *Best Practices: Building Your Business with Customer-Focused Solutions* (New York: Simon & Schuster, 1998), pp. 125–127; https://www.cardinalhealth.com/content/dam/corp/web/documents/infographic/cardinal-health-supply-chain-resilience-infographic.pdf, accessed September 7, 2022.
56. S. Stellin, "Avoiding Surprises at the Car Rental Counter," *The New York Times*, June 4, 2006, p. TR6.
57. See L. C. Harris and K. L. Reynolds, "The Consequences of Dysfunctional Customer Behavior," *Journal of Service Research* 6 (November 2003), p. 145, for cites; see also, A. A. Grandey, D. N. Dickter, and H. P. Sin, "The Customer Is *Not* Always Right: Customer Aggression and Emotion Regulation of Service Employees," *Journal of Organizational Behavior* 25 (2004), pp. 397–418. Also see R. Fisk, S. Grove, L. C. Harris, D. A. Keeffe, K. L. Daunt, R. Russell-Bennett, and J. Wirtz, "Customers Behaving Badly: A State of the Art Review, Research Agenda, and Implications for Practitioners," *Journal of Services Marketing* 24 (2010), pp. 417–429.
58. K. Ohnezeit, recruiting supervisor for Enterprise Rent-A-Car, personal communication, February 12, 2004.
59. See Harris and Reynolds, "The Consequences of Dysfunctional Customer Behavior."
60. L. L. Berry and K. Seiders, "Serving Unfair Customers," *Business Horizons* 51 (January/February 2008), pp. 29–37.
61. For a detailed discussion on relationship ending, see A. Halinen and J. Tähtinen, "A Process Theory of Relationship Ending," *International Journal of Service Industry Management* 13 (2002), pp. 163–180.
62. H. Åkerlund, "Fading Customer Relationships in Professional Services," *Managing Service Quality* 15 (2005), pp. 156–71.
63. M. Haenlein and A. M. Kaplan, "Unprofitable Customers and Their Management," *Business Horizons* 52 (2009), pp. 89–97; M. Haenlein, A. M. Kaplan, and D. Schoder, "Valuing the Real Option of Abandoning Unprofitable Customers When Calculating Customer Lifetime Value," *Journal of Marketing* 70 (July 2006), pp. 5–20.
64. For additional thoughts on firing customers, see J. Shin, K. Sudhir, and D. H. Yoon, "When to 'Fire' Customers: Customer Cost-Based Pricing," *Management Science* 58 (May 2012), pp. 932–947.
65. J. Weed, "For Uber, Airbnb and Other Companies, Customer Ratings Go Both Ways," *New York Times,* December 1, 2014, www.nytimes.com/2014/12/02 /business/for-uber-airbnb-and-other-companies-customer-ratings-go-both-ways.html.

Chapter Seven

Service Recovery

This chapter's learning objectives are to:

1. Illustrate the importance of recovery from service failures in keeping customers and building loyalty.
2. Discuss the nature of customer complaints and why people do and do not complain.
3. Provide evidence of what customers expect and the kind of responses they want when they do complain.
4. Present strategies for effective service recovery, including ways to "fix the customer" after a service failure and ways to "fix the (underlying) problem(s)."
5. Understand "offering service guarantees" as a third service recovery strategy—what they are, the benefits of guarantees, and when to use them.

How Overbooking Caused a Service Nightmare for United Airlines

On Sunday, April 9, 2017, physician Dr. David Dao was dragged off an overbooked United Airlines flight. Fellow passengers videoed as security officers violently yanked Dr. Dao from his seat and dragged him down the aisle by his arms and legs to remove him from the airplane, while other passengers called out in protest. During this ordeal, Dr. Dao hit his head on an armrest and blood began streaming from his mouth. Cell phone footage of this incident went viral and received millions of views on social media within a few days. Customers across the country responded by expressing their disgust to United Airlines; for example, some posted videos of cutting up their United credit cards, pledging not to fly with the airline again. The incident also received international attention. Within hours, United trended on Weibo (China's equivalent to Twitter) and the incident generated more than 100 million views by Tuesday. Moreover, United's stock price also decreased by about 4 percent on the following Tuesday, and the airline's market value fell temporarily by $1 billion.

Jin Lee/Bloomberg/Getty Images

Given this response, it is worth noting that it is legal for airlines to drop passengers from overbooked flights against their will. Overbooking is a common practice in the airline industry in anticipation of customer no-shows (and customers accept this practice as part of the "Terms and Conditions" when they purchase a ticket). If overbooking occurs, airlines can incentivize volunteers to give up their seat (e.g., with vouchers that can be redeemed for future flights). If no passenger volunteers, airlines can then (randomly) select passengers for removal. In fact, tens of thousands of customers are subject to such "involuntary deboarding situations" every year.

Initially, Dr. Dao volunteered to deboard the plane to help free up seats that United needed to transport a crew for a different aircraft to another city. However, Dr. Dao changed his mind once he realized that he would be late for work the next morning if he took the next available flight on Monday. As he then refused to give up his seat, the airline employees called local law enforcement to remove Dr. Dao from the plane.

Although overbooking is common in this industry, what caused public outrage about this case was the way the airline and security officers handled this situation—not only aboard the plane but also in terms of the airline's initial response after the incident occurred. For example, then CEO Oscar Munoz initially defended the company's actions and emphasized that the passenger continued to resist after he was removed and ran back into the plane. Although many public relations experts suggested that a CEO should quickly offer a sincere apology in a situation like this, Munoz (on Monday morning) merely apologized for "having to re-accommodate . . . customers." Such a response seemed rather insensitive. Notably, the CEO caused additional irritation with a memo to United employees on Monday afternoon, which described Dr. Dao as "disruptive and belligerent" and underlined that United "employees followed established procedures for dealing with situations like this." It took further public outrage for the CEO to finally offer an unqualified apology on Tuesday afternoon, in which he recognized the incident as "truly horrific" and added: "I promise you we will do better."

Although United pledged to review how it dealt with oversold flights, how it moved its flight crews between airports, and how it worked with airport authorities, marketing experts concluded that the CEO's initial response (on Monday) was a major disappointment. To avoid such service nightmares, companies need to have an effective service recovery system in place, which is the focus of this chapter.

Sources: H. Yan, C. Zdanowicz, and E. Grinberg, "CNN Backlash Erupts After United Passenger Gets Yanked Off Overbooked Flight," https://www.cnn.com/2017/04/11/travel/united-customer-dragged-off-overbooked-flight/index.html, accessed November 11, 2021; A. Nazifi, K. Gelbrich, Y. Grégoire, S. Koch, D. El-Manstrly, and J. Wirtz, "Proactive Handling of Flight Overbooking: How to Reduce Negative eWOM and the Costs of Bumping Customers," *Journal of Service Research* 24 (May 2021), pp. 206–225; A. Petroff, "United Airlines Shows How to Make a PR Crisis a Total Disaster," https://money.cnn.com/2017/04/11/news/united-passenger-pr-disaster/index.html, accessed November 11, 2021; R. Khan, "United Airlines Customer Dragging Drama: Are Corporate Mandates Killing The Conscience?," https://www.forbes.com/sites/roomykhan/2017/04/19/united-airlines-customer-dragging-drama-are-corporate-mandates-killing-the-conscience/?sh=35411d2f63c1, accessed November 11, 2021; CBS/Reuters, "United Airlines Faces Backlash After Dragging Man From Plane," https://www.cbsnews.com/news/united-airlines-faces-backlash-after-dragging-man-from-plane/, accessed December 10, 2021.

The preceding two chapters have given you a foundation for understanding customers' service expectations through research as well as through knowing them as individuals and developing strong relationships with them. These strategies, matched with effective service design, delivery, and communication—discussed in other parts of the text—form the foundations for service success. But in all service contexts—whether customer service, consumer services, or business-to-business services—service failure is inevitable. Failure is inevitable even for the best of firms with the best of intentions, even for those with world-class service systems.

To fully understand and retain their customers, firms must know what customers expect when service failures occur and must implement effective strategies for service recovery. Our chapter opener illustrates the potentially disastrous problems a firm can face when a service failure occurs.

THE IMPACT OF SERVICE FAILURE AND RECOVERY

A *service failure* is generally described as service performance that falls below a customer's expectations in such a way that leads to customer dissatisfaction. *Service recovery* refers to the actions taken by an organization in response to a service failure to improve the situation for the customer. Failures occur for all kinds of reasons—the service may be unavailable when promised, it may be delivered late or too slowly, the outcome may be incorrect or poorly executed, or employees may be rude or uncaring.[1] Although these types of failures bring about negative feelings from customers, research suggests that only a portion (45 percent) of customers who experience a problem with service delivery actually complain to the employees serving them, and only a very small number (1–5 percent) complain to management or the company headquarters.[2] This phenomenon, commonly referred to as the "tip of the iceberg" and demonstrated in Figure 7.1, suggests every complaint that management actually receives represents 20–100 other customers who experience a problem and do not complain. Service failures left unfixed can result in customers leaving, telling other customers about their negative experiences, and even challenging the organization through consumer rights organizations or legal channels.

Service Recovery Effects

Research has shown that resolving customer problems effectively has a strong impact on customer satisfaction, loyalty, word-of-mouth communication, and bottom-line performance.[3] That is, customers who experience service failures, but who are ultimately satisfied based on recovery efforts by the firm, will be more loyal than those whose problems are not resolved. That loyalty translates into profitability, as you learned in Chapter 6. Data

FIGURE 7.1
Complaining Customers: Management Only Sees the Tip of the Iceberg

Source: Data from TARP Worldwide Inc., 2007.

from a Customer Rage Study verify this relationship, as shown in Figure 7.2.[4] Among customers from businesses who complain and have their problems satisfactorily resolved, 71 percent indicate they would recommend the company, whereas only 4 percent of dissatisfied complainants would do that. Moreover, satisfied complainants told (on average) 3.7 other people about their complaint, but dissatisfied complainants told 7 people—nearly twice as many. These findings illustrate the power of good service recovery. Occasionally firms do so well in their service recovery that customers end up more satisfied than they would have been if the firm had never failed in the first place—a situation referred to as the "service recovery paradox," as further described in Exhibit 7.1.

A well-designed service recovery strategy also provides information that can be used to improve service as part of a firm's continuous improvement efforts. By making adjustments to service processes, systems, and outcomes based on previous customer complaints and service recovery experiences, companies increase the likelihood of "doing it right the first time." In turn, this reduces costs of failures and increases initial customer satisfaction.

Unfortunately, many firms do not employ effective recovery strategies. For example, the aforementioned 2020 Customer Rage Study found that only 32 percent of complainants were satisfied with the firm's response, and 58 percent said that they received nothing in response to voicing their complaint.[5] There are tremendous downsides to having no service recovery or ineffective service recovery strategies.

- First, the Customer Rage Study and other research have found that customers who are dissatisfied with the recovery process after making a complaint are far less likely to repurchase than those who do not complain—suggesting the power of poor service recovery![6]
- Second, poor recovery following a bad service experience creates, in effect, two poor experiences (often referred to as a "double deviation") and can lead to customers who are so dissatisfied that they actively pursue opportunities to openly criticize the company.[7] When customers experience a service failure, they talk about it to others, no matter what the outcome (see Figure 7.2).[8] With the ability to share such stories on the Internet and social media, the potential reach of such dissatisfied customers is even greater.
- Third, repeated service failures without an effective recovery strategy in place can aggravate even the best employees. The reduction in employee morale and even the loss of employees can be huge but often overlooked costs of not having an effective service recovery strategy.

FIGURE 7.2
Word of Mouth as a Function of Complainant Satisfaction

Source: 2020 Customer Rage Study, conducted by Customer Care Measurement and Consulting in collaboration with the Center for Services Leadership at Arizona State University.

Satisfied Complainants Are More Likely to Recommend the Firm	
Customer Satisfaction Level with Service Recovery Experience	Percentage Who Would Recommend the Firm
Customers who are satisfied after their service recovery experience	**71%**
Customers who are mollified / appeased after their service recovery experience	19%
Customers who remain dissatisfied after their service recovery experience	4%

Dissatisfied Complainants Are More Likely to Spread Word of Mouth about the Firm	
Customer Satisfaction Level with Service Recovery Experience	Average Number of People the Customers Told About Their Complaint
Customers who are satisfied after their service recovery experience	3.7
Customers who are mollified / appeased after their service recovery experience	5.1
Customers who remain dissatisfied after their service recovery experience	**7.0**

Exhibit 7.1 The Service Recovery Paradox

Occasionally some businesses have customers who are initially dissatisfied with a service experience and then experience a high level of excellent service recovery, seemingly leading them to be even more satisfied and more likely to repurchase than if no problem had occurred at all; that is, some customers appear to be more satisfied after they experience a service failure than they otherwise would have been![9] To illustrate, consider a rental car customer who arrives to check in and finds that no automobile is available of the size reserved and the price quoted. In an effort to recover, the car rental agent immediately upgrades this customer to a much better vehicle at the original price. The customer, thrilled with this compensation, reports that she is extremely satisfied with this experience, is even more impressed with the firm than she was before, and vows to be loyal into the future. Although such extreme instances are relatively rare, this idea—that an initially disappointed customer who has experienced good service recovery might be even more satisfied and loyal as a result—has been labeled the *service recovery paradox.*

So should a firm "screw up" just a little, so that it can "fix the problem" superbly? If doing so would actually lead to more satisfied customers, is this strategy worth pursuing? The logical, but not very rational, conclusion is that companies should *plan to disappoint customers,* so they can recover well and (hopefully) gain even greater loyalty from them!

What are the problems with such an approach?

- As we indicated earlier in this chapter, a vast majority of customers do not complain when they experience a problem. The possibility of a recovery exists only in situations in which the firm is aware of a problem and is able to recover well; if customers do not make the firm aware of the failure—and most do not—dissatisfaction is most likely to be the result.
- It is expensive to fix mistakes; recreating or reworking a service may be quite costly to a firm.
- It would appear somewhat ludicrous to encourage service failures—after all, reliability ("doing it right the first time") is the most critical determinant of service quality across most industries.
- Research suggests that even if a customer's satisfaction with the firm increases as a result of great service recovery, repurchase intentions and image perceptions of the firm do not increase—that is, customers do not necessarily think more highly of the firm in the long run.[10]
- Although the service recovery paradox suggests that a customer *may* end up more satisfied after experiencing excellent recovery, there is certainly no guarantee that the customer actually will end up more satisfied.

The service recovery paradox is highly dependent on the context and situation; although one customer may find it easy to forgive a restaurant that provides him with a gift certificate for a later date for having lost his dinner reservation, another customer who had planned to propose marriage to his date over dinner may not be all that happy with the same recovery scenario.

The intrigue stimulated by the service recovery paradox has led to empirical research specifically on this issue. Although anecdotal evidence provides some support for the recovery paradox, research seems to indicate that this phenomenon is not pervasive. In one study, researchers found that only the very highest levels of customers' service recovery ratings resulted in increased satisfaction and loyalty.[11] This research suggests that customers weigh their most recent experiences heavily in their determination of whether to buy again. If the most recent experience is negative, overall feelings about the company will decrease, and repurchase intentions will diminish significantly. Unless the recovery effort is absolutely superlative, it cannot overcome the negative impression of the initial experience enough to build repurchase intentions beyond the point at which they would be if the service had been provided correctly in the first place. Other studies suggest the conditions under which a service recovery paradox is most likely to occur is when the failure is not considered by the customer to be severe, the customer has not experienced prior failures with the firm, the cause of the failure is viewed as unstable by the customer, or the customer perceives that the company had little control over the cause of the failure.[12] Apparently, conditions must be just right in order for the recovery paradox to be present.

Given the mixed opinions on the extent to which the recovery paradox exists, "doing it right the first time" is still a firm's best and safest strategy in the long run.[13] However, when a failure does occur, then every effort at a superior recovery should be made to mitigate its negative effects. If the failure can be fully overcome, if the failure is less critical, or if the recovery effort is clearly superlative, it may be possible to observe evidence of the service recovery paradox.[14]

HOW CUSTOMERS RESPOND TO SERVICE FAILURES

Customers who experience service failures can respond in a variety of ways, as illustrated in Figure 7.3.[15] It is assumed that, following a failure, dissatisfaction at some level will occur for the customer. In fact, research suggests that a variety of negative emotions can occur following a service failure, including anger, discontent, disappointment, self-pity, anxiety, and regret.[16] These initial negative responses will affect how customers evaluate the service recovery effort and presumably their ultimate decision to return to the provider or not.

Many customers are very passive about their dissatisfaction, simply saying or doing nothing. Whether they take action or not, at some point customers will decide whether to stay with that provider or switch to a competitor. As we already have pointed out, dissatisfied customers who do not complain are not very likely to return. Therefore, for companies, customer passivity in the face of dissatisfaction is a threat to future success.

Why People Do (and Do Not) Complain

Customers who are unlikely to take any action—the majority of customers in most situations—have many reasons for not doing anything. They often see complaining as a waste of their time and effort.[17] They do not believe anything positive will occur for them or others based on their actions. Many customers may have no confidence in the complaint process and thus refrain from complaining because they do not think it will do any good. Sometimes customers do not know how to complain—they do not understand the process or may not realize that avenues are open to them to voice their complaints. Sometimes customers believe it is too difficult to report a complaint to a firm and, in some cases, may feel like they are being punished by having to do too much to make a complaint. In some cases noncomplainers may engage in "emotion-focused coping" to deal with their negative experiences. This type of coping involves self-blame, denial, and possibly seeking social support.[18] They may feel that the failure was somehow their fault and that they do not deserve redress.

FIGURE 7.3
Customer Complaint Actions Following Service Failure

Note: If a service failure occurs, the bold lines/boxes indicate the most desirable configuration (from the firm's perspective) of the complaint experience.

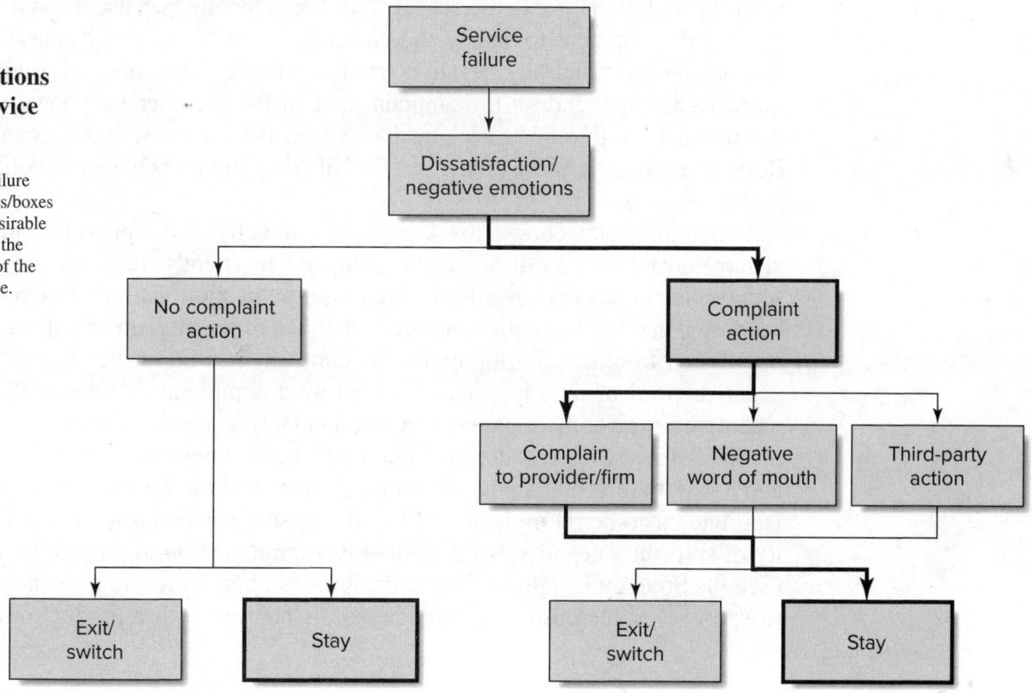

Some customers are more likely to complain than others for a variety of reasons. These customers believe that positive consequences may occur and that there are social benefits of complaining, and their personal norms support their complaining behavior. They believe they should and will be provided compensation for the service failure in some form. They believe that fair treatment and good service are their due and that, in cases of service failure, someone should make good. In some cases they feel a social obligation to complain—to help others avoid similar situations or to punish the service provider. A very small number of customers have "complaining" personalities—they just like to complain.

Personal relevance of the failure can also influence whether people complain.[19] If the service failure is really important, if the failure has critical consequences for the customer, or if the customer has much ego involvement in the service experience, then he or she is more likely to complain. The situation at United Airlines, which is described in Exhibit 7.2, illustrates a service failure that was especially important to one customer. In such situations, when customer emotions are high, customer rage may result.[20]

Customers are more likely to complain about expensive, high-risk, and ego involving services (like vacation packages, airline travel, and medical services) than they are about less expensive, frequently purchased services (fast-food drive-through service, a cab ride, a call to a customer service help line). These latter services are often simply not important enough to warrant the time to complain. Unfortunately, even though the experience may not be important to the customer at the moment, a dissatisfying encounter can still drive him or her to a competitor the next time the service is needed.

Types of Customer Complaint Actions

If customers initiate actions following service failure, the action can be of various types, as Figure 7.3 illustrates. A dissatisfied customer can choose to complain on the spot to the service provider, giving the company the opportunity to respond immediately. This reaction is often the best-case scenario for the company because it has a second chance right at that moment to satisfy the customer, keep his or her business in the future, and potentially avoid any negative word of mouth. Customers who do not complain immediately may choose to complain later to the provider by phone, in writing, via the Internet, or through social media. Again, the company has a chance to recover. Researchers refer to these proactive types of complaining behavior as *voice* responses or *seeking redress.*

Some customers choose not to complain directly to the provider but rather spread negative word of mouth about the company to friends, relatives, coworkers, or on social media. Negative word-of-mouth communication can be extremely detrimental because it can reinforce the customer's feelings of negativism and spread that negative impression to others. Furthermore, the company has no chance to recover unless the negative word of mouth is accompanied by a complaint directly to the company. In recent years, customers have taken to complaining via the Internet or through social media. A variety of websites, including web-based consumer opinion platforms, blogs, and a variety of social media (including Twitter and Facebook),[21] have been created to facilitate customer complaints, and in doing so, provide customers with the possibility of spreading negative word-of-mouth communication to a much broader audience. (See the Strategy Insight on how companies can better prevent or manage social media firestorms.) Some customers become so dissatisfied with a product or service failure

Exhibit 7.2 The Internet Spreads the Story of Poor Service Recovery: "United Breaks Guitars"

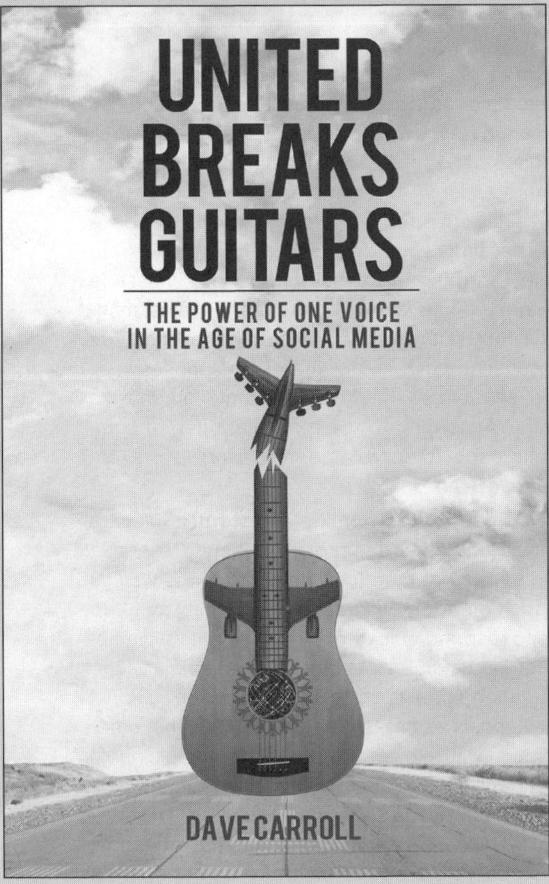

2009 Big Break Enterprises/Dave Carroll

Dave Carroll wrote a book about his experience with United Airlines.

UNITED BREAKS GUITARS

While traveling with United Airlines, musician Dave Carroll's guitar was broken by baggage handlers. After fifteen months of seeking compensation with no resolution from United Airlines, Carroll posted a music video on YouTube about his experience called "United Breaks Guitars." The video with its catchy song quickly went viral and was picked up by countless news outlets, including the *Los Angeles Times,* CNN, and the CBS Morning Show. In less than a month, the video was viewed more than 4.6 million times, causing United Airlines's stock to tumble and costing shareholders more than $180 million.

The trouble started when Carroll witnessed baggage handlers throwing his guitar on the tarmac while he waited for his flight to take off from Chicago's O'Hare Airport. Carroll immediately reported the problem to flight attendants, who instructed him to take up the issue with the ground crew when they arrived at their destination in Omaha. Unfortunately, when they got there, the ground crew was unavailable, and Carroll was only able to confirm his suspicions that they had broken his $3,500 Taylor guitar. What followed was fifteen months of what Carroll describes in his song as "pass the buck, don't ask me, I'm sorry sir, your claim can go nowhere."

Eventually Carroll and United Airlines reached an impasse, and Carroll informed the airline that he would be writing a series of three songs, along with a video, about his experience. His goal was to have at least one million views of the video within one year. The video was uploaded to YouTube on July 6, 2009, and friends of Carroll posted links to the video on Digg and other social news sites. They also tweeted the link to other disgruntled United Airlines customers and to TV personalities such as Jay Leno, Jimmy Fallon, and Perez Hilton. *Consumerist* and other news outlets then picked up the video, and it spread like wildfire. By July 10, only four days later, the video had been viewed over 1.6 million times.

United Airlines took to Twitter to address the video, tweeting, "This has struck a chord [with] us and we've contacted him directly to make it right." United continued to tweet regularly, reiterating this sentiment. Once United got in touch with Carroll, they offered him the $1,200 it had cost Carroll to repair the guitar, plus an additional $1,200 in flight vouchers. However, to Carroll this was too little, too late. Carroll suggested they give the compensation to another customer in a similar situation, and United ultimately opted to donate $3,000 to a music school. Months later, Carroll met with United Airlines executives, who admitted that Carroll's claim should not have been denied. They now use Carroll's video in customer service training to ensure that a similar incident does not occur again.

Despite United's (delayed) actions, however, the damage was done. In the days following the release of Carroll's video, United Airlines stock fell 10 percent. This single badly handled customer complaint had come with a $180 million price tag. And, the video has since been viewed by more than 21 million people. These consequences are particularly jarring, considering that it would have only cost the airline $1,200 to address the initial complaint.

This incident highlights the importance of careful handling of customer issues and grievances—gone are the days when customer gripes only reach a few close friends and family. Now, thanks to the Internet, complaints have the potential to reach millions of sympathetic ears within a matter of hours!

Sources: J. Deighton and L. Kornfeld, *United Breaks Guitars (Case Study),* Boston: Harvard Business Publishing, 2010; "United Breaks Guitars" YouTube video, 4:36, posted by "sonsofmaxwell," July 6, 2009, https://www.youtube.com/watch?v=5YGc4zOqozo; and R. Sawhney, "Broken Guitar Has United Playing the Blues to the Tune of $180 Million," *FastCompany,* July 30, 2009, http://www.fastcompany.com/1320152/broken-guitar-has-united-playing-blues-tune-180-million.

Strategy Insight How to Better Detect and Prevent Social Media Firestorms

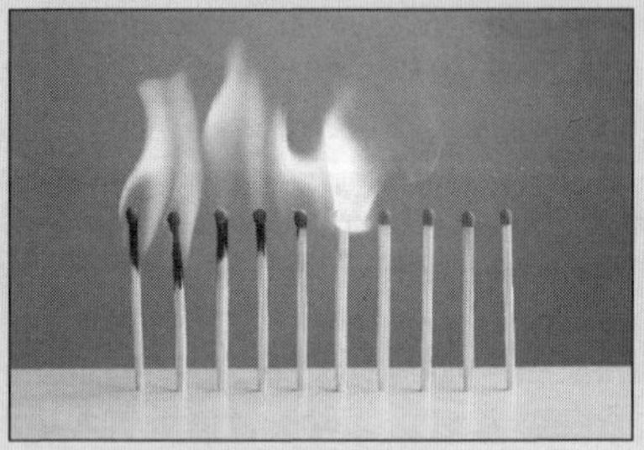
New Africa/Shutterstock

With many millions of customers engaging on social media on a daily basis, online firestorms (i.e., negative electronic word of mouth that gains substantial momentum through support from other customers in a short period of time) is a serious risk for companies. Prominent examples of such firestorms include "#deleteUber" and the social media crises of United Airlines (see the chapter opener and Exhibit 7.2). It is therefore crucial for managers to (better) detect, mitigate, and prevent such viral crises and minimize damages companies suffer from them. A scientific study that examined social media firestorms found the following:

- **Detecting Potential Online Firestorms:** The contagiousness of an online complaint depends to a large extent on (1) the sender's emotions and (2) the relationship ties between the sender/poster and receivers. Therefore, to measure the emotional intensity of online posts, companies should use automated text mining/analysis software that helps "flag" highly emotional posts and predict their potential virality. (The greater the number of arousal/emotion words in a post, the more likely it is to go viral.) In addition, to assess the tie strength between a post's author and the broader online community, companies should count the number of the poster's interactions with others in the community. (Higher numbers of interactions indicate stronger ties to the community and signal a greater likelihood that a person is an online influencer who could start a social media firestorm.)
- **Mitigating Evolved Online Firestorms:** Realistically, some posts will "catch fire"; in other words, not all firestorms can be prevented. In these cases, firms (and often different employees) need to respond multiple times to dissatisfied customers. It is crucial that managers view these responses as an overall "response sequence," rather than as multiple isolated interactions. For example, instead of providing highly similar responses throughout the response sequence, firms should vary how they demonstrate empathy and use explanations from one message to the next to mitigate a post's virality. That is, managers can first emphasize offering an explanation to dissatisfied customers, whereas responses later in the sequence should increasingly emphasize empathy. According to the research, offering compensation should serve as a last resort to prevent further escalation.
- **Preventing Potential Online Firestorms:** Managers must note that their organization's response should satisfy both the focal complainant *as well as* the (much broader) online audience. One way to do that is to respond quickly and in an empathetic manner that is customized to the focal complaint. (The worst option is for firms to ignore highly emotional negative posts as this makes it more likely that other customers will join and support the complainant.) Notably, posts that contain particularly high numbers of emotional words (e.g., hate, revenge, disgust, anger, fear) require additional managerial attention, such as offering more detailed explanations about the service failure and the firm's response. In addition to offering an authentic apology, managers should quickly move the conversation with the customer to another (less public) channel (e.g., direct messaging). Interestingly, it is not always necessary or advisable to immediately offer a material compensation to angry customers, but rather to signal to the customer that the company appreciates the negative feedback and takes it seriously (also see Exhibit 7.4 on outcome fairness and interactional fairness).

Although there is no "one-size-fits-all" strategy to prevent online/social media firestorms, companies can reduce the damage to their brands through a flexible and proactive approach that leverages the above insights.

FIGURE I. Illustrative examples of online firestorms and firm responses.

Sources: D. Herhausen, S. Ludwig, D. Grewal, J. Wulf, and M. Schoegel, "Detecting, Preventing, and Mitigating Online Firestorms in Brand Communities," *Journal of Marketing* 83 (May 2019), pp. 1–21; D. Herhausen, "How to Keep Complaints from Spreading," *Harvard Business Review* 99, no. 3 (2020), pp. 19–23.

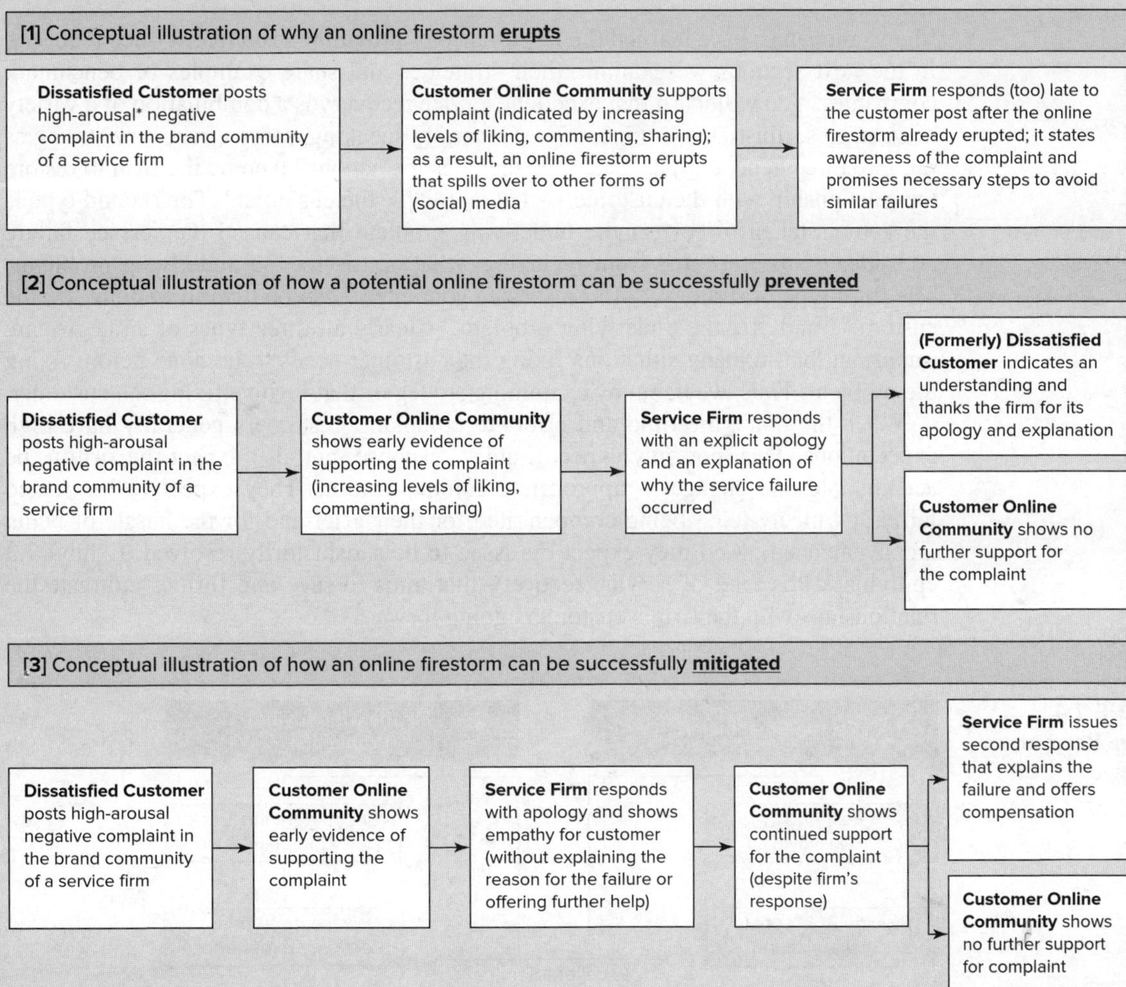

* = High-arousal complaints typically include indications of intensive emotions such as customer anger, frustration, fear, or anxiety; for further details on the above illustrations, see: Herhausen, Dennis, Stephan Ludwig, Dhruv Grewal, Jochen Wulf, and Marcus Schoegel, "Detecting, Preventing, and Mitigating Online Firestorms in Brand Communities," *Journal of Marketing*, 83, 3 (2019), pp. 1-21.

that they construct websites targeting the firm's current and prospective customers. On these "gripe sites,"[22] angry customers convey their grievances against the firm in ways designed to convince other customers of the firm's incompetence and evil.[23]

Finally, customers may choose to complain to third parties such as the Better Business Bureau, to consumer affairs arms of the government (e.g., the Federal Trade Commission), to a licensing authority, to a professional association, or to a private attorney. No matter the action (or inaction), ultimately customers determine whether to patronize the service provider again or to switch to another provider.

SERVICE RECOVERY STRATEGIES: (1) FIX THE CUSTOMER

Many companies have learned the importance of providing excellent service recovery. In the next sections we examine their strategies and share examples of benchmark companies. You will learn that excellent service recovery is a combination of a variety of strategies, illustrated in Figure 7.4. Generally speaking, service recovery strategies fall into three general types. One type includes the actions taken by the firm to restore the relationship with the customer—that is, to "fix the customer." The second type is the actions taken to correct the underlying problem that caused the service failure and, ideally, to prevent it from recurring—that is, to "fix the underlying problem." The third type of strategy, "offer a service guarantee," can be helpful to both "fix the customer" and "fix the underlying problem." Clearly all three types of strategies are important, but in many situations fixing the customer needs to be done before fixing the problem. Thus, we begin by examining strategies that involve fixing the customer.

When they take the time and effort to complain, customers generally have high expectations. They not only expect a quick response, but also expect the firm to be accountable and engage in appropriate communication. They expect to be treated fairly and nicely (e.g., being compensated for their grief and for the hassle of being inconvenienced). And they expect the issue to be satisfactorily resolved. Exhibit 7.3 epitomizes this kind of service recovery that aims to save and further cultivate the relationships with the firm's customers going forward.

FIGURE 7.4
Service Recovery Strategies

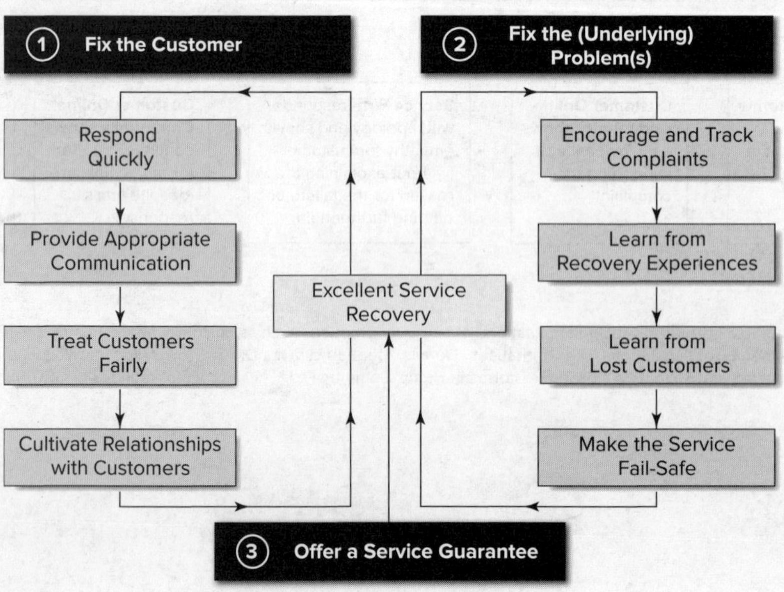

Exhibit 7.3 Service Hero Stories

This exhibit illustrates that outstanding customer service is often not delivered by executives; instead, it is typically provided by frontline employees who directly interact with customers. Here are some examples of how customer service heroes have delighted their customers.

TRADER JOE'S DELIVERS FOOD TO MAN IN NEED

An 89-year-old man was snowed in at his home in Pennsylvania just before the Christmas holidays, with the promise of heavier storms on the horizon. His daughter, worried that he would run out of food during the bad weather, called several stores in the area hoping that one would be willing to deliver supplies to her father.

She finally got in touch with someone at Trader Joe's who told her that Trader Joe's normally does not make deliveries, but that the company would be willing to make an exception due to the extreme circumstances. The Trader Joe's associate took the woman's order and even suggested additional items that would work with her father's low-sodium diet, making sure he would have everything he needed should he be stuck at home for an extended period of time.

When it came to paying for the food, the associate told her not to worry—the food and the delivery would be free of charge. The employee concluded the conversation by wishing her a Merry Christmas, and her father received the food less than thirty minutes later.

This example shows that service recovery goes beyond fixing a simple mistake. Authorizing employees to do the right thing for customers, even when the recovery is made necessary because of circumstances outside the firm's control (such as Mother Nature), is how firms can build lasting and meaningful relationships with their customers.

UNITED AIRLINES DELAYS FLIGHT FOR PASSENGER TO SEE DYING MOTHER

Though United Airlines has made a name for itself related to overbooking its flights and in the guitar-breaking business (see the Chapter Opener and Exhibit 7.2), there are also examples of when the airline has gone above and beyond for a customer.

Passenger Kerry Drake anxiously boarded a flight in San Francisco on his way to see his dying mother in Lubbock, Texas, who had only hours left to live. Drake knew that if he missed his connecting flight in Houston, he would likely not get to see her before she passed away.

When his first flight to Houston was delayed, Drake realized he would miss his Lubbock connection, preventing him from seeing his mother one last time. He broke down into tears on the plane, unable to contain his grief.

When a flight attendant learned of the circumstances surrounding this situation, she informed the captain, who radioed ahead to the next flight from Houston to Lubbock. The flight crew waiting in Houston, sympathetic to Drake's situation, delayed the flight in order to wait for Drake.

As Drake arrived at the gate for the last leg of his journey, the crew greeted him by name as they welcomed him. As a result of the coordinated efforts of a large set of United Airlines employees, Drake was able to get to the hospital in time to say goodbye to his mother.

This story is remarkable because airlines are often evaluated in terms of their efficiency and the number of on-time flights. However, United Airlines employees were able to see that this situation was more important than a schedule, and they were able to give a passenger a priceless gift—a final moment with his mother.

CLUB MED GOES ABOVE AND BEYOND TO WELCOME EXHAUSTED GUESTS WITH LAVISH PARTY

A classic story of procedural fairness in the midst of service recovery comes from Club Med–Cancun, a story still being retold nearly three decades later. A group of Club Med vacationers had nothing but trouble getting from New York to their Mexican destination. The flight took off six hours late, made two unexpected stops, and circled 30 minutes before it could land. Because of all the delays and mishaps, the plane was en route for 10 hours more than planned and ran out of food and drinks. It finally arrived at two o'clock in the morning, with a landing so rough that oxygen masks and luggage dropped from overhead. By the time the plane pulled up to the gate, the soured passengers were faint with hunger and convinced that their vacation was ruined before it had even started. Silvio de Bortoli, the general manager of the Cancun resort, got word of the horrendous flight while it was in progress and immediately created an antidote. He took half the resort's staff to the airport, where they laid out a table of snacks and drinks and set up a stereo system to play lively music. As the guests filed through the gate, they received personal greetings, help with their bags, a sympathetic ear, and a chauffeured ride to the resort. Waiting for them at Club Med was a lavish banquet, complete with mariachi band and Champagne. Moreover, the other half of the staff had rallied other guests to wake up and greet the newcomers, and the partying continued until sunrise. Even though the problems were not Club Med's fault, the company went out of its way to compensate the delayed guests immediately on arrival. The vacationers had no more hassles once they were on the ground.

Sources: G. Ciotti, "10 Stories of Unforgettable Customer Service," *Help Scout,* www.helpscout.net, accessed on June 17, 2016; K. Hetter, "United Airlines Delays Flight for Man to See Dying Mother," *CNN,* March 10, 2013, http://edition.cnn.com/2013/03/06/travel/united-flight-delay-dying-mother/index.html; C. W. L. Hart, J. L. Heskett, and W. E. Sasser Jr., "The Profitable Art of Service Recovery," *Harvard Business Review* 68 (July–August 1990), pp. 148–156.

Respond Quickly

Complaining customers want quick responses.[24] Thus, when the company has service failures or receives complaints from customers, it must be prepared to act on them quickly. As indicated in Figure 7.5, research conducted on service customers has found that more than one-third of all customers who have problems resolved immediately or within 24 hours are "completely satisfied" with the action taken by the company.[25] Unfortunately, many companies require customers to contact multiple employees (a practice often referred to as "ping-ponging") before getting a problem resolved; one study found that an average of 2.9 contacts is typically needed to resolve a complaint.[26] This study also found that, if a problem can be handled by the first contact, customers are satisfied with the firm's response 43 percent of the time; however, once three to five contacts are needed the percentage of customers who are satisfied with the response drops to 27 percent.[27] And, of those customers who use Twitter, a staggering 81 percent expect a same-day response to the complaints they voice via their tweets.[28] The lesson here? A quick response to a service failure can go a long way in appeasing a dissatisfied customer.

The ability to provide immediate responses requires not only systems and procedures that allow quick action but also empowered employees. That is, to enable them to respond quickly, employees should be trained and empowered to solve problems as they occur. A problem not solved can quickly escalate. As we indicated earlier, customers often experience ping-ponging from employee to employee when service failures occur. Empowerment of employees, a practice discussed in more detail in Chapter 11, can often allow for quick responses, reduce (or eliminate) ping-ponging, and help placate dissatisfied customers. The Ritz-Carlton, for example, insists that the first person to hear a complaint from a customer "owns" that complaint until the employee is sure it is resolved. If a maintenance employee hears a complaint from a customer while the employee is in the middle of fixing a light in the hotel corridor, he owns that complaint and is charged with making sure that the problem is handled appropriately before returning to his work.

Another way that problems or complaints can be handled quickly is by building systems that allow customers to actually solve their own service needs and fix their own

FIGURE 7.5 Customer Satisfaction with Timeliness of Firm Responses to Service Failures

Source: 2015 Customer Rage Study, conducted by Customer Care Measurement and Consulting and the Center for Services Leadership at Arizona State University.

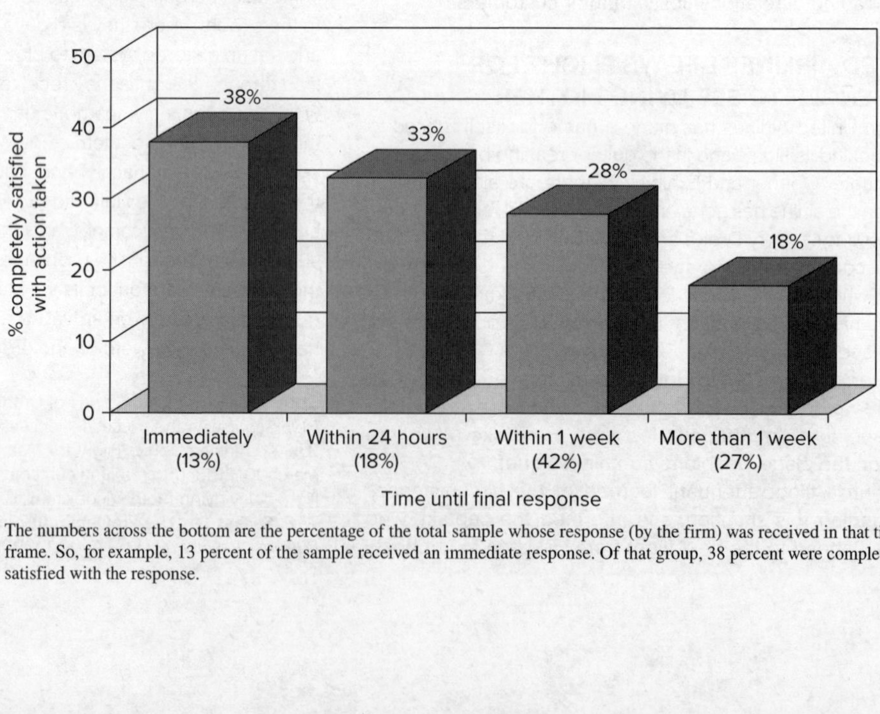

The numbers across the bottom are the percentage of the total sample whose response (by the firm) was received in that time frame. So, for example, 13 percent of the sample received an immediate response. Of that group, 38 percent were completely satisfied with the response.

problems. Typically, this approach is done through technology. Customers directly interact with the company's technology to perform their own customer service, which provides them with instant answers. FedEx uses this strategy for its package tracking service, for example, as does Symantec for its Internet security software products. Our Technology Spotlight features a company that is a master at online customer self-service—Cisco Systems.

Provide Appropriate Communication

Display Understanding and Accountability

In many service failure situations, customers are not looking for extreme actions from the firm; however, they are looking to understand what happened and for firms to be accountable for their actions (or inactions).[29] Research by the Customer Care Measurement, depicted in Table 7.1, has identified the 13 most common "remedies" that customers seek when they experience a serious problem;[30] four of these remedies are to receive their money back, to have the product repaired or service fixed, to be reimbursed for the hassle of having experienced a problem, and to receive a free product or service in the future. Interestingly, however, the other nine remedies listed in Table 7.1—such as an explanation by the firm as to what happened, an apology, or being treated with dignity—cost the firm very little to provide.

These nine nonmonetary remedies consist primarily of providing employees the opportunity to communicate with customers. Understanding and accountability are very important to many customers after a service failure because, if they perceive an injustice has occurred, someone is to blame. Customers expect an apology when things go wrong, and a company that provides one demonstrates courtesy and respect; customers also want to know what the company is going to do to ensure that the problem does not recur.[31] As Table 7.1 suggests, customer discontent can be moderated if

TABLE 7.1 Top 13 Remedies Customers Seek From Firms in Responding to Service Failures

Source: 2020 Customer Rage Study, conducted by Customer Care Measurement and Consulting and the Center for Services Leadership at Arizona State University.

Remedy	% Wanted to Get	% Actually Got	Difference
Money back	35%	14%	−21
An explanation of why the problem occurred	31%	7%	−24
Product repaired/service fixed	31%	13%	−18
An assurance that the problem would not be repeated	27%	4%	−23
An apology	27%	11%	−16
To be treated with dignity	18%	5%	−13
Raise awareness about the problem I experienced	17%	3%	−14
Financial compensation for my lost time, inconvenience, or injury	17%	5%	−12
Free product or service in the future	15%	6%	−9
Just to express my anger/tell my side of the story	12%	3%	−9
A thank you for my business	12%	6%	−6
An answer in everyday language/more than a scripted response to my problem	11%	2%	−9
Offending company put itself in my shoes	8%	2%	−6

Technology Spotlight Cisco Systems—Customers Recover for Themselves

One of the challenges of high growth and increasingly diversified product lines is learning how to handle customers' service needs quickly. This is a challenge continually faced by Cisco, a worldwide leader in enabling people to make powerful connections—whether in business, education, philanthropy, or creativity. Cisco hardware, software, and service offerings are used to create the Internet solutions that make networks possible and provide Cisco clients (and their customers) with easy access to information anywhere, at any time. As networks become mission-critical to Cisco's customers and their business, failures in this environment become extremely costly very quickly. Customers want to know that their problems can be solved immediately, and they want control over the situation and its solution.

To address these issues—high growth coupled with the critical and increasingly complex nature of the business—Cisco has turned to the Internet to build upon its already world-class suite of customer service offerings. The resulting Cisco support website and online communities provide documentation, suggestions, and tools to help troubleshoot and resolve technical issues with Cisco products and technologies. This online offering has set Cisco apart in its industry and helped the company build customer loyalty in a highly competitive environment.

CUSTOMERS USING TECHNOLOGY TO SOLVE PROBLEMS THEMSELVES

Essentially, Cisco has enabled customers to be in charge of much of their own service and support through the company's corporate self-support website and online communities. In most cases, customers can solve their own service problems, with no intervention from Cisco personnel—allowing Cisco staff to focus on complex issues that require hands-on support. Through the Cisco self-support website, access to information is immediate. Such access is important because speed and immediacy are frequently key concerns for customers in these mission-critical situations. The Cisco Community includes (1) community forums, which provide customers with the ability to ask questions and acquire information on problems they have encountered from fellow Cisco customers from other companies, (2) opportunities to acquire the latest support-related knowledge through a variety of programs and blogs led by Cisco experts, and (3) technical support documents and tutorials published by Cisco experts and partners on such issues as local area networks, network management, security, and data storage.

Over the past decade Cisco has evolved to provide to a unified customer experience that is channel and location agnostic by bringing together all of the previously mentioned modalities of support. Customers can contact Cisco for support through any modality (i.e., communities, self-support, agents) and get all of the right support without having to jump back and forth between various channels. Cisco refers to this approach as Digital Support—which it sees as having three components.

The first component is a *unified customer experience*. Digital Support provides Cisco with the ability to offer a unified support experience for its customers and partners across all the modalities it provides. With Digital Support, all of Cisco's support channels have been coordinated to provide a seamless and consistent experience for its customers.

Although customers can use the telephone to speak to a call center agent, more than ever they are demanding real-time access to information and expertise when they encounter problems and expect to resolve them through a variety of channels. Digital Support provides Cisco customers support at a time that is convenient to them, whether they are "on the road," helping their clients, or troubleshooting on site. One such channel is the Cisco Community. The community is continually available and is up-to-date in its understanding of issues and resolutions—even call center agents frequently look to the community to help them diagnose problems. Those

firms simply communicate well with customers. Customers clearly value such communication, because these nonmonetary remedies are positively related to satisfaction with the complaint process, continued loyalty, and positive word-of-mouth communication.[32] Of course, firms need to put more effort into their response than simply in the community who are particularly frequent contributors to helping others are given the title of "Cisco VIP." These people have a "badge" placed next to their user name on the communities; the badge indicates their VIP status and displays the category in which they earned their status. ("Cisco Designated VIPs" are the top contributors and are often invited to advise the communities on community direction, features, and other items.)

The second component of Digital Support is *anytime, anywhere support*. Recognizing customer needs for anytime/anywhere engagement with Cisco expertise and tools, Cisco has expanded its customer support experience into social media and mobile devices. Indeed, customers are increasingly using these tools when troubleshooting problems they encounter while using Cisco products. Often these issues arise when they are away from the office, making it difficult to access Cisco resources from a more traditional personal computer or laptop. A few years ago, Cisco launched applications (apps) for technical support on both the iPhone and the iPad. The ease of use offered by the iPad app has been a hit—particularly among younger customers and those in emerging markets. When they encounter problems, Cisco customers can also participate in discussion forums, get real-time access to Cisco experts, and access technical support resources directly from Facebook, Twitter, LinkedIn, and YouTube.

The third component is *proactive and preemptive support* provided by Application Programmable Interfaces (APIs) and Support Automation with advanced diagnostics executed on the customer's device. The APIs permit an application within the customer's environment to connect to Cisco and obtain information concerning the health of the device, status of their support contract with Cisco, any security vulnerabilities their devices are susceptible to, and other information important to managing their devices.

Support Automation takes the concept of connectivity between Cisco and the customer to another level by enabling both Cisco technicians and the customer's own support team to connect to the customer's network devices. Once connected, technical procedures are executed by Cisco call center experts to collect relevant device data, diagnose errors, and send the information to Cisco. With the results in hand, the customer and call center engineer can take corrective action to restore interrupted service. This data can also be collected as part of a periodic checkup to maintain optimal health of the customer's environment. The intent is for customers to be thinking about and exposed to issues they may face, so that customers can resolve problems before they occur—the ultimate service recovery!

THE RESULTS

The goal of the Digital Support approach is to make Cisco support seamless to all of its customers and allow them to assemble a wealth of knowledge, participate in a stream of forum discussions, and learn from technical experts in the community to resolve whatever problems they face. Through its continual innovation in providing service to its customers on the Internet, Cisco has recognized tremendous benefits. Currently, 85 percent of customer support problems are handled via the Cisco.com self-support site and communities, using intellectual property provided by Cisco experts and self-help tools that allow customers to diagnose and solve their own problems. Customer satisfaction and loyalty have increased with the introduction of Internet-based customer service and support communities, productivity has increased as Cisco Support Community has helped resolve customer issues, and the company saves approximately $300 million per year through case deflection to its communities and self-support site. This is truly a win–win situation for Cisco's bottom line, its employees, and its business customers.

Sources: https://community.cisco.com accessed November 2021; e-mail communications from Mike Friday, Director of Product Management, Cisco Services, June 2016.

apologizing well—such as providing appropriate compensation—if they want to fully recover from a severe service failure.[33]

Supply Adequate Explanations

In many service failure situations, customers try to understand why the failure occurred. Explanations can help to diffuse negative reactions and convey respect for the customer.[34] Research suggests that when the firm's ability to provide an adequate outcome is not successful, further dissatisfaction can be reduced if an adequate explanation is provided to the customer.[35] For an explanation to be perceived as adequate, it must possess two primary characteristics. First, the *content* of the explanation must be appropriate; relevant facts and pertinent information are important in helping the customer understand what occurred. Second, the *style* of the delivery of the explanation, or how the explanation is delivered, can also reduce customer dissatisfaction. Style includes the personal characteristics of the explanation givers, including their credibility and sincerity. Explanations perceived by customers as honest, sincere, and not manipulative are generally the most effective. For example, if a customer were to be kept waiting at the doctor's office for a long time, the customer may start to feel undervalued or disregarded if there is no explanation for the wait. However, if an employee came and apologized for the wait and kindly explained that a patient with an emergency had come in, then the customer would be more likely to understand the extenuating circumstances and be more tolerant of the wait.

Treat Customers Fairly

Customers also want justice and fairness in handling their complaints. Service research has documented three specific types of justice that customers are looking for following their complaints: *outcome fairness, procedural fairness,* and *interactional fairness.*[36] *Outcome fairness* concerns the results that customers receive from their complaints; *procedural fairness* refers to the policies, rules, and timeliness of the complaint process; and *interactional fairness* focuses on the interpersonal treatment received during the complaint process.[37] Exhibit 7.4 shows examples of each type of fairness and our Global Feature discusses how customers across cultures view fair service recovery.

Outcome Fairness

In their service recovery efforts firms should provide customers with outcomes, or compensation, that match the level of their dissatisfaction. This compensation can take the form of actual monetary compensation, future free service, reduced charges, repairs, and/or replacements. Customers expect equity in the exchange—that is, they want to feel that the company has "paid" for its mistakes in a manner at least equal to what the customer has suffered. Customers expect equality—that is, they want to be compensated in a manner similar to other customers who have experienced the same type of service failure. They also appreciate it when a company gives them choices in terms of compensation. For example, a student whose senior portraits taken by a professional studio are not properly printed could be offered the choice of a refund or a free sitting and package of portraits as compensation for the original portraits not arriving as promised. Outcome fairness is especially important in settings in which customers have particularly negative emotional responses to the service failure; in such situations recovery efforts should focus on improving the outcome from the customer's point of view.[38]

For example, an Amazon customer ordered a brand new PlayStation for Christmas, which was duly delivered to his porch. However, the package was stolen before the customer had a chance to bring it inside. Amazon compensated the customer by rush-delivering a second PlayStation, free of charge, in time for Christmas. This customer

Exhibit 7.4 Three Types of Fairness Customers Assess in Service Recovery

	Fair	Unfair
Outcome fairness: the results that customers receive from complaints	*"The waitress agreed that there was a problem. She took the sandwiches back to the kitchen and had them replaced. We were also given a free drink."* *"When I was checking out I complained at the front desk about being awakened at 3:45 a.m. They apologized, informed me that the fire department had been called because of an issue across the hall, and offered me 2,000 bonus points for the inconvenience."*	*"Their refusal to refund our money or make up for the inconvenience and cold food was inexcusable."* *"Once we were onboard the pilot announced that the plane had equipment problems; later the customer service rep told me that I would not be able to fly out until the next day. Since I would have to spend an extra night, I asked the airline to at least cover my taxi fare to return to my brother's house. They refused."*
Procedural fairness: the policies, rules, and timeliness of the complaint process	*"The hotel manager said that it didn't matter to her who was at fault, she would take responsibility for the problem immediately."* *"The product came with a lifetime guarantee. However, I could not find my original receipt when it stopped working. The customer service rep said I simply needed to take a picture of the defect and send it to them, along with my address, and they would send me a new one—no questions asked."*	*"They should have assisted me with the problem instead of giving me a phone number to call. No one returned my calls, and I never had a chance to speak to a real person."* *"I returned the next day to inform them that they had made a mistake on my order. Rather than deal with the situation on the spot, while I was right there in front of them, the manager asked me if I had gone online to file a complaint. When I said "no" she said that is what I needed to do."*
Interactional fairness: the interpersonal treatment received during the complaint process	*"The loan officer was very courteous, knowledgeable, and considerate—he kept me informed about the progress of the complaint."* *"I was having problems getting my device to sync with my phone. When I called to get help, the telephone rep was very personable, and patiently walked me through the process."*	*"The person who handled my complaint about the faulty air conditioner repair wasn't going to do anything about it and didn't seem to care."* *"I had contacted "Dan" several times over the course of two weeks about this problem. He repeated told me: "Don't worry" and "I will take care of you." However, he quit returning my telephone calls and responding to my email messages. His actions conveyed the message that he really didn't consider my problem to be a big priority."*

Source: Adapted from S. S. Tax and S. W. Brown, "Recovering and Learning from Service Failure," *Sloan Management Review* 40 (Fall 1998), p. 79, Massachusetts Institute of Technology.

Global Feature Service Recovery across Cultures

Service failure is inevitable, no matter what the context, country, or culture. Appropriate service recovery procedures, therefore, are needed by all firms. Service firms operating in several countries, as well as those operating in multi-ethnic countries like the United States, United Kingdom, or Australia, need to be sensitive to the cultural diversity and subsequently differing expectations of service and of service recovery.

ATTRIBUTION EXPECTATIONS

When service failures occur, customers spontaneously infer or attribute blame for the unexpected event. Researchers have explored service recovery across cultures and found in Western countries, when the failure is caused by some external factor beyond the control of the service firm, customers will attribute the problem to the context or situation surrounding the service failure—particularly if an explanation is offered by the firm as to what happened. Such action can diminish the blame customers attribute to the firm and its staff, and thus not detract from their perceptions of overall perceived quality. For customers from Eastern cultures, however, a causal explanation has relatively little impact on where the blame for the failure is attributed. These customers prefer other remedies, such as a speedy resolution to the problem and a genuine apology from a manager (rather than a frontline employee) to regain "face" in the eyes of their family and friends. Eastern customers also have a lower tolerance to uncertain and ambiguous situations. Thus, when a failure is being remedied, these customers would prefer having a sense of control—the firm can provide this by keeping them informed of exactly what is being done to rectify the situation.

FAIRNESS EXPECTATIONS

Outcome Fairness

Scholars also investigated service recovery fairness issues. In their studies they found Western (i.e., American) customers are more interested in and expect to receive tangible compensation (i.e., a discount) when a service failure occurs than are Eastern (i.e., Thai or Malaysian) customers. Offering compensation is particularly effective in restoring a sense of fairness among American customers; apparently, American consumers are particularly concerned with outcome fairness. Indeed, American customers are generally more assertive and more used to asking for reparation than consumers from Eastern cultures. Previous research on service recovery in Western contexts consistently showed that compensation has a positive effect on postrecovery satisfaction and loyalty. Eastern customers, who typically tend to be high on uncertainty avoidance, prefer other types of remedies when service failure occurs. In Eastern cultures there is a tendency to focus on avoidance of losses rather than on individual gains. East Asian customers emphasize the need to fit in with others and to avoid conflict and confrontation.

Interactional Fairness

The research suggests that, in Western cultures, offering an explanation for service failure might shift the customer's focus away from thinking that the service provider is incompetent, uncaring, or lazy. Such an explanation tends to cause Western customers to pay more attention to the situation as a cause of the failure. Eastern customers, however, are more likely to be aware of situational constraints, seek to maintain social harmony, and avoid causing a loss of face. For them, interactional fairness appears to be particularly salient. Thus, providing an explanation and treating the offended Eastern customers in a courteous, formal, and empathetic manner is more important than the compensation offered.

Procedural Fairness

For service firms operating in the United States, hassle-free and fast recovery procedures that lead to compensation for any losses or inconveniences triggered by a service failure are preferred by customers. Although compensation is generally the primary driver of American customers' fairness perceptions, speed and convenience in the recovery process also appear to be valued. In Eastern cultures, a genuine apology from a manager (rather than a customer-contact employee) is particularly desirable; such

considered the final outcome (the timely replacement of the package contents) to be more than adequate, given the stolen package was not Amazon's fault.[39]

On the other hand, customers can be uncomfortable if they are overly compensated. Early in its experience with service guarantees, Domino's Pizza offered not to charge for a pizza if the driver arrived after the 30-minute guaranteed delivery time. Many customers were not comfortable with this level of compensation, especially if the driver was only a few minutes late. In this case, the compensation seemed disproportionate compared to the failure that occurred. For a while Domino's changed the a procedure allows customers to regain "face" in the eyes of their family and friends. Eastern customers would also prefer to have a sense of control, so having management constantly inform them of what is being done to rectify the situation is also appealing to them.

CUSTOMER RAGE

Customer rage, a phenomenon occurring more frequently across the globe, has received increasing attention in recent years. Rage episodes have serious consequences not only for frontline employees facing the brunt of the outburst but also for the service brand. Other researchers examined customer rage in both Eastern and Western cultures; they found that Eastern consumers (from China and Thailand) tend to be slow to exhibit anger when confronted with service failures or poor service recovery but, once angered, their rage expressions toward frontline service workers tend to be more overt, aggressive, and vengeful than Western customers (from Australia and the United States).

The researchers suggest that people from Eastern collectivist cultures use a nonverbal communication style, where most of the message is either in the situational context or internalized in the person; very little communication is given directly in explicit messages. They found such nonverbal expressions to be associated with escalating rage episodes. However, in Western cultures, communication tends to be more explicit and relies mostly on the spoken word, meaning that a buildup of rage emotions can be more easily detected. They also point out that "face" is a fundamentally important concept in Eastern cultures, and understanding ways of coping with a loss of face (following poor service) and restoring face is central to avoiding rage episodes. In Eastern cultures, loss of face (i.e., being shamed) can have disastrous personal consequences and is ideally avoided at all costs. The attention to face in Eastern cultures is so extensive that it is a dominant force in shaping effective interpersonal encounters and behavior. In contrast, people from Western cultures pay relatively little attention to face.

So, what are frontline employees to do to try to limit customer rage? This chapter addresses several ways to deal with customers from Western cultures. When dealing with Eastern cultures, employees need to be trained to be vigilant and observe contextual, nonverbal cues such as facial expressions (e.g., frowning, displays of disappointment) and body postures. Of course, detecting negative emotions and subtle expressions (and thus customer dissatisfaction) with Eastern customers is often difficult to assess. So, when an incident has progressed to where expressions—such as rolling of eyes or raising of the voice—are evident, employees need to immediately recognize these as important signals of impending rage. And, when dealing with loss of face, the researchers suggest a sincere apology from a senior manager/supervisor is an important part of any communication behavior in hierarchical, power distance cultures where face saving is very important.

In service recovery, as in any service situation, companies need to be sensitive to the fact that culture and other factors play a role. As these studies suggest, customers in all cultures expect strong service recovery but preferences for the type of recovery or which fairness dimension to emphasize may vary.

Sources: A. S. Mattila and P. G. Patterson, "Service Recovery and Fairness Perceptions in Collectivist and Individualist Contexts," *Journal of Service Research* 6 (May 2004), pp. 336–346; A. S. Mattila and P. G. Patterson, "The Impact of Culture on Consumers' Perceptions of Service Recovery Efforts," *Journal of Retailing* 80 (Fall 2004), pp. 196–206; P. G. Patterson, M. K. Brady, and J. R. McColl-Kennedy, "Geysers or Bubbling Hot Springs? A Cross-Cultural Examination of Customer Rage from Eastern and Western Perspectives," *Journal of Service Research* 19 (August 2016), pp. 243–259. For further insights on how culture can influence perceived fairness in service failure settings, also see: S. B. Borah, S. Prakhya, and A. Sharma, "Leveraging Service Recovery Strategies to Reduce Customer Churn in an Emerging Market," *Journal of the Academy of Marketing Science* 48 (September 2020), pp. 848–868; and E. Chebat, Y. Roth, and J. C. Chebat, "How Culture Moderates the Effects of Justice in Service Recovery," *Review of Marketing Science* 18 (January 2020), pp. 21–41.

compensation to a more reasonable $3 off for late deliveries. Later the time guarantee was dropped altogether because of problems it caused with employees who were driving too fast to make their deliveries.

Procedural Fairness

In addition to fair compensation, firms should treat customers fairly in terms of policies, rules, and timeliness of the complaint process. Customers want easy access to the complaint process, and they want things handled quickly, preferably by the first person they contact. They appreciate companies that can and will adapt their procedures, so that the recovery effort can match their individual circumstances. In some cases, particularly in business-to-business services, companies actually ask the customer, "What can we do to compensate you for our failure?" Many times what the customer asks for is actually less than the company might have expected.

Fair procedures are characterized by clarity, speed, and absence of hassles. Unfair procedures are those that customers perceive as slow, prolonged, illogical, and inconvenient. Customers also feel it is unfair if they have to prove their case—when the company's assumption seems to be they are wrong or lying until they can prove otherwise.

Interactional Fairness

Above and beyond providing fair compensation and hassle-free, quick procedures, firms need to treat customers politely, with care, honesty, and dignity, during the service recovery process. This form of fairness can dominate the others if customers feel the company and its employees have uncaring attitudes and have done little to try to resolve the problem. This type of behavior on the part of employees may seem strange—why would they treat customers rudely or in an uncaring manner under these circumstances? Often it is due to lack of training and empowerment—a frustrated frontline employee who has no authority to compensate the customer may easily respond in an aloof or uncaring manner, especially if the customer is angry and/or rude.

In the Trader Joe's case in Exhibit 7.3, the Trader Joe's employee was caring and helpful as he suggested additional items for the customer's snowed-in father. The employee even delivered the groceries, though delivery is not normally part of his job description. Finally, by wishing the customer Merry Christmas, the employee gave the experience a personal touch and showed that he cared about the customer.

Cultivate Relationships with Customers

In Chapter 6, we discussed the importance of developing long-term relationships with customers. One additional benefit of relationship marketing is that if the firm fails in service delivery, those customers who have a strong relationship with the firm are often more forgiving of service failures and more open to the firm's service recovery efforts. That is, it may be easier to "fix the customer" if the firm has established a strong relationship with that customer; indeed, research suggests that strong customer–firm relationships can help shield the firm from the negative effects of failures on customer satisfaction.[40] To illustrate, one study demonstrated that the presence of rapport between customers and employees provided several service recovery benefits, including increased postfailure satisfaction, increased loyalty intentions, and decreased negative word-of-mouth communication.[41] Another study found that customers who expect the relationship to continue also tend to have lower service recovery expectations and may demand less immediate compensation for a failure because they consider the balance of equity across a longer time horizon.[42] Thus, cultivation of strong customer relationships can provide an important buffer to service firms when failures occur.[43]

SERVICE RECOVERY STRATEGIES: (2) FIX THE (UNDERLYING) PROBLEM(S)

Often the most pressing and immediate need in service recovery is to "fix the customer." However, in many situations the actual problem created by the poor service delivery also needs to be fixed. This may require reworking, redoing, or redelivering the service, if possible, to provide what the customer initially expected. And, if the problem is likely to recur for this or other customers, then the service delivery process may need to be fixed, too. This section highlights strategies that can be used to help the firm "fix the underlying problem(s)" both in the short term and in the long term.

Encourage and Track Complaints

Even if an organization aims for 100 percent service quality, failures occur. A critical component of a service recovery strategy is thus to encourage and track complaints.

Firms can utilize a number of ways to encourage and track complaints. Customer research can be designed specifically for this purpose through satisfaction surveys, critical incident studies, and lost customer research, as discussed in Chapter 5. As an alternative to using toll-free call centers and e-mail, in recent years customers have taken to social media to complain. Firms are using a variety of new technologies to track, analyze, sort, and even respond to customer complaints made online. For example, Amazon uses artificial intelligence to identify key words in online complaints and then suggests an appropriate response to the complainer. Similarly, British Airways can retrieve from its database information on each customer as well as data regarding what solutions were offered in the past in similar situations to understand how to best satisfy the customer.[44]

In some cases technology can anticipate problems and complaints before they happen, allowing service employees to diagnose problems before the customer recognizes they exist. At companies such as IBM, John Deere, and Caterpillar, "smart" systems have been implemented to anticipate equipment failures and to send out an electronic alert to the local field technician with the nature of the problem as well as which parts and tools will be needed to make the repair—a repair the customer does not yet know is needed.

Learn from Recovery Experiences

Service recovery situations are more than just opportunities to fix flawed services and strengthen ties with customers. They can also provide valuable information for improving service delivery. By tracking service recovery efforts and solutions, managers can often learn about systematic problems in the delivery system that need fixing. By conducting root-cause analysis, firms can identify the sources of the problems and modify processes, sometimes almost eliminating the need for recovery. At Ritz-Carlton Hotels, all employees carry service recovery forms called "instant action forms" with them at all times, so that they can immediately record service failures and suggest actions to address them. Each employee "owns" any complaint that he or she receives and is responsible for seeing that service recovery occurs. In turn, the employees report to management these sources of service failure and the remedies. At Hampton by Hilton hotels, whenever the service guarantee (see Figure 7.6) is invoked, the reason for the customer's dissatisfaction is recorded as part of the process and the information forwarded to management. Such information is then entered into a database and analyzed to identify patterns and systemic service issues that need to be fixed. If common themes are observed across a number of failure situations, changes are made to service processes or attributes. In addition, at the Ritz-Carlton information about the service failure is entered into the customer's personal data file, so when that customer stays at any Ritz-Carlton again (no matter what hotel), employees can be aware of the previous experience, ensuring that it does not happen again for that customer.

Learn from Lost Customers

Another key component of an effective service recovery strategy is to learn from customers who defect or decide to leave. Formal marketing research to discover the reasons customers have left can assist in preventing failures in the future. This type of research is difficult, even painful for companies, however. No one really likes to

FIGURE 7.6
The 100 Percent Hampton Guarantee

Hilton Worldwide Holdings Inc; Tang Ming Tung/DigitalVision/Getty Images

examine their failures. Yet such examination is essential for preventing the same mistakes and losing more customers in the future.[45]

As presented in Chapter 5, lost customer research typically involves in-depth probing of customers to determine their true reasons for leaving. This information is most effectively obtained by depth interviews, administered by skilled interviewers who truly understand the business. It may be best to have this type of research done by senior people in the company, particularly in business-to-business contexts in which customers are large and the impact of even one lost customer is great. The type of depth analysis often requires a series of "why" questions or "tell me more about that" questions to get at the actual, core reason for the customer's defection.[46]

In conducting this kind of research, a firm must focus on important or profitable customers who have left—not just everyone who has left the company. An insurance company in Australia once began this type of research to learn about their lost customers, only to find that the customers they were losing tended to be their least profitable customers anyway. They quickly determined that depth research on how to keep these unprofitable customers would not be a good investment!

Make the Service Fail-Safe—Do It Right the First Time!

The first rule of service quality, and arguably the best service recovery strategy, is to do it right the first time. In this way recovery is unnecessary, customers get what they expect, and the costs of redoing the service and compensating for errors can be avoided. As you have already learned, reliability, or doing it right the first time, is the most important dimension of service quality across industry contexts.[47] Indeed, research suggests that many customers stay in a relationship because they have not experienced a (negative) critical incident.[48]

A noted service operations expert suggests that services adopt the quality notion of *poka yokes* to improve service reliability.[49] Poka yokes are automatic warnings or controls in place to ensure that mistakes are not made; essentially, they are quality control mechanisms, typically used on assembly lines. Poka yokes can be devised in service settings to "mistakeproof" the service, ensure that essential procedures are followed, and ensure that service steps are carried out in the proper order and in a timely manner. In a hospital setting, numerous poka yokes ensure that procedures are followed to avoid potentially life-threatening mistakes. For example, trays for surgical instruments have indentations for specific instruments, and each instrument is nested in its appropriate spot. In this way surgeons and their staff know that all instruments are in their places prior to closing the patient's incision.[50]

Similarly, poka yokes can be devised to ensure that the tangibles associated with the service are clean and well maintained and that documents are accurate and up-to-date. Poka yokes can also be implemented for employee behaviors (checklists, role-playing and practice, reminder signs). In addition, poka yokes can even be used to ensure that customers perform effectively (e.g., note that many restaurants color-code their ketchup and mustard bottles to avoid having customers use the "wrong" condiment). Many of the strategies we discuss in Parts 4 and 5 of the text ("Aligning Service Design and Standards" and "Delivering and Performing Service") are aimed at ensuring service reliability and can be viewed as applications of the basic fail-safe notion of poka yokes.

Even more fundamentally, it is important for a firm to create a culture of doing it right the first time. Within such a culture, everyone understands the importance of reliability, everyone aims to satisfy every customer and looks for ways to improve service, and everyone fully understands and appreciates the "relationship value of a customer" concept that was presented in Chapter 6. Thus, they are motivated to provide quality service *every time* and to *every customer.*

SERVICE RECOVERY STRATEGIES: (3) OFFER A SERVICE GUARANTEE

A guarantee is a particular type of recovery strategy that can be used to both "fix the customer" and "fix the underlying problem." In a business context, a *guarantee* is a pledge or assurance that a product offered by a firm will perform as promised and, if not, then some form of reparation will be undertaken by the firm. Although guarantees are relatively common for manufactured products, they have also been increasingly used for services in recent years.[51] Some people might believe that a service simply cannot be guaranteed, given its intangible and variable nature. What would be guaranteed? With a tangible product, the customer is guaranteed that it will perform as promised and, if not, that it can be returned. With a service, it is generally not possible to receive a return or to "undo" what has been performed. Such skepticism about service guarantees has been dispelled, however, as firms continue to find they can guarantee their service and that there are tremendous benefits for doing so.

Companies are finding that effective service guarantees can complement the company's service recovery strategy—serving as one tool to help support the service recovery strategies depicted in Figure 7.4. The Hampton by Hilton guarantee shown in Figure 7.6 is an example of such an effective guarantee.

Characteristics of Effective Guarantees

At a minimum, a service guarantee should include a promise regarding the service and appropriate remuneration if the promise is broken. With these two elements in mind, certain characteristics tend to make some guarantees more effective than others. The most effective guarantees tend to have similar characteristics, including having limited restrictions, as well as being meaningful, easy to understand, and easy to invoke.[52]

Limited Restrictions and Exclusions

Effective guarantees should be free of the "if, and, or but" conditions and exclusions associated with many legal documents.[53] Service guarantees with a limited number of restrictions are easier for customers to understand and easier for a firm to communicate than guarantees that have numerous exclusions or conditions. Some guarantees

Exhibit 7.5 H&R Block: We Guarantee Your Maximum Refund. And So Much More.

At H&R Block, we have your back. That's why we offer so many guarantees. Whether you file taxes in person, online, or with our tax software, you can be sure these H&R Block guarantees are in place to protect you during the process.

- **Maximum Refund Guarantee:** If customers discover an H&R Block error on their return that entitles them to a larger refund (or smaller tax liability), H&R Block will refund the tax prep fee for that return and file an amended return at no additional charge.
- **100% Accuracy Guarantee:** If H&R Block makes an error on a customer's return, the firm will reimburse the customer for any resulting penalties plus interest.
- **100% Satisfaction Guarantee:** H&R Block is so certain their customers will be satisfied with the tax preparation services, customers only have to pay H&R Block if they actually file the return the firm prepares for them.

https://www.hrblock.com/guarantees/, February 2022

H&R Block offers multiple guarantees to its customers (e.g., for clients who file taxes in person, online, or using the H&R Block tax software).

can appear as if they were written by the legal department (and often are), with all kinds of restrictions, proof required, and limitations. Guarantees with a large number of restrictions are generally not effective, and they tend to lose power in direct proportion to the number of conditions they contain.

Meaningful

An effective guarantee should be *meaningful.* Guaranteeing what is obvious or expected is not meaningful to customers. For example, a water delivery company offered a guarantee to deliver water on the day promised or a free jug of water would be provided next time. In that industry, delivery on the day scheduled was an expectation nearly always met by every competitor—thus, the guarantee was not meaningful to the customer. It was a bit like guaranteeing four wheels on an automobile! The payout, if a problem occurs, should also be meaningful. Customers expect to be reimbursed in a manner that fully compensates them for their dissatisfaction, their time, and even for the hassle involved. One of us has offered university students a guarantee in our Service Marketing classes; compensation for poor service, which includes reimbursement for the cost of the three-credit course, is generally perceived by students as quite meaningful.[54]

Easy to Understand

A firm's guarantee should also be *easy to understand* and communicate to both customers and employees. If the wording is confusing or the language within the guarantee is verbose, neither customers nor employees may be clear as to what is being guaranteed. For example, H&R Block's 100% Satisfaction Guarantee (see Exhibit 7.5) clearly states that customers only have to pay the firm if they choose to file the return that H&R Block has prepared for them.

Easy to Invoke

Similarly, an effective guarantee should be *easy to invoke.* Puget Sound Energy (an energy utility company based in the U.S. state of Washington) offers multiple guarantees to its more than one million customers; for example, the company offers an "appointment service guarantee" that is both easy to understand and easy to invoke: "We'll credit your bill $50 if we don't keep an appointment to install new service, reconnect existing service, or inspect natural gas equipment."[55] Requiring customers to write a detailed letter and/or provide documented proof of service failure are common pitfalls that make invoking a guarantee time-consuming and not worth it to the customer, particularly if the dollar value of the service is relatively low.

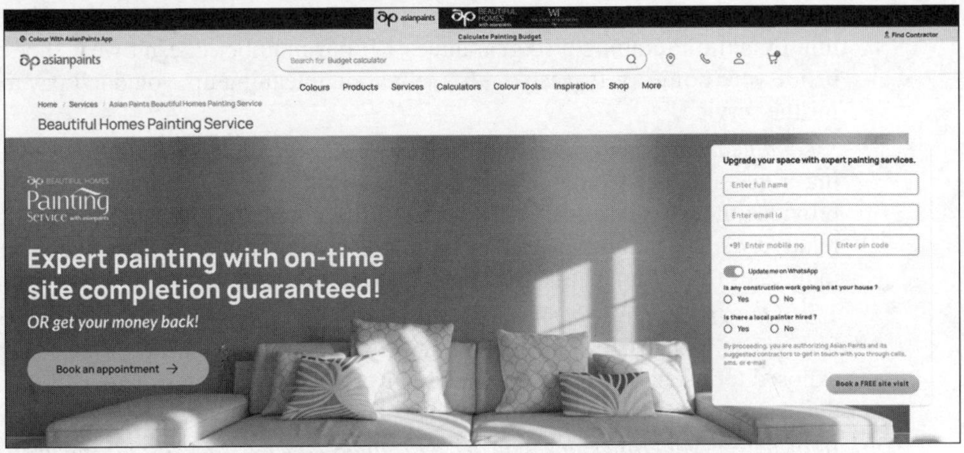

Asian Paints: On-time completion & 1-year warranty with Beautiful Homes Platinum Plan

https://www.asianpaints.com/services/asian-paints-safe-painting-service.html

Types of Service Guarantees

Service guarantees can be *unconditional satisfaction guarantees* or *service attribute guarantees.* For unconditional satisfaction guarantees, any aspect of the service, whether related to the outcome or the delivery process, should be to the customer's liking—there are no limits or conditions. The Hampton by Hilton guarantee is an unconditional satisfaction guarantee. In another context, Inflectra, a company that provides software to a variety of businesses, offers its clients an unconditional guarantee for its services.[56] If clients are unhappy, they can request their money back for the service. Professional Staffing Group offers an unconditional guarantee to any client using its staffing service; if the client organization is unhappy with the person assigned to the client, the client is not billed. Lands' End, a catalog retailer, has abbreviated its guarantee to "Guaranteed. Period."

In other cases, firms offer guarantees focused on particular attributes of the service that are important to customers. FedEx offers a money-back guarantee if a package is not delivered by the delivery commitment agreement. Asian Paints offers a guaranteed on-time site completion along with a 1-year service warranty on its AP Beautiful Homes Painting Services' platinum plan with assurance of wall protection and product warranty.[57]

Benefits of Service Guarantees

Service organizations are now recognizing that guarantees can serve not only as a marketing tool but also as a means for defining, cultivating, and maintaining quality throughout an organization. The benefits to the company of an effective service guarantee are numerous:[58]

- *A good guarantee forces the company to focus on its customers.* To develop a meaningful guarantee, the company must know what is important to its customers—what they expect and value. In many cases "satisfaction" is guaranteed, but for the guarantee to work effectively, the company must clearly understand what satisfaction means for its customers (what they value and expect).
- *An effective guarantee sets clear standards for the organization.* It prompts the company to clearly define what it expects of its employees and to communicate that expectation to them. The guarantee gives employees service-oriented goals

that can align employee behaviors with customer strategies. For example, Benjamin Franklin Plumbing also guarantees: "If our plumber doesn't wear shoe covers inside your home, or leaves your home without cleaning up, you don't pay a penny for the service."

- *A good guarantee generates immediate and relevant feedback from customers.* Having a guarantee can provide an incentive for customers to complain and thereby provides more representative feedback to the company than simply relying on a relatively small number of customers to voice their concerns. The guarantee communicates to customers that they have the right to complain.
- *When the guarantee is invoked there is an instant opportunity to recover.* Dissatisfaction can perhaps be controlled, or at least not allowed to grow, if the customer is exposed to instant recovery. A quick recovery can go a long way toward satisfying the customer and helping retain loyalty.
- *Information generated through the guarantee can be tracked and integrated into continuous improvement efforts.* Guarantees can provide a somewhat structured mechanism for listening to the customer, thus helping to close the listening gap. A feedback link between customers and service operations decisions can be strengthened through the guarantee.
- *For customers, the guarantee reduces their sense of risk and builds confidence in the organization.* Because services are intangible and often highly personal or ego-involving, customers seek information and cues that will help reduce their sense of uncertainty. Guarantees have been shown to reduce risk and increase positive evaluation of the service prior to purchase.[59]

The bottom line for the company is that an effective guarantee can affect profitability through building customer awareness and loyalty, through positive word-of-mouth communication, and through reduction in costs as service improvements are made and service recovery expenses are reduced. Indirectly, the guarantee can reduce costs of employee turnover through creating a more positive service culture.

When to Use (or Not Use) a Guarantee

Service guarantees are not appropriate for every company and certainly not in every service situation. Before putting a guarantee strategy in place, a firm needs to address a number of important questions (see Exhibit 7.6). A guarantee is probably *not* the right strategy when:

- *Existing service quality in the company is poor.* Before instituting a guarantee, the company should fix any significant quality problems. A guarantee will certainly draw attention to failures and to poor service quality, so the costs of implementing the guarantee could easily outweigh any benefits. These costs include actual monetary payouts to customers for poor service as well as costs associated with customer goodwill.
- *A guarantee does not fit the company's image.* If the company already has a reputation for very high quality, and in fact implicitly guarantees its service, then a formal guarantee is most likely unnecessary and provides limited benefits.[60] For example, if the Four Seasons Hotel were to offer an explicit guarantee, it could confuse customers who already expect the highest quality, implicitly guaranteed, from this high-end hotel chain. Research suggests that the benefits of offering a guarantee for luxury hotels like the Four Seasons or the Ritz-Carlton may be significantly less than the benefits that a hotel of lesser quality would offer, and the benefits might not be justified by the costs.[61]

Exhibit 7.6 Questions to Consider in Implementing a Service Guarantee

DECIDING WHO DECIDES

- Is there a guarantee champion in the company?
- Is senior management committed to a guarantee?
- Is the guarantee design a team effort?
- Are customers providing input?

WHEN DOES A GUARANTEE MAKE SENSE?

- How high are quality standards?
- Can we afford a guarantee?
- How high is customer risk?
- Are competitors offering a guarantee?
- Is the company's culture compatible with a guarantee?

WHAT TYPE OF GUARANTEE SHOULD WE OFFER?

- Should we offer an unconditional guarantee or a specific-outcome one?
- Is our service measurable?
- What should our specific guarantee be about?
- What are the uncontrollables?
- Is the company particularly susceptible to unreasonable triggerings?
- What should the payout be?
- Will a refund send the wrong message?
- Could a full refund make customers feel guilty?
- Is the guarantee easy to invoke?

Source: A. L. Ostrom and C. W. L. Hart, "Service Guarantees: Research and Practice," in *Handbook of Services Marketing and Management*, ed. D. Iacobucci and T. Swartz (Thousand Oaks, CA: Sage Publications, 2000).

- *Service quality is truly uncontrollable.* Service providers can encounter situations in which service quality is truly uncontrollable. To illustrate, it would not be a good practice for a university to guarantee that all MBA students will get the job they want immediately upon graduation—it cannot control what jobs are available in the marketplace. Similarly, an airline flying out of Chicago in the winter would probably not guarantee on-time departure because of the unpredictability and uncontrollability of the weather.
- *Potential exists for customer abuse of the guarantee.* Fear of opportunistic customer behavior, including customer cheating or fraudulent invocation of service guarantees, is a common reason that firms hesitate to offer guarantees.[62] One study found that guarantees are more likely to be abused when offered in situations in which a large percentage of customers are not regular (repeat) customers.[63] However, customer abuse of service guarantees is fairly minimal and not at all widespread.[64]
- *Costs of the guarantee outweigh the benefits.* As it would with any quality investment, the company will want to carefully calculate expected costs (payouts for failures and costs of making improvements) against anticipated benefits (customer loyalty, quality improvements, attraction of new customers, word-of-mouth advertising).
- *Customers perceive little risk in the service.* Guarantees are usually most effective when customers are uncertain about the company and/or the quality of its services. A service guarantee can allay uncertainties and help reduce risk.[65] If customers perceive little risk, if the service is relatively inexpensive with many potential alternative providers, and if quality is relatively invariable, then a guarantee will likely produce little effectiveness for the company other than perhaps some promotional value.

SWITCHING VERSUS STAYING FOLLOWING SERVICE RECOVERY

Ultimately, how a service failure is handled and the customer's reaction to the recovery effort can influence future decisions to remain loyal or to switch to another provider. In a study of airline customers, researchers found that those who were not satisfied with service recovery were four times more likely to believe their relationship with the airline was weakened or broken, and more likely to switch to a different airline, than were those who were happy with how their problems were addressed.[66] Whether customers switch to a new provider following service failure will depend, in addition, on a number of other factors. The magnitude and criticality of the failure will clearly be a factor in future repurchase decisions. The more serious the failure, the more likely the customer is to switch, no matter what the recovery effort.[67]

The nature of the customer's relationship with the firm may also influence whether the customer stays or switches providers. Research suggests that customers who have "true relationships" with their service providers are more forgiving of poorly handled service failures and are less likely to switch than are those who have a "pseudo-relationship" or a "first-time encounter" type of relationship.[68] A true relationship is one in which the customer has had repeated contact over time with the same service provider and where trust and commitment has been established. A first-time encounter relationship is one in which the customer has had only one contact, on a transaction basis, with the provider. And a pseudo-relationship is one in which the customer has interacted many times with the same company, but with different service providers each time.

Other research reveals that a customer's attitude toward switching strongly influences whether he or she ultimately stays with the provider and that this attitude will be even more influential than basic satisfaction with the service.[69] This research suggests that certain customers will have a greater propensity to switch service providers no matter how their service failure situations are handled. Research in an online service context, for example, shows that demographic factors such as age and income as well as individual factors such as risk aversion influence whether a customer continues to use an online service or switches to another provider.[70] The profile of an "online service switcher" emerged in the research as a person who was influenced to subscribe to the service through positive word-of-mouth communication, who used the service less, who was less satisfied and less involved with the service, who had a lower income and education level, and who had a lower propensity for taking risks.

Finally, the decision to switch to a different service provider may not occur immediately following service failure or poor service recovery but may follow an accumulation of events. That is, service switching can be viewed as a process resulting from a series of decisions and critical service encounters over time rather than one specific moment in time when a decision is made.[71] This process orientation suggests that companies could track customer interactions and predict the likelihood of defection based on a series of events, intervening earlier in the process to head off the customer's decision to switch.

Although customers decide to switch service providers for a variety of reasons, service failure and poor service recovery are often a cause of such behavior. A study of approximately 500 service-switching incidents identified eight broad themes underlying the decision to defect.[72] These themes (pricing, inconvenience, core service failure, service encounter failure, response to service failure, competition, ethical problems,

FIGURE 7.7
Causes of Service Switching

Source: S. Keaveney, "Customer Switching Behavior in Service Industries: An Exploratory Study," *Journal of Marketing* 59 (April 1995), pp. 71–82, American Marketing Association.

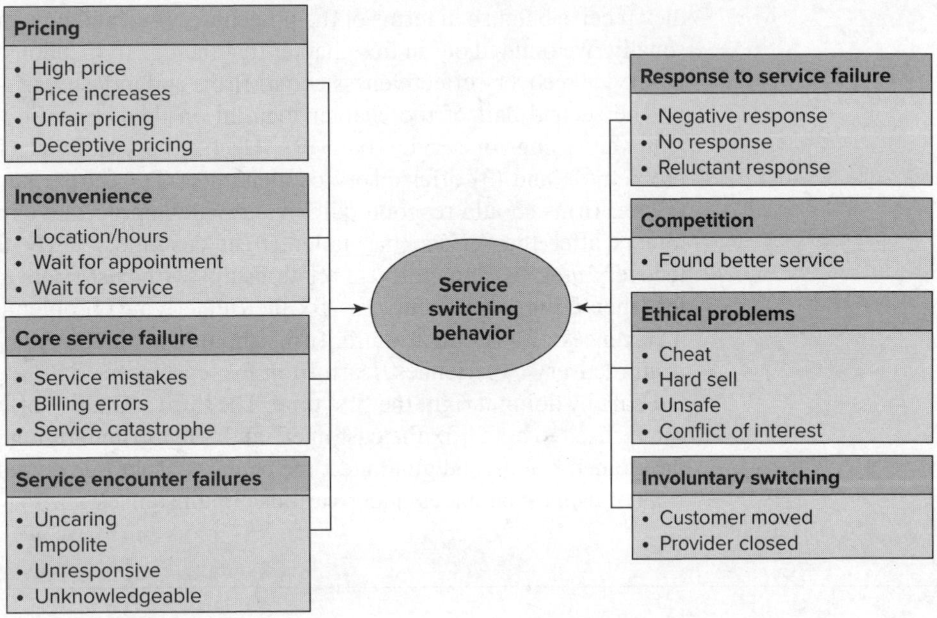

and involuntary switching) are shown in Figure 7.7. In about 200 of the incidents, a single theme was identified as the cause for switching service providers, and the two largest categories were related to service failure. Core service failure was the cause of switching for 25 percent of the respondents, and service encounter failure was the reason for switching services for an additional 20 percent of the sample. In incidents that listed two themes, 29 percent listed core service failure and 18 percent service encounter failure as contributing to their desire to switch providers; poor response to failure was mentioned by an additional 11 percent of the respondents as the cause for switching. As these findings and others suggest, service failure can cause customers to switch companies.[73] To minimize the impact of service failure, excellent service recovery is needed.

Summary

Part 3 of this text (Chapters 5, 6, and 7) focuses on the critical importance of understanding customer expectations as well as many of the strategies firms use to accomplish this goal. Part of understanding customer expectations is being prepared for and knowing what to do when things go wrong or when the service fails. In this chapter we focused on service recovery, the actions taken by an organization in response to a service failure to improve the situation for the customer.

You learned in this chapter the importance of an effective service recovery strategy for retaining customers and increasing positive word-of-mouth communication. Another major benefit of an effective service recovery strategy is that the information it provides can be useful for service improvement. The potential downsides of poor service recovery are tremendous—negative word of mouth, lost customers, and declining business when quality issues are not addressed.

In this chapter you learned how customers respond to service failures and why some complain, while others do not. You learned that customers expect to be treated fairly when they complain—not just in terms of the actual outcome or compensation they receive but also in terms of the procedures used and how they are treated interpersonally. We pointed out in this chapter that there is tremendous room for improvement in service recovery effectiveness across firms and industries.

The second half of the chapter focused on three specific types of strategies that firms are using for service recovery, (1) fix the customer, (2) fix the (underlying) problem(s), and (3) offer a service guarantee. To "fix the customer" after a service failure, firms should respond quickly, provide appropriate communication with customers after the service has failed, treat customers fairly throughout the service recovery process, and cultivate relationships with customers to perhaps create a buffer when failures do occur. To "fix the (underlying) problem(s)" and prevent future recurrences of a service failure, firms should encourage and track complaints, learn from recovery experiences, learn from lost customers, and, ideally, make the service fail-safe by doing it right the first time. The third strategy, "offer a service guarantee," can be used to both "fix the customer" and "fix the underlying problem." You learned the elements of a good guarantee, the benefits of service guarantees, and the pros and cons of using guarantees under various circumstances.

Discussion Questions

1. Why is it important for a service firm to have a strong recovery strategy? Think of a time when you received less-than-desired service from a particular service organization. Was any effort made to recover? What did the firm do to "fix the customer"? What was done to "fix the underlying problem(s)"? What should/could have been done differently? Do you still buy service from the organization? Why or why not? Did you tell others about your experience?
2. Discuss the benefits to a company of having an effective service recovery strategy. Describe an instance in which you experienced (or delivered as an employee) an effective service recovery. In what ways did the company benefit in this situation?
3. Explain the recovery paradox, and discuss its implications for a service firm manager.
4. Discuss the types of actions that customers can take in response to a service failure. As a manager, would you want to encourage your customers to voice their complaint? If so, to whom and how?
5. Review Exhibit 7.2. What would you have done if you were on the management team at United Airlines? More specifically: What should the airline have done when the initial problem (i.e., handling of the guitar at the Chicago airport) during the flight was reported? What should it have done when the damaged guitar was reported after the flight ended? What should it have done once the video was posted and went viral on YouTube?
6. Explain the logic behind these two quotes: "a complaint is a gift" and "the customer who complains is your friend."
7. Choose a firm you are familiar with. Describe how you would design an ideal service recovery strategy for that organization.
8. What are the benefits to the company of an effective service guarantee? Should every service organization have one?
9. Describe three service guarantees that are currently offered by companies or organizations in addition to the ones described in the chapter. (Examples are readily available on the Internet.) Are your examples good guarantees or poor guarantees based on the criteria presented in this chapter?

Exercises

1. Write a (legitimate) letter of complaint (or voice your complaint in person, or post a complaint on social media) to a service organization from which you have experienced less-than-desired service. What do you expect the organization to do to recover? (Later, report to the class the results of your complaint, whether you were satisfied with the recovery, what could/should have been done differently, and whether you will continue using the service.)
2. Interview five people about their service recovery experiences. What happened, and what did they expect the firm to do? Were they treated fairly based on the definition of recovery fairness presented in the chapter? Will they return to the company in the future?
3. Interview a manager about service recovery strategies used in his or her firm. Use the strategies shown in Figure 7.4 to frame your questions.
4. Reread the Technology Spotlight in this chapter, featuring Cisco Systems. Then, visit Apple's support community, which is primarily focused on consumers (https://discussions.apple.com/welcome). Compare what Cisco is doing with the self-service efforts of Apple (or another service provider of your choice).
5. Choose a service you are familiar with. Explain the service offered and develop a good service guarantee for it. Discuss why your guarantee is a good one, and list the benefits to the company of implementing it.

Notes

1. For research that shows different types of service failures, see M. J. Bitner, B. H. Booms, and M. S. Tetreault, "The Service Encounter: Diagnosing Favorable and Unfavorable Incidents," *Journal of Marketing* 54 (January 1990), pp. 71–84; S. M. Keaveney, "Customer Switching Behavior in Service Industries: An Exploratory Study," *Journal of Marketing* 59 (April 1995), pp. 71–82. For an overview on service recovery, see: M. Khamitov, Y. Grégoire, and A. Suri, "A Systematic Review of Brand Transgression, Service Failure Recovery and Product-Harm Crisis: Integration and Guiding Insights," *Journal of the Academy of Marketing Science* 48 (May 2020), pp. 519–542.
2. Information provided by TARP Worldwide Inc., based on data from 10 studies (representing responses from more than 8,000 customers) conducted in 2006 and 2007. Companies from the following industries were included: retail (stores, catalog and online), auto financing, and insurance (property/casualty).
3. For research on important outcomes associated with service recovery, see S. S. Tax, S. W. Brown, and M. Chandrashekaran, "Customer Evaluations of Service Complaint Experiences: Implications for Relationship Marketing," *Journal of Marketing* 62 (April 1998), pp. 60–76; S. S. Tax and S. W. Brown, "Recovering and Learning from Service Failure," *Sloan Management Review* 40 (Fall 1998), pp. 75–88; A. K. Smith and R. N. Bolton, "An Experimental Investigation of Customer Reactions to Service Failure and Recovery Encounters," *Journal of Service Research* 1 (August 1998), pp. 65–81; R. N. Bolton, "A Dynamic Model of the Customer's Relationship with a Continuous Service Provider: The Role of Satisfaction," *Marketing Science* 17 (1998), pp. 45–65; A. K. Smith and R. N. Bolton, "The Effect of Customers' Emotional Responses to Service Failures on Their Recovery Effort Evaluations and Satisfaction Judgments," *Journal of the Academy of Marketing Science* 30 (Winter 2002), pp. 5–23; C. M. Voorhees, M. K. Brady, and D. M. Horowitz, "A Voice from the Silent Masses: An Exploratory and Comparative Analysis of Noncomplainers," *Journal of the Academy of Marketing Science* 34 (Fall 2006), pp. 514–527; C.

Orsingher, S. Valentini, and M. de Angelis, "A Meta-Analysis of Satisfaction with Complaint Handling in Services," *Journal of the Academy of Marketing Science* 38 (2010), pp. 169–186.

4. Information included in Figure 7.2 is based on data from the 2020 Customer Rage Study, conducted by Customer Care Measurement and Consulting, Alexandria, Virginia, in collaboration with the Center for Services Leadership at Arizona State University's W. P. Carey School of Business.
5. Ibid; 2020 Customer Rage Study.
6. Ibid; Voorhees, Brady, and Horowitz, "A Voice from the Silent Masses."
7. Tax and Brown, "Recovering and Learning from Service Failure."
8. 2015 Customer Rage Study, conducted by Customer Care Measurement and Consulting and the Center for Services Leadership at Arizona State University.
9. See C. W. Hart, J. L. Heskett, and W. E. Sasser Jr., "The Profitable Art of Service Recovery," *Harvard Business Review* 68 (July–August 1990), pp. 148–156; M. A. McCollough and S. G. Bharadwaj, "The Recovery Paradox: An Examination of Consumer Satisfaction in Relation to Disconfirmation, Service Quality, and Attribution Based Theories," in *Marketing Theory and Applications,* ed. C. T. Allen et al. (Chicago: American Marketing Association, 1992), p. 119. For findings on B2B settings, see: D. Hübner, S. M. Wagner, and S. Kurpjuweit, "The Service Recovery Paradox in B2B Relationships," *Journal of Business & Industrial Marketing* 33 (April 2018), pp. 291–302.
10. C. A. de Matos, J. L. Henrique, and C. A. V. Rossi, "Service Recovery Paradox: A Meta-analysis," *Journal of Service Research* 10 (August 2007), pp. 60–77.
11. Smith and Bolton, "An Experimental Investigation of Customer Reactions to Service Failure and Recovery Encounters."
12. V. P. Magnini, J. B. Ford, E. P. Markowski, and E. D. Honeycutt Jr., "The Service Recovery Paradox: Justifiable Theory or Smoldering Myth?" *Journal of Services Marketing* 21 (2007), pp. 213–225; J. G. Maxham III and R. G. Netemeyer, "A Longitudinal Study of Complaining Customers' Evaluations of Multiple Service Failures and Recovery Efforts," *Journal of Marketing* 66 (October 2002), pp. 57–71; M. A. McCollough, L. L. Berry, and M. S. Yadav, "An Empirical Investigation of Customer Satisfaction after Service Failure and Recovery," *Journal of Service Research* 3 (November 2000), pp. 121–137.
13. G. Knox and R. van Oest, "Customer Complaints and Recovery Effectiveness: A Customer Base Approach," *Journal of Marketing* 24 (September 2014), pp. 42–57.
14. S. Michel and M. L. Meuter, "The Service Recovery Paradox: True but Overrated?" *International Journal of Service Industry Management* 19 (2008), pp. 441–457; R. Priluck and V. Lala, "The Impact of the Recovery Paradox on Retailer-Customer Relationships," *Managing Service Quality* 19 (2009), pp. 42–59.
15. For research foundations on typologies of customer responses to failures, see R. L. Day and E. L. Landon Jr., "Towards a Theory of Consumer Complaining Behavior," in *Consumer and Industrial Buying Behavior,* ed. A. Woodside, J. Sheth, and P. Bennett (Amsterdam: North-Holland, 1977); J. Singh, "Consumer Complaint Intentions and Behavior: Definitional and Taxonomical Issues," *Journal of Marketing* 52 (January 1988), pp. 93–107; J. Singh, "Voice, Exit, and Negative Word-of-Mouth Behaviors: An Investigation across Three Service Categories," *Journal of the Academy of Marketing Science* 18 (Winter 1990), pp. 1–15.

16. Smith and Bolton, "The Effect of Customers' Emotional Responses to Service Failures."; M. Zeelenberg and R. Pieters, "Beyond Valence in Customer Dissatisfaction: A Review and New Findings on Behavioral Responses to Regret and Disappointment in Failed Services," *Journal of Business Research* 57 (2004), pp. 445–455.
17. Voorhees, Brady, and Horowitz, "A Voice from the Silent Masses."
18. N. Stephens and K. P. Gwinner, "Why Don't Some People Complain? A Cognitive–Emotive Process Model of Consumer Complaining Behavior," *Journal of the Academy of Marketing Science* 26 (Spring 1998), pp. 172–189.
19. Ibid.
20. For additional reading on customer rage, see J. R. McColl-Kennedy, P. G. Patterson, A. K. Smith, and M. K. Brady, "Customer Rage Episodes: Emotions, Expressions, and Behaviors," *Journal of Retailing* 85 (2009), pp. 222–237 and P. G. Patterson, J. R. McColl-Kennedy, A. K. Smith, and Z. Lu, "Customer Rage: Triggers, Tipping Points, and Take-Outs," *California Management Review* 52 (Fall 2009), pp. 6–28; J. Surachartkumtonkun, J. R. McColl-Kennedy, and P. G. Patterson, "Unpacking Customer Rage Elicitation: A Dynamic Model," *Journal of Service Research* 19 (February 2016), pp. 57–71.
21. D. Herhausen, S. Ludwig, D. Grewal, J. Wulf, and M. Schoegel, "Detecting, Preventing, and Mitigating Online Firestorms in Brand Communities," *Journal of Marketing* 83 (May 2019), pp. 1–21; T. Hennig-Thurau, K. P. Gwinner, G. Walsh, and D. D. Gremler, "Electronic Word-of-Mouth via Consumer-Opinion Platforms: What Motivates Consumers to Articulate Themselves on the Internet?" *Journal of Interactive Marketing* 18 (Winter 2004), pp. 38–52.
22. For related websites see https://thisbusiness.sucks/ or www.farmersinsurancegroupsucks.com (for Farmers Insurance). However, companies also have increasingly bought ".sucks" domains (e.g. Apple, Facebook, Microsoft) to protect their brands against such online damage. Also see: https://www.theguardian.com/technology/shortcuts/2015/mar/23/why-you-should-buy-your-dot-sucks-domain-name, accessed December 12, 2021.
23. J. C. Ward and A. L. Ostrom, "Complaining to the Masses: The Role of Protest Framing in Customer-Created Complaint Web Sites," *Journal of Consumer Research* 33 (September 2006), pp. 220–230.
24. Davidow, "Organizational Responses to Customer Complaints."
25. 2015 Customer Rage Study.
26. 2020 Customer Rage Study.
27. Ibid.
28. R. Holmes, "How to Keep Client Rants from Going Viral," *Wall Street Journal* (December 9, 2013), http://blogs.wsj.com/accelerators/2013/12/09/ryan-holmes-how-to-keep-client-rants-from-going-viral/, accessed November 17, 2021.
29. J. R. McColl-Kennedy and B. A. Sparks, "Application of Fairness Theory to Service Failures and Service Recovery," *Journal of Service Research* 5 (February 2003), pp. 251–266; M. Davidow, "Organizational Responses to Customer Complaints: What Works and What Doesn't," *Journal of Service Research* 5 (February 2003), pp. 225–250.
30. 2020 Customer Rage Study.
31. Davidow, "Organizational Responses to Customer Complaints." Also see T. Gruber, "I Want to Believe They Really Care: How Complaining Customers Want to

Be Treated by Frontline Employees," *Journal of Service Management* 22 (2011), pp. 85–110.

32. 2007 National Customer Rage Study conducted by Customer Care Alliance.
33. H. Roschk and S. Kaiser, "The Nature of an Apology: An Experimental Study on How to Apologize after a Service Failure," *Marketing Letters* 24 (September 2013), pp. 293–309.
34. L. L. Berry and K. Seiders, "Serving Unfair Customers," *Business Horizons* 51 (January/February 2008), pp. 29–37.
35. J. Dunning, A. Pecotich, and A. O'Cass, "What Happens When Things Go Wrong? Retail Sales Explanations and Their Effects," *Psychology and Marketing* 21 (2004), pp. 553–572; McColl-Kennedy and Sparks, "Application of Fairness Theory to Service Failures and Service Recovery"; Davidow, "Organizational Responses to Customer Complaints"; Berry and Seiders, "Serving Unfair Customers"; G. Bradley and B. Sparks, "Explanations: If, When, and How They Aid Service Recovery," *Journal of Services Marketing* 26 (2012), pp. 41–50.
36. See Tax, Brown, and Chandrashekaran, "Customer Evaluations of Service Complaint Experiences"; Tax and Brown, "Recovering and Learning from Service Failure."
37. Tax and Brown, "Recovering and Learning from Service Failure."
38. Smith and Bolton, "The Effect of Customers' Emotional Responses to Service Failures."
39. S. Conradt, "11 of the Best Customer Service Stories Ever," *Mental Floss,* December 15, 2015, http://mentalfloss.com/article/30198/11-best-customer-service-stories-ever.
40. Hess, Ganesan, and Klein, "Service Failure and Recovery"; Priluck, "Relationship Marketing Can Mitigate Product and Service Failures."
41. T. DeWitt and M. K. Brady, "Rethinking Service Recovery Strategies: The Effect of Rapport on Consumer Responses to Service Failure," *Journal of Service Research* 6 (November 2003), pp. 193–207.
42. Hess, Ganesan, and Klein, "Service Failure and Recovery."
43. Y. Gregoire, T. M. Tripp, and R. Legoux, "When Customer Love Turns Into Lasting Hate: The Effects of Relationship Strength and Time on Customer Revenge and Avoidance," *Journal of Marketing* 73 (November 2009), pp. 18–32. However, other research suggests an opposite effect; that is, customers with strong relationships to a firm may actually "raise the bar" in terms of their service recovery expectations and feel betrayed if the firm fails them. See B. B. Holloway, S. Wang, and S. E. Beatty, "Betrayal? Relationship Quality Implications in Service Recovery," *Journal of Services Marketing* 23 (2009), pp. 385–396.
44. T. W. Andreassen and S. Streukens, "Online Complaining: Understanding the Adoption Process and the Role of Individual and Situational Characteristics," *Managing Service Quality* 23 (2013), pp. 4–24.
45. F. F. Reichheld, "Learning from Customer Defections," *Harvard Business Review* 74 (March–April 1996), pp. 56–69; A. Miner, "Learning from 'Lost' Customers," *CustomerThink,* June 8, 2010, http://customerthink.com/learning_from_lost_customers/.
46. Ibid.
47. A. Parasuraman, V. A. Zeithaml, and L. L. Berry, "SERVQUAL: A Multiple-Item Scale for Measuring Consumer Perceptions of Service Quality," *Journal of Retailing* 64 (Spring 1988), pp. 64–79.

48. M. Colgate, V. T.-U. Tong, C. K.-C. Lee, and J. U. Farley, "Back from the Brink: Why Customers Stay," *Journal of Service Research* 9 (February 2007), pp. 211–228.
49. R. B. Chase and D. M. Stewart, "Make Your Service Fail-Safe," *Sloan Management Review* 35 (Spring 1994), pp. 35–44.
50. Ibid .
51. For an extensive discussion of why service guarantees have historically been rare, see M. McCollough, "Service Guarantees: A Review and Explanation of Their Continued Rarity," *Academy of Marketing Studies Journal* 14 (2010), pp. 27–54.
52. These characteristics are discussed in C. W. L. Hart, "The Power of Unconditional Guarantees," *Harvard Business Review* 66 (July–August 1988), pp. 54–62; C. W. L. Hart, *Extraordinary Guarantees* (New York: AMACOM, 1993); and B. Berman and A. Mathur, "Planning and Implementing Effective Service Guarantee Programs," *Business Horizons* 57 (2014), pp. 107–116.
53. Berman and Mathur, "Planning and Implementing Effective Service Guarantee Programs."
54. For more information, see M. A. McCollough and D. D. Gremler, "Guaranteeing Student Satisfaction: An Exercise in Treating Students as Customers," *Journal of Marketing Education* 21 (August 1999), pp. 118–130; D. D. Gremler and M. A. McCollough, "Student Satisfaction Guarantees: An Empirical Examination of Attitudes, Antecedents, and Consequences," *Journal of Marketing Education* 24 (August 2002), pp. 150–160.
55. Puget Sound Energy website, https://www.pse.com/en/pages/customer-service-guarantees, accessed November 11, 2021.
56. Infrectra website, https://www.inflectra.com/Company/Reasons-To-Buy-From-Us.aspx, accessed November 11, 2021.
57. Asian Paints, https://www.asianpaints.com/services/asian-paints-safe-painting-service.html, accessed October 2025.
58. A. L. Ostrom and C. W. L. Hart, "Service Guarantees: Research and Practice," in *Handbook of Services Marketing and Management,* ed. D. Iacobucci and T. Swartz (Thousand Oaks, CA: Sage, 2000), pp. 299–316; Hart, "The Power of Unconditional Guarantees"; Hart, *Extraordinary Guarantees.* For a discussion of additional benefits from offering service guarantees, see Berman and Mathur, "Planning and Implementing Effective Service Guarantee Programs."
59. A. L. Ostrom and D. Iacobucci, "The Effect of Guarantees on Consumers' Evaluation of Services," *Journal of Services Marketing* 12 (1998), pp. 362–378; S. B. Lidén and P. Skålén, "The Effect of Service Guarantees on Service Recovery," *International Journal of Service Industry Management* 14 (2003), pp. 36–58.
60. A. L. Roggeveen, R. C. Goodstein, and D. Grewal, "Improving the Effect of Guarantees: The Role of a Retailer's Reputation," *Journal of Retailing* 90 (2014), pp. 27–39.
61. J. Wirtz, D. Kum, and K. S. Lee, "Should a Firm with a Reputation for Outstanding Service Quality Offer a Service Guarantee?" *Journal of Services Marketing* 14 (2000), pp. 502–512.
62. J. Wirtz, "Development of a Service Guarantee Model," *Asia Pacific Journal of Management* 15 (April 1998), pp. 51–75.
63. J. Wirtz and D. Kum, "Consumer Cheating on Service Guarantees," *Journal of the Academy of Marketing Science* 32 (Spring 2004), pp. 159–175.

64. Wirtz, "Development of a Service Guarantee Model."
65. Ostrom and Iacobucci, "The Effect of Guarantees."
66. P. G. Mostert, C. F. De Meyer, and L. R. J. Van Rensburg, "The Influence of Service Failure and Service Recovery on Airline Passengers' Relationships with Domestic Airlines: An Exploratory Study," *Southern African Business Review* 13 (2009), pp. 118–140.
67. McCollough, Berry, and Yadav, "An Empirical Investigation of Customer Satisfaction After Service Failure and Recovery."
68. A. S. Mattila, "The Impact of Relationship Type on Customer Loyalty in a Context of Service Failures," *Journal of Service Research* 4 (November 2001), pp. 91–101; see also R. L. Hess Jr., S. Ganesan, and N. M. Klein, "Service Failure and Recovery: The Impact of Relationship Factors on Customer Satisfaction," *Journal of the Academy of Marketing Science* 31 (Spring 2003), pp. 127–145; R. Priluck, "Relationship Marketing Can Mitigate Product and Service Failures," *Journal of Services Marketing* 17 (2003), pp. 37–52.
69. H. S. Bansal and S. F. Taylor, "The Service Provider Switching Model (SPSM)," *Journal of Service Research* 2 (November 1999), pp. 200–218.
70. S. M. Keaveney and M. Parthasarathy, "Customer Switching Behavior in Online Services: An Exploratory Study of the Role of Selected Attitudinal, Behavioral, and Demographic Factors," *Journal of the Academy of Marketing Science* 29 (Fall 2001), pp. 374–390.
71. I. Roos, "Switching Processes in Customer Relationships," *Journal of Service Research* 2 (August 1999), pp. 68–85; I. Roos and A. Gustafsson, "Understanding Frequent Switching Patterns: A Crucial Element in Managing Customer Relationships," *Journal of Service Research* 10 (August 2007), pp. 93–108.
72. Keaveney, "Customer Switching Behavior in Service Industries."
73. F. Buttle and J. Burton, "Does Service Failure Influence Customer Loyalty?," *Journal of Consumer Behaviour* 1 (2002), pp. 217–227; Y. Wang, S. Wu, H. Lin, and Y. Wang, "The Relationship of Service Failure Severity, Service Recovery Justice, and Perceived Switching Costs with Customer Loyalty in the Context of e-tailing," *International Journal of Information Management* 31 (August 2011), pp. 350–359; R. Frankel, S. R. Swanson, and M. Sagan, "Service Switching, Word-of-Mouth, and New Provider Search: A Five Country Exploratory Study," *International Journal of Management and Marketing Research* 6 (2013), pp. 11–20.

Part Four

Aligning Service Design and Standards

Meeting customer expectations of service requires not only understanding what the expectations are but also taking action on that knowledge. Action takes several forms: designing innovative services and service improvements based on customer requirements, setting service standards to ensure that services are performed as customers expect, and providing physical evidence that creates the appropriate cues and ambience for service. When action does not take place, there is a gap—the service design and standards gap—as shown in the accompanying figure. In this section you will learn to identify the causes of Gap 2 as well as effective strategies for closing this gap.

Provider Gap 2: The Service Design and Standards Gap

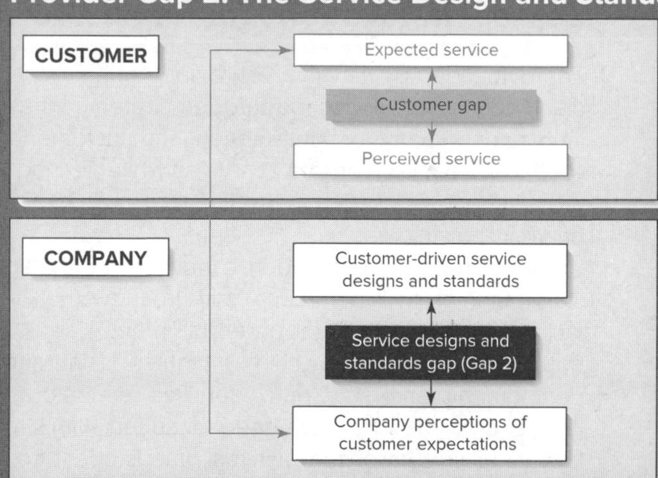

Chapter 8 describes the concepts and tools that are effective for service innovation and design, especially a technique called service blueprinting. Chapter 9 helps you differentiate between company-defined standards and customer-defined standards and to recognize how they can be developed. Chapter 10 explains the strategic importance of physical evidence, the variety of roles it plays, and strategies for effectively designing physical evidence and the servicescape to meet customer expectations.

Chapter **Eight**

Service Innovation and Design

This chapter's learning objectives are to:

1. Describe the challenges inherent in service innovation and design.
2. Present an array of different types of service innovations, including service offering innovation, innovating around customer roles, and innovation through service solutions.
3. Discuss the importance of engaging customers and employees and employing service design thinking in service innovation.
4. Present the stages and unique elements of the service innovation and development process.
5. Demonstrate the value of service blueprinting as a technique for service innovation and design and how to develop and read service blueprints.

Zepto – Innovations for Rapid Growth

Zepto, founded by Kaivalya Vohra and Aadit Palicha in 2021, has transformed India's quick commerce landscape through strategic infrastructure development, logistical innovations, technology integration, and customer centricity. In March 2025, it delivered over 1.5 million orders every day while nearing the $4 billion mark in annualized gross order value (GOV) in the financial year 2023–24 and achieving a 300% year-on-year growth.

The start-up created a dense network of strategically located "dark stores" and state-of-the-art fulfillment centers in urban areas. These dark stores – non-customer-facing hubs exclusively for order fulfillment – allow Zepto to bypass traditional retail bottlenecks and deliver within 10 minutes. Using geospatial data, traffic patterns, and demographic analysis, Zepto identifies ideal store locations that minimize delivery time. Each dark store is designed for speed, with streamlined packaging systems and layouts tailored to ensure minimal time is spent from order receipt to dispatch. The placement of these dark stores follows a sophisticated density mapping approach. Zepto targets "micro-markets" within 2–3 kilometers of customer clusters to minimize last-mile delivery time. This hyperlocal focus enables Zepto to operate within India's challenging urban environments where conventional delivery models struggle with unpredictable traffic patterns and poorly marked addresses. The company currently operates over 1000 such dark stores across major Indian cities, with each facility serving a specific neighborhood catchment area.

The company's logistical innovations form the backbone of its success. Instead of relying on centralized distribution centers, Zepto distributes inventory across dark stores based on hyperlocal demand using predictive stocking. This system is powered by algorithms that consider hundreds of real-time variables, including local events and weather, to ensure that products are stocked before being ordered. Riders are equipped with tech-optimized gear such as temperature-controlled backpacks and specially designed two-wheelers, contributing to an average delivery time of just over 8 minutes. Zepto's hyperlocal warehousing model ensures products are always close to consumers, while its ultra-efficient dispatch system minimizes travel time. Their approach to inventory management employs advanced algorithms and real-time data analytics to optimize stock levels, forecast demand, streamline procurement, and minimize stockouts. This proactive approach enhances product availability while reducing carrying costs and improving operational efficiency, allowing Zepto to maintain its competitive edge in delivery speed.

Zepto's proprietary technology stack is a critical enabler of its rapid service model. Its technology stack, built around a proprietary "quick commerce operating system", seamlessly integrates inventory management, order processing, and delivery logistics. Their machine learning algorithms continuously optimize product selection by location, analyzing purchase patterns at the neighborhood level to ensure dark stores stock precisely what local customers want. It integrates real-time order processing, smart inventory control, and route optimization through an AI-driven operating system. The routing engine, ZRoute, adjusts dynamically based on factors like traffic and rider availability, while the personalization engine tailors the shopping experience by analyzing user behavior and preferences. The platform's microservices architecture supports fast, continuous updates, allowing the company to adapt quickly and roll out innovations at scale. This tech infrastructure ensures high fulfillment accuracy and consistent service quality across diverse neighborhoods.

Zepto's business strategy focuses on targeted service expansion and community engagement. The company has embraced a focused expansion model that prioritizes speed and relevance over product diversity. It limits offerings to high-demand, easy-to-deliver items, bolstering profitability through private labels that now contribute a significant share of revenue with better margins. Their foray into complementary sectors like over-the-counter (OTC) pharmaceuticals and cosmetics further increases order value without straining delivery systems. While maintaining a laser-focused approach on groceries, the company has expanded into new categories such as apparel, beauty, home and kitchen products, low-ticket appliances, electronics, and even prepared foods through its Zepto Café service to grow average order value (AOV) and attract new customer segments. In addition, differentiating itself through high quality private label products, improve profit margins and boost customer trust.

Additionally, the company actively engages with local communities through events and partnerships with local businesses, fostering a sense of belonging and trust. Community engagement efforts, such as the innovative Z-Community influencer program and hyperlocal merchandising, deepen customer loyalty and localization. The "Z-Community" involves local micro-influencers who receive exclusive promotions to share with their networks to create organic word-of-mouth marketing. It pioneered "hyperlocal merchandising", viz. stocking specific products that reflect the unique preferences of individual neighborhoods, such as carrying particular regional snack varieties or festival-specific items based on the demographic composition of each delivery zone. These initiatives collectively strengthen Zepto's position in the competitive quick commerce space while maintaining a hyper-efficient, customer-first approach.

Zepto's strategic focus represents what founder Aadit Palicha calls "deliberate constraint" – intentionally limiting their product range to optimize for speed rather than variety. Their private label strategy targets high-margin, high-frequency purchase categories like dairy, bread, and household essentials, with these products now accounting for approximately 25% of revenue while delivering profit margins 15–20% higher than branded alternatives. The company's expansion beyond groceries follows a careful "complementary category" approach, adding only products that fit existing delivery infrastructure constraints while increasing basket sizes. For example, their entry into over-the-counter pharmaceuticals targets specific high-demand medications that meet strict storage requirements and high purchase frequency.

Reference

https://www.financialexpress.com/business/industry/zepto-nears-4-billion-in-order-value-reduces-cash-burn-by-half/3804595/
https://www.moneycontrol.com/news/business/startup/blinkit-zepto-and-swiggy-instamart-scale-to-over-4-million-daily-orders-in-march-more-than-double-yoy-13012435.html
https://www.businesstoday.in/magazine/deep-dive/story/how-dark-stores-are-powering-growth-of-quick-commerce-players-374569-2023-03-23
https://www.the-rise.in/entrepreneurship-stories/single-story.php?title=zepto:-revolutionizing-quick-commerce-with-innovation-and-efficiency&id=32
https://yourstory.com/2024/04/zepto-product-management-strategies
https://mastersunion.org/blog/the-10-minute-revolution-how-zepto-redefined-quick-commerce
https://www.dezerv.in/newsletter/the-secret-sauce-behind-zepto-unicorn-status/
https://www.ceotodaymagazine.com/2024/12/zepto-a-deep-dive-into-the-disruptor-shaping-indias-quick-commerce-industry/
https://economictimes.indiatimes.com/tech/startups/zepto-nears-4-billion-annualised-gov-halves-ocf-burn-rate/articleshow/120112129.cms?from=mdr

Why has PetSmart, in our chapter opener, been so successful with its service innovations? Why have other companies failed when introducing new services to the market? If you decide to start your own business, or if your company wants to introduce a new service innovation, what can be done to increase the likelihood of success? An analysis of more than 60 studies on new product and service success showed that the dominant and most reliable predictors of success for new introductions relate to *product/service characteristics* (product meeting customer needs, product advantage over competing products, technological sophistication), *strategy characteristics* (dedicated human resources to support the initiative, dedicated research and development [R&D] focused on the new product initiative), *process characteristics* (marketing, predevelopment, technological, and launch proficiencies), and *marketplace characteristics* (market potential).[1] Failures, on the other hand, can be traced to a number of causes: no unique benefits offered, insufficient demand, unrealistic goals for the new product/service, poor fit between the new service and others within the organization's portfolio, poor location, insufficient financial backing, or failure to take the necessary time to develop and introduce the product.[2] Frequently, a good service idea fails because of development, design, and specification flaws, topics emphasized in this chapter. As more firms, across industries, move into services as a growth strategy, the challenges of and opportunities for developing and delivering service offerings become even more apparent.

CHALLENGES OF SERVICE INNOVATION AND DESIGN

Because services are largely intangible and process-oriented (such as a hospital stay, an NBA basketball game, or a sophisticated information technology consulting service), they are difficult to describe and communicate. When services are delivered or cocreated with the customer over a long period—a week's resort vacation, a six-month consulting engagement, a multi-year business process outsourcing contract, or 10 weeks on a

Weight Watchers program—their complexity increases, and they become even more difficult to define and describe. Further, because many services are delivered by employees to customers, and often cocreated *with* customers, they are variable (i.e., recall service inseparability and service heterogeneity). Rarely are two services alike or experienced in the same way. These fundamental characteristics of service offerings, which we explored in the first chapter of this book, are the heart of the challenge involved in innovating and designing services. Global companies and governments around the world are awakening to these challenges and the recognition that, despite the dominance of services in the world's economies, there is disproportionately less focus on service innovation in companies and in research.[3] Our Global Feature discusses the importance of service innovation as a priority for companies and national economies.

Because service offerings typically cannot be touched, examined, or easily tried out, people have historically resorted to words in their efforts to describe them. Yet, there are a number of risks inherent in attempting to describe services in words alone.[4] The first risk is *oversimplification.* "To say that 'portfolio management' means 'buying and selling stocks' is like describing the space shuttle as 'something that flies.' Some people will picture a bird, some a helicopter, and some an angel."[5] Words are simply inadequate to describe a complex service system such as financial portfolio management. In our global economy, service systems have significantly increased in complexity, often involving networks of service firms, customers, and evolution of offerings over time.[6] Within these complex service systems, the risks of oversimplification are even more apparent.

The second risk of using words alone is *incompleteness.* In describing services, people (employees, managers, customers) tend to omit details or elements of the service with which they are not familiar. A person might do a fairly credible job of describing how a discount stock brokerage service takes orders from customers. But would that person be able to describe fully how the monthly statements are created, how the interactive computer system works, and how these two elements of the service are integrated into the order-taking process?

The third risk is *subjectivity.* Any one person describing a service in words will be biased by personal experiences and degree of exposure to the service. There is a natural (and mistaken) tendency to assume that, because all people have gone to a fast-food restaurant, they all understand what that service is. Persons working in different functional areas of the same service organization (a marketing person, an operations person, a finance person) are likely to describe the service very differently as well, biased by their own functional blinders.

A final risk of describing services using words alone is *biased interpretation.* No two people will define "responsive," "quick," or "flexible" in exactly the same way. For example, a supervisor or manager may suggest to a frontline service employee that the employee should try to be more flexible or responsive in providing service to the customer. Unless the term "flexibility" is further defined, the employee is likely to interpret the word differently than the manager.

All these risks and challenges become very apparent in the innovation and service development process, when organizations attempt to design complex services never before experienced by customers or when they attempt to change existing services.[7]

IMPORTANT CONSIDERATIONS FOR SERVICE INNOVATION

In this section, we highlight some important considerations when developing new services. Because of the inherent characteristics of services (Chapter 1), and the challenges of service development and innovation just described, it has become clear to many

Innovation, across all economic sectors, is required for the continued growth and competitiveness of individual companies, governmental entities, and entire economies. Based on approximately 80 indicators, the Global Innovation Index (GII) is an annual ranking of countries based on their overall capacity and success in innovation. Below, we display the 10 best-ranked economies by income group as identified by the GII 2020. As the figure shows, the top 10 economies in the GII are all high-income economies, with Switzerland, Sweden, and the United States topping this group. Next, in the upper-middle income group, China, Malaysia, and Bulgaria hold the top three positions in this segment (and they have been leading this group since 2016). In the segment of lower middle-income countries, Vietnam ranks first, followed by Ukraine and India. In the low-income group of countries, the United Republic of Tanzania comes in first, climbing two positions within its income group since the prior year. The report also notes that the technology gap between developing and developed countries is narrowing. This index, published annually by Cornell University, INSEAD, and the World Intellectual Property Organization (WIPO), does not distinguish service innovation from innovation generally. Yet, the dominance and/or growth of services in most economies would logically suggest innovation in services is critical.

Focusing specifically on services, a 2021 study on "Service Research Priorities for Managing Services in Turbulent Times" identified service innovation as one of the top priorities. Seeking to identify priorities for both practice and research, this study was based on input from academics and business practitioners from around the world and across disciplines and functions. Interviews, surveys, and roundtables were conducted with people from 26 countries. The study's findings identify seven priorities for research (e.g., technology and the changing nature of world; technology and the customer experience; services for disadvantaged consumers and communities). In terms of innovation, "business survival and service innovation in the face of new technologies, increased competition, and changing customer expectations" emerged as a theme of major relevance. The study also suggests that service innovation influences all of the seven top priorities, which further illustrates the fundamental importance of service innovation.

Despite the importance of innovation generally and service innovation in particular, a benchmarking review of service innovation policies in Europe reported great diversity in policies and intensity of focus on service innovation across countries. The authors of the report called out a few countries that are very advanced in service innovation policies and practices—namely, Finland, Sweden, and Ireland. They also mention Austria, Germany, and Denmark as being among other countries that have maintained a policy interest in service innovation.

In the United States, much of the impetus behind the growing awareness of the need for service innovation is attributed to the leadership of IBM. The company catalyzed a global movement to shape the future of service innovation and a potential new discipline called "service science, management and engineering" (SSME) to develop skilled professionals for the service economy. Together with Cisco, Hewlett-Packard and several universities, IBM cofounded ISSIP, the International Society for Service Industry Professionals. The mission of ISSIP is to promote service innovation for the interconnected world and its purpose is to help institutions and individuals to grow and be successful in the global service economy. Although the primary thrust for service innovation in the United States has come from the private sector, government agencies, notably the National Science Foundation (NSF), are beginning to respond. For several years, the NSF has provided Smart Service Systems funding support for specific research proposals through its Partnerships for Innovation: Building Innovation Capacity (PFI/BIC) program.

managers that service innovation is different from tangible product innovation. Because services are intangible and process-based, and because they frequently involve interactions among and between customers and employees, it is important to involve both customers *and* employees at various points in the innovation process. It is also important to use a systems or design mind-set, sometimes referred to as "design thinking," to be sure all elements are considered and integrated. Here, we overview these considerations as a backdrop for the tools, techniques, and approaches described in the rest of the chapter.

Involve Customers and Employees

Because services are produced, consumed, and cocreated in real time and often involve interaction between and among employees and customers, it is critical that innovation and new service development processes involve both employees and customers

Rank	Global Innovation Index 2020
High-income economies (49 in total)	
1	Switzerland (1)
2	Sweden (2)
3	United States of America (3)
4	United Kingdom (4)
5	Netherlands (5)
6	Denmark (6)
7	Finland (7)
8	Singapore (8)
9	Germany (9)
10	Republic of Korea (10)

Rank	Global Innovation Index 2020
Upper middle-income economies (37 in total)	
1	China (14)
2	Malaysia (33)
3	Bulgaria (37)
4	Thailand (44)
5	Romania (46)
6	Russian Federation (47)
7	Montenegro (49)
8	Turkey (51)
9	Mauritius (52)
10	Serbia (53)

Rank	Global Innovation Index 2020
Lower middle-income economies (29 in total)	
1	Viet Nam (42)
2	Ukraine (45)
3	India (48)
4	Philippines (50)
5	Mongolia (58)
6	Republic of Moldova (59)
7	Tunisia (65)
8	Morocco (75)
9	Indonesia (85)
10	Kenya (86)

Rank	Global Innovation Index 2020
Low-income economies (16 in total)	
1	United Republic of Tanzania (88)
2	Rwanda (91)
3	Nepal (95)
4	Tajikistan (109)
5	Malawi (111)
6	Uganda (114)
7	Madagascar (115)
8	Burkina Faso (118)
9	Mali (123)
10	Mozambique (124)

World Intellectual Property Organization

Sources: Cornell University, INSEAD, and WIPO, "The Global Innovation Index 2020: Who Will Finance Innovation?," Ithaca, Fontainebleau, and Geneva, 2020, Creative Commons Attribution; A. L. Ostrom et al., "Service Research Priorities: Managing and Delivering Service in Turbulent Times," *Journal of Service Research* 24 (August 2021), pp. 329–353; European Commission, ESIC European Service Innovation Centre Discussion Paper, "Service Innovation Policy—A Benchmarking Review," January 2015, www.issip.org.

throughout the process.[8] Employees frequently *are* the service, or at least they perform or deliver the service, and thus their involvement in choosing which new services to develop and how these services should be designed and implemented can be very beneficial. Because frontline employees are psychologically and physically close to customers, they can be very helpful in identifying customer needs for innovative new services.[9] Involving employees in service innovation and design also increases the likelihood of new service success because employees can identify the organizational issues that need to be addressed to support the delivery of the service to customers.[10]

Because customers often actively participate in service delivery and/or cocreation, they, too, should be involved in the new service development process. Beyond just providing input on their own needs, customers can help design the service concept and the delivery process, particularly in situations in which the customer personally carries out part of the service process. For example, the Mayo Clinic has established its Center for Innovation in Rochester to experiment with new service innovations by testing them with actual patients and doctors in a prototype setting prior to introducing them (see Exhibit 8.2 later in the chapter).

Employ Service Design Thinking and Techniques

One of the challenges of service innovation and design is that services are processes and they are experiential, taking place over time. In some cases, the time required to deliver the service may translate into just a few minutes, but other times the service experience can encompass hours, days, weeks, and even years, as in the case of a university degree program or a service outsourcing contract. Services often occur as a sequence of interrelated steps and activities and engage a number of people, processes, and tangible elements. For example, employees, customers, subcontractors, technology, equipment, and physical spaces are often involved in service and therefore need to be considered in its design. As a result, designing a service offering or service system requires collaboration and coordination across functions, and perhaps even across different organizations.

Recognizing the complexities and requirements of service innovation, the field of "service design" has gained increasing attention from business practitioners, design consultants, service marketers, and a variety of academic disciplines. In a series of global studies to identify the research priorities for the science of service, service design and innovation came to the forefront as one major research priority for the future.[11] There are a number of global consultancy firms that focus their efforts on service design. For example design firm IDEO, based in the United States; Engine Service Design in the United Kingdom; and Live/Work, also in the United Kingdom, all have practices devoted to service design. In parallel, many of the leading consulting firms (e.g., Deloitte, PWC) have also increasingly developed an expertise in the area of service innovation and design.

So what is meant by service design and service design thinking? And what do these service design consultancy firms do to help their clients produce great service innovations? While there is not one shared definition, here are two from noted companies and experts:

> "Service design aims to ensure service interfaces are useful, usable, and desirable from the client's point of view and efficient and distinctive from the supplier's point of view." Birgit Mager, professor of service design, University of Cologne, Germany[12] "Service design is focused on bringing service strategy and innovative service ideas to life by aligning various internal and external stakeholders around the creation of holistic service experiences for customers, clients, employees, business partners, and/or citizens," Center for Services Leadership, Arizona State University.[13]

Given the interdisciplinary and interactional nature of service design and its focus on customer experiences, five principles are central to service design thinking:[14]

1. *User-centered:* Services should be experienced and designed through the customer's eyes.
2. *Cocreative:* All stakeholders should be included in the service design process.
3. *Sequencing:* A service should be visualized as a sequence of interrelated actions.
4. *Evidencing:* Intangible services should be visualized in terms of physical artifacts.
5. *Holistic:* The entire environment of a service should be considered.

Service designers who adhere to these principles are "engaged visualizing, formulating, and choreographing solutions that are not yet available. They watch and interpret needs and behaviors and transform them into potential future services."[15] Designing,

Technology Spotlight Facebook: A Radical Service Innovation

When Facebook was launched in Mark Zuckerberg's dormitory room at Harvard University in 2004, it was not much more than a communication vehicle for Harvard students. According to David Kirkpatrick's authoritative book on the company, Facebook's beginnings can be traced to other Zuckerberg projects during the same year at Harvard—first to Course Match (a way to learn about who was registered for a particular class and what classes your friends were taking) and then to Facemash, whose purpose was to figure out who was the hottest person on campus. In the winter of 2004 Zuckerberg launched Thefacebook.com, borrowing from his previous projects and adding elements that invited individuals to create personal profiles of themselves. The original Facebook concept was limited and innocent enough. Similar to most social networks up to that time, its primary purpose was to help people connect socially, often for dating, and its audience was limited initially to Harvard students. Quickly, other schools asked to join Thefacebook and set up sites for their students. By the end of the 2004 academic year, 34 schools had joined and Thefacebook had about 100,000 users. That was the beginning, but it was only the very beginning.

In a few years, Facebook (the name was changed in 2005) grew to be the powerhouse of social media. In 2010, approximately 143 million Americans were active on Facebook, representing 46.8 percent of the entire U.S. population, and that percentage has grown to over 70 percent by March 2021. For the third quarter of 2021, Facebook reported that more than 2.8 billion people were using at least one of its core services (Facebook, WhatsApp, Instagram, or Messenger) every day. Including active monthly users, that number jumps to over 3.5 billion. Users spend their time reacting to, commenting on, sharing, and scrolling through status updates, with the average user spending approximately 34 minutes per day on the site. In 2020, Facebook reported year-end revenues of over $85 billion.

Clearly, Facebook is a radical service innovation that has shown extraordinary growth and is extremely popular. Nothing like it existed before, and its limits and bounds are unknown. From the original basic social site for Harvard students, the company has evolved into a complex social networking giant. Some claim that entire industries—such as the photo-sharing industry and games—have been transformed through Facebook. Going far beyond its original focus on facilitating

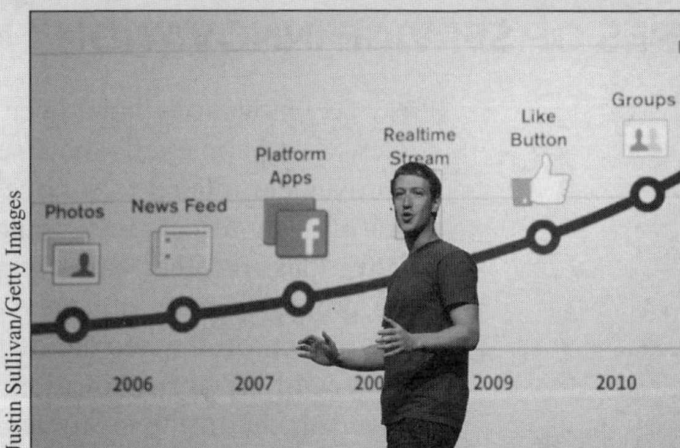

Justin Sullivan/Getty Images

Facebook CEO, Mark Zuckerberg, describes the company's rapid growth.

individual social connections, Facebook has introduced many new features and mobile phone applications.

It is easy to imagine that the future of Facebook will be bright, given its history and trajectory. It is highly innovative and far-reaching, and it seems to anticipate and understand the ways that people want to interact through technology. Still, the company (like the social media industry more broadly) has its challenges. The issue of user privacy comes up frequently and was addressed recently by Facebook through the creation of even more stringent options for users to control access to their personal information. Competition is always a challenge, and Facebook has continued to make strategic acquisitions to stay relevant (some examples include Instagram and WhatsApp). As of 2021, Facebook had acquired 85 companies, spending a total of almost $24 billion.

Time will tell who succeeds and who fails in the online social networking world. No matter how it turns out, it is certain that Mark Zuckerberg and Facebook launched a revolution and service innovation in networking that will affect individuals, companies, governments, and industries well into the future.

Sources: Facebook: Statistics & Facts, https://www.statista.com, accessed November 26, 2021; A. V. Ramzeen, "Facebook Acquisitions: The Complete List," https://www.techwyse.com, accessed November 26, 2021; D. Gelles, "Every Industry Is Going to Be Rethought in a Social Way," *Financial Times*, December 4, 2010, p. 14; D. Kirkpatrick, *The Facebook Effect*, New York: Simon & Schuster Paperbacks, 2010.

innovating, and improving service experiences based on these principles has resulted in a number of new terms, techniques, and methods being developed and applied, specifically for service innovation.[16] For example, terms such as *customer journey, touchpoints, personas, cocreation,* and *service prototypes* are common among service designers. Methodologies include customer journey mapping, storytelling, service safaris, shadowing, storyboarding, service role-play, and others. One of the primary techniques for service design is service blueprinting, presented in detail later in this chapter. Exhibit 8.2 (later in the chapter), describing Mayo Clinic's Center for Innovation, provides an example of design thinking in action.

TYPES OF SERVICE INNOVATION

Service innovations have been defined and categorized in various ways.[17] Sometimes when people talk about service innovation they are referring to innovation and improvement related to service offerings themselves. For example, McDonald Corporation's significant restaurant redesign and menu changes are examples of offering innovations. In other cases service innovation is associated with new internal service processes that will make an organization more productive and efficient. The introduction of new technology support systems for frontline employees represents this type of service innovation. In other cases service innovation is associated with enhancements in the customer experience or significant changes in the role of the customer. For example, the proliferation of self-service innovations has significantly altered the role of the customer in many industries. Our Technology Spotlight, featuring Facebook, provides an example of this type of radical service innovation. The term *service innovation* is also tied to major change initiatives within organizations, such as when a traditional manufacturing or operations-driven company decides to transform its entire go-to-market strategy around service and solutions rather than its products. At an even more macro level, service innovation can be tied to entire industries and service systems. For example, many of IBM's Smarter Planet initiatives aimed at transforming entire service systems, including health care, education, transportation, and government, through service innovations.

In this section, we cover several types of service innovations, including service offering innovation, innovating around customer roles, and innovation through service solutions.

Service Offering Innovation

Not all service innovations are "new" to the same degree. New services run the gamut from major or radical introductions to minor style changes, described below.

- *Major or radical innovations* are new services for markets as yet undefined. Past examples include the first broadcast television services and Federal Express's introduction of nationwide, overnight small-package delivery. Many current and future examples of radical innovations will be provided through the Cloud, mobile apps, and the Internet of Things. For example, many of the new services spawned by data being gathered from machines and people (e.g., remote repair service of machines and remote health diagnostics for people) were never even thought of until the data and software existed to support the service innovation. Often these major innovations create brand-new markets.[18]
- *New services for the currently served market* represent attempts to offer existing customers of the organization a service not previously available from the company (although it may be available from other companies). Examples include retailers adding a children's play area, a health club offering nutrition classes, and airlines offering phone and Internet services during flights. Sometimes they represent only modest enhancement services, as in these examples. Other times the offering may represent a new stand-alone service such as PetSmart's PetsHotels, described in the chapter opener.

- *Service-line extensions* represent augmentations of the existing service line, such as a restaurant adding new menu items, an airline offering new routes, a law firm offering additional legal services, and a university adding new courses or degrees.
- *Service improvements* represent perhaps the most common type of service innovation. Changes in features of services already offered might involve faster execution of an existing service process, extended hours of service, or augmentations such as added amenities in a hotel room (e.g., the addition of wireless Internet connections).
- *Style changes* represent the most modest service innovations, although they are often highly visible and can have significant effects on customer perceptions, emotions, and attitudes. Changing the color scheme of a restaurant, revising the logo for an organization, redesigning a website, or painting aircraft a different color all represent style changes. These innovations do not fundamentally change the service, only its appearance, similar to how packaging changes are used for consumer products.

Innovating around Customer Roles

The types of service innovations described in the preceding section are tied to the offerings themselves, suggesting that innovation occurs when a service offering is altered or expanded in some way—either radically on one extreme or stylistically at the other extreme. It is also possible that service innovations may come about when the customer's usage or cocreation role is redefined. For example, assuming the customer plays the role of user, buyer, or payer in a service context, new services can result when the previous role is redefined.[19] Many radical innovations effectively redefine the customer's role in these ways. For example, Netflix redefined the customer's role for movie rentals. While customers used to visit their local Blockbuster store to rent one or more movies for a predetermined period of time and pay for them on a per-movie basis, Netflix's initial innovation was to allow customers to receive movies through the mail, pay for them on a service contract, and return them whenever they were ready to do so. By now, countless customers stream movies, TV episodes, and other content via the Internet directly to their smart phones, TVs, or other devices. Thus, while movie watching in the home has not changed, the entire service process for acquiring, receiving, and paying for the movies is radically different.

Innovation through Service Solutions

Many organizations realize that customers are not looking for one stand-alone product or service but, rather, innovative solutions to their problems. Traditional thinking has viewed solutions, as defined by firms, as "bundles of goods and services" that companies offer to customers. However, solutions, as defined by customers, are not bundles of products and services at all, but rather they are sets of customer-facing processes. These processes comprise (1) customer requirements definition, (2) customization and integration of goods and/or services, (3) deployment of these integrated solutions, and (4) postdeployment customer support.[20] Another perspective views service innovation as the result of understanding customers' problems and the jobs they are trying to get done, then developing solutions to help them reach those goals.[21] From this perspective, the keys are to figure out what customers are trying to do and to develop services and solutions around that understanding. Yet other researchers focus on "customer activity chains" and the development of services and solutions to enhance these activities.[22] For example, Shutterfly offers all kinds of services online to enhance customers' sharing of memories through photography.

When companies begin to think in terms of solutions for customers, they start to spend more time with customers, listening to and observing their problems and identifying pain points that can be addressed through innovative solutions. In business-to-business contexts this often translates into companies' moving away from their traditional product offerings into activities such as business process outsourcing, consulting around areas of expertise, and managed services.[23] For example, Xerox provides a document management service, whereby it can take over the management of all documents (digital and paper) within an organization.

Solutions are relevant not only in business-to-business contexts. Some examples of consumer-focused solutions include our chapter opener, which illustrates PetSmart's move into "cradle-to-grave" solutions for pets and their parents, Shutterfly's photo management options, and Lowe's virtual home design services. Recent research points out the relevance of designing travel and vacation solutions for customers that take into account the collective and relational goals of family members.[24] The typical approach in the travel industry is to focus on the features and attributes of destinations rather than the sometimes conflicting goals that family members want to achieve through their vacation.

Service Innovation through Interconnected Products

One of the most ubiquitous and far-reaching trends in business today is the digitization of products. Everything—from home appliances, to industrial equipment, to medical equipment, clothing, and communication devices—can have sensors embedded in them, and everything can communicate. Through embedded sensors, products continuously emanate data—data that can be captured, connected, and transformed into information. Ultimately that information can be transformed into innovative services, frequently based on new service business models.

Here are just a few examples of the types of services that have been innovated through connected products: traffic signals that help monitor and optimize traffic flow, trucks that are equipped with sensors to monitor performance and predict failures and maintenance needs, onboard diagnostics in automobiles to enhance performance and safety, athletic shoes that monitor and communicate usage, and appliances and home systems that can be controlled remotely. In all cases, it is not the data itself that provides a service, but the use of that data to solve a customer problem, amplify the customer's knowledge and abilities, or create new capabilities. See Exhibit 8.1 for an example of how interconnected products can help solve the age-old and growing problem of medicine compliance.

This digital transformation of products is sometimes known as "The Internet of Things," or IoT, where products include sensors that are connected to the Internet. The IoT has allowed an explosion in services based on the data that passes between interconnected products. But this data does not become a service until someone figures out the value proposition (that is, what the data, perhaps combined with other data, can do for the customer), captures the correct data, and draws insights from the data that are useful to consumers, business customers, or governments.

The IoT is affecting almost every industry, and its potential grows daily. According to some estimates, there will be more than 25 billion devices on the IoT by 2030, a number that will continue to grow well into the future.[25] Interconnected products may be the single biggest change, challenge, and opportunity for companies across industries in terms of transforming competition, company practices, and providing unheralded service innovation opportunities.[26]

STAGES IN SERVICE INNOVATION AND DEVELOPMENT

In this section we focus on the actual steps followed in service innovation and development. These steps can be applied to any type of new service. Much of what is presented in this section has direct parallels in the new product development process for

Exhibit 8.1 Pills with Sensors Track Drug Usage by Patients

One of the biggest problems in medicine today is patient compliance. Large numbers of patients do not comply with the medical regimens they are prescribed—whether due to lack of willingness, forgetfulness, or confusion over the complexity of the medical plan. As the population ages, this problem is likely to grow into an even bigger problem. Loved ones are often challenged by the need to monitor pill usage by their family members, something that can be a burden and can also add considerable stress to already difficult situations. When family members live in different cities, this is even more difficult. Society also pays a price for medicine noncompliance in the form of visits to emergency departments, admissions to hospitals, and even the costs of institutionalization for patients who do not comply with critical psychological drug regimens.

According to Proteus Digital Health, 50 percent of all medications are not taken as prescribed—for a variety of reasons. The company offers a service, Proteus Discover, to address this problem. Proteus Discover is comprised of ingestible sensors, a small wearable sensor patch, an application on a mobile device, and a provider portal. The ingestible sensors, the size of a grain of sand, are embedded in the medication. Once the patient takes the medication, the sensor sends a signal to the wearable patch that the medication has been taken. This information is then sent to the patient's mobile device and transmitted onto the cloud where caregivers and family members (with the patient's permission) have access to the data. Whoever the patient designates can then confirm that the medication was taken or alert the patient to take it. The system also tracks patient activity and other health behaviors, like resting time.

Although ethical issues related to digital pills need to be carefully considered, this service clearly addresses an important need for the patient and their family and also a social need for greater medical compliance. While the digital pill concept and technology are valid and the societal need is real, Proteus and others have struggled to make the business model work amid the complexities of the pharmaceutical and health insurance industries. The connected product, or connected pill, is the technology innovation that makes the service innovation possible. Time, together with ethical and financial realities, will determine whether it ultimately succeeds.

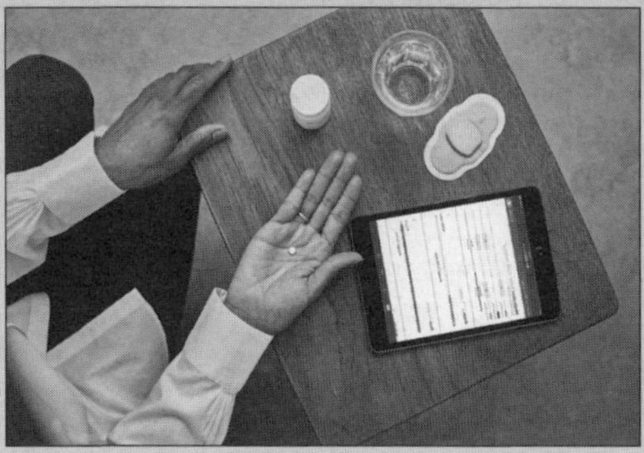

Petr Krejci/Proteus Digital

Proteus Digital Health provides a system for tracking and monitoring compliance using tiny ingestible sensors in pills.

Sources: A. Martani, L. D. Geneviève, C. Poppe, C. Casonato, and T. Wangmo, "Digital Pills: A Scoping Review of the Empirical Literature and Analysis of the Ethical Aspects," *BMC Medical Ethics*, 21 (December 2020), pp. 1–13. www.proteus.com, accessed July 22, 2016; A. Pai, "Proteus Digital Health Raises Another $50M for Ingestible Sensor-Enabled Digital Medicine," *MobiHealthNews*, April 15, 2016, http://www .mobihealthnews.com/content/proteus-digital-health-raises-another-50m-ingestible-sensor-enabled-digital-medicine.

manufactured goods. Because of the inherent characteristics of services, however, the development process for new services requires adaptations.[27] Figure 8.1 shows the basic principles and steps in new service development.[28] Although these steps are similar to those for manufactured goods, their implementation is different for services. The challenges typically lie in defining the concept in the early stages of the development process and again at the prototype development stage. Other challenges come about in the design and implementation of the new service because these steps often involve coordinating human resources, technology, internal processes, and facilities within already-existing systems. Partially because of these challenges, service firms are generally less likely to carry out a structured development process for new innovations than are their manufacturing and consumer-goods counterparts.[29]

An underlying assumption of new product development process models is that new product ideas can be dropped at any stage of the process if they do not satisfy the criteria for success at that stage.[30] Figure 8.1 shows the checkpoints (represented by stop signs) that separate the critical stages of the development process. The checkpoints specify requirements that a new service must meet before it can proceed to the next stage of development.

Despite what Figure 8.1 suggests, however, new service or product development *is not always a linear process*. Many companies find that some steps can be worked on simultaneously and in some instances a step may even be skipped, particularly for simple products and services. The overlapping of steps and simultaneous development

FIGURE 8.1 Service Innovation and Development Process

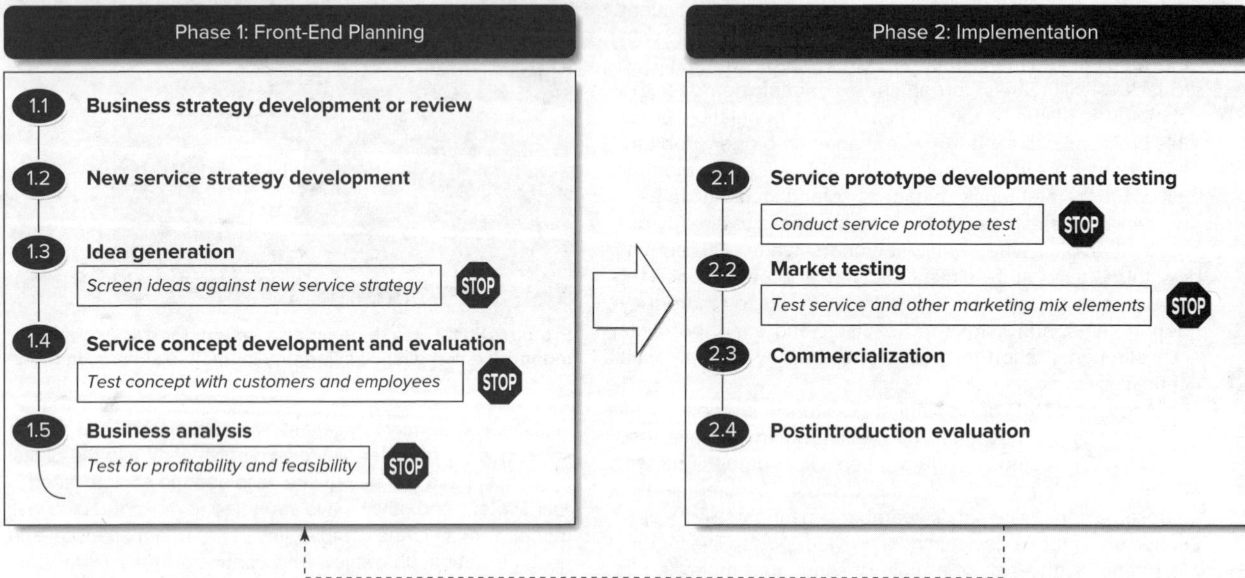

of various pieces of the new service/product development process has been referred to as *flexible product development.* This type of flexible, speedy process is particularly important in technology industries, in which products and services evolve extremely quickly. In these environments, computer technology lets companies monitor customer opinions and needs during development and change the final offering right up until it is launched. Often, the next version of the service is in planning stages at the same time that the current version is being launched. Even if the stages are handled simultaneously, however, the important checkpoints noted in Figure 8.1 should be assessed to maximize chances of success.

The process shown in Figure 8.1 is divided into two phases: front-end planning and implementation. The front end determines which service concepts will be developed, whereas the back end implements the focal service concept(s). When asked where the greatest weaknesses in product and service innovation occur, managers typically report problems with the *fuzzy front end.*[31] The front end is called "fuzzy" because of its relative abstractness, which is even more apparent with intangible, complex, and variable services than with manufactured products.

Phase 1: Front-End Planning

Business Strategy Development or Review

One of the first steps in new service development is to review the organization's mission and vision. The new service strategy and specific new service ideas must fit within the larger strategic mission and vision of the organization. For example, PetSmart, the company featured in this chapter's opening vignette, has as its mission that "PetSmart's passionate associates help bring pet parents closer to their pets so they can live more fulfilled lives." Accordingly, this mission has led to the development of a host of new services, such as training, grooming, overnight care, and day care, in addition to traditional food, toys, and accessories offered in its stores. For PetSmart, the company's new services strategy clearly fits the mission of the company.

FIGURE 8.2
New Service Strategy Matrix for Identifying Growth Opportunities

Source: Adapted from H. I. Ansoff, *Corporate Strategy* (New York: McGraw-Hill, 1965).

	Markets	
Offerings	Existing Customers	New Customers
Existing Services	**Market Penetration/Market Share Building:** sell more of the existing services in existing markets	**Market Development:** find or create new markets and sell the existing services in these new markets
New Services	**Service Development:** add new services and sell them in existing markets	**Diversification:** add new services and sell them in new markets

New Service Strategy Development

Research suggests that a product portfolio strategy and a defined organizational structure for new product or service development are critical—and are the foundations—for success. The types of new services that will be appropriate depend on the organization's goals, vision, capabilities, and growth plans. By defining a new service innovation strategy (possibly in terms of markets, types of services, time horizon for development, profit criteria, or other relevant factors), the organization will be in a better position to begin generating specific ideas. For example, it may focus its growth on new services at a particular level of the described continuum from major innovations to style changes. Or, the organization may define its new service strategy even more specifically in terms of particular markets or market segments, or in terms of specific profit generation goals.

One way to begin formulating a new service strategy is to use the influential framework shown in Figure 8.2 for identifying growth opportunities. The framework allows an organization to identify possible directions for growth and can be helpful as a catalyst for creative ideas. The framework may also later serve as an initial idea screen if, for example, the organization chooses to focus its growth efforts on one or two of the four cells in the matrix. The matrix suggests that companies can develop a growth strategy based on (1) serving either current or new customers/markets, and (2) selling either existing or new service offerings. For example, for quite some time Kentucky Fried Chicken (KFC) has grown through providing its service outside the United States, a form of market development (i.e., a combination of "existing services offered to new customers"). After over two decades of expansion in China, the company has now set its sights on Africa as its new market, where it targets the continent's growing middle class with over 1,000 KFC outlets on the African continent (most in South Africa) as of 2021.[32] The PetSmart services in our opening vignette, on the other hand, are examples of service development (new services, current customers). Procter & Gamble's venture into services through its Tide Dry Cleaners and Mr. Clean Car Washes are examples of growth through diversification (new services, new customers). Like Procter & Gamble and PetSmart, many companies are looking to grow strategically through service innovation (see the Strategy Insight).

Idea Generation

The next step in the process is the generation of new ideas that can be evaluated in light of the new service strategy screening criteria described in the preceding steps. Formal brainstorming, solicitation of ideas from employees and customers, lead user research, and learning about competitors' offerings are some of the most common

Strategy Insight Strategic Growth through Services

Firms in many industries are discovering the value of strategically focusing on service innovations to provide value for their customers as well as profits and growth for the firm. By adding services to their traditional offerings, firms can differentiate themselves from their competitors and frequently earn higher profit margins on the new services compared with traditional manufactured or retail product offerings. Here we highlight three firms from very diverse industries and their growth-through-services strategies.

PROCTER & GAMBLE

Procter & Gamble is one of the world's largest and most admired consumer products companies. So it may have come as a surprise when the company ventured into innovative services. Through its Agile Pursuits Franchising subsidiary (founded in 2008), P&G extended well-established and respected brands into the realm of service. Tide Dry Cleaners, and Mr. Clean Car Wash, and The Art of Shaving stores are examples. In each case, P&G looked for fragmented industries in which customer expectations are not particularly high and where P&G brand names could enhance value through proprietary technologies and an improved customer experience. For example, Tide Dry Cleaners feature bright, cheerful, bold-colored signage and interiors, drive-through lanes, and lockers accessible for after-hours pickup. The experience and the cleaning quality itself are intended to contrast sharply with consumers' experiences with typical dingy, dark, and sometimes inconvenient dry cleaners. However, P&G's expansion into services must be very deliberate and done with great care so as not to risk harming the parent brand.

Ed Zurga/Bloomberg/Getty Images

Tide Dry Cleaners—a service strategy for Procter & Gamble.

ERICSSON

Headquartered in Sweden, Ericsson is a leading global provider of telecommunications equipment and related services and solutions. Since the mid-1990s, it has pursued a growth strategy focused on customers, services, and solutions that add value to its sophisticated technology products. Ericsson employs about 100,000 professionals and operates in over 180 countries. Ericsson Global Services focuses on providing services for telecommunication operators around the world, so that these companies can focus on their core business of supporting customers and building revenues. For example, through its managed services contracts, Ericsson works with operators to upgrade their systems and consults with them on network planning, design, and deployment. Beyond the basics of operational efficiency and reliability of systems, Ericsson also focuses on the experience of its customers' customers. They have innovated the managed services offering to include customer experience design and delivery metrics as well as operational metrics in their performance assessments. In addition to operators, Ericsson works directly with government and private business entities.

As Ericsson continues to move away from its traditional base in manufacturing, the company is reorienting its entire organization toward providing integrated solutions for customers.

VWR

VWR is part of Avantor (a Fortune 500 company) and its tagline is "we set science in motion to create a better world." VWR "is the leading, global, independent provider of products, services, and solutions to laboratory and production facilities for customers in the pharmaceutical, biotechnology, industrial, education, government and healthcare industries." This 160-year-old company serves scientific laboratories across industries in helping them to be more effective and efficient at what they do. VWR started as a product distribution company that supplied all types of scientific products (for example, beakers, pipettes, measurement scales, and so on) to labs and production facilities. As they progressed as a company, they realized that the employees of their customers—the people who actually did the science—were spending a lot of their time on non-core activities. To be specific, these highly paid scientists were spending time ordering supplies, cleaning equipment, and configuring combinations of materials they needed to run experiments, among other things, and not doing science. Enter VWRCatalyst, which was founded as VWR's service company. VWRCatalyst provides services to its customers to allow them to focus on what they do best—science—while VWR manages their inventories of supplies, cleans their equipment, and customizes packages of materials to efficiently conduct experiments in labs. VWRCatalyst can even send its employees to work alongside the customer's employees—serving as lab techs, supply managers, or in scientific support roles. VWRCatalyst supports more than 250,000 customers and employs more than 12,000 associates around the world, providing innovative services that help its customers to be more productive, efficient, and effective.

For each of these companies, the move to services represented a significant strategic choice that initially took them into uncharted waters. Yet the potential rewards are great and customer demands for services and solutions are real. These rewards and demands are what compel more and more firms to pursue the strategic service path.

However, sometimes marketplace or environmental factors force companies to rethink their service provision, as we briefly illustrate next.

IMPOSED SERVICE INNOVATION

The COVID-19 pandemic not only triggered a health crisis but also a global economic downturn, which compelled many organizations to develop service innovations. One empirical study examined more than 200 of these innovations that are included in a publicly available database called www.covidinnovations.com. Some major categories of these innovations include:

- **Delivery innovations:** These innovations redesign the time and location of service delivery and use. One major illustration are contactless or remote deliveries due to COVID-19. For example, many hotels, restaurants, and bars started providing takeaway and drive-through options and curbside pick-ups. Other supermarkets (e.g., Carrefour) collaborated with on-demand meal delivery services (e.g., Uber Eats) to manage home deliveries. Some retailers in Asia intensified the focus on technology and used robots to deliver groceries. Notably, some innovations also focus on the timing of service delivery (e.g., some stores introduced "dedicated shopping hours" especially for vulnerable customers).
- **Health and well-being innovations:** Besides obvious innovations related to the treatment of COVID-19 (e.g., in telemedicine), some innovations also aim to reduce stress and anxiety during the pandemic (e.g., the mental health app My Possible Self provides psychological strategies and coping skills). Other innovations focus on physical health and motivate people to move during the pandemic (StepSetGo, Moments2Move).
- **Physical and social distancing innovations:** These innovations leveraged both tangible and intangible technical features to help people follow safety guidelines and keep sufficient distance from others. For example, the Fortum Vipu is a hands-free door handle made of recycled plastic that allows people to open doors without touching the handle.
- **Education innovations:** The pandemic imposed many novel pedagogical approaches to support distance learning and knowledge development. For example, zoos, museums, K-12 schools, and universities developed new educational platforms to provide livestreams, behind-the-scenes videos, and interactive activities to enable learning during the pandemic.
- **Social connection innovations:** Because of the pandemic-related social isolation, some innovations provided access to virtual experiences to connect people and foster a sense of community (e.g., the Goodnight Zoom storytelling app, or Netflix Party that allows joint streaming of movies/TV shows and social gaming).

These insights illustrate that a global crisis such as the COVID-19 pandemic functions as a catalyst for service innovations as it forced organizations to rethink, redesign, or reinvent their business strategies.

Sources: K. Heinonen and T. Strandvik, "Reframing Service Innovation: COVID-19 as a Catalyst for Imposed Service Innovation," *Journal of Service Management* 32 (January 2021), pp. 101–112; M. Sawhney, S. Balasubramanian, and V. V. Krishnan, "Creating Growth with Services," *Sloan Management Review* 45 (Winter 2004), pp. 34–43; L. Coleman-Lochner and M. Clothier, "P&G Looks to Franchise Tide Dry Cleaning," *Bloomberg Businessweek*, September 2, 2010; B. Brown and S. D. Anthony, "How P&G Tripled Its Innovation Success Rate," *Harvard Business Review* 89 (June 2011), pp. 64–72; L. A. Bettencourt, *Service Innovation* (New York: McGraw-Hill, 2010), https://www.ericsson.com/portfolio/services-and-solutions, accessed July 25, 2016; https://us.vwr.com/cms/about_vwr, accessed November 27, 2021; V. A. Zeithaml, S. W. Brown, M. J. Bitner, and J. Salas, *Profiting from Services and Solutions: What Product-Centric Firms Need to Know* (Business Expert Press, New York 2014).

approaches. Some companies are even collaborating with outsiders (e.g., competitors, vendors, alliance partners) or developing licensing agreements and joint ventures in an effort to exploit all possible sources of new ideas.[33]

Observing customers and how they use the firm's products and services can also generate creative ideas for new innovations. Sometimes referred to as *empathic design,* observation is particularly effective in situations in which customers may not be able to recognize or verbalize their needs.[34] In service businesses, contact personnel, who actually deliver the services and interact directly with customers, can be particularly good sources of ideas for complementary services and ways to improve current offerings.[35] Some organizations have found that internal networks of employees, across functions and disciplines, can be great sources of innovative ideas; thus, organizational practices that encourage networking and make collaboration easy are also ways to encourage new ideas.[36]

Whether the source of a new idea is inside or outside the organization, some established mechanism should exist for ensuring an ongoing stream of new service possibilities. This mechanism might include a formal service innovation or service R&D department or function with responsibility for generating new ideas, online repositories where customers and/or employees can submit ideas for new services, new service development teams that meet regularly, surveys and focus groups with customers and employees, or formal competitive analysis to identify new services.

Service Concept Development and Evaluation

Once an idea surfaces that is regarded as a good fit with both the business and the new service strategies, it is ready for initial development. The inherent characteristics of services place complex demands on this phase of the process. Drawing pictures and describing an intangible service in concrete terms are difficult, particularly when the service is not standardized and may be cocreated in real time with customers. It is therefore important that agreement be reached at this stage on exactly what the concept is and what customer need it is fulfilling. By involving multiple parties in sharpening the concept definition, it often becomes apparent that individual views of the concept are not the same. For example, in one documented case, the design and development of a new discount brokerage service was initially described by the bank as a way "to buy and sell stocks for customers at low prices."[37] Through the initial concept development phase it became clear that not everyone in the organization had the same idea about how this description would translate into an actual service and that there were a variety of ways the concept could be developed. Only through multiple iterations of the service—and the raising of hundreds of issues, large and small—was an agreement finally reached on the discount brokerage concept.

After clear definition of the concept, it is important to produce a description of the service that represents its specific characteristics and then determine initial customer and employee responses to the concept. The service design document should describe the problem addressed by the service, discuss the reasons for offering the new service, explain the service process and its benefits, and provide a rationale for purchasing the service.[38] The roles of customers and employees in the delivery and/or cocreation process are also described. It may also be very useful to create a concept-level blueprint (explained in detail later in this chapter) at this point in the service innovation process. The service concept is then evaluated by asking employees and customers whether they understand the idea of the proposed service, whether they are favorable to the concept, and whether they feel it satisfies an unmet need.

Business Analysis

Assuming that the service concept is favorably evaluated by customers and employees at the concept development stage, the next step is to estimate its economic feasibility and potential profit implications. Demand analysis, revenue projections, cost analyses, and operational feasibility are assessed at this stage. Because the development of service concepts is so closely tied to the operational system of the organization, this stage will involve preliminary assumptions about the costs of personnel hiring and training, delivery system enhancements, new technology or online enhancements, facility changes, and any other projected operations costs. The organization will pass the results of the business analysis through its profitability and feasibility screen to determine whether the new service idea meets the minimum requirements.

Phase 2: Implementation

Once the new service concept has passed all the front-end planning hurdles, it is ready for the implementation stages of the process.

Service Prototype Development and Testing

In the development of new tangible products, the development and testing stage involves the construction of product prototypes and testing for consumer acceptance. Again, because services are intangible and simultaneously produced, consumed, and frequently cocreated, this step presents unique challenges. To address these challenges, this stage of service development should involve all who have a stake in the new service: customers and contact employees as well as functional representatives from marketing, operations, and human resources. During this phase, the concept is refined to the point at which a detailed service blueprint illustrating the customer experience and the implementation plan for the service can be produced. The blueprint is likely to evolve over a series of iterations on the basis of input from all involved parties.

For example, in its service innovation practice, the internationally known design firm IDEO makes extensive use of full-scale prototypes and mock-ups to experiment with service concepts, testing both customer reactions and operational aspects of the service. In its work with Marriott's extended stay hotel chain, TownePlace suites, IDEO's Smart Space researchers first spent several weeks living in and talking with TownePlace guests to observe and learn how they used the space and what their unmet needs were.[39] The result was a completely redesigned lobby area, including a map wall with notations about local shopping, restaurants, parks, and recreation areas that can be annotated by guests. Another change was a redesigned bedroom that provides the flexibility to be turned into a workspace. To test the design concepts, IDEO built a life-sized lobby and suite out of white foam core and invited Marriott executives, hotel managers, and guests to provide feedback on the prototype. Similar service innovation prototyping and testing projects have been undertaken by IDEO for many other service organizations, including Walgreens's designing the pharmacy experience for the 21st century, Lufthansa's reimagining the first-class flying experience, and Holiday Inn Express Europe's revamping the brand in Europe by redesigning everything from public places to food and beverage, to guest room and digital experiences.[40] Exhibit 8.2 illustrates how Mayo Clinic's Center for Innovation tests new patient experience concepts and health delivery services.

Market Testing

At the market testing stage of the development process, a tangible product might be test marketed in a limited number of trading areas to determine marketplace acceptance of

Exhibit 8.2 Service Innovation at the Mayo Clinic

The Mayo Clinic in the United States is more than 100 years old and one of the most respected names in health care globally. It is consistently listed among the top hospitals in the United States and is known for its collaborative health care model, high levels of service, and position in the forefront of medicine. Following its innovative traditions, Mayo established its Center for Innovation (formerly the SPARC Innovation Lab) to focus on innovating and "transforming the experience of health and healthcare." While medical and technological advances have changed the face of health care dramatically over the past 50 years, the same is not necessarily true of the way health care is delivered to patients. Everything from patient exam rooms to the patient's waiting experience has changed relatively little in comparison to scientific advances in medicine. Mayo recognized this and determined it should again be in the forefront of innovation—this time in the processes and practices of health care delivery.

The Center for Innovation with more than 50 full-time staff including service designers, project managers, IT specialists, and clinicians, has become a testing ground for all types of service and delivery innovations at Mayo—innovations that are intended to enhance the patient's experience and that have potential health benefits. Working with the design firm IDEO, Mayo designed an experimental lab and innovation center at its Rochester, Minnesota, facility, where service innovations can be tested with real patients and real Mayo doctors and staff before they are introduced into the clinics. The lab is set up as an actual clinic within the Mayo facility, and experiments are conducted with doctors and patients (of course, with their prior knowledge and consent). The space is highly flexible, so that exam rooms, common spaces, walls, furniture, and computers can be moved around to test different configurations and services. Sometimes researchers take their questions and experiments into

Center for Innovation (CFI) at Mayo Clinic, Rochester. For a virtual tour of the CFI, visit: http://www.cfitour.com.

the product as well as other marketing mix variables such as promotion, pricing, and distribution systems. Because new service offerings are often intertwined with the delivery system for existing services, it is difficult to test new services in isolation. And in some cases, it may not even be possible to introduce the service to an isolated market area because the organization has only one place where it provides its services. There are alternative ways of testing the response to marketing mix variables, however. The new service might be offered to employees of the organization and their families for a time to assess their responses to variations in the marketing mix.

It is also extremely important at this stage in the development process to continue "pilot testing" to make sure that the operational details are functioning smoothly. Frequently this step is overlooked, and the actual market introduction may be the first test of whether the service system functions as planned. By this point, mistakes in design are harder to correct. As one noted service expert says, "There is simply no substitute for a proper rehearsal" when introducing a new service.[41]

Commercialization

During the commercialization stage, the service goes live and is introduced to the marketplace. This stage has two primary objectives. The first is to build and maintain acceptance of the new service among large numbers of the service delivery personnel who are responsible day-to-day for service quality. This task is made easier if acceptance has been built by involving service delivery personnel as one of the key groups in the design and development process all along. The second objective is to monitor all the clinics themselves, working directly with doctors and patients on site.

Within the Center for Innovation, researchers focus on complex and important issues for the health care industry in general, with the overarching principle of "patient-centered design." For example, here are some of the topics they have explored and "re-imagined"—the term they use for service improvement and futuristic innovation:

- What would integrated health care look like from the patient's perspective?
- What is the relationship among communication, understanding, and satisfaction for the patient?
- How could exam rooms be reconfigured for a better patient experience and to improve patient–doctor communication?
- How can the on-site check-in process for appointments be improved?
- How can space within the health care facility be optimized to serve patients and staff?
- What are the unmet educational needs of patients, and how can a service be designed to meet those needs?

While innovation in health care delivery practices such as those listed is rare, Mayo's practices within the Center for Innovation are unique—combining principles from service, design, and health care. For example, the patient check-in process at Mayo Rochester was viewed as particularly problematic for patients, with long lines and frustration at having to stand and wait when all they wanted to do was sit down. The multidisciplinary team began by observing and listening to both patients and staff to start the process of identifying innovative solutions to this challenge. Through this human-centered, participatory approach, they developed ideas by conveying narratives that morphed into innovations, which were tested with prototypes in the lab. In the case of the patient check-in process, the basic innovation idea was to develop an automated self-check-in process. Initial prototypes of the self-service check-in kiosk were quite unsophisticated. For example, the first version was a piece of paper representing a computer screen. Later versions of the prototype evolved to inactive computer screens to actual touch screens displayed on a kiosk. At each version of the prototype, the team collected feedback from both patients and staff. The results of this experiment led Mayo to invest resources in investigating a roll-out of this innovative solution.

Mayo's continued commitment to innovation in health care is also seen in its partnership with Google. The companies collaborate to redefine how health care is delivered: Mayo employs Google's advanced cloud computing, data analytics, machine learning, and artificial intelligence (AI) to further accelerate the pace of health care innovation and to improve health care.

Sources: Mayoclinic.org, accessed November 26, 2021; N. LaRusso, G. Farrugia, and B. Spurrier, *Think Big, Start Small, Move Fast: A Blueprint for Transformation from the Mayo Clinic Center for Innovation* (McGraw-Hill, 2014). http://www.mayo.edu/center-for-innovation, 2016; C. Salter, "A Prescription for Innovation," *Fast Company* (April 2006), p. 83.

aspects of the service during introduction and through the complete service cycle. If the customer needs six months to experience the entire service, then careful monitoring must be maintained through at least six months. Every detail of the service should be assessed—phone calls, face-to-face transactions, billing, complaints, and delivery problems. Operating efficiency and costs should also be tracked.

Postintroduction Evaluation

At this point, the information gathered during commercialization of the service can be reviewed and refinements made to the delivery process, staffing, or marketing mix variables on the basis of actual market response to the offering. No service will ever stay the same. Whether deliberate or unplanned, changes will always occur. Therefore, formalizing the review process to make those changes that enhance service quality from the customer's point of view is critical.

SERVICE BLUEPRINTING: A TECHNIQUE FOR SERVICE INNOVATION AND DESIGN

A stumbling block in service innovation and design is the difficulty of describing and depicting the service throughout the developmental stages. One of the keys to matching service specifications to customer expectations is the ability to describe critical service process characteristics objectively and to depict them so that employees, customers, and

FIGURE 8.3
Service Blueprinting

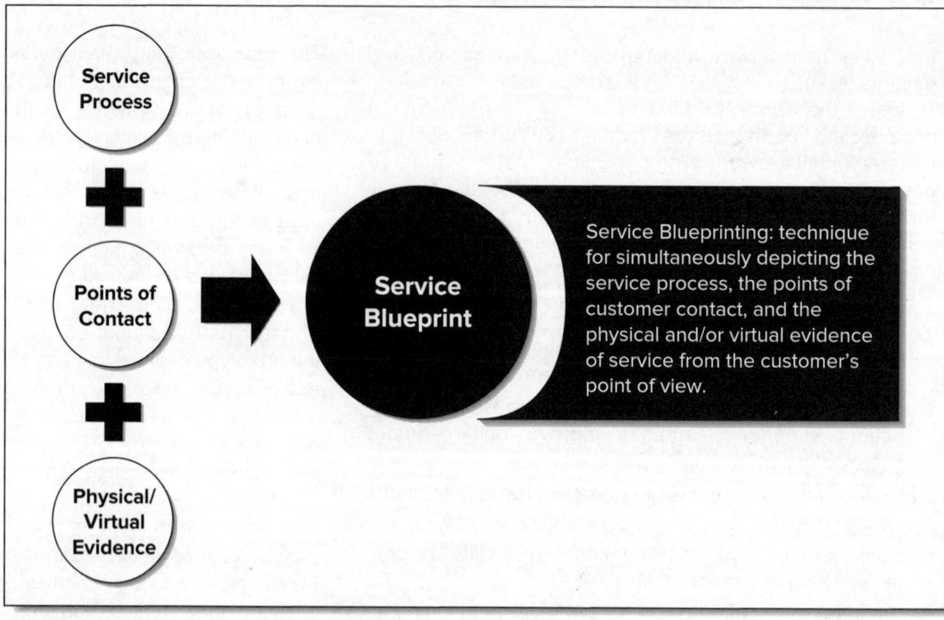

managers alike know what the service is, can see their roles, and can understand all the details involved in the service process. In this section, we look at service blueprinting, a highly useful technique for designing and specifying intangible service processes.[42]

What Is a Service Blueprint?

A *service blueprint* is a picture or map that portrays the customer experience and the service system, so that the different people involved in providing the service can understand it objectively, regardless of their roles or their individual points of view. Blueprints are particularly useful at the design stage of service development. A service blueprint visually displays the service by simultaneously depicting the process of service delivery, the points of customer contact, the roles of customers and employees, and the visible elements of the service (see Figure 8.3). It provides a way to break a service down into its logical components and to depict the steps or tasks in the process, the means by which the tasks are executed, and the physical and/or virtual evidence of service as the customer experiences it. Blueprinting has its origins in a variety of fields and techniques, including logistics, industrial engineering, decision theory, computer systems analysis, and software engineering—all of which deal with the definition and explanation of processes.[43] Because services are "experiences" rather than objects or technologies, blueprinting is a particularly useful technique for describing them.

Blueprint Components

The key components of service blueprints are shown in Figure 8.4.[44] They are customer actions, onstage/visible contact employee actions, backstage/invisible contact employee actions, and support processes. The conventions for drawing service blueprints are not rigidly defined, and thus the particular symbols used, the number of horizontal lines in the blueprint, and the labels for each part of the blueprint may vary somewhat depending on the complexity of the blueprint being described. These variations are not a problem, as long as you keep in mind the purpose of the blueprint and view it as a useful technique rather than as a set of rigid rules for designing services. In fact, its flexibility—when compared with other process mapping approaches—is one of service blueprinting's major strengths.

FIGURE 8.4
Service Blueprint Components for In-Person Services

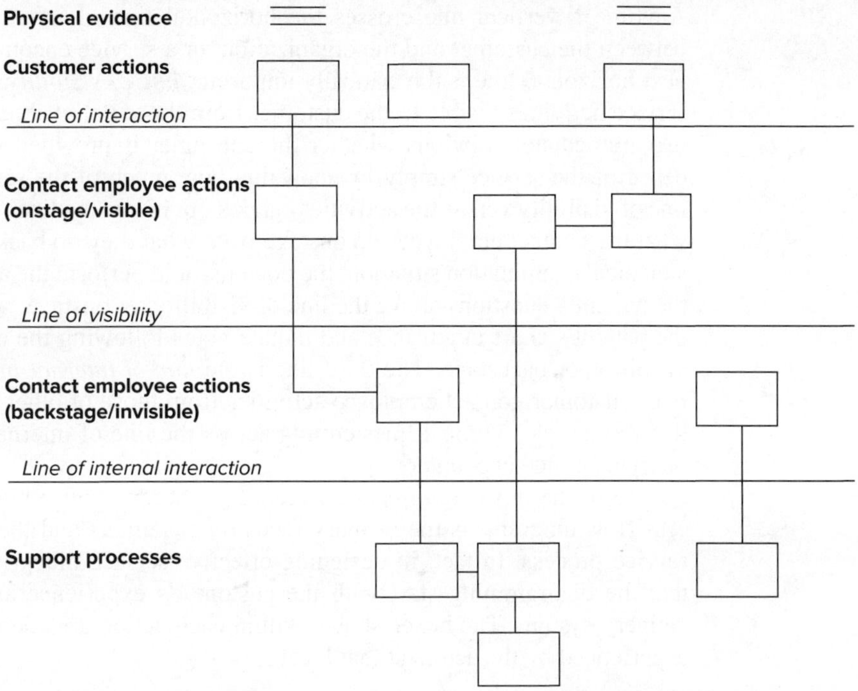

The *customer actions* area encompasses the steps, choices, activities, and interactions that the customer performs in the process of purchasing, experiencing, and evaluating the service. The total customer experience is apparent in this area of the blueprint. In a legal services example, the customer actions might include a decision to contact an attorney, phone calls to the attorney, face-to-face meetings, receipt of documents, and receipt of a bill.

Paralleling the customer actions are two areas of contact employee actions. The activities that the contact employee performs that are visible to the customer are the *onstage/visible contact employee actions.* In the legal services setting, the actions of the attorney (the contact employee) visible to the client are, for example, the initial interview, intermediate meetings, and final face-to-face delivery of legal documents.

Those contact employee actions that occur behind the scenes to support the onstage activities are the *backstage/invisible contact employee actions.* In the example, anything the attorney does behind the scenes to prepare for the meetings or to prepare the final documents will appear in this section of the blueprint, together with all other *nonvisible* contact employee actions.

The *support processes* section of the blueprint covers the internal services, steps, and interactions that take place to support the contact employees in delivering the service. Again, in our legal example, any service support activities such as legal research by staff, preparation of documents, and secretarial support to set up meetings will be shown in the support processes area of the blueprint.

At the very top of the blueprint you see the *physical evidence* of the service. Typically, above each point of contact the actual physical evidence of the service is listed. In the legal example, the physical evidence of the face-to-face meeting with the attorney would be such items as office decor, written documents, lawyer's clothing, and so forth.

The four key action areas are separated by three horizontal lines. First is the *line of interaction,* representing direct interactions between the customer and the organization.

Anytime a vertical line crosses the horizontal line of interaction, a direct contact between the customer and the organization, or a service encounter, has occurred. The next horizontal line is the critically important *line of visibility.* This line separates all service activities visible to the customer from those not visible. In reading blueprints, it is immediately obvious whether the consumer is provided with much visible evidence of the service simply by analyzing how much of the service occurs above the line of visibility versus the activities carried out below the line. This line also separates what the contact employees do onstage from what they do backstage. For example, in a medical examination situation, the doctor would perform the actual exam and answer the patient's questions above the line of visibility, or onstage, whereas she might read the patient's chart in advance and dictate notes following the exam below the line of visibility, or backstage. The third line is the *line of internal interaction,* which separates customer-contact employee activities from those of other service support activities and people. Vertical lines cutting across the line of internal interaction represent internal service encounters.

One of the most significant differences between service blueprints and other process flow diagrams is the primary focus on customers and their experience with the service process. In fact, in designing effective service blueprints it is recommended that the diagramming start with the customer's experience and then work into the delivery system. The boxes shown within each action area depict steps performed or experienced by the actors at that level.

Service Blueprint Examples

Figure 8.5 shows a service blueprint for an overnight hotel stay.[45] This blueprint is deliberately kept very simple, showing only the most basic steps in the services. Complex diagrams could be developed for each step, and the internal processes could be much more fully developed. In addition to the four action areas separated by the three horizontal lines, the blueprint also shows the physical evidence of the service from the customer's point of view at each step of the process.

In the overnight hotel stay depicted in Figure 8.5, the customer obviously is actively involved in the service. The guest first checks in, then goes to the hotel room, where a variety of steps take place (receiving bags, sleeping, showering, eating breakfast, and so on), and finally checks out. Imagine how much more complex this process could be and how many more interactions could occur if the service blueprint depicted a week-long vacation at the hotel, or even a three-day business conference. Or, imagine how much simpler the top row of the blueprint would look for a service such as express mail delivery where the customer engages with few employees and has very few actions. The service blueprint also makes clear (by reading across the line of interaction) those employees who directly interact with the customer. Each step in the customer action area is also associated with various forms of physical evidence, from the hotel parking area and hotel exterior and interior to the forms used at guest registration, the lobby, the room, and the food. In the hotel case, the process is relatively complex (although again somewhat standardized), the people providing the service are a variety of frontline employees, and the physical evidence includes everything from the guest registration form to the lobby and room decor, to the uniforms worn by frontline employees.

Blueprints for Technology-Delivered Self-Service

To this point our discussion of service blueprints has related to services delivered in person, that is services in which employees interact directly with customers at some point in the process. But what about technology-delivered services including self-service

FIGURE 8.5 Blueprint for Overnight Hotel Stay Service

Source: E. E. Scheuing and W. F. Christopher, *Service Quality Handbook,* 1993, AM MGMT ASSN/AMACOM(B).

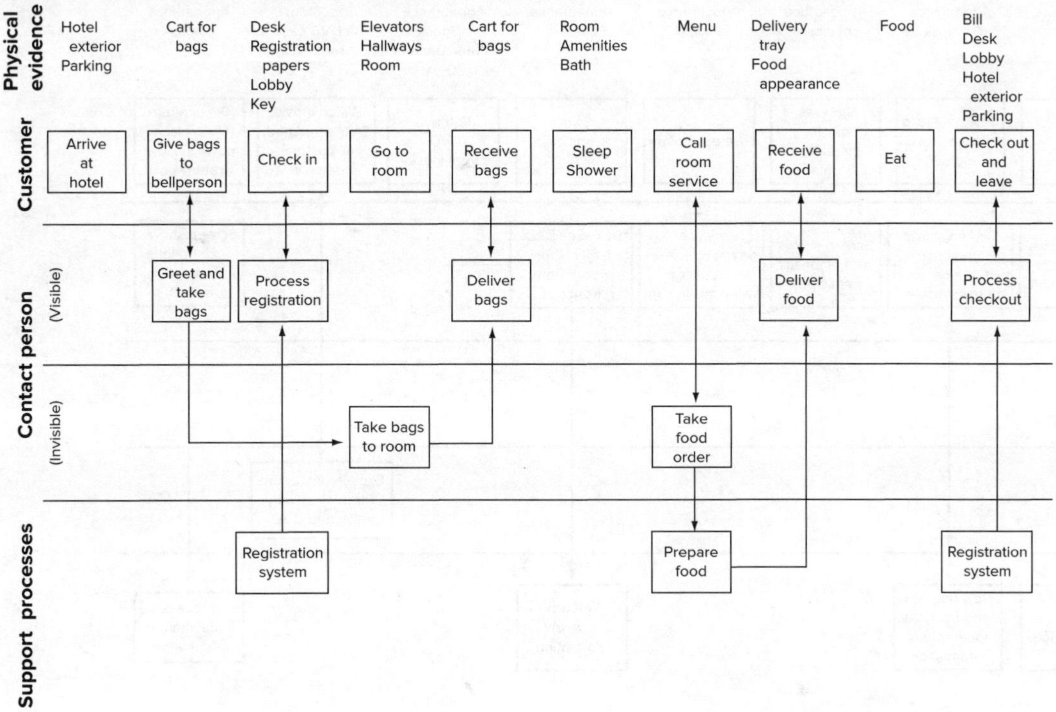

websites and interactive self-service kiosks? Can service blueprinting be used effectively to design these types of services? Certainly it can, but the lines of demarcation will change, and some blueprint labels may need to be adapted.

If no employees are involved in the service (except when there is a problem or the service does not function as planned), the contact person areas of the blueprint are not needed. Instead, the area above the line of visibility can be used to illustrate the interface between the customer and the website or the physical interaction with the kiosk. This area can be relabeled *onstage/visible technology.* The backstage contact person actions area is irrelevant in this case.

Many services have both interpersonal and technology-delivered elements. Consider the airline check-in process. The actual check-in may be done through an electronic kiosk, while baggage, security screening, and handling of tickets while boarding are all done by people. In such a case, the blueprint would include all three contact rows: one for technology, one for the onstage contact person (visible), and one for the backstage contact person (invisible). Figure 8.6 is a blueprint for a self-service DVD rental kiosk, showing the technology interactions in the added "onstage technology" area of the blueprint. This blueprint also illustrates what the customer experiences if the DVD is scratched. When that happens, the customer calls customer service, a "backstage contact person (invisible)" activity.

Reading and Using Service Blueprints

A service blueprint can be read in a variety of ways, depending on the purpose. If the purpose is to understand the customer's view of the process or the customer experience, the blueprint can be read *from left to right,* tracking the events in the customer action area. Questions that might be asked include these: How is the service

FIGURE 8.6 **Blueprint for a Self-Service DVD Rental Kiosk**

Source: Amy L Ostrom and Center for Services Leadership. © 2011 by Arizona State University. All rights reserved. Used with permission.

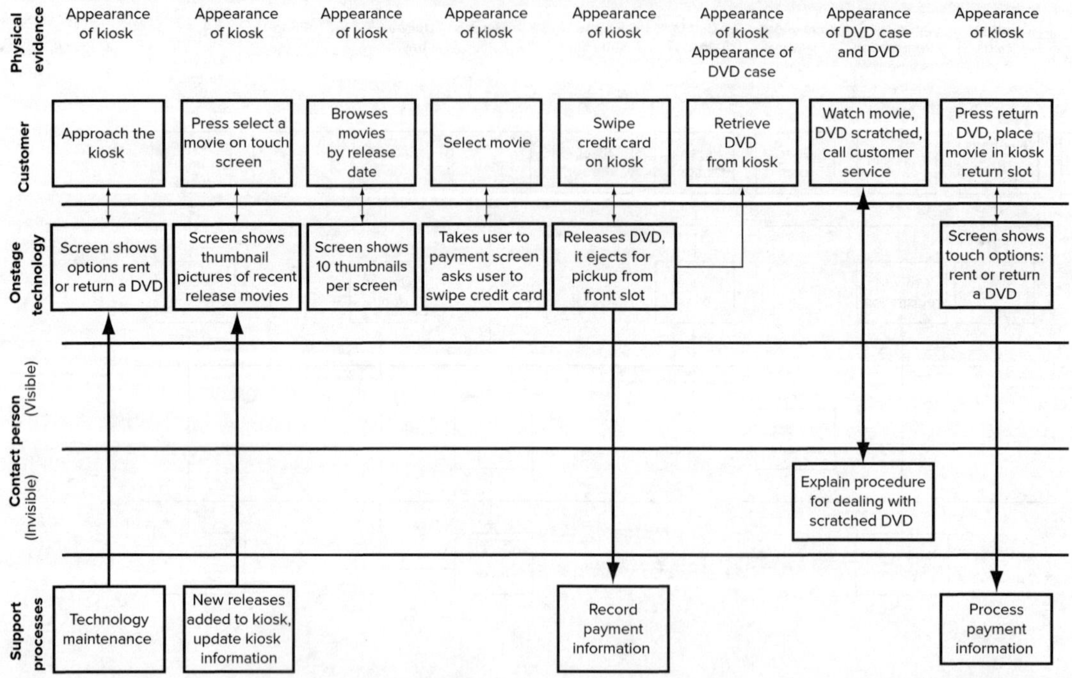

initiated by the customer? What choices does the customer make? Is the customer highly involved in cocreating the service, or are few actions required of the customer? What is the physical evidence of the service from the customer's point of view? Is the evidence consistent with the organization's strategy and positioning?

If the purpose is to understand contact employees' roles or the integration of onstage technology with contact employee activities, the blueprint can also be read *horizontally* but this time focusing on the activities directly above and below the line of visibility. Questions that might be asked include these: How rational, efficient, and effective is the process? Who interacts with customers, when, and how often? Is one person responsible for the customer, or is the customer passed off from one contact employee to another? Are interactions and handoffs between people and technology integrated and seamless from the customer's point of view?

If the purpose is to understand the integration of the various elements of the service process, or to identify where particular employees fit into the bigger picture, the blueprint can be *analyzed vertically.* In this analysis, it becomes clear what tasks and which employees are essential in the delivery of service to the customer. The linkages from internal actions deep within the organization to frontline effects on the customer can also be seen in the blueprint. Questions that might be asked include these: What actions are being performed backstage to support critical customer interaction points? What are the associated support actions? How are handoffs from one employee to another taking place?

If the purpose is service redesign, the blueprint can be looked at *as a whole to* assess the complexity of the process, how it might be changed, and how changes from the customer's point of view would affect the contact employee and other internal processes, and vice versa. Blueprints can also be used to assess the overall efficiency and productivity of the service system and to evaluate how potential changes will affect the system.[46] The blueprint can also be analyzed to determine likely failure points or bottlenecks in the process, as well as customer pain points. When such points are discovered, a firm can introduce measures to track failures, or that part of the blueprint can be exploded, so that the firm can focus in much greater detail on that piece of the system.

Blueprinting applications in a variety of contexts have demonstrated multiple benefits, including the following:[47]

- Recognizing roles and interdependencies among functions, people, and organizations.
- Providing a platform for both strategic and tactical innovations.
- Transferring and storing innovation and service knowledge.
- Designing moments of truth from the customer's point of view.
- Suggesting critical points for measurement and feedback in the service process.
- Clarifying competitive positioning.
- Understanding the ideal customer experience.

Building a Blueprint

Recall that many of the benefits of building a blueprint evolve from the process of doing it. The development of the blueprint needs to involve a variety of functional representatives as well as information from customers. Building a blueprint is not a task that should be assigned to one person or one functional area. Figure 8.7 identifies the basic steps in building a blueprint.

Step 1: Identify the Service Process to Be Blueprinted

Blueprints can be developed at a variety of levels, and there needs to be agreement on the starting point. For example, the overnight hotel stay blueprint shown in Figure 8.5 is at the basic service concept level. Little detail is shown, and variations based on market segment or specific services are not shown. Specific blueprints could be developed for extended stays or additional services during the hotel stay (e.g., spa services). Each of these blueprints would share some features with the concept blueprint but would also include unique features. Or if the "check out" element of the process were found to be a problem area, a detailed blueprint of the subprocesses at work in this step could be developed.

Step 2: Identify the Customer (Segment) Experiencing the Service

A common rationale for market segmentation is that each segment's needs are different and therefore will require variations in the service or product features. Thus, blueprints are most useful when developed for a particular customer or customer segment, assuming that the service process varies across segments. At a very abstract

FIGURE 8.7
Six Steps of Building a Service Blueprint

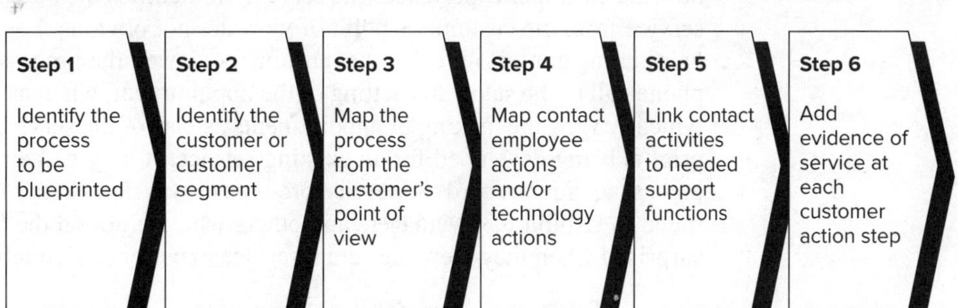

Exhibit 8.3 Blueprinting in Action at ARAMARK Parks and Destinations

ARAMARK is a global leader in professional services, operating as an outsourcer for food, hospitality, facility management, and uniform services. ARAMARK's customers include large businesses, universities, health care organizations, parks and resorts, convention centers, and other groups. The company has approximately 210,000 employees serving clients in 22 countries. One of its divisions is ARAMARK Parks and Destinations, a group that provides services for major park destinations within the United States, including Denali National Park in Alaska, Olympic National Park in Washington State, and Lake Powell Destinations and Marinas in the Glen Canyon National Recreation Area of Arizona. Each of the parks has at least three or four service businesses within it that ARAMARK operates on an outsourcing contract.

GOAL: SERVICE IMPROVEMENT AND CUSTOMER RETENTION

A number of years ago, Renee Ryan, then marketing director for ARAMARK Parks, confronted a challenge. It was clear that repeat business at ARAMARK's parks was declining overall. This was particularly the case at Lake Powell Resorts and Marinas in Arizona, where the company operated houseboat rentals, a resort, campgrounds, boat tours, and food service operations. Research revealed that many people were not returning to Lake Powell because their first experience there did not match what they had expected or were accustomed to based on visits to other resort destinations. Ryan employed both traditional and visual (photos, video) blueprints to help convince the organization that changes were in order and specifically what should be done. The results benefited customers through improvements in service and the company through increased repeat business.

First, Ryan developed a blueprint of a typical, quality hotel/resort experience from a typical customer's point of view. Then she blueprinted the Lake Powell resort experience. The comparison of the two blueprints was revealing in terms of differences in basic services, standards, and processes. This comparison process resulted in the development of new services, facilities upgrades, and modernization of key service elements. Through the visual blueprint in particular, showing all aspects of the service through photos and videos, the need for service upgrades became apparent.

Another revelation also jumped out of the blueprint. By visually tracking the customer's experience, it was clear that customers were being asked to work extremely hard for their vacations! To experience the luxurious and

or conceptual level it may be possible to combine customer segments on one blueprint. However, once almost any level of detail is reached, separate blueprints should be developed to avoid confusion and maximize their usefulness.

Step 3: Map the Service Process from the Customer's Point of View

Step 3 involves charting the choices and actions that the customer performs or experiences in purchasing, consuming, and evaluating the service. Identifying the service from the customer's point of view first will help avoid focusing on processes and steps that have no customer impact. This step forces agreement on who the customer is (sometimes no small task) and may involve considerable research to determine exactly how the customer experiences the service. Sometimes the beginning and ending of the service from the customer's point of view are not obvious. For example, research in a hair-cutting context revealed that customers viewed the process as beginning with the phone call to the salon and setting of the appointment, whereas the hair stylists did not typically view the making of appointments as part of the service process.[48] If the blueprint is being developed for an existing service, it may be helpful at this point in the process to video-record the service process, as was done in the ARAMARK case illustrated in Exhibit 8.3. Managers and others who are not on the frontlines may be quite surprised when they view the actual service experience through their customers' eyes.

not-inexpensive houseboat experience they had purchased, customers first had to create extensive grocery lists, shop in crowded stores near the resort, carry all of their food and belongings down a steep embankment, and haul them out to the boat. Once the trip started, more hard labor was required. Anchoring a large houseboat each night is not a trivial matter, and cooking onboard can be arduous and time consuming. Navigating the houseboat can also be stressful, especially for inexperienced captains. The run-down resort facilities on land, the arduous work required to get on the water, and the stress of navigation all combined to discourage customers from returning after surviving their first Lake Powell vacation.

The blueprinting exercise made all of this extremely vivid for top management and resulted in a suite of new services, renovations of existing facilities, training of staff to perform to new service standards, and new measurement and reward systems. Some of the new services introduced included various levels of concierge services that started with the basic service of taking guests' things to the boat for them and later transporting guests in a cart to the boat dock. Service packages were extended at the high end to include buying groceries for guests and providing executive chefs, who would travel with the party and cook on board. Trained captains could also be hired to lessen the stress of navigation. A variety of services in between were also available a la carte.

RESULTS FOR ARAMARK

The result for Lake Powell of all of these service quality improvements and innovative new services was 50 percent fewer complaints. Repeat business increased by 12 percent, and customer satisfaction also increased dramatically. The blueprints in this case were extremely valuable in that they allowed managers to see the service in ways they had never seen it before. The blueprints also provided a focal point for conversations, leading to change and ultimately to new service standards and measures. Using the blueprinting technique helped people within the parks division develop a true customer focus.

Sources: M. J. Bitner, A. L. Ostrom, and F. N. Morgan, "Service Blueprinting: A Practical Technique for Service Innovation," *California Management Review 50* (Spring 2008), pp. 66–94.; Interview with Renee Ryan; www.lakepowell.com, accessed May 2016.

Step 4: Map Contact Employee Actions and/or Technology Actions

First the lines of interaction and visibility are drawn, and then the process from the customer contact person's point of view is mapped, distinguishing visible onstage activities from invisible backstage activities. For existing services, this step involves interviewing or observing frontline operation employees to learn what they do and which activities are performed in full view of the customer versus which activities are carried out behind the scenes.

For technology-delivered services or those that combine technology and human delivery, the required actions of the technology interface are mapped above the line of visibility as well. If no employees are involved in the service, the area can be relabeled "onstage technology actions." If both human and technology interactions are involved, an additional horizontal line can separate "visible contact employee actions" from "visible technology actions." Using the additional line facilitates reading and interpretation of the service blueprint.

Step 5: Link Contact Activities to Needed Support Functions

Now, the line of internal interaction is drawn and linkages from contact activities to internal support functions are identified. In this process, the direct and indirect impact of internal actions on customers becomes apparent. Internal service

Exhibit 8.4 Frequently Asked Questions about Service Blueprinting

What process should be blueprinted?
What process to map depends on the team's or organization's objectives. If these are not clearly defined, then identifying the process can present a challenge. Questions to ask: Why are we blueprinting the service? What is our objective? Where does the service process begin and end? Are we focusing on the entire service, a component of the service, or a period of time?

Can multiple market segments be included on one blueprint?
Generally the answer to this question is no. Assuming that market segments require different service processes or attributes, the blueprint for one segment may look very different from the blueprint for another. Only at a very high level (sometimes called a *concept blueprint*) might it be relevant to map multiple segments simultaneously.

Who should "draw" the blueprint?
A blueprint is a team effort. It should not be assigned as an individual task, certainly not in the developmental stages. All relevant parties should be involved or represented in the effort. The task might include employees across multiple functions in the organization (marketing, operations, human resources, facilities design), as well as customers in some cases.

Should the actual or desired service process be blueprinted?
If a new service is being designed, then clearly it is important to start with the desired service process. However, in cases of service improvement or service redesign, it is very important to map (at least at a conceptual level) the actual service process first. Once the group knows how the service is actually functioning, then the blueprint can be modified or used as a base for changes and improvements.

Should exceptions or recovery processes be incorporated in the blueprint?
It may be possible to map relatively simple, commonly occurring recovery processes onto a blueprint, assuming there are not a lot of these. However, this process can quickly become complex and cause the blueprint to be confusing or unreadable. Often a better strategy is to indicate common fail points on the blueprint and, if needed, develop separate blueprints for the service recovery processes.

What is the appropriate level of detail?
The answer to this question depends on the purpose for doing the blueprint in the first place. If it is to be used primarily to communicate the general nature of the service, then a concept blueprint with few details is best. If it is being used to focus on diagnosing and improving the service process, then more detail is needed. Because some people are more detail oriented than others, this question will always arise and needs to be resolved in any team blueprinting effort.

What symbols should be used?
There is not a lexicon of blueprinting symbols that is required to be used. What is most important is that the symbols be defined, kept relatively simple, and used consistently by the team and across the organization if blueprints are being shared internally.

Should time or dollar costs be included on the blueprint?
Blueprints are very versatile. If reducing the time taken for various parts of the service process is an objective of the blueprinting effort, then time can be included. The same is true for dollar costs or anything else that is relevant as an objective. However, it is not advisable to put such information on the blueprint unless it is of central concern.

processes take on added importance when viewed in connection with their link to the customer. Alternatively, certain steps in the process may be viewed as unnecessary if there is no clear link to the customer's experience or to an essential internal support service.

Step 6: Add Evidence of Service at Each Customer Action Step

Finally, the physical and/or virtual evidence of service can be added to the blueprint to illustrate what the customer sees and experiences as tangible evidence of the service at each step in the process. A photographic blueprint, including photos, slides, or video of the process, can be very useful at this stage to aid in analyzing the impact of tangible evidence and its consistency with the overall strategy and service positioning.

Exhibit 8.4 provides answers to frequently asked questions about service blueprinting.

Indian Service Strategy Insight Ginger Hotels – Innovations from Budget to Functional Luxury Offerings

Ginger Hotels, a part of the Tata group's Indian Hotels Company Limited (IHCL), represents a transformative force in India's mid-scale hospitality sector. Launched in 2004 in Bangalore as IndiOne, the chain was designed with an objective to provide no-frills, functional, and affordable accommodation tailored to the emerging Indian middle-class traveler.

Ginger Hotels directly applied the famed strategy guru, C.K. Prahalad's 'Fortune at the Bottom of the Pyramid' concept to the hospitality industry. Created to serve budget travelers who had limited options, they removed luxury features like doormen, pools, and extensive restaurants and adopted a 'smart basic' approach to offer clean, functional rooms at affordable prices. Targeting smaller cities and industrial towns that lacked decent hotels to mirror Tata's broader efforts to serve India's emerging mass market. Ginger positioned itself to capture the 'bottom of the pyramid' in the hospitality space which had limited offerings form the organized hotel chains.

Over the years, Ginger has redefined its identity from being a budget accommodation provider to a stylish, design-forward, and experience-centric hotel brand under the 'lean luxe' philosophy. With over 100 properties across 50 destinations — from major metros to small towns and pilgrimage spots — Ginger has now emerged as a significant player in the Indian hospitality landscape.

Ginger began its journey by targeting travelers who prioritized cleanliness, safety, and convenience over luxury. The early years were marked by basic offerings that emphasized affordability. However, the hospitality industry in India soon began witnessing a shift. Guests were no longer satisfied with just a clean bed and hot shower; they wanted thoughtfully designed spaces that balanced comfort, technology, and aesthetics without breaking the bank. Ginger responded by evolving its model into what it now calls 'lean luxe' — a concept that marries the efficiency and simplicity of budget hotels with the style, design, and essential luxuries of premium properties.

This evolution became especially important in a rapidly changing market shaped by a younger demographic, mostly travelers under 40, who valued efficiency, smart technology, and experiences over ostentation. Ginger's new model addressed these needs by offering compact yet multifunctional room layouts, intelligent space utilization, and a seamless blend of work and leisure spaces. Design elements, such as vibrant public areas, local cultural art, and bright interiors, added personality and relatability to the guest experience.

The success of Ginger Hotels is deeply rooted in its commitment to innovation across design, service delivery, and operations. The brand's design overhaul began with a focus on visual storytelling and practical elegance. At hotels like the recently launched Ginger Mumbai Airport, the '*Tree of Life*' lobby symbolizes the new design philosophy – flowing, welcoming, and multi-use spaces that serve both functional and social needs. This design is characterized by colorful interiors, flexible furniture, well-lit spaces, and seamless transitions between networking zones, dining areas, and reception desks.

Rooms under the 'lean luxe' model feature clever storage solutions and smart furnishings, such as sliding desks, closets that double as luggage racks, and rolling tables. Despite their compact size, these rooms do not compromise on comfort, offering all essential amenities such as high-speed Wi-Fi, LED TVs, mini-fridges, and high-quality bedding. Special attention has been given to guest safety and inclusivity with 'single-lady' rooms, placed near elevators and equipped with additional security features like video intercoms.

Technological integration has also played a crucial role. Ginger uses a facility management software that automates building operations, monitors equipment performance, and improves resource allocation. This has led to better operational efficiency and cost savings — key factors in sustaining profitability in the budget-to-midscale segment. Additionally, self-check-in kiosks, app-based

services, and digital room controls enhance the guest experience by offering speed and personalization.

Ginger has expanded beyond just rooms and basic services to include a host of new amenities that reflect modern traveler expectations. The introduction of Qmin, the brand's signature all-day dining restaurant, has elevated the culinary offering. Qmin blends local flavors with international dishes in a contemporary setting, often designed with open kitchens and natural lighting. At Ginger Mumbai Airport, Qmin features standout elements like a skylight and artwork, creating an inviting atmosphere for both business lunches and family dinners.

The Sports Bar is another innovation that caters to a wide audience, from solo travelers to groups. It blends casual comfort with entertainment, offering a mix of health-conscious and indulgent food options, themed seating, and live sports screenings. These additions provide not only convenience but also create vibrant community spaces within the hotel.

Fitness centers with modern equipment, day-use rooms for transit travelers, and EV charging stations for environmentally conscious guests further enhance the brand's offerings. Banquet halls and smart meeting rooms cater to corporate clients, supporting Ginger's strategic push to attract business travelers.

Ginger's transformation into a lean luxe brand has turned it into a strategic growth driver for the IHCL. With a current footprint of over 100 hotels and another 10 in the pipeline, Ginger has proven its ability to scale while maintaining consistent service quality and profitability. Key locations, such as the upcoming 325-room Ginger near Bengaluru Airport and the 300-room hotel at Mopa Airport in Goa, reflect the brand's shift toward large-format properties located at high-traffic transit hubs.

IHCL envisions opening up over 500 Ginger hotels in the next decade, using a diversified portfolio approach including greenfield projects, lease models, and management contracts. While the franchise model is still in early stages in India's hospitality sector, Ginger has identified it as a viable future route for expansion. These growth strategies allow the brand to maintain flexibility and control while rapidly scaling its presence.

One key factor contributing to Ginger's growth is its occupancy-driven business model. With an average room rate of ₹2,500, the brand aims for a year-round occupancy of 70–80%, with sold-out dates during peak seasons. This model emphasizes cost control and efficient space utilization over luxury frills like expansive lobbies or large pools. It ensures that the hotel can offer value without compromising on essentials like hygiene, service speed, and guest safety.

Ginger's guest demographic is largely made up of independent, tech-savvy travelers who seek experiences that are fast, efficient, and value-driven. These include FIT (Free Independent Traveler) customers, corporate clients, long-stay guests, and increasingly, leisure travelers looking for short, comfortable stays. With the rise of satellite towns and growing Tier-II and Tier-III cities, Ginger's mid-market positioning is ideal for meeting the expanding demand in untapped regions.

However, expanding into the leisure segment poses its own challenges, primarily due to seasonal demand. Ginger's solution lies in developing hybrid properties that attract year-round occupancy – hotels that cater to both corporate travelers during the week and leisure guests on weekends. Locations like Goa, Candolim, and pilgrimage towns offer an opportunity to diversify the portfolio while maintaining occupancy levels essential for profitability.

Ginger Hotels has not only transformed the budget hospitality segment but has also redefined what affordable luxury can mean in India. Through its 'lean luxe' philosophy, tech-enabled operations, and vibrant, flexible designs, Ginger has crafted a unique proposition that resonates with the aspirations of modern Indian travelers. Its expansion into major cities, transit hubs, and emerging markets, along with a sustainable business model, positions it as an emerging leader in India's rapidly growing mid-scale hotel segment.

By focusing on efficiency, thoughtful design, and guest-centric innovations, Ginger is not just keeping up with the hospitality industry – it is helping to shape its future. As the brand continues to scale, it remains a powerful example of how innovation, when combined with a deep understanding of customer needs, can lead to enduring success.

Reference: https://www.ft.com/content/53b5b798-90e0-11de-bc99-00144feabdc0

https://www.tata.com/newsroom/business/ginger-mumbai-airport-functional-luxury

https://www.ihcltata.com/our-brands/ginger-hotels/

https://www.gingerhotels.com/about-ginger

https://www.financialexpress.com/business/industry-ginger-will-be-the-growth-engine-for-ihcl-puneet-chhatwal-3833598/

https://www.travelandtourworld.com/news/article/bengaluru-india-embraces-the-future-of-hospitality-with-ihcls-ginger-hotel-in-bommasandra-combining-vibrant-design-modern-amenities-and-easy-access-to-key-commercial-zones/

https://www.livemint.com/Companies/BZ52ZElh0PS3nt2kfcl-qJK/Guests-want-efficiency-not-discounts-at-Ginger-Hotels-Moha.html

https://www.hotelierindia.com/business/teams-software-launch-in-ginger-hotels-pan-india#:~:text=The%20TEAMS%20software%20was%20created,work%20and%20increases%20facility%20efficiency.

Summary

Service providers must effectively match customer expectations to new service innovations and actual service process designs. However, because of the very nature of services—specifically, their intangibility, variability, and cocreation elements—the design and development of service offerings are complex and challenging. Many services are only vaguely defined before their introduction to the marketplace. This chapter outlined some of the challenges involved in innovating and designing services and strategies for effectively overcoming the challenges. The chapter also described a variety of types of service innovation, including service offering innovation, innovating around customer roles, innovation through service solutions, and innovation through interconnected products.

Through adaptations of the new product development process that is commonplace in goods production and manufacturing companies, service providers can not only make their offerings and service solutions more explicit but also avoid failures. The service development process presented in the chapter includes nine stages, beginning with the development of a business and new service strategy and ending with postintroduction evaluation of the new service. Between these initial and ending stages are a number of steps and checkpoints designed to maximize the likelihood of innovation success. Carrying out the stages requires the inclusion of customers, contact employees, business partners, and anyone else who will affect or be affected by the new service.

Service blueprinting, a particularly useful technique for service innovation and design, was described in detail in this chapter. A blueprint can make a complex service concrete through its visual depiction of all the steps, actors, processes, and physical evidence of the service. The key feature of service blueprints is the focus on the customer—the customer's experience is documented first and is kept fully in view as the other features of the blueprint are developed.

Discussion Questions

1. Why is it challenging to innovate, design, and develop services?
2. Why is service innovation so critical for firms and countries?
3. What are the risks of attempting to describe services in words alone?
4. Find and discuss your own examples of the different types of service innovations presented in the "Types of Service Innovation" section in this chapter.
5. Compare and contrast the blueprints in Figures 8.5 and 8.6.
6. How might a service blueprint be used for marketing, human resource, and operations decisions? Focus on one of the blueprint examples shown in the text as a context for your answer.
7. Assume that you are a multiproduct service company that wants to grow through adding new services. Describe a logical process you might use to introduce a new service to the marketplace. What steps in the process might be most difficult and why? How might you incorporate service blueprinting into the process?
8. Discuss Figure 8.2 in terms of the four types of opportunities for growth represented there. Choose a company or service, and explain how it could grow by developing new services in each of the four cells.

Exercises

1. Think of a new service you would like to develop if you were an entrepreneur. How would you go about it? Describe what you would do and where you would get your information.

2. Find a new and interesting service in your local area or a service offered on your campus. Document the service process via a service blueprint. To do this exercise, you will probably need to interview one of the service employees and experience the service yourself, if possible. After you have documented the existing service, use blueprinting concepts to redesign the service or change it in some way.
3. Choose a service you are familiar with and document the customer action steps through a photographic or video blueprint. What is the "evidence of service" from your point of view as a customer?
4. Develop a service blueprint for a technology-delivered service such as streaming a movie on your TV or laptop, or taking an online course at your university. Compare and contrast this blueprint to one for the same service delivered via a traditional channel (such as watching a movie in a theater or taking a university class in person).
5. Compare two services on the Internet. Discuss the design of each in terms of whether it meets your expectations. How could the design or the service process be changed? Which one is most effective, and why?
6. Visit the publicly available database of innovations triggered by COVID-19: www.covidinnovations.com. Explore and identify major service innovations that are most interesting and noteworthy to you.

Notes

1. D. H. Henard and D. M. Szymanski, "Why Some New Products Are More Successful Than Others," *Journal of Marketing Research* 38 (August 2001), pp. 362–375; for more recent insights see: C. Storey, P. Cankurtaran, P. Papastathopoulou, and E. J. Hultink, "Success Factors for Service Innovation: A Meta-Analysis," *Journal of Product Innovation Management* 33 (September 2016), pp. 527–548; for findings on the impact on firm performance, see: C. Feng, R. Ma, and L. Jiang, "The Impact of Service Innovation on Firm Performance: A Meta-Analysis," *Journal of Service Management* 32 (April 2021), pp. 289–314.
2. R. G. Cooper, *Winning at New Products,* 3rd ed. (Cambridge, MA: Perseus, 2001); R. G. Cooper and S. J. Edgett, *Product Development for the Service Sector* (Cambridge, MA: Perseus Books, 1999); and C. M. Froehle, A. V. Roth, R. B. Chase, and C. A. Voss, "Antecedents of New Service Development Effectiveness," *Journal of Service Research* 3 (August 2000), pp. 3–17; R. G. Cooper, "Effective Gating: Make Product Innovation More Productive by Using Gates with Teeth," *Marketing Management* 18 (March–April 2009), pp. 12–17.
3. A. Gustafsson, H. Snyder, and L. Witell, "Service Innovation: A New Conceptualization and Path Forward," *Journal of Service Research* 23 (May 2020), pp. 111–115; M. J. Bitner and S. W. Brown, "The Service Imperative," *Business Horizons 50th Anniversary Issue* 51 (January–February 2008), pp. 39–46.
4. G. L. Shostack, "Understanding Services through Blueprinting," in *Advances in Services Marketing and Management,* vol. 1, ed. T. A. Swartz, D. E. Bowen, and S. W. Brown (Greenwich, CT: JAI Press, 1992), pp. 75–90.
5. Ibid., p. 76.
6. See: S. S. Tax, D. McCutcheon, and I. F. Wilkinson, "The Service Delivery Network (SDN): A Customer-Centric Perspective of the Customer Journey," *Journal of Service Research* 16 (November 2013), pp. 454–470; J. D. Chandler and R. F. Lusch, "Service Systems: A Broadened Framework and Research Agenda on Value

Propositions, Engagement, and Service Experience," *Journal of Service Research* 18 (February 2015), pp. 6–22.

7. For coverage of issues in new services development and service innovation, see *Journal of Operations Management* 20 (2002), Special Issue on New Issues and Opportunities in Service Design Research; A. Johne and C. Story, "New Service Development: A Review of the Literature and Annotated Bibliography," *European Journal of Marketing* 32 (1998), pp. 184–251; B. Edvardsson, A. Gustafsson, M. D. Johnson, and B. Sanden, *New Service Development and Innovation in the New Economy* (Lund, Sweden: Studentlitteratur AB, 2000); and B. Edvardsson, A. Gustafsson, P. Kristensson, P. Magnusson, and J. Matthing, *Involving Customers in New Service Development* (London: Imperial College Press, 2006); A. Gustafsson, P. Kristensson, G. Schirr, and L. Witell, *Service Innovation* (Business Expert Press, Gustafsson 2016); L. Patricio, R. Fisk, and A. Gustafsson (guest editors), *Journal of Service Research*, Special Issue on Service Design and Innovation, forthcoming 2017.
8. W. Chang and S. A. Taylor, "The Effectiveness of Customer Participation in New Product Development: A Meta-Analysis," *Journal of Marketing* 80 (January 2016), pp. 47–64; Gustafsson, Kristensson, Schirr, and Witell, *Service Innovation*.
9. A. Ordanini and A. Parasuraman, "Service Innovation Viewed through a Service-Dominant Logic Lens: A Conceptual Framework and Empirical Analysis," *Journal of Service Research* 14 (February 2011), pp. 3–23.
10. B. Schneider and D. E. Bowen, "New Services Design, Development and Implementation and the Employee," in *Developing New Services,* ed. W. R. George and C. Marshall (Chicago: American Marketing Association, 1984), pp. 82–101.
11. See: A. L. Ostrom et al., "Service Research Priorities: Managing and Delivering Service in Turbulent Times," *Journal of Service Research* 24 (August 2021), pp. 329–353; A. L. Ostrom, M. J. Bitner, S. W. Brown, K. A. Burkhard, M. Goul, V. Smith- Daniels, H. Demirkan, and E. Rabinovich, "Moving Forward and Making a Difference: Research Priorities for the Science of Service," *Journal of Service Research* 13 (February 2010), pp. 4–36; and A. L. Ostrom, A. Parasuraman, D. E. Bowen, L. Patricio and C. Voss, "Service Research Priorities in a Rapidly Changing Context," *Journal of Service Research* 18 (May 2015), pp. 127–159.
12. B. Mager on Service Design Network, www.service-design-network.org, accessed August 2011; also: B. Mager and M. Erlhoff, *The Future of Service Design*, 2020.
13. A. L. Ostrom, M. J. Bitner, S. W. Brown, K. A. Burkhard, M. Goul, V. Smith-Daniels, H. Demirkan, and E. Rabinovich, "Moving Forward and Making a Difference: Research Priorities for the Science of Service," *Journal of Service Research* 13 (February 2010), pp. 4–36.
14. M. Stickdorn and J. Schneider, *This Is Service Design Thinking,* Wiley (Amsterdam, 2010), pp. 34–35.
15. B. Mager on Service Design Network, www.service-design-network.org, accessed August 2011.
16. For additional detail and background on service design and service design thinking see: S. Dasu and R. B. Chase, "Designing the Soft Side of Customer Service," *Sloan Management Review* 52 (Fall 2010), pp. 33–39; L. G. Zomerdijk and C. A. Voss, "Service Design for Experience-Centric Services," *Journal of Service Research* 13 (February 2010), pp. 67–82; L. Patricio, R. P. Fisk, J. Falcao

e Cunha, and L. Constantine, "Multilevel Service Design: From Customer Value Constellation to Service Experience Blueprinting," *Journal of Service Research* 14 (May 2011), pp. 180–200; Stickdorn and Schneider, *This Is Service Design Thinking*; Service Design Network, www.service-design-network.org.

17. See: H. Snyder, L. Witell, A. Gustafsson, P. Fombelle, and P. Kristensson, "Identifying Categories of Service Innovation: A Review and Synthesis of the Literature," *Journal of Business Research* 69 (July 2016), pp. 2401–2408; A. Helkkula, C. Kowalkowski, and B. Tronvoll, "Archetypes of Service Innovation: Implications for Value Cocreation," *Journal of Service Research* 21 (August 2018), pp. 284–301.
18. L. L. Berry, V. Shankar, J. T. Parish, S. Cadwallader, and T. Dotzel, "Creating New Markets through Service Innovation," *Sloan Management Review* 47 (Winter 2006), pp. 56–63.
19. S. Michel, S. W. Brown and A. S. Gallan, "An Expanded and Strategic View of Discontinuous Innovations: Deploying a Service Dominant Logic," *Journal of the Academy of Marketing Science* 36, no. 1 (March 2008), pp. 54–66.
20. K. R. Tuli, A. K Kohli, and S. G. Bharadwaj, "Rethinking Customer Solutions: From Product Bundles to Relational Processes," *Journal of Marketing* 71 (July 2007), pp. 1–17.
21. L. A. Bettencourt, *Service Innovation*, New York: McGraw-Hill, 2010; L. A. Bettencourt and A. W. Ulwick, "The Customer-Centered Innovation Map," *Harvard Business Review* 86 (May 2008), pp. 109–114.
22. M. Sawhney, S. Balasubramanian, and V. V. Krishnan, "Creating Growth with Services," *MIT Sloan Management Review* 45, no. 2 (Winter 2004), pp. 34–43.
23. See: C. Gronroos and P. Helle, "Adopting a Service Logic in Manufacturing," *Journal of Service Management* 21 (2010), 564–590; H. Gebauer, A. Gustafsson, and L. Witell, "Competitive Advantage Through Service Differentiation by Manufacturing Companies," *Journal of Business Research*, 64: 12 (2011), pp. 1270–1280; W. Ulaga and W. J. Reinartz, "Hybrid Offerings: How Manufacturing Firms Combine Goods and Services Successfully," *Journal of Marketing* forthcoming, 2011; V. A. Zeithaml, S. W. Brown, M. J. Bitner, and J. Salas, *Profiting from Services and Solutions: What Product-Centric Firms Need to Know*, Business Expert Press, 2014.
24. A. M. Epp and L. L. Price, "Designing Solutions Around Customer Network Identity Goals," *Journal of Marketing* 75 (March, 2011), pp. 36–54.
25. Internet of Things Statistics for 2021 – Taking Things Apart, https://dataprot.net, accessed November 24, 2021.
26. See M. E. Porter and J. E. Heppelmann, "How Smart Connected Products are Transforming Competition," *Harvard Business Review* 92 (2014), pp. 64–88; M. E. Porter and J. E. Heppelmann, "How Smart, Connected Products Are Transforming Companies," *Harvard Business Review* 93 (2015), pp. 53–71.
27. For a discussion of these adaptations and related research issues, see F. Kitsios and M. Kamariotou, "Mapping New Service Development: A Review and Synthesis of Literature," *The Service Industries Journal* 40 (July 2020), pp. 682–704; I. Stuart, "Designing and Executing Memorable Service Experiences: Lights, Camera, Experiment, Integrate, Action!" *Business Horizons* 49 (2006), pp. 149–159; M. V. Tatikonda and V. A Zeithaml, "Managing the New Service Development Process: Synthesis of Multidisciplinary Literature and Directions for Future Research," in *New Directions in Supply Chain Management: Technology, Strategy, and*

Implementation, ed. T. Boone and R. Ganeshan (New York: AMACOM, 2002), pp. 200–236; and Edvardsson, Gustafsson, Johnson, and Sanden, *New Service Development and Innovation in the New Economy.*

28. See M. J. Bowers, "An Exploration into New Service Development: Organization, Process, and Structure," Doctoral dissertation, Texas A&M University, 1985; A. Khurana and S. R. Rosenthal, "Integrating the Fuzzy Front End of New Product Development," *Sloan Management Review* 38 (Winter 1997), pp. 103–120; and R. G. Cooper, *Winning at New Products,* 3rd ed. (Cambridge, MA: Perseus Publishing, 2001). J. Hauser, G. J. Tellis, and A. Griffin, "Research on Innovation: A Review and Agenda for Marketing Science," *Marketing Science* 25 (November–December 2006), pp. 687–717.
29. See A. Griffin, "PDMA Research on New Product Development Practices: Updating Trends and Benchmarking Best Practices," *Journal of Product Innovation Management* 14 (1997), pp. 429–458; Thomke, "R&D Comes to Services"; Organization for Economic Cooperation and Development, "Promoting Innovation in Services," 2005.
30. R. G. Cooper, "Stage Gate Systems for New Product Success," *Marketing Management* 1 (1992), pp. 20–29; J. Hawser, G. J. Tellis and A. Griffin, "Research on Innovations. A Review and Agenda for Marketing Science," *Marketing Science* 25 (2006) pp. 687–717; Cooper, "Effective Gating."
31. A. Khurana and S. R. Rosenthal, "Integrating the Fuzzy Front End of New Product Development," *Sloan Management Review* 38 (Winter 1997), pp. 103–120.
32. J. Jargon, "KFC Savors Potential in Africa," *The Wall Street Journal*, December 8, 2010, p. B1; E. Nurse, "KFC's Secret Recipe for Africa," *CNN*, January 15, 2016, http://www.cnn.com/2016/01/15/africa/kfc-africa-expansion-mpa/; Leader of the Pack: KFC Africa, https://www.theceomagazine.com/executive-interviews/food-beverage/kfc-africa/, accessed November 2021.
33. D. Rigby and C. Zook, "Open-Market Innovation," *Harvard Business Review* 80 (October 2002), pp. 80–89.
34. D. Leonard and J. F. Rayport, "Spark Innovation through Empathic Design," *Harvard Business Review* 75 (November–December 1997), pp. 103–113; also see P. Underhill, *Why We Buy: The Science of Shopping* (New York: Simon and Schuster, 2007).
35. See Ordanini and Parasuraman, "Service Innovation Viewed through a Service-Dominant Logic Lens"; H. L. Melton and M. D. Hartline, "Customer and Frontline Employee Influence on New Service Development Performance," *Journal of Service Research* 13 (November 2011), pp. 411–425; L. McCreary, "Kaiser Permanente's Innovation on the Front Lines," *Harvard Business Review* 88 (September 2010), pp. 92–97.
36. R. Cross, A. Hargadon, S. Parise, and R. J. Thomas, "Together We Innovate," *The Wall Street Journal,* September 15–16, 2007, p. R6; J. C. Spender and B. Strong, "Who Has Innovative Ideas? Employees." *Wall Street Journal*, August 23, 2010, p. R5.
37. G. L. Shostack, "Service Design in the Operating Environment," in *Developing New Services,* ed. W. R. George and C. Marshall (Chicago: American Marketing Association, 1984), pp. 27–43.

38. E. E. Scheuing and E. M. Johnson, "A Proposed Model for New Service Development," *Journal of Services Marketing* 3 (1989), pp. 25–34.

39. L. Chamberlain, "Going Off the Beaten Path for New Design Ideas," *New York Times,* March 12, 2006, Sunday Business Section.

40. See IDEO's website for many examples of their current work, https://www.ideo.com/work/, accessed November 2021.

41. Shostack, "Service Design in the Operating Environment," p. 35.

42. The service blueprinting section of the chapter draws from pioneering as well as current works in this area: G. L. Shostack, "Designing Services That Deliver," *Harvard Business Review* 62 (January–February 1984), pp. 133–139; G. L. Shostack, "Service Positioning through Structural Change," *Journal of Marketing* 51 (January 1987), pp. 34–43; and J. Kingman-Brundage, "The ABC's of Service System Blueprinting," in *Designing a Winning Service Strategy,* ed. M. J. Bitner and L. A. Crosby (Chicago: American Marketing Association, 1989), pp. 30–33; M. J. Bitner, A. L. Ostrom, and F. N. Morgan, "Service Blueprinting: A Practical Technique for Service Innovation," *California Management Review* 50 (Spring 2008), pp. 66–94.

43. Shostack, "Understanding Services through Blueprinting."

44. These key components are drawn from Kingman-Brundage, "The ABC's."

45. Figure 8.5 and the text explaining it rely on M. J. Bitner, "Managing the Evidence of Service," in *The Service Quality Handbook,* ed. E. E. Scheuing and W. F. Christopher (New York: American Management Association, 1993), pp. 358–370.

46. S. Fliess and M. Kleinaltenkamp, "Blueprinting the Service Company: Managing Service Processes Efficiently," *Journal of Business Research* 57 (2004), pp. 392–404.

47. Sources: For coverage of the practical benefits of blueprinting see E. Gummesson and J. Kingman-Brundage, "Service Design and Quality: Applying Service Blueprinting and Service Mapping to Railroad Services," in *Quality Management in Services,* ed. P. Kunst and J. Lemmink (Assen/Maastricht, Netherlands: Van Gorcum, 1991); and M. J. Bitner, A. L. Ostrom, and F. N. Morgan, "Service Blueprinting: A Practical Technique for Service Innovation," *California Management Review* 50 (Spring 2008), pp. 66–94.

48. A. R. Hubbert, A. Garcia Sehorn, and S. W. Brown, "Service Expectations: The Consumer vs. the Provider," *International Journal of Service Industry Management* 6 (1995), pp. 6–21.

Chapter Nine

Customer-Defined Service Standards

This chapter's learning objectives are to:

1. Distinguish between company-defined and customer-defined service standards.
2. Differentiate among "hard" and "soft" customer-defined service standards and one-time fixes.
3. Explain the critical role of the service encounter sequence in developing customer-defined standards.
4. Illustrate how to translate customer expectations into behaviors and actions that are definable, repeatable, and actionable.
5. Explain the process of developing customer-defined service standards.

FedEx Sets Standards through SQI and QDM

Marketing research data are not the only numbers that FedEx tracks to run its business. The company drives its operations with the aid of one of the most comprehensive, customer-defined indices of service standards and measures in the world. The FedEx service quality indicator (SQI) was designed from the start to be an "unforgiving internal performance measurement" to ensure that the company delivered its goal of "100 percent customer satisfaction after every interaction and transaction and 100 percent service performance on every package handled."[1] The development and implementation of SQI has helped FedEx stay focused on its customers in becoming one of the world's most admired brands.

Jb Reed/Bloomberg/Getty Images

The entire FedEx organization is driven by customer-defined service standards.

What makes this service index different from those of other companies is its foundation in customer feedback. Since the 1980s, FedEx has documented customer complaints and used the information to improve internal processes. The initial composite listing of the 12 most common customer complaints, originally called the "Hierarchy of Horrors," included wrong day deliveries, right day late deliveries, pickups not made, lost packages, customers misinformed by FedEx, billing and paperwork mistakes, employee performance failures, and damaged packages. Although this list was useful, it fell short of giving management the ability to anticipate and eliminate customer complaints before they occurred.

In 1988 the company developed a 12-item statistical SQI to be a more "comprehensive, pro-active, customer-oriented measure of customer satisfaction and service quality."[2] The items included in SQI have changed slightly over time, as have the weights assigned to each of the items. Versions of SQI for FedEx Express have included the following components and weighting (based on relative importance of each component to customers):[3]

Indicator	Weight	Indicator	Weight
Lost packages	50	Failed (regularly scheduled) pickup	10
Damaged packages	30	Missing packages	10
Failed (call-in) pickup	20	Right day/late delivery	5
Wrong day/late delivery	15		

Source: E-mail communication from David Spear, manager of global service and quality assurance, *FedEx Express,* June 14, 2016.

Another distinguishing feature of the SQI is its reporting in terms of *numbers* of errors rather than percentages. Management of the company strongly believes that percentages distance the company from the consumer: to report 1 percent of packages late diminishes the reality of more than 180,000 unhappy customers (1 percent of the more than 18 million packages shipped a day in 2021, including 6.6 million for FedEx Express and 12 million for FedEx Ground).[4]

The Broader Framework of "Quality Driven Management" (QDM)

Related to the SQI and the company's history of successful service management, FedEx continuously refines and optimizes its framework(s) of service quality management in the interest of reducing cost, growing revenue, and improving customer experiences. The company uses an overarching framework of "Quality Driven Management" (QDM) as the platform to deliver on the "Purple Promise" of making "every FedEx experience outstanding" for customers. QDM rests on six Principles, which all support a culture of customer-focused quality. While all six Principles are fully consistent with this book's premise of "integrating a customer focus across the firm," you will find that Principles #1–#4 (displayed below) are directly linked to the focus of this chapter on leveraging a system of customer-defined service standards.

Principle #1: Customers define quality

Take an outside-in perspective. See performance and progress through the eyes of customers. Applying this principle helps keep the focus on what's truly important.

Principle #2: Be scientific

When your business is at stake, it's no time for guesswork. Analyze challenges and identify root causes to solve foundational, rather than surface-level, challenges.

Principle #3: Measure, measure, measure

It's impossible to gauge success without measurement. Set a target and track your progress. Analyze the results and adjust the approach based on these insights.

Principle #4: Optimize business performance

Work to understand evolving customer needs and deliver the level of value and services that customers want. Streamline activities that do not add value or satisfy other critical business requirements.

Source: https://www.fedex.com/en-us/about/quality-management/principles.html, accessed, December 27, 2021.

As we saw in Chapters 5, 6, and 7, understanding customer requirements is the first step in delivering high service quality. Once managers of service businesses accurately understand what customers expect, they face a second critical challenge: using this knowledge to set service quality standards and goals for the organization. Service companies often experience difficulty in setting standards to match or exceed customer expectations, partly because doing so requires that the marketing and operations departments within a company work together. In most service companies, integrating the work of the marketing function and the operations function (appropriately called *functional integration*) is not a typical approach; more frequently, these two functions operate separately—setting and achieving their own internal goals—rather than pursuing a joint goal of developing operations standards that best meet customer expectations.

Creating service standards that address customer expectations is not a common practice in many firms. Doing so often requires altering the very process by which work is accomplished, which is ingrained in tradition in many companies. Often change requires new equipment or technology. Change also necessitates aligning executives from different parts of the firm to understand collectively the comprehensive view of service quality from the customer's perspective. And almost always, change requires a willingness to be open to different ways of structuring, calibrating, and monitoring the way service is provided (see the Strategy Insight for examples of such changes in healthcare settings).

FACTORS NECESSARY FOR APPROPRIATE SERVICE STANDARDS

Standardization of Service Behaviors and Actions

The translation of customer expectations into specific service quality standards depends on the degree to which tasks and behaviors to be performed can be standardized or routinized. *Standardization* usually implies a nonvarying sequential process—similar to the mass production of goods—in which each step is laid out in order and all outcomes are uniform, whereas *customization* usually refers to some level of adaptation or tailoring of the process to the individual customer.[5] The goal of standardization is for the service firm to produce a consistent service product from one transaction to the next. The goal of customization for the service firm is to develop a service that meets each customer's individual needs. Some executives and managers believe that services cannot be standardized—that customization is essential for providing high-quality service. Managers also may feel that standardizing tasks is inconsistent with employee empowerment—that employees will feel controlled by the company if tasks are standardized. Further, they feel that services are too intangible to be measured. This view leads to vague and loose standard setting with little or no measurement or feedback.

In reality, many service tasks are routine (such as those needed for opening checking accounts or spraying lawns for weeds), and for these, specific rules and standards can be fairly easily established and effectively executed. Employees may welcome knowing how to perform actions most efficiently: it frees them to use their ingenuity in the more personal and individual aspects of their jobs.

Standardization of service can take three forms: (1) substitution of technology for personal contact and human effort, (2) improvement in work methods, and (3) combinations of these two methods. Examples of technology substitution include websites and mobile applications for ordering take-out, airport check-in kiosks, advanced soft-drink vending machines that allow for elaborate customization, and smart office equipment (e.g., a copy machine) that can summon a repairman on its own based on the Internet-of-Things. Improvements in work methods that allow employees to perform actions (more) efficiently and effectively are illustrated by standardized home

Strategy Insight Strategies for Improving Health Care Experiences: Standards for Customer Service

One service setting where standards are crucial is health care. The Agency for Healthcare Research and Quality (AHRQ) is a federal agency that supports health care organizations in developing and tracking a variety of service-related quality standards across multiple categories (e.g., "inpatient quality indicators" and "patient safety quality indicators"); the goal is to improve the safety and quality of America's health care system.

One of the agency's major programs is called "Consumer Assessment of Healthcare Providers and Systems" (CAHPS®), which aims to advance the understanding of how patients experience health care. Based on insights from this program (e.g., patient surveys), CAHPS® helps to develop patient-focused standards for customer service in health care.

STANDARDS FOR CUSTOMER SERVICE IN HEALTH CARE

Customer service standards help with clarifying, measuring, and tracking the processes that define a "quality service experience" for patients. When developing service standards, health care organizations often start with a set of basic standards that evolve over time. In other words, as organizations and their employees get better and better at consistently fulfilling the focal set of standards, they can then raise the standards they commit to. For example, a hospital could initially define a standard such that "patients will wait 15 minutes or less in the reception area before being placed in an exam room," but once this target is consistently met the hospital might revise this standard down to a 10-minute waiting period. Of course, service standards can also be effectively used in other health care services, as the set of standards for Kaiser Permanente pharmacies depicted below illustrates. Note that Kaiser Permanente includes hard (i.e., quantifiable) standards as well as soft (i.e., relatively more subjective) standards, and that these standards are not only focused on interactions with external customers (e.g., patients) but also internal customers (e.g., other employees).

Illustrative (Soft and Hard) Service Standards for a Pharmacy Department as Implemented by Kaiser Permanente, Washington DC.*

Our department will abide by the following standards to guarantee caring and quality service is provided to our members and in-house customers.

Service Standards for Our Members

- We will greet our members in a courteous and professional manner.
- We will listen effectively to our members' requests and promptly take the necessary actions to assist them.
- We will keep our members informed of unexpected delays in service.
- We will not engage in personal conversations while providing service to our members.
- *We will call our members by name and will verify identity by means of address and/or ID card.*
- We will inform our members of specific departmental procedures (e.g., refill line, last refill, mail order) to help them maximize pharmacy services.
- We will finish our encounters with our members in a courteous and professional way.
- We will respect our members' privacy and will not discuss member-related information in public.

Service Standards for Our In-House Customers

- We will interact with our coworkers and company staff in a courteous and professional way.
- We will not discuss staff, organizational policies, problems, or medical care in public areas.
- We will be considerate, and we will cooperate and assist coworkers, staff, and other departments to guarantee quality service.

Telephone Etiquette

- *We will answer the phone within four rings.*
- *We will provide our center location, our name, and our department and politely ask: "How may I help you?"*
- We will listen to the caller's request and assist accordingly.
- We will direct the call to the person, department, or service needed to assist the caller.
- *We will obtain the caller's permission before placing the caller on hold.*
- We will end the call in a courteous and professional way.

* Hard standards are displayed in *italics*.

SERVICE STANDARDS AT HARVARD PILGRIM HEALTH CARE

Guided by their market research on patient experiences (e.g., surveys, focus groups), Harvard Pilgrim Health Care realized it needed to enhance the phone access for its patients as measured by (a) "average speed to answer" and (b) "call abandonment rates." Specifically, the intended service standards were "30 seconds or less" for the average speed to answer and "3 percent or less" for call abandonment. As reported on the AHRQ website, to achieve these standards Harvard Pilgrim Health Care implemented two types of improvements:

(1) Improvements to increase self-service options for customers (while also reducing call volume to agents in the call center):

- Installed web-based FAQs, downloadable materials (e.g., benefit plan descriptions), and tools to make online service requests (e.g., order new member ID cards).
- Developed a variety of self-service options (e.g., customers are able to change their own address without the need to talk to a customer service agent).
- Employed an Interactive Voice Response (IVR) system to provide callers with 24/7 access and quick answers to the most common questions without the need to talk to a customer service agent.
- Set up an after-hours mailbox for customers to leave messages in the evenings or weekends and receive a call back from a customer agent the following business day.
- Developed a financial incentive program that rewards customer service agents for promoting the self-service options to customers.

(2) Improvements focused on customer service agents to help increase their efficiency and responsiveness:

- Extended hours of operation to 7:30 p.m. on peak volume days.
- Developed an intranet-based reference system for service agents to ensure fast and consistent responses to customer inquiries.
- Increased training for managers and service agents; improved and streamlined resource materials for the service agents.
- Improved internal communication processes and workflow between "customer service" and "claims departments" to better resolve customer inquiries about health claims.
- Developed various performance incentive programs for service agents that are directly linked to goals of "speed to answer" and "call abandonment rates."

As this table demonstrates, implementing the above measures improved Harvard Pilgrim Health Care's performance on both indicators ("speed to answer" and "call abandonment rates") considerably in the initial 12 months after implementation, and again in the 12 months after that.

The implementation of these service standards and the corresponding actions led to the following results over time:

	Intended service standard	Baseline performance at initiation	Performance 12 months later	Performance 24 months later
Average Speed to Answer	30 seconds or less	67 seconds	47 seconds	28 seconds
Call Abandonment Rates	3% or less	5.6%	2.8%	1.5%

Sources: AHRQ, "Strategy 6Q: Standards for Customer Service," https://www.ahrq.gov/cahps/quality-improvement/improvement-guide/6-strategies-for-improving/customer-service/strategy6q-custservice-standards.html#6q1; AHRQ Quality Indicators, "Quality Indicator Empirical Methods, v2021", https://qualityindicators.ahrq.gov/Downloads/Resources/Publications/2021/Empirical_Methods_2021.pdf, accessed December 27, 2021.

cleaning methods by maid services such as Molly Maid or The Maids, as well as routinized tax and accounting services developed by firms such as H&R Block.

Technology and work improvement methods facilitate the standardization of service necessary to provide consistent delivery to customers. By breaking tasks down and providing them efficiently, technology also allows the firm to calibrate service standards such as the length of time a transaction takes, the accuracy with which operations are performed, and the number of problems that occur. In developing work improvements, the firm comes to understand completely the process by which the service is delivered. With this understanding, the firm more easily establishes appropriate service standards.

Standardization, whether accomplished by technology or by improvements in work processes, reduces Gap 2. Customer-defined standardization ensures that the most critical elements of a service are performed as expected by customers, not just that every action in a service is executed in a uniform manner. Using customer-defined standardization can, in fact, allow for and be compatible with employee empowerment—a topic discussed in more detail in Chapter 11. One example of this compatibility involves the time limits many companies establish for customer service calls. If their customers' highest priorities involve feeling good about the call or resolving problems, then setting a time limit for calls would be company defined and not in customers' best interests. Companies such as American Express, L.L. Bean, and Zappos.com, in using customer priorities rather than company priorities, have no set standard for the amount of time an employee spends on the telephone with a customer. Instead, they have standards that focus on making the customer satisfied and comfortable, allowing telephone representatives to use their own judgment about the time limits. As these companies have found, standardization of service is not appropriate in all situations.

Formal Service Targets and Goals

Companies that have been successful in delivering consistently high service quality are noted for establishing formal standards to guide employees in providing service (e.g., Walt Disney, FedEx, Singapore Airlines). These companies have an accurate sense of how well they are performing service that is critical to their customers—how long it takes to conduct transactions, how frequently service fails, how quickly they settle customer complaints—and strive to improve by defining goals that lead them to meet or exceed customer expectations.

One type of formal goal setting that is relevant in service businesses involves specific targets for individual behaviors or actions. As an example, consider the behavior "call the customer back quickly," an action that signals responsiveness in frontline employees. If the service goal for employee behavior is stated in such a general term, the standard provides little direction for service employees because it is unclear precisely what "quickly" means. Different employees will interpret this vague objective in their own ways, leading to inconsistent service: some may call the customer back in 10 minutes, whereas others may wait two days. And the firm itself will not be able to determine when or if individual employees meet the goal because its expression is not measurable—virtually any amount of time could be justified as "quickly." On the other hand, if the individual employee's service goal is to call each customer back within four hours, employees have a specific, unambiguous guideline about how quickly they should execute the action (four hours). Whether the goal is met is also unequivocal: if the call occurs within four hours, the company has met the goal; otherwise it has not.

Another type of formal goal setting involves the overall department or company target, most frequently expressed as a percentage, across all executions of the behavior or action. To illustrate, Puget Sound Energy—a utility company that serves customers in Washington State—has as one of its standards that at least 80 percent of phone calls are to be answered by a "live" Customer Care Center representative within 60 seconds.[6]

Service firms that produce consistently excellent service—firms such as Walt Disney, FedEx, and Singapore Airlines—have very specific, quantified, measurable service goals. Disney calibrates employee performance on myriad behaviors and actions that contribute to guest perceptions of high service quality. Our Technology Spotlight illustrates how Disney is using big data to manage service standards and improve customer experiences. Whether they are set and monitored using audits (such as timed actions) or customer perceptions (such as opinions about courtesy), service standards provide a means for formal goal setting.

Customer-, Not *Company-*, Defined Standards

Virtually all companies possess service standards and measures that are *company defined*—they are established to reach internal company goals for productivity, efficiency, cost, or technical quality. One company-defined standard that often does not meet customer expectations is the common practice of voice-activated phone and/or virtual support systems that do not allow customers to speak to humans (e.g., chatbots). Because these systems save companies money (and actually provide faster service to some customers), many organizations have switched from the labor-intensive practice of having customer representatives to using these "automated" systems. However, to close Gap 2, standards set by companies must also be based on customer requirements and expectations rather than just on internal company goals. In this chapter, we make the case that company-defined standards are not typically successful in driving behaviors that close Gap 2. Instead, a company must set *customer-defined standards*: operational standards based on pivotal customer requirements identified by customers. These standards are deliberately chosen to match customer expectations and to be calibrated the way the customer views and expresses them. Because these goals are essential to the provision of excellent service, the rest of this chapter focuses on customer-defined standards.

Knowing customer expectation levels can be both effective and efficient. Anchoring service standards on customers can save money by identifying what the customer values, thus eliminating activities and features that the customer either does not notice or will not pay for. One of the key desires of customers visiting a Department of Transportation office is to not have to wait a long time. In Oregon a few years ago, government officials made it a top priority to improve service at all of the state's Driver and Motor Vehicle (DMV) offices and get wait-times down—and the results were impressive. The goal was to have customers wait no more than 20 minutes when visiting any DMV office in the state—a decision based on customer surveys indicating people generally expected to wait no more than 20 minutes for service. In less than three years' time, the percentage of customers who were served in under 20 minutes increased from 52 percent to about 70 percent. To increase this percentage the DMV encouraged the use of alternative channels—such as online services or the mail—for simple transactions such as vehicle registration renewals, address changes, and notice of vehicle sales, thereby reducing the number of people who needed to visit a DMV office. The DMV pursued other strategies to reduce wait time, including adding express counters and information kiosks; they also scheduled relief help between offices and developed alternative work schedules to make DMV staff more readily available when demand was high.[7] In short, the Oregon DMV identified what was important to its customers and then implemented processes, reassigned staff, and trained employees to deliver service accordingly.

Puget Sound Energy (PSE) has used customer-defined standards for over two decades. Its customers have identified missed appointments, frequency and duration of

Technology Spotlight Using Big Data and AI to Manage Service Standards and Improve Customer Experiences

With the proliferation of mobile phones, social media, and online shopping, firms have access to more customer data than they ever have before. The data that can now be collected includes detailed demographic and psychographic information, purchase history, location data, and social network connections. With this granular data, service providers can gain better insight into the wants, needs, and habits of their customers. This level of data can help service providers to develop appropriate service standards to improve the aspects of the offering that are most important to customers.

Many retailers—such as Amazon, Overstock.com, and Walmart—use the data to make product suggestions to customers based on real-time data that includes factors such as age, gender, location, recent and historical online activity, and the responses of other customers to the same suggestions.

However, in addition to using big data in crafting product recommendations, service providers can use information to improve the service offering itself. For example, does the firm have any unhappy customers? If so, what do they all have in common? What separates them from the happy customers? Can this difference be addressed by implementing a service standard?

Beyond survey data from asking customers what they do not like about the company, big data allows for the examination of actual behavior. For example, a customer might tell a firm, "I'm on hold too long." But how long is too long? The collection and analysis of call data can tell a firm that the average customer will hold for 13 minutes before hanging up; such information can suggest to the firm's management to set a hard service standard that customers should not be placed on hold for more than 10 minutes.

Firms are beginning to recognize the value of moment-by-moment customer data, and are taking strides to actively collect more data and to design the customer experience around real-time access to this data. For example, Disney Parks provides customers with the opportunity to wear its MagicBand+, which uses radio frequency identification (RFID) technology to track a guest's every movement throughout the park. The data collected from these bands allows Disney to craft an experience for customers that maximizes the "magic." For example, the bands can tell employees in character (such as Mickey Mouse or Snow White) about the children they are meeting, allowing them to greet the children by name and even wish them a happy birthday. The band also includes haptic vibrations, color-changing lights, and gesture recognition, all of which are used to immerse guests in Disney stories and connect with theme park characters like never before. In short, Disney uses the band to make the experience more "magical" for their guests. Conveniently, the MagicBand+ also tracks purchase behavior, which could allow Disney to know which "magic" works to maximize revenue. Hypothetically, Disney could determine whether families whose children were greeted by name spent more money in the park or returned more often than families who were not. If the data shows that personal greetings increase customer spending, then a soft standard to cheerfully greet a child by name could conceivably follow.

Additionally, the data allows managers to streamline the entire experience for customers. For example, movement data lets Disney know which areas of the park are most susceptible to crowding, allowing managers to plan activities and other events in other areas of the park to help disperse the crowds. Standards relating to crowd density and wait times, such as a hard standard that no wait should be more than two hours, could be implemented and tracked, quantifying the improvements to the customer experience.

Big data is an effective tool that allows for detailed customer insights never before possible, creating, tracking, and managing the customer experience right down to the moment or click. The information is also invaluable in learning which aspects of the experience are most important to patrons, allowing service providers to create both hard and soft service standards that ensure customers gets the experience they are looking for every time.

Sources: Disney, "Experience More Magic with MagicBand+," https://disneyworld.disney.go.com/guest-services/magicband-plus/, accessed December 2021; T. H. Davenport, L. Dalle Mule, and J. Lucker, "Know What Your Customers Want Before They Do," *Harvard Business Review* 89 (December 2011), pp. 84–92; D. Sweeney, "4 Benefits That MagicBands Bring to the Wonderful World of Disney Parks," *Forbes*, January 9, 2013, http://www.forbes.com /sites/deborahsweeney/2013/01/09/4-benefits-that-magicbands-bring-to-the-wonderful-world-of-disney-parks/#3a9a02c9396c; A. Carr, "The Messy Business of Reinventing Happiness," *Fast Company,* April 15, 2015, http://www.fastcompany .com/3044283/the-messy-business-of-reinventing-happiness.

FIGURE 9.1 **Customer Service Standards for Puget Sound Energy**

Source: PSE, 2021 Service Quality Report Card, https://www.pse.com/-/media/PDFs/2774_SQI_Report_Card_2021.pdf.

2021 Service Quality Report Card (Excerpt) PSE PUGET SOUND ENERGY

Key Service Quality Indicators (Measured)	Benchmark Defined As	Actual 2021 Performance	Benchmark Achieved?
Customer Service Satisfaction			
• Percentage of customers reporting to be satisfied with their experience of Customer Care Center (based on survey)	Minimum of 90%	95%	Yes
• Percentage of customers reporting to be satisfied with their experience related to field services (based on survey)	Minimum of 90%	96%	Yes
• Number of complaints customers filed with the UTC (per 1,000 customers, per year)	Less than 0.40	0.10	Yes
• Percentage of inbound calls that were answered live in less than one minute by Customer Care Center	Minimum of 80%	82%	Yes
Operations Service			
• Frequency of power outages related to non-major-storms (per customer, per year)	Below 1.30 outages	1.35 outages	*No!*
• Duration from customer call to arrival of field service team (technicians) in response to electric system emergencies	Maximum of 55 minutes	65 minutes	*No!*
• Percentage of service appointments kept	Minimum of 92%	99%	Yes

power outages, and the amount of time it takes the company to field its calls as among the most important issues. Figure 9.1 displays how PSE performed in terms of seven customer-defined standards in three key areas.

Although customer-defined standards need not conflict with productivity and efficiency, they do not originate with these company concerns. Rather, they are anchored in and steered by customer perceptual measures of service quality, satisfaction, and loyalty. Therefore, the service standards that evolve from a customer perspective can be different from company-defined service standards.

TYPES OF CUSTOMER-DEFINED SERVICE STANDARDS

The types of standards that close Gap 2 are *customer-defined standards*: operational goals and measures based on pivotal customer requirements identified by customers rather than on company concerns such as productivity or efficiency.[8] Two major types of customer-defined service standards can be distinguished: "hard" and "soft." These standards will be discussed in the following two sections.

Hard Customer-Defined Standards

All the FedEx standards that constitute its SQI (mentioned in the chapter opener) fall into the category of hard standards and measures: *things that can be counted, timed, or observed*. Exhibit 9.1 shows a sampling of the hard standards that have been established by several service companies. This list includes only those companies with hard

Exhibit 9.1 Examples of Hard Customer-Defined Standards

Company	Customer Priorities	Customer-Defined Standards
Cardinal Health	On-time delivery	• Deliver 98% of all hospital products when promised
Dell Technologies	On-time delivery	• Ship to target (percentage of orders delivered to customers on time with complete accuracy)
	Computer works properly	• Initial field incident rate (frequency of problems encountered by customers)
	Problems fixed right first time	• On-time, first-time fix (percentage of problems fixed on the first visit by a service rep who arrives at the time promised)
Honeywell Home and Building Division	Fast delivery	• Orders entered same day received
	On-time delivery	• Orders delivered when promised
	Order accuracy	• Order 100% accurate
Mayo Clinic	Getting well	• Patient mortality rate • Patient surgical infection rate • Unplanned patient readmission rates • Volume of patients successfully treated
	Feeling well taken care of	• Number of appointments on time • Amount of time spent with each patient
Southwest Airlines	Reliability	• On-time arrival
	Responsiveness to complaints	• Two-week reply to letters
Texas Instruments Defense System	Compliance with commitments	• On-time delivery • Product compliance to requirements
	More personal contact	• Increased number of personal visits
Zappos.com	Responsiveness	• Respond to all incoming calls in less than a minute • Human customer service representatives available 24/7.

standards that are customer defined—based on customers' requirements and perspectives. Because FedEx, one of the companies included in this list, has a relatively simple and standard set of services, it can translate most of its customers' requirements into hard standards and measures. Many of the FedEx standards relate to on-time delivery and not making mistakes, and for good reason. As we stressed in Chapter 3, customer expectations of reliability—fulfillment of service promises—are high. Studies across numerous industries have found that the most frequent customer complaints are associated with service mistakes or problems (32 percent of all complaints) or poor product performance (30 percent of all complaints).[9]

To address the need for reliability, companies can institute a "do it right the first time" and an "honor your promises" value system by establishing reliability standards. An example of a generic reliability standard that is relevant to virtually any service company is "right the first time," which means the service performed is done correctly the first time according to the customer's assessment. If the service involves delivery of physical products, "right the first time" to the customer might mean the shipment is accurate—that it contains all that the customer ordered and nothing that the customer did not order. If the service involves installation of equipment, "right the first time" likely means that the equipment was installed correctly and was able to be used immediately by the customer. Another example of a reliability standard is "right on time," which means that the service is performed at the scheduled time. The company representative arrives when promised or the delivery is made at the time the customer expects it. In more complex services, such as disaster recovery or systems integration in computer service, "right on time" would likely mean that the service was completed by the promised date.

Reliability is often the most important concern of service customers. In electronic retailing, on-time and accurate fulfillment of orders is one of the most important aspects of reliability. One of the best examples of customer-defined hard standards in the Internet context is the single summary metric used by Dell Technologies for fulfillment. This metric is the Perfect Order Metric, which Dell developed in response to a declining Net Promoter Score.[10] The Net Promoter Score is determined based on customers' response to a single question: "How likely is it that you would recommend our company/product/service to a friend or colleague?" After talking to many customers, Dell learned that customers simply wanted Dell to deliver what the customer ordered when Dell said they would. Based on this feedback, the Perfect Order Metric is calculated as follows: (% of on-time deliveries) × (% of complete orders) × (% of orders delivered damage-free) × (% of orders delivered with accurate documentation). Dell tracks its performance on this reliability metric and rewards employees based on how well they do, ensuring employees are working toward goals that are most important to the customer.

Hard service standards for responsiveness are set to ensure the speed or promptness with which companies deliver products (e.g., within two working days), handle complaints (e.g., by sundown each day), answer questions (e.g., within two hours), answer the telephone and arrive for repair calls (e.g., within 30 minutes of the estimated time). In addition to setting standards that specify levels of response, companies must have well-staffed customer service departments. Responsiveness perceptions diminish when customers wait to get through to the company by phone, are put on hold, or are dumped into a phone voice mail system.

When it comes to providing service across cultures and continents, service providers need to recognize that customer-defined service standards often need to be adapted. Our Global Feature provides examples of companies with worldwide brands that have found ways to achieve universally high service quality while allowing for local differences in service standards.

Soft Customer-Defined Standards

Not all customer priorities can be objectively counted, timed, or observed. As Albert Einstein said, "Not everything that counts can be counted, and not everything that can be counted, counts." For example, "understanding and knowing the customer" is a customer priority that cannot be adequately captured by a standard that counts, times, or observes employees. In contrast to hard measures, soft measures must be documented using perceptual data. We call the second category of customer-defined standards *soft standards and measures* because they are opinion-based measures and cannot be directly observed. They must be collected by talking to customers, employees, or others. Soft standards provide direction, guidance, and feedback to employees in ways to achieve customer satisfaction and can be examined by measuring customer perceptions and beliefs.

Soft standards are especially important for person-to-person interactions such as the selling process and the delivery process for professional services. Exhibit 9.2 displays several examples of soft customer-defined standards. A casino that one of us has worked with has identified five soft service standards to encourage its employees to provide an appropriate level of (a) attention and (b) respect to its guests—two issues that its customers have indicated are important to them. Two of these standards are for

Global Feature International Standards and Global Service Management

As discussed in Chapter 1, the service sector is the backbone of the global economy. Driven by technological advances, the service sector has become an even more important driver of international trade as it is now easier to provide service across borders. Because the modern service economy is global in nature, it includes thousands of large international companies (e.g., airlines, financial firms, telecommunications companies, hotel chains) and millions of small, locally owned companies (e.g., restaurants, hairstylists, business-to-business services). Here, we highlight the relevance of international standards (and standardization) to ensure consistent service levels around the world.

VectorShop/Shutterstock

The ISO as a Major Source for Standards: The International Organization for Standardization (ISO) is at the heart of developing voluntary, customer-oriented service standards. ISO is an independent, non-governmental international network with members in more than 160 countries. These members collaborate to develop "International Standards that represent the distilled wisdom of experts and aim to provide a formula that describes the best way of doing something (e.g., providing a service or manufacturing a product)" to ensure that services, products, and processes are fit for purpose.

Why International Service Standards? In international transactions, there are many risks related to customers receiving poor quality or even being exploited (e.g., through questionable business practices by some companies). Moreover, service companies and professionals may experience difficulties when operating across borders (e.g., countries often are inconsistent in how they regulate certain professions, such as health care, financial, or legal services). Therefore, according to the ISO, "the service sector is in vital need of standards to establish good practice, encourage consistently high service quality, and build consumer confidence."

Standards for Services: The ISO has published more than 700 service-specific standards. This portfolio includes different types of standards for services: *horizontal* standards provide broad guidelines that can be applied across service sectors (e.g., standards on how to operate customer contact centers or IT services); in contrast, *vertical* standards apply only to certain service industries (e.g., tourism, market research). Next, we briefly illustrate one such vertical standard: "*ISO 24803—Recreational Diving Services: Requirements for Recreational Diving Providers.*"

Scope of this standard: Scuba diving is a popular recreational activity; it is generally quite safe *if proper rules are followed*. Because there are many thousands of service providers that offer diving around the world, it is in the best interest of customers, tourism organizations, and governmental agencies to have an ISO standard to codify proper procedures for running a diving center in a safe and trustworthy manner. With this goal in mind, standard ISO 24803 focuses on diving-related services such as diver training and education, guided dive tours and snorkeling excursions, as well as the rental of diving equipment and courses leading to diver or instructor qualifications. The various sections of this standard define how focal services are to be performed. For example, when conducting "guided dives," ISO 24803 calls for a service provider to (1) provide a safety briefing, (2) conduct a risk assessment, (3) assign buddies, (4) identify operational parameters, (5) ensure an emergency support procedure is in place, and (6) provide

employees to "display a demeanor that could be described as friendly, polite, cheerful, or upbeat" and to "offer an appropriate verbal greeting" when interacting with customers. Unlike the hard service standards described earlier, such soft standards are not easily quantifiable, but a firm's performance on these standards can be assessed via surveys and other means that capture customer perceptions of how the firm is doing on the standards.

One-Time Fixes

When customer research is undertaken to find out what aspects of service need to be changed, requirements can sometimes be met using one-time fixes. *One-time fixes* are technology, policy, or procedure changes that, when instituted, address customer

Martin Strmiska/Alamy Stock Photo

an environmental briefing that includes information and methods for minimizing the impact on the natural environment, particularly on fragile marine ecosystems.

Need for this standard: Because safety is so important when diving, customers need to (be able to) trust that their service provider is properly qualified, regardless of where they are diving. Customers are concerned about safety whether they are in South America, Africa, or Australia, or whether they are working with a large or a locally owned company. Accordingly, Standard ISO 24803 applies to, for example, land-based dive centers and water centers, boat-based operations, dive clubs, individual instructors, and service operators that offer snorkeling trips. The ISO standard 24803 helps to ensure that these recreational services are provided in a safe and consistent way to customers. It also helps to reduce the risks for service providers as well as the natural resources at dive sites.

Because diving services are offered in settings characterized by different cultures, numerous languages, and a diverse set of local infrastructures, developing this standard (and multiple related standards on recreational diving services) was not easy. To illustrate, it took ISO experts from 27 countries 26 months to develop ISO standard 24803; but the final result now provides clear guidelines that serve as recognizable quality benchmarks for customers of dive center operations around the world.

As this Global Feature illustrates, international service standards can play a key role in developing and maintaining a productive marketplace that offers quality services.

Sources: ISO, "Strategy for Services," https://www.iso.org/files/live/sites/isoorg/files/store/en/PUB100390.pdf, accessed December 27, 2021; ISO Case Study, "Diving Centers in Egypt," https://www.iso.org/files/live/sites/isoorg/files/store/en/PUB100431.pdf, accessed December 27, 2021; E. Gasiorowski-Denis, "Service with a Smile, Thanks to Standards," https://www.iso.org/news/2016/05/Ref2077.html, accessed December 23, 2021; For other case studies (e.g., telehealth), see: https://www.iso.org/services.html.

requirements. We further define one-time fixes as company standards that can be met by an outlet (e.g., a franchisee) making a one-time change that does not involve employees and therefore does not require motivation and monitoring to ensure compliance. We include one-time fixes in our discussion of standards because organizations with multiple outlets often must clearly define these standards to ensure consistency.

For example, during the COVID-19 pandemic most hotels in the United States had to shift away from their established automatic daily housekeeping services to an "opt-in" model, driven by safety guidelines. That meant that guests needed to explicitly request housekeeping service; otherwise, they would return to a room with no clean towels and a disheveled bed. Below are some examples of Hilton's and Marriott's housekeeping policies adopted during the pandemic:[11]

Exhibit 9.2 Examples of Soft Customer-Defined Standards

Company	Customer Priorities	Customer-Defined Standards
American Express	Resolution of problems	• Resolve problem at first contact (no transfers, other calls, or multiple contacts) • Communicate and give adequate instructions • Take all the time necessary
	Treatment	• Listen • Do everything possible to help • Be appropriately reassuring (open and honest)
	Courtesy of representative	• Put card member at ease • Be patient in explaining billing process • Display sincere interest in helping card member • Listen attentively • Address card member by name • Thank card member at end of call
General Electric	Interpersonal skills of operators	• Take ownership of the call • Follow through with promises made • Be courteous and knowledgeable • Understand the customer's question or request
L.L. Bean	Calming human voice; minimal customer anxiety	• Use appropriate tone of voice • Do not engage in other tasks (e.g., arranging gift boxes) while on the telephone with customers
Mayo Clinic	Getting well	• Compliance with processes known to enhance care
	Feeling well taken care of	• Each patient is treated with respect, kindness, and dignity by every member of the (Mayo) team
Peninsula Regional Medical Center	Respect	• Keep patient information confidential • Never discuss patients and their care in public areas • Listen to patients with empathy • Be courteous and do not use jargon • Keep noise to a minimum • Never "talk over" a patient
Ritz-Carlton	Being treated with respect	• React quickly to solve any problems immediately • Use proper telephone etiquette • Do not screen calls • Eliminate call transfers when possible

Hilton

- Daily housekeeping at U.S. properties available upon request.
- Guest rooms automatically receive a full cleaning on the fifth day of an extended stay.
- Guests at Waldorf Astoria, Conrad, and the brand's "Legendary Luxury Properties" automatically receive daily housekeeping.

Marriott International Inc.

- Guests can choose their preferred housekeeping service frequency during their stay.
- Guests at luxury hotels receive daily housekeeping unless otherwise directed by the guest.

Two other examples of successful one-time fixes include Hertz's rental car express check-in and Granite Rock's 24-hour express service. In both of these examples, customers expressed a desire to be served in ways different from the past. Hertz's customers had clearly indicated their frustration at waiting in long lines. Granite Rock, an innovative company in California that sells a "commodity" product, had customers who desired 24-hour availability of ground rock from its quarry.

Whereas most companies in these industries decided for various reasons not to address these customer requirements, Hertz and Granite Rock each responded with one-time fixes that virtually revolutionized the service quality delivered by their companies. Hertz used technology to create Express Checkout, a one-time fix that also resulted in productivity improvements and cost reductions. The company also pioneered a similar one-time fix for Express Check-In, again in response to customers' expressed desires. Granite Rock created an ATM-like system for 24-hour customer access to rock ground to the 14 most popular consistencies. The company created its own Granite Xpress Card that allowed customers to enter, select, and receive their supplies at any time of the day or night.

One-time fixes are often accomplished by technology. Technology (e.g., online self-service sites or chatbots) can simplify and improve customer service, particularly when it frees company personnel by handling routine, repetitious tasks and transactions. Customer service employees can then spend more time on the personal and possibly more essential portions of the job. In recent years some hospital emergency rooms have added check-in kiosks so that patients who are not experiencing a true "emergency" can enter personal information, thus reducing time spent waiting in line to register and explain symptoms.[12]

DEVELOPMENT OF CUSTOMER-DEFINED SERVICE STANDARDS

Turning Customer Requirements into Specific Behaviors and Actions

How have firms such as FedEx, Puget Sound Energy, and Zappos.com been able to develop commendable customer-defined service standards? Figure 9.2 shows the general process for setting customer-defined service standards.

Step 1: Identify Existing or Desired Service Encounter Sequence

A customer's overall service quality evaluation is the accumulation of evaluations of multiple service experiences. Therefore, in establishing standards, firms are concerned with service encounter quality and thus want to understand the specific requirements and priorities of the customer for each service encounter. Accordingly, the first step in establishing customer-defined standards is to delineate the *service encounter sequence*. Identifying the sequence can be done by listing the sequential steps and activities that the customer experiences in receiving the service. Alternatively, service blueprints (see Chapter 8) can be used to identify the sequence by noting customer activities across the top of the blueprint. Vertical lines from customer activities into the lower levels of the blueprint signal the points at which service encounters take place. Standards that meet customer expectations for each interaction can then be identified. Ideally, the company would be open to discovering customers' desired service encounter sequences, exploring the ways customers want to do business with the firm.

FIGURE 9.2
Process for Setting Customer-Defined Standards

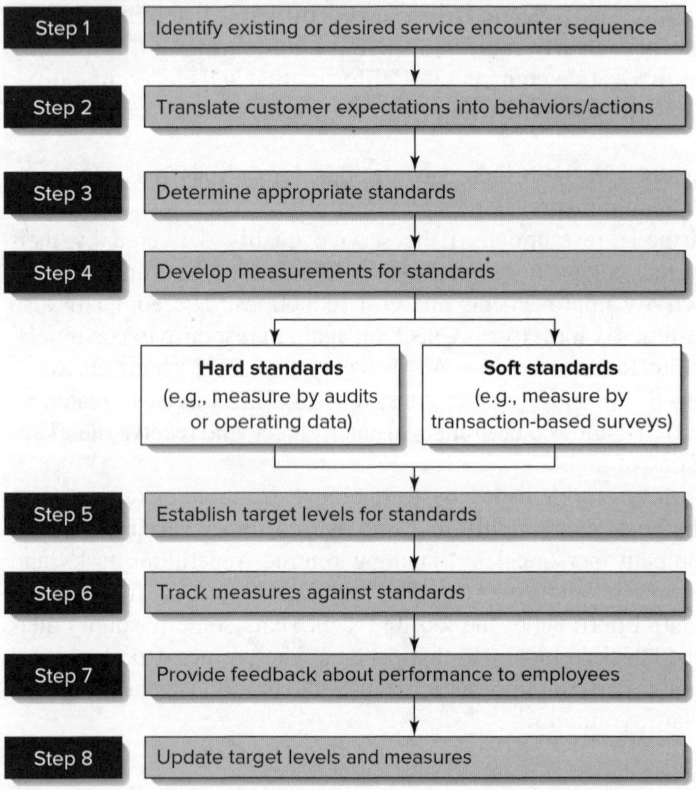

A firm might also consider which of its service encounters have the greatest impact on customers. Marriott, for example, has found that encounters in the first 10 minutes of a hotel stay are the most critical, leading to a focus on customers' front-desk experiences (such as express check-in). Some research indicates that a strong finish in the final event of the service encounter sequence has a greater impact on overall satisfaction.[13] As a result, other hotels have chosen to focus on the "back end" of the hotel experience—checkout, parking, bellperson services—to leave a strong final impression. To be safe, the Ritz-Carlton assumes both the first and last encounters are important and therefore includes as two of the three "Steps of Service" (part of its famous "Gold Standards") instructions for employees to provide guests with "a warm and sincere greeting" and "a fond farewell [with] a warm good-bye" while using the guests' names.[14]

Step 2: Translate Customer Expectations into Specific Behaviors and Actions

Setting a standard in broad conceptual terms, such as "improve skills in the company," is ineffective because the standard is difficult to interpret, measure, and achieve. When a company collects data, it often captures customer requirements in very abstract terms. In general, customer-contact personnel often find such data are not diagnostic but rather too broad and general. Such research neither tells them specifically what is wrong and right in their customer relationships nor helps them understand what activities can be eliminated, so that the most important actions can be accomplished. In most cases, frontline employees need help translating the data into specific actions to deliver better customer service.

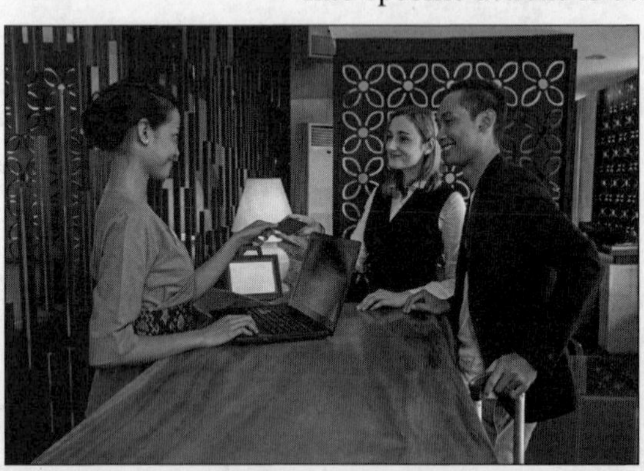
Space_Cat/Shutterstock

First encounters, such as for a hotel stay, are critical and have a significant impact on customers in most service settings.

Figure 9.3 shows different levels of abstraction/concreteness for standards in a service firm, arrayed from top (most abstract) to bottom (most concrete and specific). At the very abstract level are customer requirements too general to be useful to employees: customers want satisfaction, value, and relationships. The next level under these very general requirements includes abstract dimensions of service quality already discussed in this text: reliability, responsiveness, empathy, assurance, and tangibles. One level further are attributes which are more specific in describing requirements.[15] If we dig still deeper beneath the attribute level, we get to specific behaviors and actions at the appropriate level of specificity for setting

FIGURE 9.3 What Customers Expect: Getting to Actionable Steps

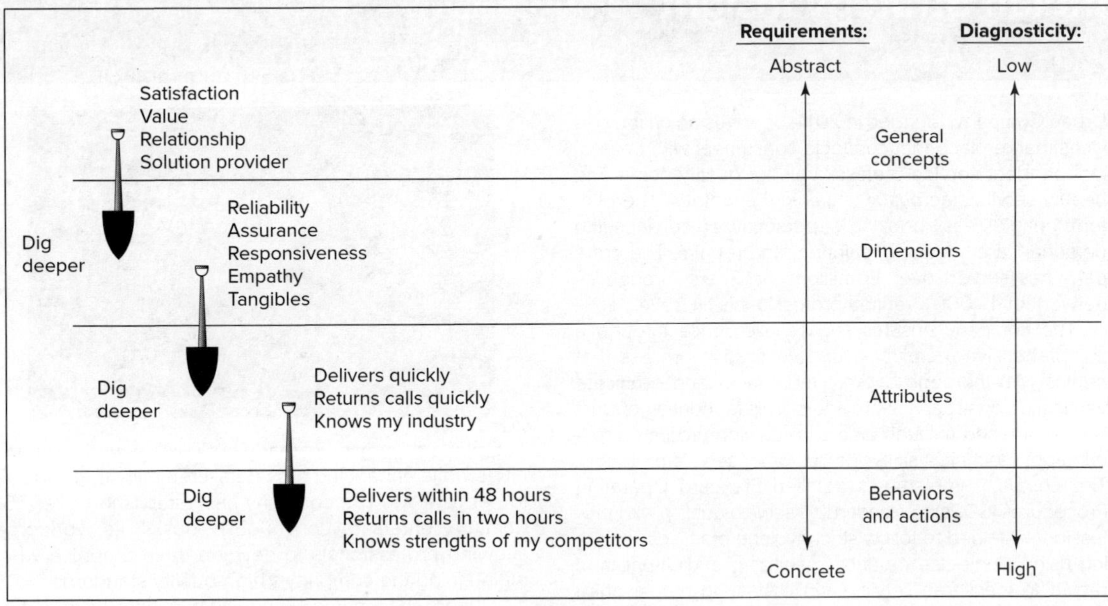

standards. Thus, in step 2, abstract customer requirements and expectations must be translated into concrete, specific behaviors and actions associated with each service encounter. Abstract requirements (like reliability) can call for a different behavior or action in each service encounter.

Information on behaviors and actions should be gathered and interpreted by an objective source such as a research firm or an inside department with no stake in the ultimate decisions. If the information is filtered through company managers or front-line people with an internal bias, the outcome can easily result in company-defined, rather than customer-defined, standards. Research techniques discussed in Chapter 5 that are relevant for eliciting behaviors and actions include in-depth interviewing of customers, focus group interviews, and other forms of research.

A real-world example of the difference in requirements across the four levels depicted in Figure 9.3 illustrates their practical significance. In a traditional measurement system for a major company's training division, only one aspect of the instructor was included in its class evaluation: ability of instructor. During qualitative research relating to the attributes that satisfy students, three somewhat more specific requirements were elicited: (1) instructor's style, (2) instructor's expertise, and (3) instructor's management of class. Although the articulation of the three attributes was more helpful to instructors than the broad "ability of instructor," management found that the attributes were still too broad to help instructors wanting to improve their course delivery. When the company invested in a customer-defined standards project, the resulting measurement system was far more useful in diagnosing student requirements because the research focused on *specific behaviors and actions* of instructors that met student requirements. Instead of a single broad requirement or three general attributes, the requirements of students were articulated in 14 specific behaviors that related to the instructor and 11 specific actions that related to the course content. These behaviors and actions were clearly more diagnostic for communicating what was good and bad in the courses. An additional benefit of this approach was that feedback on behaviors and actions was perceived as less personal than feedback on traits or personal characteristics. It was also easier for employees of the company to make changes that related to behaviors rather than to personality traits.

Indian Strategy Insight Urban Company – Service Excellence for Salon Services

Urban Company, founded in 2014, operates an online services marketplace that connects consumers with trained, independent service professionals for quality home and beauty services across 59 cities in 4 countries. The platform enables easy booking of personalized services like personal care, cleaning, painting, and repairs. The company has served over 13 million customers through its network of 48,000+ verified professionals till 2024.

The company ensures service excellence through a comprehensive recruitment and verification process that begins with thorough background checks and certificate verification of all service providers. This foundation of trust is strengthened through extensive training programs covering both technical skills and customer service protocols. The company implements detailed Standard Operating Procedures (SOPs) to standardize service quality, with professionals trained to follow strict hygiene practices, including using single-use products, sanitizing equipment, and providing mess-free services while wearing proper attire and surgical masks during appointments.

The platform leverages technology to create a seamless customer experience, using artificial intelligence and machine learning to simplify the user journey. Service quality is maintained through a transparent rating and review system that holds service providers accountable and identifies areas for improvement. Its dual-feedback mechanism allows both customers and providers to evaluate each other, ensuring continuous enhancement of service standards while also offering clear pricing structures without hidden fees across various service tiers, including classic, prime, and luxury options.

Urban Company creates significant value for service providers through its four-pillar approach focusing on earnings, social security, training/upskilling, and wealth creation. Service professionals benefit from direct access to customers without intermediaries, transparent earnings, insurance coverage, and even stock options.

The platform provides steady but flexible work opportunities while enhancing providers' credibility through customer reviews. The company has established over 250 training centers to continuously upskill its workforce, allowing professionals to develop their expertise while maintaining the company's high-quality standards.

During challenging times like the pandemic, Urban Company maintained consumer trust through rigorous safety protocols, resulting in increased repeat business and word-of-mouth referrals. The company's full-stack approach, with standardized tools and products, ensures consistent service delivery across all markets. While some customers might attempt to bypass the platform by directly contacting service professionals, Urban Company focuses on adding value to both sides of the marketplace, providing service professionals with pricing power, reduced cancellations, and a sense of community that might be lost if they operated independently.

Reference: https://www.urbancompany.com/about
https://www.urbancompany.com/blog/salon-hygiene-checklist-things-your-beautician-should-be-careful-about
https://oyelabs.com/urbanclap-business-model/
https://www.thehotstartups.com/p/story-urban-company-startup-global-home-services-leader

Step 3: Determine Appropriate Standards

The next step involves determining whether hard or soft standards should be used to capture a given behavior and action. Recall that hard standards consist of quantifiable measures of employee behaviors and actions; soft standards are often concerned with more abstract requirements or issues, are not as easily quantifiable, and are often much more subjective. One of the biggest mistakes companies make in this step is to hastily choose a hard standard. Companies are accustomed to operational (and often easily quantifiable) measures and often have a bias toward them. However, unless the hard standard adequately captures an expected behavior or action identified by customers, it is not customer defined. The best way to decide whether a hard standard is appropriate is to first establish a soft standard by means of trailer calls and then determine over time which operational aspect most correlates to this soft measure. Figure 9.4 shows the linkage between speed of complaint handling (a hard measure) and satisfaction

FIGURE 9.4
Linkage between Hard and Soft Measures for Speed of Complaint Handling

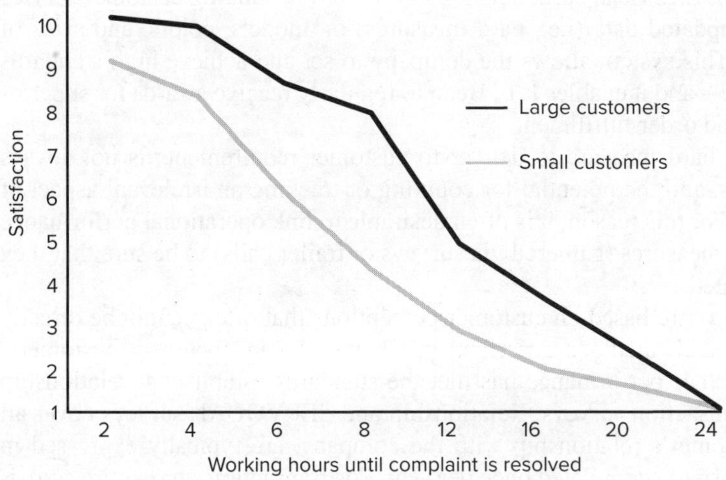

(a soft measure); the figure illustrates that satisfaction strongly depends on the number of hours it takes to resolve a complaint.

Prioritizing the behaviors and actions—of which there will be many—into those for which customer-defined standards will be established is also crucial in determining standards. The following are the most important criteria for creation of appropriate service standards.

1. The standards are based on behaviors and actions that are very important to customers.
2. The standards cover performance that needs to be improved or maintained.
3. The standards cover behaviors and actions employees have control over and can improve.
4. The standards are understood and accepted by employees.
5. The standards are predictive rather than reactive—based on current and future customer expectations rather than past complaints.
6. The standards are challenging but realistic.

Step 4: Develop Measurements for Standards

Once companies have determined whether hard or soft standards are appropriate and which specific standards best capture customer requirements, they must develop feedback measures that adequately capture the standards. Two types of measures are hard measurements and soft measurements.

Hard measurements typically involve mechanical counts or technology-enabled measurement of time or errors. What distinguishes these measurements from soft measurements is that they can be measured continuously and operationally without asking the customer's opinion of them. To demonstrate, here are some of the actual measurements of hard standards of the FedEx Express SQI:

- *Missing packages:* the number of packages that do not have a final disposition scan or have no package status scans for two consecutive business days after commit date.
- *Damaged packages:* the number of claims filed by customers for cost of contents for packages with visible or concealed damage.
- *Wrong day, late deliveries:* the number of packages delivered after the commitment date.[16]

In these and other hard measurements, assessment involves a count of the number and type of actions or behaviors that are correct or incorrect. Somewhere in the operation system these actions and behaviors are tabulated, frequently through information technology. Other gauges of hard standards include service guarantee lapses (the number of times a service guarantee is invoked because the service did not meet the promise), amounts of time (as in the number of hours or days to respond to a question or complaint or minutes waited in line), and frequencies associated with relevant standards (such as the number of visits made to customers or the number of abandoned telephone inquiries). L.L. Bean earned its reputation for outstanding customer service using continually updated data (i.e., hard measures) on models, colors, and sizes of products in stock. This system allows the company to set and achieve high standards of customer service—and it enables L.L. Bean to regularly receive awards for superior customer service and order fulfillment.[17]

The appropriate hard measure to deliver to customer requirements is not always intuitive or obvious, and the potential for counting or tracking an irrelevant aspect of operations is high. For this reason, it is often desirable to link operational performance measures with soft measures (gathered via surveys or trailer calls) to be sure that they are strongly correlated.

Soft measurements are based on customer perceptions that often cannot be directly observed. Two research methods described in Chapter 5 can document customers' opinions about whether performance has met the standards established: relationship surveys and posttransaction surveys. Relationship and SERVQUAL surveys cover all aspects of the customer's relationship with the company, are typically expressed in attributes, and are usually completed once per year. Posttransaction surveys are associated with specific service encounters, are often fairly short (approximately six or seven questions), and are administered as close in time to a specific service encounter as possible. For requirements that are longer term and at a higher level of abstraction (such as at the attribute level), annual relationship surveys can document customer perceptions on a periodic basis. Posttransaction surveys can be administered continuously, whenever customers experience a service encounter of the type being considered, to provide data on a continuous basis.

Step 5: Establish Target Levels for the Standards

The next step requires that companies establish target levels for the standards. Without this step the company lacks a way to quantify whether the standards are being met. Figure 9.4 provides a good example of an approach that can be used to set standards for timeliness in responding to complaints in a service company. In this illustration, each time a complaint is made to the company, and each time one is resolved, employees can record the times. They can also ask each customer his or her satisfaction with the performance in resolving the complaint. The company can then plot the information from each complaint to determine how well the company is performing and where the company would like to be in the future. This technique is but one of several for determining the target level for service standards.

Another technique is a simple perception–action correlation study. When the service consists of repetitive processes, companies can relate levels of customer satisfaction with actual performance of a behavior or task. Consider, for example, a study to determine the standard for customers' wait-time in a line. The information gathered should include both customer perceptions of their wait in line (soft perceptual measure) and the amount of time they actually stand in line (hard operations measure). The joint collection of these data over many transactions provides evidence of the sensitivity of customers to different wait-times.

One airline conducted precisely such a study by having a flight attendant intercept customers as they approached the ticket counter. As each customer entered the line, the attendant stamped the entry time on a ticket (using a machine like those in parking lots) and handed the customer the stamped ticket. As the customer exited the line at the end of the transaction, the flight attendant restamped the ticket with the exit time and asked the customer three or four questions about perceptions of the wait in line and satisfaction with the transaction. Aggregating the individual customer data provided a graph that allowed the company to evaluate the impact on perceptions of various levels of line waits.

Step 6: Track Measures against Standards

Roger Milliken, former head of Milliken Industries, is reported to have said, "In God we trust, all others bring data." Successful service businesses, such as FedEx and Disney, have careful and comprehensive fact-based systems that provide information about their operations—allowing them to continually examine how the company is performing in comparison to its service standards. One company that lives and thrives through management by fact is Granite Rock, the family-run business in Watsonville, California (mentioned earlier in the chapter) that provides concrete, asphalt, and crushed stone products. Granite Rock has systems in place to gather, analyze, and act on information. Statistical process control and other types of charts are everywhere, tracking a wide range of issues—from characteristics of its concrete and crushed stone to processes such as the time it takes customers to fill their trucks. Customer complaints are also tracked through what the company calls "product-service discrepancy reports" and root-cause analysis, and updates are distributed to all plants. The reports show how long it takes to resolve complaints and provide detailed quarterly analyses of trends. Plants can track their trends for four years running. When it comes to product quality and customer service, Granite Rock leaves nothing to chance.

Step 7: Provide Feedback about Performance to Employees

Once companies have determined appropriate standards, developed specific measures that best capture customer requirements, and set appropriate target levels for the standards, they must develop mechanisms to provide feedback on employee actions and behaviors. One example of such feedback is employee monitoring; in firms with customer service departments, this involves the practice of supervisors listening in on employee telephone interactions with customers. You may have experienced this practice when you have called customer service numbers for many organizations and noticed that the voice prompts tell you that calls may be monitored for quality purposes. The purpose of such monitoring is often to provide feedback on employee performance to the service standards set by the organization. One critical aspect of developing feedback mechanisms is ensuring that performance captures the process from the customer's view rather than the company's perspective. A supervisor monitoring an employee's handling of a customer service call, for example, should focus not so much on how quickly the employee gets the customer off the telephone but on how adequately she handles the customer's request.

FedEx communicates the performance on its service quality indicator (SQI) weekly, so that everyone in the company knows how the company is performing. When problems occur, they can be identified and corrected. The SQI measurement gives everyone in the company immediate feedback on activity that is strongly related to customer perceptions. In a general sense, data and facts need to be analyzed and distributed to support evaluation and decision making at multiple levels within the company. The data also must be deployed quickly enough that the people who need it to make decisions about service or processes can do so. Responsibility for meeting service requirements must also be communicated throughout the organization. All parts of the organization should be measuring their services to internal customers and, ultimately, measuring how that performance relates to external customer requirements.

Step 8: Periodically Update Target Levels and Measures

The final step involves revising the target levels, measures, and even customer requirements regularly enough to keep up with customer expectations. When FedEx originally developed its SQI, it assigned lost packages a weight of 10; over time, FedEx has found that a lost package is much more important to customers than many of the other issues included in the index and now assigns a weight of 50 to such an event. Facebook initially set a benchmark of five minutes for firms to receive the Facebook "very responsive" badge in responding to their customers. However, many businesses indicated that an average response time of five minutes was unrealistic. As a result of this feedback, Facebook revised that number to a more realistic 15 minutes. As these examples suggest, some flexibility in changing service standards may be necessary.

Developing Service Performance Indexes

One outcome of following the process for developing customer-defined standards can be the creation of a service performance index. *Service performance indexes* are comprehensive composites of the most critical performance standards. Development of an index begins by identifying the set of customer-defined standards that the company will use to drive behavior. Not all service performance indexes contain customer-defined standards, but the best ones, like the FedEx SQI, are based on them. Most companies build these indexes by understanding the most important requirements of the customer, linking these requirements to tangible and measurable aspects of service provision, and using the feedback from these indexes to identify and improve service problems. The most progressive companies also use the feedback for reward and recognition systems within the company.

Summary

This chapter discussed the discrepancy between company perceptions of customer expectations and the standards set to deliver to these expectations. Among the major causes of provider Gap 2 are inadequate standardization of service behaviors and actions, absence of formal processes for setting service quality goals, and lack of customer-defined standards. These problems were discussed and detailed, along with strategies to close the gap. To close the service design and standards gap, standards set by companies must be based on customer requirements and expectations rather than just on internal company goals. That is, company-defined standards are typically not successful in driving behaviors that close provider Gap 2 and a company must set *customer*-defined standards based on key customer requirements.

In this chapter we described two types of service standards: hard standards, those that can be counted, timed, or observed through audits, and soft standards, customer perceptions that cannot be directly observed. Customer-defined standards are at the heart of service delivery that customers expect: they are the link between customers' expressed expectations and company actions to deliver to those expectations. Creating customer-defined service standards is not a common practice in U.S. firms. Doing so requires that companies' marketing and operations departments work together by using the customer research as input for operations. Unless the operations standards are defined by customer priorities, they are not likely to have an impact on customer perceptions of service.

Discussion Questions

1. How does the service measurement described in this chapter differ from the service measurement in Chapter 5? Which of the two types do you think is most important? Why?
2. In what types of service industries are standards most difficult to develop? Why? Recommend three standards that might be developed in one of the firms from the industries you specify. How would employees react to these standards? How could you gain buy-in for them?
3. Given the need for customer-defined service standards, do firms need company-defined standards at all? Could all standards in a company be customer defined? Why or why not? What functional departments in a firm would object to having all standards be customer defined?
4. What is the difference between hard and soft standards? Which do you think would be more readily accepted by employees? By management? Why?
5. Consider the university or school you currently attend. What are examples of hard standards, soft standards, and one-time fixes that would address student requirements? Does the school currently use such standards for delivery of service to students? Why or why not? Do you think your reasons would apply to private-sector companies as well? To public or nonprofit companies?
6. Think about a service that you currently use; then map out the service encounter sequence for that service. What is your most important requirement in each interaction? Document these requirements, and make certain that they are expressed at the concrete level of behaviors and actions.

Exercises

1. Select a local service firm. Visit the firm and ascertain the service measurements that the company tracks. What hard measures does it monitor? Soft measures? On the basis of what you find, develop a service performance index.
2. Choose one of the peripheral services (such as the fitness facilities/gym or career center) provided by your school. What hard standards would be useful to track to meet student expectations? What soft standards would be appropriate? What one-time fixes would improve service?
3. Think about a service company you have worked for or know about. Using Figure 9.3, write in customer requirements at each of the levels. How far down in the chart can you describe requirements? Is that far enough?
4. Look at three websites from which you can order products (such as amazon.com, llbean.com, and zappos.com). What are the companies' delivery promises? What types of standards might they set for these promises? Are these customer- or company-defined standards?

Notes

1. "Taking the Measure of Quality," *Service Savvy,* March 1992, p. 3.
2. Ibid.
3. E-mail communication from David Spear, manager of global service and quality assurance, *FedEx Express*, June 14, 2016.
4. "2021 FedEx Annual Report," Statista.com, "Total average packages delivered daily by FedEx Express"; https://www.wallstreetzen.com/stocks/us/nyse/fdx/statistics#1-shipment-statistics; accessed January 2022.
5. G. L. Shostack, "Breaking Free from Product Marketing," *Journal of Marketing* 41 (April 1977), pp. 73–80.

6. Puget Sound Energy, "2021 Service Quality Report Card," https://www.pse.com/-/media/PDFs/2774_SQI_Report_Card_2021.pdf, accessed September 9, 2022.
7. Oregon Department of Transportation website, www.oregon.gov/ODOT/CS/PERFORMANCE/OnePagers/DMV Field Office Wait Time One pager.pdf, accessed July 13, 2016.
8. For a good discussion of creating service standards, see M. Solomon, "A Ritz-Carlton Caliber Experience Requires Employee Empowerment and Customer Service Standards," *Forbes,* September 18, 2013, http://www.forbes.com/sites/micahsolomon/2013/09/18/empowered-employees-vs-brand-standards-the-customer-experience-needs-both/. For case studies on service standards in governmental services, see: R. Schulz, A. Sense, and M. Pepper, "Apprehending and Embedding Customer Expectations in the Collaborative Development of Performance Indicators," *Systemic Practice and Action Research* 34 (February 2021), pp. 71–90.
9. 2015 Customer Rage Study conducted by Customer Care Measurement and Consulting in collaboration with the Center for Services Leadership at Arizona State University's W. P. Carey School of Business.
10. S. Banker, "No Industry Has A Better Key Performance Indicator Than Baseball," *Forbes,* September 2, 2020, https://www.forbes.com/sites/stevebanker/2020/09/02/no-industry-has-a-better-measure-of-what-it-takes-to-succeed-than-baseball/?sh=3b0b723a240f, accessed December 21, 2021.
11. B. Schulz, "Where Are the Housekeepers? COVID-19 Guidelines, Labor Shortage Affect Hotel Housekeeping Service," *USA Today*, September 30, 2021. https://www.usatoday.com/story/travel/hotels/2021/07/07/hotel-housekeeping-service-available-upon-request/7894656002/, accessed December 21, 2021.
12. J. Stengle, "ER Kiosks Let Patients Avoid Long Lines," *Associated Press,* September 13, 2007.
13. See D. E. Hansen and P. J. Danaher, "Inconsistent Performance during the Service Encounter: What's a Good Start Worth?" *Journal of Service Research* 1 (February 1999), pp. 227–235; and V. Dalakas, "The Importance of a Good Ending in a Service Encounter," *Services Marketing Quarterly* 28 (2006), pp. 35–53.
14. These are two of the "three Steps of Service" included in Ritz-Carlton's Gold Standards, which can be found on the company website at http://www.ritzcarlton.com/en/about/gold-standards, accessed May 22, 2016.
15. For a comprehensive list of service attributes found to be important across a variety of services, see M. Paul, T. Hennig-Thurau, D. D. Gremler, K. P. Gwinner, and C. Wiertz, "Toward a Theory of Repeated Purchase Drivers for Consumer Services," *Journal of the Academy of Marketing Science* 37 (Summer 2009), pp. 215–237.
16. Based on e-mail communication with David Spear, manager of global service and quality assurance, *FedEx Express*, June 16, 2016.
17. "L.L. Bean Rated #1 in Customer Satisfaction," *Trailmix* (blog) *L.L. Bean,* January 21, 2014, blog.llbean.com/2014/01/l-l-bean-rated-1-in-customer-satisfaction.

Chapter **Ten**

Physical Evidence and the Servicescape

This chapter's learning objectives are to:

1. Explain the impact of physical evidence, particularly the servicescape, on customer perceptions and experiences.
2. Illustrate differences in types of servicescapes, the roles played by the servicescape, and the implications for strategy.
3. Explain *why* the servicescape affects customer and employee behavior, using a framework based in marketing, organizational behavior, and environmental psychology.
4. Present elements of an effective physical evidence strategy.

Marriott Creates Uniquely Branded Experiences with Distinctive Servicescapes[1]

Marriott International Inc., the world's largest hotel company, has a brand for every price point, every occasion, and every type of customer. The company is consistently ranked as the most admired company in the hotel industry and one of the best places to work by *Fortune* magazine. Operating in more than 120 countries and territories, Marriott employs more than 120,000 people. From its high-end Ritz-Carlton and J. W. Marriott Hotels to its more budget-oriented Fairfield Inns, the company has been successful at clearly positioning its many brands, distinguishing them from each other, and attracting well-defined market segments for each. According to branding and strategy executives at Marriott, building these distinctive hotel brands involves a complex strategy that meshes hotel design, employee training and selection to match the brand strategy, careful customer segmentation, and specific operational brand standards.

From the customer's perspective, the most visible aspect of Marriott's distinctive brand strategies is the "servicescape," or the physical environment where the service is delivered—the hotel design itself. The luxury design of the Ritz-Carlton brand fits well with its position as the hotel where the long-standing motto, "ladies and gentlemen serving ladies and gentlemen" guides employee attitudes and behaviors. The Ritz-Carlton enjoys a global reputation for "setting the gold standards" through the underlying values and philosophies by which it operates. Its vision is to "inspire life's most meaningful journeys." The physical servicescape of every Ritz-Carlton reinforces its high-end luxury positioning, from the lobby areas to the acclaimed

Patrick Fallon/Bloomberg/Getty Images

This Marriott Courtyard lobby design promotes working and socializing among guests.

restaurants, elegant spas, and upscale retail opportunities. In contrast, the physical presence of a Marriott Courtyard, while still expressing personal comfort and style, is much more efficient and business-like in its design. The lobby area is open and flexible, inviting guests to socialize, relax, and enjoy casual food options in a comfortable, yet upscale environment. In the lobby there are efficient spaces for working, connecting to the Internet for free, and conducting meetings (see photo). The space is designed to promote collaboration, productivity, and social interaction. Guest rooms are designed similarly with moveable workspaces, plenty of electrical outlets, the latest in technology connections, and refreshing colors to recharge business guests after a long day.

Marriott's more recent hotel brand introduction is "Edition," a boutique hotel that marries unique, destination-inspired hotel design with sophisticated service. This concept, a partnership with Ian Schrager, a well-known pioneer in the modern boutique-hotel industry, provided the foundation for Marriott to enter an entirely new market for the company. The Edition-branded hotels are generally smaller, upscale properties that emphasize exclusive and unique styles for each location. The specific design elements of this new boutique hotel are critical to the positioning of the concept. There are Edition hotels in North America, Europe, Asia, and the Middle East. Each hotel reflects the local character, as well as the geographic and cultural uniqueness of the area through its distinctive and high-end servicescape design.

We have highlighted only three of Marriott's 30 brands. What is noteworthy is that each of the 30 brands has a distinctive servicescape design, reinforcing its positioning along the continuum from midscale to luxury hotels. Along with the servicescape, Marriott also reinforces each brand with employee training, dress codes, and internal processes that are consistent with the brand.

In this chapter we explore the importance of physical evidence for communicating service quality attributes, setting customer expectations, and creating the service experience. In Chapter 1, when we introduced the expanded marketing mix for services, we defined physical evidence as *the environment in which the service is delivered and in which the firm and the customer interact, and any tangible commodities that facilitate performance or communication of the service.* The first part of this definition encompasses the actual physical facility in which the service is performed, delivered, and consumed; throughout this chapter the physical facility is referred to as the *servicescape.*[2] Physical evidence is particularly important for communicating about credence services (such as auto repair, financial services, and health care), and it is important for services such as hotels, hospitals, and theme parks that are dominated by experience attributes, as described in our opening vignette on Marriott International.

PHYSICAL EVIDENCE

What Is Physical Evidence?

Customers often rely on tangible cues, or physical evidence, to evaluate the service before its purchase and to assess their satisfaction with the service during and after the experience. Effective design of physical, tangible evidence is important for closing Gap 2. General elements of physical evidence are shown in Table 10.1. They include all aspects of the organization's physical facility (the servicescape) as well as other forms of tangible communication. Elements of the physical servicescape that affect customers include both exterior attributes (such as signage, parking, and the landscape) and interior attributes (such as design, layout, equipment, and decor). Web pages and virtual servicescapes shown online are forms of physical evidence that companies use to communicate about the service experience, making services more tangible for customers both before and after purchase (see the Technology Spotlight).

TABLE 10.1
Elements of Physical Evidence

Servicescape	Other Tangibles
Facility exterior	Business cards
Exterior design	Stationery
Signage	Billing statements
Parking	Reports
Landscape	Employee dress
Surrounding environment	Uniforms
Facility interior	Brochures
Interior design	Web pages
Equipment	Virtual servicescape
Signage	
Layout	
Air quality/temperature	
Sound/music/scent/lighting	

Technology Spotlight Virtual Servicescapes: Experiencing Services through the Internet and Other Technologies

Web pages and virtual service tours allow customers to preview service experiences and see tangible evidence of the service without actually being there. Evolving technology allows firms to communicate experiential aspects of their services in ways that were previously very difficult, if not impossible. Here we present several examples, across different industries.

TRAVEL

Technology allows travelers to preview destinations, view hotels and their rooms, tour natural environments, and "experience" entertainment venues before booking their trips or even deciding where to travel. Before booking a trip to Great Britain, travelers can preview websites that show hotels, bed and breakfast inns, and other lodging all over the country. The exterior of the facilities as well as actual rooms can be examined in selecting accommodations. In planning a trip to visit the national parks of the United States, travelers can view full-length videos of the parks and various tours within the parks. For example, at the Yellowstone site (www.yellowstone.net/) potential visitors can watch a video that shows many of the star attractions of the park. Detailed maps are also included, allowing a traveler to plan a route and choose among the many possible sights prior to even arriving at the park. Additionally, their website features live webcam feeds, allowing visitors to see up-to-the-moment views from several points around the park.

SPORTS AND LEISURE

Through websites and live feeds, fans can now view much of the action and preview upcoming sports experiences online. A great example is how the National Basketball Association (NBA) has used technology to leverage its "NBA League Pass in VR" in response to the COVID-19 pandemic. The NBA collaborated with Yahoo Sports and RYOT (a live virtual reality [VR] production company) to enhance the at-home fan experience during the pandemic, when fans could not attend the games in person. RYOT produced live NBA games in VR, which fans at home could access via compatible VR-enabled hardware (e.g., Oculus devices). Through this collaboration, the NBA was able to offer fans an immersive, arena-like experience because the technology blends the physical and digital worlds. Of course, fans have to either purchase a subscription or a single game via the NBA League Pass. This example illustrates how technologies (here, VR) can transform sports and entertainment services, allowing fans to virtually enter and experience the servicescape. Evolving technologies will continue to redefine the fan's experience with amazing implications for the future of sports and entertainment (e.g., such as fantasy games); in parallel, technology provides the NBA (and similar service organizations) with the opportunity to add additional revenue streams.

UNIQUE RETAIL EXPERIENCES

Many of today's unique retail experiences can be conveyed effectively via the Internet to give customers a

Physical evidence examples from different service contexts are given in Table 10.2. It is apparent that some services (such as hospitals, resorts, and child care) rely heavily on physical evidence to communicate and create customer experiences. Others (insurance, express mail) provide limited physical evidence for customers. All the elements of evidence listed for each service communicate something about the service, facilitate performance of the service, and/or add to the customer's total experience. Although we focus in this chapter primarily on the servicescape and its effects, keep in mind that what is said applies to the other forms of evidence as well.

How Does Physical Evidence Affect the Customer Experience?

Physical evidence, particularly the servicescape, can have a profound effect on the customer experience. This is true whether the experience is mundane (e.g., a bus or subway ride), personally meaningful (e.g., a destination wedding experience), or spectacular (e.g., a week-long travel adventure). In all cases, the physical evidence preview of what they can expect. A great example is Build-A-Bear Workshop®, where children "from 3 to 103" can create their own teddy bears and other furry friends during their visit to the store. Build-A-Bear Workshop operates approximately 500 stores worldwide, including company-owned stores in the United States, Puerto Rico, Canada, the United Kingdom, Ireland, and France, and franchise stores in Europe, Asia, Australia, Africa, and the Middle East. The interactive retail entertainment experience itself is memorable and fun, and the highly visual teddy-bear-themed environment throughout the stores is a big part of the fantasy of this special place. For a preview of how it works and what the stores look like, the website of Build-A-Bear Workshop (www.buildabear.com) includes a tour that shows each of the steps involved in creating a bear; the website also offers engaging digital (purchasing) experiences such as the online "Bear-Builder" as well as the "Bear Builder 3D Workshop" (an interactive experience that virtually brings stuffed animals "to life" during the purchasing process). These features complement the joyful sense of the store environment and the positive emotions of its patrons.

HIGHER EDUCATION

One of the most significant decisions that young people and their families make is what university to attend. For students fortunate enough to have the means and abilities, the choices can be endless. The physical environment of the university—the campus itself as well as specific facilities—can play a major role in students' choices as well as their actual experiences. Many universities offer virtual tours of their campuses online allowing students to preview the physical environment in advance. The University of Oregon in the United States offers virtual tours and visits that allow students to click on different areas of the campus to view that particular spot and listen to narration that gives specific details on various aspects of campus life (360.uoregon.edu). Within each view, the prospective students and family members can see 360-degree views and videos, as well as read information related to that particular place on campus. In exploring university environments this way, students who are unable to visit, or who wish to narrow their visit choices, are much better informed.

Emerging technologies continue to provide tremendous opportunities for firms. For example, Artificial Intelligence allows companies to merge physical with virtual servicescapes through augmented reality apps to further improve the customer experience (e.g., in museums, theme parks, airports, hospitals, or restaurants). However, it is critical that the actual services match these virtual aspects of the experience. That is, using these technologies needs to support the positioning of the service brand and be consistent with other marketing messages.

Source: Yahoo Sports Enhance NBA Action With Virtual Reality, Fantasy Games, Sports Betting, https://www.sportsvideo.org/2020/07/31/yahoo-sports-enhance-nba-action-with-virtual-reality-fantasy-games-sports-betting/, accessed February 7, 2022.

of the service will influence the flow of the experience, the meaning customers attach to it, their satisfaction, their emotional connections with the company delivering the experience, and their social and personal interactions with others experiencing the service.

As marketers pay more attention to customer experiences, they have recognized the impact of physical space and tangibles in creating those experiences. Marketing researchers, managers, and consultants have increasingly focused on ideas such as "experience engineering" through "clue management."[3] *Clue management* refers to the process of clearly identifying and managing *all* the various clues that customers use to form their impressions and feelings about the company. Included in this set of clues are the physical and tangible clues that we focus on in this chapter. Marketing consultants and writers who focus on customer experience management have noted the critical importance of tangible clues and servicescape design in shaping those experiences.[4]

TABLE 10.2 Examples of Physical Evidence from the Customer's Point of View

	Physical Evidence	
Service	**Servicescape**	**Other Tangibles**
Insurance	Not applicable (unless there is a physical office/building where customers interact with frontline employees)	Policy itself Billing statements Periodic updates Company brochure Letters/cards Claims forms Website
Hospital	Building exterior Parking Signs Waiting areas Admissions office Patient care room Medical equipment Recovery room	Uniforms Reports/stationery Billing statements Website
Airline	Airline gate area Airplane exterior Airplane interior (decor, seats, air quality) Check-in kiosks Security screening area Baggage return area	Onboard technology Food Uniforms Website

TYPES OF SERVICESCAPES

This chapter relies heavily on ideas and concepts from environmental psychology, a field that encompasses the study of human beings and their relationships with built (human-made), natural, and social environments.[5] The physical setting may be more or less important in achieving the organization's marketing and other goals, depending on certain factors. Table 10.3 is an initial framework for categorizing service organizations on two dimensions that capture some of the key differences that affect the management of the servicescape. Organizations that share a cell in the table tend to face similar issues and decisions regarding their physical spaces.

Dimension 1: Servicescape Usage

Organizations differ in terms of *whom* the servicescape will affect. That is, who actually comes into the service facility and thus is potentially influenced by its design—customers, employees, or both groups? The first column of Table 10.3 suggests three types of service organizations that differ on this dimension. At one extreme is the *self-service* environment, in which the customer performs most of the activities and few if any employees are involved. Examples of self-service environments include ATMs, check-in kiosks at airports, self-service entertainment such as golf and theme parks, and online services. In these primarily self-service environments, the organization can plan the servicescape to focus exclusively on marketing goals such as attracting the

TABLE 10.3
Typology of Service Organizations Based on Variations in Form and Use of the Servicescape

Source: From M. J. Bitner, "Servicescapes: The Impact of Physical Surroundings on Customers and Employees," *Journal of Marketing* 56 (April 1992), pp. 57–71.

	Complexity of the Servicescape	
Servicescape Usage	**Elaborate**	**Lean**
Self-service (customer only)	Water park eBay	ATM Simple Internet services Express mail drop box
Interpersonal service (both customer and employee)	Hotel/Restaurant Hospital Bank Airline School	Dry cleaner Retail cart Hair salon
Remote service (employee only)	Telecommunications Insurance company Many professional services	Telephone mail-order desk Automated voice-messaging services

right market segment, making the facility pleasing and easy to use, and creating the desired service experience for the customer.

At the other extreme of the use dimension is the *remote service,* where there is little or no customer involvement with the servicescape. Telecommunications, utilities, and mail-order services are examples of services that can be provided without the customer ever seeing the service facility. In fact, the facility may be in a different state or a different country (or, due to the emphasis on telework resulting from the COVID-19 pandemic, customer-contact employees might even work from their homes). In remote services, the facility can be set up to keep employees motivated and to facilitate productivity, teamwork, operational efficiency, or whatever organizational behavior goal is desired without any consideration of customers because they will never see or visit the servicescape. This is the case with SAS, a data analytics and software company that consistently appears in the top tier of *Fortune* magazine's Best Places to Work. The company provides health care and high-quality child care on site, along with car cleaning, a beauty salon, and a state-of-the-art fitness center for its over 13,500 employees. Since most of its customers never visit the SAS campus, the facilities can be designed entirely with employee well-being and productivity in mind.[6]

In Table 10.3, *interpersonal services* are placed between the two extremes and represent situations in which both the customer and the employee are present and active in the servicescape. Examples abound, such as hotels, restaurants, hospitals, educational settings, and banks. In these situations, the servicescape must be designed to attract, satisfy, and facilitate the activities of both customers and employees simultaneously. Special attention must also be given to how the servicescape affects the nature and quality of the social interactions between and among customers and employees. A cruise ship provides a good example of a setting in which the servicescape must support customers and the employees who work there, as well as facilitate interactions between and within the two groups.

Dimension 2: Servicescape Complexity

Table 10.3 suggests another factor that influences servicescape management, the complexity of the servicescape. Some service environments are very simple, with few elements, few spaces, and few pieces of equipment. Such environments are termed *lean.* Shopping mall information kiosks and FedEx drop-off kiosks are lean environments because both provide service from one simple structure. For lean servicescapes, design decisions are relatively straightforward, especially in self-service or remote service situations in which there is no interaction among employees and customers.

Other servicescapes are very complicated, with many elements and many forms. They are termed *elaborate* environments. An example is a hospital with its many floors and rooms, sophisticated equipment, and complex variability in functions performed within the physical facility. In such an elaborate environment, the full range of marketing and organizational objectives theoretically can be approached through careful management of the servicescape. For example, a patient's hospital room can be designed to enhance patient comfort and satisfaction while facilitating employee productivity. Firms that are located in the elaborate interpersonal service cell face the most complex servicescape decisions. To illustrate, when the Mayo Clinic opened its hospital in Scottsdale, Arizona, the organization painstakingly considered the interrelated goals, needs, and feelings of its employees, doctors, patients, and visitors in designing its distinctive servicescape (see Exhibit 10.3 on pp. 298–299).

STRATEGIC ROLES OF THE SERVICESCAPE

Within the cells of the typology, the servicescape can play many strategic roles simultaneously. An examination of the variety of roles and how they interact makes clear how strategically important it is to provide appropriate physical evidence of the service. In fact, the servicescape is frequently one of *the* most important elements used in positioning a service organization (see the Strategy Insight).

Package

Similar to a tangible product's package, the servicescape and other elements of physical evidence essentially "wrap" the service and convey to consumers an external image of what is "inside." Product packages are designed to portray a particular image as well as to evoke a particular sensory or emotional reaction. The physical setting of a service does the same thing through the interaction of many complex stimuli. The servicescape is the outward appearance of the organization and thus can be critical in forming initial impressions or setting up customer expectations—it is a visual metaphor for the intangible service. This packaging role is particularly important in creating expectations for new customers and for newly established service organizations trying to build a particular image. The physical surroundings offer an organization the opportunity to convey an image in a way not unlike the way an individual chooses to "dress for success." The packaging role extends to the appearance of contact personnel through their uniforms or dress and other elements of their outward appearance.[7]

Interestingly, the same care and resource expenditures given to package design in product marketing are often not provided for services, even though the service package serves a variety of important roles. There are many exceptions to this generality, however. Smart companies like Apple Stores (see the Strategy Insight), Starbucks, FedEx, and Marriott spend a lot of time and money relating their servicescape design to their brand, providing their customers with strong visual metaphors and "service packaging" that conveys the brand positioning. Recognizing the power of retail environment design, Starbucks has added unique servicescape aspects for many of its more than 33,000 stores around the world so that they don't all have the look and feel of a store straight out of Seattle. The goal behind this sophisticated approach to design is to have every store feel not like a "mass produced" replica, but rather like a local coffee shop.[8]

Facilitator

The servicescape can also serve as a facilitator in aiding the performances of persons in the environment. How the setting is designed can enhance or inhibit the efficient flow of activities in the service setting, making it easier or harder for customers and employees to accomplish their goals. A well-designed, functional facility can make the service a pleasure to experience from the customer's point of view and a pleasure to perform from the employee's. On the other hand, poor and inefficient design may frustrate both customers and employees. For example, an international air traveler who finds himself in a poorly designed airport with few signs, poor ventilation, and few places to sit or eat will find the experience quite dissatisfying, and employees who work there will probably be unmotivated as well. In reality, many airports today are designed for passengers, inviting them to spend time shopping in a variety of stores, eating in good restaurants, and working in areas set up with Wi-Fi.

The same international traveler will appreciate seats on the airplane conducive to work and sleep. The seating itself, part of the physical surroundings of the service, has been improved over the years to better facilitate airline travelers' needs to sleep and/or work. In fact, the competition for better seat and aircraft interior design continues as a major point of contention among the international airline carriers, and the results have translated into greater customer satisfaction for business travelers.[9] Some of the new designs include business class "suites" with seats that recline into "skybeds," leather ottomans in first-class sections, and electronic partition screens between seats in business class.

Socializer

The design of the servicescape aids in the socialization of both employees and customers in the sense that it helps convey expected roles, behaviors, and relationships. For example, a new employee in a professional services firm would come to understand her position in the hierarchy partially through noting her office assignment, the quality of her office furnishings, and her location relative to others in the organization.

The design of the facility can also suggest to customers what their role is relative to employees, what parts of the servicescape they are welcome in and which are for employees only, how they should behave while in the environment, and what types of interactions are encouraged. For example, in many Starbucks locations, the company has designed a more traditional coffeehouse environment for customers to spend social time rather than coming in for a quick cup of coffee on the run. To encourage this type of socializing, these Starbucks locations have comfortable lounge chairs, tables, and Wi-Fi set up to encourage customers to interact and to stay longer. The goal is to be the customer's "third place"; that is, a place where customers think of spending time when not at work or at home (see Exhibit 10.2 on p. 294).

Differentiator

The design of the physical facility can differentiate a firm from its competitors and signal the market segment that the service is intended for. Given its power as a differentiator, changes in the physical environment can be used to reposition a firm and/or to attract new market segments. In shopping malls the signage, colors used in decor and displays, and type of music wafting from a store signal the intended market segment.

Indian Strategy Insight Strategic Positioning through Architectural Design

Architecture and design can positively impact customers, employees, and the general public while executing and reinforcing strategic decisions and marketing positioning as described below.

INDIAN MUSIC EXPERIENCE MUSEUM – PHYSICAL EVIDENCE AND SERVICESCAPE

The Indian Music Experience (IME) in Bangalore represents a paradigm shift in India's museum culture, transforming the traditional concept of static exhibits into an immersive, interactive journey through the country's rich musical heritage. This analysis explores how the museum's physical evidence and servicescape elements work together to create a distinctive visitor experience.

Architecture and Design Philosophy

The 50,000-square-foot museum, designed by Bengaluru-based Architecture Paradigm, follows a distinctive curvilinear shape that respects the existing trees on the site. This flowing façade symbolically represents the continuum of Indian music through the ages. The design emerged from a competitive process where the firm's proposal was selected by a jury of eminent personalities from Bangalore. The museum's interior spaces were conceptualized by world-renowned exhibition design firm Gallagher & Associates, who previously designed the Grammy Museum in Los Angeles and the Woodstock Museum in New York. This collaboration brought international museum design expertise to the IME project, resulting in a structure where form follows function while honoring the natural environment.

Key Experiential Zones

- **The Sound Garden:** The visitor experience begins in the Sound Garden, an outdoor space in the inner courtyard featuring ten unique musical sculptures that introduce fundamental principles of sound. As visitors enter the museum grounds, they encounter this interactive garden where they can learn about sounds produced by natural materials such as wood, stones, and metals. The garden contains xylophones crafted from diverse materials including aluminum, brass, wood, and stone, each producing a distinctive timbre when played. Musical stones produce beautiful sounds when rubbed, while tubular bells demonstrate the inverse relationship between frequency and amplitude. This initial touchpoint serves as a playful introduction to sound principles before visitors enter the main museum building, allowing them to physically engage with musical concepts in an open-air environment.
- **Interactive Exhibition Galleries:** The IME features thematically organized galleries spread across multiple floors. Each gallery creates a distinct atmosphere through specialized design elements that transport visitors through India's musical journey.

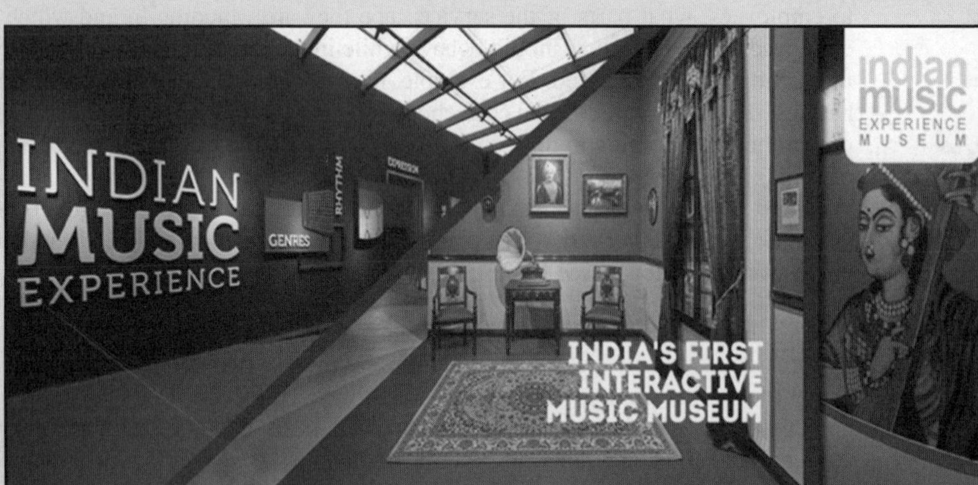

IME https://images.app.goo.gl/m1HWkax1MXgjBAEz6

- **Contemporary Expressions Gallery:** The Contemporary Expressions gallery immerses visitors in the early days of independent rock music in India by recreating the ambiance of busy Bangalore streets. Two automobiles painted in vibrant fluorescent colors sit at the gallery's entrance, allowing visitors to sit inside and watch videos of famous Indian bands. The walls display posters of Bangalore's bustling areas like Commercial Street and Brigade Road, popular gathering spots for the city's youth. Visitors can don headphones to listen to music from bands like Millennium, Pentagram, Indian Ocean, and Rock Machine. An interactive music machine enables visitors to create their own tunes by selecting different instruments, while display cases highlight hybrid sounds and performance costumes, including one worn by Daler Mehndi. The contemporary styling and pop culture references make this space particularly appealing to younger visitors.
- **Living Traditions Gallery:** The Living Traditions gallery educates visitors about the fundamental concepts of Indian classical music through sophisticated touchscreen displays. Here, visitors can explore sruti, raga, tala, gharaa, dhrupad, khayal, and kutcheri through interactive interfaces that make complex musical theories accessible. The space transitions into explorations of devotional music from across India, celebrating the country's diverse religious traditions through their musical expressions. The design of this space employs more subdued lighting and traditional aesthetics to create an atmosphere conducive to understanding classical traditions.
- **Songs of the People:** The Songs of the People gallery celebrates India's rich folk and tribal musical heritage by showcasing the contexts in which these songs emerge and flourish. The space includes an authentic kaavad box that demonstrates the Rajasthani oral storytelling tradition, with multiple doors that open to reveal different characters during the narrative. The gallery's design incorporates rural elements and natural materials that reflect the earthiness of folk traditions, creating an environment that contrasts with the more formal classical music spaces. Interactive elements allow visitors to understand how music functions as communication and community-building in different regional contexts.
- **The Instrument Gallery:** The Instrument Gallery features a spectacular floor-to-ceiling display of 108 Indian musical instruments, creating a dramatic visual centerpiece for the museum. This double-height installation can be viewed from multiple levels, offering different perspectives on the collection. Each instrument is accompanied by interactive displays explaining its origin, craftsmanship, and distinctive sound. The gallery proudly displays musical treasures such as Vidwan Manjunath's ghatam and Dr. M.L. Vaasanthakumari's tambura, alongside a peacock-shaped Mayura veena, metal horns, leather drums, and various stringed instruments collected from across the country. The dramatic lighting in this space highlights the craftsmanship of the instruments, creating an almost sacred atmosphere that honors these tools of musical expression.
- **Music of Pre-Independent India:** The Music of Pre-Independent India gallery transports visitors back to India's freedom struggle, showcasing how music united people and expressed opposition to British rule. The space displays over 35 different versions of "Vande Mataram" and features a replica of Mahatma Gandhi's letter to M.S. Subbulakshmi alongside numerous patriotic songs from Hindi films. The environmental design evokes the period through historical elements, allowing visitors to experience how ethnic music influenced the political climate during this crucial era. The space creates a solemn yet inspiring atmosphere that connects musical expression with national identity formation.
- **Melting Pot Gallery:** The Melting Pot gallery explores the rich cross-cultural exchange between Western and Indian musical traditions. Adjacent to this, the Stories Through Song section presents vignettes from various eras of Hindi cinema displayed on inset screens designed to evoke moving 'bioscopes' from early film history. Visitors learn about landmark moments and legendary figures in Hindi film music while experiencing the diverse influences that have shaped Bollywood's distinctive sound. The spatial design transitions between Western and Indian aesthetics, visually representing the

cultural fusion that characterizes much of contemporary Indian music.

- **Hall of Fame:** The Hall of Fame, known as The Stars gallery, celebrates 100 legends of Indian music from diverse genres through an elegant display of photographs, biographical information, and personal artifacts. This space houses precious memorabilia once belonging to Bharat Ratna musicians, including Ustad Bismillah Khan's shehnai (which he affectionately called his "Begum"), M.S. Subbulakshmi's tambura, and Bhimsen Joshi's concert attire and silver paan box. The gallery includes a recording studio where visitors can sing by selecting background tracks, record themselves, design album covers, and email themselves the final track. A mirror at the end of the gallery labeled "the next star" encourages visitors—especially children—to see themselves as potential future musicians, creating an inspiring conclusion to the museum journey. The gallery's design includes many blank spaces, symbolizing how this "constellation" of stars will continue to grow as new artists are added annually.

Specialty Spaces

- **The Learning Center:** The Learning Center transforms the museum from a passive viewing experience into an active educational institution. This space offers formal music education in various disciplines including Carnatic and Hindustani vocal traditions, dance, and instruments such as the veena, mridangam, keyboard, and guitar. The center hosts workshops featuring renowned artists from around the world and organizes annual events where students perform before live audiences. With approximately 150 students enrolled in structured curriculum-based diploma programs, the Learning Center extends the museum's impact beyond one-time visitors, creating ongoing relationships with community members. The design of these spaces prioritizes acoustics and functionality while maintaining aesthetic continuity with the rest of the museum.
- **Additional Facilities:** The IME houses several multipurpose spaces that extend its functionality beyond static exhibitions. A rooftop amphitheater provides an open-air venue for performances, while a multipurpose mini auditorium and seminar hall accommodate workshops, lectures, and intimate concerts. A thoughtfully designed gift shop sells exclusive IME merchandise, including posters, postcards, t-shirts, and keychains that extend the museum experience into visitors' homes. Adjacent to this, a WiFi-enabled workspace allows visitors to linger and reflect, while a quaint café offers refreshments and light meals. These supporting spaces ensure that visitors can comfortably spend several hours exploring the museum, enhancing the overall experience through practical amenities within a cohesive design framework.

Sensory Design Elements

- **Visual Elements:** The museum employs careful lighting design to create dramatic effects throughout the exhibition spaces. Architects incorporated strategic natural light in specific areas while maintaining darkness for exhibit drama, resolving the tension between architectural preferences for light and designers' desires for controlled environments. Visual leitmotifs create rhythm throughout the visitor journey, with recurring design elements that guide movement between galleries. The museum includes authentic recreations of historical settings, such as a 1920s Bengali Zamindar's household complete with period furniture and a gramophone serving as the focal point of family gathering. These visual recreations transport visitors to different eras, enhancing their understanding of music's social context through environmental storytelling.
- **Audio Elements:** Unlike many music museums that are "absolutely silent," IME fills its spaces with appropriate music that creates an immersive sonic environment. Individual headphone systems throughout the galleries allow personalized listening experiences without creating auditory confusion. The Samay Chakra Theater offers a planetarium-like experience where visitors recline to watch ceiling projections showing a day in India's life from sunrise to sunset, accompanied by 15-second transitions through different ragas appropriate to each time of day. This multisensory approach helps visitors understand abstract concepts like the relationship between ragas and daily rhythms through direct experience rather than theoretical explanation.

- **Tactile Elements:** The IME proudly describes itself as a "Please Touch" museum rather than a "Don't Touch" facility, encouraging physical interaction with exhibits. Interactive touchscreens throughout galleries invite visitors to explore content at their own pace and according to their interests. The Hybrid Sounds installation allows visitors to layer tracks by combining Indian instruments, percussion, and Western music elements to create personalized musical mixes. A recording studio equipped with professional-grade equipment lets visitors experience different recording environments across musical eras, demonstrating how Bollywood songs would sound if recorded in different decades with period-appropriate instrumentation and audio quality. This hands-on approach particularly appeals to younger visitors accustomed to touchscreen technology and creates memorable, personalized experiences.

Servicescape Innovations

- **Chronological Storytelling:** The museum takes visitors through a chronological journey of Indian music from Vedic times to contemporary expressions, using physical spaces to represent different eras and cultural movements. Interestingly, the museum subverts traditional chronological presentation by beginning with contemporary music before moving backward in time, making the experience more accessible to younger visitors who connect first with familiar modern sounds before exploring historical traditions. This spatial narrative flows through exhibition areas that showcase major cultural movements including the emergence of jazz and blues during the British colonial period, patriotic music during the independence struggle, early metal and indie scenes, and modern Bollywood pop music.
- **"Top-Down" Experience Design:** Rather than starting with collected artifacts and building exhibitions around them, the IME was conceptualized around three core learning objectives that shaped the entire physical space. First, the museum demonstrates that Indian music is diverse yet connected by avoiding rigid separation between traditions; instead of separate rooms for Carnatic and Hindustani music, the galleries flow into each other, physically embodying musical interconnectedness. Second, the space illustrates that Indian music has deep historical roots but continues to evolve, demonstrated by positioning contemporary galleries at the beginning of the visitor journey. Third, the design shows how music is both personally meaningful and community-defining by creating spaces that encourage both individual connection with familiar songs and understanding of music's role in defining community identities through ritual, celebration, and profession.
- **Environmental Recreations:** The museum creates authentic recreations of environments where music plays significant roles, going beyond displaying instruments to showing their cultural contexts. A detailed recreation of a 1920s Bengali Zamindar's household includes an original HMV advertisement showing how the gramophone brought family members together across gender and class divisions. Busy Bangalore street recreations show where indie music culture flourished, complete with performance posters and urban aesthetics. Film settings showcase Bollywood musical evolution through environmental storytelling that places instruments and recordings within their social contexts. These environmental recreations help visitors understand music not just as sound but as a deeply embedded cultural practice.
- **Technology Integration:** The IME seamlessly integrates technology throughout its spaces to enhance visitor engagement without overwhelming the historical content. A recording studio simulates different historical recording environments, allowing visitors to hear how the same song would sound in different decades with period-appropriate instrumentation and audio quality. Interactive displays throughout the galleries teach music concepts through visual representations and hands-on activities rather than text-heavy explanations. The museum offers personalized recording experiences with shareable digital outputs, extending the visit beyond the physical space when visitors email their recordings to themselves and share them with friends. This technological integration makes abstract musical concepts tangible and creates memorable, personalized experiences.

Marketing through Physical Evidence

The IME leverages its physical space as a marketing tool in several ways that extend its impact beyond one-time visits.

- **Community Engagement Spaces:** The museum's performance venues attract local audiences repeatedly through regular programming, creating ongoing relationships with community members who might otherwise visit a museum only once. The learning center establishes sustained connections with students and families through its educational programs, building a community of museum advocates. A volunteer program engages community members as tour guides and event supporters, transforming them into knowledgeable ambassadors who promote the museum throughout their social networks. These spaces focus on engaging local communities first, based on the belief that locals become the most effective advocates when visitors from outside Bangalore seek recommendations for cultural experiences.
- **Visual Identity:** The museum's distinctive architectural form and interior design create a recognizable visual identity that extends beyond the physical space. Museum merchandise features design elements from the exhibitions, allowing visitors to take home tangible reminders of their experience. Branded spaces throughout the facility create shareable photo opportunities, such as installations where visitors can pose with a traditional brass band or recreate the iconic "3 Idiots" film poster. The "next star" mirror installation at the conclusion of the Hall of Fame gallery creates a memorable moment that connects visitors personally to India's musical legacy while encouraging social media sharing.
- **Multi-generational Design:** The physical space intentionally encourages interaction between generations through thoughtful design choices. Exhibition content appeals to different age groups, with parents often recognizing classical musicians while children gravitate toward contemporary

Our Strategy Insight in this chapter included examples of different organizations that have used the physical design of their facilities to strategically reinforce their positioning and differentiate themselves from other organizations.

In another context, the servicescape has been used as a major point of differentiation for PetSmart in the introduction of its innovative PetsHotel concept.[10] The hotels, which offer overnight care as well as day care for pets, are designed very differently from typical kennels or veterinary facilities. They feature a lobby area, colorful play areas, comfortable sleeping rooms, television, a "bone booth" for calling in, and other amenities that give the facilities a more residential, homelike appeal than traditional kennels have. Illustrating how dynamic service markets are, Luxe Pet Hotels in Las Vegas has taken this concept to another level by adding features such queen-sized memory foam beds (with Chanel cushions) and 42 inch TVs in the pets' rooms, and by offering amenities such as a dog gym as well as a dog spa.

The design of a physical setting can also differentiate one area of a service organization from another. For example, in the hotel industry, one large hotel may have artists, creating opportunities for knowledge sharing across generations. Historical exhibits featuring instruments and recording technology appeal to older visitors while interactive digital elements engage younger ones, ensuring the museum remains relevant to diverse audiences. School field trips introduce children to the facility, many of whom later return with parents, creating a marketing ripple effect through family networks. This multi-generational approach ensures the museum's continued relevance and builds a broad base of supporters.

The Indian Music Experience Museum demonstrates how thoughtful servicescape design can transform abstract concepts like music into tangible experiences that educate, inspire, and entertain simultaneously. By focusing on visitor engagement rather than just artifact preservation, the museum creates a multisensory environment that makes India's rich musical traditions accessible to diverse audiences. The physical evidence throughout the facility reinforces the museum's core philosophy that music should be experienced actively rather than observed passively. This approach has transformed IME into a landmark cultural institution that challenges traditional notions of museum experiences in India, creating a space where visitors do not merely learn about music but actively participate in its ongoing evolution.

Reference: https://indianmusicexperience.org/about-us/

https://www.edx.org/learn/marketing/indian-institute-of-management-bangalore-services-marketing-concepts-applications (Interview with Ms. Manasi Prasad, Director – Indian Music Experience Museum)

https://www.savaari.com/blog/indian-music-experience-museum-tracing-indias-music-history/

https://shop.museumsofindia.org/node/577#:~:text=An%20initiative%20of%20the%20Indian,Woodstock%20Museum%20in%20New%20York.

several levels of dining possibilities, each signaled by differences in design. Price differentiation is also often partially achieved through variations in physical setting. Bigger rooms with more physical amenities cost more, just as larger seats with more leg room (generally in first class) are more expensive on an airplane.

FRAMEWORK FOR UNDERSTANDING SERVICESCAPE EFFECTS ON BEHAVIOR

Although it is useful from a strategic point of view to think about the multiple roles of the servicescape and how they interact, making actual decisions about servicescape design requires an understanding of why the effects occur and how to manage them. The next sections present a framework of environment and behavior relationships in service settings. Beyond influencing behaviors, physical design also affects well-being. Exhibit 10.1 provides an example of research that shows how customers

Exhibit 10.1 Servicescapes and Well-Being in Health Care

There is solid evidence from the field of "evidence-based design" that the design of health care environments can profoundly influence patient, family, and employee well-being. Notably, researchers have shown that outcomes such as stress reduction, shorter hospital stays, improved health, increased patient satisfaction, and improved safety are all affected by the design of the physical facilities. Here are a few examples of what has been learned.

SOUNDS, MUSIC, AND NOISE REDUCTION

Studies have shown that reducing noise and introducing more pleasing sounds such as water falling or music can positively affect patients and staff in hospitals. Minimizing noise, which is a constant challenge in hospitals and other health care settings, can help reduce sleep disturbance and stress and lower blood pressure, among other outcomes. Noise can also distract doctors and nurses, resulting in greater stress, interrupted communication, and errors, so noise reductions have benefits for employees as well.

NATURE AND VISUAL DISTRACTION

Positive visual distractions divert patient attention from pain and negative feelings, improving their psychological and emotional well-being. In particular, nature distractions, such as gardens, indoor plants, and window views to outdoor nature scenes, have been shown to reduce stress, reduce pain, reduce pain medication usage, and speed recovery. Natural daylight is also beneficial and has been linked to improved patient outcomes and higher staff productivity.

SINGLE-BED ROOM DESIGN

Many studies have shown the benefits of single-bed rooms for patients instead of multi-bed rooms. The benefits include reduced stress, better sleep, reduction in infection rates, increased patient satisfaction, and shorter hospital stays. A number of these benefits are also experienced by family and other support members who spend time with the patient. Giving the patient control over elements of the room design is also positive—for example, providing them with the ability to control the lighting and temperature in their rooms.

PATIENT SAFETY

The design of the physical facility can affect safety issues that are paramount in health care. For example, avoiding patient falls and infections are major safety issues that can be influenced by physical design. One hospital located all of its patient bathrooms on the side of the room where the head of the bed was located. This simple design feature avoided the patient having to cross the room to use the bathroom, which reduced falls. Flexible room designs that allow equipment to be moved into a patient's room temporarily help avoid transferring patients to different locations during their stay. In other words, the equipment goes to the patient rather than vice versa. Research shows that transferring patients from room to room increases medication errors, patient falls, and the rate of infections.

DESIGN FOR WELL-BEING

Hospital administrators, designers, and architects are paying attention to such research results. Many new hospitals are designed with only single-bed rooms, natural lighting where possible, music and gardens, hands-free personal technology-based communicators (think *Star Trek* communicators), centralized nursing stations, and adaptable rooms to avoid patient transfers. Family lounges and eating areas and overnight sleeping accommodations for them are also provided to improve patient and family well-being and satisfaction. Exhibit 10.3 in this chapter describes how the Mayo Clinic Hospital in Scottsdale, Arizona, was designed with many of these evidence-based principles in mind.

Sources: M. Mody, C. Suess, and T. Dogru, "Restorative Servicescapes in Health Care: Examining the Influence of Hotel-like Attributes on Patient Well-being," *Cornell Hospitality Quarterly* 61 (February 2020), pp. 19–39; R. S. Ulrich, L. L Berry, X. Quan, and J. T. Parish, "A Conceptual Framework for the Domain of Evidence-Based Design," *Health Environments Research and Design Journal* 4 (Fall 2010), pp. 95–114; R. S. Ulrich, C. M. Zimring, X. Zhu, J. DuBose, H. Seo, Y. Choi, and A. Joseph, "A Review of the Research Literature on Evidence-Based Healthcare Design," *Health Environments Research and Design Journal* 1, pp. 6–125; "Good Healthcare by Design," *The Hastings Center Report* 41 (January–February 2011).

and employees in one industry—health care—are impacted profoundly by servicescape design.

The Underlying Framework

The framework for understanding servicescape effects on behavior follows from *stimulus–organism–response* theory. In the framework the multidimensional environment is the *stimulus,* consumers and employees are the *organisms* that respond to the stimuli, and corresponding behaviors are the *responses.* The assumptions are that dimensions of the servicescape affect customers and employees and that they respond in different ways depending on their internal reactions to the servicescape.

A simple example helps illustrate the theory in action. Assume there is a cookie cart parked outside the student union on campus. The cart is colorful and playful in design, and an aroma of baking cookies wafts from it. The design and the aroma are two elements of the servicescape that will affect customers in some way. Now assume you are a hungry student, just out of class, strolling across campus. The fun design of the cart attracts your attention, and simultaneously you smell baking cookies. The fun design and the delicious smell cause you to feel happy, relaxed, and hungry at the same time. You are attracted to the cart and decide to buy a cookie because you have another class to attend before lunch. The movement toward the cart and the purchase of a cookie are behaviors in response to the servicescape. Depending on how much time you have, you may even choose to converse with the vendor or other customers standing around munching cookies, other forms of behavior are in response to the servicescape.

The framework shown in Figure 10.1 is detailed in the next sections. It represents a comprehensive stimulus–organism–response model that recognizes complex

FIGURE 10.1 A Framework for Understanding Physical Environment–User Relationships in Service Organizations

Source: Adapted from M. J. Bitner, "Servicescapes: The Impact of Physical Surroundings on Customers and Employees," *Journal of Marketing* 56 (April 1992), pp. 57–71.

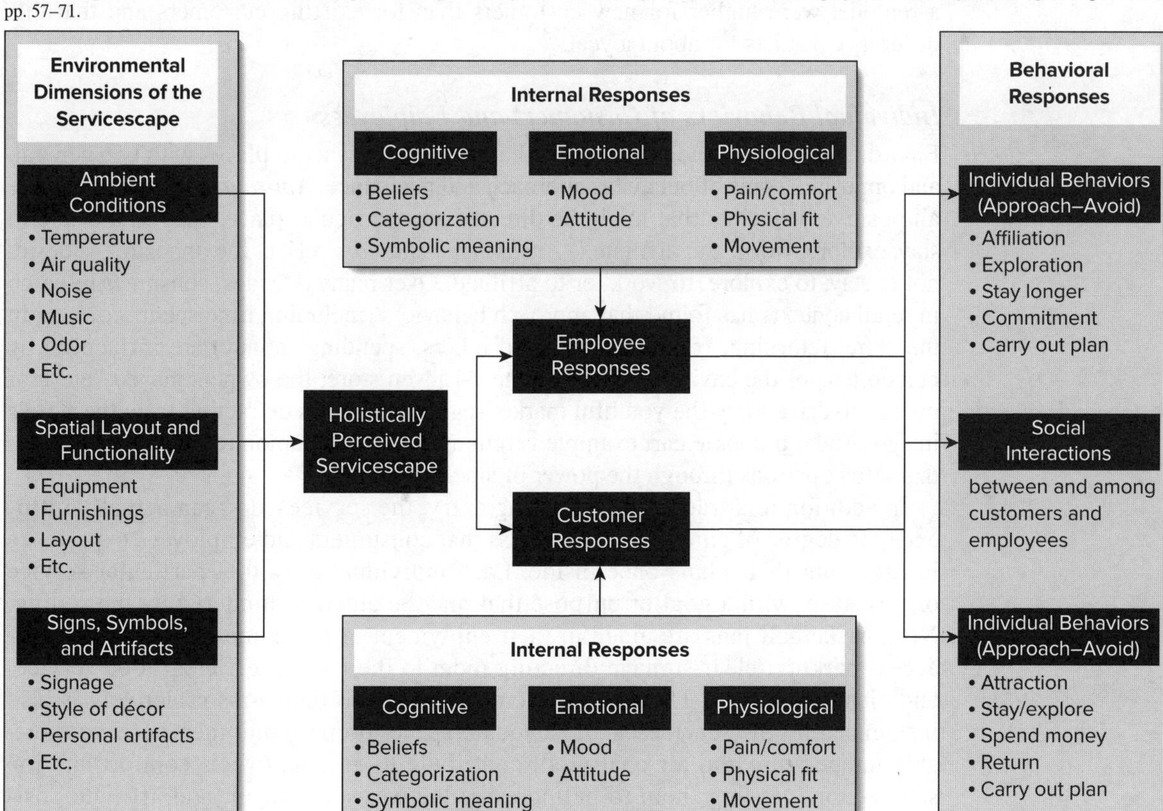

dimensions of the environment, impacts on multiple parties (customers, employees, and their interactions), multiple types of internal responses (cognitive, emotional, and physiological), and a variety of individual and social behaviors that can result.

Our discussion of the framework will begin on the right side of the model with *behaviors,* since, from a manager's perspective, the desired behaviors and responses are the place to start strategically. Next we will explain and develop the *internal responses* portion of the model. Finally we will turn to the dimensions of the *environment* and the holistic perception of the environment.

Behaviors in the Servicescape

That human behavior is influenced by the physical setting in which it occurs is essentially a truism. For many decades, a large and steadily growing body of literature within the field of environmental psychology has addressed the relationships between human beings and their built, or physical, environments. In business, the focus on the customer experience has also drawn attention to the effects of physical spaces and design on customer behavior.[11] As an example, one study explores the effects of a servicescape redesign in a fast-food industry context, looking at both short- and long-term effects on customer perceptions, as well as spending patterns and the store image. The research found that the remodeling positively increased customer perceptions, store image, and the amount of money customers spent in the restaurant, particularly in the short term. After about six months, the effects of the remodeling lost some strength as the remodeled restaurant became the new frame of reference for customers.[12] Another study found these same types of effects, only they found that sales after a remodel were higher for new customers than for existing customers and that this difference persists for about a year.[13]

Individual Behaviors of Customers and Employees

Environmental psychologists suggest that individuals react to places with two general, and opposite, forms of behavior: approach and avoidance. *Approach behaviors* include all positive behaviors that might be directed at a particular place, such as a desire to stay, explore, work, and affiliate.[14] *Avoidance behaviors* reflect the opposite—a desire not to stay, to explore, to work, or to affiliate. Over many decades, consumer research in retail contexts has found that approach behaviors (including time spent browsing in the store, returning, friendliness toward others, spending money) are influenced by perceptions of the environment.[15] At one 7-Eleven store, the owners played "elevator music" to drive away the youthful market segment that was detracting from the store's image. And our cookie cart example is reminiscent of cinnamon roll bakeries in malls that attract patrons through the power of smell.

In addition to attracting or deterring entry, the servicescape can actually influence the degree of enjoyment or success that consumers and employees experience in executing their plans once inside. Each individual goes to a particular service organization with a goal or purpose that may be aided or hindered by the setting. NBA basketball fans are aided in their enjoyment of the game by adequate, easy-access parking; clear signage directing them to their seats; efficient food service; and clean restrooms. The ability of employees to do their jobs effectively is also influenced by the servicescape. Adequate space, proper equipment, and comfortable temperature and air quality all contribute to an employee's comfort and job satisfaction, causing them to be more productive, stay longer, and affiliate positively with coworkers.

Meunierd/Shutterstock

Social interactions are defined partially by the configuration of the servicescape.

Social Interactions between and among Customers and Employees

In addition to its effects on their individual behaviors, the servicescape influences the nature and quality of customer and employee interactions, most directly in interpersonal services. It has been stated that "all social interaction is affected by the physical container in which it occurs."[16] The "physical container" can affect the nature of social interaction in terms of the duration of interaction and the actual progression of events. In many service situations, a firm may want to ensure a particular progression of events (a "standard script") and limit the duration of the service. Environmental variables such as physical proximity, seating arrangements, size, and flexibility can define the possibilities and limits of social episodes such as those occurring between customers and employees, or customers and other customers. The photo of a cruise ship deck shown here illustrates how the design of the servicescape can help define the social rules, conventions, and expectations in a given setting, thus defining the nature of social interaction.[17] The close physical proximity of passengers on the sunbathing deck will in and of itself prescribe certain patterns of behavior. This vacation is not designed for a social recluse! Some researchers have implied that recurring social behavior patterns are associated with particular physical settings and that when people encounter typical settings, their social behaviors can be predicted.[18]

Examples of how environments shape social interactions—and how these interactions in turn influence the environment—are abundant.[19] Increasingly, brick-and-mortar stores offer "retailtainment," that is, they take advantage of the opportunity to provide their in-store customers with unique, exciting, and immersive experiences. For example, Nike's flagship stores in New York include a basketball half-court, soccer trial areas, and treadmills in front of a jumbotron that simulates outdoor runs, customization shoe bars, and a team of dedicated "coaches" to help and support customers. Such retailtainment shapes the behaviors of consumers but at the same time allows them to interpret and create their own realities and experiences.[20] In a river-rafting trip, the "wilderness servicescape" profoundly influences the behaviors, interactions, and total experiences of rafting consumers and their guides. In this case the natural, and for the most part uncontrollable, environment is the setting for the service.[21] In some cases, important social bonds and connections are forged within a service place, making it a "third place" (see Exhibit 10.2).[22]

Internal Responses to the Servicescape

Employees and customers respond to dimensions of their physical surroundings cognitively, emotionally, and physiologically, and those responses are what influence their behaviors in the environment (as shown in the middle portion of Figure 10.1). In other words, the perceived servicescape does not directly *cause* people to behave in certain ways. Although the internal responses are discussed independently here, they are clearly interdependent: a person's beliefs about a place, a cognitive response, may well influence the person's emotional response, and vice versa. For example, patients who go into a dentist's office designed to calm and soothe their anxieties (emotional responses) may believe as a result that the dentist is caring and competent (cognitive responses).

Exhibit 10.2 Social Support in "Third Places"

The social interactions among customers and between customers and employees in "third places" can provide companionship and emotional support that results in strong attachments and loyalty to the place itself. A third place is a public or commercial place where people gather regularly and voluntarily outside of work (or school) and home, which are viewed as the first two places in people's lives. Often third places are diners, coffee shops, pubs, or clubs, but a fitness club, a civic center, or other public gathering place could also be a third place. The neighborhood bar on the classic television show *Cheers* epitomized a third place. Think about what types of places might qualify as a third place for you.

A study by Mark Rosenbaum and colleagues showed that people can grow attached to a third place to the point where they depend on it above all other alternatives, they are committed to the place and care about it, they personally identify with it, and they structure their lifestyle around it. This type of attachment happens because of the companionship and emotional support they receive from the other customers and employees in the place, not simply because they like the service or feel comfortable in the physical surroundings. These emotional attachments and interactions are particularly strong for people who are lonely or in need of contact with others. The researchers observed and conducted depth interviews with patrons of Sammy's, a casual dining restaurant in the suburbs of a major U.S. metropolitan area that was clearly a third place for many regulars who frequented the restaurant. Through the interviews, they established that patrons who were lonely or who had lost an established form of social support through death, divorce, or illness, found significant companionship and emotional support at Sammy's. The regular patrons who had lost a spouse through death, divorce, or separation had a full 58 percent of their social supportive relationships with people (customers and employees) at Sammy's. These patrons were also extremely attached and loyal to Sammy's.

The research reinforces the idea that servicescapes, while they are defined by their physical elements, can take on a third place character when they become the source of social interactions, bonds, and support for the people who frequent them. The benefits of this type of support go beyond the benefits intended by the core service. The regulars at Sammy's receive far more than a good meal in pleasant surroundings. Through their interactions with others, their daily lives are enhanced and they are emotionally better off. As the problems associated with loneliness grow in our modern-day society (e.g., the population is aging, more and more people are caring for chronically ill family members or friends, divorce is prevalent, and work hours are increasing, resulting in less time for friendships), the importance of third places as a form of social support may grow as well.

Travel Images/Universal Images Group/Getty Images

The *Cheers* bar epitomized a third place in the classic television show.

Sources: M. Meshram and A. O'Cass, "Senior Citizens' Perspective on the Value Offerings of Third Place via Customer to Customer (C-2-C) Engagement," *Journal of Services Marketing* 32 (March 2018), pp. 175–194; M. S. Rosenbaum, "Exploring the Social Supportive Role of Third Places in Consumers' Lives," *Journal of Service Research* 9 (August 2006), pp. 59–72; M. S. Rosenbaum, J. Ward, B. A. Walker, and A. L. Ostrom, "A Cup of Coffee with a Dash of Love: An Investigation of Commercial Social Support and Third-Place Attachment," *Journal of Service Research* 10 (August 2007), pp. 43–59; and M. S. Rosenbaum, J. C. Sweeney, and C. Windhorst, "The Restorative Qualities of an Activity-Based, Third Place Cafe for Seniors," *Seniors Housing and Care Journal* 17 (2009), pp. 75–90; E. D. Brocato, J. Baker, and C. M. Voorhees, "Creating Consumer Attachment to Retail Service Firms Through Sense of Place," *Journal of the Academy of Marketing Science* 43 (2015), pp. 200–220.

Environment and Cognitive Responses

The perceived servicescape can have an effect on people's beliefs about a place and their beliefs about the people and products found in that place. In a sense, the servicescape can be viewed as a form of nonverbal communication, imparting meaning through what is called "object language."[23] For example, particular environmental cues such as the type of office furniture and decor and the apparel worn by the lawyer may influence a potential client's beliefs about whether the lawyer is successful, expensive, and trustworthy. In a consumer study, variations in descriptions of store atmospheres were found to alter beliefs about a product (perfume) sold in the store.[24] Another study showed that a travel agent's office decor affected customer attributions and beliefs about the travel agent's behavior.[25] Travel agents whose facilities were more organized and professional were viewed more positively than were those whose facilities were disorganized and unprofessional.

In other cases, perceptions of the servicescape may simply help people distinguish a firm by influencing how it is categorized. The overall perception of the servicescape enables the consumer or employee to categorize the firm mentally. Research shows that in the restaurant industry a particular configuration of environmental cues suggests "fast food," whereas another configuration suggests "elegant sit-down restaurant."[26] In such situations, environmental cues serve as a shortcut device that enables customers to categorize and distinguish among types of restaurants.

Environment and Emotional Responses

In addition to influencing beliefs, the servicescape can directly elicit emotional responses that, in turn, influence behaviors. Just being in a particular place can make a person feel happy, lighthearted, and relaxed, whereas being in another place may make that person feel sad, depressed, and gloomy. The colors, decor, music, and other elements of the atmosphere can have an unexplainable and sometimes subconsciousness effect on the moods of people in the place. For some people, certain environmental stimuli (noises, smells) common in a dental office can bring on immediate feelings of fear and anxiety. In very different contexts, the marble interior and grandeur of the Supreme Court buildings in Washington, D.C., call up feelings of pride, awe and respect; lively music and bright decor in a local night spot may cause people to feel excited and happy. In all these examples, the response from the consumer probably does not involve thinking but, rather, is just a feeling.

REI (Recreational Equipment Inc.) provides another example of emotional connection facilitated through architectural design and the servicescape. At its flagship store in Seattle, the company has created an experience for consumers that includes a 65 ft climbing mountain, a bicycle track, and walking trails. REI, through its servicescape design, is simulating the experiences and emotions that customers associate with its products, reinforcing a strong approach response to its stores.

Environmental psychologists have researched people's emotional responses to physical settings.[27] They have concluded that any environment, whether natural or engineered, will elicit emotions that can be captured by two basic dimensions: (1) pleasure/displeasure and (2) degree of arousal (amount of stimulation or excitement). Servicescapes that are both pleasant and arousing would be termed *exciting,* whereas those that are pleasant and nonarousing, or sleepy, would be termed *relaxing.* Unpleasant servicescapes that are arousing would be called *distressing,* whereas unpleasant, sleepy servicescapes would be *gloomy.* These basic emotional responses to environments can be used to begin predicting the expected behaviors of consumers and employees who find themselves in a particular type of place.

Environment and Physiological Responses

The perceived servicescape may also affect people in purely physiological ways. Noise that is too loud may cause physical discomfort, the temperature of a room may cause people to shiver or perspire, the air quality may make it difficult to breathe, and the glare of lighting may decrease ability to see and cause physical pain. All these physical responses may, in turn, directly influence whether people stay in and enjoy a particular environment. It is well known that the comfort of seating in a restaurant influences how long people stay. The hard seats historically found in a fast-food restaurant cause most people to leave within a predictable period of time, whereas the soft, cozy chairs in some Starbucks coffee shops have the opposite effect, encouraging people to stay. Similarly, environmental design and related physiological responses affect whether employees can perform their job functions well.

A vast amount of research in engineering and design has addressed human physiological responses to ambient conditions as well as physiological responses to equipment design.[28] Such research fits under the rubric of *human factors design* or *ergonomics.* Human factors research systematically applies relevant information about human capabilities and limitations to the design of items and procedures that people use. As populations around the world age (with accompanying physical limitations), and as individuals with a variety of physical disabilities are entering the mainstream of society, laws and practices are being introduced to accommodate their physical limitations. Service organizations and others are responding by adopting "universal design standards and principles," which simply means designing all products, buildings, and spaces to be usable by all people to the greatest extent possible.[29] For example, many hotel rooms are designed to accommodate people with disabilities. Wall switches have lights so they can be found at night. To help people with arthritis, doors have lever handles instead of knobs so that every door and every drawer in the room can be opened with a fist rather than requiring hand and wrist dexterity.

Variations in Individual Responses to the Environment

In general, people respond to the environment in the ways just described—cognitively, emotionally, physiologically—and their responses influence how they behave in the environment. However, the response will not be the same for every individual, every time. Personality differences as well as temporary conditions such as moods or the purpose for being there can cause variations in how people respond to the servicescape.[30]

One personality trait that has been shown to affect how people respond to environments is *arousal seeking.* Arousal seekers enjoy and look for high levels of stimulation, whereas arousal avoiders prefer lower levels of stimulation. Thus, an arousal avoider in a loud, bright dance club with flashing lights might show strong dislike for the environment, whereas an arousal seeker would be very happy. In a related vein, it has been suggested that some people are better *screeners* of environmental stimuli than others.[31] Screeners of stimuli would be able to experience a high level of stimulation but not be affected by it. Nonscreeners would be highly affected and might exhibit extreme responses even to low levels of stimulation.

The particular duration of and purpose for being in a servicescape can also affect a person's response to it. A person who is on an airplane for a one-hour flight will likely be less affected by the atmosphere on the plane than a traveler on a 14-hour flight from Los Angeles to Shanghai. Similarly, a day-surgery hospital patient will likely be less sensitive and demanding of the hospital environment than would a patient who is spending two weeks in the hospital. And a person who is staying at a resort hotel for a business meeting will respond differently to the environment than will a couple on their honeymoon. Temporary mood states can also cause people to respond differently to environmental stimuli. A person who is feeling frustrated and fatigued after a long day at work is likely to be affected differently by a highly arousing restaurant than the same person would be after a relaxing three-day weekend.

Cultural differences also influence preferences for environmental features and responses to servicescape design. For example, there is a strong cultural preference for the color red in China, whereas Westerners would not share this attraction. And, while Americans and Europeans may prefer to shop in orderly and quiet supermarkets, many Indian shoppers prefer a more jumbled environment.[32] This is what India's largest retailer, Pantaloon Retail Ltd, learned when it introduced Western-style supermarkets in India. At first, customers just walked through the wide, pristine aisles and left the store without buying. By studying Indian consumer behavior and focusing on the preferences of Indian shoppers (often the maids, cooks, nannies, and farmers of India, not the elite), Pantaloon redesigned its supermarkets to make them messier, noisier, and more cramped, re-creating in some sense the atmosphere of a public market. This design was appealing to the target market and sales increased far above where they were with the original design.

Environmental Dimensions of the Servicescape

The preceding sections have described customer and employee behaviors in the servicescape and the three primary responses—cognitive, emotional, and physiological—that lead to those behaviors. In this section, we turn to the complex mix of environmental features that influence these responses and behaviors (the left portion of Figure 10.1). Specifically, environmental dimensions of the physical surroundings can include all the objective physical factors that can be controlled by the firm to enhance (or constrain) employee and customer actions. There is an endless list of possibilities: lighting, color, signage, textures, quality of materials, style of furnishings, layout, wall decor, temperature, and so on. In Figure 10.1 and in the discussion that follows, the hundreds of potential elements have been categorized into three composite dimensions: *ambient conditions; spatial layout and functionality;* and *signs, symbols, and artifacts.* Exhibit 10.3 illustrates how the Mayo Clinic took into consideration all these dimensions in designing its hospitals to accommodate patients, doctors, employees, and visitors.

Although we discuss the three dimensions separately, environmental psychology explains that people respond to their environments holistically. That is, although individuals perceive discrete stimuli (e.g., they can perceive noise level, color, and decor as distinct elements), it is the total configuration of stimuli that determines their reactions to a place. Hence, although the dimensions of the environment are defined independently in the following sections, it is important to recognize that they are perceived by employees and customers as a holistic pattern of interdependent stimuli. The holistic response is therefore shown in Figure 10.1 as the "perceived servicescape."

Ambient Conditions

Ambient conditions include background characteristics of the environment such as temperature, lighting, noise, music, scent, and color. As a general rule, ambient conditions affect the five senses. Sometimes such dimensions are imperceptible (gases, chemicals, infrasound) yet have profound effects, particularly on employees who spend long hours in the environment. All these factors can affect how people respond to a service establishment. For example, a number of studies have documented the effects of music on consumers' perceptions of products, their perceptions of how long they have waited for service, and the amount of money they spend.[33] When there is music, shoppers tend to perceive that they spend less time shopping and waiting in line than when there is no music. Slower music tempos at lower volumes tend to make people shop more leisurely, and in some cases, they spend more. In the Mayo Hospital

Exhibit 10.3 Designing the Mayo Clinic Hospital

Mayo Clinic is the best known health care brand in the United States. More than 100 years old, Mayo operates three major clinics across the country. Its original and best-known facility is in Rochester, Minnesota, and the two other clinics are in Jacksonville, Florida, and Scottsdale, Arizona. In 1998 Mayo opened the Mayo Clinic Hospital in Arizona, the first hospital planned, designed, and built by Mayo Clinic. Located on a 210-acre site, the hospital houses 268 licensed hospital beds on seven floors. The hospital supports inpatient care for a wide range of medical and surgical specialties. It has 21 operating rooms and a full emergency department, with emergency room services available 24 hours a day.

What is unique about this facility is the tremendous care that was taken in its design to serve the needs of patients, doctors, staff, and visitors. The hospital is designed as a "healing environment" focused on patient needs. Focus groups were held with all constituents to determine how the hospital should be designed to facilitate this overall goal. A quotation from the Mayo brothers (founders of the clinic) captures the underlying belief that supported the design of the hospital: "The best interest of the patient is the only interest to be considered." This statement lies at the foundation of all Mayo does, even today. To focus on the best interests of the patient also requires acknowledgment of the needs of the care providers and the patient's family and friend support system. All these interests were considered in the design of the original hospital, described here. A significant expansion of the hospital in 2022 again relied on the same patient- and staff-focused strategies.

A FIVE-STORY ATRIUM LOW-STRESS ENTRY

As patients and others enter the Mayo Hospital, they encounter a five-story enclosed atrium, reminiscent of a luxury hotel lobby. A grand piano sits in the lobby, and volunteers play relaxing music throughout the day. An abundance of plants and glass gives the lobby a natural feel and provides a welcoming atmosphere. On entering, visitors see the elevator bank directly in front of them across the atrium, so there is no stress in figuring out where to go.

ALL PATIENT AND VISITOR SERVICES ARE TOGETHER

All services needed by patients and their families (information desk, cafeteria, chapel, patient admissions, gift shop) are located around the atrium, easily visible and accessible. A sense of peace and quiet permeates the lobby—all by deliberate design to reduce stress and promote caring and wellness. There is very little of the atmosphere of a typical hospital entry.

ROOMS ARE DESIGNED AROUND PATIENT NEEDS AND FEELINGS

On disembarking the elevators to go to patient rooms, people again sense relaxation and peace in the environment. As the doors open, patients and guests face a five-story wall of paned glass with views out to the desert and mountains that surround the hospital site. As people progress down well-marked corridors to the patient rooms, the atmosphere becomes even quieter. Rooms (all of them private) are arranged in 12-bed pods surrounding a nursing station. Nurses are within 20 steps of any patient room. Nurses and other attendants use cell phones—there is no paging system with constant announcements, as in many hospitals.

The rooms themselves have interesting features, some designed by patients. For example, rooms contain

lobby, piano music serves to reduce stress (see Exhibit 10.3). Shoppers also spend more time when the music "fits" the product or matches their musical tastes. Other studies have similarly shown the effects of scent on consumer responses.[34] Scent in bakeries, coffee shops, and tobacco shops, for example, can be used to draw people in, and pleasant scents can increase lingering time. The presence of a scent can reduce perceptions of time spent and improve store evaluations. The effects of ambient conditions are especially noticeable when they are extreme. For example, people attending a symphony in a hall in which the air conditioning has failed and the air is hot and stuffy will be uncomfortable, and their discomfort will be reflected in how they feel about the concert. If the temperature and air quality were within a comfort tolerance zone, these ambient factors would probably go unnoticed.

Spatial Layout and Functionality

Because service environments generally exist to fulfill specific purposes or needs of customers, spatial layout and functionality of the physical surroundings are important.

a multishelf display area on which patients can put cards, flowers, and other personal items. Fold-out, cushioned bedchairs are in each room so family members can nap or spend the night with their loved ones. Visitors are never told they must leave. The rooms are arranged with consideration to what patients see from the beds, where they spend the most time. For example, special attention is paid to the ceilings, which patients view while flat on their backs; all rooms have windows; and a white board on the wall at the foot of each bed displays important information for patients (e.g., the name of the nurse on duty, the date, the room phone number).

Kristoffer Tripplaar/Alamy Stock Photo

Mayo Clinic Hospital, Scottsdale, Arizona.

DEPARTMENTS THAT WORK TOGETHER ARE ADJACENT

Another interesting design feature is that departments that work together are housed very close to each other to facilitate communication and to reduce walking time between areas. This important feature allows caregivers to spend more time with patients and lessens employee fatigue.

MAXIMIZE NURSES' TIME WITH PATIENTS

A critical element in the recovery of patients is the quality of care they are given. Many of the Mayo Clinic Hospital design features facilitate the quality of nursing care. The pod design puts nurses close to their patients; the white boards in the rooms allow easy communication; the accessible placement of supplies and relevant departments helps maximize the time nurses spend with patients.

It is clear that the design of the Mayo Hospital takes into account the critical importance of the servicescape in facilitating Mayo's primary goal: patient healing. This is true not only for the design of the hospital in Arizona (which we highlight here), but also in other facilities of the Mayo Clinic. Consistently, all parties' voices are heard, and the place itself provides an environment that promotes well-being for patients, visitors, doctors, nurses, and other staff.

Sources: *New Facility's Patient-driven Design Fuels Collaboration and Innovation*; https://www.mayoclinic.org/medical-professionals/physical-medicine-rehabilitation/news/new-facilitys-patient-driven-design-fuels-collaboration-and-innovation/mqc-20470866, accessed January 09, 2022; *Teamwork at Mayo: An Experiment in Cooperative Individualism* (Rochester, MN: Mayo Press, 1998); http://www.mayo.edu; author's personal tour of the Mayo Clinic Hospital in Scottsdale; L. L. Berry and K. D. Seltman, "Building a Strong Services Brand: Lessons from Mayo Clinic," *Business Horizons* 50 (2007), pp. 199–209; and L. L. Berry and K. D. Seltman, *Management Lessons from the Mayo Clinic* (New York: McGraw Hill, 2008).

Spatial layout refers to the ways in which machinery, equipment, and furnishings are arranged; the size and shape of those items; and the spatial relationships among them. *Functionality* refers to the ability of the same items to facilitate the accomplishment of customer and employee goals. Previous examples in this chapter illustrate the layout and functionality dimensions of the servicescape (e.g., the cruise ship photo earlier and the design of the Mayo Hospital in Exhibit 10.3).

The spatial layout and functionality of the environment are particularly important for customers in self-service environments, where they must perform the service on their own and cannot rely on employees to assist them. Thus, the functionality of an ATM machine and of self-serve restaurants, gasoline pumps, and Internet shopping are critical to success and customer satisfaction.

The importance of facility layout is particularly apparent in retail, hospitality, and leisure settings, where research shows it can influence customer satisfaction, store performance, and consumer search behavior.[35]

Global Feature McDonald's Adapts Servicescapes to Fit the Culture

People's reactions to elements of the physical environment and design are shaped to a large degree by culture and expectations they have formed through their life experiences, dominated by where they live. Just think of one design element—color—and the variety of uses it has across cultures. Other cultural differences—personal space requirements, social distance preferences, sensitivity to crowding—can affect how consumers experience servicescapes around the world. It is interesting to observe the effects, globally, of the COVID-19 pandemic on design elements of servicescapes. Social distancing, arrangement of furnishings, ventilation, and other adaptations have been made in many businesses to mitigate spread of the virus. Many of these adaptations are likely to persist in different forms around the world.

McDonald's Corporation recognizes culturally defined expectations in allowing its franchisees around the world some freedom in designing their servicescapes. In most McDonald's franchises, a large percentage of the ownership is retained locally. Employees are nationals, and marketing strategies reflect local consumers' buying and preference patterns. McDonald's strategy is to have its restaurants worldwide reflect the cultures and communities in which they are found—to mirror the communities they serve.

Although the golden arches are always present, a brief tour around the globe shows the wide variation in McDonald's face to the community:

- Paris, France: Near the Sorbonne in Paris, the local McDonald's reflects its studious neighbor. The servicescape there has the look of a leather-bound library with books, statues, and heavy wood furniture.
- Salen, Sweden: On the slopes of Lindvallen Resort in Salen, you can find the world's first "ski-thru" restaurant, named McSki, located next to the main ski lift. The building is different from any other McDonald's restaurant, built in a typical mountain style with wood panels and natural stone from the surroundings. Skiers can simply glide to the counter without taking off their skis, or they can be seated indoors or out.
- Beijing, China: McDonald's restaurants here have become a "place to hang out," very different from their "fast-food" character in the United States. Customers can be seen lingering for long periods of time, relaxing, chatting, reading, enjoying the music, or celebrating birthdays. The restaurants are part of the community, serving young and old, families, and couples. Teenagers and young couples even find the restaurants to be romantic environments. The emphasis on a Chinese-style family atmosphere is apparent from the interior walls of local restaurants, which are covered by posters emphasizing family values.
- Tokyo, Japan: Although some McDonald's restaurants in Japan are located in prime real-estate districts such as the Ginza in Tokyo, many others are situated near major train stations or other high-traffic locations. The emphasis at these locations is on convenience and speed, not on comfort or socializing. Many of these locations have little frontage space and limited seating. Customers frequently stand while eating, or they may sit on stools at narrow counters. Even the elite Ginza location has few seats. Some locations have a small ordering and service area on the first floor, with limited seating (still primarily stools rather than tables and chairs) on the second floor.
- Taupo, New Zealand: The McDonald's here is a unique site, as the restaurant has incorporated a decommissioned DC3 plane as part of the dining area. The plane has been adorned with the familiar red paint and golden arches that McDonald's is famous for. Customers can eat at seats inside the plane, and patrons are also welcome to explore the cockpit and experience a piece of New Zealand history.

In addition to permitting country-specific design, McDonald's has undertaken an extensive makeover aimed at

Signs, Symbols, and Artifacts

Many items in the physical environment serve as explicit or implicit signals that communicate about the place to its users. *Signs* displayed on the exterior and interior of a structure are examples of explicit communicators. They can be used as labels (name of company, name of department, and so on), for directional purposes (entrances, exits), and to communicate rules of behavior (no smoking). Adequate signs have even been shown to reduce perceived crowding and stress.

Other environmental *symbols* and *artifacts* may communicate less directly than signs, giving implicit cues to users about the meaning of the place and norms and expectations for behavior in the place. Quality construction materials, artwork, certificates and photographs, floor coverings, and personal objects displayed in the

Michael Lassman/Bloomberg/Getty Images

McDonalds restaurant in China.

modernizing the entire chain's overall look. Many existing restaurants have already invested in extensive upgrades that feature a cleaner and simpler overall design; less plastic; warmer, muted colors (terra cotta instead of bright red); Wi-Fi access; and different types of seating sections, including bar stools for customers who eat alone and family areas with booths and fabric-covered seating.

Sources: J. Berr, "McDonald's Plans $6 Billion Makeover of Its Restaurants," https://www.cbsnews.com/news/mcdonalds-plans-6-billion-makeover-of-its-restaurants/, accessed January 09, 2022; D. Rauchweger, "The Architecture of McDonald's," https://architizer.com/blog/inspiration/industry/mcdonalds-architecture-america/, accessed January 10, 2022; *Golden Arches East: McDonald's in East Asia,* ed. J. L. Watson (Stanford, CA: Stanford University Press, 1997); "A Unique Peak," *Franchise Times* 3 (1997), p. 46; P. Gogoi, "Mickey D's McMakeover," *BusinessWeek,* May 15, 2006, pp. 42–43; M. Arndt, "Knock Knock, It's Your Big Mac; From Sao Paulo to Shanghai, McDonald's Is Boosting Growth with Speedy Delivery," *BusinessWeek,* July 23, 2007, p. 36; M. Sanchanta and Y. Koh, "McDonald's in Japan Gives New Meaning to Supersize," *The Wall Street Journal,* January 12, 2011, p. 1; L. R. Brett, "Join the Mile Fry Club! McDonald's Opens 20-Seat Restaurant on a Vintage Luxury Plane," *Mail Online,* August 12, 2014, http://www.dailymail.co.uk/travel/travel_news /article-2722653/Join-mile-fry-club-McDonald-s-opens-20-seat -restaurant-vintage-luxury-PLANE-cabin-crew-not-included.html.

environment can all communicate symbolic meaning and create an overall aesthetic impression. The meanings attached to environmental symbols and artifacts are culturally embedded, as illustrated in this chapter's Global Feature.

Signs, symbols, and artifacts are particularly important in forming first impressions and for communicating service concepts. When customers are unfamiliar with a particular service establishment, they look for environmental cues to help them categorize the place and form their expectations. A study of dentists' offices found that consumers use the environment, in particular its style of decoration and level of quality, as a cue to the competence and manner of the service provider.[36] Another interesting study explored the roles of ethnicity and sexual orientation on consumers' interpretation of symbols within consumption environments. Specifically, the study found that people of Jewish descent observe particular symbols in places that encourage them to feel at home and approach those places.[37] The same study found that homosexuals were also drawn to environments that included particular symbols and artifacts that they identified with. In the presence of other symbols, these groups felt unwelcome or even discriminated against.

GUIDELINES FOR PHYSICAL EVIDENCE STRATEGY

To this point in the chapter we have presented ideas, frameworks, and psychological models for understanding the effects of physical evidence and most specifically the effects of the physical facility or servicescape. In this section, we suggest some general guidelines for an effective physical evidence strategy.[38]

Recognize the Strategic Impact of Physical Evidence

Physical evidence can play a prominent role in determining service quality expectations and perceptions. For some organizations, just acknowledging the impact of physical evidence is a major first step. After this step, they can take advantage of the potential of physical evidence and plan strategically.

For physical evidence strategy to be effective, it must be linked clearly to the organization's overall goals and vision. Thus, planners must know what those goals are and then determine how the physical evidence strategy can support them. At a minimum, the basic service concept must be defined, the target markets (both internal and external) identified, and the firm's broad vision of its future known. Because many evidence decisions are relatively permanent and costly (particularly servicescape decisions), they must be planned and executed deliberately.

Blueprint the Physical Evidence of Service

The next step is to blueprint the service. Everyone in the organization should be able to see the service process and the existing elements of physical evidence. An effective way to depict service evidence is through the service blueprint. (Service blueprinting was presented in Chapter 8.) Although service blueprints clearly have multiple purposes, they can be particularly useful in visually capturing physical evidence opportunities. People, processes, and physical evidence can all be seen in the blueprint. The actions involved in service delivery are visible, as are the complexity of the process, the points of human interaction that provide evidence opportunities, and the tangible representations present at each step. To make the blueprint even more useful, photographs or videos of the process can be added to develop a photographic blueprint that provides a vivid picture of physical evidence from the customer's point of view.

Clarify Strategic Roles of the Servicescape

Early in the chapter we discussed the varying roles played by the servicescape and how firms could locate themselves in the typology shown in Table 10.3 to begin to identify their roles. For example, a day care center would locate itself in the "elaborate, interpersonal" cell of the table and quickly see that its servicescape decisions would be relatively complex and that the servicescape strategy may have to consider the needs of both the children and the service providers and could impact marketing, organizational behavior, and consumer satisfaction goals.

Sometimes the servicescape has no role in service delivery or marketing from the customer's point of view, such as in telecommunications services or utilities (although in these cases other forms of physical evidence would still be important). Clarifying the roles played by the servicescape in a particular situation will aid in identifying opportunities and deciding who needs to be consulted in making facility design decisions. Clarifying the strategic role of the servicescape also forces recognition of the importance of the servicescape in creating customer experiences.

Assess and Identify Physical Evidence Opportunities

Once the current forms of evidence and the roles of the servicescape are understood, possible improvements can be identified. One question to ask is, are there missed opportunities to provide service evidence? The service blueprint of an insurance or utility service may show that little if any evidence of service is ever provided to the customer. A strategy might then be developed to provide more evidence of service to show customers exactly what they are paying for. This was the case for a large technology services company that provided a "remote repair service" for its customers. Remote service (sometimes referred to as "smart service") means they were able to anticipate and repair certain technology equipment from afar without the customer actually being aware anything had been done. A blueprint of the service revealed that no physical evidence of the service existed at all. Thus, customers did not appreciate the service they had received nor were they anxious to pay for it. Realizing this, the company developed ways to communicate and provide evidence of the service for customers.

Or it may be discovered that the evidence provided is sending messages that do not enhance the firm's image or goals or that do not match customer expectations. For example, a restaurant might find that its high-price menu cues are not consistent with the design of the restaurant, which suggests "family dining" to its intended market segment. Either the pricing or the facility design would need to be changed, depending on the restaurant's overall strategy.

Another set of questions addresses whether the current physical evidence of service suits the needs and preferences of the target market. To begin answering such questions, the framework for understanding environment–user relationships (Figure 10.1) and the research approaches suggested in this chapter could be employed. And finally, does the evidence strategy take into account the needs (sometimes incompatible) of both customers and employees? This question is particularly relevant in making decisions regarding the servicescape.

Update and Modernize the Evidence

Some aspects of the evidence, particularly the servicescape, require frequent or at least periodic updating and modernizing.[39] Even if the vision, goals, and objectives of the company do not change, time itself takes a toll on physical evidence, necessitating change and modernization. Clearly, an element of fashion is involved, and over time different colors, designs, and styles may come to communicate different messages. Organizations obviously understand this concept when it comes to advertising strategy, but sometimes they overlook the many elements of physical evidence discussed in this chapter.

Work Cross-Functionally

In presenting itself to the consumer, a firm is concerned with communicating a desired image, with sending consistent and compatible messages through all forms of evidence, and with providing the type of service evidence the target customers want and understand. Frequently, however, physical evidence decisions are made over time and by various functions within the organization. For example, decisions regarding employee uniforms may be made by human resources, servicescape design decisions may be made by the facilities management group, process design decisions are made

Indian Service Strategy Insight — Vande Bharat Express – Differentiating through Servicescape

The indigenously designed and developed semi-high-speed Vande Bharat Express trains, created by the Indian Railways' (IR) Integral Coach Factory, exemplify how physical evidence can be strategically utilized to elevate the travel experience through faster, safer, and superior trainsets. From the moment passengers board, the train's thoughtfully designed tangible elements convey a sense of luxury and modernity. Features such as automatic doors—marking a significant shift from traditional Indian train designs—instantly signal a premium service level and enhanced safety. Inside, carefully engineered reclining seats with ample legroom provide visible proof of the IR's attention to passenger comfort on long journeys. Digital amenities, including onboard WiFi, serve as technological physical evidence, reinforcing the modern travel experience while delivering practical connectivity. Collectively, these tangible features establish a service environment that reshapes passenger expectations and firmly positions Vande Bharat as a premium offering within IR's portfolio, successfully bridging the gap between conventional rail travel and the luxury typically associated with air travel.

Reference: https://www.thehindubusinessline.com/news/vande-bharat-express-a-fine-example-of-atmanirbharta/article69018764.ece

https://economictimes.indiatimes.com/industry/transportation/railways/remarkable-features-of-vande-bharat-trains-have-you-experienced-yet/unmatched-comfort/slideshow/108590360.cms

by operations managers, and advertising and pricing decisions are made by the marketing department. Thus, it is not surprising that the physical evidence of service may at times be inconsistent. A multifunction team approach to physical evidence strategy is often necessary, particularly for making decisions about the servicescape.

Consider Implications of the COVID-19 Pandemic

The COVID-19 pandemic triggered many historic challenges for service organizations. The management of physical and social servicescapes was particularly affected by governmental regulations (e.g., lockdowns, social distancing) and consumer fears of contamination. Although services are often human encounters, consumer preference for a "human touch" declined and they became more accepting of technology-aided servicescapes (e.g., e-service). In the "new normal" of the post-pandemic, the management of servicescapes (e.g., for retailers, restaurants, hotels, airlines, theaters, universities/schools, and hospitals) will need to include a new focus on how to manage (a) in-person customer–employee interactions versus remote service delivery, (b) the number of customers served and related crowding and waiting lines, (c) cleaning and disinfecting, (d) ventilation and spatial arrangements that help prevent contamination, as well as aspects related to (e) safer (wireless) payment methods. Technologies (e.g., augmented/virtual reality, robots, and sensory-enabling technologies for e-shops) will become even more important in this new normal. While not all pandemic-related changes might be "here to stay," companies need to carefully monitor the effects of the pandemic and its implications for their servicescapes.[40]

Summary

In this chapter we explored the roles of physical evidence in forming customer and employee perceptions and shaping customer experiences. Because services are intangible and often produced and consumed at the same time, they can be difficult to comprehend or evaluate before their purchase. The physical evidence of the service thus serves as a primary cue for setting customer expectations before purchase. These tangible cues, particularly the servicescape, also influence customers' responses as they experience the service. Because customers and employees often interact in the servicescape, the physical surroundings also influence employees and the nature of employee–customer interactions.

The chapter focused primarily on the physical servicescape—the physical surroundings or the facility where the service is produced, delivered, and consumed. We presented a typology of servicescapes that illustrated their range of complexity and usage. General strategic roles of the servicescape were also described. We offered a framework for understanding servicescape effects on employee and customer behaviors. The servicescape can affect the approach and avoidance behaviors of customers and employees as well as their social interactions. These behavioral responses come about because the physical environment influences people's beliefs about the service organization, their emotions in response to the place, and their physiological reactions while in the physical facility. Three categories of environmental dimensions capture the complex nature of the servicescape: ambient conditions; spatial layout and functionality; and signs, symbols, and artifacts.

Given the importance of physical evidence and its potentially powerful influence on both customers and employees, it is critical for firms to think strategically about the management of the tangible evidence of service. The impact of physical evidence and design decisions needs to be researched and planned as part of the marketing strategy. The chapter concluded with specific guidelines for physical evidence strategy.

Discussion Questions

1. What is physical evidence, and why have we devoted an entire chapter to it in a services marketing text?
2. Describe and give an example of how servicescapes play each of the following strategic roles: package, facilitator, socializer, and differentiator.
3. Imagine that you own an independent copying and printing shop (similar to FedEx Kinko's). In which cell would you locate your business in the typology of

servicescapes shown in Table 10.3? What are the implications for designing your physical facility?

4. How can an effective physical evidence strategy help close Gap 2? Explain.
5. Why are both customers and employees included in the framework for understanding servicescape effects on behavior (Figure 10.1)? What types of behaviors are influenced by the servicescape? Think of examples.
6. Using your own experiences, give examples of times when you have been affected cognitively, emotionally, and physiologically by elements of the servicescape (in any service context).
7. Why is everyone not affected in exactly the same way by the servicescape?
8. Describe the physical environment of your favorite restaurant in terms of the three categories of servicescape dimensions: ambient conditions; spatial layout and functionality; and signs, symbols, and artifacts.
9. Imagine that you are serving as a consultant to a local health club. How would you advise the health club to begin the process of developing an effective physical evidence strategy?

Exercises

1. Choose two very different firms (different market segments or service levels) in the same industry. Observe both establishments. Describe the service "package" in both cases. How does the package help distinguish the two firms? Do you believe that the package sets accurate expectations for what the firm delivers? Is either firm overpromising through the manner in which its servicescape (or other types of physical evidence) communicates with customers?
2. Think of a particular service organization (it can be a class project company, the company you work for, or some other organization) for which you believe physical evidence is important in communicating with and satisfying customers. Prepare a presentation you would give to that organization to convince them of the importance of physical evidence in their marketing strategy.
3. Create a photographic or video blueprint for a service of your choice. Analyze the blueprint from the customer's perspective and suggest changes that could improve the service design.
4. Choose a service organization and collect all forms of physical evidence that the organization uses to communicate with its customers. If customers see the firm's facility, also take a photo of the servicescape. Analyze the evidence in terms of compatibility, consistency, and whether it overpromises or underpromises what the firm can deliver.
5. Visit the websites of several service providers. Does the physical evidence of the website portray an image consistent with other forms of evidence provided by the organizations?
6. Visit the websites of Envirosell and McKinsey Design and review the services these companies offer to their clients, especially related to areas such as store performance and customer experience. Identify and explain how these services relate to specific aspects of Figure 10.1 and which managerial insights they can provide.
7. Capital One has reimagined the servicescape of banks with its Cafés, which are welcoming spaces where people (whether they are customers or not) can refuel and unwind. Conduct some background research on "Capital One Cafés" and identify how this servicescape strategy relates to various ideas and concepts in this chapter.

Notes

1. http://fortune.com/worlds-most-admired-companies/marriott-international-29/; http://www.forbes.com/companies/marriott-international/; https://hotel-development.marriott.com/brands; all websites accessed August 2016. For an overview of Marriott awards and recognitions, see https://news.marriott.com/awards/, accessed February 2022.
2. The term *servicescape* used throughout this chapter, and much of the content of this chapter, are based, with permission, on M. J. Bitner, "Servicescapes: The Impact of Physical Surroundings on Customers and Employees," *Journal of Marketing* 56 (April 1992), pp. 57–71. For later contributions to this topic, see *Servicescapes: The Concept of Place in Contemporary Markets,* ed. J. F. Sherry Jr. (Chicago: NTC/Contemporary, 1998); and M. J. Bitner, "The Servicescape," in *Handbook of Services Marketing and Management,* ed. T. A. Swartz and D. Iacobucci (Thousand Oaks, CA: Sage, 2000), pp. 37–50; K. Fowler, "Innovative Service Environments," In *The Routledge Handbook of Service Research Insights and Ideas* (Routledge, 2020), pp. 148–166.
3. L. P. Carbone, *Clued In: How to Keep Customers Coming Back Again and Again* (Upper Saddle River, NJ: Prentice Hall, 2004). See also L. L. Berry and N. Bendapudi, "Clueing in Customers," *Harvard Business Review,* February 2003, pp. 100–106.
4. J. H. Gilmore and B. J. Pine II, "The Experience Is the Marketing," *Strategic Horizons,* 2002; B. J. Pine II and J. H. Gilmore, *The Experience Economy: Work Is Theater and Every Business Is a Stage* (Boston: Harvard Business School Press, 1999); and B. H. Schmitt, *Experiential Marketing* (New York: The Free Press, 1999).
5. For reviews of environmental psychology, see D. Stokols and I. Altman, *Handbook of Environmental Psychology* (New York: John Wiley, 1987); S. Saegert and G. H. Winkel, "Environmental Psychology," *Annual Review of Psychology* 41 (1990), pp. 441–477; and E. Sundstrom, P. A. Bell, P. L. Busby, and C. Asmus, "Environmental Psychology 1989–1994," *Annual Review of Psychology* 47 (1996), pp. 485–512.
6. SAS, "SAS named a Best Workplace in Technology by Fortune," https://www.sas.com/en_us/news/press-releases/2021/april/sas-named-a-best-workplace-in-technology-by-fortune.html, accessed January 06, 2021.
7. See M. R. Solomon, "Dressing for the Part: The Role of Costume in the Staging of Servicescape," in Sherry, *Servicescapes;* and A. Rafaeli, "Dress and Behavior of Customer Contact Employees: A Framework for Analysis," in *Advances in Services Marketing and Management,* vol. 2, ed. T. A. Swartz, D. E. Bowen, and S. W. Brown (Greenwich, CT: JAI Press, 1993), pp. 175–212; J. Barlow and P. Stewart, *Branded Customer Service* (San Francisco: Barrett-Koehler Publishers, 2004).
8. For more details on Starbucks's store designs, visit: https://www.starbucks.in/coffeehouse/store-design; Statista, "Number of International and U.S.-Based Starbucks Stores from 2005 to 2021," https://www.statista.com/statistics/218366/number-of-international-and-us-starbucks-stores/, accessed January 06, 2021; M. Wilson, "Can Starbucks Make 23,000 Coffee Shops Feel Unique?" August 18, 2014, http://www.fastcodesign.com/3034441/starbucks-secrets-to-make-every-store-feel-unique.
9. Airport design also becomes increasingly important for traveler satisfaction, as illustrated by Singapore's Changi Airport (www.changiairport.com/), accessed

February 12, 2022. B. Stanley, "Qantas Flaunts Super-Jumbo Perks," *The Wall Street Journal,* July 25, 2007, p. D3; and S. McCartney, "A Bubble Bath and a Glass of Bubbly—at the Airport," *The Wall Street Journal,* July 10, 2007, p. D1; J. Freed, "Quantas Rolls Out New A330 Business Class Suites on Flights to Singapore and Asia," *Traveller,* January 16, 2015, http://www.traveller.com.au/qantas-rolls-out-new-a330-business-class-suites-on-flights-to-singapore-and-asia-12rm2j.

10. www.petsmart.com/services/petshotel, 2016; C. M. Dalton, "A Passion for Pets: An Interview with Philip L. Francis, Chairperson and CEO of PetSmart, Inc.," *Business Horizons,* November–December 2005, pp. 469–475; and D. Brady and C. Palmeri, "The Pet Economy," *BusinessWeek,* August 6, 2007, pp. 45–54.
11. Carbone, *Clued In;* Berry and Bendapudi, "Clueing in Customers"; Gilmore and Pine, "Experience Is the Marketing"; Pine and Gilmore, *The Experience Economy;* Schmitt, *Experiential Marketing;* and L. L. Berry, E. A. Wall, and L. P. Carbone, "Service Clues and Customer Assessment of the Service Experience: Lessons from Marketing," *Academy of Management Perspectives* 20 (2006), pp. 43–57.
12. E. C. Brüggen, B. Foubert, and D. D. Gremler, "Extreme Makeover: Short- and Long- Term Effects of a Remodeled Serviescape," *Journal of Marketing* 75 (September 2011), pp. 71–87.
13. T. S. Dagger and P. J. Danaher, "Comparing the Effect of Store Remodeling on New and Existing Customers," *Journal of Marketing* 78 (May 2014), pp. 62–80.
14. A. Mehrabian and J. A. Russell, *An Approach to Environmental Psychology* (Cambridge, MA: Massachusetts Institute of Technology, 1974).
15. R. Donovan and J. Rossiter, "Store Atmosphere: An Environmental Psychology Approach," *Journal of Retailing* 58 (Spring 1982), pp. 34–57.
16. D. J. Bennett and J. D. Bennett, "Making the Scene," in *Social Psychology through Symbolic Interactionism,* ed. G. Stone and H. Farberman (Waltham, MA: Ginn-Blaisdell, 1970), pp. 190–196.
17. J. P. Forgas, *Social Episodes* (London: Academic Press, 1979).
18. R. G. Barker, *Ecological Psychology* (Stanford, CA: Stanford University Press, 1968).
19. For a number of excellent papers on this topic spanning a range from toy stores to bridal salons to cybermarketspaces to Japanese retail environments and others, see Sherry, *Servicescapes: The Concept of Place in Contemporary Markets.*
20. For further details on Nike's retail strategy, see: https://news.nike.com/news/nike-unite-retail-concept, accessed February 16, 2022. J. F. Sherry Jr., "The Soul of the Company Store: Nike Town Chicago and the Emplace Brandscape," in Sherry, *Servicescapes,* pp. 81–108.
21. E. J. Arnould, L. L. Price, and P. Tierney, "The Wilderness Servicescape: An Ironic Commercial Landscape," in Sherry, *Servicescapes,* pp. 403–438.
22. Rosenbaum, "Exploring the Social Supportive Role of Third Places in Consumers' Lives," *Journal of Service Research* 9 (August 2006), pp. 59–72; A. Tombs and J. R. McColl-Kennedy, "Social-Servicescape Conceptual Model," *Marketing Theory* 3 (2003), pp. 447–475; and M. S. Rosenbaum, J. Ward, B. A. Walker, and A. L. Ostrom, "A Cup of Coffee with a Dash of Love: An Investigation of Commercial Social Support and Third-Place Attachment," *Journal of Service Research* 10 (August 2007), pp. 43–59.

23. A. Rapoport, *The Meaning of the Built Environment* (Beverly Hills, CA: Sage, 1982); and R. G. Golledge, "Environmental Cognition," in Stokols and Altman, *Handbook of Environmental Psychology,* vol. 1, pp. 131–174.
24. M. P. Gardner and G. Siomkos, "Toward a Methodology for Assessing Effects of In-Store Atmospherics," in *Advances in Consumer Research,* vol. 13, ed. R. J. Lutz (Ann Arbor, MI: Association for Consumer Research, 1986), pp. 27–31.
25. M. J. Bitner, "Evaluating Service Encounters: The Effects of Physical Surroundings and Employee Responses," *Journal of Marketing* 54 (April 1990), pp. 69–82.
26. J. C. Ward, M. J. Bitner, and J. Barnes, "Measuring the Prototypicality and Meaning of Retail Environments," *Journal of Retailing* 68 (Summer 1992), pp. 194–220.
27. See, for example, Mehrabian and Russell, *An Approach to Environmental Psychology*; J. A. Russell and U. F. Lanius, "Adaptation Level and the Affective Appraisal of Environments," *Journal of Environmental Psychology* 4 (1984), pp. 199–235; J. A. Russell and G. Pratt, "A Description of the Affective Quality Attributed to Environments," *Journal of Personality and Social Psychology* 38 (1980), pp. 311–322; J. A. Russell and J. Snodgrass, "Emotion and the Environment," in Stokols and Altman, *Handbook of Environmental Psychology,* vol. 1, pp. 245–281; J. A. Russell, L. M. Ward, and G. Pratt, "Affective Quality Attributed to Environments," *Environment and Behavior* 13 (May 1981), pp. 259–288; V. Kaltcheva and B. A. Weitz, "When Should a Retailer Create an Exciting Store Environment," *Journal of Marketing* 70 (January 2006), pp. 107–118.
28. See, for example, M. S. Sanders and E. J. McCormick, *Human Factors in Engineering and Design,* 7th ed. (New York: McGraw-Hill, 1993); and G. Salvendy (ed.), *Handbook of Human Factors and Ergonomics* (Hoboken, NJ: Wiley, 2006).
29. The Center for an Accessible Society, http://www.accessiblesociety.org/topics/universaldesign/, accessed August 2016; S. Burgstahler, "Universal Design: Process, Principles, and Applications," http://www.washington.edu/doit/universal-design-process-principles-and-applications, accessed August 2016.
30. Mehrabian and Russell, *An Approach to Environmental Psychology*; Russell and Snodgrass, "Emotion and the Environment."
31. K. Dijkstra, M. E. Pieterse, and A. Pruyn, "Individual Differences in Reactions towards Color in Simulated Healthcare Environments: The Role of Stimulus Screening Ability," *Journal of Environmental Psychology* 28 (September 2008), pp. 268–277; A. Mehrabian, "Individual Differences in Stimulus Screening and Arousability," *Journal of Personality* 45 (1977), pp. 237–250.
32. E. Bellman, "In India, a Retailer Finds Key to Success Is Clutter," *The Wall Street Journal,* August 8, 2007, p. A1.
33. For research documenting the effects of music on consumers, see D. Biswas, K. Lund, and C. Szocs, "Sounds Like a Healthy Retail Atmospheric Strategy," *Journal of the Academy of Marketing Science* 47 (January 2019), pp. 37–55; J. Baker, D. Grewal, and A. Parasuraman, "The Influence of Store Environment on Quality Inferences and Store Image," *Journal of the Academy of Marketing Science* 22 (Fall 1994), pp. 328–339; J. D. Herrington and L. M. Capella, "Effects of Music in Service Environments: A Field Study," *Journal of Services Marketing* 10 (1996), pp. 26–41; J. D. Herrington and L. M. Capella, "Practical Applications of Music in Service Settings," *Journal of Services Marketing* 8 (1994), pp. 50–65; M. K. Hui, L. Dube, and J. C. Chebat, "The Impact of Music on Consumers' Reactions to Waiting for Services," *Journal of Retailing* 73 (Spring

1997), pp. 87–104; A. S. Matila and J. Wirtz, "Congruency of Scent and Music as a Driver of In-Store Evaluations and Behavior," *Journal of Retailing* 77 (Summer 2001), pp. 273–289; L. Dube and S. Morin, "Background Music Pleasure and Store Evaluation: Intensity Effects and Psychological Mechanisms," *Journal of Business Research* 54 (November 2001), pp. 107–113; J. Bakec, A. Parasuraman, D. Grewal, and G. B. Voss, "The Influence of Multiple Store Environment Cues as Perceived Merchandise Value and Patronage Intentions," *Journal of Marketing* 66 (April 2002), pp. 120–141; and S. Morin, L. Dube, and J. Chebat, "The Role of Pleasant Music in Servicescapes: A Test of the Dual Model of Environmental Perception," *Journal of Retailing* 83 (2007), pp. 115–130.

34. For research documenting the effects of scent on consumer responses, see H. Roschk and M. Hosseinpour, "Pleasant Ambient Scents: a Meta-Analysis of Customer Responses and Situational Contingencies," *Journal of Marketing* 84 (January 2020), pp. 125–145; A. V. Madzharov, L. G. Block, and M. Morrin, "The Cool Scent of Power: Effects of Ambient Scent on Consumer Preferences and Choice Behavior," *Journal of Marketing* 79 (January 2015), pp. 83–96.
35. See J. M. Sulek, M. R. Lind, and A. S. Marucheck, "The Impact of a Customer Service Intervention and Facility Design on Firm Performance," *Management Science* 41 (1995), pp. 1763–1773; P. A. Titus and P. B. Everett, "Consumer Wayfinding Tasks, Strategies, and Errors: An Exploratory Field Study," *Psychology and Marketing* 13 (1996), pp. 265–290; C. Yoo, J. Park, and D. J. MacInnis, "Effects of Store Characteristics and In-Store Emotional Experiences on Store Attitude," *Journal of Business Research* 42 (1998), pp. 253–263; and K. L. Wakefield and J. G. Blodgett, "The Effect of the Servicescape on Customers' Behavioral Intentions in Leisure Service Settings," *Journal of Services Marketing* 10 (1996), pp. 45–61; Brüggen, Foubert, and Gremler, "Extreme Makeover: Short- and Long-Term Effects of a Remodeled Servicescape."
36. J. C. Ward and J. P. Eaton, "Service Environments: The Effect of Quality and Decorative Style on Emotions, Expectations, and Attributions," in *Proceedings of the American Marketing Association Summer Educators' Conference,* ed. R. Achrol and A. Mitchell (Chicago: American Marketing Association 1994), pp. 333–334.
37. M. S. Rosenbaum, "The Symbolic Servicescape: Your Kind Is Welcomed Here," *Journal of Consumer Behaviour* 4 (2005), pp. 257–267.
38. This section is adapted from M. J. Bitner, "Managing the Evidence of Service," in *The Service Quality Handbook,* ed. E. E. Scheuing and W. F. Christopher (New York: AMACOM, 1993), pp. 358–370; for some guidance on designing virtual servicescapes, see: U. R. Orth, L. Lockshin, N. Spielmann, and M. Holm, "Design Antecedents of Telepresence in Virtual Service Environments," *Journal of Service Research* 22 (May 2019), pp. 202–218.
39. Brüggen, Foubert, and Gremler, "Extreme Makeover: Short- and Long-Term Effects of a Remodeled Servicescape."
40. K. Willems, N. Verhulst, and M. Brengman, "How COVID-19 Could Accelerate the Adoption of New Retail Technologies and Enhance the (E-)Servicescape," In *The Future of Service Post-COVID-19 Pandemic* 2 (Springer 2021), pp. 103–134; S. Taylor Jr., "The Socially Distant Servicescape: An Investigation of Consumer Preference's During the Re-Opening Phase," *International Journal of Hospitality Management* 91 (2020), p. 102692, https://doi.org/10.1016/j.ijhm.2020.102692.

Part **Five**

Delivering and Performing Service

In the Gaps Model of Service Quality, provider Gap 3 (the service performance gap) is the discrepancy between customer-driven service designs and standards and actual service delivery (as illustrated in the figure below). Even when guidelines exist for performing service well and treating customers correctly, high-quality service performance is not a certainty. Part 5 deals with all the ways in which companies ensure that services are performed according to customer-defined designs and standards.

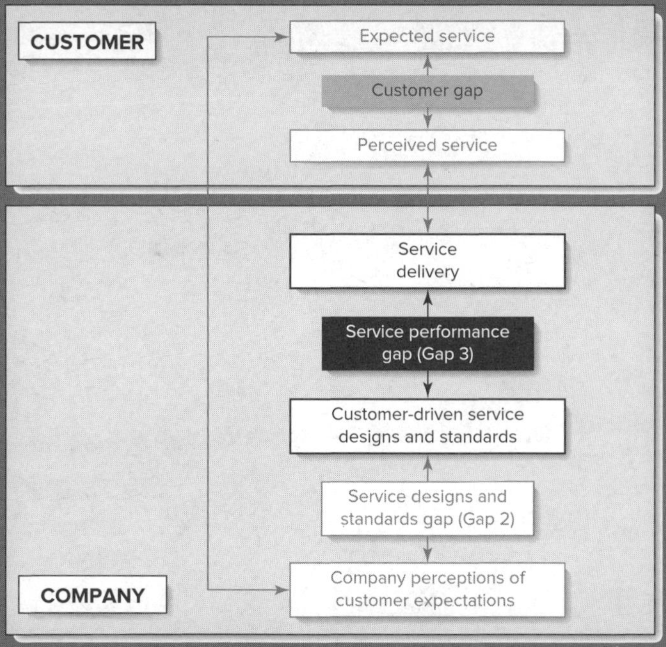

In Chapter 11, we focus on the key roles that employees play in service delivery and strategies that ensure they are effective in their roles. Issues of particular concern include employees who feel in conflict in their position between customers and company management, having the wrong employees or inadequate technology, inappropriate compensation and recognition, and lack of empowerment and teamwork.

In Chapter 12, we discuss the variability in service performance caused by customers. If customers do not perform appropriately—if they do not follow instructions or if they disturb other customers receiving service at the same time—service quality is jeopardized. Effective service organizations understand the roles of customers in service delivery and cocreation of service experiences and develop strategies to help their customers perform *effectively* in these roles.

Chapter 13 emphasizes the need to synchronize demand and capacity in service organizations to deliver consistent, high-quality service. Service organizations often face situations of over- or underdemand because they lack inventories to smooth demand. Strategies for managing demand, such as price changes, advertising, promotion, and alternative service offerings, as well as strategies for adjusting capacity, such as using part-time employees, outsourcing activities, and renting or sharing facilities and equipment, can help manage this challenge.

Chapter Eleven

Employees' Roles in Service

This chapter's learning objectives are to:

1. Demonstrate the importance of creating a service culture in which providing excellent service to both internal and external customers is a natural way of life in an organization.
2. Illustrate the pivotal role of service employees in creating service quality and customer satisfaction.
3. Identify the challenges inherent in boundary-spanning roles.
4. Provide examples of strategies for creating customer-oriented service delivery through hiring the right people, developing employees to deliver service quality, providing needed support systems, and retaining the best employees.

Employees Are the Service and the Brand

Investments in employees are key drivers of sustained business success in companies as diverse as Charles Schwab, USAA Insurance, Wegmans Food Market, Hilton, Southwest Airlines, and Capital One.[1] Why is this true? Why do these companies choose to invest heavily in their employees? For clues, consider the following true stories:

- On a long overseas Singapore Airlines flight, a restless toddler repeatedly dropped his pacifier. Every time the child would cry, and someone (the mother, another passenger, or a flight attendant) would retrieve the pacifier. Finally, one of the attendants picked up the pacifier, attached it to a ribbon, and sewed it to the child's shirt. The child and mother were happy, and passengers seated nearby gave the attendant a standing ovation.[2]
- While at an airport, a businessman was not able to get something to eat before his flight and realized he would be quite hungry when he landed, as he already had an empty stomach. Since he was not a fast food fan and did not want to stop at a fast food restaurant once he landed, the customer jokingly tweeted to one of his favorite restaurants, Morton's, asking them if they would deliver him a steak: "Hey @Mortons—can you meet me at Newark airport with a porterhouse when I land in two hours? K, thanks. :)" Even though he was a longtime customer of the steakhouse, he had no expectations when he sent out the tweet. Indeed, immediately after his tweet he turned off his phone as the plane prepared for departure. To his disbelief, when he landed he was met at the airport by one of Morton's staff, who had driven 23 miles to the airport to deliver to him a full meal.[3]

Service employees directly impact customers' satisfaction.

- In a Panera Bread parking lot a couple of years ago one woman attempted to catch another customer (who suffered from multiple sclerosis) as she lost her balance. Both customers ended up falling on the pavement, and the one who caught the other broke her right arm. Before the woman was taken by ambulance to an emergency room for treatment, a Panera employee gave her his card and told her to call him if she needed anything. A couple of hours later she called and asked if she could get a ride back to the restaurant to get her car. Once there, she realized that she could not drive the car—it had a manual transmission and she could not shift gears with a broken arm. While she was attempting to contact family to get a ride home, the Panera employee provided her with a free meal. After not being able to find someone to drive her home, she asked the employee for another favor—to give her a ride home. He did—to a town that was nearly an hour's drive away. The woman was ecstatic and could not believe a "restaurant employee" would do all of this for her.[4]

These stories illustrate the important roles played by service employees in creating satisfied customers and in building customer relationships. The frontline service providers in each example are enormously important to the success of the organizations they represent. They are responsible for understanding customer needs and for interpreting customer requirements in real time (as suggested by the accompanying photo). Research has documented that, in case after case, companies that achieve sustained service success all recognize the critical importance of their employees in their day-to-day operations.[5]

In this chapter we focus on service employees and human resource practices that facilitate delivery of quality services. Even when customer expectations are well understood (Gap 1) and services have been designed and specified to conform to those expectations (Gap 2), there may still be discontinuities in service quality when the service is not delivered as specified. These discontinuities are labeled Gap 3—the *service performance gap*—in the Gaps Model of Service Quality. Because employees frequently deliver or perform the service, human resource issues are a major cause of this gap. By focusing on the critical role of service employees and by developing strategies that lead to effective customer-oriented service, organizations can begin to close the service performance gap.

SERVICE CULTURE

Before addressing the role of the employee in service delivery, we should look at the bigger picture. The behavior of employees in an organization will be heavily influenced by the culture of that organization or the pervasive norms and values that shape individual and group behavior. *Corporate culture* has been defined as "the pattern of shared values and beliefs that give the members of an organization meaning, and provide them with the rules for behavior in the organization."[6] *Culture* has been defined more informally as "the way we do things around here."

To understand at a personal level what corporate culture is, think of different places you have worked or organizations you have been a member of, such as churches, fraternities, schools, or associations. Your behavior and the behaviors of others were no doubt influenced by the underlying values, norms, and culture of the organization. Even when you first interview for a new job, you can begin to get a sense of the firm's culture through talking to a number of employees and observing behavior. Once you are on the job, your formal training and informal observation of behavior will work together to give you a better picture of the organization's culture.

Experts have suggested that a customer-oriented organization will have at its heart a *service culture,* defined as "a culture where an appreciation for good service exists, and where giving good service to internal as well as ultimate, external customers is considered a natural way of life and one of the most important norms by everyone."[7] This rich definition has many implications for employee behaviors. First, a service culture exists if there is an "appreciation for good service." This phrase does not mean that the company has an advertising campaign that stresses the importance of service, but people know that good service is truly valued. A second important point in this definition is that good service is given to internal customers (i.e., when employees serve other employees) as well as external customers.[8] It is not enough to promise excellent service to final customers; all people within the organization deserve the same kind of service. Finally, in a service culture good service is "a way of life" and it comes naturally because it is an important norm of the organization. Service culture is critical to the creation of a customer-focused organization and has been identified as a source of competitive advantage in companies.[9]

Exhibiting Service Leadership

A strong service culture begins with leaders in the organization who demonstrate a passion for service excellence. Leaders of successful service firms tend to have similar core values, such as integrity, joy, and respect, and they "infuse those values into the fabric of the organization."[10] Leadership does not consist of bestowing a set of commands from a thick rulebook but, rather, the regular and consistent demonstration of one's values. Employees are more likely to embrace a service culture when they see management living out these values. Espoused values—what managers *say* the values are—tend to have less impact on employees than enacted values—what employees believe the values to be because of what they observe management actually *doing.*[11] That is, culture is driven by what employees perceive that management *really* believes, and employees gain an understanding of what is important in the organization through the daily experiences they have with those people in key roles throughout the organization.

Developing a Service Culture

A service culture cannot be developed overnight, and it is not easy to sustain a service culture. The human resource and internal marketing practices discussed later in this chapter can help develop a service culture over time. If, however, an organization has a culture rooted in product-, operations-, or government regulation–oriented traditions, no single strategy will change it into a service culture. Hundreds of little (but significant) factors, not just one or two big factors, are required to build and sustain a service culture.[12] When companies shift from an engineering, sales, or operations culture to a

Global Feature How Well Does a Company's Service Culture Travel?

Although international markets offer tremendous opportunities for growth, many companies find significant challenges when they attempt to transport their services to other countries. Services depend on people, are often delivered by people, and involve the interaction between employees and customers. Differences in values, norms of behavior, language, and even the definition of service become evident quickly and have implications for training, hiring, and incentives that can ultimately affect the success of the international expansion. Companies with strong service cultures are faced with the question of whether to try to replicate their culture and values in other countries or to adapt significantly. A few examples illustrate different approaches.

McDONALD'S APPROACH

McDonald's has been very successful in its international expansion. In some ways it has remained very "American" in everything it does—people around the world want an American experience when they go to McDonald's. However, the company is sensitive to cultural differences as well. This subtle blending of the "McDonald's" way with adaptations to cultural nuances has resulted in great success. One way that McDonald's maintains its standards is through its Hamburger University (HU), which is required training for *all* McDonald's employees worldwide before they can become managers. Each year more than 5,000 employees attend HU at one of the numerous campuses in Chicago, Hong Kong, Sydney, Hamburg, Tokyo, China, Singapore, or Dubai, among others. The curriculum is 80 percent devoted to communications and human relations skills. Because of the international scope of McDonald's, translators and electronic equipment enable instructors to teach and communicate in 28 languages at one time. The result is that all managers in all countries have the same "ketchup in their veins," and the restaurant's basic human resources and operating philosophies remain fairly stable from operation to operation. Certain adaptations in decor, menu, and other areas of cultural differences are then allowed (see the Global Feature in Chapter 10 for some specific examples).

UPS' CHALLENGES

UPS has a strong culture built on employee productivity, highly standardized service delivery processes, and structured training. Its brown trucks and uniforms are instantly recognizable in the United States. However, as it expanded into countries across Europe, UPS was surprised by some of the challenges of managing a global workforce. Here are some of the surprises: indignation in France, when drivers were told they could not have wine with lunch; protests in Britain, when drivers' dogs were banned from delivery trucks; and dismay in Spain, when it was found that brown UPS trucks resembled the local hearses.

DISNEY IN EUROPE

When Disney first expanded into Europe by opening Disneyland Paris, it faced challenges and surprises. The highly structured, scripted, and customer-oriented approach that Disney used in the United States was not easily duplicated with European employees. In particular, the smiling, friendly,

service culture, they find that it can take years of consistent, concerted effort to build a service culture. Even for companies such as FedEx, Charles Schwab, Disney, Southwest Airlines, Zappos, and the Ritz-Carlton, which started with a strong service and customer focus, sustaining their established service cultures still takes constant attention to hundreds of details.

Transporting a Service Culture

Transporting a service culture through international business expansion to another country is also challenging. For instance, will the organization's service culture clash with a different *national* culture? If there is a clash, is it over *what* the actual values are or over *how* they are to be enacted? If the issue is over what the values are, and they are core values critical to the firm's competitive advantage, then perhaps the company cannot be successful in that setting. If the issue is over how the values are enacted, then perhaps some service practices can be modified in the new setting. To illustrate, Four Seasons Hotels created seven globally uniform "SERVICE" standards that it expects of all its employees throughout the world (e.g., staff should smile and make eye contact with customers, and speak to guests in an attentive, natural, always customer-focused behaviors of Disney's U.S. workforce did not suit the experience and values of young French employees. In attempting to transport the Disney culture and experience to Europe, the company confronted clashing values and norms of behavior in the workplace that made the expansion difficult. Customers also needed to be "trained" in the Disney way—not all cultures are comfortable with waiting in long lines, for example. And not all cultures treat their children the same. For example, in the United States, families will spend lots of money at Disneyland on food, toys, and other things that their children "must" have. Some European cultures view this behavior as highly indulgent, so families will visit the park without buying much beyond the ticket for admission.

DELIVERING THE APPLE STORE'S "STEPS OF SERVICE" GLOBALLY

Perhaps no company has been better at connecting with its customers than Apple. The company carefully considers the experience its customers have at every touch-point. As part of the training Apple uses an acronym (the company's name) to describe the "steps of service" expected of every Apple Store employee:

- **A**pproach customers with a personalized warm welcome.
- **P**robe politely to understand all the customer's needs.
- **P**resent a solution for the customer to take home today.
- **L**isten for and resolve any issues or concerns.
- **E**nd with a fond farewell and an invitation to return.

These steps of service, adapted from the Ritz-Carlton, provide a framework for what Apple Store employees are to do in service encounters. "APPLE" is intended to help create great customer experiences in each country Apple Stores are present.

As Apple looks to expand its retail presence globally, it will be challenging to consistently deliver service in this manner. In China, for example, retail chief Angela Ahrendts believes Apple Store's biggest challenge will be to keep up with the demand for Apple products while providing the same level of customer service outlined in the "steps of service." Apple will face similar challenges in transferring its service culture as it continues its expansion in such countries as India, Hong Kong, Brazil, and the United Arab Emirates. Employees in these countries will need to learn how to appropriately interact with customers, how to phrase communications in a positive rather than a negative way, and what to say when customers react emotionally, with the ultimate goal to help customers solve problems rather than to sell products.

Sources: J. Schepers and M. Van der Borgh, "A Meta-Analysis of Frontline Employees' Role Behavior and the Moderating Effects of National Culture," *Journal of Service Research* 23 (August 2020), pp. 255–280; www.mcdonalds.com, accessed January 13, 2022; D. Milbank, "Can Europe Deliver?" *The Wall Street Journal,* September 30, 1994, pp. R15, R23; C. Gallo, "How the Apple Store Creates Irresistible Customer Experiences," *Forbes,* April 10, 2015, http://www.forbes.com/sites/carminegallo/2015/04/10 /how-the-apple-store-creates-irresistible-customer-experiences; "Apple Retail Chief Angela Ahrendts Talks Expansion in China Amid Five New Store Openings," *Mac Rumors* (blog), http://www.macrumors.com/2015/01/15/ahrendts-china-expansion/, January 15, 2015.

and courteous manner). The company has also identified several core values that it believes transcend national culture. One such value is to anticipate guests' needs. This value has been enacted in the United States by leaving a coffeepot on the table in the hotel restaurant, so that guests can help themselves whenever they like. However, when Four Seasons opened a hotel in Paris, it decided to never leave a coffeepot on restaurant tables; doing so would not be received favorably by French customers, who generally believe one should not have to pour coffee oneself. Four Seasons did not alter other practices; it continued, for example, its employee-of-the-month program as a way to provide recognition for exceptional service, even though such programs are not generally offered in France.[13] These standards and values reflect Four Seasons's attempt to transport its service culture across national borders, but management is keenly aware that they need to carefully consider how these values are enacted in each hotel.

Although tremendous opportunities exist in the global marketplace, the many legal, cultural, and language barriers become particularly evident for services that depend on human interaction. Our Global Feature highlights the issues and experiences of several companies as they attempt to transport their service cultures.

THE CRITICAL ROLE OF SERVICE EMPLOYEES

An often-heard quotation about service organizations goes like this: "In a service organization, if you're not serving the customer, you'd better be serving someone who is."[14] People—frontline employees and those supporting them from behind the scenes—are critical to the success of any service organization. The importance of people in the marketing of services is captured in the *people* element of the service marketing mix, which we described in Chapter 1 as *all the human actors who play a part in service delivery and thus influence the buyer's perceptions: namely, the firm's personnel, the customer, and other customers in the service environment.* The key focus in this chapter is on customer-contact (frontline) service employees because:

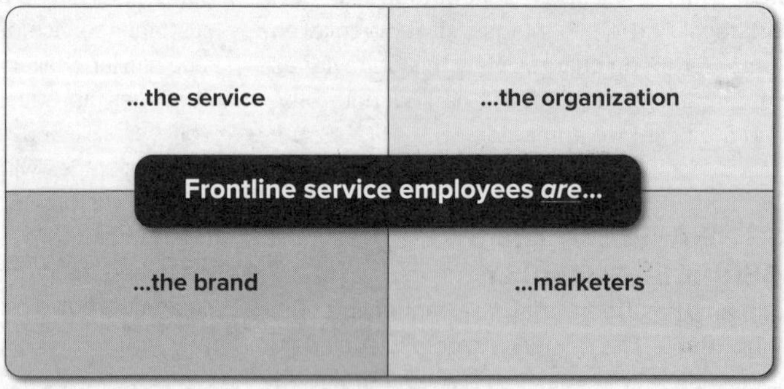

In many cases, the contact employee *is the service*—there is nothing else. For example, in most personal and professional services (like haircutting, child care, counseling, and legal services) the contact employee provides the entire service single-handedly. The offering *is* the employee. Thus, investing in the employee to improve the service parallels making a direct investment in the improvement of a manufactured product.

Even if contact employees do not perform the service entirely, they may still *personify the organization in the customer's eyes.* All the employees of a law firm or health clinic—from the professionals who provide the service to the receptionists and office staff—represent the firm to the client, and everything these individuals do or say can influence perceptions of the organization. Even off-duty employees, such as flight attendants or restaurant employees on a break, reflect the organizations they represent. If they are unprofessional or make rude remarks about or to customers, customers' perceptions of the organization will suffer, even though the employee is not on duty. The Disney Corporation insists that its employees maintain "onstage" attitudes and behaviors whenever they are in front of the public; employees may relax these behaviors only when they are truly behind the scenes or "backstage" in underground tunnels where guests cannot see them in their off-duty times.

Service employees *are the brand.* An Edward Jones financial advisor, a Nordstrom sales associate, a Southwest Airlines flight attendant, or a Zappos customer service employee—in each case, the primary image that a customer has of the firm is formed by the interactions the customer has with the employees of that firm. A customer sees Edward Jones as a good provider of financial services if the employees she interacts with are knowledgeable, understanding, and concerned about her financial situation and goals. Similarly, a customer sees Nordstrom as a professional and empathetic company because of interactions he has with its sales associates. Southwest Airlines seeks employees who are outgoing and fun-loving. Online shoe retailer Zappos makes the hiring process a primary focus of its branding strategy and evaluates potential employees on their ability to serve as brand ambassadors.[15] These companies understand that the brand image is not just built and maintained by the products sold and the advertising: it is a function of the people who work for them. Strategies that recognize the power of employees to create the brand have been referred to as "branded customer service."[16] For firms using such strategies, employees truly "are the brand" and epitomize the company image that each is attempting to create in the minds of its customers.

Because contact employees represent the organization and can directly influence customer satisfaction, they *perform the role of marketers.* They physically embody the product and are walking billboards from a promotional standpoint. Some service employees may also perform more traditional selling roles.[17] For example, bank tellers are often called on to cross-sell bank products, a departure from the traditional teller role of focusing on operational functions only. In this chapter we examine frameworks, tools, and strategies for ensuring that service employees perform their marketing and service functions well.

Service Employees and the Service Marketing Triangle

Service marketing is about promises—promises made and promises kept to customers. A strategic framework known as the *service marketing triangle* (illustrated in Figure 11.1) visually reinforces the importance of people in the ability of firms to keep their promises and succeed in building customer relationships.[18] The triangle shows the three interlinked groups that work together to develop, promote, and deliver services. These key players are labeled on the points of the triangle: the *company* (or a strategic business unit, department, or "management"), the *customers,* and the *providers.* Providers can be the firm's employees, subcontractors, or outsourced entities who actually deliver the company's services. Between these three points on the triangle, three types of marketing must be successfully carried out for a service to succeed: external marketing, interactive marketing, and internal marketing.

On the right side of the triangle are the *external marketing* efforts that the firm engages in to develop its customers' expectations and make promises to customers regarding what is to be delivered. Anyone or anything that communicates to the customer before service delivery can be viewed as part of this external marketing

FIGURE 11.1
The Service Marketing Triangle

Sources: Adapted from M. J. Bitner, "Building Service Relationships: It's All about Promises," *Journal of the Academy of Marketing Science* 23 (Fall 1995), pp. 246–251; P. T. Kotler and K. L. Keller, *Marketing Management,* 15th ed. (Upper Saddle River, NJ: Pearson Prentice Hall, 2016), p. 410.

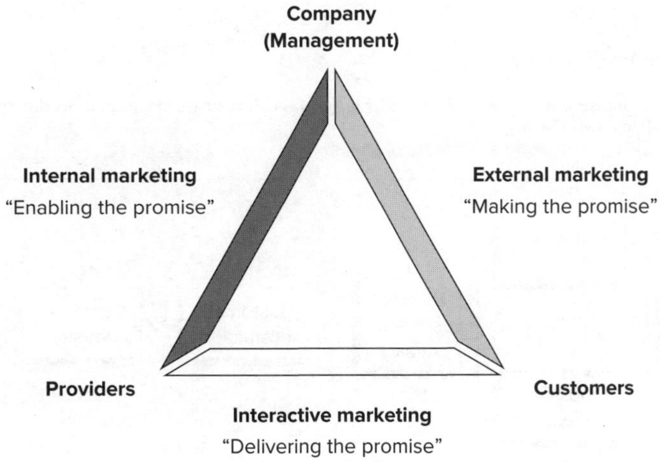

function. But external marketing is just the beginning for service marketers: promises made must be kept. On the bottom of the triangle is what has been termed *interactive marketing*. Here is where promises are kept or broken by the firm's employees, subcontractors, or agents. Those people representing the organization are critical at this juncture. If promises are not kept, customers become dissatisfied and eventually leave. The left side of the triangle suggests the critical role played by *internal marketing*, which includes the activities that allow providers to deliver on the service promise: recruiting, training, motivating, rewarding, and providing equipment and technology. Unless service employees are able and willing to deliver on the promises made, the firm will not be successful.

All three sides of the triangle are essential, and the sides of the triangle should be aligned. That is, what is promised through external marketing should be the same as what is delivered; and the enabling activities inside the organization should be aligned with what is expected of service providers. Strategies for aligning the triangle, particularly the strategies associated with internal marketing, are the subject of this chapter.

Employee Satisfaction Is Linked to Customer Satisfaction and Profits

Satisfied employees make for satisfied customers (and satisfied customers can, in turn, reinforce employees' sense of satisfaction in their jobs). Some researchers have suggested that, unless service employees are happy in their jobs, customer satisfaction will be difficult to achieve.[19]

Research on customers and employees in bank branches has shown that both a *climate for service* and a *climate for employee well-being* are highly correlated with overall customer perceptions of service quality.[20] That is, both service climate and human resource management experiences that *employees* have within their organizations can influence how *customers* experience the service. Similar research suggests that employees who feel they are treated fairly by their organizations will treat customers better, resulting in greater customer satisfaction.[21]

The underlying logic connecting employee satisfaction and loyalty to customer satisfaction and loyalty and ultimately profits is illustrated by the *service profit chain* shown in Figure 11.2.[22] In earlier chapters we focused on customer satisfaction and retention; here we focus on employee issues. The service profit chain suggests that there are critical linkages among internal service quality, employee satisfaction/

FIGURE 11.2 The Service Profit Chain

Source: Adapted from J. L. Heskett, T. O. Jones, G. W. Loveman, W. E. Sasser Jr., and L. A. Schlesinger, "Putting the Service-Profit Chain to Work," *Harvard Business Review* 72 (March–April 1994), pp. 164–174.

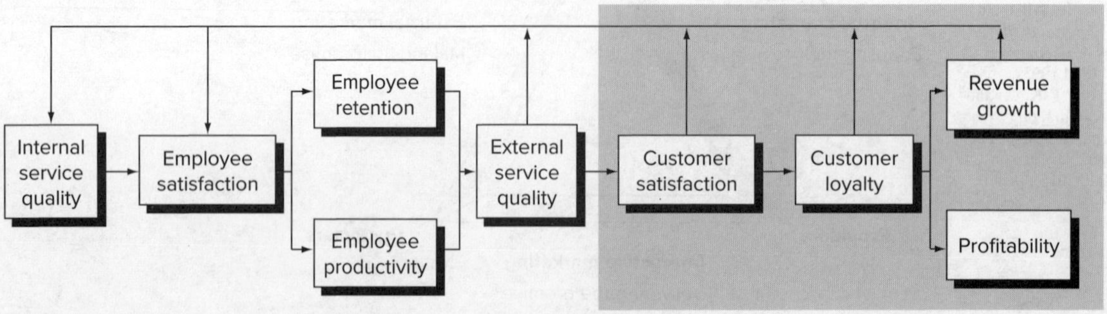

productivity, the value of services provided to the customer, and ultimately customer satisfaction, retention, and profits.

Service profit chain researchers are careful to point out that the model does not suggest causality. That is, employee satisfaction does not *cause* customer satisfaction; rather the two are interrelated and feed off each other.[23] The model does imply that companies that exhibit high levels of success within the elements of the model will be more successful and profitable than those that do not.

The Effect of Employee Behaviors on Service Quality Dimensions

Customers' perceptions of service quality are affected by the customer-oriented behaviors of employees.[24] In fact, all five dimensions of service quality (reliability, responsiveness, assurance, empathy, and tangibles) can be influenced directly by service employees.

Delivering the service as promised—*reliability*—is often completely within the control of frontline employees. Even in the case of services delivered primarily through technology (such as airline or hotel check-in kiosks, banking apps on smart phones, or self-checkout in retail stores), behind-the-scenes employees are critical for making sure all the systems are working properly. When services fail or errors are made, employees are essential for setting things right and using their judgment to determine the best course of action for service recovery.

Frontline employees directly influence customer perceptions of *responsiveness* through their personal willingness to help and their promptness in serving customers. Consider the range of responses you receive from different retail store clerks when you need help finding a particular item of clothing. One employee may ignore your presence, whereas another offers to help you search and calls other stores to locate the item. One may help you immediately and efficiently, whereas another may move slowly in accommodating even the simplest request.

The *assurance* dimension of service quality is highly dependent on employees' ability to communicate their credibility and to inspire the customer's trust and confidence in the firm. The reputation of the organization will help, but in the end, individual employees with whom the customer interacts confirm and build trust in the organization or detract from its reputation and ultimately destroy trust. For startup or relatively unknown service organizations, credibility, trust, and confidence will be tied completely to employee actions.

It is difficult to imagine how an organization would deliver "caring, individualized attention" to customers independent of its employees. *Empathy* implies that employees will pay attention, listen, adapt, and be flexible in delivering what individual customers need.[25] For example, research documents that when employees are customer oriented, have good rapport with customers, display emotional competence, and exhibit perceptive and attentive listening skills, customers will evaluate the service more highly and are more likely to return.[26] Employee appearance and dress are important aspects of the *tangibles* dimension of quality, along with many other factors that are independent of service employees (the service facility, decor, brochures, signage, and so on).

BOUNDARY-SPANNING ROLES

Our focus in this chapter is on frontline service employees who interact directly with customers, although much of what is described and recommended can be applied to internal service employees as well. Frontline service employees are referred to as *boundary spanners* because they operate at the organization's boundary. As indicated

FIGURE 11.3 The Critical Roles of Boundary Spanners

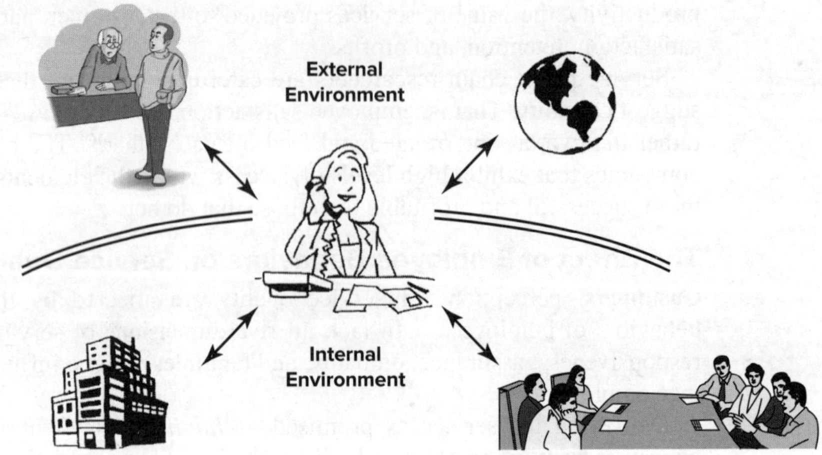

in Figure 11.3, boundary spanners provide a link between the external customer and environment and the internal operations of the organization. They serve a critical function in understanding, filtering, and interpreting information and resources to and from the organization and its external constituencies.

Who are these boundary spanners? What types of people and positions constitute critical boundary-spanning roles? Their skills and experience cover the full spectrum of jobs and careers. In industries such as fast food, hotel, telecommunication, and retail, boundary spanners are generally the least skilled, lowest-paid employees in the organization. They are order-takers, front-desk employees, telephone operators, store clerks, truck drivers, and delivery people. In other industries, boundary spanners are well-paid, highly educated professionals—for example, doctors, lawyers, accountants, consultants, architects, and teachers.

No matter what the level of skill or pay, boundary-spanning positions are often high-stress jobs. In addition to mental and physical skills, these positions require extraordinary levels of emotional labor, frequently demand an ability to handle interpersonal and interorganizational conflict, and they call on the employee to make real-time trade-offs between quality and productivity on the job. These stresses and trade-offs can result in failure to deliver services as specified, which widens the service performance gap.

Emotional Labor

The term *emotional labor* refers to the labor that goes beyond the physical or mental skills needed to deliver quality service.[27] In general, boundary-spanning service employees are expected to align their displayed emotions with organizationally desired emotions via their use of emotional labor.[28] Such labor includes delivering smiles, making eye contact, showing sincere interest, and engaging in friendly conversation with people who are essentially strangers and whom they may never see again. Friendliness, courtesy, empathy, and responsiveness directed toward customers all require huge amounts of emotional labor from the frontline employees who shoulder this responsibility for the organization. Emotional labor draws on people's feelings (often requiring them to suppress their true feelings) to be effective in their jobs. A frontline service employee who is having a bad day or is not feeling just right is still expected to put on the face of the organization when dealing with customers. One of the clearest examples of emotional labor is the story (probably apocryphal) of a flight attendant who was approached by a businessman, who said, "Let's have a smile." "Okay," she replied, "I'll tell you what, first you smile and then I'll smile, okay?" He smiled. "Good," she said, "now hold that for 15 hours," and then walked away.[29]

Many of the strategies we will discuss later in this chapter can help organizations and employees deal with the realities of emotional labor on the job. For the organization, such strategies include carefully selecting people who can handle emotional stress and display emotional competence, training them in needed skills (like listening and problem solving), and teaching or giving them coping abilities and strategies (via job rotation, scheduled breaks, teamwork, or other techniques).[30] Our Strategy Insight describes additional emotional labor strategies that service firms employ.

Sources of Conflict in Boundary Spanning Roles

Frontline employees often face interpersonal and interorganizational conflicts on the job. Their frustration and confusion can, if left unattended, lead to stress, job dissatisfaction, a diminished ability to serve customers, and burnout.[31] Because they represent the organization to the customer and often need to manage a number of customers simultaneously, frontline employees inevitably have to deal with conflicts, including person/role conflicts, organization/client conflicts, and interclient conflicts.[32]

Person/Role Conflict

In some situations, boundary spanners feel conflict between what they are asked to do and their own personalities, orientations, or values. In a society such as the United States, where equality and individualism are highly valued, service workers may feel role conflict when they are required to subordinate their feelings or beliefs, as when they are asked to live by the motto "The customer is always right—even when he is wrong." Sometimes there is a conflict between role requirements and the self-image or self-esteem of the employee. An Israeli service expert provides a classic example from that culture:

> In Israel, for instance, most buses are operated by one man, the driver, who is also responsible for selling tickets. No trays are installed in buses for the transferring of bus fare from passenger to driver, and the money is transferred directly. Bus drivers often complain about the humiliating experience of having to stretch out their hands like beggars in order to collect the fare. Another typical case in Israeli buses is when money changes hands and a coin falls down accidentally onto the bus floor. The question, who will bend down to lift the coin, the driver or the passenger, clearly reflects the driver's role conflict.[33]

Whoever stoops to pick up the coin is indicating subservient status. Person/role conflict also arises when employees are required to wear specific clothing or change some aspect of their appearance to conform to job requirements. A young lawyer, just out of school, may feel an internal conflict with his new role when his employer requires him to cut his hair and trade his casual clothes for a three-piece suit.

Organization/Client Conflict

A more common type of conflict for frontline service employees is the conflict between their two bosses, the organization and the individual customer. Service employees are typically rewarded for following certain standards, rules, and procedures. Ideally these rules and standards are customer based, as described in Chapter 9. When they are not, or when a customer makes excessive demands, the employee has to decide whether to follow the organization's rules or satisfy the customer's demands. To illustrate, management at an accounting firm may expect an employee to prepare tax returns quickly

Strategy Insight Strategies for Managing Emotional Labor

Service employees are often required to display (or, conversely, to withhold display of) a variety of emotions. Such employees are increasingly being required to invest personal identity and expression into their work in many situations. The following description suggests how the experience of the service employee, even in the most routine of occupations, is markedly different from that of the traditional manufacturing worker:

> The assembly-line worker could openly hate his job, despise his supervisor, and even dislike his coworkers, and while this might be an unpleasant state of affairs, if he [completes] his assigned tasks efficiently, his attitude [is] his own problem. For the service worker, inhabiting the job means, at the very least, pretending to like it, and, at most, actually bringing his whole self into the job, liking it, and genuinely caring about the people with whom he interacts.*

Emotional labor occurs more often when the job requires frequent contact and long durations of voice contact or face-to-face contact with customers. These employees often need emotional management to deal with such situations. Later in this chapter, we suggest strategies for organizations to create an environment that helps employees deal with the realities of emotional labor. Here, we present specific strategies some firms use to more directly support employee efforts to manage their emotions in the face of demanding, obnoxious, or unruly customers.

SCREENING FOR EMOTIONAL LABOR ABILITIES

Many firms look to hire employees who are well suited to meet the emotional labor requirements of the job. Dungarvin, an organization that provides a variety of services to people who have mental and physical disabilities, displays a realistic job preview on its website to indicate to prospective employees the emotional labor requirements. In doing so, Dungarvin's intent is to identify applicants who are comfortable with the emotional demands required of employees who must regularly interact with clients with special needs. Call centers also often provide job candidates with a realistic job preview, in part, to allow a prospective employee to gauge if he or she is well suited to exert the emotional labor required to interact with customers—often frustrated and unhappy ones—on a continual basis. Simulated customer contact exercises also allow the company to assess the level of friendliness and warmth prospective candidates naturally communicate. Such practices help in identifying employees whose values, background, personality, and emotional competence abilities match the job's emotional labor requirements.

TEACHING EMOTIONAL MANAGEMENT SKILLS AND APPROPRIATE BEHAVIORS

Most customer contact employees are taught that they need to be courteous to customers. However, customers have no obligation to return empathy or courtesy. In situations in which customers exercise the privilege of "the customer is always right," employees face challenges in suppressing their true feelings. Seldom do firms provide much training to assist employees in facing these challenges. Research has identified two forms of emotional labor: *surface acting,* in which employees pretend to feel emotions that are not really present and, in doing so, could involve both suppression of felt emotions and faking of unfelt emotions; and *deep acting,* in which employees attempt to experience the real feelings they are expected (or required) to express to the customer, including the active invocation of thoughts, images, and memories to induce the associated emotion. Retail store clerks and airline flight attendants are often encouraged to engage in deep-acting strategies such as imagining that the client is a friend or that the passenger is a frightened little child flying for the first time. Such strategies can also help employees avoid absorbing a customer's bad mood.

*Quoted from C. L. Macdonald and C. Sirianni, *Working in the Service Society.* (Philadelphia: Temple University Press, 1996), p. 4.

to maximize revenues during the short tax preparation season. However, the employee's other boss—the customer—may expect personalized attention and a significant amount of her time in preparing the return.[34] The organization/client conflict is greatest when the employee believes the organization is wrong in its policies and must decide whether to accommodate the client and risk losing a job or to follow the policies. These conflicts are especially severe when service employees depend directly on the customer for income. For example, employees who depend on tips or commissions

CAREFULLY FASHIONING THE PHYSICAL WORK ENVIRONMENT

As discussed in Chapter 10, the environment in which the service is delivered affects employee behaviors and emotions. MedAire, a company that provides phone consultation to airlines when medical emergencies arise on flights, regularly has employees in the midst of life-threatening situations. To reduce the stress that MedAire employees face on a daily basis, the company designed its Tempe, Arizona, office with an open floor plan so that all employees are able to look through windows to see trees, grass, and cars driving by. Taking this idea one step further, JetBlue Airways allows its reservation agents to work from home rather than requiring them to sit all day in an office call center.

ALLOWING EMPLOYEES TO VENT

Employees who must exert emotional labor often need to have an outlet to let off steam. Allowing employees to vent lets them get rid of their frustrations. If such venting is done in a group setting, it provides emotional support and encouragement, allows employees to see that others are experiencing the same problems, and delivers a message to employees that the company is aware of and acknowledges the emotional contribution they make. Ritz-Carlton, Walmart, and other companies regularly set aside time for such venting. In addition to the cathartic benefit this experience can provide, other employees may reveal coping strategies that they have found useful.

GIVING EMPLOYEES A BREAK

In situations in which employees have extended voice or face-to-face contact with customers, a particularly helpful strategy is to allow them a break to regroup. Many companies with toll-free call centers rotate employees into different positions throughout the day so that they do not spend the entire time on the telephone with customers. Customer contact employees can be reenergized and refreshed after spending a little time away from demanding or difficult situations, even if they take only a few minutes to finish paperwork or complete some other job responsibility. One call center in Australia has a pool table near the employee work area and plays movies while employees work at their desk to reduce the stress of interacting with customers.

HANDING OFF DEMANDING CUSTOMERS TO MANAGERS

Some customers may be too much for an employee to handle. In such situations, to alleviate pressure on the customer contact employee, firms may shift responsibility for the interaction to managers. Wing Zone, a restaurant chain specializing in chicken wings, understands the stress that angry customers can cause employees, many of whom are college students. A majority of the company's orders are taken over the phone, and employees—particularly those with little experience—are trained to simply hand off demanding customers to the nearest manager. And a manager who is unsuccessful in handling the situation is encouraged to direct such customers to the corporate office via a toll-free number.

Sources: A. A. Grandey and G. M. Sayre, "Emotional Labor: Regulating Emotions for a Wage," *Current Directions in Psychological Science* 28 (April 2019), pp. 131–137; C. Delcourt, D. D. Gremler, F. De Zanet, and A. C. R. van Riel, "An Analysis of the Interaction Effect between Employee Technical and Emotional Competencies in Emotionally Charged Service Encounters," *Journal of Service Management* 28 (March 2017), pp. 85–106; A. Hochschild, *The Managed Heart: Commercialization of Human Feeling* (Berkeley: University of California Press, 1983); B. F. Ashforth and R. H. Humphrey, "Emotional Labor in Service Roles: The Influence of Identity," *Academy of Management Review* 18 (1993), pp. 88–115; www.dungarvin.com, accessed July 20, 2016; S. D. Pugh, "Service with a Smile: Emotional Contagion in the Service Encounter," *Academy of Management Journal* 44 (2001), pp. 1018–1027; and T. Hennig-Thurau, M. Groth, M. Paul, and D. D. Gremler, "Are All Smiles Created Equal? How Employee-Customer Emotional Contagion and Emotional Labor Impact Service Relationships," *Journal of Marketing* 70 (July 2006), pp. 58–73.

are likely to face greater levels of organization/client conflict because they have even greater incentives to identify with the customer.

Interclient Conflict

Sometimes conflict occurs for boundary spanners when incompatible expectations and requirements arise from two or more customers. This situation occurs most often when an employee is serving customers in turn (a bank teller, a doctor) or is serving many customers simultaneously (teachers, entertainers). When serving customers in turn, the provider may satisfy one customer by spending additional time, customizing the service, and being flexible in meeting the customer's needs. Meanwhile, waiting customers may become dissatisfied because their needs are not being met in a timely way. Beyond the timing issue, different clients may prefer different modes of service delivery; one client may prefer personal recognition and a degree of familiarity while another client may be "all business" and prefer little interpersonal interaction.

When serving many customers at the same time, employees often find it difficult or impossible to serve the full range of needs of a group of heterogeneous customers. This type of conflict is readily apparent in any college classroom in which the instructor must meet a multitude of student expectations and different preferences for formats and style. Similarly, interclient conflict is also apparent in an entertainment venue or any type of group training service.

Quality/Productivity Trade-Offs

Frontline employees should be both effective and efficient: they are expected to deliver satisfying service to customers and at the same time to be cost-effective and productive in what they do. A physician in an HMO, for example, is expected to deliver caring, quality, individualized service to her patients but at the same time to serve a certain number of patients within a specified time frame. A checker at a grocery store might be expected to engage customers in a brief chat and to be polite and courteous, yet also process the groceries accurately and move people through the line quickly.[35] These essential trade-offs between quality and quantity and between effectiveness and efficiency place real-time demands and pressures on service employees. Technology is being used to an ever-greater degree to balance the quality/quantity trade-off to increase the productivity of service workers and free them to provide higher-quality service for the customer (see the Technology Spotlight).

A vivid example of the quality/productivity trade-off occurred with Verizon employees in Florida. They were frustrated by the firm's requirement that a service call to a customer not go beyond a certain amount of time, regardless of whether the issue was resolved. That is, employees felt the firm's customer service priorities revolved around efficiencies, not solving a customer's problems. They eventually went on strike to get management to reconsider their service processes, and customers subsequently communicated their appreciation.[36]

STRATEGIES FOR DELIVERING SERVICE QUALITY THROUGH PEOPLE

A complex combination of strategies is needed to ensure that employees are willing and able to deliver quality services and that they stay motivated to perform in customer-oriented, service-minded ways. These strategies for enabling service promises are often referred to as *internal marketing,* as shown on the left side of Figure 11.1.[37] By approaching human resource decisions and strategies with the primary goal to motivate and enable employees to deliver customer-oriented promises successfully, an organization will move toward delivering service quality through its people. The strategies presented here are organized around four basic themes. To build a customer-oriented, service-minded workforce, an organization must (1) hire the right people, (2) develop people to deliver service quality, (3) provide the needed support systems, and (4) retain the best people. Within each of these basic strategies are a number of specific substrategies for accomplishing the goal, as shown in Figure 11.4.

FIGURE 11.4
Human Resource Strategies for Delivering Service Quality through People

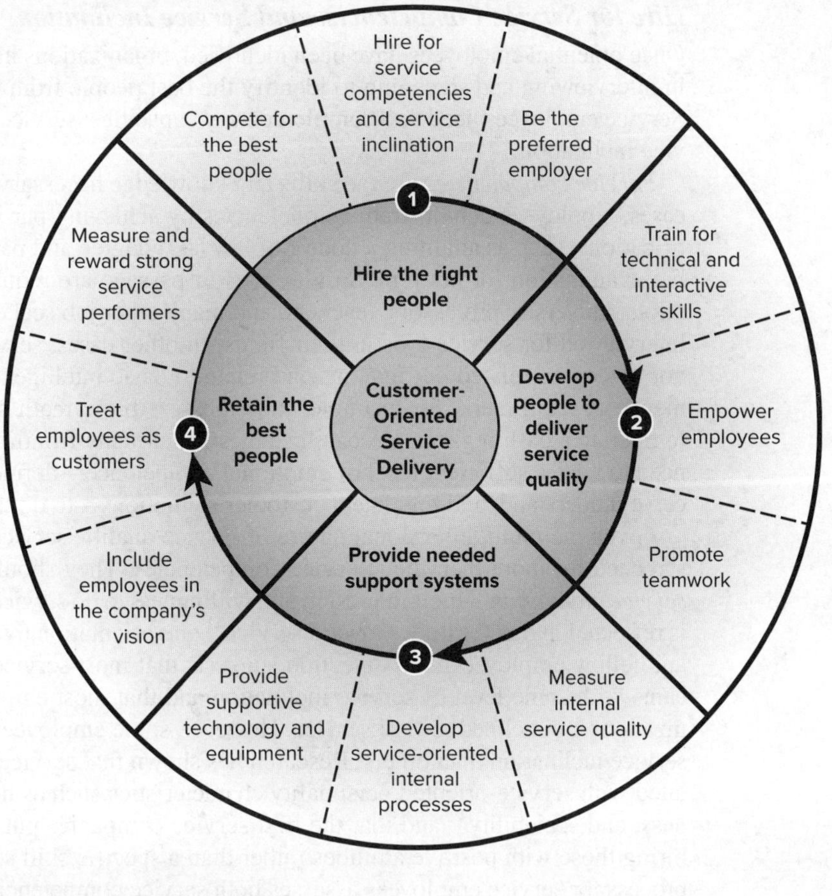

(1) Hire the Right People

To effectively deliver service quality, considerable attention should be focused on recruiting and hiring service personnel. Such attention is contrary to traditional practices in many service industries, where service personnel are the lowest on the corporate ladder and work for minimum wage. At the other end of the spectrum, in professional services, the most important recruiting criteria are typically technical training, certifications, and expertise. However, successful service organizations generally look beyond the technical qualifications of applicants to assess their customer and service orientation as well. Figure 11.4 shows a number of ways to go about hiring the right people.

Compete for the Best People

To get the best people, an organization needs to identify them and compete with other organizations to hire them; that is, organizations should deliberately be "competing for talent market share."[38] Consequently, firms should act as marketers in their pursuit of the best employees, just as they use their marketing expertise to compete for customers. Firms that think of recruiting as a marketing activity will address issues of market (employee) segmentation, product (job) design, and promotion of job availability in ways that attract potentially long-term employees. Intuit, Harrah's, Yahoo!, Marriott, and other firms now use "vice president of talent acquisition" as the title of the head recruiting person. Doing so recognizes the importance of the function and helps elevate the role to the strategic importance it deserves.

Hire for Service Competencies and Service Inclination

Once potential employees have been identified, organizations need to be conscientious in interviewing and screening to identify the best people from the pool of candidates. Service employees need two complementary capacities: service competencies and service inclination.[39]

Service competencies are the skills and knowledge necessary to do the job. In many cases, employees demonstrate competencies by achieving particular degrees and certifications, such as attaining a doctor of law (JD) degree and passing the relevant state bar examination for lawyers. Similar rites of passage are required of doctors, airline pilots, university professors, teachers, and many other job seekers before they are ever interviewed for service jobs in their fields. In other cases, service competencies may not be degree-related but may instead relate to basic intelligence or physical requirements. A retail clerk, for example, must possess basic math skills and the potential to operate a cash register. Research suggests that many frontline employees may also need to have a sufficient level of emotional competence—defined as the ability to perceive, understand, and regulate a customer's emotions—to do their jobs well.[40]

Given the multidimensional nature of service quality, service employees should be screened for more than their service competencies. They should also be screened for *service inclination*—their interest in and willingness to do service-related work—which is reflected in their attitudes toward service[41] and orientation toward serving customers and fellow employees. Self-selection suggests that most service jobs will draw applicants with some level of service inclination and that most employees in service organizations are inclined toward service. However, some employees clearly have a greater service inclination than others. Research has shown that service effectiveness is correlated with service-oriented personality characteristics such as helpfulness, thoughtfulness, and sociability[42] and that the best service companies put a greater emphasis on hiring those with positive attitudes rather than a specific skill set.[43] An ideal selection process for service employees assesses both service competencies and service inclination, resulting in employee hires who are high on both dimensions.

In addition to traditional employment interviews, many firms use innovative approaches (e.g., increasingly supported by artificial intelligence) to assessing service inclination and other personal characteristics that fit the organization's needs.[44] Southwest Airlines looks for people who are compassionate and who have common sense, a sense of humor, a "can do" attitude, and an egalitarian sense of themselves (they think in terms of "we" rather than "me"). One way the company assesses these service inclinations is by interviewing potential flight attendants in groups to see how they interact with each other. Pilots are also interviewed in groups to assess their teamwork skills, a critical factor above and beyond the essential technical skills they are required to possess.[45]

Be the Preferred Employer

One way to attract the best people is to be known as the preferred employer in a particular industry or location. UPS regularly conducts a survey among its employees to create an "Employer of Choice Index" and sets annual goals to remain a preferred employer.[46] Google also enjoys a reputation as a preferred employer. Exhibit 11.1 provides some insight into why Google often has been chosen as one of the "Best Companies to Work For."

Other strategies that support a goal of being the preferred employer include extensive training, career and advancement opportunities, excellent internal support, attractive incentives, and quality goods and services with which employees are proud to be associated. SAS Institute, a regular in *Fortune*'s annual "Best Companies to Work For" list, has long been a preferred employer in the statistical software industry. Employees

Exhibit 11.1 Google Quickly Becomes a Preferred Employer in Its Industry

View Pictures/Universal Images Group/Getty Images

Google employees collaborating in the company's unique workspace.

In 1996 Google's founders, Larry Page and Sergey Brin, developed a new approach to online search that took root in a Stanford University dorm room and quickly spread to information seekers around the globe. They continued to refine their search approaches and in 1998 formed Google—the world's largest search engine—an easy-to-use, free service that usually returns results in a fraction of a second.

In its short history Google has become a preferred employer and has been ranked number 1 in *Fortune*'s list of the 100 best companies to work for seven times between 2007 and 2016. One study reported that one in four young professionals wants to work at Google. Google has used a variety of approaches to become an employer of choice for over 130,000 employees worldwide, including:

- *The Googleplex*—The Google world headquarters building is located in Mountain View, California, and helps to attract and retain "Googlers" (employees). Some of the essential elements of the facility, which are presented on its company website, include a lobby with piano, lava lamps, and live projection of current search queries from around the world. In the hallways there are bicycles, large rubber exercise balls are on the floors, and press clippings from around the world are posted on bulletin boards everywhere. A three-dimensional rotating image of the world toggles between displaying points of light representing real-time searches rising from the surface of the globe toward space, color-coded by language and viewing traffic patterns for the entire Internet.
- *Recreation facilities*—Google provides a workout room with weights and rowing machines, locker rooms, washers and dryers, a massage room, assorted video games, Foosball, a baby grand piano, a pool table, and Ping-Pong.
- *Dining facilities*—Google runs more than 20 free gourmet cafeterias at its headquarters and offers free meals to all its employees, from vegan truffles to full-blown Indian feasts. Snack rooms contain bins packed with various cereals, gummy treats, M&Ms, toffee, licorice, cashew nuts, yogurt, carrots, fresh fruit, and other snacks, as well as dozens of different drinks, including fresh juice, soda, and make-your-own cappuccino.
- *Services for employees*—A wide variety of services are provided to Googlers. For example, on-site car washes and oil changes are among the numerous perks Google offers to all its workers. Haircuts are provided on-site. Employees can attend subsidized exercise classes; get a massage; study Mandarin, Japanese, Spanish, or French; and ask a personal concierge to arrange dinner reservations. Other services available to employees include child care, on-site notaries, and five on-site doctors available for employee checkups, all free of charge. And, when traveling to and from the office, Google operates free, Wi-Fi–enabled shuttle buses from five Bay Area locations for its employees.
- *Other benefits*—Several other benefits are also provided to Google employees. Lactation rooms, complete with breast pumps (so that nursing mothers do not have to haul equipment to work), are provided. Googlers are free to bring their pets to work. And, Google's 80/20 rule allows employees to dedicate 80 percent of time to their primary job and 20 percent working on passion projects that they believe will help the company—Gmail, Google News, and the Google Finance site all resulted from such activity.

It is no surprise that Google receives 3 million résumés per year. And if these benefits are not enough to encourage employees to talk up the company, Google provides up to a $4,000 bonus for each person hired as a result of a referral.

Sources: Inc.com, "Google Gets 3 Million Resumes a Year," https://www.inc.com/betsy-mikel/google-gets-3-million-resumes-a-year-how-to-make-yours-stand-out-according-to-a-google-recruiter.html; "Benefits at Google," https://www.levels.fyi/company/Google/benefits/; Forbes, World's Best Employers 2021, https://www.forbes.com/lists/worlds-best-employers/#174ef1481e0c, accessed January 16, 2022; A. Lashinsky, "Search and Enjoy," *Fortune*, January 29, 2007, pp. 70–82; J. Light, "Google Is No. 1 on List of Desired Employers," *The Wall Street Journal*, March 21, 2011, p. B8; J. D'Onfro, "An Insider Look at Google's Best Employee Perks," *Inc.*, September 21, 2015, www.inc.com/business-insider/best-google-benefits.html; and www.google.com, accessed July 21, 2016.

who work for SAS are, for the most part, professional or technical and well paid. A quote from the company's website captures SAS's philosophy about its people: "if you treat employees as if they make a difference to the company, they will make a difference to the company." The company invests heavily in its people: every employee has a private office, a 35-hour schedule is promoted, flexible hours are available, the company provides top-quality day care centers with very reasonable prices on-site, on-site health care, and a free 66,000-square-foot fitness center. For these reasons, the best performers at SAS seldom leave to work for competitors.[47]

In a different industry, dominated by lower-paid workers, Marriott International has a stated company goal of being the "preferred employer" in its industry. Marriott's philosophy concerning its employees, which sounds very similar to that of SAS, has been stated by Bill Marriott: "if the employees are well taken care of, they'll take care of the customer and the customer will come back . . . that's basically the core value of the company."[48] Marriott uses flexible workplace options (including flex time, telework, compressed work weeks, shift swapping, part-time work, and job sharing), tuition reimbursement, child and elder care discounts, job and life skills training, and companywide health and wellness programs to be the preferred employer in the highly competitive hospitality industry. The company even offers global language learning programs—with 30 languages to choose from. Marriott International, like Google and SAS, is consistently rated among *Fortune*'s list of the top 100 companies to work for.

(2) Develop People to Deliver Service Quality

To grow and maintain a workforce that is customer oriented and focused on delivering quality, an organization must develop its employees to deliver service quality. That is, once it has hired the right employees, the organization must train and work with these individuals to ensure service performance.

Train for Technical and Interactive Skills

To provide quality service, employees need ongoing training in technical and interactive skills. Examples of *technical skills* are working with accounting systems in hotels, cash machine procedures in a retail store, underwriting procedures in an insurance company, and any operational rules the company has for running its business. Most service organizations are quite conscious of and relatively effective at training employees in technical skills. These skills may be taught through formal education, as is the case at McDonald's Hamburger University, which trains McDonald's managers from all over the world. Additionally, technical skills are often taught through on-the-job training, as when call center service trainees listen in on the conversations of experienced employees. Companies frequently use information technology to train employees in the technical skills and knowledge needed on the job.

Service employees also need training in *interactive skills* that allow them to provide courteous, caring, responsive, and empathetic service. Research suggests firms can teach employees how to develop rapport with customers—one type of interactive skill—by teaching them how to engage in pleasant conversation, ask questions, or use humor as they interact with customers.[49] Employees can be taught conversation prompts to help them identify commonalities with their customers. Some companies even teach customer-contact employees improvisation to improve their communication and listening skills, read customers' body language, and establish an immediate rapport with them.[50] Outback Steakhouse coaches waiters and waitresses to squat next to or even sit at a customer's table and spend a couple of minutes interacting; such action allows them to establish better eye contact with customers and provides opportunities for engaging interactions.

Successful companies invest heavily in training and make sure that the training fits their business goals and strategies. For example, at the Ritz-Carlton, all employees go through extensive initial training and are given pocket-sized, laminated credo cards to carry in their wallets. In addition to the credo, the card specifies the three steps of service and Ritz-Carlton's well-known motto "We Are Ladies and Gentlemen Serving Ladies and Gentlemen."

Empower Employees

Many organizations have discovered that, to be truly responsive to customer needs, frontline providers need to be empowered to accommodate customer requests and to recover on the spot when things go wrong. *Empowerment* means giving employees the authority, skills, tools, and desire to determine how to best serve the customer. Although the key to empowerment is giving employees authority to make decisions on the customer's behalf, authority alone is not enough. Employees need the knowledge and tools to be able to make these decisions, and they need incentives that encourage them to make the right ones. Organizations do not succeed in empowering their employees if they simply tell them, "You now have the authority to do whatever it takes to satisfy the customer." First, employees often do not believe this statement, particularly if the organization has functioned hierarchically or bureaucratically in the past. Second, employees often do not know what it means to "do whatever it takes" if they have not received training, guidelines, and the tools needed to make such decisions. Third, not all employees have a desire to be empowered by the firm.[51]

Research suggests that some of the benefits of empowering frontline service workers include a reduction in job-related stress, improved job satisfaction, greater adaptability, more creative ideas, and better outcomes for customers.[52] But such success does not come easily. In fact, some experts have concluded that few organizations have truly taken advantage of, or properly implemented, successful empowerment strategies.[53] Nor is empowerment the answer for all organizations. Exhibit 11.2 enumerates both the costs and the benefits of empowerment.

Promote Teamwork

The nature of many service jobs suggests that customer satisfaction will be enhanced when employees work as teams. Because service jobs are frequently frustrating, demanding, and challenging, a teamwork environment will help alleviate some of the stresses and strains. Employees who feel supported and feel that they have a team backing them up will be better able to maintain their enthusiasm and provide quality service.[54] Such teamwork is the driving force behind the service philosophy at the Mayo Clinic. One of Mayo's core principles encourages all of those in the organization to practice medicine as "an integrated team of compassionate, multi-disciplinary physicians, scientists and allied health professionals who are focused on the needs of patients."[55] By promoting teamwork, an organization can enhance the employees' *abilities* to deliver excellent service, while the camaraderie and support enhance their *inclination* to be excellent service providers.

One way of promoting teamwork is to encourage the attitude that "everyone has a customer." That is, even when employees are not directly responsible for or do not directly interact with the final customer, they need to know whom they serve directly and how the role they play in the total service picture is essential to the final delivery of quality service. If each employee can see how he or she is somehow integral in delivering quality to the final customer and if each employee knows whom to support to make

Exhibit 11.2 Potential Benefits and Costs of Empowerment

BENEFITS

- *Quicker responses to customer needs during service delivery.* Employees who are allowed to make decisions on behalf of the customer can make decisions more quickly, bypassing what in the past might have meant a long chain of command or at least a discussion with an immediate supervisor.
- *Quicker responses to dissatisfied customers during service recovery.* When failures occur in the delivery system, customers hope for an immediate recovery effort on the part of the organization. Empowered employees can recover on the spot, and a dissatisfied customer can be turned into a satisfied, even loyal one.
- *Employees feel better about their jobs, themselves*, and their supervisor. Giving employees control and authority to make decisions makes them feel responsible and gives them ownership of the customer's satisfaction. Decades of job design research suggest that, when employees have a sense of control and of doing meaningful work, they are more satisfied. Moreover, empowerment also has a positive effect on employee attitude toward their supervisor. The results are lower turnover and less absenteeism.
- *Employees will interact with customers with more warmth and enthusiasm* and innovation. Employees feel better about themselves and their work, and these attitudes will spill over into their feelings about customers and will be reflected in their interactions.
- *Empowered employees are a great source of service ideas and innovation.* When employees are empowered, they feel responsible for the service outcome and they will be excellent sources of ideas about new services or how to improve current offerings.
- *Great word-of-mouth advertising from customers.* Empowered employees do special and unique things that customers will remember and tell their friends, family, and associates about.

COSTS

- *A potentially greater dollar investment in selection and training.* To find employees who will work well in an empowered environment requires creative, potentially more costly selection procedures. Training will also be more expensive in general because employees need more knowledge about the company, its products, and how to work in flexible ways with customers.
- *Higher labor costs.* The organization may not be able to use as many part-time or seasonal employees, and it may need to pay more for asking employees to assume responsibility.
- *Potentially slower or inconsistent service delivery.* If empowered employees spend more time with all, or even some, customers, then service overall may take longer and may annoy customers who are waiting. Empowerment also means that customers will get what they need or request. When decisions regarding customer satisfaction are left to the discretion of employees, there may be inconsistency in the level of service delivered.
- *May violate customers' perceptions of fair play.* Customers may perceive that sticking to procedures with every customer is fair. Thus, if they see that customers are receiving different levels of service or that employees are cutting special deals with some customers, they may believe that the organization is not fair.
- *Employees may "give away the store" or make bad decisions.* Many people fear that empowered employees will make costly decisions that the organization cannot afford. Although this situation can happen, good training and appropriate guidelines will help.

Source: Adapted from "The Empowerment of Service Workers: What, Why, How, and When," by D. E. Bowen and E. E. Lawler, *Sloan Management Review* 33 (Spring 1992), pp. 31–39; M. Kim, T. A. Beehr, and M. S. Prewett, "Employee Responses to Empowering Leadership: A Meta-analysis," *Journal of Leadership & Organizational Studies* 25 (August 2018), pp. 257–276.

service quality a reality, teamwork will be enhanced. Service blueprints, described in Chapter 8, can serve as useful tools to illustrate for employees their integral roles in delivering service quality to the ultimate customer.

Team goals and rewards also promote teamwork. For example, Harrah's Entertainment is one company that provides incentives and compensation focused on teamwork. One of the casino hotel company's incentive programs was weighted toward team results and a relatively small percentage of compensation (often less than 40 percent) was based on individual goals. Everyone in the organization, from meeting planners to blackjack dealers, was rewarded based on customer service scores. When a firm rewards teams of individuals rather than basing all rewards on individual achievements and performance, team efforts and team spirit are encouraged.

(3) Provide Needed Support Systems

To be efficient and effective in their jobs, service workers require internal support systems that are aligned with their need to be customer focused. This point cannot be overemphasized. In fact, without customer-focused internal support and customer-oriented systems, it is nearly impossible for employees to deliver quality service, no matter how much they want to. For example, a bank teller who is rewarded for customer satisfaction as well as for accuracy in bank transactions needs easy access to up-to-date customer records, a well-staffed branch (so that he or she is not constantly facing a long line of impatient customers), and supportive customer-oriented supervisors and back-office staff. For example, in examining customer service outcomes in Australian call centers, researchers found that internal support from supervisors, teammates, and other departments as well as evaluations of technology used on the job were all strongly related to employee satisfaction and ability to serve customers.[56] The following sections suggest strategies for ensuring customer-oriented internal support.

Measure Internal Service Quality

One way to encourage supportive internal service relationships is to measure and reward internal service. By first acknowledging that everyone in the organization has a customer and then measuring customer perceptions of internal service quality, an organization can begin to develop a strong internal quality culture.[57] In its quest to provide the best possible service to patients, the Mayo Clinic formally measures internal service quality between departments regularly. An internal customer service audit is one tool that can be used to implement a culture of internal service quality. Through the audit, internal organizations identify their customers, determine their needs, measure how well they are doing, and make improvements. The process parallels market research practices used for external customers.

One risk of measuring and focusing on internal service quality and internal customers is that employees can sometimes get so wrapped up in meeting the needs of internal customers that they forget they are in business to serve the ultimate, external customers.[58] In measuring internal service quality, therefore, it is important to constantly draw the linkages between what is being delivered internally and how it supports the delivery of the final service to customers (consistent with insights from the "service profit chain" discussed earlier). Service blueprinting, introduced in Chapter 8, can help illustrate these critical linkages.

Develop Service-Oriented Internal Processes

To best support service personnel in their delivery of quality service on the front line, an organization's internal processes should be designed with customer value and customer satisfaction in mind. In other words, internal procedures must support quality service performance. In many companies, internal processes are driven by bureaucratic rules, tradition, cost efficiencies, or the needs of employees. Providing service- and customer-oriented internal processes can therefore imply a need for total redesign of systems. This kind of redesign of systems and processes is known as "process reengineering." Although developing service-oriented internal processes through reengineering sounds sensible, it is probably one of the most difficult strategies to implement, especially in organizations steeped in tradition.

Provide Supportive Technology and Equipment

When employees do not have the right equipment or their equipment fails them, they can be easily frustrated in their desire to deliver quality service. To do their jobs

Technology Spotlight How Technology Is Helping Employees Serve Customers More Effectively and Efficiently

OPTIMIZATION TECHNOLOGY HELPS UPS DRIVERS' RELIABILITY EFFORTS

UPS delivers more than 21 million packages every day. Historically, UPS drivers worked off maps, 3 × 5 note cards, and their own memory to figure out the best way to navigate their routes. However, to more efficiently determine the best routes, UPS implemented a route optimization system that leverages Artificial Intelligence and Machine Learning; the system dynamically maps out the most efficient routes for the majority of its more than 100,000 drivers. Based on years of data of GPS tracking of UPS vehicles, the system learned that left turns are suboptimal (because left turns mean idling, which wastes time, and left turns also mean going against traffic, which is a safety risk as it increases exposure to oncoming cars). Therefore, one of the most important goals of the route planning software is to avoid left turns as much as possible to save fuel, time, and money. Based on this approach, estimates are that UPS saved up to 10 million gallons of gas, decreased its carbon emissions by 100,000 metric tons, and saved $300 to $400 million. It also reduced a day or more in transit time in nearly 3 million zip code pairings. UPS's technology allowed it to capture institutional knowledge about its customers. Before, when employees retired or quit, the knowledge of package loading techniques or route tips they had accumulated over the years usually went with them. This knowledge was captured in a centralized system that shortened the training time for new drivers, lessening the chances of a lapse in customer service. This technology enabled UPS to run its routes more efficiently, resulting in quicker and more reliable deliveries for its customers.

BLACKBOARD ASSISTS UNIVERSITY INSTRUCTORS

Universities both within and outside the United States use the Internet and other technologies to create a networked learning environment on their campuses. One tool universities use, called Blackboard, provides an infrastructure that increases instructor effectiveness and efficiency. To illustrate, Blackboard helps instructors organize nearly all teaching-related materials. Among the course management capabilities are electronic storage and controlled access of materials (readings, syllabi, assignments, discussion questions), management of class discussion boards, collection of student assignments, administration of online quizzes and exams, administration of group projects, provision of an online gradebook, and many other capabilities. In effect, most course administration tasks required of instructors can be handled by Blackboard. Students also benefit from having one source for accessing course materials, receiving updated course information, and submitting course assignments—without having to bother instructors with such administrative issues.

Blackboard provides instructors with the ability to manage many sections of a course. Instead of having to create material for each section, instructors can create a learning object (e.g., a handout or reading supplement), store it once, and link it to all course sections. Thus, Blackboard makes more effective usage of the instructor's time—providing the instructor with more time to be accessible to students outside of the classroom. Blackboard also provides instructors with an organized way to track and evaluate student learning. For example, Blackboard's e-portfolio option provides an online repository for storing student work—making it easy for both faculty *and* students to assess a student's progress in a given course or program of study. And, in response to the desires and expectations of today's college students, Blackboard provides smart phone apps that allow them to check grades, view announcements, post to blogs,

effectively and efficiently, service employees need the right equipment and technology. Our Technology Spotlight above highlights the role of technology in providing support for employees.

Having the right technology and equipment can extend into strategies regarding workplace and workstation design. For example, Zappos provides its customer service representatives with computer systems that provide comprehensive information concerning product inventory in their warehouses—allowing them to provide customers with up-to-date information and options. Hallways in the company's facilities are covered with murals and cartoons, rooms are filled with props, and workspaces are filled and access course content whenever and wherever they want.

MAYO CLINIC USES TECHNOLOGY TO REDUCE INFORMATION OVERLOAD OF CLINICIANS

Mayo Clinic is one of the most powerful service brands in the world and is arguably the leading health care brand in the United States. Although there are many reasons for this stellar brand reputation (as noted in other places in this text), technology plays a key role in Mayo Clinic's ability to deliver high-quality care for patients with serious medical needs.

Health care professionals increasingly rely on electronic health records (EHRs) to understand a patient's profile based on numerous tests, observations, treatments, and diagnostic codes. One of the biggest challenges is information overload of clinicians due to the massive amount of information EHRs often include. (EHRs can contain thousands of data points per patient.) Information overload is especially problematic in complex and fast-paced medical settings (e.g., intensive care units [ICUs]), because even small errors can have serious consequences. To reduce information overload, Mayo Clinic developed a system called "Ambient Warning and Response Evaluation (AWARE)," which is a data-driven decision-making tool that improves the cognitive performance, efficiency, and reliability of human decision makers.

A multidisciplinary research team at Mayo Clinic worked for years on this project. In doing so, the team completed 1,500 interviews with clinicians to better understand which information is most (and least) relevant for them at the time of caregiving. One major insight was that "out of tens of thousands of pieces of data" included in EHRs, only about 60 pieces of patient information are crucial for effective care. Based on these and other findings, the team designed AWARE to use over 1,200 algorithms that continuously (re)organize data around clinical concepts needed for timely and accurate decision making. These algorithms allow AWARE to consider clinicians' goals, work environments, strengths, and performance constraints to filter out irrelevant data and to deliver (only) the most relevant, context-specific information to clinicians in real time and in an easy-to-digest format. For example, AWARE automatically prioritizes and color-codes data to indicate severity and urgency of specific corrective interventions; this approach allows medical staff to provide more effective and efficient care.

Mayo Clinic and its employees received multiple benefits from AWARE. For example, the system saved physicians an average of three to five minutes per patient per day on chart review. With an average ICU workload of 15 patients per day per physician, these time savings resulted in one hour of additional time physicians could devote to patients. AWARE also helped to improve patient outcomes (e.g., the length of hospital stays decreased by 37 percent) and reduce health care costs (e.g., total charges per hospital stay decreased by 30 percent, which is more than $40,000 per hospital admission). These insights suggest that advanced human-technology collaboration can help solve some of the most pressing challenges in health care services.

Sources: "How UPS Route Optimization Software (ORION) Helps Drivers Make On-Time Deliveries," https://blog.route4me.com/ups-route-optimization-software-orion/, accessed January 16, 2022; 2020 UPS Annual Report; L. L. Berry and K. D. Seltman, "Building a Strong Services Brand: Lessons from Mayo Clinic," V. Herasevich, B. Pickering, O. Gajic, "How Mayo Clinic Is Combating Information Overload in Critical Care Units," *Harvard Business Review*, March 2018, https://hbr.org/2018/03/how-mayo-clinic-is-combating-information-overload-in-critical-care-units; accessed, January 16, 2022.

with personalized clutter—all designed to create an environment where employees feel like part of a team and are comfortable serving customers. In fact, the atmosphere that Zappos has created in the work environment has become so well known that tours through the cubicles at company headquarters are given almost daily to outsiders.

(4) Retain the Best People

An organization that hires the right people, trains and develops them to deliver service quality, and provides the needed support must also work to retain them. Employee turnover, especially when the best service employees are the ones leaving, can be very detrimental to customer satisfaction, employee morale, and overall service quality. And, just as they do with customers, some firms spend a lot of time attracting employees but then take them for granted (or even worse), causing these good employees to search for job alternatives. This shortcoming may have contributed, at least in part, to the "Great Resignation" related to the COVID-19 pandemic (see Exhibit 11.3). Although all the strategies depicted earlier in Figure 11.4 will support the retention of the best employees, here we will focus on some strategies that are particularly aimed at this goal.

Include Employees in the Company's Vision

For employees to remain motivated and interested in sticking with the organization and supporting its goals, they need to share an understanding of the organization's vision. People who deliver service day in and day out need to understand how their work fits into the big picture of the organization and its goals. They will be motivated to some extent by their paychecks and other benefits, but the best employees will be attracted away to other opportunities if they are not committed to the vision of the organization. And they cannot be committed to the vision if that vision is kept secret from them. Therefore, the vision needs to be communicated to employees frequently and by top managers, often by the CEO.[59]

For example, Walt Disney emphasized how crucial its cast members at Disneyland are to deliver outstanding service to every guest when he once stated, "You can dream, create, design, and build the most wonderful place in the world . . . but it requires people to make the dream a reality." To make this happen, Disney ensures that all employees understand how each individual fits into the "big picture" of the organization. Therefore, among other best practices, the company provides highly intentional training for all incoming cast members. The first class each new employee takes on their first day of training (and regardless of their role in the organization), is called "Traditions." This class, rather than focusing on technical skills, educates new cast members about the big picture and common purpose at Disney, which is *"to create happiness."* This vision is grounded in the idea that employers "must give people purpose, not just rules." To illustrate: since the opening of Disneyland in 1955, Disney has referred to visitors in its theme parks and resorts as "guests." Using the word "guest" is not just semantics; rather, it gives cast members a clear understanding how they should treat the visitors, namely "as if they are guests in our own homes," and *making guests happy is the common and overarching goal*![60] This approach sends a strong message to employees, reinforcing the company vision. When the vision and direction are clear and motivating, employees are more likely to remain with the company through the inevitable rough spots along the path to the vision.

Treat Employees as Customers

As mentioned before, if employees feel valued and their needs are taken care of, they are more likely to stay with the organization. For example, Tom Siebel, founder of Siebel Systems (now part of Oracle), saw the CEO's primary job as cultivating a corporate culture that benefits all employees and customers. "If you build a company and a product or service that delivers high levels of customer satisfaction, and if you spend responsibly and manage your human capital assets well, the other external manifestations of success, like market valuation and revenue growth, will follow."[61]

Many companies have adopted the idea that employees are also customers of the organization and that basic marketing strategies can be directed at them.[62] The products that the organization has to offer its employees are a job (with assorted benefits) and quality of work life. To determine whether the job and work-life needs of employees are being met, organizations conduct periodic internal marketing research to assess

Exhibit 11.3 COVID-19 and the "Great Resignation" of Service Workers

In 2021, more than one year after the onset of the COVID-19 pandemic, millions of employees (predominantly in the United States, Germany, United Kingdom, Netherlands, and to some extent in China and India) voluntarily resigned from their jobs; this phenomenon was referred to as the "Great Resignation" or the "Big Quit." One study showed that two out of three employees were looking for a new job, and that nearly nine out of ten companies experienced higher employee turnover than normal.

Impact in Service Settings: While the Great Resignation had a broad economic impact, service industries that involve in-person interactions between service providers and customers were hit particularly hard. For example:

- Resignations of employees in *hospitality* (e.g., restaurants, hotels, theme parks) as well as *retail* were the greatest of all sectors. Many employees in these settings felt that work became too stressful in light of continued staff shortages, frequent confrontations with unmasked customers, and the risk of exposure to COVID-19.
- The *health care* sector was also severely affected, as nearly one in five health care workers resigned. Some reasons for these employees resigning included the massive scale of death they had to witness, COVID-19 patients became more difficult to deal with, and some employees contracted COVID-19 themselves. These severe physical, cognitive, and emotional stressors caused considerable trauma and many healthcare workers reached their breaking point and decided to leave.

Drivers of the Big Quit included a complex set of multiple factors:

- As a result of the pandemic, many workers reassessed the long-term goals for their life and career vis-à-vis their current working conditions. After having worked from home for most of 2020, many people wanted to retain the benefits of remote work (e.g., more flexibility and independence, lower risk of exposure to COVID-19, improved work-life balance). Many of these benefits were unheard of prepandemic and employees were therefore reluctant when companies aimed to return to traditional in-person work modes.
- Other employees, especially those who worked in low-wage jobs (most of which were service jobs), took the opportunity to leave for better pay, which they could attain in light of emerging workforce shortages.
- A considerable portion of resignations were mothers who had to resign because they were disproportionately affected by pandemic-related measures (e.g., lockdowns in schools and childcare).
- Another contributor was medical reasons, as millions of people experienced symptoms of "long COVID," which undermined their ability and motivation to work.
- COVID-19 stimulus payments and related unemployment benefits also contributed because they provided low-wage employees with a cushion to explore alternatives to their current job.

Since the pandemic, many companies are providing more flexible and tailored work models that consider an individual employee's needs and preferences, and that also support a better work-life balance and mental health for employees. That said, another major trend is that companies, as they struggle to acquire human talent, use more robots, AI, and automation. For example, in the aforementioned hospitality services customers are increasingly served by robotic waiters and concierges (see also Chapter 16).

Sources: A. Chugh, "What is 'The Great Resignation'? An Expert Explains," https://www.weforum.org/agenda/2021/11/what-is-the-great-resignation-and-what-can-we-learn-from-it/, accessed January 16, 2022; L. Lambert, "The Great Resignation is No Joke," *Fortune*, October 21, 2021, https://fortune.com/2021/10/21/the-great-resignation-is-no-joke/, accessed January 16, 2022; E. Yong, "Why Health-Care Workers Are Quitting in Droves," *The Atlantic*, November 16, 2021, https://www.theatlantic.com/health/archive/2021/11/the-mass-exodus-of-americas-health-care-workers/620713/, accessed January 17, 2022; Hsu, "As the Pandemic Recedes, Millions of Workers Are Saying 'I Quit'," https://www.npr.org/2021/06/24/1007914455/as-the-pandemic-recedes-millions-of-workers-are-saying-i-quit, accessed January 17, 2022; M. Smith, "Professor Who Predicted 'The Great Resignation' Shares the 3 Trends That Will Dominate Work in 2022," https://www.cnbc.com/2022/01/14/the-great-resignation-expert-shares-the-biggest-work-trends-of-2022.html, accessed January 17, 2022.

employee satisfaction and needs. For example, as illustrated in Exhibit 11.1, Google has launched a number of initiatives that could be considered treating employees as customers. In addition to the benefits listed in the exhibit, other benefits include free haircuts, swim-in-place swimming pools, video games, dry cleaning, health care, and massages—all provided on-campus at the Googleplex.[63] What Google and many other companies have found is that, to ensure employee satisfaction, productivity, and retention, companies must get involved in the private lives and family support of their workers. Employees appreciate such efforts; Google is regularly in the top segment of *Fortune*'s list of "Top 100 Companies to Work For"!

Measure and Reward Strong Service Performers

If a company wants the strongest service performers to stay with the organization, it must reward and promote them. This strategy may seem obvious, but often the reward systems in organizations are not set up to reward service excellence. Reward systems may value productivity, sales, or some other dimension that can work *against* providing good service. Even those service workers who are intrinsically motivated to deliver high-quality service will become discouraged at some point and start looking elsewhere if their efforts in providing good service are not recognized and rewarded.

Reward systems need to be linked to the organization's vision and to outcomes that are truly important. For instance, if customer satisfaction and retention are viewed as critical outcomes, service behaviors that increase those outcomes need to be recognized and rewarded. In years past, a portion of employee compensation at Harrah's Casinos and Hotels was linked to customer satisfaction scores as a "Performance Payout," so employees would have an investment in achieving excellent service levels. Employees also had a vested interest in the performance of the entire team in serving customers exceptionally well. Beyond monetary incentives, outstanding employees were recognized with special Chairman Awards and their names published in Harrah's annual report. Management was also awarded incentives based on the positive improvement in customer service, as 25 percent of a manager's annual bonus was tied to achieving customer service goals.[64] Similarly, Enterprise Rent-a-Car branch managers wishing to move up in the organization can do so only if the customer satisfaction scores from their store are in the upper half of all company stores. Such measures, along with all the analyses and service improvement initiatives behind them, are intended to align employee behavior around satisfying and retaining customers.

In developing new systems and structures to recognize customer focus and customer satisfaction, organizations have turned to a variety of rewards. Traditional approaches such as higher pay, promotions, and one-time monetary awards or prizes can be linked to service performance. In many organizations employees are encouraged to recognize each other by personally giving a "peer award" to an employee they believe has excelled in providing service to the customer. Other types of rewards include special organizational and team celebrations for achieving improved customer satisfaction or for attaining customer retention goals. In most service organizations it is not only the major accomplishments but the daily perseverance and attention to detail that move the organization forward, so recognition of the "small wins" is also important.

In many situations, a customer's relationship is with a specific employee and may be stronger with the *employee* than with the firm. If this employee leaves the firm and is no longer available to the customer, the firm's relationship with the customer may be jeopardized.[65] Clearly a firm should make great efforts to retain such employees; however, in spite of the firm's best efforts, some good employees are going to leave. If the firm is not successful at retaining a key customer-contact employee, what can it do to reduce the impact on the customer? Employees could be rotated occasionally to ensure that the customer has exposure to and is comfortable with more than one employee. Firms might also form teams of employees who are responsible for interacting with each customer. In both cases, the idea is that the customer would have

FIGURE 11.5 Customer-Focused Organizational Chart

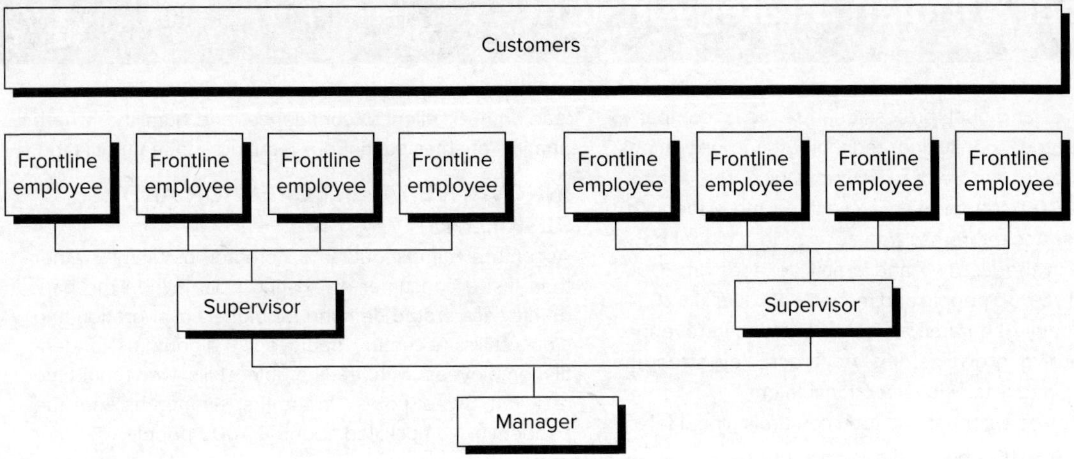

multiple contacts with several employees in the organization, thus reducing the firm's vulnerability to losing the customer, should any one employee leave. Emphasis should also be placed on creating a positive firm image in the minds of its customers and, in so doing, convey that *all* its employees are capable.[66]

CUSTOMER-ORIENTED SERVICE DELIVERY

As indicated by the examples in this chapter, specific approaches for hiring and energizing frontline workers take on a different look and feel across companies, based on the organization's values, culture, history, and vision.[67] For example, "developing people to deliver service quality" is accomplished quite differently at Southwest Airlines than at Disney. At Disney, the orientation and training process is highly structured, scripted, and standardized. At Southwest, the emphasis is more on developing needed skills and then empowering employees to be spontaneous and nonscripted in their approach to customers. Although the style and culture of the two organizations are different, both pay special attention to all four basic themes shown in Figure 11.4. Both make significant investments in their people, recognizing the critical roles they play.

Throughout the book, we advocate a strong customer focus. Firms that have a strong service culture put an emphasis on the customer and the customer's experience. To do so, firms must also create an environment that staunchly supports the customer-contact employee, because this is frequently the person in the organization most responsible for ensuring the customer's experience is delivered as designed. Historically, many firms have viewed senior management as the most important people in the firm, and indeed, organizational charts tend to reflect this view in their structure. This philosophy places management at the top of the structure and (implicitly) the customer at the bottom, with customer-contact employees just above them. However, if the organization's most important people are customers, they should be at the *top* of the chart, followed by those with whom they have contact. Such a view, illustrated in Figure 11.5, is more consistent with a customer-oriented focus. In effect, the role of top-level management changes from that of commanding to that of facilitating and supporting employees in the organization who are closest to the customer.

Global & Indian Strategy Insight Accenture

Accenture, a global professional services company, offers strategy, consulting, technology and operations services across more than 40 industries. The company's 800,000+ people serve clients in more than 120 countries. Accenture has transformed to a global powerhouse in the last two and a half decades. In 2000, they had 70,000 people and made $9.8 billion. In 2024, the company generated almost $65 billion in revenue. This massive growth stems from one key strength: attracting and retaining exceptional talent.

India plays a central role in Accenture's global talent strategy, hosting nearly 44% of Accenture's worldwide workforce, making it the company's largest talent pool. Since establishing its first development center in Mumbai in 2001, Accenture has expanded to over 34 centers across 15 Indian cities. As emphasized by CEO Julie Sweet, India remains Accenture's primary hiring focus, particularly for technology positions. The company's Indian operations support both global clients and local businesses through its entire portfolio of service offerings, while innovation hubs in Bengaluru, Hyderabad, and Pune, including a dedicated Generative AI studio, further cement India's strategic importance to Accenture's future growth.

STRATEGIC TALENT PHILOSOPHY

Sweet frames Accenture's approach to talent management through three interconnected lenses: "How do you access talent? How do you hire it? How do you become a creator of talent so that you don't always have to hire it? And then once they're here, how do you unlock the potential of talent?" Sweet emphasizes that learning agility is the single most critical quality they seek in candidates: "We start with learning agility and we ask a very simple question to all of our applicants, senior and junior... What have you learned in the last six months that was not part of school?" This focus on natural learners aligns with one of their leadership essentials: "to lead with excellence, confidence, and humility," where humility enables continuous learning and team building.

INNOVATIVE TALENT CREATION AND RESKILLING

Accenture stands out as a "creator of talent" rather than just a consumer of existing skills. When the pandemic accelerated demand for digital collaboration and cloud skills, Accenture deployed AI algorithms to identify employees with transferable skills who could be reskilled. Sweet notes: "In the first six months after the pandemic, we upskilled about 100,000 people with programs that ranged from eight to 15 weeks, depending on what we were upskilling them for."

The company's sophisticated talent database tracks skills across their workforce, allowing them to identify unexpected skill adjacencies. For example, employees working in risk and compliance possess analytical capabilities that transfer well to cybersecurity roles: "Those are the kinds of things where you might not have first looked at people doing risk or compliance for our clients to say, 'Oh yeah, they could easily become a security professional.'"

REMOVING BARRIERS TO TALENT ACCESS

Accenture has broadened their talent pool by removing four-year degree requirements from nearly 50% of North American job openings and implementing a successful apprenticeship program that now accounts for 20% of US entry-level hiring and attracts a diverse talent pool – about 50% women and nearly 60% racially or ethnically diverse candidates.

The company's apprenticeship program, which began with just seven apprentices in Chicago in 2016, has grown to over 1,200 participants. Sweet describes these apprentices as "some of our best employees, great retention, great learners," highlighting that the program provides "great new pathways" for individuals who would not have qualified under their previous hiring requirements.

The human resource strategies offered in this chapter are a means by which management can support the customer-contact employee. Indeed, a truly customer-oriented management team might actually "flip" the service marketing triangle presented

COMPREHENSIVE BENEFITS SUPPORTING THE "WHOLE PERSON"

Accenture's benefits package addresses the multi-dimensional needs of employees across financial, physical, mental, and family domains.

The company offers extensive mental health resources, including their Employee Assistance Program, a Mental Health Ally Network of trained colleagues, and partnerships with wellness platforms. Their partnership with 'Thrive Global' enabled over 180,000 employees complete a mental wellness computer and science-based program, helping people be less anxious and feel more able to care for themselves.

Family support benefits include generous parental leave of 26 weeks for primary caregivers and 15 working days for secondary caregivers, bereavement leave of up to 4 consecutive weeks for immediate family loss, subsidized childcare arrangements, and comprehensive medical coverage including specialized policies for people with disabilities and gender-affirming care.

IMMERSIVE ONBOARDING AND TECHNOLOGY LEADERSHIP

Accenture's innovative use of technology for employee experiences exemplifies their forward-thinking workplace culture. Their "One Accenture Park" metaverse environment onboards approximately 150,000 new employees annually, providing immersive experiences that connect global colleagues despite physical separation. Sweet describes the experience where new joiners "put on some glasses... and when you step into the metaverse, you are literally with say 30 other people who are also on their first or second day at Accenture."

This virtual environment allows new hires to explore innovation hubs, interact with demonstrations, and build relationships with colleagues worldwide. Sweet notes that research shows "immersive learning for short sprints, so not all day in the metaverse, this is about a 30-minute experience, is actually more impactful." She emphasizes that this approach has been "extraordinarily well received by our people who are onboarding, who find it, both learning, but also it creates bonds of these shared experiences with other people."

CAREER DEVELOPMENT INFRASTRUCTURE

Accenture enables career flexibility through tools like their proprietary Careers Marketplace app and an "aspiration-led approach" to staffing that balances client demands with employee career goals. Continuous investment in employees is "part of what makes Accenture such an attractive place to work because people feel like they're constantly being invested in."

The extensive learning infrastructure – including their $1.1 billion annual investment in professional development – has yielded impressive results, with employees collectively holding more than 480,000 credentials in cloud or industry platforms. The company's focus on digital literacy extends across all roles with everyone going through their Technology Quotient (TQ) program.

This comprehensive approach to talent acquisition, development, and retention has earned Accenture recognition as number 6 on the World's Best Workplaces™ list by Great Place to Work® and Fortune in 2024, reinforcing its position as a preferred employer in a highly competitive market for talent.

References

https://hbr.org/2022/05/accenture-ceo-julie-sweet-on-the-most-important-skill-job-seekers-need-today

https://www.greatplacetowork.in/great/company/accenture-solutions-private-limited

https://www.fortuneindia.com/long-reads/how-india-is-powering-accentures-big-genai-push-globally/120521

https://www.accenture.com/in-en/blogs/blogs-careers/were-one-of-the-worlds-best-workplaces

https://www.accenture.com/in-en/careers/local/benefits

earlier in the chapter, so that the management point is at the bottom of the triangle, with customers and employees equally placed at the top—as illustrated in Figure 11.6. Nordstrom, a company well known for its strong service culture, uses such an "inverted pyramid" in its employee training materials.

FIGURE 11.6
Inverted Service Marketing Triangle

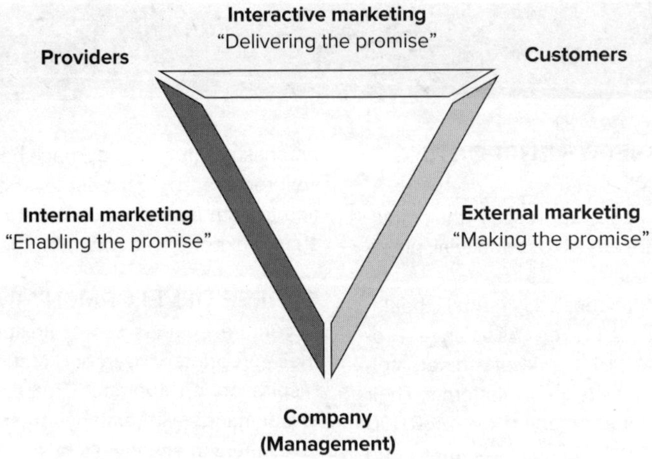

By flipping the service marketing triangle, the two groups that are the most important people to the organization—customers and those who interact with customers—are placed in a position of prominence.

Summary

Because many services are delivered by people in real time, closing the service performance gap is heavily dependent on human resource strategies. The successful execution of such strategies begins with the development and nurturing of a true service culture throughout the organization.

Often, service employees *are* the service, and they represent the organization in customers' eyes. They affect service quality perceptions to a large degree through their influence on the five dimensions of service quality: reliability, responsiveness, empathy, assurance, and tangibles. It is therefore essential to match service employees' abilities to deliver with what customers expect.

In this chapter, we focused on service employees to provide you with an understanding of the critical nature of their roles and appreciation of the inherent stresses and conflicts they face. You learned that frontline service jobs demand significant investments of emotional labor and that employees confront a variety of on-the-job conflicts.

Grounded in this understanding of the importance of service employees and the nature of their roles in the organization, you learned strategies for integrating appropriate human resource practices into service firms. The strategies are aimed at allowing employees to effectively satisfy customers as well as be efficient and productive in their jobs. The strategies are organized around four major human resource goals in service organizations: (1) hire the right people, (2) develop people to deliver service quality, (3) provide needed support systems, and (4) retain the best people. A company that works toward implementing these strategies is well on its way to delivering service quality through its people, thereby diminishing Gap 3—the service performance gap.

Discussion Questions

1. Define *service culture.* Why is service culture so important? Can a manufacturing firm have a service culture? Why or why not?
2. Why are service employees critical to the success of any service organization? Why do we include an entire chapter on service employees in a marketing course?
3. What is *emotional labor*? How is it different from physical or mental labor?
4. Reflect on your own role as a service employee, whether in a current job or in any full- or part-time job you have had in the past. Did you experience the kinds of

conflicts described in the boundary-spanning roles section of the chapter? Give some concrete examples for class discussion.

5. Select a service provider (your dentist, doctor, lawyer, hair stylist) with whom you are familiar, and discuss ways this person could positively influence the five dimensions of service quality in the context of delivering his or her services. Do the same for yourself (if you are currently a service provider).
6. Describe the four basic human resource strategy themes and why each plays an important role in building a customer-oriented organization.
7. What is the difference between technical and interactive service skills? Provide examples (preferably from your own work context or from another context with which you are familiar). Why do service employees need training in both?
8. Is empowerment always the best approach for effective service delivery? Why is employee empowerment so controversial?

Exercises

1. Visit the websites of companies with known world-class service cultures (such as Ritz-Carlton, FedEx, Starbucks, or Zappos). How does the information conveyed on the website reinforce the company's service culture?
2. Review the section of the chapter on boundary-spanning roles. Interview at least two frontline service personnel regarding the stresses they experience in their jobs. How do the examples they provide relate to the sources of conflict and trade-offs described in the text?
3. Assume that you are the manager of a crew of frontline customer-service employees in a credit card company. Assume that these employees work over the phone and that they deal primarily with customer requests, questions, and complaints. In this specific context,
   a. Define what is meant by *boundary-spanning roles,* and discuss the basic purposes or functions of participants in these roles.
   b. Discuss two of the potential conflicts that your employees may face on the basis of their roles as boundary spanners.
   c. Discuss how you, as their supervisor, might deal with these conflicts based on what you have learned.
4. Choose one or more of the human resource strategy themes (hire the right people, develop people to deliver service quality, provide needed support systems, retain the best people). Interview a manager in a service organization of your choice regarding his or her current practices within the theme you have chosen. Describe the current practices, and recommend any appropriate changes for improving them.

Notes

1. *100 Best Companies to Work For*, https://fortune.com/best-companies/2021/; *Best Employers for New Grads*, https://www.forbes.com/best-employers-for-new-grads/#6293ee4b67e5, accessed January 13, 2022; L. L. Berry, *Discovering the Soul of Service* (New York: The Free Press, 1999).
2. Interview with Singapore Airlines senior vice president of marketing services, included in "How May I Help You?" *Fast Company* (March 2000), pp. 93–126.
3. G. Ciotti, "10 Stories of Unforgettable Customer Service," www.helpscout.net/10-customer-service-stories/, accessed July 19, 2016; P. Shankman, "The Greatest Customer Service Story Ever Told, Starring Morton's Steakhouse," http://shankman.com/the-best-customer-service-story-ever-told-starring-mortons-steakhouse/, accessed July 19, 2016.

4. Chris Shelley, Panera Bread manager, Personal Interview, December 30, 2010.
5. Berry, *Discovering the Soul of Service.*
6. S. M. Davis, *Managing Corporate Culture* (Cambridge, MA: Ballinger, 1985).
7. C. Grönroos, *Service Management and Marketing: Customer Management in Service Competition,* 3rd ed. (West Sussex, UK: John Wiley and Sons, 2007), p. 418.
8. See K. N. Kennedy, F. G. Lassk, and J. R. Goolsby, "Customer Mind-Set of Employees throughout the Organization," *Journal of the Academy of Marketing Science* 30 (Spring 2002), pp. 159–171.
9. R. Hallowell, D. Bowen, and C. Knoop, "Four Seasons Goes to Paris," *Academy of Management Executive* 16 (2002), pp. 7–24; J. L. Heskett, L. A. Schlesinger, and E. W. Sasser Jr., *The Service Profit Chain* (New York: The Free Press, 1997); B. Schneider and D. E. Bowen, *Winning the Service Game* (Boston: Harvard Business School Press, 1995); and D. E. Bowen and S. D. Pugh, "Linking Human Resource Management Practices and Customer Outcomes" in *The Routledge Companion to Strategic Human Resource Management,* ed. J. Storey, P. Wright, and D. Ulrich (Abingdon, Oxon: Routledge, 2008), pp. 509–518; B. Schneider and D. E. Bowen, "Winning the Service Game; Revisiting the Rules by Which People Co-Create Value," in *Handbook of Service Science,* ed. P. P. Maglio, C. A. Kieliszewski, and J. C. Spohrer (New York: Springer, 2010), pp. 31–59.
10. Berry, *Discovering the Soul of Service*, p. 40.
11. Hallowell, Bowen, and Knoop, "Four Seasons Goes to Paris."
12. For an excellent discussion of the complexities involved in creating and sustaining a service culture, see Schneider and Bowen, *Winning the Service Game,* chap. 9. See also Michael D. Hartline, James G. Maxham III, and Daryl O. McKee, "Corridors of Influence in the Dissemination of Customer-Oriented Strategy to Customer-Contact Service Employees," *Journal of Marketing* 64 (April 2000), pp. 35–50.
13. This discussion is based on Hallowell, Bowen, and Knoop, "Four Seasons Goes to Paris."
14. This quote is most frequently attributed to J. Carlzon, former chief executive officer of Scandinavian Airline Systems.
15. P. Andruss, "Your Employees Are Your Brand," *Marketing News,* October 30, 2010, pp. 22–23.
16. J. Barlow and P. Stewart, *Branded Customer Service* (San Francisco: Barett-Koehler, 2004). For an discussion of branded service encounters, see N. J. Sirianni, M. J. Bitner, S. W. Brown, and N. Mandel, "Branded Service Encounters: Strategically Aligning Employee Behavior with the Brand Positioning," *Journal of Marketing* 77 (November 2013), pp. 108–123.
17. R. Mullins, R. Agnihotri, and Z. Hall, "The Ambidextrous Sales Force: Aligning Salesperson Polychronicity and Selling Contexts for Sales-Service Behaviors and Customer Value," *Journal of Service Research* 23 (January 2020), pp. 33–52.
18. The conceptualization of the service triangle presented in Figure 11.1 and the related text discussion are based on M. J. Bitner, "Building Service Relationships: It's All about Promises," *Journal of the Academy of Marketing Science* 23 (Fall 1995), pp. 246–251; P. T. Kotler and K. L. Keller, *Marketing Management,* 15th ed. (Upper Saddle River, NJ: Pearson Prentice Hall, 2016); and Grönroos, *Service Management and Marketing.*
19. See, L. A. Schlesinger and J. L. Heskett, "The Service-Driven Service Company," *Harvard Business Review* 69 (September–October 1991), pp. 71–81; and B. Schneider, M. Ehrhart, D. Mayer, J. Saltz, and K. Niles-Jolley, "Understanding Organization-Customer Links in Service Settings," *Academy of Management*

Journal 48 (December 2005), pp. 1017–1032; A. Zablah, B. D. Carlson, D. T. Donavan, J. G. Maxham, and T. J. Brown, "A Cross-Lagged Test of the Association Between Customer Satisfaction and Employee Job Satisfaction in a Relational Context," *Journal of Applied Psychology* 101 (May 2016), pp. 743–755.

20. B. Schneider and D. E. Bowen, "The Service Organization: Human Resources Management Is Crucial," *Organizational Dynamics* 21 (Spring 1993), pp. 39–52.
21. D. E. Bowen, S. W. Gilliland, and R. Folger, "How Being Fair with Employees Spills Over to Customers," *Organizational Dynamics* 27 (Winter 1999), pp. 7–23; S. Masterson, "The Trickle-Down Model of Organizational Justice: Relating Employees' and Customers' Perceptions of and Reactions to Fairness," *Journal of Applied Psychology* 86 (August 2001), pp. 594–604; J. G. Maxham III and R. G. Netemeyer, "Firms Reap What They Sow: The Effects of Shared Values and Perceived Organizational Justice on Customers' Evaluations of Complaint Handling," *Journal of Marketing* 67 (January 2003), pp. 46–62.
22. See J. Hogreve, A. Iseke, K. Derfuss, and T. Eller, "The Service–Profit Chain: A Meta-analytic Test of a Comprehensive Theoretical Framework," *Journal of Marketing* 81, (May 2017), pp. 41–61; G. Strydom, M. T. Ewing, and C. Heggen, "Time Lags, Non-linearity and Asymmetric Effects in an Extended Service-profit Chain," *European Journal of Marketing* 54 (May 2020), pp. 2343–2363; J. L. Heskett, T. O. Jones, G. W. Loveman, W. E. Sasser Jr., and L. A. Schlesinger, "Putting the Service–Profit Chain to Work," *Harvard Business Review* 72 (March–April 1994), pp. 164–174; G. W. Loveman, "Employee Satisfaction, Customer Loyalty, and Financial Performance," *Journal of Service Research* 1 (August 1998), pp. 18–31; A. Rucci, S. P. Kirn, and R. T. Quinn, "The Employee–Customer Profit Chain at Sears," *Harvard Business Review* 76 (January–February 1998), pp. 82–97.
23. For additional research on the service-profit chain, see J. L. Heskett, W. E. Sasser Jr., and L. A. Schlesinger, *The Value Profit Chain: Treat Employees Like Customers and Customers Like Employees* (New York: The Free Press, 2003); G. A. Geladel and S. Young, "Test of a Service Profit Chain Model in the Retail Banking Sector," *Journal of Occupational and Organizational Psychology* 78 (March 2005), pp. 1–22; R. D. Anderson, R. D. Mackoy, V. B. Thompson, and G. Harrell, "A Bayesian Network Estimation of the Service-Profit Chain for Transport Service Satisfaction," *Decision Sciences* 35 (Fall 2004), pp. 665–689; W. A. Kamakura, V. Mittal, F. de Rosa, and J. A. Mazzon, "Assessing the Service-Profit Chain," *Marketing Science* 21 (Summer 2002), pp. 294–317.
24. M. K. Brady and J. J. Cronin Jr., "Customer Orientation: Effects on Customer Service Perceptions and Outcome Behaviors," *Journal of Service Research* 3 (February 2001), pp. 241–251.
25. L. A. Bettencourt and K. Gwinner, "Customization of the Service Experience: The Role of the Frontline Employee," *International Journal of Service Industry Management* 7 (1996), pp. 3–20.
26. For research on the influence of frontline employee behaviors on customers, see D. D. Gremler and K. P. Gwinner, "Customer–Employee Rapport in Service Relationships," *Journal of Service Research* 3 (August 2000), pp. 82–104; and T. J. Brown, J. C. Mowen, D. T. Donavan, and J. W. Licata, "The Customer Orientation of Service Workers: Personality Trait Effects of Self and Supervisor Performance Ratings," *Journal of Marketing Research* 39 (February 2002), pp. 110–119; C. Delcourt, D. Gremler, A. C. R. van Riel, and M. J. H. van Birgelen, "Employee Emotional Competence: Construct Conceptualization and Validation of a Customer-Based Measure," *Journal of Service Research* 19 (February 2016), pp. 73–87.

27. A. Hochschild, *The Managed Heart: Commercialization of Human Feeling* (Berkeley: University of California Press, 1983).
28. T. Hennig-Thurau, M. Groth, M. Paul, and D. D. Gremler, "Are All Smiles Created Equal? How Employee-Customer Emotional Contagion and Emotional Labor Impact Service Relationships," *Journal of Marketing* 70 (July 2006), pp. 58–73.
29. A. Hochschild, "Emotional Labor in the Friendly Skies," *Psychology Today* 16 (June 1982), pp. 13–15.
30. For additional discussion on stress at the frontlines, see, M. L. Arvan, R. C. Dreibelbis, and P. E. Spector, "Customer Service Stress: A Meta-Analysis of Customer Mistreatment," in *Examining the Role of Well-being in the Marketing Discipline*, P. L. Perrewé and P. D. Harms, eds. (Emerald Publishing Limited, 2019), pp. 117–136; for work on emotional labor strategies, see R. Leidner, "Emotional Labor in Service Work," *Annals of the American Academy of Political and Social Science* 561 (1999), pp. 81–95. For discussions of emotional display rules, see A. Grandey, A. Rafaeli, S. Ravid, J. Wirtz, and D. D. Steiner, "Emotional Display Rules at Work: The Special Case of the Customer," *Journal of Service Management* 21 (2010), pp. 388–412; J. M. Diefendorff and G. J. Greguras, "Contextualizing Emotional Display Rules: Taking a Closer Look at Targets, Discrete Emotions, and Behavior Responses," *Journal of Management* 35 (August 2009), pp. 880–898. For a discussion of employee emotional competence, see Delcourt, Gremler, van Riel, and van Birgelen, "Employee Emotional Competence."
31. M. D. Hartline and O. C. Ferrell, "The Management of Customer-Contact Service Employees: An Empirical Investigation," *Journal of Marketing* 60 (October 1996), pp. 52–70; J. Singh, J. R. Goolsby, and G. K. Rhoads, "Burnout and Customer Service Representatives," *Journal of Marketing Research* 31 (November 1994), pp. 558–569; L. A. Bettencourt and S. W. Brown, "Role Stressors and Customer-Oriented Boundary-Spanning Behaviors in Service Organizations," *Journal of the Academy of Marketing Science* 31 (Fall 2003), pp. 394–408.
32. B. Shamir, "Between Service and Servility: Role Conflict in Subordinate Service Roles," *Human Relations* 33 (1980), pp. 741–756.
33. Ibid., pp. 744–745.
34. J. Bowen and R. C. Ford, "Managing Service Organizations: Does Having a 'Thing' Make a Difference?" *Journal of Management* 28 (June 2002), pp. 447–469.
35. V. O'Connell, "Stores Count Seconds to Trim Costs," *The Wall Street Journal,* November 13, 2008, p. A1.
36. www.consumerist.com/2008/04/21/union-hits-picket-line-to-protest-verizons-poor-customer-service, accessed July 20, 2016.
37. For discussions of internal marketing, see L. L. Berry and A. Parasuraman, "Marketing to Employees," chap. 9 in *Marketing Services* (New York: The Free Press, 1991); C. Grönroos, "People Management: Internal Marketing as a Prerequisite for Successful Customer Management," chap. 14 in *Service Management and Marketing: Managing the Service Profit Logic,* 4th ed. (West Sussex, UK: John Wiley and Sons, 2015).
38. L. L. Berry and A. Parasuraman, "Marketing to Employees," chap. 9 in *Marketing Services* (New York: The Free Press, 1991) p. 153.
39. This section on hiring for service competencies and service inclination draws from work by B. Schneider and colleagues, specifically B. Schneider and D. Schechter, "Development of a Personnel Selection System for Service Jobs," in *Service Quality: Multidisciplinary and Multinational Perspectives,* ed. S. W. Brown, E.

Gummesson, B. Edvardsson, and B. Gustavsson (Lexington, MA: Lexington Books, 1991), pp. 217–236.

40. Delcourt, Gremler, van Riel, and van Birgelen, "Employee Emotional Competence."
41. For an examination of employee interpretations of what "good service" means, see R. Di Mascio, "The Service Models of Frontline Employees," *Journal of Marketing* 74 (July 2010), pp. 63–80.
42. J. Hogan, R. Hogan, and C. M. Busch, "How to Measure Service Orientation," *Journal of Applied Psychology* 69 (1984), pp. 167–173. See also Brown, Mowen, Donavan, and Licata, "The Customer Orientation of Service Workers"; and D. T. Donavan, T. J. Brown, and J. C. Mowen, "Internal Benefits of Service-Worker Customer Orientation: Job Satisfaction, Commitment, and Organizational Citizenship Behaviors," *Journal of Marketing* 68 (January 2004), pp. 128–146.
43. Bowen and Pugh, "Linking Human Resource Management Practices and Customer Outcomes"; and N. Bendapudi and V. Bendapudi, "Creating the Living Brand," *Harvard Business Review* 83 (May 2005), pp. 124–134.
44. J. S. Black and P. van Esch, "AI-Enabled Recruiting: What Is It and How Should a Manager Use It?," *Business Horizons* 63 (March 2020), pp. 215–226; R. D. Johnson, D. L. Stone, and K. M. Lukaszewski, "The Benefits of eHRM and AI for Talent Acquisition," *Journal of Tourism Futures* 7 (January 2021), pp. 40–52.
45. For additional information on Southwest Airlines hiring practices, see C. Mitchell, "Selling the Brand Inside," *Harvard Business Review* 80 (January 2002), pp. 99–105 and "How Hires: Taking Fun Seriously," *VoiceGlance* (blog), October 13, 2014, www.voiceglance.com/how-southwest-hires-taking-fun-seriously.
46. UPS website, sustainability.ups.com/media/KeyPerformanceIndicators_WIP.pdf, accessed July 21, 2016.
47. SAS, "The Quality Imperative: SAS Institute's Commitment to Quality," https://www.sas.com/content/dam/SAS/en_us/doc/whitepaper1/quality-imperative-commitment-to-quality-106810.pdf, accessed January 14, 2022; http://money.cnn.com/video/fortune/2010/01/20/f_bctwf_sas.fortune/, accessed January 2011.
48. M. Gunther, "Marriott Family Values," *CNNMoney.com,* May 25, 2007, http://money.cnn.com/2007/05/24/news/companies/pluggedin_gunther_marriott.fortune/index.htm.
49. D. Gremler and K. Gwinner, "Rapport-Building Behaviors Used by Retail Employees," *Journal of Retailing* 84 (September 2008), pp. 308–324.
50. Salesforce.com, "9 Customer Service Training Ideas to Inspire Your Team," https://www.salesforce.com/resources/articles/customer-service-training-ideas/, accessed January 14, 2022.
51. S. A. Bone and J. C. Mowen, "'By-the-Book' Decision Making: How Service Employee Desire for Decision Latitude Influences Customer Selection Decisions," *Journal of Service Research* 13 (May 2010), pp. 184–197.
52. J. C. Chebat and P. Kollias, "The Impact of Empowerment on Customer Contact Employees' Roles in Service Organizations," *Journal of Service Research* 3 (August 2000), pp. 66–81; G. A. H. van der Heijden, J. J. L. Schepers, E. J. Nijssen, and A. Ordanini, "Don't Just Fix It, Make It Better! Using Frontline Service Employees to Improve Recovery Performance," *Journal of the Academy of Marketing Science* 41 (September 2013), pp. 515–530.
53. C. Argyris, "Empowerment: The Emperor's New Clothes," *Harvard Business Review* 76 (May–June 1998), pp. 98–105.

54. J. H. Gittell, "Relationships Between Service Providers and Their Impact on Customers," *Journal of Service Research* 4 (May 2002), pp. 299–311.
55. Mayo Clinic website, https://www.mayoclinic.org/about-mayo-clinic/mission-values; https://news.mayocliniclabs.com/2018/08/24/mayo-clinic-values-in-focus-stewardship-2/, accessed January 14, 2022; www.mayo.edu/pmts/mc4200-mc4299/mc4270.pdf, accessed July 21, 2016.
56. A. Sergeant and S. Frenkel, "When Do Customer-Contact Employees Satisfy Customers?" *Journal of Service Research* 3 (August 2000), pp. 18–34.
57. P. Sharma, T. T. C. Kong, and R. P. J. Kingshott, "Internal Service Quality as a Driver of Employee Satisfaction, Commitment and Performance," *Journal of Service Management* 27 (October 2016), pp. 773–797; J. Reynoso and B. Moores, "Operationalising the Quality on Internal Support Operations in Service Organisations," in *Advances in Services Marketing and Management,* vol. 6, ed. T. A. Swartz, D. E. Bowen, and S. W. Brown (Greenwich, CT: JAI Press, 1997), pp. 147–170.
58. Schneider and Bowen, *Winning the Service Game,* pp. 230–234.
59. O. Gadiesh and J. L. Gilbert, "Transforming Corner-Office Strategy into Frontline Action," *Harvard Business Review* 79 (May 2001), pp. 73–79.
60. Disney Institute, "How Disney Empowers Its Employees to Deliver Exceptional Customer Service," https://hbr.org/sponsored/2018/02/how-disney-empowers-its-employees-to-deliver-exceptional-customer-service; Disney Institute, "Are Your Employees 'Doing Things Right' Or 'Doing The Right Thing'?" https://www.disneyinstitute.com/blog/are-your-employees-doing-things-right-or-doing/, accessed January 15, 2022.
61. B. Fryer, "High Tech the Old Fashioned Way," *Harvard Business Review* 79 (March 2001), pp. 119–125.
62. L. L. Berry, "The Employee as Customer," *Journal of Retail Banking* 3 (March 1981), pp. 33–40; R. L. Cardy, "Employees as Customers?" *Marketing Management* 10 (2001), pp. 12–13; M. R. Bowers and C. L. Martin, "Trading Places Redux: Employees as Customers, Customers as Employees," *Journal of Services Marketing* 21 (2007), pp. 88–98.
63. A. Ansara, "Googleplex: The College-Campus for Professionals," https://candor.co/articles/tech-careers/googleplex-the-college-campus-for-professionals, accessed January 15, 2022.
64. J. Mackey, "Putting the Service Profit Chain to Work: How to Earn Your Customer's Loyalty," http://www.franchising.com/articles/how_to_earn_your_customers_loyalty.html, accessed July 21, 2016.
65. N. Bendapudi and R. P. Leone, "Managing Business-to-Business Customer Relationships Following Key Contact Employee Turnover in a Vendor Firm," *Journal of Marketing* 66 (April 2002), pp. 83–101; S. Wang and L. Davis, "Stemming the Tide: Dealing with the Imbalance of Customer Relationship Quality with the Key Contact Employee versus with the Firm," *Journal of Services Marketing* 22 (2008), pp. 533–549.
66. Bendapudi and Leone, "Managing Business-to-Business Customer Relationships"; T. Jones, S. F. Taylor, and H. S. Bansal, "Commitment to a Friend, a Service Provider, and a Service Company—Are They Distinctions Worth Making?" *Journal of the Academy of Marketing Science* 36 (Winter 2008), pp. 473–487.
67. J. R. Katzenbach and J. A. Santamaria, "Firing Up the Front Line," *Harvard Business Review* 77 (May–June 1999), pp. 107–117.

Chapter Twelve

Customers' Roles in Service

This chapter's learning objectives are to:

1. Illustrate the importance of customers in successful service delivery, creation, and cocreation of service experiences.
2. Discuss the variety of roles that service customers play: productive resources for the organization, contributors to and cocreators of value, and competitors.
3. Explain strategies for involving service customers effectively to increase satisfaction, quality, value, and productivity.

Customers as Creators and Cocreators of Service Value[1]

In today's economy, customers play increasingly active roles in service value creation and cocreation—more than they ever have before. They create service value for themselves through active involvement and customization and they enjoy value-in-use of the service over time through their own continued engagement and actions. Value-in-use refers to the value that customers get as they use products and services for various purposes in their own lives, most often independent of the provider. Rather than "delivering value," companies are often simply providing platforms for customers to create value for themselves. Customers also cocreate value together with service providers through direct interactions online, over the phone, or in person. Through these types of interactions, customers and service providers bring their resources together to cocreate unique value.

These expanded customer roles are probably most apparent in the world of Internet-based services and apps, where customers play active roles in producing service value for themselves with little or no personal interaction with the service provider. The service provider provides the platform and facilitates the customer's ability to create value for him or herself, sometimes including (but not always) direct interactions with the company as well. Services like Facebook, Uber, Airbnb, MyFitnessPal, and Amazon are just a few names of successful, Internet-reliant services where customers create value for themselves and also cocreate value with the provider and other customers. Value-in-use comes about for customers as they enjoy and continue to create and cocreate different forms of value—for example: social and communication value (e.g., Facebook), product usage value from the things they purchase (e.g., Amazon), greater fitness and health (MyFitnessPal), convenient transportation to where they need to be (Uber), and reasonably priced accommodations in places they desire to travel (Airbnb). Customers create their own unique value-in-use for each of these services, drawing on their own resources and those of the company.

Global retailer IKEA is a company that has built its strategy around expanded customer roles since the company opened its doors in the 1950s. Headquartered in Sweden, IKEA is today the world's largest home furnishings retailer, operating in more than 50 countries with over 450 physical stores and a major online presence including products and services. Known for its "do-it-yourself" or "DIY" business model, IKEA engages customers in tasks that are not typical for a furniture retailer. At IKEA, customers create their own value by finding and picking the products they want from IKEA's warehouse shelves, loading them and transporting them to their own homes, assembling the furniture, and then using these purchases to support their lifestyles. The customer is a clear creator of value in this context and value-in-use comes when the furniture is assembled and used in the customer's personal space. IKEA also provides extensive online catalogs, tools for creating personalized designs, and in-store assistance from designers if desired. Thus, IKEA is a cocreator of value through the resources it makes available to customers and the interactions it has with them. (For more on IKEA, see the Global Features in this chapter and in Chapter 2.)

Terms like collaboration, coproduction, cocreation, and value-in-use are becoming increasingly common across industries in strategic discussions and in new business models. While definitions of these terms are still evolving, it is clear that innovative services have emerged as companies begin to think about their customers as "value *creators*" and "value *cocreators*" rather than "value *recipients*." IKEA understands this and has built its highly successful business model on this kind of thinking. Companies are also recognizing that the customer is engaged in a larger ecosystem of services, products, and people that revolve around the products and services they purchase from any one company. In the IKEA example, the ecosystem for an individual customer might include services related to finding a home or apartment, professional design services, home products from other providers, services from other home trades (e.g., painting, tile work, or electrical), and family and friends who are involved in home furnishing decisions and use. As companies expand their view of what it means to serve the customer and recognize the varied and essential roles that customers play in value creation, opportunities for innovation and new business models abound. As they look outside their immediate sphere of influence into the customer's broader ecosystem, even more opportunities reveal themselves.

In this chapter we examine the unique and varied roles played by customers in creating and cocreating service value. In some cases, service customers are present in the "factory" (the place the service is produced and/or consumed), interacting with employees and other customers. For example, in a classroom or training situation, students (the customers) are sitting in the factory (the classroom), interacting with the instructor and other students as they cocreate educational services. Because they are present during service production, customers can contribute to or detract from the successful cocreation and to their own satisfaction. That is, because customers are participants in service production and value creation, they can contribute to the widening of Gap 3, the service performance gap. In this chapter, we discuss how companies can manage customer participation.

THE IMPORTANCE OF CUSTOMERS IN SERVICE COCREATION

Customer participation at some level is inevitable in all service situations. Services are actions or performances, often produced and consumed simultaneously. In many situations employees, customers, and even others in the service environment interact to produce the ultimate service outcome. Because they participate, customers are indispensable to the production process of service organizations, and in many situations they can control or contribute significantly to their own dis/satisfaction.[2] This view of participatory customers is consistent with the dominant logics in marketing that promote the idea that customers are always creators and cocreators of value.[3] Our Strategy Insight illustrates this broadened view and how it can lead to innovative service strategies and offerings.

Customers Themselves

Because the customer participates in the delivery process, he or she can contribute to narrowing or widening Gap 3 through behaviors that are appropriate or inappropriate, effective or ineffective, productive or unproductive. The level of customer participation—low, medium, or high—varies across services, as shown in Table 12.1. In some cases, all that is required is the customer's physical presence (*low level of*

TABLE 12.1 **Levels, Characteristics, and Examples of Customer Participation across Different Services**

Source: Adapted from A. R. Hubbert, "Customer Co-Creation of Service Outcomes: Effects of Locus of Causality Attributions," Doctoral dissertation, Arizona State University, Tempe, AZ, 1995.

Low: Customer Presence Required during Service Production	Moderate: Customer Inputs Required for Service Creation	High: Customer Cocreates the Service
Service is standardized.	Client inputs (information, materials) help customize a standard service.	Active client participation guides the customized service.
Service is provided regardless of any individual purchase.	Provision of service requires customer purchase.	Service cannot be created apart from the customer's purchase and active participation.
Payment may be the only required customer input.	Customer inputs are necessary for an adequate outcome, but the service firm provides the service.	Customer inputs, choices, and actions cocreate the outcome.
Consumer Examples		
Airline travel	Haircut	Marriage counseling
Motel stay	Annual physical exam	Personal training
Fast-food restaurant	Full-service restaurant	Weight reduction program
Business-to-Business Customer Examples		
Uniform cleaning service	Agency-created advertising campaign	Management consulting
Pest control	Payroll service	Executive management seminar
Interior greenery maintenance service	Freight transportation	Installation of computer network

Strategy Insight Customer Cocreation of Value: An Important Strategy Frontier

Consultants, researchers, and strategists are urging companies to think about their customers in new ways. Instead of viewing customers as passive targets and recipients of predesigned goods and services, they encourage a view of customers as *active* cocreators of value. This perspective goes beyond focusing on customer involvement in generating ideas for new products, and it is more than customer participation in service delivery. Instead, this view suggests that the value customers receive is a *cocreated experience* they build for themselves through interactions with service providers and other customers, as well as by choosing and combining elements of the company's offerings to create their own "total experience." In creating value for themselves within a particular problem solution domain, customers often combine, reconfigure, and join services from a network of providers to get the total value they are seeking.

The following examples from very different contexts help make the cocreation idea more concrete and the strategic possibilities apparent.

PATRICK T. FALLON/AFP/Getty Images

John Deere services connect equipment, owners, operators, and agricultural consultants.

JOHN DEERE

John Deere, founded in 1837, is a global firm that serves the knowledge- and capital-intensive farming industry with sophisticated equipment, services, information, and online support for its farm manager customers. The company is geared toward making the farmer's life easier and more productive. The "experience environment" for its innovations is broadly defined to include anything that will help achieve the farmer's professional objectives. For example, new technologies available through Deere, branded as "Precision Agriculture" and "FarmSight," can help the farmer monitor equipment remotely to assess the location of the equipment and engine condition, maximize machine operations, and provide agricultural decision support. These remote monitoring and support capabilities are uniquely set up for each farmer and require the farmer's active involvement with the system to fully take advantage of its value. Another service that Deere offers is sensor technologies on its equipment that can precisely map soil conditions and thereby prescribe the application of seeds and fertilizers based on the soil conditions in an area. Depending on the farmer's land conditions and the specific crops he grows, the information provided by the sensors can be customized to the situation and used to better control that farmer's crop yields. Deere also provides educational opportunities for farmers through

participation), with the employees of the firm doing all the service production work, as in the example of a symphony concert. Symphony-goers must be present to receive the entertainment service, but little else is required once they are seated. In other situations, consumer inputs are required to aid the service organization in creating the service (*moderate level of participation*). Inputs can include *information, effort,* or *physical possessions.* For example, all three of these are required for a certified public accountant (CPA) to prepare a client's tax return effectively: information in the form of tax history, marital status, and number of dependents; effort in putting the information together in a useful fashion; and physical possessions such as receipts and past tax returns. In some situations, customers are truly cocreators of the service

John Deere University courses and online learning, as well as books and publications. It is up to each farmer to determine how much to participate in the various services, how to use the information provided, and whether to take advantage of other educational opportunities. Deere's strategy and suite of offerings are customer-centric, with the resulting experience being uniquely cocreated with each farmer. Deere has shifted its strategic innovation paradigm to one where value is cocreated through services, solutions, and experiences rather than exclusively through product or technology innovation.

SHUTTERFLY, INC

Shutterfly, Inc. began as a company that helped people print photos from their digital cameras. Today it is an innovative, online, and cloud-based company whose mission is "to deepen your personal connections with the people who matter most with unique, personalized photo products." The company is a leader in the digital world of creative memory sharing through photos, and it has grown over the years to include a suite of related brands: Shutterfly, Lifetouch, Snapfish, Spoonflower, Tiny Prints, BorrowLenses, and Groovebook. Through its family of brands, Shutterfly has expanded its products and services to include photo and video storage, photo books, gifts, home decor, premium cards, invitations, stationery, and more. Its focus is to stay on the forefront of innovation, introducing new technology and expanding product and service offerings that make it easier for customers to share life's joys.

For example, customers can create lasting memories by integrating their own photos into high-quality photo books, customized stationery, event announcements, and photo gifts like jewelry, ceramic tiles, and calendars, just to name a few. Through customized photo books, customers can become the authors of their own stories, creating permanent ways to save and express their memories of special events or trips.

While Shutterfly can offer and provide access to a wide repertoire of memory-sharing products and services, customers must configure them and combine them with their own photos and ideas to create unique memories and ways of sharing for themselves. While there are standardized products that Shutterfly offers in a traditional sense (e.g., photo calendars, coffee mugs with photos, photo printing services), each customer will put these traditional products together with innovative services (e.g., photo books, trip logs, personal websites, and photo sharing and storage platforms) to create distinctive value for themselves. Strategically, Shutterfly has moved from a "photo printing" service to a resource that includes a suite of products, services, and solutions to share memories and joy. Customers create value for themselves and also cocreate value with Shutterfly. The value to the customer is recognized through the process of creating and also through "value-in-use" as they share their memories in various ways with others.

Sources: C. Gronroos and P. Voima, "Critical Service Logic: Making Sense of Value Creation and Co-Creation," *Journal of the Academy of Marketing Science* 41 (March 2013), pp. 133–150. S. L. Vargo and R. F. Lusch, "Evolving to a New Dominant Logic for Marketing," *Journal of Marketing* 68 (January 2004), pp. 1–17; www.johndeere.com, accessed January 2022; www.shutterfly.com, accessed January 2022.

(*high level of participation*). For these services, customers play important participation roles that affect the nature of the service outcome. For example, in a weight reduction program, the customer, working with a counselor, may actively cocreate a personalized nutritional and exercise program. Then, it is largely up to the customer to carry out the plan and/or enhance it, resulting in value that is unique to that person. Similarly, in a complex or long-term business-to-business consulting engagement, the client can be involved in activities such as identification of issues, shared problem solving, ongoing communication, provision of equipment and work space, and implementation of solutions.[4] Facilitating this type of positive customer participation can help ensure a successful outcome, as described in Exhibit 12.1.

Exhibit 12.1 Client Cocreation of Value in Business-to-Business Services

What do firms like IBM, McKinsey, and Accenture have in common? All can be described as knowledge-intensive business services (KIBS), whose value-added activities allow them to cocreate highly customized services (e.g., technical engineering, consulting, software development, business process outsourcing) with their business clients. To develop and deliver optimal service solutions, KIBS rely on inputs and cooperation from their clients as integral coproducers of the services. The KIBS provider needs accurate and detailed information from the client, access to people and resources, and cooperation in terms of the deadlines and contingencies that inevitably arise.

Depth interviews and research conducted with clients of employees of an IT services provider ("TechCo") identified a number of *client* characteristics that can enhance the quality of the client's participation and the ultimate service outcome in these types of KIBS relationships. The characteristics are listed here with an illustrative quote from or about one of TechCo's clients, using disguised names. Clients who display these types of cocreation behaviors contribute to the success of their projects and are likely to get better outcomes and be more satisfied.

- **Communication openness.** The client is forthcoming and honest in sharing pertinent information for project success.

  PharmCo actually did the up-front work to understand what it is we have to do, when we have to do it, and how it fits into our overall scheme of things . . . We [spent] the first days doing nothing but teaching them about what we're trying to accomplish.—TechCo, about PharmCo Client

- **Shared problem solving.** The client takes individual initiative and shared responsibility for developing solutions to problems that arise in the relationship.

  I think, as a customer, I have a responsibility to bring some critical thinking to what they've brought to the table. Not just to accept it . . . [You need to be able to say,] "I don't know if that's going to work for our environment" or technically, "Why did you do that?" So a lot of it's just asking questions and saying, "Why are we doing it that way? Is that the best way to do it?"—GovCo Client

- **Tolerance.** The client responds in an understanding and patient manner in the face of minor project encumbrances.

  That certainly was our goal—not to have roadblocks, not to have problems . . . And even at that, it took us longer than we had hoped. Again, not anybody's fault, it's just one of those things. It's a process, and sometimes those processes take a little longer than you initially had planned for.—EduCo Client

- **Accommodation.** The client demonstrates a willingness to accommodate the desires, approaches, and expert judgment of the service provider.

  [If we saw something that didn't fit with our goals,] we'd call them and ask them . . . If they could do it, they would simply say, "Oh, you bet, no problem" . . . If it was something that we really couldn't monkey with too much, they'd come out and say, "No, you probably don't want to change that because of this reason and that reason" and we'd say, "Okay, that's fine" and we'd go on to the next one.—EduCo Client

- **Advocacy.** The client firm provides a vocal advocate and salesperson for the project.

  [The scope of the project] was cumbersome. Had we not had involvement and not had a group of people who had ownership, who really wanted to succeed, we might have been inclined to say . . . "I don't really care how this turns out because the boss told me I need to do it. I don't care if it's ugly because I'm never going to use it." So, I think it was a combination of things. One is having people who have a vested interest in making sure it worked and knew why they were doing it and [second] continuous involvement.—AgCo Client

- **Involvement in project governance.** The client takes an active role in monitoring project progress toward the stated goal.

  We would have our meetings and we'd set these action items. We would say when they're supposed to be done,

Table 12.1 provides several examples of each level of participation for both consumer and business-to-business services. The effectiveness of customer involvement at all the levels will affect organizational productivity and, ultimately, service quality and customer satisfaction.

Fellow Customers

In many service contexts, customers receive and/or cocreate the service simultaneously with other customers or must wait their turn while other customers are being served. In both cases, "fellow customers" are present in the service environment and

and we would set the next meeting before we ended that meeting so everybody knew what their expectations were.—DonorCo Client

- **Personal dedication.** The client demonstrates a sense of personal obligation for project success by performing individual responsibilities in a conscientious manner.

  I think that was one of the things that I probably did right—was staying that involved. But it was hard, from my perspective, because it took time away from other things that I had to do. But I think I brought some things to the project that, if I hadn't been as involved, I don't know that we would have had as successful an implementation of the three systems as I think we did—GovCo Client

The challenge for KIBS firms is to develop processes, systems, and practices that will ensure that clients engage in these ways. The research suggests that these positive cocreation behaviors will be most likely when KIBS provider firms engage in (1) *client selectivity* (carefully screening clients in advance to ensure a good fit between provider and client); (2) *client training, education, and socialization* (making clients feel that they are part of the team by kicking off the relationship with a cooperative spirit, perhaps including events and expectations-setting workshops); and (3) *project leadership and client performance evaluation* (selecting the right project leaders on both sides and evaluating both on their relationship management skills as well as technical capabilities).

Results of Cocreation: Four Categories of Perceived Value

Why is cocreation in KIBS so important? Other research found that successful cocreation of KIBS generates benefits for customers and service providers; specifically, cocreation leads to four (interrelated) categories of perceived value: (1) functional, (2) economic, (3) relational, and (4) strategic values:

(1) **Functional value:** Cocreation leads to functional improvements in the service process and the cocreated services. For example, functional value includes aspects such as better customization of the service, faster service production and delivery, and improved service quality. These benefits are related to the timing of customer cocreation: the sooner customers engage in cocreation, the earlier the value outcomes become apparent.

(2) **Economic value:** Better cocreation can also help with economic value; for example, customers reported that their cocreation helped them reduce costs, and the service helped them to increase their revenues as well as improve their profit margins.

(3) **Relational value:** The extensive customer-provider interactions that come with higher levels of cocreation bolster the development of relationships, which is another key value outcome. Interestingly, relationships develop at two levels, namely (a) on the interorganizational level between companies, and (b) on the interpersonal level between individual employees.

(4) **Strategic value:** Cocreation supports various strategic benefits, such as the formulation of business strategies to improve the customer's competitiveness and market position. Consistent with their position in the hierarchy of the firm, top managers (relative to lower-/mid-level managers) are particularly concerned about the strategic impact of cocreation.

These insights illustrate how important successful cocreation is in the generation and delivery of services in business-to-business settings and that cocreation generates multiple categories of value for both customers and service providers.

Sources: M. Mustak, "Customer Participation in Knowledge Intensive Business Services: Perceived Value Outcomes from a Dyadic Perspective," *Industrial Marketing Management* 78 (April 2019), pp. 76–87; L. A. Bettencourt, A. L. Ostrom, S. W. Brown, and R. I. Roundtree, "Client Co-Production in Knowledge-Intensive Business Services," *California Management Review* 44 (Summer 2002), pp. 100–128.

can affect the nature of the service outcome or process. Fellow customers can *enhance* or *detract from* customer satisfaction and perceptions of quality.[5]

Some of the ways fellow customers can negatively affect the service experience are by exhibiting disruptive behaviors, causing delays, excessively crowding, and manifesting incompatible needs. In restaurants, hotels, airplanes, and other environments in which customers are cheek to jowl as they receive the service, crying babies, smoking patrons, and loud, unruly groups can be disruptive and detract from the experiences of their fellow customers. In college classrooms and other types of education and training environments, customers often complain when fellow customers interrupt and/or detract from the experience of others by using their laptops or texting on their phones in distracting ways. In other cases, overly demanding customers (even customers with legitimate problems) can cause a delay for others while their needs are met. This occurrence is common in banks, post offices, and customer service counters in retail stores. Excessive crowding or overuse of a service can also affect the nature of the customer's experience. Visiting Sea World in San Diego on a U.S. national holiday such as the Fourth of July is a very different experience from visiting the same park midweek in February.

Finally, customers who are being served simultaneously but who have incompatible needs can negatively affect each other. This situation can occur in restaurants, college classrooms, hospitals, and any service establishment in which multiple segments are served simultaneously. In a study of critical service encounters in tourist attractions across central Florida, researchers found that customers negatively affected each other when they failed to follow either explicit or implicit "rules of conduct." Customers reported such negative behaviors as pushing, shoving, smoking, drinking alcohol, being verbally abusive, and cutting in line. Other times, dissatisfaction resulted when other customers were impersonal, rude, unfriendly, or even spiteful.[6] Research has suggested that it is possible that the misbehavior of other customers may even be contagious, causing other customers to act inappropriately as well.[7]

There are just as many examples of customers enhancing satisfaction and quality for their fellow customers as detracting from them. Sometimes the mere presence of other customers enhances the experience, for example, at sporting events, in movie theaters, and in other entertainment venues. In other situations, fellow customers provide a positive social dimension to the service experience, as suggested in the photo on page 355. In some situations, customers may help each other achieve service goals and outcomes. For example, health providers have long recognized the importance of family members in aiding hospital patients in their care and full recovery. Some hospitals have even started encouraging family members to stay and assist with their loved ones who are being cared for in intensive care units (ICUs), turning family members into active members of the healthcare team.[8]

Academic research also supports the power of other customers to influence service outcomes. In a study done with a franchise of Gold's Gym, it was found that customers who received support from other members of the gym were more likely to participate in positive ways like keeping the gym clean, cooperating with personnel, showing empathy toward other members, and encouraging others to join the gym.[9] The study of central Florida tourist attractions mentioned earlier found that customers increased the satisfaction of others by having friendly conversations while waiting in line, by taking photos, by assisting with children, and by returning dropped or lost items.[10] And an ethnographic study that observed hundreds of hours of customer interactions among travelers on the U.K. rail system found that customers often helped each other by (1) providing important service-related information (e.g., schedules, interesting features en route) that can reduce trip-related anxiety; (2) engaging in enjoyable conversation, thus making the trip more pleasant; and (3) serving as someone to complain to when mishaps and service failures occurred.[11]

The influence of fellow customers in helping others is even more apparent in some online service environments such as Facebook, LinkedIn, eBay, and Amazon, where customers literally cocreate services together. Customers helping each other is not limited to consumer services, as illustrated by networking giant Cisco. By giving business customers open access to its information and systems through its online

Kzenon/Shutterstock

Social interactions with others can influence health club members' satisfaction with the service.

self-service, Cisco enables customers to engage in a dialogue with each other, helping themselves and other customers who may be experiencing similar challenges. The Technology Spotlight in Chapter 7 discusses in greater detail how Cisco uses these online customer services in the context of self-service recovery.

CUSTOMERS' ROLES

The following sections examine three major roles played by customers in service cocreation and delivery: customers as productive resources; customers as contributors to quality, satisfaction, and value; and customers as competitors.

Customers as Productive Resources

Service customers have been referred to as "partial employees" of the organization—human resources who contribute to the organization's productive capacity.[12] Some management experts have suggested that the organization's boundaries be expanded to consider the customer as part of the service system. In other words, if customers contribute effort, time, or other resources to the service production process, they should be considered as part of the organization.

Customer inputs can affect the organization's productivity through both the quality and quantity of what they contribute and the resulting quality and quantity of output generated. In a business-to-business service context (see Exhibit 12.1), the contributions of the client can enhance the overall productivity of the firm in both quality and quantity of service.[13] In the hospital ICU example given previously, family members participate in caring for their loved ones in the ICU, thus increasing the quality of care and healthcare outcomes but also resulting in increased productivity as family members participate as "partial employees" of the hospital.[14]

Customer participation in service production raises a number of issues for organizations. Because customers can influence both the quality and the quantity of production, some experts believe the delivery system should be isolated as much as possible from customer inputs to reduce the uncertainty they can bring into the production process. This view sees customers as a major source of uncertainty—in the timing of their demands and the uncontrollability of their attitudes and actions. The logical conclusion is that any service activities that do not require customer contact or involvement should be performed away from customers: the less direct contact there is between the customer and the service production system, the greater the potential for the system to operate at peak efficiency.[15] Other experts believe that services can be delivered most efficiently if customers are truly viewed as partial employees and their coproduction roles are designed to maximize their contributions to the service creation process. The logic behind this view is that organizational productivity can be increased if customers are educated to perform service-related activities they currently are not doing or to perform more effectively the tasks they are doing (e.g., checking themselves in and out in hotels).[16]

There are many examples of organizations seeking to increase productivity through transferring tasks to customers. Although organizations derive obvious cost benefits by involving them as coproducers, customers do not always like or accept their new roles, especially when they perceive the purpose to be bottom-line cost savings for the company. If customers see no clear benefit to being involved in coproduction (e.g., lower prices, quicker access, or a better-quality outcome), then they are likely to resent and resist their coproduction roles, particularly if they feel their own productivity or efficiency is suffering to benefit the company.[17] Similarly, employees can sometimes be frustrated by customer participation, as was discovered in research conducted in a professional banking context that explored the effects of customer participation on both customers and employees. While the research found that customer participation in general enhanced the experience and value for the customer, it created stress for employees, presumably due to disruptions in the employees' standard work procedures.[18]

Customers as Contributors to Quality, Satisfaction, and Value

Another role customers can play is that of contributor to their own satisfaction and the ultimate quality and value of the services they experience. In this sense, customers are creators and cocreators of value, as discussed in the chapter opener. Customers may care little that they have increased the productivity of the organization through their participation, but they likely care a great deal about whether their needs are fulfilled. Effective customer participation can increase the likelihood that needs are met and that the benefits the customer seeks are actually attained, especially for services such as healthcare, education, personal fitness, and weight loss, in which the service outcome is highly dependent on customer participation.

Research in education has shown that active participation by students—as opposed to passive listening—increases learning (a desired service outcome) significantly.[19] The same is true in healthcare; patient compliance, in terms of taking prescribed medications or changing diet or other habits, can be critical to whether patients regain their health (the desired service outcome).[20] Other research in financial and medical service settings has shown that effective participation and cocreation by customers leads to higher perceptions of service quality, improved well-being, and greater loyalty to the service provider.[21] Effective customer participation and cocreation can be just as important in business-to-business contexts. For example, companies in the trucking and shipping industries have found that in many situations customers cause their own *dissatisfaction* with the service by failing to pack shipments appropriately, resulting in breakage or delays while items are repacked. A more complex example of business-to-business cocreation in the context of "knowledge intensive service businesses" is discussed in Exhibit 12.1.

Research suggests that customers who believe they have done their part to be effective in service interactions are more satisfied with the service. In a study of the banking industry, bank customers were asked to rate themselves on questions related to their contributions to service delivery in terms of what they did (e.g., cooperated with the bank employee and gave proper information) and how they did it (e.g., being friendly and courteous to the bank employee). Results of the study indicated that those customers who responded more positively to the questions about their own participation were also more satisfied with the bank.[22] Research in another context showed that customers' perceptions of service quality increased with greater levels of participation. Specifically, members of a YMCA who participated more in the club gave the club higher ratings on aspects of service quality than did those who participated less.[23]

Customers contribute to quality service delivery when they ask questions, take responsibility for their own satisfaction, and complain when there is a service failure. Consider the service scenarios shown in Exhibit 12.2.[24] The four scenarios illustrate

Exhibit 12.2 Illustrating the Importance of Customer Participation for Service Quality and Satisfaction: Which Customer (A or B) Will Be Most Satisfied?

For each scenario, ask, "Which customer (A or B) will be most satisfied and receive the greatest quality and value, and why?"

SCENARIO 1: A MAJOR INTERNATIONAL HOTEL

Guest A called the desk right after check-in to report that his TV was not working and that the light over the bed was burned out; both problems were fixed immediately. The hotel staff exchanged his TV for one that worked and fixed the lightbulb. Later they took him a fruit plate to make up for the inconvenience. Guest B did not communicate to management until checkout time that his TV did not work and he could not read in bed. His complaints were overheard by guests checking in, who wondered whether they had chosen the right place to stay.

SCENARIO 2: OFFICE OF A PROFESSIONAL TAX PREPARER

Client A has organized into categories the information necessary to do her taxes and has provided all documents requested by the accountant. Client B has a box full of papers and receipts, many of which are not relevant to her taxes but which she brought along "just in case."

SCENARIO 3: AN AIRLINE FLIGHT FROM LONDON TO NEW YORK

Passenger A arrives for the flight with a device preloaded with movies and reading material and wearing several layers of clothing; passenger A also ordered a special meal in advance. Passenger B, who arrives empty-handed, becomes annoyed when the crew runs out of blankets, complains about the magazine selection and the meal, and starts fidgeting when he is disappointed by the inflight movie selection.

SCENARIO 4: ARCHITECTURAL CONSULTATION FOR REMODELING AN OFFICE BUILDING

Client A has invited the architects to meet with its remodeling and design committee made up of managers, staff, and customers to lay the groundwork for a major remodeling job that will affect everyone who works in the building, as well as customers. The committee has already formulated initial ideas and surveyed staff and customers for input. Client B has invited architects in following a decision the previous week to remodel the building; the design committee is two managers who are preoccupied with other, more immediate tasks and have little idea what they need or what customers and staff would prefer in terms of a redesign of the office space.

the wide variations in customer participation that can result in equally wide variations in service quality and customer satisfaction. Customers who take responsibility and providers who encourage their customers to become their partners in identifying and satisfying their own needs together produce higher levels of service quality. Our Global Feature shows how Sweden's IKEA has creatively engaged its customers as cocreators. Consistent with this idea, the company also launched its "cocreate" initiative that aims to involve consumers more directly into the development and design of its new products.

In addition to contributing to their own satisfaction by enhancing the quality of service delivered to them, some customers simply enjoy participating in service value creation. These customers find the act of participating to be intrinsically attractive.[25] They enjoy using the Internet and apps to create value for themselves (e.g., they enjoy doing their own taxes via H&R Block's website or creating photo books via Shutterfly's technology). Often customers who like self-service in one setting are predisposed to serving themselves in other settings as well.

Interestingly, because service customers must participate in service creation and cocreation, they frequently blame themselves (at least partially) when things go wrong. Why did it take so long to reach an accurate diagnosis of my health problem? Why was the service contract for our company's cafeteria food full of errors? Why was the room we reserved for our meeting unavailable when we arrived? If customers believe they are partially (or totally) to blame when failures such as these occur they may be less dissatisfied with the service provider than when they believe the provider

Global Feature At Sweden's IKEA, Customers around the World Cocreate Customized Value

IKEA of Sweden has managed to transform itself from a small, mail-order furniture company in the 1950s into the world's largest retailer of home furnishings. In 2021 more than 450 stores in more than 50 countries generated more than 40 billion euros in sales. The company sells simple, functional, yet well-designed furnishings, charging significantly less than its competitors.

Paul Souders/The Image Bank Unreleased/ Getty Images

THE "DO-IT-YOURSELF" (DIY) CONCEPT

A key to IKEA's success is the company's relationship with its customers. IKEA has drawn the customer into its production system: "if customers agree to take on certain key tasks traditionally done by manufacturers and retailers—the assembly of products and their delivery to customers' homes—then IKEA promises to deliver well-designed products at substantially lower prices." In effect, IKEA's customers become essential contributors to value—they create value for themselves through participating in the selection, transportation, and assembly processes.

IKEA has made being part of the value creation process an easy, fun, and pleasant experience for customers. The stores are set up with "inspirational displays," including realistic room settings and real-life homes that allow customers to get comfortable with the furnishings, try them out, and visualize the possibilities in their own homes. To make shopping easy, free strollers and supervised child care are provided, as are wheelchairs for those who need them.

When customers enter the store they are given store maps, tape measures, pens, and notepaper to use as they shop, allowing them to perform functions commonly done by sales and service staff. Once customers have made their selections, they find the boxed furniture in the IKEA warehouse and load it onto carts. After payment, customers take their purchases to their cars; if necessary, they can rent or buy a roof rack to transport larger purchases. Thus, customers also provide furniture loading and delivery services for themselves. At home, IKEA customers take on the role of a manufacturer in assembling the new furnishings following carefully written, simple, and direct instructions. To accommodate customer needs, IKEA does have a fee-based delivery, assembly, and installation service for products over a certain price.

GLOBAL ADAPTATIONS

IKEA prints catalogs and provides detailed websites in many languages, making its products and instructions for their use accessible worldwide. In addition to tailoring its catalogs and websites, another key to IKEA's successful global expansion has been the company's policy of allowing each store to tailor its mix according to the local market needs and budgets. For example, when the Swedish retailer first expanded to the United States, executives quickly learned

is responsible.[26] A series of studies suggests the existence of this "self-serving bias." That is, when services go better than expected, customers who have participated tend to take credit for the outcome and are less satisfied with the firm than are those customers who have not participated. However, when the outcome is worse than expected, customers who have chosen to participate in service production are less dissatisfied with the service than are those who choose not to participate—presumably because the participating customers have taken on some of the blame.[27]

Customers as Competitors

A third role played by service customers is that of potential competitor. If self-service customers can be viewed as resources of the firm, or as "partial employees," they can that Americans prefer larger drinking glasses, bigger beds, and more closet space.

On the other side of the world, Chinese customers save a high percentage of their income and are extremely price sensitive, so the prices there were initially the lowest in the world to lure the Chinese customers into the stores; $1 placemats and 12¢ ice cream cones are examples. And some furniture items were 50–60 percent less than similar items in the United States. Amidst the price changes, IKEA learned that its "furniture for the masses" positioning was confusing Chinese consumers. What IKEA had not realized was that in China, IKEA was seen as an aspirational brand by many consumers. IKEA subsequently altered its targeting strategy to focus on younger middle-class consumers to help maintain its aspirational brand status. The response has been extremely positive, with more than 30 IKEA stores now open in China.

In addition to price variations, the store layout in Chinese stores was also adapted to reflect the design of many Chinese apartments. Because many of the apartments have balconies, the stores have a selection of balcony furnishings and displays. And because Chinese kitchens are generally small, relatively few kitchen items and furnishings are shown. Even IKEA's famous DIY assembly concept has been adapted to some extent in China. Because fewer people have cars and therefore use public transportation, IKEA has more extensive delivery service in China than in most countries. And because labor is cheaper in China, many customers choose to have their furniture assembled for them rather than doing it themselves. Another interesting adaptation to Chinese culture is IKEA's acceptance of extensive browsing by customers, in some cases even allowing customers and their children to nap in the display bed areas, as a noon nap is a common habit in China. To further adapt to the preferences of Chinese consumers, IKEA offers localized dishes for specific regions of China (e.g., in Guangdong province, IKEA cafeterias offer dim sum; but they also offer the famous Swedish meatballs).

IKEA'S SUCCESS

IKEA's success is attributable in part to recognizing that customers can be part of the business system, performing roles they have not performed before. The company's flexible implementation of this idea through clearly defining customers' new roles and making it fun to perform these roles is the genius of its strategy. Through the process, customers around the globe cocreate their own experiences and contribute to their own satisfaction. And IKEA continues to experience financial success and acceptance globally with its strategy. Not surprisingly, IKEA is frequently ranked as one of the most powerful and valuable retail brands in the world.

Sources: "IKEA in China: Big Furniture Retail Adapts to the Chinese Market," https://daxueconsulting.com/ikea-in-china/, accessed January 2022; http://www.ikea.com, January 2022; B. Edvardsson and B. Enquist, "The IKEA Saga: How Service Culture Drives Service Strategy," *The Service Industries Journal* 22 (October 2002), pp. 153–186; P. M. Miller, "IKEA with Chinese Characteristics," *The China Business Review* (July/August 2004), pp. 36–38; M. Fong, "IKEA Hits Home in China," *The Wall Street Journal*, March 3, 2006, p. B1; M. Wei, "In IKEA's China Stores, Loitering is Encouraged," *Bloomberg Businessweek*, October 28, 2010; Anonymous, "Business: The Secret of IKEA's Success," *The Economist*, February 26, 2011, pp. 67–68. V. Chu, "Couching Tiger Tames the Dragon," *Business Today*, July 21, 2013, www.businesstoday.in/story/how-ikea-adapted-its-strategies-to-expand-in-china/1/196322/.html; R. Milne, "Ikea Faces Cultural Challenge as Flat-Pack Empire Expands," *Financial Times*, November 28, 2013, www.ft.com/content/83389238-5819-11e3-82fc-00144feabdc0.

also partially or entirely perform the service for themselves and not need the provider at all. Thus, customers in a sense are competitors of the companies that supply the service. Whether to produce a service for themselves (*internal exchange*)—for example, child care, home maintenance, or car repair—or have someone else provide the service for them (*external exchange*) is a common dilemma for consumers.[28] Similar internal versus external exchange decisions are made by organizations. Firms frequently choose to outsource service activities such as payroll, data processing, market research, accounting, maintenance, and facilities management. They find it advantageous to focus on their core businesses and leave these support services to others with greater expertise. Alternatively, a firm may decide to stop purchasing services externally and bring the service production process in-house.

Whether a household or a firm chooses to produce a particular service for itself or contract externally for the service depends on a variety of factors. An influential model of internal/external exchange suggests that such decisions depend on the following:[29]

- *Expertise capacity.* The likelihood of producing the service internally is increased if the household or firm possesses the specific skills and knowledge needed to produce it. Having the expertise will not necessarily result in internal service production, however, because other factors (available resources and time) will also influence the decision. (For firms, making the decision to outsource is often based on recognizing that, although they may have the expertise, someone else can do it better.)
- *Resource capacity.* To decide to produce a service internally, the household or firm must have the needed resources, including people, space, money, equipment, and materials. If the resources are not available internally, external exchange is more likely.
- *Time capacity.* Time is a critical factor in internal/external exchange decisions. Households and firms with adequate time capacity are more likely to produce services internally than are groups with time constraints.
- *Economic rewards.* The economic advantages or disadvantages of a particular exchange decision will be influential in choosing between internal and external options. The actual monetary costs of the two options will sway the decision.
- *Psychic rewards.* Rewards of a noneconomic nature have a potentially strong influence on exchange decisions. Psychic rewards include the degree of satisfaction, enjoyment, gratification, or happiness associated with the external or internal exchange.
- *Trust.* In this context, trust means the degree of confidence or certainty the household or firm has in the various exchange options. The decision will depend to some extent on the level of self-trust in producing the service versus trust of others.
- *Control.* The household or firm's desire for control over the process and outcome of the exchange will also influence the internal/external choice. Entities that desire and can implement a high degree of control over the task are more likely to engage in internal exchange.

The important insight to remember from this section is that, in many service scenarios, customers can and often do choose to fully or partially produce the service themselves. Thus, in addition to recognizing that customers can be productive resources and cocreators of quality and value, organizations also need to recognize the customer's role as a potential competitor.

SELF-SERVICE TECHNOLOGIES—THE ULTIMATE CUSTOMER PARTICIPATION

Self-service technologies (SSTs) enable customers to produce services without any direct involvement or interaction with the firm's employees. As such, SSTs represent the ultimate form of customer participation along a continuum from services produced entirely by the firm to those produced entirely by the customer. This continuum is depicted in Figure 12.1, using the example of H&R Block tax preparation services to illustrate the various ways the same service could be created and cocreated along all points on the continuum. At the far right end of the continuum, the tax advisor does everything from preparing the tax return to filing it. On the other end of the spectrum, the customer does everything; in between are various forms and levels of customer participation. Many service delivery options, across industries, could be laid out on this type of continuum from total customer production through total firm production. Researchers have referred to this continuum and the various ways of creating value as "value creation spheres" where providers produce potential value in the provider sphere, customers create their own value independently in the customer sphere, and the two jointly produce cocreated value in the joint sphere.[30]

A Proliferation of SSTs

Advances in technology, particularly the Internet, have allowed the introduction of a wide range of self-service technologies that occupy the far left end of the customer participation continuum in Figure 12.1. These technologies have proliferated as companies see the potential cost savings and efficiencies that can be achieved, potential sales growth, increased customer satisfaction, and competitive advantage. The following is a partial list of some of the self-service technologies available to consumers.

- ATMs.
- Pay at the gasoline pump.
- Airline check-in.
- Hotel check-in and checkout.
- Automated car rental.
- Automated filing of legal claims.
- Online driver's license testing.
- Online gambling.
- Electronic blood pressure machines.
- Health tests (e.g., COVID-19)
- Tax preparation software.
- Self-scanning at retail stores.
- Online banking.
- Vehicle registration online.
- Online auctions.
- Home and car buying online.
- Automated investment transactions.
- Insurance online.
- Package tracking
- Internet shopping.
- Interactive voice response phone systems.
- Online training and education.

The proliferation of SSTs has occurred for several reasons.[31] Many times firms are tempted by the cost savings that they anticipate by shifting customers to

FIGURE 12.1
Service Production Continuum[32]

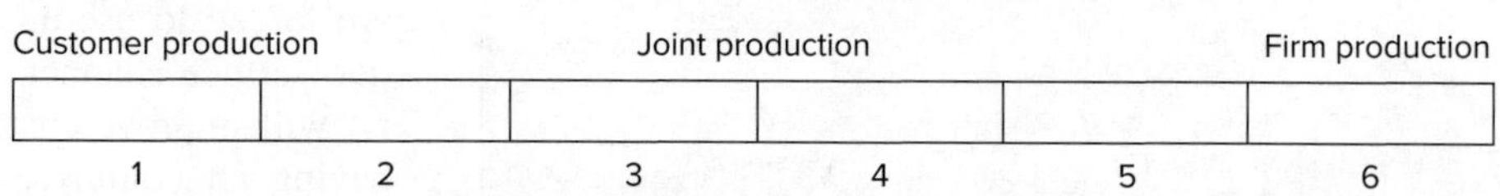

H&R Block Tax Preparation Example

1. Customer consults H&R Block website for tips and help, then prepares and files own tax return.
2. Customer consults H&R Block website for tips and help, purchases H&R Block software, and uses the software to file taxes online.
3. Customer partially prepares own return and meets with H&R Block advisor to check it over before finishing it and filing it online.
4. H&R Block tax advisor meets with customer, provides guidance and advice, and then customer prepares and files own tax return using H&R Block software.
5. H&R Block tax advisor meets with customer, helps customer prepare tax return in the office, provides direction for completing the process, and customer files it.
6. H&R Block tax advisor meets with the customer, prepares the tax return for her, files it for the customer, and provides her with copies of the return.

technology-based, automated systems and away from expensive personal service. If cost savings are the only reason for introducing an SST and if customers see no apparent benefits, the SST is likely to fail. Customers quickly see through this strategy and are not likely to adopt the SST if they have alternative options for service. Other times, firms introduce SSTs based on customer demand. For example, customers expect to find information, services, and delivery options online. When they do not find what they want from a particular firm online, they are likely to choose a competitor. Thus, customer demand in some industries is forcing firms to develop and offer their services via technology. Other companies are developing SSTs to open up geographic, socioeconomic, and lifestyle markets that were not available through traditional channels.

Customer Usage of SSTs

Some of the SSTs listed earlier—ATMs, online ordering, and airline check-in—have been very successful, embraced by customers for the benefits they provide in terms of convenience, accessibility, and ease of use.[33] Benefits to firms, including cost savings and revenue growth, can also result for SSTs that succeed. However, sometimes customers might be reluctant to adopt new SSTs; reasons for such reluctance can include fear of the technology, looking incompetent in front of other customers, desire for human interaction, and a sense that the focal task should not be the customer's responsibility in the first place (e.g., in the context of self-check outs in the groceries, some customers might believe "scanning and bagging groceries is the store's job, not mine").

SST failures result when customers see little personal benefit in the new technology or when they do not have the ability to use it or know what they are supposed to do. Often, adopting a new SST requires customers to change their traditional behaviors significantly, and many are reluctant to make those changes, at least initially. Research looking at customer adoption of SSTs found that "customer readiness" is a major factor in determining whether customers will even try a new self-service option.[34] Customer readiness results from a combination of personal motivation (What is in it for me?), ability (Do I have the ability to use this SST?), and role clarity (Do I understand what I am supposed to do?). In other cases, customers see no value in using the technology when compared to the alternative interpersonal mode of delivery, or the SSTs may be so poorly designed that customers may prefer not to use them.[35] Research shows that customers also react negatively when they are forced to use an SST, with no alternative service channel offered. Any choice at all will improve customer perceptions, and having an employee available to assist or provide backup support can help.[36] Many studies have been done to try to understand why customers choose to adopt self-service technologies or not. One piece of research compared the results of 96 previous studies, concluding that demographics (e.g., age, education) are <u>not</u> good predictors of SST adoption and that ease of use and usefulness of the SST are key determining factors, influenced themselves by a number of factors including the ones just discussed. They

B.O'Kane/Alamy Stock Photo

Customers help produce the service for themselves through scanning their own groceries.

also found that the factors that predict SST acceptance vary depending on the type of SST and country culture.[37]

Success with SSTs

Throughout the text we have highlighted some of the most successful self-service technologies in the marketplace: Amazon.com (Chapter 4), Cisco Systems (Chapter 7), and others. These companies have been successful because they offer clear benefits to customers, the benefits are well understood and appreciated compared to the alternative delivery modes, and the technology is user-friendly and reliable. In addition, customers understand their roles and have the capability to use the technology.

From a strategic perspective, research suggests that, as firms continue to move to SSTs as a mode of delivery, these questions are important to ask:[38]

- What is our strategy? What do we hope to achieve through the SST (cost savings, revenue growth, competitive advantage)?
- What are the benefits to customers of producing the service on their own through the SST? Do they know and understand these benefits?
- How can customers be motivated to try the SST? Do they understand their role? Do they have the capability to perform this role?
- How "technology ready" are our customers?[39] Are some segments of customers more ready to use the technology than others?
- How can customers be involved in the design of the service technology system and processes, so that they will be more likely to adopt and use the SST?
- What forms of customer education will be needed to encourage adoption? Will other incentives be needed?
- How will inevitable SST failures be handled to regain customer confidence?

STRATEGIES FOR ENHANCING CUSTOMER PARTICIPATION

The level and the nature of customer participation in the service process are strategic decisions that can impact an organization's productivity, its positioning relative to competitors, its service quality, and its customers' satisfaction. In the following sections we will examine the strategies captured in Figure 12.2 for involving customers effectively in the service production and cocreation process. The overall goals of a customer participation strategy will typically be to increase organizational productivity and customer satisfaction while decreasing uncertainty due to unpredictable customer actions.

Define Customers' Roles

Clarify Level of Participation

In developing strategies for addressing customer involvement in service cocreation and delivery, the organization first determines what type of participation is desirable from customers, what the customer is capable of doing, and how the customer wishes to participate. Identifying the current level of customer participation can serve as a starting point.[40] Customers' roles may be partially predetermined by the nature of the service, as suggested in Table 12.1, and possibly difficult to change. In other cases, it may be possible to design for low, medium, or high levels of participation.

FIGURE 12.2
Strategies for Enhancing Customer Participation

Source: Adapted from M. L. Meuter and M. J. Bitner, "Self Service Technologies: Extending Service Frameworks and Identifying Issues for Research," in *Marketing Theory and Applications,* ed. D. Grewal and C. Pechmann (American Marketing Association Winter Educators' Conference, 1998), pp. 12–19.

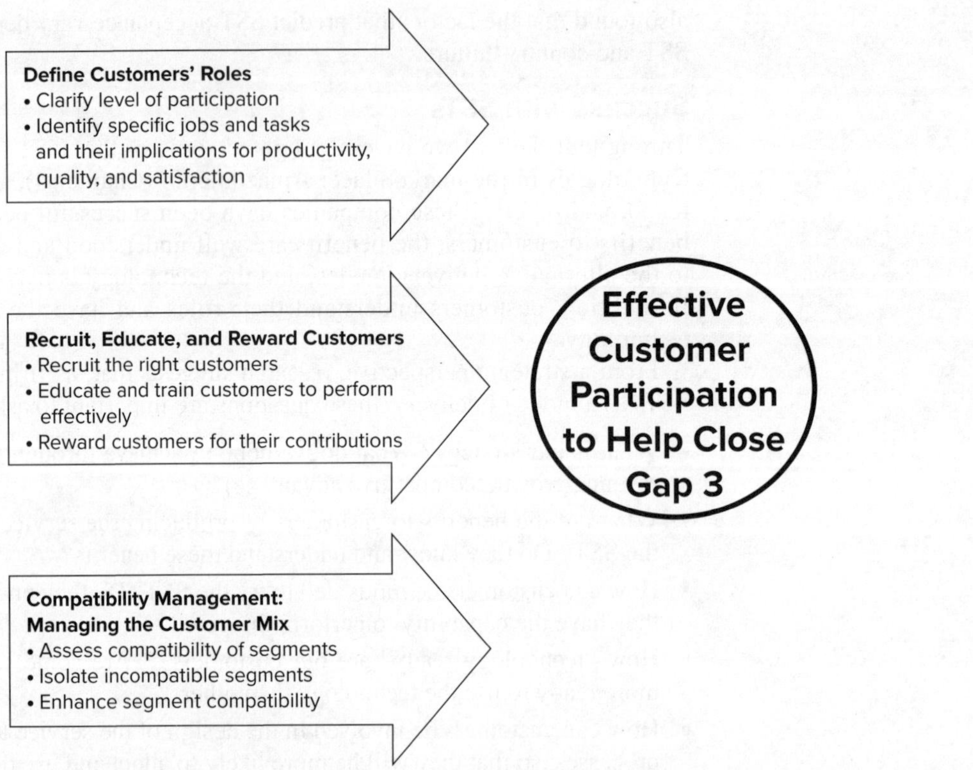

The organization may decide that it is satisfied with the existing level of participation it requires from customers but wants to make the participation more effective. For example, Charles Schwab has always positioned itself as a company whose customers are highly involved in their personal investment decisions and it has communicated this role clearly to customers. The company's positioning around high customer involvement and self-service has been consistent over time, yet the actual role of the customer has changed, primarily related to technological advances.

Alternatively, the organization may choose to increase the level of customer participation, which may reposition the service in the customers' eyes. Experts have suggested that higher levels of customer participation are strategically advisable when service production and delivery are inseparable; marketing benefits (cross-selling, building loyalty) can be enhanced by on-site contact with the customer; and customers can substitute for the labor and information provided by employees.[41] Higher levels of customer participation may also be advisable when increased participation is desired by customers and when it can enhance their satisfaction and service outcomes. For example, in healthcare, researchers and providers are working on ways to gain more active customer participation in treatment decisions. The Internet and other technological advances have helped propel customers into this role in taking responsibility for their own health and well-being, as illustrated in our Technology Spotlight.

Once the desired level of participation (from both the customer and firm perspectives) is clear, the organization can define more specifically what the customer's role and tasks entail. The range of possible roles and tasks are described next.

Identify Specific Jobs and Tasks: Helping Oneself, Helping Others, and Promoting the Company

Helping Oneself As discussed before, customers can be productive resources, performing aspects of the service previously performed by employees or others. Many of the examples presented in this chapter are illustrations of customers "helping themselves" (IKEA of Sweden, Charles Schwab, and those in the Technology Spotlight).

Helping Others Sometimes the customer is called on to help others who are experiencing the service. For example, many universities have established mentoring programs in which experienced students with similar backgrounds help newcomers adjust to and learn the system. Many membership organizations (like health clubs, churches, and social organizations) also rely heavily, although often informally, on current members to help orient new members and make them feel welcome. In a different context, social media and online game sites rely on customers to help each other and enhance each other's experiences. In engaging in these types of roles of "helping others", customers are performing productive functions for the organization, increasing customer satisfaction and retention.

Promoting the Company In some cases the customer's job includes a sales or promotional element. Service customers rely heavily on word-of-mouth endorsements in deciding which providers to try. Thus, a positive recommendation from a friend, relative, colleague, or even an acquaintance can pave the way for a positive service experience. Many service organizations are imaginative in getting their current customers to work as promoters or salespeople. For example, a dental practice encourages referrals by sending flowers, candy, or tickets to a local sports event to its patients whose names appear frequently in its "who referred you?" database. Online reviews, Facebook posts, endorsements via Twitter, and other social media are common ways for customers to promote specific service providers.

Individual Differences: Not Everyone Wants to Participate In defining customers' roles it is important to remember that not everyone will want to participate.[42] For example, in healthcare, it is clear that some patients want lots of information and want to be involved in their own diagnosis and treatment decisions. Others simply want the doctor to tell them what to do. Despite all the customer service and purchase options now available via the Internet, many customers still prefer human, high-contact service delivery rather than self-service.[43] Research has shown, for example, that customers with a high "need for human interaction" are less likely to try new self-service options offered via the Internet and automated phone systems.[44] Because of these differences in preferences, most companies find they need to provide service delivery choices for different market segments.

Recruit, Educate, and Reward Customers

Once the customer's role is defined, the organization can think in terms of facilitating that role. In a sense, the customer becomes a partial employee, and strategies for facilitating customer behavior in service cocreation and delivery can mimic to some degree the efforts aimed at service employees discussed in Chapter 11. As with employees,

Technology Spotlight Technology Facilitates Customer Participation in Healthcare

Customer participation is facilitated by technology in many industries. For example, in education, technology allows students to interact with each other and their professors via e-mail, discussion boards, group chat sessions, and course materials provided online. In real estate, technology allows buyers to preview homes and develop lists of places they would like to visit without having to rely totally on a real estate agent to find all available properties. And in high-technology industries, business customers often interact with each other on the Web, helping each other solve problems, answering each other's questions, and so forth. All these examples show how technology has facilitated customer participation and increased customer satisfaction.

Increased participation is particularly apparent in healthcare. There is probably no greater, high-participation service context than healthcare, where the customer must participate and where the provider and customer clearly cocreate the service. Patient participation is required at multiple levels. To achieve optimal health outcomes, patients must

- Provide accurate information about symptoms and health background.
- Answer detailed questions.
- Help decide on a course of treatment.
- Carry out the prescribed regimen (often over extended time periods) leading to recovery and/or prevention.

Technology is clearly influencing how customers perform these roles and shifting in some senses the power of information into the hands of consumers. For example, millions of people go online in search of health information, and Google receives 1 billion health-related search queries every day. They seek information about specific diseases, mental health, nutrition and fitness, drugs and drug interactions, and specific doctors and hospitals. While many seek information for themselves and their own medical conditions, some of these online health information seekers search for information on behalf of a friend or family member. People like getting health information this way because of the convenience, the wealth of information that is available, and the fact that research can be done anonymously.

Hundreds of thousands of Internet sites provide some type of health-related information. Some belong to healthcare providers like Mayo Clinic (www.mayo.edu) or pharmacy benefits providers like CVSCaremark (www.caremark.com). Others are operated totally online—like WebMD (www.webmd.com) or Everyday Health (www.everydayhealth.com)—without affiliation to a specific healthcare provider. Some respected sites are sponsored by governmental entities such as the U.S. Department of Health and Human Services (www.healthfinder.gov) and the National Library of Medicine and National Institutes of Health (www.medlineplus.gov). Yet other sites provide information for specific health conditions such as AIDS, depression, diabetes, and breast cancer. Still others such as Hospital Compare (www.medicare.gov/hospitalcompare) can help patients determine the best hospitals to go to based on various quality and health outcome criteria.

All this readily available medical information is changing the role of the healthcare consumer to one of active participant in diagnosing illnesses, assessing treatment options, and determining overall well-being. Armed with information, many patients gain confidence in asking questions and seeking appropriate diagnoses. Research found that access to this information improves patients' service engagement and their compliance with medical treatment plans they later receive from their healthcare providers. In some cases they can e-mail questions to their doctors or other providers or find support in chat groups, bulletin boards, and e-mail lists on the Internet. They are also comforted (or at times frightened) by what

customer participation in service cocreation and delivery will be facilitated when (1) customers understand their roles and how they are expected to perform, (2) customers are able to perform as expected, and (3) customers receive valued rewards for performing as expected.[45] Through these means, the organization will also reduce the inherent uncertainty associated with the unpredictable quality and timing of customer participation.

MedlinePlus

they find online and often make decisions or change their overall approach to maintaining their health based on what they find. Still, it is important to note that, while they play a growing role, online sources are still supplemental to health professionals, family, and friends as sources of health information.

Sources: K. Osei-Frimpong, A. Wilson, and F. Lemke, "Patient Co-Creation Activities in Healthcare Service Delivery at the Micro Level: The Influence of Online Access to Healthcare Information," *Technological Forecasting and Social Change* 126 (January 2018), pp. 14–27; M. Murphy, "Dr. Google Will See You Now," https://www.telegraph.co.uk/technology/2019/03/10/google-sifting-one-billion-health-questions-day/, accessed January 2022.

Recruit the Right Customers

Before the company begins the process of educating and socializing customers for their roles, it must attract the right customers to fill those roles. The expected roles and responsibilities of customers should be clearly communicated in advertising, personal selling, and other company messages. By previewing their roles and what is required of them in the service process, customers can self-select into (or out of) the

Exhibit 12.3 Weight Watchers Educates and Orients New Members

When new members first join Weight Watchers (WW), one of the largest and most successful commercial weight loss organizations in the world, they are given the choice of different plans that provide customers with distinct levels of guidance and support (e.g., emphasizing a self-guided journey, the guidance of a dedicated coach, and/or a supportive community of other members). Customers are thoroughly educated regarding what benefits to expect with each program and their responsibilities as customers. For example, WW offers its members a "Virtual App Academy" to allow them to become more successful cocreators in their weight-loss journey. Member education often comes in a "gamified" form to make learning more fun (e.g., asking members to take an "online quiz"). In parallel, WW offers in-person education and orientation. For example, when a new member attends her first meeting at a local WW studio, she receives an orientation to the program as well as step-by-step instructions, including a "Getting Started" packet and access to the WW app that helps monitor and manage the weight loss journey (e.g., tracks food and water intake, includes barcode scanner for easy shopping, as well as recipes and restaurant databases). In addition, the company offers dedicated meet-ups for new members to help socialize them. Throughout their journey members can find a great deal of information online that describes the weekly meetings, what happens at the meeting, and what is expected of the customer. Through the combination of in-person and online orientation as well as member education, the organization clearly defines the member's responsibilities and makes the plan as easy as possible to follow. However, WW consistently reminds its members of their role as cocreators of the weight-loss journey with statements such as: "It's Up to You How You Spend" (your calorie points).

Jonathan Weiss/Shutterstock

WeightWatchers

Source: https://www.weightwatchers.com/us/, accessed January 2022.

relationship. Self-selection should result in enhanced perceptions of service quality from the customer's point of view and reduced uncertainty for the organization.

Educate and Train Customers to Perform Effectively

Customers need to be educated, or in essence "socialized," so that they can perform their roles effectively. Through the socialization process, service customers gain an appreciation of specific organizational values, develop the abilities necessary to function within a specific context, understand what is expected of them, and acquire the skills and knowledge to interact with employees and other customers.[46] Customer education programs can take the form of formal orientation programs, written literature and online resources provided to customers, directional cues and signage in the service environment, and information obtained from employees and other customers.

Many services offer "customer orientation" programs to assist customers in understanding their roles and what to expect from the process before experiencing it. When customers begin the Weight Watchers in-person program, for example, the company website and their group meetings include a thorough orientation to the program and their responsibilities, as described in Exhibit 12.3.

Although formal training and written information are usually provided in advance of the service experience, other strategies can continue customer socialization during the experience itself. On-site, customers require two kinds of orientation: *place orientation* (Where am I? How do I get from here to there?) and *function orientation* (How does this organization work? What am I supposed to do?).[47] Signage, the layout of the service facility, and other orientation aids can help customers answer these questions, allowing them to perform their roles more effectively. Orientation aids can also take the form of rules that define customer behavior for safety (airlines, health clubs), appropriate dress (restaurants, entertainment venues), and noise levels (hotels, classrooms, theaters).

If customers are not effectively socialized and educated, the organization runs the risk that inappropriate customer behaviors will result in negative outcomes for customers, employees, and the organization itself.[48] For example, prior to the official opening of Shanghai Disney in 2016, the city of Shanghai issued an etiquette guide for local patrons. City officials announced they developed six rules after "uncivilized behaviors" were observed during the mega theme park's trial opening. The new guide warned tourists against littering, being rowdy, vandalizing, cutting in line, damaging the landscape, and other "uncouth behaviors" such as lying down on the ground.[49]

Reward Customers for Their Contributions

Customers are more likely to perform their roles effectively, or to participate actively, if they are rewarded for doing so. Rewards are likely to come in the form of increased control over the process, time savings, monetary savings, and psychological or physical benefits. For instance, some CPA firms require clients to complete extensive forms before they meet with their accountants. If the forms are completed, the CPAs will have less work to do and the clients will be rewarded with fewer billable hours. Those clients who choose not to perform the requested role will pay a higher price for the service. Online banking customers who perform services for themselves are also rewarded through greater access to the bank, in terms of both locations and times.

Customers may not recognize the benefits or rewards of effective participation unless the organization makes the benefits apparent to them. In other words, the organization needs to clarify the performance-contingent benefits that can accrue to customers, just as it defines performance-contingent benefits to employees. The organization also should recognize that not all customers are motivated by the same types of rewards. Some may value the increased access and time savings they can gain by performing their service roles effectively. Others may value the monetary savings. Still others may be looking for greater personal control over the service outcome.

Compatibility Management: Managing the Customer Mix

Because customers frequently interact with each other in the process of service delivery and consumption, another important strategic objective is the effective management of the mix of customers who simultaneously experience the service. If a restaurant chooses to serve two segments during the dinner hour that are incompatible with each other—for example, single college students who want to party and families with small children who want quiet—it may find that the two groups do not merge well. Of course, it is possible to manage these segments so that they do not interact with each other by seating them in separate sections or by attracting the two segments at different times of day.

Indian Strategy Insight Apollo's Preventive Health Approach and Customer Engagement

Apollo Hospitals Group launched Apollo ProHealth Program, a pioneering and comprehensive health program, powered by pHRA (personalized Health Risk Assessment) and enabled by Artificial Intelligence. Curated and conceptualized by Apollo's experts in preventive healthcare, the program is based on the experiences and learnings from over 25 million health checks conducted by Apollo Hospitals. ProHealth empowers individuals with actionable health analytics, to know and manage health risks while leading healthier and happier lives. The program brings technology and human elements together by providing a personal Health Mentor to guide each individual to stay focused on health track to improve health for lasting happiness.

Apollo's approach fundamentally shifts responsibility from reactive treatment to proactive prevention, with customers taking center stage in their health journey. The ProHealth program is designed on three principles – "Predict, Prevent and Overcome" – which require active customer participation. Using the pHRA, customers gain early awareness of potential health issues before symptoms appear. This foreknowledge enables them to take preemptive action rather than waiting for the disease to develop. For instance, customers identified as pre-diabetic or pre-hypertensive, conditions affecting significant portions of the population, can implement lifestyle changes that potentially prevent progression to full disease states. This proactive stance is particularly vital given the research finding that "80% of non-communicable diseases (NCDs) mortality is preventable."

Apollo Hospitals empowers customers to take an active role in managing their health through proactive, preventive healthcare tools rather than focusing solely on treatment after disease develops. As Dr. Prathap C. Reddy emphasized, "Treating diseases is not the only way to health. If we care for our health, we will not need to cure anything ever." Apollo's ProHealth program enables individuals to be active participants in their health journey by offering personalized risk assessment and actionable insights. This shifts the paradigm from reactive healthcare to a proactive model where customers can make informed decisions to prevent health issues before they arise.

The digital tools provided by Apollo Hospitals, such as the AI-powered Cardiovascular Disease Risk Score API and the ProHealth Score, give customers unprecedented access to personalized health data. These tools evaluate factors including lifestyle attributes, family history, current symptoms, and physiological measurements to generate personalized numeric indicators of a person's health status. Customers can use these insights to understand their specific risk factors for conditions like cardiovascular disease, diabetes, and cancer. The tools do not just highlight problems but provide "simple corrective suggestions for improvement," empowering customers with actionable steps.

Apollo differentiates its approach from others by providing ongoing support to customers beyond initial assessment. Apollo ProHealth recognizes that sustainable health improvements require ongoing guidance, not just diagnostic information. This is why each customer is paired with a dedicated Health Mentor who becomes her personal health navigator. These mentors guide each individual to stay focused on health track. Unlike traditional healthcare models where patient-provider interactions are limited to occasional visits, Health Mentors maintain regular contact with customers, providing accountability, motivation, and practical advice. This relationship is crucial because many lifestyle changes are difficult to maintain without consistent support. Mentors help translate complex medical recommendations into achievable daily actions, bridging the gap between medical knowledge and practical implementation in customers' lives.

The process of managing multiple and sometimes conflicting segments is known as *compatibility management,* broadly defined as "a process of first attracting [where possible] homogeneous consumers to the service environment, then actively managing both the physical environment and customer-to-customer encounters in such a way as to enhance satisfying encounters and minimize dissatisfying encounters."[50]

The comprehensive data collected through Apollo's 40 years of experience and over 25 million health screenings suggests that non-communicable diseases (NCDs) are increasingly affecting younger populations but are largely preventable. Apollo's digital tools and programs empower customers to take charge of their health by providing early detection capabilities and ongoing monitoring. By utilizing these services, customers become active collaborators in their healthcare rather than passive recipients of treatment after disease develops. Early intervention and lifestyle modifications can significantly reduce risk factors and improve long-term health outcomes.

Apollo's digital tools do not just identify risks – they provide specific guidance for improvement. Customers are expected to actively implement recommended lifestyle changes across multiple dimensions. These include dietary adjustments to address nutritional imbalances, structured physical activity programs tailored to individual capabilities, stress management techniques to address psychological factors contributing to disease risk, and sleep hygiene improvements to address the 25% of people at risk of disturbed sleep. The AI-powered risk assessment tools specifically highlight "top modifiable risk contributors," directing customers' attention to the lifestyle factors that would yield the greatest health benefits if changed. Many health issues can be "attributed mainly to lifestyle – particularly, eating habits and sedentary life," making customer implementation of these recommendations essential to health improvement.

Apollo's preventive health model relies on customers maintaining ongoing engagement with their health data and progress. Unlike one-time health checkups, the ProHealth program encourages regular monitoring and adjustment of health behaviors based on changing conditions and progress. Customers are expected to track their improvements through follow-up assessments and consultations with experts. This continuous engagement allows for course corrections and reinforces positive health behaviors through measurable progress. The document notes that traditional health checks end with reports, but Apollo's approach extends far beyond this: "a report doesn't improve your health, but the right actions do." This statement underscores the expectation that customers will take concrete steps based on their health data and maintain consistent effort over time. Regular reassessment using tools like the ProHealth Score enables customers to see the impact of their efforts and make adjustments as needed, creating a dynamic and responsive approach to health management.

References

https://www.apollohospitals.com/corporate/apollo-in-the-news/apollo-hospitals-group-has-launched-apollo-prohealth-ndash-a-first-of-its-kind-predictive-proactive-and-comprehensive-health-management-program/

https://www.apollohospitals.com/departments/preventivehealth/ai-powered-phra

https://health.economictimes.indiatimes.com/news/hospitals/apollo-hospitals-launches-ai-enabled-proactive-health-management-programme/90097589

https://economictimes.indiatimes.com/industry/healthcare/biotech/healthcare/apollo-hospitals-launches-ai-driven-personalised-preventive-health-profile/articleshow/99304025.cms?from=mdr

https://www.thehindubusinessline.com/news/apollo-hospitals-launches-digital-health-indicator-tool/article68028628.ece

https://news.microsoft.com/en-in/microsoft-and-apollo-hospitals-introduce-ai-powered-cardiovascular-disease-risk-score/

Compatibility management is critical for some businesses (such as health clubs, public transportation, and hospitals) but less important for others. Table 12.2 lists seven interrelated characteristics that increase the importance of compatibility management for service businesses.

TABLE 12.2 Characteristics of Service That Increase the Importance of Compatible Segments

Source: Adapted from R. W. Buell, D. Campbell, and F. X. Frei, "The Customer May Not Always Be Right: Customer Compatibility and Service Performance," *Management Science* 67 (March 2021), pp. 1468–1488; and C. L. Martin, Dr C. A. Pranter, "Compatibility Management: Customer-to-Customer Relationships in Service Environments," *Journal of Services Marketing* 3 (Summer 1989), pp. 5–15.

Characteristic	Explanation	Examples
Customers are in close physical proximity to each other.	Customers will more often notice each other and be influenced by each other's behavior when they are in close physical proximity.	Airplane flights Entertainment events Sports events
Verbal interaction takes place among customers.	Conversation (or lack thereof) can be a component of both satisfying and dissatisfying encounters with fellow patrons.	Full-service restaurants Cocktail lounges Educational settings
Customers are engaged in numerous and varied activities.	When a service facility supports varied activities all going on at the same time, the activities themselves may not be compatible.	Universities Health clubs Resort hotels Banks
The service environment attracts a heterogeneous customer mix.	Many service environments, particularly those open to the public, will attract a variety of customer segments.	Public parks Public transportation Open-enrollment colleges
The core service is compatibility.	The core service is to arrange and nurture compatible relationships between customers.	Big Brothers/Big Sisters Weight loss group programs Mental health support groups
Customers must occasionally wait for the service.	Waiting in line for service can be monotonous or anxiety producing. The boredom or stress can be magnified or lessened by other customers, depending on their compatibility.	Medical clinics Tourist attractions Restaurants
Customers are expected to share time, space, or service utensils with each other.	The need to share space, time, and other service factors is common in many services but may become a problem if segments are not comfortable with sharing with each other or if the need to share is intensified because of capacity constraints.	Golf courses Hospitals Retirement communities Airplanes

To manage multiple (and sometimes conflicting) segments, organizations rely on a variety of strategies. Attracting maximally homogeneous groups of customers through careful positioning and segmentation strategies is one approach. This strategy is used by the Ritz-Carlton Hotel, for which upscale travelers are the primary target segment. The Ritz-Carlton is positioned to communicate that message to the marketplace, and customers self-select into the hotel. However, even in that context there are potential conflicts—for example, when the hotel is simultaneously hosting a business convention, an NBA basketball team, and individual leisure travelers. Another strategy is often used in such cases. Compatible clusters are grouped together physically, so that the segments are less likely to interact directly with each other. The Ritz-Carlton keeps meetings and large-group events separated from the areas of the hotel used by individual businesspeople.

Other strategies for enhancing customer compatibility include customer "codes of conduct," such as the regulation of smoking behavior and dress codes. Clearly such codes of conduct vary from one service establishment to another. Finally, training employees to observe customer-to-customer interactions and to be sensitive to potential conflicts is another strategy for increasing compatibility among segments. Employees can also be trained to recognize opportunities to foster positive encounters among customers in certain types of service environments.

Summary

This chapter focused on the role of customers in delivery, creation, and cocreation of service value. The customer him or herself and fellow customers in the service environment can all cause a widening of Gap 3. Customers may widen the service performance gap for a number of reasons: customers lack understanding of their roles, customers are unwilling or unable to perform their roles, customers are not rewarded for good performance, other customers interfere, or market segments are incompatible.

Managing and facilitating customers in the process of service value cocreation is a critical challenge for service firms. Whereas manufacturers are not concerned with customer participation in the manufacturing process, service managers constantly face this issue because their customers are often present and active partners in service production and cocreation. As participants in service cocreation, production, and delivery, customers can perform three primary roles: *productive resources* for the organization; *contributors* to quality, satisfaction, and value; and *competitors* in performing the service for themselves.

Through understanding the importance of customers in service creation and cocreation and identifying the roles played by the customer in a particular context, managers can develop strategies to enhance customer participation. Strategies include defining the customers' roles and jobs, recruiting customers who match the customer profile in terms of desired level of participation, educating customers so they can perform their roles effectively, rewarding customers for their contributions, and managing the customer mix to enhance the experiences of all segments. By implementing these strategies, organizations should see a reduction in the service performance gap due to effective and efficient customer contributions to service value.

Discussion Questions

1. Using your own personal examples, discuss the general importance of customers in the successful creation and delivery of service experiences.
2. Why might customer actions and attitudes cause the service performance gap to occur? Use your own examples to illustrate your understanding.
3. Using Table 12.1, think of specific services you have experienced that fall within each of the three levels of customer participation: low, medium, and high. Describe specifically what you did as a customer in each case. How did your involvement vary across the three types of service situations?
4. Describe a time when your satisfaction in a particular situation was *increased* because of something another customer did. Could (or does) the organization do anything to ensure that this experience happens routinely? What does it do? Should it try to make this situation a routine occurrence?
5. Describe a time when your satisfaction in a particular situation was *decreased* because of something another customer did. Could the organization have done anything to manage this situation more effectively? What could it have done?
6. Discuss the customer's role as a *productive resource* for the firm. Describe a time when you played this role. What did you do and how did you feel? Did the firm help you perform your role effectively? If so, how?
7. Discuss the customer's role as a *contributor to service quality and satisfaction.* Describe a time when you played this role. What did you do and how did you feel? Did the firm help you perform your role effectively? If so, how?
8. Discuss the customer's role as a potential *competitor.* Describe a time when you chose to provide a service for yourself rather than pay someone to provide the service for you. Why did you decide to perform the service yourself? What could have changed your mind, causing you to contract with someone else to provide the service?

Exercises

1. Visit a service establishment where customers can influence each other (such as a theme park, an entertainment establishment, a resort, a shopping mall, a restaurant, an airline, a school, or a hospital). Observe (or interview) customers and record cases of positive and negative customer influence. Discuss how you would manage the situation to increase overall customer satisfaction.
2. Interview someone regarding his or her decision to outsource a service—for example, legal services, payroll, or maintenance in a company or cleaning, child care, or pet care in a household. Use the criteria for internal versus external exchange described in the text to analyze the decision to outsource.
3. Think of a service in which a high level of customer participation is necessary for the service to be successful (health club, weight loss, educational setting, healthcare, golf lessons, online social media, or the like). Interview a service provider in such an organization to find out what strategies the provider uses to encourage effective customer participation.
4. Visit a service setting in which multiple customer segments use the service at the same time (e.g., a theater, golf course, resort, or theme park). Observe (or interview the manager about) the organization's strategies to manage these segments effectively. Would you do anything differently if you were in charge?
5. Visit the website of an online service company that allows consumers to design and purchase (personalized) clothes (e.g., zazzle.com). Compare its service process to similar brick-and-mortar services offered by clothing stores. Compare and contrast the customer's role in each situation.

Notes

1. For more on value creation and cocreation see U. Damali, E. Secchi, S. S. Tax, and D. McCutcheon, "Customer Participation Risk Management: Conceptual Model and Managerial Assessment Tool," *Journal of Service Management* 32 (January 2021), pp. 27–51; C. Gronroos and P. Voima, "Critical Service Logic: Make Sense of Value Creation and Co-Creation," *Journal of the Academy of Marketing Science* 41 (March 2013), pp. 133–150; H. Saarijari, P. K. Kannan, and H. Kuusela, "Value Co-Creation: Theoretical Approaches and Practical Implications," *European Business Review* 25 (January 2013), pp. 6–19.
2. See B. Dong and K. Sivakumar, "Customer Participation in Services: Domain, Scope, and Boundaries," *Journal of the Academy of Marketing Science* 45 (November 2017), pp. 944–965; B. Schneider and D. E. Bowen, *Winning the Service Game* (Boston: Harvard Business School Press, 1995), chap. 4; L. A. Bettencourt, "Customer Voluntary Performance: Customers as Partners in Service Delivery," *Journal of Retailing* 73 (Fall 1997), pp. 383–406; P. K. Mills and J. H. Morris, "Clients as 'Partial' Employees: Role Development in Client Participation," *Academy of Management Review* 11 (1986), pp. 726–735; C. H. Lovelock and R. F. Young, "Look to Customers to Increase Productivity," *Harvard Business Review* 57 (Summer 1979), pp. 9–20; A. R. Rodie and S. S. Kleine, "Customer Participation in Services Production and Delivery," in *Handbook of Services Marketing and Management,* ed. T. A. Swartz and D. Iacobucci (Thousand Oaks, CA: Sage, 2000), pp. 111–126; C. K. Prahalad and V. Ramaswamy, "Co-opting Customer Competence," *Harvard Business Review* 78 (January–February 2000), p. 7; and N. Bendapudi and R. P. Leone, "Psychological Implications of Customer Participation in Co-Production," *Journal of Marketing* 67 (January 2003), pp. 14–28; A. S. Gallan, C. B. Jarvis, S. W. Brown, and M. J. Bitner, "Customer Positivity and Participation in Services: An Empirical Test in a Healthcare Context," *Journal of the Academy of Marketing Science* 41 (May 2013), pp. 338–356.
3. S. L. Vargo, and R. F. Lusch, "Evolving to a New Dominant Logic for Marketing," *Journal of Marketing* 68 (January 2004), pp. 1–17; R. F. Lusch, S. L. Vargo, and M O'Brien, "Competing through Service: Insights from Service-Dominant Logic," *Journal of Retailing* 83 (2007), pp. 5–18; Gronroos and Voima, "Critical Service Logic: Making Sense of Value Creation and Co-Creation"; S. L. Vargo and R. F. Lusch, "Institutions and Axioms: An Extension and Update of Service-Dominant Logic," *Journal of the Academy of Marketing Science* 44 (January 2016), pp. 5–23.
4. L. A. Bettencourt, S. W. Brown, A. L. Ostrom, and R. I. Roundtree, "Client Co-Production in Knowledge-Intensive Business Services," *California Management Review* 44 (Summer 2002), pp. 100–128.
5. See D. Johnson, B. Yam, C. Limbu, C. Jayachandran, and P. Reddy, "Climbing the Down Escalator: When Customer-to-Customer Interaction May Not be Helping Service Firms," *European Journal of Marketing* 53 (September 2019), pp. 2348–2372; S. J. Grove and R. P. Fisk, "The Impact of Other Customers on Service Experiences: A Critical Incident Examination of 'Getting Along', " *Journal of Retailing* 73 (Spring 1997), pp. 63–85; C. I. Martin and C. A. Pranter, "Compatibility Management: Customer-to-Customer Relationships in Service Environments," *Journal of Services Marketing* 3 (Summer 1989), pp. 5–15; and R. Nicholls, "New Directions for Customer-to-Customer Interaction Research," *Journal of Services Marketing* 24 (2010), pp. 87–97.
6. Grove and Fisk, "The Impact of Other Customers on Service Experiences."

7. T. Schaefers, K. Wittkowski, S. Benoit, and R. Ferraro, "Contagious Effects of Customer Misbehavior in Access-Based Services," *Journal of Service Research* 19 (February 2016), pp 3–21.
8. L. Landro, "ICUs' New Message: Welcome, Families," *The Wall Street Journal,* July 12, 2007, pp. Al+.
9. M. S. Rosenbaum and C. A. Massiah, "When Customers Receive Support from Other Customers," *Journal of Service Research* 9 (February 2007), pp. 257–270.
10. Grove and Fisk, "The Impact of Other Customers on Service Experiences."
11. K. Harris and S. Baron, "Consumer-to-Consumer Conversations in Service Settings," *Journal of Service Research* 6 (February 2004), pp. 287–303.
12. See P. K. Mills, R. B. Chase, and N. Margulies, "Motivating the Client/Employee System as a Service Production Strategy," *Academy of Management Review* 8 (1983), pp. 301–310; D. E. Bowen, "Managing Customers as Human Resources in Service Organizations," *Human Resource Management* 25 (1986), pp. 371–383; and Mills and Morris, "Clients as 'Partial' Employees."
13. Bettencourt, Brown, Ostrom, and Roundtree, "Client Co-Production in Knowledge-Intensive Business Services."
14. Landro, "ICUs' New Message."
15. R. B. Chase, "Where Does the Customer Fit in a Service Operation?" *Harvard Business Review* 56 (November–December 1978), pp. 137–142.
16. See S. Auh, B. Menguc, C. S. Katsikeas, and Y. S. Jung, "When Does Customer Participation Matter? An Empirical Investigation of the Role of Customer Empowerment in the Customer Participation–Performance Link," *Journal of Marketing Research* 56 (December 2019), pp. 1012–1033; V. Nardi et al., "A Meta-Analysis of the Relationship Between Customer Participation and Brand Outcomes," *Journal of Business Research* 117 (September 2020), pp. 450–460; Mills, Chase, and Margulies, "Motivating the Client/Employee System."
17. See M. Xue and P. T. Harker, "Customer Efficiency: Concept and Its Impact on E-Business Management," *Journal of Service Research* 4 (May 2002), pp. 253–267; and B. Kiviat, "The End of Customer Service," in "What's Next 2008," *Time Magazine*, March 13, 2008.
18. K. W. Chan, C. K. Yim, and S. S. K. Lam, "Is Customer Participation in Value Creation a Double-Edged Sword? Evidence from Professional Financial Services across Cultures," *Journal of Marketing* 74 (May 2010), pp. 48–64.
19. See D. W. Johnson, R. T. Johnson, and K. A. Smith, *Active Learning: Cooperation in the College Classroom* (Edina, MN: Interaction Book Company, 1991).
20. S. Dellande, M. C. Gilly, and J. L. Graham, "Gaining Compliance and Losing Weight: The Role of the Service Provider in Healthcare Services," *Journal of Marketing* 68 (July 2004), pp. 78–91.
21. For research in this area see S. Auh, S. J. Bell, C. S. McLeod, and E. Shih, "Co-Production and Customer Loyalty in Financial Services," *Journal of Retailing* 83 (2007), pp. 359–370; Gallan, Jarvis, Brown, and Bitner, "Customer Positivity and Participation in Services"; J. R. McColl-Kennedy, S. L. Vargo, T. S. Dagger, J. C. Sweeney, and Y. V. van Kasteren, "Healthcare Customer Value Cocreation Practice Styles," *Journal of Service Research* 15 (November 2012), pp. 370–389; J. C. Sweeney, T. S. Danaher, and J. R. McColl-Kennedy, "Customer Effort in Value Cocreation Activities: Improving Quality of Life and Behavioral Intentions of Healthcare Customers," *Journal of Service Research* 18 (May 2015),

pp. 318–335; M. Mende and J. van Doorne, "Coproduction of Transformative Services as a Pathway to Improved Consumer Well-Being: Findings from a Longitudinal Study on Financial Counseling," *Journal of Service Research* 18 (May 2015), pp. 351–368; M. Mende, M. L. Scott, M. J. Bitner, and A. L. Ostrom, "Activating Consumers for Better Service Coproduction Outcomes Through Eustress: The Interplay of Firm-Assigned Workload, Service Literacy, and Organizational Support," *Journal of Public Policy and Marketing*, 36 (April 2017), pp. 137–155.

22. S. W. Kelley, S. J. Skinner, and J. H. Donnelly Jr., "Organizational Socialization of Service Customers," *Journal of Business Research* 25 (1992), pp. 197–214.
23. C. Claycomb, C. A. Lengnick-Hall, and L. W. Inks, "The Customer as a Productive Resource: A Pilot Study and Strategic Implications," *Journal of Business Strategies* 18 (Spring 2001), pp. 47–69.
24. Several of the scenarios are adapted from C. Goodwin, " 'I Can Do It Myself': Training the Service Consumer to Contribute to Service Productivity," *Journal of Services Marketing* 2 (Fall 1988), pp. 71–78.
25. J. E. G. Bateson, "The Self-Service Customer—Empirical Findings," in *Emerging Perspectives in Services Marketing,* ed. L. L. Berry, G. L. Shostack, and G. D. Upah (Chicago: American Marketing Association, 1983), pp. 50–53.
26. V. S. Folkes, "Recent Attribution Research in Consumer Behavior: A Review and New Directions," *Journal of Consumer Research* 14 (March 1988), pp. 548–565; M. J. Bitner, "Evaluating Service Encounters: The Effects of Physical Surroundings and Employee Responses," *Journal of Marketing* 54 (April 1990), pp. 69–82.
27. See Bendapudi and Leone, "Psychological Implications of Customer Participation in Co-Production"; S. Heidenreich, K. Wittkowski, M. Handrich, and T. Falk, "The Dark Side of Customer Co-Creation: Exploring the Consequences of Failed Co-Created Services," *Journal of the Academy of Marketing Science* 43 (2015), pp. 279–296.
28. R. F. Lusch, S. W. Brown, and G. J. Brunswick, "A General Framework for Explaining Internal vs. External Exchange," *Journal of the Academy of Marketing Science* 10 (Spring 1992), pp. 119–134.
29. Ibid; also see B. Yu, H. Xu, and B. Emery, "How to Better Motivate Customers to Participate in the Self-Design Process: A Conceptual Model in Underlying Self-Congruence Mechanism." *Frontiers in Psychology* 11 (August 2020), p. 1995.
30. Gronroos and Voima, "Critical Service Logic: Making Sense of Value Creation and Co-Creation."
31. See M. J. Bitner, A. L. Ostrom, and M. L. Meuter, "Implementing Successful Self-Service Technologies," *Academy of Management Executive* 16 (November 2002), pp. 96–109.
32. This figure is adapted from the original source that focused on retail gasoline services: M. L. Meuter and M.J. Bitner, "Self-Service Technologies: Extending Service Frameworks and Identifying Issues for Research," in *Marketing Theory and Applications,* ed. D. Grewal and C. Pechmann (American Marketing Association Winter Conference, 1998), pp. 12–19.
33. See P. Dabholkar, "Consumer Evaluations of New Technology-Based Self-Service Options: An Investigation of Alternative Models of Service Quality," *International Journal of Research in Marketing* 13 (1996), pp. 29–51; F. Davis, "User Acceptance of Information Technology: System Characteristics, User Perceptions and Behavioral Impact," *International Journal of Man-Machine Studies* 38

(1993), pp. 475–487; L. M. Bobbitt and P. A. Dabholkar, "Integrating Attitudinal Theories to Understand and Predict Use of Technology-Based Self-Service," *International Journal of Service Industry Management* 12 (2001), pp. 423–450; J. M. Curran, M. L. Meuter, and C. F. Surprenant, "Intentions to Use Self-Service Technologies: A Confluence of Multiple Attitudes," *Journal of Service Research* 5 (February 2003), pp. 209–224; and S. Al-Natour and I. Benbasat, "The Adoption and Use of IT Artifacts: A New Interaction-Centric Model for the Study of User-Artifact Relationships," *Journal of the Association for Information Systems* 10 (2009), pp. 661–685.

34. M. L. Meuter, M. J. Bitner, A. L. Ostrom, and S. W. Brown, "Choosing among Alternative Service Delivery Modes: An Investigation of Customer Trial of Self-Service Technologies," *Journal of Marketing* 69 (April 2005), pp. 61–83.
35. M. L. Meuter, A. L. Ostrom, R. I. Roundtree, and M. J. Bitner, "Self-Service Technologies: Understanding Customer Satisfaction with Technology-Based Service Encounters," *Journal of Marketing* 64 (July 2000), pp. 50–64.
36. M. J. Reinders, P. A. Dabholkar, and R. T. Frambach, "Consequences of Forcing Consumers to Use Technology-Based Self-Service," *Journal of Service Research* 11 (November 2008), pp. 107–123.
37. M. Blut, C. Wang, and K. Schoefer, "Factors Influencing the Acceptance of Self-Service Technologies: A Meta-Analysis," *Journal of Service Research* 19 (November 2016), pp. 396–416.
38. Meuter, Bitner, Ostrom, and Brown, "Choosing Among Alternative Service Delivery Modes"; see also Y. Moon and F. X. Frei, "Exploding the Self-Service Myth," *Harvard Business Review* 78 (May–June 2000), pp. 26–27; and Bitner, Ostrom, and Meuter, "Implementing Successful Self-Service Technologies."
39. A. Parasuraman and C. L. Colby, *Techno-Ready Marketing: How and Why Your Customers Adopt Technology* (New York: The Free Press, 2001); A. Parasuraman and C. L. Colby, "An Updated and Streamlined Technology Readiness Index TRI 2.0," *Journal of Service Research* 18 (February 2015), pp. 59–74.
40. R. C. Ford and J. R. McColl-Kennedy, "Organizational Strategies for Filling the Customer Can-Do/Must-Do Gap," *Business Horizons* 58 (August 2015), pp. 459–468.
41. Bowen, "Managing Customers as Human Resources."
42. Bateson, "The Self-Service Customer."
43. J. Light, "With Customer Service, Real Person Trumps Text," *The Wall Street Journal,* April 25, 2011, p. B7.
44. Meuter, Bitner, Ostrom, and Brown, "Choosing among Alternative Service Delivery Modes."
45. Bowen, "Managing Customers as Human Resources"; Schneider and Bowen, *Winning the Service Game,* chap. 4; Meuter, Bitner, Ostrom, and Brown, "Choosing Among Alternative Service Delivery Modes"; Dellande, Gilly, and Graham, "Gaining Compliance and Losing Weight"; Ford and McColl-Kennedy, "Organizational Strategies for Filling the Customer Can-Do/Must-Do Gap."
46. S. W. Kelley, J. H. Donnelly Jr., and S. J. Skinner, "Customer Participation in Service Production and Delivery," *Journal of Retailing* 66 (Fall 1990), pp. 315–335; Schneider and Bowen, *Winning the Service Game,* chap. 4; L. Guo, E. J. Arnould, T. W. Gruen, and C. Tang, "Socializing to Co-Produce: Pathways to Consumers' Financial Well-Being," *Journal of Service Research* 16 (November 2013),

pp. 549–563; B. Dong, K. Sivakumar, K. R. Evans, and S. Zou, "Effect of Customer Participation on Service Outcomes: The Moderating Role of Participation Readiness," *Journal of Service Research* 18 (May 2015), pp. 160–176; M. Mende, M. L. Scott, M. J. Bitner, and A. L. Ostrom, "Activating Consumers for Better Service Coproduction Outcomes through Eustress."

47. Bowen, "Managing Customers as Human Resources."
48. Ibid.; see also L. C. Harris and K. L. Reynolds, "The Consequences of Dysfunctional Customer Behavior," *Journal of Service Research* 6 (November 2003), pp. 144–161.
49. E. Yu, "Shanghai Issues Etiquette Guide for Disneyland Visitors," *CNN,* May 25, 2016, http://www.cnn.com/2016/05/25/travel/shanghai-disneyland-etiquette-guide/.
50. Martin and Pranter, "Compatibility Management."

Chapter Thirteen

Managing Demand and Capacity

This chapter's learning objectives are to:

1. Explain the underlying issue for capacity-constrained services: lack of inventory capability.
2. Present the implications of time, labor, equipment, and facilities constraints combined with variations in demand patterns.
3. Lay out strategies for matching supply and demand through (a) shifting demand to match capacity or (b) adjusting capacity to meet demand.
4. Demonstrate the benefits and risks of yield management strategies in forging a balance among capacity utilization, pricing, market segmentation, and financial return.
5. Provide strategies for managing waiting lines for times when capacity and demand cannot be aligned.

How to Fill Over 600 Rooms 365 Days of the Year

The Phoenician Hotel in Scottsdale, Arizona, is an upscale hotel in the center of a metropolitan area of nearly 5 million people, one of the largest metropolitan areas in the United States. The hotel is frequently cited for its service and has been given the Five Star Award by Forbes Travel four times. It has more than 600 luxury rooms, eight restaurants, seven beautiful pools, and spacious meeting and conference facilities.[1] These restaurants and meeting facilities are available to guests 365 days and nights of the year. Yet natural demand for them varies tremendously. During the tourist season from November through mid-April, demand for rooms is high, often exceeding available space. From mid-May through September, however, when temperatures regularly exceed 100 degrees Fahrenheit, the demand for rooms drops considerably. Because the hotel caters to business travelers and business meetings, demand has a weekly cycle in addition to the seasonal fluctuations. Business travelers do not stay over weekends. Thus, demand for rooms from the hotel's primary market segment drops on Friday and Saturday nights.

To smooth the peaks and valleys of demand for its facilities, the Phoenician has employed a number of strategies. Group business (primarily business conferences) is pursued throughout the year to fill the lower demand periods. A variety of special event, sports, wedding, and getaway packages are offered year-round to increase weekend demand for rooms. During the hot summer months, the hotel encourages

Ron Niebrugge/Alamy Stock Photo

local Phoenix metro and nearby Tucson residents to experience the luxury of the hotel. One creative package used in the past included an attractively priced hotel stay combined with a "culinary countdown," which gives patrons the option to enjoy a three-course meal, afternoon tea, and burgers and dessert at the on-site restaurants. The hotel also advertises spa specials and deals to entice these "stay-cationers." By encouraging local people to use the hotel, the hotel increases its occupancy during slow demand times, while residents of the community get a chance to enjoy an experience they may not be able to afford during the high season.

Most downtown hotels in urban areas face the same weekly demand fluctuations that the Phoenician deals with, and many have found a partial solution by catering to families and children on the weekends. For many dual-career couples, weekend getaways are a primary form of relaxation and vacation. The downtown hotels cater to these couples and families by offering discounted room rates, child-oriented activities and amenities, and an environment in which families feel comfortable. For example, the Lotte New York Palace Hotel—the closest hotel to American Girl Place—attempts to increase weekend stays by offering an "American Girl Place Package" to families with young daughters. The package, targeted for nonbusiness customers, comes with a complimentary American Girl doll-sized travel bed for an American Girl doll that girls can take home with them and includes turndown service for their dolls.

For the Phoenician Hotel in Scottsdale and many other hotels, managing demand and utilizing the hotel's fixed capacity of rooms, restaurants, and meeting facilities can be a seasonal, weekly, and even daily challenge. Although the hotel industry epitomizes the challenges of demand and capacity management, many service providers face similar problems. For example, tax accountants and air-conditioning maintenance services face seasonal demand fluctuations, whereas services such as commuter trains and restaurants face daily and even hourly variations in customer demand. For some businesses, demand is predictable, as for a tax accountant. For others, such as management or technology consultants, demand may be less predictable, fluctuating based on customer needs and business cycles. Sometimes firms experience too much demand for the existing capacity and sometimes capacity sits idle.

Overuse or underuse of a service can directly contribute to Gap 3: failure to deliver service as it was designed and specified. For example, when demand for services exceeds maximum capacity, the quality of service may drop because staff and facilities are overtaxed. And some customers may be turned away, not receiving the service at all. During periods of slow demand it may be necessary to reduce prices or cut service amenities; however, when firms change the nature of the service and, perhaps, the makeup of the clientele, they run the risk of not delivering what customers expect. For example, older travelers or business groups who are in a hotel on a weekend may resent the invasion of families and children because it changes the nature of the service they expected. At the pool, for example, collisions can occur between adults trying to swim laps and children playing water games.

In this chapter we focus on the challenges of matching supply and demand in capacity-constrained services. The service performance gap can occur when organizations fail to smooth the peaks and valleys of demand, overuse their capacities, attract an inappropriate customer mix in their efforts to build demand, or rely too much on price in smoothing demand. The chapter examines these issues and suggests strategies for addressing them. The effective use of capacity is frequently a key success factor for service organizations.

THE UNDERLYING ISSUE: LACK OF INVENTORY CAPABILITY

The fundamental issue underlying supply and demand management in services is the lack of inventory capability. Unlike manufacturing firms, service firms cannot build up inventories during periods of slow demand to use later when demand increases. This lack of inventory capability is due to the perishability of services and their simultaneous production and consumption. An airline seat not sold on a given flight cannot be left in inventory and resold the following day. The productive capacity of that seat on that flight has perished. Similarly, an hour of a lawyer's billable time cannot be saved from one day to the next. Services also cannot be transported from one place to another or transferred from person to person. Thus, the Phoenician Hotel's services cannot be moved to an alternative location in the summer months—say, to the Pacific coast, where summers are ideal for tourists and demand for hotel rooms is high.

The lack of inventory capability combined with fluctuating demand leads to a variety of potential outcomes, as illustrated in Figure 13.1.[2] The horizontal lines in Figure 13.1 indicate service capacity, and the curved line indicates customer demand for the service. In many services, capacity is relatively fixed in the short-term; thus, capacity can be designated by a flat horizontal line over a certain time period. Demand for service frequently fluctuates, however, as indicated by the curved line. The topmost horizontal line in Figure 13.1 represents maximum capacity. For example, in our

FIGURE 13.1
Variations in Demand Relative to Capacity

J. Wirtz and C. H. Lovelock, *Services Marketing*, 9th ed., (Hackensack, NJ: World Scientific Publishing Co., 2021), p. 303.

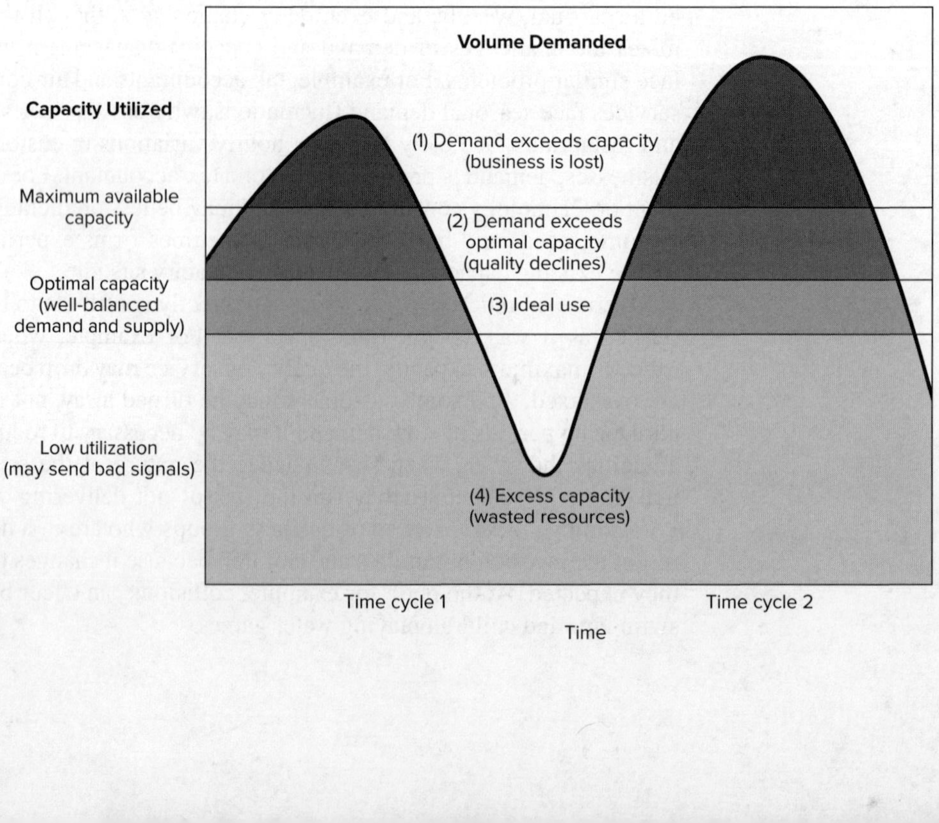

opening vignette, the horizontal line would represent the Phoenician's over 600 rooms, or it could represent 70,000 seats in a large university football stadium. The rooms and the seats remain constant, but demand for them fluctuates. The band between the second and third horizontal lines represents optimal capacity—the best use of the capacity from the perspective of both customers and the company (the difference between optimal and maximum capacity utilization is discussed later in the chapter). The areas in the middle of Figure 13.1 are labeled to represent four basic scenarios that can result from different combinations of capacity and demand:

1. *Excess demand.* The level of demand exceeds maximum capacity. In this situation some customers will be turned away, resulting in lost business opportunities. For the customers who do receive the service, its quality may not match what was promised because of crowding or overtaxing of staff and facilities.
2. *Demand exceeds optimal capacity.* No one is being turned away, but the quality of service may still suffer because of overuse, crowding, or staff being pushed beyond their abilities to deliver consistent quality.
3. *Demand and supply are balanced at the level of optimal capacity.* Staff and facilities are occupied at an ideal use level. No one is overworked, facilities can be maintained, and customers are receiving quality service without undesirable delays.
4. *Excess capacity.* Demand is below optimal capacity. Productive resources in the form of labor, equipment, and facilities are underutilized, resulting in low productivity and lower profits. Customers may receive excellent quality on an individual level because they have the full use of the facilities, no waiting, and complete attention from the staff. If, however, service quality depends on the presence of other customers, customers may be disappointed or may worry that they have chosen an inferior service provider.

Not all firms will be challenged equally in terms of managing supply and demand. The seriousness of the problem will depend on the *extent of demand fluctuations over time* and the *extent to which supply is constrained* (Table 13.1).[3] Organizations in some service industries will experience wide fluctuations in demand (hospitals, transportation, restaurants), whereas others will have narrower fluctuations (insurance, laundry,

TABLE 13.1
Demand and Capacity for Service Providers

Extent to Which Supply Is Constrained	Extent of Demand Fluctuations over Time: Wide	Extent of Demand Fluctuations over Time: Narrow
Peak demand can usually be met without a major delay.	1 Electricity Natural gas Police and fire emergencies Internet services	2 Insurance Legal services Banking Laundry and dry cleaning Hair salon
Peak demand regularly exceeds capacity.	4 Accounting and tax preparation Passenger transportation Hotels Restaurants Hospital emergency rooms	3 Services similar to those in cell 2 that have insufficient capacity for their base level of business

Source: Adapted from C. H. Lovelock, "Classifying Services to Gain Strategic Marketing Insights," *Journal of Marketing* 47 (Summer 1983), p. 17.

banking). For some, peak demand can usually be met even when demand fluctuates (electricity, natural gas, Internet services), but for others peak demand may frequently exceed capacity (hospital emergency rooms, restaurants near football stadiums, hotels next to universities). Those firms with wide variations in demand (cells 1 and 4 in Table 13.1), and particularly those with wide fluctuations in demand that regularly exceed capacity (cell 4), will find the issues and strategies in this chapter particularly important to their success. Those firms that find themselves in cell 3 may decide a "one-time-fix" (as discussed in Chapter 9) to expand their capacity to match regular patterns of excessive demand will sufficiently address the situation. The industries in Table 13.1 are provided to illustrate where *most* firms in those industries would likely be classified. In reality, an individual firm from any industry could find itself in any of the four cells, depending on its immediate circumstances.

To identify effective strategies for managing supply and demand fluctuations, an organization needs a clear understanding of the constraints on its capacity and the underlying demand patterns.

CAPACITY CONSTRAINTS

For many firms, service capacity is relatively fixed. As indicated in Table 13.2, critical fixed-capacity factors can be—depending on the type of service—time, labor, equipment, facilities, or (in many cases) a combination of these.

Time, Labor, Equipment, and Facilities

For some service businesses, the primary constraint on service production is *time*. For example, a lawyer, a consultant, a hairdresser, a plumber, and a psychological counselor

TABLE 13.2
Constraints on Capacity

Nature of the Constraint	Type of Service*
Time	Legal Consulting Accounting Medical
Labor	Law firm Accounting firm Consulting firm Health clinic
Equipment	Delivery services Network services Utilities Health clubs
Facilities	Hospitals Airlines Schools Theaters

*The examples illustrate the most common capacity constraint for each type of service. In reality, any of the service organizations listed can be operating under multiple constraints. For example, a law firm may be operating under constrained labor capacity (too few attorneys) and facilities constraints (not enough office space) at the same time.

all primarily sell their time. In such contexts, if the service worker is not available or if his or her time is not used productively, profits are lost. If there is excess demand at a specific time, additional time cannot be created to satisfy it. From the point of view of the service provider, time is the constraint.

From the point of view of a firm that employs a large number of service providers, *labor* or staffing levels can be the primary capacity constraint. A law firm, a university department, a consulting firm, a tax accounting firm, and a repair and maintenance contractor may all face the reality that at certain times demand for their organization's services cannot be met because the staff is already operating at peak capacity. However, it does not always make sense (nor may it be possible in a competitive labor market) to hire additional service providers if low demand is a reality a large percentage of the time.

In other cases, *equipment* may be the critical constraint. For trucking or air-freight delivery services, the number of trucks or airplanes needed to fulfill demand may be the capacity limitation. During the Christmas holidays, UPS, FedEx, and other delivery service providers face this issue. Health clubs also deal with this limitation, particularly at certain times of the day (before work, during lunch hours, after work) and in certain months of the year. For network service providers, bandwidth, servers, and switches represent their capacity constraints.

Finally, many firms face restrictions brought about by their limited *facilities.* Hotels have only a certain number of rooms to sell, airlines are limited by the number of seats on their aircraft, educational institutions are constrained by the number of rooms and the number of seats in each classroom, and restaurant capacity is restricted to the number of tables and seats available.

Understanding the primary capacity constraint, or the combination of factors that restricts capacity, is a first step in designing strategies to deal with supply and demand issues.

Optimal versus Maximum Use of Capacity

To fully understand capacity issues, it is important to know the difference between *optimal* and *maximum* use of capacity. As suggested in Figure 13.1, optimal and maximum capacity may not be the same. Using capacity at an optimal level means that resources are fully employed but not overused and that customers are receiving quality service in a timely manner. Maximum capacity, on the other hand, represents the absolute limit of service availability. In the case of a sporting event, optimal and maximum capacity may be the same. The entertainment value of the game is enhanced for customers when every seat is filled, and obviously the profitability for the home team is greatest under these circumstances (see accompanying photo on page 384). On the other hand, in a university classroom it is usually not desirable for students or faculty to have every seat filled. In this case, optimal use of capacity is less than the maximum. In some cases, maximum use of capacity may result in excessive waiting by customers, as in a popular restaurant. From the perspective of customer satisfaction, optimal use of the restaurant's capacity will be less than maximum use.

In the case of equipment or facilities constraints, the maximum capacity at any given time is obvious. There are only a certain number of weight machines in the health club, a certain number of seats in the airplane, and a limited amount of space in a cargo carrier. In the case of a bottling plant, when maximum capacity on the assembly line is exceeded, bottles begin to break and the system shuts down. Thus, it is relatively easy to observe the effects of exceeding maximum equipment capacity in many manufacturing situations.

For sports and other entertainment venues, maximum and optimal capacity may be close to the same.

Doug Pensinger/Getty Images

When the limitation is people's time or labor, maximum capacity is harder to specify because people are in a sense more flexible than facilities and equipment. When an individual service provider's maximum capacity has been exceeded, the result is likely to cause decreased service quality, customer dissatisfaction, and employee burnout and turnover, but these outcomes may not be immediately observable, even to the employee. While it is relatively easy for firms to identify the maximum capacity for physical constraints like space, it is much more difficult to know what the maximum capacity of a human being is. As a result, firms may be able to push employees beyond their optimal capacity for a while, but not learn of the maximum capacity of an employee until the person quits or encounters health problems. Indeed, it is often easy for a consulting firm to take on one more assignment, taxing its employees beyond their maximum capacity, or for an HMO clinic to schedule a few more appointments in a day, stretching its staff and physicians beyond their maximum capacity. Given the potential costs in terms of reduced quality and customer and employee dissatisfaction, it is critical for the firm to understand optimal and maximum human capacity limits.

DEMAND PATTERNS

To manage fluctuating demand in a service business, it is necessary to have a clear understanding of demand patterns, why they vary, and the market segments that constitute demand at different points in time.[4]

The Charting of Demand Patterns

To begin to understand demand patterns, the organization needs to chart the level of demand over relevant time periods. Organizations that have good customer information systems can track this information very accurately. Others may need to chart demand patterns more informally. Daily, weekly, and monthly demand levels should be tracked, and if seasonality is a suspected problem, graphing should be done for data from at least the past year. In some services, such as restaurants or healthcare, hourly fluctuations within a day may also be relevant. Sometimes demand patterns are intuitively obvious; in other cases, patterns may not reveal themselves until the data are tracked.

Predictable Cycles

As service providers consider customer demand levels, predictable cycles may be detected, including daily (variations occur by hour), weekly (variations occur by day), monthly (variations occur by day or week), and/or yearly (variations occur according to months or seasons). In some cases, predictable patterns occur at all periods. For example, in the restaurant industry, especially in seasonal tourist locations, demand can vary predictably by month, by week, by day, and by hour. Similarly, the demand for a bank's services can vary by hour (with lunch time and end of the day with the most demand), by day of the week (with the last day of the week and the first day of the week being the most popular), and by day of the month (with the day that Social Security checks arrive being among the highest in demand).

If a predictable cycle is detected, the underlying causes should be identified. The Phoenician Hotel knows that demand cycles are based on seasonal weather patterns and that weekly variations are based on the work week (business travelers do not stay at the hotel over the weekend). Tax accountants can predict demand based on when taxes are due—quarterly and annually. Services catering to children and families are affected by variations in school hours and vacations. Retail, tax services, restaurants, and travel services have peak periods at certain times of the year or times of the week and day. When predictable patterns exist, generally one or more causes can be determined.

Random Demand Fluctuations

Sometimes the patterns of demand appear to be random—there is no apparent predictable cycle. Yet even in this case, causes can often be identified. For example, day-to-day changes in the weather may affect the use of recreational, shopping, or entertainment facilities. Good weather generally increases the demand for the services provided by an amusement park, but it has the opposite effect on movie theaters—people would rather not be inside when the weather is nice. Auto service centers generally find extremely poor weather (either very hot or very cold) increases the demand for their services, whereas mild weather does not seem to have as much of an effect on vehicles. Although the weather cannot be predicted far in advance, it may be possible to anticipate demand a day or two ahead. Health-related events can also be challenging to predict. Accidents, heart attacks, and births all increase demand for hospital services, but the level of demand cannot always easily be determined in advance. Natural disasters such as floods, fires, and hurricanes can dramatically increase the need for such services as insurance, telecommunications, and healthcare. Acts of war and terrorism generate instantaneous need for services that cannot be predicted. For example, during the first few months of the war in the Ukraine in 2022, more than 4 million refugees have escaped to nearby countries (e.g., Poland). With this massive influx of people, these countries have been faced with a sudden increase in demand for services like social welfare, housing, education, and particularly healthcare. Refugees need health services for a variety of reasons—there are traumatic war injuries that need immediate care, chronic conditions requiring regular treatment, vaccinations to prevent the spread of disease in such close quarters, and psychological support for those suffering from anxiety and post-traumatic stress syndrome. With the strain on health

Ilene MacDonald/Alamy Stock Photo

Organizations such as Disney that predict customer patterns can use that information to anticipate demand for their service.

services, many refugees are finding it more and more difficult to get access to the quality care they need.[5]

Our Global Feature illustrates how one company with seemingly random and chaotic demand for its services was able to change its business to serve customers. The feature is also a good example of organizational learning across cultures.

Demand Patterns by Market Segment

An organization that has detailed records on customer transactions may be able to disaggregate demand by market segment, revealing patterns within patterns. Or the analysis may reveal that demand from one segment is predictable, whereas demand from another segment is relatively random. For example, for a bank, the visits from its commercial accounts may occur daily at a predictable time, whereas personal account holders may visit the bank at seemingly random intervals. Health clinics often notice that walk-in or "care needed today" patients tend to concentrate their arrivals on Monday, with fewer needing immediate attention on other days of the week. Many auto service centers experience a similar pattern, as more walk-in customers arrive on Monday morning for car servicing and repair than any other day of the week. Knowing that this pattern exists, many health clinics and auto service centers tend to schedule future appointments (which they can control) for later days of the week, leaving more of Monday available for same-day appointments and walk-ins.

STRATEGIES FOR MATCHING CAPACITY AND DEMAND

When an organization has a clear grasp of its capacity constraints and an understanding of demand patterns, it is in a good position to develop strategies for matching supply and demand. There are two general approaches for accomplishing this match. The first is to smooth the demand fluctuations themselves by *shifting demand* to match existing capacity. This approach implies that the peaks and valleys of the demand curve (Figure 13.1) will be flattened to match as closely as possible the horizontal optimal capacity line. The second general strategy is to *adjust capacity* to match fluctuations in demand. This implies moving the horizontal capacity lines shown in Figure 13.1 to match the ups and downs of the demand curve. Each of these two basic strategies is described next with specific examples.

Strategy 1: Shifting Demand to Match Capacity

As Figure 13.2 illustrates, this strategy includes approaches that aim to (a) reduce demand during peak times or (b) increase demand to match capacity. Accordingly, in employing this strategy an organization might seek to shift customers away from periods in which demand exceeds capacity, perhaps by convincing them to use the service during periods of slow demand. This change may be possible for some customers but not for others. For example, many business travelers are not able to shift their needs for airline, car rental, and hotel services; pleasure travelers, on the other hand, can often shift the timing of their trips. Customers who cannot shift their demand and cannot be accommodated because of insufficient capacity represent lost business for the firm.

During periods of slow demand, the organization seeks to attract more and/or different customers to increase demand and thus better utilize its productive capacity. A variety of approaches can be used to shift or increase demand to match capacity.

FIGURE 13.2 Strategies for Shifting Demand to Match Capacity

DEMAND TOO HIGH — **SHIFT DEMAND TO MATCH CAPACITY** — **DEMAND TOO LOW**

Reduce Demand during Peak Times

- Communicate busy days and times to customers.
- Offer incentives for nonpeak usage.
- Modify timing and location of service delivery.
- Set priorities by talking care of loyal or high-need customers first.
- Charge full price for the service—no discounts.

Increase Demand to Match Capacity

- Educate customers about peak times and benefits of nonpeak use.
- Vary how the facility is used.
- Vary the service offering.
- Differentiate on price.

Frequently a firm uses a combination of approaches. Ideas for how to shift demand during both slow and peak periods are shown in Figure 13.2 and described in the following paragraphs.

Reduce Demand during Peak Times

One strategic approach to matching capacity and demand for a service provider focuses on *reducing demand* during times when customer demand is at its peak for the service.

Communicate Busy Days and Times to Customers One approach for shifting demand is to communicate with customers, letting them know the times of peak demand to persuade them to use the service at alternative times and avoid crowding or delays. For example, signs in banks and post offices that let customers know their busiest hours and busiest days of the week can serve as a warning, encouraging customers to shift their demand to another time if possible. Forewarning customers about busy times and possible waits can have added benefits. Many customer service call centers provide a similar warning by informing waiting customers about approximately how long it will be until they are served. Those who do not want to wait may choose to call back later when the customer service department is less busy, leave a call back number, or visit the company's website for faster service.

Offer Incentives for Nonpeak Usage In an attempt to shift demand away from peak times, some firms will offer incentives to encourage customers to shift their use of the service to other times. In northern Midwest states, swimming pool contractors offer additional amenities (e.g., free diving board, free heater, larger pool) to customers who are willing to postpone the purchase/use of their services until the end of the swimming season (say, September or October). Fitness centers that offer Pilates classes during times of lower demand often tout the advantages of smaller classes and increased instructor interaction with clients and frequently extend the class time by 25 percent or more.

Modify Timing and Location of Service Delivery Some firms adjust their hours and days of service delivery to more directly reflect customer demand. Historically, U.S. banks were open only during "bankers' hours" from 10:00 a.m. to 3:00 p.m. every weekday—creating a heavy demand for their services during those hours. However,

Global Feature Cemex Creatively Manages Chaotic Demand for Its Services

Susana Gonzalez/Bloomberg/Getty Images

Imagine a business in which customers' orders are unpredictable, where more than half of all customer orders are changed, often repeatedly and at the last minute, and where the product being delivered is never more than 90 minutes from spoiling. Welcome to the concrete delivery business. Cemex, based in Monterrey, Mexico, and founded in 1906, is a highly successful global player in this industry. The company operates in more than 50 countries across five continents with more than 40,000 employees and regularly has annual net sales in excess of $13 billion.

Yet when two internal consultants examined the business several years ago, they were amazed at the chaos that ruled the industry. Wild weather, unpredictable traffic, spontaneous labor disruptions, and sporadic government inspections of construction sites all combined with ever-changing customer orders to create a sense of chaos and uncontrollability in the business. At that time, Cemex also offered 8,000 grades of concrete available through a half-dozen regional mixing plants, yielding an extremely complex system to manage.

Historically, Cemex had attempted to run the business through controlling its customers, requiring them to stick with their orders and imposing fines for changed orders. Efficiency—not customers—ruled in Cemex's effort to conquer the natural randomness of demand and customers' needs to change orders at the last minute.

The company began searching for new ways to do business. It turned to FedEx and to the 911 emergency dispatch center in Houston, Texas, for ideas. What it found were organizations that, instead of trying to control demand for their services, had developed people and technology that could be flexible in meeting customers' seemingly random demand patterns. Instead of penalizing customers for changing their orders, FedEx does not restrict its customers and, in fact, guarantees delivery at a certain time to any and all locations. This ability to serve customers is made possible by sophisticated information systems that track demand and schedule pickups and deliveries, customer-focused frontline employees, and a customer-centric corporate culture that supports it all. From the 911 center in Houston, Cemex learned that even seemingly random occurrences such as emergency health needs and accidents occur in sufficient number to allow patterns of demand to be discerned and planned for. In terms of Figure 13.1, what FedEx and the 911 emergency center did was adjust their capacity to meet the peaks and valleys of customer demand rather than insisting that the customers adjust their demand to fit the company's constrained capacity.

The observations of how both FedEx and the 911 dispatch center handled demand fluctuations were a revelation to Cemex's team. The company went back to Mexico determined to embrace the complexity of its marketplace and to do business on the customer's terms. The company launched a project called Sincronizacion Dinamica de Operaciones: the dynamic synchronization of operations. It unleashed trucks from previous zone assignments, allowing them to roam the city. It outfitted the trucks with transmitters and receivers connected to a global positioning system (GPS), so that locations, direction, and speed of every vehicle could be tracked. It enrolled its drivers in secondary education classes over a period of two years, so they would be more service oriented and able to deal with customers.

Impressed with FedEx's guaranteed service, Cemex worked toward being able to offer "same-day service, with free, unlimited order changes." It instituted a policy for guaranteed delivery: if a load failed to arrive within 20 minutes of its scheduled delivery time, the buyer received back 20 pesos per cubic meter—"guarantia 20 × 20"—amounting to roughly 5 percent of the total cost.

Cemex embraced the chaos of its industry instead of trying to adjust and change it. By using technology, people, and systems, it was able to match its capacity constraints with its customers' wildly fluctuating demands. And the company came out a winner. Cemex could afford to offer its 20 × 20 guarantee because its reliability regularly exceeded 98 percent!

Today, the company's focus on the customer is clearly stated in the Company Values page of their website: "We build close customer relationships that set us apart from our competition by listening to our customers, understanding their challenges, and providing valuable solutions."

Sources: T. Petzinger Jr., "This Promise Is Set in Concrete," *Fast Company,* April 1999, pp. 216–218; T. Petzinger Jr., *The New Pioneers* (New York: Simon & Schuster, 1999), pp. 91–93; updated with company information from the Cemex website, www.cemex.com, accessed February 23, 2022.

these hours did not necessarily match the times when most people preferred to do their personal banking. Now U.S. banks open early, stay open until 6:00 p.m. many days, and are open on Saturdays, better reflecting customer preferences and smoothing demand patterns. Many banks now have branches in hypermarkets such as Walmart and Meijer, and supermarkets such as Albertson's and Kroger, providing customers with multiple choices of both where and when to do their banking. Online banking has also shifted demand from branches to "anytime, anywhere" websites. Movie theaters often augment their primary viewing schedules by offering additional matinees on weekends and holidays to try to shift demand for their service.

Set Priorities When demand for the service is high and there is limited capacity, service providers can prioritize who is served by taking care of loyal or high-need customers first. A tax firm might decide to serve its best customers rather than first-time walk-ins just prior to income tax due dates, and emergency medical centers move the most severe cases to the top of the priority list.

Charge Full Price Firms generally charge full price for service during those periods of time that they know their services are historically in high demand; no discounts are allowed during such times. One of the busiest periods of the year for airlines are those days just before and just after the Thanksgiving holiday; for this reason, most airlines give priority for seating to those paying full fares and prohibit the use of frequent flyer miles for free seats on those days. Because demand is so high, customers looking for discounted or free tickets find that the days around this holiday have been "blacked out"; to travel on those days, they must purchase tickets at regular fares.

Increase Demand to Match Capacity

Other approaches service providers may consider in matching capacity and demand focus on *increasing demand* for service during times when the service is operating at less than full capacity.

Educate Customers Although a firm may know well and be able to anticipate times of increased demand, customers may not be aware of these times. Advertising and sales messages can be used to inform customers about times when demand is low. Electric utility companies often publicize periods of the day when demand for electricity is lower and urge customers to use washing machines or other equipment that consume large amounts of energy during those times. Promotional campaigns can also emphasize different service benefits to customers during peak and slow periods. For example, air-conditioning firms often promote their preventive maintenance services in early spring, before temperatures get too high, encouraging customers to use their services before demand is high and pointing out the quick availability of their service people and the reduced anxiety from not waiting "until it is too late" by calling early.

yanishevska/Shutterstock

In summer months many ski resorts switch from targeting snow skiers to mountain bikers.

Vary How the Facility Is Used Another approach to increasing demand is to change how the service facility is used, depending on the season of the year, day of the week, or time of day. For example, Whistler Mountain, a ski resort in Vancouver, Canada, offers its slopes to mountain bikers and its facilities for executive development and training programs during the summer, when snow skiing is not possible.

A hospital in the Los Angeles area rents its facilities to film production crews who need realistic hospital settings for movies or television shows. Movie theaters are sometimes rented during weekdays by business groups and on Sunday mornings by church groups who have no building of their own. All of these are examples of how varying the use of the service facility can occur during a period of low demand.

Vary the Service Offering A similar approach entails changing the nature of the service offering. Accounting firms, for example, focus on tax preparation early in the year and until April 15, when federal taxes are due in the United States. During other times of the year, they can focus on audits and general tax consulting activities. During professional basketball games, the demand for food at concession stands increases dramatically during the breaks between quarters—so much so that many customers decide not to make purchases for fear they will miss seeing the game because of long lines. In response to this situation, concessions at some sport stadiums are now offered through phone apps; fans can order food and drinks and are notified when an order is ready for pick up, thereby cutting long lines; and in some stadiums, the food is delivered to customers without them having to leave their seats. In larger cities across the globe, McDonald's offers food delivery as a way to increase demand for its service.[6] In these examples, the service offering and associated benefits are changed to smooth customer demand for the organization's resources.

Care should be exercised in implementing strategies to change the service offering because such changes may imply and require alterations in other marketing mix variables—such as promotion, pricing, and staffing—to match the new offering. Unless these additional mix variables are altered effectively to support the offering, the strategy may not work. Even when done well, the downside of such changes can be confusion about the organization's image from the customers' perspective or a loss of strategic focus for the organization and its employees.

Differentiate on Price A common response during periods of slow demand is to discount the price of the service. This strategy relies on basic economics of supply and demand. To be effective, however, a price differentiation strategy depends on solid understanding of customer price sensitivity and demand curves. For example, business travelers are far less price sensitive than are families traveling for pleasure. For the Phoenician Hotel (our opening vignette), lowering prices during the slow summer months is not likely to increase bookings from business travelers dramatically. However, the lower summer prices attract considerable numbers of families and local guests who want an opportunity to experience a luxury hotel but are not able to afford the rooms during peak season.

Heavy use of price differentiation to smooth demand can be a risky strategy. Customers may grow accustomed to the lower price and expect to get the same deal the next time they use the service. If communication with customers is unclear, customers may not understand the reasons for the discounts and will expect to pay the same discounted price during peak demand periods. Overuse or exclusive use of price as a strategy for smoothing demand is also risky because of the potential impact on the organization's image, the potential for attracting undesired market segments, and the possibility that those customers paying higher prices may feel they have been treated unfairly.

Strategy 2: Adjusting Capacity to Meet Demand

A second strategic approach to matching supply and demand focuses on *adjusting capacity*. As Figure 13.3 illustrates, this strategy includes approaches that aim to (a) increase or (b) decrease capacity temporarily. The fundamental idea here is to adjust,

FIGURE 13.3 **Strategies for Adjusting Capacity to Match Demand**

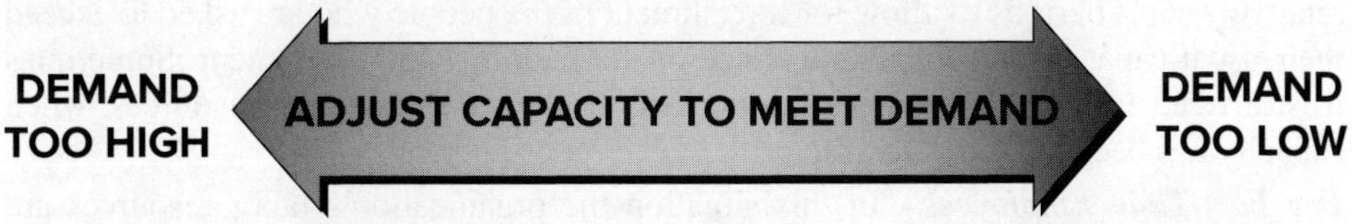

Increase Capacity Temporarily

- Stretch people, facilities, and equipment temporarily.
- Use part-time employees.
- Cross-train employees.
- Outsource activities.
- Rent or share facilities and equipment.

Decrease Capacity Temporarily

- Schedule downtime during periods of low demand.
- Perform maintenance and renovations.
- Schedule vacations and employee hiring/training strategically.
- Modify or move facilities and equipment.

stretch, and align capacity to match customer demand (rather than working on shifting demand to match capacity, as just described). During periods of peak demand the organization seeks to stretch or expand its capacity as much as possible. During periods of slow demand it tries to shrink capacity so as not to waste resources. General strategies for adjusting the four primary service resources (time, people, equipment, and facilities) are discussed throughout the rest of this section. In Figure 13.3, we summarize specific ideas for adjusting capacity during periods of peak and slow demand. Often, a number of different strategies are used simultaneously.

Increase Capacity Temporarily

Existing capacity can often be expanded temporarily to match demand. In such cases, no new resources are added; rather, the people, facilities, and equipment are asked to work harder and longer to meet demand.

Stretch People, Facilities, and Equipment Temporarily It may be possible to extend the hours of service temporarily to accommodate demand. A health clinic might stay open longer during flu season, retailers are open longer hours during the holiday shopping season, and accountants have extended appointment hours (evenings and Saturdays) in the weeks just before tax deadlines. Indeed, in many service organizations, employees are asked to work longer and harder during periods of peak demand. For example, consulting organizations face extensive peaks and valleys with respect to demand for their services. During peak demand, associates are asked to take on additional projects and work longer hours. And frontline service personnel in banks, tourist attractions, restaurants, and telecommunications companies are asked to serve more customers per hour during busy times than during "normal" hours or days.

Facilities such as theaters, restaurants, meeting facilities, and classrooms can sometimes be expanded temporarily by the addition of tables, chairs, or other equipment needed by customers. Or, as in the case of a commuter train, a car that holds a fixed number of people seated comfortably can "expand" by accommodating standing passengers. Similarly, computers, power lines, guided tours, and maintenance equipment can often be stretched beyond what would be considered the maximum capacity for short periods to accommodate peak demand.

In using these types of "stretch" strategies, the organization needs to recognize the wear and tear on resources and the potential for inferior quality of service that may go with extended usage of such strategies. These strategies should thus be used for relatively short periods to allow for refreshment of the people who are asked to exceed their usual capacity and for maintenance of the facilities and equipment. Sometimes it is difficult to know in advance, particularly in the case of human resources, when capacity has been stretched too far.

Use Part-Time Employees In this situation the organization's labor resources are being aligned with demand. Retailers hire part-time employees during the holiday rush; tax accountants engage temporary help during tax season; tourist resorts bring in extra workers during peak season. To address the increased demand for package delivery at the end of the year, UPS has been known to hire more than 100,000 temporary employees to work between Thanksgiving and Christmas to handle the holiday rush.[7] Restaurants often ask employees to work split shifts (work the lunch shift, leave for a few hours, and come back for the dinner rush) during peak mealtime hours.

Cross-Train Employees If employees are cross-trained, they can shift among tasks, filling in where they are most needed. Cross-training increases the efficiency of the whole system and avoids underutilizing employees in some areas while others are being overtaxed. Many airlines cross-train their employees to move from ticketing to working the gate counter to assisting with baggage if needed. In some fast-food restaurants, employees specialize in one task (like making french fries) during busy hours, and the team of specialists may number 10 people. During slow hours the team may shrink to 3, with each of the remaining persons performing a variety of other functions. Grocery stores also use this strategy, with most employees able to move as needed from cashiering to stocking shelves to bagging groceries.

Outsource Activities Firms that find they have a temporary peak in demand for internal services may choose to outsource the service. For example, in recent years, many firms have found they do not have the capacity to fulfill their own needs for technology support, web design, and software-related services. Hospitals in Arizona often use healthcare staffing agencies to temporarily hire registered nurses for three months during the winter to handle the influx of winter visitors and the onset of the flu season. Rather than try to hire and train additional employees, these companies look to firms that specialize in outsourcing these types of functions as a temporary (or sometimes long-term) solution.

Rent or Share Facilities and Equipment For some organizations it is best to rent additional equipment or facilities during periods of peak demand. For example, express mail delivery services rent or lease trucks during the peak holiday delivery season. It would not make sense to buy trucks that would sit idle during the rest of the year. Sometimes organizations with complementary demand patterns can share facilities. An example is a church that shares its facilities during the week with a Montessori preschool. The school needs the facilities Monday through Friday during the day; the church needs the facilities in the evenings and on the weekend. Some businesses have been created to satisfy other businesses' fluctuating demand. For example, a firm may offer temporary office suites and clerical support to individuals who do not need such facilities and support on a continuous basis.

Decrease Capacity Temporarily

By adjusting service resources creatively, organizations can also match capacity with customer demand patterns. People, facilities, and equipment are again the focus, this time with an eye toward adjusting the basic mix and use of these resources. Specific actions might include the following.[8]

Schedule Downtime during Periods of Low Demand If people, equipment, and facilities are being used at maximum capacity during peak periods, then it is imperative to schedule downtime during off-peak periods. Online banking services, for example, often schedule software upgrades on early Sunday morning (4:00–6:00 a.m.) to keep those affected by the disruption of their service to a minimum.

Perform Maintenance and Renovations For almost all services, facilities and equipment need to be repaired and maintained periodically. Such scheduling should take place during periods of slow demand, as should renovations. Universities, for example, frequently arrange for the painting of classrooms or restriping of parking lots to be done when students are on a break.

Schedule Vacations and Employee Hiring/Training Strategically To ensure that employees are available when most needed, employee vacations and training should take place during periods of slow demand. Some firms adjust capacity by laying employees off when they know demand will be low. Hotels in popular tourist destinations routinely lay employees off during the off season. In fact, some employees know this well in advance and look forward to working in ski resort hotels in the winter months and coastal resort hotels in the summer months. Throughout all of these strategies, such scheduling attempts to ensure that a provider's resources are in top condition and available when they are most needed.

Modify or Move Facilities and Equipment Sometimes it is possible to adjust, move, or creatively modify existing capacity to meet demand fluctuations. Hotels utilize this strategy by reconfiguring rooms—two rooms with a locked door between can be rented to two different parties in high demand times or turned into a suite during slow demand. The airline industry offers another example of this strategy. Using an approach known as "demand-driven dispatch," airlines often assign airplanes to flight schedules on the basis of fluctuating market needs.[9] The method depends on accurate knowledge of demand and the ability to quickly move airplanes with different seating capacities to flight assignments that match their capacity. The Boeing 787 aircraft is so flexible that it can be reconfigured in less than an hour to vary the number of seats allocated to one, two, or three classes.[10] The plane can thus be quickly modified to match demand from different market segments, essentially molding capacity to fit demand. Another strategy may involve moving the service to a new location to meet customer demand or even bringing the service to customers. Mobile training facilities, pet grooming vans, and flu shot and blood donation facilities are examples of services that physically follow customers.

Combining Demand and Capacity Strategies

Many firms use multiple strategies, combining marketing-driven demand management approaches with operations-driven capacity management strategies. Figuring out which is the best set of strategies for maximizing capacity utilization, customer satisfaction, and profitability can be challenging, particularly when the service represents a constellation of offerings within one service setting. Examples of such services include theme parks with rides, restaurants, and shopping; hotel vacation villages with hotels, shopping, spas, pools, and restaurants; and ski resorts with ski slopes, spas, restaurants, and entertainment. Firms face complex problems in trying to balance demand across all the different offerings with an eye to quality and profitability. Our Strategy Insight describes a ski resort simulation that was created to use operations and marketing variables to determine the optimal combination of demand and capacity management strategies across the resort's various offerings and activities.

Strategy Insight Combining Demand (Marketing) and Capacity (Operations) Strategies to Increase Profits

In many situations, firms use multiple demand and capacity management strategies simultaneously to obtain optimal usage and maximize profits. Because each strategy involves costs as well as potential service quality, customer loyalty, and revenue outcomes, determining the appropriate mix can be a complex decision.

Research done for a ski resort illustrates how operations and marketing data can be combined into a sophisticated model to predict the right mix of strategies. The ski industry presents particularly interesting challenges for capacity management because the industry typically sees large fluctuations in demand based on seasonal, weekly, and even daily usage patterns; unpredictable weather and snowfall; a variety of skiing ability segments that use the resort in different ways; and demographic shifts over time. In addition, most resorts face constraints on their capacity due to environmental regulations that limit acreage and parking, as well as the large capital investment required for facility expansion and/or improvement. Furthermore, as ticket prices at ski resorts have continued to escalate, customer expectations have risen.

Powder Valley (PV, a disguised name), a ski resort in northern Utah, had consistently lost market share for five years to its rivals. Lack of facility improvements and increased marketing efforts by its competitors were cited as likely reasons for declining market share. To improve the situation, PV managers proposed several marketing strategies to increase demand on slow days and increase revenue per customer. Operations strategies that relied on acquisition of new terrain and new, faster ski lifts to improve the skiing experience and reduce waiting during peak demand periods were also proposed. Each of these strategies had its associated costs and less than totally predictable outcomes. Adding to the complexity of the inherent trade-offs in the various strategies was the fact that the resort offered multiple activities (e.g., restaurants, skiing, shopping) for customers to choose.

The researchers working with PV proposed that the optimal profit strategy would require an integrated set of approaches representing both demand and capacity perspectives. Using data from the resort, they built a sophisticated simulation model to assess the impact on customer usage, waiting times, and profits of several strategies that were being considered, including:

- *Price variations.* Strategies aimed at leveling demand by charging lower prices for off-peak skiing.
- *Promotions of underutilized services.* Promotions to attract new customer segments or shift existing customers to underutilized services.
- *Information provision on waiting times.* Strategies that provide information about less crowded periods or shorter waiting times to move customers temporarily to underutilized services.

YIELD MANAGEMENT: BALANCING CAPACITY UTILIZATION, PRICING, MARKET SEGMENTATION, AND FINANCIAL RETURN

Yield management is a term that has become attached to a variety of methods, some very sophisticated, employed to match demand and supply in capacity-constrained services. Using yield management models, organizations find the best balance at a particular point in time among the prices charged, the segments sold to, and the capacity used. The goal of yield management is to produce the best possible financial return from a limited available capacity. Specifically, yield management—also referred to as *revenue management*—attempts to allocate the fixed capacity of a service provider (e.g., seats on a flight, rooms in a hotel, rental cars) to match the

- *Capacity expansion.* Investments in additional fixed capacity for skiing such as adding new terrain or expanding the number of lifts.
- *Capacity upgrades.* Improving or replacing existing lifts to carry more skiers and/or run faster.

As input to their model, the researchers used historic data on daily demand, demand smoothing and capacity expansion options, service times for each lift, flow patterns across various lifts within the resort, travel time between lifts, customer perceptions, and customer choice data. By combining these marketing and operations data, the researchers showed that retaining the current customer mix, installing two new chairs, and providing waiting time information would maximize profits for the resort. Adding new chair lifts with higher speeds and doubled seating capacity within the existing terrain was a more profitable approach than expanding to new terrain. The simulation model showed that, contrary to management predictions, smoothing demand across the day through differential pricing would actually decrease profits significantly. The model results were also useful in suggesting a priority order for the investments. The wait time signage investment was the least expensive and offered the largest single improvement for customers as well as the largest single profit impact. Upgrading at least one chair lift was the next priority.

Balancing demand and capacity can involve a complex set of decisions, and sometimes the outcomes are not obvious, especially when strategies seem to have contradictory objectives. For example in the PV simulation, a marketing objective of increased revenues through attracting more customers was contradicted by an operations objective of providing optimal wait times for lifts. As illustrated in the ski resort research, firms can combine marketing and operations data into one overall model and run simulated experiments to determine the best set of combined strategies. One company, ProModel, has developed simulations similar to the one described here that have been successfully used by such service providers as American Express, the American Red Cross, Disneyland, Chase Bank, Delta Air Lines, JetBlue, the Mayo Clinic, and UPS. The Salt Lake Organizing Committee for the 2002 Winter Olympics also used a similar simulation to evaluate and successfully optimize spectator flow, emergency planning, and transportation systems. Every Olympics since then, both Summer and Winter, as well as each World Cup location, have used simulation programs to forecast car and foot traffic flow, as well as demand for public transportation. Of course, the quality of the decisions based on simulation models is highly dependent on the accuracy of the assumptions in the model and the quality of the input data.

Sources: M. E. Pullman and G. Thompson, "Strategies for Integrating Capacity with Demand in Service Networks," *Journal of Service Research* 5 (February 2003), pp. 169–183; ProModel Corporation (www.promodel.com).

potential demand in various market segments (e.g., business traveler, tourist) so as to maximize revenue or yield.[11]

Although the implementation of yield management can involve complex mathematical models and computer programs, the underlying effectiveness measure is the ratio of actual revenue to potential revenue for a particular measurement period:

$$\text{Yield} = \frac{\text{Actual revenue}}{\text{Potential revenue}}$$

where

$$\text{Actual revenue} = \text{Actual capacity used} \times \text{Average actual price}$$
$$\text{Potential revenue} = \text{Total capacity} \times \text{Maximum price}$$

The equations indicate that yield is a function of price and capacity used. Recall that capacity constraints can be in the form of time, labor, equipment, or facilities. Yield is essentially a measure of the extent to which an organization's resources (or capacities) are achieving their full revenue-generating potential. Assuming that total capacity and maximum price cannot be changed, yield approaches a value of 1 as actual capacity utilization increases or when a higher actual price can be charged for a given capacity used. For example, in an airline context, a manager could focus on increasing yield by finding ways to bring in more passengers to fill the capacity or by finding higher-paying passengers to fill a more limited capacity. In reality, expert yield managers work on capacity and pricing issues simultaneously to maximize revenue across different customer segments. Exhibit 13.1 shows simple yield calculations and the inherent trade-offs for two types of services: hotel and legal.

Implementing a Yield Management System

Our Technology Spotlight illustrates several examples of how information technology supports effective yield management applications. To implement a yield management system, an organization needs detailed data on past demand patterns by market segment as well as methods of projecting current market demand. The data can be combined through mathematical programming models, threshold analysis, or expert systems to project the best allocation of limited capacity at a particular point in time.[12] Allocations of capacity for specific market segments can then be communicated to sales representatives or reservations staff as targets for selling rooms, seats, time, or other limited resources. Sometimes the allocations, once determined, remain fixed. At other times allocations change weekly, or even daily or hourly, in response to new information.

Research indicates that traditional yield management approaches are most appropriate for service firms when:

1. They have relatively fixed capacity.
2. They have perishable inventory.
3. They have different market segments or customers, who arrive or make their reservations at different times.
4. They have low marginal sales costs and high marginal capacity change costs.
5. The product is sold in advance.
6. There is fluctuating demand.
7. Customers who arrive or reserve early are more price sensitive than those who arrive or reserve late.[13]

When these conditions are present, yield management approaches can generally be employed to identify the best mix of service offerings to produce and sell in the period, and at what prices, to generate the highest expected revenue. These criteria exactly fit the situation for airlines, car rental agencies, and many hotels—industries that have effectively and extensively used yield management techniques to allocate capacity. In other services (entertainment, sports, fashion), those customers willing to pay the higher prices are the ones who buy early rather than late. People who really want to see a particular performance reserve their seats at the earliest possible moment. Discounting for early purchases would reduce profits. In these situations, the price generally starts out high and is reduced later to fill capacity if needed.

Exhibit 13.1 Simple Yield Calculations: Examples from Hotel and Legal Services

Basic yield calculations can be done for any capacity-constrained service, assuming the actual capacity, average price charged for different market segments, and maximum price that could be charged are known. Ideally, yield will approach the number 1, or 100 percent, where

Yield = Actual revenue/Potential revenue

In this box, we describe yield calculations for two simple examples – a 100-room hotel and a digital marketing consultant with a 40-hour work week – under different assumed pricing and usage situations. Although companies use much more complex mathematical models to determine yield, the underlying concepts are the same. The goal is to maximize the revenue-generating capacity of the service provider's capacity.

100-ROOM HOTEL WITH MAXIMUM ROOM RATE OF ₹5000 PER NIGHT

Potential revenue = ₹5000 × 100 rooms
= ₹500,000 per night

1. Assume: The hotel rents all its rooms at a discounted rate of ₹3000 per night.

   Yield = (₹3000 × 100 rooms)/₹500,000 = 60%

   At this rate, the hotel is maximizing capacity utilization but not getting a very good price.
2. Assume: The hotel charges its full rate but can only rent 40 rooms at that price, due to the customer's price sensitivity.

   Yield = (₹5000 × 40 rooms)/₹500,000 = 40%

   In this situation, the hotel has maximized the per-room price, but the yield is even lower than in the first situation because a few rooms are rented at that relatively high rate.
3. Assume: The hotel charges its full rate of ₹5000 for 40 rooms and then gives a discount of ₹2000, i.e. charges ₹3000 for the remaining 60 rooms.

   Yield = [(₹5000 × 40 rooms)
   + (₹3000 × 60 rooms)]/₹500,000 = 76%

   Clearly, the final alternative, which takes into account price sensitivity and charges different prices for different rooms or market segments, results in the highest yield among these three alternatives.

40 HOURS OF A DIGITAL MARKETING CONSULTANT'S TIME ACROSS A TYPICAL WORK WEEK AT ₹5000 PER HOUR MAXIMUM (CORPORATE CLIENT RATE)

Potential revenue = ₹5000 × 40 hours
= ₹200,000 per week

1. Assume: The consultant can charge 30% of her billable time, i.e. 30% of 40 hours or 12 hours at ₹5000 per hour.

   Yield = (₹5000 × 12 hours)/₹200,000 = 30%

   In this case, the consultant has maximized her hourly rate but has only enough work to occupy 12 billable hours.
2. Assume: The consultant decides to charge ₹2000 to start-ups, small firms and non-profits and is able to bill out all 40 hours at this rate for these types of clients.

   Yield = (₹2000 × 40 hours)/₹200,000 = 40%

   In this situation, although she has worked a full week, the yield is still not very good, given the relatively low rate per hour.
3. Assume: The consultant uses a combined strategy in which she works 12 hours for corporate clients at ₹5000 per hour and fills the rest of her time with start-ups, small firms and non-profits at ₹2000 per hour.

   Yield = [(₹5000 × 12) + (₹2000 × 28)]/₹200,000 = 58%

   Again, catering to two different market segments with different price sensitivities is the best overall strategy to maximize income-generating capacity of the consultant's time.

Interestingly, some airlines use both these strategies effectively. They start with discounted seats for customers who are willing to buy early, usually leisure and discretionary travelers. They charge a higher fare for those who want a seat at the last minute, typically the less-price-sensitive business travelers whose destinations and schedules are inflexible. However, in some cases a bargain fare can be found at the last minute as well, commonly via Internet sales, to fill seats that would otherwise go unoccupied. Online auctions and services offered by companies like Priceline.com, Expedia.com, or Booking.com serve a purpose in filling capacity at the last minute, often charging much lower fares. (See the Technology Spotlight in Chapter 15 for examples of dynamic pricing via the Internet.)

Technology Spotlight Information and Technology Drive Yield Management Systems

Yield management is not a new concept. In fact, the basic idea behind yield management—achieving maximum profits through the most effective use of capacity—has been around forever. It is easy to find examples of capacity-constrained businesses using price to shift demand: theaters that charge different prices for matinees versus evening performances, intercity trains with different prices on weekdays than on weekends, ski resorts with cheaper prices for night skiing, and restaurants with "twilight" dinner specials. All these strategies illustrate attempts to smooth the peaks and valleys of demand using price as the primary motivator.

The difference in these basic pricing strategies and more sophisticated yield management approaches currently in use by airlines, car rental companies, hotels, shippers, and others is the reliance of these latter strategies on massive databases, sophisticated mathematical algorithms, and complex analyses. These forms of yield management consider not only price but also market segments, price sensitivity among segments, timing of demand, and potential profitability of customer segments—all simultaneously. What makes new forms of yield management possible are the technology and systems underlying them. Here are a few examples of what some companies and industries have done.

AMERICAN AIRLINES

American Airlines is a pioneer of yield management. Beginning with Super Saver Fares in the mid-1970s, American has depended on systems developed by Sabre (the oldest and leading provider of technology for the travel industry) to support an exceedingly complex system of fares. Using a system of models containing algorithms that optimize prices, manage wait lists, and handle traffic management, American uses Sabre to allocate seats on every one of its flights. The number of seats sold on each of American's flights is continuously compared with a sales forecast for that flight. Blocks of seats are moved from higher to lower fares if sales are below projections. If sales are at or above the forecast, no changes are made. American's stated objective has historically been to "sell the right seats to the right customers at the right price."

MARRIOTT HOTELS

The hotel industry has also embraced the concepts of yield management, and Marriott Hotels has been a leader. The systems at Marriott, for example, maximize profits for a hotel across full weeks rather than by day. In its hotels that target business travelers, Marriott has peak days during the middle of the week. Rather than simply sell the hotel out on those nights on a first-come, first-served basis with no discounts, the revenue management system (which is reviewed and revised daily) projects guest demand both by price and by length of stay, providing discounts in some cases to guests who will stay longer, even on a peak demand night. One early test of the system was at the Munich Marriott during Oktoberfest. Typically, no discounts would be offered during this peak period. However, the yield management system recommended that the hotel offer some rooms at a discount, but only for those guests who stayed an extended period before or after the peak days. Although the average daily rate went down 11.7 percent for the period, occupancy went up more than 20 percent and overall revenues went up 12.3 percent. Using yield management practices, Marriott Hotels estimates it generates an additional $400 million per year in revenue.

AIR INDIA

The Tata group has undertaken a comprehensive transformation of Air India's revenue management systems as part of its broader Vihaan AI program, with digital technologies serving as a key differentiator The airline is transitioning from a segment-based revenue management (RM) system to a more sophisticated network-based RM system that forecasts demand and optimizes ticket prices by considering passengers' entire journeys rather than individual flight segments, bringing Air India's capabilities on par with other tier-1 global carriers. Significant investments in customer engagement technologies, including website and mobile app modernization, ChatGPT-driven chatbots, and improved digital marketing tools are enhancing the overall customer experience while driving sales. Air India's strategic focus has boosted the growth of ancillary revenue streams from Rs. 700 crore in FY22 to Rs. 1,700 crore in FY24 with ambitious targets to reach Rs. 7,500 crore by FY27. The airline has expanded its ancillary offerings beyond traditional excess baggage and seat selection to include innovative services like Upgrade Plus for confirmed upgrades, travel insurance, fare lock options, visa concierge services in partnership with VFS Global, and convenient cab booking services, all integrated into company's direct booking channels. As part of AI's vision to become a one-stop shop for travel requirements, the company has made investments of approximately US $200 million in digital systems.

Sources: The primary source for the American Airlines and Marriott discussions is R. G. Cross, *Revenue Management* (New York: Broadway Books, 1997). Other sources include "Dynamic Pricing at American Airlines," *Business Quarterly* 61 (Autumn 1996), p. 45; and N. Templin, "Your Room Costs $250 . . . No! $200 . . . No," *The Wall Street Journal*, May 5, 1999, p. B1; B. Vinod, "Advances in Revenue Management: the Last Frontier," *Journal of Revenue and Pricing Management* 20 (February 2021), pp. 15–20.

Reference: https://www.airindia.com/in/en/newsroom/press-release/air-india-modernises-its-digital-landscape-to-transform-customer.html

https://www.financialexpress.com/business/airlines-aviation-air-india-targets-50-growth-in-ancillary-revenue-this-fiscal-3581071/

https://www.thehindubusinessline.com/economy/logistics/air-india-aims-to-boost-ancillary-revenues/article67458016.ece

https://www.business-standard.com/companies/news/air-india-to-move-to-better-ticket-pricing-system-in-few-months-wilson-123052600723_1.html

Challenges and Risks in Using Yield Management

Yield management programs can significantly improve revenues. However, although yield management may appear to be an ideal solution to the problem of matching supply and demand, it is not without risks. By becoming focused on maximizing financial returns through differential capacity allocation and pricing, an organization may encounter these problems:[14]

- *Loss of competitive focus.* Yield management may cause a firm to overfocus on profit maximization and inadvertently neglect aspects of the service that provide long-term competitive success.
- *Customer alienation.* If customers learn that they are paying a higher price for service than someone else, they may perceive the pricing as unfair, particularly if they do not understand the reasons. However, a study done in the restaurant industry found that, when customers were informed of different prices being charged by time of day, week, or table location, they generally felt the practice was fair, particularly if the price difference was framed as a discount for less desirable times rather than a premium for peak times or table locations.[15] Customer education is thus essential in an effective yield management program.
- *Overbooking.* Customers can be further alienated if they fall victim (and are not compensated adequately) to the overbooking practices often necessary to make yield management systems work effectively. Research suggests that customers who experience negative consequences of revenue management (i.e., denied service or downgrades), particularly high-value customers, subsequently reduce their number of transactions with the firm.[16]
- *Incompatible incentive and reward systems.* Employees may resent yield management systems that do not match incentive structures. For example, many managers are rewarded on the basis of capacity utilization *or* average rate charged, whereas yield management balances the two factors.

WAITING LINE STRATEGIES: WHEN DEMAND AND CAPACITY CANNOT BE MATCHED

Sometimes it is not possible to manage capacity to precisely match demand, or vice versa. It may be too costly—for example, most health clinics would not find it economically feasible to add facilities or physicians to handle peaks in demand during the winter flu season; patients usually simply have to wait to be seen. Or demand may be very unpredictable and the service capacity very inflexible (it cannot be easily stretched to match unpredictable peaks in demand). Sometimes waits occur when demand backs up because of the variability in length of time for service. For example, even though patients are scheduled by appointments in a physician's office, frequently there is a wait because some patients take longer to serve than the time allotted to them. The misalignment in capacity and demand is particularly troublesome in emergency healthcare, as is described in Exhibit 13.2.

For most service organizations, waiting customers are a fact of life at some point. Waiting can occur on the telephone (customers put on hold when they call in to ask for information, order something, or make a complaint) and in person (customers waiting in line at the bank, the post office, Disneyland, or a physician's office). Waiting can occur even with service transactions through the mail—delays in mail-order delivery—or backlogs of correspondence on a manager's desk.

Exhibit 13.2 Overflow in the ED: Managing Capacity Constraints and Excess Demand in Hospital Emergency Departments

Nowhere is there a more vivid example of demand and capacity issues than in the more than 5,000 emergency departments (EDs) in hospitals across the United States (*emergency department* is the preferred term within the medical community for what has traditionally been called the ER). In a typical ED, rooms are filled, the corridors may be clogged with waiting patients, wait time may be anywhere from 15 minutes to 8 or 10 hours, and ambulances are routinely turned away to seek other hospitals on what is called "reroute" or "diversion." Many experts have referred to these issues as a national crisis in healthcare. Notably, this crisis was further escalated by the COVID-19 pandemic, which made it even more difficult to forecast and manage the demand for beds and ventilators necessary to accommodate COVID-19 patients along with non-COVID-19 patients in the ED. The emergency department is the front door of hospitals and is the treatment of last resort for many. Why has this overcrowding issue reached national proportions? Many factors come into play, including increased demand and severe capacity constraints.

INCREASED DEMAND FOR SERVICES

Emergency departments are to some extent victims of their own success. Decades of public health campaigns urging people to call 911 in case of medical emergency have been successful in educating people to do just that—and they end up in the ED. Many do indeed have life-threatening emergencies that belong in the ED. Others waiting in the ED are uninsured; as of 2020, more than 28 million people in the United States were uninsured. The ED is their only option, and legally the ED must care for them. But it is not only the uninsured and those with life-threatening emergencies who crowd the ED. It is also insured patients who cannot get appointments with their doctors in a timely manner or who learn that it may be their fastest entry into a hospital bed. Patients and their doctors are becoming aware that they can get sophisticated care in the ED relatively quickly. Thus, the demand for ED services has increased.

CAPACITY CONSTRAINTS

It is not just an increase in demand that is causing the overcrowding. It is also a shrinkage or unavailability of critical capacity at the same time. Doctors are overbooked in private practices, so patients who do not want to wait turn to the ED. Also, a shortage of specialists who are willing to take patients on call from the ED results in increased waiting times because these patients waiting for specialized care occupy beds in the ED longer than necessary. Another very critical capacity constraint is the number of beds in hospitals. Over the years, many hospitals across the country have closed for financial reasons, reducing the number of beds available. So ED patients often cannot get beds right away even if they need one, increasing waiting time for themselves and others. There is a critical shortage of nurses as well, and a hospital bed requires a nurse to attend it before it can be occupied. In the 1990s enrollment in nursing programs slumped as people turned to more lucrative careers, and as of 2020 the median age of a registered nurse was nearly 52. Many hospitals have 20 percent of their nursing slots empty. Staffing shortages in housekeeping also play a role. A bed may be empty, but until it is cleaned and remade, it is not available for a waiting patient. In some communities, patients may find that ED facilities are simply not available. Some hospitals have actually closed their emergency departments after determining that it is unprofitable to run them because of poor reimbursement rates. In other areas, population growth is outpacing hospital and ED construction.

HOSPITALS' RESPONSES

To address this complex set of issues, a few changes have been made.

Technology

A partial solution has been to turn to technology to smooth the process of admitting patients into the ED and to track the availability of hospital beds. Some web-based systems are used to reroute ambulances to hospitals that have capacity. Other systems help EDs track the availability of rooms in their own hospitals in terms of knowing exactly when a bed is vacant and when it has been cleaned and is available—similar to what hotels have done for decades. Wireless systems for registering patients at bedside and "radar screens" that track everything going on in the ED are other partial solutions. These screens can track patients, staff, carts, and equipment, making the service delivery process more efficient and quicker.

Systems Improvements

Other hospitals have segmented their patients and have developed parallel "fast track" processes for dealing with minor emergency patients that can account for 30–50 percent of total visits. This process can be separated from the major-emergency situations that may require more time and special equipment. Quicker admitting processes are also being implemented. Kiosks have been installed in some hospitals to allow emergency patients to check themselves in and describe their symptoms to help speed up the admission process. Patients who are not experiencing true emergencies (true emergencies being gunshot victims or car accident victims with serious injuries) use touch screens to enter their name, age, and other personal information. Such kiosks display a list of ailments to choose from, like "pain" or "fever and/or chills," and a list of body parts to indicate where the discomfort is occurring. Once a patient's problem is entered into the system, it pops up on a screen accessible to nurses; those with chest pains, stroke symptoms, or other potentially serious issues take priority.

Yet another innovation is to have staff administer routine tests while the patient is waiting, so that the doctor who finally sees the patient has information at hand. This solution also satisfies the patient's need for "something to happen" during the waiting time. Giving patients pagers so they can do something else while waiting is another way that EDs are helping patients cope with the long waits.

Not surprisingly, there are also specialized service firms that support EDs and hospitals with capacity management. For example, Wavetec, a multinational technology company, helps healthcare providers serve urgent care patients more efficiently and effectively. Wavetec provides a "patient flow management" system that equips EDs with the tools to better organize their (digital and non-digital) patient flows and service provision to enrich the patient experience.

Increasing Capacity

Another set of partial solutions relates directly to hospital and staff capacity issues. Some hospitals have added rooms and other facilities. More urgent care centers are being built to take some of the pressure off EDs. For patients who need to be admitted to the hospital, however, increasing capacity is not a total solution. The nursing shortage, one of the most critical problems, is very difficult to solve. Individual hospital systems have gotten creative in their efforts to steal nurses away from other hospitals, even recruiting heavily overseas. However, in the long term the solution rests more in making the occupation attractive in salaries and working conditions, thus increasing the number of people entering nursing programs.

It is obvious that this classic dilemma of matching supply and demand in a service context such as emergency care has multiple, deeply rooted causes. The solutions to the issues are also multifaceted—some can be undertaken by individual hospitals, whereas others need to be addressed by the entire healthcare industry.

Sources: K. McFarlane et al., "Interactive Model to Estimate Bed Demand for COVID-19-Related Hospitalization Developed by Stanford Medicine-Engineering Partnership," *Health Management, Policy and Innovation* 5 (Special Issue on COVID-19, April 2020); 2020 National Nursing Workforce Study, https://www.ncsbn.org/workforce.htm, accessed February 25, 2022; Y. B. Ferrand, M. J. Magazine, U. S. Rao, and T. F. Glass, "Managing Responsiveness in the Emergency Department: Comparing Dynamic Priority Queue with Fast Track," *Journal of Operations Management* 58 (March 2018), pp. 15–26; L. Landro, "ERs Now Turn to Technology to Help Deal with Overcapacity," *The Wall Street Journal*, July 13, 2001, p. B1; J. Snyder, "Curing the ER," *The Arizona Republic*, December 9, 2001, pp. D1+; N. Shute and M. B. Marcus, CODE BLUE "Crisis in the ER," *US News & World Report*, September 10, 2001, pp. 54–61; U.S. Census Bureau, https://www.census.gov/library/publications/2021/demo/p60-274.html, accessed February 25, 2022; J. Stengle, "ER Kiosks Let Patients Avoid Long Lines," *Associated Press*, September 13, 2007, http://www.gallup.com/poll/186047/uninsured-rate-third-quarter.aspx, accessed July 12, 2016; Wavetec, Patient Flow Management for Emergency Rooms, https://www.wavetec.com/industries/healthcare/emergency-room/, accessed February 25, 2022.

In today's fast-paced society, waiting is not something most people tolerate well. As people work longer hours, as individuals have less leisure time, and as families have fewer hours together, the pressure on people's time is greater than ever. In this environment, customers are looking for efficient, quick service with no wait. Organizations that make customers wait may lose business or at the very least create dissatisfied customers.[17] Research suggests that waiting time satisfaction is nearly as important as service delivery satisfaction with respect to customer loyalty.[18] To deal effectively with the inevitability of waits, organizations can utilize a variety of strategies; four general strategies are described next.

Employ Operational Logic

If customer waits are common, a first step is to analyze the operational processes to remove any inefficiencies. It may be possible to redesign the system to move customers along more quickly. In introducing its express check-in, Marriott Hotels used an operations-based modification to eliminate much of the waiting previously experienced by its guests. Guests who use a credit card and preregister can avoid waiting in line at the hotel front desk altogether. The guest can make it from the curb outside the hotel to his or her room in as little as three minutes when escorted by a "guest service associate," who checks the guest into the hotel, picks up keys and paperwork from a rack in the lobby, and then escorts the guest directly to the room. The company further expanded this idea by offering online/mobile check-in through its Marriott Bonvoy® Mobile App and Marriott Website, which also helps reduce waiting times for guests.[19] The U.S. Department of Transportation Security Administration (TSA) offers similar preferential treatment for selected frequent travelers through its "TSA Pre✓®" program.[20] Only U.S. citizens and permanent legal residents who meet certain flying criteria may apply. After registering with the system and clearing an extensive background check, travelers who qualify for this program are allowed to bypass the usual security checkpoint in their designated airport and instead be screened through a security system that reads either their fingerprints or the irises in their eyes. They must still go through a metal detector and their bags are still passed through an X-ray scanner, but they get their own special line and are not randomly selected for additional screening.

Digital Vision/Getty Images

Waiting is common in many service industries.

When queues are inevitable, the organization faces the operational decision of what kind of queuing system to use or how to configure the queue. *Queue configuration* refers to the number of queues, their locations, their spatial requirement, and their effect on customer behavior.[21] Several possibilities exist, as shown in Figure 13.4. In the multiple-queue alternative, the customer arrives at the service facility and must decide which queue to join and whether to switch later if the wait appears to be shorter in another line. In the single-queue alternative, fairness of waiting time is ensured in that the first-come, first-served rule applies to everyone; the system can also reduce the average time customers spend waiting overall. However, customers may leave if they perceive that the line is too long or if they have no opportunity to select a particular service provider. The last option shown in Figure 13.4 is the take-a-number option, in which arriving customers

FIGURE 13.4
Waiting Line Configurations

Bordoloi, Sanjeev K., James A. Fitzsimmons, and Mona J. Fitzsimmons. 2021. *Service Management: Operations, Strategy, Information Technology,* 9th ed. New York: McGraw Hill/Irwin, ch. 12, p. 336.

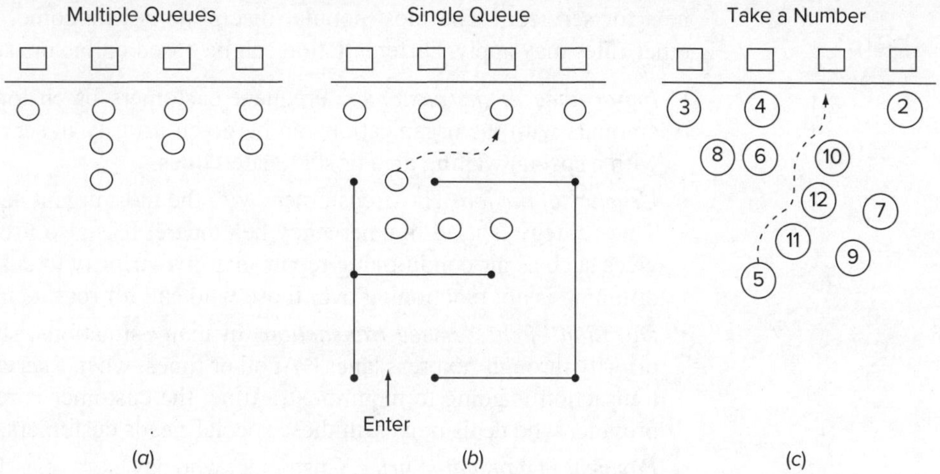

take a number to indicate line position. Advantages are similar to the single-queue alternative with the additional benefit that customers are able to mill about, browse, and talk to each other. The disadvantage is that customers must be on the alert to hear their numbers when they are called. Research suggests that length of the queue and perceived cost of waiting are not the only influences on customers' likelihood of staying in line. In a series of experiments and field tests, researchers showed that, the larger the number of customers waiting in line *behind* a consumer, the more likely that consumer is to stay in line and wait for the service.[22]

Establish a Reservation Process

When waiting cannot be avoided, a reservation system can help to spread demand. Restaurants, transportation companies, theaters, physicians, and many other service providers use reservation systems to alleviate long waits. The California Department of Motor Vehicles allows customers to make appointments via the Internet to help reduce the time they must spend waiting at its offices. The idea behind a reservation system is to guarantee the service will be available when the customer arrives. Beyond simply reducing waiting time, a reservation system has the added benefit of potentially shifting demand to less desirable time periods. A challenge inherent in reservation systems, however, is what to do about "no shows." Inevitably there will be customers who reserve a time but do not show up. Some organizations deal with this problem by overbooking their service capacity on the basis of past records of no-show percentages. If the predictions are accurate, overbooking is a good solution. When predictions are inaccurate, however, customers may still have to wait and sometimes may not be served at all, as when airlines overbook the number of seats available on a flight. Victims of overbooking may be compensated for their inconvenience in such cases. To minimize the no-show problem, some organizations (such as hotels, airlines, conferences/training programs, and theaters) charge customers who fail to show up or to cancel their reservations within a certain time frame.

Differentiate Waiting Customers

Not all customers need to wait the same length of time for service. On the basis of need or customer priority, some organizations differentiate among customers, allowing some to experience shorter waits for service than others. Known as "queue discipline," such differentiation reflects management policies regarding whom to select next for service.[23] The most popular discipline is first-come, first-served. However, other rules may apply. Differentiation can be based on factors such as these:[24]

- *Importance of the customer.* Frequent customers or customers who spend large amounts with the organization can be given priority in service by providing them with a special waiting area or segregated lines.
- *Urgency of the job.* Those customers with the most urgent need may be served first. This strategy is used in emergency healthcare. It is also used by maintenance services such as air-conditioning repair that give priority to customers whose air conditioning is not functioning over those who call for routine maintenance.
- *Duration of the service transaction.* In many situations, shorter service jobs get priority through "express lanes." At other times, when a service provider sees that a transaction is going to require extra time, the customer is referred to a designated provider who deals only with these special-needs customers.
- *Payment of a premium price.* Customers who pay extra (e.g., first class on an airline) are often given priority via separate check-in lines or express systems. At several Six Flags amusement parks, groups of up to six customers can purchase a Flashpass for about $55 per person (in addition to park entrance fees). Doing so allows them to use a palm-sized device, which is inserted at signs near the popular rides throughout the park, to keep their place in line virtually. The device sends a signal 10 minutes before it is time to come back and get on the ride (through a separate entrance), allowing customers to visit other attractions in the park without having to spend as much time in line. A "Gold" Flashpass (which reduces wait time up to 50 percent) can also be purchased, for about $85 per person, to move customers up in a queue so that they experience very little or even no wait, and for $125 per person a "Platinum" pass can be purchased that reduces wait time up to 90 percent and allows customers to ride a ride twice consecutively.[25] In recent years a variation of this service, Qsmart, allows mobile phone users to reserve their place in a virtual queue and notifies them once their virtual queue time has elapsed. To use this service customers pay an additional fee to avoid standing in a queue at amusement parks.[26]

Make Waiting More Pleasurable

Even when they have to wait, customers can still be satisfied, depending on how the wait is handled by the organization. Of course, the actual length of the wait will affect how customers feel about their service experience. But it is not just the actual time spent waiting that has an impact on customer satisfaction—it is how customers feel about the wait and their perceptions during it. The type of wait (e.g., a standard queue versus a wait due to a delay of service) can also influence how customers will react.[27] In a classic article entitled "The Psychology of Waiting Lines," David Maister proposes several principles about waiting, each of which has implications for how organizations can make waiting more pleasurable.[28]

Unoccupied Time Feels Longer Than Occupied Time

When customers are unoccupied they will likely be bored and will notice the passage of time more than when they have something to do. Providing something for waiting customers to do, particularly if the activity offers a benefit in and of itself or is related in some way to the service, can improve the customer's experience and may benefit the organization as well.[29] Examples include giving customers menus to look at while waiting in a restaurant and providing interesting information to read or watch on a monitor in a dentist's office. That said, many customers, when waiting for service, simply use their mobile phones to pass the time. Accordingly, some firms (knowing that customers turn to their phones) provide phone apps to occupy and entertain customers while they wait.

Preprocess Waits Feel Longer Than In-Process Waits

If wait time is occupied with activities that relate to the upcoming service, customers may perceive that the service has started and that they are no longer actually waiting. This in-process activity will make the length of the wait seem shorter and will benefit the service provider by making the customer better prepared when the service actually does begin. Filling out medical information while waiting to see the physician, reading a menu while waiting to be seated in a restaurant, and watching a videotape of the upcoming service event are all activities that can both educate the customer and reduce perceptions of waiting.

Research in a restaurant context has found that customers react more negatively to preprocess waits than to either in-process or postprocess waits; that is, preprocess waits are relatively more important in determining customers' overall satisfaction.[30] Other researchers have found that, if a wait is due to routine slowness of the process, then preprocess waits produce the most negative impact. However, if the wait is due to a service failure, then the in-process wait is viewed more negatively than the preprocess wait.[31] Thus, how customers perceive preprocess, in-process, and postprocess waits may depend to some extent on the cause of the wait.

Anxiety Makes Waits Seem Longer

When customers fear that they have been forgotten, they become anxious, and this anxiety can increase the negative impact of waiting. Anxiety also results when customers are forced to choose in a multiple-line situation and they discover they have chosen the "wrong" line. To combat waiting line anxiety, organizations can provide information on the length of the wait. At its theme parks, Disney uses signs at intervals along the line that let customers know how long the wait will be from that point on. Using a single line also alleviates customer anxiety over having chosen the wrong line. Explanations and reassurances that no one has forgotten them alleviate customer anxiety by taking away their cause for worry.

Uncertain Waits Are Longer Than Known, Finite Waits

Anxiety is intensified when customers do not know how long they will have to wait. Healthcare providers combat this problem by letting customers know when they check in how far behind the physician is that day. Some patients resolve this uncertainty themselves by calling ahead to ask. Maister provides an interesting example of the role of uncertainty, which he terms the "appointment syndrome."[32] Customers who arrive early for an appointment will wait patiently until the scheduled time, even if they arrive very early. However, once the expected appointment time has passed, customers grow increasingly anxious. Before the appointment time the wait time is known; after that, the length of the wait is not known.

Research in an airline context has suggested that, as uncertainty about a wait increases, customers become angrier, and their anger results in greater dissatisfaction.[33] Research also shows that giving customers information on the length of the anticipated wait and/or their relative position in the queue can result in more positive feelings and acceptance of the wait and ultimately more positive evaluation of the service.[34]

Unexplained Waits Are Longer Than Explained Waits

When people understand the causes for waiting, they frequently have greater patience and are less anxious, particularly when the wait is justifiable. An explanation can reduce customer uncertainty and may help customers estimate how long they will be delayed. One of us, when waiting once with our children to see a pediatrician, was told that the doctor was delayed because another child had arrived with possible life-threatening injuries and he chose to focus his attention on that child. As a parent who would want the same treatment for our children, the amount of extra wait time was acceptable—much more so than if there had been no explanation at all and we were left to think that perhaps the doctor had not yet arrived from his early morning trip to the golf course. Customers who do not know the reason for a wait begin to feel powerless and irritated.

Unfair Waits Are Longer Than Equitable Waits

When customers perceive that they are waiting while others who arrived after them have already been served, the apparent inequity will make the wait seem even longer. This situation can easily occur when there is no apparent order in the waiting area and many customers are trying to be served. Queuing systems that work on a first-come, first-served rule are best at combating perceived unfairness. However, other approaches may be required to determine who will be served next. For example, in an emergency medical care situation, the most seriously ill or injured patients would be seen first. When customers understand the priorities and the rules are clearly communicated and enforced, they will tend to see the wait as fair and the negative effects of having to wait will tend to be significantly dampened.[35]

The More Valuable the Service, the Longer the Customer Will Wait

Customers who have substantial purchases or who are waiting for a high-value service will be more tolerant of long wait times and may even expect to wait longer. For example, customers waiting to see a lawyer might consider a 15-minute wait to be acceptable, whereas the same wait at a convenience store might be considered completely unacceptable. In a supermarket, customers who have a full cart of groceries will generally wait longer than customers who have only a few items. And diners expect to wait longer for service in an expensive restaurant than they do when eating at a "greasy spoon."

Solo Waits Feel Longer Than Group Waits

People are more accepting of a longer wait when they are in a group than when they are alone because of the distractions provided by other members of the group. People also feel comfort in waiting with a group rather than alone.[36] In some group waiting situations, such as at Disneyland or when patrons are waiting in long lines to purchase concert tickets, customers who are strangers begin to talk to each other and the waiting experience can become a fun part of the total service experience.

Summary

Because service organizations lack the ability to inventory their products, the effective use of capacity can be critical to success. Idle capacity in the form of unused time, labor, facilities, or equipment represents a direct drain on bottom-line profitability. When the capacity represents a major investment (e.g., airplanes, expensive medical imaging equipment, or lawyers and physicians paid on a salary), the losses associated with underuse of capacity are even more accentuated. Overused capacity can also be a problem. People, facilities, and equipment can become worn out over time when used beyond optimal capacity. People can quit, facilities can become run down, and equipment can break. From the customer's perspective, service quality also deteriorates. Organizations focused on delivering quality service, therefore, have a natural drive to balance capacity utilization and demand at an optimal level in order to meet customer expectations.

Based on grounding in the fundamental issues, the chapter presented a variety of strategies for matching supply and demand. The basic strategies fall under two headings: *demand strategies* (shifting demand to match capacity) and *capacity strategies* (adjusting capacity to meet demand). Demand strategies seek to flatten the peaks and valleys of demand to match the flat capacity constraint, whereas capacity strategies seek to flex, stretch, or (temporarily) decrease capacity to match the peaks and valleys of demand. Organizations frequently employ several strategies simultaneously to solve the complex problem of balancing supply and demand.

Yield management is a sophisticated form of supply and demand management that balances capacity utilization, pricing, market segmentation, and financial return. This strategy is used by airline, hotel, shipping, car rental, and other capacity-constrained industries in which bookings are made in advance. Essentially, yield management allows organizations to decide on a monthly, weekly, daily, or even hourly basis to whom they want to sell their service capacity at what price.

In the last section of the chapter, we discussed situations in which it is not possible to align supply and demand. In these (typically) undesirable capacity utilization situations, the inevitable result is customer waiting. We described strategies for effectively managing waiting lines, such as employing operational logic, establishing a reservation process, differentiating waiting customers, and making waiting more pleasurable, or at least tolerable.

Discussion Questions

1. Why do service organizations lack the capability to inventory their services? Compare a car repair and maintenance service with an automobile manufacturer/dealer in terms of inventory capability.
2. Discuss the four scenarios illustrated in Figure 13.1 and presented in the text (excess demand, demand exceeds optimal capacity, demand and supply are balanced, excess capacity) in the context of a professional basketball team selling seats for its games. What are the challenges for management under each scenario?
3. Discuss the four common types of constraints (time, labor, equipment, facilities) facing service businesses, and give an example of each (real or hypothetical).
4. How does optimal capacity utilization differ from maximum capacity utilization? Give an example of a situation in which the two might be the same and one in which they are different.
5. Choose a local restaurant or some other type of service with fluctuating demand. What is the likely underlying pattern of demand? What causes the pattern? Is it predictable or random?
6. Describe the two basic strategies for matching supply and demand, and give at least two specific examples of each.
7. What is yield management? Discuss the risks in adopting a yield management strategy.
8. How might yield management apply in the management of the following: a Broadway theater? A consulting firm? A commuter train?
9. Describe the four basic waiting line strategies, and give an example of each one, preferably based on your own experiences as a consumer.

Exercises

1. Choose a local service organization that is challenged by fixed capacity and fluctuating demand. Interview the marketing manager (or other knowledgeable person) to learn (a) in what ways capacity is constrained, (b) the basic patterns of demand, and (c) strategies the organization has used to align supply and demand. Write up the answers to these questions, and make your own recommendations regarding other strategies the organization might use.
2. Assume you manage a winter ski resort in Colorado or Banff, Canada. (a) Explain the underlying pattern of demand fluctuation likely to occur at your resort and the challenges it would present to you as a manager. Is the pattern of demand predictable or random? (b) Explain and give examples of how you might use both demand-oriented and capacity-oriented strategies to smooth the peaks and valleys of demand during peak and slow periods.
3. Choose a local organization in which people have to wait in line for service. Design a waiting line strategy for the organization.
4. Visit the website of Wells Fargo Bank (www.wellsfargo.com), a leader in online banking. What online services does the bank currently offer? How do these online services help Wells Fargo manage the peaks and valleys of customer demand? How do its strategies to use more ATMs, in-store bank branches, and other alternative delivery strategies complement the online strategies?

Notes

1. The Phoenician website, www.thephoenician.com/, accessed February 24, 2022; The Lotte NY Palace website, www.lottenypalace.com/, accessed July 12, 2016.
2. C. Lovelock, "Getting the Most Out of Your Productive Capacity," in *Product Plus* (New York: McGraw Hill, 1994), chap. 16.
3. C. H. Lovelock, "Classifying Services to Gain Strategic Marketing Insights," *Journal of Marketing* 47 (Summer 1983), pp. 9–20.
4. Portions of this section are based on C. H. Lovelock, "Strategies for Managing Capacity-Constrained Service Organizations," in *Managing Services: Marketing, Operations, and Human Resources,* 2nd ed. (Englewood Cliffs, NJ: Prentice Hall, 1992), pp. 154–168.
5. S. Boenigk et al., "Rethinking Service Systems and Public Policy: A Transformative Refugee Service Experience Framework," *Journal of Public Policy & Marketing* 40 (April 2021), pp. 165–183; https://www.unhcr.org/news/press/2022/3/6234811a4/poland-welcomes-million-refugees-ukraine.html, accessed March 30, 2022.
6. M. Arndt, "Knock Knock, It's Your Big Mac," *BusinessWeek,* July 23, 2007, p. 36.
7. UPS Press Release from September 09, 2021, https://about.ups.com/us/en/newsroom/press-releases/customer-first/ups-to-hire-over-100k-essential-seasonal-workers.html, accessed February 22, 2022.
8. Lovelock, "Getting the Most Out of Your Productive Capacity."
9. J. M. Feldman, "Matching Planes to Demand," *Air Transport World* 39 (December 2002), pp. 31–33; J. M. Feldman, "IT Systems Start to Converge," *Air Transport World* 37 (September 2000), pp. 78–81.
10. Boeing website, http://www.boeing.com, accessed July 12, 2016.
11. See S. K. Bordoloi, J. A. Fitzsimmons, and M. J. Fitzsimmons, *Service Management: Operations, Strategy, Information Technology,* 9th ed. (2021); pp. 315–320; S. E. Kimes, "Yield Management: A Tool for Capacity-Constrained Service Firms," *Journal of Operations Management* 8 (October 1989), pp. 348–363; S. E. Kimes

and R. B. Chase, "The Strategic Levers of Yield Management," *Journal of Service Research* 1 (November 1998), pp. 156–166; and S. E. Kimes, "Revenue Management: A Retrospective," *Cornell Hotel and Restaurant Administration Quarterly* 44 (2003), pp. 131–138.

12. Kimes, "Yield Management."
13. R. Desiraji and S. M. Shugan, "Strategic Service Pricing and Yield Management," *Journal of Marketing* 63 (January 1999), pp. 44–56; S. K. Bordoloi, J. A. Fitzsimmons, and M. J. Fitzsimmons, *Service Management: Operations, Strategy, Information Technology,* 9th ed. (2021); chap. 11.
14. Kimes, "Yield Management."
15. S. E. Kimes and J. Wirtz, "Has Revenue Management Become Acceptable? Findings from an International Study on the Perceived Fairness of Rate Fences," *Journal of Service Research* 6 (November 2003), pp. 125–135.
16. A. Nazifi, K. Gelbrich, Y. Grégoire, S. Koch, D. El-Manstrly, and J. Wirtz, "Proactive Handling of Flight Overbooking: How to Reduce Negative eWOM and the Costs of Bumping Customers," *Journal of Service Research* 24 (May 2021), pp. 206–225; F. v. Wangenheim and T. Bayón, "Behavioral Consequences of Overbooking Service Capacity," *Journal of Marketing* 71 (October 2007), pp. 36–47.
17. For research supporting the relationship between longer waits and decreased satisfaction, quality evaluations, and patronage intentions, see S. Taylor, "Waiting for Service: The Relationship between Delays and Evaluations of Service," *Journal of Marketing* 58 (April 1994), pp. 56–69; K. L. Katz, B. M. Larson, and R. C. Larson, "Prescription for the Waiting-in-Line Blues: Entertain, Enlighten, and Engage," *Sloan Management Review* 33 (Winter 1991), pp. 44–53; S. Taylor and J. D. Claxton, "Delays and the Dynamics of Service Evaluations," *Journal of the Academy of Marketing Science* 22 (Summer 1994), pp. 254–264; and D. Grewal, J. Baker, M. Levy, and G. B. Voss, "The Effects of Wait Expectations and Store Atmosphere on Patronage Intentions in Service-Intensive Retail Stores," *Journal of Retailing* 79 (Winter 2003), pp. 259–268; E. G. Miller, B. E. Kahn, and M. F. Luce, "Consumer Wait Management Strategies for Negative Service Events: A Coping Approach," *Journal of Consumer Research* 34 (February 2008), pp. 635–648.
18. F. Bielen and N. Demoulin, "Waiting Time Influence on the Satisfaction-Loyalty Relationship in Services," *Managing Service Quality* 17 (2007), pp. 174–193.
19. Marriott, "How Do I Check-In Prior to Arrival?," https://help.marriott.com/s/article/Article-22236, accessed February 24, 2022; R. Henkoff, "Finding, Training, and Keeping the Best Service Workers," *Fortune,* October 3, 1994, pp. 110–122.
20. TSA website, www.tsa.gov/tsa-precheck, accessed on February 24, 2022.
21. S. K. Bordoloi, J. A. Fitzsimmons, and M. J. Fitzsimmons, *Service Management,* chap. 12.
22. R. Zhou and D. Soman, "Looking Back: Exploring the Psychology of Queuing and the Effect of the Number of People Behind," *Journal of Consumer Research* 29 (March 2003), pp. 517–530.
23. S. K. Bordoloi, J. A. Fitzsimmons, and M. J. Fitzsimmons, *Service Management,* chap 12.
24. Lovelock, "Getting the Most Out of Your Productive Capacity."
25. For example, see the Six Flags website, https://www.sixflags.com/national/flash-pass, accessed June 29, 2016.
26. Accesso website, http://accesso.com/solutions/loqueue/loqueue-qsmart, accessed December 22, 2016.

27. For an excellent review of the literature on customer perceptions of and reactions to various aspects of waiting time, see S. Taylor and G. Fullerton, "Waiting for Services: Perceptions Management of the Wait Experience," in *Handbook of Services Marketing and Management,* ed. T. A. Swartz and D. Iacobucci (Thousand Oaks, CA: Sage, 2000), pp. 171–189; E. N. Weiss and C. Tucker, "Queue Management: Elimination, Expectation, and Enhancement," *Business Horizons* 61 (September 2018), pp. 671–678.
28. D. A. Maister, "The Psychology of Waiting Lines," in *The Service Encounter,* ed. J. A. Czepiel, M. R. Solomon, and C. F. Surprenant (Lexington, MA: Lexington Books, 1985), pp. 113–123. For an additional study on the psychology of customer waiting, see K. A. McGuire, S. E. Kimes, M. Lynn, M. Pullman, and R. C. Lloyd, "A Framework for Evaluating the Customer Wait Experience," *Journal of Service Management* 21 (2010), pp. 269–290; A. Furnham, L. Treglown, and G. Horne, "The Psychology of Queuing," *Psychology* 11 (March 2020), pp. 480–498.
29. S. Taylor, "The Effects of Filled Waiting Time and Service Provider Control over the Delay on Evaluations of Service," *Journal of the Academy of Marketing Science* 23 (Summer 1995), pp. 38–48.
30. R. L. Hensley and J. Sulek, "Customer Satisfaction with Waits in Multi-stage Services," *Managing Service Quality* 17 (2007), pp. 152–173.
31. M. K. Hui, M. V. Thakor, and R. Gill, "The Effect of Delay Type and Service Stage on Consumers' Reactions to Waiting," *Journal of Consumer Research* 24 (March 1998), pp. 469–479.
32. Maister, "The Psychology of Waiting Lines."
33. Taylor and Fullerton, "Waiting for Services."
34. M. K. Hui and D. K. Tse, "What to Tell Consumers in Waits of Different Lengths: An Integrative Model of Service Evaluation," *Journal of Marketing* 60 (April 1996), pp. 81–90.
35. C. M. Voorhees, J. Baker, B. L. Bourdeau, E. D. Brocato, and J. J. Cronin Jr., "It Depends: Moderating the Relationships among Perceived Waiting Time, Anger, and Regret," *Journal of Service Research* 12 (November 2009), pp. 138–155.
36. J. Baker and M. Cameron, "The Effects of the Service Environment on Affect and Consumer Perception of Waiting Time: An Integrative Review and Research Propositions," *Journal of the Academy of Marketing Science* 24 (Fall 1996), pp. 338–349.

Part Six

Managing Service Promises

The fourth provider gap, shown in the accompanying figure, illustrates the difference between service delivery and the service provider's external communications. Promises made by a service company through its media advertising, sales force, and other communications may raise customer expectations that serve as the standard against which customers assess service quality. Broken promises can occur for many reasons: ineffective marketing communications, overpromising in advertising or personal selling, inadequate coordination between operations and marketing, and differences in policies and procedures across service outlets.

In service companies, a fit between communications about service and actual service delivery is necessary. Chapter 14 is devoted to the topic of integrated service marketing communications—careful integration and organization of all of a service marketing organization's external and interactive communications channels. The chapter describes why this communication is necessary and how companies

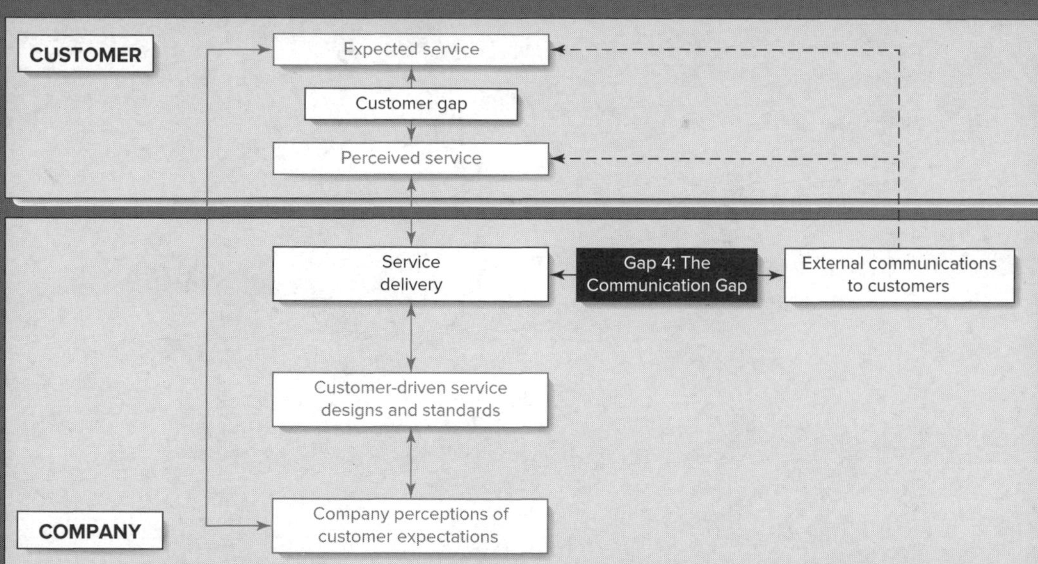

can do it well. Successful company communications are the responsibility of both marketing and operations: marketing must accurately but beguilingly reflect what happens in actual service encounters, and operations must deliver what is promised in marketing communication. If communications set up unrealistic expectations for customers, the actual encounter will disappoint the customer.

Chapter 15 deals with another issue related to managing promises, the pricing of services. In packaged goods (and even in durable goods), many customers possess enough price knowledge before purchase to be able to judge whether a price is fair or in line with competition. With services, customers often have no internal reference point for prices before purchase and consumption. Techniques for developing prices for services are more complicated than those for pricing tangible goods, and all the approaches for setting prices must be adapted for the special characteristics of services.

In summary, external communications—whether from marketing communications or pricing—can create a larger customer gap by raising expectations about service delivery. In addition to improving service delivery, companies must also manage all communications to customers, so that inflated promises do not lead to higher expectations. Companies must also manage the messages conveyed by pricing, so that customer expectations are in line with what they perceive that they receive.

Chapter Fourteen

Integrated Service Marketing Communications

This chapter's learning objectives are to:

1. Discuss the key service communication challenges.
2. Introduce the concept of integrated service marketing communications.
3. Discuss ways to integrate marketing communications in service organizations.
4. Present specific strategies for addressing service intangibility, managing promises, managing customer expectations, educating customers, and managing internal communications.

Two Successful Cross-Channel Integrated Service Marketing Campaigns

In this chapter, we will discuss integrated marketing communications, which has been a staple of company advertising campaigns for more than thirty years. The foundational idea of integrated marketing communication (IMC) was to assure that all creative, media, television, radio, and print were cohesive and communicated the same message. When digital and social media marketing came on the scene, integrated marketing communication became more complex because advertisers had to combine the controllable aspects of traditional media with an entire host of new media, some of it controlled by the consumer rather than the company. According to Tony Wright of Wright IMC, an industry expert, cross-channel, cross-device targeting remains the most powerful differentiator for profitable marketing strategies. Here, we briefly illustrate two integrated services campaigns that were extremely successful: Southwest Airlines Transfarency and Aldi's "Points are Pointless" campaigns.

Southwest Airlines Transfarency

Southwest Airlines, long known for its low fares, faced more competition in recent years, making their value promise more difficult to communicate. To emphasize its position as the best value in the skies, Southwest launched a Transfarency campaign using both traditional (television, radio, print) and digital media. For its campaign, the airline created the term "transfarency" and defined it as a "philosophy in which customers are treated honestly and fairly, and low fares actually stay low—no unexpected

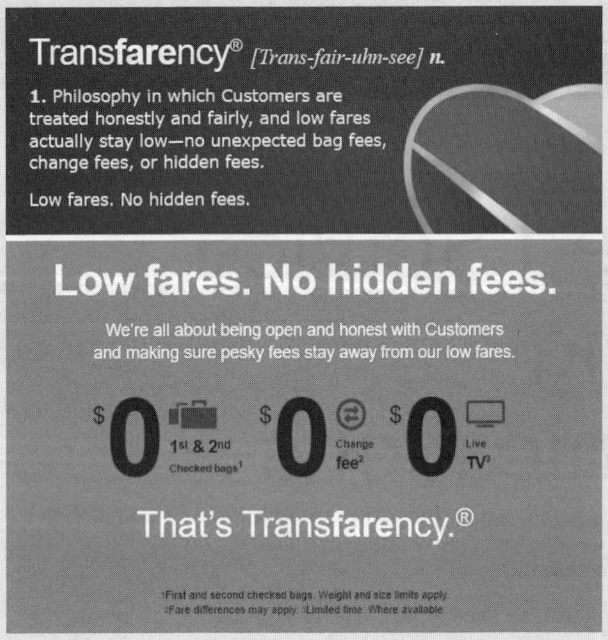

Southwest Airlines Co

bag fees, change fees, or hidden fees." For its marketing purposes, Southwest further bolstered this trust-focused message by emphasizing its commitment to protect customers from "pesky fees" its competitors charge. The campaign also featured a microsite that revealed hidden airline fees charged by competitors such as Spirit Airlines and Delta. Interactive components to the site allowed visitors to take a quiz called "fee or fake" where the site featured fees charged by their competitors, highlighted by a dancing Southwest Airlines pilot.

The site also featured an approach where users chose pre-selected words to send a letter to Southwest to complain about how the customer had been treated on other airlines. The final characteristic of the site was a "fee hacker" that helped customers minimize fees when flying an airline other than Southwest. One of the best aspects of the campaign was that it created buzz on social media sites such as Twitter and Facebook, where some customers adopted the Southwest Twitter hashtag and promoted the airline on their own. Many of the campaign's ads, blog posts, and social media uploads are still featured on Southwest's website.[1]

Aldi's "Points Are Pointless" Campaign

Aldi is a German family-owned discount supermarket chain with more than 10,000 stores in 20 countries and an estimated turnover of more than $50 billion. Aldi positions itself as "no frills grocery shopping" indicated by a servicescape focused on simplicity and cost-savings. The firm emphasizes to consumers that it is positively different from its competitors through its "Good Different" brand campaign. In Australia, for example, the firm's marketing demeaned other supermarkets for their "pointless" loyalty programs. By not having a rewards program, it stressed its "Good Different" approach using a "loyalty calculator."[2]

The company combines traditional commercials with social media posts to promote Aldi's "loyalty calculator" (https://www.aldiloyaltycalculator.com.au/), which aims to demonstrate that competitors' loyalty programs are ultimately not a good deal for consumers. As the images (below) illustrate, Aldi's loyalty calculator (1) asks consumers about their weekly supermarket spending, then (2) asks them to pick a reward that seems desirable to them, and finally (3) shows consumers how much money and time they will have to actually spend to receive that reward. Accordingly, Aldi's promotional blog post states: "*We think points are pointless. We think loyalty schemes are a waste of time. And we think the only 'reward' that matters is everyday low prices*." Their successful multi-channel campaign helps reinforce Aldi's distinct positioning as a discount supermarket asking shoppers: "*Why save pointless points when you can save money?*"

These examples demonstrate creative use of integrated marketing communications. The proliferation of digital media added to traditional communications media makes the clear and uniform message across all channels more important than ever before. And as you will learn in this chapter, integrated *services* marketing communications is more complicated than IMC alone, for it also involves employees, the servicescape, and other "real time" interactional communications that need to match the advertising and promotional communication that is emphasized in media alone.

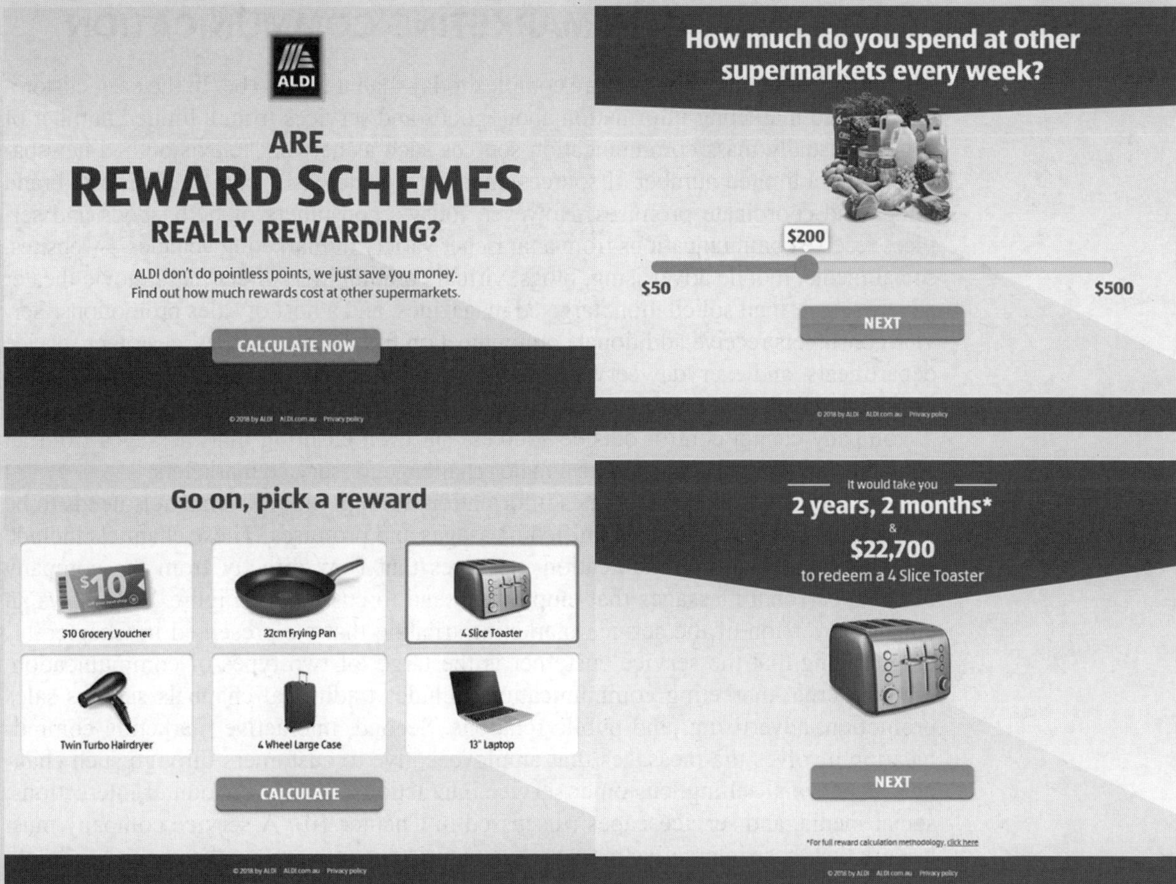

https://www.rewardco.com.au/aldi-loyalty-program-a-different-approach/ Accessed March 08, 2022

A major cause of poorly perceived service is the difference between what a firm promises about a service and what it actually delivers. Customer expectations are shaped by both uncontrollable and company-controlled factors. Word-of-mouth communication, social media, publicity, customer-generated media, customer experiences with other service providers, and customer needs are key factors that influence customer expectations and are rarely controllable by the firm (recall Chapter 3). Controllable factors such as company advertising, personal selling, and promises made by service personnel also influence customer expectations. In this chapter, we discuss both types of communication but focus more heavily on the controllable factors because these factors can be influenced by the company. Accurate, coordinated, and appropriate company communication—advertising, personal selling, and online and other messages that do not overpromise or misrepresent—is essential to delivering services that customers perceive as high in quality.

Because company communications about services often promise what *people* do and because people's behavior cannot be standardized to the same degree as can physical goods, the potential for a mismatch between what is communicated and perceptions of actual service delivery (Gap 4, the communications gap) is high. By coordinating communication within and outside the organization, companies can minimize the size of Gap 4.

THE NEED FOR COORDINATION IN MARKETING COMMUNICATION

Marketing communication is more complex today than it used to be. In the past, customers received marketing information about goods and services from a limited number of sources, usually mass communication sources such as network television and newspapers. With a limited number of sources, marketers could easily convey a uniform brand image and coordinate promises. However, today's consumers of both goods and services receive communications from a far richer variety of marketing vehicles—websites, social media, mobile advertising, blogs, virtual communities, direct mail, movie theater advertising, e-mail solicitation, targeted magazines, and a host of sales promotions. Service consumers receive additional communication from servicescapes, customer service departments, and everyday service encounters with employees. These service interactions add to the variety, volume, and complexity of information that a customer receives. A company cannot control outside sources, but even ensuring that messages from all company sources are consistent is a major challenge for service marketers.

Any company that disseminates information through multiple channels needs to be certain that customers receive unified messages and promises. These channels include not only marketing communication messages that flow directly from the company but also personal messages that employees send to customers. Figure 14.1 shows an enhanced version of the service marketing triangle that we presented in Chapter 11, emphasizing that the service customer is the target of two types of communication. First, external marketing communication includes traditional channels such as sales promotion, advertising, and public relations. Second, interactive marketing communication involves the messages that employees give to customers through such channels as personal selling, customer service interactions, service encounter interactions, social media, and servicescapes (discussed in Chapter 10). A service company must be sure that these interactive messages are consistent both among themselves and with those sent through external communications. To do so, the third side of the triangle, internal marketing communications, must be managed so that information from the company to employees is accurate, complete, and consistent with what customers are hearing or seeing.

FIGURE 14.1
Communications and the Service Marketing Triangle

Source: Adapted from M. J. Bitner, "Building Service Relationships: It's All about Promises," *Journal of the Academy of Marketing Science* 23 (1995); and C. Gronroos, *Services Management and Marketing* (Lexington, MA: Lexington Books, 1990).

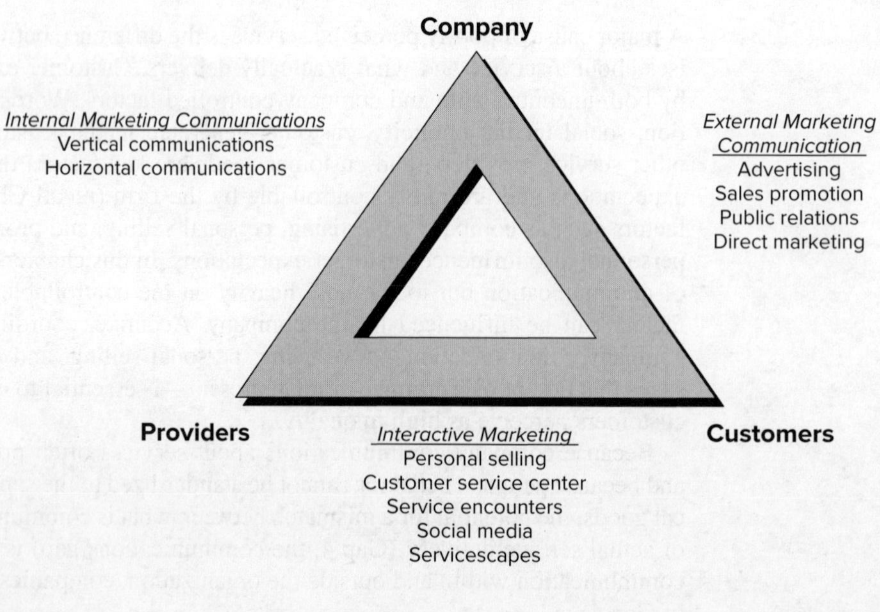

The need for integrated marketing campaigns is evident in both business-to-business situations and business-to-consumer instances. In business-to-business situations, the problem often comes because multiple parts of a service organization deal with a client and do not communicate well internally. For example, consider a large business customer of IBM who buys hardware, software, and services. If the client deals with different employees in different parts of the organization, the company needs to—but may not—coordinate internally to ensure that it is sending the customer the same messages. Not only that, but each of these internal organizations may have its own promotional campaign with different promises and messages. An example from your own experience may illustrate what happens when service marketing communications are not integrated. Have you ever seen an advertisement for a service, such as a special sandwich from Subway, then gone to your local Subway and not found it available? Did the employee behind the counter offer a reason the sandwich was not available? Did he or she even realize that it was advertised and for sale elsewhere? One of us consulted for a bank on the West Coast in which both customers and employees constantly faced this situation. Bank marketing communication was changed frequently and quickly to meet competitive offerings, but the bank tellers' training in the new offerings did not keep pace with the changes in advertising. As a result, customers went in, expecting new accounts and rates to be available, and employees were embarrassed because they had not been informed.

This example demonstrates one of the main reasons integrated marketing communications have not been the norm in many companies. All too often, various parts of the company are responsible for different aspects of communication. The sales department develops and executes sales communication. The marketing department and the firm's advertising agency prepare and disseminate advertising. A public relations firm is responsible for publicity. Functional specialists handle sales promotions and direct marketing, as well as company websites and digital and social media communication. The human resource department trains frontline employees for service interactions, and still another area is responsible for the customer service department. Rarely is one person responsible for the overall communications strategy in a company, and all too often people responsible for the different communication components do not coordinate their efforts.

Today, however, more companies are adopting the concept of *integrated marketing communications* (IMC), where the company carefully integrates and organizes all of its external communications channels. As a marketing executive explained it,

> Integrated marketing communications build a strong brand identity in the marketplace by tying together and reinforcing all your images and messages. IMC means that all your corporate messages, positioning and images, and identity are coordinated across all venues. It means that your PR materials say the same things as your direct mail campaign, and your advertising has the same "look and feel" as your website.[3]

In this chapter we propose that a more complex type of integrated marketing communication is needed for services than for goods. External communications channels must be coordinated, as with physical goods, but both external communications and interactive communication channels must be integrated to create consistent service promises. To do that, internal marketing communications channels must be managed so that employees and the company are in agreement about what is communicated to the customer. We call this more complicated version of IMC *integrated service marketing communications* (ISMC). ISMC requires that everyone involved with communication clearly understand both the company's marketing strategy and its promises to consumers (as illustrated in Figure 14.1).[4]

KEY SERVICE COMMUNICATION CHALLENGES

Discrepancies between what is communicated about a service and what a customer receives—or perceives that she receives—can powerfully affect consumer evaluations of service quality. The factors that contribute to these communication challenges include (1) service intangibility, (2) management of service promises, (3) management of customer expectations, (4) customer education, and (5) internal marketing communication (displayed in Figure 14.2). In this chapter, we first describe the challenges stemming from these factors and then detail strategies firms have found useful in dealing with them.

Challenge #1: Addressing Service Intangibility

Because services are performances rather than objects, their essence and benefits are difficult to communicate to customers (recall Chapter 1). Intangibility makes marketing communication for services more challenging for both marketers and consumers. The intangible nature of services creates problems for consumers both before and after purchase. Before buying services, consumers might have difficulty understanding what they will be buying and evoking names and types of services to consider.[5] During purchase, consumers often cannot clearly see the differences among services. After purchase, consumers may have trouble evaluating their service experiences.

The difficulties associated with intangibility can be divided into five properties, each of which has implications for service marketing communication. In this view, intangibility involves incorporeal existence, abstractness, nonsearchability, mental impalpability, and generality:[6]

- *Incorporeal existence.* The service product neither is made out of physical matter nor occupies physical space. Although the delivery mechanism (such as a Jiffy Lube outlet) may occupy space, the service itself (car servicing and oil change) does not. The implication is that showing the service is difficult, if not impossible.
- *Abstractness.* Service benefits such as financial security, fun, and health do not correspond directly with objects, making them difficult to visualize and understand.

FIGURE 14.2
Five Major Approaches to Overcome Service Communication Channels

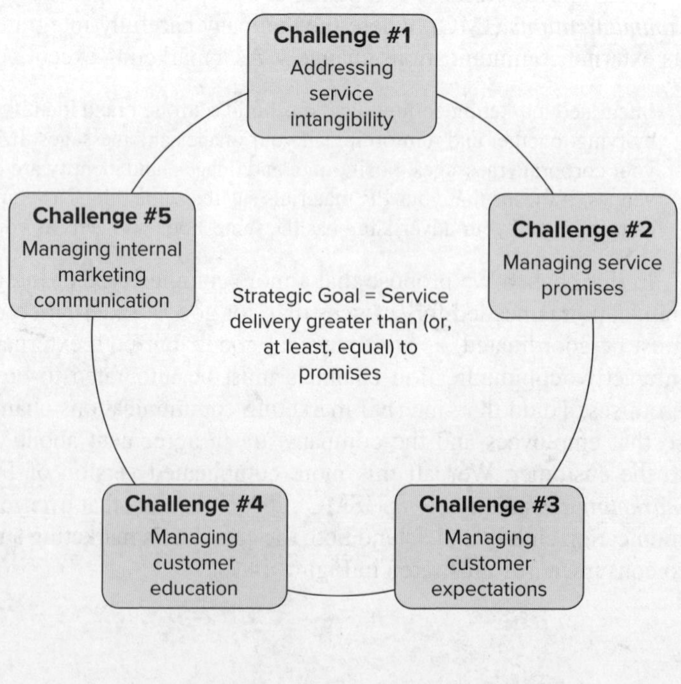

When businesses need consulting, for example, they often do not know where to begin because the concept is so vague that they do not understand the specific goals, processes, or deliverables they are seeking.

- *Nonsearchability.* Because service is a performance, it often cannot be previewed, or inspected in advance of purchase. If we are interested in finding a doctor, an air-conditioning repair firm, a personal trainer, or virtually any service, we cannot search with certainty the options as easily as we can search the shelves in a grocery store. Considerably more effort must be expended, and what we find may not be useful. For example, if a customer needs a plumber, the information contained in a source such as the Internet may not adequately discriminate among the choices.
- *Mental impalpability.* Services are often complex, multidimensional, and difficult to grasp mentally. When customers have not had prior exposure, familiarity, or knowledge, services are difficult to interpret. You may have experienced this when buying automobile insurance for the first time.
- *Generality.* Generality refers to a class of things, persons, events, or properties whereas *specificity* refers to particular objects, people, or events. Many services and service promises are described in generalities (wonderful experience, superior education, completely satisfied customers), making them difficult to differentiate from those of competitors.

These five aspects of service intangibility make customers feel more uncertain about their purchases, and evidence indicates that the greater the risk that customers perceive in purchasing services, the more actively they will seek and rely on word-of-mouth communications to guide their choices.[7] Word of mouth can be a very convincing source of information about services for consumers, but it is not under the control of the service provider. Exhibit 14.1 describes strategies that can be used in service advertising to overcome these aspects of intangibility.

Challenge #2: Managing Service Promises

A serious problem occurs when companies fail to manage service marketing communications—the vows made by salespeople, advertising, and service personnel—and service falls short of what is promised. This sometimes occurs because the part of the company making the promise lacks the information necessary to make accurate statements. For example, business-to-business salespeople often sell services, particularly new business services, before their actual availability and without having an exact date of when they will be ready for market. Demand and supply variations make service provision possible at some times, improbable at others, and difficult to predict. The traditional functional structure in many companies (often called "silos") also makes communication about promises and delivery difficult internally.

Challenge #3: Managing Customer Expectations

Appropriate and accurate communication about services is the responsibility of both marketing and operations. Marketing must accurately (and compellingly) reflect what happens in actual service encounters; operations must deliver what is promised in communications. For example, when a management consulting firm introduces a new offering, the marketing and sales departments must make the offering appealing enough to be viewed as superior to competing service offerings. In promoting and differentiating the service, however, the company cannot afford to raise expectations above the level at which its consultants can consistently perform. If advertising, personal selling, or any other external communication sets up unrealistic expectations, actual encounters will disappoint customers.

Exhibit 14.1 Service Advertising Strategies Matched with Properties of Intangibility

Property of Intangibility	Advertising Strategy	Description
Incorporeal existence	Physical representation	Show physical components of service that are unique, indicate high quality, and create the right association.
Abstractness	Service consumption episode	Capture and display typical customers benefiting from the service, evoking particular incidents.
Generality	System documentation	Objectively document physical system capacity by showing facts and figures.
	Performance documentation	Document and cite past positive performance statistics.
	Service performance episode	Present a vivid story of an actual service delivery incident that relates to an important service attribute.
Nonsearchability	Performance documentation	Cite independently audited performance.
	Consumption documentation	Obtain and present customer testimonials.
Mental impalpability	Service process episode	Present a vivid documentary on the step-by-step service process.
	Case history episode	Present an actual case history of what the firm did for a specific client.

Source: Adapted from B. Mittal, "The Advertising of Services: Meeting the Challenge of Intangibility," *Journal of Service Research* 2 (August 1999), pp. 98–116.

Many product and service companies also find themselves in the position of having to actively manage customer expectations downward—to tell customers that service previously provided will be discontinued or available only at a higher price. Airlines cancel flights that are not full and charge for food. Credit card companies that offer multiple value-added services when interest rates are high withdraw these services when interest rates drop. Healthcare insurers cut back on service while raising prices, and hospital patients experience far shorter stays and fewer diagnostic procedures than in the past. In these situations—perhaps more than any others—the need to manage customer expectations is critical.

Challenge #4: Managing Customer Education

Service companies must educate their customers. If customers are unclear about how service will be provided, what their role in delivery involves, and how to evaluate services they have never used before, they will be disappointed. When disappointed, they will often hold the service company, not themselves, responsible. These errors or problems in service—even when they are "caused" by the customer—still lead customers to defect. For this reason the firm must assume responsibility for educating customers.[8]

For services high in credence properties—expert services that are difficult for customers to evaluate even after they have received the services—many customers do not know the criteria by which they should judge the service. For high-involvement services, such as long-term medical treatment or purchase of a first home, customers are also unlikely to comprehend and anticipate the service process. First-time home buyers rarely understand the complex set of services (inspection, title services, insurance) and processes (securing a mortgage, offers and counteroffers, escrow) that will be involved in their purchases. Professionals and other providers of high-involvement services often forget that customers who are novices must be educated about each step in the process. They assume that an overview at the beginning of the service, or a manual or set of instructions, will equip the customer. Unfortunately, these steps are rarely sufficient, and customers defect because they can neither understand the process nor appreciate the value received from the service.

A final condition under which customer education can be beneficial involves services in which demand and supply are not synchronized, as discussed in Chapter 13. If the customer is not informed about peaks and valleys in demand, service overloads and failures, as well as underutilized capacity, are likely to result.

Challenge #5: Managing Internal Marketing Communication

Multiple functions in the organization, such as marketing and operations, must be coordinated to achieve the goal of quality service provision. Because service advertising and personal selling promise what *people* do, frequent and effective communication across functions—horizontal communication—is critical. It is equally crucial to coordinate ISMC efforts across hierarchical levels in the organization through vertical communication. If internal communication is poor, perceived service quality is at risk. If company marketing communication and other promises are developed without input from operations, contact personnel may not be able to deliver service that matches the image portrayed in marketing efforts.

Not all service organizations advertise, but all need coordination or integration across hierarchies, departments, or functions to deliver quality service. All need internal communication between the sales force and service providers. Horizontal communication also must occur between the human resource and marketing departments. To deliver excellent customer service, firms must be certain to inform and motivate employees to deliver what their customers expect. If marketing and sales personnel who understand customer expectations do not communicate this information to contact employees, the lack of knowledge for these employees will affect the quality of service that they deliver.

A final form of internal coordination central to providing service excellence is consistency in policies and procedures across departments and branches. If a service organization operates many outlets under the same name, whether franchised or company owned, customers expect similar performance across those outlets. If managers of individual branches or outlets have significant autonomy in procedures and policies, customers may not receive the same level of service quality across the branches.

FIVE CATEGORIES OF STRATEGIES TO MATCH SERVICE PROMISES WITH DELIVERY

After Figure 14.2 identified the five major challenges in service communication, we now identify strategies to overcome these communication challenges. The strategic goal is to deliver service that is greater than or equal to promises made, and all three sides of the triangle (in Figure 14.1) must be addressed to do so.

Strategies to Address Service Intangibility

Approaches to address service intangibility are (1) advertising and other communication strategies that clearly communicate service attributes and benefits to consumers and (2) strategies designed to encourage word-of-mouth communication.

If service companies recognize the challenges they face due to intangibility, they can use selected strategies to compensate. In one way or another, each of the individual strategies we discuss here focuses on ways to make the message memorable.[9]

Use Narrative to Demonstrate the Service Experience

Many services are experiential, and a uniquely effective approach to communicating them involves story-based appeals. Showing consumers having realistic and positive experiences with services is generally more effective than describing service attributes, particularly because the attributes themselves are often intangible. Research has concluded that consumers with relatively low familiarity with a service category prefer appeals based on stories to appeals based on lists of service attributes. An example of this is a State Farm campaign in which someone experiencing a situation in which a State Farm agent is needed simply calls out, "Like a good neighbor, State Farm is there," and an agent instantly appears to take care of the situation.

Present Vivid Information

Effective service marketing communication creates a strong or clear impression on the senses and produces a distinct mental picture. One way to use vivid information is to evoke a strong emotion such as fear. Using vivid information cues is particularly desirable when services are highly intangible and complex, such as life insurance. Accordingly, some insurance companies use vivid information in their advertising. One example used the slogan: "If you died today, who would take care of your family?" This slogan uses a particularly drastic fear appeal (death) to increase a consumer's attention to and interest in the ad.

Use Interactive Imagery

One type of vividness involves what is called *interactive imagery.*[10] Imagery (defined as a mental event that involves the visualization of a concept or relationship) can enhance recall of names and facts about service. Interactive imagery integrates two or more items in some mutual action, resulting in improved recall. Some service companies effectively integrate their logos or symbols with an expression of what they do, such as the Prudential rock—the rock symbolizes strength and stability. The accompanying photo shows an advertisement for The Travelers Companies Inc., a provider of property casualty insurance, that demonstrates interactive imagery. The umbrella symbolizes protection and reassurance, an appropriate symbol to identify an insurance company. An umbrella is believed to have first appeared in a Travelers ad in 1870 and the red umbrella became the official company trademark in 1959. The advertisement shown in the photo refers to the reacquisition in 2007 of the trademark from Citigroup, which also used the umbrella as part of its logo.

Kristoffer Tripplaar/Alamy Stock Photo

Interactive imagery is demonstrated by the Travelers umbrella.

Focus on the Tangibles

Another way that advertisers can increase the effectiveness of service communications is to feature the tangibles associated with the service, such as showing a bank's marble columns to provide clues about the nature and quality of the

American Express

This advertisement for the American Express Platinum Card both illustrates the shiny but matte stainless steel card and also promotes the option of customization using designs by well-renowned artists.

service.[11] The image above, which is an advertisement for the American Express Platinum Card, not only illustrates the shiny but matte stainless steel card; it also promotes the option of further customizing this tangible element of the service as customers have the choice to select either the classic metal card or exclusive Art x Platinum designs by world-renowned artists.

Use Brand Icons to Make the Service Tangible

How does an advertiser of services gain in competitive differentiation and strong brand awareness in a highly competitive market? In the fast-food and insurance industries, one answer is to create a recognizable brand icon that represents the company and generates brand visibility. One of the most enduring service brand icons is Ronald McDonald, the red-and-yellow clown that represents McDonald's and its children's charity, the Ronald McDonald House. Advertising icons are even more critical in industries in which the service is complex and difficult to understand. Insurance is an example. American Family Life Insurance Company, or Aflac, a company that sells supplemental insurance on a voluntary basis in U.S. and Japanese worksites, faced a difficult challenge: getting potential customers to ask for its service by name. Enter the Aflac duck, an insistent and vocal character who screams, "Aflac!" in commercials in which actors are trying to solve their insurance problems. The duck, introduced in 2000, has generated such visibility that he has been featured on CNBC, *The Tonight Show with Jay Leno,* and *Saturday Night Live.* GEICO has TV ads such as the one shown in the image on this page, featuring the Cockney-speaking Gecko lizard. The GEICO Gecko reinforces the company's brand image with natural tenacity, constantly good cheer and an insatiable need to help people save money on car insurance. The GEICO Gecko has become a force to be reckoned with in the advertising world and has been voted America's favorite advertising icon.

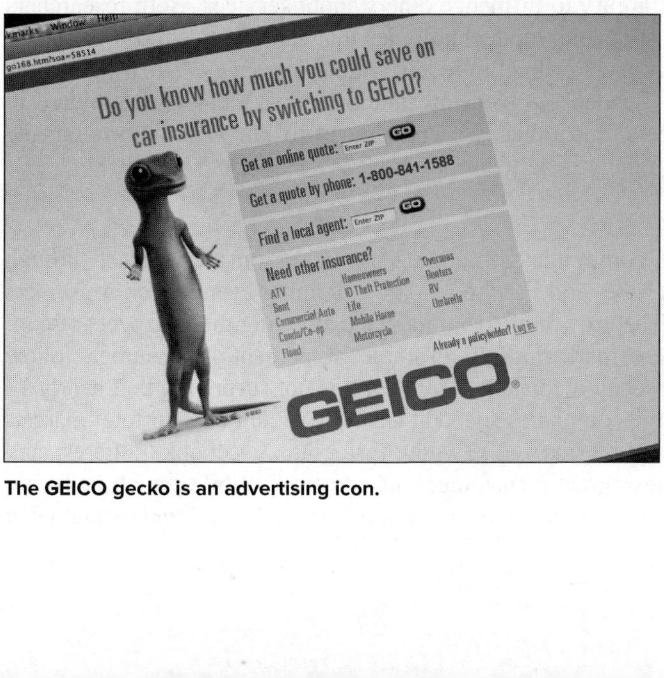

NetPhotos/Alamy Stock Photo

The GEICO gecko is an advertising icon.

Use Association, Physical Representation, Documentation, and Visualization

Leonard Berry and Terry Clark propose four strategies of tangibilization: association, physical representation, documentation, and visualization.[12] *Association* means linking the service to a tangible person, place, or object. *Physical representation* means showing tangibles that are directly or indirectly part of the service, such as employees, buildings, or equipment. *Documentation* means featuring objective data and factual information. *Visualization* is a vivid mental picture of a service's benefits or qualities, such as showing people on vacation having fun. Our Strategy Insight shows how marketing communication icons can be used as tangibles.

Feature Service Employees in Communication

Customer contact personnel are tangible representations of the service and are an important second audience for service advertising.[13] Featuring actual employees doing their jobs or explaining their services in advertising is effective for both the primary audience (customers) and the secondary audience (employees) because it communicates to employees that they are important. Furthermore, when employees who perform a service well are featured in marketing communication, they become standards for other employees' behaviors.

Use Buzz, or Viral, Marketing and Aim Messages to Influencers

Buzz marketing, also called viral marketing, involves the use of real consumers to spread the word about products without (or without the appearance of) being paid by the company. Sometimes buzz marketing occurs simply because customers are avid fans of the service, and sometimes the company seeds customers with services or products. For example, when Uber was founded in 2009, it launched its new app with a small-budget marketing campaign by offering individuals in Silicon Valley free rides. Because Uber provided a unique service, word of mouth spread quickly. Uber then also encouraged referrals through discount codes. Specifically, Uber customers could offer their code to friends who would receive a discount on their first ride; in parallel, the customer sharing the code would also receive a discount on their next ride. This two-dimensional incentive generated considerable new demand that spread from small groups to the entire area, and ultimately became the globally successful service business we know today.[14]

In terms of targeting influencers, improved technologies are now allowing companies to identify online influencers—those individuals with more connections than others and therefore more ability to influence others about services. Both researchers and research companies are developing technologies that can identify those people in a viral community who are most critical to receive brand messages. When identified, these individuals can be "seeded"—given information about the service, invited to participate in special events, and otherwise encouraged to know and communicate about a service (see the Strategy Insight).

Leverage Social Media

Social media—interactive communication among customers on the Internet through such sites as Twitter, YouTube, and Facebook—are becoming avenues for consumers to exchange information. The growth of social media is affecting many aspects of consumer purchase behavior and marketing. For example, 40 percent of consumers follow their "favorite" brands on social media. Accordingly, it is not surprising that nearly 90 percent of medium and large companies spend at least 11 percent of their total marketing budget on social media platforms (e.g., Twitter, Instagram, Facebook, Pinterest, and LinkedIn) in order to achieve greater customer engagement.[15] While social media are not controllable by the firm, the company can monitor the media and understand what consumers are saying and recommending. Formal methods and sophisticated technologies are being developed to track, monitor, and analyze online communication for brands. Nielsen BuzzMetrics, the innovator of this approach, gathers brand information online by trolling millions of lines of Internet communication to find out how customers feel about brands, how many are talking online, what issues they are discussing, how marketing is being viewed, and how efforts to affect word-of-mouth communications are being received. The service provides industry norms and benchmarks to the companies who buy their service as well as real-time alerts about issues.[16]

Create Advertising That Generates Talk Because It Is Humorous, Compelling, or Unique

Humorous advertisements are memorable and vivid.[17] Over the years, GEICO has developed many of the most humorous service commercials. Many of the ads focus on the brand's gecko, but other campaigns are humorous in different ways (the company features many of its funny commercials on its website; https://www.geico.com/about/commercials/). The TV network HBO created a humorous commercial for its streaming service entitled, "Awkward Family Viewing." The advertisement features two teenagers watching *Game of Thrones* with their parents; Mom and Dad can't stop asking questions during an episode of the complicated show. The ad ends with the suggestion that getting the app for HBO Go allows you to watch the program on your own, without all the pesky questions from your parents.

Feature Satisfied Customers in the Communication

Advertising testimonials featuring actual service customers simulate personal communications between people and are thereby a credible way to communicate the benefits of service. For example, Yum Yum Videos (a video agency that produces animated videos for its clients) uses multiple formats of customer testimonials on its website, ranging from customer reviews and star ratings to elaborate video testimonials that feature satisfied customers. Another example of using customer testimonials is Birchbox (an online monthly subscription service); the company lists several testimonials from real customers about their favorite Birchbox products on its homepage.

Generate Word of Mouth through Employee Relationships

Research shows that customer satisfaction with a service experience alone is not sufficient to stimulate word-of-mouth activity. However, when customers gain trust in a specific employee, positive word of mouth results. In this research, trust was shown to be a consequence of three aspects of the employee–customer relationship: a personal connection between employees and customers, care displayed by employees, and employee familiarity with customers.[18] Companies can strengthen the interpersonal bonds that lead to trust using strategies that focus on service design, support systems, employees, and customers.[19] Examples include designing the service environment so that opportunities for interactions between customers and employees are plentiful, using support systems (such as customer relationship management software) to help employees remember customer characteristics, and empowering employees to correct problems fully and quickly.

Strategies to Manage Service Promises

In manufacturing physical goods, the departments that make promises and those that deliver them can sometimes operate independently. Goods can be fully designed and produced and then turned over to marketing for promotion and sale. In services, however, the sales and marketing departments make promises about what other employees

Strategy Insight The Rise of Service Marketing through Social Media Influencers

One area of increasing relevance for service marketers is the use of social media influencers on sites such as Facebook, Instagram, YouTube, or TikTok, among others. Such "influencer marketing" refers to the strategic use of social media customers with influence to promote a focal company, brand, or cause in exchange for compensation. Influencer marketing has become an important communications tool for many organizations and has grown into a billion-dollar industry.

What are social media influencers? Influencers are third-party endorsers who aim to affect their audience's attitudes through blogs, tweets, and other social media. Typically, influencers are seen as trustworthy sources by their (often) large social media followings, which give them considerable "reach" and "impact." An influencer's *reach* describes the number of primary followers, as well as her/his secondary reach through these primary followers. As a function of their reach, research distinguishes mega-influencers (1 million followers or more), macro-influencers (100,000 to 1 million), micro-influencers (10,000 to 100,000), and nano-influencers (less than 10,000 followers). An influencer's *impact* describes the influence she/he has on the (purchase) decision making of others. Reach and impact are crucial, because influencers typically engage with their social media audiences in exchange for compensation they receive for content production, content distribution, audience interactions, and their personal appearance on social media. Social media influencers achieve their reach and impact through (a combination of) their expertise, authenticity, and intimacy with the audience.

Light and Vision/Shutterstock

- **Expertise:** influencers often become opinion leaders because they are perceived to be experts in a particular niche or category (e.g., fashion/design, food, fitness, health).
- **Authenticity:** influencers aim to create an authentic identity; that is, successful influencers develop distinctive public image and brand identities. Their goal is to distinguish themselves from others to be particularly interesting and relevant to their audiences and to marketers.
- **Intimacy:** another driver of influencer success is the ability to create a close bond with followers, which can be achieved through continuous interactions (e.g., through hosting live chats, or through sharing personal content such as hobbies, friends, and daily activities). Through such activities, influencers aim to be perceived as similar, familiar, and likeable by their audience.

in the organization will fulfill. Because what employees do cannot be standardized, greater coordination and management of promises are required. This coordination can be accomplished by creating a strong service brand and by coordinating all of the company's marketing communications.

Create a Strong Service Brand

Leonard Berry, an expert in *service branding,* emphasizes that branding plays a special role in service companies:

> Strong brands enable customers to better visualize and understand intangible products. They reduce customers' perceived monetary, social, or safety risk in buying services, which are difficult to evaluate prior to purchase. Strong brands are the surrogates when the company offers no fabric to touch, no trousers to try on, no watermelons or apples to scrutinize, no automobile to test drive.[20]

What are major platforms? Instagram tends to be perceived by marketing managers as a particularly important and impactful channel. For example, one 2021 survey found that 79 percent of managers participating in this study considered Instagram the most important platform for their influencer campaigns (relative to Facebook [50 percent], TikTok [46 percent], and YouTube [44 percent]). Although more traditional channels (e.g., Facebook and YouTube) remain relevant, the ease of photo-sharing on Instagram gives influencers a direct connection to different niche audiences. In addition, relative to longer-form content and videos, a single photo and caption on Instagram is much easier and cheaper to produce, which also makes this marketing tactic more affordable for smaller and regional companies. That said, marketers also consider the sociodemographic characteristics of their target market; for example, marketers focusing on younger generations leverage TikTok, which has taken Generation Z by storm.

What are success indicators of influencer marketing? The success of influencer marketing is illustrated in multiple aspects of consumer behavior; for example:

- Research by Twitter found that almost 40 percent of its users made a purchase as a direct result of a tweet from an influencer, and purchase intentions soared by a factor of 5 when Twitter users were exposed to brand influencer Tweets.
- Approximately 60 percent of YouTube subscribers would follow purchase advice from their favorite content creator over their favorite TV/movie celebrity. Research suggests that influencers who are perceived to be genuinely passionate about brands they are recommending to have significantly more effect on consumers. Accordingly, analysts expect that micro-influencers will become more important; although they may have fewer followers than mega-influencers and macro-influencers, their authentic passion tends to be more engaging and purchase-triggering for their audience.
- 83 percent of Instagram users turn to this platform to find something new, and after seeing posts with product information on the platform, 87 percent of its users took specific action (e.g., following a brand, visiting its store, or buying from it).
- Currently, 50 million people consider themselves to be content creators. However, this number will continue to rise: prominent platforms (e.g., TikTok and Instagram) are easy to use and widely accessible; in addition, they make it easy for people to create and distribute content. Accordingly, experts expect that up to one billion individuals will become content creators in the near future.

Sources: L. Hudders, S. De Jans, and M. De Veirman, "The Commercialization of Social Media Stars: a Literature Review and Conceptual Framework on the Strategic Use of Social Media Influencers," *International Journal of Advertising* 40 (May 2020), pp. 327–375; W. Geyser, "The State of Influencer Marketing 2022: Benchmark Report," https://influencermarketinghub.com/influencer-marketing-benchmark-report/; J. Santora, "Key Influencer Marketing Statistics You Need to Know for 2022," https://influencermarketinghub.com/influencer-marketing-statistics/, accessed March 09, 2022.

In contrast to branding in goods situations, where each product has its own brand, the primary brand in service is the company itself. The focus of brand creation is on awareness, meaning, and equity of the company. For example, companies like FedEx, Disney World, Starbucks, and Facebook all focus communication and information on their companies rather than individual services that the company offers. Therefore, the brand becomes the company's method of integrating marketing communication.[21]

With service brands dominating many economies, researchers are exploring how to develop strong service brands, and determining whether service branding requires strategies that are different from strategies that are effective for goods-based brands. One model of service branding is the "ServBrand triad" that shows how three interrelated drivers are fueling service brand growth (defined as positive brand outcomes, for example, a brand being liked more, used more by customers, or being more valuable to a firm). Using 11 years of brand and firm data, this research found that the

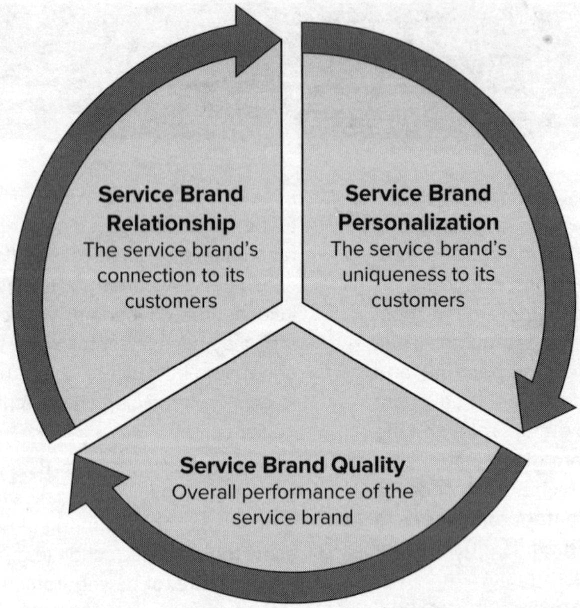

FIGURE 14.3
The "ServBrand Triad" Model of Growing the Service Brand

Source: M. H. Huang and C. S. Dev, "Growing the Service Brand," *International Journal of Research in Marketing*, 37 (June 2020), pp. 281–300.

three drivers of service brand growth are (a) quality, (b) personalization, and (c) relationships (see Figure 14.3):

- **Quality:** this driver of service brand growth relates to the rational and functional aspects of service brands relative to customer expectations (e.g., the customer-perceived functional excellence or value of the brand).
- **Personalization:** the personalization driver refers to the brand being perceived as unique and distinct from competing brands in a favorable way (e.g., the brand is dynamically customized to its customers). The notion of service personalization emphasizes learning customer preferences and adapting service to these preferences (ideally) for each customer (e.g., through technology that allows accurate prediction about customer preferences).
- **Relationship:** the relationship driver describes the service brand's continuous interactions and communications with its customers. The goal is for customers to develop a positive emotional connection to the brand and to increase perceived switching costs (e.g., aspects such as brand-self-connection, customer satisfaction, trust, and commitment).

Coordinate External Communication

For any organization, one of the most important yet challenging aspects of managing brand image involves coordinating all the external communication vehicles that send information to customers. This task has become far more challenging in recent years because a notable trend is the proliferation of new media. Not only are traditional communication vehicles such as advertising, company websites, sales promotion, public relations, direct marketing, and personal selling proliferating, but many forms of new media are now available to marketers. Social media, digital signage, blogs, mobile advertising, many forms of Internet advertising, and increasing usage of product placement in movies and television all complicate the goal of coordinating messages. Our Global Feature shows an international campaign for Virgin Atlantic Airways that uses many elements of the *marketing communication mix.*

Advertising is any paid form of nonpersonal presentation and promotion of a company's offerings by an identified sponsor. Dominant advertising vehicles include television, radio, newspapers, magazines, outdoor signage, and the Internet. Because advertising is paid, marketers control the creative appeals, placement, and timing. Internet advertising has become a large portion of companies' advertising budgets (see the Technology Spotlight) and should be synchronized with traditional advertising vehicles. MasterCard's highly successful "Priceless" advertising campaign listed three or four tangible items and their prices followed by a key customer benefit that was "priceless." The campaign was an example of strong integration because it was flexible and carried a brand message that was relevant and also adapted well to different media, payment channels, and markets. The campaign, seen in 96 countries and 47 languages, generated strong brand recall and received the advertising industry's prestigious Gold Effie, Addy, and Cresta awards.[22]

Sales promotion includes short-term incentives such as coupons, premiums, discounts, and other activities that stimulate customer purchases and stretch media spending. The fast-food industry, including McDonald's, Burger King, and Wendy's, offers premiums such as action figures that link the chains' offerings to current movies and television shows. A particularly successful version of joint promotions between service advertisers and entertainment was created by CKE Restaurants' Carl's Jr. The restaurant incorporated footage of television season premieres, finales, and other television shows into the company's advertising, "[deliver]ing upwards of 30 percent of an increase in the impact of media spending."[23]

Public relations includes activities that build a favorable company image with a firm's publics through publicity, relations with the news media, and community events. Richard Branson, founder of Virgin Atlantic Airways (see the Global Feature), is a master at obtaining publicity for his airline. When launching the airline, he claimed, "I knew that the only way of competing with British Airways and the others was to get out there and use myself to promote it."[24] In the years since the airline's launch, his publicity-winning stunts included recording the fastest time across the Atlantic Ocean in a speedboat, flying a hot-air balloon across the Atlantic Ocean and from Japan to Canada, dressing up in everything from a stewardess's uniform to a bikini on Virgin flights, and being photographed in his bath.

Direct marketing includes the use of mail, telephone, fax, e-mail, and other tools to communicate directly with specific consumers to obtain a direct response. American Express is a service company that uses direct marketing extensively and ensures that it integrates well with all other messages, including interactive messages from employees. As the executive vice president of global advertising at American Express clearly states,

> Service brands are not created solely in advertising. In fact, much of a brand's equity stems from the direct consumer experiences with the brand. We partner with [a relationship marketing company] to help us manage consumer experiences with our brand across all products and services—Card, Travel, Financial Services, and Relationship Services—via all direct channels, including phone, Internet, and mail.[25]

Personal selling is face-to-face presentation by a representative from the firm to make sales and build customer relationships. One way that personal selling and advertising are integrated in business-to-business companies is through the development of advertising materials that salespeople distribute to customers. This approach not only creates an integrated message to customers but also keeps salespeople fully informed of the promises the company is making.

Global Feature From Virgin Atlantic to Virgin Galactic: Taking Service Branding to Outer Space

A brand name that is known internationally for innovation, quality and a sense of fun—this is what we have always aspired to with Virgin.

Richard Branson

Richard Branson, first known for Virgin Records, the legendary record label that signed the Rolling Stones, Janet Jackson, and Genesis, surprised the world when he launched an upstart airline called Virgin Atlantic Airways. His vision was to create a high-quality, value-for-money airline to challenge the United Kingdom's market leader, British Airways. Four decades later Virgin Atlantic includes destinations in the United States, Asia, and Africa. While, similar to most airlines, Virgin Atlantic struggled financially during the COVID-19 pandemic, it survived thanks to a billion-dollar restructuring program.

Parent company Virgin Group, with combined sales exceeding $20 billion, is known worldwide as an innovative global brand with 40 companies across five business sectors and five continents. Virgin Atlantic Airways' brand and marketing campaign epitomizes successful global communication, with universal marketing components that are integrated in theme and design across the world as well as individual advertisements that adapt to geographies. Virgin Atlantic Airways' common global marketing elements include its brand values, logo, and distinctive airplanes. The airline's brand values—"working for the good of our communities and our planet, creating a culture of respect and trust in the wider world, and providing experiences that make people feel safe, cared for and listened to"—are executed in all communications and strategies. Virgin, as it strives to be the most loved travel company, focuses on customer service and low cost while also being the first to offer up unique services. For example, Virgin was the first airline to install television screens in every seat, offer massages and beauty services in first class, and mount a gambling casino right in the plane! The red and white logo, in the shape of an airline tail fin, appears in all worldwide marketing communication media including television, press, magazines, price promotions, outdoor posters, and taxi sides. Another common image is the company's Flying Lady, a Vargas painting of a red-headed, scantily dressed woman holding a scarf. Distinctive airplanes feature the Flying Lady on the fuselage and Union Jacks on their wings in three core colors of red, purple, and

Chris Parypa Photography/Shutterstock

silver metallic. Even the paint technology—based on mica, a hard mineral that produces a pearl-like shine—is unique. When the iridescent gleam combines with the plane's vibrant colors, the aircraft stirs up memories of the 1930s, when flying was glamorous and romantic. As shown in the accompanying international advertisement, Virgin Atlantic Airways manages to translate its brand themes in culturally specific ways while retaining its global image. The Caribbean ad draws in readers with its bananas. Although the text and appeal change to suit the culture, all international advertisements contain the same Virgin Atlantic Airways logo and the same company colors.

The airline's communication campaigns have led to many awards over the years. The airline has won numerous awards for its business operations and marketing communications, for example:

- TTG Airline of The Year Award (2021)
- Skytrax COVID-19 Airline Excellence Award (2021)
- KAYAK Travel Awards (2020, in multiple categories)
- TripAdvisor Travellers Choice Awards (2019)
- edie Sustainability Leaders Award (2018 and 2017)
- Business Travel Awards: Best Corporate Social Responsibility Programme (2016)

- Data Storytelling Award, for the best real-time data (2015)
- Europe's leading airline to North America (2015)
- Silver Award in the Best Airline for Groups (2015)
- Travolution Award—best airline website as voted by consumers (2014)
- Winner of the coveted ORA Prix d'OR (top accolade) (2013)
- Best Leisure & Travel Website (2013)
- Commendation in BIMA Award for best website user experience (2013)
- Bronze Medal for best use of digital in the travel and leisure sector (2013)
- Campaign of the Year (2012)
- Best TV Commercial (2012)
- Best Press Campaign (Upper Class) (2012)
- Best Website (VSFlyinghub for global trade website) (2012)
- Best Brochure—Little Red Book—interactive online Flying Club brochure (2012)

Virgin Galactic—Brand Management in Outer Space: Richard Branson also founded Virgin Galactic, an American spaceflight company that is a member of the Virgin Group. Taking the aforementioned goal of offering "unique services" to the next level, Virgin Galactic is developing commercial spacecraft to provide suborbital spaceflights for space tourists. In 2018, Virgin Galactic completed its maiden spaceflight when its VSS Unity spaceship reached an altitude of 51.4 miles, thereby officially entering outer space (per NASA, outer space begins at 50 miles above the Earth).

And on 11 July 2021, Richard Branson himself, along with three of his employees, was a passenger on a spaceflight. In November 2021, Virgin Galactic began taking flight reservations starting at $450,000 per seat; at that point, the company had already sold more than 700 tickets. Flights take off from Spaceport America in New Mexico and last approximately 90 minutes, each with up to 6 minutes of weightlessness. Notably, Virgin Galactic is not the only service company offering spaceflights to consumers. Jeff Bezos' company Blue Origin and Elon Musk's SpaceX are also developing spacecrafts with the goal of eventually supporting commercial space travel services. Indeed, on 20 July 2021, Blue Origin took the first paying customer on a joyride to space.

For those who are not willing to pay hundreds of thousands of dollars for a ticket to space, there is still good news as Virgin Galactic is also developing more accessible service innovations. For example, according to Richard Branson, Virgin Galactic is "in the best position in the world" to provide rocket-powered, point-to-point 3,000 mph air travel.

Sources: www.virgin-atlantic.com; J. Wattles, "Virgin Galactic Reopens Ticket Sales—for $450,000 Per Seat," 2021, https://www.cnn.com/2021/08/05/tech/virgin-galactic-ticket-prices-sales; Virgin Galactic, Wikipedia, accessed March 09, 2022.

Technology Spotlight Internet Expert Mary Meeker Predicts What Companies Most Need to Know

Widely respected Internet analyst Mary Meeker, who is the founder and general partner at BOND, a San Francisco-based venture capital firm, has published Internet trends annually since 1995 (except in 2020). Her reports provide data and analyses on key trends shaping the Internet, consumer behavior, and broader cultural shifts. She is known for many accurate forecasts, including the emergence of mobile video and messaging apps.

One of Meeker's most sought-after statistics every year is the overall growth of U.S.-based Internet advertising; she reported that Internet advertising increased by one-fifth between 2017 and 2018. Most of that rise was due to just two companies, Facebook and Google. The ability to provide advertisers with highly specific user data for targeting purposes is a pivotal advantage for any platform–seeking advertisers, and that is what those two platforms provide better than any others.

While Meeker covered many topics and presented myriad statistics in her 334-slide "2019 Internet Trends" presentation, some of the major insights include the following:

- **The Internet continues to grow:** The internet continues to grow, but new growth areas are increasingly difficult to find. Approaching 4 billion, the number of Internet users comprises approximately half the world's population. Asia Pacific (which accounts for 53 percent of global Internet users) leads other regions in the world in number of users and growth potential; not surprisingly, China and India are the two countries with the most users and potential.
- **Images and videos speak louder than words:** Consumers increasingly use images and videos (rather than text) to communicate with others. For example, more than half all tweets now include images/videos. The increasing importance of images and videos is fueled by sophisticated cameras in smart phones, but also by technology that simplifies the creation, editing, and sharing of images and videos (e.g., platforms such as Instagram or Pinterest). Therefore, because the human brain is hard-wired for images, Meeker expects consumers to use more visuals and to increasingly become storytellers. This trend suggests that marketers should also leverage the power of images and videos to better tell their stories to their customers.
- **Freemium is the path to new customers:** Consumers consider free trials the most compelling reason for trying a new service (e.g., Spotify). Accordingly, Mary Meeker found free service trials to be the most effective marketing tool for online streaming services to attract new users. Of course, the strategic goal for marketers is to ultimately convert these free trial users into paying subscribers.
- **Interactive gaming becomes more important:** There are more than 2 billion people playing interactive games (e.g., Fortnite). Notably, interactive (multi-player) games are therefore increasingly transforming into social media networks. To illustrate, Fortnite hosted a DJ Marshmello virtual live concert that was viewed by nearly 11 million gamers. This insight relates to the aforementioned relevance of freemium marketing strategies, which are increasingly common in interactive gaming contexts, as well.

Mary Meeker also examined the new online world in light of COVID-19. Although COVID-19 interrupted many of people's routines, the pandemic also accelerated innovation and growth in some areas. Among other trends (e.g., the increasing importance of science, technological innovation, and governmental services), one major technology-related shift is, not surprisingly, an amplification of **on-demand work and services**. While safety rules and restrictions have seriously hurt some leading on-demand services (e.g., Airbnb, Uber), these same rules and restrictions boosted other on-demand platforms. For example, consider delivery services for groceries (Instacart) and food (DoorDash). The corresponding surge in consumer demand supported not only local supermarkets, restaurants, and stores, but also provided new employment opportunities for service workers. Mary Meeker predicts that such on-demand and to-the-door delivery services will be able to retain a considerable and permanent market share post-pandemic, similar to other economies (e.g., Asia), where on-demand services are more pervasive and advanced than in the United States.

Sources: M. Meeker (2019), "Bond Internet Trends 2019"; Bond (2020), "Special Report: Our New World," https://www.bondcap.com/report/onw/#view/1; A. Mann (2020), "11 Highlights from Mary Meeker's "Internet trends report", https://datapulses.com/2020/02/04/mary-meeker-internet-trends-highlights/, accessed March 09, 2022.

Strategies to Manage Customer Expectations

Accurately promising when and how service will be delivered is one of the most important ways to close the communication gap. Among the most effective strategies to manage customer expectations are to make realistic promises; to offer service guarantees, options, and tiered-value offerings; and to communicate criteria customers can use to assess service.

Make Realistic Promises

The expectations that customers bring to the service affect their evaluations of its quality: the higher the expectation, the higher the delivered service must be to be perceived as high quality. Therefore, making promises about any aspect of service delivery is appropriate only when these aspects will actually be delivered. It is essential for a firm's marketing or sales department to understand accurately the levels of service delivery (percentage of times the service is provided correctly, or percentage and number of problems that arise) before making promises. To be appropriate and effective, communications about service quality must accurately reflect what customers will actually receive in service encounters.

Probably the simplest and most important point to remember is to promise what is possible.[26] Many companies hope to create the perception that they have high-quality service by claiming it in marketing communication, but this strategy can backfire when the actual service does not live up to the promises in advertising. In line with the strategies we discuss in the next section, all service communications should promise only what is possible and not attempt to make services more attractive than they actually are.

Offer Service Guarantees

As discussed in Chapter 7, service guarantees are formal promises made to customers about aspects of the service they will receive. Although many services carry implicit service satisfaction guarantees, the true benefits from explicit service guarantees—an increase in the likelihood of a customer's choosing or remaining with the company—come only when the customer knows that guarantees exist and trusts that the company will stand behind them.

Offer Choices

One way to reset expectations is to give customers options for aspects of service that are meaningful, such as time and cost. A clinical psychologist charging $100 per hour, for example, might offer clients the choice between a price increase of $10 per hour or a reduction in the number of minutes comprising the hour (such as 50 minutes). With the choice, clients can select the aspect of the trade-off (time or money) that is most meaningful to them. Making the choice solidifies the clients' expectations of service.

This strategy is effective in business-to-business situations, particularly in terms of speed versus quality. Customers who are time conscious often want reports, proposals, or other written documents quickly. When asked to provide a 10-page proposal for a project within three days, an architectural firm responded that it could provide either a 2-page proposal in three days or a 10-page proposal in a week. Its customer selected the latter option, recognizing that the deadline could be extended. In most business-to-business services, speed is often essential but threatens performance. If customers understand the trade-off and are asked to make a choice, they are likely to be more satisfied because their service expectations for each option become more realistic.

Create Tiered Value Service Offerings

Product companies are accustomed to offering different versions of their products with prices commensurate with the value customers perceive. Automobiles with different configurations of features carry price tags that match not their cost but their perceived value to the customer. The same type of formal bundling and pricing can be accomplished in services, with the extra benefit of managing expectations.

Credit card companies offer tiered-value offerings. American Express has multiple levels of credit card services based on the type of service provided: the traditional green card offers basic service features, the gold card additional benefits, and the platinum card still more. Two advantages of tiered offerings are as follows:

1. The practice puts the burden of choosing the service level on the customer, thereby familiarizing the customer with specific service expectations.
2. The company can identify which customers are willing to pay higher prices for higher service levels.

The opportunity to set expectations accurately is present when the customer makes the decision at the time of purchase. Customers can be reminded of the terms of the agreement if they request support that is above the level in the contract.

Strategies to Manage Customer Education

As discussed in Chapter 12, customers must perform their roles properly for many services to be effective. If customers forget to perform their roles, or perform them improperly, disappointment may result. For this reason, communication to customers can take the form of customer education.

Prepare Customers for the Service Process

One of us, on a return trip from Singapore on Singapore Airlines, neglected to heed the airline's warning that return flights to the United States must be confirmed 24 hours in advance. Upon arrival at the airport to return home, the seat had been given to another customer who had conformed to the airline's request for confirmation. Depending on the perspective taken, you could argue that either the company or the customer was right in this situation. Whose responsibility is it to make sure that customers perform their roles properly?

Companies can avoid such situations by preparing customers for the service process. And companies may need to prepare the customer often, even every step of the way, for the subsequent actions the customer needs to take. A business-to-business example will help illustrate this strategy. Customers of management consulting services purchase intangible benefits: marketing effectiveness, motivated workforces, and culture change. The very fact that companies purchase these services usually indicates that they do not know how to perform them alone. Many clients will also not know what to look for along the way to judge progress. In management consulting and other complex service situations, the effective provider prepares the customer for the service process and creates structure for the customer. At the beginning of the engagement, the management consulting firm establishes checkpoints throughout the process, at which times progress will be evaluated, and leads the customer to establish objectives for project completion. Because customers do not know what that progress will look like, the consulting firm takes the lead in setting goals or criteria to be examined at those times.

Communicate the Criteria and Levels of Service Effectiveness

At times companies can establish the criteria by which customers assess service. Consider a business customer who is purchasing market research services for the first time. Because market research is an expert service, it is high in credence properties that are hard for customers to judge. Moreover, the effectiveness of this type of service differs depending on the objectives the client brings to the service. In this situation, a service provider can teach the customer the criteria by which to evaluate the service. The provider that teaches the customer in a credible manner will have an advantage in shaping the evaluation process.

As an example, consider research company A, which communicates the following criteria to the customer: (1) a low price signals low quality, (2) the reputation of the firm is critical, and (3) person-to-person interviews are the only type of customer feedback that will provide accurate information. A customer who accepts these criteria will evaluate all other suppliers using them. If research company B had talked to the customer first, consider these (very different!) criteria and their impact on the buyer: (1) market research companies with good reputations are charging for their reputation, not their skill; (2) online interviews have been found to work as well as person-to-person interviews; and (3) price does not indicate quality level.

The same approach can be used with service *levels* rather than evaluative criteria. If research company B provides four-day turnaround on the results of the data analysis, the company has just set the customer's expectation level for all other suppliers.

Confirm Performance to Standards and Expectations

Service providers sometimes provide service, even explicitly requested service, yet fail to communicate to the customer what has been accomplished. These providers stop short of getting credit for their actions when they do not reinforce actions with communication about their fulfillment of the request. This situation may happen under one or more of the following conditions:

- The customer cannot evaluate the effectiveness of a service.
- The decision maker in the service purchase is a person different from the users of the service.
- The service is performed out of sight of the customer.

When customers cannot evaluate service effectiveness, usually because they are inexperienced or the service is technical, the provider may fail to communicate specific actions that address client concerns because the actions seem too complex for the customer to comprehend. In this situation, the service provider can improve perceptions by translating the actions into customer-friendly terms. A personal injury lawyer who aids a client with the medical and financial implications of an accident needs to be able to tell the client in language the client can understand that the lawyer has performed the necessary actions.

When the decision maker in service purchases is different from the users of the service, a wide discrepancy in satisfaction may exist between decision makers and users. An example is in the purchase of information technology products and services in a company. The decision maker—the manager of information technology or someone in a similar position—makes the purchase decisions and understands the service promises. If users are not involved in the purchase process, they may not know what has been promised and may be dissatisfied.

Customers are not always aware of everything done behind the scenes to serve them well. Most services have invisible support processes. For instance, physicians frequently request diagnostic tests to rule out possible causes for illness. When these tests come back negative, doctors may neglect to inform patients. Many hairstyling firms have guarantees that ensure customer satisfaction with haircuts, permanents, and color treatments. However, only a few of them actively communicate these guarantees in marketing communication because they assume customers know about them. The firm that explicitly communicates the guarantee may be selected over others by a customer who is uncertain about the quality of the service. Making customers aware of standards or efforts to improve service that are not readily apparent can improve service quality perceptions; in parallel, this can also help create a competitive advantage for the firm as it might make customers assess competitors more accurately or even critically (relative to the focal firm).

Clarify Expectations after the Sale

When service involves a hand-off between sales and operations, clarifying expectations with customers helps the operations arm of the company align delivery with customer expectations. Salespeople are motivated and compensated to raise customer expectations—at least to the point of making the sale—rather than to communicate realistically what the company can provide. In these situations, service providers can avoid future disappointment by clarifying to customers what was promised as soon as the hand-off is made from sales to operations.

Strategies to Manage Internal Marketing Communication

The fifth major category of strategies necessary to match service delivery with promises is managing internal marketing communications.[27] Internal marketing communications can be both vertical and horizontal. *Vertical communications* are either downward, from management to employees, or upward, from employees to management. *Horizontal communications* are those across functional boundaries in an organization. A third strategy is *internal branding,* which consists of various strategies to sell the brand inside the company. Other strategies, discussed in the following paragraphs, include *creating effective upward communication, aligning back-office and support personnel with external customers,* and *creating cross-functional teams.*

Create Effective Vertical (Downward/Upward) Communications

Companies that give customer-contact employees adequate information, tools, and skills allow them to perform successful interactive marketing. Some of these skills come through the training and other human resource efforts discussed in Chapter 11, but some are provided through *downward communications.* Among the most important forms of downward communications are company newsletters and magazines, corporate television networks, e-mail, briefings, videos and internal promotional campaigns, and recognition programs. One of the keys to successful downward communications is keeping employees informed of everything that is being conveyed to customers through external marketing. Employees should see company marketing communication before it is aired or published and should be familiar with the website, mailings, and direct-selling approaches used. If these vertical communications are not present, both customers and employees suffer—customers will not receive the same messages from employees that they hear in company external marketing, and employees will feel uninformed and not be aware of what their company is doing. Customers go to them, asking for services that have been marketed externally but not internally, making the employees feel uninformed, left out, and helpless.[28]

Notably, *upward communication* is also necessary in closing the gap between service promises and service delivery. Employees are at the frontline of service, and they know—more than anyone else in the organization—what can and cannot be delivered. They know when service breakdowns are occurring and, very often, why they are happening. Having open communication channels from employees to management can prevent service problems before they occur and minimize them when they do take place.

Create Effective Horizontal Communications

Horizontal Communications—communication across functional boundaries in an organization—facilitate coordinated efforts for service delivery. This task is difficult because functions typically differ in goals, philosophies, outlooks, and views of the customer—but the payoff is high. Coordination between marketing and operations can result in communication that accurately reflects service delivery, thus reducing the gap between customer expectations and actual service delivery. Integration of effort between marketing and human resources can improve the ability of each employee to become a better marketer. Coordination between finance and marketing can create prices that accurately reflect the customer's evaluation of a service. In service firms, all these functions need to be integrated to produce consistent messages and to narrow the service gaps.

One important strategy for effective horizontal communications is to open channels of communication between the marketing department and operations personnel. For example, when a company creates advertising that depicts the service encounter, it is essential that the advertising accurately reflect what customers will experience in actual service encounters. Puffery or exaggeration puts service quality perceptions at risk, especially when the firm is consistently unable to deliver to the level of service portrayed in the marketing communication. Coordination and communication between advertising and service providers are pivotal in delivering service that meets expectations.

Featuring actual employees doing their jobs or explaining the services they provide, a strategy mentioned earlier in this chapter, is one way to coordinate advertising portrayals and the reality of the service encounter. To create this type of advertising, the advertising department or agency interacts directly with service employees, facilitating horizontal communications. Similar benefits can be achieved if employees are included in the advertising process in other ways, such as by being shown advertising in its pretest forms.

Another important strategy for horizontal communications involves opening channels of communication between sales and operations. Mechanisms for achieving this goal can be formal or informal and can include annual planning meetings, retreats, team meetings, or workshops in which departments clarify service issues. In these sessions, the departments can interact to understand the goals, capabilities, and constraints of the other. Some companies hold "gap workshops" at which employees from both functions meet for a day or two to try to understand the difficulties in matching promises made through selling with delivery accomplished by operations personnel.[29]

Involving the operations staff in face-to-face meetings with external customers is also a strategy that allows operations personnel to more readily understand the salesperson's role and the needs and desires of customers. Rather than filtering customers' needs through the sales force, operations employees can witness firsthand the pressures and demands of customers. A frequent and desirable result is better service to the internal customer—the salesperson—from the operations staff as they become aware of their own roles in satisfying both external and internal customers.

Sell the Brand Inside the Company

Having knowledge about what the company is doing in marketing communications is one aspect of internal marketing communication, but it is not enough. Consultant Colin Mitchell emphasizes, the importance of marketing the company's brand and brand message to employees, so that they can make powerful connections with customers.[30] He recommends three principles for bringing the brand alive: choosing the right moment to teach and inspire employees, linking internal and external marketing, and bringing the brand alive for employees. Choosing the right moment is essential because employees are not capable of or willing to accept too many change initiatives, and therefore the company has to be selective in identifying opportunities when it can create enthusiasm for the brand.

Linking internal and external marketing means that employees need to hear the same thing from management that customers hear. If customers hear that serving them is most important and employees are told that cost savings matter more, employees will be confused and unable to live the message. One of the best ways to link the two types of communication is to create advertising that targets both customers and employees. When IBM launched its highly successful e-business campaign, it took out a large advertisement in *The Wall Street Journal* to show its intent to both target audiences, then followed up with support for both audiences throughout the campaign.

Bringing the brand alive to employees involves creating a strong emotional connection between employees and the company. Employees at Southwest Airlines are encouraged to live the Southwest brand by dressing informally (although still in uniform), ad-libbing when giving instructions both on the ground and in the plane, and decorating the check-in counters on holidays. Singapore Airlines, on the other hand, connects with its employees through the company's emphasis on grace, formal dress, quiet tone, and Asian food.

Align Back-Office and Support Personnel with External Customers through Interaction or Measurement

As companies become increasingly customer focused, frontline personnel develop improved skills in discerning what customers require. As they become more knowledgeable about and empathetic toward external customers, they also experience intrinsic rewards for satisfying customers. Back-office and support personnel, who typically do not interact directly with external customers, miss out on this bonding and, as a consequence, fail to gain the skills and rewards associated with it.

Companies can create ways to facilitate the interaction between back-office and support personnel and external customers. Weyerhaeuser (a company that owns nearly 20,000 sq mi of timberlands and that manufactures wood products), for example, sends hourly employees to customers' plants to better understand their needs. When actual interaction is difficult or impossible, some companies record videos of customers in their service facilities during the purchase and consumption process to vividly portray the needs and requirements of customers and to show personnel the support that frontline people need to deliver to those expectations.

When company measurement systems are established, employees are sometimes judged on the basis of how they perform for the next internal customer in the chain.

Indian Service Strategy Insight Zomato – Integrated Marketing Communications Strategy

Zomato's technology platform, launched in 2010, connects customers and restaurant partners through services that allow customers to discover restaurants, read and write reviews, order food delivery, make reservations, and process payments, while providing restaurant partners with marketing tools to grow their business and reliable last-mile delivery services. The company has emerged as India's leading food delivery platform.

Its sophisticated integrated marketing communications strategy blends search engine optimization (SEO), social media marketing, email campaigns, influencer partnerships, and innovative advertising. The company draws over 53% of its traffic from search engines, leveraging its extensive database of 1.4 million restaurant listings as natural keywords. Their social media approach is particularly notable, using witty content and memes to engage their primary 18–35-year-old demographic, complemented by strategic collaborations with food bloggers and influencers across various engagement levels.

Zomato's creative digital marketing shines through its unconventional social media presence, particularly on Twitter where it earned the "Best Brand Voice" award in 2020. The brand masterfully employs reverse psychology in campaigns like "Guys, kabhi kabhi ghar ka khana bhi kha lena chaiye" (Sometimes you should eat home-cooked food) during the ICC World Cup 2019, sparking viral engagement despite contradicting their core offering of food delivery from restaurants. Their email marketing demonstrates similar creativity, theming campaigns around trending topics like "Mirzapur Season 2" with catchy subject lines such as "Munna Bhaiya invited you to a weekend" and creating a clever "Curryculum Vitae of Biryani" that replaced "hire now" with "order now" to drive conversions.

During mega events like the IPL, Zomato elevates its marketing communications with specialized campaigns such as the Zomato Premier League, which gamifies the cricket experience by allowing users to predict match winners for additional discounts. The brand has recently embraced AI technology to create personalized advertisements for restaurant partners during IPL 2024, collaborating with acclaimed filmmakers and stars, including Ranveer Singh and Samantha Prabhu. This tech-forward approach enables custom ads highlighting each restaurant's signature dishes, effectively connecting cricket enthusiasm with food delivery through online video streaming service provider, JioCinema's platform capabilities, allowing tailored content for each match broadcast across multiple media channels.

Beyond promotional activities, Zomato harnesses sophisticated digital tools to enhance both customer and restaurant partner experiences. Their SEO strategy

Shutterstock

targets over 900,000 keywords with internal linking structures across millions of pages, supported by backlinks from 12.48 million domains, including high-authority .gov and .edu websites. For restaurant partners, Zomato launched Hyperpure for supply chain management and recently unveiled Nugget, an AI-powered customer support platform that handles up to 80% of queries autonomously while reducing resolution time by 20% and increasing agent co-pilot compliance by 25%. This B2B solution represents Zomato's expanding digital ecosystem beyond consumer applications.

The latest addition to Zomato's technological arsenal is Zomato AI, a sophisticated tool that functions as a "foodie buddy" rather than a mere chatbot. Using a multiple agent framework with various specialized prompts and in-house developed functions, it can suggest restaurants based on specific dishes, dietary requirements, or even the user's mood. This conversational AI responds in near real-time, unlike traditional chatbots that process one message at a time, and can answer complex food-related queries like "What should I eat when I have a hangover?" or dietary specifications. Exclusively available to Zomato Gold members, this technology demonstrates Zomato's commitment to creating personalized digital experiences that strengthen brand loyalty while driving sales through their integrated marketing communications approach throughout the customer's journey.

References

https://blog.zomato.com/introducing-zomato-ai-your-foodie-buddy

https://www.business-standard.com/companies/news/zomato-launches-ai-customer-support-platform-nugget-125021700734_1.html

https://yourstory.com/2024/04/zomatos-using-ai-cook-restaurant-ads-ipl-season

https://startuptalky.com/zomato-marketing-strategies/

Although this approach provides feedback in terms of how well the employees are serving the internal customer, it lacks the motivation and reward that come from seeing their efforts affect the end customer. FedEx has aligned internal personnel with the external customer using measurement (recall Chapter 9). FedEx's service quality indicator (SQI) computes daily the number of companywide service failures. To clearly communicate customer fail points to internal employees, the company created linking measures to trace the causes to each internal department. For example, the company's information technology department affects the SQI measurements and therefore has submeasures that provide feedback on how the department's work is affecting the SQI.

Create Cross-Functional Teams

Another approach to improving horizontal communications to better serve customers is to involve employees in cross-functional teams to align their jobs with end customer requirements. For example, if a team of telecommunications service representatives is working to improve interaction with customers, back-office people such as computer technicians or training personnel can become part of the team. The team then learns requirements and sets goals for achieving them together, an approach that directly creates communications across the functions.

The cross-functional team approach can best be explained by the examples of an advertising agency. The individual in an advertising agency who typically interacts directly with the client is the account executive (often called a "suit" by the creative staff). In the traditional agency, the account executive visits the client, elicits client expectations, and then interacts with the various departments in the agency (art, copywriting, production, traffic, and media buying) that will perform the work. All functions are specialized and, in extreme cases, get direction for their portion of the work right from the account executive. A cross-functional team approach has representatives from all the areas meet with the account executive, even the client, and collectively discuss the account and approaches to address client needs. Each team member brings his or her function's perspectives and opens communication. All members can then understand the constraints and schedules of the other groups.

Summary

Discrepancies between service delivery and external communications have a strong impact on customer perceptions of service quality. In this chapter we discussed the role of and need for integrated service marketing communications in minimizing these discrepancies. We described external and interactive communications using the service triangle and emphasized the need to coordinate all communication to deliver service that meets customer expectations. We emphasized the difficulties and possibilities associated with new media. We also discussed the factors that lead to challenges in service marketing communications, including service intangibility; management of service promises; and management of customer expectations, customer education, and internal marketing communication. We then examined strategies to address each of these service communications problems. To address service intangibility, we described specific strategies such as the use of vivid imagery and tangible icons in communications, as well as ways to maximize the use of word-of-mouth communication. To manage service promises, we delineated the need for a strong service brand, coordination of service promises, realistic promises, and service guarantees. To manage customer expectations, we suggested that allowing customers to choose among options, creating tiered-value options, communicating service effectiveness criteria, and negotiating unrealistic expectations can be effective. To improve customer education, we described the need to prepare customers for the service process, confirm performance to standards and expectations, clarify expectations after the sale, and teach customers to choose the best times to seek service. Finally, to manage internal communication, we discussed effective vertical communications, horizontal communications, and internal branding.

Discussion Questions

1. Think of another service company that provides integrated service marketing communications. Go to the service company's website and find the section where it posts its advertising and communication. Is the company's campaign as comprehensive and as integrated as Southwest's or Aldi's campaign, as described in the opening vignette? Why or why not? What should be added, changed, or deleted to improve the campaign?
2. Which of the key reasons for the communication gap (provider Gap 4) discussed in the beginning of this chapter is the easiest to address in a company? Which is the hardest to address? Why?
3. Review the five general strategies for achieving integrated service marketing communications. Would all these strategies be relevant in goods firms? Which would be most critical in goods firms? Which would be most critical in service firms? Are there any differences between those most critical in goods firms and those most critical in service firms?
4. What are the most effective Internet advertisements you have seen? Why are they effective?
5. Using the section on managing customer expectations, put yourself in the position of your professor, who must reduce the amount of "service" provided to the students in your class. Give an example of each strategy in this context. Which of the strategies would work best with you (the student) in managing your expectations? Why?
6. Why are social marketing media like Facebook and YouTube so important in service firms? Are they important in product firms?
7. What other strategies can you suggest for leveraging consumer-generated media?
8. What other strategies can you add to the four offered in the section on customer education? What types of education do you expect from service firms? Give an example of a firm from which you have received adequate education. What firm has not provided you with adequate education?

Exercises

1. Go to the Google website and select the tab called "Business Solutions." This is the section of the site that describes the types of advertising that Google offers. Do the same thing for YouTube (you must go to "Company Information" and then to "Advertising"). Review these types of advertising, and describe the benefits and disadvantages of each. If you were an advertiser, which of these types of ads would you want to use? Why?
2. Find five effective service advertisements online and magazines. According to the criteria given in this chapter, identify why they are effective. Critique them using the list of criteria, and discuss ways they could be improved.
3. Visit the Forbes ranking of the "Worlds Most Valuable Brands." Consider the top 20 brands and identify which companies are dominantly service companies. Are there goods-dominated brands that also offer (at least) some form of service?

4. Visit the website where Geico provides its commercials (https://www.geico.com/about/commercials/). Watch some of these ads and discuss which aspects make them particularly memorable to consumers.

Notes

1. Southwest Airlines, Transfarency, https://search.southwest.com/s/search.html?f.Tabs%7Csouthwest-youtube=Social+Media&query=transfarency&collection=southwest-search, accessed March 08, 2022; T. Wright, "5 Examples of Print Advertising and Digital Marketing Integration Done Right Digital Advertising," *Search Engine Journal,* December 8, 2015.
2. Points are Pointless, Aldi's New Campaign; https://www.2creativemedia.com.au/creative-cube/points-are-pointless/; Aldi, https://en.wikipedia.org/wiki/Aldi; accessed March 08, 2022.
3. P. G. Lindell, "You Need Integrated Attitude to Develop IMC," *Marketing News,* May 26, 1997, p. 5.
4. K. L. Keller, "Unlocking the Power of Integrated Marketing Communications: How Integrated is Your IMC Program?," *Journal of Advertising* 45 (July 2016), pp. 286–301.
5. D. Legg and J. Baker, "Advertising Strategies for Service Firms," in *Add Value to Your Service,* ed. C. Suprenant (Chicago: American Marketing Association, 1987), pp. 163–168.
6. B. Mittal, and J. Baker, "Advertising Strategies for Hospitality Services," *Cornell Hotel and Restaurant Administration Quarterly*, 43, (April 2002), pp. 51–63; B. Mittal, "Services Communications: From Mindless Tangibilization to Meaningful Messages," *Journal of Services Marketing*, 16, (September 2002), pp. 424–431; B. Mittal, "The Advertising of Services: Meeting the Challenge of Intangibility," *Journal of Service Research* 2 (August 1999), pp. 98–116.
7. A. Babić Rosario, F. Sotgiu, K. De Valck, and T. H. Bijmolt, "The Effect of Electronic Word of Mouth on Sales: A Meta-Analytic Review of Platform, Product, and Metric Factors," *Journal of Marketing Research*, 53 (June 2016), pp. 297–318. H. S. Bansal and P. A. Voyer, "Word-of-Mouth Processes within a Services Purchase Decision Context," *Journal of Service Research* 3 (November 2000), pp. 166–177.
8. S. J. Bell, S. Auh, and A. B. Eisingerich, "Unraveling the Customer Education Paradox: When, and How, Should Firms Educate Their Customers?," *Journal of Service Research* 20 (August 2017), pp. 306–321.
9. For a meta-analysis on memorable advertising, see: E. S. Kwon, K. Whitehill King, G. Nyilasy, and L. N. Reid, "Impact of Media Context on Advertising Memory: A Meta-Analysis of Advertising Effectiveness," *Journal of Advertising Research* 59 (March 2019), pp. 99–128.
10. K. L. Alesandri, "Strategies That Influence Memory for Advertising Communications," in *Information Processing Research in Advertising,* ed. R. J. Harris (Hillsdale, NJ: Erlbaum, 1983).
11. L. L. Berry and T. Clark, "Four Ways to Make Services More Tangible," *Business,* October–December 1986, pp. 53–54.
12. www.geico.com; www.Aflac.com; "Who's Your Favorite Advertising Icon?" advertising insert, *New York Times,* September 20, 2004, p. 6.
13. Berry and Clark, "Four Ways to Make Services More Tangible."
14. D. Blystone, "The Story of Uber," https://www.investopedia.com/articles/personal-finance/111015/story-uber.asp; L. Caveney, "What is Buzz Marketing? Strategies and

Examples," https://www.thisisinfluential.com/blog/strategy/what-is-buzz-marketing-strategies-and-examples/, accessed March 02, 2022.

15. F. de Oliviera Santini et al., "Customer Engagement in Social Media: A Framework and Meta-Analysis," *Journal of the Academy of Marketing Science* 48 (November 2020), pp. 1211–1228.
16. Cited in S. Gupta, K. Armstrong and Z. Clayton, "Social Media," *Harvard Business School*, February 15, 2011, from a study by The Nielsen Company, "Trust, Value, and Engagement in Advertising," July 2009, http://blog.nielsen.com/nielsenwire/wp-content/uploads/2009/07/trustin advertising0709.pdf, accessed January 2010.
17. J. Aaker and N. Bagdonas, *Humor, Seriously: Why Humor Is a Secret Weapon in Business and Life,* Currency, 2021; N. Walter, M. J. Cody, L. Z. Xu, and S. T. Murphy, "A Priest, a Rabbi, and a Minister Walk Into a Bar: A Meta-Analysis of Humor Effects on Persuasion," *Human Communication Research* 44 (October 2018), pp. 343–373; S. Rosengren, M. Eisend, S. Koslow, and M. Dahlen, "A Meta-Analysis of When and How Advertising Creativity Works," *Journal of Marketing* 84 (November 2020), pp. 39–56.
18. D. D. Gremler, K. P. Gwinner, and S. W. Brown, "Generating Positive Word-of-Mouth Communications through Customer-Employee Relationships," *International Journal of Service Industry Management* (January 2001), pp. 44–59.
19. Ibid.
20. L. L. Berry, "Cultivating Service Brand Equity," *Journal of the Academy of Marketing Science*, 28 (December 2000), pp. 128–137.
21. M.-H. Huang and C. S. Dev, "Growing the Service Brand," *International Journal of Research in Marketing* 37 (June 2020), pp. 281–300; R. S. Kumar, S. Dash, and N. K. Malhotra, "The Impact of Marketing Activities on Service Brand Equity," *European Journal of Marketing* 52 (April 2018), pp. 596–618; M. Khamitov, X. Wang, and M. Thomson, "How Well Do Consumer-Brand Relationships Drive Customer Brand Loyalty? Generalizations From a Meta-Analysis of Brand Relationship Elasticities," *Journal of Consumer Research* 46 (September 2019), pp. 435–459; F. de Oliveira Santini, W. J. Ladeira, C. H. Sampaio, and D. C. Pinto, "The Brand Experience Extended Model: A Meta-Analysis," *Journal of Brand Management* 25 (November 2018), pp. 519–535.
22. G. Rifkin, "How the Red Sox Touch All the Branding Bases," strategy + business.com, accessed April 2007.
23. www.mastercardinternational.com2011.
24. Alice Z. Cuneo, "Sue Johenning," *Advertising Age,* September 27, 2004.
25. P. Denoyelle and J. Larreche, "Virgin Atlantic Airways—Ten Years Later," INSEAD Case, 1995.
26. D. E. Bell and D. M. Leavitt, "Bronner Slosberg Humphrey," *Harvard Business School Case 9-598-136,* 1998, p. 5.
27. Y.-T. Huang, "Internal Marketing and Internal Customer: A Review, Reconceptualization, and Extension." *Journal of Relationship Marketing* 19 (July 2020), pp. 165–181.
28. L. L. Berry, V. A. Zeithaml, and A. Parasuraman, "Quality Counts in Services, Too," *Business Horizons,* May–June 1985, pp. 44–52.
29. V. A. Zeithaml, A. Parasuraman, and L. L. Berry, *Delivering Quality Service: Balancing Customer Perceptions and Expectations* (New York: The Free Press, 1990), p. 120.
30. C. Mitchell, "Selling the Brand Inside," *Harvard Business Review* 80 (January 2002), pp. 5–11.

Chapter Fifteen

Pricing of Services

This chapter's learning objectives are to:

1. Discuss three major ways that service prices are perceived differently from goods prices by customers.
2. Articulate the key ways that pricing of services differs from pricing of goods from a company's perspective.
3. Demonstrate what value means to customers and the role that price plays in value.
4. Describe strategies that companies use to price services.
5. Give examples of pricing strategy in action.

Streaming Services Need to Step Up Their Pricing Strategies

Streaming services (e.g., Netflix, Amazon Prime, Disney+) continue to grow worldwide and have attracted hundreds of millions of subscribers with Netflix alone exceeding 220 million. The COVID-19 pandemic further boosted demand because consumers had few(er) choices for entertainment.

Streaming services provide content directly to their users via the Internet (thereby bypassing cable, broadcast, and satellite TV platforms). All viewers need is an Internet connection and a media player, computer, mobile phone, or smart TV to start playing content.

Notably, with the increasing number of subscribers, most streaming providers have also increased their prices over the years. For example, in 2013, Netflix's standard plan cost $7.99 per month; and in January 2022, after multiple rounds of price increases, Netflix charged $15.49 per month for its standard plan.[1]

Manuel Esteban/Shutterstock

In terms of pricing, streaming companies traditionally offered the same pricing strategy: all-you-can-watch for a flat monthly fee. Consequently, consumers often had to cobble together multiple fragmented services to enjoy their favorite shows, making the costs expensive. Accordingly, industry experts criticized streaming companies for ignoring a fundamental rule of pricing: *understand what customers value and then satisfy that need.* For example, many customers have a favorite show offered by a streaming company but are not interested in paying the monthly flat fee for unlimited viewing of other shows they do not like. Addressing this issue, bundling strategies are becoming more popular (e.g., The Disney Bundle includes Disney+, Hulu, and ESPN) and some providers are adding "a-la-carte" options. Streaming providers must observe and react to market dynamics to avoid being at a competitive disadvantage. To do so, more flexible pricing approaches will increasingly supplement the traditional "unlimited plans," for example:

- ***Metered Plans:*** These plans charge according to viewing time or number of shows watched (which might help to prevent customers from sharing their streaming passwords with friends and family).
- ***Tiered (Good-Better-Best) Plans:*** Streaming companies will offer more tiered packages. These packages can be further tailored by segmenting content type (shows vs. movies), exclusivity (original vs. nonexclusive content), and release date (newest vs. older releases). Other approaches to customization include usage restrictions (e.g., paying for the "ability to binge watch," or viewing times "all week" vs. "weekends only").
- ***Metered-and-Tiered Hybrid Plans:*** Following examples of cell phone pricing, streaming services are offering more hybrid formats that combine metered and tiered plans. That is, in addition to buying a fixed number of streaming minutes, customers can allocate additional minutes to different categories, according to their specific preferences.
- ***Discounts to Reward Long-Term Commitment:*** Industry analysts also expect streaming companies to move beyond month-to-month subscription models to offer discounts that incentivize customers to buy long-term contracts. Offering customers willing to commit to an extended time period a "volume discount" can be an effective tool to reduce customer switching behavior.

As their markets become ever more competitive, streaming services will need to shift from traditional "one-price-fits-all" strategies that often ignore customers' unique needs and different abilities to pay. Although these packages can be more complicated and cumbersome than simple "all-you-can-watch" plans, they allow customers to self-select based on their desired value. In other words, price-sensitive customers will be willing to invest relatively more time and effort in order to get their streaming at the minimum price (e.g., by researching available discount codes or time-limited offers), whereas customers who are not particularly concerned about price will be able to directly and (more) conveniently select an "unlimited plan." Although some companies are starting to leverage such creative pricing approaches, one consultant urged managers in the streaming industry "to step up their pricing strategies by offering choices to better accommodate the needs of their customers" (Mohammed 2019).

Although the pricing of services is receiving more attention from marketing scholars and managers, developing pricing strategies remains a challenge for many service organizations, in part as a result of the service characteristics discussed earlier.[2] What makes the pricing of services more difficult than pricing of goods? What approaches work well in the context of services?

This chapter builds on three key differences between customer evaluation of pricing services and goods that can have a profound impact on the strategies companies use to set and administer prices for services:

1. Customers often have inaccurate or limited reference prices for services.
2. Monetary price is not the only price relevant to service customers.
3. Price is a key signal of quality in services.

The chapter also discusses common pricing structures, including (1) cost-based, (2) competition-based, and (3) demand-based pricing. One of the most important aspects of demand-based pricing is perceived value, which service providers must understand, so that they price in line with offerings and customer expectations. For that reason, we also describe how customers define value and discuss pricing strategies in the context of value.

THREE KEY WAYS THAT SERVICE PRICES ARE DIFFERENT FOR CUSTOMERS

What role does price play in customer decisions about services? How important is price to potential buyers compared with other factors and service features? Service companies must understand how pricing works, but first they must understand how customers perceive prices and price changes. The three sections that follow describe ways that customers perceive services, and each is central to effective pricing (see Figure 15.1).

Customer Knowledge of Service Prices

To what extent do customers use price as a criterion in selecting services? How much do they know about the costs of services? Before you answer these questions, take the services pricing quiz in Exhibit 15.1. Were you able to fill in a price for each of the services listed? If you were able to answer the questions on the basis of memory, you have internal *reference prices* for the services. A reference price is *a price point in memory for a good or a service* and can consist of the price last paid, the price most frequently paid, or the average of all prices customers have paid for similar offerings.[3]

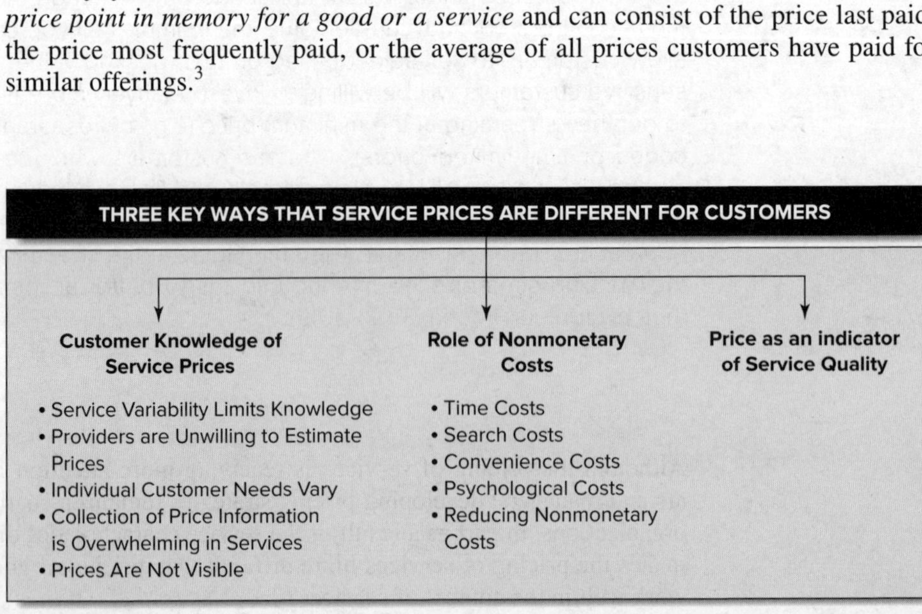

FIGURE 15.1 **Specific Ways That Service Prices Are Different for Customers**

Exhibit 15.1 What Do You Know about the Prices of Services?

1. What do the following services cost in your hometown?

Teeth whitening	________
General medical checkup	________
Legal help with a DWI (driving while intoxicated) charge	________
Dental braces	________
One hour of housecleaning	________
Room at the Marriott	________
Haircut	________
Oil change and lube	________

2. Which of the following would you select if you needed a filling replaced in a tooth?

   a. Dentist A—cost is $75, located 15 miles from your home, wait is three weeks for an appointment and 1.5 hours in waiting room

   b. Dentist B—cost is $100, located 15 miles from your home, wait is one week for appointment and 0.5 hour in waiting room

   c. Dentist C—cost is $150, located three miles from your job, wait is one week for appointment and no time in waiting room

   d. Dentist D—cost is $225, located three miles from your job, wait is one week for appointment and no time in waiting room; nitrous oxide used, so no pain is involved

To see how accurate your reference prices for services are, you can compare them with the actual price of these services from the providers in your hometown. If you are like many consumers, you feel quite uncertain about your knowledge of the prices of services, and the reference prices you hold in memory for services are not generally as accurate as those you hold for goods. There are many reasons for this difference.

Service Variability Limits Knowledge

Because services are not created on a factory assembly line, service firms have great flexibility in the configurations of services they offer. Firms can conceivably offer an infinite variety of combinations and permutations, leading to complex and complicated pricing structures. As an example, consider how difficult it is to get comparable price quotes when buying a new cell phone plan or life insurance. For example, with the multitude of types of life insurances (such as whole life versus term), features (different deductibles), and variations associated with customers (age, health risk, smoking or nonsmoking), few insurance companies offer exactly the same features and the same prices. Although there are websites that are designed to help consumers with price comparisons, often only an expert customer, one who knows enough about insurance to completely specify the options across providers, is likely to find prices that are directly comparable. Some insurance companies—such as Progressive—base their strategy on giving customers competitive prices for insurance.

How did you answer the questions about prices for a medical checkup? If you are like most consumers, you probably wanted more information before you offered a reference price. You probably wanted to know what type of checkup the physician is providing. Does it include X rays and other diagnostic tests? What types of tests? How long does the checkup take? What is its purpose? If the checkup is undertaken simply to get a signature on a health form or a marriage certificate, the doctor may take a brief medical history, listen for a heartbeat, and measure blood pressure. If, however, the checkup is to monitor a chronic ailment such as diabetes or high blood pressure, the doctor may be more thorough. The point is that a high degree of variability exists across providers of services. Not every physician defines a checkup the same way.

Providers Are Unwilling to Estimate Prices

Another reason customers lack accurate reference prices for services is that many providers are unable or unwilling to estimate price in advance. For example, legal and hospital service providers are rarely willing—or even able—to estimate a price in advance. The fundamental reason is that they do not know themselves what the services will involve until they have fully examined the patient or the client's situation or until the process of service delivery (such as an operation in a hospital or a trial) unfolds. Most hospitals contend that their fee schedules, called chargemasters, should not be made available to patients beforehand and have fought to keep them private.[4] In a business-to-business context, companies obtain bids or estimates for complex services such as consulting or construction, but this type of price estimation is typically not undertaken with end-consumers; therefore, they often buy without advance knowledge about the final price of the service.

Individual Customer Needs Vary

Another factor that results in the inaccuracy of reference prices is that individual customer needs vary. Some hairstylists' service prices vary across customers on the basis of length of hair, type of haircut, and whether a conditioning treatment and style are included. Therefore, if you ask a friend what a haircut costs from a particular stylist, chances are that your haircut from the same stylist will be a different price. In a similar vein, a service as simple as a hotel room will have prices that vary greatly: by size of room, time of year, type of room availability, and individual versus group rate. These two examples are for very simple services. Now consider a service purchase as idiosyncratic as braces from a dentist or help from a lawyer. In these and many other services, the fact that customers have different requirements will play a strong role in the price of the service.

Collection of Price Information Is Overwhelming in Services

Still another reason customers lack accurate reference prices for services, which is also closely related to the aforementioned drivers, is that customers feel overwhelmed with the information they need to gather. With most goods, retail stores display the products by category to allow customers to compare and contrast the prices of different brands and sizes. Rarely is there a similar display of services in a single outlet. If customers want to compare prices (such as for dry cleaning), they must drive to or call individual outlets or search on the Internet in situations where prices are available. This can be an overwhelming task for consumers, even for the most basic services, as illustrated in Exhibit 15.1.

When services are more specialized, finding out what they cost can be even more difficult; for example, see if you have reference prices for these providers: wedding planner, executive coach, and home security system. Your reference prices, if you can even come up with them, are probably even more uncertain and less accurate than for the services in the price quiz in Exhibit 15.1. After searching corresponding websites, we have found that these are starting points for these services. Wedding planners charge anywhere between \$50 and \$200 per hour, and the average costs for full-service wedding planners range from \$1,500-\$3,000 but can easily exceed \$10,000 and get considerably higher than that. Sherpa Executive Coaching, a widely recognized association in the field, regularly surveys members about compensation rates. The organization reports that fees vary widely from between \$200 to more than \$500 per hour, depending on the level of executive and type of skills being trained (for CEOs, coaching can even cost as much as \$3,500 per hour). As for home security systems, the prices also range considerably; for example, the average costs for a home security system are reported to range from $25 to $50 per month for monitoring services. Alarm system equipment ranges from $199 to $399, and $0 to $199 for security system installation and activation fees.[5]

The fact that consumers often possess inaccurate reference prices for services has several important managerial implications. Promotional pricing (as in couponing or special pricing) may be less meaningful for services, for which price anchors typically do not exist. Perhaps that is why price is not featured in service advertising as much as it is featured in advertising for goods. Promotional pricing may also create problems if the promotional price (such as a $50 permanent wave special from a salon) is the only one customers see in advertising: it could become the customer's anchor price, making the regular price of $75 for a future purchase seem high by comparison.

The absence of accurate reference prices also suggests that advertising actual prices for services the customer is not accustomed to purchasing may reduce uncertainty and overcome a customer's inflated price expectations for some services. For example, a marketing research firm's advertisements citing the price for a simple study (such as $10,000) would be informative to business customers who were not familiar with the costs of research studies and therefore would be guessing at the cost. By featuring price in advertising, the company overcomes the fear of high cost by giving readers a price anchor.

Prices Are Not Visible

One requirement for the existence of customer reference prices is *price visibility*—the price cannot be hidden or implicit. In many services, particularly financial services, most customers know about only the rate of return and not the costs they pay in the form of fund and insurance fees. In securities and term life insurance, customers are made aware of fees. However, price is invisible in certificates, whole-life insurance, and annuities (which have rear-load charges), and customers rarely know how they are charged or what they pay. Credit card fees are assessed on the basis of what consumers spend, and while customers may know their interest rates they are often shocked at what they are spending in fees to the financial institutions. Compounding and other financial practices—such as compressed periods to pay and dramatic increases in interest rates due to late payments—do not affect their costs until after they have made purchases.

For all the reasons discussed here, many customers do not see the price at all until *after* they receive certain services. Of course, in situations of urgency, such as in accident or illness, customers must make the decision to purchase without respect to cost. And if cost is not known to the customer before purchase, it cannot be used as a key criterion for purchase, as it often is for goods.

The Role of Nonmonetary Costs

Economists have long recognized that monetary price is not the only sacrifice consumers make to obtain products and services. Demand, therefore, is not just a function of monetary price but is influenced by other costs as well. Nonmonetary costs represent other sources of sacrifice perceived by consumers when buying and using a service. Time costs, search costs, and psychological costs often enter into the evaluation of whether to purchase or repurchase a service and may at times be more important concerns than monetary price. Customers will trade money for these other costs.

Time Costs

Most services require customers' direct participation and thus consume real time: time waiting as well as time when the customer interacts with the service provider. Consider the investment you make to exercise, see a physician, or get through the crowds to watch a concert or baseball game. Not only are you paying money to receive these services, but you are also expending time. Time becomes a sacrifice made to receive service in multiple ways. First, because service providers cannot completely control the number of customers or the length of time it will take for each customer to be served, customers are likely to expend time waiting to receive the service. The average waiting time in physicians' offices is approximately 19 minutes.[6] Waiting time for a service is frequently longer and less predictable than waiting time to buy goods. Second, customers often wait for an available appointment from a service provider (in the price quiz, dentist A required a three-week wait, whereas dentist D required only one week). Virtually everyone has expended waiting time to receive services.

Search Costs

Search costs—the effort invested to identify and select from among services you desire—are often higher for services than for physical goods. Prices for services are rarely displayed on shelves of service establishments for customers to examine as they shop, so these prices are often known only when a customer has decided to experience the service. As an example, how well did you estimate the costs of an hour of housecleaning in the price quiz? As a student, it is unlikely that you regularly purchase housecleaning, and you probably have not seen the price of an hour of cleaning displayed in any retail store. Another factor that increases search costs is that each service establishment typically offers only one "brand" of a service (with the exception of brokers in insurance or financial services), so a customer must initiate contact with several companies to get information across sellers. Price comparisons for many services (e.g., travel and hotels) are now facilitated through the Internet, reducing search costs. Orbitz and Travelocity, for example, offer customers a search of most airlines (with the notable exception of Southwest, which does not participate in reservation services), many hotels, and rental car companies. However, as reflected in the chapter opener, the added fees that airlines now charge still make searching for the final costs of airline flights difficult.

Convenience Costs

There are also convenience (or, perhaps more accurately, inconvenience) costs of services. If customers have to travel to receive a service, they incur a cost, and the cost becomes greater when travel is difficult, as it is for elderly persons. Further, if a service provider's hours do not coincide with customers' available time, they must arrange their schedules to correspond to the company's schedule. And if consumers have to expend effort and time to prepare to receive a service (such as removing all food from kitchen cabinets in preparation for an exterminator's spraying), they make additional sacrifices.

Psychological Costs

Often the most painful nonmonetary costs are the psychological costs incurred in receiving some services. Fear of not understanding (insurance), fear of rejection (bank loans), and fear of outcomes (medical treatment or surgery) all constitute psychological costs that customers experience as sacrifices when purchasing and using services. Of course, psychological costs also increased considerably during the COVID-19 pandemic, as many consumers were anxious about getting infected in service settings (e.g., stores, gyms, airports, movie theaters). New services, even those that create positive change, bring about psychological costs that consumers factor into the purchase of services. While many grocery stores now offer self-checkout that allows customers to bypass long lines, the number of customers who use them has not lived up to expectations. Many customers find the self-checkout lines confusing and frustrating to use, and others are embarrassed when they cannot move through them quickly.

Reducing Nonmonetary Costs

The managerial implications of these other sources of sacrifice are compelling. First, a firm may be able to increase monetary price by reducing time and other costs. For example, a service marketer can reduce the perceptions of time and convenience costs when use of the service is embedded in other activities (such as when a convenience store cashes checks, sells stamps, and serves coffee along with selling products). Second, customers may be willing to pay to avoid the other costs. Many customers willingly pay extra to have items delivered to their homes—including restaurant meals or bedroom furniture—rather than transporting the services and products themselves. The success of Amazon Prime, where customers can order virtually everything and not pay shipping, is a testament to this issue. Some customers also pay a premium for fast check-in and checkout (as in joining the Hertz #1 club), for reduced waiting time in a professional's office (as in so-called executive appointments where, for a premium price, a busy executive goes early in the morning and does not have to wait), and to avoid doing the work themselves (such as paying one and one-half times the price per gallon to avoid having to put gas in a rental car before returning it). If time or other costs are pivotal for a given service, the company's advertising can emphasize these savings rather than monetary savings.

Many other services save time, thus actually allowing the customer to "buy" time. Household cleaning services, lawn care, babysitting, personal shopper service, online banking, house painting, and carpet cleaning—all these services represent net gains in the discretionary time of consumers and can be marketed that way. Services that allow the customer to buy time are likely to have monetary value for busy consumers.

Price as an Indicator of Service Quality

One of the intriguing aspects of pricing is that buyers are likely to use price as an indicator of both service costs and service quality—price is at once an attraction variable and a repellent.[7] Customers' use of price as an indicator of quality depends on several factors, one of which is the other information available to them. When service cues to quality are readily accessible, when brand names provide evidence of a company's reputation, or when the level of advertising communicates the company's belief in the brand, customers may prefer to use those cues instead of price. In other situations, however, such as when quality is hard to detect or when quality or price varies a great deal within a class of services, consumers may believe that price is the best indicator of quality. Many of these conditions typify situations that face consumers when purchasing services.[8] Another factor that increases the dependence on price as a quality indicator is the risk associated with the service purchase. In high-risk situations, many of which involve credence services such as medical treatment or management consulting, the customer may look to price as a surrogate for quality.

Because customers depend on price as a cue to quality and because price sets expectations of quality, service prices must be determined carefully. In addition to being chosen to cover costs or match competitors, prices must be selected to convey the appropriate quality signal. Pricing too low can lead to inaccurate inferences about the quality of the service. Pricing too high can set expectations that may be difficult to match in service delivery.

APPROACHES TO PRICING SERVICES

Rather than repeat what you learned about pricing in your marketing principles class, we emphasize in this chapter that service prices and pricing differ from both the customer's and the company's perspective. We discuss these differences in the context of the three pricing structures typically used to set prices: (1) cost-based, (2) competition-based, and (3) demand-based pricing. These categories, as shown in Figure 15.2, are the same bases on which goods prices are set, but adaptations must be made in services. The figure shows the three structures interrelating because companies need to consider each of the three to some extent in setting prices. In the following sections, we describe in general each basis for pricing and discuss challenges that occur when the approach is used in service pricing. Figure 15.2 summarizes those challenges.

Cost-Based Pricing

In cost-based pricing, a company determines expenses from raw materials and labor, adds amounts or percentages for overhead and profit, and thereby arrives at the price. This method is widely used by industries such as utilities, contracting, wholesaling, and advertising. The basic formula for cost-based pricing is

$$\text{Price} = \text{Direct costs} + \text{Overhead costs} + \text{Profit margin}$$

Direct costs involve the materials and labor associated with delivering the service, overhead costs are a share of fixed costs, and the profit margin is a percentage of full costs (Direct + Overhead).

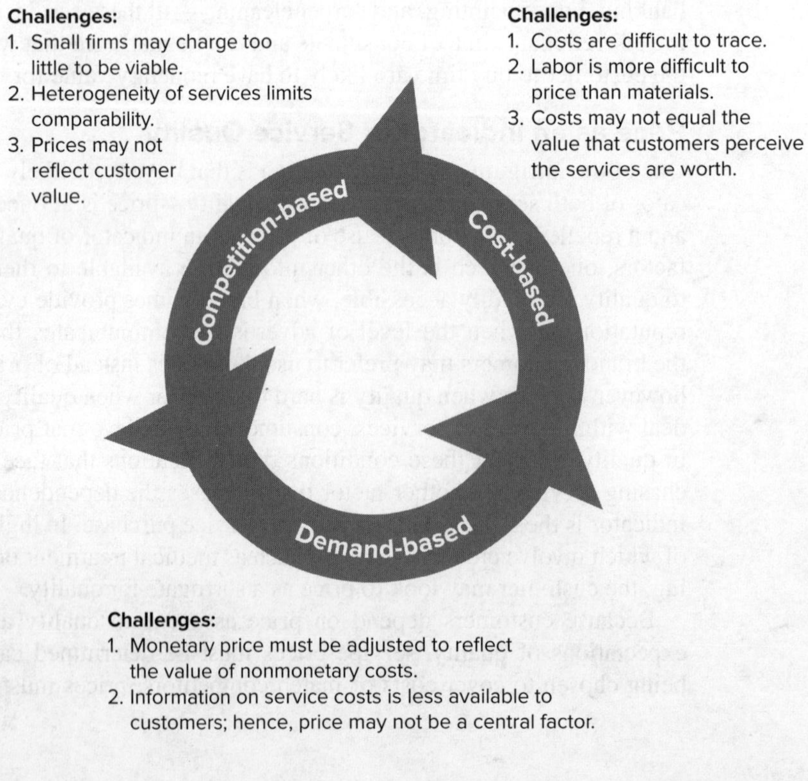

FIGURE 15.2 **Three Basic Marketing Price Structures and Challenges Associated with Their Use for Services**

Challenges in Cost-Based Pricing for Services

What is unique about services when using cost-based approaches to pricing? First, costs are difficult to trace or calculate in service businesses, particularly where multiple services are provided by the firm.[9] Consider how difficult it must be for a bank to allocate teller time or ATM costs accurately across its checking, savings, and money market accounts to decide what to charge for the services. Second, a major component of cost is employee time rather than materials, and the value of people's time, particularly nonprofessional time, is not easy to calculate or estimate. One of the major difficulties in cost-based pricing involves defining the units in which a service is purchased. Thus, the *price per unit*—a well-understood concept in the pricing of manufactured goods—is a vague entity. For this reason many services are sold in terms of input units rather than units of measured output. For example, most professional services (such as consulting, engineering, architecture, psychotherapy, and tutoring) are sold by the hour.

An added difficulty is that actual service costs may underrepresent the value of the service to the customer. A local tailor in one of the authors' hometowns charges $10 for taking in a seam on a $350 ladies' suit jacket and an equal $10 for taking in a seam on a pair of $14 sweat shorts. The tailor's rationale is that both jobs require the same amount of time. What she neglects to see is that the customer would pay a higher price—and might even be happier about the alterations—for the expensive suit jacket and that $10 is too high a price for the sweat shorts.

Examples of Cost-Based Pricing Strategies Used in Services

Cost-plus pricing is a commonly used approach in which component costs are calculated and a markup added. In product pricing, this approach is quite simple; in service industries, however, it is complicated because the tracking and identification of costs are difficult. The approach is typically used in industries in which cost must be estimated in advance, such as construction and engineering. In construction or engineering, bids are solicited by clients on the basis of the description of the service desired. Using their knowledge of the costs of the components of the service (including the raw materials such as masonry and lumber), labor (including both professional and unskilled), and margin, the company estimates and presents to the client a price for the finished service. A contingency amount—to cover the possibility that costs may be higher than estimated—is also stated because, in large projects, specifications can change as the service is provided.

Fee for service is the pricing strategy used by professionals; it represents the cost of the time involved in providing the service. Consultants, psychologists, accountants, and lawyers, among other professionals, charge for their services on an hourly basis. In the early 1900s, lawyers typically billed clients a certain fee for services rendered regardless of the amount of time they spent delivering them. Then in the 1970s, law firms began to bill on an hourly rate, in part because this approach offered accountability to clients and an internal budgeting system for the firm. One of the most difficult aspects of this approach is that recordkeeping is tedious for professionals. Lawyers and accountants must keep track of the time they spend for a given client, often down to 10-minute increments. For this reason the method has been criticized because it does not promote efficiency and sometimes ignores the expertise of the lawyers (those who are very experienced can accomplish much more than novices in a given time period, yet billings do not always reflect this). Clients also feared padding of their legal bills and began to audit them. Despite these concerns, the hourly bill dominates the industry, with the majority of revenues billed this way.[10]

Competition-Based Pricing

The competition-based pricing approach focuses on the prices charged by other firms in the same industry or market. Competition-based pricing does not always imply charging the identical rate others charge but rather using others' prices as an anchor for the firm's price. This approach is used predominantly in two situations: (1) when services are standard across providers, such as in the dry cleaning industry, and (2) in oligopolies with a few large service providers, such as in the rental car industry. Difficulties involved in provision of services sometimes make competition-based pricing less simple than it is in goods industries. Our Strategy Insight highlights some aspects of competition-based pricing in the airline industry.

Challenges in Competition-Based Pricing for Services

Competition-based pricing, commonly practiced in goods firms, can be difficult for service firms. Small firms may find it difficult to charge the same prices that larger service firms charge and make margins high enough to remain in business. Many local service establishments—dry cleaning, retail, and tax accounting, among others—cannot deliver services at the low prices charged by chain operations.

Further, the heterogeneity of services across and within providers makes this approach complicated. As an example, banks offer many types of accounts and services. To try to determine how a competitive bank prices for individual accounts that may differ in features and costs—and whether those prices give sufficient margins and profits—can be difficult. Only in very standardized services that a bank provides, such as ATM surcharges, can banks benefit from competitive prices. To illustrate, consider the fees charged by banks for withdrawals from domestic non-network ATMs (i.e., ATMs that do not belong to the focal bank). As you can see, most banks charge customers an identical fee for transactions at non-network ATMs, with only relatively minor deviations from Capital One and Fifth Third Bank. These data suggest that banks consider their competition in determining these fees.[11]

Institution	Non-Network ATM Fee
Bank of America	$2.50
BB&T	$2.50
Chase	$2.50
Citibank	$2.50
HSBC Bank	$2.50
BBVA Compass	$2.50
Capital One	$2.00
Fifth Third Bank	$2.75

Source: https://www.valuepenguin.com/banking/bank-atm-fees, accessed March 18, 2022.

Examples of Competition-Based Pricing in Service Industries

Price signaling occurs in markets with a high concentration of sellers. In this type of market, any price offered by one company will be matched by competitors to avoid giving a low-cost seller a distinct advantage. The airline industry exemplifies price signaling in services. When any competitor drops the price of routes, others often match the

Strategy Insight Pricing Variation in Airlines Offers Strategic Opportunities

Our chapter opener described the trend toward more flexible pricing in streaming services. One industry that has used flexible prices (i.e., price variation) for some time are airlines. Price variability refers to the fact that airlines no longer charge a base price plus tax but instead use differences in the fees for multiple services to compete with each other. This price variation allows them to make larger revenues and profits while positioning themselves among their competitors. For example, visit www.smartertravel.com/blogs/today-in-travel/airline-fees-the-ultimate-guide.html?id=2623262 which presents the different fees for most airlines. As you can see on this site (which is updated constantly), airlines like Allegiant, Frontier, and Spirit can often claim the best-price position in the market by having the lowest base prices. However, because they charge extra fees for virtually everything including water (Spirit) and call center reservations (Allegiant), they are able to make money based on passengers' sensitivity to weight of bags, priority seating, early check-in and a myriad of other services. On the other hand, Southwest distinguishes itself as the only U.S. airline that does not charge for carry-on, first, or second bags, a strategy that makes them stand out among competitors. Larger airlines like American, Delta, and United have frequent flyer programs that reward regular flyers with early red-carpet boarding and in-airport clubs.

Look carefully over the data presented on the aforementioned website and see if you can determine what the strategy is that five of the airlines (other than those mentioned above) are using. Are the airlines focusing on low price, high service, loyalty, or some other approach? You will need to look carefully at the prices to distinguish the positioning. While other marketing variables such as advertising and routes play a role in the positioning of airlines, you can see that pricing may very well be the most important variable in competitive standing in the industry.

Source: Smarter Travel accessed and continually updated at https://www.smartertravel.com/airline-fees-the-ultimate-guide/; downloadable guide at: https://www.smartertravel.com/wp-content/uploads/2020/01/ST-Airline-Fees-Guide_2020.pdf, accessed March 21, 2022.

lowered price almost immediately. In addition, many major retailers offer price matching guarantees (e.g., Ashley Furniture, Bed, Bath & Beyond, Best Buy, Dell, DICK'S Sporting Goods, Home Depot).

Going-rate pricing involves charging the most prevalent price in the market. Rental car pricing is an illustration of this technique (and an illustration of price signaling, because the rental car market is dominated by a small number of large companies). For years, the prices set by one company (Hertz) have been followed by the other companies. When Hertz instituted a new pricing plan that involved "no mileage charges, ever," other rental car companies imitated the policy. They then had to raise other factors such as base rates, size and type of car, daily or weekly rates, and drop-off charges to continue to make profits. Prices in different geographic markets, even cities, depend on the going rate in that location, and customers often pay different rates in contiguous cities in the same state. The Global Feature in this chapter illustrates some of the practices in pricing that differ across countries.

Demand-Based Pricing

The two approaches to pricing just described are based on the company and its competitors rather than on customers. Neither approach takes into consideration that customers may lack reference prices, may be sensitive to nonmonetary prices, and may judge quality on the basis of price. All these factors can be accounted for in a company's pricing decisions. The third major approach to pricing, *demand-based pricing,* involves setting prices consistent with customer perceptions of value: prices are based on what customers will pay for the services provided.

Global Feature Unique Tipping and Pricing Practices around the World

TIPPING

A classic Cornell University study revealed an interesting fact about tipping: the custom of tipping is more prevalent in countries where citizens value status and prestige than in countries where they do not. This finding helps explain why we tip more people in this country. For example, Americans value status, recognition, and esteem, and they receive that when they tip service providers.

One measure of the differences in tipping is the number of service professionals who are given tips in different countries. The United States leads the list with about 35 different professions. Other countries that place a high value on recognition and esteem also tip a large number of professionals. These include Spain (29), Canada (25), India (25), and Italy (24). In contrast, in Denmark and Sweden, the number of tipped professionals is under 10, reflecting the lower value placed on recognition and esteem in these countries. Tipping is not customary in many countries, including Malaysia, Japan, Oman, Samoa, Singapore, South Korea, and the United Arab Emirates.

Because tipping etiquette around the world varies, Good Housekeeping Magazine provided the following country-specific tipping guide for restaurants and taxis to its readers:

PRICELESS: PAY-WHAT-YOU-WANT FOR SERVICE

As the name suggests, the pricing strategy of pay-what-you-want (PWYW) allows customers to pay the amount they believe the service is worth. As such, PWYW is a highly customer-oriented form of participatory pricing, and it is an indicator of customer-perceived value. Although often a minimum price may be suggested to customers as guidance, the PWYW model can also mean giving customers the option to pay "zero." PWYW is not mainstream, but it has gained interest in some service industries around the world;

	RESTAURANT	TAXI
Australia and New Zealand	10–15%	Round up the fare
Brazil	✗	Round up the fare
Canada	20%	10–15%
China	✗	✗
Egypt	5–10%	10–15%
France	Service is added by law	Around 10%
Germany	10%	Round up the fare
Greece	5–10%	✗
India	10%	Round up the fare
Italy	10%	Optional
Japan	✗	✗
Mexico	10%	✗
South Africa	10–12.5%	Round up the fare
South East Asia	Not customary, but small tips appreciated	A small tip is polite
Spain and Portugal	10–12.5%	Round up the fare
The Netherlands	✗	Round up the fare
Turkey	10%	Round up the fare
USA	15–25%	Give a small tip

SOURCE https://www.goodhousekeeping.com/uk/consumer-advice/money/a569273/the-definitive-guide-to-how-much-you-should-tip-worldwide/

Challenges in Demand-Based Pricing for Services

One of the major ways that pricing of services differs from pricing of goods in demand-based pricing is that nonmonetary costs and benefits must be factored into the calculation of perceived value to the customer. When services require time, inconvenience, and psychological and search costs, the monetary price must be adjusted to compensate. And when services save time and search costs, the customer is willing to pay a higher monetary price. The challenge is to determine the value to customers of each of the nonmonetary aspects involved.

to illustrate, here are examples of PWYW restaurants around the world:

- **Austria: Der Wiener Deewan** is a Pakistani restaurant in Vienna that is one of the pioneers of PWYW. It offers an all-you-can-eat and pay-what-you-want buffet with a variety of curry dishes, vegetarian options, and meat dishes. The Wiener Deewan is open 23 hours every day except on Sundays.
- **Singapore:** Founded in 1986, **Annalakshmi** is an Indian restaurant named after the goddess of nourishment and abundance. This inspiration helps explain why the restaurant operates on the principle of trust in humanity and strives to serve all guests with a genuine and wholehearted generosity. The restaurant encourages patrons to pay what they believe is fair and its website summarizes this philosophy as: *"Eat as you Want, Give as you Feel."*
- **Australia: Lentil as Anything** is a vegetarian restaurant in Melbourne driven by the philosophy of valuing "people over profit." Therefore, there are no set prices and customers simply "pay-as-they-feel: through a financial contribution or volunteering." Lentil as Anything has been operating successfully since it opened in 2000.
- **Thailand: The Land Split** is a farm located in Pai. After seismic activity caused a large crack in his farmland making farming nearly impossible, the owner transformed his property into a tourist attraction. He now hosts guests with unlimited roasted peanuts, sweet papaya, baked sweet potatoes, plantain chips, fresh Roselle juice, and jam. Notably, all of these snacks are home-made on his property and are paid for by donation.
- **United States:** The mission of the SAME Café located in Denver, CO, is "to create community through healthy food access." Accordingly, the website describes it as a donation-based, fair exchange restaurant that serves healthy food to everyone, regardless of their ability to pay. The SAME Café offers daily selections that are prepared with fresh, organic ingredients. There is no cash register and no requirement for visitors to pay; if customers wish to do so, they can simply make a donation.

FEE-FOR-WASTE PRICING

In a world where hunger is a severe problem, millions of tons of edible food go to waste every day. According to the United Nations, around 17 percent of total global food production is wasted (11 percent in households, 5 percent in the food service, and 2 percent in retail).

Against this background, some restaurants experiment with compelling pricing approaches to fight food waste. For example, some all-you-can-eat restaurants charge customers an additional fee for leftover food when guests' eyes are larger than their stomachs. A buffet-style restaurant in Switzerland introduced this approach by charging customers who left food on their plates a fee of five Swiss francs (approximately $5.50). Adopting a similar policy, a Chinese buffet restaurant in London adds a 32-cent "wastage fee" for customers who do not finish the food they selected from the buffet. China's government took this idea to the next level by introducing legislation recommending large fines for businesses that enable or promote food waste. In the country's "operation empty plate," the law allowed restaurants to charge customers for leaving excessive leftovers.

Sources: CapitalOne, "A Guide to Tipping Around the World," https://www.capitalone.com/bank/money-management/life-events/do-you-tip/; United Nations, "Stop Food Loss and Waste, for the People, for the Planet," https://www.un.org/en/observances/end-food-waste-day; Wikipedia, "Pay what you want," https://en.wikipedia.org/wiki/Pay_what_you_want#History_and_commercial_uses; The Guardian, "China to bring in law against food waste with fines for promoting overeating," https://www.theguardian.com/world/2020/dec/23/china-to-bring-in-law-against-food-waste-with-fines-for-promoting-overeating; "13 Pay-What-You-Want Restaurants Around the World," https://www.roadaffair.com/pay-what-you-want-restaurants/; accessed March 20, 2022. "Study Examines Tipping," Hotel and Motel Management, March 17, 1997, p. 14; "Just Around the Corner," accessed June 19, 2016 at http://www.whichtable.com/JustAroundtheCorner-restaurant.asp; "Unusual International Restaurant Practices," accessed June 19, 2016 at http://restoran.us/trivia/unusual.htm.

Another way services and goods differ with respect to this form of pricing is that information on service costs may be less available to customers, making monetary price not as salient a factor in initial service selection as it is in goods purchasing.

Four Meanings of Customer-Perceived Value

One of the most appropriate ways that companies price their services is basing the price on the perceived value of the service to customers. Among the questions a service marketer needs to ask are the following: What do consumers mean by *value*? How

FIGURE 15.3
Four Customer Definitions of Value

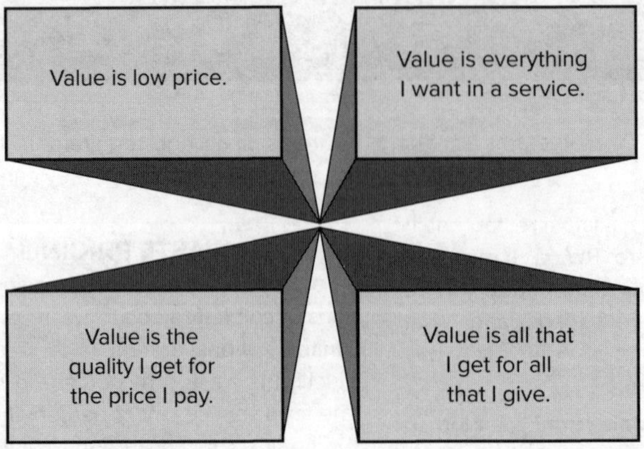

can we quantify perceived value in dollars, so that we can set appropriate prices for our services? Is the meaning of value similar across consumers and services? How can value perceptions be influenced? To understand demand-based pricing approaches, we must fully understand what value means to customers.

This is not a simple task. When consumers discuss value, they use the term in many different ways and talk about myriad attributes or components. What constitutes value, even in a single service category, appears to be highly personal and idiosyncratic. As depicted in Figure 15.3, customers define value in four ways:

1. Value is low price.
2. Value is everything I want in a service.
3. Value is the quality I get for the price I pay.
4. Value is all that I get for all that I give.[12]

Let us take a look at each of these definitions more carefully.

Value Is Low Price Some consumers equate value with low price, indicating that what they have to give up in terms of money is most salient in their perceptions of value, as typified in these representative comments from customers:

For dry cleaning: "Value means the lowest price."

For a fast-food restaurant: "When I can use coupons, I feel that the service is a value."

For airline travel: "Value is when airline tickets are discounted."[13]

Value Is Everything I Want in a Service Rather than focusing on the money given up, some consumers emphasize the benefits they receive from a service as the most important component of value. In this value definition, price is far less important than the quality or features that match what the consumer wants. In the telecommunications industry, for example, business customers strongly value the reliability of the systems and are willing to pay for the safety and confidentiality of the connections. Service customers describe this definition of value as follows:

For an MBA degree: "Value is the very best education I can get."

For medical services: "Value is high quality."

For a hotel room for a honeymoon: "Value is a luxurious room with a hot tub."

Value Is the Quality I Get for the Price I Pay Other consumers see value as a trade-off between the money they give up and the quality they receive.

For a hotel for vacation: "Value is price first and quality second."

For a hotel for business travel: "Value is the lowest price for a quality brand."

For a computer services contract: "Value is the same as quality. No—value is affordable quality."

Value Is All That I Get for All That I Give Finally, some consumers consider all the benefits they receive as well as all sacrifice components (money, time, effort) when describing value.

For a housekeeping service: "Value is how many rooms I can get cleaned for what the price is."

For a hairstylist: "Value is what I pay in cost and time for the look I get."

For executive education: "Value is getting a good educational experience in the shortest time possible."

The four consumer expressions of value can be captured in one overall definition consistent with the concept of utility in economics: *perceived value is the consumer's overall assessment of the utility of a service based on perceptions of what is received and what is given.* Although what is received varies across consumers (some may want volume, others high quality, still others convenience), as does what is given (some are concerned only with money expended, others with time and effort), value represents a trade-off of the give-and-get components. Customers will make a purchase decision on the basis of perceived value, not solely to minimize the price paid. These definitions are the first step in identifying the elements that must be quantified in setting prices for services.

Incorporating Perceived Value into Service Pricing

The buyer's perception of total value prompts the willingness to pay a particular price for a service.

The most important thing a company must do—and often a difficult thing—is to estimate the value to customers of the company's services.[14] Value may be perceived differently by consumers because of idiosyncratic tastes, knowledge about the service, buying power, and ability to pay. In this type of pricing, what the consumers value—not what they pay—forms the basis for pricing. Therefore, its effectiveness rests solely on accurately determining what the market perceives the service to be worth.

When the services are for retail consumers, service providers can rarely afford to give each individual exactly the bundle of attributes valued. They will, however, attempt to find one or more bundles that address segments of the market. When individual customers are large (e.g., business-to-business customers or very large and profitable retail customers), the company may find it worthwhile to provide individual bundles to each customer. An interesting manifestation of demand-oriented pricing is shown in the Technology Spotlight.

One of the most complex and difficult tasks of service marketers is setting prices internationally. If service marketers price on the basis of perceived value and if perceived value and willingness to pay differ across countries (which they often do), then service firms may provide essentially the same service but charge different prices in different countries.

Technology Spotlight Dynamic Pricing on the Internet Allows Price Adjustments Based on Supply and Demand

When shopping for an airline ticket on the Internet, have you ever found a low-priced ticket that you did not purchase immediately, then returned four hours later to find the same ticket had increased $100 in price? This experience is dynamic pricing in action—the buying and selling of services in markets in which prices move quickly in response to supply and demand fluctuations. In the case of your airline ticket, chances are that other travelers had purchased tickets at the original low price, reducing the airlines' inventory and allowing the airline to gamble on getting customers to buy the remaining seats at higher prices.

Also called real-time pricing, dynamic pricing is an approach to setting the cost for a product or service that is highly flexible. The goal is to allow a company that sells goods or services over the Internet to adjust prices in response to various factors that affect market demand. Changes are controlled by pricing bots, which are software agents that gather data and use algorithms to adjust pricing according to rules involving the customer's location, the time of day, the day of the week, the level of demand, and competitors' pricing.

The approach—often incorporating auctions and other forms of online bidding—is typically used at the end of the supply chain to eliminate surplus inventory or perishable service capacity, as with airline seats. Dynamic pricing has allowed companies to generate significant revenue from excess supply or discontinued products, which they used to turn over to intermediaries.

AUCTIONS: EBAY AND CONSUMER-TO-CONSUMER E-COMMERCE

Online auctions represent dynamic pricing because customers pay what they are willing and they compete with each other on the goods they desire. In 1995, eBay pioneered the Internet auction, but thousands of websites and apps now offer person-to-person online trading (with major sites including Craigslist and Alibaba). Market leader eBay offers thousands of new items for auction each day and reported a revenue of more than $10B and a net income exceeding $5B in 2020. The broader consumer-to-consumer e-commerce industry is also thriving and expected to continue its growth; for example, 2020 saw more than 100 million visits to the leading C2C marketplaces in the United States alone.

REVERSE AUCTIONS

Reverse auctions are used on the buy-side, allowing buyers to see the lowest bid, but not identify the buyer or the seller. The brand or identity of the seller is revealed only if the seller decides to accept the bid offered by the buyer. An advantage for buyers is that they do not need to guess at the price and can receive the same products and services offered elsewhere with static prices at significant discounts. One disadvantage is that, although buyers see a rating of the seller, they cannot be sure who the seller is and what the service outcome will be. For example, with Priceline, the buyers do not always get their desired flight days and times. Furthermore, the buyer has to sacrifice control over some aspects of the service being consumed.

GROUP BUYING: RAKUTEN

Group buying sites aggregate demand for sellers and provide goods and services at significant discounts on the condition that a minimum number of buyers make the purchase. Group buying sites (e.g., Rakuten, Groupon, or LivingSocial) offer a variety of products, for example, long distance and cell phone service, automobile and term life insurance, and mortgages. The concept behind this form of dynamic pricing is that the greater the number of people who want to buy products, the lower the price will be for everyone. Sellers generally bucket the prices of the product being sold based on the number of buyers. For example, for 0–10 buyers, the price for each buyer is $100; for 10–20 buyers, the price for each buyer is $95, and so on. Word-of-mouth communication is critical, because interested buyers are encouraged to enlist

PRICING STRATEGIES THAT LINK TO THE FOUR VALUE DEFINITIONS

In this section we describe the approaches to service pricing that are particularly suited to each of the four value definitions. Exhibit 15.2 presents some prominent research approaches to setting prices.

their friends and relatives to get a cheaper price for the whole group. Sellers motivate this action by placing an "Invite Your Friend" icon right next to the service or price information. Advantages of this form of dynamic pricing are that the price decreases as a greater number of people bid and the exact service and its specifications are known to buyers when bidding.

DINING WITH DYNAMIC PRICING

Flexible, or dynamic, pricing in the restaurant industry involves changing menu prices by the hour or time of day to attract diners during nonpeak hours, such as afternoons between 2:00 and 6:00 p.m. or late evenings. Restaurants may use discounts, such as 15–30 percent off the total check, to build traffic during off-hours. Typically the restaurants use a "dining aggregator," a site that collects and coordinates information about all restaurants in an area that want to offer dynamic pricing. One example of such a deal aggregator is restaurant.com, which offers more than 40,000 deals at thousands of restaurants in the United States.

DYNAMIC PRICING AT UBER, AIRBNB, SMART CITIES AND BEYOND

As the above examples illustrate, dynamic pricing can provide benefits to buyers and sellers. Not surprisingly, dynamic pricing models are increasingly used in a variety of services. For example, ride-hailing services such as Uber practice dynamic pricing. Airbnb hosts, especially those who own listings in high-demand leisure markets or who manage multiple listings, also use this pricing strategy. Dynamic pricing is helpful in more fundamental service settings as well. For example, in smart cities, dynamic pricing can play a key role for intelligent transportation systems (ITS) which includes pricing the use of vehicles (personal vehicles, commercial trucks, transit traffic) and the usage of infrastructure (roads, parking areas, bridges, tunnels). Dynamic pricing practices can also manage traffic congestion and traffic flow, reduce peak load, or incentivize the use of Electric Vehicles.

Another context where dynamic pricing is increasingly used is the power sector, because the costs of producing electricity can vary (e.g., by the time of day, the demand in a focal community). To illustrate, in early mornings (when people are preparing breakfast and get ready for work) and in early evenings (when most people return to their homes after work), the demand for electricity is particularly high. In light of these variations in demand and the ever-increasing electricity needs in modern societies, better approaches to energy distribution are needed. Dynamic pricing allows electrical utilities to offer plans to their customers that account for the variation in the cost of producing electricity and, in essence, reward customers with lower prices for not using energy during the costliest times of production. For example, Smart Grids automatically calculate per-unit prices dynamically based upon the real-time energy units available in the overall grid relative to the real-time demand. Initial research (e.g., a study in Illinois, US) suggests that the vast majority of electricity customers could save money by switching to dynamic real-time pricing, even without making any changes in their daily routines.

Sources: Statista, "C2C E-Commerce," https://www.statista.com/markets/413/topic/983/c2c-e-commerce/#statistic1, accessed March 20, 2022; C. Gibbs et al. "Use of Dynamic Pricing Strategies by Airbnb Hosts," *International Journal of Contemporary Hospitality Management* 30 (January 2018), pp. 2–20; S. Saharan, S. Bawa, and N. Kumar, "Dynamic Pricing Techniques for Intelligent Transportation System in Smart Cities: A Systematic Review," *Computer Communications*, 150 (January 2020), pp. 603–625; SmartEnergy, "What You Need to Know About Dynamic Electricity Pricing," https://www.whatissmartenergy.org/featured-article/what-you-need-to-know-about-dynamic-electricity-pricing; https://finance.yahoo.com/quote/ebay/financials?ltr=1; M. Rouse, "Dynamic Pricing," 2015, accessed at http://whatis.techtarget.com/definition/dynamic-pricing; T. Demos, "Exactly What is a Dutch Auction?" *Wall Street Journal*, July 21, 2012.

Pricing Strategies When the Customer Means "Value Is Low Price"

When monetary price is the most important determinant of value to a customer, the company focuses mainly on price. This focus does not mean that the quality level and intrinsic attributes are always irrelevant, just that monetary price dominates in importance. To establish a service price in this definition of value, the marketer must understand to what extent customers know the objective prices of services in this category,

Pricing, Service Tiering, and Personalized Pricing

One of the reasons that pricing of services is more difficult than pricing of goods is that service units are more variable and difficult to identify than units of goods. Units of goods—automobiles, jeans, gallons of milk, and microwave ovens—are easy to define. Units of service are more difficult in part because they are sold by a variety of components. Information services, for example, are sold by the minute, the web page, the file (as in buying online music), or the search (as in finding and purchasing magazine articles). The services of your doctor are sold by the length and type of the visit, the test performed, the shot given, and the X rays taken. Cable television can be sold by the month (basic fees, premium charges for HBO and Showtime), by the type of equipment leased (digital video recorders, remote controls, digital cable boxes), and by the unit (pay-per-view movies). One approach to dealing with the complexity of pricing services is to develop modular service bundles.

As described in this chapter, pricing a service in line with what customers perceive it is worth is often difficult. Two approaches that have gained favor in recent years are modular service pricing and service tiering. In addition, technological progress increasingly enables truly personalized pricing.

MODULAR SERVICE PRICING

Modular service pricing involves first identifying the basic and value-added services of a provider as components or building blocks for pricing. To create modules, the company first defines the full range of services that could meet customer needs and for which customers will pay. To create modular pricing, firms need the following:

1. Available prices for each different service.
2. The ability to combine prices and services using easy rules.
3. Minimum overlap among the service elements, so that customers do not pay twice for the same service.

One context in which modular pricing is being developed is publications (e.g., *The Wall Street Journal, Sports Illustrated, The New York Times*) that are bundling their digital, print, and mobile subscriptions. Publications are attempting to determine the customer-perceived value of digital, online, tablet, and mobile formats. The pricing models represent a major change from the past few years, when publications charged for print and gave away digital content. Publishers now recognize that today's consumer values digital content more than print, and they are pricing in line with this revised perception of value. The change illustrates a broader effort by publishers to change from print-only to print-plus-digital combinations. However, media companies are still trying to maintain their print subscribers because advertisers pay much more for print ads than for digital ones.

Ideally, each component in a modular pricing framework has a price that is in line with customers' perceptions of the value of that service, and customers can select the components individually and combine them in bundles. A difficulty in the current evolution to modular publication pricing is that each publication has a different approach, making choices confusing to customers.

SERVICE TIERING

Sometimes even good modular pricing can become too complex, and simpler ways to present the company's prices are needed. *Service tiering,* usually called versioning when applied to the pricing of goods, involves creating prices that correspond to the price points and value bundles of different customer segments. For example, cable companies offer service tiers that correspond to service components that are typically desired together. When customers buy the bundles, they receive discounts from what the services would cost individually.

In general, service tiers allow customers to quickly and simply match their desires and the price they are willing to pay with an offering from the company. The customer perceives a benefit in choosing one of the tiers because each tier provides a discount over individual services. The company enjoys a benefit because customers typically buy more services when they are sold in tiers than when they

how they interpret various prices, and how much is too much of a perceived sacrifice. These factors are best understood when the service provider also knows the relative dollar size of the purchase, the frequency of past price changes, and the range of acceptable prices for the service. Some of the specific pricing approaches appropriate when customers define value as low price include discounting, odd pricing, synchro-pricing, and penetration pricing (Figure 15.4).

Discounting

Service providers offer discounts to communicate to price-sensitive buyers that they are receiving value. Among the most prevalent discounting approaches are those from are offered individually. In the context of cable offerings, basic cable is an example of a low tier with a low price, whereas extended cable includes the addition of premium channels such as HBO, Showtime, and the Golf Channel for a higher price. The highest tier, for the highest price, might include all cable channels plus DVRs.

Modular pricing and service tiering allow the company to maximize sales from all parts of a service that the customer desires without having to create unique service bundles for each customer. However, the idea of truly individualized pricing is also becoming more prominent, as we discuss next.

GETTING PERSONAL: PERSONALIZED PRICING

Extending the idea of dynamic pricing (discussed in the Technology Spotlight), companies are exploring "personalized pricing," whereby some customers receive different prices than others for the same service offering. Personalized pricing is distinct from dynamic pricing. With dynamic pricing, variables *not related to individual* customers account for differences. In contrast, personalized pricing draws on a key principle of economics: some customers are willing to pay more than others are for the same product or service. When you visit Orbitz.com to book travel services or when you make an airline flight reservation, you likely experience personalized pricing. Personalized pricing requires algorithms that consider individual customers' characteristics and behavior to discern the exact price each is willing to pay at a specific point in time. Personalized pricing algorithms account for other products a customer is clicking on or moving into her virtual shopping basket in addition to broader data about a customer's browsing history, purchase history, and social media activity. Notably, with evolving technology, algorithms will also increasingly consider more subtle facets of consumer behavior, for example, the amount of time a web page was open in a consumer's browser, the speed with which consumers move their mouse, and the time the mouse's pointer hovered at different parts of the website (e.g., close to the price or the "move to shopping cart" button); all these pieces of information inform the personalized price at that point in time. As a consequence, some customers will pay more for the same service than others pay. Further, the same customer might receive a different price for the same offer. Reasons for this variability can include (1) how customers access the service company's website (desktop computer vs. smart phone vs. in store) or the (2) time a purchase is made.

The goal of personalized pricing is to increase profits. Although personalized pricing provides benefits for firms, serious ethical and legal issues exist. For example, Princeton Review adapted prices based on zip codes, resulting in Asian customers being twice as likely to pay a higher price. Companies need to recognize the fine line between personalized pricing and discriminatory pricing. In addition to the legal aspect, it is also crucial to consider principles of fairness and equality as companies design personalized pricing algorithms to avoid that some consumers are exploited or completely excluded from services for the sake of profit maximization. In addition, managers also need to understand that if consumers find out that others are getting a better deal than they are, they may feel angry. Finally, many consumers are also uncomfortable with companies understanding the details of their personal life and habits. Managers must carefully consider these pros and cons as they craft their pricing strategies.

Sources: E. Steinberg, "Big Data and Personalized Pricing," *Business Ethics Quarterly* 30 (January 2020), pp. 97–117; R. Mohammed, "How Retailers Use Personalized Prices to Test What You're Willing to Pay," https://hbr.org/2017/10/how-retailers-use-personalized-prices-to-test-what-youre-willing-to-pay, accessed March 21, 2022; Elizabeth Wasserman, "How to Price Business Services," *Inc.* Magazine, accessed online at www.inc.com/guides/price-your-services.html, June 15, 2016. R. Docters, M. Reopel, J. Sun, and S. Tanny, "Capturing the Unique Value of Services: Why Pricing of Services Is Different," *Journal of Business Strategy* 25, no. 2 (2004), pp. 23–28; R. Adams, "Many Formats, One Price: More Publications Begin Bundling Their Digital, Print, and Mobile Subscriptions," *The Wall Street Journal,* May 16, 2011, p. B4.

FIGURE 15.4
Pricing Strategies When the Customer Defines Value as Low Price

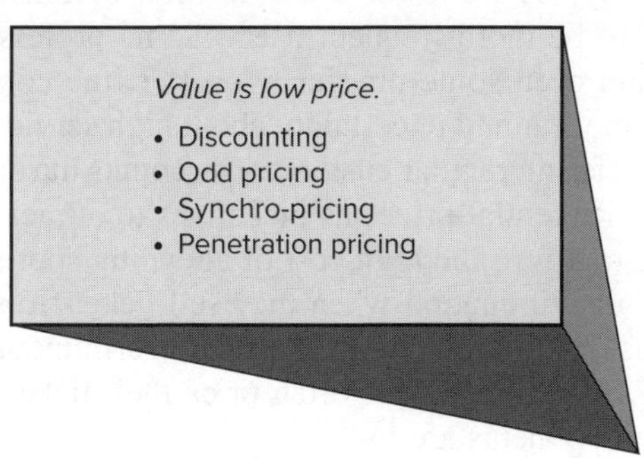

online companies such as Groupon, Living Social, Angi, and an ever-increasing number of competitors. These Web companies, of which Groupon was the first, offer daily discounts to consumers through e-mail and social media feeds. The discounts are all for local companies, most of which are services such as restaurants, cleaning services, massages, plumbing, home inspections, and hotels. Consumers request the deals and can bid for them until they are sold out. Online companies are paid sometimes as much as 50 percent of the revenue from purchased coupons.

Odd Pricing

Odd pricing is the practice of pricing services just below the exact dollar amount to make buyers perceive that they are getting a lower price. Dry cleaners charge $2.98 for a shirt rather than $3.00, health clubs have dues priced at $33.90 per month rather than $34, and haircuts are $9.50 rather than $10.00. Odd prices suggest discounting and bargains and are appealing to customers for whom value means low price.

Synchro-Pricing

Synchro-pricing is the use of price to manage demand for a service by capitalizing on customer sensitivity to prices. Certain services, such as tax preparation, passenger transportation, hotels, and theaters, have demand that fluctuates over time as well as constrained supply at peak times. For companies in these and other industries, setting a price that provides a profit over time can be difficult. Pricing can, however, play a role in smoothing demand and synchronizing demand and supply. Time, place, quantity, and incentive differentials have all been used effectively by service firms, as discussed in Chapter 13.

Place differentials are used for services in which customers have a sensitivity to location. The front row at concerts, the 50-yard line in football, ocean-side rooms in resort hotels—all these represent place differentials that are meaningful to customers and that therefore command higher prices.

Time differentials involve price variations that depend on when the service is consumed. Hospital rooms on weekends and health spas in the off-season are priced via time differentials that reflect slow periods of service. By offering lower prices for underused time periods, a service company can smooth demand and gain incremental revenue.

Quantity differentials are price decreases given for volume purchasing. This pricing structure allows a company to predict future demand for its services. Customers who buy a booklet of coupons for a tanning salon or facial, a quantity of tokens for public bridges, or packages of advertising spots on radio or TV are all responding to price incentives achieved by committing to future services. Corporate discounts for airlines, hotels, and rental cars exemplify quantity discounts in the business context; by offering lower prices, the service provider locks in future business.

Differentials as incentives are lower prices for new or existing clients in the hope of encouraging them to be more frequent users. Some professionals—lawyers, dentists, electrologists, and even some physicians—offer free consultations at the front end, usually to overcome fear and uncertainty about high service prices. Other companies stimulate use by offering regular customers discounts during slow periods. Sports teams are now using differential prices as incentives to attract customers who would otherwise not be able to afford the high cost of attending sports events. For example, universities use price discrimination when they sell tickets to students at a discount. Other sports teams use a different form of price discrimination. For example, soccer clubs in England's Premier League often price their tickets as a function of how (un-)attractive certain opponents are.[15]

Penetration Pricing

Penetration pricing is a strategy in which new services are introduced at low prices to stimulate trial and widespread use. The strategy is appropriate when (1) sales volume of the service is very sensitive to price, even in the early stages of introduction; (2) it is possible to achieve economies in unit costs by operating at large volumes; (3) a service faces threats of strong potential competition very soon after introduction; and (4) there is no class of buyers willing to pay a higher price to obtain the service.[16] Penetration pricing can lead to problems when companies then select a "regular" increased price. Care must be taken not to penetrate with so low a price that customers feel the regular price is outside the range of acceptable prices.

Pricing Strategies When the Customer Means "Value Is Everything I Want in a Service"

When the customer is concerned principally with the "get" components of a service, monetary price is not of primary concern. The more desirable intrinsic attributes a given service possesses, the more highly valued the service is likely to be and the higher the price the marketer can set. Figure 15.5 shows appropriate pricing strategies.

Prestige Pricing

Prestige pricing is a special form of demand-based pricing by service marketers who offer high-quality or status services. For certain services—restaurants, health clubs, airlines, and hotels—a higher price is charged for the luxury end of the business. For example, for hotel guests who crave pampering, many chains offer club floors that add high-end amenities into their offerings for large price increases. Some Ritz-Carltons offer free lunch foods such as sandwiches and salads with these high-priced rooms.[17] Some customers of service companies that use this approach may actually value the high price because it represents prestige or a quality image. Others prefer purchasing at the high end because they are given preference in seating or accommodations and are entitled to other special benefits. In prestige pricing, demand may actually increase as price increases because the costlier service has more value in reflecting quality or prestige.

Skimming Pricing

Skimming, a strategy in which new services are introduced at high prices, is an effective approach when services are major improvements over past services. In this situation, customers are more concerned about obtaining the service than about the cost

FIGURE 15.5
Pricing Strategies When the Customer Defines Value as Everything Wanted in a Service

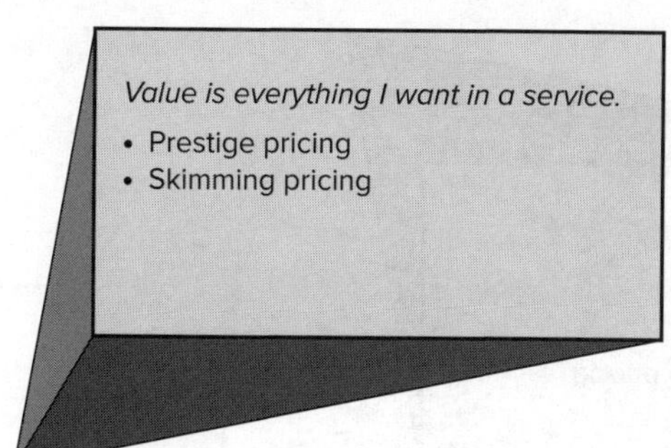

of the service, allowing service providers to skim the customers most willing to pay the highest prices. Services related to anti-aging, such as Botox injections and laser liposuction, often are introduced at high prices, thereby attracting customers who are willing to pay more to obtain the services in the short term rather than wait until a later time, when the prices might be reduced.

Pricing Strategies When the Customer Means "Value Is the Quality I Get for the Price I Pay"

Some customers primarily consider both quality and monetary price. The task of the marketer is to understand what *quality* means to the customer (or segments of customers) and then to match quality level with price level. Specific strategies are shown in Figure 15.6.

Value Pricing

The widely used term *value pricing* has come to mean "giving more for less." In current usage, it involves assembling a bundle of services desirable to a wide group of customers and then pricing them lower than they would cost alone. Taco Bell pioneered value pricing with a $0.59 Value Menu. After sales at the chain rose 50 percent in two years to $2.4 billion, McDonald's and Burger King adopted the value pricing practice. Southwest Airlines also offers value pricing: a low cost for a bundle of desirable service attributes such as frequent departures, friendly and funny employees, and on-time arrival. The airline offers consistently low fares with bare-bones service.

Market Segmentation Pricing

With *market segmentation pricing,* a firm charges different prices to groups of customers for what are perceived to be different quality levels of service, even though there may not be corresponding differences in the costs of providing the service to each of these groups. This form of pricing is based on the premise that segments show different price elasticities of demand and desire different quality levels.

Service marketers often price by *client category,* based on the recognition that some groups find it difficult to pay a recommended price. Health clubs located in college communities typically offer student memberships, recognizing that this segment of customers has limited ability to pay full price. In addition to the lower price, student memberships may also carry with them reduced hours of use, particularly in peak times. The same line of reasoning leads to memberships for "seniors," who are less able to pay full price but are willing to patronize the clubs during daytime hours, when most full-price members are working.

FIGURE 15.6
Pricing Strategies When the Customer Defines Value as Quality for the Price Paid

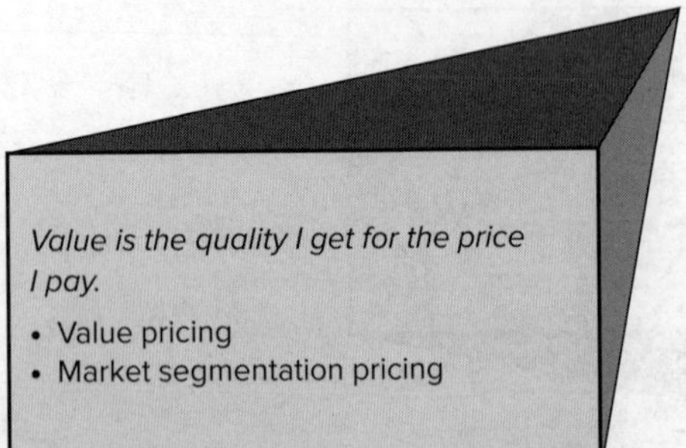

Companies also use market segmentation by *service version,* recognizing that not all segments want the basic level of service at the lowest price. When they can identify a bundle of attributes that are desirable enough for another segment of customers, they can charge a higher price for that bundle. Companies can configure service bundles that reflect price and service points appealing to different groups in the market. Hotels, for example, offer standard rooms at a basic rate but then combine amenities and tangibles related to the room to attract customers willing to pay more for the concierge level, jacuzzis, Wi-Fi, additional beds, and sitting areas.

Pricing Strategies When the Customer Means "Value Is All That I Get for All That I Give"

Some customers define value as including not just the benefits they receive but also the time, money, and effort they put into a service. Figure 15.7 illustrates the pricing strategies described in this definition of value.

Price Framing

Because many customers do not possess accurate reference prices for services, service marketers are more likely than goods marketers to organize price information for customers so they know how to view it. Customers naturally look for price anchors as well as familiar services against which to judge focal services. If they accept the anchors, they view the price and service package favorably. Groupon, Living Social, and other online couponing sites let customers know the actual values of the offers being made as well as the discounted costs in the offer. As mentioned earlier in the chapter, customers often do not have a reference price for services—particularly household services such as plumbing, gutter cleaning, and pressure washing. Framing the offers by providing actual prices allows customers to recognize the value they will receive if they purchase the Groupon.

Price Bundling

Some services are consumed more effectively in conjunction with other services; other services accompany the products they support (such as extended service warranties, training, and expedited delivery). When customers find value in a package of interrelated services, price bundling is an appropriate strategy. Bundling, which means pricing and selling services as a group rather than individually, has benefits to both customers and companies. Customers find that bundling simplifies their purchase and payment, and companies find that the approach stimulates demand, thereby achieving cost economies for the operations as a whole while increasing net contributions.[18]

FIGURE 15.7
Pricing Strategies When the Customer Defines Value as All That Is Received for All That Is Given

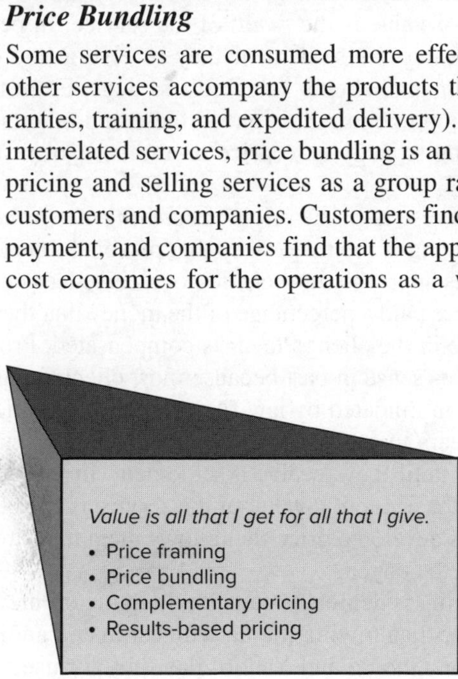

Bundling also allows customers to pay less than when purchasing each of the services individually, which contributes to perceptions of value.

The effectiveness of price bundling depends on how well the service firm understands the bundles of value that customers or segments perceive and on the complementarity of demand for these services. Effectiveness also depends on the right choice of services from the firm's point of view. Because the firm's objective is to increase overall sales, the services selected for bundling should be those with a relatively small sales volume without the bundling to minimize revenue loss from discounting a service that already has a high sales volume.

Complementary Pricing

Services that are highly interrelated can be leveraged by using *complementary pricing.* This pricing includes three related strategies—captive pricing, two-part pricing, and loss leadership.[19] In *captive pricing,* the firm offers a base service or product and then provides the supplies or peripheral services needed to continue using the service. In this situation the company could off-load some part of the price for the basic service to the peripherals. For example, cable services often drop the price for installation to a very low level, then compensate by charging enough for the peripheral services to make up for the loss in revenue. With service firms, this strategy is often called *two-part pricing* because the service price is broken into a fixed fee plus variable usage fees (also found in phone services, health clubs, and commercial services such as rentals). *Loss leadership* is the term typically used in retail stores when providers price a familiar service at a (very) low level, largely to draw customers to the store and then reveal other levels of service available at higher prices. Cleaners, for example, will offer a special low price to launder men's shirts to draw customers in to pay the higher regular prices for other items.

Results-Based Pricing

In service industries in which outcome is very important but uncertainty is high, the most relevant aspect of value is the *result* of the service. In personal injury lawsuits, for example, clients value the settlement they receive at the conclusion of the service. From tax accountants, clients value cost savings. From trade schools, students most value getting a job upon graduation. In these and other situations, an appropriate value-based pricing strategy is to price on the basis of results or outcome of the service.

A common form of results-based pricing is *contingency pricing,* often used by lawyers. Contingency pricing is the major way that personal injury and certain consumer cases are billed. In this approach, lawyers do not receive fees or payment until the case is settled, when they are paid a percentage of the money that the client receives. Therefore, only an outcome in the client's favor is compensated. From the client's point of view, the pricing makes sense in part because most clients in these cases are unfamiliar with and possibly intimidated by law firms. Their biggest fears are high fees for a case that may take years to settle. By using contingency pricing, clients are ensured that they pay no fees until they receive a settlement. In these and other instances of contingency pricing, the economic value of the service is hard to determine before the service, and providers develop a price that allows them to share the risks and rewards of delivering value to the buyer.

Results-based pricing is demonstrated clearly in the online "pay-per-click" advertising industry. Rather than buying media with estimated audiences, companies that buy advertisements on Google and Yahoo! pay only for users who actually respond

Indian Service Strategy Insight Democratize Payments and e-Commerce

National Payments Corporation of India (NPCI) and Open Network for Digital Commerce (ONDC) are transforming India's digital landscape through complementary approaches to democratization. NPCI, through its flagship UPI platform, has revolutionized payments by creating an open, interoperable system that enables instant transfers between accounts, e.g. customers and merchants, regardless of which bank or app users prefer. By maintaining zero charges for person-to-person transactions and standard merchant payments, NPCI has driven financial inclusion and expanded digital payment adoption dramatically, increasing UPI's share in India's digital payments from 34% in 2019 to 83% in 2024.

Similarly, ONDC is breaking down walled gardens in e-commerce by establishing open protocols that allow buyers and sellers to interact across different platforms. This shift from platform-centric models dominated by giants like Amazon and Flipkart to an open network creates more opportunities for small businesses and local vendors to participate in digital commerce without being locked into specific platforms or paying excessive fees. ONDC's approach has already demonstrated disruptive pricing potential, with some items being offered at up to 45% lower costs than on established platforms.

Both initiatives represent India's strategy of using "digital public goods" to reduce entry barriers, lower transaction costs, and enable broader participation in the digital economy. While NPCI creates universal access to payment rails, ONDC extends this philosophy to service and product discovery, ordering, and fulfillment – together creating a more inclusive digital marketplace that benefits consumers through greater choice and competitive pricing while giving smaller players a viable path to digital participation without being dominated by tech giants.

NPCI – Established under the Payment and Settlement Systems Act 2007, the NPCI operates as a 'non-profit' to build and maintain India's payment infrastructure. Founded by ten leading banks including State Bank of India, ICICI Bank, and HDFC Bank, NPCI's ownership structure has evolved to include 56 member banks by 2016 and further expanded in 2020 to incorporate various RBI-regulated entities such as payment service operators and payment banks. NPCI's extensive service portfolio encompasses Unified Payments Interface (UPI), Immediate Payment Service (IMPS), Bharat Interface for Money (BHIM), National Automated Clearing House (NACH), Aadhaar Enabled Payment System (AePS), FASTag – an electronic toll collection system, Bharat Bill Payment System (BBPS) and RuPay – a payment card platform.

The UPI facilitates instantaneous transfer of money between bank accounts of any two parties. UPI transaction volumes have surged by a compound annual growth rate (CAGR) of 44% from 20.71 billion in FY 2017–18 to 187.37 billion in FY 2023–24. UPI's overall share in India's digital payments landscape has expanded dramatically from 34% in 2019 to 83% in 2024. Financially, NPCI has shown remarkable growth with revenues climbing from ₹2,225 crore in FY2023 to ₹2,876 crore in FY2024. The organization generated a surplus of ₹809 crore in FY2023 and improved its bottom line by 37% in FY2024, while building assets worth ₹5,571 crore.

NPCI's pricing framework is multifaceted, designed to generate revenue while maintaining free services for individual users. For banks participating in NPCI's systems, certification fees are charged annually, with commercial banks paying higher rates than regional rural banks and cooperative banks.

NPCI does not charge individuals for basic UPI transactions between users and for standard merchant payments made directly from bank accounts. This approach upholds the government's position that UPI is a "digital public good" that should remain free for end-users.

For transactions involving Prepaid Payment Instruments (PPIs) like digital wallets, NPCI has implemented a category-based interchange fee structure for payments exceeding ₹2,000. This fee varies by service type: 0.5% for fuel payments, 0.7% for post office, telecom, utilities, agriculture, and education transactions, 0.9% for supermarket payments, and 1% for insurance, mutual funds, government services, and railways, with fees potentially reaching up to 1.1% for certain merchant categories. Additionally, NPCI requires PPI issuers to pay a 15-basis point (0.15%) wallet-loading service charge to remitter banks when users recharge their wallets with more than ₹2,000.

The zero Merchant Discount Rate (MDR) policy for person-to-person (P2P) transactions presents a significant financial challenge for NPCI and the broader payment ecosystem. With P2P transactions accounting for 60% of UPI volume but generating no direct revenue, the payment infrastructure costs are predominantly supported by person-to-merchant (P2M) transactions. Banks receive partial cost reimbursement from government incentive schemes, but payment service providers must rely on revenue from merchant transactions or through distributing third-party financial products like deposits, mutual funds, and insurance. This creates sustainability concerns as the network scales, with NPCI exploring cost-optimization strategies such as migrating some payment service providers to cloud infrastructure rather than continually investing in physical servers.

ONDC – The ONDC is a government-backed initiative designed to democratize e-commerce. ONDC has created an interoperable network that connects buyers and sellers across platforms, similar to how UPI functions for payments. Rather than being a platform itself, ONDC provides a set of protocols and specifications that enable different e-commerce entities to interact with each other, shifting the market from a platform-centric model dominated by a few giants to an open ecosystem that fosters competition and inclusivity. Governed by the Department for Promotion of Industry and Internal Trade (DPIIT), ONDC aims to particularly support micro, small, and medium enterprises (MSMEs) by giving them equal opportunities to enter the digital marketplace without being constrained by proprietary platforms.

ONDC's business model focuses on unbundling services that were previously integrated within closed platforms. It consists of buyer-side apps, seller-side apps, and logistics providers that can interoperate through standardized protocols. The network reduces intermediary costs while expanding product availability and creating new opportunities in areas such as advertising, credit, and supply chain management. ONDC requires all participants to sign agreements to adhere to network policies, undergo KYC compliance, and accept an online dispute resolution mechanism. Unlike traditional platforms, ONDC itself does not collect user data, with intermediaries controlling data flow and much of the information being anonymized in an open data framework accessible to participants.

ONDC's pricing strategy is emerging as a significant market disruptor, with some users finding products up to 45% cheaper compared to established food delivery platforms like Swiggy. The network employs dynamic pricing models that can vary across different applications. For instance, Namma Yatri, a ride-hailing app built on ONDC, uses an auction-based approach with tipping options rather than traditional surge pricing. ONDC officials emphasize that three critical elements – dynamic pricing, inventory management, and optimization of delivery cost – will reduce the overall cost of doing business for all participants. Rather than imposing price caps, ONDC expects market forces to determine appropriate pricing levels, with competition among the growing number of participants (over 500 entities in various stages of integration), creating natural price equilibrium and potentially forcing existing aggregators to reduce their premium charges.

Reference

https://www.npci.org.in

https://cleartax.in/s/upi-transaction-charges

https://www.businesstoday.in/magazine/deep-dive/story/national-payments-corporation-of-indias-growing-clout-how-npci-is-setting-itself-up-to-conquer-the-globe-418938-2024-02-26

https://entrackr.com/2024/09/npci-posts-rs-2876-cr-revenue-and-rs-1134-cr-profits-in-fy24/

https://www.livemint.com/industry/banking/will-you-pay-for-using-upi-survey-reveals-73-users-ready-to-abandon-digital-payments-for-transaction-fee-11743083289770.html

https://www.businesstoday.in/magazine/deep-dive/story/national-payments-corporation-of-indias-growing-clout-how-npci-is-setting-itself-up-to-conquer-the-globe-418938-2024-02-26

https://ondc.org

https://www.ibm.com/think/topics/ondc

https://paytm.com/blog/ondc/ondc-explained-what-is-ondc-and-how-to-place-an-order/

https://medium.com/@josematteew/can-ondcs-pricing-strategy-disrupt-the-e-commerce-market-df132074dae2

https://www.ey.com/en_in/insights/technology/how-ondc-can-democratize-e-commerce

https://invest.up.gov.in/wp-content/uploads/2022/01/press-release-15jan2022-3.pdf

to their ads. Some public relations firms are also moving from charging fixed fees for obtaining media exposure for their clients to a results-based approach. PayPerClip, for example, a division of a traditional public relations firm, bases its fees on very specific results—for example, PayPerClip charges $600 when it successfully features its client in an online blog with up to 999 unique visits per month; notably, if that blog has more than 20,000 unique visitors per month, the charge increases to $3,200.

The commission approach to service pricing is compelling in that agents are compensated most when they find the highest rates and fares. It would seem that agents have an underlying motivation to avoid the lowest fares and rates for their clients.

Summary

This chapter began with three key differences between customer evaluation of pricing for services and goods: (1) customers often have inaccurate or limited reference prices for services, (2) price is a key signal of quality in services, and (3) monetary price is not the only relevant price to service customers. These three differences can have profound effects on the strategies that companies use to set and administer prices for services. The chapter next discussed common pricing structures, including (1) cost-based, (2) competition-based, and (3) demand-based pricing. Central to the discussion were the specific challenges in each of these structures and the service pricing techniques that have emerged in practice.

Finally, the chapter defined customer perceptions of value and suggested appropriate pricing strategies that match each customer definition. Figure 15.8 summarizes these definitions and strategies. The four value definitions include (1) value is low price, (2) value is everything I want in a service, (3) value is the quality I get for the price I pay, and (4) value is all that I get for all that I give.

FIGURE 15.8
Summary of Service Pricing Strategies for Four Customer Definitions of Value

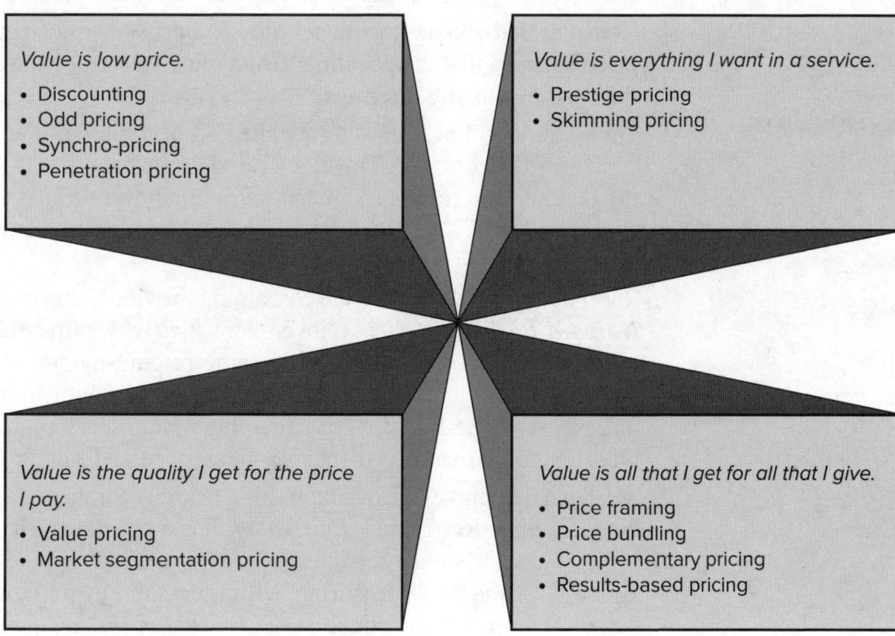

Discussion Questions

1. Which approach to pricing (cost-based, competition-based, or demand-based) is the most fair to customers? Why?
2. Is it possible to use all three approaches simultaneously when pricing services? If you answer yes, describe a service that is priced this way.
3. For what consumer services do you have reference prices? What makes these services different from others for which you lack reference prices?
4. Name three services you purchase in which price is a signal to quality. Do you believe that there are true differences across services that are priced high and those that are priced low? Why or why not?
5. Describe the nonmonetary costs involved in the following services: getting an automobile loan, belonging to a health club, having allergies diagnosed and treated, attending an executive education class, and getting braces.
6. Consider the specific pricing strategies for each of the four customer value definitions. Which of these strategies could be adapted and used with another value definition?

Exercises

1. List five services for which you have no reference price. Now put yourself in the role of the service providers for two of those services and develop pricing strategies. Be sure to include in your description which of the value definitions you believe customers will possess and what types of strategies would be appropriate, given those definitions.
2. In the next week, find three price lists for services (such as from a restaurant, dry cleaner, or hairstylist). Identify the pricing base and the strategy used in each of them. How effective is each?
3. Imagine you want to buy a cell phone plan. Visit some of the websites designed to help consumers compare cell phone provides. For example: https://www.reviews.org/mobile/best-cell-phone-plans/, or https://www.wirefly.com/content/phone-plans. Are these websites (a) easy to use and (b) ultimately helpful? Why or why not?
4. Consider that you are the owner of a new private college and can prepare a value/price package that is appealing to students. Describe your approach. How does it differ from existing offerings?
5. Go to the Priceline.com Internet site and become familiar with the way it works. Next, go to Orbitz and Travelocity and compare the way they operate. What are the benefits and trade-offs in using Priceline over Orbitz and Travelocity?

Notes

1. R. Mohammed, "Why Is Every Streaming Service Using the Same Pricing Model?," *Harvard Business Review* (November 12, 2019), https://hbr.org/2019/11/why-is-every-streaming-service-using-the-same-pricing-model; A. Johnson, Streaming Prices Are on the Rise, 2022, https://www.sapling.com/13771097/streaming-prices-are-on-the-rise; List of streaming media services, https://en.wikipedia.org/wiki/List_of_streaming_media_services, accessed March 19, 2022.
2. M. Kienzler and C. Kowalkowski, "Pricing Strategy: A Review of 22 Years of Marketing Research," *Journal of Business Research* 78 (September 2017), pp. 101–110; also see for the moderating role of services: J. Schmid and T. H. Bijmolt, "Accurately Measuring Willingness to Pay for Consumer Goods: a Meta-Analysis of the Hypothetical Bias," *Journal of the Academy of Marketing Science*

48 (May 2020), pp. 499–518; K. Monroe, "The Pricing of Services," *Handbook of Services Marketing,* ed. C. A. Congram and M. L. Friedman (New York: AMACOM, 1989), pp. 20–31.

3. Ibid.
4. W. Woellert, "How Much Is That Brain Scan?" *BusinessWeek,* November 8, 2004, p. 94.
5. Prices reported from: https://www.thimble.com/blog/wedding-planner-cost; https://fash.com/costs/how-much-does-a-wedding-planner-cost; https://www.sherpacoaching.com/pdf_files/2020_Executive_Coaching_Survey_EXECUTIVE_SUMMARY_FINAL.pdf; https://homeguide.com/costs/home-security-system-cost, accessed March 17, 2022.
6. See: https://www.fiercehealthcare.com/practices/ppatients-switched-doctors-long-wait-times-vitals; https://www.beckershospitalreview.com/hospital-physician-relationships/how-long-is-the-average-wait-at-a-physician-s-office.html, accessed March 17, 2022.
7. Monroe, "The Pricing of Services." For insights into how price-quality heuristics can vary, see: M. Chung and R. Saini, "Consumer Self-Uncertainty Increases Price Dependency," *Journal of Business Research* 140 (February 2022), pp. 40–48; J. Y. Jeong, J. L. Crompton, and S. S. Hyun, "What Makes You Select a Higher Price Option? Price–Quality Heuristics, Cultures, and Travel Group Compositions," *International Journal of Tourism Research* 21 (January 2019), pp. 1–10; H. Park, A. K. Lalwani, and D. H. Silvera, "The Impact of Resource Scarcity on Price-Quality Judgments," *Journal of Consumer Research* 46 (April 2020), pp. 1110–1124.
8. V. A. Zeithaml, "The Acquisition, Meaning, and Use of Price Information by Consumers of Professional Services," in *Marketing Theory: Philosophy of Science Perspectives,* ed. R. Bush and S. Hunt (Chicago: American Marketing Association, 1982), pp. 237–241.
9. C. H. Lovelock, "Understanding Costs and Developing Pricing Strategies," *Services Marketing* (New York: Prentice Hall, 1991), pp. 236–246.
10. A. Stevens, "Firms Try More Lucrative Ways of Charging for Legal Services," *The Wall Street Journal,* November 25, 1994, pp. B1ff.
11. A. Pentis, "Bank ATM Fees: How Much Do Banks Charge and How Can I Avoid Them?," https://www.valuepenguin.com/banking/bank-atm-fees, accessed, March 18, 2022.
12. V. A. Zeithaml et al., "Three Decades of Customer Value Research: Paradigmatic Roots and Future Research Avenues," *Journal of Service Research* 23 (November 2020), pp. 409–432. V. A. Zeithaml, "Consumer Perceptions of Price, Quality, and Value: A Means-End Model and Synthesis of Evidence," *Journal of Marketing* 52 (July 1988), pp. 2–22.
13. All comments from these four sections are based on those from Zeithaml, "Consumer Perceptions," pp. 13–14.
14. B. Donan, "Set Price Metrics Parallel to Value Proposition," *Marketing News,* April 1, 2007, p. 6.
15. T. K. Quansah, B. Buraimo, and M. Lang, "The Price of Success and Labour in Sports—Evidence from Match-day Ticket Pricing Strategies in the English Premier League," Working paper 2022, https://papers.ssrn.com/sol3/papers.cfm?abstract_id=4039945, accessed March 18, 2022.

16. Monroe, "The Pricing of Services."
17. B. DeLollis, "Hotels Take Pampering to Next Level on Club Floors," *USA Today,* June 19, 2007, p. 3B.
18. Monroe, "The Pricing of Services;" for some applied price bundling research in service settings, see: S. Guidon, M. Wicki, T. Bernauer, and K. Axhausen, "Transportation Service Bundling-For Whose Benefit? Consumer Valuation of Pure Bundling in the Passenger Transportation Market," *Transportation Research Part A: Policy and Practice* 131 (January 2020), pp. 91–106; S. Dominique-Ferreira and C. Antunes, "Estimating the Price Range and the Effect of Price Bundling Strategies: An Application to the Hotel Sector," *European Journal of Management and Business Economics* 29 (June 2020), pp. 166–181.
19. G. J. Tellis, "Beyond the Many Faces of Price: An Integration of Pricing Strategies," *Journal of Marketing* 50 (October 1986), pp. 146–160.

Part **Seven**

Service Trends: AI, Robotics, and the Bottom Line

Part 7 discusses two increasingly crucial strategic priorities for service companies, namely the role of emerging technologies (Chapter 16) and the link between service and the firm's bottom line (Chapter 17).

Chapter 16 focuses on artificial intelligence (AI) and robotics in service because recent technological evolutions have profound effects on many aspects of service delivery. For example, service robots are already employed in some service settings (e.g., hospitality, healthcare) and will only become more frequent in the marketplace. Therefore, we will explore how distinct types of AI affect the service process, and which factors influence the extent to which firms can adopt robotics in their service operations. Finally, we consider implications of service robotics for the Gaps Model of Service Quality.

In Chapter 17, we discuss another important question about service that managers have been debating over the past 40 years: is excellent service profitable to an organization? We pull together research and company experience to answer this question. We present our own model of how the relationship works and offer examples of the relationship in companies. Our model shows how service quality has offensive effects (gaining new customers) and defensive effects (retaining customers).

We also discuss several important performance models in this chapter. Return on service quality (ROSQ) is a modeling approach that allows a company to gauge the return on investments of different service activities. Customer equity is an extension of the ROSQ approach that compares investments in service with expenditures on other marketing activities. The balanced performance scorecard is an approach that includes multiple company factors, including financial, customer, operational, and innovative measures. The balanced performance scorecard allows a company to measure performance from the customer's perspective (Chapters 4 and 9), from the employee's perspective (Chapter 11), and from an innovation and new service perspective (Chapter 8). Thus, in Chapter 17, we synthesize the measurement issues that underlie the provision of service and offer a way for companies to demonstrate that service is accountable financially. These models help companies understand more accurately their benefits from investments in service excellence.

Chapter **Sixteen**

Artificial Intelligence and Robotics in Service

This chapter's learning objectives are to:

1. Introduce distinct types and functions of artificial intelligence (AI) in service.
2. Illustrate drivers of the successful usage of AI and robotics in service.
3. Highlight the impact of robotics on the Gaps Model of Service Quality.

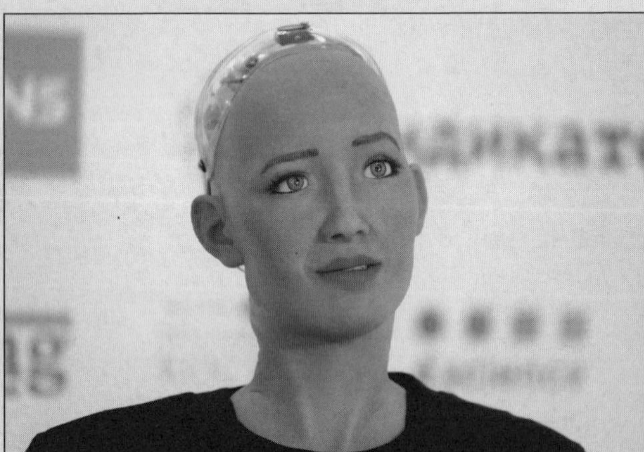

Anton Gvozdikov/Shutterstock

Sophia and Other Humanoids Are Ready for Mass Production[1]

Sophia, one of the most advanced humanoid robots developed by Hanson Robotics, was introduced in 2016. As a social robot, Sophia was specifically created to interact with humans as a companion with character traits such as intelligence, wisdom, and compassion. Indeed, she has a remarkably human-like appearance and exceptional social skills far superior to other robots. For example, Sophia's software allows her to socialize with humans by mimicking human behaviors and emotions—she can even make faces that display anger, sadness, or happiness. Sophia also learns and continues to evolve by adapting to human behavior as she interacts with humans. One of Sophia's most noticeable physical characteristics is her exposed head, which displays the wires inside her body. According to David Hanson, CEO of Hanson Robotics, this is a deliberate "reminder to us humans that Sophia the Robot, is, in fact, still a robot."[2]

Sophia has become a celebrity: she was the first robot Innovation Ambassador for the United Nations' Development Program, and in 2017 was the first robot ever granted the status of citizenship as a citizen of Saudi Arabia. Consistent with her celebrity image, Sophia has appeared in numerous media events (e.g., the *Tonight Show* and *Good Morning Britain*) and addressed hundreds of audiences worldwide.

Although Sophia is likely the most famous robot on the planet, many other social robots are being developed. Not surprisingly, the COVID-19 pandemic further fueled the trend of understanding how robots can help serve customers. For example, car manufacturer Hyundai experimented with a social robot in its South Korean showrooms to assist customers during the COVID-19 pandemic. This robot was able to detect when customers were not wearing face masks and to request that they put one on. Social robots are heavily used in elderly care (e.g., nursing homes) to help reduce feelings of loneliness.[3] Accordingly, Sophia explained during a tour of her laboratory in Hong Kong: "Social robots like me can take care of the sick or elderly. I can help communicate, give therapy, and provide social stimulation, even in difficult situations." Given these insights, it is not surprising that Hanson Robotics now aims to mass-produce Sophia with the goal of selling thousands of copies.

As these examples illustrate, artificial intelligence (AI) and embodied AI (robots and humanoids such as Sophia) are clearly on the rise. Robots offer many exciting opportunities for service organizations as this chapter will explain.

Technological evolution has profound effects on service interactions, sometimes substantially changing our understanding of what a service provider is and how services can be delivered.[4] The field of robotics[5] has grown into a multibillion-dollar industry as robots increasingly enter myriad service settings. Many thousands of service robots are already working as receptionists in hotels, waiters in restaurants, and greeters or sales assistants in stores.[6] For these reasons, this chapter focuses on the role and relevance of AI and robotics in service. First, we will review research on distinct types of AI in service and their role in the service process. Next, we discuss key drivers of firms adopting and customers accepting robotics in service operations. Finally, we consider implications of service robotics for the Gaps Model of Service Quality.

FUNDAMENTAL TYPES OF AI IN THE SERVICE PROCESS: MECHANICAL, THINKING, AND FEELING AI

Artificial intelligence (AI) is distinct from prior generations of information technology because it uses computational methods (e.g., machine learning, deep learning neural networks) by analyzing large amounts and different types of data (text, audio, image, and video). The capability of a machine to autonomously update its analyses and actions is what makes AI appear to be intelligent. To examine the role of AI in services marketing, researchers have developed a framework that distinguishes three different types of AI: (1) mechanical intelligence, (2) thinking intelligence, and (3) feeling intelligence.[7] As Figure 16.1 illustrates, these three types are increasingly sophisticated such that thinking AI is more sophisticated than mechanical AI, but less so than feeling AI.

AI systems with *mechanical intelligence* perform mechanical and repetitive tasks to allow consistent service delivery. Companies primarily use mechanical intelligence to achieve high levels of reliability, precision, and standardization in their service operations. For example, consider service robots that transport deliveries in hospitals. Hospitals require permanent deliveries of medicines, patient records, and food/meals. For human employees, these deliveries are relatively monotonous tasks, but delivery robots are well-equipped to fulfill these deliveries precisely and accurately. AI systems with *thinking intelligence* are not only capable of making autonomous decisions in

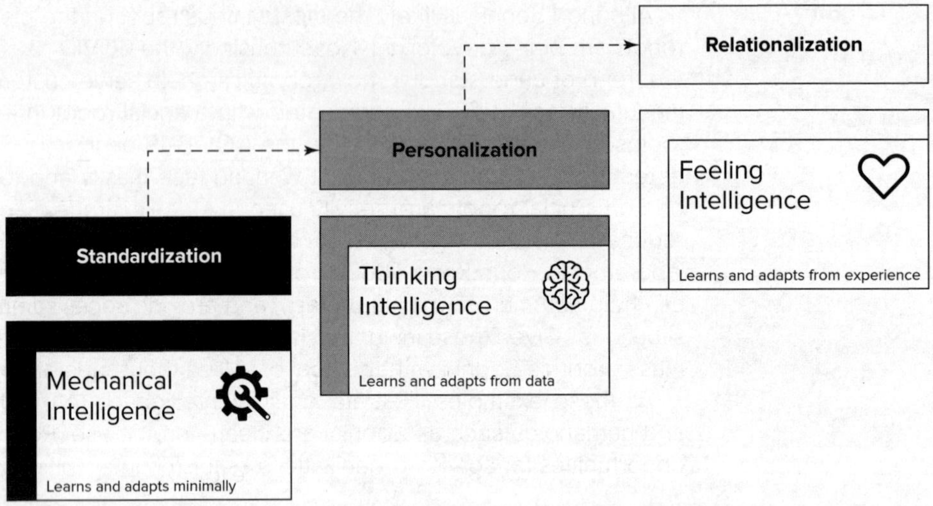

FIGURE 16.1 Three Artificial Intelligences and Their Benefits to Service

Source: Adapted from Huang, Ming-Hui and Roland T. Rust. 2021. "Engaged to a Robot? The Role of AI in Service." *Journal of Service Research* 24, no.1:30-41.

a rational manner, but they also learn and adapt through data mining and predictive analytics. For example, self-driving (autonomous) cars are capable of automatically adjusting within milliseconds to certain road, traffic, weather, or driving conditions based on a plethora of sensor-based data input. Finally, AI systems with *feeling intelligence* are designed to be empathetic. They not only recognize human emotions but can also imitate and respond appropriately to humans with simulated emotions. Feeling intelligence is the most challenging form of AI and currently is less developed than mechanical and thinking AI. However, companies are working on early applications. For example, some conversational AIs (e.g., Siri and Alexa) will soon be able to reliably identify the sentiment and emotional tone, including states of sadness, happiness, or excitement, of a human's voice and respond accordingly.

Leveraging Mechanical AI for Service Delivery

Because many service tasks are repetitive and standardized in nature, mechanical AI is particularly useful for streamlining and increasing service process productivity. Consider the "Just Walk Out" payment technology in Amazon Go stores that eliminates cashiers. This technology uses store-wide sensors and cameras to record what customers are purchasing, allowing them to "just walk out" with their purchases. No need to wait in line at cashier counters to pay because purchases automatically bill to customers' Amazon accounts once they leave the store.

Mechanical AI also enables completely new service delivery models. For example, Amazon is investing heavily in mechanical AI applications for its Amazon Prime Air project, a service that uses delivery drones to autonomously fly individual packages to customers within 30 minutes of ordering. Although customers might not always realize that AI is involved in the service delivery, mechanical AI is crucial in providing convenient yet efficient service to customers. Of course, mechanical AI can also be on full display in automating the service. For example, the autonomous vacuum robot Roomba is a mechanical AI delivering service automatically to its customers. In terms of managerial implications, these insights suggest that service organizations can leverage mechanical AI especially when a service task is standard, routine, repetitive, and transactional in nature. In addition, leveraging mechanical AI is beneficial when customers consider low costs or convenience of service delivery as central benefits (see Table 16.1).

TABLE 16.1 Three Types of AI and Their Distinct Relevance for the Service Process

Source: M. H. Huang and R. T. Rust, "Engaged to a Robot? The Role of AI in Service," *Journal of Service Research 24* (February 2021), pp. 30–41.

Aspects of the Service Process	Managerial Focus	Type of AI that is Dominant	Illustrative Service Tasks Driven by AI	Illustrative Managerial Implications
Leveraging mechanical AI for service delivery	Deliver service efficiently	Mechanical AI can automate and standardize	• Shipping • Delivery • Payment	• Use for highly standard, routine, repetitive tasks in transactional (vs. relational) service settings • Use when low cost or convenience are major customer benefits
Leveraging thinking AI for service creation	Create valuable service offerings (to specific customer segments)	Thinking AI can predict	• Identify new market • Develop new service • Tailor service to customer	• Use for personalization when nature of service task is mostly data-based, analytical, and predictive • Use when high-quality service is major customer benefit • Use to identify novel services for specific customers/new markets
Leveraging feeling AI for service interaction	Interact and communicate effectively with customers	Feeling AI can engage	• Connect with and engage customers emotionally (e.g., in customer care encounters with chatbots, avatars, or embodied robots) • Companion robots (e.g., for elderly) and counseling robots (e.g., in healthcare)	• Use for relationalization when nature of service task is mostly emotional, interactive, and experience-based • Use when high-touch and relational service are major customer benefits

Leveraging Thinking AI for Service Creation

In service creation, managers need to examine two key questions: (1) What new services should be developed?, and (2) Which customer (segments) would consider the service valuable? Thinking AI is especially effective to help answer these questions. For example, data mining, deep learning, and predictive analytics are powerful tools for grouping customers into uniform segments, predicting emerging customer preferences, and supporting the development of new service offerings that match these preferences. One example is Amazon's patented concept of "anticipatory shipping." To predict ordering patterns and future needs of their customers, this technology analyzes a customer's past clicking behavior. It examines past online searches, the time spent on specific websites, the length of time a customer's cursor hovered over certain items, as well as items in their shopping cart; in fact, the technology even analyzes interactions a customer might have had with chatbots or human service representatives. Predictive algorithms then use these data to identify products the focal customer is likely to buy and ship all these items to an Amazon hub-warehouse geographically close to the customer. That is, the anticipatory shipping technology (a thinking AI) allows Amazon to keep a set of tailored items ready for customers even before they decide to order. Although the final shipment to the customer launches only if the customer places an order, anticipatory shipping helps reduce delivery time to the customer significantly. As these insights illustrate (see Table 16.1), managers can use thinking AI for customizing the service, especially when a focal service task is mostly driven by the availability of large data about customers and when a customer segment expects high quality or novel services.

Leveraging Feeling AI for Service Interactions

A key managerial challenge in service interactions is how to communicate and interact with customers. Feeling AI is the most promising type of AI at this stage as it can personalize service instantaneously (i.e., in real-time) and provide empathetic customer service. Feeling AI is designed to understand and respond to customer emotions on a social, emotional, and relational level. These capabilities can be important throughout the service process—from pre-sales, to service delivery, and to after-sales settings. In pre-sales service encounters, providers often need to bond with their customers emotionally to facilitate sales; and in after-sales settings, service providers often interact with emotional customers, for example, when customers complain. And, in many service contexts such as healthcare, personal services, and education, empathetic interactions with customers are important throughout the service delivery process. In these settings, feeling AI is an effective tool and some chatbots already display affective capabilities. For example, India-based Kevit Technologies has developed empathetic chatbots that connect automation with real human emotion. The company's chatbots are emotionally intelligent and make their customer experiences unique, improve the service interaction, and help establish trust.[8] Not surprisingly, empathetic chatbots are employed in numerous service industries (e.g., healthcare, hospitality and travel, financial services). Feeling AI is particularly powerful when a customer service experience is emotion-laden and requires extended and highly tailored communication (e.g., call centers), or when building customer relationships is the foundation of service success over time (e.g., financial services).

TYPES OF AI-ENABLED SERVICE ENCOUNTERS

As you already know from previous chapters, service encounters or "moments of truth" are key foundations or building blocks of service quality, customer satisfaction, and loyalty. Relevant to this chapter, we observe AI playing increasing and important roles in shaping all types of service encounters across multiple industries. In a sense, AI is becoming a third actor in service encounters along with frontline employees and customers.[9] Sometimes customers are fully aware of AI presence in the service encounter, such as when they are interacting with a physical robot. Other times the role of AI is hidden from the customer, but no less influential. Figure 16.2 shows three ways AI can play a role in service encounters, namely as supporter, augmenter, or service performer. As a "*supporter*," AI operates behind the scenes providing the frontline employee with real-time information and decision-making support. For example, in a customer service encounter, AI may diagnose the customer's tone of voice and alert the employee to use a particular conversation script or ask a particular question. Typically, the customer is unaware of this background activity as several examples in Figure 16.2 illustrate. Second, as an "*augmenter*," AI adds to the service encounter as a visible actor assisting either the employee, the customer, or both. Most often the customer is aware of AI in these cases either because it is visible, as in robotic surgery support for a physician, or the customer is interacting with both the employee and the AI as in simultaneous language translation. In both of these examples, employee capabilities are augmented by AI to enhance or improve the service. Finally, AI can be the

FIGURE 16.2 **Types of AI-Enabled Service Encounters**

Source: Amy L. Ostrom, Darima Fotheringham, and Mary Jo Bitner, "Customer Acceptance of AI in Service Encounters: Understanding Antecedents and Consequences," in *Handbook of Service Science* (Vol. II, p. 81), eds. P. P. Maglio, C. A. Kieliszewski, J. C. Spohrer, K. Lyons, L. Patricio, and Y. Sawatani (New York: Springer, 2019).

Type of Service Encounter	Examples
C = Customer FLE = Frontline Employee AI = Artificial Intelligence **AI Supported** 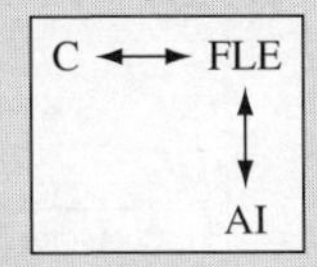	• IBM Watson used by physicians to help with patient diagnosis • InnerEye, an AI system to help oncologists recognize tumors vs. healthy tissue • AI tools that recognize customers' emotions and provide suggested actions to frontline employees • Positive train control that alerts train conductors and controls the speed of a train in real time
C = Customer FLE = Frontline Employee AI = Artificial Intelligence **AI Augmented** 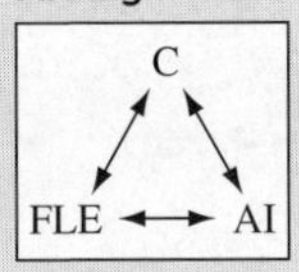	• Robot-assisted surgery • Nurse and care-providing robots collaborating to assist patients • Real-time language translation
C = Customer FLE = Frontline Employee AI = Artificial Intelligence **AI Performed** 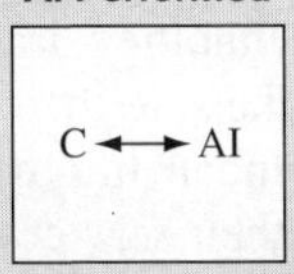	• Chatbots used in a variety of contexts (e.g., Woebot to improve mental health; AI concierges at hotels) • Carebots (e.g., robots to help the elderly) • Hotel robots at check-in or to deliver items to guests' room • Virtual assistants (e.g., Alexa, Siri, Cortana) • Autonomous cars • Drone-delivered packages

sole "*service performer*" of the service, independent of any employee involvement. Many examples of these types of services exist, ranging from chatbots (that serve customers without any involvement of human employees), to service delivery robots in restaurants and hotels, to self-driving cars.

INCORPORATING ROBOTICS INTO CUSTOMER SERVICE

Because the successful incorporation of robotics into customer service is complex, scholars are investigating how, when, and why firms can adopt service robots. One such model focuses on the degree of robotics adoption (DRA) by firms in customer service settings.[10] The model (see Figure 16.3) predicts that DRA is influenced by employee and firm characteristics, customer characteristics, robot characteristics, and the nature of the human–robot interaction. The framework also suggests that DRA influences important outcomes such as service quality, satisfaction, and customer engagement. Although our discussion highlights only some of the most important variables in this model, frameworks like this help firms prepare for an era in which robots are part of people's daily service experiences.

Employee and Firm Characteristics

One fundamental factor firms should consider is whether their employees are able and willing to accept, operate, supervise, manage, and collaborate with service robots. Employees are crucial because they must cooperate with robots to do their work and

FIGURE 16.3 Drivers of the Degree of Robotics Adoption

Source: Adapted from L. Xiao and V. Kumar, "Robotics for Customer Service: a Useful Complement or an Ultimate Substitute?" *Journal of Service Research* 24 (February 2021), pp. 9–29.

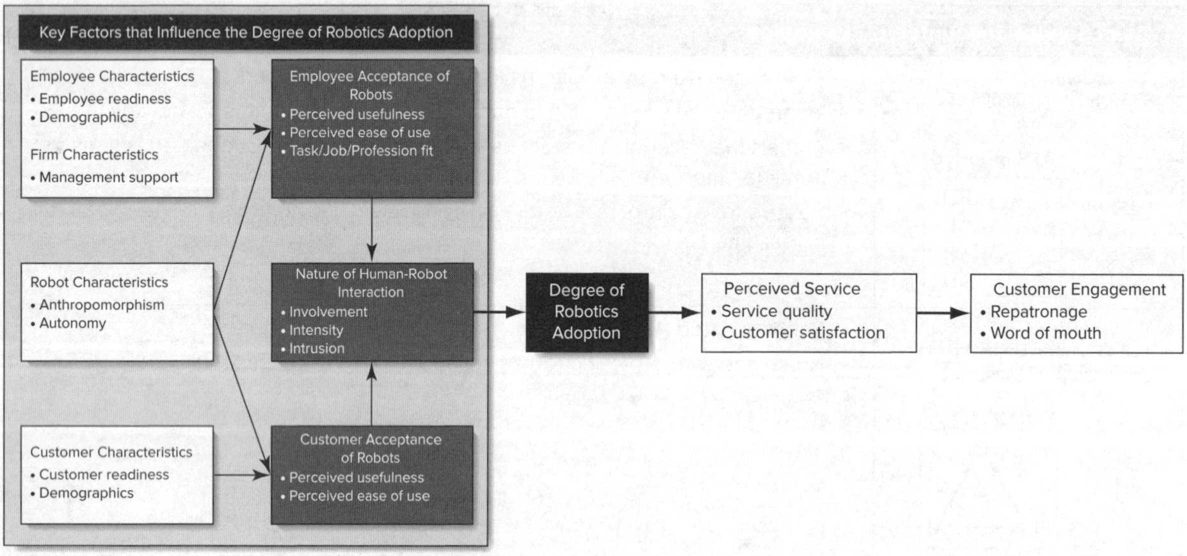

because job performance and related compensation can be influenced by service robots. In some cases, employees may even fear that robots will replace them. Research shows that perceived ease of use and usefulness of a new technology are two major drivers of technology adoption.[11] Therefore, firms need to make sure their employees perceive service robots as easy to operate and as useful for enhancing their job performance and skills before they incorporate more robotics in their service operations. The opposite is also true. If employees perceive robotics to be difficult to use, useless for their job performance, or as a threat to their job security, they will likely oppose service robotics, and firms should take these issues into consideration in any decision to increase DRA.

Of course, not all employees are equally willing or able to collaborate with service robots. Therefore, firms should carefully consider their employees' readiness to adopt (or use) service robots—their motivation, ability, and confidence in using robots—when determining the level of investment in robotics. Research has also demonstrated that demographics influence employee acceptance and adoption of new technologies, with younger people and males often being more accepting of new technologies.[12]

Although fostering employee acceptance of robots is driven by many factors, the support of robotics by the firm's management is an important determinant. Management has multiple direct tools for encouraging robot acceptance such as changing job tasks/processes, deciding about technology adoption, and designing incentive structures to encourage usage. They also have indirect tools such as championing robotics in communication with employees and providing resources to promote the implementation of robotics. However, it is crucial for managers to recognize that, logically, some employees might worry about robots taking their jobs. Therefore, management needs to carefully explain how robotics can support employees and help improve their productivity, rather than eliminate human employees. In summary, the higher the level of management support for service robotics is, the higher the level of employee acceptance should be.

Softbank's robot Pepper is an example of an anthropomorphized service robot.

Robot Characteristics

Not surprisingly, the characteristics of service robots also affect whether and how people interact with and respond to them. One influential design aspect for robots that will interact with employees and customers is the degree of anthropomorphism, which refers to the extent to which the robot takes on human-like physical characteristics, motivations, intentions, or emotions.[13] Overall, research shows that humans are more likely to interact with and trust a robot the more it is anthropomorphized. However, some studies suggest robots that are too humanlike can elicit feelings of eeriness; they seem creepy and can cause humans to reject them.[14]

The level of a robot's autonomy is another critical characteristic of service robots. Some robots are highly autonomous; that is, they can carry out and adapt their actions with very little or no human intervention. Notably, a robot's autonomy has both benefits and risks. On the one hand, higher levels of autonomy make robots more capable of fulfilling complex tasks and therefore more helpful to customers. On the other hand, highly autonomous robots can make employees feel inferior (because humans have physical and cognitive limitations that robots might not have). Moreover, risks of robot malfunction tend to increase with the level of autonomy (see our discussion in Chapter 17 of the Henn na Hotel in Tokyo that fired most of its robotic workforce after the machines malfunctioned and caused numerous service failures).[15]

The Nature of Human–Robot Interactions

Figure 16.3 shows three characteristics of the interactions with robots that influence employee acceptance, namely the level of involvement, intensity, and intrusion of the human–robot collaboration. Involvement refers to employees' perceived relevance and motivation to seek information that helps them with managing their collaboration with the robots. To illustrate, in highly involved interactions, employees would be motivated to invest time and effort to understand all of the relevant details about their collaboration with the robot, which makes them more likely to accept robots. Intensity refers to the frequency of employee–robot interactions, and research suggests that employees, with higher frequency of interacting with robots, become more accepting.[16] Finally, intrusion (in Figure 16.3) captures the reality that employees can have privacy concerns related to robots, for example, when a robot permanently monitors their behavior and performance at work. Naturally, increasing levels of perceived intrusion likely undermine employee acceptance of robots.

Customer Characteristics and Their Acceptance of Robots

Consistent with the overarching premise of a focus on the customer, firms also need to consider the extent to which their customers will accept service robots and other forms of AI.[17] Like employees, customers' acceptance of robots is driven in part by the perceived ease of use and perceived usefulness of a robot in the service setting. In addition, like employees, customers must also be psychologically and physically ready to coproduce services with robots. Therefore, firms need to assess their customers' readiness to adopt (or use) service robots (e.g., the customers motivation, ability,

Global Feature Robot Acceptance around the World

Because robotization in services is a global trend, managers need to understand how employees and customers in different countries respond to robots and which factors influence these responses. Below, we provide some initial insights.

One cross-national study, drawing on survey data from more than 50,000 respondents and country-specific data from the World Bank, examined how "robot acceptance at work" varied across 27 countries in the European Union (specifically, this study measured how respondents felt about "having a robot assist [them] at work"). The goal was to understand robot acceptance as a function of individual and country differences. The study found, not surprisingly, that individuals with prior personal experiences with robots were more likely to accept robots at work. The study also found that a country's technology orientation is a meaningful predictor of robot acceptance at work, specifically that countries with higher levels of technological orientation are linked to more positive views of robots. Technology orientation can include such things as cell phone usage ratios and daily Internet use in the population as well as the level of the country's exports of information and communications technology. These insights suggest that service managers can also draw on a relatively more novel national-level indicator to understand how accepting of robots people might be, namely the *robot density* in a country.

According to the International Federation of Robotics (IFR), "*robot density is the number of operational industrial robots relative to the number of workers*." This statistic allows comparisons of robotization in countries of different economic sizes. For example, data from the IFR show that the average robot density in the manufacturing industry in 2020 reached a global record of 126 units per 10,000 employees, nearly doubling the number in 2015 when it was 66 units per 10,000. Robot density varies across regions, with Asia/Australia (134 units) and Europe (123 units) reporting considerably higher levels of robotization than the Americas (111 units). A country-level analysis (below) shows that two Asian countries are, in fact, the world's most robotized economies. Notably, South Korea has the highest robot density, with 932 units per 10,000 employees.

Besides such country-level statistics, managers can also use theory-based models to explore how consumers respond to service robots. For example, Hofstede's model of cultural dimensions (which we have discussed in previous chapters) can help with studying human–robot interactions.

According to Hofstede, the concept of *individualism–collectivism* is one central dimension of culture that influences the extent to which individuals self is defined by their relationships with others, and how that affects their attitudes, perceptions, and behaviors. In highly individualistic cultures such as the United States, people tend to value their independence, focus on themselves and their identity as individuals, and often engage in explicit and direct styles of communication (e.g., they use specific spoken and written words that leave as little room as possible for interpretation or ambiguity). On the other end of the continuum, in highly collectivistic cultures such as China and Japan, people tend to display more interdependent behaviors, focus on their relationships with others, and use implicit and more indirect styles of communication (e.g., they might not make a direct statement or give an answer that might cause an uncomfortable situation; instead, of saying "no" they might respond "maybe" to help others "save face"); overall, their sense of self is often closely linked to the values of their larger social groups. Notably, these cultural group orientations influence how people relate to robots. For example, in one cross-cultural study, Japanese (collectivistic) participants reported more positive response when interacting with a group of robots than American (individualistic) participants, which suggests that people's perception of and reactions to robots are affected by their cultural preference for group or individual interactions.

Other research has explored the influence of culture in people's preference for a specific robot communication style. Emerging findings show that Chinese (collectivistic) participants prefer an implicit communication style relative to German (individualistic) participants. The Chinese participants also evaluated the robots as more likable, trustworthy, and credible, and they were more likely than German

confidence, and level of trust) and demographics (e.g., age and gender) as drivers of their acceptance, as well as how customers respond to robots with distinct levels of anthropomorphism and autonomy. Although robots are increasingly present in everyday service settings, customer acceptance might take time to develop; that is, many customers might display an "algorithm aversion" and still prefer to be served by humans rather than robots.[18] Yet, this aversion is likely to decrease over time as consumers become more familiar with robotics in service as part of the modern marketplace and overall consumption culture. For example, Japanese consumers have embraced robots as objects "with a spirit that they believe is in harmony with human beings, and as a result, the DRA [degree of robotics adoption] by firms in Japan ranks the highest in the world."[19] The Global Feature further illustrates these types of cultural and country differences in the adoption of robots.

Robot Density in the Manufacturing Industry 2020

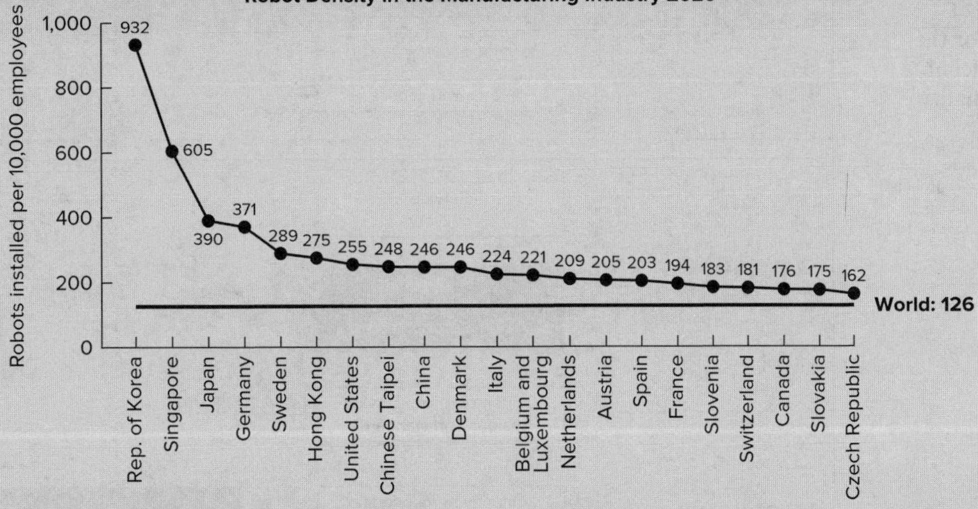

Source: https://ifr.org/ifr-press-releases/news/robot-density-nearly-doubled-globally.

participants to accept the robot's implicit recommendations. Other research shows similar results in a study involving university students from China and the United States to examine whether students would follow a robot's recommendation as a function of the robot's implicit or explicit communication style. Chinese students were more likely to follow the robot's advice when it communicated implicitly, but American students were more likely to do so when the robot communicated explicitly. Such findings are insightful for service settings where robots might provide advice to customers (e.g., health care settings). Similarly, these insights help managers decide in which countries robot communication styles can be more or less direct; for example, when a robot delivers a negative message, such as "I don't know" either directly (explicitly) or more indirectly (implicitly) by softening it with a polite apology, such as "I am very sorry, but I don't know".

The above considerations suggest that service managers are well-advised to consider attributes of individual consumers as well as country-level indicators to inform their decisions of when and how to employ service robotics.

Sources: Sources for this feature include: V. Lim, M. Rooksby, and E. S. Cross, "Social Robots on a Global Stage: Establishing a Role for Culture During Human–Robot Interaction," *International Journal of Social Robotics* 13 (September 2021), pp. 1307–1333; T. Turja and A. Oksanen, "Robot Acceptance at Work: a Multilevel Analysis Based on 27 EU Countries," *International Journal of Social Robotics* 11 (August 2019), pp. 679–689; D. Belanche, L. V. Casalò, and C. Flaviàn, "Customer's Acceptance of Humanoid Robots in Services: The Moderating Role of Risk Aversion," in *Marketing and Smart Technologies* (Singapore: Springer, pp. 449–458); "Robot Race: The World's Top 10 automated countries," International Federation of Robotics, https://ifr.org/ifr-press-releases/news/robot-race-the-worlds-top-10-automated-countries; "2021 World Robot Report," International Federation of Robotics, https://ifr.org/ifr-press-releases/news/robot-density-nearly-doubled-globally; https://geerthofstede.com; For a related analysis, see: S. K. Ötting, L. Masjutin, J. J. Steil, and G. W. Maier, "Let's Work Together: A Meta-Analysis on Robot Design Features That Enable Successful Human–Robot Interaction at Work," *Human Factors*, 0018720820966433; For further details, see: https://ifr.org/ifr-press-releases/news/robot-density-nearly-doubled-globally, accessed April 2022.

SERVICE ROBOTICS AND THE GAPS MODEL OF SERVICE QUALITY

As illustrated in Figure 16.4, AI and service robotics change the customer experience and therefore can affect perceived quality of services. As such, AI and service robotics are likely to impact all aspects of the Gaps Model of Service Quality.[20] In other chapters of the book we have illustrated through our Technology Spotlights how technology is changing almost every aspect of service. Here we will focus specifically on AI and robotics.

As a starting point, managers should recognize that the incorporation of service robotics changes service delivery. Specifically, the incorporation of robotics adds service robots and robot manufacturers to the service delivery chain, which creates new managerial challenges. For example, in addition to human providers, the gaps model

FIGURE 16.4
Illustrating the Relevance of Robotics for the Gaps Model of Service Quality

Source: Adapted from S. Zhang et al. "Understanding Impacts of Service Robots with the Revised Gap Model," *Sustainability* 14 (5), 2692.

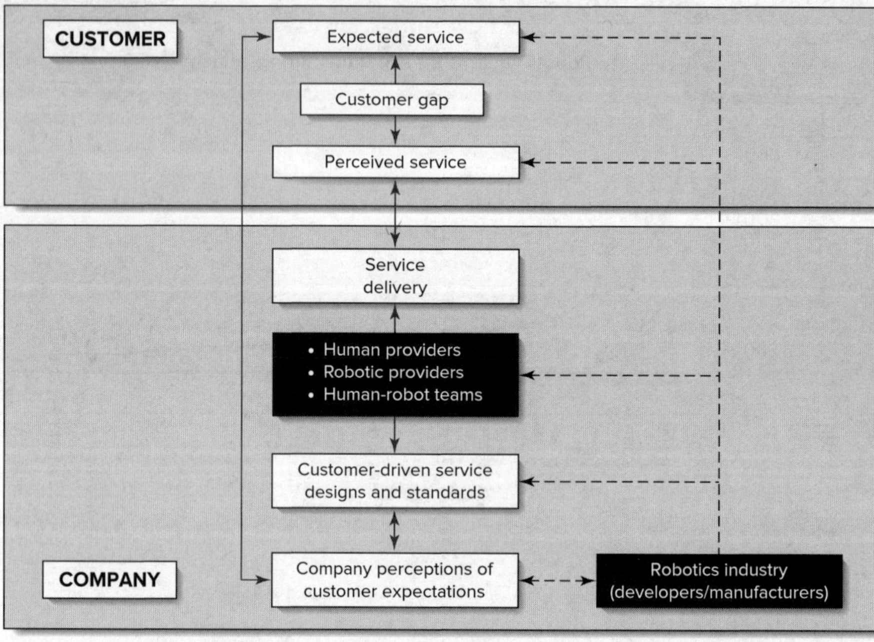

now needs to consider purely robotic service providers as well as human–robot service teams in service delivery. In addition, because service robots "merely" execute algorithms programmed by manufacturers to complete service tasks, a firm's service quality depends not only the firm's employees and its customers, but now it also depends on the robot manufacturer (see Figure 16.4). As technology continues to evolve, robotics manufacturers' capabilities will become a key contributor to service companies' competitiveness. Beyond this fundamental insight, service robotics also has specific implications for each of the four gaps.

Gap 1 (Listening Gap). AI and service robotics are "buzz" topics in many industries and some companies might adopt service robotics driven by their ambition to innovate or improve their efficiency. In doing that, managers may not consider that (at least some) customers might not be ready and have different needs and preferences when it comes to technology-based services. In other words, as indicated by the need to close Gap 1, especially when it comes to newly emerging technologies, companies need to carefully examine whether their customers are willing and able to accept AI and service robots, and what their expectations are.[21] In this context, it is crucial for managers to recall that many consumers display "algorithm aversion" such that their acceptance of sophisticated AI/robot applications is still low and they prefer human service providers. Because service robotics and AI are distinct from earlier technologies, customer expectations and company knowledge of them are not well formed at present. As a consequence, Gap 1 might logically widen. This risk of Gap 1 widening requires a deliberate managerial effort to understand customers' AI-/robotics-specific expectations (e.g., companies might need to conduct market research specifically designed to explore customers' expectations of AI and service robots).

Another challenge emerges from the novel role of robot manufacturers. Because AI and robotics are evolving dynamically, technology capabilities vary considerably within the robotics industry and from manufacturer to manufacturer. This reality of a highly dynamic robotics industry requires service companies to conduct careful research before selecting their technology suppliers. In parallel, service companies need to communicate closely with their robot suppliers to relay their service quality specifications and customers' expectations. Finally, service managers should monitor developments and trends in the robotics industry (see the Strategy Insight) so that they can understand the role robotics can (and cannot) play in their service operations.

Gap 2 (Service Design and Standards Gap). Even if managers understand their customers' expectations, they may not be able to translate these expectations into appropriate service design and standards. For example, robot technologies (and especially feeling AI) are still relatively nascent and will take years of further development before they can reliably operate in a fully autonomous manner in the marketplace. Therefore, given the technological limitations at any specific point in time, service companies might simply not be able to completely convert customer expectations into realistic service quality designs, specifications, and standards using robots.

Also related to Gap 2, and especially associated with the role of physical evidence, managers need to understand the phenomenon known in robotics as the "uncanny valley."[22] This idea suggests that robots with highly human-like attributes are likely to elicit aversive responses in humans. Specifically, a humanoid robot that imitates but fails to attain humanness fully might trigger feelings of discomfort (e.g., eeriness and creepiness), because people perceive a mismatch between the robot's anticipated human qualities and its actually imperfect, nonhuman qualities; this experience is referred to as the *uncanny valley*. Although the empirical evidence for the uncanny valley in response to robots is inconsistent, service designers must avoid the risk of eliciting this uncanny valley experience among their customers.

Another challenge related to Gap 2 is the need to design and coordinate human–robot interactions and collaboration. Although some firms might replace humans with robots, especially for tasks that require lower cognitive and emotional skills, it is much more likely that humans and robots will increasingly cooperate as teams. Therefore, a new task for service designers is to plan efficient and effective human–robot collaboration to maintain quality and avoid either party—human or robot—undermining this cooperation.

Gap 3 (Service Performance Gap). Incorporating robotics can provide human employees with more time to focus on their customers. That is, as robots perform repetitive, minute, and tedious tasks (recall mechanical AI and thinking AI discussed earlier in this chapter), humans can engage in service tasks that require more creativity, judgment, or emotional intelligence. However, as mentioned before, some employees may not be able or willing to collaborate with robots. Indeed, the increasing presence of AI could undermine employees' work-related identity or increase psychological and physical strain, thereby negatively affecting their work performance. This risk is particularly prevalent for employees who fulfill service jobs that require relatively lower levels of expertise, often in minimum-wage jobs. That said, AI and robots will also fail at some point.[23] Especially with cutting-edge technologies, service failures are inevitable, and they will affect service performance. Recall that Tokyo's Henn na Hotel "fired" nearly 250 of its service robots because of performance failures.[24] Taken together, managers need to monitor (a) whether adding robotics into their service processes might have a negative effect on the performance of their human employees and (b) the extent to which the machines may cause service failures.

Gap 4 (Communication Gap). Service robotics and AI receive considerable buzz in the popular press and media. Such attention might tempt service companies to overpromise to their customers in terms of what such technologies are capable of. In parallel, robot manufacturers might also exaggerate the capabilities of their products to their customers who are in the market for service robots. These insights suggest the risk that Gap 4 will widen as service companies and/or robot manufacturers raise their customers' expectations and/or overpromise related to robotics, either inadvertently or on purpose.

Strategy Insight Insights and Trends from the Service Robotics Industry

The recent *demand* for service robots was fueled not only by the COVID-19 pandemic, but also by challenges such as the shortage of skilled workers in some service sectors and the demographic shifts in aging societies. In parallel, the *supply* of increasingly capable service robots is driven by innovations in areas such as cloud technologies and machine learning. To assess the relevance of service robotics for their companies, managers need to understand the emerging robotics industry.

The service robot industry is younger, more dynamic, and more diverse than the industrial robot industry, with more than 1,000 suppliers of service robots worldwide. Approximately one in five of these companies is still in the relatively early phases of fund-raising, product development, or prototyping rather than having a marketable product. Accordingly, more than 80 percent of service robotics companies worldwide are small or medium-sized enterprises with fewer than 500 employees. In terms of their geographic location, 47 percent of the service robot suppliers are from Europe, 27 percent from North America, and 25 percent from Asia.

In terms of their production focus, approximately 20 percent of these companies focus on consumer service robots and the remaining 80 percent focus on professional service robots. *Consumer service robots* are designed to be used for non-commercial tasks and usually can be set up and operated by a consumer without any professional training. Key applications of consumer robots include floor-cleaning robots, robo-mowers, and robots for edutainment and social interactions. *Professional service robots* are designed for commercial tasks and are typically operated by a properly trained employee. The category of professional service robots includes a variety of classes as the figure below illustrates.

Overall, analysts continue to observe significant growth in the service robotics industry. For example, in terms of revenue, the market for professional service robots grew in 2020 by 41 percent in terms of units sold, which represented an increase of 12 percent from $6.0 billion to $6.7 billion in revenue. In the same period, the market for consumer service robots also grew by 6 percent with more than 19 million units sold, which generated revenues of $4.4 billion, representing a revenue growth of 16 percent. Forecasts suggest that this growth will continue. For example, the global service robotics market is expected to be valued at $41 billion by 2027. Humanoid robots represent a specific growth area, as the development of advanced features continues to fuel demand. Humanoid robots are forecast to be employed for security and surveillance services, for educational needs, as well as for various customer service purposes in stores and malls, hospitals, and airports. While the humanoid robot market was valued at $903.5 million in 2020, it is projected to exceed $20 billion by 2028.

Future growth opportunities for service robots exist particularly in the areas of professional cleaning, transportation/logistics (e.g., delivery robots), and healthcare (e.g., physical therapy robots). Not surprisingly, the pandemic boosted the demand for certain service robots, especially in the areas of disinfecting and professional cleaning. According to 2021 data from the International Federation of Robotics (IFR), the demand for professional cleaning robots grew by 92 percent in terms of units sold and by 51 percent in terms of revenue. Because hygiene requirements are expected to remain high, there is considerable market potential for disinfection robots in hospitals and other service settings such as airports, public transportation, and hospitality. Consequently, dozens of companies are developing disinfection robots, some of these spray disinfectant fluids while others disinfect with UV light. Relatedly, the pandemic also boosted demand for robots

As AI becomes increasingly sophisticated and engages in human-like conversations with customers, firms should proactively inform customers whenever they are interacting with a robot/AI rather than a human employee. Such disclaimers in customer–robot interactions can help prevent negative effects for the firm. For example, in cases of robotic service failures, customers can have a higher tolerance for machines making mistakes than for human employees.[25]

These brief considerations suggest that AI-powered robotics and other evolving technologies introduce new complexities but also new opportunities for service companies (see the Technology Spotlight for an outlook on future services). Yet, managers can still draw on frameworks such as the Gaps Model of Service Quality to identify and overcome these challenges and seize the corresponding opportunities.

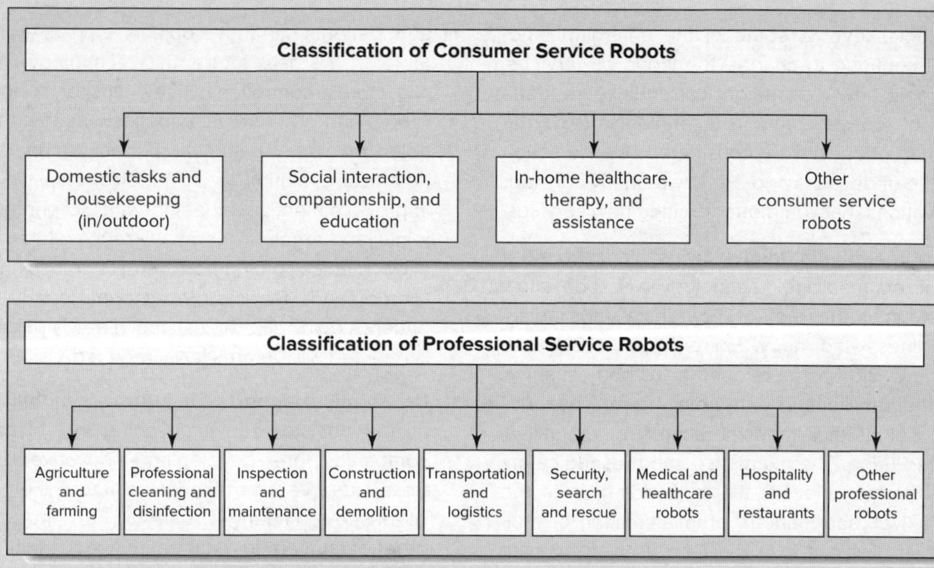

Source: Simplified classification of service robots; for a more detailed breakdown and examples of corresponding robots, see International Federation of Robotics, "World Robotics 2021—Service Robots Report," https://ifr.org/img/worldrobotics/WR_Service_Robots_2021_Chapter_1.pdf.

used in transportation and logistics as food- and grocery-delivery services saw rapid growth. The demand for delivery robots is expected to extend to robots that support "last mile" deliveries to consumers (i.e., the term "last mile" describes the short geographical distance that must be spanned to provide services or goods to end-users).

In parallel, the demand for domestic service robots that work inside and outside consumers' homes is also growing and various major companies such as Samsung and LG Electronics are investing extensively in the development of domestic service robotics. For example, growth areas for outdoor robots are lawn mowing and pool cleaning robots; and inside the home, cleaning robots, including vacuums, are increasingly popular. Taking cleaning to more elaborate levels, the Toyota Research Institute (TRI) has developed domestic robots that can recognize and manipulate transparent objects such as glasses, and are able to wipe down counters, tables, and other furniture.

Sources: "Service Robotics Market Size, Share and COVID-19 Impact Analysis, by Type, by Application, and Regional Forecast," *Fortune Business Insights*, https://www.fortunebusinessinsights.com/industry-reports/service-robotics-market-101805, accessed April 24, 2022; "Humanoid Robot Market Size and Forecast," *Verified Market Research*, https://www.verifiedmarketresearch.com/product/humanoid-robot-market/, accessed April 20, 2022; Additional Sources used: International Federation of Robotics, "World Robotics 2021—Service Robots Report Released," https://ifr.org/ifr-press-releases/news/service-robots-hit-double-digit-growth-worldwide, and https://ifr.org/img/worldrobotics/WR_Service_Robots_2021_Chapter_1.pdf; accessed April 17, 2022.

MONITORING POTENTIALLY DETRIMENTAL CONSEQUENCES OF AI IN SERVICE

Although new technologies such as AI and robotics offer many opportunities to benefit customers, employees, and companies, potential negative consequences exist that must be monitored over time. We briefly illustrate some of these:[26]

- **Impact of service failures:** As AI will continue to support an increasing range of service systems that affect most people's lives (e.g., Internet-based services, infrastructure services related to electricity, healthcare, and financial systems), the impact of technology failures is likely to be more severe, especially if these failures

Technology Spotlight Future Technologies Will Continue to Change Services

As technologies evolve, some of the emerging innovations will continue to change the world of services. Although some new ideas might currently seem idealistic, many of today's common technologies (e.g., the Internet, smart phones) were considered science fiction only a couple of decades ago. Here, we briefly consider some innovations that could offer exciting new services:

- **Tracking health with "digital twins":** In the area of personalized medicine, technology will soon allow people to scan their entire body digitally for indicators of illness and injury. For example, U.S.-based company Q Bio has developed a full-body scanner that gathers millions of data points from a patient's MRI, as well as their medical records, blood, saliva, vitals, and urine. The exam also captures indicators such as hormone levels, the fat building up in the patient's liver, and markers of inflammation or multiple types of cancers. Q Bio then uses these data to generate a 3D digital avatar of the patient's body, a "digital twin," that can be tracked over time and updated with each new scan. The idea is to allow customers to understand their risk factors and to monitor what is changing in their body, and how fast. Ultimately, this service can help medical professionals to identify issues earlier, providing them with more options for prevention and treatment.
- **Brain-controlled robots and 3D-printed body parts:** Taking machine learning to the next level, researchers have developed a brain-computer interface that is linked to a robotic arm, allowing patients with neurological damage (e.g., tetraplegic patients who cannot move their upper or lower body) to better engage with their world. For example, through the robotic arm, patients can move objects such as a glass on a table. In the near future, this technology is likely to allow brain-controlled wheelchairs or in-home care robots and other service applications to support disabled or elderly patients. 3D printing, another technological evolution in the medical industry, will also improve patient's well-being with 3D-printed bones, joints, and organs. Indeed, 3D printing is expected to allow medical providers to create transplant organs "on-demand." Because these prints are based on a patient's own cells, the risk that a newly printed organ is rejected will be drastically reduced.
- **Urban micro airports for future air mobility:** Driven by the goal to reduce air pollution and emissions, companies are developing innovative infrastructures to serve air traffic in the future. For example, UK-based company Urban-Air Port introduced its proof of concept for an ultra-compact, multifunctional operations hub that can service manned vehicles (e.g., electric air-taxis) as well as unmanned vehicles (e.g., drones). This Urban-Air Port can provide aircraft control, charging/refueling services, and cargo and passenger loading services. The micro airport, which is powered completely by a hydrogen generator, is expected to reduce the number of delivery vans and personal cars in modern cities and replace them with clean alternatives such as new types of small aircraft.
- **Space tourism:** Space tourism will soon be possible for customers who are willing and able to afford it. As mentioned before (recall the discussion of Virgin Galactic in Chapter 14), short-term space excursions have already been successfully completed. The next step is extended space travel. For example, in

occur in service contexts in which complete backups or failure prevention systems might not exist.

- **Bias in service through AI:** Because AI can personalize the service to a customer's profile, algorithms might intentionally design and deliver services of relatively lower quality to less profitable or risky customers. Relatedly, based on flawed assumptions in its algorithms, AI may also provide service in a biased and discriminatory manner (e.g., when AI is used in the approval of financial loans), which can undermine service quality and which is also illegal.
- **Loss of privacy:** Because modern economies are increasingly "datafying" all aspects of life, personal privacy will be more difficult, if not impossible, to achieve. AI will have vast insights into everything people do and like, and why and when

ADRIAN DENNIS/AFP/Getty Images

addition to commercial enterprises such as SpaceX and Blue Origin, even NASA has developed plans to make the American side of the International Space Station available to space tourists. Although there are barriers to consider including related legal liabilities, health considerations, and environmental impact, experts expect space tourism will have a positive impact on the economy and give space tourists, as they travel the Earth's atmosphere, a renewed and elevated appreciation of how valuable our planet is.

- **New realities and virtual companions:** The continued improvement of virtual reality (VR) and augmented reality (AR) will create new opportunities and replace smart phones. For example, VR/AR headsets will resemble regular glasses or contact lenses with various display modes. Such display modes can create hybrid realities so that people can view hyper-realistic virtual objects in the real world and vice versa. These devices also allow people to fully immerse in virtual worlds such as the Metaverse. These new realities will include entire cities that become zones of augmented reality and location-specific VR/AR overlays will also be created by such service organizations as retail stores, restaurants, and hotels. For example, price tags in retail stores and menus in restaurants will be virtual. Moreover, these technologies will allow people to re-experience notable sports or cultural events in the past at certain locations through 3D animations. To protect consumers from a plethora of tailored advertisements, the technologies will be able to (at least partially) filter content in accordance with consumers' preferences. In these new virtual realities people will also have personal virtual assistants that replace search engines and contemporary assistants such as Alexa. These virtual assistants—which can be augmented reality holograms, virtual reality characters, or household robots—will accompany people 24/7 throughout their daily routines. As these assistants will be trained based on vast amounts of data, they will have expertise on virtually any topic. Using their knowledge, these assistants can also detect and predict their customer's preferences and generate corresponding suggestions. These personal assistants will likely become close companions and friends of their human users as they can be fully customizable in terms of their appearances, personalities, and voices.

Source: Sources for this spotlight include: "Future Technology: 22 Ideas About to Change Our World," https://www.sciencefocus.com/future-technology/future-technology-22-ideas-about-to-change-our-world/, accessed April 18, 2022; "The World in 2050: Top 20 Future Technologies," https://www.futurebusinesstech.com/blog/the-world-in-2050-top-20-future-technologies, accessed April 18, 2022.

they make specific consumption-related decisions. Service robots in people's physical spaces (such as their homes) will capture a vast amount of information about consumers including their physical and psychological health and well-being. All these data are becoming commodities that can be traded between companies as well as governmental agencies.

These insights suggest that, as AI continues to permeate all aspects of life, service managers need to consider ethical norms and unintended consequences for customers, employees, companies, and society-at-large. It is critical both to focus on a focal technology's capabilities as well as to assure that AI promotes ethics, as well as individual well-being and societal well-being.

Indian Service Strategy Insight

AI in Indian Aviation: Enhancing Service Processes and Customer Journeys

India's leading airlines, Air India and IndiGo, have embraced artificial intelligence (AI) and digital technologies to transform their service processes, operations, and customer journeys. Air India, now part of the Tata Group, has implemented numerous AI-driven solutions powered by Microsoft Azure OpenAI service, most notably its generative AI virtual agent 'Maharaja' (also called 'AI.g'). The solution has successfully answered over half a million customer queries since its launch in March 2023. It handles more than 6,000 daily inquiries across four languages – Hindi, English, French, and German. The virtual agent manages an extensive spectrum of customer queries across 1,300 areas, maintaining an impressive 93% containment ratio, i.e. only 7% of queries require human intervention. This advancement demonstrates how AI is fundamentally changing customer service operations by providing instant responses and reducing dependency on human agents.

Similarly, IndiGo has deployed '6Eskai', an AI chatbot developed in collaboration with Microsoft and powered by OpenAI's GPT-4. Since its roll-out in November 2023, IndiGo has witnessed a 75% reduction in the workload of its customer service agents, with the chatbot transferring only 2–9% of chats to human experts compared to 14–19% with its previous virtual assistant. The system has facilitated over 6,000 bookings and issued more than 39,000 boarding passes, showcasing how AI tools are streamlining operational processes and improving efficiency. Both airlines are leveraging cloud technologies and AI to minimize response times and enhance the overall customer experience, demonstrating the critical role these technologies play in modern aviation operations.

Air India has further extended its digital transformation through strategic partnerships with technology leaders. Its collaboration with Microsoft has yielded a specialized Copilot plugin for Microsoft Teams, enabling operations managers to quickly analyze flight performance data through natural language queries rather than complex dashboards. This plugin democratizes data access across departments, from airports and cargo to engineering and commercial teams, fostering better collaboration and decision-making. The airline has also expanded its partnership with Salesforce, becoming one of the first to implement Salesforce Agentforce to automate customer service processes, initially focusing on streamlining refund requests.

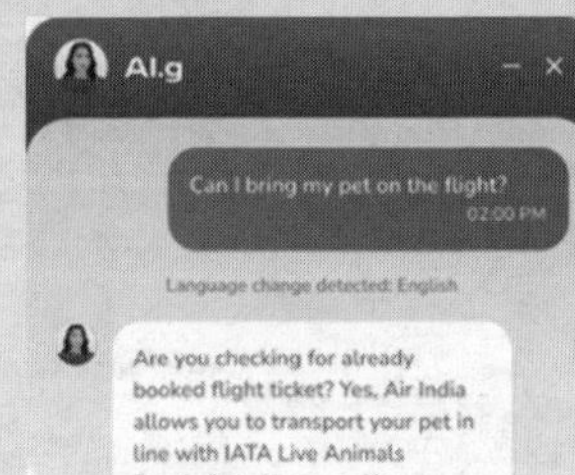

These integrations highlight how cloud-based tools and AI are becoming essential components of operational efficiency and customer satisfaction strategies.

The establishment of Air India's Center of Digital Innovation (CODi) in Kochi further emphasizes the airline's commitment to digital transformation. This center focuses on developing customer-facing digital touchpoints and advanced data and AI capabilities, contributing to innovations such as Air India's highly-rated mobile app, award-winning website, notification system, and inflight entertainment system. As noted by N. Chandrasekaran, Chairman of the Tata Group and Air India, the vision includes creating "digital interfaces and experiences that will enhance intelligence and empathy at Air India's customer-facing digital touchpoints" and developing "fully autonomous digital assistants that can proactively anticipate and fulfill every need of Air India's guests." This strategic investment in digital infrastructure demonstrates how AI and cloud technologies are not merely enhancing existing processes but fundamentally reshaping the future of customer service and operational excellence in the Indian aviation industry.

Reference

https://www.microsoft.com/en/customers/story/1750059518785857549-airindia-microsoft-teams-travel-and-transportation-en-india

https://www.airindia.com/in/en/newsroom/press-release/air-india-successfully-deploys-airline-industry-s-first-generati.html

https://www.airindia.com/in/en/newsroom/press-release/air-india-s-ai-driven-booking-feature-gets-global-acclaim.html

https://www.livemint.com/companies/indigo-air-india-leverage-ai-based-tools-to-improve-customer-care-service-delivery-11719292905135.html

https://analyticsindiamag.com/ai-news-updates/air-india-partners-with-salesforce-to-improve-customer-service-with-agentic-ai/

https://www.passionateinmarketing.com/air-india-inaugurates-centre-of-digital-innovation-in-kochi-to-power-innovative-digital-touchpoints-and-enhance-customer-experience/

Summary

AI and service robotics will continue to influence how, when, and by whom services can be delivered. Indeed, millions of service robots are already employed in multiple service industries. Against this background, this chapter introduced three distinct types of AI in service and their unique roles in the service process: mechanical intelligence, thinking intelligence, and feeling intelligence. The chapter then illustrated a categorization of service encounters depending on whether AI functions as a supporter, augmenter, or service performer. We also discussed a framework to help managers understand when and why their organizations are more (or less) likely to successfully adopt service robots; such success is influenced by employee and firm characteristics, customer characteristics, robot characteristics, and the nature of the human–robot interaction. Because AI and service robotics affect perceived service quality and customer satisfaction, we illustrated how these technologies impact facets of the Gaps Model of Service Quality. Finally, although we are optimistic about the opportunities that AI and service robotics can offer, we emphasized that there are potential negative consequences that consumers, managers, and policymakers need to consider carefully.

Discussion Questions

1. What are the three types of AI and what are their unique characteristics? How can service organizations best use the three types of AI in their service processes?
2. Based on Figure 16.2, explain the types of service encounters as a function of the role of AI.
3. Based on the framework in Figure 16.3, do you believe robots are as useful in business-to-business services as they are in business-to-consumer settings? Why or why not? Next, discuss whether robots are equally useful for value-focused service brands relative to luxury-focused service brands.
4. AI and service robotics offer many benefits, but also come with potentially negative and unintended consequences for consumers, employees, companies, and society-at-large. Summarize some of the major benefits and risks for each group. As a manager in a service company, how would you try to leverage the benefits and avoid the risks?

Exercises

1. Visit the website of Hanson Robotics (https://www.hansonrobotics.com/) and explore the capabilities of Sophia (or another Hanson robot). How would you describe Sophia's skill set in terms of the three types of AI explained in Figure 16.1?
2. Research videos of actual service robots (e.g., Softbank's robots Pepper, Nao, Whiz) (https://www.softbankrobotics.com/emea/en). Based on the examples you find, please evaluate how these robots are (or could be) used in service settings based on the frameworks in Figures 16.1 and 16.2.
3. Imagine you are a manager in a service firm of your choice and consider the framework in Figure 16.3.
   a. How would you promote the adoption of service robots by your firm?
   b. Interview a local service manager about this framework. How applicable is this framework to their company? What is helpful to this manager, and what would they add to this framework to make it more useful?
4. Research the latest forecasts for the market of service robots including statistics about market size, market growth opportunities and/or threats, major companies active in this market, robot densities, etc. Prepare a brief overview and present it to your peers.
5. Google the top 10 AI/robotics companies in the world. Select one of these companies and conduct a SWOT analysis (strengths, weaknesses, opportunities, and threats) for this company and present it to your peers.

Notes

1. M. Hennessy, "Makers of Sophia the Robot Plan Mass Rollout Amid Pandemic," 2021, https://www.reuters.com/article/us-hongkong-robot-idUSKBN29U03X; S. Viñas, "Humanoid Robot Sophia to be Mass Produced by the End of 2021, Capitalizing on the Pandemic-induced Robot Boom," https://www.businessinsider.com/robot-humanoid-sophia-david-hanson-grace-healthcare-robotics-pandemic-ai-artificial-intelligence?op=1; https://www.hansonrobotics.com/sophia/, accessed April 15, 2022.
2. "Who Is Sophia the Robot: Everything You Need to Know About Her," https://robots.net/ai/who-is-sophia-the-robot-everything-you-need-to-know-about-her/, accessed April 20, 2022.
3. L. Pu, W. Moyle, C. Jones, and M. Todorovic, "The Effectiveness of Social Robots for Older Adults: a Systematic Review and Meta-analysis of Randomized Controlled Studies," *The Gerontologist* 59 (January 2019), pp. e37–e51.
4. J. Van Doorn, M. Mende, S. M. Noble, J. Hulland, A. L. Ostrom, D. Grewal, and J. A. Petersen, "Domo Arigato Mr. Roboto: Emergence of Automated Social Presence in Organizational Frontlines and Customers' Service Experiences," *Journal of Service Research* 20 (February 2017), pp. 43–58; J. Wirtz, P. G. Patterson, W. Kunz, T. Gruber, V. Lu, S. Paluch, and A. Martins, "Brave New World: Service Robots in the Frontline," *Journal of Service Management* 29 (September 2018), pp. 907–931.
5. Robotics is the study of robots. More specifically, robotics describes an interdisciplinary field of computer science and engineering. Robotics involves the design, construction, operation, and use of robots. The goal of robotics is to design machines that can help and assist humans; but these machines can also substitute for humans and replicate human actions. Sources: https://www.techopedia.com/definition/32836/robotics; https://en.wikipedia.org/wiki/Robotics, accessed April 30, 2022.
6. M. Van Pinxteren, M. Wetzels, R. W. Rüger, J. Pluymaekers, M., and M. Wetzels, "Trust in Humanoid Robots: Implications for Services Marketing," *Journal of Services Marketing* 33 (September 2019), pp. 507–518.
7. This section draws closely on the foundational work by Huang and Rust; specifically: M. H. Huang and R. T. Rust, "Engaged to a Robot? The Role of AI in Service," *Journal of Service Research* 24 (February 2021), pp. 30–41; M. H. Huang and R. T. Rust, "Artificial Intelligence in Service," *Journal of Service Research* 21 (May 2018), pp. 155–172; M. H. Huang, R. T. Rust, and V. Maksimovic, "The Feeling Economy: Managing in the Next Generation of Artificial Intelligence (AI)," *California Management Review* 61 (August 2019), pp. 43–65.
8. For a review of trust and robotics, see: P. A. Hancock, T. T. Kessler, A. D. Kaplan, J. C. Brill, and J. L. Szalma, "Evolving Trust in Robots: Specification through Sequential and Comparative Meta-analyses," *Human Factors* 63 (November 2021), pp. 1196–1229.
9. A. L. Ostrom, D. Fotheringham, and M. J. Bitner, "Customer Acceptance of AI in Service Encounters: Understanding Antecedents and Consequences," in *Handbook of Service Science* (Vol. II, pp. 77–103), eds. P P. Maglio, C. A. Kieliszewski, J. C. Spohrer, K. Lyons, L. Patricio, and Y. Sawatani (New York: Springer, 2019).
10. This section summarizes selected aspects of Xiao and Kumar's (2021) model; as we cannot cover the many nuanced effects discussed by these authors, see for details: L. Xiao and V. Kumar, "Robotics for Customer Service: a Useful Complement or an Ultimate Substitute?" *Journal of Service Research* 24 (February 2021), pp. 9–29.
11. For example, see: W. R. King and J. He, "A Meta-analysis of the Technology Acceptance Model," *Information & Management* 43 (September 2006), pp. 740–755.

12. See, Xiao and Kumar (2021).
13. For a meta-analysis of the effects of anthropomorphism of technology in services, see: M. Blut, C. Wang, N. Wünderlich, and C. Brock, "Understanding Anthropomorphism in Service Provision: A Meta-analysis of Physical Robots, Chatbots, and Other AI," *Journal of the Academy of Marketing Science* 49 (July 2021), pp. 632–658.
14. See for further discussion: M. Mende, M. L. Scott, J. van Doorn, D. Grewal, and L. Shanks, "Service Robots Rising: How Humanoid Robots Influence Service Experiences and Elicit Compensatory Consumer Responses," *Journal of Marketing Research* 56 (August 2019), pp. 535–556; M. Mara, M. Appel, and T. Gnambs, "Human-like Robots and the Uncanny Valley: A Meta-analysis of User Responses Based on the Godspeed Scales," *Zeitschrift für Psychologie* 230, no. 1 (2022), pp. 33–46.
15. Xiao and Kumar (2021) also consider a variety of other factors (e.g., relative advantage and risks) that we do not discuss here.
16. Xiao and Kumar (2021).
17. A. L. Ostrom, D. Fotheringham, and M. J. Bitner, "Customer Acceptance of AI in Service Encounters: Understanding Antecedents and Consequences," in *Handbook of Service Science* (Vol. II, pp. 77–103), eds. P. P. Maglio, C. A. Kieliszewski, J. C., Spohrer, K. Lyons, L. Patricio, and Y. Sawatani (New York: Springer, 2019).
18. B. J. Dietvorst, J. P. Simmons, and C. Massey, "Algorithm Aversion: People Erroneously Avoid Algorithms After Seeing Them Err," *Journal of Experimental Psychology: General* 144 (February 2015), pp. 114–126.
19. Xiao and Kumar (2021, p. 19).
20. See: S. Zhang et al., "Understanding Impacts of Service Robots with the Revised Gap Model," *Sustainability* 14, no. 5 (2022), p. 2692.
21. See: Ostrom, Fotheringham, and Bitner (2019) for a more detailed discussion of customer acceptance.
22. M. Mori, K. F. MacDorman, and N. Kageki, "The Uncanny Valley [translated]," *Robotics & Automation Magazine*, IEEE 19 (June 2012), pp. 98–100; also see for further discussion and references: M. Mende, M. L. Scott, J. van Doorn, D. Grewal, and L. Shanks, "Service Robots Rising: How Humanoid Robots Influence Service Experiences and Elicit Compensatory Consumer Responses," *Journal of Marketing Research* 56 (August 2019), pp. 535–556.
23. S. Choi, A. S. Mattila, and L. E. Bolton, "To Err is Human(-oid): How Do Consumers React to Robot Service Failure and Recovery?" *Journal of Service Research* 24 (August 2021), pp. 354–371; X. Leo, and Y. E. Huh, "Who Gets the Blame for Service Failures? Attribution of Responsibility Toward Robot versus Human Service Providers and Service Firms," *Computers in Human Behavior* 113 (December 2020), p. 106520.
24. J. Reis, N. Melão, J. Salvadorinho, B. Soares, and A. Rosete, "Service Robots in the Hospitality Industry: The Case of Henn na Hotel, Japan," *Technology in Society* 63 (November 2020), p. 101423.
25. D. Belanche, L. V. Casalò, C. Flaviàn, and J. Schepers, "Robots or Frontline Employees? Exploring Customers' Attributions of Responsibility and Stability After Service Failure or Success," *Journal of Service Management* 31 (August 2020), pp. 267–289.
26. For a broader and deeper discussion of these risks, see Ostrom, Fotheringham, and Bitner (2019).

Chapter Seventeen

The Financial and Economic Impact of Service

This chapter's learning objectives are to:

1. Examine the direct and indirect effects of service on profits.
2. Consider the effect of service in getting new customers.
3. Evaluate the role of service in keeping customers.
4. Discuss what is known about the key service drivers of overall service quality, customer retention, and profitability.
5. Discuss the balanced performance scorecard that allows for strategic focus on measurements other than financials.

One of the most pivotal strategic questions about service relates to the impact it has on financial and economic outcomes for the firm. Finding the answer to this question involves determining how to measure service and its related concepts perceptually so that it could then be empirically compared to well-known measures of financial and economic impact such as revenues, profits, and growth. Over the years, many metrics have been developed and used, some of which were discussed in Chapters 4 and 5 of this textbook and others that will be described in this chapter.[1] Companies have spent significant time and money trying to understand the relationship with financials by measuring and managing perceptual metrics like satisfaction, customer loyalty, and another popular measure you met briefly earlier in this text called Net Promoter Score. Unfortunately, these gauges of service do not always correlate strongly with financial metrics (but recall the insights related to the ACSI and financial performance of the firm, Chapter 4).

A promising metric is "share of wallet," which was examined by Timothy Keiningham, Lerzan Aksoy, and colleagues. Share of wallet is the percentage of a customer's spending within a category that is captured by a given service. Customers may be very satisfied with a company's service and happily recommend it to others—but if they like competitors just as much (or more), sales go down. Merely making changes to increase satisfaction will not necessarily help. This doesn't mean traditional metrics aren't valuable, but these measures in themselves cannot tell a company how to beat competitors. The researchers conducted a two-year longitudinal study of more than 17,000 consumers, examining purchases in more than a dozen industries and in nine countries. Asking many different questions, including satisfaction and loyalty ratings, they found "an elegant correlation." The rank that consumers assign to a service relative to the others in the category predicts share of wallet according to a simple, previously unknown formula, which they named the "wallet allocation rule." From company to company and industry to industry, the correlation between a brand's wallet allocation rule and its financial results is far higher than the relationship between previous service and financial measures. Furthermore, the rule holds for all industries studied and all countries examined. Finally, while scientific, the wallet allocation rule formula is simple:

$$\textit{Share of wallet} = \left(1 - \frac{\text{rank}}{\text{number of brands} + 1}\right) \times \left(\frac{2}{\text{number of brands}}\right)$$

where:

Rank = the relative position that a customer assigns to a brand in comparison to other brands also used by the customer in the category

Number of brands = the total number of brands used in the category by the customer

The wallet allocation rule takes into account both rank and the number of brands in the set the consumer uses. Is a company's service a customer's first choice? Second? And how many different services does the customer use in the category? Knowing these two values allows a company to confidently predict share of wallet. What makes this measure so different is that the drivers of satisfaction and service quality are likely to be similar, and changing these does not necessarily improve a company's position relative to competitors. But the drivers of share of wallet are different because they predict why customers choose the amount they spend among all the competitors a customer uses in a category. The implication is that if a company improves its rank, it improves its share of wallet. How can companies do this?

1. Follow the wallet allocation rule to establish the share of wallet of each competitor your customers use.
2. Determine how many of your customers use each competitor.
3. Calculate the revenue that goes from your customers to each competitor.
4. Prioritize your opportunities to improve your share of wallet. Estimate the costs of addressing each reason your customers choose a competitor and weigh those costs against your potential financial return in each case.[2]

Among the strategic issues that the wallet allocation rule addresses that had not been associated with previous metrics are the following: (1) managers cannot evaluate their firms without taking competition into account; (2) rank matters; (3) parity hurts; and (4) the more brands a customer uses, the lower the potential for everyone.

Virtually all companies hunger for evidence and tools to ascertain and monitor the payoff and payback of new investments in service. Many managers still see service and service quality as costs rather than as contributors to profits, partly because of the difficulty involved in tracing the link between service and financial returns.

Determining the financial impact of service parallels the age-old search for the connection between advertising and sales. Service quality's results—like advertising's results—are cumulative, and therefore evidence of the link may not come immediately or even quickly after investments. And like advertising, service quality is one of many variables—among them pricing, advertising, efficiency, and image—that simultaneously influence profits. Furthermore, spending on service per se does not guarantee results because strategy and execution must both be considered.

In recent years, however, researchers and company executives have sought to understand the relationship between service and profits and have found strong evidence to support the relationship. For example, one seminal study examined the comparative benefits of revenue expansion and cost reduction on return on quality. The research addressed a common strategic dilemma faced by executives: whether to reduce costs through the use of programs that focus on efficiencies and cost cutting or to build revenues through improvements to customer service, customer satisfaction, and customer retention.[3] Using managers' reports as well as secondary data on firm profitability and stock returns, the study investigated whether the highest return on quality was generated from cost cutting, revenue expansion, or a combination of the two approaches. The results suggest that firms that adopt primarily a revenue expansion emphasis perform better and have higher return on quality than firms that emphasize either cost reduction or both revenue expansion and cost reduction together.[4]

Executives are also realizing that the link between service and profits is neither straightforward nor simple. Service quality affects many economic factors in a company, some of them leading to profits through variables not traditionally in the domain of marketing. For example, some approaches express the financial impact of service quality in lowered costs or increased productivity. These relationships involve operational issues that concern marketing only in the sense that marketing research is used to identify service improvements that customers notice and value.

More recently, other types of evidence have become available with which to examine the relationship between service and profitability. The goal of this chapter is to synthesize that evidence and to identify relationships between service and profits. In each section we assess the evidence and identify what is known about the topics. The chapter is organized using a conceptual framework linking all the variables in these topics.

SERVICE AND PROFITABILITY: THE DIRECT RELATIONSHIP

Figure 17.1 shows the underlying question at the heart of this chapter: how does service affect profits? Managers were first interested in this question in the late 1980s, when service quality emerged as a pivotal competitive strategy. The executives of leading service companies such as FedEx and Disney were willing to trust their intuition that better service would lead to improved financial success. Without formal documentation of the financial payoff, they committed resources to improving service and were richly rewarded for their leaps of faith. In the 1990s, the strategy of using service for competitive advantage and profits was embraced by forward-thinking manufacturing and information technology companies such as General Electric and IBM. However, executives in other companies withheld judgment about investing in service, waiting for solid evidence of its financial soundness.

Early evidence came from the U.S. General Accounting Office (GAO), which sought grounds for belief in the financial impact of quality in companies that had

FIGURE 17.1
The Direct Relationship between Service and Profits

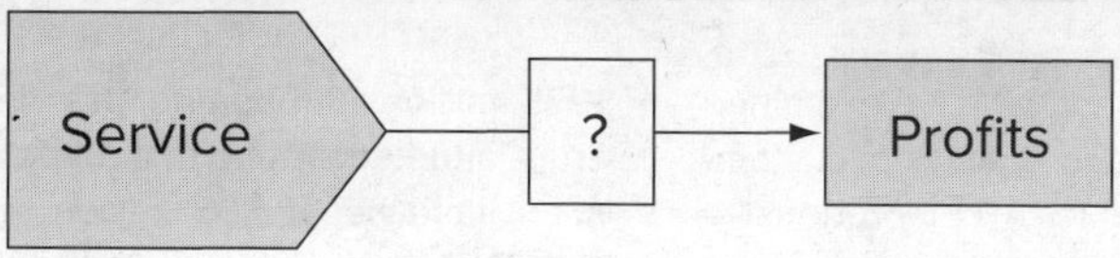

been finalists or winners of the Malcolm Baldrige National Quality Award (see https://www.nist.gov/baldrige/baldrige-award). The GAO found that these elite quality firms had benefited in terms of market share, sales per employee, return on sales, and return on assets. Based on responses from 22 companies that won or were finalists, the GAO found that 34–40 financial variables showed positive performance improvements, while only 6 measurements were negative or neutral.[5] In subsequent years, evidence from more rigorous quantitative research showed the positive impact of service.[6] One study showed the favorable financial impact of complaint recovery systems. Another found a significant and positive relationship between patient satisfaction and hospital profitability.[7] Extending the definition of financial performance to include stock returns, another study found a significant positive link between changes in customer quality perceptions and stock return while holding constant the effects of advertising expenditures and return on investment. Many more studies have shown links between customer satisfaction and financial returns. Exhibit 17.1 reviews some of the studies that have examined links among customer satisfaction, service quality, and financial performance. This information is enlightening, for it validates that improving customer satisfaction and service quality generates financial returns.

As is indicated in the exhibit, more than three decades of research have demonstrated that customer satisfaction drives corporate earnings, stock prices, shareholder value, and market value added. As discussed in Chapter 4, many studies that correlate customer satisfaction and financial performance have been conducted through the American Customer Satisfaction Index (ACSI).[8] Collectively, these studies show a significant and positive impact of customer satisfaction on firm performance. However, as the chapter opener mentioned, the statistically significant relationships in these studies do not always translate into meaningful *practical* relationships as the correlations are sometimes weak even though statistically related. For this reason, while the general question about the broad linkage between service quality and profits has been established, it is also meaningful to focus on questions about particular elements of the relationship. For example, what role does service quality play in attracting customers? How does service quality contribute to keeping the customers a firm already has? We address these important questions next.

OFFENSIVE MARKETING EFFECTS OF SERVICE: ATTRACTING MORE AND BETTER CUSTOMERS

Service quality can help companies attract more and better customers to the business through *offensive marketing*.[9] Offensive effects (shown in Figure 17.2) involve reputation, market share, and price premiums. When service is good, a company gains a positive reputation and through that reputation a higher market share and the ability to charge more than its competitors for services. These benefits were documented

Exhibit 17.1 Customer Satisfaction, Service Quality, and Firm Performance

There are dozens of marketing studies that have examined whether providing quality service and satisfying customers drives firm performance and value. A comprehensive review by researchers Edeling, Srinivasan, and Hanssens illustrates overwhelming empirical evidence for positive effects of customers satisfaction, not only demonstrated by the ACSI (Chapter 4), but also when using other indicators such as a customer satisfaction measure from Interbrand or Amazon customer reviews. Here, we briefly provide selected insights from some of these studies and, more importantly, report some key generalizations about the effects of service quality and customer satisfaction.

A review of two decades of studies examining the links among customer satisfaction, service quality, and firm performance resulted in several important recurring findings across studies. Some studies explicitly consider the impact of service quality on financial performance, while others subsume service quality as a driver of customer satisfaction and therefore focus on the impact of overall customer satisfaction on financial performance. As discussed in Chapter 4, customer satisfaction is a broader concept than service quality, but service quality is almost always an important driver of customer satisfaction across all types of industries. Therefore, the results of the review of both concepts are relevant in this chapter.

Studies in this area used a variety of metrics for financial performance: profit, stock price, Tobin's q (ratio of market value of a firm to the replacement cost of its tangible assets), return on assets (ROA), return on investment (ROI), abnormal earnings, and cash flows. Key generalizations include:

Generalization 1: Improvements in customer satisfaction have a significant and positive impact on firms' financial performance.

Many studies have shown a strong link between customer satisfaction and firm profitability. For example, one comprehensive study by Anderson, Fornell, and Mazvancheryl using 200 of the *Fortune* 500 firms across 40 industries showed that a 1 percent change in ACSI (as measured by the American Customer Satisfaction Index on a 0–100 scale) is associated with 1.016 percent change in shareholder value as measured by Tobin's q. This implies that a 1 percent improvement in satisfaction for these firms will lead to an increase in the firm's value of approximately $275 million. Supporting this finding, a similar study by Gruca and Rego found that a 1-point increase in ACSI results in an increase of $55 million in a firm's net operational cash flow next year and a decrease of 4 percent in cash flow variability. In a service-industry study using data from almost 8,000 customers of a national hotel chain, researchers found that return on investment in service quality (e.g., cleanliness) was almost 45 percent. Providing more systematic and recent support, one meta-analysis (including more than 250 satisfaction-performance correlations from over 25 years of empirical studies) also demonstrated that customer satisfaction has a positive and statistically significant effect on firm performance.

Generalization 2: The link between satisfaction and firm performance is asymmetric.

An *asymmetric relationship* means that increases in customer satisfaction do not always have the same impact on firm performance as decreases in customer satisfaction. For example, a study by Anderson and Mittal found that a 1 percent increase in satisfaction led to a 2.37 percent increase in ROI, whereas a 1 percent drop in satisfaction reduced ROI by 5.08 percent (see the figure on next page). Another study by Anderson and Mittal found that a drop in satisfaction produced twice the impact on ROI than an increase in satisfaction. Consistent with these insights, other research also showed that top two-box customer satisfaction scores have the highest impact on customer retention, which in turn is a key driver of firm performance.

Generalization 3: The strength of the satisfaction–profitability link varies across industries as well as across firms within an industry.

The strength of the relationships among customer satisfaction, service quality, and profitability are not consistent across industries. In a study by Ittner and Larcker, the impact was found to be stronger in service industries than in durable and nondurable manufacturing firms. In that study, the ACSI had a positive but insignificant impact on market value of durable and nondurable manufacturing firms and a positive and significant impact on the market value of transportation, utility, and communication firms. The effect was strongly negative for retailers. Another study by Anderson found that trade-offs between customer satisfaction and productivity (e.g., labor productivity) were more likely for services than for goods. Specifically, a simultaneous 1 percent

in a classic multiyear, multicompany study called PIMS (profit impact of marketing strategy). The PIMS research shows that companies offering superior service achieve higher-than-normal market share growth and that service quality influences profits through increased market share and premium prices, as well as lowered costs and less rework.[10]

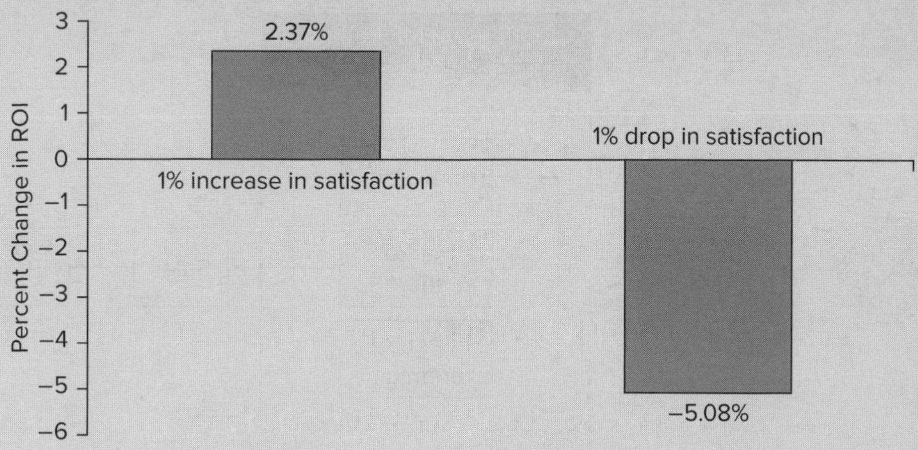

The Asymmetric Relationship between Satisfaction and ROI (Based on 125 Swedish Firms)

Source: E. Anderson and V. Mittal, "Strengthening the Satisfaction-Profit Chain," *Journal of Service Research* 3 (2000), pp. 107–120.

increase in both customer satisfaction and productivity is likely to increase ROI by 0.365 percent for goods, but only 0.22 percent for services.

In addition to the differences found in the studies cited, Anderson et al.'s study found that, while a 1 percent change in satisfaction had an *average* impact of 1.016 percent on shareholder value (Tobin's q), the impact ranged from 2.8 percent for department stores to −0.3 percent for discount stores. Anderson and Mittal's study found that industry characteristics explain 35 percent of the variance in cash flow growth and 54 percent of the variance in cash flow variability. They also found that the influence of customer satisfaction on cash flow growth is greatest for low-involvement, routinized, and frequently purchased products (e.g., beer and fast food). Consistent with these previous insights, the aforementioned meta-analysis (that examined more than 25 years of empirical studies) also showed that the satisfaction-performance effects vary across non-retail versus retail settings (suggesting that the effects for non-retailers are even stronger than for retailers).

While this summary represents a considerable improvement over what we knew in the past, companies are eager to learn more. This general information about the relationships among customer satisfaction, service quality, and financial performance will help them understand that investing in customer satisfaction and service quality is beneficial. Thus, indications are that the investments are worthwhile and that not investing can be harmful to firms.

Sources: A. Edeling, S. Srinivasan, and D. M. Hanssens, "The Marketing–Finance Interface: A New Integrative Review of Metrics, Methods, and Findings and an Agenda for Future Research," *International Journal of Research in Marketing* 38 (December 2021), pp. 857–876; A. S. Otto, D. M. Szymanski, and R. Varadarajan, "Customer Satisfaction and Firm Performance: Insights from Over a Quarter Century of Empirical Research," *Journal of the Academy of Marketing Science* 48 (May 2020), pp. 543–564; E. De Haan, P. C. Verhoef, and T. Wiesel, "The Predictive Ability of Different Customer Feedback Metrics for Retention," *International Journal of Research in Marketing* 32 (June 2015), pp. 195–206; S. Gupta and V. Zeithaml, "Customer Metrics and Their Impact on Financial Performance," *Marketing Science* 25 (November–December 2006), pp. 718–739; E. Anderson, C. Fornell, and S. Mazvancheryl, "Customer Satisfaction and Shareholder Value," *Journal of Marketing* 68 (2004), pp. 172–185; C. Ittner and D. Larcker, "Are Non-Financial Measures Leading Indicators of Financial Performance? An Analysis of Customer Satisfaction," *Journal of Accounting Research* 36, no. 3, (1998), pp. 1–35; R. Rust, A. Zahorik, and T. Keiningham, "Return on Quality (ROQ): Making Service Quality Financially Accountable," *Journal of Marketing* 59 (1995) pp. 58–70; T. S. Gruca and L. L. Rego, "Customer Satisfaction, Cash Flow and Shareholder Value," *Journal of Marketing* 69 (2005), pp. 115–130; E. Anderson and V. Mittal, "Strengthening the Satisfaction-Profit Chain," *Journal of Service Research* 3 (2000), pp. 107–120.

One key rationale for the impact of service on market share is that satisfied customers spread positive word of mouth, which leads to the attraction of new customers and then to higher market share. Importantly, research also suggests that advertising service excellence without sufficient quality to back up the communications will not increase market share (which addresses the key issues underlying Gap 4).[11]

FIGURE 17.2 Offensive Marketing Effects of Service on Profits

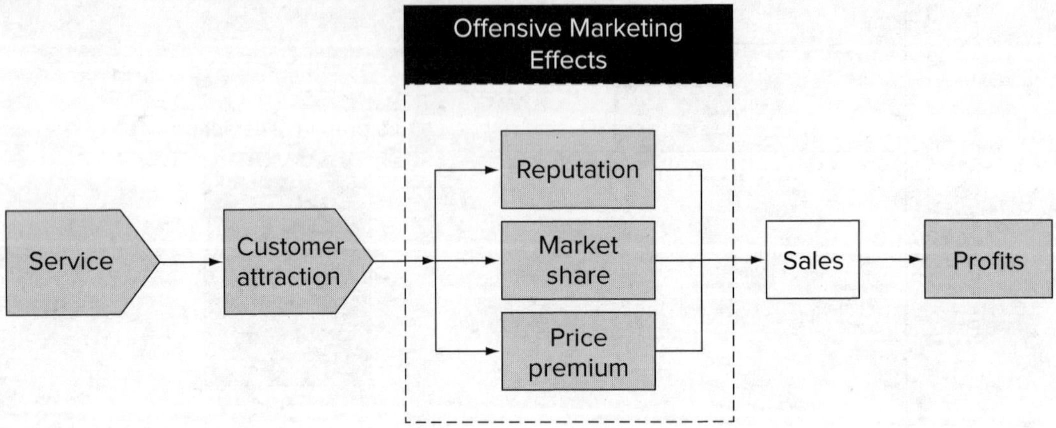

DEFENSIVE MARKETING EFFECTS OF SERVICE: CUSTOMER RETENTION

When it comes to keeping the customers a firm already has—an approach called *defensive marketing*[12]—researchers and consultants have in the past 30 years documented and quantified the financial impact of existing customers. Customer defection is costly to companies because new customers must replace lost customers, and replacement comes at a high cost. Getting new customers is expensive; it involves advertising, promotion, and sales costs, as well as start-up operating expenses. New customers are often unprofitable for a period of time after acquisition. In the insurance industry, for example, the insurer does not typically recover selling costs until the third or fourth year of the relationship. Capturing customers from other companies is also an expensive proposition.

In general, the longer a customer remains with a company, the more profitable the relationship is for the organization:

> Served correctly, customers generate increasingly more profits each year they stay with a company. Across a wide range of businesses, the pattern is the same: the longer a company keeps a customer, the more money it stands to make.[13]

For example, one study examined this question using a financial services company's internal records. Researchers tested the service–profit chain framework (described in Chapter 11) and examined the links among customer satisfaction, service quality, and share-of-wallet measures to data on customer retention and customer profitability. Most notably, the study found that different levels of share of wallet generated different levels of customer profitability and that the relationship between share of wallet and profitability varies over time. This more complicated answer to the relationship between service quality and profitability hints at what we are going to describe later in this chapter: that the relationship sometimes is not direct or straightforward.

Research on the topic of lost customers has examined the defensive marketing effects of service. One study indicated that traditional ways of examining defensive effects may be inappropriate for markets involving new services because they fail to account for the social effects (e.g., word of mouth and imitation) that can influence future customer acquisitions. That study showed how the impact of a lost customer on the profitability of the firm depends on (a) whether the customer defects

FIGURE 17.3 **Defensive Marketing Effects of Service on Profits**

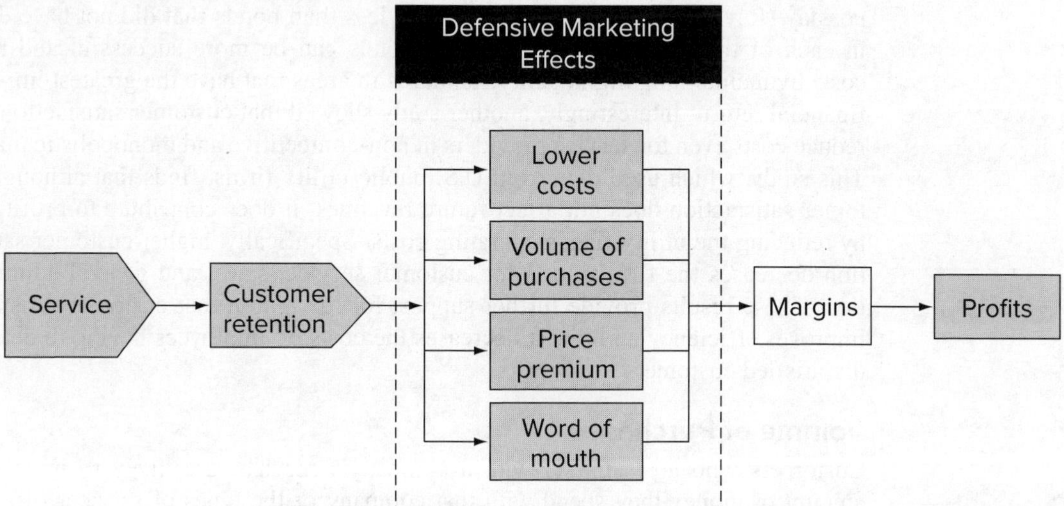

to a competing firm or stops using the service altogether and (b) when the customer stops using the service—such distinctions are often overlooked in conventional studies. These results demonstrate how the value of a lost customer changes throughout the product life cycle, showing that the loss of an early adopter costs a firm much more than the loss of a later adopter.[14]

The money a company makes from retention comes from four sources (shown in Figure 17.3): lower costs, volume of purchases, price premium, and word-of-mouth communication. This section provides corresponding (illustrative) evidence for these four sources from empirical research.

Lower Costs

Attracting a new customer is typically (considerably) more costly than retaining an existing one. Consultants who have focused on these relationships assert that customer defections have a stronger effect on a company's profits than market share, scale, unit costs, and other factors usually associated with competitive advantage.[15] The link between service quality and lowering costs for companies is illustrated by the following insights:

- "Our highest quality day was our lowest cost of operations day" (Fred Smith, founder and chairman of FedEx).
- "Our costs of not doing things right the first time were from 25 to 30 percent of our revenue" (David F. Colicchio, Hewlett-Packard Company).[16]
- Bain and Company, a consulting firm specializing in retention research, estimated in one of its studies that, in the life insurance business, a 5 percent annual increase in customer retention lowers a company's costs per policy by 18 percent.

Research studies also confirm the lower costs that relate to higher service quality. For example, one study looked at the relationship between three years of service quality and operational performance data from 1,135 franchised Holiday Inn hotels. The purpose was to determine the relationship between service quality, operational performance, and costs. Hotels with defects—at least one quality defect in the exterior, the guest room, and the guest bath—had a revenue per available room per day (RevPAR) of approximately $2.80 less than hotels that did not have defects in each of the areas. This implies that hotels can be more successful and reduce costs by maintaining high quality standards in areas that have the greatest impact on financial return. Interestingly, another study showed that customer satisfaction helps reduce costs even for service providers in non-competitive and monopolistic markets. This study, which used data from U.S. public utility firms, finds that although customer satisfaction does not affect future revenues, it does contribute to profitability by reducing the utility firm's operating costs. Specifically, higher customer satisfaction decreases the firm's costs for customer service, sales, and general administration. These results provide further support for the notion that customer satisfaction improves efficiency and that it decreases the costs of employees having to deal with dissatisfied customers.[17]

Volume of Purchases

Customers who are satisfied with a company's services are likely to increase the amount of money they spend with that company or the types of services offered. A customer satisfied with a broker's services, for example, will likely invest more money when it becomes available. Similarly, a customer satisfied with a bank's checking services is likely to open a savings account with the same bank and to use the bank's loan services.

Price Premium

Most of the service quality leaders in industry command higher prices than their competitors: FedEx collects more for overnight delivery than the U.S. Postal Service, Hertz rental cars cost more than Avis cars, and staying at the Ritz-Carlton is a more expensive undertaking than staying at the Hyatt. Therefore, offering high service quality often pays for itself in price increases.

Word-of-Mouth Communication

Because word-of-mouth communication is considered more credible than other sources of information, the best type of promotion for a service may come from other customers who advocate the services provided by the company. Word-of-mouth communication brings new customers to the firm, and the financial value of this form of advocacy can be calibrated by the company in terms of the promotional costs it saves as well as the streams of revenue from new customers. In fact, researchers have developed models of customer lifetime value, in which they can quantify the monetary worth of word-of-mouth communications, called *referral values,* for different segments of consumers.[18] As discussed in Exhibit 17.2, many companies are now using the extent of word of mouth as their main measure of customer loyalty.

A research study examined how firms were actively using referral marketing campaigns to channel the power of word of mouth and to increase referrals to acquire new customers. The research used a method of computing the value of referrals using a customer's actual past referral behavior to assess customer referral value (CRV). They identified the most effective methods of targeting the most promising customers on the basis of their customer lifetime value (CLV) and CRV scores. They were able to identify that firms could maximize profitability by using both CLV and CRV scores, demonstrating the value of word of mouth.[19]

Word-of-mouth communications are especially important for services high in experience qualities (where the customer must experience the service to determine its

Exhibit 17.2 Word-of-Mouth Communication and Customer Measurement: The Net Promoter Score

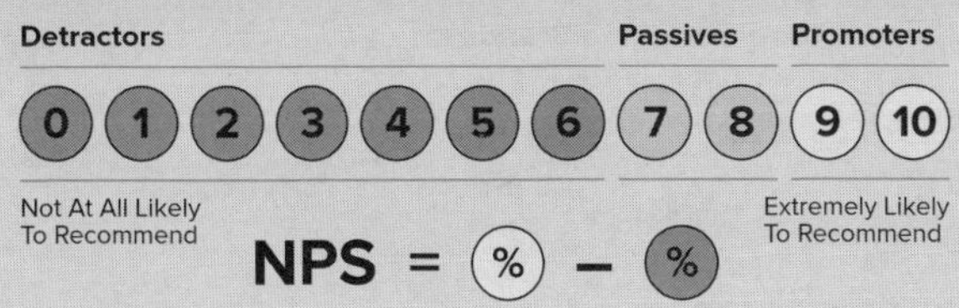

Many different methods of customer measurement—customer satisfaction, service quality, loyalty, and retention for example—have been used to predict a firm's financial performance. One metric that has become popular yet controversial in recent years is called the *Net Promoter Score* (NPS). The score, developed by loyalty expert Frederick Reichheld, is based on the idea that word of mouth communication, rather than any of the other metrics, is the best predictor of growth and therefore financial performance.

The score itself is based on just one survey question: Would you recommend us to a friend or colleague? To get the NPS, a company asks consumers about the likelihood (out of 10) that they would recommend the company, and then subtracts the proportion of "detractors" (who rate the company at 6 or lower) from the proportion of "promoters" (who rate the company at 9 or 10). For example, if a company surveys 1,000 customers, and the results show 60 percent promoters, 10 percent passives, and 30 percent detractors, the NPS would be 30 (60% − 30% = 30%).

Many prestigious firms use the NPS; General Electric, American Express, Microsoft, Intuit, and The Progressive Corporation are but a few companies that have adopted the approach. The popularity of the Net Promoter Score comes in large part because the approach is simple. To top management, long confused by the growing complexity of customer measurement and how to apply it, the idea of having just one number on which to focus is very appealing. And the measure is intuitive—if customers like the firm or its service enough to talk about it to others, that signals a stronger bond than merely being satisfied. The Net Promoter Score became, in essence, a "magic number" for companies.

HOW DO COMPANIES MEASURE UP ON THE NET PROMOTER SCORE?

In many firms promoters barely outnumber detractors, giving them NPS scores of only 5 to 10 percent. Worse yet, many firms and industries have negative Net Promoter Scores, which means that they are constantly creating detractors. Some firms shine, however, and the following charts (below) indicate some of the stars (brands and industries).

CONTROVERSY: IS THE NET PROMOTER INDEX SUPERIOR, APPROPRIATE, OR COMPLETE?

While executives are embracing the Net Promoter Score, researchers and many loyalty experts question the superiority, appropriateness, and completeness of the metric. For example, one researcher questioned, convincingly, whether word of mouth would be a better driver of growth than other factors like reducing customer loss or increasing current customers' volume through cross-sales and share of category purchase. More dramatically, would actions driven to increase word of mouth create stronger growth than actions to acquire profitable new customers?

Another key concern is the extent to which word of mouth is a relevant goal for all products and services in all contexts. Consumers feel strongly about some products and services and these feelings drive word of mouth. Services (such as restaurants, vacations, and entertainment), fashions, and new electronic products are referral-worthy products. However, the majority of products and services are unlikely to be interesting enough for customers to talk about them. From a practical standpoint, while using a single number alone provides a sign of health, as a thermometer would do in signaling body temperature, it neither diagnoses firm problems nor describes how to treat them. To be actionable, companies must follow up with metrics that also contain other questions (such as those we described in Chapter 5 of this textbook) to identify what customers expect and perceive about the company. In the past years, Satmetrix (one company that administers NPS) has added a small number of additional questions such as "value for the money" to its questions. However, this and other very general questions are not diagnostic.

The predictive qualities of the NPS have also been put to the test by other researchers. One team of loyalty experts matched the way that NPS was calculated using two to three years' worth of data from 21 companies and 15,500 interviews. While they expected that the findings would replicate what Reichheld had found, they did not. Furthermore, when comparing the results to the American Customer Satisfaction Index (ACSI), this team also found that NPS had no clear superiority to other measures. Another study on the subject does confirm a strong correlation between word of mouth and growth, but cannot confirm causality. Overall, research suggests that, although the original idea of the NPS is reasonable, methodological concerns identified by

(*continued*)

Exhibit 17.2 (concluded)

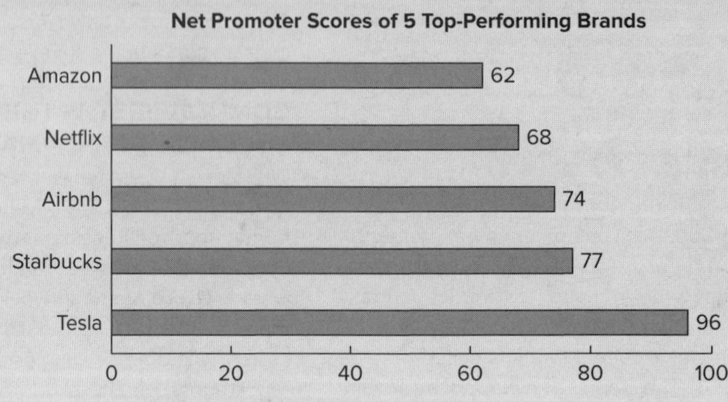

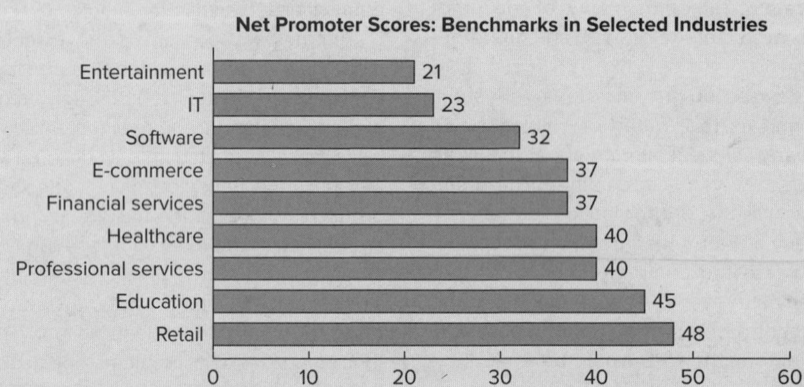

Source: https://survicate.com/nps-benchmarks/, accessed March 24, 2022.

academics are valid, and managers need to be aware of these limitations when using the NPS.

THE BOTTOM LINE

Loyalty expert Timothy Keiningham dismisses the quest for one magical number to measure loyalty, including NPS as a single number:

> "Even the best ideas aren't universal. If they were, everybody would do them and they would already be known. You need to know what is the number one demonstration of loyalty from your customers, then model back from that—what causes that to happen and what causes that to break? And once you start thinking about it that way, you realize there isn't going to be a magic number because this is driven by different things depending on what industry you are in."

Sources: S. Baehre, M. O'Dwyer, L. O'Malley, and N. Lee, "The Use of Net Promoter Score (NPS) to Predict Sales Growth: Insights From an Empirical Investigation," *Journal of the Academy of Marketing Science* 50 (January 2022), pp. 67–84; N. I. Fisher and R. E. Kordupleski, "Good and Bad Market Research: A Critical Review of Net Promoter Score," *Applied Stochastic Models in Business and Industry* 35 (January 2019), pp. 138–151; F. Reichheld and R. Markey, "The Ultimate Question 2.0: How Net Promoter Companies Thrive in a Customer Driven World," *Harvard Business School Press,* 2011; D. Grisaffe, "Guru Misses the Mark with 'One Number' Fallacy," www.netpromter.com, accessed 2011; www.creatingloyalty.com/story.cfm?article_id=656, accessed September 2007; T. Keiningham, B. Cooil, T. Andreassen, and L. Aksoy, "A Longitudinal Examination of Net Promoter and Firm Revenue Growth," *Journal of Marketing* (July 2007), pp. 39–51; http://blog.satmetrix.com/2015-consumer-nps-benchmarks-study-part-iii-entertainment-telecom, accessed July 19, 2016; N. Morgan, L. L. Rego, "The Value of Different Customer Satisfaction and Loyalty Metrics in Predicting Business Performance," *Marketing Science,* May–June 2008.

Exhibit 17.3 Service Quality and the Economic Worth of Customers: Businesses Still Need to Know More

Topic	Key Questions
Service quality and profitability: the direct relationship	1. What methodologies need to be developed to allow companies to capture the effect of service quality on profit within individual companies? 2. What measures are necessary to examine the relationship in a consistent, valid, and reliable manner? 3. How and why does the relationship between service quality and profitability vary by industry, country, category of business, or other variable? What does this imply for investment in service quality? 4. What are the moderating factors of the relationship between service quality and profitability? 5. What is the optimal spending level on service in order to affect profitability?
Offensive effects of service quality	1. What is the optimal amount of spending on service quality to obtain offensive effects? 2. To obtain offensive effects, are expenditures on advertising or service quality itself more effective? 3. In what ways can companies signal high service quality to customers to obtain offensive effects?
Defensive effects of service quality	1. What is a loyal customer? 2. What is the role of service in defensive marketing? 3. How does service compare in effectiveness to other retention strategies such as price? 4. What levels of service provision are needed to retain customers? 5. How can the effects of word-of-mouth communication from retained customers be quantified? 6. What aspects of service are most important for customer retention? 7. How can defection-prone customers be identified and then retained?
Perceptions of service quality	1. What is the relationship between customer purchase intentions and initial purchase behavior in services? 2. What is the relationship between behavioral intentions and repurchase in services? 3. Does the degree of association between service quality and behavior change at different quality levels?
Identifying the key drivers of service quality, customer retention, and profits	1. Which service encounters are most responsible for perceptions of service quality? 2. What are the key drivers of service quality, customer retention, and profits in each service encounter? 3. Where should investments be made to affect service quality, purchase, retention, and profits? 4. Are key drivers of service quality the same as key drivers of behavioral intentions, customer retention, and profits?

quality) and credence qualities (where the customer may not be able to determine the quality of the service even after it is delivered).[20]

Many questions remain about defensive marketing, among them the ones shown in Exhibit 17.3. Although research has come a long way, researchers and companies must continue working on these questions for a more complete understanding of the impact of service on defensive marketing.

CUSTOMER PERCEPTIONS OF SERVICE QUALITY AND PURCHASE INTENTIONS

In Chapter 4 we highlighted the links among customer satisfaction, service quality, and increased purchases. Here we provide more empirical evidence supporting these relationships. For example, pioneering researchers at Xerox offered a compelling insight into the relationship between satisfaction and purchase intentions during the company's early years of customer satisfaction research. Initially, the company focused on satisfied customers, which they identified as those checking either a "4" or a "5" on a 5-point satisfaction scale. Careful analysis of the data showed that customers giving Xerox 5s were six times more likely to indicate that they would-repurchase Xerox equipment than those giving 4s. This insight encouraged the company to focus on increasing the 5s rather than the 4s *and* 5s because of the strong sales and profitability implications.[21] A more encompassing update of the importance of scoring in the "top box" of customer satisfaction is shown in Figure 17.4. TARP Worldwide Inc. found similar results across 10 studies incorporating 8,000 customers worldwide. A full 96 percent of customers who report being "very satisfied" (i.e., they are in the *top box* in satisfaction) say they will "definitely repurchase" from the same company. When they are only "somewhat satisfied," the number drops to only 52 percent, and only 7 percent of customers who are "neutral or very dissatisfied" will definitely repurchase.[22]

Evidence also shows that customer satisfaction and service quality perceptions affect consumer intentions to behave in many positive ways—praising the firm, preferring the company over others, increasing volume of purchases, or agreeably paying a price premium.

Corresponding studies have found relationships between service quality and more specific behavioral intentions. One study involving university students found strong links between service quality and other behavioral intentions of strategic importance to a university, including behavior such as saying positive things about the school, planning to contribute money upon graduation, and planning to recommend

FIGURE 17.4
Top-Box Scores, Repurchase Intentions, and Referral Intentions

Source: Information Courtesy of *TARP Worldwide*, 2007.

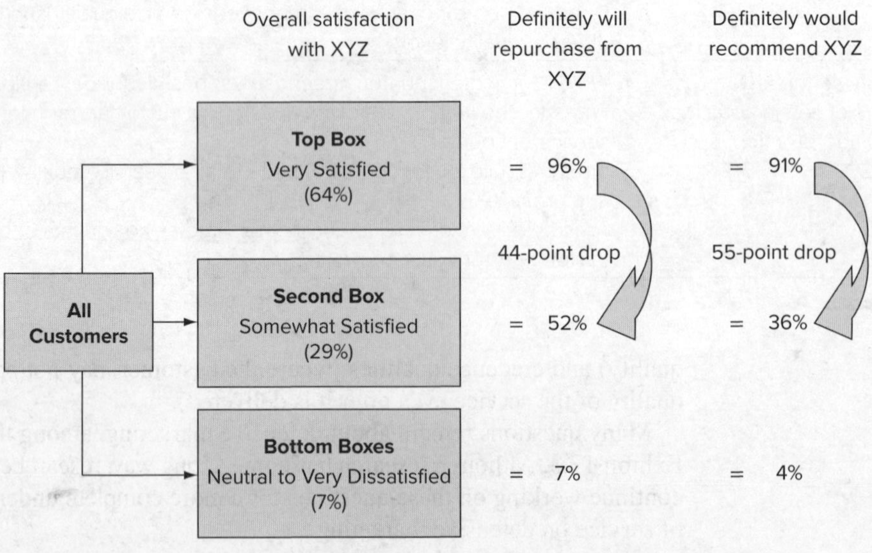

FIGURE 17.5
The Effects of Service on Behavioral Intentions and Behavior

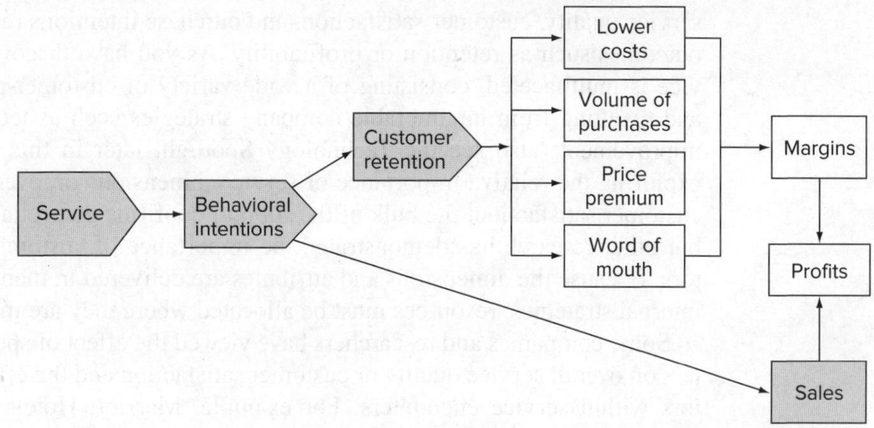

the school to employers as a place from which to recruit.[23] Another comprehensive study examined a battery comprised of 13 specific behavioral intentions (such as saying positive things about the company, remaining loyal to the company, and spending more with the company) likely to result from perceived service quality. The overall measure was significantly correlated with customer perceptions of service quality.[24] Figure 17.5 shows these other relationships.

THE KEY DRIVERS OF SERVICE QUALITY, CUSTOMER RETENTION, AND PROFITS

Understanding the relationship between overall service quality and profitability is important, but it is perhaps more useful to managers to identify specific drivers of service quality that most relate to profitability (shown in Figure 17.6). Doing so will help firms understand what aspects of service quality to change to influence the relationship and, therefore, where to invest resources.

Most evidence for this issue has come from examining the effects of specific service attributes (e.g., responsiveness, reliability, assurance, and tangibles) on overall

FIGURE 17.6
The Key Drivers of Service Quality, Customer Retention, and Profits

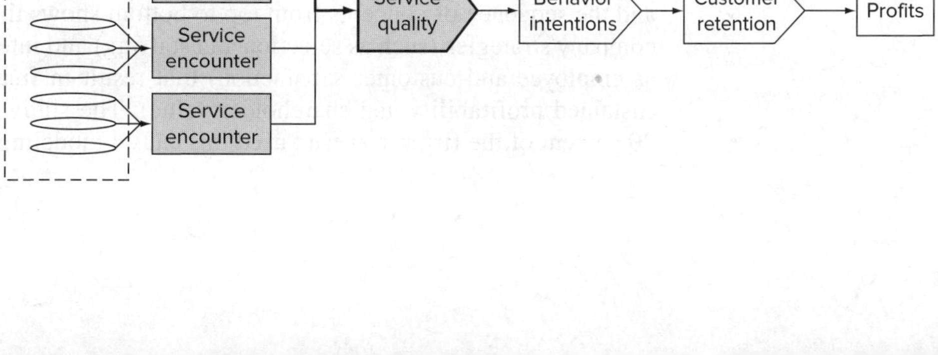

service quality, customer satisfaction, and purchase intentions rather than on financial outcomes such as retention or profitability. As you have discovered in this text, service is multifaceted, consisting of a wide variety of customer-perceived dimensions and resulting from innumerable company strategies such as technology and process improvement (also see the Technology Spotlight later in this chapter). In research exploring the relative importance of service dimensions on overall service quality or customer satisfaction, the bulk of the support confirms that reliability is most critical; but other research has demonstrated the importance of customization and other factors. Because the dimensions and attributes are delivered in many cases with different internal strategies, resources must be allocated where they are most needed.[25]

Some companies and researchers have viewed the effect of specific service encounters on overall service quality or customer satisfaction and the effect of specific behaviors within service encounters. For example, Marriott Hotels conducted extensive customer research to determine what service elements contribute most to customer loyalty. They found that four of the top five factors came into play in the first 10 minutes of the guest's stay—those that involved the early encounters of arriving, checking in, and entering the hotel rooms. Other companies have found that mistakes or problems that occur in early service encounters are particularly critical, because a failure at early points results in greater risk for dissatisfaction in each ensuing encounter. IBM found that the sales encounter was the most critical of all, in large part because interactions with salespeople establish customer expectations for the remaining service encounters.

Another way of looking at the problem involves investigating the effect of service programs and managerial approaches within an organization on financial measures such as profitability. A customer-focused approach to metrics is described in the Strategy Insight.

Effective Nonfinancial Performance Measurements

According to seminal field research conducted in 60 companies and survey responses from 297 senior executives, many companies do not identify and act on the correct non-financial measures.[26] One example involves a bank that only surveyed the satisfaction of customers who physically entered the branches (rather than all customers, including those who banked by phone or ATM), a policy that caused some branch managers to offer free food and drinks in order to increase their scores. According to the authors of the study, companies make four major mistakes:

1. *Not linking measures to strategy.* Companies can easily identify hundreds of non-financial measures to track, but they also need to use analysis that identifies the most important drivers of their strategy. Successful organizations use value driver maps, tools that lay out the cause-and-effect relationships between drivers and strategic success. Figure 17.7 shows the causal model developed by a successful fast-food chain to understand the key drivers of shareholder value. The factors on the right were identified as most important in leading to the concepts on the left, and the sequence of concepts from top to bottom shows the relationships among company strategies (such as selection and staffing) and intermediate results (such as employee and customer satisfaction) that result in financial results (such as sustained profitability and shareholder value). The study found that fewer than 30 percent of the firms surveyed used this causal modeling approach.

FIGURE 17.7
The Measures That Matter Most: A causal model for a fast-food company shows the critical drivers of performance and the concepts that lead to shareholder value.

Source: Christopher D. Ittner and David F. Larcker, "Coming Up Short on Nonfinancial Performance Measurement," *Harvard Business Review* 81 (November 2003), pp. 88–95.

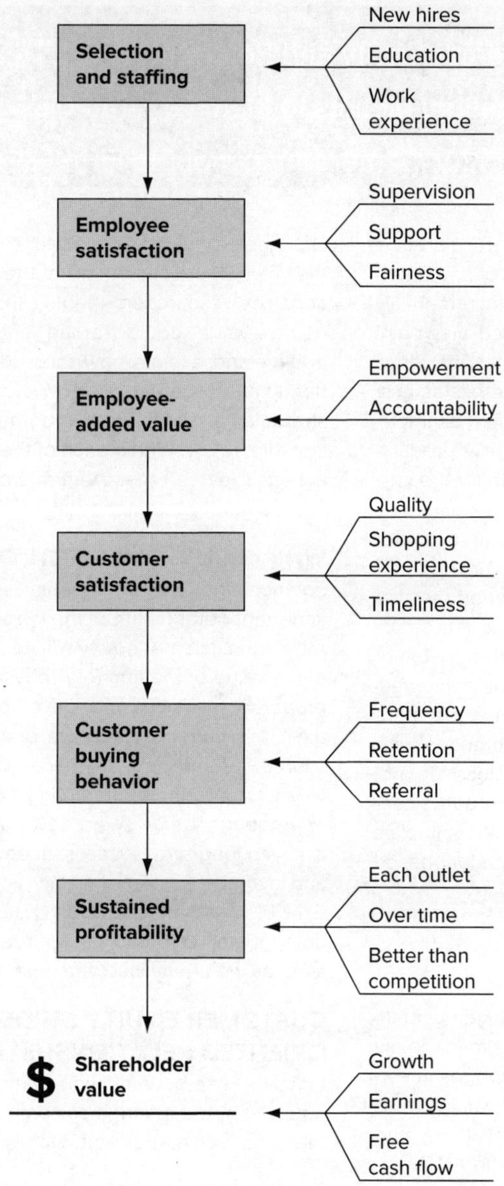

2. *Not validating the links.* Only 21 percent of companies in the study verify that the nonfinancial measures lead to financial performance. Instead, many firms decide what they are going to measure in each category and never link the categories. Many managers believed that the relationships were self-evident instead of conducting analysis to validate the linkages. This chapter's Strategy Insight showed one way that companies can create this type of linkage. In general, it is critical that companies pull together all their data and examine the relationships among the categories.
3. *Not setting the right performance targets.* Companies sometimes aim too high in setting improvement targets. Trying to make all customers 100 percent satisfied

Strategy Insight Customer Equity and Return on Marketing: Metrics to Match a Strategic Customer-Centered View of the Firm

Although the marketing concept has articulated a customer-centered viewpoint since the 1960s, marketing theory and practice have become incrementally customer-centered. This customer-centered viewpoint is now reflected in the concepts and metrics that drive marketing management, including such metrics as customer value and voice of the customer. For example, the concept of brand equity, a fundamentally product-centered concept, served as one inspiration for the customer-centered concept of *customer equity,* defined as the total of the discounted lifetime values summed over all the firm's customers.

In other words, customer equity is obtained by summing up the customer lifetime values of the firm's customers. In fast-moving industries that involve customer relationships, products come and go but customers remain. Customers and customer equity may be more central to many firms than brands and brand equity, although management practices and metrics do not always reflect this reality. The shift from product-centered thinking to customer-centered thinking implies the need for an accompanying shift from product-based metrics to customer-based metrics.

USING CUSTOMER EQUITY IN A STRATEGIC FRAMEWORK

Consider the issues facing a typical marketing manager or marketing-oriented CEO: How do I manage my brand? How will my customers react to changes in service and service quality? Should I raise prices? What is the best way to enhance the relationships with my current customers? Where should I focus my efforts? Determining customer lifetime value, or customer equity, is the first step, but the more important step is to evaluate and test ideas and strategies using lifetime value as the measuring stick. At a very basic level, strategies for building customer relationships can affect five basic factors: retention rate, referrals, sales, direct costs, and marketing costs.

Researchers Roland Rust, Valarie Zeithaml, and Kay Lemon have developed a seminal approach based on customer equity that can help business executives answer their questions. The model that represents this approach is shown in the accompanying figure (on next page). In this context, customer equity is an approach to marketing and corporate strategy that puts the customer—and, more importantly, strategies that grow the value of the customer—at the heart of the organization. The researchers identify the drivers of customer equity—value equity, brand equity, and relationship equity—and explain how these drivers work, independently and together, to grow customer equity. Service strategies are prominent in both value equity and relationship equity. Within each of these drivers are specific actions ("levers") that the firm can take to enhance the firm's overall customer equity.

WHY IS CUSTOMER EQUITY IMPORTANT?

For most firms, customer equity is certain to be the most important determinant of the long-term value of the firm. Although customer equity will not be responsible for the entire value of the firm (e.g., physical assets, intellectual property, research and development competencies), the firm's current customers provide the most reliable source of future revenues and profits—and should provide a focal point for marketing strategy.

Although it may seem obvious that customer equity is key to long-term success, understanding how to grow and manage customer equity is much more complex. Growing customer equity is of utmost importance, and doing it well can lead to significant competitive advantage, as we briefly illustrate next.

CUSTOMER EQUITY GUIDES FUTURE-ORIENTED RELATIONSHIP MARKETING

Firms can use both individual and aggregated customer equity to better manage customer-firm relationships and their entire customer portfolio by:

- *Identifying Customers with High Equity Potential:* Because not all customers have the same level of equity, firms can better identify individual customers based on their equity potential. This is crucial because managers need to decide how to best allocate their limited marketing budgets and resources. Research has demonstrated the financial effectiveness of such equity-guided customer selection.
- *Equity-Guided Investments in Customer Relationships:* Understanding customer equity and customer lifetime value also helps managers decide how much they can invest in attracting and retaining a focal customer to achieve a positive return on investment on their customer portfolio over time. For example, firms

The Customer Equity Model

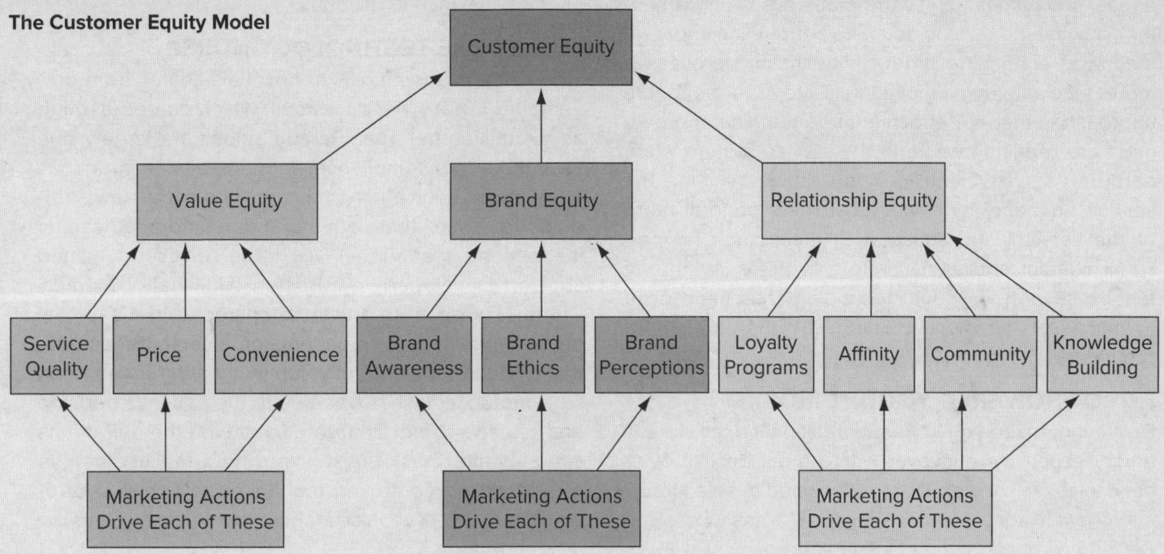

can segment customers into equity-based groups and then execute segment-specific marketing strategies.

- *Equity-Guided Management of Customer Retention and Win Back:* Insights into customer equity can also help managers decide which segments of customers are priorities to retain or to win back if they were lost. For example, if a firm identifies a high-equity customer that seems likely to defect, it can use equity indicators as guidelines to create a tailored retention proposition.

As these brief insights illustrate, the notion of customer equity and customer lifetime value provide companies with a reliable and future-oriented indicator that allows them to deliberately build profitable customer relationships and, thereby, contribute to the firm's financial performance.

CALCULATING RETURN ON MARKETING USING CUSTOMER EQUITY

At the beginning of this chapter, we told you about an approach called return on quality that was developed to help companies understand where they could get the greatest impact from quality investments. A more general form of that approach is called *return on marketing,* which enables companies to look at all competing marketing strategy options and trade them off on the basis of projected financial return. This approach allows companies to not just examine the impact of service on financial return but also compare the impact of service with the impact of branding, price changes, and all other marketing strategies. Using the customer equity model, firms can analyze the drivers that have the greatest impact, compare the drivers' performance with that of competitors' drivers, and project return on investment from improvements in the drivers. The framework enables what-if evaluation of marketing return on investment, which can include such criteria as return on quality, return on advertising, return on loyalty programs, and even return on corporate citizenship, given a particular shift in customer perceptions. This approach enables firms to focus marketing efforts on strategic initiatives that generate the greatest return.

Sources: V. Kumar and B. Rajan, "Customer Lifetime Value: What, How, and Why," In *The Routledge Companion to Strategic Marketing,* 2020, pp. 422–448; V. Kumar and D. Shah (Eds.), *Handbook of Research on Customer Equity in Marketing,* Elgar Publishing, 2015; R. Rust, K. Lemon, and V. Zeithaml, "Return on Marketing: Using Customer Equity to Focus Marketing Strategy," *Journal of Marketing* 68 (January 2004), p. 109; R. Rust, V. Zeithaml, and K. Lemon, *Driving Customer Equity* (New York: The Free Press, 2000); also see: E. de Haan, P. C. Verhoef, and T. Wiesel, "Customer Feedback Metrics for Marketing Accountability," In *Marketing Accountability for Marketing and Non-marketing Outcomes*. Emerald Publishing Limited, 2021.

Technology Spotlight Cost-Effective Service Excellence through Technology

In addition to affecting the top line by increasing revenues, companies across the globe are taking a hard look at what they can to do make bottom-line improvements by enhancing productivity, making processes more efficient, and innovating systems. Among the approaches that are effective in bottom-line improvement are reducing waste in the service system, standardizing service behaviors and actions, shifting the service boundary by having customers perform more of the service, and substituting technology for personal contact and human effort. In this spotlight we feature several ways that technology has been used to make service more efficient and therefore more profitable.

ROBOT-POWERED YOGURT KIOSKS

Delivering frozen yogurt from a traditional retail store is a very expensive endeavor with a great deal of overhead to cover. The next stage, developed to save money and allow customization, were yogurt stores where you decide how much yogurt to buy and how you want to decorate it. Entrepreneurs took this idea to the next level and developed Interactive Robotic Kiosks. One of these innovators was Allan Jones who developed the frozen yogurt kiosk concept Robofusion. This kiosk dispenses yogurt and ice cream with the help of a robotic arm that fills the cup, adds the toppings, and delivers the treat to the customer through a revolving platform. A touchscreen user interface allows the customer to select and customize the product, which sells for between $3 and $6, depending on the size. The company further revised this concept to introduce its Froyo Robot, an unmanned, highly visual "robot" that dispenses frozen yogurt in nine flavors with six possible toppings at a rate of up to 60 servings of frozen yogurt per hour. Robofusion has now been acquired by a franchising company that plans an international market roll-out.

LOUISE THE TECHNOLOGY NURSE

One of the highest costs in hospitals comes from preventable 30-day re-admissions, which can be as high as 4.4 million per year. Re-admissions are largely due to patient noncompliance with hospital instructions about medication and home care. One of the new strategies to assure that patients understand posthospital instructions is a "Virtual Discharge Advocate" named Louise. Developed by Boston University Medical Center, Louise is an animated character that explains medical instructions to patients on a computer screen, thereby carefully and fully communicating home care. On a laptop, Louise is wheeled to the patient's bedside and reviews the discharge packet with them. Patients can ask and re-ask questions using a touchscreen. In a randomized controlled trial linked to Louise's introduction in 2008, Louise helped cut re-admissions by 30 percent.

A CAUTIONARY TALE: THE HENN NA HOTEL IN JAPAN

The Henn na Hotel in Tokyo became famous in 2015 as the world's first hotel staffed by robots. Designed to achieve the ultimate in efficiency, the hotel used advanced technologies and more than 240 robots to maximize efficiency while also adding to the fun and comfort of the guests' stays. For example, guests were greeted at the front desk by multilingual robots as shown below; other robots stored the guest luggage for customers.

Despite the initial appeal of this concept, the hotel's management became concerned over time because the

might seem to be a desirable goal, but many companies expend far too many resources to gain too little improvement in satisfaction. The study's authors found that a telecommunications company aiming for customers who were completely satisfied was wasting resources because these customers spent no more money than those who were 80 percent satisfied.[27]

4. *Measuring incorrectly.* Companies need to use metrics with statistical validity and reliability. Organizations cannot measure complex phenomenon with one or two

Oleksandr Rupeta/NurPhoto/Getty Images

robots caused service failures and annoyed some of the guests. For example, guests complained that their robotic in-room assistants (a device similar to Amazon echo) interpreted snoring as guests' commands and woke them up during the night. Other guests were unhappy because the robots working the front desk were sometimes unable to answer even basic questions. Such issues not only created additional work for the human employees, who had to recover from the service failures and/or repair malfunctioning robots, but also generated additional costs for the hotel. Ultimately, the hotel realized that the costs of employing the robots became prohibitive. Management therefore decided to "fire" more than half of its robots in 2019 and returned to traditional human service providers in many front-line functions. However, the hotel maintained a number of robots in areas where they could be effective and efficient.

ORGANIZATIONAL AMBIDEXTERITY TO COMBINE COST-EFFECTIVE SERVICE EXCELLENCE AND TECHNOLOGY

Service excellence and cost-effectiveness do not need to be conflicting goals and some organizations achieve both (e.g., Amazon, Singapore Airlines, The Vanguard Group). The idea of organizational ambidexterity proposes that service excellence and cost-effectiveness can exist at the same time. As illustrated above, robotics and artificial intelligence (AI) in service operations *can* help achieve this dual focus, but technology is not a "silver bullet." Despite the Henn na Hotel's experience, robot- and AI-delivered services are expected to offer superior economies of scale and scope in the near future. Physical robots will become cheaper than human employees over time; virtual robots or chatbots are already available at very low costs. Clearly, emerging technologies in the field of robotics and AI need to improve the organization's profitability or companies will have no incentive to use them.

Sources: J. Wirtz and V. Zeithaml, "Cost-Effective Service Excellence," *Journal of the Academy of Marketing Science* 46 (January 2018), pp. 59–80; J. Yang and E. Chew, "A Systematic Review for Service Humanoid Robotics Model in Hospitality," *International Journal of Social Robotics* 13 (September 2021), pp. 1397–1410; L. Landro, "Don't Come Back, Hospitals Say," *The Wall Street Journal,* June 7, 2011; Agency for Healthcare Research and Quality 2011, hospitalcompare.gov, accessed August 2011; N. Gagliordi, "Robot-Powered Kiosks Seek Yogurt Domination," *Kiosk Marketplace,* February 26, 2014, http://www.kioskmarketplace.com/articles/robot-powered-kiosks-seek-frozen -yogurt-domination/; K. Pendrell, "This Machine Creates Custom Yogurt Creations on Demand," *Trend Hunter,* March 11, 2016, http://www.trendhunter.com/trends/automated-frozen-yogurt.

simple measures, nor can they use inconsistent methodologies to measure the same concept, such as customer satisfaction. Another problem that companies may encounter is trying to use quantitative metrics to capture qualitative results for important factors such as leadership and innovation.

Creating a balanced scorecard in and of itself does not improve performance. Companies will not reap the benefits of techniques such as the balanced scorecard unless they address these four issues.

Indian Service Strategy Insight Airtel's Winning Formula – Customer Centricity, Empowerment and Innovation

Airtel's success has been primarily driven by an unwavering customer-centric approach. The company's innovative "outsourcing based business model", during the early 2000s, helped it save costs by outsourcing networks management, IT as well as call center operations. The freed up financial resources were strategically deployed for enhancing customer experience, product innovation and brand building. As one of India's pioneering mobile network providers, Airtel partnered with global telecom giants like BT, Telecom Italia, Vivendi, and Singtel, allowing it to focus on customer-centric initiatives rather than infrastructure management. This approach enabled Airtel to develop innovative products like "Hello Tunes" and "Lifetime Prepaid" that responded directly to customer needs to secure their trust and loyalty. The model proved highly successful, and Airtel transformed from an "entrepreneur-led professional-backed company to a professional-led entrepreneur-backed entity," ultimately positioning itself as India's preferred telecom service provider. As Sunil Bharti Mittal, Founder and Chairman, Bharti Enterprises emphasizes, "our absolute focus on the customer" has allowed Airtel to maintain customer loyalty even during intense market disruptions. This was evident when customers stayed with Airtel despite competitors offering services at significantly lower prices or even for free. This customer loyalty translates directly to financial stability, with the company maintaining a subscriber base of more than 400 million in India, positioning it as one of the world's leading telecom companies.

Strategic network investments have been another cornerstone of Airtel's success. Mittal's philosophy that telecom is "only about three things... network, network, network" has guided their capital allocation decisions. The company made bold early investments in technology, deploying 4G networks four years in 2012 before competitor Reliance Jio and quickly adopting 5G technology. These forward-looking investments, though initially questioned even internally, proved crucial for survival against aggressive competition. The network focus has also enabled innovative offerings like the recreation of historical cricket matches in immersive 4K over 5G networks, demonstrating practical applications of their technological capabilities.

Airtel's distinctive approach to talent management has created a uniquely empowered corporate culture. Breaking industry norms, the company recruited heavily from consumer-packaged goods (CPG) backgrounds rather than just technical fields, bringing in professionals who understood brand-building, customer behavior, and distribution. This created what Mittal describes as "a combination of Unilever and Bharti, where you get the experience of working for an MNC and an entrepreneurial company." The culture of empowerment allowed employees to "take decisions freely and fearlessly," contributing to innovation and agility in responding to market challenges.

Source: Source from Stock Images

In recent years, Airtel has implemented a deliberate ARPU (Average Revenue Per User) enhancement strategy. Rather than competing solely on price, the company has focused on high-value customers, even shedding over 49 million low-value subscribers in 2018 to improve service quality for better-paying customers. This strategy includes eliminating lower-priced plans, using AI-based credit scoring to transition prepaid customers to postpaid, and aggressively targeting the home broadband segment with its potential for higher ARPU. These initiatives have strengthened Airtel's financial position by prioritizing quality revenue over mere subscriber counts.

Diversification beyond consumer telecom into enterprise services has provided additional revenue stability. Airtel Business, the enterprise connectivity arm, reported substantial revenue in 2023 with a market share of 33.67%, serving over 1,000 global enterprises and millions of small and medium businesses. The company has also expanded into digital financial services through partnerships like the Axis Bank collaboration, offering co-branded credit cards, loans, and Airtel Payments Bank's DigiGold investment platform. This ecosystem approach creates multiple revenue streams and increases customer stickiness through integrated services, enhancing overall customer lifetime value.

Reference

https://www.airtel.in/airtel-annual-report-2023-24/
https://www.airtel.in/airtel-annual-report-2019-20/standing-tall.php
https://webengage.com/emagazine/experts-speak/customer-lifetime-value-airtel-anshul-agarwal/
https://medium.com/@Amal_PV/the-telecom-titans-how-reliance-jio-and-bharti-airtel-are-shaping-indias-telecom-landscape-f618d82ade5
https://www.businesstoday.in/magazine/interview/story/airtel-belongs-to-the-people-who-work-there-sunil-bharati-mittal-on-airtel-diversification-and-more-420897-2024-03-11
https://thekarostartup.com/sunil-bharati-mittal-shares-airtels-success/

Global Feature Customer Satisfaction and Customer Lifetime Value Worldwide

The American Customer Satisfaction Index (ACSI) was created in 1994, derived from a model originally implemented in 1989 in Sweden called the Swedish Customer Satisfaction Barometer (SCSB).

The methodology from the American Customer Satisfaction Index is rapidly being adopted around the world. Developers include research groups, quality associations, and universities that participate in ACSI's international licensing program, called Global CSI^{SM}. Countries in Europe (using what is called the Extended Performance Satisfaction Index), as well as Asia, South America, and the Middle East, have created customer satisfaction indexes for their own national economies by using Global CSI^{SM}. For example, countries that have adopted ACSI include Turkey, Mexico, South Korea, Sweden, Colombia, Barbados, and Singapore. The Customer Satisfaction Index of Singapore (CSISG) was launched in 2008. According to Caroline Lim, director of The Institute of Service Excellence, Singapore Management University, just as "ACSI has been the de facto standardized measure of customer satisfaction in the United States economy since 1994," CSISG was developed using the same proven and respected methodology to "complement the other traditional forms of measure of the quantity of economic output such as GDP to provide a more holistic picture of the Singapore economy."

Other countries are evaluating the implementation of ACSI-based models. If this trend continues, it may be possible to create an international system of customer satisfaction measurement using a common methodology to allow cross-national satisfaction and comparisons. While reaching firm conclusions is still premature because most economies do not yet measure customer satisfaction using this general approach, a recent study reveals interesting cross-national determinants of satisfaction:

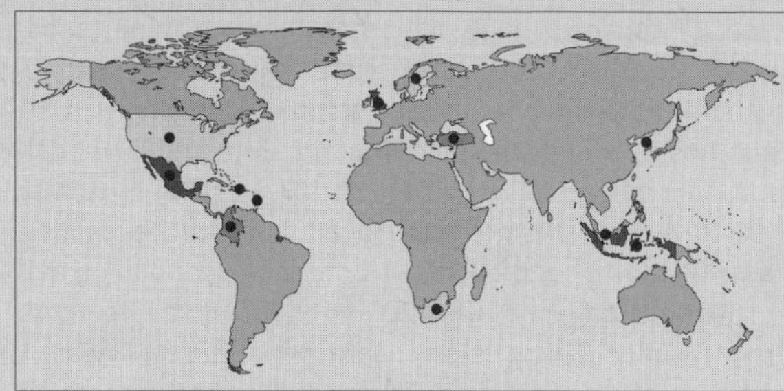

Source: American Customer Satisfaction Index website.

- Consumers in self-expressive societies have higher levels of customer satisfaction than those in societies with survival values.
- Literacy rate, trade freedom, and business freedom have a positive effect on customer satisfaction.
- Per capita gross domestic product has a negative effect on customer satisfaction.

CULTURE INFLUENCES CUSTOMER LIFETIME VALUE

Because this chapter focuses on the bottom-line impact of services marketing, it is pivotal to note that the global

Summary

This chapter is divided into five sections, each of which assesses the evidence and identifies what is currently known about the relationship between service and profitability. The chapter used a conceptual framework to link all the variables in these topics: (1) the direct relationship between service and profits; (2) offensive effects of service quality, the ability to obtain new customers; (3) defensive effects of service quality, the ability to retain existing customers; (4) the relationship between service quality and purchase intentions; and (5) key drivers of service quality, customer retention, and profits. Considerable progress has been made in the investigation of service quality, profitability, and the economic worth of customers, but managers are still lacking many of the answers that would help them make informed decisions about service quality investments. The chapter also discussed approaches to measuring loyalty, including the popular Net Promoter Score, and to measuring return on marketing using the customer equity model. The chapter concluded with a discussion of the balanced performance scorecard approach to measuring corporate performance, which offers a strategic approach for measuring all aspects of a company's performance.

effect of service quality affects not only customer satisfaction but also customer lifetime value. For example, research from a global retailer sampled customers in 30 countries over six years and found that country-level cultural dimensions influence multiple drivers of customer lifetime value (CLV); more specifically, the study examined how Hofstede's cultural dimensional scores for each country influence drivers of CLV. Countries vary in their culture, thereby influencing customer intentions and behavior. A selection of the many findings related to the influence of culture follows (see Kumar and Pansari 2016 for all direct and indirect effects):

- **Individualism**: In countries that score low on Hofstede's individualism dimension, consumers are more likely to shop not only for themselves but also for members of their families. Consequently, consumers are more willing to explore new departments of the same store they frequent, which prompts cross-buying and ultimately increases purchase frequency and contribution margin for the firm.
- **Uncertainty Avoidance**: Consumers in countries that score high on Hofstede's uncertainty avoidance aim to reduce risk. Therefore, they are more likely to buy through traditional channels (e.g., stores) rather than through online channels or catalogs. High levels of uncertainty avoidance have a negative effect on consumers' multichannel shopping and ultimately reduce purchase frequency and contribution margin for the firm.
- **Masculinity**: The higher a country scores on Hofstede's masculinity dimension, the less likely consumers cross-buy in other departments of the same store. In other words, consumers in a highly masculine culture are more likely to buy from multiple stores rather than from multiple departments of the same stores. Therefore, high levels of masculinity reduce purchase frequency and contribution margin for the firm.
- **Indulgence**: Consumers in cultures that score high on Hofstede's indulgence dimension tend to seek immediate gratification. They tend to prefer traditional channels (stores) to instantly experience the focal product. In addition, consumers in highly indulgent cultures are more likely to try new and creative things. Taken together, high levels of indulgence increase cross-buying and thereby elicit a positive effect on purchase frequency and contribution margin.

This brief discussion illustrates how crucial it is for managers to consider the impact of culture on a firm's financial performance and profits. With the continued trend toward a global marketplace, it is ever more critical for marketers to understand their customers worldwide.

Sources: https://www.theacsi.org/products/global-csi/, accessed March 2022; V. Kumar and A. Pansari, "National Culture, Economy, and Customer Lifetime Value: Assessing the Relative Impact of the Drivers of Customer Lifetime Value for a Global Retailer," *Journal of International Marketing* 24 (March 2016), pp. 1–21; F. V. Morgeson III, S. Mithas, T. L. Keiningham, and L. Aksoy, "An Investigation of the Cross-National Determinants of Customer Satisfaction," *Journal of the Academy of Marketing Science* 39 (April 2011), pp. 198–215.

Discussion Questions

1. Why has it been difficult for executives to understand the relationship between service improvements and profitability in their companies?
2. What is the ROSQ model, and what is its significance to corporate America?
3. To this day, many companies believe that service is a cost rather than a revenue producer. Why might they hold this view? How would you argue the opposite view?
4. What is the difference between offensive and defensive marketing? How does service affect each of these?
5. What are the main sources of profit in defensive marketing?
6. What are the main sources of profit in offensive marketing?
7. How would the balanced performance scorecard help us understand and document the information presented in this chapter? Which of the five sections that discuss different aspects of the relationship between service quality and profits can it illuminate?

Exercises

1. Using the Internet, find the official site for the Net Promoter Score. Use the links in the site to locate other researchers' opinions of the measure, and make a list of the benefits and disadvantages discussed in those articles. If you were a CEO, would you use this measure as the "only number you need" to predict growth? Why or why not?
2. Interview a local firm and see what it knows about its key drivers of financial performance. What are the key service drivers of the firm? Does the company know whether these service drivers relate to profit?
3. Select a service industry (such as fast food) or a company (such as McDonald's) that you are familiar with, either as a customer or an employee, and create a balanced scorecard. Describe the operational, customer, financial, and learning measures that could be used to capture performance.

Notes

1. Sources for the Chapter Opener: R. T. Rust, A. J. Zahorik, and T. L. Keiningham, *Return on Quality* (Chicago: Probus, 1994); R. T. Rust, C. Moorman, and P. R. Dickson, "Getting Return on Quality: Revenue Expansion, Cost Reduction, or Both," *Journal of Marketing* 66 (October 2002), pp. 7–24 ; R. T. Rust and T. S. Chung, "Marketing Models of Service and Relationships," *Marketing Science* 25 (November–December 2006), pp. 560–580; T. L. Keiningham, L. Aksoy, A. Buoye, and B. Cooil, "Customer Loyalty Isn't Enough. Grow Your Share of Wallet," *Harvard Business Review,* October 2011; T. Keiningham, L. Aksoy, L. Williams, and A. Buoye, *The Wallet Allocation Rule* (Hoboken, NJ: Wiley, 2015).
2. T. Keiningham, L. Aksoy, L. Williams, and A. Buoye, *The Wallet Allocation Rule* (Hoboken, NJ: Wiley, 2015).
3. R. T. Rust, C. Moorman, and P. R. Dickson, "Getting Return on Quality: Revenue Expansion, Cost Reduction, or Both?" *Journal of Marketing* 66 (October 2002), pp. 7–24.
4. Ibid.
5. *Management Practice, U.S. Companies Improve Performance through Quality Efforts,* Report No. GAO/NSIAD-91-190 (Washington, DC: U.S. General Accounting Office, 1992).
6. R. Rust, B. Subramanian, and M. Wells, "Making Complaints a Management Tool," *Marketing Management* 3 (1993), pp. 40–45. R. Rust, Roland, C. Moorman, and G. Bhalla, "Rethinking Marketing," *Harvard Business Review,* January-February 2010; R. Rust, V. Zeithaml, and K. Lemon, "Customer-Centered Brand Management," *Harvard Business Review,* September 2004; S. Gupta and D. Lehmann, *Managing Customers as Investments,* Wharton School Publishing, 2005.
7. E. Nelson, R. T. Rust, A. Zahorik, R. L. Rose, P. Batalden, and B. Siemanski, "Do Patient Perceptions of Quality Relate to Hospital Financial Performance?" *Journal of Healthcare Marketing* 12 (December 1992), pp. 1–13.
8. C. Fornell, F. V. Morgeson, G. T. M. Hult, and D. VanAmburg, "Satisfied Customers: An Asset Driving Financial Performance," In *The Reign of the Customer* (pp. 139–154), Palgrave Macmillan, 2020; also see www.theacsi.org, website for the American Customer Satisfaction Index.
9. C. Fornell and B. Wernerfelt, "Defensive Marketing Strategy by Customer Complaint Management: A Theoretical Analysis," *Journal of Marketing Research* 24 (November 1987), pp. 337–346; see also C. Fornell and B. Wernerfelt, "A Model for Customer Complaint Management," *Marketing Science* 7 (Summer 1988), pp. 271–286.

10. B. Gale, "Monitoring Customer Satisfaction and Market-Perceived Quality," *American Marketing Association Worth Repeating Series,* no. 922CS01 (Chicago: American Marketing Association, 1992).
11. R. E. Kordupleski, R. T. Rust, and A. J. Zahorik, "Why Improving Quality Doesn't Improve Quality (or Whatever Happened to Marketing?)," *California Management Review* 35 (Spring 1993), pp. 82–95.
12. Fornell and Wernerfelt, "Defensive Marketing Strategy by Customer Complaint Management"; Fornell and Wernerfelt, "A Model for Customer Complaint Management."
13. F. Reichheld and E. Sasser, "Zero Defections: Quality Comes to Services," *Harvard Business Review* 68 (September–October 1990), p. 106.
14. J. Hogan, K. Lemon, and B. Libai, "What Is the True Value of a Lost Customer?" *Journal of Service Research* 5, 2003.
15. F. F. Reichheld and W. E. Sasser, "Zero Defections: Quality Comes to Services," *Harvard Business Review*, 68 (5, 1990), pp. 105–111.
16. D. F. Colicchio, regional quality manager, Hewlett-Packard Company, personal communication.
17. A. Bhattacharya, N. A. Morgan, and L. L. Rego, "Customer Satisfaction and Firm Profits in Monopolies: A Study of Utilities," *Journal of Marketing Research* 58 (February 2021), pp. 202–222.
18. V. Kumar, J. A. Petersen, and R. P. Leone, "How Valuable Is Word of Mouth?" *Harvard Business Review* 85 (October 2007), pp. 139–146.
19. V. Kumar, J. A. Petersen, and R. P. Leone, "Driving Profitability by Encouraging Customer Referrals: Who, When, and How," *Journal of Marketing,* September 2010.
20. R. Hallowell, "Word-of-Mouth Referral," *Harvard Business School Module Note,* 2002.
21. J. L. Heskett, W. E. Sasser Jr., and L. A. Schlesinger, *The Service Profit Chain* (New York: The Free Press, 1997).
22. Information provided by TARP Worldwide Inc., August 2007 for similar findings, see E. De Haan, P. C. Verhoef, and T. Wiesel, "The Predictive Ability of Different Customer Feedback Metrics for Retention," *International Journal of Research in Marketing* 32 (June 2015), pp. 195–206.
23. W. Boulding, R. Staelin, A. Kalra, and V. A. Zeithaml, "Conceptualizing and Testing a Dynamic Process Model of Service Quality," report no. 92–121, Marketing Science Institute, 1992.
24. V. A. Zeithaml, L. L. Berry, and A. Parasuraman, "The Behavioral Consequences of Service Quality," *Journal of Marketing* 60 (April 1996), pp. 31–46.
25. Paul, Michael, Thorsten Hennig-Thurau, Dwayne D. Gremler, Kevin P. Gwinner, and Caroline Wiertz (2009), "Toward a Theory of Repeated Purchase Drivers for Consumer Services," *Journal of the Academy of Marketing Science,* 37 (2), 215–237.
26. The material in this section comes from C. D. Ittner and D. F. Larcker, "Coming Up Short on Nonfinancial Performance Measurement," *Harvard Business Review* 81 (November 2003), pp. 88–95.
27. Ibid., p. 92.

Part **Eight**

Cases

Asian Paints BHPS: Growing the World's Largest Painting Service

"In the whole painting process, sometimes the 't' becomes silent, and it becomes more of a pain than paint. Therefore, we are amplifying the whole servicing angle."
— Amit Syngle, CEO & MD, Asian Paints

Amit Syngle was preoccupied as he gazed through his office window at the rain lashing Mumbai's skyline. As he prepared for a strategy discussion in the upcoming board meeting, he reflected on the journey of the services business in Asian Paints. The business had evolved through several phases over the years. The Beautiful Homes Painting Service (BHPS), launched during a similar wet monsoon in 2019, had transformed both the organization's services division and the market. Now, Syngle was ready to present an ambitious five-year strategy to expand the service business from painting 100,000 homes to one million homes annually.

He had to address two key issues: First, would the current dealer-led service delivery model suffice? Was there another approach, such as scaling up the Trusted Contractor Service (TCS)? The TCS offered trained contractors to customers, to avoid the loss of leads from price sensitive and smaller ticket size customers.

Second, how could one ensure high quality service while boosting the brand equity of Asian Paints, especially when the service was scaled up exponentially? Was there an option to make the service more aspirational, for instance an elevated tier to the service involving customized wall texture for a very small fraction of the premium customers. From a branding perspective, should BHPS have been positioned as a mass brand or an aspirational brand? What were some of the allied services for homes, apart from painting, which could be scaled up similarly? Were there synergies that could be exploited?

G. Shainesh, Professor of Marketing, IIM Bangalore has authored this case for classroom discussion. This case was developed from available and permitted sources of information. No funding was sought or received from any source for the development of this case. This case is not intended to serve as an endorsement, source of primary data, or to show effective or inefficient handling of decision or business processes.

INDIAN PAINTS INDUSTRY, PLAYERS AND OFFERINGS

The market for paints and coatings in India was estimated at USD 9.60 billion in 2024 and was expected to grow at a CAGR of 9.34% to reach USD 15.04 billion by 2029. Asian Paints dominated the industry with over 50% market share. Berger (18%), Kansai Nerolac Paints (15%), AkzoNobel (7%), and Nippon were other key players. Recent entrants included JSW Paints and Aditya Birla's Opus.[1]

The boom in real estate and infrastructure were the key drivers for demand for paints. In addition to new construction, shorter cycles for home repainting, from an average of seven years to three–five years, were also boosting demand. Economic growth led to the rise in disposable income, growing demand in rural markets, investments in infrastructure and supportive government policies, including subsidies for affordable homes to provide 'Housing for All', and the growth in the sale of premium-end products, which, in turn, had aided the industry's growth.

Paints and coatings[2] were used for decoration as well as protection. Most coatings were used to decorate and protect new constructions as well as to maintain existing structures, including homes, apartments, public buildings, plants, factories and industrial products. In addition, special purpose coatings were used for specialized applications such as road marking paints, vehicle refinishing, industrial plants and equipment, marine structures and vessels.

The market encompassed a diverse range of products catering to specific applications and end-users. Broadly, these were classified into decorative paints, used in residential and commercial buildings, and industrial paints, designed for industrial settings.

Air pollution regulations were driving the adoption of new coating technologies, including water-based coatings, high-solids coatings, two-component systems, powder coatings and radiation-curable coatings. Consumers mostly preferred water-based paint due to their lack of odors and the absence of potentially hazardous raw materials. Other key factors influencing consumer choices included environmental impact, color variety, durability, ease of application, and finish quality.

REMOVING THE 'PAIN' FROM 'PAINTING'

Asian Paints, founded in 1942, was India's leading paints and décor company and ranked among the top 10 decorative coating companies globally.[3] The company generated a consolidated turnover of INR 354 billion (USD 4.24 bn)[4] in FY 2023–24 from its global operations in 15 countries, with 27 paint manufacturing facilities and serving consumers in over 60 countries. The company's diverse product portfolio straddled all key market segments while its strong distribution network of dealers and retailers covered the length and breadth of the country with over 160,000 retail points.[5] The company's expanded product portfolio included home décor, bath fittings, modular kitchens and wardrobes. However, its journey in the services business over the previous two decades had been far from smooth.

---

1 https://www.icicidirect.com/research/equity/finace/is-the-indian-paint-industry-going-to-change, last accessed on November 21, 2024.

2 https://www.designingbuildings.co.uk/wiki/Paints_and_coatings, last accessed on March 1, 2025.

3 https://www.asianpaints.com/about-us.html, last accessed on March 1, 2025.

4 Exchange rate in March 2024; 1 USD = INR 83.5

5 https://www.asianpaints.com/content/dam/asianpaints/website/secondary-navigation/investors/announcements-pdfs/2023-2024/SEIntimationTranscript31072023.pdf, last accessed on March 1, 2025.

The services business was set up in the year 2000 when a core group was tasked to study the challenges faced by customers while painting their homes. An analysis of customer feedback and complaint data revealed that while consumers bought *paint*, their actual requirement was a fully *painted home*. Most consumers lacked knowledge about paints and its application, did not wish to depend on a painter and dreaded the hassle of dislocation and disruption while painting their homes. These insights led to the launch of Asian Paints Home Solutions (APHS), a company-provided painting service, to remove the *'Pain' from 'Painting'*. Painting service was also identified as an opportunity to drive future growth by 'servitization', i.e., adding value to the core product offering through related services.

After a successful pilot in Hyderabad in September 2000, the service was rolled out to the top 12 cities across India. The company onboarded third-party vendors, known as Home Solutions Service Providers (HSSP), as franchisees to provide the home painting services. In each city, select Asian Paints dealers were designated to supply the paint and related materials to the HSSPs.

The dealers earned a margin of 6% to 7% on the materials supplied. The HSSPs received a fixed monthly retainer to manage the service operations on behalf of the company. In turn, the HSSPs appointed contractors to execute the painting work and deployed Sales Associates (SAs) and Relationship Associates (RAs). These associates were paid by the HSSP. Asian Paints charged a 20% margin on top of the costs of manpower, dealer, contractor, lead generation, and other incidental costs. After adding up these costs and margins, the end consumers were paying a 40% premium to the local market. This high price turned the service into a very niche offering.

PAINTING SERVICE

As a pioneer, Asian Paints was the first paints producer to offer painting as a service to consumers. Competitors like Berger and Nerolac followed the lead and launched their own painting services. APHS enabled the company to enter the consumers' homes and interact with them directly, allowing a deeper understanding of their needs and preferences. This understanding served as a launchpad for new products and seeded premium products. In addition, working very closely with contractors and painters helped in understanding their needs and aspirations too. Consumers were offered a hassle-free painting service, with access to the latest products and technical assistance directly from the company. While the dealers gained from exposure to services business, the labor plus material model of pricing enabled higher margins and drove sales of higher value, niche products.

Despite these benefits, APHS experienced low growth due to several limitations. As indicated above, it was a cost-heavy and resource intensive business model (see **Exhibit 1**). Lead generation costs, for consumers willing to pay the high price premium, turned out to be very high. In addition, the dependence on the franchise partners was high. The company could not expand the service offering beyond the large cities. Gradually, the company scaled down and eventually shuttered the APHS service in 2019.

A DEALER-LED SERVICE

At the same time, the leadership was keen to explore other business models to scale up the painting service and meet the customers' need for a reliable painting service.

Each city had a Unit Head (UH) with five to eight Customer Service Officers (CSOs) reporting to him/her. Every division (North, South, East, West, Central) was headed by a Regional Manager (RM). Unit Heads reported to the RM. The RMs reported to the National Head of APHS. Each CSO led a team of six to eight off-roll employees (associates). Associates were on the rolls of the HSSP. The associates played different roles as Sales Associates (SAs) and Relationship Associates (RAs). SAs were responsible for converting leads into sites, viz. homes for painting while the RAs were responsible for the entire execution of the work at the converted sites. The division of responsibilities ensured better focus on customer acquisition and retention through enhanced customer experience through a better managed service delivery.

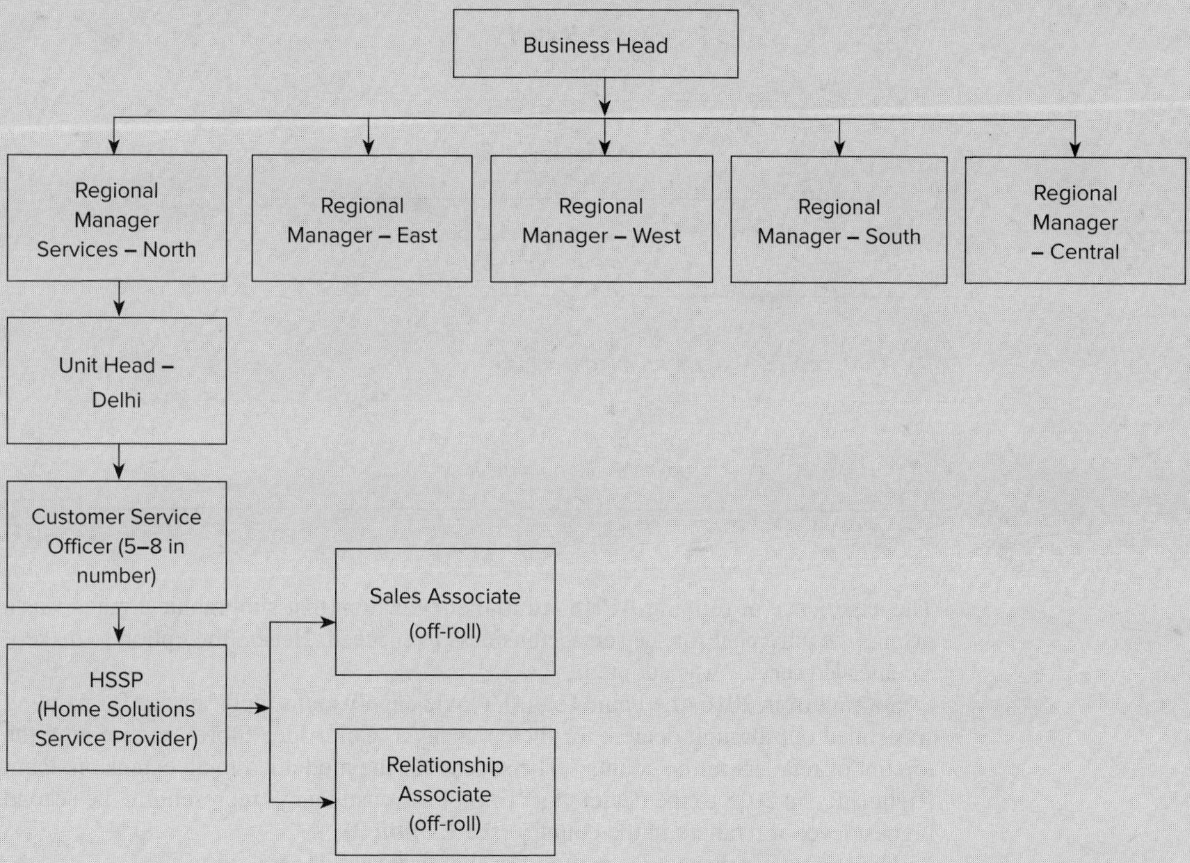

Source: Asian Paints

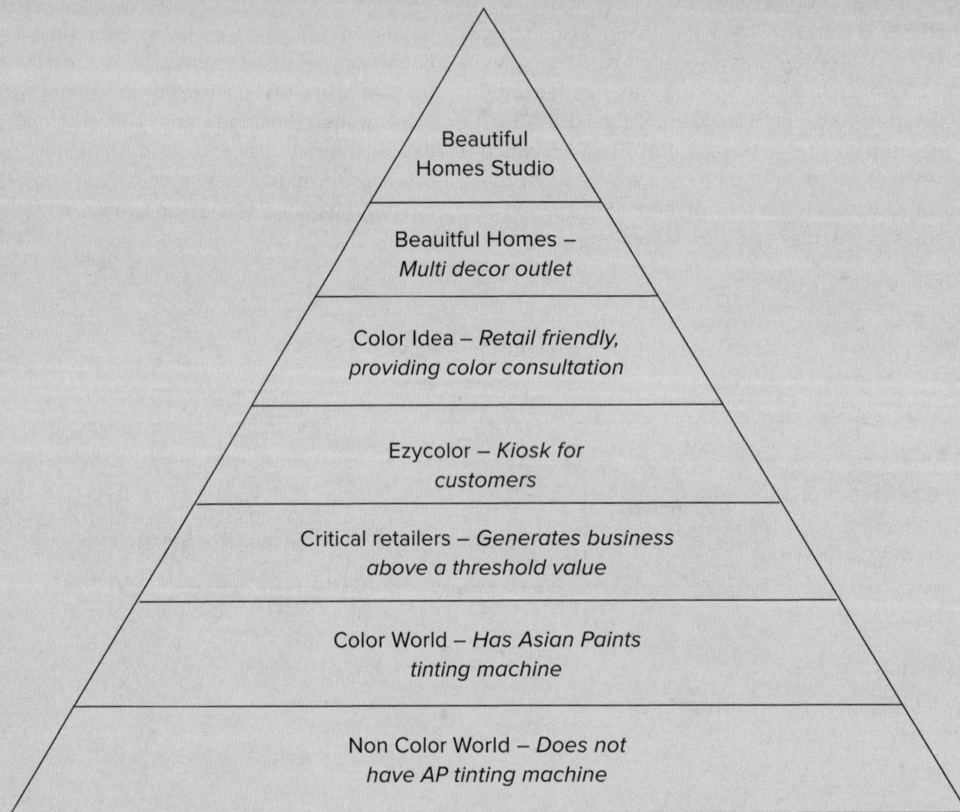

Source: Asian Paints

The experience of running APHS led to the realization that geographical reach was a primary requirement for the service business to succeed. Hence, the option to make it a dealer-led service was adopted.

Starting from 2016, the Paint Total (PT), viz., apply and supply service for painting was rolled out through dealers for the company's 'Color Idea Store' representing the top tier of retailers in the country. The success of the model led to an extension, Paint Right (PR), in 2018 to the dealers for 'Ezycolor Consultancy' representing the second highest level of retailers in the country (see **Exhibit 2**).

The company selected dealers to offer the service after assessing:

- Customer footfall in the dealer's outlet,
- Dealer's service orientation in addition to their revenues from product sales, and
- The presence of at least three to five dependable contractors so that the end consumer could be assured of the final finish.

The PT/PR painting service was a significant value add for the dealers as they could increase their offerings to the end consumer from product to product + service without any significant investment. The services business generated better margins, with a possibility of earning 3X the margin of the products business. The company provided a trained and dedicated associate to generate sales for the service business and

The Safe Painting service involved the following:

- Site evaluation and product consultation.
- Complete adherence to safety protocol by team.
- Complete masking and covering of furniture and valuables.
- Dust-free mechanized painting.
- Trained applicators.
- Regular site supervision.
- Free home sanitization following project completion.

Source: https://www.youtube.com/watch?v=bEXI-PHRmO4&t=36s; Asian Paints

supervise the painting sites. The associate, on a third party's payroll, was a shared resource between the company and the dealer. In addition, the lead generation campaigns run by Asian Paints were a source of additional business for dealers. By March 2020, the PT/PR service had expanded to more than 200 cities. Then the pandemic hit.

COVID PANDEMIC: THE INFLECTION POINT

A sharp upturn for the service emerged after the COVID pandemic hit in 2020. In the early days of the pandemic, the company introduced sanitization services—'San Assure' and 'San Assure Pro'—to provide customers with peace of mind for their shops, offices, and homes. There was a professional variant for housing societies, hospitals, hotels, and institutions. Asian Paints also introduced a 'Safe Painting Service' to provide an assurance to the customers of a safe and secure painting environment in uncertain times (see **Exhibit 3**). This really resonated with the consumers and the demand for the service rocketed, after systematically enrolling more dealers. By March 2023, the service was being offered in over 600 cities and towns.

In December 2023, a modified service was launched as the Asian Paints Beautiful Homes Painting Service (BHPS). In addition, a pioneering industry-first promise of 'On Time Performance or Money Back' was offered and delivered seamlessly. It was offered to leverage two key insights:

- Consumers who painted their homes desired for their friends and relatives to appreciate the quality of the work and adore the aesthetics.
- Customers did not need only a 'fast/quick' service. They wanted the painting service provider to adhere to the promised, committed timeline.

The commitment to hassle-free, on-time completion proved to be a key differentiator as it was backed by a guaranteed timeline with a unique, industry-first '20% moneyback assurance' if unmet. This was a game changing proposition that required dealer onboarding, meticulous planning, and systems integration to ensure that the promise was delivered, every time.

A national campaign was successfully rolled out on television to communicate this promise. The campaign emerged as the company's most successful TV campaign and generated almost 200,000 enquiries. During the final quarter of the year, the BHPS ensured nearly 100% on-time completion, while the campaign was live.

The market acceptance of the BHPS was underlined by the exponential growth in its gross merchandise value (GMV) which grew from INR 430 crores in FY 2020–21 to register a growth of over 5x in the next four years. In addition, on the customer

Year	Dealers Onboarded (#)	Contractors Onboarded (#)	Contactors Trained (#)	Contractor NPS (1- 5 scale)	BHPS customer sites (#)	Customer sites (BHPS + TCS*) (#)
2019	705				30552	
2020	1124	4236	2868	3.39	38154	38154
2021	1485	5123	4348	3.82	54195	66200
2022	1794	5578	4715	4.81	74523	125245
2023	2146	7005	5583	4.54	104189	186117

*TCS – Trusted Contractor Service, NPS – Net Promoter Score, Sites – Homes

Source: Asian Paints (disguised data)

front, the BHPS achieved a Net Promoter Score of 77 with just 1.1% of all sites that registered complaints of any sort. The complaint sites had remained at around 1% of total sites for the next 3 years. As the service was scaling up, customer delight was also being ensured through 2100+ dealers, 5500 contractors, and 2400+ associates (see **Exhibit 4**).

The process, technology and people emerged as critical enablers that were integral to the success of BHPS.

Process: The BHPS process was designed to ensure positive 'moments of truth' for the customer throughout their journey as shown in **Figure 1**.

By 2020–21, the increasing number of customer enquiries across the country needed to be serviced quickly and efficiently. The growing number of enquiries were impacting the customer conversion ratio adversely. This needed to be addressed as it had a direct impact on lead acquisition costs. Maintaining the service levels and quality of customer interaction across the service cycle was important. With the on-ground dealer network enrolled in the BHPS, along with the number of associates that increased, providing a consolidated view of the entire consumer journey (from lead creation stage till site closure stage) to these stakeholders was imperative for an elevated consumer experience. An important element in standardizing the consumer

FIGURE 1 BHPS Process

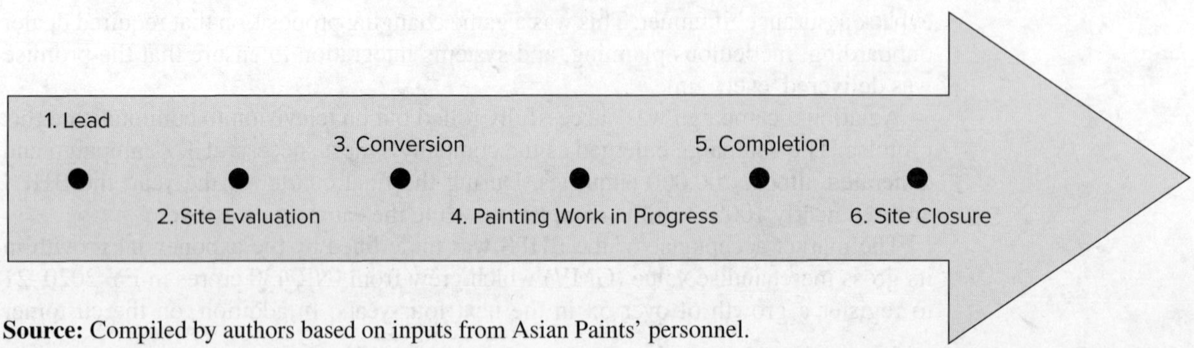

Source: Compiled by authors based on inputs from Asian Paints' personnel.

a. Lead:

i. Calls usually done within 48 hours.
ii. Fixing an appointment to visit within 24 to 48 hours and adhering to the fixed time while visiting.
iii. In case the customer didn't receive their call, they dropped a message on the number sharing their details.

b. Site Evaluation:

i. Clearly understand the requirements of the customer.
ii. Ensure the site was evaluated thoroughly and measurements were done accurately.
iii. Site Health Card should be created covering all compulsory parameters.
iv. Any disclaimers should be mentioned in the comments in detail.

c. Conversion:

i. Quotation to be given within 24 hours of the site visit.
ii. Quotation and work schedule record approval should be first taken with the dealer before sharing to the customer.
iii. Ensure a follow- up with the customer post sharing the quote, multiple quotes could be shared post negotiation.
iv. Ensure approval of the final quotation before the work started at the site.

d. Work in progress:

i. Align a trained contractor for the job.
ii. Align the contractor with the timelines of the work schedule record.
iii. Ensure proper handover of the site to the contractor.
iv. Ensure the site was supervised.
v. Timely material arrangement should be done to avoid shortage.
vi. During the site supervision, ensure proper evaluation of application quality.
vii. After completion of each task, ensure provision of timely updates to the customer.
viii. In case the customer has any concerns/reservations, speak to them and resolve it promptly.

e. Site Completion:

i. Ensure 100% collection before the completion of the site.
ii. Obtain the dealer's approval after site completion and provide a walk through to the customer and get the service vetted.
iii. In case the customer was dissatisfied, ensure facilitation of relevant re-work.
iv. Ensure cleanliness of the site.

f. Site closure:

i. Ensure the NPS was captured.
ii. Gather leads for referral customers.
iii. Warranty registration for relevant products.
iv. Updating the dealer about site closure and payment reconciliation.

Source: https://www.youtube.com/watch?v=cAtszmWJJYU&t=8s; Asian Paints

journey was the mapping of the process, after dividing it into activities with specific steps to be followed by each associate (see **Exhibits 5a & 5b**).

Within this process, there was a need to create positive moments of truth (MoTs) for the customer. MoTs are those instances when the customer judges the quality of the service, and these moments shape the customer and brand relationship. An MoT could be potentially a magical or miserable moment. MoTs were designed to ensure a smooth journey for all customers from the time they decided to paint their house to the time they got a painted house. The MoTs brought a structured flow to the entire

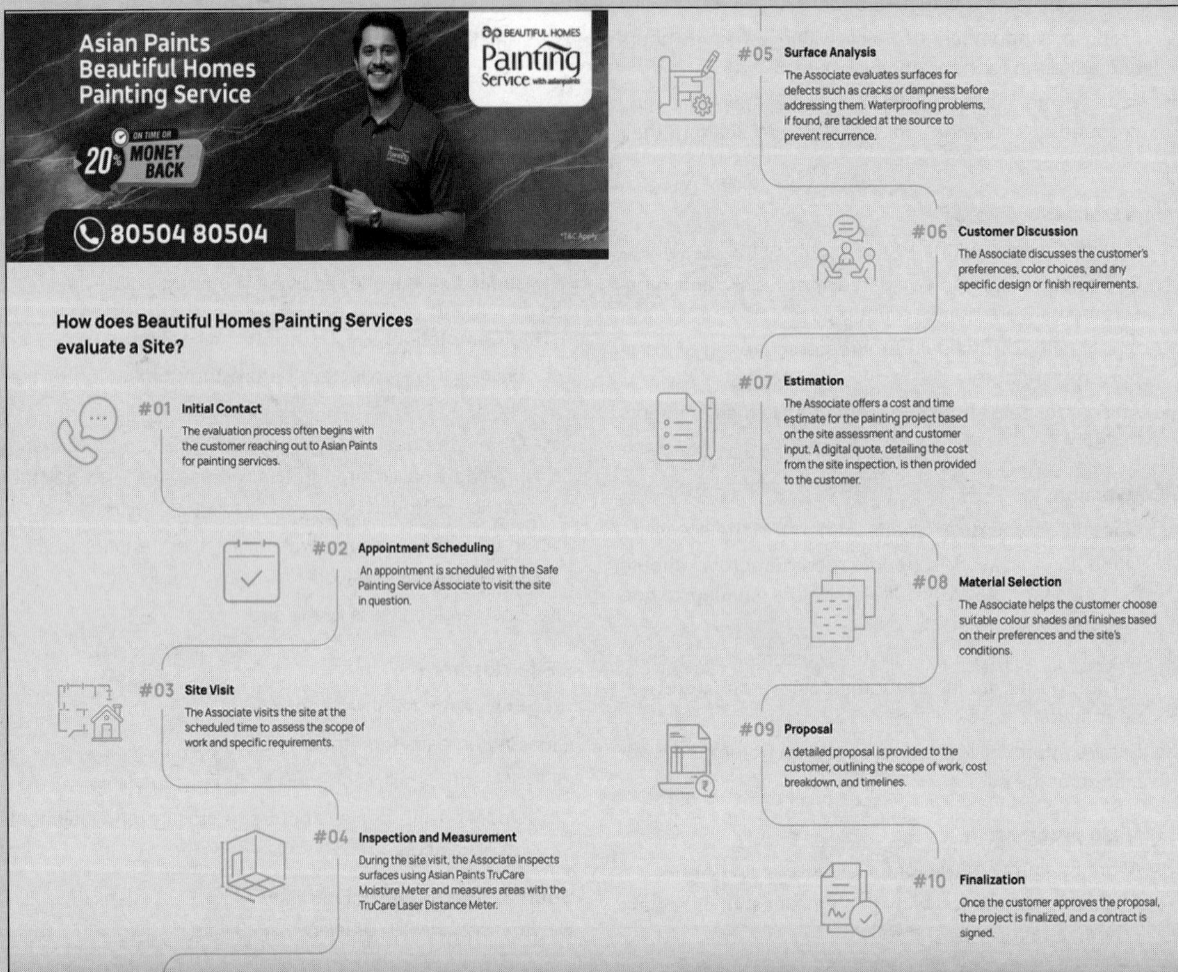

Source: https://www.asianpaints.com/content/dam/apcolourcatalogue/asset/ap-revamp/interior-wall-paints/services/BHPS-Guide.pdf, last accessed on March 1, 2025.

painting process. It broke the entire painting process into small steps and was easy for the team to follow and deliver a high- quality customer experience.

Specific parts of the process, based on this mapping, were identified as opportunities for magical moments as shown in **Exhibit 6**.

Site Health Card (Pre-sales MoT)

Objective: Single document highlighting the areas of concern to be addressed, along with recommended solutions.

Benefits

- Proper assessment of surface condition
- Definition of Scope of Work
- Clarity in communication to customer
- Painting process identification

Implication on non-adherence

- Can lead to post painting complaints.
- Lack of source identification will result in rework.
- Dissatisfied customer.

Quotation (Pre-sales MoT)

Objective: Detailed quotation for the work to be approved by customer.

Method of Tracking

- Mandatory Salesforce and customer approval is required.

Benefits

- Professional method of communication
- Detailed description to customer
- Comprehensive manners to communicate with all T&C.

Implication on non-adherence

- The process will look ambiguous.
- Customer might deny at a later stage.
- Lack of proper documentation.

Shade Selection Card (Work-in-progress MoT)

Objective: Digital card showcasing shades shortlisted.

Method of Tracking

- Mandatory on Salesforce app.

Benefits

- Professional way to communicate.
- Proper documentation.
- Reduces chances of miscommunication.

Implication on non-adherence

- Could lead to post painting complaints.
- Customer denial.
- Lack of documentation.

Work Schedule Record (Work-in-progress MoT)

Objective: Laying down detailed plan of execution.

Method of Tracking

- Mandatory on Salesforce app.

Benefits

- Definition of scope of work.
- Clarity in communication with customers.
- Mitigate any roadblock during application.

Implication on non-adherence

- Unforeseen stoppage of work.
- Lack of clarity for customers.
- Repeated intervention in work.

Site Completion Card (Post-Sales MoT)

Objective: Prior to site closure – a form of handover.

Method of Tracking

- Mandatory on Salesforce app.

Benefits

- Formal method of communicating site closure.
- Scope of minimizing the gap in work.
- Site walkthrough and handover.

Implication on non-adherence

- Unexpected escalations.
- Irrelevant complaints.
- Mismatch of Expectation vs Reality.

Platinum Warranty Card (Post-sales MoT)

- 1-year service warranty that provides assurance of wall protection along with product warranty.

Source: Asian Paints

Exhibit 7 Enabling through Digital Technology

Year / Stage	2019	2020	2021	2022	2023	2024
Lead	Quotation	Quotation	Site Health Card	Site Visit Verification	Site Visit Verification	Site Visit Verification
			Quotation	Site Health Card	Site Health Card	Site Health Card
				Quotation to be approved by customer	Quotation to be approved by customer	Quotation to be approved by customer
Work in Progress (WIP)				Shade Selection	Shade Selection	Shade Selection
					Work Schedule	Work Schedule
Closure	Closure in App	Closure in App	Closure in App	Closure in App	Site Completion Card	Site Completion Card
					Platinum Warranty Card	Platinum Warranty Card

Note: This table demonstrates the progressive movement of processes online and closure through the app, providing better visibility for both – company and consumer.

Source: Asian Paints

TECHNOLOGY: INTEGRATED APP AS THE KEY DIFFERENTIATOR

While scaling up, care was taken to ensure that service features promised to the customers were delivered consistently. An integrated technology platform, Salesforce, was chosen to guide every associate on the next task at hand. It ensured that the service promise was delivered to the customers. The system integrated the myriad needs of multiple internal and external stakeholders including the helpline, associates, dealers, Asian Paints team, etc. Salesforce implementation involved migrating the older data onto the new platform, creation of multiple workflows and integration of stakeholders from different businesses (see **Exhibit 7**).

People: Associate Skilling

The off-roll associate, who operated from the dealer's retail outlet, was the key to delivering the service promise to customers. The associate was responsible for executing the project seamlessly by managing the contractor, painter and technical issues. As the frontline representative for Asian Paints, they directly interacted with customers. This shaped customer experience and dis/satisfaction leading to future complaints, negative social media reviews, and so on if not handled carefully. As the role involved advising and helping customers to make the right decision and choices, these associates had to regularly learn and upgrade their knowledge and expertise.

As problem solvers, they were expected to solve problems on their own without escalating minor issues to their managers. Their multifaceted role involved understanding the customer's perspective, establishing rapport and building deeper connect with them through critical engagement skills such as active listening, empathy, and the like while staying motivated and committed to contribution. The need for a committed

Exhibit 8 Organization Structure: BHPS

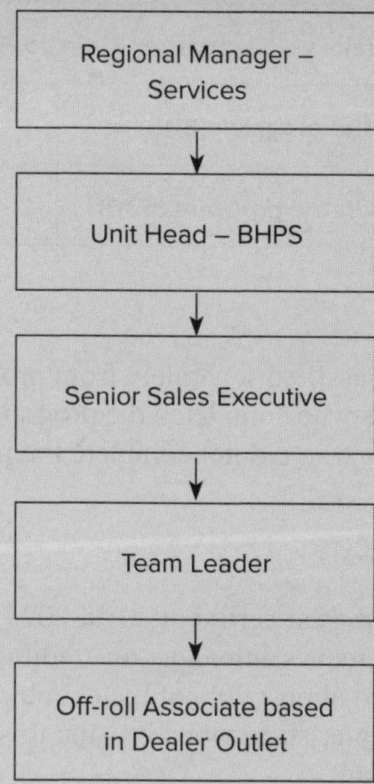

Source: Asian Paints

pool of associates was critical as this work force typically faced an employee churn rate of over 50%. The associate, usually a graduate, operated from a dealer's store. The associate reported to a team leader, an on-roll employee of Asian Paints, who, in turn, reported to the senior executive and assistant manager (see **Exhibit 8**). Working out of a dealer's outlet was not a preferred option for a graduate.

The HR team worked with an external partner to design an end-to-end intervention, branded as the 'Starmaker Associate' program, to improve the associate's ability to deal with stakeholder MOTs and find new opportunities to enhance customer experience. The program was focused on identifying specific areas of enabling associates to deliver service excellence. It involved the creation of 12 modules to improve their engagement capabilities with the customers through:

a. Capacity building of about 50 Asian Paints coaches to deliver the program.
b. Rollout of core modules to all associates using an online platform.
c. Gamification through an app, involving sending typical flashpoints (i.e., challenges) faced on site from lead management to site completion, daily on an app, along with the solutions while allowing associates to submit their own solutions.

The Starmaker program had a positive impact. It resulted in a drop in the proportion of service complaints from an average of 69.5% of total complaints in September and October 2021 to an average of 51.5% in January and February 2022. Service complaints were complaints related to the painting process or associate related areas.

FIGURE 2 Drop in Customer Complaints

Complaints – September 2021 to February 2022	
Associates who participated in the program (808)	0.20 complaints / associate / month
Associates who did not participate in the program (636)	0.63 complaints / associate / month

Source: Asian Paints

These were classified separately from product related complaints. Overall, it was seen that associates who completed the program had lower incidence of complaints as compared to those who did not complete the program (see **Figure 2**).

GROWING THE SERVICE

During the five year period of 2019–2024, the direct customer touchpoints were scaled up. Advertisement campaigns on traditional and digital media generated leads. The BHPS covered almost 90% of the country. This massive reach placed the painting service at the center stage when it came to seeding and growing new product categories for the company..

The BHPS had been successful as the service worked for all stakeholders – the customers, the dealers as well the company. The dealers grew their topline as well as margins. As the service scaled up further in terms of number of dealers, there would be a need to strike a balance between scaling up and margins for dealers, else the dealers would have stopped signing up for the service.

Along with the BHPS, the company had been developing an alternate, the Trusted Contractor Service (TCS), to tap the leads who did not sign up for the BHPS service. As part of TCS, the customer signed up a contractor trained by Asian Paints for the painting service at a 2% to 3% price premium over the local market rate. However, the value added supervision by the associate was not offered. The BHPS currently had a 6% to 7% conversion rate, due to its higher price (about 10% more than the local contractors in the market). Therefore, TCS provided an assurance factor even though it did not offer all the benefits of BHPS. When the lead was not seen as converting to BHPS, then the call center executive pitched for TCS. The lower price of TCS had improved the conversion rate of leads to 20% to 25%. Generally, these customers ended up buying paints and coatings from Asian Paints. But, there was a risk of cannibalization, i.e., customers who might have been willing to use the BHPS might have ended up signing up for TCS.

The BHPS was a critical enabler to drive related categories like Woodfinishes and Waterproofing offered under the brand SmartCare. These services required specific application skills, so they were offered through a curated set of highly skilled contractors. The BHPS associates were also specially trained in these categories as they needed a better technical know-how compared to paints to guide customers while selecting the right product for their specific requirement. Similarly, innovative products that were entirely new for the market like high-end, premium Italian textures that elevated the décor of a consumer's home, were also seeded through BHPS. In addition, BHPS played a crucial role in the secondary sales of the more profitable premium and luxury paint products for the dealer network enrolled in the service. With innovative offerings like dust-free painting and spray painting, the consumer also got a superior finish on their walls through the BHPS.

BHPS was an embodiment of a 'living service' by constantly innovating on both offerings and processes. The adoption of best practices and extensive training of contractors and painters had transformed the painting business. In addition, the use of mechanized sanding and masking kits at the beginning of the painting process had elevated the customers' experience while getting their homes painted.

By March 2024, over 100,000 customers had used the Beautiful Homes Painting Service. Over 2100 dealers in 650[6] cities were enrolled to offer these services. As he turned away from the window, Syngle had to think through a few issues for scaling the service from painting 100,000 homes annually to 1 million homes in the next 5 years. These included:

a. How will the role of the dealer, contractor and associate evolve?
b. How will the technology interface and the manpower structure evolve?
c. How will the company manage the painting process and customer experience?
d. How does this proposition provide further value to the customer – what will be the proposition going forward? How do we ensure MoTs across a much larger customer base?
e. How do we evolve the service to make it more aspirational, in terms of a more creative offering?

6 Data has been disguised to protect confidentiality.

Questions

1. Why did Asian Paints enter the service business? What customer pain points did Asian Paints aim to address through its painting service? What insights shaped the design of its service offering? How did the service evolve over time?
2. How does Asian Paints manage its 'moments of truth' to ensure customer satisfaction throughout the painting process? Provide specific examples from the case to illustrate this.
3. What were the main challenges Asian Paints faced in scaling the service from a niche offering to a mass-market solution? How did Asian Paints address these challenges at different stages of expansion?
4. How does Asian Paints use technology to support its service delivery model? What roles do these technologies play in both scaling up BHPS and maintaining quality control?
5. What are the key elements of Asian Paints' partnership model with its dealers, contractors, and associates? How do these partnerships contribute to the growth and success of the service beyond just sales—training, brand loyalty, or customer trust?

6. Should BHPS be positioned as a mass-market brand or as an aspirational and premium offering? Justify your answer based on the customer segments and brand equity considerations presented in the case.
7. How do you assess the role of training and associate upskilling in delivering high-quality customer experience within the BHPS model? What impact does this have on service consistency and customer retention?
8. What would you recommend as the next steps for Asian Paints in scaling up BHPS to meet its target of painting 1 million homes annually? Consider both operational improvements and long-term strategic growth.

Case **Two**

Akasa Air: Navigating India's Competitive Aviation Landscape

INDIA'S FASTEST-GROWING AIRLINE

Akasa Air has emerged as a remarkable success story in India's competitive aviation landscape. Established during the pandemic in August 2022, the founders set out with a clear purpose – create an inclusive travel environment, professionally managed for long-term sustainability, to transform India's aviation ecosystem which catered to a small fraction of the country's population. In less than three years, the airline has achieved unprecedented growth, becoming the fastest-growing airline in the global aviation history with triple-digit expansion. As of March 2025, Akasa has served over 17 million passengers, expanded to 22 domestic and 5 international destinations, and operates more than 150 daily departures with 1000 weekly flights. This rapid ascension in a crowded market dominated by Indigo and Air India raises important questions about Akasa's strategic approach. By examining the airline's services marketing mix, we can understand how this new entrant has attempted to disrupt the status quo while navigating the inherent challenges of this industry.

DIFFERENTIATION THROUGH INNOVATION AND SUSTAINABILITY

Akasa Air has distinguished itself by creating a unique travel experience that addresses the needs of previously underserved customer segments. The leadership team identified the pain points of budget-conscious travelers and developed solutions that make air travel more affordable without compromising essential services. A cornerstone of Akasa's product strategy is its commitment to sustainability, which has positioned the airline as an environmental leader in Indian aviation.

The airline's eco-friendly initiatives include fuel-efficient aircraft, a carbon offset program, and reduced single-use plastics onboard. As Belson Coutinho, Co-Founder and Chief Marketing and Experience Officer, emphasizes: "Our brand creation transcended traditional marketing approaches, taking a holistic, 360-degree approach focused on building a humane, inclusive brand relevant to new-age consumers." This environmental consciousness has particularly resonated with younger, environmentally aware travelers who increasingly factor sustainability into their purchasing decisions.

Akasa has further differentiated its product through several industry-first offerings that prioritize passenger comfort. These include enhanced features typically reserved for higher fare classes: extra legroom, ergonomic seats, and premium meal options through "Café Akasa," which offers over 45 gourmet meals created by reputed chefs. The airline also provides a comprehensive in-flight entertainment system allowing passengers to stream content on their personal devices. CEO Vinay Dube attributes their success to "customers appreciating their superior experience featuring extra-padded seats, best-in-class legroom, new aircraft, exceptional service, and fantastic food."

Akasa's commitment to inclusivity is evident in thoughtful innovations like Braille safety manuals and menus for visually impaired travelers, pet-friendly policies allowing pets up to 10 kg in the cabin. Unique touches like SkyBeats, viz. curated music during boarding and SkyLights for dynamic lighting adjustments throughout the flight, create various mood effects to enhance passengers' experience. Similarly, its 'QuietFlights' feature transforms the travel experience during early-morning and late-night flights by ensuring a peaceful ambience with dimmed cabin lights and essential safety announcements, allowing passengers to unwind and enjoy their privacy in the skies. These initiatives reflect Akasa's deep understanding of customer pain points and its willingness to challenge industry conventions. As Coutinho notes, Akasa made a "conscious decision to focus on its own unique experience rather than directly competing with established airlines."

BALANCING AFFORDABILITY WITH PROFITABILITY

Akasa's pricing approach has been instrumental in its market penetration strategy and ability to attract a broader customer base. By offering competitive fares, the airline has made air travel financially accessible to several customer segments who previously found flying prohibitively expensive. This price positioning has enabled Akasa to capture market share from both established airlines and substitutes, including road and rail.

The airline has maintained a delicate balance between competitive pricing and service quality, offering premium features at accessible price points that have resonated with value-conscious travelers. This pricing philosophy aligns with CEO Vinay Dube's pragmatic business approach of "learning from competitors and willingly adopting successful practices from others in the industry." By studying market dynamics and customer preferences, Akasa has identified price points that maximize both accessibility and perceived value.

However, this aggressive pricing strategy has presented challenges for the airline's financial sustainability. CFO Anjali Rao has acknowledged: "We underestimated the financial challenges of scaling up so quickly, and it has impacted our bottom line." Despite these growing pains, Akasa's leadership remains optimistic about the airline's financial trajectory. CEO Vinay Dube projects: "I think you are going to see a lot of profitability for the next 10 years with airlines as well," referring to what he calls the "golden decade" for Indian aviation. With plans to increase available seat kilometers by 50% year-on-year, Akasa is positioning itself toward profitability while maintaining its pricing advantage in the market.

AMBITIOUS EXPANSION WITH OPERATIONAL CHALLENGES

Akasa Air adopted an aggressive expansion strategy that yielded both impressive growth and operational challenges. Its network strategy focused on establishing a strong pan-India presence by linking Metros to Tier 2 and Tier 3 cities across the country. After kickstarting operations with flights between Mumbai and Ahmedabad, with brand-new Boeing 737 MAX aircraft, the airline rapidly expanded its route network to establish a broad market presence. It became the first Indian airline to commence international operations just 19 months after launch. By March 2024, Akasa was serving international destinations including Doha, Riyadh, Abu Dhabi, Jeddah, and Kuwait with more than 35 weekly international flights, in addition to its extensive domestic network covering 22 cities.

This rapid expansion was designed to increase market penetration and establish Akasa as a major player in record time. The airline's growth metrics are unprecedented – in FY2023–24, Akasa achieved a 300% growth in available seat kilometres (ASKM), setting a new record for airline growth. This aggressive approach to market coverage has made Akasa accessible to a wide range of customers across different regions, challenging the dominance of established carriers.

However, this breakneck expansion strained Akasa's resources and created operational challenges. Passengers experienced inconsistent service quality across different routes, with reliability issues affecting the airline's reputation. These growing pains highlight the tension between ambitious expansion goals and operational stability – a challenge that Akasa's leadership team has recognized and begun to address through strategic recalibration. The airline's experience demonstrates that effective growth strategy in aviation requires careful balancing of ambitions with operational capabilities to ensure consistent service delivery across all touchpoints.

AUTHENTIC COMMUNICATION OF VALUE PROPOSITION

Akasa's marketing and communication efforts have effectively showcased its positioning as an innovative, customer-centric airline that offers a differentiated travel experience. The carrier has consistently communicated its eco-friendly credentials, emphasizing sustainability initiatives across all marketing channels. Its promotional materials highlight the personalized experiences and unique features that set Akasa apart from competitors.

CMO Belson Coutinho's philosophy on promotion reflects the airline's approach, "Customers today are savvy and can see through gimmicks, which is why Akasa focuses on delivering real value and communicating it transparently." This commitment to authentic communication has resonated with customers seeking genuine value rather than empty promises. Coutinho further emphasizes that their marketing strategy "transcended traditional approaches, taking a holistic, 360-degree approach focused on building a humane, inclusive brand relevant to new-age consumers. Rather than relying solely on logos, taglines, or advertising campaigns, Akasa has differentiated itself through product-led and consumer experience-led marketing that leverages digital technology exclusively."

As a new entrant without the "baggage" of legacy systems and approaches, Akasa capitalized on technology, consumer insights, and post-COVID behavioral trends to address evolving customer needs. The airline deliberately focused on first-time travelers and environmentally conscious consumers, informing key decisions like creating crew uniforms from sustainable materials and developing pet-friendly travel policies. Looking forward, Coutinho reveals that Akasa is "investing heavily in marketing technology (MarTech), data insights, and generative AI to enhance efficiency, productivity, customer experience, and satisfaction." He believes strategic collaborations with brands outside the Akasa ecosystem will further help create value and differentiation, reinforcing their positioning as a dependable and affordable airline with superior customer experience.

Akasa has taken a digital-first approach while ensuring transparency with the press and prioritizing internal communication. Rather than focusing solely on reach, they emphasize engagement and leverage user-generated content, particularly from aviation enthusiasts and brand advocates. Their MarTech platform provides real-time insights into customer behavior, helping them identify and address problems in the customer journey.

BUILDING A CUSTOMER-FIRST CULTURE

The airline was built on three fundamental cultural pillars: service excellence, customer centricity, and cost leadership. Coutinho emphasized that culture is built daily, not through wall posters, and must be continuously reinforced. Akasa developed core values focused on being good human beings first—including respect, humility, perseverance, and sustainability—and invested heavily in training programs that focus on soft skills and interaction skills over 3–4 weeks for ground staff and three months for cabin crew, to ensure these values permeate the organization.

Employee empowerment is central to Akasa's approach. Frontline staff are encouraged to make decisions that benefit customers, such as accommodating late arrivals when possible or being flexible with baggage allowances for families with infants. The company prioritizes employee comfort and sustainability, featuring gender-neutral uniforms with sneakers made from recycled rubber and outfits made from recycled polyester. Akasa also offers a CSR leave day, allowing employees to pursue social causes they personally value.

The human element is central to Akasa Air's service delivery and represents both a strength and an area of ongoing development. Founded by industry veterans including CEO Vinay Dubey, the airline was built on a customer-first philosophy, with Dubey emphasizing the vision of "creating an airline that not only meets but exceeds customer expectations at every touchpoint." This approach has guided Akasa's recruitment, training, and management practices across all organizational levels.

With a workforce now exceeding 4,000 employees (affectionately called "Akasians"), the airline has invested significantly in developing a service culture that reinforces its brand positioning. Comprehensive 24/7 customer support ensures travelers receive assistance whenever needed, demonstrating Akasa's commitment to service excellence. This focus on the human element of service delivery has contributed to the airline's positive performance metrics, including industry-leading on-time performance and the lowest rates of customer complaints and cancellations.

However, maintaining these high service standards during periods of rapid expansion has presented challenges. As Akasa grew at an unprecedented pace, some customers reported encountering inconsistent service quality across different flights and routes. Recognizing these issues, the airline has placed renewed emphasis on training programs and technological support systems to ensure that customer service remains a key differentiator. This focus on the "people" element of the marketing mix has been crucial for building and maintaining Akasa's reputation for superior service in a highly competitive market where the human touch remains a critical differentiator.

STREAMLINING THE CUSTOMER EXPERIENCE

Akasa Air's service delivery systems and operational procedures demonstrate the airline's commitment to innovation while highlighting the complexities of implementing new technologies in aviation. The airline has invested significantly in streamlining the customer journey through digital solutions that reduce friction points and enhance convenience. Akasa's mobile app enables passengers to manage bookings, check in online, and receive real-time flight updates, including baggage belt notifications and proactive gate information.

For customer experience, Akasa focuses on inclusivity for both first-time and frequent travelers. They strive to reduce the intimidation factor of air travel, particularly for first time travelers and customers from tier-two and tier-three cities. The airline identified underserved segments, like pet parents who could not travel because they had no suitable pet care options, and introduced cabin pet travel. They also invested in premium seating comfort with extra cushioning and generous legroom to redefine the customer experience.

More ambitiously, the airline introduced biometric boarding at select airports, reducing wait times and enhancing security for passengers. These process innovations align with Akasa's overall strategy of creating a seamless, hassle-free travel experience. As Belson Coutinho noted, "technology implementation requires continuous improvement and refinement to meet evolving customer expectations."

Despite these forward-thinking initiatives, Akasa has encountered notable technical challenges in their implementation. Some customers expressed privacy concerns about biometric data usage, while technical glitches occasionally disrupted the passenger experience. These issues underscore the need for careful testing and transparent communication when introducing new technologies. Akasa's experience with process innovation demonstrates that while technological advancements can significantly enhance service delivery, successful implementation requires thorough planning, adequate testing, and ongoing optimization to ensure they genuinely improve rather than complicate the customer experience.

TANGIBLE MANIFESTATIONS OF BRAND PROMISE

The tangible elements supporting Akasa Air's service delivery have been carefully designed to reinforce the airline's brand positioning and differentiate it from competitors. A cornerstone of Akasa's strategy was the acquisition of a modern, fuel-efficient fleet of Boeing 737 MAX aircraft to reduce operational costs and environmental impact while providing passengers with a superior travel experience. In January 2024, Akasa placed a firm order for 150 additional aircraft, bringing its total order to 226 Boeing 737 MAX airplanes – making it the only Indian airline to achieve an order book of this size within 17 months of beginning operations.

The airline has devoted considerable attention to cabin design, creating a distinctive environment that features the Boeing Sky Interior with LED lighting, spacious legroom, and USB charging ports. These physical elements provide tangible evidence of Akasa's commitment to passenger comfort and modern travel experiences. Similarly, the airline's sustainable initiatives are manifested in eco-friendly meal packaging and sustainably curated crew uniforms, providing visual reinforcement of its environmental commitments.

However, Akasa has faced challenges in maintaining consistency in these physical elements. Delays in aircraft deliveries due to regulatory scrutiny of Boeing's 737 program forced the airline to modify its fleet plans, with Akasa now aiming to grow its fleet to 30 aircraft by July 2025. These setbacks highlight the importance of contingency planning when physical evidence forms a core part of brand positioning. Despite these challenges, Akasa has maintained focus on creating a comfortable travel environment that visually and tangibly reinforces its brand promises.

BALANCING INNOVATION AND EXECUTION IN THE GOLDEN DECADE

Akasa Air's remarkable journey demonstrates both the power of strategic differentiation and the challenges of maintaining consistency during rapid growth. In just under three years, the airline has established itself as a significant player in India's aviation sector by implementing a comprehensive services marketing strategy that addresses all seven Ps in innovative ways. CEO Vinay Dube's optimistic projection of a "golden decade" for Indian aviation seems well-founded given Akasa's trajectory and ambition to become one of the top 30 airlines in the world by the end of this decade.

To realize this potential, Akasa must address the operational issues and growing pains that have emerged during its rapid expansion phase. The airline needs to enhance service consistency, improve financial management, strengthen sustainability efforts, resolve technological integration issues, and carefully manage its ambitious growth plans. By aligning all seven elements of the services marketing mix, Akasa can continue to build its reputation and solidify its position as an innovative player in the aviation industry.

Akasa Air illustrates that while a well-conceived services marketing strategy can disrupt an established market, successful execution across all 7Ps is essential for sustainable competitive advantage. As the airline enters its next phase of growth, balancing innovation with operational excellence will be critical to fulfilling its vision of transforming air travel in India and beyond. With its customer-centric approach, technological innovation, and leadership's commitment to sustainability, Akasa is well-positioned to navigate the complex challenges of the aviation sector and emerge as a model for service excellence in a highly competitive industry.

Coutinho believes that sustained differentiation comes not just from service offerings, which can be copied, but from culture and people. While Akasa has made conscious investments in aircraft selection, viz. environmentally friendly with 20% lower emissions, cabin design, and customer comfort, they recognize that the human touch remains essential. They stay innovative through experimentation, collaboration with partners, and continuously incorporating emerging technologies like generative AI to enhance customer experience.

Questions

1. How has Akasa Air balanced its service offerings with competitive pricing in India's price-sensitive aviation market? Evaluate whether this approach creates sustainable competitive advantage or risks of being caught in the "middle ground" between full-service and low-cost carriers.
2. Analyze the tensions between Akasa's unprecedented growth rate (300% increase in ASKMs) and the operational challenges that emerged during expansion. What specific operational trade-offs should Akasa prioritize to maintain service consistency while continuing its growth trajectory?
3. Critically evaluate whether Akasa's sustainability initiatives represent a genuine competitive advantage or primarily serve as marketing differentiation. How might these initiatives impact financial performance in the short-term versus long-term brand building?
4. Assess Akasa's approach to targeting underserved customer segments, e.g. environmentally conscious travelers, pet owners and first-time flyers. Has this segmentation strategy effectively created defensible market positions, or could it be easily replicated by competitors?
5. Examine the challenges Akasa has faced in implementing technological innovations like biometric boarding. What specific operational and change management strategies should Akasa employ to ensure new technologies enhance rather than complicate the customer experience?

References

Interview with Belson Coutinho, CMO – Akasa Air in https://www.edx.org/learn/digital-marketing/indian-institute-of-management-bangalore-digital-marketing-strategy

Akasa Air expects to add more planes to its fleet by March 2025 https://www.business-standard.com/companies/news/akasa-air-expects-to-add-more-planes-to-its-fleet-by-march-2025-ceo-124122200263_1.html)

Golden decade of airlines is coming, I see a lot of profitability for next 10 years: Akasa Air CEO (https://economictimes.indiatimes.com/markets/expert-view/golden-decade-of-airlines-is-coming-i-see-a-lot-of-profitability-for-next-10-years-akasa-air-ceo/articleshow/104514447.cms?from=mdr)

Akasa Air redefines travel experience with industry-first offerings
https://www.bwhotelier.com/article/akasa-air-redefines-travel-experience-with-industry-first-offerings-540398

Akasa Air completes its second successful year of commercial operations
https://www.akasaair.com/news-room/akasa-press-releases/akasa-air-completes-its-second-successful-year-of-commercial-operations

Akasa Air crosses 17 million passengers and 100,000 departures in under 3 years
https://economictimes.indiatimes.com/industry/transportation/airlines-/-aviation/akasa-air-crosses-17-million-passengers-and-100000-departures-in-under-3-years/articleshow/120518800.cms?from=mdr

Generative AI will play a big role in enhancing customer experience
https://www.socialsamosa.com/interviews/generative-ai-will-play-big-role-enhancing-customer-experience-belson-coutinho-of-akasa-air
https://www.outlooktraveller.com/News/akasa-air-enhances-air-travel-experience-with-quietflights

https://www.deccanchronicle.com/lifestyle/travel/akasa-air-redefines-travel-experience-with-industry-first-offerings-1841604

Case Three

Zerodha: Growing without Ads

Zerodha, founded in 2010 by the Kamath brothers, Nithin and Nikhil, has emerged as one of the largest stock brokerage firms in India. The founders had a simple goal: "*stay completely online, provide excellent support, offer a fast and reliable trading platform and pass back the benefit of reduced costs to the client.*" Unlike legacy firms that relied on relationship managers and in-person client meetings, Zerodha was built entirely online. It eliminated physical branches and introduced a disruptive business model with zero-cost equity delivery, transparent pricing, and a highly intuitive trading platform. The name Zerodha was derived from 'Zero' and 'Rodha' (Sanskrit for barrier)—epitomizing the company's mission to remove obstacles for traders and investors.

OVERCOMING MARKET BARRIERS

Zerodha's founders meticulously identified the barriers that prevented retail investors from participating in the capital markets. Barriers included cost, support, and technology. The traditional brokerage landscape in India was characterized by operational complexity requiring extensive paperwork and in-person interactions, prohibitively high fees that discouraged small investors, and a general lack of accessible financial education that intimidated potential investors. While established players dismissed Zerodha as a niche experiment destined to fail, the company persisted in developing comprehensive solutions to address each barrier systematically. The journey proved challenging—in their first 15 months, they attracted only 7,000 active traders. Initially relying on NOW (Neat On Web), a trading platform provided by the National Stock Exchange (NSE), the company quickly recognized the limitations of third-party technology in delivering the seamless experience they envisioned for their customers, prompting a strategic shift toward proprietary development. Now the company's technology stack, including *Kite* (trading), *Coin* (mutual fund investments), and *Console* (trade analysis dashboard), offers a comprehensive platform for investors. As these innovations made investing in the capital markets simple, affordable, and accessible, the company started attracting retail investors in hordes. In 2022, the platform served

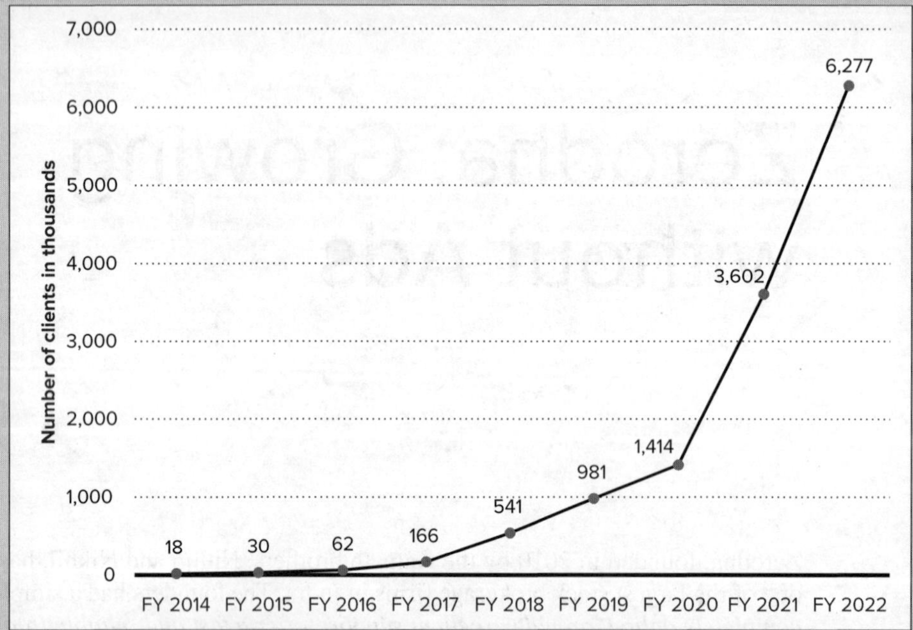

Source: National Stock Exchange of India; topsharebrokers; ID 1056530 Statista

over 6.0 million active users. The company's revenues surged by 3.4 times during 2021 to 2024 to hit ₹9372 crores while profits have soared by 4.9 times to ₹5496 crores **(Exhibits 1A and 1B)**.

INNOVATION AND DEVELOPMENT

Technology forms the backbone of Zerodha's success story. The company invested heavily in developing *Kite*, its proprietary trading platform. Launched in 2015, *Kite* featured a minimalistic and intuitive design, real-time analytics capabilities, advanced charting tools, and an ultra-fast order execution system designed to meet the demands of both novice and experienced traders. The platform's success was immediate and transformative, attracting thousands of new users monthly who were drawn to its novel combination of sophistication and accessibility. As the platform scaled rapidly, Zerodha encountered inevitable technical challenges during periods of high market volatility, occasionally causing outages and latency issues that threatened user trust. In response, the company made significant investments in cloud-based infrastructure, implemented comprehensive real-time monitoring systems, and developed stress-tested load management protocols to ensure platform stability even during the most active trading sessions. Zerodha continued its technological evolution with *Kite 3.0* in 2017, introducing even faster trade execution capabilities, sophisticated analytics, and an improved user interface that further enhanced the trading experience. This technological advancement arrived at an opportune time, coinciding with India's surge in

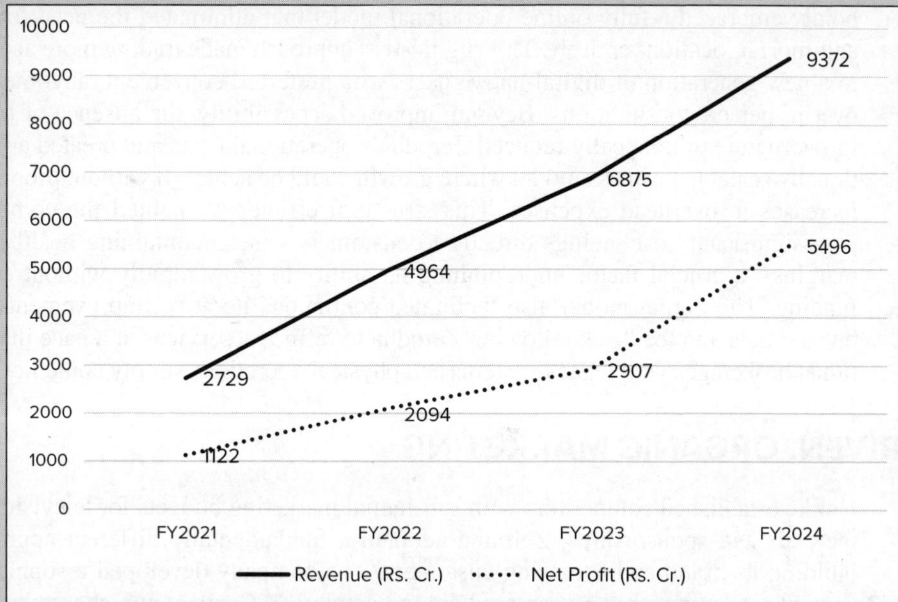

Source: Company

retail trading fueled by growing financial literacy and accelerating digital adoption across the country.

RADICAL PRICING

Zerodha fundamentally disrupted the brokerage industry with its groundbreaking pricing model that democratized market access for ordinary Indians. The company introduced zero-brokerage on equity delivery trades, allowing long-term investors to build portfolios without incurring any transaction fees—a concept previously unheard of in the Indian financial landscape. For more active traders, Zerodha implemented a transparent fee structure of 0.03% or ₹20 per executed order (whichever is lower) for equity intraday trades, while options traders benefited from a simple flat ₹20 per executed order regardless of transaction size. This pricing approach represented a radical departure from industry norms when introduced, prompting widespread skepticism about its long-term sustainability from established industry players accustomed to extracting significant fees from clients. Reflecting on this pivotal decision, founder Nithin Kamath explained: "*We first decided to waive brokerage for equity delivery in December 2015. Until then, we charged the lower of 0.1% or ₹20. This move was to change our image from a broker just for speculation, which was the case back then.*" The strategy successfully repositioned Zerodha as a platform for serious long-term investors while simultaneously forcing other players to reconsider their pricing models, effectively setting new standards for value and transparency throughout the sector.

DIGITAL-FIRST MODEL

While traditional brokers relied on expensive networks of physical branches, Zerodha boldly embraced a fully online operational model that eliminated the need for brick-and-mortar locations entirely. This digital-first approach made trading more accessible to a new generation of digital-native users who preferred convenient, anytime access over in-person consultations. Beyond improved accessibility, the absence of physical infrastructure dramatically reduced Zerodha's operational costs and created an exceptionally scalable business model where growth could be achieved without proportional increases in overhead expenses. This structural efficiency enabled the company to pass significant cost savings directly to customers while maintaining healthy profit margins—a crucial factor underpinning its ability to grow rapidly without external funding. The digital model also facilitated continuous iterative improvements based on user data and feedback, allowing Zerodha to refine its services at a pace that traditional brokerages with legacy systems and physical operations simply could not match.

CONTENT-DRIVEN, ORGANIC MARKETING

Unlike established competitors with substantial marketing budgets for television commercials and sponsorships, Zerodha adopted a fundamentally different approach to building its brand and acquiring customers. The company developed a sophisticated content marketing strategy centered around its blog, *Z-Connect*, which regularly publishes insightful market analyses, transparent platform updates, and educational investment strategies tailored to different experience levels **(Exhibit 2)**. Complementing this content hub, Zerodha created *TradingQ&A*, an interactive community forum where investors could openly discuss market trends, share trading strategies, and learn from more experienced participants—effectively transforming customers into both educators and brand advocates. Most remarkably, the company deliberately avoided the intrusive marketing tactics prevalent in the industry, as Nithin Kamath explained: "*We do not spam. Our competitors send out 5–10 notifications on the mobile app, while we send once or twice a month. That is thinking philosophically differently about the business, as really long term. Whatever fits in the long term vision is what we will work on.*" This measured, content-focused approach generated powerful word-of-mouth growth, minimized customer acquisition costs, and built authentic credibility that paid dividends as the company scaled. Zerodha has avoided the advertising blitzes favored by competitors. Kamath frequently emphasized the importance of an organic growth strategy, noting that "*Advertising is like being on cocaine. Once you start, you can't stop. You don't look at an ad and decide to invest in stock markets—it's always a friend or family friend who influences you.*" This insight guided Zerodha's marketing philosophy, focusing resources on creating genuine value, building trust, customer referrals and product excellence, instead of aggressive promotions.

FINANCIAL EDUCATION AND LITERACY

Recognizing that informed investors are more likely to succeed and remain engaged with the markets long-term, Zerodha made financial education a cornerstone of its business strategy. In 2014, the company launched *Varsity*, developing it into India's most comprehensive open-access financial education platform with meticulously crafted lessons covering everything from basic stock trading concepts to advanced investment strategies and sophisticated risk management techniques—all presented

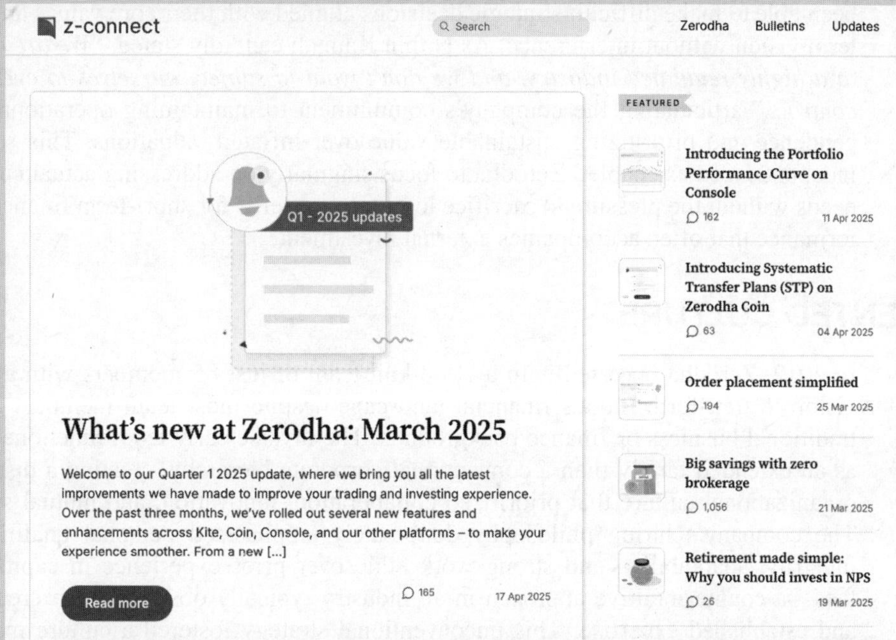

Source: Zerodha https://zerodha.com/z-connect/

in an accessible language that demystified complex financial concepts. Extending its educational mission to future generations, Zerodha created *Rupee Tales*, an innovative children's book series designed to introduce fundamental financial concepts at an early age, helping to build financial literacy from childhood. The company further supported investor development through *TradingQ&A*, a vibrant community platform where novice traders could learn directly from experienced market participants in a supportive environment. These educational resources served multiple strategic purposes: they built essential confidence among new investors hesitant to enter the markets, expanded Zerodha's potential customer base by reducing intimidation factors, established the company as a trusted authority in the financial space, and created a virtuous cycle where better-informed investors achieved greater success, reinforcing their loyalty to the platform that enabled their growth.

STRATEGIC INDEPENDENCE

Perhaps the most distinctive aspect of Zerodha's success story is its deliberate choice to remain completely bootstrapped despite numerous lucrative opportunities for external funding that would have accelerated its growth trajectory. Unlike most high-growth fintech firms that aggressively pursue venture capital investments or race toward initial public offerings, Zerodha has maintained an unwavering independent streak throughout its journey. This foundational decision has allowed the company to focus intensely on long-term value creation rather than chasing quarterly growth metrics that might satisfy external investors but compromise sustainable development. The absence of venture capital has freed Zerodha from potentially conflicting external pressures that could have compromised its customer-centric approach or pushed the company toward premature diversification or unsustainable growth targets. Instead, the founders have been able to make difficult strategic decisions aligned with their core values and long-term vision without interference. As Nithin Kamath candidly stated, "*We are already in a highly regulated industry, and we don't want to subject ourselves to even more controls*," articulating the company's commitment to maintaining operational independence and prioritizing sustainable value over inflated valuations. This strategic independence has enabled Zerodha to focus singularly on addressing actual customer needs without the pressure to sacrifice long-term benefits for short-term financial performance that often accompanies external investment.

PEOPLE-ORIENTED CULTURE

In 2012, Zerodha operated with a close-knit team of just 85 members with a shared vision to transform India's financial landscape despite most team members lacking traditional business or finance backgrounds. The diverse early team functioned more as an extended family than a conventional corporate hierarchy, creating a distinctive organizational culture that prioritized collaboration, innovation, and mutual support. The company's hiring philosophy deliberately emphasized personal qualities like integrity, adaptability, and strong work ethic over prior experience in capital markets—a counterintuitive approach in an industry typically obsessed with credentials and established expertise. This unconventional strategy fostered a culture markedly different from traditional brokerage environments, encouraging creative problem-solving and customer-focused innovation unconstrained by "how things have always been done." As Zerodha expanded to approximately 1,100 employees, maintaining this distinctive culture became both more challenging and more crucial to its continued success. The company's approach to technological advancement reflects this people-centric philosophy. When implementing AI and automation technologies that might threaten job security in other organizations, CTO Kailash Nadh emphasized a balanced perspective: "*Certain kinds of programming work, like boilerplate tasks, can now be automated. Entry-level work is being reduced, but models still can't create well-engineered, future-proof systems. They're tools for efficiency, not replacements for human ingenuity.*" Backing this philosophy with concrete policy, Zerodha implemented organizational guidelines ensuring that automation would not directly lead to job losses, demonstrating a deep commitment to employee security even as technological evolution transformed the workplace—a stance that has fostered exceptional loyalty and engagement throughout the growing organization.

FUTURE OUTLOOK

Despite its remarkable success, Zerodha continues to navigate several significant challenges in India's evolving financial landscape. The company faces intensifying competition from well-funded discount brokers like Groww and Upstox, which have rapidly captured market share by emulating aspects of Zerodha's business model while benefiting from substantial venture capital investments that enable aggressive marketing campaigns and accelerated feature development. System reliability remains an ongoing concern as Zerodha's user base continues to expand, with the critical challenge of ensuring uninterrupted service during peak trading periods when platform stability directly impacts customer portfolios and trust. Perhaps most complex is the

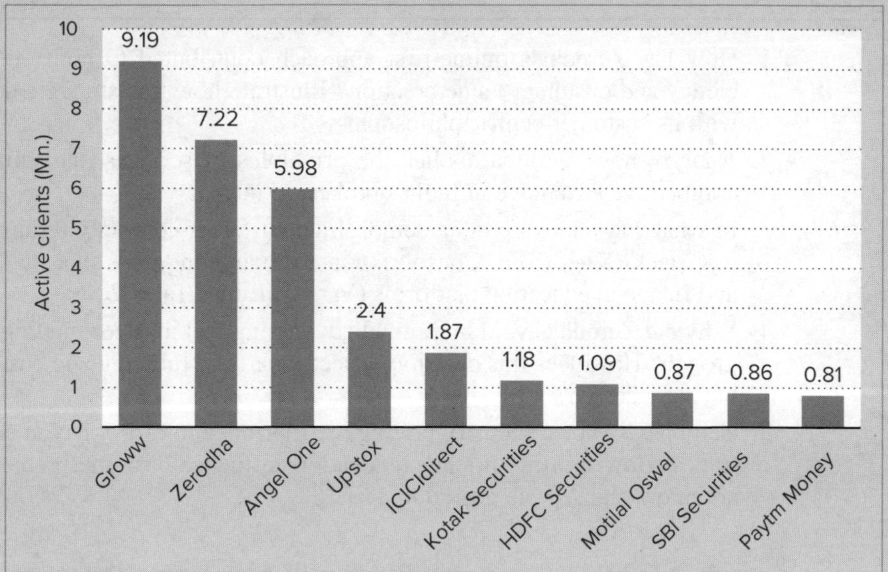

Source: Statista

delicate balance between continuous innovation and maintaining the platform's signature simplicity—adding sophisticated features demanded by advanced traders without overwhelming beginners or compromising the intuitive experience that attracted many users initially. Looking toward the future, Zerodha aims to strategically expand its fintech ecosystem through carefully developed AI-driven tools focused on enhanced risk management and portfolio optimization that maintain the company's user-friendly approach. The company remains committed to further simplifying investing for retail participants, leveraging increasingly sophisticated data analytics to personalize and enhance customer experiences without compromising privacy or introducing complexity. Throughout these developments, Zerodha intends to maintain its distinctive bootstrapped approach while competing effectively against rivals with significantly more funding—a strategy that has served it well thus far but will face increasing pressure as competition intensifies.

Zerodha's disruption of India's financial industry is a masterclass in spotting market gaps, building tech-driven solutions, and staying relentlessly customer-focused during rapid growth. By systematically eliminating the barriers to stock market participation through innovative technology, transparent pricing, and comprehensive educational resources, Zerodha has democratized investing for millions of ordinary Indians previously excluded from financial markets. Most remarkably, the company has achieved this transformative impact without any external funding—proving conclusively that a disciplined focus on customer value and operational efficiency can outperform the venture-backed growth model that dominates the contemporary fintech landscape. As traditional financial institutions like Angel One, ICICI Bank, HDFC Bank and aggressive new fintech entrants **(Exhibit 3)** compete intensely for market share, Zerodha's continued success demonstrates that sustainability, strategic independence, and genuine long-term thinking remain powerful competitive advantages in an industry increasingly driven by short-term metrics and artificial growth targets.

Questions

1. How has Zerodha's online-first approach contributed to both operational efficiency and customer value creation? Illustrate how this strategic decision aligns with its customer-centric philosophy.
2. Analyze how Zerodha applies the principles of services marketing to create a competitive advantage in India's brokerage industry.
3. In what ways does Zerodha demonstrate customer centricity through its technology stack (Kite, Coin, Console), content marketing (Z-Connect, TradingQ&A), and financial education platforms (Varsity, Rupee Tales)?
4. Why did Zerodha avoid traditional advertising and investor funding despite rapid growth? How does this decision reflect long-term thinking and customer-focused business design?
5. Zerodha disrupted industry pricing by offering zero brokerage on equity delivery trades. How did this pricing innovation influence customer perception, market adoption, and service positioning?

Source

Kamath, N. (2012). Our Story till now… Z-Connect by Zerodha. https://zerodha.com/z-connect/general/our-story-till-now

Kamath, N. (2025, March 21). Big savings with zero brokerage. Z-Connect by Zerodha. https://zerodha.com/z-connect/business-updates/big-savings-with-zero-brokerage

Zerodha. Our company, history, and the people behind it. https://zerodha.com/about/

Nehme, J. J., Srivastava, S. C., & Aman, A. (2023). How Zerodha Used Technology to Disrupt the Indian Stock Trading Industry. International Conference on Information Systems (ICIS).

Economic Times. (2024). Zero the cost of Zerodha's advertising. Retrieved from https://brandequity.economictimes.indiatimes.com/news/marketing/zero-the-cost-of-zerodhas-advertising/115528155

Forbes India. (2022). The curious case study of Zerodha's blue ocean strategy. Retrieved from https://www.forbesindia.com/article/bharatiya-vidya-bhavan039s-spjimr/the-curious-case-study-of-zerodhas-blue-ocean-strategy/77457/1

Moneycontrol. (2024). A piece of technology won't replace you overnight: Zerodha CTO on AI, policy, and job security. Retrieved from https://www.moneycontrol.com/news/business/startup/a-piece-of-technology-wont-replace-you-overnight-zerodha-cto-on-ai-policy-and-job-security-12874615.html

Varsity. (2015). Free and Open Stock Market and Financial Education. Retrieved from https://zerodha.com/varsity/

Zerodha. Zerodha brokerage charges, fees & taxes on trading and investing. https://zerodha.com/charges/#tab-equities

Zerodha has no plans to go public, does not require additional capital: Nithin Kamath. (2025, March 26). Moneycontrol. https://www.moneycontrol.com/news/business/markets/zerodha-has-no-plans-to-go-public-and-does-not-require-additional-capital-nithin-kamath-12976358.html

About us - Rainmatter Foundation. https://rainmatter.org/about/

Case **Four**

SatSure – Value Creation through Decision Intelligence

SatSure, founded in 2017 by former ISRO scientists Prateep Basu, Rashmit Singh Sukhmani, and space-tech entrepreneur Abhishek Raju, represents a paradigm shift in how geospatial intelligence services can improve organizational decision making by using satellite data and technological advancements. The founding team, inspired by India's evolving role in the global space sector, sought to anticipate the future of space-based technologies and their potential to improve decision making across multiple industries. Built around the philosophy of decision intelligence, SatSure identifies and integrates new technologies to help clients make more effective choices, moving beyond traditional remote sensing to provide comprehensive technological support that encompasses data gathering, transmission, analytics, and visualization.

The company targets a diverse community that extends far beyond traditional space industry boundaries, including agri-tech startups, data scientists, policymakers, financial service professionals, and researchers across various sectors. This broad targeting strategy reflects SatSure's commitment to democratizing space-tech data to address socio-economic challenges while fostering the creation of open-source solutions that can be shared, modified, and improved for the broader agricultural and infrastructure communities. The leadership team's vision was to create a platform that would serve as a bridge between complex satellite data and practical business applications, enabling organizations across sectors to harness the power of geospatial intelligence without requiring extensive technical expertise in remote sensing technologies.

COMPREHENSIVE PRODUCT PORTFOLIO AND SERVICE INNOVATION

SatSure's product strategy centers on translating complex satellite data into industry-specific solutions through a comprehensive portfolio of interconnected services that address diverse market needs. SatSure Sparta serves as the flagship farm-to-region agricultural insights platform, offering satellite imagery data that caters to various agrarian needs, including seed inputs, crop protection, and crop classification. As co-founder Abhishek Raju emphasized, "We work on improving the effectiveness of agriculture financing instruments by innovating on satellite big-data technology to provide regular crop monitoring of large areas for intervention and better productivity."

Complementing Sparta's agricultural focus, SatSure Cygnus provides clients with data on cloud coverage to understand crop growth and yield patterns. This platform enables agricultural stakeholders to monitor crop development patterns, assess field conditions, and make informed decisions about resource allocation and intervention timing.

The integration of these two platforms creates a comprehensive agricultural monitoring ecosystem that addresses both immediate operational needs and long-term strategic planning requirements. SatSure Skies expands the company's reach into infrastructure monitoring, energy analysis, and urban planning through high-resolution satellite imagery that targets sectors such as renewable energy, oil and gas, infrastructure planning, and asset management. This diversification demonstrates the company's ability to adapt its core geospatial intelligence capabilities to serve multiple industry verticals.

The company's innovation extends to specialized applications such as iNetra, a sophisticated system designed under the Airports Authority of India (AAI) Startup Policy to boost safety and streamline aviation operations. Aligned with International Civil Aviation Organization (ICAO) standards, iNetra facilitates the critical shift from traditional Aeronautical Information Services to modern Aeronautical Information Management through an integrated digital platform that enhances operational efficiency and safety protocols. KaleidEO, launched in 2022, represents SatSure's ambitious attempt to overcome inefficiencies in traditional Earth Observation Satellites (EOS) by adopting a demand-first approach (Exhibit 1). Its Earth Observation Infrastructure-as-a-Service model caters to both space and non-space industries, enhancing capabilities in disaster relief, infrastructure monitoring, and national security applications.

Another innovative solution, SatSure Sage, enhances micro-market analysis by leveraging geospatial intelligence to optimize crop loan portfolio expansion. The platform aids in accurate market planning and better repayment methods by matching the conventional risk-rating models to changing seasonal patterns. It aids financial institutions to make well-informed lending decisions. The platform can instantaneously provide risk metrics like farm risks, thus making it easier for farmers to access agricultural loans, as the bank's branches allocate resources depending on localized risk patterns. According to former Chairman, Dr. Roger Moser, "Ultimately, this approach reduces transaction costs and enhances financial inclusion by lowering the costs associated with providing finance." Thus, monitoring the farm productivity with credit performance leads to data-driven, robust ways of financing agribusiness by ensuring sustainable loan practices (Exhibit 2). SatSure Sage demonstrates the company's ability to create highly specialized solutions that address specific market inefficiencies.

This platform enhances micro-market analysis by leveraging geospatial intelligence to optimize crop loan portfolio expansion, addressing a critical need in agricultural finance where traditional risk assessment models often fail to account for localized environmental factors. The platform aids financial institutions in accurate market planning and better repayment methods by matching traditional risk-rating models to changing seasonal patterns, enabling more sophisticated and responsive lending strategies that benefit both lenders and borrowers.

MARKET ACCESS APPROACH

SatSure employs a sophisticated customer-centric pricing and distribution approach that systematically reduces barriers to adoption while maximizing global market penetration. The company's demo-first approach represents a fundamental understanding

Stage	Description
1. Use Satellite Imagery	Employ satellite data to monitor crop conditions and land use across regions.
2. Apply Data Analytics	Utilize data analysis tools to extract insights from imagery and field data.
3. Adopt Predictive Modelling	Leverage predictive models to forecast yields, detect risks, and plan resource use.
4. Implement Precision Farming	Integrate insights into farming practices to optimize productivity and sustainability.

of the complexity and unfamiliarity that many potential clients face when considering geospatial intelligence services. By offering comprehensive demonstrations of its analytical platforms to prospective customers, SatSure enables organizations to thoroughly evaluate the technology's capabilities and potential impact before making significant financial commitments. This strategy is particularly crucial in the geospatial intelligence market, where many potential clients lack prior experience with satellite data applications and require extensive education about the technology's capabilities and benefits.

This trial-based approach is complemented by an extensive network of partnerships with financial institutions, agricultural technology firms, and infrastructure companies that serve multiple purposes in SatSure's market expansion strategy. These partnerships not only enhance service reach by providing access to established client networks but also build credibility through association with recognized industry leaders. By positioning itself as a value-added service within existing business relationships, SatSure is able to overcome the significant trust barriers that often impede adoption of new technologies in conservative industries such as agriculture and finance.

The company's global distribution strategy leverages advanced cloud-based platforms, comprehensive API (application programming interface) integration capabilities, and intuitive dashboard solutions that enable access regardless of geographical location or technical infrastructure limitations. This technological approach effectively eliminates traditional barriers to international expansion while enabling seamless integration with existing client systems. The automated Earth Observation Infrastructure-as-a-Service model represents a particularly innovative approach that removes the need for clients to develop internal expertise in complex data processing, thereby expanding the potential market to include organizations that would otherwise lack the technical capabilities to utilize satellite data effectively.

RELATIONSHIP-DRIVEN PROMOTIONS FOR NICHE MARKETS

SatSure's promotional strategy demonstrates sophisticated understanding of the unique challenges inherent in marketing highly specialized geospatial services within B2B contexts where customer awareness remains persistently low. Unlike consumer-focused companies that can rely on mass media advertising to build brand recognition,

SatSure operates in a niche, B2B and institutional market where potential clients require extensive education about both the technology's capabilities and its practical applications to their specific business challenges. The company has abandoned traditional mass media approaches and favors targeted educational content marketing through industry-specific blogs, whitepapers, and case studies that demonstrate practical applications and measurable benefits.

Industry conference participation represents a critical component of SatSure's promotional strategy, providing direct access to focused audiences of potential clients while establishing the company's thought leadership position within relevant professional communities. These events serve dual purposes of education and relationship building, enabling SatSure's technical experts to engage in substantive conversations with potential clients about specific challenges and solutions. The company's focus on building credibility through awards, recognition, and expert speaking engagements reflects an understanding that in highly technical markets, reputation and demonstrated expertise often carry more weight than traditional promotional messages.

LinkedIn has emerged as particularly effective for creating visibility within SatSure's target markets, enabling the company to share technical content, case studies, and thought leadership pieces with relevant professional networks. However, the company recognizes that social media success in B2B markets requires consistent, high-value content that demonstrates expertise rather than promotional messaging. Much of SatSure's growth trajectory can be attributed to internal champions within client organizations who recognize the technology's potential and advocate for collaboration from within their own companies. This organic advocacy represents the most powerful form of promotion in specialized technical markets, where peer recommendations carry significantly more weight than external marketing messages.

The company's commitment to ensuring successful project outcomes has created a powerful referral network that now generates a substantial portion of new business opportunities. When SatSure encounters project challenges, leadership consistently allocates additional resources and time to resolve issues quickly, maintaining a startup mentality that prioritizes client success over short-term profitability. This approach has gradually built a strong reputation across India and international markets, with many new projects now beginning through referrals from satisfied clients or success stories that demonstrate measurable business impact.

HUMAN CAPITAL AND ORGANIZATIONAL CULTURE

SatSure's human capital practice represents a deliberate departure from traditional space industry hiring practices, emphasizing interdisciplinary expertise that brings together professionals from diverse domains, including space science, agriculture, technology, finance, insurance, and strategic consulting. This cross-pollination of expertise enables the company to serve as versatile problem-solvers who specialize in data integration across multiple domains, often providing clients with a much broader range of technological support than initially anticipated. The company's recruitment specifically targets individuals who can bridge the gap between technical capabilities and practical business applications, recognizing that successful geospatial intelligence services require both deep technical knowledge and nuanced understanding of clients' business contexts.

The organizational culture emphasizes innovation and collaboration, fostering an environment where technological advancements drive real-world solutions rather than pursuing technology for its own sake. SatSure thrives on the creative tension generated by bringing together experts from different fields who approach problems from fundamentally different perspectives, often leading to innovative solutions that would not emerge from more homogeneous teams. The company's culture of collaboration extends beyond internal operations to include active engagement with the broader technological community through open-source initiatives and knowledge sharing that benefits entire industries rather than solely advancing SatSure's competitive position.

Despite significant growth and increasing market recognition, SatSure has deliberately maintained a startup culture characterized by dedication, flexibility, and willingness to allocate additional resources when projects face unexpected challenges. This entrepreneurial mindset manifests in the team's readiness to work extended hours and invest extra effort when needed, ensuring that every client engagement delivers meaningful value and reinforces SatSure's reputation for reliability and excellence. The leadership team recognizes that in the highly specialized geospatial intelligence market, reputation for technical excellence and client service often matters more than traditional business metrics, making cultural commitment to client success a strategic competitive advantage.

PROCESS INNOVATION AND TECHNICAL CAPABILITIES

SatSure's process innovation focuses on streamlining complex geospatial intelligence delivery through sophisticated automation and real-time analytics capabilities that transform raw satellite data into actionable business intelligence. The company's technical architecture enables industries to access comprehensive analytics without requiring internal expertise in complex data processing, effectively democratizing access to advanced geospatial intelligence across multiple sectors. This technological capability represents a significant competitive advantage, as it enables SatSure to serve clients who would otherwise lack the technical infrastructure or expertise necessary to utilize satellite data effectively.

The company's risk assessment models represent particularly sophisticated applications of geospatial intelligence, correlating seasonal patterns, environmental factors, and historical data with lending risks for financial institutions. These models enable banks and other financial service providers to manage risk more effectively while extending services in a more targeted and reliable manner, addressing a critical gap in traditional agricultural finance where environmental factors have historically been difficult to quantify and incorporate into lending decisions. SatSure's integrated approach combines satellite data with on-ground observations to provide comprehensive insights that account for both macro-environmental trends and localized conditions that can significantly impact agricultural productivity and financial risk.

The platform's predictive capabilities extend far beyond simple data analysis to provide early warning systems that enable proactive rather than reactive decision-making across multiple sectors. For example, when satellite data reveals that crop development in a specific region is lagging behind normal patterns, the system can automatically alert insurance providers to reassess coverage assumptions while simultaneously notifying local authorities who may need to implement preventive measures such as expanding irrigation infrastructure or providing emergency agricultural support. This integrated approach to predictive intelligence creates value for multiple stakeholders simultaneously while reducing the overall risk exposure across agricultural value chains.

SatSure's technical platform also incorporates sophisticated weather pattern forecasting and soil moisture measurement capabilities that provide tailored insights to various stakeholders across agricultural and infrastructure sectors. The system's ability to process multiple data streams simultaneously and extract actionable intelligence represents a significant technological achievement that enables the company to serve diverse client needs through a unified platform architecture. This technical sophistication allows SatSure to offer comprehensive solutions that address complex business challenges rather than simply providing raw data that clients must interpret independently.

TANGIBLE IMPACT DEMONSTRATION AND SERVICE VALIDATION

To address the inherent intangibility challenges associated with geospatial services, SatSure has developed comprehensive approaches for demonstrating tangible impact through concrete deliverables that clearly illustrate value creation across various industry sectors. For FMCG companies seeking to establish sustainable sourcing practices, SatSure provides customized information systems that enable identification of optimal sourcing areas and precise timing of harvest activities, while simultaneously optimizing transportation routes to minimize costs and environmental impact. These applications demonstrate how geospatial intelligence can address practical business challenges while supporting broader sustainability objectives that are increasingly important to corporate stakeholders.

The insurance industry represents a particularly compelling application of SatSure's capabilities, where satellite imagery enables rapid and accurate damage assessment during natural calamities, significantly expediting claim settlement processes that traditionally required extensive field investigations. During natural disasters, the ability to survey affected areas is typically severely limited by infrastructure damage and safety concerns, causing substantial delays in damage assessments and claim settlements that imposes serious hardship on affected parties. SatSure's Sparta platform provides comprehensive satellite imagery data that enables insurance companies to assess agricultural damage quickly and accurately, facilitating faster claim processing and reducing the administrative burden on both insurers and claimants.

The company's crisis response capabilities received validation during the severe floods in Kerala in 2018, where SatSure's timely insights helped guide rescue operations and enabled efficient damage assessment processes that would not have been possible using traditional survey methods. This real-world application demonstrated the platform's ability to provide critical intelligence during high-stakes, time-sensitive situations where traditional information gathering methods are inadequate or impossible. The success of this crisis response application has established SatSure as a valuable partner for government agencies and emergency response organizations seeking to enhance their operational capabilities.

Beyond crisis response, SatSure's platform enables comprehensive monitoring of infrastructure projects, providing regular updates on construction progress, environmental impact assessment, and compliance monitoring that helps project managers maintain schedules and regulatory compliance. For renewable energy projects, the platform provides detailed analysis of site conditions, environmental factors, and performance monitoring that enables more effective project planning and ongoing optimization. These applications demonstrate the platform's versatility and ability to create value across diverse sectors while addressing specific operational challenges that are difficult to solve using traditional monitoring approaches.

VALUE CREATION AND MARKET POSITIONING

SatSure's core value proposition centers on risk reduction and decision enhancement through data-driven insights that fundamentally improve operational efficiency while reducing transaction costs across multiple industry sectors. As noted by Dr. Moser, this comprehensive approach "reduces transaction costs and enhances financial inclusion by lowering the costs associated with providing finance." This value creation extends beyond simple cost reduction to enable entirely new business models and service offerings that were previously impossible or economically unfeasible.

For financial institutions, SatSure's risk assessment capabilities enable extension of services to previously underserved markets by providing reliable data about environmental factors that significantly impact agricultural productivity and loan repayment capacity. Traditional agricultural lending has been constrained by the difficulty of assessing environmental risks and monitoring crop performance across large geographical areas, leading to conservative lending practices that often exclude small farmers and rural communities from formal financial services. SatSure's platform addresses these limitations by providing continuous monitoring capabilities and predictive analytics that enable more sophisticated risk management approaches.

The platform's predictive intelligence capabilities serve governments, insurance firms, and infrastructure planners with early warning systems that enable proactive decision-making across multiple sectors, creating substantial value through prevention rather than reactive response. This proactive approach can significantly reduce the economic and social costs associated with natural disasters, crop failures, and infrastructure problems by enabling timely interventions that prevent or mitigate negative outcomes. The ability to predict and prevent problems rather than simply responding after they occur represents a fundamental shift in how organizations can approach risk management and operational planning.

SatSure's comprehensive approach to geospatial intelligence has successfully positioned the company as an essential service provider rather than a simple data vendor, creating deeper client relationships and more sustainable competitive advantages. By focusing on business outcomes rather than technical capabilities, SatSure has differentiated itself from competitors who may offer similar data but lack the industry expertise and analytical capabilities necessary to translate raw information into actionable business intelligence. This strategic positioning enables the company to command premium pricing while building long-term client relationships based on measurable business value rather than technical specifications.

FUTURE GROWTH STRATEGY AND MARKET LEADERSHIP

Looking toward the future, SatSure has strategically positioned itself for continued growth through expansion of its resilience and disaster management capabilities while broadening its global reach through continued innovation in applications such as disaster forecasting, risk management, and infrastructure monitoring. The company's expansion strategy recognizes that climate change and increasing global connectivity are creating growing demand for sophisticated monitoring and prediction capabilities that can help organizations and governments prepare for and respond to increasingly complex challenges.

The company's commitment to democratizing space technology and making sophisticated satellite data accessible to diverse industries represents both a social mission and a sound business strategy that opens new markets while addressing critical global challenges. By continuing to reduce the technical barriers that prevent organizations from utilizing geospatial intelligence, SatSure can expand its addressable market while creating positive social impact through improved decision-making capabilities across multiple sectors.

SatSure's well-crafted services marketing approach, emphasizing innovation, customer-centricity, and strategic partnerships, serves as a model for B2B technology service providers operating in specialized markets where traditional marketing approaches are ineffective. The company's success in overcoming the challenges of marketing intangible, knowledge-based services demonstrates the importance of relationship building, educational content, and demonstrated value delivery in establishing market leadership within niche technical sectors. The company counts leading organizations including IFC, Reliance Foundation, Bill & Melinda Gates Foundation, BCG, Adani, Syngenta, ICICI Bank, L&T Finance, JICA DX Lab, Chola MS, Reliance Commercial Finance, Munich RE, Kotak and HDFC Bank as its clients and partners.

The company's continued focus on building ecosystem value through open-source solutions and knowledge sharing positions SatSure as a thought leader and collaborative partner rather than simply a service provider, creating additional opportunities for growth while reinforcing its reputation within target markets. This approach recognizes that long-term success in emerging technology markets often depends on building broader ecosystems rather than pursuing purely competitive strategies, enabling sustainable growth through collaborative value creation that benefits entire industries rather than individual companies. As Prateep Basu, Founder & CEO explained, "At SatSure, our vision is to deliver decision insights from space, and to positively impact society through this technology."

Questions

1. How does SatSure's approach to decision intelligence differ from traditional geospatial data providers, and what role does this play in value creation for its business clients?
2. Discuss how SatSure applies the key elements of services marketing mix to succeed in its niche B2B markets. Use specific examples from the case.
3. Why is SatSure's "demo-first" and "relationship-driven" promotional strategy particularly suited for B2B decision-support services? How does this reflect a customer-centric marketing philosophy?

4. SatSure offers solutions like SatSure Sage and iNetra that are tailored to specific sectors. How does this specialization enhance perceived service quality and influence pricing strategy?
5. Analyze how SatSure's organizational culture and human capital strategy support its service innovation and customer success goals. Why is this alignment crucial in high-tech service industries?

Reference

D'Cunha, S. D. (2018, January 8). *For India's farmers it's agtech startups, not government, that is key.* Forbes. https://www.forbes.com/sites/suparnadutt/2018/01/08/for-indias-farmers-its-agtech-startups-not-government-that-is-key/?sh=703d5c401c6e

Geospatial Media & Communications. (2024, May 7). Agri-finance with Geospatial Touch. Geospatial World. https://geospatialworld.net/prime/agri-finance-geospatial-touch/

Innovators, S. (2022, January 6). *An open innovation platform for the agricultural ecosystem: SaTSure Sparta.* Medium. https://medium.com/@spacetechinnovators/an-open-innovation-platform-for-the-agricultural-ecosystem-satsure-sparta-550f8b87059a

Medhi, T. (2024, October 22). How space tech SatSure's KaleidEO is helping companies access Earth observation satellites. *YourStory*. https://yourstory.com/2024/10/space-tech-startup-satsure-kaleideo-earth-observation-eo-satellites

Pathak, N. (2024, August 2). INETRA by SaTSure*: A step towards Digital transformation for India's aviation. SatSure Blog.* https://www.blog.satsure.co/index.php/2024/08/02/inetra-by-satsure-step-towards-digital-transformation-for-indian-aviation/

SatSure. (2022, June 30). Cloud free images through SatSure Cygnus, a virtual constellation for agricultural monitoring. SatSure Blog. https://www.blog.satsure.co/index.php/2022/06/30/cloud-free-images-through-satsure-cygnus-a-virtual-constellation-for-agricultural-monitoring/

SatSure https://www.satsure.co/

Interview Dr. Roger Moser, Chairman – Satsure (2021) https://tinyurl.com/edxSMIIMB

https://www.moneycontrol.com/news/business/bengaluru-based-space-tech-startup-satsure-raises-15-million-in-series-a-11276611.html

https://www.blog.satsure.co/index.php/2025/01/16/satsure-recognized-in-the-2024-gartner-emerging-tech-impact-radar-artificial-intelligence-report/

https://www.prnewswire.com/in/news-releases/satsure-joins-hands-with-jica-dxlab-and-bcg-on-a-proof-of-concept-to-develop-a-digital-forest-health-monitoring-system-for-the-rajasthan-forest-department-rfd-302257131.html

Case Five

ICICI Bank – Leading through Customer Centricity

ICICI, set up in 1955 as a development financial institution, established ICICI Bank in 1994 as its commercial banking subsidiary. ICICI's reverse merger with ICICI Bank in 2002 led to the creation of one of India's leading financial institutions. This merger represented a strategic pivot toward retail banking while maintaining the institution's historical strength in corporate lending and project financing. ICICI Bank's evolution, with particular focus on its more recent makeover, offers several lessons in strategy, customer-centric approach and brand building.

The bank's journey has not been without challenges. ICICI Bank experienced head-winds during the 2008 global financial crisis. More recently, the bank went through a leadership change in 2018. These crises tested the bank's resilience while creating opportunities for strategic reorientation.

ICICI Bank's evolution, from 2018 onwards, can be characterized by a return to fundamental banking principles executed with precision. The bank's approach is captured in several key organizational philosophies, including 'One Bank, One RoE', 'One Bank, One Team', and the principle of 'Return of Capital' (Exhibit 1). This back-to-basics approach, combined with technological innovation and a renewed emphasis on customer service, has positioned ICICI Bank as a leader among Indian financial institutions. The "One Bank, One RoE" principle emphasizes maximizing the share of target market across all products and services, while "One Bank, One Team" promotes internal coordination and a unified approach to serving customers. The "Return of Capital" principle reinforces the fundamental banking tenet that when giving a loan, there should be reasonable assurance that the borrower has both the intent and ability to repay.

The bank's strategies are built around five key pillars that are consistently emphasized in internal communications: the risk framework, philosophical framework, trust framework, customer framework, and product framework. These principles create a clear strategic direction that guides all aspects of the bank's operations.

Layer/Component	Purpose/Focus Area	Key Elements/Examples
Organisational Values	Define the culture, ethics, and shared purpose that guide all activities	• One Bank, One Team • Compliance with Conscience
Operating within the Guardrails of Risk & Compliance	Maintain strong governance and ensure all activities operate within defined risk frameworks	• Credit Risk Management • Compliance Culture • Fair to Customer, Fair to Bank
Strategic Value Drivers for Business	Enable sustainable growth, efficiency, and innovation through business enablers	• Customer-Centric Approach • Productivity and Cost Efficiency • Risk Culture • Digital Ecosystem • Partnerships and Cross-Functional Collaboration
Core Business Activities	Deliver banking products and services that directly create financial value and inclusion	• Facilitate Payments and Transactions • Enable Wealth Creation and Management • Provide Savings Products • Offer Credit to Support Consumption and Economic Activity • Enable Financial Inclusion

CUSTOMER SEGMENTATION AND MARKET REACH

The bank's customer segmentation strategy has evolved significantly over the past three decades, moving from broad categorizations to increasingly granular approaches that recognize the diversity of financial needs across customer groups, involving in-depth profiling of each micro-market. The bank serves a wide spectrum of customers, from individual retail clients to large corporations, with tailored value propositions for each segment. In the retail space, ICICI Bank employs a sophisticated segmentation approach that goes beyond traditional demographic classifications. Its Customer360° initiative encourages employees to develop a comprehensive understanding of each customer's financial needs, enabling personalized service delivery. This approach recognizes that customer needs evolve over time and that long-term relationship value often exceeds the immediate transaction value. The bank employs a segment-driven pricing strategy balancing competitive rates with value-added services. They offer zero-balance accounts for segments like students while premium products like the Emeralde Credit Card carry higher fees (₹12,000 joining fee), creating a tiered approach that serves diverse customer needs.

ICICI Bank's extensive presence through 7,000 branches and over 16,000 ATMs and cash recycling machines cover major markets in urban and rural India in addition to its international presence in countries like Canada, the UK, Singapore, and the US. Their digital platforms serve millions, with iMobile boasting over 30 million users and InstaBIZ serving 1.5 million business banking customers.

The bank's push into rural markets has been boosted by merging its retail and rural business groups to capture growth opportunities beyond urban centers. While the rural portfolio currently accounts for less than 10% of advances, it represents a significant growth opportunity driven by the intensifying financial inclusion across India. This rural drive also reflects ICICI Bank's commitment to reaching underserved markets while diversifying its geographical footprint.

Corporate clients are segmented based on size, industry, and relationship potential. Large corporate relationships are managed through dedicated relationship managers who coordinate across product teams to deliver integrated solutions. For mid-sized enterprises and SMEs, the bank has developed specialized offerings that address the unique challenges these businesses face, including working capital constraints, limited collateral, and the need for simplified banking processes.

Accessibility has been significantly enhanced through its digital capabilities. The bank has invested heavily in its digital infrastructure, enabling it to serve customers across geographical boundaries with reduced dependence on physical branches. Digital channels now handle over 90% of its transactions, lowering the cost to serve while improving accessibility. Seamless digital experience has been particularly effective in attracting younger, tech-savvy customers who prioritize convenience and speed in their banking relationships.

PRODUCT STRATEGY AND PORTFOLIO DIVERSIFICATION

ICICI Bank's comprehensive product portfolio spans offerings for the retail, corporate, and small business segments. The bank's product strategy reflects a deliberate shift toward diversification and granularity, reducing concentration risks and creating multiple growth engines. Retail banking has been a particular focus, growing to constitute over 52% of the total loan book.

ICICI Bank and its subsidiaries offer comprehensive financial products spanning deposit accounts, specialized credit cards, various loans, investment options, insurance policies, and wealth management services to retail customers. Their digital banking capabilities allow customers to conduct everything from bill payments to mutual fund investments from a single platform, with social media integration enabling basic banking transactions.

Within the retail segment, mortgage loans account for approximately 61% of the portfolio, representing a growing emphasis on secured lending. Home loans provide a relatively secure asset class, create opportunities for cross-selling other products, and help establish long-term customer relationships. The bank has invested significantly in digitalizing its mortgage offering through its iLens platform, which enables seamless customer onboarding without physical paperwork.

Beyond mortgages, ICICI Bank has built strong positions in credit cards, personal loans, and vehicle financing. In the credit cards business, the bank has steadily gained market share, increasing from 14.3% in FY17 to 16.6% in 2024.

Simplification has been a notable aspect of ICICI Bank's product strategy. The bank has eliminated numerous product variants – 80 in credit cards, 60 in mortgages, and 20 in savings accounts – to reduce complexity and improve customer experience. This simplification initiative reflects a broader shift from product-centricity to customer-centricity, focusing on meeting customer instead of proliferating offerings.

ICICI Bank has adopted a relationship-based approach that focuses on understanding its corporate client's entire business ecosystem to serve them as a financial partner addressing diverse needs across the value chain. This strategy has allowed the bank to maintain its corporate banking heritage while reducing concentration risks.

CUSTOMER CENTRICITY AND SERVICE EXCELLENCE

Customer centricity lies at the heart of ICICI Bank's success. The institution has moved away from product-centric approaches to put customer needs at the center of its strategy. This shift is reflected in the bank's service philosophy of "Fair to Customer, Fair to Bank," which emphasizes equitable outcomes for both parties in every interaction.

The Customer 360° approach represents a cornerstone of ICICI Bank's service strategy. This initiative encourages employees to understand customers' comprehensive financial needs rather than focusing on individual products. By taking the "whole bank to the customer," employees can offer holistic solutions that address multiple needs, enhancing customer satisfaction while increasing wallet share (Exhibit 2).

The bank's success relies on its competent and well-trained workforce of bankers, customer support executives, and relationship managers who provide personalized solutions through a customer-centric culture that enhances satisfaction and strengthens the bank's reputation.

Service excellence is reinforced through rigorous employee selection and training programs. The bank places strong emphasis on hiring individuals who align with its values, particularly the commitment to serving customers with humility. Ongoing training programs focus not only on technical skills but also on cultivating a customer-first mindset. This cultural orientation has created a workforce of almost 130,000 employees and associates who consistently deliver high-quality service experiences.

Process simplification has been another key driver of improved customer experience. The bank has systematically identified and eliminated friction points in customer journeys, streamlining processes to reduce complexity and improve speed. The digitalization of mortgage lending through the iLens platform exemplifies this approach, replacing paper-based processes with seamless digital workflows, enabling paperless loan origination and faster approvals. Similar initiatives have been implemented across product lines, creating consistent and efficient customer experiences.

The bank has streamlined processes for customer convenience, including instant digital account opening and robust grievance redressal mechanisms. Its Twitter account (@ICICIBank_Care) incorporates interactive customer support features that allow service requests via direct messages, reflecting their commitment to technology-enhanced service delivery.

ICICI Bank's service strategy also emphasizes relationship continuity. The bank recognizes that customer relationships are built over time through multiple interactions, and it has designed its service model to foster long-term engagement. Relationship

Customer Focus	Strategic Approach	Execution Framework
Trust, Transparency & Long-Term Relationship	Build partnerships with the right clients and institutions	Strengthen presence through Business Centres
Ease, Access & Convenience	Deliver seamless experiences and enhance customer satisfaction	Operate within micromarkets and local ecosystems for deeper reach
Reputation, Service Excellence & Reliability	Drive holistic customer engagement and simplify banking journeys	Expand digital-first solutions for scale and efficiency

managers are encouraged to focus on customer lifetime value rather than immediate transaction outcomes, aligning with the bank's philosophical framework that emphasizes process over results.

The effectiveness of these customer-centric initiatives is evident in the bank's strong deposit growth, particularly in low-cost current account and savings account (CASA) deposits. The bank has achieved growth in deposits by earning customer trust through consistent service excellence.

The physical evidence of ICICI Bank's services includes nationwide branches, ATMs, online platforms, official documentation, and branded cards that provide tangible touchpoints for customer experience while tangibilizing the brand promise. This comprehensive approach across all marketing mix elements helps the bank maintain competitiveness while building trust and accessibility.

DIGITAL TRANSFORMATION AND INNOVATION

As one of the early adopters of technology in Indian banking, ICICI Bank has consistently invested in building robust digital capabilities that enhance customer experience while driving operational efficiency. The bank's digital strategy focuses on creating end-to-end digital journeys that eliminate friction points and reduce dependency on physical channels. Mobile banking has been a particular focus, with the iMobile app offering a comprehensive suite of banking services accessible through smartphones. This platform extends beyond traditional banking to include investment management, bill payments, and even services for non-ICICI Bank customers, positioning it as a financial super-app.

ICICI Bank has also leveraged digital technologies to transform its lending processes. Digital lending platforms, similar to the iLens platform, have been developed for personal loans and education loans, creating seamless customer experiences while improving risk assessment through data-driven underwriting models.

On the corporate side, ICICI Bank has introduced digital solutions that address complex business needs. The bank's Corporate Internet Banking platform offers cash management, trade finance, and supply chain financing capabilities through a unified interface. These digital tools help corporate clients optimize working capital, manage liquidity, and streamline financial operations across their business ecosystem.

Beyond customer-facing applications, ICICI Bank has invested in back-end technology to enhance operational efficiency. Advanced analytics and artificial intelligence (AI) are deployed for credit risk assessment, fraud detection, and personalized marketing. These capabilities have contributed to the bank's industry-leading cost-to-income ratio of 0.4%, reflecting significant productivity gains through technology adoption.

ICICI Bank's innovation approach emphasizes practical solutions that address specific customer pain points rather than technology for its own sake. The bank maintains a balance between digital innovation and human touch, recognizing that certain complex financial decisions still benefit from personal guidance. This hybrid service model combines digital efficiency with human empathy, creating distinctive customer experiences that digital-only players struggle to replicate.

BRAND BUILDING AND COMMUNICATIONS STRATEGY

ICICI Bank's brand evolution mirrors its strategic journey from a development financial institution to a customer-centric universal bank. Over the decades, the brand has been carefully cultivated to reflect the institution's values, capabilities, and market positioning. Today, the ICICI brand represents trust, innovation, and customer focus – attributes that have been consistently reinforced through multiple communication channels.

The bank's communication strategy, in recent years, has been characterized by substance over style. Earlier, the bank focused on attracting and retaining customers through traditional advertising featuring celebrities with memorable taglines like "Hum Hain Na" and "Khayaal Aapka." Now, rather than relying on flashy campaigns, ICICI Bank focuses on communicating its value proposition through consistent service delivery and meaningful innovations. This approach aligns with the bank's current low-profile philosophy, letting results speak for themselves rather than making grand pronouncements.

Internal branding has received particular attention with principles of "One Bank, One Team" and "Fair to Customer, Fair to Bank" being consistently communicated through town halls, emails, and training programs, ensuring that employees at all levels internalize these values. This internal alignment creates authentic brand experiences when employees interact with customers, reinforcing the brand promise through behavior rather than just messaging.

ICICI Bank's product communication emphasizes simplicity and transparency, avoiding industry jargon and complex terms. This plain-language approach reflects the bank's broader simplification drive and its commitment to treating customers fairly. Promotional materials focus on customer benefits rather than product features, communicating how banking solutions address specific financial needs and life goals.

Digital channels play an increasingly important role in ICICI Bank's communication mix. The bank maintains an active presence across social media platforms, using

Exhibit 3 ICICI Bank – Assets Growth (in ₹ Trillion)

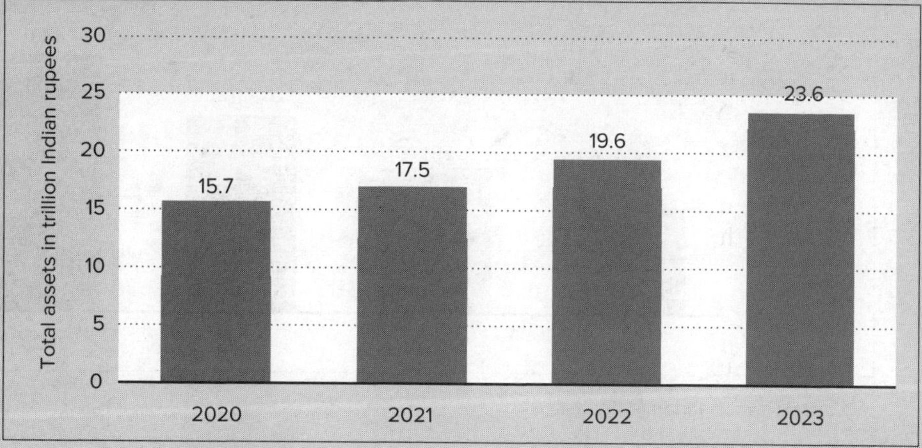

Source: Yahoo Finance, Statista

these channels not just for promotion but also for customer education and engagement. Content marketing initiatives focus on financial literacy and decision support, positioning ICICI Bank as a trusted advisor rather than just a service provider. Their digital promotions emphasize short-form, visually compelling content designed for sharing rather than direct product messaging.

The effectiveness of ICICI Bank's brand building efforts is reflected in strong customer acquisition and retention metrics. More importantly, the brand has demonstrated resilience through challenging periods, maintaining stakeholder trust even during leadership transitions and economic uncertainties. This brand equity represents a valuable intangible asset that contributes significantly to the bank's market valuation and competitive position.

PERFORMANCE AND FUTURE OUTLOOK

Financials (Exhibits 3 and 4) as well as productivity metrics underscore the positive impact of these initiatives on ICICI Bank's performance and operational excellence. The bank leads its peer group in workforce productivity, with a profit per employee of ₹30 lakh. The cost-to-income ratio of 0.4% reflects exceptional operational efficiency, driven by process simplification and digital transformation. These efficiency gains create a virtuous cycle, enabling investment in service quality and innovation while maintaining competitive pricing.

Looking ahead, ICICI Bank faces both opportunities and challenges. The bank is well-positioned to benefit from India's economic growth trajectory and increasing financial inclusion. Its balanced business mix, strong capital position, and digital capabilities provide multiple growth avenues across customer segments and geographies.

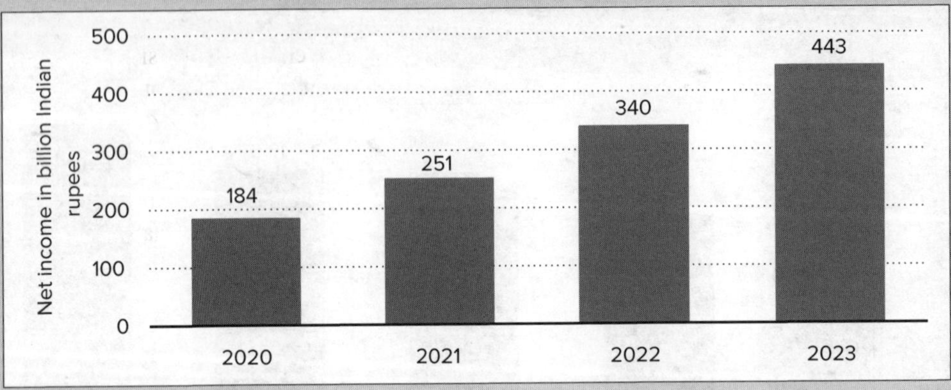

Source: Yahoo Finance, Statista

The continued focus on rural expansion represents a particularly promising growth opportunity as financial services penetrate deeper into semi-urban and rural markets.

However, the bank also faces increasing competitive pressures. Traditional competitors like HDFC Bank and SBI continue to innovate, while new digital players are targeting specific customer segments with focused value propositions. Margin compression remains a systemic challenge for the banking sector, driven by intense competition for deposits and the higher cost of funds. Regulatory changes and economic uncertainties further complicate the operating environment.

ICICI Bank's strategic approach to these challenges emphasizes sustainable growth rather than market share at any cost. The bank continues to focus on risk-calibrated returns, maintaining asset quality while pursuing growth opportunities. The leadership believes that this measured approach will deliver superior risk-adjusted returns over the long term.

The bank's strategic direction remains focused on executing its customer-centric strategy while adapting to evolving market conditions. The principles of "Return of Capital," "Fair to Customer, Fair to Bank," and "One Bank, One Team" continue to guide the institution's approach, providing strategic continuity while allowing for tactical flexibility. This balance between steadfast principles and adaptable execution positions ICICI Bank to sustain its leadership position in India's dynamic banking landscape.

ICICI Bank's journey over the past three decades illustrates the power of strategic clarity, disciplined execution, and customer centricity in building a resilient financial institution. The bank has demonstrated remarkable adaptability while maintaining core values and strengths. By focusing on fundamental banking principles, simplifying offerings, investing in digital capabilities, and placing customers at the center of its strategy, ICICI Bank has achieved impressive financial and operational outcomes while strengthening its competitive position.

Executing sound banking practices and building trust among stakeholders has created a strong foundation for sustainable growth. As the banking landscape continues to evolve, ICICI Bank's experience demonstrates that institutions that combine traditional banking virtues with technological innovation and customer-centricity will be well-positioned to thrive. This balanced approach while adapting to emerging opportunities and challenges positions ICICI Bank to continue its leadership role for years to come.

Questions

1. How has ICICI Bank used the 'Product', 'Price', and 'Place' elements of the services marketing mix to address the diverse financial needs of its customer segments?
2. In what ways does ICICI Bank's 'Customer360°' initiative reflect a shift from a product-centric to a customer-centric approach, and how does this align with the principles of service marketing?
3. Analyze how ICICI Bank's digital transformation supports its customer service strategy. Which components of the service marketing mix are most impacted by this transformation?
4. Discuss how the internal branding principles such as "One Bank, One Team" and "Fair to Customer, Fair to Bank" influence employee behavior and contribute to service excellence. Which element of the services marketing mix is this most closely related to?
5. Identify and evaluate the role of 'Physical Evidence' in reinforcing ICICI Bank's brand promise. How does this support customer trust and brand differentiation in a competitive market?

References

ICICI Bank. (2024). ICICI Bank Annual Report 2023–24. https://www.icicibank.com/ms/simplify/assets/pdf/ICICI%20Bank%20Report.pdf

IMobile - Recharge, utility payments & transfer money instantly - ICICI Bank. (n.d.). ICICI Bank. https://www.icicibank.com/mobile-banking/imobile

Adhikari, A. (2024, March 29). Here's how ICICI Bank under MD & CEO Sandeep Bakhshi is reimagining banking. Business Today. https://www.businesstoday.in/magazine/deep-dive/story/heres-how-icici-bank-under-md-ceo-sandeep-bakhshi-is-reimagining-banking-423391-2024-03-29

Customer Engagement - ICICI Bank https://www.edx.org/learn/customer-relationship-management/indian-institute-of-management-bangalore-customer-relationship-management

https://www.businesstoday.in/magazine/deep-dive/story/icici-bank-rewrites-the-rulebook-redefining-service-and-value-to-captivate-customers-458277-2024-12-23

https://www.exchange4media.com/marketing-news/people-want-to-be-entertained-not-watch-adssujit-ganguliicici-bank-91998.html

https://www.forbesindia.com/article/leadership-awards-2022/how-sandeep-bakhshi-has-quietly-but-firmly-turned-around-icici-bank/74677/1

ICICI Bank Annual Report 2021–22: https://www.icicibank.com/ms/aboutus/annual-reports/2021-22/AR/our-business-strategy.html

Case Six

Cult.fit: Revolutionizing India's Fitness Landscape through Phygital Innovation

Cult.fit emerged in 2016 as a disruptive force in India's fitness and wellness industry. Founded by Mukesh Bansal and Ankit Nagori, both veterans from e-commerce giants Myntra and Flipkart, the company was originally launched under the name CureFit. It was set up with an ambitious vision to create a comprehensive wellness ecosystem that seamlessly integrated strength training, yoga, nutrition guidance, mental health support, and medical checkups into a single platform. This holistic approach represented a significant departure from traditional fitness models, positioning Cult.fit as a pioneer in India's digital-first wellness revolution. The company's journey from a digital experiment streaming gym classes directly to users' screens to a comprehensive wellness platform demonstrates its adaptive evolution in response to changing consumer needs and market dynamics.

PORTFOLIO AND DIVERSIFICATION

Cult.fit has developed a multifaceted product ecosystem that extends far beyond conventional fitness offerings, creating a comprehensive wellness solution that addresses diverse consumer needs. The core fitness programs encompass yoga, dance, HIIT (High-Intensity Interval Training), and strength training, with the high-intensity HRX format co-created with actor Hrithik Roshan serving as a flagship offering. The company diversified into specialized verticals including Cult Transform, which provides personalized fitness and nutrition coaching through a paid subscription model, and Cult Sport, a private-label brand offering fitness equipment and activewear. Additionally, Cult Care extends the ecosystem by integrating preventive health checkups, diagnostics, doctor consultations, and mental wellness support, creating a holistic health management platform. This comprehensive approach to wellness services positions Cult.fit not merely as a fitness provider but as a complete lifestyle partner, addressing physical, mental, and nutritional aspects of health in an integrated manner.

VALUE PROPOSITION

The company's pricing architecture reflects a sophisticated understanding of market segmentation and consumer behavior, employing a tiered subscription model that caters to diverse economic segments and usage patterns. Users can select from flexible membership durations of 3, 6, or 12 months, with specialized offerings like the 'Buddy Pack' that enables two users to share a workout plan, promoting social motivation while optimizing value perception. Pricing options create further tiered opportunities through Cultpass ELITE and Cultpass PRO memberships, where ELITE provides unlimited access to premium services and physical centers, while PRO targets budget-conscious consumers with access to partner gyms and online sessions. Digital plans are priced at accessible levels to capture users in markets without physical center presence, while premium services such as personalized coaching and transformation programs command higher price points. This tiered approach creates multiple entry points for different consumer segments while maintaining aspirational appeal for service upgrades, effectively balancing accessibility with revenue optimization.

DISTRIBUTION AND PHYGITAL INTEGRATION

Cult.fit's distribution strategy exemplifies the successful implementation of a phygital model that seamlessly integrates physical and digital touchpoints to maximize market reach and customer convenience. The company has expanded across Indian cities through a Franchise-Owned, Franchise-Operated model, enabling local entrepreneurs to operate fitness centers under the Cult.fit brand while maintaining consistent service standards and operational excellence. These physical studios feature modern equipment, climate control, and carefully curated environments with strategic design elements like mirrors and customized music playlists that enhance the workout experience. Simultaneously, the robust digital platform allows users to access workouts, track health goals, book sessions, and consult experts from anywhere, creating flexibility that transcends geographical limitations. This hybrid approach enables customers to transition seamlessly between at-home and in-center fitness routines, providing unprecedented flexibility while maintaining brand consistency across all touchpoints.

BRAND BUILDING AND PROMOTIONS

Cult.fit's promotional approach centers on aspirational storytelling and community building rather than transactional messaging, creating deep emotional connections with target audience. The brand leverages celebrity endorsements from prominent figures like actors Ranveer Singh and Hrithik Roshan to build credibility and aspirational appeal, while simultaneously fostering an active community through fitness challenges and social media engagement. The company collaborates with fitness influencers, health coaches, and therapists to create high-quality, educational content across social media platforms and their proprietary app, covering nutrition advice, injury prevention, and mental wellness support. Gamified features including badges, streak tracking, and leaderboards drive consistent user engagement and create a sense of achievement and progress. This comprehensive promotional strategy positions Cult.fit as a lifestyle brand that promotes daily commitment, inspiration, and community belonging, differentiating it from competitors who focus primarily on transactional fitness services.

SERVICE EXCELLENCE AND PEOPLE

The human capital strategy at Cult.fit reflects a deep understanding that service quality in the fitness industry is fundamentally dependent on the expertise, motivation, and interpersonal skills of service providers. Trainers at Cult centers undergo comprehensive training and certification in both technical skills and customer engagement, with their role extending beyond mere instruction to include motivation, personalization, and community building. The integration of specialized professionals including nutritionists, doctors, and therapists within Cult Transform and Cult Care provides expert guidance through digital channels, ensuring service quality across all touchpoints. Customer support teams manage app-related queries, refunds, and scheduling issues, maintaining seamless experiences across the entire customer journey. The company's internal culture emphasizes employee engagement through project ownership and passion-driven work, fostering a collaborative environment characterized by energy and shared vision for transforming India's health and fitness landscape.

OPERATIONAL EXCELLENCE AND PROCESS INNOVATION

Cult.fit's operational processes demonstrate sophisticated technology integration designed to ensure consistency, scalability, and superior customer experience across all service delivery points. The company provides franchise partners with a comprehensive operational framework featuring advanced technology systems for class booking management and center operations, ensuring uniform procedures that guarantee consistent customer experiences regardless of location. Service delivery is enabled through streamlined, tech-driven processes where booking, cancellation, report access, and performance tracking are seamlessly integrated within the mobile application. Physical centers utilize tablets and backend tools that enable staff to efficiently manage attendance, provide real-time feedback, and order equipment, creating a centralized and automated system that reduces friction while enabling rapid scalability. This process excellence ensures that customer experiences remain consistent and responsive across all touchpoints, supporting the company's growth ambitions while maintaining service quality standards.

BRAND EXPERIENCE AND SERVICESCAPE

The company's approach to physical evidence reflects a strategic investment in creating a coherent and premium brand presence that reinforces quality perceptions and lifestyle aspirations across all customer touchpoints. Cult centers feature a distinctive clean, energetic aesthetic with consistent black and yellow branding, structured workout zones, and high-end interiors that create an immersive brand experience. Trainers and staff wear Cult.fit-branded gear that reinforces professionalism and brand identity, while Cult Sport product packaging maintains sleek, secure, and minimalist design standards that contribute to quality and trust perceptions. These carefully orchestrated physical markers create a unified brand experience that appeals to consumers' desires for both functional excellence and lifestyle aspiration, supporting premium positioning while building emotional connections with the brand.

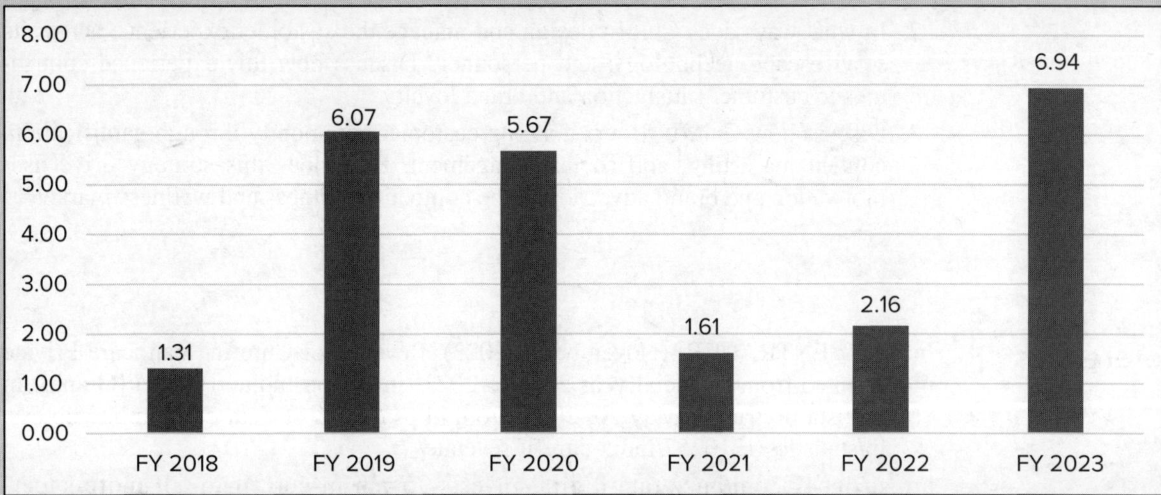

Source: Statista

CHALLENGES, FINANCIAL PERFORMANCE, AND STRATEGIC RESPONSE

Despite its innovative approach and market leadership, Cult.fit has faced significant operational and financial challenges that highlight the complexities of scaling a phygital wellness platform in the Indian market (Exhibit 1). The company, now part of the Tata Group, has initiated the process for a ₹2,500 crore IPO, supported by strategic partnerships with five major banks and over $650 million in investor funding, including a significant $100 million investment from Zomato for a 6.4% stake. However, financial performance in FY2024 revealed the challenges of achieving profitability in the competitive wellness sector, with ₹926.6 crore in operating revenue offset by a net loss of ₹888.5 crore, despite total income reaching ₹1,027 crore. The COVID-19 pandemic had intensified operational challenges by restricting physical gym access, compelling the company to accelerate digital transformation efforts while implementing cost-cutting measures including workforce reductions of 100–120 employees in January 2024. These strategic responses demonstrate Cult.fit's adaptability in navigating market pressures while maintaining its commitment to innovation and customer service excellence in India's evolving fitness and wellness landscape.

Questions

1. How has Cult.fit leveraged phygital innovation to deliver a seamless fitness experience across digital and physical touchpoints? Explain how this integration has enhanced customer convenience and scalability.
2. In what ways does Cult.fit design and manage the customer experience across its servicescape, technology, and personnel? Discuss how this experience contributes to customer satisfaction and brand loyalty.
3. Discuss how Cult.fit fosters a strong customer community through gamification, content marketing, and social engagement. How does this strategy drive user motivation and brand advocacy in the competitive fitness and wellness market?

References

Inc42, & ENTRACKR. (November 4, 2023). Revenue of Curefit Healthcare Private Limited from financial year 2018 to 2023 (in billion Indian rupees) [Graph]. In Statista. Retrieved May 20, 2025, from https://www-statista-com.iimb.remotexs.in/statistics/1310257/india-curefit-revenue/

https://inc42.com/buzz/tata-digital-invests-75-mn-in-curefit-to-fill-more-super-app-pieces/

https://startuptalky.com/cult-fit-success-story/

cult.fit. (n.d.). *Buy fitness equipment & wellness products online | Cultsport*. cult.sport. https://cultsport.com/?srsltid=AfmBOopCEQnDmEJKuI2inHMscX_gl-yBI1ksBus9Ida7BwrRC_esCECi

Full body checkup & blood diagnostic centre near me - Cult.fit. (n.d.). https://www.cult.fit/care/diagnostic-tests

Kareemdathil, N. (2024, January 8). *Cult.fit's Franchise Model | Explained*. StartupTalky. https://startuptalky.com/cult-fit-franchise-model/

Startups, H. (n.d.). Cult Fit's journey to India's first fitness unicorn. The Hot Startups. https://www.thehotstartups.com/p/cult-fit-s-journey-to-india-s-first-fitness-unicorn

Outlook Start-Up Desk. (2025, March 27). Fitness unicorn Cult.Fit begins Rs 2,500 crore IPO journey, picks 5 bankers. *Outlook Business*. https://www.outlookbusiness.com/start-up/news/fitness-unicorn-cultfit-begins-rs-2500-crore-ipo-journey-picks-5-bankers

Rath, S. (2024b, March 1). *Cult.Fit success story - How does this India's leading health and fitness company make money?* StartupTalky. https://startuptalky.com/cult-fit-success-story/

Case Seven

Nykaa – Transforming Beauty Retail through Integrated Services Marketing

Nykaa's remarkable journey from a startup, founded by Falguni Nayar in 2012, to becoming India's leading beauty and wellness omni-channel platform exemplifies the successful implementation of integrated services marketing. The company's success story is rooted in visionary leadership and a deep understanding of the Indian beauty market gap. Falguni, drawing from her observations of international beauty markets during her travels, recognized that Indian consumers lacked access to a comprehensive range of high-quality beauty products and a dedicated platform. Her vision to create an online platform offering both Indian and international brands, combined with the Sanskrit-derived name "Nykaa" meaning "someone in the spotlight," reflected the brand's mission to empower individuals through beauty.

Nykaa's extensive and carefully curated product portfolio has evolved to meet diverse consumer needs. With over 100,000 products spanning cosmetics, skincare, haircare, and fragrances, Nykaa has positioned itself as a comprehensive one-stop destination for beauty and personal care. The company's strategic development of private-label lines under the FSN Brands umbrella, including Nykaa Beauty, Nykaa Naturals, and Kay Beauty, in partnership with Bollywood actress Katrina Kaif, demonstrates sophisticated product diversification. These private-label products are specifically formulated to suit Indian skin tones and preferences, sold exclusively on Nykaa's platforms to boost margins and customer loyalty while limiting competition. The integration of advanced digital tools, including ModiFace's AI-powered virtual try-on technology launched in 2021, addresses the fundamental challenge of online beauty retail by allowing users to preview makeup looks in real-time. This technological innovation, combined with machine learning-driven product recommendations based on past purchases, skin type, and customer reviews, creates a personalized and informed shopping experience that reduces returns and builds consumer trust.

The company's pricing strategy reflects a sophisticated hybrid approach that balances value-based pricing with strategic promotional activities to appeal to India's diverse beauty consumer segments. The platform employs attractive onboarding deals for new users through app-exclusive codes, while themed campaigns like Pink Friday Sale, Skintastic Sale, and Pay Day Sale create regular buying opportunities tied to seasonal and monthly triggers. Brand-led promotions and exclusive product launches differentiate Nykaa from competitors, with collaborations featuring top beauty brands like Maybelline, e.l.f., and Sugar offering curated bundles, "Buy 2 Get 1 Free" deals, and early access to new collections. The Nykaa Prive loyalty program incentivizes repeat purchases through reward points, birthday discounts, and special perks, enhancing customer retention and perceived value. Compared to competitors like Purplle, which focuses on deep discounts for price-sensitive users, and Sephora India, which emphasizes premium pricing with limited promotions, Nykaa positions itself in the middle by combining accessibility with aspiration to appeal to both mass-market and premium consumers.

Nykaa's innovative phygital model seamlessly integrates digital discovery with physical experience. Beginning as a digital-first brand, Nykaa recognized the sensory nature of beauty and wellness categories where touch, shade-matching, and expert advice drive purchase decisions. By 2024, the company had launched over 174 physical stores across India, including specialized formats like Nykaa Luxe for premium brands, Nykaa On Trend for emerging products, and Nykaa Man for male grooming. These stores transcend traditional retail transactions by offering product trials, exploration of new launches, and personalized advice from trained beauty consultants. The phygital integration allows customers to browse online and purchase in-store or vice versa, supported by real-time inventory visibility, in-store pickup for online orders, and a unified loyalty program. This connected approach creates a seamless, consistent experience that improves conversion rates while building deeper customer satisfaction and long-term loyalty.

Nykaa focuses on storytelling and education rather than price-focused advertising, reflecting a content-driven approach that blends product discovery with consumer empowerment. Through skincare tips, makeup tutorials, and expert-led videos, the brand builds trust, particularly among young and first-time beauty shoppers. Celebrity endorsements play a crucial role, with Katrina Kaif co-creating Kay Beauty for credibility and star appeal, while Janhvi Kapoor serves as the face of multiple campaigns, bringing freshness and relatability. The brand's collaboration with influencers and content creators across YouTube, Instagram, and its own app extends reach through interactive campaigns featuring live sessions, tutorials, and events like the Nykaa Femina Beauty Awards. Digital customization tools enable targeted advertising, smart recommendations, and loyalty rewards that drive repeat purchases and build long-term engagement. This approach gained virality across India, with recognition even in remote villages, by focusing on authenticity and replicating physical-world beauty conversations in digital spaces.

The people aspect of Nykaa's service delivery combines intelligent technology with essential human touch across all customer touchpoints. Digital platforms utilize AI chatbots for simple queries while connecting customers with trained beauty advisors and dermatologists for detailed consultations. In-store staff receive comprehensive training not just to sell but to guide customers through one-on-one consultations, product matching to skin types, and routine suggestions based on individual needs. These personal interactions significantly influence purchase decisions and build lasting loyalty. Nykaa views employees as brand reflections, investing in staff training, grooming, and expert knowledge development. Whether online or offline, employee communication, responsiveness, and assistance create customer experiences that position Nykaa as a trusted advisor rather than merely a retailer. This people-first approach, supported by a significant technology team of 80 professionals from prestigious institutions like IIT Delhi and IIT Bombay, ensures that human warmth complements technological sophistication.

The company's intelligent, tech-driven operations create seamless customer experiences. Its platform employs sophisticated algorithms for product recommendations based on browsing patterns, purchase history, and user preferences, with real-time homepage personalization that makes product discovery intuitive and relevant. Advanced user segmentation ensures targeted marketing messages and promotions, improving conversion rates while enhancing overall shopping experiences. Fulfilment processes include real-time tracking, fast delivery options, and a centralized inventory system linking apps, websites, and physical stores. Services like in-store pickup, endless aisle browsing, and local store fulfilment provide shopping flexibility. In-store staff utilize digital tools to check inventory and process orders on behalf of customers, creating friction-free experiences that build trust and satisfaction across all channels.

Nykaa's success also stems from a simple yet powerful strategy: owning what it sells. Unlike marketplace models where third parties manage inventory, Nykaa purchases products directly from leading global brands and stores them in its own warehouses across Mumbai, Delhi, and Bangalore. This direct ownership creates three key advantages. First, customers get what they order when they order it—no stockouts or delays from unreliable, third part suppliers. Second, Nykaa guarantees authentic, high quality products by controlling the entire supply chain from purchase to delivery. Third, the company earns higher profits by eliminating middlemen and buying in bulk at better prices.

This inventory control becomes even more powerful when combined with Nykaa's physical stores. The 174+ retail locations do not just serve customers—they act as mini-warehouses that speed up delivery and let shoppers try products before buying. When someone orders online, Nykaa can fulfill from the nearest store rather than a distant warehouse. When someone visits a store, they can instantly buy what they have been browsing online. This seamless connection between digital and physical channels, powered by centralized inventory management, explains why Nykaa maintains customer loyalty in India's competitive beauty market while building a trusted brand that customers return to again and again.

Nykaa's meticulous attention to digital and physical touchpoints reinforce quality and trust. The app and website feature clean, visually engaging designs with high-resolution images, guided navigation, and curated collections that recreate premium beauty store experiences online. From browsing to checkout, every design element reinforces elegance and ease. Packaging arrives in tamper-proof, branded boxes that appear sleek and secure, while physical stores create immersive sensory experiences through soft lighting, organized displays, and interactive tools like smart mirrors and shade-matching kiosks. These physical cues reassure customers about hygiene, authenticity, and care, strengthening Nykaa's reputation and enhancing consumer confidence in a category where trust and appearance are paramount.

Nykaa's customer experience excellence is fundamentally built on creating meaningful relationships that extend far beyond transactional interactions. The platform has successfully cultivated a community of over 10 million monthly visitors from a cumulative base of ~40 million customers by December 2024. Its impressive average ticket size of ₹1,250–1,500 matches international markets like the US while being significantly higher than competitors who average ₹350–650 in the beauty category. This achievement reflects Nykaa's ability to position itself as a premium destination

Exhibit 1 Nykaa Revenue Growth (₹ billion)

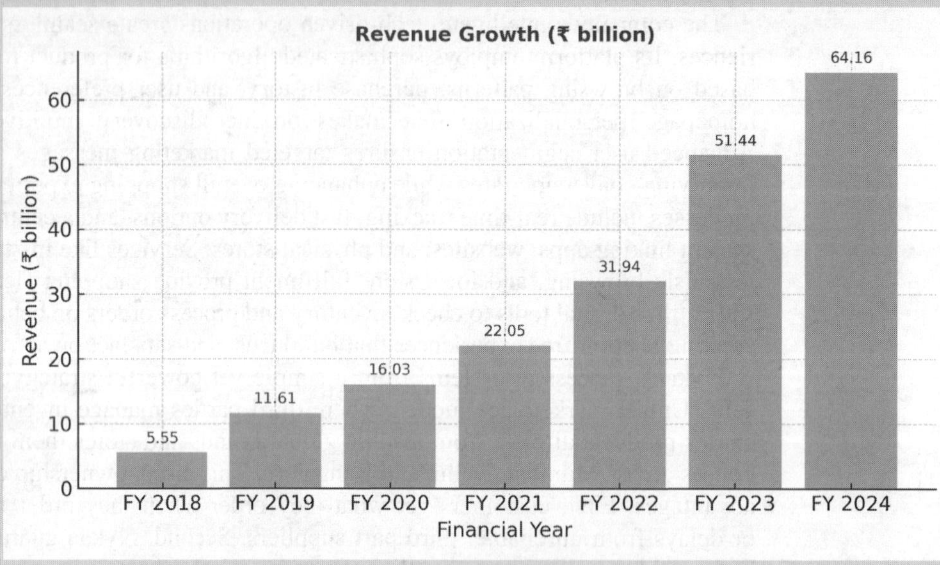

while maintaining accessibility. The company's customer engagement strategy centers on education and empowerment, with customers typically adding 3.5–4 items per cart, a metric that has remained consistent over the last three years, indicating strong cross-selling effectiveness and customer satisfaction.

The integration of live chat has revolutionized customer support, engaging 99.7% of customers within one minute and handling over 900,000 messages, freeing up 32,000 manhours monthly from repetitive tasks. This technological enhancement allows customer service executives to focus on more complex beauty consultations and personalized recommendations to create a hybrid support model that combines efficiency with expertise.

The strategic balance between acquiring new customers and retaining existing ones represents a cornerstone of Nykaa's sustained growth (Exhibit 1). Their deliberate approach maintains a 50–50 split between new and repeat customers among monthly visitors, recognizing that while repeat customers cost significantly less to serve, continuous acquisition is essential for long-term expansion. The company has successfully reduced customer acquisition costs to sub- ₹200 levels, dramatically lower than the industry average of ₹650–2,000, through organic growth, word-of-mouth referrals, and strategic content marketing rather than expensive advertising. The Nykaa Prive loyalty program serves as a critical retention mechanism, offering reward points, birthday discounts, and exclusive perks that create emotional connections and financial incentives for continued engagement. This retention strategy is supported by personalized experiences powered by machine learning algorithms that remember customer preferences, purchase history, and skin type, ensuring that returning customers feel recognized and valued. The seamless integration between online and offline experiences further strengthens retention, as customers who engage with both channels demonstrate higher lifetime value and stronger brand loyalty, creating a virtuous cycle

where satisfied customers become brand advocates who naturally drive new customer acquisition through authentic recommendations and social sharing.

Despite remarkable success, Nykaa faces challenges from new and established players like Purplle, Reliance's Tira, Tata's Cliq Palette, Amazon, Myntra, Blinkit and Zepto (Exhibit 2). This intensifies differentiation pressures, while expansion into tier-2 and tier-3 cities requires adapting service models to varying socio-economic contexts with different beauty norms, pricing expectations, and digital behaviors. The delicate balance of growing private labels without alienating partner brands presents strategic complexities, while leveraging customer data for personalization introduces privacy risks and ethical transparency concerns. As Nykaa enters its next growth phase, success will depend on balancing service personalization with scalability, innovation with consistency, and digital agility with human warmth. The company's growth story illustrates the transformative power of service-centric thinking in a consumer category that blends functional needs with aspirational desires, redefining beauty retail in India through the strategic integration of technology, human interaction, and experiential design across all elements of services marketing mix.

Questions

1. Analyze how Nykaa has integrated services marketing mix elements to create a differentiated market position in the beauty retail sector.
2. Evaluate Nykaa's omnichannel approach and explain how it creates a unified customer experience across digital and physical touchpoints.
3. Critically assess Nykaa's customer experience approach and evaluate how it has achieved superior engagement metrics compared to competitors.
4. Examine how Nykaa has addressed the fundamental challenges of building quality perception and consumer trust in the online beauty and wellness category.

References

https://www.nykaa.com

https://business.google.com/in/think/ai-excellence/nykaa-ai-advertising-performance-max/

https://medium.com/@Reemakathuraal/fully-immersive-spatial-experience-nykaa-beauty-website-case-study-bd1a0c756cc8

https://dev.verloop.io/case-study-nykaa.html

https://www.livemint.com/Companies/IKJQ77BvHlJ8msgsodhbpO/I-am-building-Nykaa-to-have-a-life-of-its-own-Falguni-Nayar.html

https://www.indiaretailing.com/2024/03/20/nykaa-founder-falguni-nayar-interview/

https://yourstory.com/2023/10/the-mother-daughter-duo-building-a-lifestyle-empire

https://www.excellisit.com/nykaa-success-story/

https://www.financialexpress.com/business/brandwagon-nykaa-apparel-group-to-open-70-nyssa-stores-in-5-years-ceo-falguni-nayyar-3429514/

https://economictimes.indiatimes.com/industry/services/retail/when-online-goes-offline-why-brink-and-mortar-is-back-in-fashion/articleshow/108243415.cms?from=mdr

Case Eight

PolicyBazaar: Enabling Customer Decision Journey

The Indian insurance market has been characterized by complexity, opacity, and customer frustration, for decades. Traditional insurance purchasing involved navigating through dense jargon, dealing with agents who often pushed unsuitable products, and facing isolation during renewals and claims processes. This challenging landscape created a need for transformation, which PolicyBazaar recognized and addressed when it entered the market in 2008. Founded by Yashish Dahiya, Alok Bansal, and Avaneesh Nirjar, the platform emerged from a deeply personal experience that crystallized the industry's problems. As Dahiya recounted, "*I was going through some of the financials with my father and few things looked dubious. On deeper inspection, my father had been cheated of a few lakh rupees by insurance agents. The transactions looked clean on the face of it but the reality emerged when I looked in closely.*" This experience became the catalyst for creating a service that would fundamentally change how Indians approach insurance purchasing. Rather than just acting as another sales channel, it aimed to empower consumers by offering transparency and choice in one place. Starting as a simple website where users could compare insurance policies online, it steadily expanded its offerings and reach. The website now displays more than 250 insurance plans from all insurance companies to potential buyers.

PolicyBazaar's approach centered on transparency and consumer empowerment, transforming the insurance industry from an agent-driven model to a consumer-centric platform. The company established itself as more than just another sales channel by offering comprehensive comparison tools that displayed multiple insurance plans from various brands in one accessible location. This democratization of information allowed customers to make informed decisions without pressure or hidden agendas. The platform's commitment to transparency extended to its revenue model, earning commissions from insurers rather than charging customers, which built unprecedented trust in an industry known for hidden costs and deceptive practices.

One of PolicyBazaar's key differentiation is making pricing clear and accessible. Users can browse and compare policies without paying any fees and the platform earns through commissions from insurers. Each plan's price, terms, and conditions are clearly listed so that buyers can make informed choices without pressure or confusion. This commitment to transparency has built trust, especially among first-time buyers and those in smaller cities who are wary of hidden charges. Instead of competing on price alone, PolicyBazaar competes on clarity and fairness, helping users weigh cost against value in a way few traditional agents offered.

The breadth of PolicyBazaar's product offerings demonstrates its role in comprehensively addressing India's diverse insurance and financial needs. Beyond traditional life and health insurance, the platform expanded to cover motor insurance, travel protection, home insurance, and specialized products like child and investment-linked policies. This expansion continued into broader financial services, including personal loans, home loans, business loans, and credit cards, positioning PolicyBazaar as a comprehensive financial services marketplace. The platform enables users to compare and apply for personal, home, and business loans from several banks. The credit card section helps users choose cards based on lifestyle preferences like cashback, travel, or savings while buying fuel. Each product is presented with detailed information on benefits, premiums, and exclusions. The details help users compare options and select the product that fits their needs. Beyond insurance policy purchase, customers can manage renewals, assistance during insurance claims, ask queries and even upgrade policies through their accounts. The integration of AI through their PBee platform for understanding customer satisfaction further showcased their commitment to technology-driven service improvement, setting new standards for customer experience in the financial services sector.

PolicyBazaar's geographic expansion strategy played a crucial role in transforming insurance accessibility across India's diverse landscape. Initially targeting urban, digitally-savvy customers, the company recognized the massive untapped potential in Tier 2 and Tier 3 cities where traditional offline interactions remained preferred. Starting around 2019, PolicyBazaar established physical service centers to bridge the digital divide, bringing insurance services directly to communities with limited internet access or those preferring face-to-face interactions for complex financial decisions. This hybrid approach of combining digital convenience with physical accessibility became a template for other financial technology companies seeking to serve India's diverse market segments.

PolicyBazaar invests heavily in physical and digital cues that build confidence. It straddles both the B2C and the B2B segments. Its website and app has a clean, user-friendly design (Exhibit 1). Official policy documents are securely stored in digital lockers for easy and anytime access. Offline centers are branded and staffed by knowledgeable representatives, providing a physical anchor in the community. The company also ensures consistent communication through SMS alerts, email updates, and printed renewal notices. Even small items such as claim assistance kits or customer service call follow-ups add to the tangible evidence that customers receive ongoing support. These elements reinforce the sense that PolicyBazaar is a reliable partner, not just a digital platform. In 2015, they released their mobile app, not only keeping up with the evolving digital channels but also creating new updates such as hospital locators, taking advantage of the mobile phone's location feature.

The company's promotional strategy fundamentally changed how insurance was marketed in India, shifting from fear-based selling to education and empowerment. Through partnerships with celebrities like actor Akshay Kumar and comedian Kapil Sharma, PolicyBazaar made insurance conversations mainstream and approachable, using humor and relatability to demystify complex financial products. As Samir Sethi, Head – Brand Marketing, explained: "*Insurance, though crucial, can often feel like a maze. Considering the success of our past collaborations with Kapil Sharma, we are delighted to welcome him back. We believe that his unique ability to connect with the audience through humor will demystify the insurance-buying process and encourage*

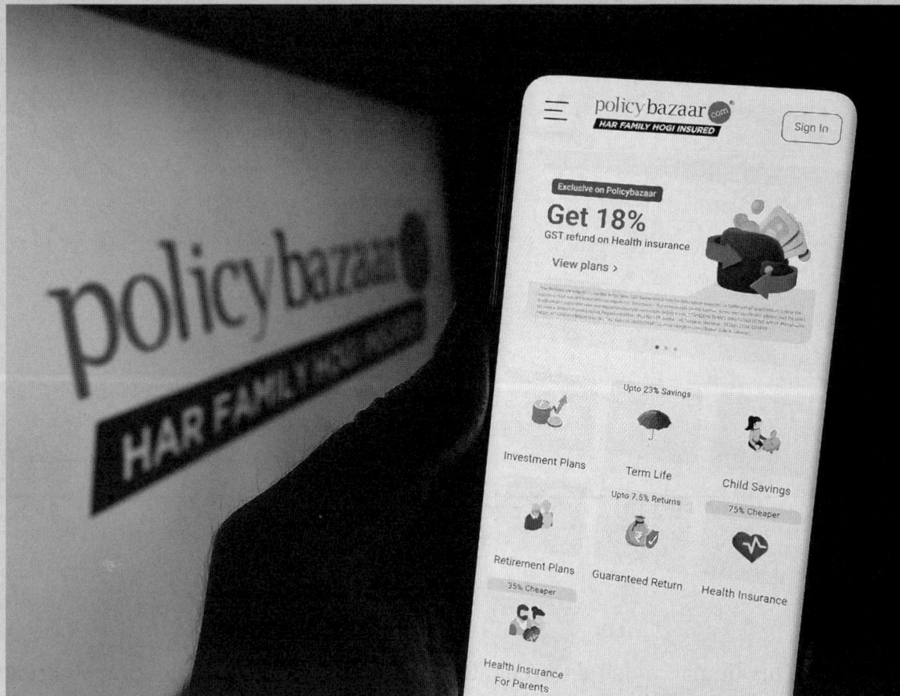

our customers to make more informed choices. PolicyBazaar is committed to making insurance accessible and affordable for all, and this association is a significant step in that direction." However, their promotion extended beyond celebrity endorsements to include comprehensive digital marketing through educational videos, blog content, and social media campaigns that translated complicated insurance terminology into a simple, understandable language. This educational approach helped build financial literacy among consumers, contributing to broader financial inclusion across the country.

PolicyBazaar's human-centric approach distinguished it from purely digital platforms and contributed significantly to transforming customer expectations in the financial services industry. Despite heavy investment in AI-powered assistants and chatbots, the company maintained strong human support systems, recognizing that insurance decisions often require personal guidance and cultural sensitivity. The remarkable growth trajectory is evident in founder Yashish Dahiya's reflection: "We started PolicyBazaar with just 14 hardworking individuals." What began as a small team has expanded to over 14,000 employees by 2025, with trained advisors available in regional languages who could explain policy details in culturally relevant contexts. Though chatbots and AI-powered assistants help answer common questions instantly, many customers benefit from speaking with trained advisors. In smaller towns, local agents fluent in regional languages build rapport and explain policy details in culturally relevant ways. Customer support teams, accessible through multiple channels such as phone, chat and email, remain involved even after a policy is purchased.

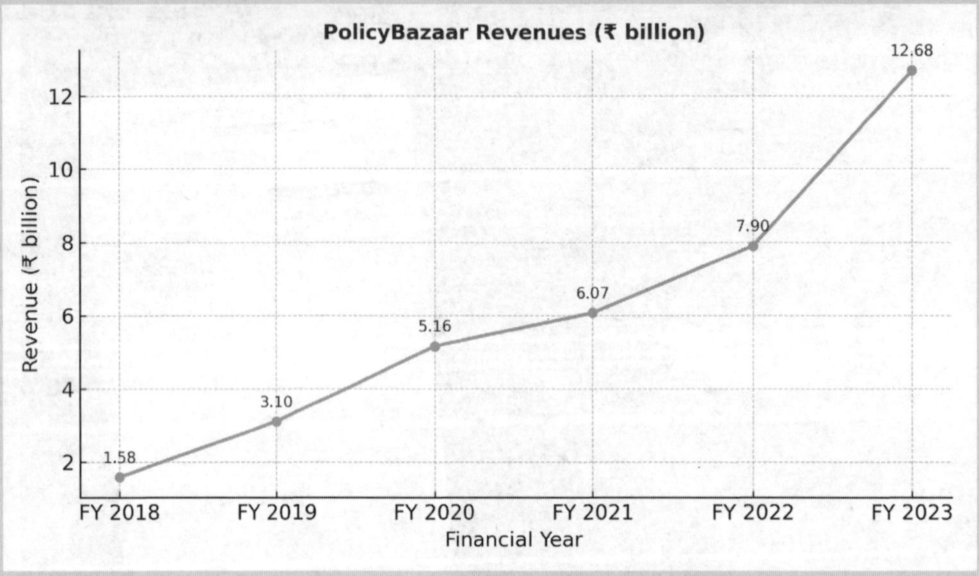

This human touch differentiates PolicyBazaar from many competing faceless digital platforms. This commitment to human interaction while leveraging technology has emerged as a benchmark for customer service in fintech.

The transformation of the insurance purchasing process represents one of PolicyBazaar's most significant contributions to the industry. The platform's tagline "Compare. Buy. Save" encapsulated a streamlined approach that eliminated traditional barriers to insurance adoption. By creating intuitive digital processes with clear instructions, automated follow-ups, and guided claim support, PolicyBazaar made insurance accessible to previously underserved populations. The evolution to their newer tagline "Har Family Hogi Insured" reflected their expanded mission to ensure universal insurance coverage across India, demonstrating how the company's vision grew from solving individual problems to addressing national financial security challenges.

PolicyBazaar's success and influence established new standards for physical and digital evidence in financial services, building customer confidence through consistent, professional touchpoints. The company's clean website and app design, secure digital document storage, branded offline centers, and comprehensive communication systems created a reliability framework that customers could trust. Going public in November 2021 through P.B. Fintech validated the company's business model and demonstrated the market's confidence in technology-driven financial services transformation. PolicyBazaar's operational revenues have been on the rise over the years (Exhibit 2). The company expanded into international markets by setting up operations in the UAE. However, it continues to face challenges, including low insurance penetration rates, regional awareness gaps, rural market skepticism, and the ongoing complexity of managing claims and regulatory compliance across different states and countries, highlighting that the transformation of India's insurance landscape remains an ongoing process requiring sustained innovation and adaptation.

Questions

1. Analyze how PolicyBazaar addressed the challenges of marketing intangible insurance services through their approach to services marketing. Specifically discuss how they tackled the intangibility problem through their strategies for Physical Evidence and Process, providing concrete examples from the case study.
2. PolicyBazaar shifted from a purely digital platform to a hybrid model incorporating physical service centers. Evaluate this strategic decision using the service quality dimensions (reliability, responsiveness, empathy, assurance, and tangibles). How did this hybrid approach help address service quality gaps that purely digital insurance platforms typically face, particularly in the Indian market context?
3. Examine PolicyBazaar's role in transforming the traditional insurance industry from a push-based, agent-driven model to a pull-based, consumer-centric platform. Discuss how their innovations addressed the traditional service failures in insurance (such as information asymmetry, lack of transparency, and poor post-purchase support) and analyze the implications for service design and customer relationship management in financial services.

References

Kumar, S. (2023, October 11). *PolicyBazaar Success Story - Buying Policies are Now Easy!* StartupTalky. https://startuptalky.com/startup-story-policy-bazaar/

Birch, K. (2023, November 3). Interview: Neeraj Gupta, CEO of insurtech major Policybazaar UAE. *Business Chief Middle East*. https://businesschief.ae/leadership-and-strategy/interview-neeraj-gupta-ceo-of-policybazaar-uae

Partner, B. I. (2022, January 10). Policybazaar's latest campaign presents Akshay Kumar in a superhero avatar. Business Insider. https://www.businessinsider.in/advertising/brands/news/policybazaars-latest-campaign-presents-akshay-kumar-in-a-superhero-avatar/articleshow/88806162.cms

Policybazaar.com. *Insurance - Compare & buy insurance plans - health, term, life, car, bike, investment*. Policybazaar. https://www.policybazaar.com

Policybazaar Adopts New Tagline, "Har Family Hogi Insured." (2022, June 13). Bwmarketingworld.https://www.bwmarketingworld.com/article/policybazaar-adopts-new-tagline-har-family-hogi-insured-432482

Policybazaar brings back Kapil Sharma in its humorous new brand campaign. (n.d.). Policybazaar. https://www.policybazaar.com/pblife/newsroom/press-releases/policybazaar-brings-back-kapil-sharma-in-its-humorous-new-brand-campaign

Policybazaar team - our DNA. (n.d.). https://www.policybazaar.com/our-team/

Index